# Financial Accounting
*Basic Concepts*

# Financial Accounting
*Basic Concepts*

**Fifth Edition**

**Earl A. Spiller, Jr.**
*Ph.D., CPA*
*Professor of Accounting*
*School of Accounting*
*University of South Carolina*

**Phillip T. May**
*Ph.D., CPA*
*Professor of Accounting*
*School of Accountancy*
*Wichita State University*

**IRWIN**

Homewood, IL 60430
Boston, MA 02116

Senior sponsoring editor: Ron M. Regis
Project editor: Margaret A. Schmidt
Production manager: Bette K. Ittersagen
Compositor: Beacon Graphics Corporation
Typeface: 10½/12 Times Roman
Printer: R. R. Donnelley & Sons Company

**Library of Congress Cataloging-in-Publication Data**

Spiller. Earl A.
    Financial accounting.

    1. Accounting.   I. May, Phillip T.   II. Title.
HF5635.S787   1990          657        89-19788
ISBN 0-256-06637-X

*Printed in the United States of America*
1 2 3 4 5 6 7 8 9 0 D O 7 6 5 4 3 2 1 0

# PREFACE

This fifth edition of *Financial Accounting: Basic Concepts* began as a traditional updating of material. It quickly evolved into a substantial modification. Added emphasis has been placed on improving the text's readability for the student and teachability for the instructor.

This edition retains its basic thrust, however, as it addresses the same audiences and embraces the same educational objectives as its predecessors. The book introduces financial accounting to those whose backgrounds include little or no prior knowledge of the subject. It is particularly suitable for a one-semester course offered to MBA students or highly motivated undergraduate students. The text is also appropriate for professional courses taught in schools of law or public administration, in executive MBA programs, and in management development programs for security analysts, credit evaluators, and other users of financial statements.

This edition maintains the same conceptual-analytical approach that was the hallmark of previous editions. However, we have tried to apply that approach more frequently to real-world situations and other events likely to be encountered by financial-statement readers.

The primary aim of the book is to develop the reader's ability to understand, interpret, and analyze the financial statements of business organizations. Several secondary objectives support the achievement of this overall goal:

1. Familiarity with accounting terminology to understand and communicate using the language of accounting.
2. Knowledge of the measurement rules and disclosure regulations governing the recording and reporting of business activity.
3. Understanding the impact that alternative accounting principles have on the financial statements, so that their various meanings can be interpreted.
4. Ability to use the conceptual structure of financial accounting as a benchmark for evaluation.
5. Acquiring a working knowledge of the accounting process to allow the use of the logical framework of accounting as an analytical tool.

## CHANGES IN THE FIFTH EDITION

The use of an actual annual report as an integrated teaching device was a successful innovation in the fourth edition. This feature has been retained. Most of the 1987 Annual Report of Kimberly-Clark Corporation is reproduced in an Appendix to Chapter 6. Each chapter thereafter ends with a discussion that relates the material of that chapter to the reporting practices of Kimberly-Clark in 1987. These sections in Chapters 6 to 18 feature an in-depth analysis of Kimberly-Clark's financial statements and notes. They help relate the textbook concepts and procedures to real-world situations and increase the reader's confidence in his or her ability to understand actual corporate financial reports.

At the suggestion of a number of instructors, we have included a second annual report as a source of problem material. The annual report of Georgia-Pacific Corporation is reproduced in an Appendix at the end of the book. Most chapters have a major assignment concerning the Georgia-Pacific financial statements. In this way, instructors may employ a continuing problem assignment from chapter to chapter.

Other significant changes in the text of the fifth edition include the following:

1. Rewriting all chapters to simplify the writing style and eliminate unnecessary jargon.
2. Attention focused on conceptual and analytical aspects directly relevant to the financial statements that readers see and the financial analyses that they will be required to complete.
3. Introduction of some appropriate financial statement ratios in a number of early chapters. This enhances the relevance of the early chapters and allows the chapter on Analysis of Financial Statements to serve a summary role and to contain more interpretative discussions.
4. Increased discussion of income flows vis-à-vis cash flows throughout the text.
5. Incorporation of the latest accounting thought and pronouncements.
6. Division of the introduction to financial accounting and its conceptual framework into two chapters. This change makes the first bite of financial accounting smaller and more interesting for first-time readers. The new Chapter 1, for example, relates accounting functions to the everyday experiences of the readers. It introduces them at the outset to the importance of accounting and to the information contained in financial statements.
7. Elimination of the appendix on manual bookkeeping procedures. The material on internal control previously contained in that appendix plus some discussion of information systems have been moved into the body of the chapter.

8. Expansion of the use of appendixes to enhance the instructor's flexibility in the choice of material. The appendixes on lower-of-cost-or-market, group depreciation procedures, and the time value of money have been retained. New appendixes cover installment sales, accounting for bonds as investments, accounting for leases by lessors, and the worksheet approach to consolidated statement preparation.

9. Greater discussion of LIFO liquidations and their effect on the financial statements in the chapter on inventories.

10. Reorganization of the material on bonds and notes. A new section discussing the relationship of bond prices and interest rates has been added. The section on "non-interest-bearing" or discount notes has been deleted (they rarely are used in financial practice) and is replaced by a discussion and illustration of installment notes. Brief analyses of zero-coupon bonds, debt-equity swaps, and in-substance defeasance have been added.

11. Simplification of the discussion and combination of leases and pensions in a single chapter with two underlying themes. One is the use of present value concepts and procedures in complex areas of liability measurement. The second discusses difficulties that arise in applying the definitions and measurement rules for liabilities.

12. A complete rewriting of Chapter 13 on income taxes to explain and illustrate the liability approach to deferred taxes as called for by the standards contained in *FASB Statement No. 96*.

13. Interchange of the material on foreign currency transactions and contingencies. The latter moves from Chapter 14 on Stockholders' Equity to Chapter 16 on Disclosure Issues. The former moves in the other direction. We believe the new placement of these sections provides a more logical cohesiveness to both chapters.

14. Use of a direct approach, unencumbered by worksheet forms, for the initial discussion of consolidated statements. The direct approach builds the consolidated statements from the basic concept of what the statements should show if there were just a single company. A modern integrated worksheet is discussed in an appendix for those interested in greater procedural depth.

15. Extensive revision of Chapter 17 to emphasize the cash definition of funds flows and the reporting formats of *FASB Statement No. 95*.

## Problem Material

The major reworking of the text material extends also to the problem material. The number of problems has been expanded by a third. Over half of them are totally new or significantly changed. Some of the long problems have been cut back in length or divided into two problems. The problems are ordered generally in terms of increasing difficulty and/or length. Lower numbered problems follow directly from the text discussions or illustrate basic material. A short description has been added as a title to each problem to aid in quickly identifying its major thrust. Most of the problems continue to stress the application of conceptual knowledge and the development of analytical skills.

An innovation in this edition is the inclusion of casettes (as in "small cases"). Each chapter contains from one to four casettes. Many of these come from the annual reports of actual companies. They tend to be longer, more challenging, and more thought-provoking than the regular problems. They often contain questions requiring a discussion of rationale or motivation or an evaluation or comparison of accounting practices. We hope the casettes will provide an interesting and relevant challenge for students where time allows an in-depth exploration of a topic.

## Other Features

The book is organized in four sections. The first six chapters, comprising Section I, establish the fundamental concepts and procedures of financial accounting and reporting. Sections II and III discuss selected areas involved in the measurement of assets and equities. The material in these sections builds on the conceptual-analytical framework in the first section. Current accounting principles and procedures are explained and examined critically. Section IV contains four chapters which concern problems of analysis, disclosure, and interpretation in the financial statements.

A glossary, containing more than 300 technical terms and phrases used in financial accounting and their definitions, appears at the end of the book. The items are arranged in alphabetical order for easy reference by the user. Each entry contains a clear, concise definition of the term and a reference to the first text chapter in which the item is discussed in depth.

An instructor's manual containing solutions to all problems is available to adopters. However, we have tried to make it more than just a solutions manual. It contains outlines of each chapter and some short suggestions or teaching hints to assist the instructor. Some sample examinations and lists of check figures are included for instructors to copy and distribute if they desire.

A computer diskette to be used by those having interest in and access to microcomputers accompanies the instructor's manual. The diskette contains spreadsheet templates that can be used to solve many of the problems in the text.

## ACKNOWLEDGMENTS

A notable change in this edition has been the replacement of Professor Martin Gosman as coauthor with Professor Phillip May. The press of other duties prevented Professor Gosman from continuing with this edition. We acknowledge with gratitude his innovations and contributions to the fourth edition which we have carried forward.

We have been fortunate to receive a number of comments and suggestions from users of the fourth edition. We are grateful for their input. Three faculty members deserve a special mention of appreciation. Professor Janet D. Daniels (University of Hartford), Professor Randall B. Hayes (College of William and Mary), and Professor Charles Tritschler (Purdue University) provided detailed reviews of the fourth edition. Professor Hayes, for example, gave us 13 pages of suggestions covering organizational improvements, topic coverage, and writing style. Professor Daniels made a number of valuable suggestions to improve the book's readability, particularly for use in executive programs. Professor Tritschler's insights, gained from many years of experience with the text, aided immeasurably in keeping us on target with respect to the major thrust and audience for the book. Both Professors Daniels and Tritschler, in addition, critically evaluated our revision plan and helped us to resolve some thorny issues of coverage and organization. Many of the changes in the fifth edition outlined earlier grew out of the comments of these three people to whom we are deeply indebted.

Professor David Gotlob (University of Wisconsin at Oshkosh) read the entire revised manuscript. He corrected our errors, suggested material in need of clarification, class-tested some new chapters, and generally provided assurance that the changes implemented in this edition were indeed improvements.

Professor Leland Mansuetti of Sierra College prepared the computer diskette. His mastery of computer worksheet preparation and of problem-solving analysis has added a significant feature to the book.

We were aided by some very able graduate assistants. Michael McCartney at Indiana University and Robin Gerety at Wichita State University verified references and numbers, checked all calculations, critiqued text and problem material, and provided other valuable assistance.

We are grateful to Kimberly-Clark Corporation and Georgia-Pacific Corporation for allowing us to reproduce their annual reports.

All of the foregoing people share in the completion of this book and in any improvements it contains. However, to our wives—Elinor and Mary—go our greatest thanks. Their encouragement, support, and assistance have made this book possible; their patience, understanding, and approval have made our efforts in writing it worthwhile; and their marginal propensities to consume have made the whole project necessary.

Comments and suggestions from users are most welcome.

**Earl A. Spiller, Jr.**
**Phillip T. May**

# CONTENTS

**SECTION IV**
**Financial Statements—Problems of Analysis, Disclosure,**
**and Interpretation**

# Fundamental Concepts and Procedures

# Chapter 1

# The World of Accounting

The word *accounting* suggests to many people a complex, detailed, and mysterious set of activities. Perhaps you also share this mental image of accounting.

Actually, you know more about accounting than you probably would guess. Your everyday contacts with the large number of businesses in our society have acquainted you with a number of accounting's functions. Consider these items:

**1.** You make a significant number of your cash disbursements by writing checks. Your checking account is best handled when you carefully keep track of individual checks in your checkbook. You record each check accurately to itemize the date, check number, payee, and dollar amount. *This is accounting*.

**2.** Each time you purchase merchandise from a business, some record is made. A sales slip may be written, a cash register receipt is printed, or a credit card invoice is prepared for you to sign. Each of these techniques is used to capture the essential data about your transaction. *This is accounting*.

**3.** Every month, before you pay your credit card bill, you compare your copies of the credit card transactions with the monthly statement. You make the comparisons to assure the accuracy of the billing. *This is accounting*.

**4.** The bank sends you a checking account statement each month. You compare the bank's account balance to your checkbook's record of your account balance. You hope they will agree, but if they do not, you identify the error and make the correction. (Did you ever notice how the mistake is usually yours and not the bank's?) *This is accounting*.

**5.** Every year, you prepare Internal Revenue Form 1040 to determine your income tax liability and whether you have satisfied this liability through tax withholdings during the year. The preparation of your tax return requires you to retrieve information concerning earnings, tax withholdings, deductible expenses, and other pertinent information. Finally, you send the form to the IRS as a statement of your tax status. *This is accounting*.

**6.** When you decide to buy a home, the cost of the purchase is not only the price you offer. You must also consider the impact of other one-time charges such as inspection costs, mortgage fees or "points," real estate commissions, special assessments for streets or sewers, and so forth. In other words, the total cost of the home is determined by adding all the relevant costs necessary to acquire the home. You must also consider recurring costs of owning the home such as property taxes, utility bills, interest charges, etc. In all of these processes, *you are doing accounting*.

These examples illustrate activities with which you are familiar, but which you have undoubtedly completed without thinking about accounting.

Look at each example. You will see that each of the accounting activities conveys some specific information about economic facts. Accounting is a system of activities devoted to the collection, processing, and communication of economic information. Accurate and timely information enables users to reach sound decisions.

In this chapter, we want to gain a general understanding of how an accounting system operates and the meaning of the reports it produces. To do this, we must first look at the tasks performed in a simple accounting system. The output of the accounting process consists of financial reports directed to various user groups. Accordingly, we then look at these groups and how they might use information about business enterprises. The third section illustrates and discusses the financial statements that accountants use to provide information. We conclude with a description of the environment in which the financial accounting process takes place.

## INTRODUCTION TO ACCOUNTING

Accounting consists of the concepts and processes by which financial and economic data are gathered, processed, and communicated. As you study further, you will see clearly that accounting is a flexible discipline that requires significant exercise of judgment. Assumptions that accounting is precise and cut-and-dried are common misunderstandings. Organizations are complex mixtures of people, resources, and procedures. Accounting for these complex mixtures is often difficult.

### The Accounting Process as a System

Let us first consider the relationship of accounting and the accounting system to the activities of a business organization. In every organization two flows occur simultaneously. First, a firm performs the activity for which it was organized. This is generally the production of a product or the delivery of a service or perhaps both. Second, as the product is completed or the service is delivered, data are generated about these activities. Accounting is the function that captures the flow of data concerning the product or service activity.

For example, at a grocery store, customers purchase meat, produce, and canned goods. The store's business purpose is to sell these products to customers. The transfer of the store's products to consumers and their transfer of cash to the grocery store represent the first business activity flow.

The flow of data parallels the physical flows of merchandise and cash. The merchant uses a cash register to capture and record sales and cash receipts. Meat, produce, and canned goods are individually coded so each item sold can be identified. In addition, the prices paid, the currency tendered by customers, and the change they receive are coded as dollars and cents. This second flow of data results when the accounting system codes the transactions in letters and digits to represent the products-to-cash transfer from the first flow. All accounting systems perform this parallel function of processing data about the activities that the business organization is completing.

Figure 1–1 enables us to visualize these two flows.

In accounting terms, each event that generates data is called a "transaction." The accounting system must be ready to capture data promptly at the point of generation. Any delay in data collection increases the possibilities of inaccuracy and omission.

At the time of data capture, the accounting system codes the transaction to permit accuracy in recording and processing the data. Generally, this means that the transaction is converted into an alphabetic or numeric form.

**FIGURE 1–1**  Parallel Activity and Information Flows

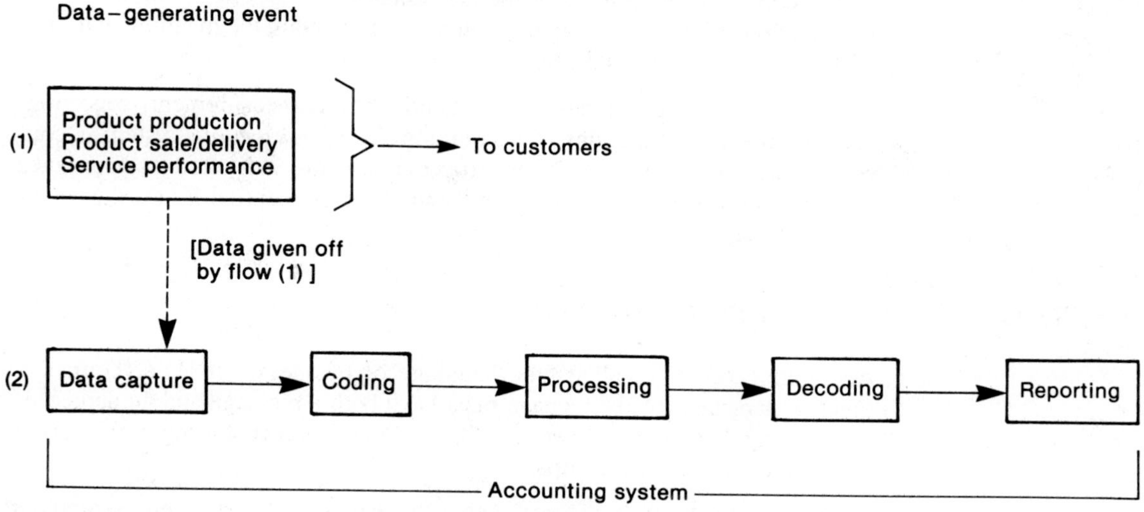

Data–generating event

Accuracy in coding data is critical to the ability of the accounting system to function effectively.

Processing in an accounting system involves a series of procedural steps to organize, store, and manipulate coded data. Processing will convert individual transaction data into meaningful combinations to satisfy the decision-making requirements of users. At this point "data" are considered to have been changed into "information."

The accounting data are not appropriately structured until they are reestablished in a form usable by decision makers. This requires two related steps. First, the information must be decoded from the form used in processing and, second, it must be placed in the appropriate report form.

In completing the accounting process, the accountant undertakes a variety of tasks, including:

1. *Identification*—selecting those transactions and events that are relevant to accounting. Criteria must be established for choosing the appropriate data to capture.
2. *Measurement*—measuring the transactions and events in monetary terms. Measurement rules must be developed for assigning dollar values to the economic transactions and events to be communicated.
3. *Recording*—using a systematic method for keeping track of the transactions. In accounting, this process is called "bookkeeping."
4. *Classification*—categorizing the captured data into a logical and useful framework so they can be reported in a meaningful way to users. Huge masses of figures have little significance unless they are ordered and their relationships highlighted.
5. *Reporting*—periodically summarizing the collected and classified financial information into statements and reports. These statements and reports are the communication tools of the accountant.
6. *Interpretation*—analyzing the statements to explain the meaning and limitations of the financial information.

In this book, we emphasize the identification, measurement, reporting, and interpretation functions of accounting. The *bookkeeping* system is concerned primarily with recording procedures. Only a limited acquaintance with its techniques is needed to understand the conceptual issues that comprise the real essence of accounting.

## USERS OF ACCOUNTING INFORMATION

Accounting often is called "the language of business." It is, of course, a financial language. Any language must have both a message and an audience. Accounting has both. However, the audience of accounting information includes many diverse groups:

1. Owners—present and prospective investors and their representatives (security analysts and investment advisors).

2. Managers and other operations personnel.
3. Creditors and lenders—suppliers of goods and services, banks, and insurance companies.
4. Employees and labor organizations.
5. Customers.
6. Taxation authorities.
7. Regulatory agencies—Securities and Exchange Commission (SEC), stock exchanges, governmental commissions, and the courts.
8. Information agencies—the financial press, trade associations, and reporting agencies.

In a broad sense, all these audiences share a common desire for information about the economic resources of an organization. The allocation of financial capital and the distribution of real resources among competing uses are basic economic decisions. Consequently, accounting for the economic resources controlled by an organization and reporting on their use to all interested parties are vital tasks. They are essential for both profit-making business ventures and nonprofit organizations such as universities and hospitals.

In another sense, however, the audiences listed above have different needs for and abilities to obtain information. Their desire for knowledge about the nature and use of an organization's resources reflects quite different objectives. For example, current and prospective owners must decide whether to increase, retain, or reduce their investment in the business. They are interested in the current state of their investment as well as information from which to forecast the future success of the business. Bankers and lenders, on the other hand, must judge whether to grant a loan and, if so, on what terms. They may be interested primarily in current financial solvency and information from which to predict the ability of a firm to pay its debts as they become due. Managers must select among alternative courses of future action relating to products, processes, and operating techniques. They need very detailed information to plan and control an organization's human and material resources effectively. Taxation authorities have a specific interest in determining how much tax the business is legally obliged to pay. Employees and their unions make decisions about whether the firm is able to pay higher wages and hire more people. The list of varying decisions and different informational needs could easily be extended for the other users on the list.

## Accounting Specialties

One result of the foregoing differences in the accounting audience has been a partitioning of the accounting process into a number of overlapping specialty areas. Each specialized accounting activity produces unique information for different users' requirements. Figure 1–2 depicts some of the major branches of the discipline of accounting, the reports prepared, and the audiences served.

**FIGURE 1–2**    The Accounting System and Accounting Specialties

| Audience | Reports | Accounting Specialties | | Reports | Audience |
|---|---|---|---|---|---|
| Federal, state, and local tax authorities | Personal/ corporate tax returns | Tax accounting | Financial accounting | Financial statements<br>- Balance sheets<br>- Income statements<br>- Statements of cash flows | Owners, creditors customers, lenders, security analysts, reporting agencies, employee groups |
| | | | Accounting system | | |
| Audience | Reports | | | Reports | Audience |
| SEC, stock exchanges, regulatory commisions, courts | Annual financial reports, Compliance reports, Statistical analyses | Regulatory accounting | Managerial accounting | Internal reports<br>- Budgets<br>- Cost analyses<br>- Control reports | All levels of management |

Note that the accounting system is central to all specialties. Each accounting specialty takes data from that system and makes a special analysis or manipulation of them to produce the information needed for its reports. Therefore, once you understand the accounting system, you will be prepared to use a number of specialized types of accounting information.

Let's look at each of the branches of accounting.

**Financial Accounting.**    Our focal point in this book will be the study of this branch of accounting. Its primary function is to provide financial information to investors and other users not directly involved in the management of the organization.

The reports from the financial accounting process are general-purpose financial statements. These statements include the balance sheet, the income statement, and the statement of cash flows. We will see shortly how each of these statements reports different important financial facts and results.

The financial statements are primarily designed for external audiences, of which stockholders and creditors are the most important. However, they are of interest to practically all audiences. Furthermore, to produce these statements, we must understand the fundamental concepts of accounting and its recording process. For these reasons, financial accounting provides a natural and logical starting point for our discussion.

**Managerial Accounting.**    Management makes decisions about the acquisition and use of resources within the entity. Management must plan for and control a firm's activities to accomplish the goals of the organization.

Therefore, in addition to the information shown on financial statements, management needs specific detailed data to control current operations and plan future operations.

The accounting information collected for financial accounting is coded so it can be reprocessed and summarized for internal management use. This managerial information comes from the same accounting system but is rearranged to provide detailed operating data and projections. For instance, in our grocery store example, a monthly income statement from financial accounting would report the total sales of products to customers during that month. However, management might also receive a weekly report detailing sales classified into such categories as meat, produce, and canned goods, and perhaps narrower subdivisions of products. This information would help management to order products and plan future purchases.

**Regulatory Accounting.**   Regulatory agencies constantly call on accountants to prepare a variety of special purpose reports. The agencies need these reports to judge whether entities are meeting their legal obligations and conforming to various social and economic regulations issued by federal, state, and local governments.

Regulatory authorities generally dictate exactly what information they desire and how it is to be arranged. The information needs of these groups require rearrangement of the data collected by the financial accounting system. In regulatory accounting, as in managerial accounting, proper coding of the data at the time of collection enables the enterprise to reprocess it to prepare the required regulatory reports.

**Tax Accounting.**   This aspect of the accounting process covers the preparation of records and reports necessary for filing specific tax returns. Most tax reporting begins with basic financial accounting data. Often, however, tax requirements call for different concepts and interpretations of those data. Therefore, accounting tax specialists are needed to reorganize the accounting data to comply with the taxation specifications.

Tax regulations are a complex set of ever changing laws and rules. Keeping up-to-date on tax regulations and their implications for business planning and decision making are critical accounting activities. Because of their different audience, their complexity, and their changeability, detailed income tax reports do not play an important role in this book. Nevertheless, we will alert you to some possible distortions caused by the intrusion of tax concepts in the measurement of business income.

## AN ILLUSTRATION OF FINANCIAL ACCOUNTING REPORTS

Financial accounting consists of the concepts and processes by which financial and economic data are captured, coded, processed, decoded, and reported to external audiences. General purpose reports or financial statements about the acquisition, financing, and use of resources are the final output of the financial accounting process.

The financial reporting package usually consists of three primary statements—a balance sheet, an income statement, and a statement of cash flows. Examples of these reports for the Kimberly-Clark Corporation, related to the quarter ending March 31, 1988, are presented on the next three pages.

The balance sheet (Figure 1–3) is a statement of financial status at a particular time. In this case, the statement shows the quantity of resources (assets), debts (liabilities), and ownership (stockholders' equity) on March 31,

---

**FIGURE 1–3**

### KIMBERLY-CLARK CORPORATION AND SUBSIDIARIES
**Consolidated Balance Sheet**
**(in millions)**

|  | March 31, 1988 | December 31, 1987 |
|---|---|---|
| **Assets** | | |
| Current assets: | | |
| Cash and cash equivalents. . . . . . . . . | $    68.8 | $    89.7 |
| Accounts receivable . . . . . . . . . . | 569.2 | 519.9 |
| Inventories . . . . . . . . . . . . . | 552.4 | 525.4 |
| Total current assets. . . . . . . . . . | 1,190.4 | 1,135.0 |
| Property, plant, and equipment . . . . . . . | 3,843.3 | 3,768.0 |
| Less: accumulated depreciation . . . . . . | (1,472.8) | (1,431.2) |
|  | 2,370.5 | 2,336.8 |
| Investments in equity companies . . . . . . | 245.3 | 264.8 |
| Other assets . . . . . . . . . . . . | 171.4 | 149.1 |
| Total assets . . . . . . . . . . . . . | $ 3,977.6 | $ 3,885.7 |
| **Liabilities and Stockholders' Equity** | | |
| Current liabilities: | | |
| Short-term debt and current portion | | |
| of long-term debt . . . . . . . . . . | $   185.7 | $   250.0 |
| Accounts payable . . . . . . . . . . | 287.9 | 281.6 |
| Other current liabilities . . . . . . . . | 517.2 | 464.5 |
| Total current liabilities . . . . . . . . | 990.8 | 996.1 |
| Long-term debt . . . . . . . . . . . | 676.6 | 686.9 |
| Deferred income taxes . . . . . . . . . | 561.3 | 548.2 |
| Minority owners' interests in subsidiaries. . . . | 88.1 | 82.6 |
| Stockholders' equity . . . . . . . . . . | 1,660.8 | 1,571.9 |
| Total liabilities and stockholders' equity . . . . | $ 3,977.6 | $ 3,885.7 |

1988. Note that the balance sheet carries a single date which is the last day of the quarter. The status of resources, debts, and ownership is also shown for December 31, 1987, the last day of the previous quarter. This presentation permits the reader to compare the change in each of the balance sheet items from the beginning to the end of the quarter.

The income statement (Figure 1–4) is a statement of performance related to a specific period of time. Kimberly-Clark's performance results cover the three-month period beginning January 1, 1988 and ending March 31, 1988. This statement reports the quantity of new resources that came into the cor-

## FIGURE 1–4

### KIMBERLY-CLARK CORPORATION AND SUBSIDIARIES
**Consolidated Income Statement**
**(in millions)**

| | *Three Months Ended March 31* | |
| --- | --- | --- |
| | *1988* | *1987* |
| Net sales. | $1,294.0 | $1,183.2 |
| Cost of products sold. | 802.6 | 729.5 |
| Distribution expense | 46.0 | 44.9 |
| Gross profit. | 445.4 | 408.8 |
| Advertising, promotion, and selling expense | 176.7 | 181.4 |
| Research expense | 24.4 | 23.6 |
| General expense. | 63.8 | 61.6 |
| Operating profit. | 180.5 | 142.2 |
| Interest income | 1.8 | 1.3 |
| Other income. | 6.3 | 4.7 |
| Interest expense. | (21.2) | (14.5) |
| Other expense. | (3.8) | (5.2) |
| Income before income taxes | 163.6 | 128.5 |
| Provision for income taxes | 65.9 | 56.3 |
| Income before. | 97.7 | 72.2 |
| Share of net income of equity companies | .2 | 5.7 |
| Minority owners' interests in subsidiaries' net income. | (4.6) | (2.8) |
| Net income. | $ 93.3 | $ 75.1 |
| Common shares outstanding—average | 80.3 | 91.9 |
| Per share of common stock | | |
| Net income. | $ 1.16 | $ .82 |
| Cash dividends declared | .40 | .36 |

poration (net sales), the resources that flowed out (costs, expenses, taxes), and the difference between the inflows and outflows (net income). Net income is the financial performance measure related to management's success in operating the enterprise. The final items on the income statement report the total dollar net income on a per share basis of ownership stock held by the investors as well as the dollar value per share of resources paid to each investor (dividends).

A third statement (Figure 1–5) called "the statement of cash flows" reveals how the firm generated and expended its cash resources during the quarter. The statement begins with the net income figure taken from the income statement and then proceeds to display the major events that increased

## FIGURE 1–5

### KIMBERLY-CLARK CORPORATION AND SUBSIDIARIES
**Consolidated Statement of Cash Flows**
**(in millions)**

|  | Three Months Ended March 31 | |
| --- | --- | --- |
|  | *1988* | *1987* |
| Operations: | | |
| Net income . . . . . . . . . . . . . . . . | $  93.3 | $   75.1 |
| Depreciation . . . . . . . . . . . . . . . | 46.4 | 44.1 |
| Other . . . . . . . . . . . . . . . . . | 39.6 | 28.4 |
| Changes in operating working capital . . . . | (14.9) | 24.5 |
| Cash provided by operations . . . . . . | 164.4 | 172.1 |
| Investing: | | |
| Capital spending. . . . . . . . . . . . | (67.7) | (39.0) |
| Disposals of property . . . . . . . . . . | 2.0 | 1.9 |
| Other . . . . . . . . . . . . . . . . . | (13.8) | (16.6) |
| Cash used for investing . . . . . . . | (79.5) | (53.7) |
| Financing: | | |
| Cash dividends paid . . . . . . . . . . | (29.5) | (28.5) |
| Acquisitions of common stock for treasury . . | (1.7) | (9.6) |
| Decrease in debt payable within one year. . . | (64.3) | (72.3) |
| Increase in long-term debt . . . . . . . . | 2.3 | 8.5 |
| Decrease in long-term debt . . . . . . . . | (12.6) | (2.9) |
| Cash used for financing . . . . . . . . | (105.8) | (104.8) |
| Increase (decrease) in cash and cash equivalents . . . . . . . . . . . . | $ (20.9) | $   13.6 |

Note: This statement has been restated in a format modified from that actually used by Kimberly-Clark. The company actually called it a statement of changes in financial position, a now obsolete title.

and decreased its cash from operating, investing, and financing activities. Notice that the net decrease in cash of $20.9 million in the quarter agrees with the decrease in cash shown on the balance sheet in Figure 1–3.

## Reading Financial Statements

Even though we have not studied the detailed accounting procedures used to convert economic transactions into financial statements, let us read the Kimberly-Clark statements to answer a few questions about the company's status and performance.

Take each of the following questions and examine the analysis employed to answer them. You will begin to see how you can use financial statement information to make judgments about a company's operations.

1. *The Balance Sheet*
    a. Have the current assets (cash, accounts receivable, inventories) increased this quarter?

       Analysis: Current assets have increased $55.4 million. At December 31, 1987 the current assets were $1,135 million, and at March 31, 1988 they were $1,190.4 million.
    b. Has the amount of total debt (current liabilities plus long-term debt) changed this quarter?

       Analysis: Total debt has decreased $15.6 million. The total of current liabilities plus long-term debt at December 31, 1987 was $1,683 million and was $1,667.4 million at March 31, 1988.
    c. Has the company increased its investment in Property, Plant, and Equipment this quarter?

       Analysis: Property, Plant, and Equipment has increased $33.7 million. The December 31st balance was $2,336.8 million and the March 31st balance was $2,370.5 million.
    d. Do the stockholders have a greater investment in the business at the end of this quarter?

       Analysis: The stockholders' ownership (equity) is greater by $88.9 million. The stockholders' equity at December 31 was $1,571.9 million and at March 31 was $1,660.8 million.
2. *The Income Statement*
    a. Has the company increased its sales of goods and services in the 1988 quarter over its sales in the 1987 quarter? What was the percentage change?

       Analysis: Sales have increased $110.8 million. Sales in this quarter, last year (1987) were $1,183.2 million and in the same quarter this year (1988) they were $1,294.0 million.
       Sales have increased 9.4% in this quarter ($110.8/$1,183.2).
    b. Has operating profit increased in the 1988 quarter over the 1987 quarter?

Analysis: Operating profit has increased $38.3 million. 1987 operating profit was $142.2 million and 1988 operating profit was $180.5 million.

c. Has net income increased in the 1988 quarter over the 1987 quarter?

Analysis: Net income has increased $18.2 million. Net income in 1987 was $75.1 million and in 1988 was $93.3 million.

d. Are operating profit and net income a higher or lower percentage of net sales in the 1988 quarter compared with the 1987 quarter?

Analysis: The percentages have increased from 1987 to 1988—operating profit +1.9% and net income +.9%

The operating profit percentages are:
1987: $142.2/$1,183.2 = 12.0%
1988: $180.5/$1,294.0 = 13.9%
Increase 13.9% − 12.0% = +1.9%
The net income percentages are:
1987: $75.1/$1,183.2 = 6.3%
1988: $93.3/$1,294.0 = 7.2%
Increase 7.2% − 6.3% = +.9%

e. Has the rate of increase in sales been more or less than the rate of change in net income?

Analysis: Sales increased by 9.4 percent, but net income increased by 24.2 percent. The percentages are calculated as:
Change in sales—($1,294.0 − $1,183.2)/$1,183.2 = 9.4%
Change in net income—($93.3 − $75.1)/$75.1 = 24.2%

3. *Statement of Cash Flows*

Before reading this statement, two items should be noted. First, this statement concentrates on explaining how the specific resource, cash, changed during the accounting period. The numbers shown in parentheses are negative values representing an outflow of cash. Second, the statement has three major sections. The top section shows cash provided from operations. The middle section shows cash changes from investing activities involving long-term assets such as equipment and buildings. The bottom section presents cash effects from financing activities during the period. Financing activities involve cash transactions with major lenders and with the owners.

a. Have the operations of Kimberly-Clark provided increased cash resources during this period?

Analysis: $164.4 million of cash was provided from operations. Net income of $93.3 million, from the income statement, was adjusted for expenses that did not require cash payments. This adjustment restates income to show the *cash* that flowed into the firm from its operations.[1]

---

[1] A detailed explanation of the statement of cash flows will be completed in Chapter 17. The necessary adjustments to provide the information used in preparing a statement like that of Kimberly-Clark will be deferred until that chapter.

b. How much has Kimberly-Clark expended in cash resources to make capital (long-term) investments this period?

   Analysis: $67.7 million was expended for capital investments. This figure is shown as a negative value indicating a cash outflow. That is the cash effect on the firm from adding to its property, plant, and equipment.

c. How much cash was paid to the stockholders for dividends this period?

   Analysis: Cash dividends paid were $29.5 million. This figure is negative to show the cash outflow as stockholders were sent dividend checks.

Now that we have completed a brief reading of several financial statements, we might ask, "What does all of this mean?" Here are a few conclusions we can draw:

**1.** The balance sheet shows an improved status measured by larger assets and reduced debt, when comparing the end of this quarter with the end of the previous quarter. In addition, the company has purchased property, plant, and equipment to use in the future production of its products. An increased asset base certainly suggests financial strength.

**2.** The income statement generally supports the balance sheet's conclusion about strength. Sales and income are both higher. The higher dollars of income explain the increased stockholders' equity on the balance sheet. Most significant is the fact that sales have increased 9.4 percent and income has increased 24.2 percent. This indicates that each dollar of sales is generating net income at a rate faster than the increase in sales. This is an impressive performance record.

**3.** The analysis of cash flows indicates that Kimberly-Clark has generated $164.4 million in cash from its business operations. In addition, $67.7 million of that cash has been invested in additional capital equipment, and $29.5 million has been used to pay dividends to the stockholders.

In summary, notice how the statements speak to you about a firm. They tell a story about the financial performance and status of the organization. Some of the items are explicit, such as dollar values for assets and income; and some items can be derived through your own analysis. This latter point was illustrated when we turned the income dollars into percentages.

The study of financial accounting will enable you to develop insights into any company's performance by analyzing its financial statements. Further, you will see how these analyses are related to the objectives of various accounting audiences.

Even now, consider the potential meaning of the Kimberly-Clark reports for each of the following audiences:

**1.** Owners—Corporate performance in the areas of income generation, dividend payout, and growth are favorable factors of Kimberly-Clark that stockholders and potential stockholders would look at in making their investment decisions.

**2.** Lenders—This audience generally is more concerned with the financial soundness of the firm than with its short-term ability to generate income. The nature and size of the resources of Kimberly-Clark, and its ability to generate cash that can be used to repay loans are of prime importance to them.

**3.** Tax authorities—Their general concern will be the income statement and the information it reveals about the current period's income. They are most interested in the calculation of the correct amounts of tax based on that income and the firm's ability, as measured by its cash flows, to pay its tax liability.

**4.** Management—Sales expansion, income growth, high levels of cash generation, and increased investments for the future represent some of management's accomplishments during the period. Management uses the financial statements as a principal means to communicate these results to external parties. Like all of us, managers are interested in what their report cards, the financial statements, reveal.

## Other Informational Disclosures

The financial statements are the most important presentations of an organization's performance and status. However, these statements often are too brief to present the detail necessary to interpret adequately the full meaning of the figures. Therefore, the accounting function provides additional information to accompany the financial statements.

**Supporting Notes.**   Accountants almost always prepare explanatory notes about financial statements. These notes inform the reader of additional information needed to properly understand the reports, and form an integral part of the statements.

Accounting regulations require certain disclosures that frequently appear in supporting notes to the statements. For instance, the basic principles used in preparing the statements must be disclosed. This would require stating how inventory was valued; how net income per share was calculated; and how, for example, the company had recorded its property, plant, and equipment. This information clarifies the methods the accountant used to develop the numbers appearing in the statements.

Additional notes may be used to explain the differences between accounting and tax treatments of transactions, to provide details concerning pension plans, to itemize categories of inventory, or to list the elements comprising the long-term debt of the firm.

**Management's Review and Disclosures.**   The chief operating officer and/or the chairman of the board of directors often present(s) a comparative analysis of the company's current period results with the results of the past period. This narrative provides an insight into the rationale behind many of the financial results depicted in the statements.

Management also is required to provide a statement acknowledging its responsibility for the preparation of the financial statements. In this disclosure, management usually tells the reader that it maintains a system to ensure reliable accounting records, selects the accounting principles used to report information, and provides a system of internal controls to safeguard the firm's resources and to ensure the integrity of the financial data. The statement also calls the reader's attention to the independent auditor's report.

**Independent Auditor's Report.**   All large publicly traded companies and many smaller privately owned firms are audited by independent public accounting firms. In an audit the certified public accountant (CPA) reviews the internal control systems of the firm, makes tests of the accounting records to determine whether the financial statements present the results of the transactions fairly, and issues a report expressing its opinion on the financial statements.

As an example, Kimberly-Clark published in its 1987 annual report the following statement issued by Deloitte Haskins & Sells, the large public accounting firm that serves as its auditor:

> We have examined the consolidated balance sheets of Kimberly-Clark Corporation and Subsidiaries as of December 31, 1987 and 1986, and the related consolidated statements of income and changes in financial position for each of the three years in the period ended December 31, 1987. Our examinations were made in accordance with generally accepted auditing standards and, accordingly, included such tests of the accounting records and such other auditing procedures as we considered necessary in the circumstances.
>
> In our opinion, such consolidated financial statements of Kimberly-Clark Corporation and Subsidiaries present fairly the financial position of the companies at December 31, 1987 and 1986, and the results of their operations and the changes in financial position for each of the three years in the period ended December 31, 1987, in conformity with generally accepted accounting principles applied on a consistent basis.

This report provides the reader with a technically proficient, independent observer's evaluation of the financial statements.[2]

## THE ACCOUNTING ENVIRONMENT

We have taken a brief look in the preceding sections at the functions of a simple accounting system and the many different audiences it serves. In addition, we reviewed a real-world set of financial accounting reports and saw

---

[2] It should be noted that a new auditor's report format is required for all statements issued after January 1, 1989. The wording of the current report is modified and expanded, but the purpose of the report remains the same.

how they can be used to communicate information. These financial statements are the focal point of our discussion in subsequent chapters.

Out of these introductory discussions should emerge the realization that accounting is a critical activity in any organization. It provides an organized recording and presentation of information about available economic resources and their use. However, to further our understanding, we need to be aware of several related elements that shape the totality of what we call "financial accounting."

## Audience Characteristics

In general, the audience for financial accounting reports consists of external users, in particular stockholders and creditors. Financial reporting assumes that this external audience cannot dictate the form of presentation or the content of the financial statements. Investors are dependent upon management to prepare reports for them and are not in a position to demand specific information or to check on its reliability.

In addition, three other characteristics of the investor audience are usually presumed:

1. *Technical competence*—statement users are presumed to be familiar with business activities and to understand accounting language and information.
2. *Comparative analyses*—statement users wish to compare one business entity with another and/or the results over successive periods of time for a single entity.
3. *Interpretive preference*—statement users prefer to complete their own interpretations of the financial information. Consequently, financial statements should present primarily factual information that is clearly distinguished from information resulting from management's interpretations, assumptions, and projections.

## Financial Reporting Objectives

The overall purpose of financial accounting is to provide useful and understandable information to its investor audience. The most recent authoritative statement about the objectives of general-purpose financial reporting lists the following three specific aims:[3]

1. To provide information that is useful to present and prospective investors, creditors, and other users in making rational investment and credit decisions.

---

[3] Financial Accounting Standards Board (FASB), *Statement of Financial Accounting Concepts No. 1,* "Objectives of Financial Reporting by Business Enterprises" (Stamford, Conn., November 1978), par. 32–53.

2. To furnish information to aid users in assessing the amounts, timing, and uncertainty of prospective cash receipts associated with investments in the enterprise.
3. To report information about the economic resources of an enterprise, the claims to those resources, and the effects of transactions and events that change those resources and any claims to them.

The first objective recognizes that financial information is essential in determining a firm's attractiveness for investment or extension of credit. Investors must be able to evaluate a firm's earnings and financial strength to rationally allocate their financial capital.

The second objective asserts that critical to these decisions is information concerning prospective cash receipts from dividends, interest, and from the proceeds associated with the sale or maturing of securities and loans. Financial accounting should supply information to allow users to predict and assess cash flows to the enterprise.

The third objective is divided into four subobjectives detailing specific information to be reported:

a. Information about a firm's economic resources, obligations, and the difference between them (which accountants call "owners' equity").
b. Information about a firm's financial performance during a period as measured by earnings.
c. Information about how a firm obtains and uses cash, how it borrows and repays, and how other factors may affect its liquidity and solvency.
d. Information about how the management of the firm has discharged its *stewardship* responsibility.

Financial accounting has three statements that respond to subobjectives (a), (b), and (c). The balance sheet displays the data required in (a). The income statement responds to (b), and the statement of cash flows presents the required data in (c). Review the information on the Kimberly-Clark statements to see how they attempt to fulfill these objectives.

Subobjective (d) arises because control over resources often rests with managers who act on behalf of the investors who furnished the resources. Those who control the resources are accountable to the investors. When appropriate reporting is made, the investors (owners) can appraise the effectiveness of management's administration of the resources.

## The Need for Accounting Principles

Financial statements, such as those you read from Kimberly-Clark, are completed in accordance with a set of basic concepts. The framework of concepts and conventions that guide the accounting process collectively are called "generally accepted accounting principles" (GAAP). They are man-made guides that determine what data are to be captured, when the data are to be recorded, how measurements are to be made, how procedures are to be applied, and how the information is to be shown on the financial statements.

Generally accepted accounting principles are widely accepted by accounting professionals, stock exchanges, the Securities and Exchange Commission, and other important users of the financial statements. All properly completed statements must comply with these principles.

Without some general standards that are consistently applied and understood, statement content, format, and meaning could vary drastically from one firm to another, from one time period to another, and from one management source to another. Accounting principles contribute to the users' understanding of financial information. Different firms use substantially uniform principles in reporting similar events, and the same firm normally does not vary its handling of similar transactions between time periods. This uniformity and consistency are absolutely essential for the comparative analyses so frequently undertaken by investors.

A careful explanation of these principles is given in Chapter 2. Throughout the rest of the chapters we will learn how to apply them in specific situations. We will quickly see that numerous alternatives are available to accountants, even within the general principles. Accountants do not record every transaction in precisely the same way under all circumstances, but all recordings do follow some basic principles.

## AUTHORITATIVE BODIES INFLUENCING ACCOUNTING THOUGHT

Generally accepted accounting principles (GAAP) have been formally identified and developed over many decades. These principles are a blend of theoretically developed procedures and practical considerations that attempt to meet the current financial reporting needs of business and society.

A number of organizations have played roles in the development of accounting principles. Currently, the two most influential bodies are the Securities and Exchange Commission (SEC) and the Financial Accounting Standards Board (FASB). These two organizations are considered to be authoritative bodies, and their pronouncements establish the principles applied in the execution of the financial accounting process.

### Securities and Exchange Commission (SEC)

The SEC is a governmental organization charged with implementing the directives specified in the securities laws of 1933 and 1934. Congress established this agency in an attempt to regulate the nation's securities markets and to ensure that investors have adequate information on which to base their decisions. The SEC's overseeing of reports applies to practically all of the large publicly traded corporations in the United States.

The regulations of the SEC contain specific reporting requirements. A major requirement is that companies must file *Form 10–K* at the end of each year. The 10–K must include a complete set of audited financial statements. In addition, other special forms and schedules are mandated periodically. The SEC has influenced accounting practices and reporting standards through its requirements found in *Regulation S–X, Financial Reporting Releases* (FRRs) since 1982, *Accounting Series Releases* (ASRs) before 1982, *Staff Accounting Bulletins* (SABs), and other enforcement documents. Through them the Commission has articulated standards for the full and fair reporting of information. The SEC places special emphasis on the fairness of the reporting displayed in the financial statements and their accompanying materials.

## Financial Accounting Standards Board (FASB)

The Financial Accounting Standards Board is a private-sector body formed to be the authoritative force in setting standards for financial accounting reports. The FASB operates independently from public accounting firms or corporations, but both groups recognize it as having the authority to set generally accepted accounting requirements and interpretations. The FASB is composed of seven members appointed by the Financial Accounting Foundation. Three are chosen from public accounting practice, and the other four are individuals who are knowledgeable in the areas of finance and accounting. They are commonly selected from industry, academia, and government.

The Financial Accounting Standards Board issues four types of accounting pronouncements:

**1.** *Statements of Financial Accounting Standards (SFAS)*—These authoritative statements spell out current generally accepted accounting principles. More than 100 of these standards have been issued.

**2.** *Statements of Financial Accounting Concepts (SFAC)*—These statements are used to present the conceptual framework of financial accounting as seen by the FASB. Although these statements provide a supporting explanation and rationale for the specification of accounting principles, they do not establish GAAP.

**3.** *Interpretations of Statements of Financial Accounting Standards*—These interpretations apply to outstanding statements and other authoritative pronouncements. These interpretations modify, clarify, and extend the meaning of outstanding pronouncements. They have the same authority as do formal Statements of Financial Accounting Standards.

**4.** *Technical Bulletins*—These bulletins provide the accounting community with guidance for applying statements and interpretations. GAAP is not established by these bulletins, but this documentation provided by the FASB staff enhances the implementation of GAAP.

Prior to the establishment of the FASB, generally accepted accounting principles were promulgated by the American Institute of Certified Public

Accountants (AICPA). This organization represents most of the professionally trained accountants responsible for issuing audit opinions on corporate financial statements. Each member of the Institute has met the educational and experiential requirements necessary to be designated a certified public accountant (CPA).

Between 1939 and 1960 the AICPA's Committee on Accounting Procedure issued over 50 Accounting Research Bulletins (ARBs) and Accounting Terminology Bulletins (ATBs). Then in 1960, the Institute created the Accounting Principles Board (APB) to issue authoritative pronouncements. Prior to its dissolution in 1973, it issued 4 statements and 31 opinions. The FASB, when it was created, recognized the ARBs and APBs still in effect as constituting generally accepted accounting principles.

The Financial Accounting Standards Board is structured to make its establishment of generally accepted accounting principles more independent, autonomous, and representative than was true previously. An essential ingredient of the FASB's method of operation is to seek extensive input from all interested parties before publishing a standard. Task forces study a problem; discussion memoranda are distributed; written comments are solicited; and public hearings are held before the issuance of a standard.

Both the AICPA and the SEC have taken formal action to increase the importance of the FASB standards. The AICPA in its *Rules of Conduct* has resolved that members generally may not opine that financial statements follow generally accepted accounting principles if, in fact, such statements vary from FASB standards. The SEC, in a similar vein, issued *Accounting Series Release No. 150,* which explicitly stated that standards and interpretations of the FASB constitute substantial authoritative support and that accounting principles contrary to FASB standards do not have such support.

## Overview of Influential Accounting Groups

In the future, generally accepted accounting principles officially will consist of *Statements of Financial Accounting Standards* issued by the FASB.[4] However, some pronouncements from earlier authorities remain in effect in their original or modified form. Current accounting practice must look, therefore, to a mixture of statements, opinions, and bulletins for its guidelines. References to many of these different authoritative pronouncements appear throughout our remaining chapters.

---

[4] Recently, the Government Accounting Standards Board (GASB) has been established to deal with the special accounting standards and problems related to the accounting process for governmental units. Through 1987 the Board has issued seven statements of standards, one concept statement, and a few technical bulletins. The problems addressed by this board are limited and will have relatively little impact on the areas of accounting we will consider.

**FIGURE 1–6**   Groups Involved in the Establishment of Accounting Principles

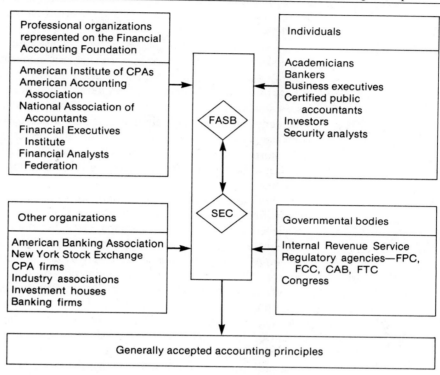

Figure 1–6 identifies various groups that influence the formulation of accounting principles and reporting standards. The SEC and FASB form the central source of authoritative pronouncements. As a rule, the former has focused on disclosure matters, and the latter has been concerned with measurement issues. However, many other groups and individuals contribute formally and informally to the deliberations. In addition, many of these groups publish research results and statements of their own which, over time, may have a subtle and continual impact on the development of accounting principles.

A detailed description of all these sources of influence is beyond our scope. Nevertheless, a few comments about some of the major professional organizations represented on the Financial Accounting Foundation may help explain the environment of financial accounting.

**1.** *American Institute of Certified Public Accountants*—This body was discussed earlier. Since authority to set standards has been transferred to the FASB, the AICPA provides extensive input through its Accounting Standards Executive Committee. It also has the major responsibility for developing *auditing* standards and overseeing the professional conduct of practicing CPAs. It publishes a monthly periodical called *The Journal of Accountancy* as well as numerous other studies and materials on accounting problems and practices.

**2.** *American Accounting Association*—This group represents primarily the views of accounting educators. Its quarterly publications, *The Accounting Review, Accounting Horizons,* and *Issues in Accounting Education,* are major outlets for writers of conceptual literature. In addition, the AAA periodically issues statements on the standards or concepts that *should* underlie financial statements and sponsors individual research projects by outstanding scholars. Both the periodic statements of standards and the research monographs tend to be normative declarations about the directions in which financial reporting should be moving and not necessarily a reflection of current accounting thought.

**3.** *National Association of Accountants*—This association represents primarily internal managerial accountants. However, in recent years it has broadened the scope of its research and educational programs to include problems of external reporting. Its monthly publication, called *Management Accounting*, is supplemented occasionally by research studies or monographs it sponsors. Its Committee on Management Accounting Practices expresses the official views of NAA on relevant accounting matters to other professional groups, including the FASB and SEC.

**4.** *The Financial Executives Institute*—Perhaps the most influential association on the management side, FEI is composed of the financial executives of large corporations. It has a direct interest in the external reporting principles imposed on businesses by the SEC and FASB. It contributes directly to discussions of accounting principles through statements from its Panel on Accounting Principles. *The Financial Executive*, its monthly publication, provides indirect input in the form of accounting literature. Also, its research arm, the *Financial Executives Research Foundation*, has sponsored several relevant and highly influential studies.

**5.** *Financial Analysts Federation*—The FAF represents a major group of users of accounting information. Composed of professional financial analysts, this organization has begun to exert influence on the development of accounting principles and reporting standards. Frequently in the past, analysts have been critical of corporate financial disclosure. The Financial Analysts Federation provides a collective voice for these criticisms. It also publishes the bimonthly *Financial Analysts Journal*.

## SUMMARY

This chapter introduces you to the basic elements in the accounting process and begins our exploration of the underlying concepts that shape financial accounting. We can summarize this chapter in these observations:

1. Accounting is a system designed to capture, process, and communicate financial information. Financial accounting is only one aspect, although a very important one, of the total discipline of accounting.
2. Financial accounting provides relevant, reliable, and timely information to an audience composed primarily of owners and creditors who are external to the management of an enterprise.
3. Financial accounting reports are comprised of three statements—a balance sheet, an income statement, and a statement of cash flows. We briefly examined all three statements for the Kimberly-Clark Corporation.
4. A balance sheet presents the status of a firm's resources, debts, and ownership. This statement permits analyses concerning the financial strength and solvency of a firm.
5. An income statement presents the performance of management in using the resources of a firm. This statement displays the new resources that have flowed into the firm, the resources used by the firm, and the net difference between the two resource flows from operating activities.
6. The cash flow statement presents the inflows and outflows of cash to a firm. It provides a bridge between the income statement and the balance sheet by relating the net income to the change in cash from operations, investing activities, and financing activities.
7. Financial statements are prepared in accordance with a set of concepts or principles called generally accepted accounting principles (GAAP). These principles promote uniformity in accounting procedures, reliability in the measurement of business transactions, and comparability among financial statements prepared by different firms and in different accounting periods.
8. Generally accepted accounting principles are currently set by the Financial Accounting Standards Board and the Securities and Exchange Commission. However, the world of accounting is shaped by a number of other organizations. Each group makes a contribution to the development of accounting and its principles.

In subsequent chapters we will continually emphasize the conceptual framework of financial accounting. However, we will also study some accounting procedures to enhance our understanding of the accounting process and to develop and hone both our analytical skills and our ability to use accounting as a tool.

By developing a sound understanding of the basic concepts of accounting, we can see how this discipline adjusts to changes in the business environment, why accurate measurement of transactions is often difficult but critical, why financial reporting is both an artform and a science, and why theory is often difficult to apply. Your understanding of these elements of accounting will enhance your ability to analyze financial information and to apply reasoned judgment in your decision-making processes.

We invite you to enter with us into this extremely important, yet elusive, world of financial accounting.

# PROBLEMS AND CASETTES

### 1–1. Users and Financial Information

A variety of users has been identified as being concerned with the messages given by the statements of financial accounting.

**Required:**

a. Identify each of the users.
b. For each user group identified in (a), specify which financial statements or elements of financial information you think would be of most importance.
c. Explain why accountants do not prepare special reports for each user group. (Before answering, consider this question: Do generally accepted accounting principles apply to everyone?)

### 1–2. Comparing Areas of Accounting

In addition to financial accounting, Chapter 1 briefly describes managerial accounting and tax accounting.

**Required:**

a. Outline the distinctions among these three areas.
b. Does a firm need to have three separate accounting systems, one for each area?
c. Why are there seemingly no generally accepted accounting principles in managerial and tax accounting?

### 1–3. Professional Organizations and Accounting Principles

A number of professional organizations were identified as having an influence on the development of accounting and accounting principles. These organizations include:

American Institute of Certified Public Accountants
American Accounting Association
National Association of Accountants
Financial Executives Institute
Financial Analysts Federation
Internal Revenue Service

**Required:**

a. Describe the composition of membership in each organization.
b. Identify whether each organization is governmental, private, or educational.
c. "The Internal Revenue Service has little influence on the development of generally accepted accounting principles. This is related to the fact that the purposes of financial accounting and tax accounting are significantly different." Explain why this statement is correct.

### 1–4. Differing Financial Reports for Different Users

The accounting department of a privately owned corporation might be called upon to prepare accounting reports for (1) a bank loan officer, (2) an agent for the Internal

Revenue Service, (3) an investor in stock of the firm, and (4) an analyst of a large insurance company that makes long-term loans to the corporation.

**Required:**

*a.* Describe how the reports presented to each of these individuals might differ and how each of them might use the accounting reports.

*b.* What role does the certified public accountant (independent auditor) play in the provision of information to each of these persons?

**1–5. Applying Accounting Tasks**

The accounting process has been described as having six tasks: (1) identification, (2) measurement, (3) recording, (4) classification, (5) reporting, and (6) interpretation.

**Required:**

Assume that you have completed the following transactions. Indicate how each of the six tasks would be involved in your personal accounting for each of the following events:

1. Purchase of an automobile after securing a loan for the purchase.
2. Preparation of your tax return for the year.
3. Payment of tuition for the school year.
4. Purchase of a microcomputer.

**1–6. Using Accounting Information**

Figure 1–2 illustrates several of the specialties found in the accounting discipline. Explain how you believe each of the four accounting specialties (tax, financial, regulatory, and managerial) would use information from each of the following transactions. (Note that some transactions may be of little import to a particular specialty.)

1. Payment of cash dividends to stockholders.
2. Expenditure for a major microwave installation by the Southwestern Bell Telephone Company to provide more efficient telephone services to its customers.
3. Borrowing $2.3 million for construction of a major new production facility by the S. S. Shipyard Company to meet the requirements of a recently signed government contract.
4. Sale of $200 million of stock by the C-R Company under a new program to raise capital.

**1–7. Steps in the Accounting Process**

The accounting process tracks economic events. Figure 1–1 illustrates five major steps related to processing accounting data associated with economic events in business. The five steps are (1) data capture, (2) coding, (3) processing, (4) decoding, and (5) reporting. Take each of the following events and describe what you do with your personal accounting system (even though it is probably informal) to complete three of the five steps.

|  | *Data Capture* | *Processing* | *Reporting* |
|---|---|---|---|

a. Pay the monthly
   telephone bill.

b. Purchase a pair of
   shoes by writing a
   check.

c. Receive and deposit
   your paycheck.

d. Make your monthly
   automobile payment.

## 1–8.  Preparing Financial Statements

Prepare financial statements from the following data, which are in random order. Use the Kimberly-Clark statements in Figures 1–3 and 1–4 as models for your statements. These statements are for the EAS Corporation and present data for the years 1989 and 1990.

a. Balance Sheets for December 31, 1989 and 1990
   (in millions)

| | |
|---|---:|
| Cash and cash investments 1989 . . . . . . . . | $ 2,721 |
| Accounts receivable 1990 . . . . . . . . . . | 7,820 |
| Accounts payable 1989 . . . . . . . . . . . | 4,600 |
| Inventories 1989 . . . . . . . . . . . . | 3,534 |
| Other current assets 1990 . . . . . . . . . | 1,631 |
| Long-term debt 1989 . . . . . . . . . . . | 7,331 |
| Accounts receivable 1989 . . . . . . . . . . | 7,566 |
| Property, plant, and equipment 1990 . . . . . . | 21,078 |
| Debt maturing within one year 1990 . . . . . . | 740 |
| Cash and cash investments 1990 . . . . . . . | 2,602 |
| Other assets 1989 . . . . . . . . . . . | 2,503 |
| Accounts payable 1990 . . . . . . . . . . | 4,625 |
| Inventories 1990 . . . . . . . . . . . . | 3,519 |
| Property, plant, and equipment 1989 . . . . . . | 20,733 |
| Common shareholders' equity 1990 . . . . . . | 14,462 |
| Payroll liabilities 1990 . . . . . . . . . . | 2,499 |
| Debt maturing within one year 1989 . . . . . . | 774 |
| Payroll liabilities 1989 . . . . . . . . . . | 2,126 |
| Other current liabilities 1989 . . . . . . . . | 3,206 |
| Other assets 1990 . . . . . . . . . . . | 2,233 |
| Deferred income taxes 1989 . . . . . . . . | 4,568 |
| Deferred income taxes 1990 . . . . . . . . | 4,488 |
| Other current assets 1989 . . . . . . . . . | 1,547 |
| Long-term debt 1990 . . . . . . . . . . . | 7,309 |
| Other current liabilities 1990 . . . . . . . . | 3,353 |
| Other liabilities 1989 . . . . . . . . . . | 1,483 |
| Other liabilities 1990 . . . . . . . . . . | 1,407 |
| Common shareowners' equity 1989 . . . . . . | 14,516 |

*b.* Income statement for the year ending December 31, 1989 and 1990 (in millions)

| | |
|---|---:|
| Sales revenue 1989 . . . . . . . . . . . . . . . | $45,628 |
| Selling expenses 1990 . . . . . . . . . . . . . | 2,595 |
| Cost of goods sold 1989 . . . . . . . . . . . . | 37,252 |
| Selling expenses 1989 . . . . . . . . . . . . . | 4,282 |
| Sales revenue 1990 . . . . . . . . . . . . . . | 43,225 |
| General and administrative expenses 1989 . . . . | 2,418 |
| Cost of goods sold 1990 . . . . . . . . . . . | 38,100 |
| General and administrative expenses 1990 . . . . | 2,584 |

### 1–9. Accounting Terminology and Definitions

Terminology is a problem in learning accounting. Many of the terms used in daily conversation are the same terms used in accounting. The accounting use, however, generally has a very specific technical meaning that varies from our more informal usage.

A number of the terms used in accounting are shown below:

1. Cash
2. Marketable securities
3. Depreciation
4. Accounts payable
5. Deferred income taxes
6. Operating profit
7. Net income
8. Current liabilities
9. Long-term debt
10. Stockholders' equity

**Required:**

Take each of the following definitions and match it with one of the terms listed above. Write the number of the term on the line to the left of the matching definition. Consult the glossary at the end of the text if necessary.

_____ *a.* A systematic process for allocating the cost of long-term plant assets over their useful lives.

_____ *b.* The final measure of a firm's success, from all sources, for a specific period of time which reflects the excess of new assets acquired during the period over the amount of assets given up in earning the new assets.

_____ *c.* An adjustment arising when the income tax expense for financial reporting purposes differs from the income tax liability payable to the governmental taxing unit.

_____ *d.* A legally enforceable claim on a firm's resources, for settlement within one year, from the purchase of goods, services, and supplies in the normal course of business.

_____ *e.* Temporary investments in traded financial securities that have a ready market for purchase and sale.

_____ *f.* A firm's obligations that are not required or are not scheduled to be paid for more than one year.

_____ *g.* Currency, coins, checks, money orders, demand deposits, cashiers' checks, bank drafts, petty cash, change funds, and savings deposits.

_____ *h.* The residual claim on a firm's assets after satisfying the claims of debt-holders.

_____ *i.* A firm's obligations to be paid within one year.

_____ *j.* The measure of a firm's success, from regular recurring operations, for a specific period of time that reflects the excess of new assets acquired during the period over the amount of assets given up in earning the new assets.

**Casette 1–1.   Analysis and Meaning of the Balance Sheet**

The following statement is the consolidated balance sheet of the First of America Bank Corporation for the second quarter of 1987.

**Consolidated Balance Sheet**
**(in thousands)**

|  | June 30, 1987 | June 30, 1986 |
|---|---|---|
| **Assets** | | |
| Cash and due from banks | $ 492,580 | $ 316,898 |
| Federal funds sold and other short-term investments | 307,197 | 132,675 |
| Investment securities | 2,153,285 | 1,444,268 |
| Loans: | | |
| Consumer | 1,389,552 | 1,091,725 |
| Commercial | 1,706,628 | 1,077,001 |
| Real estate | 1,988,982 | 1,194,895 |
| Lease financing | 6,315 | 4,663 |
| Foreign | 42,739 | 46,049 |
| Total loans | 5,134,216 | 3,414,333 |
| Less: allowance for loan losses | 96,592 | 51,675 |
| Net loans | 5,037,624 | 3,362,658 |
| Premises and equipment | 131,530 | 88,376 |
| Other assets | 280,269 | 117,065 |
| Total assets | $8,402,485 | $5,461,940 |
| **Liabilities and Shareholders' Equity** | | |
| Deposits: | | |
| Non-interest bearing | $1,320,172 | $ 922,973 |
| Interest bearing | 6,020,362 | 3,906,213 |
| Total deposits | 7,340,534 | 4,829,186 |
| Short-term borrowings | 226,690 | 166,182 |
| Long-term debt | 116,939 | 44,136 |
| Other liabilities | 115,348 | 79,676 |
| Total liabilities | 7,799,511 | 5,119,180 |
| Redeemable preferred stock | 1,729 | 1,900 |
| Shareholders' equity | 601,245 | 340,860 |
| Total liabilities and shareholders' equity | $8,402,485 | $5,461,940 |

**Required:**

*a.* Use the above statement to answer the following questions.

1. Calculate the dollar value by which the bank has increased its *Total Assets* from 1986 to 1987.

2. Calculate the dollar value by which the bank has increased its asset titled *Premises and Equipment* from 1986 to 1987.
3. Calculate the dollar value by which the bank has increased its liability titled *Long-Term Debt* from 1986 to 1987.
4. Explain the significance to the bank of each increase computed in (1), (2), and (3).

b. When reading a financial statement, you can measure the dollar amount of increase or decrease in an account. Important as that computation may be, it is also important to see whether the account has changed as a percentage of the total assets or total liabilities of the company.
1. Compute the percentage which the *Premises and Equipment* account is of *Total Assets* in both 1986 and 1987.
2. Compute the percentage which the *Long-Term Debt* is of *Total Liabilities and Shareholders' Equity* in both 1986 and 1987.

c. The financial statement presented is for a bank. How would you explain the fact that *Deposits* are shown as a liability when a bank's customers (depositors) put the asset cash in the bank?

## Casette 1–2. Analysis and Meaning of the Income Statement

The following statement is the Consolidated Statement of Earnings of AT&T and Subsidiaries for the three months ended March 31, 1987 and 1986.

### Statement of Earnings
### (in millions)

| | Three Months Ended March 31 | |
| --- | --- | --- |
| | 1987 | 1986 |
| **Revenues:** | | |
| Sales of services | $4,593 | $4,691 |
| Sales of products | 2,486 | 2,718 |
| Rental revenues | 1,042 | 1,301 |
| Total revenues | 8,121 | 8,710 |
| **Costs and expenses:** | | |
| Cost of services | 2,154 | 2,224 |
| Cost of products | 1,443 | 1,772 |
| Cost of rentals | 469 | 510 |
| Selling, general and administrative expenses | 2,720 | 2,608 |
| Research and development expense | 553 | 560 |
| Total expenses | 7,339 | 7,674 |
| Operating income | 782 | 1,036 |
| Other income—net | 64 | 59 |
| Interest expense | 149 | 176 |
| Income before income taxes | 697 | 919 |
| Provision for income taxes | 252 | 390 |
| Income before effect of a change in depreciation method | 445 | 529 |
| Cumulative effect of a change in depreciation method | — | (175) |
| Net income | $ 445 | $ 354 |

**Required:**

*a.* Use the above statement to answer the following questions:

1. Calculate the dollar amount by which the *Total Revenues* have decreased from 1986 to 1987.
2. Calculate the dollar amount by which the *Total Costs and Expenses* have decreased from 1986 to 1987.
3. Calculate the dollar amount by which the *Net Income* has increased from 1986 to 1987.
4. Explain whether the item titled *Cumulative Effect of a Change in Depreciation Method* had a positive or negative effect in determining Net income in 1986.
5. Explain how Net income can increase from 1986 to 1987 when revenues and costs and expenses each decreased.

*b.* Why would AT&T disclose sales from services, products, and rentals separately and costs of services, products, and rentals separately? Explain.

*c.* This question refers to the *Research and Development Expense*. AT&T reduced its R&D expenses by $7 million from 1986 to 1987. However, you might wonder whether AT&T was expending the same relative amount of resources on R&D. Calculate the percentage of total revenues represented by R&D by dividing the R&D expense in each year by the total revenues in each year and explain whether AT&T was expending the same relative amount on R&D in each year.

# Chapter 2

# A Conceptual Framework for Financial Accounting

Financial reporting is both an art and a science. By and large, accounting has developed as a practical art with its history dominated by the design of procedures to solve particular reporting problems. The search for basic concepts often involves generalizations derived from a study of accounting practice. In other words, accounting is what accountants do.

However, the basic structure of accounting consists of more than simple generalizations concerning accounting practice. A body of conceptual knowledge also has evolved. Rising above the myriad of specific events, theorists have set forth some basic assumptions about business activities. From these assumptions, we attempt to develop logical conclusions about what accountants should do.

This process is called "model building" and is quite similar to that employed in mathematics and economics. Accounting models are not as abstract as those in other disciplines, however. Though a number of accounting models have been advanced, this chapter describes only the conceptual framework of the conventional model, the system of reasoning that underlies present financial reporting. It provides the theoretical basis on which subsequent chapters rest.

## THE NATURE OF FINANCIAL ACCOUNTING

We saw in Chapter 1 that accounting systems communicate economic information to many different users. One of accounting's most important audiences consists of owners, creditors, and other external parties. The subset of accounting that serves these groups is called "financial accounting" and is the focal point of this book. The general-purpose reports of financial accounting provide this diverse audience with information about the economic resources of a business—what they are, how they were used, and how they were financed.

## A Hierarchy of Reporting Objectives

Owners, creditors, and other members of the external audience are assumed to share a common goal. All are interested in the ability of the entity to generate cash flows that can be used to pay dividends, interest, repay loans, and expand the business. This concern leads to the hierarchy of reporting objectives mentioned in Chapter 1 and listed in Figure 2–1.

The general reporting objectives for the enterprise (C–1 and C–2) stress the predictive ability of cash flows and accountability for resources. We can tie the specific enterprise objectives (D–1, D–2, and D–3) to predictive ability by noting that the amount of cash to be generated in the future depends on the quantity of economic resources (D–1) and how they are used and financed. Changes in resources and obligations involve direct and indirect future cash inflows and outflows. In turn, these changes in resources and obligations are caused by operating (D–2) and financing (D–3) transactions and events.

---

**FIGURE 2–1**
**Hierarchy of Financial Reporting Objectives**

**A. General User**
  Objective:   To provide information that is useful in making rational investment and credit decisions.

**B. Specific User**
  Objective:   To furnish information to aid users in assessing the amounts, timing, and uncertainty of prospective cash receipts from dividends or interest and the proceeds from the sale, redemption, or maturity of securities and loans.

**C. General Enterprise**
  Objectives:  1. To provide information to help users to predict the amounts, timing, and uncertainty of future cash flows to and from the business enterprise.
    2. To provide information about how the management of the enterprise has discharged its stewardship responsibility.

**D. Specific Enterprise**
  Objectives:  1. To report information about an enterprise's economic resources, obligations, and the difference between them (owners' equity).
    2. To report information about an enterprise's financial performance during a period as measured by earnings and its components.
    3. To report information about how an enterprise obtains and uses cash, about its borrowings and repayments, and about other factors that may affect its liquidity.

---

Accountability or stewardship becomes important when, as we noted in Chapter 1, owners and creditors do not actively manage the companies in which they have invested. Professional managers act as *agents* for the owners or *principals*. Frequently, principals cannot directly observe the actions of the agents. Principals need assurance that the necessary effort is being exerted to manage the enterprise in accordance with their objectives.

Financial accounting plays an important role in this principal-agent (owner-manager) relationship. The accounting reports become a way for owners to monitor the stewardship of the managers. Through accounting reports, owners can evaluate whether resources have been used effectively and efficiently to accomplish their objectives. In addition, financial accounting measures are often incorporated in the contracts drawn up between principals and agents. The contracts provide incentives for managers to conduct the activities of the enterprise in accordance with the wishes of the principals. These accounting measures then serve as benchmarks to determine whether management has met the terms of the contract and is thus entitled to incentive pay in the form of bonuses, profit sharing, or stock options.

## Financial Accounting Information

What accounting information and reports do users need to satisfy their objectives of predictive ability and accountability? Objectives D–1, D–2, and D–3 suggest that information about economic resources and obligations, resource usage to generate earnings, and the provision and use of cash are the most important.

It is not surprising, therefore, that the reporting function in financial accounting is centered on three primary financial statements. One statement is directed to each of these informational objectives.

The *balance sheet,* or statement of financial position, presents the financial condition of the entity as of a moment in time. It is akin to a photographer's snapshot. It portrays, in monetary terms as of a particular date, the economic resources controlled by the business and the sources of those resources as reflected in various claims and ownership interests.

In the time intervals between the issuance of statements of financial position, two major types of transactions occur that are of key interest to stockholders and creditors. One type involves the acquisition and financing of productive resources. We call these *financing-investing activities.* The other major type of transaction involves activities related to the production and sale of goods and services. We call these *operating activities.* Knowledge of both types of activities is important in assessing future cash flows associated with investments in the business enterprise.

The *income statement* summarizes the major changes in the resources of the business as a result of the operating (earning) activities. It attempts to report on the performance of the enterprise during a particular period of time.

The *statement of cash flows* discloses the major financing and investing transactions undertaken by the firm. Like the income statement, it covers a period of time. This statement shows the firm's sources of capital during the period and the major areas to which these financial resources were committed. In so doing, the statement discloses the causes of changes in cash during the period. Although it does not depict short-run operating performance as effectively as the income statement, the statement of cash flows helps its users understand the enterprise's operating performance and interpret earnings information. It also helps users evaluate the financing activities of an enterprise and assess its liquidity or solvency. For pedagogical reasons, we shall defer our detailed discussion of the statement of cash flows until Chapter 17.

In Chapter 1 we showed you the financial reporting package of Kimberly-Clark for the first quarter of 1987. Take a moment and look back to those pages. Notice that there are three major statements—the balance sheet, the statement of consolidated income, and the consolidated statement of cash flows. Observe also that the balance sheets are prepared as of specific dates—in this case on December 31, 1986 and March 31, 1987. On the other hand both the statements of flows—the income statement and the statement of cash flows—cover periods of time, the first quarters of 1986 and 1987.

Figure 2–2 shows diagramatically how these three statements are time-related for Kimberly-Clark's quarterly accounting period.

## Financial Accounting Principles

When we think about it though, how much do we really know about the amounts appearing on these statements? Consider the following questions:

1. Are the inventories on the balance sheet listed at a value for which they can be sold or at the price paid when they were purchased? Is the same valuation base used in all statements?
2. Are the resources comprising property, plant, and equipment valued at what we would have to pay for them now? What is "accumulated depreciation" and why is it subtracted on the balance sheet?
3. Does the long-term debt on the balance sheet represent the amount the company owes right now, the total amount that eventually will be paid back, or some other amount?
4. When are sales recognized on the income statement? Have these amounts actually been collected in cash? Do they include saleable goods that have been produced but not yet delivered to customers?
5. How does the company determine its deductions from sales (expenses)? Have all these items been paid in cash? Three directors retired at the end

**FIGURE 2–2**  Financial Accounting Statements

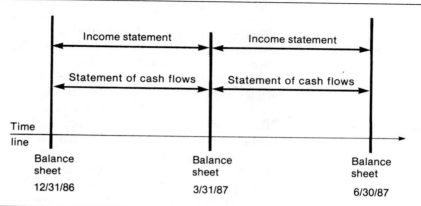

of 1986, yet we see no deduction for the loss of their services anywhere. Why?

6. Why do cash outflows for capital spending appear on the statement of cash flows and not on the income statement?

We could go on, but the point is made. The preparation and interpretation of financial accounting reports require a framework of concepts and conventions that structure the identifying, measuring, classifying, and reporting processes. With the rise of large corporations, in which absentee owners entrust operating control to professional managers, investors and creditors need what we called in Chapter 1, generally accepted accounting principles or GAAP.

GAAP is a practical attempt to reduce the misinterpretations, ambiguities, and potential biases that are inevitable when we try to capture all of the complexities of large business activities and organizations in a group of primarily quantitative reports. A framework of generally accepted accounting principles provides four general benefits.

**1.** It organizes existing ideas and practices so users can better understand them. As a result, the users' ability to analyze accounting reports as well as their confidence in them will increase.

**2.** It enhances the comparability of information among the statements of different companies. Seemingly similar items are less likely to be reported differently by different enterprises, and, if they are, users are more likely to detect the difference and be able to assess its impact.

**3.** It provides criteria for evaluating the internal consistency of accounting practice. When accounting practices are firmly rooted in a logical and coherent foundation, recommended procedures in one area are more likely to be consistent with the recommended treatments in other areas.

**4.** It supplies guidelines for resolving accounting problems as they emerge. New reporting problems, which seem to be arising with increasing frequency, can be handled more quickly and consistently.

We must remember, however, that accounting principles derive from human experience. They are not discovered; they are developed. They do not represent final precise answers; they are flexible and evolve as economic conditions and business practices change. Generally accepted accounting principles are not always based on strict logic; they are sometimes established by political compromise among conflicting parties or through the codification of practices considered "acceptable."

As noted in the last chapter, generally accepted accounting principles officially consist of *Statements of Financial Accounting Standards,* issued by the Financial Accounting Standards Board, and regulations of the Securities and Exchange Commission. However, GAAP existed long before the Board or the SEC was created. Some pronouncements from earlier authoritative bodies remain. In fact, some principles and procedures have been implicit in accounting practice for so long that it becomes difficult to compile a definitive list.[1]

## A FRAMEWORK FOR FINANCIAL ACCOUNTING PRINCIPLES

This section concerns the conceptual framework for the conventional financial accounting model. Figure 2–3 depicts the overall framework and the interrelationships of its major elements. Not all accountants or accounting organizations would agree entirely with this particular arrangement or identification of elements. Many of the ideas come from the series of *Statements of Financial Accounting Concepts* published by the Financial Accounting Standards Board. The rest reflect concepts appearing frequently in accounting literature and practice. Together they form an interrelated structure upon which we can build in subsequent chapters.

Before discussing the particular elements, let us take an overview of the entire framework in Figure 2–3. The financial accounting system seeks to record and report information about actual business transactions and economic events. In order to do so, some basic assumptions about the business environment and about the accounting process itself need to be established. From these assumptions follow some general principles and standards. These in turn lead to procedures and practices accountants use to describe real-world events as they construct financial reports.

---

[1] Two such attempts in the last 25 years were Paul Grady, *Accounting Research Study No. 7,* "Inventory of Generally Accepted Accounting Principles for Business Enterprises" (New York: AICPA, 1965); and AICPA, *APB Statement No. 4,* "Basic Concepts and Accounting Principles Underlying Financial Statements of Business Enterprises" (New York, October, 1970).

**FIGURE 2-3** A Framework for Financial Accounting Principles

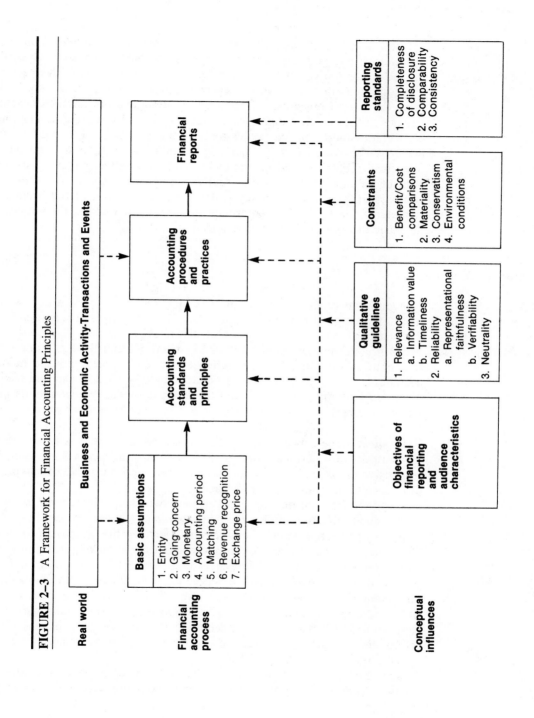

But this process of *selecting assumptions, deriving principles, applying procedures,* and *preparing reports* is not carried out in a vacuum. Overriding the whole process of financial accounting are a number of other factors and conditions that we have termed *conceptual influences* in Figure 2–3. First, the overall objectives of financial reporting and the assumed characteristics of the audience discussed earlier play a significant role in adopting particular assumptions and setting general standards. Second, two groups of normative characteristics also pervade the information process. One set—relevance, reliability, and neutrality—provide qualitative guidelines for all parts of the information process. Another set—completeness of disclosure, comparability, and consistency—affect the preparation of the financial statements. Lastly, certain environmental factors and conventions modify the basic theory or constrain its application.

## Qualitative Guidelines

Conventional financial accounting is characterized by certain normative ideas of what good reporting ought to be. These doctrines specify qualities that make reported information useful, desirable, or proper. *Relevance* and *reliability* are the paramount, although sometimes conflicting, guidelines that help accountants to judge when events should be recorded in the accounting system and what dollar values should be used to measure them. *Neutrality* attempts to assure that the choices made by accountants are guided by evenhandedness and economic facts, not by ulterior motives.

**Relevance.**    The concept of relevance is elusive because it is a subjective measure of informational content. Relevant information is that which is responsive to the audience's informational needs and is capable of making a difference to the user of the information.

To be relevant, information must possess two subqualities. First, it must have value to the user—either *predictive value* or *feedback value.* Information with predictive value improves the users' ability to make forecasts about the outcome of events of interest and is used in making decisions. Information with feedback value reduces users' uncertainty by confirming or altering their prior expectations. It is used for accountability—the evaluation and monitoring of management's stewardship.

The second subquality of relevance is *timeliness.* Timely information is reported before it ceases to affect decisions: "Timeliness alone cannot make information relevant, but a lack of timeliness can rob information of relevance it might otherwise have had."[2]

Accountants have only begun to understand what the relevance guideline means. Apart from generalized notions about the perceived needs of

---

[2] FASB, *Statement of Financial Accounting Concepts No. 2,* "Qualitative Characteristics of Accounting Information" (Stamford, Conn., May 1980), par. 56.

investors and creditors, we know little about which specific information items and measurements are relevant to users' actual or hypothesized decision models. For example, in a warehouse a steel wholesaler has 10 tons of steel that cost $60 per ton three months ago. Because of a slowdown in the economy, similar steel can be acquired from the mills at $53 per ton. Deliveries from the warehouse to retail customers have been made recently at a selling price of $68 per ton. However, recent sales activity has been sluggish, and management is considering retail price cuts in hopes of promoting sales activity. What dollar value per ton—$60, $53, $68, or some other figure—should the accountant assign to this steel in reporting to investors and creditors? Which of these figures do you think is relevant to the audience? (We will explore the financial accounting answer on the next page.)

**Reliability.**   This guideline plays the most important role in conventional accounting. Reliable financial accounting information should be accurate and unbiased. Financial statements should be based on actual verifiable events and should faithfully represent what they purport to show. In this way, they will serve an audience that we assume desires to make its own interpretations and will offer protection to an audience that we assume cannot dictate the content of financial reports.

Two major conditions contribute to the existence of reliability:

**1.** *Representational faithfulness* implies a correspondence between accounting measures and the underlying economic events they represent. Bias occurs in financial reporting when measurement methods fail to capture the essence of underlying economic variables. In pursuing representational faithfulness, accountants try to stress economic substance over legal form.

A financial statement is analogous in many ways to a map. To have representational faithfulness, the map should portray accurately what it represents. A geopolitical map cannot represent topography well, but it can and should show countries clearly. Likewise, a topographical map may not show political boundaries, but the reader should be able to depend on it to delineate correctly the mountains and river valleys.

By way of further analogy, a portrait of a person's head painted by the famous artist Picasso might show a cube-shaped head with three eyes. Whatever its artistic merits, representational faithfulness would not be one of them *if* the purpose of the painting was to depict how a human head actually appears. Similarly, representational faithfulness guards against unreasonable biases being introduced in the financial statements through the personal interpretations of the preparer.

**2.** *Verifiability* means that accounting information and measurement methods can be confirmed by other independent competent measurers. Bias can also occur in financial reporting as a result of unintentional error in an accountant's judgment. When accounting is done so that independent parties, upon examination of the same data, can reach the same conclusions or derive the same measurements, possible measurer-bias is significantly reduced. The desire for verifiability (objectivity) is one reason why accountants place great importance on transactions between independent parties, rather than relying on management's plans, expectations, or dreams of the future.

Reliability and relevance are relative concepts that are utilized in specific situations in varying degrees. Both are desirable, and more of either adds to the usefulness of accounting information. However, the accounting profession has not established how they interact or how trade-offs between them are to be made. Relevance in accounting practice more often than not takes a back seat to reliability.

As we shall see, conventional financial accounting resolves the valuation problem in our previous example of steel inventory in favor of the $60 purchase cost on the grounds of reliability and an assumption that historical cost is relevant to the investor's needs. But, because $53 and $68 more nearly reflect current values, a case can be made that they are more relevant, albeit less reliable, than the cost of $60. Perhaps the most relevant measure would be a *forecast* of what the steel will be sold for. Yet, this number would be the least reliable. Forecasts generally are not directly reported on financial statements because of their perceived lack of reliability, despite their obvious relevance for predictive purposes.

**Neutrality.** This qualitative characteristic pervades all aspects of the accounting process. "Neutrality means that either in formulating or implementing standards, the primary concern should be the relevance and reliability of the information that results, not the effect that the new rule may have on a particular interest."[3] Accounting policies should be chosen without any specific purpose other than to measure economic variables accurately. When judgments are needed to make the statements useful, those judgments should be free from any purposeful bias favoring any particular group. Financial statements should present information fairly and impartially.

Neutrality does not mean that financial statements have no purpose or that various parties may not be affected differently by their disclosures. Rather, no attempt should be made in the measuring-reporting process to influence a party's behavior in a particular direction. A road map designed to encourage people to travel on a tollroad by omitting alternative routes would not be neutral. Similarly, the choice of an accounting method solely because it would discourage (or encourage) companies from merging would not be appropriate under this standard. Neutrality attempts to minimize intentional bias in financial reporting.

## Reporting Standards

Because financial accounting serves as a communication medium, reporting considerations are intertwined with qualitative guidelines. To the extent that

---

[3] Ibid., par. 98.

reporting is a logical adjunct to the accounting process, the reporting standards are an extension of the qualitative guidelines. Three such reporting guidelines are *completeness of disclosure, comparability,* and *consistency.*

**Completeness of Disclosure.**   Completeness means that financial statements should present information thoroughly and understandably to users of the reports. A highway map that shows all roads but omits a number of thruway interchanges lacks completeness. One without scales or legends suffers similarly.

In financial accounting the term *full and fair disclosure,* which arose from the securities laws of 1933 and 1934 creating the SEC, is often used to describe this characteristic. *Full disclosure* requires that all material accounting data that might be significant to a reasonably intelligent user be disclosed. There should be no *unnecessary* summarization. Moreover, narrative explanations (notes) should supplement the quantitative information. Included would be the identification of accounting policies followed, changes in accounting procedures from one period to the next, and other supplementary data about assumptions and estimates necessary for a reader's accurate interpretation of the statements. *Fair disclosure* requires that the information given be clearly presented. Reasonable condensation is desirable; supporting schedules should be amply used. Moreover, statement titles and other terminology should be understandable.

**Comparability.**   The desire to conduct comparative analyses among firms and between accounting periods is assumed to be one of the major characteristics of the audience of financial accounting. Comparability calls for like events to be reported in the same manner and unlike events to be reported differently. Some of the obvious reporting conventions that promote comparability are uniform measurement practices; relatively standardized formats for financial statements; uniform definitions, terminology, and classifications; and reporting periods of identical length and frequency. Comparability also requires that changes in accounting principles be restricted to situations in which the new principle is *clearly preferable* to the old. When a change has been made, its nature, effect, and justification should be explained.

The application of the comparability standard sometimes becomes controversial when comparisons across firms are made. Some uniformity in accounting practices among firms is necessary. Only then will reported differences in the financial statements reflect variances in the economic circumstances of the firms. Comparative analyses may be frustrated if different accounting methods are applied to like events. On the other hand, an overly mechanistic quest for uniformity almost certainly would result in masking underlying economic differences, causing unlike items to be measured and reported as though they possessed the same characteristics.

**Consistency.**   An essential ingredient of comparability is consistency. Measurement methods and reporting procedures should be consistently applied from one report to another. The choices and judgments the accountant makes regarding alternative practices should be the same from period to period for the same enterprise. Otherwise, users will not be able to analyze trends or to discern changing relationships over time. Consistency does not bar accountants from changing to more accurate or correct procedures. However, if no change has been reported, the reader should feel secure that the same concepts and procedures underlie each period's statements. Consistency in accounting does bar indiscriminate switching from practice to practice.

## Basic Assumptions

Seven fundamental assumptions can be identified in financial accounting. Four of them—the entity concept, the going-concern concept, the monetary concept, and the accounting period concept—are *environmental* in nature. They postulate some fairly obvious, yet simplifying conditions for business activity. The other three assumptions—matching concept, revenue-recognition concept, and exchange-price concept—concern *operational* processes. They establish the proper way for accountants to carry out the major tasks of financial reporting. You can readily identify the influence of financial reporting objectives and qualitative guidelines on the selection of these assumptions.

**Entity Concept.**  This assumption states that *accounting reports and records pertain to a specifically defined business entity, separate and distinct from the people or groups concerned with it*. The accounting entity can be any identifiable organizational unit with control over resources and with economic activities of interest to someone. It is not necessarily synonymous with any specific legal or taxable organization. For example, accounting records are maintained for a one-owner business (single proprietorship), which is not recognized as a separate entity for the levying of taxes or for most legal purposes. In this situation the entity concept would direct that the accounting records reflect only the activities of the business and not the personal affairs of the owners.

Large modern corporations are recognized by legal and tax authorities as separate organizations. In this case the accounting entity and the legal entity are the same. Because of its importance, the private, profit-directed corporation is the major entity discussed in the remainder of this book. The entity concept limits our focus to accounting only for events that affect the corporation. Gains and losses of the corporation must be distinguished from gains and losses of the individual stockholders.

In Chapter 15 we will modify the single-corporation definition of the entity and look at a *consolidated entity,* a group of interrelated corporations under a single control. That discussion also explores some of the difficulties in selecting an appropriate entity.

**Going-Concern Concept.**   This assumption describes the accounting entity more fully. Under the going-concern, or *continuity* concept, *in the absence of evidence to the contrary, the entity is assumed to remain in operation sufficiently long to carry out its objectives and plans*. Thus, the accountant does not focus on liquidation values, but rather on values related to the continued operation of the firm.

Partially manufactured inventory is viewed as an economic resource because we assume it will be completed and sold in future periods. The cost of a building is allocated over its useful life because we assume the entity will be in existence at least that long. Economic resources and obligations are often classified as current and long-term. Without the going-concern assumption, everything would be current!

Of course, we are describing only an assumption, not reality for all businesses. If evidence exists that an entity will cease operations in the foreseeable future, then a different assumption should be selected and different accounting procedures developed. For instance, special accounting procedures are used for concerns in liquidation or bankruptcy. Financial accounting, however, is interested in those firms that are expected to remain in operation.

**Monetary Concept.**   This assumption contains two basic ideas about the unit of measurement used in accounting. The first states that *money, as the common denominator for the expression of economic activity, should be used to measure accounting events and transactions*. No other means of expression is so universal, simple, and adaptable. Excluded from financial accounting, however, are events that are not monetarily quantifiable—for example, a heart attack suffered by the company president, a labor dispute among the production employees, or the hiring of a charismatic sales manager. They may be of great importance but are not communicated through the accounting system.

The second part of this assumption states that *fluctuations in the value of the dollar can be ignored without significant impairment of the usefulness of the financial statements*. The size of the monetary unit, as measured by its purchasing power value, declines whenever the quantity of goods and services that people will exchange for it decreases significantly over time. We call this "inflation." The monetary concept assumes that any distortions caused by inflationary price-level changes will not undermine the reliability of the financial statements. Although soundly criticized as invalid during the last 50 years, this assumption remains an integral though contentious cornerstone of conventional accounting theory.

**Concept of the Accounting Period.**   To communicate, financial accounting must operate in a time framework. The complexity of modern business requires interim measures of economic progress. Users of financial reports rely on timely data and cannot wait until the entity's demise to ascertain net income. The *periodicity concept assumes that economic activity can be meaningfully divided into arbitrary time periods.*

Considering the continuous nature of enterprise activity, the time periods selected are to some extent artificial. Periodic reports can serve only as indicators of the stream of an entity's economic activity. Measurements of operating results for any short period of time are tentative. They involve estimates and approximations, but accountants make them to supply needed information for making current decisions.

In the employment of this concept, accountants must achieve a balance between reliability and timeliness. The accounting period must be long enough to provide reasonably accurate results yet short enough to supply currently usable information. For reporting to investors, accountants use quarterly and yearly accounting periods. Usually the time periods, which are identified in the accounting reports, are of equal length in order to facilitate comparisons.

**Matching Concept.** The general nature of business affairs can be described as an acquisition-consumption-recovery cycle. Stripped of embellishments, the conduct of any business enterprise involves acquiring economic resources in order to use them to produce a product or a service, which is then sold. A resource inflow, usually in the form of cash or claims to cash, results from the sale. Measuring accounting income involves matching against the total resource inflow (*revenues*) received from the period's operations the cost of resources (*expenses*) that were consumed in the production of the inflow.

The central operational assumption of financial accounting is that *net income is best measured by a matching of costs against the revenues to which the costs have given rise.* In this way, we are associating the resources used up in operations with the resources received from operations. Costs are divided into two groups—those applicable to the production of revenues in the current period (expenses) and those applicable to the production of revenues in future periods (assets). Costs, in theory, should be allocated between the present and the future wholly on the basis of when they contribute to the process of revenue generation.

In practice, uncertainties and difficulties in assigning costs cause departures from this theory. Nevertheless, the general concept is that a cost becomes an expense when the resource (asset) is consumed in the production of revenues. In a broad sense, revenues provide a monetary measure of the *accomplishment* of a firm in satisfying the wants and desires of consumers. Likewise, expenses can be viewed as a monetary expression of *effort,* in the sense of resources used, in satisfying consumer desires. By coupling the two flows of revenue and expense, we relate effort and accomplishment to obtain a meaningful measure of performance (net income).

This matching concept is, of course, only one possible assumption. There are other approaches to income measurement. For example, the business could be valued at the end of selected periods of time, and net income could be defined as the increase or decrease in value. Alternatively, we could employ some subjective approach to determine the present value of expected future net cash receipts.

The matching assumption is selected, however, because it incorporates greater reliability and historical perspective than do other alternatives. Although not completely free from judgmental factors, the basic information used in the matching concept—revenues and expenses—is rooted in actual market transactions and events. Its usefulness may be limited to the extent that the matching concept ignores changes in value or future expectations. Nevertheless, financial accounting currently accepts this fundamental assumption.

**Revenue-Recognition Concept.** If we are to match costs (expenses) against the revenues they generate, we need to know when to recognize the revenues themselves. Two tests are part of this concept. *Revenue should be recognized only when it has been earned and can be measured with a reasonable degree of reliability.* Revenues are effectively earned when substantially all of the activities associated with their production have been completed. In addition, the revenues must be measurable. Revenues are not always recognized as they are economically earned because of lack of reliable measurement. Instead, the accountant waits for some verifiable evidence, such as a legal sale plus the acquisition of some well-defined asset. With few exceptions, the accountant finds this evidence when transactions with outside customers are completed. In most cases, the point of sale has become the most generally accepted event for revenue recognition. Usually, both criteria are met there. We explore some ramifications of the revenue recognition concept in greater depth in Chapter 7.

**Exchange-Price Concept.** This operational assumption establishes the valuation measures to be applied as data enter the accounting process. *The resources (assets) held by a firm and the claims against those resources (liabilities) are to be recorded at the prices (values) agreed upon or inherent in the exchanges in which they originated.* Assume that a business acquired a new piece of equipment, paying $60,000 for it. To the firm, the equipment possesses greater value than $60,000 over its life; otherwise, it would not have been acquired. Once purchased and installed, it might be worth very little if the firm tried to sell it to someone else. The exchange-price concept dictates that the equipment be recorded at $60,000, its historical cost. One can see that the qualitative guideline of verifiability strongly influences the selection of this particular measurement standard. This standard also draws support from the going-concern concept.

Similar exchange-price valuations are applied to other types of accounting data. In addition, the measurement concept is extended to include transfers and exchanges not involving money prices, as in barter transactions or those between the firm and its owners. In such cases the initial valuation measure is called "fair market value" and is defined as the value that would have prevailed in a bona fide exchange.

## Constraints

Accounting practice sometimes handles items differently from the standards and principles and their underlying assumptions. Often these differences result from constraints present in the real world. This section discusses four practical influences that modify the application of the conceptual framework of financial accounting.

**Benefit/Cost Comparisons.**    Accounting information costs money to gather, process, and report. This information should be collected and disclosed only if the benefits of its use are greater than the cost of generating it. All information must attain some minimum level of relevance and reliability to be useful. However, often marginal increases in relevance or reliability can be attained only at great cost. For example, measuring current values of economic resources instead of their historic exchange prices could improve decision making. However, the cost of measurement might exceed the gains. The benefit/cost convention places a constraint of practicality on accounting measurements.

To be sure, the benefits and costs of disclosing information are difficult to quantify. Usually accountants make no explicit calculation. Rather, the constraint is considered subjectively by individual business enterprises and by the Financial Accounting Standards Board. Business entities weigh this consideration in deciding how detailed their accounting systems should be and how much information should be reported voluntarily to outside parties. The FASB should be cognizant of the benefit/cost constraint each time it mandates a change in reporting requirements. Applications of benefit/cost comparisons are particularly difficult in external reporting because the groups that benefit are different from the groups that incur the costs of reporting.

**Materiality.**    This convention both influences the manner of recording items and sets a guideline for reporting. Materiality refers to the relative importance or magnitude of a piece of accounting information. Any amount or transaction that has a significant (material) effect on the financial statements should be recorded correctly and reported. However, transactions of trivial amounts can be recorded in the most expedient way. In addition, minor items (immaterial ones) do not need to be reported in detail. For example, notice that all amounts reported in the financial statements of Kimberly-Clark in Chapter 1 are expressed in millions of dollars. The dollars and cents that may be material to us personally are not material to an interpretation of Kimberly-Clark.

Materiality serves as a threshold for the recognition of information. In the FASB's definition, an item is material if "in the light of surrounding circumstances, the magnitude of the item is such that it is probable that the judgment of a reasonable person relying upon the report would have been changed or influenced by the inclusion or correction of the item."[4] Even with this definition, decisions on what is material or immaterial vary from situation to situation and often require careful judgment based on extensive experience. An item may be material by amount or by its very nature. Bribes, for example, usually are immaterial in amount. Yet, most accountants believe they should be disclosed.

**Conservatism.**   This time-honored tradition grows out of the uncertain environment and the tentative measurements of accounting. Historically, it has been viewed, and sometimes applied, as a rule requiring understatement of income and assets. In modern financial accounting, it calls for due caution and a careful assessment of risks and uncertainties. The old adage, "Don't count your chickens before they hatch," is in keeping with the spirit of conservatism in financial reporting. When a measurement requires judgment, accountants tend to select those procedures that result in smaller amounts of resources or income. Accountants feel that the possible consequences of overstating these items (bankruptcy, loan defaults, subsequent stock market declines, lawsuits, etc.) are more severe than those associated with an understatement.

**Environmental Conditions.**   The legal environment of business includes certain precedents and procedures. In addition, practically all firms are regulated to some degree by governmental bodies. These legal and governmental influences affect the accounting procedures used in business. In the extreme situation, accounting procedures may be dictated by governmental bodies, as in the case of railroads and public utilities.

Income tax regulations are another of the environmental factors that currently play an exceedingly important role in accounting practice. Tax rulings are designed to achieve a multiplicity of political and economic purposes. Financial accounting procedures, on the other hand, attempt to achieve the proper matching of costs and revenues to measure business income. Where the two sets of concepts are not the same, the business entity faces a dilemma. Either separate records must be maintained for tax accounting and for financial accounting, with the attendant inconvenience and expense, or procedures designed to implement particular goals of taxation end up being used in the measurement of periodic business income.

One additional environmental factor should be mentioned. In some industries, particular accounting practices have evolved over the years. Most firms

---

[4] Ibid., par. 132.

in those industries conform to them, even though these historical practices may seem to depart from sound accounting concepts. For example, inventories of meat packing companies are frequently reported at selling prices, not at cost. Banks and utility companies use different classifications and orderings of items on their balance sheets than do most other companies. Eventually, many of these practices become part of GAAP, at least for those industries.

## ROLE OF THE AUDITOR

Financial accounting reports are prepared by management and presented to groups who are not directly connected with an entity's operations. At the same time, management is being judged through the reports it presents. Inherent in this situation is a potential conflict of interest, not unlike allowing a baseball pitcher to call his or her own balls and strikes. An independent attestation helps resolve this potential conflict.

The function of verifying and appraising the accuracy, integrity, and authenticity of the financial statements is called *auditing*. Auditing is a major present-day accounting activity. Certified public accountants are licensed by each state and charged with the responsibility of passing independent professional judgment on financial statements. An auditor's report accompanies the financial statements for most companies and not-for-profit organizations.

The financial statements are presentations by management; therefore, management bears the primary responsibility for their accuracy and fairness. The auditor, however, provides advice and guidance to management in matters of financial reporting and serves as an independent check on management's presentations. The auditor's report adds significantly to the credibility and, hence, usefulness of the financial information by affirming that the statements are a fair representation and have been prepared in accordance with GAAP. The standards and procedures auditors use in making these judgments form the subject matter of separate accounting courses and books in auditing.

### Unqualified Opinion

Most financial statements are accompanied by an auditor's report similar to that presented in Chapter 1 for Kimberly-Clark. Effective in 1989, the standard report form or so-called clean opinion was modified by the Auditing Standards Board of the AICPA. The new report appears in Figure 2–4.

In the introductory paragraph, the auditor indicates which financial statements have been examined and differentiates its responsibility to express an opinion on them from management's responsibility to prepare them.

**FIGURE 2–4**
**The New Standard Independent Auditor's Report**

We have audited the accompanying balance sheet of X Company as of December 31, 19XX and the related statements of income, retained earnings and cash flows for the year then ended. These financial statements are the responsibility of the Company's management. Our responsibility is to express an opinion on these financial statements based on our audit.

We conducted our audit in accordance with generally accepted auditing standards. Those standards require that we plan and perform the audit to obtain reasonable assurance about whether the financial statements are free of material misstatement. An audit includes examining, on a test basis, evidence supporting the amounts and disclosures in the financial statements. An audit also includes assessing the accounting principles used and significant estimates made by management, as well as evaluating the overall financial statement presentation. We believe that our audit provides a reasonable basis for our opinion.

In our opinion, the financial statements referred to above *present fairly, in all material respects,* the financial position of X Company as of [at] December 31, 19XX, and the results of its operation and its cash flows for the year then ended *in conformity with generally accepted accounting principles.* [Italics added].

In the second paragraph, commonly called the *scope paragraph,* the auditor states that the examination of the statements and records was conducted in accordance with professional standards. Generally accepted *auditing* standards provide the criteria for the evaluation of the competency of the auditor's work. Notice that the auditor, not management, has determined the nature and extent of the audit work performed. On the basis of this work, the auditor expresses a professional opinion on the financial statements.

The third, or *opinion paragraph,* draws a conclusion of considerable importance to the external user. Italics have been supplied to highlight the key words in this conclusion. The auditor affirms that the statements represent what they purport to represent, undistorted by the value judgments of the persons preparing them. Notice that GAAP provides the guidelines for the evaluation of fairness. To reach this conclusion, auditors must satisfy themselves that:

1. The accounting principles selected and applied have general acceptance.
2. The accounting principles are appropriate in the circumstances.
3. The financial statements, including the related notes, are informative of matters that may affect their use, understanding, and interpretation.
4. The information presented in the financial statements is classified and summarized in a reasonable manner, that is, neither too detailed nor too condensed.

5. The financial statements reflect the underlying events and transactions in a manner that presents the information within a range of acceptable limits.[5]

Under certain conditions, the auditor adds a fourth explanatory paragraph calling the readers' attention to important aspects of the statements. These conditions include among others:

1. A change in the consistent application of an accounting principle (often called a "consistency exception").
2. A desire to emphasize a particular matter such as the existence of significant related party transactions or important events occurring after the balance sheet date.
3. The existence of material uncertainties affecting the financial statements.

The third condition might involve the recoverability of certain assets, the collection of a material receivable, the existence of major income tax litigation, or other significant legal proceedings. Also a group of factors will sometimes cause the auditor to question whether the firm can continue to operate as a going concern. This going-concern uncertainty must be disclosed in the fourth paragraph even though the financial statements as presented receive a clean opinion. For example, the financial statements prepared for the Wurlitzer Company for the year ended March 31, 1985 contained an additional explanatory paragraph:

> As discussed in Note 1, there are conditions which indicate that the ability of the Company to continue as a going concern may be dependent on its ability to generate sufficient cash flows to meet its obligations and sustain its operations. The financial statements do not include any adjustments relating to the recoverability and classification of recorded asset amounts or the amounts and classification of liabilities that might be necessary should the Company be unable to continue as a going concern.

## Qualified Opinions

If the CPA cannot attest to all of the above factors or if the scope of the audit has been limited for some reason, the auditor must issue a *qualified* opinion. A qualified opinion can be issued only if the auditor believes that *overall* the financial statements are fairly stated. However, they may reflect a departure from generally accepted accounting principles, inadequate disclosure in the judgment of the auditor, or the inability of the auditor to perform some specific audit procedure. In these cases, the scope and/or opinion paragraphs are appropriately qualified with the words "except for." Also, an additional paragraph is inserted explaining the exception in greater detail.

---

[5] AICPA, *Statement on Auditing Standards No. 5*, "The Meaning of 'Present Fairly in Conformity with Generally Accepted Accounting Principles' in the Independent Auditor's Report" (New York, July 1975), par. 4.

Unqualified and qualified opinions are merely two of four different types of opinions that can be expressed by auditors, although they are the predominant types given. Based on the particular situation and its materiality, the auditor may feel it is more appropriate to issue either a *disclaimer of opinion* or an *adverse opinion*. In a disclaimer, the auditor declines to express any opinion at all, often because of serious audit scope limitations. An adverse opinion is expressed when the auditor believes that the financial statements in material respects, are *not* presented fairly in accordance with GAAP. The latter two opinions are rarely seen. Situations that would lead to either of these opinions are usually resolved by the client company changing its practices or the audit firm resigning the engagement.

Two important items should be noted. First, an unqualified opinion does not mean that the company is a good investment. A firm with losses or headed by an incompetent management team could still receive a "clean" opinion if its financial statements were fairly presented in accordance with GAAP. Second, remember that the auditor's report is a professional judgment, not a precise certification or an infallible prediction. Sometimes, although not often, the auditor's judgment is wrong. When the error results from incompetent audit work, we call it an "audit failure." You may occasionally read about lawsuits against auditors in the financial press for alleged audit failures.

Sometimes, however, the auditor is unable to predict the outcome of many uncertainties. Consider the following examples. In 1980 the auditor for Chrysler Corporation stated that they were unable to express an opinion (disclaimer) because of serious doubts about the company being a going concern. In 1981 those doubts continued; however, Chrysler received a qualified opinion regarding its going-concern status. Yet, we all know the recovery Chrysler has made since then. On the other hand, Penn Square Bank in Oklahoma City failed on July 5, 1982 in what amounted to one of the most costly failures in U.S. history. From 1976 to 1979, they received unqualified opinions. In 1980, the auditor issued a qualified opinion. Penn Square changed auditors and received an unqualified opinion on its 1981 statements. The auditor's report was dated March 19, 1982, less than four months before the bank had its doors locked by the bank examiners.

## SUMMARY

The purpose of this chapter has been to explore the conceptual setting of financial accounting. You may not fully appreciate this chapter until later in your study of accounting. You undoubtedly will want to refer back to it as we move along. We strongly encourage you to do so.

Among the general observations in this chapter are the following:

1. The inputs to the accounting process consist of a myriad of business transactions and economic events. Financial accounting has the task of presenting this information in reports that are useful in making rational

investment and credit decisions, in assessing the nature of the prospective cash receipts associated with the enterprise, in evaluating the earnings potential and financial strength of the firm, and in judging the effectiveness of management's administration of the resources of the firm.

2. The outputs of the accounting process are three financial reports or statements—a balance sheet, which provides information concerning the existing resource base of the enterprise and how the resources were financed; an income statement, which presents information about the historical results of the profit-directed activities of the enterprise; and a statement of cash flows, which relates information about liquidity and about financing-investing activities.

3. Generally accepted accounting principles and procedures rest on a network of seven underlying concepts or assumptions. Four of these concepts —entity, going concern, monetary, and accounting period—describe the business and reporting environment. The other three concepts—matching, revenue recognition, and exchange price—simply describe how accounting processes are to be completed. These assumptions rest more on their practical usefulness than on any "inherent truth."

4. The network of assumptions and the principles and procedures derived from them are interlaced with three qualitative guidelines—relevance, reliability, and neutrality—and three reporting guidelines—completeness of disclosure, comparability, and consistency. Together they exert a significant regulating influence on the totality we call accounting.

5. As a practical art, financial accounting also contains many practical conventions and environmental constraints. The need for cost/benefit comparisons, materiality, and conservatism are prominent ones.

6. Most financial reports are accompanied by an auditor's report. Auditors (CPAs) are highly educated and trained professionals who attest that the statements have been prepared in accordance with generally accepted accounting principles. In general, the auditing profession plays the role of watchdog over the reporting of financial accounting information.

## PROBLEMS AND CASETTES

### 2–1. Implications of the Reporting Period
The following quotation is attributed to one of the leaders in the development of accounting in the first half of this century: "The allocation of income to periods of time would be indefensible if it were not indispensable."

**Required:**

a. Explain the use of the term *indefensible* in relation to reliability and to the going-concern concept.

b. Explain the use of the term *indispensable* in relation to relevance and to the accounting period concept.

c. What are the advantages and disadvantages of long and short reporting periods?

## 2–2. Reporting Standards

Elan Investment Services, Inc. is a registered broker-dealer and issues a statement of financial condition (balance sheet) annually, as required by the Securities and Exchange Act of 1934. The December 31, 1986 Statement of Financial Condition showed the following two assets:

Cash . . . . . . . . . . . . . . . . . . . . . . . . . . . . . . . . . $ 63,387
Cash segregated under Federal and other regulations (note 2) . . . . .   185,771

Note 2 to the Statement of Financial Condition read:

2. Cash Segregated Under Federal and Other Regulations

Cash, which has been segregated in a special reserve bank account for the benefit of customers under Rule 15c3–3 of the Securities and Exchange Commission, was $185,771 at December 31, 1986.

### Required:

*a.* Which qualitative guidelines, constraints, and/or reporting standards are being met by Elan's reporting of their cash accounts and the accompanying note? Explain.

*b.* Is the SEC setting a generally accepted accounting principle when it requires segregation in a "special reserve bank account"? In answering this question, explain the difference between a principle and a procedure.

## 2–3. Manipulating Accounting Principles

The Tax Reform Act of 1986 included a number of tax code changes that affected both businesses and individuals. For individuals, one of the major changes was the lowering of tax rates effective for the tax year 1987.

Most individuals are "cash basis" taxpayers and recognize income (revenue) when they receive it in cash and recognize expenses when they pay them in cash. When the tax reform act was passed in 1986, most tax advisors recommended that individuals "delay receiving revenue, where possible, until next year" and "pay ahead on deductible expenses in the current year."

### Required:

*a.* Explain how the application of either or both of these procedures would lower a person's tax liability.

*b.* Which financial accounting principle(s) would be violated by the advisors' advice?

*c.* Explain why implementing the advice would not be a violation of accounting principles for tax purposes but would be a violation of accounting principles for financial accounting purposes.

## 2–4. Accounting Principle Advantages

Generally accepted accounting principles result from the interaction of reporting objectives, audience characteristics, qualitative guidelines, underlying assumptions, and practical constraints. What advantages and benefits are derived from having a broad set of reporting objectives and qualitative guidelines such as those issued by the Financial Accounting Standards Board?

## 2–5. Defining Generally Accepted Accounting Principles

The Accounting Principles Board (a forerunner of the FASB) in *Statement No. 4* indicated:

> *Generally accepted accounting principles* therefore is a technical term in financial accounting. Generally accepted accounting principles encompass the conventions, rules, and procedures necessary to define accepted accounting practice at a particular time. The standard of "generally accepted accounting principles" includes not only broad guidelines of general application, but also detailed practices and procedures.

### Required:

*a.* Explain why the APB considers *generally accepted accounting principles* as a technical term in financial accounting.

*b.* Explain what the difference is between a principle and a practice or procedure.

*c.* Explain what the meaning is of the phrase "at a particular time."

## 2–6. Materiality and Judgment

Materiality is a difficult concept to apply in making judgments affecting financial statements. The obvious extremes of materiality are rather easy to judge, and most people would substantially agree on the effect of the extremes. The most significant and difficult question is, "How do you identify that point where immateriality turns to materiality?"

Respond to the following questions by first determining whether you feel the item is material and then stating what factors you used to reach your decision.

1. You are applying for a loan, and the banker asks you to list what your salary was last year. You respond with $24,000. The loan is made and when you reach home you look at your tax return. Your salary last year was $24,100. Did you make a material error with the banker?

2. The accountant for XYZ Co. realizes that he has made a mistake in preparing the income statement for the year. He overlooked reporting $15,000 of supplies expense. This means that expenses are understated (too small) by $15,000 and income is overstated (too large) by $15,000.

   a. Without knowing anything else, do you consider this to be a material error?

   b. Suppose the size of the supplies expense reported was $5,000. Is the $15,000 material?

   c. Suppose the size of the supplies expense reported was $50,000. Is the $15,000 material?

   d. Suppose the net income reported was $375,000. Is the $15,000 material?

   e. Suppose you are president of the company and are paid a salary based on the reported net income of $150,000. Your salary is 10 percent of net income. Is the $15,000 material?

   f. Suppose you as president are paid a 10 percent bonus based on the company's reported net income which is $375,000. Your salary prior to the bonus is $680,000. Is the $15,000 material?

## 2–7. Completeness of Disclosure and Materiality

Kraft, Inc. included the following note in its 1986 Annual Report:

Note 8: Contingencies

The company and its subsidiaries are parties against which are pending a number of legal and administrative proceedings (including several private actions some seeking treble damages, based on alleged violations of the antitrust laws) which are incidental to the business. In the opinion of the company's General Counsel, the outcome of such proceedings will not materially affect the company's consolidated financial position or operations.

### Required:

*a.* Why would Kraft, Inc. feel compelled to make this disclosure? What accounting concept is being implemented by making this disclosure?

*b.* The note states that the outcome "will not materially affect" the company's position.

(1) What factors do you think the General Counsel is using to reach its "not material" conclusion?

(2) The sales for the company in the current year were $8.7 billion, and the assets at the end of the current year totaled $4.7 billion. How would this information affect your answer in (1) above? Explain.

## 2–8. Applying Principles for Revenue Recognition

An important accounting principle relates to the measurement and recognition of revenue. This principle is referred to as the *revenue recognition concept* in the text.

Companies are expected to use their revenue recognition procedures to produce consistent measurements. A financial statement reader may assume that, without information to the contrary, revenue is being recognized in a manner consistent with prior periods. In turn, any deviations in revenue recognition should be disclosed.

The First Wisconsin Corporation, a large bank holding company, included the following note in its annual report:

> Loans, which include lease financing receivables, are stated at the principal amount. Income is accrued on all loans not discounted by applying the interest rate to the amount outstanding. On discounted loans, income is recognized on a basis which results in approximately level rates of return over the term of the loans. Where it is not reasonable to expect that income will be realized, accrual of income ceases and these loans are placed on a "cash basis" for purposes of income recognition. Loans upon which borrowers have begun bankruptcy proceedings are reviewed individually as to continuation of income accrual.

### Required:

*a.* What does the bank corporation tell you about its procedure for revenue recognition when the note says, "income is recognized on a basis which results in approximately level rates of return over the term of the loans"? Explain.

*b.* What does the bank corporation tell you about its procedure for revenue recognition when the note says, "Where it is not reasonable to expect that income will be realized, accrual of income ceases and these loans are placed on a 'cash basis' for purposes of income recognition"? Explain.

*c.* Explain how your answers to (*a*) and (*b*) can be justified as procedures by the same bank. Is this not inconsistent accounting? Are there accounting principles other than revenue recognition that apply here?

## 2–9. Nonstandard Accounting Principles

The annual reports of the Wisconsin Public Service Corporation contain the following explanation in its notes to the financial statements:

Summary of Significant Accounting Policies:

Jurisdictional Accounting—The company uses jurisdictional accounting which reflects the effects of the different rate-making principles followed by the various jurisdictions regulating the company. These include the Public Service Commission of Wisconsin (PSCW), the Michigan Public Service Commission (MPSC) and the Federal Energy Regulatory Commission (FERC). The retail portion of the business is regulated by the PSCW and MPSC which make up approximately 89% and 2%, respectively, of the company's revenues. The FERC regulates the electric wholesale portion which is approximately 9% of the revenues.

### Required:

a. Why would the company make a disclosure of this type in its annual reports? Does this suggest that they are not following generally accepted accounting principles?

b. Do you think the environmental factor of regulation should determine how a firm completes its accounting? Explain.

c. Arthur Andersen & Co. performed an annual independent audit on the Wisconsin Public Service Corporation and issued a standard "clean" opinion. Does Arthur Andersen think the company has followed generally accepted accounting principles? How can you tell?

d. Arthur Andersen states that the financial statements "present fairly" the financial position and results of operations. Explain what you think "present fairly" means. Explain why Arthur Andersen did not say "present *accurately.*"

## 2–10. Accounting Principles Constraints

The framework for financial accounting principles includes constraints that might modify the application of the principles. Four possible constraints are (1) cost-benefit, (2) materiality, (3) conservatism, and (4) environmental conditions. Develop an example of each constraint and explain how it could modify the application of a basic accounting principle.

## 2–11. Applying Accounting Principles

The following items describe situations that affect the financial accounting reports.

1. A delivery truck is purchased for $18,000 in cash. At the end of the year, the accounting records show the truck at a value of $12,400, although used trucks of the same model are selling for only $10,000.

2. At the beginning of the year, a retail store bought a three-year fire insurance policy and paid $1,500 cash. During the first year, only $500 was charged as insurance expense even though the entire $1,500 had been paid in cash.

3. Sue Flay purchased 300 shares of capital stock in Eggs-n-Cakes, Inc., for $30 per share from her broker. She sold half of the shares for $48 per share during the year. Nevertheless, Eggs-n-Cakes' annual report shows no change in the 10,000 shares that have been outstanding all year and have had an average book value of $27.32 per share.

4. In 1957 a firm purchased a plot of land in Dallas for $280,000. The plan was to build its home office on the land, but home office operations have been moved to Ft. Worth. In the company's 1993 annual report, the land is still reported at $280,000, although it is located in a prime commercial area of Dallas.

5. A business firm finished remodeling all of its offices. The final step in remodeling was to purchase 20 wastebaskets for $4.95 each. The entire $99 was charged to miscellaneous expense even though the wastebaskets are expected to last at least four years.

6. Wes Harper owns a construction firm, a real estate firm, and a management consulting firm. He participates actively in each business but has a separate bank account, separate accounting records, and files a separate tax return for each company.

**Required:**

*a.* For each item, describe the assumptions and/or constraints of the financial accounting framework that would justify the action taken.
*b.* Describe how the accounting assumption(s) in each case may detract from the realism of the situation.

## 2–12. Violating Accounting Principles

Each of the following items describes a situation that *violates* one or more of the assumptions, concepts, guidelines, etc. of financial accounting.

1. A firm specializes in the construction of roller coasters for amusement parks. Each roller coaster takes about three years to build, and the firm only works on two or three at a time. The president decides, therefore, to prepare a set of financial statements only upon completion of each roller coaster.
2. Deep Drill Oil Exploration Co. prepares a set of financial statements for the year 1990 in making application for a bank loan. The company has been having difficulty due to the downturn in the oil industry. The owner is concerned that the banker may not believe the company is a solid performer. He directs the accountant to use estimated asset values for drilling rigs and estimated values for income that assume all rigs will be busy during the following year. This year, only 10 percent of the rigs have been used.
3. A business owns 500 acres of land, purchased at a cost of $300 per acre. The owner of a very similar tract of land across the road just recently sold that property for $400 per acre. Based on this evidence, the business increases the recorded value of its land from $150,000 to $200,000.
4. A firm borrowed $100,000 at a 10 percent rate of interest. The president observes that, since the date of the loan, the general price level has increased 3 percent. She says, "payback of the $100,000 will now be made with 'cheaper' dollars." Therefore, she concludes, "our interest expense should be only $7,000 this year. After all, we offset the $10,000 interest expense by gaining $3,000 in value with cheaper dollars."
5. The president and sole owner of Quick Sprint Express Co. purchases five new units to be added to the company's fleet of delivery trucks. While negotiating for the trucks, he decides to buy a van for his family use. All six vehicles were purchased with a check written on the company's bank account.
6. After considering outside bids for the construction of a new conveyer belt, Greenlee Coal Co. decides to build the conveyer belt itself. The cost is $550,000. However, the firm records the equipment at $700,000, the lowest of the outside bids received.

**Required:**

For each item, identify which accounting assumptions or qualitative guidelines have been violated.

**Casette 2–1.  Georgia Pacific Corporation**

In the appendix at the end of the book is a complete set of financial statements of Georgia-Pacific Corporation taken from its annual report of 1987.

Answer the following questions with particular reference to the application of the seven primary accounting concepts.

1. How does this report illustrate implementation of the *accounting period concept?* What is Georgia-Pacific's accounting period?
2. How does the income statement illustrate the *matching concept?* Explain.
3. How do these statements illustrate the *entity concept?* What is the accounting entity?
4. How do these statements illustrate the *monetary concept?* What limitations does this impose on the statements? How does Georgia-Pacific deal with these limitations?
5. How does the classification of liabilities into "Current" and "Long-term debt" illustrate the *going-concern concept?*
6. How does the "Property, plant, and equipment" classification illustrate the *exchange-price concept?*
7. How do these statements illustrate the *revenue recognition concept?* Explain.

**Casette 2–2.  Manipulating Accounting Principles in International Intrigue**

Time magazine carried an article in the September 21, 1987 issue titled "Beware of Machines in Disguise." The article detailed the results of an investigation by the Toshiba Corporation of its Toshiba Machine subsidiary's sale of banned advanced milling machines to the Soviet Union. The machines performed highly sophisticated milling of submarine propellers that made them super-quiet, thereby, allowing Soviet submarines to elude detection more easily.

The investigation revealed clandestine meetings between Toshiba executives and Soviet officials, secret shipments of disguised machines, relabeling equipment models to appear as more simple equipment, and demonstrations of only simple functions during normal working hours with demonstrations of the machinery's true capacity when the plant was deserted.

The article then states, "The secrecy extended even to accounting: Toshiba Machine allegedly split the proceeds from one shipment into two semi-annual periods to avoid drawing attention to the company's sales boost."

**Required:**

a. Which accounting principle(s) are involved in the Toshiba attempt to keep these transactions secret?
b. Explain which financial statements would be affected by the procedures used.
c. Explain how this situation illustrates the importance to a company of being attentive to the concepts of:
   (1) materiality
   (2) comparability
   (3) neutrality
d. What role might auditing play in uncovering these secret sales?

# Chapter 3

# Assets and Equities

In Chapter 2 we mentioned that most entities carry out two basic types of activities. They first acquire various financial and productive resources by engaging in *financing-investing activities*. Then they use these resources in *operating activities* to accomplish organizational goals. A not-for-profit organization like the Red Cross uses its resources to provide disaster relief and to support programs that promote health and alleviate human suffering. A for-profit business uses its resources to produce and sell products or provide services to satisfy the needs of consumers. The accounting system compares the cost of the resources used (expenses) with the resources received through sale (revenues), and the difference provides a measure of income under our matching concept.

Therefore, an understanding of these resources is fundamental to the study of financial accounting—what they are, where they come from, how they are valued, and how changes in their form and valuation are reported. In the technical terminology of accounting, the resources of an organization are called its *assets*. The acquisition of assets simultaneously creates financial interests on the part of those groups contributing the resources. A financial interest may be a legal claim, such as the requirement to repay a bank loan, or a residual interest, such as stock ownership in a corporation. Accountants use the term *equities* to describe all sources of assets. They use the terms *liabilities* and *owners' equity* as subdivisions of equities to indicate the financial interests of non-owner parties (creditors) and of owners, respectively.

The financial condition of a business entity consists of its assets and related equities. One major reporting task of financial accounting is to inform investors and creditors periodically of the financial position of the firm. For this purpose, a financial statement called a *balance sheet* or *position statement* is prepared as of a particular moment in time.

## BALANCE SHEET EQUATION

The elements that appear on a position statement can be arranged in the following basic equation:

$$\text{Assets} = \text{Equities}$$

This equation can be expanded, as explained above, to show the major components of equities:

$$\text{Assets} = \text{Liabilities} + \text{Owners' Equity}$$

In this manner, the balance sheet shows a dual analysis of business capital. In accordance with the monetary concept, it denotes the dollar amount of the resources a particular organization will use in conducting its activities (its assets) and also the dollar value of the financial claims or interests created by the commitment of capital to the enterprise (its liabilities and owners' equity).

The dollar value of the assets and equities have to be equal; every asset comes from somewhere. Of course, the many changes in assets and equities as a firm goes through its daily operations make it almost impossible to identify particular equities with particular assets. At the outset, however, each asset had a source; therefore, in the aggregate, resources equal sources.

The position statement provides the starting point for our discussion of financial accounting. In this chapter, our attention centers on a description and classification of these elements on the balance sheet. In addition, we tie revenue and expense, which are incorporated in the matching assumption, to changes in the accounting equation.

## ASSETS

As the term is used in financial accounting, *assets* are "probable future economic benefits obtained or controlled by a particular entity as a result of past transactions or events."[1] Assets are the forms taken by the financial capital that has been invested in the entity.

Note the following four considerations:

**1.** Assets encompass all types of economic resources. Included is physical property such as cash, land, and machinery. They also embody the right to receive services. For example, a company purchases a three-year insurance policy. This entitles the firm to transfer the risk of loss to the insurance company. The economic resource is in the form of a service to be received over a three-year period; hence, prepaid insurance qualifies as an asset.

**2.** We are concerned only with items that hold future economic benefit. These items are expected to contribute to the firm's future cash flows. Re-

---

[1] FASB, *Statement of Financial Accounting Concepts No. 3*, "Elements of Financial Statements of Business Enterprises" (Stamford, Conn., December 1980), par. 19.

sources have value, or utility, because they can be exchanged for cash or other resources or because they possess future potential for service. Thus, assets are the active ingredients in any organization; they are the where-withal for conducting the entity's business. When their service potential has been used up, they no longer appear as assets. For example, a company may have an old machine in good physical condition, but it is no longer used because of technological obsolescence. The machine is not an accounting asset because it has no future value.

**3.** Assets are acquired as a result of a specific event, called a "transaction." The transaction may result in legal ownership, as in the case of an inventory purchase, in a right to use property, as in the case of a prepayment of rent, or in a right to receive services, as in a prepayment of insurance. In all cases, the transaction culminates a process of negotiation between the accounting entity and an independent party and conveys to the entity control over a resource that will provide future economic benefit.

Two examples of items that are *not* accounting assets illustrate the importance of this consideration. First, labor services a firm will receive from its employees in future years does not represent an asset at the present time. Even though these services probably will be used productively in the future, their existence depends on a future transaction. Second, items like public streets that are enjoyed by all users do not represent accounting assets because no past transaction has resulted in a particular entity being able to benefit exclusively from the streets or to limit the access of other users to them.

**4.** Assets must be measurable in monetary terms with a reasonable degree of reliability. Some valuable resources do not entail a measurable dollar outlay. For this reason, advantages such as being located in a city with a large pool of skilled labor or with good fire and police protection would not qualify as part of a firm's accounting assets. Employee training programs over a number of years may lead to the existence of a valuable service potential. In most cases, though, the dollar amount of this benefit would be extremely difficult to quantify, so it would not appear among the assets on the balance sheet.

## Monetary and Nonmonetary Assets

The future economic benefit of an asset consists of either its exchange value (purchasing power) or its use value. Those resources providing purchasing-power value are called *monetary assets*. Included are cash, short-term securities being held as a temporary backlog for cash, and accounts and notes receivable. These assets furnish general service potential to an enterprise because they can be exchanged for cash or other productive resources. Temporary investments (called "marketable securities") can be converted into cash practically at a moment's notice. For most purposes, the business entity views them as the equivalent of cash. Receivables represent legal claims to another firm's cash. The benefit they represent is a right to receive a certain amount of purchasing power.

The largest portion of a firm's assets usually consists of *nonmonetary* items. These assets are acquired to produce products or deliver services and, in turn, to generate revenues. Each of them is valuable to the business because it possesses specific service potential to be used over a period of time. Their cost hopefully will be recovered as their stored-up services are consumed in the production of revenues. Some may be beneficial in the short term (e.g., inventories, prepaid rent, prepaid insurance, supplies). Others—such as land, buildings, vehicles, and equipment—may provide benefits over many years. These resources perform the same basic economic function, regardless of the duration; their capacity to be combined with other resources to produce and sell exchangeable goods and services gives them use value.

## Classification of Assets

When presenting assets on a balance sheet, accountants have found that some classification of the individual items enhances communication. Over the years, certain arrangements have received sanction through use in financial and accounting circles and through formal pronouncements by authoritative bodies. Normally, these classifications distinguish between current and all other assets (noncurrent).

**Current Assets.** Current assets include cash and other resources that will be converted into cash or used in the normal operations of the business within a relatively short period of time. *Cash, marketable securities, short-term receivables,* various kinds of *inventories,* and *prepayments* are primary examples of current assets. These assets are being continually turned over during the *operating cycle* of a firm. When presented on the balance sheet, these current assets are usually listed in the order of decreasing liquidity (the speed with which the item can be converted to cash or liquidated).

The operating cycle is usually described as the time needed by a business to acquire (purchase or make) a product or service, sell it, and collect the receivables. An operating cycle of a business may be depicted as follows:

$$\text{Cash} \longrightarrow \text{Inventory} \longrightarrow \text{Receivables} \longrightarrow \text{Cash}$$

Of course, for each type of business the operating cycle may be of a different length, anywhere from a few weeks to several years. Therefore, the American Institute of Certified Public Accountants (AICPA) has recommended the use of a one-year period *or* the operating cycle, whichever is longer, as the cutoff time for determining whether an asset is current. This definition prevails in current financial reporting; as a result, current assets may include inventories and prepayments applicable to time periods as long as three years. Nevertheless, in general, the definition of "a relatively short period of time" used in the identification of current assets is one year or less.

**Other Asset Categories.** Accounting practice is not so uniform in classifying noncurrent assets. However, one reasonable and fairly common subdivision includes the following three groupings:

1. *Investments*—long-term security investments (stocks and bonds of other companies), moneys restricted for special purposes, land held for future use or speculation, and long-term loans to other parties.
2. *Property, plant, and equipment*—land, buildings, machinery, equipment, furniture, and fixtures used in the business.
3. *Intangibles*—nonphysical rights and privileges such as patents, long-term prepayments, copyrights, licenses, and franchise costs.

We generally adhere to this particular classification scheme. However, remember that arrangements and terminology vary. The term *fixed assets* frequently is used synonymously for "property, plant, and equipment," and intangible assets often are lumped together in a nondescript category labeled "other assets" or "deferred charges." Statement form is primarily a matter of convention. All that can be asked is that the classification of assets be reasonable, consistent, and understandable to the reader.

## Recording of Assets

Monetary assets generally are recorded at their current cash equivalent. This measurement derives directly from their use as providers of current purchasing power.

Except in rare instances, *nonmonetary assets are recorded at their acquisition cost*. This practice follows from the exchange-price assumption of the financial accounting model discussed in Chapter 2. Moreover, adherence to this *cost principle* facilitates income measurement—the matching of dollar acquisition costs against revenues. Costs provide relevant information as monetary measures of management's effort in acquiring assets. Presumably, management decides that the estimated value in future use or sale of a particular asset is *at least* equal to its cost. Users of the statements can judge management's performance by examining how the asset costs that are used up match the related revenues reported on the income statement. In brief, recording assets at cost is assumed to meet the audience's needs for reliable information about management's accountability for financial resources.

Acquisition cost is commonly measured by the *cash paid or promised*. If asset acquisition does not involve a direct cash purchase, asset values are measured by the *cash equivalent exchanged*. For instance, if a firm purchases merchandise, paying $5,000 in cash immediately and promising to pay (incurring a liability of) $8,000 within 30 days, the proper amount of asset cost is $13,000. If a partner invests equipment having a current market value of $25,000 in the business enterprise, the asset should be entered at that amount in the accounting records. In each of these cases, the cash-equivalent figure is a measure of the values exchanged or the price inherent in the transaction between the entity and another party.

Accountants assume that the acquisition cost and fair market value of an asset are identical at the date of acquisition. Although the market value of an asset may subsequently change, normally no attempt is made in the accounting records to show such fluctuations. Similarly, transactions relating to the eventual consumption or disposition of an asset are based on its acquisition cost.

# EQUITIES

The equities of a firm represent the sources of its assets. They measure the financial investment in or claim on the business by particular groups. Equities are subdivided into two categories—liabilities and owners' equity. Liabilities indicate the financial interest of creditors (those from whom the firm has borrowed) and usually reflect some type of legal obligation. Owners' equity, on the other hand, reflects the financial investment of the owners of the business. Let us take a closer look at each of these types of equities and at some of the common items they include.

## Liabilities

Liabilities are the debts and other amounts owed by the business entity. Most liabilities represent definite amounts owed to specific groups or individuals. Such is the case with accounts payable, bank loans, mortgages payable, and so on. These liabilities arise from transactions between the business enterprise and creditors who have advanced assets to the firm. The entity's promise to repay the loans are legally enforceable claims by the creditors.

The accounting concept of a liability, however, encompasses more than just legal commitments. It includes all obligations for the future transfer of cash or other assets, including services. Constructive obligations are included. For instance, many firms have long-standing practices of granting paid vacations to their employees. Although no legal contract may require such payments, an obligation exists that entails the future sacrifice of resources. An accounting liability for employee vacation pay will be recognized in the current year.

Of course, as was the case with the definition of an asset, the concept of a liability includes only those obligations that originate from transactions that have already occurred. Liabilities are also subject to the need for reasonably accurate monetary measurements.

**Accrued Liabilities.**　The Liability for Employee Vacation Pay mentioned above is an example of an *accrued liability* (*accrued* is an accounting term meaning "to build up or accumulate"). This type of liability grows progressively until a payment date is reached, at which time the liability is liquidated. Another example is Wages Payable. Employees normally are paid after they have performed services. A liability increases each day employees work. Then, on payday, the liability is satisfied through the issuance of paychecks. Figure 3–1 illustrates this type of accrued liability.

Interest payable is another good example of an accrued liability. Interest is the charge made for the use of borrowed money. The interest owed increases as time passes, until a periodic cash payment is made for the total interest related to the elapsed time. The pattern of accumulation and payment is the same as shown in Figure 3–1.

Often it is not convenient or necessary to record the daily increase in a liability. However, if a balance sheet is to be prepared before the date of payment, we must be sure to recognize all of these accrued liabilities to the extent that they have accumulated by the balance sheet date. In Chapter 5 we explore the accounting procedures whereby the accrued claims are brought up to date and formally recognized.

**Advances.**　Most liabilities represent claims to be settled by a cash payment. Occasionally, a claim arises that will be satisfied by the delivery of a product or the performance of a service. For example, magazine subscriptions normally are paid in advance. The publisher has an obligation to provide magazines during the entire subscription period. The claim, though not for cash, is real and should be shown on the position statement. One source of the publisher's asset Cash is the liability Subscriptions Received in Advance. The liability is gradually decreased as the magazines are delivered. Such liabilities fall under the general label of *advances,* although each one usually carries a separate account title—Rent Received in Advance,

**FIGURE 3–1**　Time Pattern of Accrued Wages Payable

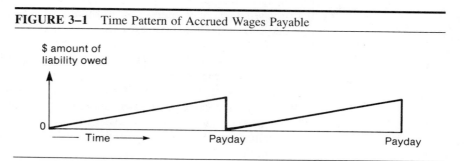

Advances by Customers, Partial Payments on Uncompleted Contracts, and so on.

**Estimated Liabilities.**    Sometimes an obligation or claim exists when the amount owed and/or the identity of the claimant is not known precisely. If the amount can be reasonably measured, it should be shown as an estimated liability. For example, a company that issues trading stamps redeemable later for various types of merchandise has a definite obligation to convey goods in the future. The number of stamps that eventually will be redeemed and the cost of the premiums to be delivered may have to be estimated. Nevertheless, a claim that arose from past sales exists now.

Similar examples of estimated liabilities include refundable deposits on beverage containers, liabilities under product warranty programs, and estimated income taxes payable. In the latter case, the payee is known, but the exact amount may be established only at a later date, perhaps after extended discussion with tax authorities. The accountant shows that a liability for taxes exists by making a reasonable estimate of the amount due.

**Executory Contracts.**    Estimated liabilities must be distinguished from potential liabilities, which are *not* recognized on the balance sheet. Potential liabilities relate solely to future events—for example, future purchases of merchandise on credit or future wage payments. No debt actually exists now because no transaction has occurred.

Also excluded from formal accounting are obligations arising from mutual promises that both parties to a contract will fulfill in the future. Consider the following two examples.

**1.** Company A signs a contract with its president agreeing to pay $100,000 each year for the next five years in exchange for the president's services. No liability is recorded for the payments to be made in the future and no asset is recorded for services to be received.

**2.** Company B signs a take-or-pay contract for three years with Company C. Under the terms of the contract, Company B must purchase 100,000 units of product from C each year or pay $200,000 a year. No liability or even offsetting asset and liability are recorded.

Generally accepted accounting principles do not require the recording of a liability when there is merely an exchange of future promises of performance. The president promises to work next year *if* he or she is paid $100,000; Company A promises to pay $100,000 next year *if* the president provides services. The contract is contingent on the mutual performance of the two sides of the contract.

In law, these arrangements often are called *executory contracts*. Such contracts are not recognized as accounting assets and liabilities unless one side has partially fulfilled its promise. Yet, as the take-or-pay contract illustrates, sometimes these arrangements closely resemble debts or other recognized liabilities.

Not surprisingly, accountants often encounter attempts to keep liabilities off of the balance sheet. Transactions for acquiring assets on credit are structured in ways that will avoid their being classified as accounting liabilities. In financial circles, these arrangements are called *off-balance-sheet financing.* The motivation to keep liabilities off the balance sheet is to show a "stronger" financial position by making liabilities appear to be lower than their actual level. This approach, of course, produces a misleading picture.

**Classification and Measurement of Liabilities.**   The arrangement of liabilities on the balance sheet closely parallels that of the assets. Liabilities are divided normally into two categories—current and long-term. The former includes amounts payable to employees (wages payable), to suppliers (accounts payable), to owners (dividends payable), to lenders (notes payable and interest payable), and to government (taxes payable). Current liabilities represent obligations that will be paid within one year or within the operating cycle of the firm, whichever is longer. The presumption is that current liabilities will be satisfied through the use of current assets or the creation of other current liabilities. Their dollar measurement is generally the amount due.

Long-term liabilities represent those debts that fall due after one year from the date of the position statement. Bonds payable and mortgage liabilities are recorded at the *present value* of the amounts due in the future. Present value is the amount that theoretically would liquidate the claim today. Procedures for its calculation are discussed in Chapter 11.

## Owners' Equity

The other major source of assets in a business entity is the equity of the owners. "Equity [owners' equity] is the residual interest in the assets of an entity that remains after deducting its liabilities. In a business enterprise, the [owners'] equity is the ownership interest."[2] If a business owns a $400,000 warehouse with a $250,000 mortgage, the warehouse is the asset, the mortgage is a liability, and the $150,000 remainder is the owners' equity in the building. Sometimes the accounting equation is reformulated to emphasize that owners' equity is the *residual interest* in assets.

$$\text{Assets} = \text{Liabilities} + \text{Owners' Equity}$$

$$\text{Assets} - \text{Liabilities} = \text{Owners' Equity}$$

$$\text{Net Assets} = \text{Owners' Equity}$$

In this text, we use the term *owners' equity* as a general description of the owners' residual interest in the business entity. When appropriate, we can

---

[2] FASB Concepts No. 3, par. 43.

restrict our reference to particular types of business organizations through the use of the terms *proprietor's equity, partners' equity,* or *stockholders' equity.* Indeed, the major differences in accounting for single proprietorships, partnerships, and corporations lie in the owners' equity section.

The same three accounting elements—assets, liabilities, and owners' equity —also exist with not-for-profit entities. These organizations employ resources, or assets, and incur accounting liabilities. Although there technically may be no "owners" of a not-for-profit entity, a residual interest in assets usually is still present. It may be labeled "Contributed Capital from City General Fund" for a municipally owned golf course, "Residual Fund Equity" for a not-for-profit community center, or simply "Fund Balance" for a university. The meaning is basically the same—the excess of assets over liabilities. Methodist Hospital of Indiana, Inc. calls its residual equity "Community Investment in Methodist Hospital (equity)."

Because corporations are the dominant form of business organization in this country, we set our discussion in this and subsequent chapters in a corporate context. Most of it, however, is equally applicable to other types of organizations.

Two prominent sources of owners' equity are present in most business enterprises. The first is the direct commitment of capital by the owners in an explicit transaction. In a corporation, shares of stock are issued to the owners as tangible evidence of their direct investment of capital. Consequently, accountants use the caption *Capital Stock* to reflect this particular equity. Any subsequent sales or exchanges of those shares among individual shareholders are irrelevant in measuring owners' equity, because they do not involve the corporate entity as one of the parties in the transaction.

Owners' equity also can increase as a result of the entity's operating activities. For instance, a firm that operates profitably experiences a net increase in assets. Assets (usually cash and accounts receivable) increase from the sale of goods and services. Assets decrease from the consumption of various productive resources. If the increases exceed the decreases, the net asset increment belongs to the owners and their total financial interest in the business rises. *Retained Earnings* is the caption used to describe the additional owners' equity arising from the retention of earned assets in the business. In this sense, retained earnings are an indirect interest, as opposed to direct capital stock investment. Alternative terms for retained earnings are *Earnings Reinvested in the Business* or *Earned Surplus,* although the latter term is rarely used now because of the erroneous impression the term *surplus* may give.

Similar sources of owners' equity exist in individual proprietorships and in partnerships. The titles used may vary in noncorporate businesses, but the concepts are the same. The owner's equity section of the position statement for Jones Drug Store might be composed of two elements: Jones, Capital, and Jones, Retained Income. These correspond roughly to Capital Stock and Retained Earnings in a corporation. However, in partnerships and proprietorships, we often find them combined into a single element representing the individual's total owner's equity. In Chapter 14 we discuss some of the legal and conceptual reasons for maintaining the distinction between capital stock and retained earnings in corporate businesses.

## RELATION OF INCOME MEASUREMENT TO ASSETS AND EQUITIES

The preceding discussion emphasizes the fact that assets come from two activity sources—capital-raising and operations. Income measurement deals only with the latter. One basic assumption of financial accounting states that net income is best measured by matching expenses against revenues. Revenues represent the total inflow of resources received by the entity as compensation for goods and services sold to customers during the period. Expenses measure the acquisition cost of the assets consumed in the process of providing goods and services. When asset increases (revenues) are greater than the asset decreases (expenses), the net increase is titled "Net Income." If expenses exceed revenues, the net asset decrease is titled "Net Loss."

When we consider revenue inflows and expense outflows in light of the basic accounting equation, an additional aspect of income transactions becomes apparent. Revenues and expenses must cause changes in owners' equity as well as in assets. For example, assume that a firm sells some merchandise it has in inventory for $800 cash. The merchandise originally cost $550. The asset inflow (cash), or revenue, from this event is $800; the asset outflow (inventory), or expense, is $550. The firm's total assets increase by the net amount of $250 ($800 − $550).

However, we cannot increase just one side of the accounting equation. Because these asset increases and decreases are unaccompanied by changes in other assets or liabilities, there has to be a corresponding change in owners' equity. This can be seen in the diagram below:

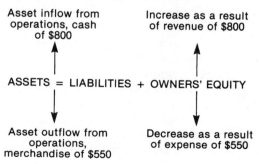

The net increase in assets of $250 is counterbalanced by a net increase in owners' equity of $250, which would appear as Retained Earnings if a position statement were prepared immediately after this event.

Most individual revenues and expenses cannot be related specifically to one another as in this example. Rather, the expenses *for the period* are matched against the revenues *for the period*. Nevertheless, every revenue causes owners' equity to increase, and every expense causes owners' equity to decrease. For this reason, retained earnings is the residual element in the accounting equation. Changes in assets (or liabilities) not offset by equal changes in other assets or liabilities cause a change in owners' equity. Consequently, throughout much of this text we focus on the measurement of assets and liabilities, knowing full well that keeping the accounting equation intact will result in the proper measurement of total owners' equity.

## BALANCE SHEET

We have now discussed in some detail the items that appear on the position statement. The basic equality of assets and equities is the reason the position statement commonly is called a "balance sheet." Its purpose, however, is to present financial information, not just to balance! (We shall use the terms *position statement* and *balance sheet* interchangeably.)

### Illustration of Balance Sheet and Income Statement

Figures 3–2 and 3–3 present financial statements of Eli Lilly and Company, taken from the company's actual 1987 annual report to shareholders.[3] Eli Lilly is an international pharmaceutical company headquartered in Indianapolis. When the *account form* is used, the position statement shows the assets on the left and the equities on the right. Often it is more convenient to show detailed classifications if the equities appear below the assets. This arrangement, called the *report form*, is used for the Eli Lilly balance sheet in Figure 3–2.

The heading of any balance sheet contains the name of the company, the name of the statement, and the date of the statement. Remember, the position statement is like a snapshot; it displays the assets on a particular date. In this case, the annual accounting period coincides with the calendar year. Some companies use a *natural* business year, which corresponds closely to the natural ebb and flow of their particular operations. For example, in a survey of 600 large companies in 1986, 219 had accounting years ending other than on December 31.[4]

A few comments about these financial statements are in order. You may want to glance back to Figures 1–3 and 1–4 in Chapter 1 and compare the

---

[3] Accompanying the financial statements in the annual report are a large number of notes that provide explanations or detailed schedules for certain items. These notes have not been reproduced.

[4] AICPA, *Accounting Trends & Techniques* (New York, 1987), p. 34.

statements of Kimberly-Clark Corporation with those of Eli Lilly. Some account names are different and the formats vary slightly, but notice the great similarities between the two sets of statements.

The balance sheet (Figure 3–2) is usually issued in comparative form, covering at least two years, so that the reader can see developing trends or major changes in the capital structure (equity sources) and in the deployment of capital among various assets. The subsidiaries referred to in the title of the balance sheet are the other corporations owned or controlled by Eli Lilly. Together they comprise the accounting entity.

Observe the equality of assets and equities on the balance sheet. The classification of assets and liabilities, particularly of the current assets and current liabilities, conforms quite closely to the traditional arrangements described earlier. Do not be concerned now with the meaning of some of the

## FIGURE 3–2

### ELI LILLY AND COMPANY AND SUBSIDIARIES
### Consolidated Balance Sheets
### (dollars in millions)

|  | December 31 | |
|---|---|---|
|  | 1987 | 1986 |
| **Assets** | | |
| Current assets: | | |
| Cash and short-term securities | $1,030.9 | $ 486.0 |
| Accounts receivable | 650.2 | 690.9 |
| Other receivables | 281.3 | 88.2 |
| Inventories | 615.5 | 694.6 |
| Prepaid expenses | 146.2 | 112.5 |
| Total current assets | 2,724.1 | 2,072.2 |
| Other assets: | | |
| Investments—at cost | 286.9 | 274.2 |
| Goodwill and other intangibles | 395.7 | 478.8 |
| Sundry | 205.7 | 243.0 |
| Total other assets | 888.3 | 996.0 |
| Property and equipment: | | |
| Land | 58.3 | 41.4 |
| Buildings | 876.3 | 779.1 |
| Equipment | 1,823.3 | 1,699.4 |
|  | 2,757.9 | 2,519.9 |
| Less allowances for depreciation | 1,115.4 | 992.3 |
| Total property and equipment | 1,642.5 | 1,527.6 |
| Total assets | $5,254.9 | $4,595.8 |

**FIGURE 3–2**   *(continued)*

| Liabilities and Shareholders' Equity | December 31 1987 | December 31 1986 |
|---|---|---|
| Current liabilities: | | |
| Loans payable. . . . . . . . . . . . . . . . . . . . . | $   238.2 | $   230.9 |
| Accounts payable . . . . . . . . . . . . . . . . . . | 164.5 | 144.6 |
| Employee compensation . . . . . . . . . . . . . | 203.0 | 200.7 |
| Dividends payable . . . . . . . . . . . . . . . . . | 80.3 | 69.5 |
| Other liabilities . . . . . . . . . . . . . . . . . . | 435.3 | 254.6 |
| Income taxes payable. . . . . . . . . . . . . . . | 231.5 | 68.7 |
| Deferred income taxes . . . . . . . . . . . . . . | 95.4 | 145.9 |
| Total current liabilities . . . . . . . . . . . | 1,448.2 | 1,114.9 |
| Long-term debt . . . . . . . . . . . . . . . . . . . | 365.7 | 395.3 |
| Deferred income taxes . . . . . . . . . . . . . . . | 297.5 | 298.4 |
| Other noncurrent liabilities . . . . . . . . . . . | 100.9 | 47.6 |
| Shareholders' equity: | | |
| Common stock . . . . . . . . . . . . . . . . . . . | 91.3 | 91.3 |
| Additional paid-in capital . . . . . . . . . . . | 48.2 | 181.8 |
| Retained earnings . . . . . . . . . . . . . . . . | 3,395.5 | 3,041.2 |
| Currency translation adjustments . . . . . . . . | 2.6 | (89.1) |
| | 3,537.6 | 3,225.2 |
| Less cost of common shares in treasury . . . . . . | 495.0 | 485.6 |
| Total shareholders' equity . . . . . . . . . . . | 3,042.6 | 2,739.6 |
| Total liabilities and shareholders' equity . . . . . . . | $5,254.9 | $4,595.8 |

special items appearing on the balance sheet, such as Allowances for Depreciation (Chapter 10), Deferred Income Taxes (Chapter 13), Additional Paid-in Capital (Chapter 14), Currency Translation Adjustments (Chapter 16), and Cost of Common Shares in Treasury (Chapter 14). They are explained in subsequent chapters.

Eli Lilly's income statement, Figure 3–3, summarizes its operating activity during each of the last two business years. The company has divided its operations into two categories. In 1987 its continuing operations generated $595.0 million of income before taxes with sales of $3,643.8 million. Like most companies, Eli Lilly highlights its income tax deduction in a separate expense category. The income generated by operations that Eli Lilly sold in 1987 or plans to sell in 1988 is reported as a single net figure of $233.2 million. At the bottom of the statement, the after-tax earnings are expressed on a per-share basis.

The net income of $643.7 million in 1987 is the amount by which net assets and retained earnings increased as a result of income-seeking activities. During the year, however, Eli Lilly distributed $289.4 million of assets to the owners (shareholders) in the form of dividends. The change in retained

---

**FIGURE 3–3**

---

### ELI LILLY AND COMPANY AND SUBSIDIARIES
**Consolidated Statements of Income**
**For the Years Ended December 31**
**(dollars in millions)**

|  | 1987 | 1986 |
|---|---|---|
| Net sales . . . . . . . . . . . . . . . . . . . | $3,643.8 | $3,322.5 |
| Costs and expenses: | | |
|   Cost of products sold . . . . . . . . . . . | 1,302.8 | 1,224.7 |
|   Research and development . . . . . . . | 466.3 | 420.3 |
|   Marketing . . . . . . . . . . . . . . . | 656.7 | 570.7 |
|   General administrative . . . . . . . . . | 362.4 | 270.2 |
|   Restructuring . . . . . . . . . . . . . | 271.9 | — |
|   Other — net . . . . . . . . . . . . . . | (11.3) | (6.8) |
| | 3,048.8 | 2,479.1 |
| Income from continuing operations before | | |
|   taxes . . . . . . . . . . . . . . . . . | 595.0 | 843.4 |
| Income taxes . . . . . . . . . . . . . . . | 184.5 | 301.9 |
| Income from continuing operations . . . . . . | 410.5 | 541.5 |
| Income from discontinued operations . . . . . | 233.2 | 16.7 |
| Net income . . . . . . . . . . . . . . . . | $ 643.7 | $ 558.2 |
| Earnings per share: | | |
|   Continuing operations . . . . . . . . . | $ 2.83 | $ 3.77 |
|   Net income . . . . . . . . . . . . . . | 4.41 | 3.89 |

earnings on the comparative balance sheet, therefore, reflects the net change of $354.3. The following reconciliation shows these changes:

| | | |
|---|---|---|
| Retained earnings 12/31/86 . . . . . . . . | | $3,041.2 |
| Add: Net income 1987 . . . . . . . . . . | $643.7 | |
| Less: Dividends paid . . . . . . . . . . | 289.4 | 354.3 |
| Retained earnings 12/31/87 . . . . . . . . | | $3,395.5 |

This agreement is one example of *articulation* between the balance sheet and the income statement. Both statements are grounded in a single conceptual model and produced by a unified reporting system.

## Uses of the Balance Sheet

The balance sheet provides information about the present resource base and the pattern of resource financing. By studying balance sheets, we can learn about management's stewardship of invested capital over time and about the solvency and liquidity of an enterprise.

A review of the equities reveals the nature of the financial commitments the entity has made and the relative interests of the owners and creditors. Such information may have a bearing on the firm's *financial strength* (ability to meet its long-term obligations) and its financial flexibility (ability to use its financial resources to adapt to changing environments). For example, financial analysts commonly look closely at the relationship of total liabilities to total assets. How much of the resource base has been financed with borrowed money? For Eli Lilly this relationship was:

|      |        | Current Liabilities | + | Long-term Debt | + | Deferred Taxes & Others | / | Total Equities |
|------|--------|---------|---|-------|---|-------|---|---------|
| 1987 | 42.1%  | (1,448.2 | + | 365.7 | + | 398.4 | / | 5,254.9) |
| 1986 | 40.4%  | (1,114.9 | + | 395.3 | + | 346.0 | / | 4,595.8) |

Generally, the lower this percentage, the stronger the firm is financially and the more flexibility it has to borrow additional money.

A companion relationship is that between the long-term debt and shareholders' equity. Of the major sources of long-term capital, who has the greatest financial interest in the enterprise? A financially sound company usually has a low ratio. A ratio greater than 1 to 1 would indicate that long-term creditors have supplied more capital than the owners. For Eli Lilly, the ratios are low in both years.

|      |           | Long-term Debt | / | Shareholders' Equity |
|------|-----------|-------|---|---------|
| 1987 | .12 to 1  | (365.7 | / | 3,042.6) |
| 1986 | .14 to 1  | (395.3 | / | 2,739.6) |

By examining the current assets and current liabilities, analysts can judge the entity's *liquidity* (ability to meet its short-term obligations). Bankers, for instance, judge a business' ability to pay its debts on time by looking at amounts and types of current assets and liabilities. Two relationships are commonly analyzed—the relationship between current assets and current liabilities and the relationship between monetary assets (cash, marketable securities, and short-term receivables) and current liabilities. The first one is called the *current ratio* and the second one, the *quick ratio*. Eli Lilly's ratios are as follows:

|                                           | *1987* | *1986* |
|-------------------------------------------|--------|--------|
| Current ratio (2,724.1/1,448.2) . . . . . . . . . . . . . . . | 1.9    |        |
| (2,072.1/1,114.9) . . . . . . . . . . . . . . . |        | 1.9    |
| Quick ratio  (1,962.4/1,448.2) . . . . . . . . . . . . . . . | 1.4    |        |
| (1,265.1/1,114.9) . . . . . . . . . . . . . . . |        | 1.1    |

The difference between current assets and current liabilities is called "working capital." It often is viewed as one measure of financial safety. Working capital provides a liquid defense against uncertain drains of financial resources in the future. The working capital for Eli Lilly on December 31, 1987 is $1,275.9 million ($2,724.1 − $1,448.2) up from $957.2 million ($2,072.1 − $1,114.9) on December 31, 1986.

In addition to serving as a source of information about solvency and liquidity, the balance sheet also provides the asset base for evaluating earnings performance. By comparing earnings from the income statement with the investment shown on the balance sheet, we can measure the past profitability of the business entity. The relationship of income to investment is called *rate of return on investment*. As one of the central measures of the earning power of the firm, it provides a benchmark for evaluating performance during a period. For Eli Lilly and Company, it would be 13.1 percent for 1987—the net income of $643.7 million divided by the *average* total assets of $4,925.35 million. A comprehensive discussion of return on investment and other financial measures occurs in Chapter 18.

## Limitations of the Balance Sheet

Before moving into Chapter 4, which deals with how assets and equities are recorded, let us consider some major limitations of the position statement. An informed reader of financial statements must be aware of what a statement does *not* show as well as what it does show.

First, the balance sheet does not indicate the current market *value* of the firm's assets or of the firm itself. The amount listed for any individual asset does not necessarily correspond to the market value of that asset. For many assets the balance sheet simply shows the remaining unexpired cost of the asset investments made by the business entity.

Likewise, owners' equity does not reflect market values either. This fact is illustrated in the case of Eli Lilly and Company. The total shareholders' equity shown on the balance sheet at December 31, 1987, is $3,042,600,000. There are 139,368,721 shares of stock outstanding; hence, the *book value per share* is about $21.83. The market value of a share of common stock on the New York Stock Exchange on that date was $78.00. Book value represents the amounts invested in the firm, (i.e., the amounts "on the books") and not the amounts the owners necessarily would get by selling it.

Second, some elements that are valuable to a business may never appear on the balance sheet because they cannot be expressed in dollars. A brand name that through the years has attracted customer loyalty, an industry's reputation for quality products, a decline in product demand, or increasing environmental regulations that could lead to the eventual closing of a productive facility are examples. The positive or negative value of these elements would rarely show explicitly on the financial statements. Yet, if one were assessing the *value* of the entity as an economic unit, these factors certainly would have to be considered.

Financial accounting attempts to record those resources representing a measurable *monetary* commitment of capital arising out of an explicit transaction. Even this attempt is frustrated when the dollar, which is used as the measuring unit, fluctuates in value. In a pure sense, many of the dollar amounts shown on the balance sheet cannot logically be added together if the resources they represent have been acquired at different times when the purchasing power (real value) of the dollars expended was varying widely.

A final limitation of the position statement is that it represents just one moment in time. A single statement may be influenced by seasonal factors or unusual circumstances occurring just before it is prepared. Although the statement may be accurate, it may not be representative of the typical assets and equities of the firm. In addition, we often are more interested in the *changes* that have occurred in balance sheet items. Even when position statements are presented in comparative form (showing the beginning and end of the year or the end of a series of years), they do not provide much detail about *why* changes occurred, particularly in the area of operations. Accordingly, the income statement and statement of cash flows are useful complements to the balance sheet.

## SUMMARY

In this chapter we establish the analytical framework for financial accounting. This framework consists of the assets and equities of the enterprise. Different assets represent varying forms of future economic benefits acquired by the firm. Equities denote sources of and claims against those assets and, therefore, the financial interest of various parties in the entity. To be recognized in financial accounting, an asset or liability must meet the definition of the element, arise from a transaction or event that has already occurred, and be measurable in dollars with a reasonable degree of reliability.

Periodically the assets and equities (liabilities and owners' equity) are formally presented on a financial statement called a "position statement" or "balance sheet." The arrangement illustrated in this chapter stresses the fundamental relationship:

$$\text{Assets} = \text{Liabilities} + \text{Owners' Equity}$$

The format and classification of items on a position statement are influenced by accounting conventions and expediency. However, reasonable subdivisions of asset, liability, and owners' equity items arranged in a clear manner can enhance the usefulness and understandability of the report.

Revenues and expenses represent the changes in assets *and* owners' equity arising from the operating activities of the firm. The income statement summarizes these changes and, in so doing, helps to explain the net increase or decrease in the retained earnings that appears on a comparative balance sheet.

The equality of assets and equities not only forms the basic structure for the position statement but also provides the foundation for the recording processes employed in accounting. Each new topic to be discussed in future chapters can be accommodated in the asset-equity classification system. The recording process of *double-entry bookkeeping* is built on that framework and is a subject in the next chapter.

## PROBLEMS AND CASETTES

### 3–1. Interpretation of Equality in the Accounting Equation

Nathan Dimlight has operated his small business for a year. At the end of the year, he presents the following information:

| | |
|---|---:|
| Assets . . . . . . . . . . . . . . . . . . . . . . . . . . . . . . | $259,000 |
| Liabilities . . . . . . . . . . . . . . . . . . . . . . . . . . . | 123,000 |
| Capital invested . . . . . . . . . . . . . . . . . . . . . . . | 100,000 |

He tells you, "Assets may equal liabilities plus owner's equity for some businesses, but it's not true for mine, unless I fudge the facts."

**Required:**

Explain why assets do not equal equities for the figures that he presents.

### 3–2. Classification of Items on Balance Sheet

Assume that Canary Clothing Company uses the following headings to classify items on its balance sheet:

| | | | |
|---|---|---|---|
| A | Current assets | E | Current liabilities |
| B | Investments | F | Long-term liabilities |
| C | Property, plant, and equipment | G | Contributed capital |
| D | Intangibles | H | Retained earnings |

**Required:**

Indicate by letter how each of the 20 items shown below should be classified. If the item should not be reported in one of the classifications indicated, use the letter X. For each of the latter items explain why you excluded it.

1. An issue of bonds payable that matures in 10 years.
2. Unexpired insurance.
3. Factory building.
4. Investment in 100,000 shares of stock of U.S. Steel Corporation.
5. Estimated liability for product warranties.
6. Shares of stock issued by Canary Clothing Company.
7. Bank account on which payroll checks are written.
8. Clothing racks, display cases, and shelving.
9. Unsettled lawsuit for damages filed by an employee who was fired.
10. Rental fees received in advance.
11. Commissions owed to sales personnel.
12. Semiannual interest due on bonds referred to in item 1.

13. Inventory of spare parts used in the maintenance of the store equipment.
14. Cost of purchasing the exclusive use of certain trademarks.
15. An extremely high credit rating assigned by the local credit agency.
16. Six-month money market certificates of deposit.
17. Company automobiles used by the merchandise buyers and sales staff.
18. Current portion of mortgage payable.
19. Unfilled customer orders.
20. A note receivable due in three years.

**3–3. Identification of Transactions**

Shown below are six abbreviated balance sheets of the Lockett Company. Each balance sheet was prepared after the company executed a business transaction.

|  | One | Two | Three | Four | Five | Six |
|---|---|---|---|---|---|---|
| **Assets:** | | | | | | |
| Cash . . . . . . . . . . . . . | $ 5 | $ 9 | $ 9 | $ 7 | $ 2 | $ 2 |
| Accounts receivable . . . . . . | 8 | 4 | 4 | 4 | 4 | 16 |
| Inventory . . . . . . . . . . | 20 | 20 | 26 | 26 | 26 | 18 |
| Equipment . . . . . . . . . . | 50 | 50 | 50 | 50 | 60 | 60 |
| Total assets . . . . . . . . | $83 | $83 | $89 | $87 | $92 | $96 |
| **Equities:** | | | | | | |
| Accounts payable . . . . . . . | $13 | $13 | $19 | $17 | $17 | $17 |
| Mortgage payable . . . . . . . | 25 | 25 | 25 | 25 | 30 | 30 |
| Capital stock . . . . . . . . . | 40 | 40 | 40 | 40 | 40 | 40 |
| Retained earnings . . . . . . . | 5 | 5 | 5 | 5 | 5 | 9 |
| Total equities . . . . . . . . | $83 | $83 | $89 | $87 | $92 | $96 |

**Required:**

Compare each balance sheet with the balance sheet that follows it. Explain the transaction that caused the change from one balance sheet to the next.

**3–4. Using the Accounting Equation**

Supply the dollar amounts indicated by the numbers (1) through (15) in the following tabulations. Each case is an independent situation.

|  | Case No. 1 | Case No. 2 | Case No. 3 | Case No. 4 | Case No. 5 |
|---|---|---|---|---|---|
| Assets, beginning . . . . . . . | $28,000 | $ (4) | $ (7) | $42,300 | $42,000 |
| Assets, end. . . . . . . . . . | 28,000 | 25,000 | 38,800 | 51,700 | (13) |
| Liabilities, beginning. . . . . . | 15,800 | 6,000 | 9,100 | (10) | 19,500 |
| Liabilities, end . . . . . . . . | (1) | (5) | 7,400 | 18,700 | 12,000 |
| Owners' equity, beginning . . . | (2) | 4,000 | 16,500 | 29,700 | (14) |
| Owners' equity, end . . . . . . | 15,000 | (6) | (8) | (11) | 22,500 |
| Additional direct investment . . . | (3) | 2,700 | (9) | 3,000 | 2,000 |
| Revenues . . . . . . . . . . | 33,000 | 29,300 | 58,300 | 21,400 | (15) |
| Expenses . . . . . . . . . . | 31,500 | 26,000 | 56,100 | (12) | 39,800 |

After you are finished, explain as succinctly as possible how net income is related to changes in assets, owners' equity (net assets), and cash.

### 3–5. Preparation of Balance Sheet

The following alphabetical listing of assets and equities is obtained from the accounting department of Litebright Corporation as of December 31, 1990:

| | |
|---|---:|
| Accounts payable | $ 32,000 |
| Accounts receivable | 12,000 |
| Accrued interest on mortgage bonds | 3,000 |
| Buildings | 160,000 |
| Capital stock | 110,000 |
| Cash | 12,600 |
| Equipment | 32,800 |
| Estimated income taxes owed | 20,600 |
| Inventories | 16,000 |
| Land | 40,000 |
| Mortgage bonds payable | 80,000 |
| Patents | 13,400 |
| Prepaid insurance | 2,200 |
| Temporary investments | 1,200 |
| Retained earnings | ? |
| Wages payable | 4,000 |

#### Required:

*a.* From the above information, prepare a balance sheet in acceptable form using appropriate headings and totals. Determine the proper amount to be shown as retained earnings.

*b.* The president is heard to comment, "Our biggest liability is our antiquated facilities, and our most important asset is our reputation for quality products." Discuss this comment in relation to the statement you prepared in part *a.*

### 3–6. Correction of Balance Sheet

The bookkeeper for Byorsell Trading Company prepared the following statement at the end of 1990.

**BYORSELL TRADING COMPANY**
**Statement of Financial Worth**
**For the Year 1990**

| | | |
|---|---:|---:|
| Current assets: | | |
| Inventory of merchandise | $ 47,900 | |
| Inventory of delivery vans | 32,000 | |
| Inventory of store fixtures | 18,000 | |
| Cash | 13,300 | $111,200 |
| Long-term assets: | | |
| Investment in marketable securities | 10,700 | |
| Notes receivable | 20,000 | 30,700 |
| Fixed assets: | | |
| Land and building | 120,000 | |
| Less mortgage payable | (80,000) | 40,000 |
| Goodwill | | 4,000 |
| | | 185,900 |
| Debts: | | |
| Serial notes payable | 50,000 | |
| Accounts payable | 18,000 | |
| Unpaid wages | 1,200 | 69,200 |
| Net worth of the stockholders | | $116,700 |

*Additional information:*

1. The inventory of merchandise includes the $3,200 cost of two barrels of spoiled merchandise that must be thrown away. Because they had not yet been discarded, the bookkeeper included them in the inventory.
2. The inventory of delivery vans represents the cost of the fleet of three new delivery trucks purchased at the end of 1990.
3. The inventory of store fixtures represents the cost of new display cabinets and shelves purchased on December 23, 1990.
4. The investment in marketable securities represents the current market value of some short-term government securities being held as a temporary backlog of cash. The securities originally cost $9,300.
5. The note receivable is from a former employee of the firm. The person was declared bankrupt last year; the court judgment indicated that the person's debts would be settled at a rate of 40 cents for every dollar.
6. The land and buildings were partially financed by borrowing from an insurance company using a 20-year mortgage note payable. The yearly interest of $9,000 on the mortgage has not been paid for 1990. At the time of purchase, it was estimated that the land was worth $20,000.
7. The goodwill represents a $4,000 payment made at the beginning of 1990 to a former owner. In exchange for the $4,000 payment, the former owner agreed not to start a competing business for four years (1990, 1991, 1992, and 1993).
8. The serial notes payable represent borrowings from a local bank. The $50,000 is to be paid in five annual installments of $10,000. The first installment is due on February 20, 1991.
9. In January 1990, 8,000 shares of stock were issued to the current owners of the company for $10 a share. The money was used to buy the assets of the former owners and to start current operations.

**Required:**

*a.* Prepare a corrected, properly classified balance sheet.
*b.* The bookkeeper notes that the value of the stockholders' interests on your balance sheet is significantly less than the market value of the 8,000 shares of stock at the *end* of 1990. Explain why this apparent discrepancy exists.

**3–7.  Identification of Items on Balance Sheet**

Indicate where you would place each of the following 10 items on a balance sheet. Explain your rationale; and, if an item should be excluded from the balance sheet, explain why.

1. Interest earned on a bank account but not yet received in cash.
2. A loan that is payable at the rate of $4,000 each year. The repayment may be in cash or equivalent service, at the option of the borrower. (Analyze from the viewpoint of the borrower.)
3. Expenditures associated with the development and installation of new service locations.
4. Gift certificates sold to customers but not yet redeemed.
5. The right to use a suite in an office building during the coming year. The rent has already been paid.

6. Amounts to be paid to key employees under the company's bonus plan. Bonuses are based on the operating results of the preceding period.
7. The legal fees that the company expects to pay its law firm to defend it in an upcoming lawsuit concerning a breach of contract.
8. An estimated value for the expressway located directly in front of the firm's manufacturing plant, thus facilitating shipment of its products by truck.
9. Investment in the securities (stocks and bonds) of another company.
10. The cost of tuition and books incurred by the vice president to obtain an M.B.A. degree in an executive management program. The company paid all costs.

### 3–8. Preparation of Comparative Balance Sheet and Ratios

The accounting records of Copy Services, Inc. show the following items arranged in alphabetical order:

|  | December 31 | |
| --- | --- | --- |
|  | 1991 | 1992 |
| Accounts payable | $14,300 | $15,400 |
| Accounts receivable | 32,000 | 34,600 |
| Advances to employees | 1,500 | 400 |
| Bank loan payable (due in 3 years) | 60,000 | 50,000 |
| Capital stock | ? | ? |
| Cash | 3,100 | 8,800 |
| Certificates of deposit (3 month) | 15,000 | 10,000 |
| Current taxes payable | 1,900 | 3,100 |
| Earnings retained in the business | 2,800 | 6,900 |
| Interest payable | 400 | 300 |
| Interest receivable | 300 | 200 |
| Investment in Xerox stock | 25,000 | 25,000 |
| Machinery | 45,000 | 40,000 |
| Salaries payable | 1,200 | 1,300 |
| Supplies inventory | 48,700 | 50,000 |
| Unrecovered portion of franchise fee paid | 10,000 | 8,000 |

**Required:**

a. From the above information, prepare a comparative balance sheet in good form and determine the proper amount to be shown as Capital Stock (Hint: the amount did not change from 1991 to 1992).
b. Calculate the following ratios on December 31, 1991 and 1992: the relationship of current assets to current liabilities (current ratio) and the relationship between total liabilities and total assets. Do these indicate an improving or deteriorating situation?
c. Net income after taxes for 1992 was $12,400. Can you explain why stockholders' equity did not increase by this amount?

### 3–9. Use of the Accounting Equation to Analyze Events

For each of the following events, indicate its effect on the elements in the accounting equation. Use +, −, and 0 to signify increase, decrease, or no effect, respectively. Use the following format:

| Event | *Current assets* + | *Noncurrent assets* = | *Current liabilities* + | *Long-term liabilities* + | *Owners' equity* |
|-------|---------|------------|-------------|--------------|--------|
| 1. | +60,000 | +100,000 | | | +160,000 |

1. In the formation of a corporation, the owners contribute a building worth $100,000 and cash of $60,000.
2. Equipment costing $10,000 is purchased. A down payment of $4,000 cash is made, with the balance due in 90 days.
3. Advertising supplies are purchased for $1,200 on account. Half of them are used immediately; the other half will be used in future periods.
4. Merchandise costing $80,000 is purchased on account.
5. Merchandise costing $46,000 is sold on account for $70,000.
6. Sales commissions of $3,200 are incurred and are still owed.
7. Marketable securities are purchased for $10,000 cash.
8. A customer makes a deposit of $3,000 cash to apply toward the purchase of merchandise next period.
9. The Department of Interior constructs a dam across a nearby stream, creating a large lake and water recreation area. The development creates a new and unforeseen market for the company's products. Anticipated sales should be at least $75,000 a year from this market alone.
10. One stockholder who originally invested $5,000 wishes to withdraw from the business. The corporation writes a check for $5,000 and retires (cancels) the stock certificate.
11. Creditors' accounts in the amount of $40,000 are paid by check.
12. The president of the corporation sold one third of her shares to the new executive vice president for $10,000 cash. The president originally had invested a total of $24,000 as part of entry 1.

### 3–10. What is an Asset and a Liability?

The following six situations have been taken from actual company records. For each situation discuss whether the company should record the item on its balance sheet.

*CBS Inc.* The company makes millions of dollars of advance royalty payments to artists in its recorded music operations. The advance royalties are deducted from future royalties due the artists on successful recordings. However, the artist usually has no obligation to return the advance royalties if the recordings are unsuccessful in the consumer market. Should the advance royalties be recognized as an asset or as an expense?

*Pennzoil Company.* The company has a number of contracts with purchasers of natural gas that contain take-or-pay provisions that obligate the purchaser to purchase (take), or pay for (if it does not take), a specified amount of gas. During the year, natural gas purchasers under many of these contracts were deficient. Pennzoil has made claims for substantial amounts under these contracts and has conducted intensive negotiations with the pipelines to obtain payment, suggesting various solutions. Active discussions are still underway. Should Pennzoil recognize a receivable for these claims?

*Inland Steel Company.* In 1984 a jury awarded the company approximately $74 million damages in a lawsuit against Koppers Company for breach of contract. In the same case, the jury awarded Koppers approximately $10 million in a counter-claim against Inland. Both awards are being appealed to the Indiana Supreme Court.

Does Inland have an asset of $74 million and a liability of $10 million, an asset of $64 million, or nothing to record?

***New York Jets.*** This professional football team signed a contract with Johnny "Lam" Jones in the late 1970s. The Jets promised to pay Jones a starting salary of $100,000 for his services as a football player. The salary escalates to $205,000 over time. In addition, he received a $250,000 signing bonus and a $200,000 loan. The contract also contains a $900,000 deferred bonus payable over 30 years starting in 1986. The Jets, however, can buy out the deferred bonus for $300,000 in 1983. Should the team show a liability for the future salary payments, the deferred bonus, or the $300,000 buy-out provision? If you answer affirmatively to any of these, would you record an offsetting asset for the services to be received? How would you record the $200,000 loan?

***Reynolds Metals Company.*** In order to assure an adequate supply of certain raw materials, the company has agreed to pay a proportionate share of the production costs of various alumina and bauxite plants. These arrangements include minimum payments of $25 million annually for four years and varying amounts totaling $166 million after that. During the last three years, Reynolds purchased $190, $159, and $141 million respectively from these plants. Should Reynolds record the $25 million or $166 million as a liability, as an offsetting asset and liability, or neither?

***United States Tobacco Company.*** In December 1983 the company agreed to become a founding sponsor of the program to restore the Statue of Liberty and Ellis Island. The company will make payments of $10 million over a ten-year period beginning in 1984. How much, if any, of the $10 million should be shown as a liability each year?

## 3–11. Preparation of Position Statement Using Account Descriptions

The following descriptions and amounts represent a complete list of assets and equities of Listless Enterprises, Inc., as of July 31, 1990:

| | |
|---|---:|
| City of Indianapolis securities maturing in 2099, held as a long-term investment | $ 35,000 |
| Vacation pay owed to employees based on time already worked | 2,000 |
| Increase in stockholders' equity from reinvestment of earned assets | 45,200 |
| Amounts due suppliers for merchandise purchases | 230,400 |
| Checking account in bank | 8,800 |
| Cost of tools, dies, and structures used in operations | 311,200 |
| Initial payments made to sales personnel to be deducted from subsequent commissions earned | 5,000 |
| Unused packing materials (boxes, cartons, bags, etc.) | 3,400 |
| Accrued interest on amounts borrowed | 7,800 |
| Amounts due from customers for products sold | 124,600 |
| Amount spent to acquire patent rights | 21,600 |
| Debt securities issued to investors, payable in installments beginning in 1995 | 125,000 |
| Interest earned on city of Indianapolis securities but not yet received in cash | 3,000 |
| Deposits received from customers to cover future servicing of products sold | 14,600 |
| Amounts paid six months in advance for rental of warehouse | 24,000 |
| Estimated amount still owed to the Internal Revenue Service for income taxes | 37,600 |
| Building location site | 60,000 |
| Finished products awaiting sale | 96,000 |
| Special bank account set aside for construction of building addition | 90,000 |
| Amounts initially contributed by stockholders | ? |

**Required:**

a. Using the preceding data, prepare a position statement in a form suitable for formal reporting. Employ appropriate account titles, subtotals, and totals.

b. Calculate the current ratio and the quick ratio on July 31, 1990.

### 3–12. Preparation of Balance Sheets at the Beginning and End of a Period

Hardy Lee Able, upon graduation from college, decided to establish a coffeehouse near his alma mater. He took his small inheritance of $50,000 and opened a bank account for the business, which he called "Cafe Grosso." On June 1, he made the following cash payments: six months' rent on a building, $18,000; kitchen supplies, $8,000; and an inventory of various blends of exotic coffees, $3,000. Also on that date he purchased $24,000 worth of furniture (tables, chairs, rugs, bamboo mats for the customers to sit on, etc.). He paid $10,000 in cash and gave a $14,000 note to the supplier for the balance.

During June, Hardy operated the coffeehouse but kept no formal accounting records. All sales and wages were received and paid in cash, as were many purchases. During the month, he invested an additional $10,000 of his own funds.

At the end of June, the bank balance stood at $16,800. All but $4,000 of the note payable had been repaid during the month. His inventories of coffees and kitchen supplies amounted to $1,400 and $3,200, respectively. He owed $600 for coffee purchases during the month which were not paid in cash, $400 to the college newspaper for advertisements run during June, and $2,400 to an electric sign company for a neon sign purchased and installed on June 30. As a promotional scheme, books of coupons that could be redeemed for various types of coffee were sold. Hardy estimated that $200 of these coupon books were still outstanding. He felt that $400 was a proper estimate of the monthly charge for the use of the furniture.

**Required:**

a. Prepare a position statement on June 1, taking into account the above data.

b. Prepare a second position statement as of June 30.

c. How successful was the venture during the month? How do you know?

### 3–13. Use of the Accounting Equation to Analyze Events

For each of the following events, indicate its effect on the elements in the accounting equation. Use +, −, and 0 to signify increase, decrease, or no effect, respectively. Use the following format:

| Event | Current assets | + | Noncurrent assets | = | Current liabilities | + | Long-term liabilities | + | Owners' equity |
|-------|------|---|------|---|------|---|------|---|------|
| 1. | +120,000 | | | | | | | | +120,000 |

1. The corporation receives $120,000 cash from investors in exchange for shares of stock of the corporation.
2. Merchandise is bought on credit for $38,000.
3. The firm acquires two plots of land for $30,000 each, paying $12,000 in cash and giving a $48,000, 20-year mortgage note for the balance.
4. Merchandise which cost the company $12,000 is sold on credit for $16,000.

5. The corporation signs a contract with a golf celebrity promising to pay her a 6 percent royalty on the sale of any products bearing her endorsement.

6. Merchandise purchased in item 2 for $4,000 is found to be the wrong color and is returned to the supplier.

7. U.S. government securities to be held as a temporary investment are purchased for $6,000 cash.

8. Salaries and wages totaling $24,000 are paid in cash.

9. One of the plots of land purchased in item 3 is sold for $36,000. The company receives $12,000 in cash, and the purchaser agrees to assume responsibility for paying $24,000 of the mortgage note.

10. The firm receives $2,400 in cash which represents its compensation for service calls made.

11. Customers pay $10,000 cash in partial settlement of their accounts.

12. Interest of $200 has built up (accrued) during the period on the U.S. government securities.

**3–14. What is an Asset and a Liability?**

The following five situations have been taken from actual company records. For each situation discuss whether the company should record the item on its balance sheet.

*John Fluke Manufacturing Company.* The 10 percent senior notes payable to banks require the company to pay interest at 115 percent of the prime rate. The amount in excess of the 10 percent rate (currently $2,009,000) is retained by the bank to be returned to the company after payment of the entire loan balance. How should this situation be reflected on the balance sheet? Is the excess really an interest expense?

*Dynamics Corporation of America.* The United States Claims Court awarded the company $11,529,195 as compensation for the government's taking of the company's patent property. Also the company is entitled to $1,403 per day for delayed payment. The government has appealed to the appellate court. Does the company have an asset now and should it accrue $1,403 per day?

*Pratt-Read Corporation.* The company is being sued for over $4,000,000 in damages in connection with the failure during recent floods of two dams owned by the corporation in the vicinity of its principal offices in Ivoryton, Connecticut. The company has insurance coverage of $3,750,000. The cases have not yet been adjudicated. What, if any, liability should be reflected on the balance sheet?

*K-Tel International, Inc.* The company made commitments to various television and radio stations to purchase $7,549,000 of advertising time for the next fiscal year. In the past six months, similar commitments for $4,900,000 have been completely utilized. Should K-Tel record these commitments as a liability? If so, what would be the corresponding change in the accounting equation?

*Caesars World, Inc.* The company has employment agreements with 19 officers and key employees that expire at various times over the next four years. The aggregate commitment for future salaries was approximately $7,400,000. The company also entered into additional agreements with 14 officers. The officers would be entitled to receive up to two times their annual compensation (aggregate amount of $4,565,000) if there is a change in control in the company and the officers are terminated. Should the company show a liability for salary payments required under either of these sets of agreements?

### 3–15. Reconstruction of Balance Sheet

You have been employed by John Bath to help organize the financial affairs of the Waters Company that he inherited from his Uncle Soapy, who kept very few formal records.

You uncover the following facts. The bank statement shows a balance of $2,700 as of August 31, 1990. No checks have been written since July, when Uncle Soapy died. Consequently, you are reasonably sure that all checks from earlier months have cleared the bank. The cash register contains $180 in currency plus two checks from customers. One check for $1,200 is dated June 28 and represents payment of an account by an excellent and major customer, Acme Toys. The other check for $375 is dated January 13, 1984, and is from a customer who died penniless in 1987.

Uncle Soapy kept a list of people who owed him money on a large piece of cardboard. When cash was received, he would cross off the customer's name; new debts would be added at the bottom of the card. As of August 31, the total amount on the card is $11,535 (the $1,200 and $375 amounts had not been crossed off because the checks had not been cashed yet). The entire $11,535 represents customers' accounts except for a $150 advance to an employee and a $1,500 note representing a loan to a manufacturer-supplier.

Also attached to the cardboard are two signed sales contracts totaling $6,000 from customers who ordered merchandise to be delivered in September.

A stack of supplier invoices is kept on a spindle. An analysis of these reveals that $9,450 is owed to suppliers for merchandise and supplies and $4,500 is owed for store equipment. The equipment had been purchased only recently and remains in the storeroom awaiting unpacking. Also on the spindle is a memo that $7,500 of merchandise has been ordered from a supplier. The order had been accompanied by a check for $1,000 as a deposit. The merchandise has not yet been received.

A careful survey of the store indicates merchandise of $70,500 and store supplies of $2,100 on hand. Store equipment *currently in use* is estimated to be $14,100. Also, advertising displays in the store are found to have been leased for one year beginning on January 1, 1990. The rental fee of $3,600 was paid in January by Uncle Soapy. The store building itself is also rented at a yearly cost of $24,000, payable semiannually. One of the last checks written was for $12,000 on June 28 to cover the second six-month period.

A cigar box full of miscellaneous documents discloses that the Waters Company owes the bank $8,000 on a short-term note. This fact is verified by the bank, which indicates that $500 in interest has accrued on the note through August 31. The box also contains an employment contract between Waters Company and a longtime employee. The contract, dated July 1, 1989, and signed by the employee and Uncle Soapy, promises the employee a salary of $15,000 a year for three years. The employee had been paid through June but had received no salary in July and August although she almost single-handedly kept the business going during those two months. Also in the box are the architects' plans for remodeling the store; Bath estimates that it would cost $6,700 to do the remodeling but that operating costs would be reduced $4,000 a year as a result. At the bottom of the box are the legal titles to a delivery truck, valued at $4,600 and used in the business, and to Uncle Soapy's car, valued at $3,300. John Bath plans to use the latter as his personal automobile.

**Required:**

*a.* Prepare a position statement for Waters Company as of August 31, 1990.

*b.* If you exclude any items from the statement, explain why.

**3–16. Effect of Errors on Balance Sheet Equation**

Each of the following independent events has been recorded in error. Indicate the effect of the error on the elements of the accounting equation. Use O, U, and N to signify overstated, understated, or no effect, respectively. Use the following format:

$$\underset{1.}{\overset{Event}{}} \qquad \underset{N}{\overset{Assets}{}} = \underset{U\ 8000}{\overset{Liabilities}{}} + \underset{O\ 8000}{\overset{Owners'\ equity}{}}$$

1. A customer delivers a check for $8,000 as a deposit on merchandise to be delivered next month. The check is recorded as a cash sale.

2. A note payable to the bank for $30,000 was paid, but the bookkeeper failed to record anything.

3. A cash investment by a stockholder of $20,000 was incorrectly recorded as a cash sale.

4. A check for $2,000 covering two months' rent was recorded entirely as rent expense for the month.

5. The bookkeeper failed to record $400 for the cost of supplies used in operations during the month. (The supplies were already on hand.)

6. Cash of $1,200 received as collection of a customer's account was recorded as revenue.

7. The collection of $5,000 cash from a note receivable was recorded as a sale (issuance) of capital stock.

8. Equipment costing $15,000 is purchased. The company makes a cash down payment of $5,000 and gives a $10,000, 90-day note payable for the balance. The bookkeeper recorded only the entry as a cash purchase of equipment for $5,000.

9. The bookkeeper failed to record the purchase of inventory on account in the amount of $3,900.

10. A total amount of $20,000 was given to two stockholders in exchange for the return of their shares of stock. The bookkeeper decreased Cash and decreased Accounts Payable.

11. A contract was signed between the company and a customer under which the company promised to sell (and the customer promised to buy) $30,000 of merchandise over the next three years. No recording was made.

12. Merchandise costing $8,000 previously purchased (and recorded) on account was returned to the supplier because it had flaws. Half of the merchandise had been paid for; the other $4,000 was unpaid. The bookkeeper, not knowing what to do, did nothing.

**Casette 3–1. Georgia-Pacific Corporation**

In the appendix at the end of the book is a complete set of financial statements of Georgia-Pacific Corporation taken from its annual report of 1987.

Answer the following questions with particular reference to its balance sheet.

1. Present the balance sheet amounts as of December 31, 1987 in the form of the following accounting equation:

$$\frac{\text{Current}}{\text{assets}} + \frac{\text{Noncurrent}}{\text{assets}} = \frac{\text{Current}}{\text{liabilities}} + \frac{\text{Long-term}}{\text{liabilities}} + \frac{\text{Stockholders'}}{\text{equity}}$$

2. How much does the company expect to collect from customers? How much has it invested in inventories and in property, plant, and equipment?
3. What valuation method is used for inventories and for property, plant, and equipment?
4. There is no asset listed for the firm's labor force. Explain why.
5. How much does the firm estimate that it owes to employees at the end of 1987?
6. Explain what bank overdrafts are. Why are they shown as a current liability? Can you follow this practice with your personal bank account?
7. By how much did working capital change from 1986 to 1987?
8. What was the amount of long-term debt on December 31, 1987? How much of the total interest actually appeared on the income statement as interest expense?
9. Did the company issue any shares of stock during 1986 or 1987? How can you tell?
10. What is the total stockholders' equity per share on December 31, 1987? Would you expect to be able to purchase shares at that price on the New York Stock Exchange on December 31?
11. Demonstrate the articulation between the income statement and the retained earnings amounts on the comparative balance sheets.
12. Calculate and compare the following ratios as of December 31, 1986 and December 31, 1987: Current ratio, quick ratio, ratio of total liabilities to total assets.
13. Calculate the company's return on investment (relationship between net income and total assets as of the end of the year) for 1987 and 1986. Which year was better?

## Casette 3–2. Establishing Needed Assets and Equities

You recently inherited a substantial sum of money. In your town there is a nine-hole, par-three golf course for sale. The course is lighted for night play. For $200,000 you can buy the grounds, clubhouse, and lighting equipment. The clubhouse contains a small snack shop, a pro shop where golf equipment would be displayed and sold, and an office. Attached to the clubhouse is a storage shed where golf carts and maintenance equipment are stored.

Assume you decide to invest in this business venture. Identify the assets and equities that you would expect to be reported on the balance sheet in future years.

## Casette 3–3. Classification of Borrowed Funds

The United Electric Company borrowed $20 million by issuing bonds payable in that amount. The $20 million was to be used over the next three years to pay for a new generating plant. The company invested the funds in U.S. Treasury notes which matured throughout the three-year period in amounts approximately equal to the payments the plant contractor required as work progressed.

Immediately after these two transactions occurred but before any construction work was started, the fiscal year ended, and the company prepared its financial statements. Three alternative suggestions were made concerning the proper place to show the Treasury notes in the balance sheet.

1. Because Treasury notes are readily marketable, they should be shown as current assets.
2. Because 20 percent of the notes would mature in the next fiscal year, $4 million should be shown among the current assets; the other $16 million should be carried as long-term investments.
3. Because they are being held to finance the new plant expansion, the entire amount should be shown as an item in the Plant and Equipment classification.

**Required:**

You, as the chief accounting officer, are asked to state the treatment you prefer. Would you use one of these or a different reporting alternative? Explain why your treatment is preferable to the ones you discard.

# Chapter 4

# *Capturing Financial Transactions*

You have seen that the analytical framework for financial accounting can be represented by the following basic equation:

$$\underbrace{\text{Assets} \quad = \quad \text{Equities}}_{\text{Liabilities} + \text{Owners' Equity}}$$

*Equities* is the accounting term for financial interests. The financial interests in (the sources of) assets consist of two groups: (1) those to whom assets are owed and (2) those who have a residual ownership claim on the firm's remaining assets. The former group we call "liabilities" and the latter group, "owners' equity."

The basic equation is used to prepare the accounting report we call "the balance sheet." The balance sheet shows the dollar amount of an organization's assets and the matching financial interests in those assets. Because every asset has some corresponding financial interest, we know that, when accounting is properly executed, both sides of the equation will have the same dollar balance.

The balance sheet shows the financial position of an entity as of a particular moment in time. Of course, business activity is not static. Assets and equities are continually changing as various business events affect a firm. The balance sheet prepared yesterday will have to be changed today to show the new status of the firm after today's activities. Tomorrow another balance sheet would be required.

Conceptually, we could prepare a new balance sheet after each business event that caused a change in the assets or equities. Of course, that would be highly impractical. Therefore, accountants have developed a series of procedures to systematically record business events. These procedures allow a firm to track the changes in assets and equities without continually preparing new balance sheets.

In order to provide information about business enterprises, the accounting system must record when a transaction occurs, the dollar amount of the change in assets and equities resulting from the transaction, and whether the changes in assets and equities were increases or decreases. Two primary records are used to capture and process transactions.

First, the accounting system uses a *journal* to record each transaction at the time it occurs. The separate record of each event provides a chronological history of a firm's transactions. In a journal, the transaction itself is the focal point. Each recording of a transaction shows the date of the event, the assets and/or equities that change, the dollar amount of the changes, and whether the changes were increases or decreases.

The second record used in accounting is called a *ledger*. It accumulates for each specific asset or equity the transaction information taken from the journal. All of the increases and decreases related to each asset and equity are collected in one place. In this way, the net change in each asset and equity can be easily computed. In a ledger, the individual assets and equities are the focal point.

Journals and ledgers constitute the *bookkeeping* instruments of accounting. Our primary interest in them, however, is not as recording devices. Therefore, we will not focus on elaborate forms. Rather, we will examine journals and ledgers only to understand their purposes and to illustrate their use in analyzing accounting information and communicating the results of those analyses.

In Chapter 1 we depicted an accounting system as containing the following elements:

Data capture $\longrightarrow$ Coding $\longrightarrow$ Processing $\longrightarrow$ Decoding $\longrightarrow$ Reporting

Journals are used in the *data capture* and *coding* stages; ledgers are used in the *processing* stage; and financial statements, in the *reporting* stage.

## LEDGER ACCOUNTS

Let us first look at the ledger. The ledger is a collection of summarizing devices called "accounts." A separate ledger account is established for each asset, each liability, and each element of owners' equity. The individual accounts serve as the mechanical media for recording increases, decreases, and resulting balances for each item in the accounting equation.

The ledger accounts comprise the heart of all accounting systems. Ultimately, all accounting changes are entered in them. When the accounts are referred to as a group, they are called a *general ledger*. In a manual accounting system, the general ledger usually consists of a binder or book (hence, the term *books* or *books of account*), with a separate page for each account. In an automated system, each account will be an electronic record in a magnetic file of accounts. The function and purpose of ledger accounts are the same in both types of recording systems.

Within a general ledger the individual accounts are identified by both title and number. Numbered accounts can be classified into various subgroupings and arranged in logical sequence. Moreover, a numbering system facilitates the recording process and is mandatory with automated recording methods.

Ledger accounts are divided so that the increases and decreases can be recorded separately. A convenient method, used especially with manual systems, divides each account into two sides. One side is used to record increases in the account, and the other side is used to record decreases.

Accounting uses terminology that identifies the *left* half of an account as the *debit* side and the *right* half as the *credit* side. It is important to note that *debit simply means left* and *credit means right*. There are no other technical meanings to these terms. To debit an account means to place an entry on the left side of the ledger account; to credit an account means the opposite—placing an entry on the right side of the account.

A formal ledger account in a simple accounting system might look like Figure 4–1. Notice that the debit and credit sides of the account are the same. Each has a place for date, explanation, posting reference (PR), and a dollar amount. The posting reference lists the source from which the entry came. This element will be explained later in this chapter.

Accountants use a shorthand method for representing ledger accounts. If you adopt the use of this shorthand, you will be able to use ledger accounts for analysis and communication without having to be concerned with their precise format. The essential element of a ledger account is the two sides, one for entering increases and the other for decreases. Consequently, a simple shorthand form, called a "T account," is used.

**Title**

| Debit | Credit |
|-------|--------|
| (left side) | (right side) |
| (Dr.) | (Cr.) |

Although the T account allows for the left- and right-side entry of accounting information, it does not show all of the information in a formal ledger account. Abbreviations for the terms debit and credit are frequently used to

**FIGURE 4–1**    Formal Ledger Account

| | | Account Title | | | | Account No. | |
|------|-------------|-----|--------|------|-------------|-----|--------|
| Date | Explanation | PR | Amount | Date | Explanation | PR | Amount |
| | | | | | | | |
| | | | | | | | |

make further shorthand use of account information. *Dr.* is used for *debit* and *Cr.* for *credit.*

## Rules for Entering Transactions

We are now ready to establish a procedure for recording in ledger accounts the increase-decrease changes to assets, liabilities, and owners' equity. The following rules regulate the entering of transactions in ledger accounts:

*Asset* accounts:

1. *Increases* are entered as *left-side* or *debit* entries.
2. *Decreases* are entered as *right-side* or *credit* entries.

*Equity* accounts (both liabilities and owners' equity):

1. *Decreases* are entered as *left-side* or *debit* entries.
2. *Increases* are entered as *right-side* or *credit* entries.

Although these rules could be changed without impairing the conceptual framework of accounting, they provide a simple, effective recording system with built-in checks and balances. The short time you need to become familiar with these rules will more than pay for itself in your added ability to understand, analyze, and communicate accounting data. Expressed in a slightly different way, the rules are:[1]

| *Debit* | *Credit* |
|---|---|
| 1. Records increases in assets. | 1. Records decreases in assets. |
| 2. Records decreases in liabilities. | 2. Records increases in liabilities. |
| 3. Records decreases in owners' equity. | 3. Records increases in owners' equity. |

## Illustration of Ledger Entries

By following the effects of various transactions on a few individual accounts, we can see how the system operates. Two different types of assets and a liability account serve as our examples.

**Inventory Account.**    Assume that the following four transactions affect this asset during the period:

1. Inventory costing $2,000 is purchased on account (payment to be made at a later date).

---

[1] It is clear from the above rules that the terms *debit* and *credit,* when used in accounting, refer only to left and right, respectively. They do not consistently indicate either increase or decrease because their effect on an individual account varies with the type of account. No favorable or unfavorable connotations should be ascribed to the terms, either. The terms can be used as verbs, as in "debit cash," as adjectives, as in "make a credit entry to accounts payable," or occasionally as nouns, as in "record a credit to cash."

2. Inventory costing $100 is found to be unsatisfactory and is returned to the supplier.
3. Additional inventory costing $800 is purchased for cash.
4. Inventory costing $1,200 is sold to customers.

These transactions would be entered in the ledger account as follows.[2]

| | Inventory | | |
|---|---|---|---|
| (1) | 2,000 | (2) | 100 |
| (3) | 800 | (4) | 1,200 |

The first and third transactions cause the asset to increase and therefore are recorded on the left or debit side. The second and fourth transactions are credited to the account, because, according to the rules, decreases in assets are recorded on the right side of the account. Of course, other accounts besides Inventory are also affected by these four transactions. For example, the first one involves an increase in a liability account, Accounts Payable (credit entry). The Cash account is credited also, as a result of transaction 3, because that asset decreases when the inventory goes up. The purpose of an individual asset or equity ledger account, however, is to record only the changes to that account caused by various transactions.

At the end of the period, the remaining inventory should appear as an asset on the position statement. We determine the amount by calculating the *balance* in the account. A comparison of the debit and credit entries reveals that the Inventory account has a debit balance of $1,500 ($2,800 − $1,300). This is to be expected. If any asset remains on hand at the end of the period, the increases (debits) must have exceeded the decreases (credits). For similar reasons, liability and owners' equity accounts normally have credit balances.

Usually once a year the ledger accounts are formally balanced and ruled. After an account is ruled, the balance is brought down on the correct side as the opening balance for the following period. This procedure is illustrated below for the Inventory account. A check mark (√) indicates that no new transaction is being recorded.

| | Inventory | | |
|---|---|---|---|
| (1) | 2,000 | (2) | 100 |
| (3) | 800 | (4) | 1,200 |
| √ Balance | 1,500 | | |

Balancing and ruling an account are mechanical processes, of course, often done by machine. They serve a useful purpose in an actual bookkeeping

---

[2] The identifying numbers in parentheses are used for illustrative purposes only and would not actually appear in practice. With T accounts, the use of key numbers and letters enables us to identify individual transactions. In a sense, they take the place of dates and other information recorded in a formal ledger account.

system by separating the entries of different accounting periods in the ledger accounts. The only *analytical* purpose served by these procedures is formally to emphasize an algebraic truism—the beginning balance plus the additions to an account equal the deductions from the account plus the ending balance (0 + $2,800 = $1,300 + $1,500). We sometimes have occasion to use this equality to reconstruct various accounts to obtain information that otherwise would not be directly available.

**Land Account.**    Increases (debits) to an asset account represent the total costs incurred in the acquisition of the asset. Decreases (credits) to an asset represent the removal of the costs associated with the portion of the asset given up. Assume, for example, that the following transactions relate to the asset land:

1. A firm purchases 20 acres of land for a price of $600,000.
2. A payment of $4,600 is made to have the land surveyed.
3. Attorney's fees of $10,500 are paid to draw up the land contract.
4. A payment of $8,300 is made for the title search and registration.
5. The firm sells 5 acres of the land.

The entries to record these transactions are shown in the following ledger account:

| | Land | | |
|---|---|---|---|
| (1) | 600,000 | (5) | 155,850 |
| (2) | 4,600 | | |
| (3) | 10,500 | | |
| (4) | 8,300 | | |
| √ Balance | 467,550 | | |

The $623,400 total cost of the asset includes all of the expenditures necessary to acquire and take title to the asset. Fees for attorneys, surveyors, and title searches are necessary to gain ownership of the land. These expenditures are added to the negotiated price paid to the former owner; all are recorded as debits. When a portion of the land is sold, the cost associated with that portion is removed from the account by means of a credit entry. In this case, the portion removed is calculated as follows:

$$\text{Original cost for 20 acres} = \$623,400/20 = \$31,170 \text{ per acre}$$

$$\text{Cost of 5 acres sold} = \$31,170 \times 5 = \$155,850$$

**Accounts Payable Account.**    One more example, an equity account, should suffice to illustrate basic ledger entries. At the beginning of the period a company owes $8,000 to its suppliers from purchases in preceding periods. During the current period the following events occur:

1. Supplies costing $4,700 are purchased on account.
2. Checks are written in payment of invoices totaling $6,400.

3. A note payable of $800 is given to one supplier to substitute for an existing account payable.

The entries necessary to record the effect of these events on the liability account Accounts Payable are shown in the following ledger account. The first entry is a credit because the liability account is increasing. The other two cause decreases in the liability and therefore are entered on the left (debit) side. The account has a credit balance of $5,500 at the end of the period.

| **Accounts Payable** | | | | |
|---|---|---|---|---|
| (2) | 6,400 | √ Balance | 8,000 |
| (3) | 800 | (1) | 4,700 |
| | | √ Balance | 5,500 |

## ACCOUNTING TRANSACTIONS

We now have both a conceptual and a procedural framework in which to record business events. The conceptual framework states that Assets = Equities; the procedural framework encompasses the system of ledger accounts and the rules for making entries in them.

*Accounting transactions* are those financial activities and events involving the business entity that cause a measurable change in asset or equity accounts. For example, offers to buy and sell (purchase orders and sales orders) normally do not constitute accounting transactions. A customer may indicate plans to buy a large quantity of merchandise. However, only the payment of cash in advance, the delivery of the merchandise, or the creation of a legal claim for payment (accounts receivable) would trigger an entry in the accounting records. Events that do not call for an accounting entry are not necessarily unimportant. A backlog of sales orders may be a significant factor for a particular business. It is one, however, that does not fit immediately into the information-reporting system of financial accounting.

Accounting transactions are of two types—external and internal. The former consists of exchanges between the business entity and an external party. Purchasing merchandise, borrowing money from a bank, and incurring a liability for labor services received are examples of external transactions. Usually they are readily apparent. Internal transactions are changes in assets and equities that do not involve an outside party. *Depreciation* (the using up of the service potential of plant assets) and the gradual expiration of prepaid insurance are examples. In this chapter, most of the accounting transactions are of the external variety. In Chapter 5, we record numerous internal transactions. Both types, however, must meet a fundamental criterion: *A measurable change in assets and/or equities must occur.*

## Nine Basic Types of Transactions

Every business transaction entered in the accounting records must maintain the basic equality of assets and equities. Inasmuch as all economic resources have corresponding sources or claims, no transaction can arise that will invalidate the equality of the two sides of the accounting equation. Among the three different types of accounts—assets, liabilities, and owners' equity—nine possible basic transactions can occur without violating the position statement equation. Some of these nine occur only infrequently. However, in order to convey a complete picture and to further our understanding of ledger account analysis, let us illustrate each of these possibilities with an actual entry. Notice that the increases and decreases in the examples have been recorded in conformity with the debit-credit rules.

**1. Asset Increase, Owners' Equity Increase.** A corporation receives cash of $60,000 from a group of investors and issues shares of stock as evidence of the ownership interest.

| Cash | | Capital Stock | |
|---|---|---|---|
| (1) 60,000 | | | (1) 60,000 |

**2. Asset Increase, Liability Increase.** The corporation buys a new piece of machinery costing $17,000 but does not pay for it immediately.

| Machinery | | Accounts Payable | |
|---|---|---|---|
| (2) 17,000 | | | (2) 17,000 |

**3. Asset Increase, Asset Decrease.** In this type of entry one asset is replaced by another asset. No change occurs in an equity account. The purchase of $9,600 of merchandise for cash is an example.

| Merchandise | | Cash | |
|---|---|---|---|
| (3) 9,600 | | 60,000 | (3) 9,600 |

**4. Asset Decrease, Owners' Equity Decrease.** Assume that $1,300 of the merchandise purchased in item (3) is destroyed by fire. The asset obviously has disappeared. Because the claims of creditors are unaffected by the inventory loss, the financial interest of the owners in the firm must correspondingly decrease. Although the account reflecting the original capital contributions could be reduced, more commonly this particular type of owners' equity decrease is reflected in the Retained Earnings account.

| Merchandise | | Retained Earnings | |
|---|---|---|---|
| 9,600 | (4) 1,300 | (4) 1,300 | |

**5. Asset Decrease, Liability Decrease.**   The company pays outstanding accounts of $2,400.

| Cash | | | | Accounts Payable | |
|---|---|---|---|---|---|
| 60,000 | | 9,600 | (5) | 2,400 | 17,000 |
| | (5) | 2,400 | | | |

**6. Liability Increase, Liability Decrease.**   This relatively rare type of transaction arises when one liability, say a note payable, is substituted for another liability, perhaps an account payable. If a $6,000 note were given to cancel an open account of the same amount, the entry would be:

| Notes Payable | | | | Accounts Payable | |
|---|---|---|---|---|---|
| | (6) | 6,000 | | 2,400 | 17,000 |
| | | | (6) | 6,000 | |

**7. Liability Increase, Owners' Equity Decrease.**   In corporations, withdrawal of assets from the business by the owners is accomplished by the payment of dividends to stockholders. Dividends are usually declared some time prior to their actual distribution in cash. At the time of *declaration* a legal liability is created. A portion of owners' equity is transformed into creditors' equity. Assume that $3,000 of dividends is declared but made payable at some later date.[3]

| Dividends Payable | | | | Retained Earnings | |
|---|---|---|---|---|---|
| | (7) | 3,000 | | 1,300 | |
| | | | (7) | 3,000 | |

Then, when the cash payment is actually made, the entry is of the type illustrated in item (5)—asset decrease, liability decrease.

**8. Owners' Equity Increase, Liability Decrease.**   Again, this transaction is rare, arising only when some element of creditors' equity is replaced by an ownership interest. Occasionally, notes or bonds payable (liability) are issued that can be exchanged for (converted into) stock at the investors' option. *If* and *when* any of the notes or bonds are converted, the liability ceases, and shares of capital stock are issued. The entry to record such a conversion of the notes issued in item (6) is:

| Capital Stock | | | | Notes Payable | |
|---|---|---|---|---|---|
| | | 60,000 | (8) | 6,000 | 6,000 |
| | (8) | 6,000 | | | |

---

[3] In most states it is illegal to decrease Retained Earnings to reflect a dividend declaration unless the account already has a credit balance. This requirement stems from the assumption that the assets to be withdrawn have arisen from profitable operations. If the firm has operated profitably, Retained Earnings will have a credit balance, as we will see shortly. For purposes of illustration, we ignore this important legal constraint here.

**9. Owners' Equity Increase, Owners' Equity Decrease.** This transaction involves the exchange of one class of capital stock for another class of capital stock. Assume that holders of capital stock are permitted to exchange their shares for a new type of Class B capital stock. This exchange would not alter assets but would convert one type of owners' equity into another type. For our illustration, assume that shareholders owning $12,000 of the capital stock exchange it for new Class B shares.

| Class B Capital Stock | | Capital Stock | | |
|---|---|---|---|---|
| | (9)  12,000 | (9)  12,000 | | 60,000 |
| | | | | 6,000 |

Table 4–1 gives a complete picture of these nine combinations of increases and decreases. Notice in each case that the two sides of the equation balance. A transaction involves either changes in the same direction affecting opposite sides of the equation or changes in opposite directions affecting the same side of the equation. As a result, the total for all nine transactions also maintains the position statement equality.

## Equality of Debits and Credits

These nine types of entries are the only possible *basic transactions* that can occur without upsetting the equality of assets and equities. Of course, many transactions are complex with multiple debits and/or credits involving a number of asset, liability, and owners' equity accounts. Nevertheless, even the most complicated accounting events can be broken down into a combination of two or more of these basic types of transactions.

A quick review of these transactions reveals one common trait: *each recording involves an equal dollar value of debits and credits.* The rules for increasing and decreasing accounts ensure that the total dollar value of left-

**TABLE 4–1**   Summary of Basic Transactions

| Transaction | Assets | = | Liabilities | + | Owners' Equity |
|---|---|---|---|---|---|
| 1. | +60,000 | | | | +60,000 |
| 2. | +17,000 | | +17,000 | | |
| 3. | +9,600; −9,600 | | | | |
| 4. | −1,300 | | | | −1,300 |
| 5. | −2,400 | | −2,400 | | |
| 6. | | | +6,000; −6,000 | | |
| 7. | | | +3,000 | | −3,000 |
| 8. | | | −6,000 | | +6,000 |
| 9. | | | | | +12,000; − 12,000 |
| Totals | 73,300 | = | 11,600 | + | 61,700 |

side entries always equals the total dollar value of right-side entries. For all of the basic types of transactions, *every debit has a corresponding credit.* Because all transactions consist of one or a combination of basic types, the total dollar value of the debits must agree with the total dollar value of the credits for any given transaction, regardless of the number of individual accounts involved. Because each transaction involves equal dollars of debits and credits, it follows that the total of all accounts with debit balances at the end of the accounting period will equal the total of all accounts with credit balances. In our example, debit-balance accounts (Cash, $48,000 + Machinery, $17,000 + Merchandise, $8,300 + Retained Earnings, $4,300) and credit-balance accounts (Accounts Payable, $8,600 + Dividends Payable, $3,000 + Capital Stock, $54,000 + Class B Capital Stock, $12,000) both total $77,600.

This particular method of recording is known as *double-entry bookkeeping,* because every transaction has at least two aspects—a debit and a credit. Compare this system with a single-entry system, which most of us practice when we keep our own checkbooks. We normally maintain a running record of the increases and decreases in our asset, Cash. However, for each change in our cash account, there exists a corresponding change in some other asset, liability, or ownership value we normally don't record. The double-entry system provides a powerful tool for ensuring that a complete analysis of each transaction is made and for checking the numerical accuracy of the analysis. The bookkeeping systems used by most businesses are based on the double-entry principle.

## TRANSACTIONS INVOLVING REVENUE AND EXPENSE

In the framework of double-entry bookkeeping, we can record any accounting transaction, including those associated with profit-seeking operations. The main objective of a business enterprise is to increase the total stock of resources by receiving more assets through the sale of products or services than are used up in providing the products or services to the customer. Let us see how this kind of activity can be analyzed with the tools we have developed to this point.

The conceptual approach to income measurement in accounting, developed in earlier chapters, is one of relating particular asset inflows (revenues) and outflows (expenses). From the standpoint of income measurement, our concern is with those asset changes during the period associated with operating activities. Remember, however, that the asset accounts will reflect *all* changes in assets from *all* activities, not just from operating activities.

*Although revenues represent a source of assets, not all inflows of assets necessarily represent revenues. Similarly, although expenses represent a use of assets, not all outflows of assets necessarily represent expenses.* If we use only asset account changes to measure net income, we would have to analyze each asset to determine which of the asset inflows and outflows were relevant to income measurement.

In Chapter 3 we observed that asset increases and decreases from revenue and expense transactions cause corresponding increases and decreases in owners' equity, specifically Retained Earnings. Therefore, whenever assets flow into the firm from the sale of products or services, an equal increase in owners' equity could be recorded by a credit to Retained Earnings. The converse is true with expenses. As an asset is consumed in the generation of revenues, the asset could be credited and Retained Earnings could be debited to reflect the equal decrease in owners' equity.

For example, the cash sale of a product would be recorded as a debit (increase) to Cash and a credit (increase) to Retained Earnings. Likewise, the payment of wages in cash would be recorded as a debit (decrease) to Retained Earnings and a credit (decrease) to Cash. At the end of the accounting period, after recording all of the respective increases and decreases in Retained Earnings, we could determine whether the firm earned an income or experienced a loss by examining the Retained Earnings account.

If a firm operates profitably, net assets will have increased. Revenues will have caused Retained Earnings to increase more than expenses will have caused it to decrease. Conversely, when a firm operates unprofitably, asset decreases will have exceeded asset increases. Accordingly, the corresponding decreases in owners' equity, which are recorded on the debit or leftside of Retained Earnings, would exceed the increases recorded on the right or credit side. On the position statement a debit balance in Retained Earnings would be subtracted from Capital Stock and is termed a *deficit*.

## Uses of Revenue and Expense Accounts

Our previous discussion makes clear that the income-measurement concept is implemented in the accounting system through a matching of increases and decreases in owners' entity. These changes in owners' equity mirror particular increases and decreases in assets, namely those related to operating activities. Entering these owners' equity changes directly in Retained Earnings is conceptually sound. However, the actual procedures used in financial accounting make use of temporary accounts called "revenue and expense accounts." They are introduced in the accounting system as subcategories of Retained Earnings to aid in keeping track of each kind of operations-related asset flow.

As assets from the sale of products and services flow in, the asset accounts are debited, with the corresponding credits going to separate *revenue* accounts. When asset outflows relating to the generation of revenues are recorded, the assets are credited and special *expense* accounts are debited. *Revenue accounts measure the relevant asset inflows, thereby reflecting the accomplishment of the firm. Expense accounts reflect the applicable asset consumptions, measuring the effort of the entity.* Therefore, revenue and expense accounts represent the tools for implementing the matching concept. Although the theory is based on asset changes, the execution occurs through owners' equity changes.

**Reasons for Revenue and Expense Accounts.**   The use of revenue and expense accounts provides more detailed and better classified information about the conduct of the periodic operating affairs of the firm. Between position statement dates, owners, creditors, managers, and others need knowledge about the nature of the changes, not just the end results. How much of the asset increase has resulted from the sale of products, from interest earned on investments, from rentals, and so forth? How does the cost of merchandise sold compare with the selling price? What is the relationship between the selling expenses and the dollar amount of sales in the current period? What other assets have been consumed during the period and in what amounts? These and similar questions cannot be answered easily when all operating activities are commingled in Retained Earnings because the detailed information necessary for the evaluation of performance is not readily available. When separate ledger accounts are maintained for each type of revenue and expense, asset flows can be usefully classified and summarized.

Revenue and expense accounts also enable us to record asset changes separately without having to match revenues and expenses on each individual sale. Even when some costs applicable to each sale can be determined, it may be very inconvenient to record the asset outflow at the time of sale. Consider the situation of a large supermarket. Crediting the Inventory account as each customer passes the checkout clerk would be too difficult and time-consuming. Instead, we measure the expense side only at the end of the accounting period.[4]

Revenue and expense accounts provide a procedure within the double-entry framework for recording each asset inflow and outflow relating to operations independently at the time it occurs or whenever it is convenient. Then net income is measured by matching revenue transactions and expense transactions for any given period.

**Illustration**

Assume that during the month of May the following transactions take place:

1. Quality Products Company is organized. Stockholders invest $12,000 in cash and receive shares of stock.
2. The company leases a building, paying $2,000 in cash for a month's rent in advance.
3. Merchandise costing $16,000 is purchased on account.
4. Two salespersons are hired at a cost of $2,500 each for the month, paid in cash.
5. The firm sells half of the merchandise, receiving $6,000 in cash and $10,000 of accounts receivable.

---

[4] We determine the cost of merchandise sold for the period by counting the inventory left at the end of the period (*taking a physical inventory*) and subtracting its cost from the total cost of inventory available for sale. More is said about this procedure in Chapter 9.

The first four transactions are relatively easy to analyze and require little explanation. Each one involves an increase in some asset, with either an accompanying increase in owners' equity (item 1), an increase in a liability (item 3), or a decrease in another asset (items 2 and 4).

Transaction 5 relates to the profit-making endeavors of the firm during the month. As a result of these activities, cash and accounts receivable flow into the business. At the same time, other resources—merchandise, prepaid rent, and salespersons' services—are given up. We could record these events directly in Retained Earnings. However, if we use revenue and expense accounts—as well as the position statement accounts—to register the transactions, we can better summarize the operating activities of the period. These accounts and the entries resulting from the transactions are shown in Table 4–2. Notice that when assets are received from operations (items 5a and 5b), a revenue account is credited. As each asset is used up during the period (items 6a, 6b, and 6c), a separate expense account is debited. In this manner, we accumulate in these special retained earnings accounts additional information about the nature of the period's activities.

**Relationship to Owners' Equity.**   We can see clearly from Table 4–2 that these new accounts are merely temporary retained earnings accounts reflecting provisional changes in owners' equity arising from periodic operations. Revenue accounts record increases in owners' equity because assets—usually cash or some type of receivable—are received from the sale of a product or service. Expense accounts, on the other hand, record the decreases in owners' equity because assets are consumed, used up, or given up in earning revenue.

**TABLE 4–2**   Use of Revenue and Expense Accounts

| Cash | | Salespersons' Services | | Sales Revenue | |
|---|---|---|---|---|---|
| (1) 12,000 | (2) 2,000 | (4) 5,000 | (6b) 5,000 | | (5a) 6,000 |
| (5a) 6,000 | (4) 5,000 | | | | (5b) 10,000 |

| Accounts Receivable | | Accounts Payable | | Cost of Goods Sold | |
|---|---|---|---|---|---|
| (5b) 10,000 | | | (3) 16,000 | (6a) 8,000 | |

| Merchandise | | Capital Stock | | Salary Expense | |
|---|---|---|---|---|---|
| (3) 16,000 | (6a) 8,000 | | (1) 12,000 | (6b) 5,000 | |

| Prepaid Rent | | Retained Earnings | | Rent Expense | |
|---|---|---|---|---|---|
| (2) 2,000 | (6c) 2,000 | | | (6c) 2,000 | |

Being owners' equity accounts, revenues and expenses follow the rules for increasing and decreasing equities. *Revenue accounts are normally credited,* inasmuch as they are positive items of owners' equity; and *expense accounts,* reflecting negative changes in owners' equity, *are normally debited.*

With the introduction of revenue and expense accounts, the accounting equation is expanded:

$$\text{Assets} = \text{Liabilities} + \text{Owners' Equity} \begin{cases} \text{Capital Stock} \\ \text{Plus} \\ \text{Retained Earnings} \end{cases} \begin{cases} \text{Revenues} \\ \text{Less} \\ \text{Expenses} \end{cases}$$

Revenue accounts temporarily substitute for the credit side of Retained Earnings; and expense accounts, for the debit side.

**Retained Earnings**

| *Decrease (Dr.)* **Expense** | | *Increase (Cr.)* **Revenue** | |
|---|---|---|---|
| *Increase (Dr.)* 8,000 5,000 2,000 | *Decrease (Cr.)* | *Decrease (Dr.)* | *Increase (Cr.)* 16,000 |

The revenue and expense accounts by nature are *single-period accounts.* Their function is to collect information applicable to the operations in one period. At the end of the period, their balances are summarized, and the net result is formally transferred to Retained Earnings in order to bring the latter account up-to-date. For this reason, they are often called "nominal" owners' equity accounts, as contrasted with Capital Stock and Retained Earnings (called "real accounts"). Referring to the distinction made in Chapters 1 and 2 between status reports (position statements) and change reports (income statements), we can say that, with respect to owners' equity, Capital Stock and Retained Earnings are the status accounts, and the revenues and expenses are the change accounts.

## Closing Entries

When the accounting process is complete for a period, the revenue and expense accounts are used to prepare the income statement. The accounts then need to be cleared to zero so that they are ready to function in the following accounting period. The process of clearing the revenue and expense accounts is called "closing the accounts." During this process, the revenue and expense accounts are reset to zero, and their balances are transferred to Retained Earnings, thereby updating its balance for income or loss of the period.

Closing the books is a technical process of transferring and summarizing balances. Accountants close each nominal account by making an entry equal in amount to the balance in the account on the side opposite from the balance. Because revenue and expense accounts are temporary retained earnings accounts, one might expect the corresponding part of the closing entry to be made to Retained Earnings. Ultimately, this is the case, but often another temporary account is used to summarize the closing process. This account, appropriately, is called the "Income Summary" account. The final summary balance in Income Summary is transferred to Retained Earnings.

The closing process for the accounts listed in Table 4–2 is illustrated in ledger form in Table 4–3. Entries (1) through (4) transfer balances to Income Summary, thereby closing the revenue and expense accounts. The credit balance of $1,000 in the Income Summary account reflects the net result of matching revenues and expenses for the period. This balance, of course, is the net income for the period. Entry (5) transfers this net increase to Retained Earnings, the owners' equity account established to reflect the results of operations.

After closing, the revenue and expense accounts show no balances. Neither does Income Summary at the end of the period. However, we have summarized in this account information concerning the period's activities. If techniques exist for summarizing information elsewhere, the nominal accounts can be closed directly without the aid of any summary account. From a mechanical standpoint, a single entry could close the books by debiting all revenue accounts, crediting all expense accounts, and debiting (net loss) or crediting (net income) the difference to Retained Earnings.

**TABLE 4–3**  Illustration of the Closing Process

| **Sales of Products** | | | | **Income Summary** | | |
|---|---|---|---|---|---|---|
| (1) | 16,000 | 16,000 | | | (1) | 16,000 |
| | | | (2) | 8,000 | | |
| | | | (3) | 5,000 | | |
| **Cost of Goods Sold** | | | (4) | 2,000 | | |
| | 8,000 | (2) | 8,000 | 15,000 | | 16,000 |
| | | | (5) | 1,000 | | |
| | | | | 16,000 | | 16,000 |
| **Salary Expense** | | | | | | |
| | 5,000 | (3) | 5,000 | **Retained Earnings** | | |
| | | | | | (5) | 1,000 |
| **Rent Expense** | | | | | | |
| | 2,000 | (4) | 2,000 | | | |

Of much greater importance than scrutinizing the mechanical process, though, is learning what accounts are closed and understanding why closing entries are made. All temporary owners' equity accounts are closed. The rationale for closing entries can be traced directly to the *concept of the accounting period*. This concept requires that regular summaries of the period's activities be made. Therefore, activities of each single period must be segregated in the ledger accounts. The closing process is merely the last logical step in a process dictated by the periodicity concept.

## The Income Statement

We have been discussing procedures for analyzing and recording those periodic activities of the business directed toward the generation of net income. The income statement is the financial report that shows the results of the matching process for the period—the amounts and kinds of revenues and costs (expenses) reasonably assignable to the revenues and the difference between them, which we call "net income" or "net loss." A simplified format for the income statement is given in Figure 4–2. The figures are based on Table 4–3.

The heading of the income statement contains the name of the business entity and the *period* covered by the statement. The latter point is particularly important. A $1,000 net income for the month of May is quite different from a $1,000 net income for the year. Every figure on the income statement, under the concept of the accounting period, relates to a particular, ascertainable time span. The length of the period may vary with the business's needs and the audience's desires.

---

**FIGURE 4–2**   Simplified Income Statement

---

### QUALITY PRODUCTS COMPANY
#### Income Statement
#### For the Month of May

| | | |
|---|---:|---:|
| Revenue: | | |
| Sales of products . . . . . . . . . . . . . . | | $16,000 |
| Expenses: | | |
| Cost of goods sold . . . . . . . . . . . . | $8,000 | |
| Salary expense . . . . . . . . . . . . . | 5,000 | |
| Rent expense . . . . . . . . . . . . . | 2,000 | |
| | | 15,000 |
| Net income . . . . . . . . . . . . . . . . | | $ 1,000 |

---

Because the income statement is a major source of information about periodic activities, it often tends to become the focal point. The amounts on the balance sheet become residuals, resulting from income determination decisions. Nevertheless, the two statements are closely related. For the owners' equity section of the position statement, the association is direct. The income statement is a summary of changes in retained earnings due to the current period's operations. Because revenues and expenses relate to asset inflows and outflows respectively, the income statement also partially explains changes in the size of assets during the period.

## Costs and Expenses

One special problem in interpretation arises from confusion among the terms *costs, assets, expenses,* and *expenditures,* which unfortunately are sometimes used interchangeably. *Cost* is the broadest term. It measures the amount of resources used or sacrificed to obtain some objective. An *expenditure* involves a monetary sacrifice to acquire a productive resource. In this context, cost is the amount of cash or cash equivalent expended to acquire economic benefits. Hence, assets acquired through expenditure decisions are sometimes called "costs."

*Expense* refers to the consumption of assets in the generation of revenues. In this context, cost is the amount of asset given up in the obtaining of revenues. Expenses can be viewed as *expired costs;* assets can be viewed as *unexpired costs*. The cost of an economic resource that benefits the future is an asset; the cost of a resource used up in generating the period's revenue is an expense.

The first step in tracing the life of an asset is to record the acquisition of the asset (incurrence of cost). After acquisition, several things can happen to an asset—nothing, conversion into another asset, use to liquidate a liability, or consumption in an attempt to generate revenue. Only in the last instance is there an expense. From the standpoint of periodic income measurement, we are concerned with two stages in the life of most assets—acquisition and consumption (expiration). When an asset is acquired, a debit entry is made to the asset account, and a corresponding credit is made, usually to cash or some liability account. When the asset is *consumed in the production of revenue,* a credit entry is made to the asset account and a debit entry to an expense account.

In the case of some assets, the period in which they are consumed in the production of revenues is the same as the period of cost incurrence. For example, the salary of a delivery person for the month of August is applicable to the revenues during that month. We cannot store these services for later use. They will be consumed, thus becoming an August expense. Similarly, the monthly rental payment on a building applies only to the particular month for which it is made. In these cases, the cost incurred during the period is the same as the cost consumed during the period.

For those assets that become expenses almost instantaneously, we can simplify the bookkeeping, with no practical objections, by recording the expense at the time the asset is acquired. If we know that an asset will in all probability become an expense during the period in which it is acquired, we often debit its cost directly to an expense account. This shortcut can be employed in the case of salespersons' services in the example in Table 4–2. When the cash is paid out, a single entry is made:

| Cash | | Salary Expense | |
|---|---|---|---|
| | 5,000 | 5,000 | |

An expense is recognized at the time of use, because use is related to the current period's revenues. A theoretical portrayal of what happens is reflected in the *two* entries in Table 4–2. An asset or productive resource is acquired; then it is consumed in the generation of revenue. The single entry, however, eliminates the formal recording of the asset acquisition. Similar examples include other types of periodic services that very probably will become expenses entirely in the period of incurrence—rent, insurance, and maybe even supplies.

Obviously, this shortcut generally would not apply to assets used in more than one accounting period (those that appear on the position statement). Buildings, equipment, and merchandise are normally handled in at least two steps—acquisition and expiration. Also, this bookkeeping shortcut should not be allowed to confuse the fundamental relationship between asset and expense. Neither the payment of cash nor the incurrence of a liability necessarily gives rise to the expense, although the shortcut recording procedure may leave that impression. "Business enterprises acquire assets not expenses to carry out their production operations; and most expenses are at least momentarily assets."[5]

# JOURNALS

Let us now turn to the other recording medium used in accounting, the journal. In the preceding section transactions are entered directly in the ledger accounts. In a more realistic situation, with hundreds of different ledger accounts, this procedure becomes unwieldy. In making entries directly in the individual ledger accounts, we lose the identity of the individual transaction. A particular ledger account contains only one part of a transaction. Consequently, relating individual debits and credits in various ledger accounts to one another in order to reconstruct the separate events of the period becomes almost an impossibility.

---

[5] FASB, *Statement of Financial Accounting Concepts No. 3,* "Elements of Financial Statements of Business Enterprises" (Stamford, Conn., December 1980), par. 64, footnote 31.

Therefore, to maintain a record of each transaction intact, we first record it in a journal. Each such recording is called a "journal entry." The use of a journal in addition to the ledger provides three benefits: (1) a chronological history of the period's activities, (2) a complete record of each transaction that can be used to trace errors, and (3) room for explanatory information about the entry.

## General Journal

Because transactions are first recorded in journals, the latter are often called *books of original entry*. Then, by a process called *posting,* the debits and credits indicated in the journal entries are entered in the respective ledger account. The simplest journal is the two-column general journal shown in Figure 4–3. We shall use the example in the preceding section to illustrate the journalizing and posting process.

When journal entries are made, the accounts to be debited are normally listed first, with the credits following and indented. When more than one account is being debited or credited, the entry is called a *compound journal entry*. The dollar amounts are entered in the respective money columns. Under each entry is an explanation giving detailed information about it. Usually the explanations are much more specific than those illustrated in Figure 4–3.

## Posting

Posting is an accounting procedure that transcribes the component parts of a journal entry from the journal to appropriate ledger accounts. Posting is strictly a transfer process and does not alter the accounting entry. The posting procedure takes the date, the account, the amount, and the debit or credit information from the journal and inserts this information in the proper ledger accounts.

In a formal accounting system, the journalizing of transactions occurs first. Posting to ledger accounts may be made at any subsequent time as the information is completely available in the journal record. Accounting systems attempt to capture and journalize transactions as they occur so as not to lose complete transactions or important related elements.

To post the journal entry that has recorded a debit to Cash for $12,000 in our example's first entry, the bookkeeper would locate the ledger page for the Cash account. The date of the transaction would be entered followed by an entry for the debit of $12,000 on the debit (left) side of the account. Also, in the posting reference column (PR) of the ledger account, an identification of the journal and the page in the journal from which the entry was taken would be entered. This provides a cross-reference back to the source of the ledger account entry.

**FIGURE 4–3**    Recording of Transactions in General Journal

## GENERAL JOURNAL                                               Page 3

| Date | Accounts | PR | Debit | Credit |
|------|----------|----|-------|--------|
| 1991<br>May   1 | Cash . . . . . . . . . . . . . . .<br>    Capital Stock . . . . . . . . . .<br>Issuance of shares to original investors. | 4 | 12,000 | 12,000 |
| 1 | Prepaid Rent . . . . . . . . . . . .<br>    Cash . . . . . . . . . . . . . .<br>One month's lease on store building on<br>Elm Street. | 4 | 2,000 | 2,000 |
| 2 | Merchandise . . . . . . . . . . . .<br>    Accounts Payable . . . . . . . .<br>Invoice No. 8079 received from Acme<br>Wholesale Suppliers. |  | 16,000 | 16,000 |
| 2 | Salary Expense . . . . . . . . . . .<br>    Cash . . . . . . . . . . . . . .<br>Two salespersons hired at a monthly<br>salary of $2,500 each. | 4 | 5,000 | 5,000 |
| 10 | Cash . . . . . . . . . . . . . . .<br>    Sales Revenue . . . . . . . . .<br>Cash sales. | 4 | 6,000 | 6,000 |
| 18 | Accounts Receivable. . . . . . . . .<br>    Sales Revenue . . . . . . . . .<br>Sales made on open account. |  | 10,000 | 10,000 |
| 31 | Cost of Goods Sold . . . . . . . . .<br>    Merchandise . . . . . . . . . .<br>Cost of the merchandise sold during May. |  | 8,000 | 8,000 |
| 31 | Rent Expense . . . . . . . . . . .<br>    Prepaid Rent . . . . . . . . . .<br>To record expiration of lease. |  | 2,000 | 2,000 |

Posting is completed by placing in the PR column (sometimes labeled LF for ledger folio) of the journal, the account number of the Cash account. This provides a forward cross-reference from the journal to the ledger and indicates that the posting procedure has been completed. The series of cross-references entered during posting are called an *audit trail* by accountants. The audit trail provides an avenue to trace, both forward and backward, the handling of a transaction.

**FIGURE 4–4**  Illustration of Posting to Ledger Account

Cash  Account No. 4

| Date | Explanation | PR | Amount | Date | Explanation | PR | Amount |
|------|-------------|----|--------|------|-------------|----|--------|
| May 1 | | J-3 | 12,000 | May 1 | | J-3 | 2,000 |
| May 10 | | J-3 | 6,000 | May 2 | | J-3 | 5,000 |
| | | | 18,000 | | | | 7,000 |
| | | | | May 31 | Balance | ✓ | 11,000 |
| | | | 18,000 | | | | 18,000 |
| June 1 | Balance | ✓ | 11,000 | | | | |

To illustrate the posting procedure, a formal ledger account for Cash (see Figure 4–4) is shown above. The *portions* of the journal entries affecting Cash have been posted. (Normally, posting would be completed entry by entry and not selectively as is shown here.) Posting to all of the other accounts would follow identical procedures.

## SUMMARY

Journals and ledger accounts are the two technical devices used in the recording process. The journal contains a chronological analysis of specific business transactions recorded intact and accompanied by explanatory information. Through the posting process, the debit and credit elements of journal entries are transferred to the ledger, where they are organized by account classification.

The ledger accounts, one for each individual asset, liability, and owners' equity element, comprise the underlying fabric of the entire accounting system. Special-purpose owners' equity accounts, called "revenues and expenses," supply us with additional valuable information. Summarized on the income statement, these accounts not only show what the net income is but give a reasonably detailed picture of how the income has been earned.

In actual business practice, the exact form of journals and ledgers varies tremendously. Only in a relatively simple, manual accounting system might they appear as illustrated in this chapter. Ledgers may consist of cards in trays (each card being a specific account), computer printout sheets, records on reels of magnetic tape or floppy diskettes, or magnetic records in a large computer database. Similarly, journals may be maintained on media ranging from bound volumes of forms to computer tapes and disks. Nevertheless, the important aspect is not the format of these devices but the particular function that each performs. They furnish an orderly record, cross-indexed by events (in journals) and accounts (in ledgers).

In subsequent chapters we use both journal and ledger entries. Both require the ability to break a business event into its component parts. The sequence in analyzing and recording a transaction is:

1. Determine how assets, liabilities, or owners' equities are affected by the transaction, remembering that the equality of assets and equities cannot be overturned.
2. Determine what particular accounts are to be increased or decreased, keeping in mind that the effects on owners' equity from operating transactions are recorded in revenue and expense accounts.
3. Translate these increases and decreases into left-side (debit) and right-side (credit) entries.
4. Record the debits and credits in journal or ledger form.
5. Verify that debits equal credits in order to check on the completeness of the analysis and on numerical accuracy.

In later chapters many additional ledger accounts are introduced. However, these will only be embellishments of the existing asset-equity system. There are only three basic types of accounts—assets, liabilities, and owners' equity. Revenue and expense accounts are subdivisions of the latter. Each new account that we encounter also will be either a subdivision or a modification of one of these three basic types. Consequently, the procedural rules for recording increases and decreases can be applied to every account, once the nature of the account is determined. The following bookkeeping rules apply to the various types of accounts introduced in this chapter:

| Type of Account | Increase | Decrease |
|-----------------|----------|----------|
| Assets | Debit | Credit |
| Liabilities | Credit | Debit |
| Owners' equity | Credit | Debit |
| Revenues | Credit | Debit |
| Expenses | Debit | Credit |

A good knowledge of these debit and credit rules, along with an understanding of the asset-equity framework, will be the basis of our further discussion. New terms, accounts, procedures, and concepts will rest on the underlying foundation established in Chapters 3 and 4.

# PROBLEMS AND CASETTES

### 4–1. Explaining Debits and Credits
Your boss is taking an accounting course to sharpen his financial analysis skills, and he asks to borrow your text. The next day he comes to you and says, "You have studied accounting. I'm confused, help me out. I was reviewing the summary

shown at the end of Chapter 4. It shows the types of accounts and how the debits or credits represent increases and decreases. They are confusing! Explain these points to me."

1. "Assets increase by means of a debit entry. Expenses, which represent asset decreases, are also debited. How can debits represent both increases and decreases in assets?"
2. "Owners' equity increases by means of a credit entry. That represents the increasing ownership of assets. When assets are decreased, the asset accounts are credited. How can a credit be used to show decreases in assets and increases in assets owned?"
3. "I just received my bank statement. Each time I make a deposit, the bank indicates that they are crediting my account. Checks I write and the bank's service charges for check printing are shown as debits. This is the opposite of what this chapter explains about the asset cash. How can this be?"

## 4–2. Determining Missing Ledger Account Values

Ledger account entries can be analyzed so that missing values are apparent. The general nature of all accounts and their increases and decreases can be expressed as:

$$\text{Beginning balance} + \text{Additions} - \text{Deductions} = \text{Ending balance}$$

For each situation below, draw a T account, insert the values you know, and determine the missing value.

1. Accounts Receivable
   a. The beginning balance is $20,000.
   b. The ending balance is $5,000.
   c. Credit sales recorded were $15,000.
   d. How much was received from cash collections of accounts receivable?
2. Supplies Inventory
   a. The beginning balance is $12,000.
   b. Supplies used amounted to $17,000.
   c. Additional supplies purchased totaled $15,000.
   d. How much was the ending balance in the Supplies account?
3. Buildings
   a. The beginning balance is $225,000.
   b. The ending balance is $240,000.
   c. New buildings totaling $62,000 were purchased.
   d. An old building, on the books at $37,000, was sold.
   e. How much depreciation was charged against the Buildings account?
4. Prepaid Rent
   a. The ending balance is $42,000.
   b. Additional payments for prepaid rent total $15,000.
   c. Expired rent is $9,000.
   d. What is the beginning balance for prepaid rent?
5. Accounts Payable
   a. The beginning balance is $83,000.
   b. Payments of $68,000 were made on outstanding accounts.
   c. The ending balance is $137,000.
   d. Additional credit purchases were made and totaled $127,000.
   e. How much credit was given for returned purchases?

### 4–3. Analyzing Both Sides of a Transaction

Every exchange transaction involves two parties (i.e., there must be a buyer for every seller). Both parties record the impact of each transaction on their assets, liabilities, and owners' equity. For each of the independent transactions below, prepare the journal entry that would be made by *each* party.

1. Acme Corporation issues shares of its stock to Hy Ball for $2,000.
2. Camelot Company receives a $500 cash payment from Deadbeat, Inc., in partial payment of an account.
3. Gates Computer Repair Company leases space from Heavenly Realty Company for $2,000 a month. Gates writes a check for $12,000 to cover the first six months' rent.
4. King Corporation borrows $50,000 on a long-term mortgage note from Last National Bank of Medusa.
5. Mammoth Motors, an automobile dealer, sells five trucks to Natural Delivery Systems, Inc., for $15,000 each. The trucks cost Mammoth Motors $9,000 apiece.

### 4–4. Determining Missing Values

Ledger account entries can be analyzed so that missing values become apparent. The general nature of all accounts and their increases and decreases can be expressed as:

$$\text{Beginning Balance} + \text{Additions} - \text{Deductions} = \text{Ending Balance}$$

Using your knowledge of how various transactions affect particular ledger accounts, determine the missing item of information in each of the five situations below (you may want to draw T accounts to aid you in analyzing the situations):

1. Accounts receivable are $32,400 and $42,800 at the beginning and end of the period, respectively. If $106,000 cash was collected from customers during the period, what were the total credit sales?
2. Accrued wages payable of $14,200 appeared on the balance sheet at the beginning of March. Wage expense for March was $37,800, and total cash payments to employees during March amounted to $33,600. How much is owed to employees at the end of the month?
3. The income statement shows a net income of $18,800. Retained earnings at the beginning and at the end of the year are $17,800 and $30,600, respectively. How much was declared in dividends during the year?
4. The position statement on November 30 shows a balance in the inventory of repair parts of $6,400, which is an increase of $4,300 since the beginning of the month. The income statement for November indicates that $9,000 of repair parts were used in making service calls. What quantity of repair parts was purchased in November?
5. A liability account, Rent Received in Advance, had a balance of $18,800 on July 1. By July 31, the balance was $8,000 higher. If rent revenue for July were $12,000, how much cash was received from rental customers during the month?

### 4–5. Determining Transactions from Account Postings

The T accounts below show the transactions of Cardinal Company during the month of May:

| Cash | | | | Accounts Payable | | | | Sales | | | |
|---|---|---|---|---|---|---|---|---|---|---|---|
| (1) | 60,000 | (2) | 600 | (8) | 29,000 | (3) | 30,700 | | | (4) | 40,900 |
| (6) | 2,500 | (5) | 12,300 | (11) | 500 | | | | | (6) | 2,500 |
| (9) | 7,800 | (7) | 1,800 | | | | | | | | |
| (13) | 33,600 | (8) | 29,000 | | | | | | | | |

| Inventory | | | | Salaries and Wages | | | | Capital Stock | | | |
|---|---|---|---|---|---|---|---|---|---|---|---|
| (3) | 30,700 | (11) | 500 | (5) | 12,300 | | | | | (1) | 60,000 |
| | | (14) | 26,500 | (15) | 700 | | | | | (10) | 4,000 |

| Depreciation | | | | Cost of Goods Sold | | | | Furniture and Fixtures | | | |
|---|---|---|---|---|---|---|---|---|---|---|---|
| (12) | 200 | | | (14) | 26,500 | | | (2) | 6,600 | (12) | 200 |

| Notes Payable | | | | Rent Expense | | | | Accounts Receivable | | | |
|---|---|---|---|---|---|---|---|---|---|---|---|
| (10) | 4,000 | (2) | 6,000 | (16) | 300 | | | (4) | 40,900 | (13) | 33,600 |

| Advances from Customers | | | | Wages Payable | | | | Unexpired Rent | | | |
|---|---|---|---|---|---|---|---|---|---|---|---|
| | | (9) | 7,800 | | | (15) | 700 | (7) | 1,800 | (16) | 300 |

### Required:

*a.* The accounts listed above show transaction postings identified with numbers (1) to (16). For each transaction:
  1. Prepare the journal entry that was posted.
  2. Explain what the underlying event was. Be as specific as possible.
*b.* Prepare an income statement and a balance sheet from the accounts shown.

### 4–6. Making Journal Entries and Posting Accounts

The General Electron Company is organized on March 1, 1990. The company completes the following transactions during March.

  1. Shares of stock are issued to various individuals who invest $150,000 in cash.
  2. Land and buildings are purchased for a total of $80,000. An appraisal allocates $10,000 to the land. Of the total purchase price, $20,000 is paid in cash and a 10-year mortgage is entered into for the remainder.
  3. A landscaping firm grades the land and installs permanent drainage at a cost of $8,000, to be paid in 30 days.
  4. A used delivery truck is purchased for cash at a price of $12,000.
  5. The delivery truck is overhauled and repainted at a cost of $1,300, which is paid in cash.
  6. Izzy Everslow is interviewed for the position of sales manager. Izzy agrees to take the position, starting April 1, at a salary of $2,000 per month.
  7. Office equipment is purchased on account for $2,200.
  8. Inventory is purchased for $40,000; cash of $15,000 is paid; and a six-month, 10 percent note for the difference is given to the supplier.

9. One of the original stockholders has a change of heart. He would prefer to loan the money to the corporation rather than own stock. The other stockholders agree to the request. Accordingly, his stock certificate for $10,000 is surrendered and canceled, and a loan agreement for $10,000 is substituted.
10. The supplier of the inventory, purchased in item 8 above, indicates that the price of the inventory was overstated by $2,000. The cost of inventory should have been only $38,000. The supplier sends a refund check for $2,000.
11. Insurance premiums of $1,800 are paid by check.
12. A check for $1,500 is received from a customer. The customer intends to complete a purchase in April and makes the advance payment to show good faith. The $1,500 will be applied to the purchase when it is completed.

### Required:

a. Prepare journal entries to record the above events.
b. Create a T account for Cash *only* and post the relevant portions of the journal entries to it. What would the Cash balance be at March 31?

### 4–7. Journalizing and Posting to Accounts

Shown below is the position statement of Neverready Delivery Service, Inc., as of April 30, 1991:

**NEVERREADY DELIVERY SERVICE**
**Statement of Financial Position**
**April 30, 1991**

| Assets | | Equities | |
|---|---:|---|---:|
| Cash . . . . . . . . . . . | $ 2,600 | Accounts payable . . . . . . . | $ 2,900 |
| Supplies . . . . . . . . . | 3,200 | | |
| Prepaid rent . . . . . . . | 3,000 | Capital stock . . . . . . . . | 15,000 |
| Equipment . . . . . . . . | 25,000 | Retained earnings . . . . . . | 15,900 |
| **Total assets** . . . . . . . | $33,800 | **Total equities** . . . . . . . . | $33,800 |

1. On May 1 the stockholders invested another $15,000 cash in the business in exchange for shares of stock.
2. The officers of the firm contacted the local bank on May 2 and arranged a line of credit whereby the business could borrow up to $200,000 as needed.
3. The business placed an order for $1,500 of supplies on May 3.
4. Accounts payable of $1,200 were paid in cash on May 7.
5. On May 15 the garage and office building, which the firm has been renting, were purchased for $12,700. The rent that had been prepaid as of April 30 was to apply against the purchase price, with the remainder paid in cash.
6. Two new employees were hired. Their salaries, beginning June 1, were to be $1,200 and $1,500 per month each. However, to be sure of their availability, each was advanced $500 on May 20.
7. The supplies ordered on May 3 were delivered on May 21 along with an invoice for $1,500.
8. An employee purchased some used equipment from the company for its book value of $3,000.

9. On May 30, a $15,000 loan was taken out at the bank under the previously arranged line of credit.

10. One third of the supplies delivered on May 21 were found to be defective and were returned to the supplier for credit.

### Required:

*a.* Prepare journal entries for the above events.

*b.* Prepare T accounts. Post the opening balances and the journal entries.

*c.* Prepare a position statement as of May 31, 1991.

*d.* Did Neverready earn any income from these transactions? Explain why or why not.

## 4–8. Reconstructing Ledger Accounts

The Shocker Co. had the following balance sheets as of December 31, 1989 and 1990 and income statement for the year 1990.

**SHOCKER COMPANY**
**Comparative Balance Sheets**
**December 31**

| | 1990 | 1989 | | 1990 | 1989 |
|---|---|---|---|---|---|
| **Assets** | | | **Liabilities** | | |
| Cash . . . . . | $ 10,000 | $ 8,000 | Bank loan payable . . . . . | $ 15,000 | $ –0– |
| Accounts receivable . . | 27,000 | 33,000 | **Stockholders' Equity** | | |
| Inventory . . . | 25,000 | 15,000 | | | |
| Prepaid insurance . . | 15,000 | 20,000 | Capital stock . . . . | 50,000 | 50,000 |
| Property & equipment . . | 27,000 | 15,000 | Retained earnings . . . . . | 39,000 | 41,000 |
| | | | Total liabilities and stockholders | | |
| Total assets . . | $104,000 | $91,000 | equity . . . . . . | $104,000 | $91,000 |

**SHOCKER COMPANY**
**Income Statement**
**For the Year Ending December 31, 1990**

| | | |
|---|---|---|
| Sales revenue. . . . . . . . . . . . . . . . . . . . . . . . . . . . . . . . . . . . . | | $12,000 |
| Expenses: | | |
| Cost of sales . . . . . . . . . . . . . . . . . . . . . . . . . . . . | $6,000 | |
| Insurance expense . . . . . . . . . . . . . . . . . . . . . . . . . . | 5,000 | |
| Depreciation expense. . . . . . . . . . . . . . . . . . . . . . . . . | 3,000 | 14,000 |
| Net loss . . . . . . . . . . . . . . . . . . . . . . . . . . . . . . . . . . . | | $ (2,000) |

**Required:**

a. Prepare a T account for each asset, liability, stockholders' equity, revenue, and expense listed on these statements. Also prepare a T account for Income Summary. Enter the balances as of January 1, 1990.

b. Use the financial statements to place the numbers in the T accounts (including the Income Summary account) that must have existed prior to the preparation of the December 31, 1990 financial statements.

c. These statements reflect the results of five separate transactions. In addition, the balance from the Income Summary was transferred. Prepare a written explanation of the five transactions and explain the transfer entry from Income Summary.

**4–9. Preparing Journal Entries and an Income Statement**

In May 1991, Andy James opened an automobile parts distributorship. He incorporated and had 100 shares of stock available for issue. The transactions for the first six months of operations are summarized below:

1. Invested $50,000 in cash, taking all 100 shares of stock.
2. Paid $36,000 rent in advance to cover 18 months.
3. Purchased storage bins and shelves costing $75,000, on account. The bins and shelves are expected to last 10 years.
4. Purchased parts for the stockroom in the amount of $30,000, all on account.
5. Received an order for $11,400 of parts to be delivered in three months. The parts cost James $7,500.
6. Purchased for cash a supply of 600 oil filters for $3 each. These filters can be sold for $14 each but are given away to the first 600 customers as a promotional scheme.
7. Sold parts for cash, $12,500, and on account, $20,600. The parts cost $22,400.
8. Paid in cash $4,800 for wages, $1,400 for advertising, and $800 for utility bills.
9. Collected $6,200 from charge customers.
10. Paid $12,300 of accounts payable and gave a $5,000 note payable in settlement of another account.
11. Delivered the parts ordered in transaction 5.
12. Accepted a used truck, to be used for parts delivery, to settle an account from a customer who owed the distributorship $5,000 for parts purchased.
13. Recognized additional unpaid liabilities at the end of the period of $900 for wages and $100 for utilities.
14. Recognized rent applicable to the current accounting period.
15. Paid $1,200 cash for an overhaul of the truck's engine ($890) and painting the firm's name on the truck ($310).

**Required:**

a. Prepare journal entries to record these transactions, employing a revenue and expense account wherever necessary.

b. Prepare an income statement for the six months ending October 31, 1991.

**4–10. Using Ledger Accounts and Statement Preparation**

The Mass-Marketers Company had the following general ledger account balances on December 31, 1990:

|                          | Debit Balances |                          | Credit Balances |
| ------------------------ | -------------: | ------------------------ | --------------: |
| Cash . . . . . . . . . . . . | $ 45,800 | Accounts payable . . . . . | $24,000 |
| Accounts receivable . . . . . . | 18,600 | Notes payable . . . . . . . | 1,600 |
| Merchandise inventory . . . . . | 15,600 | Wages payable . . . . . . | 500 |
| Supplies inventory . . . . . . . | 1,100 | Interest payable . . . . . . | 200 |
| Prepaid insurance . . . . . . . | 2,500 | Capital stock . . . . . . . | 84,000 |
| Equipment . . . . . . . . . . | 48,600 |                          |        |
| Buildings . . . . . . . . . . | 28,000 | Retained earnings . . . . . | 49,900 |
|                          | $160,200 |                          | $160,200 |

During the first quarter of 1991, the following transactions were completed by the company:

1. Purchased additional merchandise inventory on account for $82,000 and additional supplies inventory for cash of $1,500.
2. Sales during the quarter were:
    *a*. On account, $105,000.
    *b*. For cash, $5,000.
3. The cost of all inventory sold, both on account and for cash, was $57,000.
4. Other cash receipts during the quarter were:
    *a*. $9,000 when additional capital stock was issued.
    *b*. $57,400 from customers who paid their accounts.
    *c*. $5,400 from the sale of excess equipment; the equipment had a value on the books of $7,200, so the $1,800 difference is a loss and should be handled as an additional expense.
    *d*. $300 refunded by the insurance company because the policy duplicated the coverage of insurance already in force.
5. Other cash disbursements were made during the quarter to:
    *a*. Pay accounts with merchandise vendors, $47,100.
    *b*. Pay the bank for the loan outstanding plus the interest that had accrued and was shown as an expense in 1990, $1,800.
    *c*. Pay employees for their wages owed at the beginning of the quarter plus additional wages earned during the quarter, $10,500.
    *d*. Pay for additional supplies inventory, $800.
    *e*. Pay for heat, light, and other utilities, $2,500.
    *f*. Pay the local newspaper for ads it printed during the first quarter of 1991, $600.
6. Other information available on March 31 is:
    *a*. Supplies used during the quarter were $1,400.
    *b*. Insurance coverage that had expired was $500.
    *c*. Depreciation expense (cost of noncurrent asset services expired) during the quarter:
        (1) Building, $600.
        (2) Equipment, $1,900.
    *d*. Although March 31 was not a payday, the employees had earned and were owed wages of $1,100.

**Required:**

*a.* Prepare T accounts for each of the accounts listed as having balances at the beginning of the quarter and post the balances to the T accounts.

*b.* Record the events of the first quarter directly in the T accounts. Create revenue and expense accounts as you need them. (Use separate revenue accounts for cash and credit sales.)

*c.* Prepare an income statement for the quarter ended March 31, 1991. Did Mass-Marketers have an income or a loss?

*d.* Prepare an Income Summary T account and close all of the revenue and expense accounts by posting them directly to Income Summary. Then close Income Summary to Retained Earnings.

*e.* Prepare a balance sheet as of March 31, 1991.

**4–11. Journalizing, Posting, and Statement Preparation**

During the month of October the following transactions took place concerning Auntie Pasto's Pizza Parlor:

*October 1–5:*

1. The business is formed as a partnership by two brothers. One brother, I. M. Dense, contributed a restaurant location valued at $60,000. The land was appraised at $24,000, and the building at $36,000, although I. M. had originally purchased the location five years ago for only $50,000. The other brother, U. R. Dense, invested $45,000 in cash and securities having a current market value of $15,000 (original cost to U. R. was $9,000).

2. Ingredients costing $40,500 were purchased, $16,500 for cash and $24,000 on open account.

3. Mixers, ovens, and other equipment worth $30,000 were acquired on open account.

4. Circulars advertising the grand opening were printed and distributed at a cost of $600. A check for $1,200 was given to a rock band to secure its services to play each evening during opening week.

5. The brothers offered to buy for $6,700 an adjacent piece of land for a parking lot. No reply was received.

*October 6–30:*

6. Cash received in connection with pizzas served to customers was $41,500.

7. Salaries and wage costs amounting to $11,700 were incurred; $10,200 of this was paid in cash.

8. Other miscellaneous services (utilities, etc.) acquired and used during the month were $1,300, paid in cash.

9. A counteroffer from the owner of the adjacent land (see item 5) was received to sell the land for $9,000 cash. The brothers Dense accepted the offer, and title to the land passed to the business.

10. Accounts payable in the amount of $9,500 were paid in cash.

11. A refund of $100 was received from the printer for faultily printed advertising circulars (see transaction 4).

*October 31:*

12. A note payable for $30,000 was offered in payment of the open account created by the equipment purchases in transaction 3. The supplier accepts the note.
13. Pizza ingredients remaining on hand amounted to $18,600.
14. Entries were made to record the cost of asset services consumed (depreciation) during October of $300 on the restaurant building and $600 on the mixers, ovens, and other equipment.
15. Interest revenue accrued on the securities invested by U. R. amounted to $100.

**Required:**

a. Prepare journal entries for the above events.
b. Post the journal entries to ledger (T) accounts.
c. Prepare an income statement for the month of October and a position statement as of October 31.
d. Review transactions 4 and 11, regarding advertising, and answer these questions:
   (1) Should the $600 be shown as prepaid advertising?
   (2) Could the $600 be shown as advertising expense?
   (3) Is the refund in transaction 11 revenue? Is it a negative expense? Is it a negative prepaid asset? Explain.

**4–12. Recording Transactions to Ledger Accounts and Statement Preparation**
At the close of business on December 31, 1991, the accounts of the Prince Toy Company had the following balances:

|  | Debit | Credit |
|---|---|---|
| Cash | $ 52,000 | |
| Accounts receivable | 68,000 | |
| Inventory | 66,000 | |
| Office supplies | 4,100 | |
| Unexpired insurance | 1,800 | |
| Prepaid maintenance | 6,000 | |
| Store equipment | 14,000 | |
| Delivery equipment | 40,000 | |
| Accounts payable | | $ 50,000 |
| Wages payable | | 14,000 |
| Rent payable | | 36,000 |
| Capital stock | | 124,000 |
| Retained earnings | | 27,900 |
| | $251,900 | $251,900 |

The following transactions, in summary form, occurred in the calendar year 1992:

1. Purchased inventory on account, $300,000.
2. Insurance premiums paid, $800.
3. Delivery equipment purchased on account, $1,000.
4. Purchased supplies, $2,400, half for cash and half on account.

5. Wages paid in cash during the year, $46,000; wages payable on December 31, 1992, $12,000.
6. Advertising expenses paid for in cash, $3,600.
7. Payments on account, $280,000.
8. Rent paid during the year, $50,000; rent payable on December 31, 1992, $8,000.
9. Sales of toys on account, $440,000.
10. Cost of inventory sold during the year, $360,000.
11. Cash collected from customers, $346,700.
12. Toys returned by customers and accepted by Prince Toy, $6,700 selling price and $4,000 cost. The customers had not paid their accounts arising from these purchases. Prince Toy Company donates the toys to a nearby day-care center.
13. Unused supplies, $1,400.
14. Insurance expired during the year, $1,200.
15. Maintenance services used up under the maintenance contract, $3,200.

**Required:**

a. Set up ledger (T) accounts for the above accounts and enter the opening balances for 1991.
b. Make ledger entries to record the transactions for 1992, using revenue and expense accounts.
c. Prepare, in good form, an income statement for 1992 and a position statement as of December 31, 1992.

**4–13. Preparing Ledger Accounts and Financial Statements**

Leif E. Maple and his wife, Sugar, decided to open a candy store on August 1, 1991. Because this business is not a corporation, an equity account called Capital rather than Capital Stock is used for the owners' investment. The following transactions occurred in August.

1. On August 2, they deposited their savings of $18,000 in a bank account for the new firm.
2. On August 3, Leif purchased new equipment for $13,200, paying $1,200 and promising to pay the rest in 60 days.
3. Leif and Sugar leased a new building for $800 per month. The builder wanted to have new tenants as soon as possible, and so agreed that lease payments could be made on the last day of each month and that no prepayment of rent or deposit would be necessary.
4. Utilities were hooked up. The firm had to pay a $720 deposit which could be subtracted from its monthly utility bills at a rate of $60 per month until the deposit was recovered.
5. Leif had alterations and improvements made to the inside of the store building that cost $9,000 and were paid in cash (these expenditures are called Leasehold Improvements).
6. Candy was ordered and delivered to the store by a wholesaler. The cost was $5,200, payable in 30 days.
7. Candy sales for cash amounted to $1,800 during the first 15 days of August.

8. Candy, which cost $200, was returned to the wholesaler because of melting and spoilage. The wholesaler replaced the candy, which had an anticipated selling price of $300.
9. Employee salaries of $1,200 were paid for the month.
10. Additional purchases of candy during the month were $2,280, unpaid as of the end of the month.
11. Supplies costing $720 were purchased for cash. Of these, approximately two thirds were used during the month.
12. Sales in the last half of the month were $4,200. This included $2,400 of credit sales, of which $2,080 had been collected by the end of the month.
13. Leif discovered that $500 worth of candy had been wrapped incorrectly. The wholesaler agreed to take the candy back because it could be returned to the maker. Leif and Sugar's account was credited.
14. It was estimated that the cost of candy on hand on August 31 was $2,600.
15. Leif estimated that the equipment would last about 5 years or 60 months. Therefore, the cost of the equipment used up will be spread equally over this period.
16. Leif estimated that the leasehold improvements would last only 3 years. After that additional improvements would have to be made.
17. The utility bill for $540 was received. This amount, less the allocated deposit, is payable on September 10.
18. The lease payment was made on August 31.

**Required:**

*a.* Enter the above transactions in ledger accounts.
*b.* Prepare an income statement for August and a position statement as of August 31.
*c.* From these statements do you foresee any financial difficulties for the Maples? Explain.

**Casette 4–1.  Establishing Needed Revenues and Expenses**

In Casette 3–2 you were asked to identify the asset and equity accounts that you would expect to appear on the balance sheet of a golf course. Review that casette and complete the analyses requested below.

**Required:**

*a.* Identify the major revenue and expense accounts that you would expect to be reported on the annual income statements for the golf course.
*b.* The following transactions have been summarized in terms of their debit-credit impact on general classifications of accounts. Using the accounts you identified in part *a* and in Casette 3–2, describe the nature of a possible underlying event that would cause the indicated changes. Do not use the same description for more than one transaction.
  (1) Debit a current asset and credit a current liability for $6,000.
  (2) Debit a current asset and credit a temporary owners' equity account for $800.
  (3) Debit a temporary owners' equity account and credit a noncurrent asset for $400.

(4) Debit a noncurrent asset and credit a current liability for $8,000.

(5) Debit a current asset for $2,500, credit another current asset for $2,000, and make entries in two temporary owners' equity accounts—one a credit for $2,500 and another a debit for $2,000.

(6) Debit a temporary owners' equity account and credit a current liability for $1,400.

(7) Debit a current liability and credit a current asset for $700.

**Casette 4–2.  Completing the Accounting Process**

On January 1, 1991, the account balances of Luslerun Corporation were as follows:

| | Debit | Credit |
|---|---|---|
| Cash . . . . . . . . . . . . . | $ 12,600 | |
| Accounts receivable . . . . . . . . . . . . . . . . . . | 135,200 | |
| Merchandise inventory . . . . . . . . . . . . . . . . | 192,300 | |
| Supplies inventory. . . . . . . . . . . . . . . . . . . | 5,100 | |
| Prepaid insurance . . . . . . . . . . . . . . . . . . | 6,000 | |
| Land . . . . . . . . . . . . . . . . . . . . . . . | 94,500 | |
| Buildings . . . . . . . . . . . . . . . . . . . . . . | 189,000 | |
| Equipment . . . . . . . . . . . . . . . . . . . . . | 63,200 | |
| Accounts payable . . . . . . . . . . . . . . . . . . | | $157,500 |
| Salaries payable. . . . . . . . . . . . . . . . . . . | | 6,300 |
| Capital stock . . . . . . . . . . . . . . . . . . . . | | 400,000 |
| Retained earnings . . . . . . . . . . . . . . . . . . | | 134,100 |
| | $697,900 | $697,900 |

During the year the transactions summarized below took place:

Purchases on account:
| | |
|---|---|
| Merchandise inventory . . . . . . . . . . . . . . . . . . . . . . . . . . | $1,134,000 |
| Supplies inventory. . . . . . . . . . . . . . . . . . . . . . . . . . . | 8,400 |

Cash receipts:
| | |
|---|---|
| Services rendered to customers. . . . . . . . . . . . . . . . . . . . . | 147,000 |
| Collections of customers' accounts . . . . . . . . . . . . . . . . . . . | 1,260,000 |

Cash disbursements:
| | |
|---|---|
| Supplies inventory. . . . . . . . . . . . . . . . . . . . . . . . . . . | 5,500 |
| Delivery charges on merchandise sold . . . . . . . . . . . . . . . . . . | 9,300 |
| Insurance premiums . . . . . . . . . . . . . . . . . . . . . . . . . | 3,400 |
| Payments on account. . . . . . . . . . . . . . . . . . . . . . . . . | 1,197,000 |
| Salespersons' salaries . . . . . . . . . . . . . . . . . . . . . . . . | 79,400 |
| Utility services . . . . . . . . . . . . . . . . . . . . . . . . . . . | 8,900 |
| Downpayment on equipment to be delivered and installed in 1992 . . . . | 50,000 |

| | |
|---|---|
| Sales of product on account . . . . . . . . . . . . . . . . . . . . . . . | 1,442,000 |

Other information:
| | |
|---|---|
| Depreciation for year on building. . . . . . . . . . . . . . . . . . . . | 6,300 |
| Depreciation for year on equipment . . . . . . . . . . . . . . . . . . | 5,100 |
| Insurance expired during year . . . . . . . . . . . . . . . . . . . . | 5,600 |
| Supplies on hand on December 31 . . . . . . . . . . . . . . . . . . . | 3,800 |
| Merchandise on hand on December 31 . . . . . . . . . . . . . . . | 273,000 |
| Unpaid salespersons' salaries . . . . . . . . . . . . . . . . . . . . | 4,200 |

**Required:**

*a.* Prepare general journal entries to record the transactions for the year.

*b.* Open ledger (T) accounts, enter the beginning balances, and post the journal entries from *(a)*.

*c.* Prepare an income statement for the year and a position statement as of the end of the year.

**Casette 4–3. Completing the Accounting Process from Incomplete Records**

The Jones Paint Manufacturing Co. had an unfortunate event occur on June 30, 1990. The company accountant was working late to finish the preparation of the financial statements for the six months ended June 30. Unexpectedly, a mixture of paint solvents exploded. The main building, which housed both the manufacturing facility and the home office, was badly burned.

The accountant had his hands burned in the fire but was able to save the ledger and the portion of the general journal on which he was working. Unfortunately, the accountant's work was not very far along. The ledger accounts show only the May 31 balances (which are the beginning balances for June 1). He had just begun entering the journal entries, and they were only partially completed.

You are called in to complete the month's accounting and statement preparation. You find the ledger accounts and the General Journal as shown below:

| **Cash** | No. 1 | | **Accounts Receivable** | No. 3 |
|---|---|---|---|---|
| √ Bal 25,000 | | √ Bal 55,000 | |

| **Inventory** | No. 4 | | **Plant & Equipment** | No. 12 |
|---|---|---|---|---|
| √ Bal 85,000 | | √ Bal 250,000 | |

| **Land** | No. 10 | | **Accounts Payable** | No. 21 |
|---|---|---|---|---|
| √ Bal 50,000 | | | √ Bal 27,000 |

| **Bank Loan Payable** | No. 24 | | **Capital Stock** | No. 30 |
|---|---|---|---|---|
| | | | √ Bal 400,000 |

| **Retained Earnings** | No. 40 | | **Sales** | No. 50 |
|---|---|---|---|---|
| | √ Bal 38,000 | | |

| **Cost of Goods Sold** | No. 60 | | **Salaries & Wages Expense** | No. 61 |
|---|---|---|---|---|
| | | | |

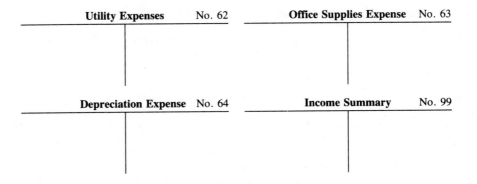

| General Journal | | | | Page 8 |
|---|---|---|---|---|
| Date | Accounts/Explanation | PR | Debit | Credit |
| June 1 | Cash | | | |
| | Bank Loan Payable | | | |
| June 5 | Cash | | | |
| | Capital Stock | | | |

You are able to determine the following information as you attempt to complete the accounting for June:

1. In checking with the bank you find that the firm had borrowed $50,000 on June 1. The firm's copy of the note signed by the president of the bank burned in the fire, but the bank sent you a photocopy to review.
2. The current owners purchased additional capital stock for $100,000 cash on June 5. The book that holds the stock certificates indicates this transaction on the duplicate pages.
3. The accountant had just finished preparing a listing of the sales invoices for the month. The listing shows:
   *a.* Sales on account for June—$195,000.
   *b.* Sales for cash for June—$15,000.
4. The warehouse foreman had been responsible for counting the inventory on June 30. Fortunately, he had not had time to give the count to the accountant before the fire. He gives you the count and, after you determine the cost for each type of inventory, you calculate the June 30 inventory as having a total cost of $265,000.
5. The accountant had also finished preparing a listing of the inventory purchase invoices for June. The total additional paint inventory purchased during June (all of which was on credit) totaled $260,000.
6. You take the checkbook and review the record of checks written. Two business expenses paid in cash were:
   *a.* Utilities—$10,000.
   *b.* Office supplies—$5,000.

7. The bank statement arrived on July 2, and you were able to determine that all of the checks for salaries and wages had been cashed. The total for June was $75,000.

8. You review the financial statements for January through May and determine that the company had been making monthly entries of $8,000 to record depreciation expense on the paint manufacturing plant and equipment.

**Required:**

a. Use the information given above and complete a general journal using the same form started by the accountant.

b. After completing the journal entries, post the entries to the ledger accounts. Cross-reference the entries between the journal and the ledger.

c. Prepare closing entries using the Income Summary account. Post the entries to the ledger.

d. Prepare in proper form a balance sheet as of June 30 and an income statement for the month of June.

# Chapter 5

# Elements of the Accounting Cycle

In Chapters 1 and 4 we discussed the major tasks the financial accounting system performs in gathering and communicating economic and financial information. Chapter 4 discussed two important accounting elements—journals and ledgers—that make the system work. Accountants record and classify the business entity's transactions in these elements. Financial statements present the results of the accounting system. They are the major vehicles of communication and represent the culmination of the accounting process.

In a sense, then, the journals and ledgers stand at the beginning of the accounting process, and the financial statements stand at the end. Accounting uses several additional procedures to complete the recording-processing-reporting link. In this chapter we will expand our understanding of the accounting process by examining some of these procedures.

The first part of the chapter discusses adjusting entries, an important procedure in the accounting system. Knowledge of this topic will increase our ability to use accounting as an analytical tool. The next section of the chapter presents all of the accounting procedures in a recurring pattern called the *accounting cycle*. An understanding of the accounting cycle will allow us to put bookkeeping and accounting procedures into perspective. Finally, one of the most critical functions of the accounting system—the exercise of accounting control—is introduced at the end of the chapter. An accounting system is useless if there is no way to assure that the financial reports are accurate and that the assets reported on the balance sheet actually do exist. Internal controls are the accountant's way of providing these assurances in the accounting system.

## ADJUSTING ENTRIES

Previously, we identified accounting transactions as being external or internal. Most of our discussion up to this point has illustrated external transactions that consist of business dealings with parties external to the entity. These parties generally are involved in transactions that result in sales, purchases, loans, stock issues, cash receipts or payments, and the like.

We did discuss one type of internal transaction—the closing entry. The closing entry is internal because it facilitates the accounting process and is not generated by any external transaction.

A much more important type of internal transaction is the *adjusting entry*. This entry also facilitates the accounting process. However, it relates either to completed external transactions or to future ones. Adjusting entries reflect changes in assets and liabilities that are taking place on a rather continuous basis but are not identified by discrete transactions with outside parties.

In Chapters 3 and 4 we illustrated a few adjusting entries without noting their special character. The following two examples explain the nature of adjusting entries:

1. Prepaid rent—an advance payment made for the use of an office building needs to be adjusted for the portion of the prepayment that expires by the end of the accounting period.
2. Accrued wages payable—the obligation to pay employees their wages accumulates daily, even though the employees are paid periodically (weekly, semi-monthly, monthly, etc.). An adjusting entry is needed to recognize the expense accumulation for wages owed to the employees but not paid at the end of the accounting period.

It would be tremendously time consuming and expensive to record these internal changes in journal entry form and to post them to the ledger accounts each day. It is easier to enter the cumulative totals periodically as part of an explicit, external transaction or as an internal account update at the end of an accounting period. For instance, in the first example, rent expense is recorded when the end of an accounting period has been reached, even though the rent was prepaid, because the rented space has been used and the value received. No external transaction occurs, but the adjusting entry will reduce the prepaid rent and record an expense in an internal transaction.

In the second example, recognition of the daily accumulation of labor costs is normally deferred until payday when the external transaction to pay employees allows us to make an entry for the entire period's cost. What happens, however, if we reach the end of an accounting period and no external transaction has occurred? An account adjustment must be made using an internal transaction to recognize the accumulation of the wage expense.

## Adjusting Entries Defined

In order to furnish audiences of financial statements with accurate and timely information, all external and internal transactions for the accounting period should be recorded prior to the preparation of the statements. Otherwise, the account balances will be incomplete and inaccurate and the financial statements, misleading. Unless all asset and equity events are recorded, the balance sheet will not portray the entity's actual financial condition at the end of the accounting period. Likewise, the income statement will not present a realistic picture of the period's operations because all revenues and expenses were not taken into consideration.

Accountants enhance accuracy and timeliness in the accounts by completing adjusting entries prior to the preparation of the financial statements. *Adjusting entries are those internal transactions recorded at the end of the accounting period to reflect events that have taken place but that have not been recorded through external transactions.*

Adjusting entries implement the concepts of *accrual accounting*. Accrual accounting requires that revenues and expenses, as well as their related effects upon the entity's financial position, be identified and reported in the period *when they occur* and not when cash receipts and disbursements are made. True, we sometimes use the cash receipt and disbursement points for recording convenience, but they do not govern which events will be presented on the financial statements.

Although a variety of financial conditions may require adjustments, there are a limited set of common types. Adjusting entries for continuous transactions involve either the allocation of an amount already recorded on the books or the accrual of an amount that has changed during the period but has not yet been recorded. Allocation and accrual apply to both revenues earned and to expenses incurred and lead to the following four possible types of adjusting transactions:

1. Allocating the consumed cost of assets previously acquired and recorded to reflect expenses for the accounting period.

   *Example:*   A business acquired trucks for $30,000 two years ago. Depreciation for the current year is $6,000. No entry will be made during the year as an external transaction. However, an internal adjusting entry at the end of the year will record the depreciation expense and the reduction in the asset account for vehicles.

2. Accruing the value of assets that expired during the accounting period (expenses) but are not yet recorded.

   *Example:*   Advertising is printed in the daily newspaper and amounts to $15,000 at year-end. The newspaper has not sent bills for the advertising, so no external transaction has occurred to recognize this expense. An internal adjusting entry will record the expense and a corresponding liability to indicate the amount payable to the newspaper.

3. Allocating the value of assets received in advance of the earning process that now have been earned as revenue.

   *Example:*   A firm produces an expensive custom product and requires purchasers to pay in advance. Last year advance payments received were $50,000. However, only $20,000 covered products completed last year; the other $30,000 covers products completed this year. Adjusting entries would be needed at the end of both years to apportion the $50,000 revenue between the two years in which it was earned.

4. Accruing the value of assets (revenues) earned during the accounting period but not yet recorded.

*Example:* On November 1, $45,000 of cash was invested in 90-day commercial paper to earn interest revenue. The commercial paper will mature on January 29 of the next year. At that time the $45,000 plus interest will be received. At year-end, December 31, $2,200 of the interest has been earned but has not been received. No external transaction has occurred. An adjusting entry is needed to record the $2,200 interest as revenue and as the asset, Interest Receivable.

As noted from the examples above, if the accounting process waits until an external transaction occurs, the accuracy of numerous transactions will be lost. Although accountants find it convenient to operate temporarily under the *cash basis of accounting,* the accounts will not accurately reflect all of the revenue that has been earned and all of the expenses that have been incurred. The *accrual basis* of accounting recognizes that earning revenue (revenue recognition) and receiving cash are not necessarily synonymous. Likewise, cash disbursement and resource consumption (expense recognition) are not the same.

Adjusting entries for allocations and accruals never feature a debit or credit to the Cash account because the effects of cash transactions are recorded only at the time they occur. Also, each adjusting entry involves at least one income statement account and at least one balance sheet account. Consequently, any failure to adjust the books properly will result in distortions to both major financial statements.

## Cost Allocations

Numerous examples of this first type of adjustment exist. Many nonmonetary assets fall into this category. They represent costs that will benefit more than one accounting period. As a portion of these assets' services is used up in each period, part of the cost is allocated as an expense to that period.

**Expenditures Initially Recorded as Assets.** Suppose that a payment for insurance during a year is recorded as follows:

| | | |
|---|---|---|
| Prepaid Insurance | 4,300 | |
|     Cash | | 4,300 |

Of course this entry results in a debit balance in the Prepaid Insurance account on December 31. A careful analysis of the insurance coverage reveals that the cost of the coverage still in force on December 31 is only $1,400. The following adjusting entry will reduce the prepaid account to $1,400 and recognize the cost of the expired insurance as $2,900:

```
Insurance Expense. . . . . . . . . . . . . . . . . . . .   2,900
        Prepaid Insurance ($4,300 − $1,400) . . . . . . . .          2,900
```

As a second example, assume that a firm orders substantial quantities of office supplies during a year. The purchases total $6,000, and they are debited to an Office Supplies Inventory account. In summary, the entries during the year would be recorded as:

```
(1)  Office Supplies Inventory . . . . . . . . . . . . .   6,000
          Cash . . . . . . . . . . . . . . . . . . . . .          6,000
```

During the year, most of the supplies are consumed; however, at year-end a count indicates that $400 of supplies are on hand. The asset account must be reduced to $400 and the difference, $5,600, should be recorded as an expense. The adjusting entry to accomplish this would be:

```
(2)  Office Supplies Expense . . . . . . . . . . . . . .   5,600
          Office Supplies Inventory . . . . . . . . . .          5,600
```

If we examine the ledger accounts they would appear as:

| Office Supplies Inventory | | | | Office Supplies Expense | |
| --- | --- | --- | --- | --- | --- |
| *(1)* | 6,000 | *(2)* | 5,600 | *(2)* | 5,600 |
| | √ 400 | | | | |

Similar adjustments would be required for such assets as prepaid rent, merchandise inventory, and other assets paid for in advance of their consumption.

**Depreciation Expense.** Depreciation expense is a special example of the cost allocation process because it uses a unique account to record the expired portion of the asset. Depreciation expense is an estimate of the cost of a long-lived asset's services used during the period in generating revenues. Although a firm continuously utilizes assets such as buildings, equipment, furniture and fixtures, and vehicles, a daily recording of depreciation is unnecessary and probably quite inaccurate. Rather, the firm makes an adjusting entry at the end of the accounting period.

For example, a company acquires store equipment at a cost of $35,000. The entry would be:

```
(1)  Store Equipment . . . . . . . . . . . . . . . . .   35,000
          Cash (or Accounts Payable). . . . . . . . . .          35,000
```

The equipment is expected to last 5 years. At the end of each year an entry would be necessary to reflect the expiration of a year's service value:

```
Depreciation Expense . . . . . . . . . . . . . . . . .   7,000
        Store Equipment ($35,000/5 years). . . . . . . .          7,000
```

In accounting practice, the credit entry almost universally is made to a separate account called *Accumulated Depreciation* (or *Allowance for Depreciation*) so the entry would appear as:

```
(2)  Depreciation Expense . . . . . . . . . . . . . .   7,000
         Accumulated Depreciation—Store
             Equipment. . . . . . . . . . . . . . .              7,000
```

If we viewed the ledger accounts, they would appear as:

| Store Equipment | | Accumulated Depreciation | | Depreciation Expense | |
|---|---|---|---|---|---|
| *(1)* 35,000 | | | *(2)* 7,000 | *(2)* 7,000 | |

The Accumulated Depreciation account is called a *contra asset* account.[1] It becomes an integral part of the asset and appears as a deduction from the asset on the position statement. For example, at the end of the year this equipment would be reported as follows:

```
Store equipment . . . . . . . . . . . . . . . . . . . .   $35,000
    Less: Accumulated depreciation . . . . . . . . . .     7,000   $28,000
```

Conceptually, making direct credits to the asset account would be a perfectly sound procedure. Although the asset may not appear to have changed physically, economically a portion of its service potential has expired. By using the contra account, we are able to report more information on the balance sheet—the original cost of the asset still in use, the estimated portion used, and the unexpired cost applicable to future periods. Depreciation, at best, is an estimate and its placement in a contra account allows the reader roughly to judge the adequacy of the provision for depreciation and to know the general age of the asset. One could not do so if the asset were reported simply at $28,000.

**Assets Initially Recorded as Expenses.** An interesting twist on the problem of recording and adjusting for consumed assets occurs when an initial payment is recorded as an expense rather than as an asset. Assume that in the insurance example earlier, the $4,300 payment is debited directly to the Insurance Expense account. The entry would be:

```
(1)  Insurance Expense . . . . . . . . . . . . . . . .   4,300
         Cash . . . . . . . . . . . . . . . . . . . .              4,300
```

---

[1] This is our first contact with some special accounts called *valuation* accounts. Their purpose is to modify the amounts entered in some other account to which they apply. Valuation accounts are of two general types—*contra accounts* to record downward modifications to the main ledger account and *adjunct accounts* to record upward modifications. Contra and adjunct accounts can be used in conjunction with any kind of account where there is a need to segregate particular kinds of increases or decreases. The complete record of the particular item is thus divided between two accounts. Part of it is in the main ledger account, while the rest has been isolated in a contra account (in the case of offsets) or adjunct account (in the case of additions).

At the end of the year, only $2,900 should be recorded as Insurance Expense. The remaining $1,400 should be in an asset account, Prepaid Insurance. An adjusting entry would be necessary to establish these amounts.

(2)   Prepaid Insurance. . . . . . . . . . . . . . . . . . 1,400
            Insurance Expense  . . . . . . . . . . . . .        1,400

Viewing the ledger accounts shows how these transactions are initially recorded and adjusted under this alternative approach:

| Insurance Expense | | Prepaid Insurance | |
|---|---|---|---|
| *(1)*    4,300 | *(2)*    1,400 | *(2)*    1,400 | |
| ✓ 2,900 | | | |

The direct debit to an expense account is used when there is a high probability that the total amount of the asset value will be consumed during the period. If a part of the asset does remain unused at the end of the period, then expenses are overstated and assets are understated.

*No matter how the initial entry is made, the end results have to be the same. All that must be determined is how much of the cost eventually should end up in the expense and asset accounts by the end of the period.* In the insurance example, both recording and adjusting options result in a $1,400 balance in Prepaid Insurance and a $2,900 balance in Insurance Expense.

**Expense Accrual**

This type of adjustment is necessary whenever an asset (usually some type of service) is used during the period but the consumption is not recorded at the time it occurs. Rather, the entries are deferred for clerical convenience until the service is actually paid for in cash. Wages and salaries are a good case in point.

Assume that salespersons' salaries are $4,000 per month, payable on the 10th of the following month. At the end of the current accounting period, December 31, the salaries for December have not been recorded, even though the firm owes the salaries and the expense has been incurred. On December 31, this expense should be recorded and the liability for the salaries should be recognized to permit preparation of accurate financial statements for the current period. The adjusting entry needed to bring the accounts to their correct balances is:

Dec. 31   Salary Expense. . . . . . . . . . . . . . . . . 4,000
                 Salaries Payable* . . . . . . . . . . . .        4,000

*At times this account is called "Accrued Salaries Payable." The term *accrued* is unnecessary as both accounts indicate the existence of a liability. The term *accrued* usually signifies an account arising from an adjusting entry.

On January 10 of the next year, the payment of these salaries will be recorded with the following entry:

Jan. 10   Salaries Payable. . . . . . . . . . . . . . . .   4,000
             Cash. . . . . . . . . . . . . . . . . . . . .             4,000

When the payment is made on January 10, no additional expense is recorded; only the liability is eliminated by disbursing cash. The cash payment did *not* determine the recognition of the expense. The expense was recorded in the period in which it was incurred using an adjusting entry.

For another illustration, assume that the company leases a photocopy machine for the office. The rental cost is based on the number of copies made at a rate of 5 cents per copy. Payments are made every other month, based on a metered count of the copies. On December 31, the meter shows that 8,000 copies have been made since the last payment. These 8,000 copies are an expense of the current accounting period and the following adjusting entry would be made:

Office Expense . . . . . . . . . . . . . . . . . . . .   400
     Equipment Rentals Payable . . . . . . . . . . . . .        400

## Revenue Allocations

When customers make advance payments as a condition for future delivery of goods and services, the firm receiving the payment has a corresponding liability equal to the amount of the payment. At the time of service or product delivery, the cash payment will have been earned. Thus, the liability no longer exists, and the amount of revenue now earned must be recognized.

Assume that a firm leases a portion of its warehouse for 12 months beginning September 1 at a monthly rate of $200. The renter pays the annual rental of $2,400 in advance on September 1. The following entry recording the advance would be made on September 1:

Sept. 1   Cash . . . . . . . . . . . . . . . . . . . .   2,400
            Liability for Advanced Rent . . . . . . . .        2,400

At year-end, December 31, four months of the lease have expired, and the firm has earned $200 for each month. These revenues will be recorded in the current year when the following *adjusting entry* is made:

Dec. 31   Liability for Advanced Rent . . . . . . . . .   800
            Rent Revenue. . . . . . . . . . . . . . .        800

**Liability Initially Recorded as Revenues.**   We saw that assets could initially be recorded as expenses, and an adjusting entry would be used to restate the account balances so that they correctly reflect assets and expenses. Similarly, the entire advance payment might have been recorded as a revenue. Then an adjusting entry would be needed to restate the liability and revenue accounts at the end of the accounting period.

Assume in the example above that the total advance had been recorded as revenue. The initial entry would have been:

| | | |
|---|---|---|
| Sept. 1 | Cash . . . . . . . . . . . . . . . . . . . . | 2,400 |
| | Rent Revenue . . . . . . . . . . . . . | 2,400 |

At year-end, the adjusting entry needed to establish the liability as $1,600 (8 months × $200 per month) would be:

| | | |
|---|---|---|
| Dec. 31 | Rent Revenue . . . . . . . . . . . . . . | 1,600 |
| | Liability for Advanced Rent . . . . . . . | 1,600 |

If we view the ledger accounts, as shown on Figure 5–1, it will be apparent that both methods produce the same results.

*Whether the allocation is from a liability account to a revenue account, as in the first example, or from a revenue account to a liability account, the purpose and end result are the same. The underlying analysis involves determining the amount applicable to products and services rendered this period and the amount applicable to future periods.*

## Revenue Accrual

This fourth common type of adjustment is similar to the second. For clerical convenience, the recording of revenue may sometimes be deferred until cash is collected. However, if the revenue is earned in one accounting period

---

**FIGURE 5–1**  Comparison of Adjustments to Alternative Recording of Advance Payments

| Initial Advance Recorded as a Liability | | | Initial Advance Recorded as Revenue | | |
|---|---|---|---|---|---|
| **Cash** | | | **Cash** | | |
| *9/1* | 2,400 | | *9/1* | 2,400 | |
| **Liability for Advanced Rent** | | | **Liability for Advanced Rent** | | |
| *12/31* | 800 | *9/1* 2,400 | | | *12/31* 1,600 |
| | | √ 1,600 | | | |
| **Rent Revenue** | | | **Rent Revenue** | | |
| | | *12/31* 800 | *12/31* 1,600 | *9/1* 2,400 | |
| | | | | √ 800 | |

and the cash collection will occur in the next, an adjustment is necessary to reflect the revenue and related asset claim. For instance, interest is earned with the passage of time, but it is not recorded every day. If a finance company lends $10,000 at 12 percent interest to a manufacturer for six months beginning on December 1, one month's interest revenue of $100 ($10,000 × 0.12 × 1/12) is applicable to the accounting period that ends on December 31. The finance company's claim has grown from $10,000 to $10,100. The adjusting entry shown below would be made on the records of the finance company to establish correct balances for assets and revenues:

| | | |
|---|---|---|
| Interest Receivable . . . . . . . . . . . . . . . . . . | 100 | |
| Interest Revenue . . . . . . . . . . . . . . . . . . | | 100 |

Any revenue-producing activity that is performed during the period but will be paid for later may be subject to the same type of adjustment. For instance, a typewriter distributorship might receive a 10 percent commission from a manufacturer on all new typewriters sold to customers. If, during December, new typewriters having a $23,000 retail price are sold, the firm should make the following adjusting entry, even though the cash may not be received until sometime in January:

| | | |
|---|---|---|
| Commissions Receivable . . . . . . . . . . . . . . . | 2,300 | |
| Commission Revenue . . . . . . . . . . . . . . | | 2,300 |

This basic introduction to some of the more common types of adjusting entries does not exhaust the subject. Throughout the remaining chapters, we will encounter other adjusting entries, as well as new examples of the basic ones discussed here. Practically any entry could be subject to later adjustment. Fundamentally, adjusting entries encompass all those entries necessary at the end of the accounting period to ensure that asset, liability, revenue, and expense accounts are as accurate as possible.

## CASH VERSUS ACCRUAL INCOME STATEMENTS

Now that we have explored the mechanics and function of adjusting entries, let us see how they can be used to convert cash basis accounting to accrual basis accounting. Recall that with cash basis accounting, revenues and expenses are recorded at the time cash amounts are either received or paid. Accrual basis accounting records revenues when they are earned and expenses when they are incurred, regardless of when cash is received or paid.

The following example illustrates the differences between these two accounting bases and shows the impact of the two methods on the preparation of the income statement.

Assume that a small regional newspaper published in Midwest City has the following transactions for the first quarter of 1991:

1. Subscriptions for the quarter ending March 31:
    *a.* Total received in cash, $25,000.
    *b.* Amount remaining in force into the following quarter, $2,000.

2. Newsprint and ink used for printing the newspaper:
   a. Total paid for during the quarter, $13,000.
   b. Amount on hand at March 31, $3,000.
3. Wages for the quarter:
   a. Wages paid in cash, $4,000.
   b. Wages owed at the end of the quarter, $1,000.
4. Six-month fire insurance policy:
   a. Premium paid on January 1, $5,000.
   b. Unexpired insurance on March 31, $2,500.
5. Office supplies:
   a. Total paid during the quarter, $1,500.
   b. Supplies on hand at March 31, $900.
6. Utilities for the quarter:
   a. Utilities paid on March 31, $500.

## Cash Basis Income Statement

The preparation of an income statement using the cash basis would recognize all of the cash receipts and payments in the six transactions as revenues and expenses. The statement would appear as shown in Figure 5–2.

## Accrual Basis Income Statement

The net income shown below includes revenues that will not be earned until the following accounting period (quarter), shows expenses for items that have

---

**FIGURE 5–2**   Cash Basis Income Statement

### MIDWEST CITY PUBLICATIONS
### Income Statement (Cash Basis)
### For the Quarter Ending March 31, 1991

| | | |
|---|---:|---:|
| Subscription revenue . . . . . . . . . . . . . . . . . . | | $25,000 |
| Expenses: | | |
| Newsprint and ink . . . . . . . . . . . . . . . . | $13,000 | |
| Wages . . . . . . . . . . . . . . . . . . . . . . | 4,000 | |
| Insurance . . . . . . . . . . . . . . . . . . . . | 5,000 | |
| Supplies . . . . . . . . . . . . . . . . . . . . . | 1,500 | |
| Utilities . . . . . . . . . . . . . . . . . . . . . | 500 | |
| Total expenses . . . . . . . . . . . . . . . . | | 24,000 |
| Net income . . . . . . . . . . . . . . . . . . . . . | | $ 1,000 |

---

not been consumed (newsprint, insurance, and supplies), and fails to show an expense that has been incurred (wages). Accounting under the accrual basis converts the cash basis values by using the following adjusting journal entries:

1. To adjust revenues:

| | | |
|---|---|---|
| Subscription Revenue . . . . . . . . . . . . . . | 2,000 | |
|     Unexpired Subscriptions . . . . . . . . . . . | | 2,000 |

2. To adjust newsprint and ink:

| | | |
|---|---|---|
| Newsprint and Ink Inventory . . . . . . . . . . . | 3,000 | |
|     Newsprint and Ink Expense . . . . . . . . . . | | 3,000 |

3. To adjust wages:

| | | |
|---|---|---|
| Wages Expense. . . . . . . . . . . . . . . . . | 1,000 | |
|     Wages Payable . . . . . . . . . . . . . . . | | 1,000 |

4. To adjust insurance:

| | | |
|---|---|---|
| Prepaid Insurance . . . . . . . . . . . . . . . | 2,500 | |
|     Insurance Expense . . . . . . . . . . . . . | | 2,500 |

5. To adjust supplies:

| | | |
|---|---|---|
| Supplies Inventory . . . . . . . . . . . . . . | 900 | |
|     Supplies Expense . . . . . . . . . . . . . | | 900 |

6. To adjust utilities: none needed as the payment made was only for the first quarter's utilities. This example shows how it is possible, on occasion, for the cash basis and the accrual basis of accounting to be in agreement.

We can summarize the adjustments to the revenue and expense accounts as follows:

| | Cash-Basis Value | Adjustment | Accrual-Basis Value |
|---|---|---|---|
| Revenues . . . . . . . . . . . . | $25,000 | $(2,000) | $23,000 |
| Newsprint and ink . . . . . . . . . | 13,000 | (3,000) | 10,000 |
| Wages . . . . . . . . . . . . . | 4,000 | 1,000 | 5,000 |
| Insurance . . . . . . . . . . . | 5,000 | (2,500) | 2,500 |
| Supplies . . . . . . . . . . . . | 1,500 | (900) | 600 |
| Utilities . . . . . . . . . . . . | 500 | –0– | 500 |

An income statement prepared on the accrual basis would appear as shown in Figure 5–3.

Notice that the accrual income is higher, in this case, because several expenses were overstated on the cash basis. Revenues were also overstated on the cash basis but not by enough to offset the overstatement of expenses. The cash basis does not present economic performance as accurately as does the accrual basis. When using the cash basis method, a number of items

---

**FIGURE 5–3**   Accrual Basis Income Statement

---

**MIDWEST CITY PUBLICATIONS**
**Income Statement (Accrual Basis)**
**For the Quarter Ending March 31, 1991**

| | | |
|---|---:|---:|
| Subscription revenue . . . . . . . . . . . . . . . . . . | | $23,000 |
| Expenses: | | |
| Newsprint and ink . . . . . . . . . . . . . . . | $10,000 | |
| Wages . . . . . . . . . . . . . . . . . . . . | 5,000 | |
| Insurance . . . . . . . . . . . . . . . . . . . | 2,500 | |
| Supplies . . . . . . . . . . . . . . . . . . . | 600 | |
| Utilities . . . . . . . . . . . . . . . . . . . | 500 | |
| Total expenses . . . . . . . . . . . . . . | | 18,600 |
| Net income . . . . . . . . . . . . . . . . . . | | $ 4,400 |

---

(newsprint and ink, insurance, and supplies) will be consumed in future periods without the need to record any expense. Wages in the next period, by contrast, will be charged with $1,000 of this period's expense under the cash basis.

# THE ACCOUNTING CYCLE

You have been introduced to a number of accounting processes and functions—preparing statements, recording in ledgers, journalizing transactions, and developing adjusting entries. These procedures in an accounting system are interrelated and performed in an established order called the *accounting cycle*. Presented in the sequence in which they normally are performed, the steps in the accounting cycle are:

1. Recording transactions in a journal.
2. Posting journal entries to ledger accounts.
3. Preparing a trial balance.
4. Journalizing and posting adjusting entries.
5. Preparing an adjusted trial balance.
6. Preparing financial statements.
7. Journalizing and posting closing entries.

The first two steps make up most of the *bookkeeping* activity *during* the accounting period. The other five steps are performed at the *end* of the accounting period. Together, they summarize the accounting process from the initial recording function to the final reporting function. Now we are ready to make a somewhat more detailed examination of these elements and to consider the function of the entire accounting system.

## Recording Transactions in a Journal

This task begins the basic recording function in accounting. It involves recognizing the occurrence of a valid transaction, separating the transaction into its component parts (asset and equity changes), and recording that analysis in the systematic debit-credit framework we discussed in the previous chapter. The journal entry provides the original record of the events of the period, usually in chronological order. Hence, a journal is called a "record of original entry." True to the entity concept, we record only those transactions involving the business enterprise.

**Source Documents.**   Before a transaction can be entered formally in any type of journal, there must be an indication that the transaction has occurred. Until the advent of widespread computer processing, most journal entries were based on data collected on some document devoted to capturing the transaction. Documents still remain as the primary data collection devices in a vast majority of businesses, but computer systems have become capable of "paperless" data capture. Examples of this include automated teller machines at banks, airline reservations made over the phone, gasoline pumps started with credit cards, and so on. Although computerized systems often provide a printed copy of the transaction, the accounting system in these cases does not need a document to begin the recording process.

Consider systems that do use source documents. A business form flows to the accounting department to trigger the analysis and recording necessary for journalizing. Source documents include purchase invoices, bills of sale, check copies, cash register tapes, labor time summaries, legal documents, receiving reports, and so on. What forms are used, who initiates them, how they are routed, and how their accuracy is assured must be considered in the design of any accounting and data processing system used by a company.

Often the source documents supporting an entry are referenced in the explanation accompanying the formal journal entry. The documents are systematically filed to allow easy retrieval when details concerning a transaction are needed. The references between the documents and the journal entries are called an *audit trail*. With these references, management and auditors can trace transactions to determine whether the entries are supported by proper underlying documents. Without an audit trail, errors may not be found or corrected, and accounting control over the recording process is certainly weakened.

**Special Journals.**   All of our journal entries have used the general journal format. This form is suitable for any type of entry but requires significant clerical effort to write and post each entry. When the volume of transactions accelerates, the general journal is not suitable because of the required increased clerical effort. To speed up the journalizing and posting process and to allow for a division of accounting labor, modifications are made to the simple journal system. A number of separate books of original entry, called *special journals,* are introduced. These journals are tailored to efficiently handle high-volume transactions of specific types such as cash disbursements, cash receipts, sales, or purchases on account. When special journals are used, a general journal continues to be used for entries that do not fit into special journals.

Special journals bring efficiency to recording and posting by using special debit and credit columns to record individual transaction data. These journals record the repeated debits and credits by entering the dollar amounts in the special columns, thereby eliminating the need to write out the name of the accounts with each entry. Greater posting efficiency is achieved by transferring only the column totals, rather than each debit and credit, to the ledger. The number of special journals used depends on the nature and frequency of the accounting transactions for each firm.

## Posting Journal Entries to Ledger Accounts

Posting is the process of transferring the individual debit and credit changes from the journal to the ledger accounts. The process of posting in a manual system was discussed in Chapter 4. Posting with the use of an automated or electronic process does not change the purpose or function of this step. Posting is the beginning of the *classifying* process in accounting. It involves fitting the recorded data into a logical, useful framework of assets and equities.

**Chart of Accounts.**   The ledger accounts used by different companies vary according to the nature of their business activities and the degree of reporting detail they desire. The accounts required by a particular company are listed to show the account titles, account numbers, and classifications (current, noncurrent, etc.). This listing is called a "chart of accounts." Often the chart of accounts is expanded to include policies for completing entries in each account. When the expanded chart of accounts is organized and used to standardize the accounting process, it is called an "accounting manual."

Account identification normally uses a numerical coding system. A series of digits identifies each account, and each digit has a specific meaning. For example, the first digit might indicate a general classification such as "1" for current assets, "2" for noncurrent assets, "3" for current liabilities, and so on. Subsequent digits signify various subclassifications such as departments, facilities, and contracts. A carefully worked-out coding system provides ready identification and an orderly arrangement by financial statement grouping for ledger accounts. Moreover, the account numbering system allows easy adoption of electronic data processing.

**Subsidiary Ledgers.** Our discussion of ledger accounts and posting has dealt only with a single main set of accounts called the *general ledger*. When a large quantity of detailed information about a particular general ledger account exists, a separate set of accounts, called *subsidiary ledger* accounts, is used.

As is implied by their name, subsidiary ledger accounts support general ledger accounts. The general ledger accounts show, in summary form, what the subsidiary accounts show in detail. Because the general ledger accounts each contain the total of a group of supporting subsidiary accounts, they are called *control accounts*.

Any general ledger account may serve as a control account, but the most common ones are Accounts Receivable and Accounts Payable. For Accounts Receivable, a separate subsidiary account is maintained for each individual who owes the firm for sales made on account. For Accounts Payable, a separate subsidiary account shows to whom the firm owes money. Other general ledger accounts that frequently use subsidiary accounts are Inventory, Equipment, Sales Revenues, Notes Receivable and Payable, and Capital Stock.

Data is captured in detail in the subsidiary ledger and in total in the general ledger control account. For example, a total of each day's credit sales (or cash collections from customers) would be journalized and posted to the Accounts Receivable general ledger account. Duplicate copies of the sales invoices (or cash remittance forms) would be sorted and posted to the individual subsidiary ledger accounts. There are no offsetting debits and credits to the amounts entered in the subsidiary ledger accounts because they simply reflect in detail what is already recorded in total in the general ledger accounts. Only general ledger entries require the equality of debits and credits.

Subsidiary ledgers provide numerous advantages. Operationally, they allow for distribution and specialization of the clerical tasks of bookkeeping. The general ledger is more compact and can be maintained by one person (or machine). A number of subsidiary ledgers containing the bulk of the detailed information can be assigned to different individuals. Perhaps the major contribution of subsidiary ledgers is their aid in error identification. Because the total in control accounts should be the same as the detail in the subsidiary accounts, periodic comparisons (called "reconciliations" or "proving" the subsidiary ledgers) between the subsidiary and general ledgers will reveal errors if the accounts disagree.

Table 5–1 illustrates the relationships between general and subsidiary ledger accounts for Accounts Receivable and Notes Payable.

At the end of the accounting period, a schedule (see Table 5–2) can be prepared listing each subsidiary account that supports a given general ledger account. A comparison can then be made between the totals to check the accuracy of the records.

**TABLE 5–1**    General Ledger and Subsidiary Ledger Accounts

## General Ledger

| Accounts Receivable | | Notes Payable | | |
|---|---|---|---|---|
| ✓  120,000 | 40,000 | 300,000 | ✓  650,000 | Control accounts |
| | 60,000 | | | |
| ✓   20,000 | | | ✓  350,000 | |

## Subsidiary Ledger

| Adams Company | | 8.0%—10-Year Note | | |
|---|---|---|---|---|
| ✓   62,000 | 25,000 | 200,000 | ✓  300,000 | |
| | 25,000 | | ✓  100,000 | |
| ✓   12,000 | | | | |

| Baker Company | | 9.5%—12-Year Note | | |
|---|---|---|---|---|
| ✓    2,000 | | 100,000 | ✓  300,000 | |
| | | | ✓  200,000 | |

| Denison Company | | 5.5%—Revolving Note | | Supporting detail accounts |
|---|---|---|---|---|
| ✓   10,500 | 5,000 | | ✓   50,000 | |
| | 5,000 | | | |
| ✓      500 | | | | |

| Edwards Company | |
|---|---|
| ✓   45,500 | 10,000 |
| | 30,000 |
| ✓    5,500 | |

**TABLE 5–2**    Schedule of Accounts Receivable (per the subsidiary ledger)

|  |  |  |
|---|---|---|
| Adams Company . . . . | $12,000 | |
| Baker Company  . . . . | 2,000 | |
| Denison Company  . . . | 500 | |
| Edwards Company  . . . | 5,500 | |
| Total . . . . . . . . . | $20,000 | (compare to control account) |

## Preparing a Trial Balance

The first step of the accounting cycle performed at the *end* of the accounting period is the preparation of a *trial balance*. It is a listing of ledger account titles and their balances (debit or credit). A trial balance provides a summary of accounts for use in making adjustments and in preparing the financial statements. It also serves as a test check of the numerical accuracy of the journalizing and posting process—the total of all debits should equal the total of all credits.

The actual preparation of a trial balance is a routine task that simply requires transcribing, often electronically onto preprinted forms, the titles and balances from the general ledger. Table 5–3 illustrates a hypothetical trial balance for the Hoosier Company.

The trial balance should "balance" (have equal debits and credits). Also, the control accounts in the trial balance should agree with the schedules of their subsidiary ledgers. If the trial balance does not balance, some recording error must have been made. On the other hand, the converse is not necessarily true. A trial balance that balances simply indicates that the debit balances equal the credit balances. It does not prove that the proper accounts were debited and credited or that the correct amounts were recorded. The task of correcting wrong account balances or bringing them up-to-date falls to the adjusting entries, the next step in the accounting cycle.

**TABLE 5–3**  Hypothetical Trial Balance

**HOOSIER COMPANY**
**Trial Balance**
**December 31, 1991**

| | Debit | Credit |
|---|---|---|
| Cash | 13,000 | |
| Accounts receivable | 20,000 | |
| Inventory | 16,000 | |
| Accounts payable | | 15,200 |
| Capital stock | | 20,000 |
| Retained earnings | | 3,900 |
| Sales revenue | | 28,300 |
| Commission revenue | | 1,700 |
| Cost of goods sold | 9,250 | |
| Salary expense | 5,700 | |
| Rent expense | 2,000 | |
| Supplies expense | 280 | |
| Delivery expense | 2,870 | |
| | 69,100 | 69,100 |

## Journalizing and Posting Adjusting Entries

Determining what adjustments are necessary to the accounts listed in the trial balance is one of the primary duties of the accountant, as contrasted with the bookkeeper. Entries to adjust the accounts at the end of the period normally require the analytical abilities of someone familiar with the operation of the system, the types of accounts used, and the interrelationships among them. Once entries are determined, the adjusting entries are journalized and posted to the appropriate ledger accounts.

The need for adjusting entries arises from the periodicity and matching concepts. However, there are no underlying documents that automatically signal that an adjusting entry must be made. Accountants have to generate the necessary information for the adjusting entries from a study of the trial balance, a review of the accounting system, and an analysis of information sources outside the accounting records themselves.

## Preparing an Adjusted Trial Balance

The adjusting entry step may be followed by the preparation of another trial balance, called the "adjusted trial balance." The primary use of the adjusted trial balance is in statement preparation. From this listing, the accountant can arrange the account names and balances in proper formats for the income and position statements.

## Preparing the Financial Statements

The next step in the accounting cycle is reporting the accumulated accounting information to various audiences through the financial statements. This stage represents the fulfillment of the reporting function and the beginning of the interpretive function. Formats for these statements have been illustrated previously. The asset, liability, and owners' equity accounts appear on the balance sheet and are called "real accounts." The revenue and expense accounts, called "nominal accounts," appear on the income statement.

## Journalizing and Posting Closing Entries

The form and purpose of closing entries was discussed in Chapter 4. Recall that revenue and expense accounts used in the current accounting period are cleared to zero so that they are ready to function in the next period. In the process of closing revenue and expense accounts, the net difference between their totals is posted to Retained Earnings.

# THE ACCOUNTING INFORMATION SYSTEM AND INTERNAL CONTROL

We have examined the basic steps in completing the accounting cycle. These steps involve recording, processing, and reporting financial accounting information. The accounting system, however, has a broader scope than just the accounting cycle. In Figure 1–1, we itemized several specialty areas of accounting. When we consider all of these areas as a coordinated group, we are dealing with the *accounting information system.*

An accounting information system (1) has a formal design; (2) is procedurally specific, as seen in the accounting cycle; (3) is concerned with the economic impact of events; (4) generates data expressed primarily in economic terms; and (5) is oriented to provide financial information to various users. Accounting information can be characterized as *scorekeeping* (how much), *attention directing* (comparisons of actual performance to the plan), and *decision making* (the effects of different alternatives on financial results).

The accounting information system may be the most important of a firm's information systems, but it is a subset of the total *management information system*. The management information system includes other information flows within a firm related to marketing, production, engineering, personnel, and the like. Clearly, there is an overlap between the accounting and management information systems, with each system transferring information to and from the other.

## Internal Accounting Control

All accounting systems operate as accurately as possible. Inevitably, however, errors arise that may decrease the accuracy or timeliness of accounting data. All systems operate within a set of limitations called "risk exposures." Risks fall into two broad categories described in the accounting profession as *errors* and *irregularities*. Errors are defined as unintentional mistakes that cause inaccurate processing of accounting data. These mistakes are most commonly caused by mistaken judgment, carelessness, misunderstood instructions, fatigue, and the like. Mistakes due to these causes can be damaging to the ultimate goals of accounting but are typically random and isolated.

Irregularities are intentional mistakes introduced into the accounting system to gain some advantage—such as stealing assets, authorizing erroneous transactions, creating data that will be misinterpreted, or disclosing confidential information. When two or more employees introduce intentional mistakes, it is called "collusion." The most serious irregularity occurs when management overrides the system controls. This condition is referred to as "management fraud."

Internal accounting controls serve to detect and correct the unintentional mistakes (errors) and to reduce the opportunities for intentional mistakes (irregularities) in an accounting system. The American Institute of Certified Public Accountants has identified a series of elements composing the internal control structure of an entity as:

1. The control environment
2. The accounting system
3. Control procedures[2]

The control environment refers to those managerial conditions established to promote effective control over financial operations and their execution. The control environment includes factors such as the management's philosophy and operating style, the entity's organizational structure, the functioning of the board of directors, the methods for assigning authority and responsibility, the methods for monitoring controls, personnel policies, and outside environmental influences—such as regulation.[3] Effective managerial attention to these factors provides the organizational underpinning for sound accounting system controls.

The accounting system refers to the methods for recording, processing, and reporting financial information. An effective system identifies and records only valid transactions, classifies and reports information on a timely basis, completes proper measurements of transaction values, determines the appropriate time periods in which transactions are influential, and properly presents transactions in financial statements.[4]

Control procedures are specific control tasks to ensure that the entity's objectives will be achieved. These procedures pertain to proper transaction authorization, segregation of duties to reduce the likelihood of concealed errors and irregularities, the use of well-designed documents for transaction processing, maintenance of safeguards over the access to and use of assets and records, and the completion of performance checks on the operation of the system of controls.[5]

Establishing and reviewing internal control is a management responsibility. Internal control needs to be continuously supervised by management. Accounting systems do not inherently provide controls. Accounting systems provide measurements and reports, but control is accomplished only when management takes appropriate action to adjust conditions which are out of balance.

---

[2] American Institute of Certified Public Accountants, *Statement on Auditing Standards No. 55*, "Consideration of the Internal Control Structure in a Financial Statement Audit," (New York: AICPA, 1988), p. 5. In addition, it should be noted that the Foreign Corrupt Practices Act (1977), as passed by the Congress, directs corporations that are subject to the Securities and Exchange Act of 1934 to devise and maintain adequate systems of internal control.

[3] Ibid., par. 9.

[4] Ibid., par. 10.

[5] Ibid., par. 11.

Internal accounting controls can be classified in one of the following six categories:

1. **Organizational Controls.** These controls concern a firm's organizational structure and its lines of authority and responsibility. They relate primarily to the control environment. Control is enhanced when the lines of authority are clear, responsibility is known, and there is organizational independence among the functions and departments within the firm.

   *Example 1:*   Clear lines of organizational separation should prevent an employee in the sales function from approving sales on credit—a finance activity. No one employee should handle all facets of a single transaction. This would permit an employee to enter into unauthorized and unverifiable transactions.

   *Example 2:*   The organizational structure should separate the treasurer's function from the controller's function. The treasurer is responsible for custody of financial assets whereas the controller is responsible for the records reflecting the assets. Separation of these functions would enhance the accuracy of cash transactions because each function could independently verify its work against the work of the other function.

2. **Asset Security Measures and Accountability Controls.** These control procedures attempt to restrict unauthorized access to the firm's assets. Two primary control procedures must be implemented. First, assets must be protected physically through the use of protective devices (cash registers, locked storage areas, fences with monitored points for entry, etc.). Second, control over the movement of assets must be accomplished through specific authorization for asset usage, prompt recording of asset movement, and regular comparisons of the physical assets with the records (reconciliations).

   *Example 1:*   Petty cash should be assigned to one individual as custodian. This clearly identifies responsibility, and a reconciliation with the assigned dollar amount is possible at any time. Responsibility for the protection of the cash asset is placed with the custodian.

   *Example 2:*   When inventory is shipped via common carrier, the release of the inventory to the carrier should be evidenced by having the carrier indicate the assumption of responsibility with a signature.

3. **Documentation Controls.** These controls involve the display and distribution of firm policies and directives. They are elements of the control

environment and the accounting system mentioned earlier. Clear, complete, and understandable documentation includes organization charts, written job descriptions, procedure manuals, charts of accounts, and referencing requirements that provide audit trails of transactions.

*Example 1:*    Each employee should be responsible to only one supervisor. Clear understanding of organizational reporting responsibilities is shown through the preparation of a formal organization chart.

*Example 2:*    An accounting manual establishes the procedures to be followed by all accounting employees. The manual documents procedures, includes instructions on account usage, and encourages standardized and consistent practices from period to period.

4. **Management Practices.**    This control is part of the control environment as influenced by the operational style of management. All management practices, whatever their specific form, set the direction for an organization. Sound planning and control practices are important to the success of internal controls. These practices set the firm's goals, project the budgeted or targeted levels of performance, and permit the accounting measurement process to compare actual performance with the targets. Management practices also cover personnel policies including employee selection, training, and evaluation. Quality employees combined with quality personnel policies enhance internal control.

*Example 1:*    Personnel should be hired and assigned to appropriate positions only after their skills have been verified and qualifications established. A personnel function responsible for these tasks provides the basis for a proficient work force.

*Example 2:*    Managerial use of budgeting enhances the general understanding of the firm's goals and operational expectations. Budgets also provide a standard against which actual performance may be measured to gauge achievement.

5. **Authorization Controls.**    The safeguarding and physical control of assets can be accomplished only when any changes involving the assets require proper authorization within the accounting system. The specific form by which authorization is evidenced varies with the assets and functions being controlled, but written evidence should be required wherever possible. Written evidence (initials, signatures, etc.) accomplishes two control objectives. First, it acknowledges performance by a specific individual. Second, it provides a clear trail concerning the transfer of asset responsibility between individuals or organizational units. Management's ability to identify individuals normally enhances their performance and, in turn, internal control.

*Example 1:*　Require that all checks disbursing cash be prepared only after a review of all supporting documentation. The review should be evidenced by a written authorization. Maximum control is enhanced if the approval and check-preparation functions are organizationally separated.

*Example 2:*　Require that all inventory released from the warehouse be acknowledged by signature. This provides a trail of the movements of and responsibilities for the assets.

6. **Transaction Controls.**　These specific control procedures cover the handling of transaction data within the accounting system. They provide reasonable assurance that transactions have been authorized, accurately recorded, and properly reported. As transactions move through the accounting system, from recording to reporting, several types of control will be applied:

a. *Input*—controls to provide assurance that transactions are promptly recorded, are accurately and completely coded, and are valid transactions of the accounting period.

*Example 1:*　Prior to processing, prepare a total of the transaction items to be processed, such as the total dollar value of the transactions. This provides a known amount that can be compared with the transactions entered into the accounting system to identify agreement or discrepancies.

*Example 2:*　Verify the hours being entered for employees against a standard such as 40 hours, 45 hours, etc. This will identify apparently erroneous values, such as 80 hours, before they are entered into the accounting system.

b. *Processing*—controls to assure that data moving from the input stage are processed without loss, erroneous addition, or unauthorized alteration. Control totals passed down from the input stage, documented logs of the accomplished processing, and management reconciliations are the most common and appropriate controls at this stage in handling transactions.

*Example 1:*　Reject and control each erroneous transaction to preclude its being processed and to permit its correction and reprocessing. For instance, all transactions with erroneous account numbers should be rejected, corrected, and resubmitted.

*Example 2:*　Verify that all transactions entered into the system were processed. Pass a control value from the input stage to the processing stage to verify that the same values were processed as were entered.

c. *Output*—controls to verify the quality of the data processed and passed down from the processing stage. These controls involve review and verification of output by an organizational unit other than those that input or process the transactions. Output requiring controlled distribution will be monitored through the use of distribution logs, signatures to evidence receipt of output, and passwords or access controls for security in electronic systems.

*Example 1:* After printing reports, but prior to their distribution, an independent review should be made of the reports. The review should be completed by a unit organizationally separate from the input or processing functions to determine the reasonableness of the output and to identify obvious discrepancies.

*Example 2:* Have a copy of the disbursement list sent directly to the audit department after completing check preparation. This will enable the audit department to reconcile the bank account independently without being dependent on the treasurer's or controller's records. This will provide an independent check on both organizational functions.

Accounting internal control is a pervasive element in all reliable accounting systems. As you study accounting, numerous examples of control opportunities will be presented. Each control plays some part in the ultimate quality of the accounting process and, hence, its information.

## SUMMARY

This chapter concludes a preliminary discussion of the procedural aspects of accounting. In it we examine the primary types of adjusting entries used to correctly state account balances at the end of an accounting period. We explore the conceptual reasoning that makes adjustments necessary and develop some analytical skills to make them. Also, we see how the difference between cash basis and accrual basis accounting affects the income statement.

The second major topic concerns the elements of the accounting cycle and the relationships between different procedural techniques in the cycle. The normal progression of these functions is:

1. *Journalizing*—analyzing data from source documents and recording them chronologically.
2. *Posting*—transferring debits and credits to individual accounts.
3. *Preparing the trial balance*—summarizing the general ledger accounts to test equality of debits and credits and proving any subsidiary ledgers.
4. *Adjusting*—analyzing, recording, and posting entries necessary to correct or update all accounts.
5. *Preparing the adjusted trial balance*—assembling the general ledger account balances to facilitate the preparation of financial statements.
6. *Preparing the financial statements*—organizing summarized reports of income-seeking activity and financial position.

7. *Closing*—zeroing out all nominal accounts, transferring their summarized balances to Retained Earnings, and balancing and ruling the real accounts to prepare for the new accounting period.

Finally, we conclude the chapter by introducing an expanded concept of the accounting information system. Although the accounting cycle is at the heart of financial accounting, the objectives of the accounting process extend far beyond transaction processing. All aspects of accounting provide information for either the scorekeeping, attention-directing, or decision-making functions of management.

We also discuss how accounting information systems include internal control procedures to enhance the accuracy and validity of processed data. Internal accounting control includes proper organizational structure, sound management policies, and monitored transaction processing. Proper control that is embedded in an accounting system assures that the accounting information will be meaningful and useful.

A basic knowledge of how the parts of an accounting system are interrelated will contribute to your understanding of accounting's end result—the financial reports—and enable you to *use* accounting as an analytical tool.

# PROBLEMS AND CASETTES

## 5–1. Preparing Original and Adjusting Journal Entries
The following information pertains to the Regent Company:

1. Prepaid rent on January 1, 1991, was $1,200. On July 1, an additional $2,400 was paid to cover the rent through June 30, 1992; the amount was debited to the prepaid account.
2. Accrued wages owed to employees as of December 31, 1991, amounted to $5,000.
3. The Supplies Inventory account had a balance of $600 on January 1, 1991. On May 15, the company purchased (for cash) $1,800 of supplies, which were recorded in the inventory account. On December 31, only $500 of supplies were unused.
4. Utility bills were received at the end of December. These included charges for electric service, $600, and for telephone service, $240. The bills have not yet been recorded.
5. Cash of $1,800, received from customers for goods to be delivered in 1992, was credited to the Sales Revenue account on December 15, 1991.
6. On January 1, 1991, the company loaned $5,000 to a supplier, receiving a two-year, 10 percent note. The annual interest for 1991 has not yet been received or recorded.

### Required:

a. For each of the above items, prepare the original (nonadjusting) journal entry, *if any*, that would have been made by Regent Company during 1991 but prior to December 31.
b. For each of the above items, prepare the adjusting journal entry, *if any*, that should be made by Regent Company on December 31, 1991.

### 5–2. Preparing Closing Entries

Use the following trial balance for the Ajar Door Company and prepare the necessary closing entries. What was the net income for the period?

| | Debit | Credit |
|---|---:|---:|
| Cash | 275,500 | |
| Accounts receivable | 250,000 | |
| Supplies | 15,600 | |
| Investments | 120,000 | |
| Prepaid insurance | 2,500 | |
| Inventory | 385,250 | |
| Land | 50,000 | |
| Buildings | 465,250 | |
| Machinery | 1,289,300 | |
| Office equipment | 85,600 | |
| Vehicles | 167,250 | |
| Cost of goods sold | 2,355,685 | |
| Salaries expense | 560,500 | |
| Selling expense | 354,865 | |
| Insurance expense | 45,300 | |
| Interest expense | 69,400 | |
| Depreciation expense | 195,500 | |
| Supplies expense | 15,600 | |
| Property tax expense | 6,800 | |
| Income tax expense | 9,700 | |
| Accumulated depreciation—buildings | | 50,600 |
| Accumulated depreciation—machinery | | 325,800 |
| Accumulated depreciation—equipment | | 49,500 |
| Accumulated depreciation—vehicles | | 120,500 |
| Accounts payable | | 218,800 |
| Notes payable | | 1,500,000 |
| Unearned revenue | | 68,400 |
| Common stock | | 650,000 |
| Retained earnings | | 54,600 |
| Sales revenue | | 3,522,900 |
| Interest revenue | | 158,500 |
| | 6,719,600 | 6,719,600 |

### 5–3. Preparing Original and Adjusting Journal Entries

The Floss-n-Toss Company manufactures a disposable flossing product for dentists. The controller is concerned about the accuracy of the accounting records and tells the bookkeeper to "simplify the recording process by charging (debiting) all cash payments to expense accounts and crediting all cash receipts to revenue accounts." The following items relate to business transactions in 1992.

1. The company purchases its first 30-month casualty insurance policy on April 1. The premium paid is $1,500.
2. The company's machines require compressed air to operate. The air is delivered in pressurized containers that require a cash deposit of $20 per container. A refund of $18 per container is paid to the company in cash when the containers

are returned. The company had 7 containers on hand at the beginning of the year, paid for 38 containers on June 30, and had 12 on hand on December 31.

3. Office supplies purchased and paid for on September 20 amounted to $1,950. Supplies on hand at the beginning and end of the year were $400 and $600, respectively.

4. Floss-n-Toss subscribed to two industry trade magazines in 1992. All subscriptions were paid in cash. One subscription was for 24 months, was subscribed for on May 1 for $120, and delivery began on June 1. The other subscription was for 36 months, was subscribed for on October 1 for $432, and delivery began on December 1.

5. The company is heavily promoting its product in the *Journal of the American Dental Association (ADA)*. Monthly ads cost $2,500. A company must run ads for a minimum of six months and payment must be made in advance. Floss-n-Toss decides to run six months of ads and makes payment on March 15. The ads will begin appearing with the November issue of the ADA journal.

6. The firm arranges for a $30,000 line of credit with the Left Bank & Trust Co. The line of credit is available July 1 and simply requires the company to request the bank to deposit funds in their cash account. As of December 31, no request has been made.

**Required:**

a. For each of the above items, prepare the original (nonadjusting) journal entry, *if any,* that would have been made by the Floss-n-Toss bookkeeper during 1992, but prior to December 31, to comply with the controller's directions.

b. For each of the above items, prepare the adjusting journal entry, *if any,* that should be made by the controller on December 31, 1992.

## 5–4. Adjusting Ledger Accounts and Preparing Financial Statements

The following trial balance is prepared from the accounts of Heritage Restaurant, Inc., on December 31, 1992—the end of the first year of operations.

|  | Debit | Credit |
|---|---|---|
| Cash | 20,800 | |
| Food inventory | 25,000 | |
| Operating supplies | 3,000 | |
| Equipment | 16,500 | |
| Accumulated depreciation | | –0– |
| Wage expense | 13,500 | |
| Rent expense | 8,000 | |
| Utilities expense | 3,600 | |
| Insurance expense | 1,500 | |
| Customer receipts | | 58,600 |
| Accounts payable | | 13,300 |
| Capital stock | | 20,000 |
| | 91,900 | 91,900 |

### Additional Information:

1. Inventories of food and operating supplies are $2,500 and $800, respectively, on December 31, 1992.
2. Wage expense averages $1,125 per month. All employees are paid on the 15th of the month. No expense has been recorded for the period from December 15 to December 31.
3. Utility bills received for December services are $500. These have not been paid or recorded.
4. Rent expense is $500 per month, payable six months in advance on June 30 and December 31. The December payment was made and recorded.
5. Customer receipts include $600 received from the December sale of dinner tickets that may be exchanged for meals anytime during 1993.
6. There are two insurance policies on hand on December 31: a one-year policy purchased on September 1 for $600 and a two-year policy purchased on July 1 for $900.
7. Depreciation on the equipment for the year amounts to $1,750.

### Required:

*a.* Set up ledger (T) accounts for each account in the trial balance and enter the amounts.
*b.* Record all necessary adjusting entries directly in the ledger accounts. Set up additional accounts where needed.
*c.* Prepare an income statement for the year and a balance sheet as of December 31, 1992.

### 5–5. Preparing Original and Adjusting Journal Entries

The Harrison Civic Theater group puts on dramas and concerts. One attraction is featured each month over the nine-month season, which begins in September. The following data relate to the first month of operations in the 1991–1992 season.

1. Rented the Orpheum Theatre. The lease agreement required rent of $2,400 per month, paid three months in advance. In addition, with the first payment must be a payment for the last month to serve as a deposit. A check for the first three-months' rent and the last month was written.
2. Sent out direct-mail announcements and placed newspaper advertisements telling of the entire season's programs and soliciting season ticket orders. The cost of $13,500 was paid in cash.
3. Contracted with the Lincoln Concessionaires to operate the refreshment stand. The Civic Theater group is to receive 15 percent of all gross sales of refreshments. The amount for sales during the preceding month is to be remitted on the 10th of the month.
4. Received cash of $33,500 for season tickets to all nine scheduled attractions.
5. Purchased a specially designed insurance policy for $8,100 cash. The policy provides fire, theft, and public liability coverage during the nine months the group is active.
6. Sold individual tickets for $7,100 for September's performances.
7. Incurred monthly salary and wage costs of $9,500, payable the fifth of the following month.

8. Printed program notes for the September performances at a cost of $2,600 paid in cash.

9. Received a report from Lincoln Concessionaires that September's refreshment sales were $6,100.

**Required:**

a. Assume that the group prepares monthly financial statements. Prepare journal entries to record the above transactions *as well as* any adjusting entries necessary on September 30, 1991.

b. Asquith Penn, the theater group's bookkeeper, makes the following statement: "The matching concept and the going concern concept are in conflict here. Matching would require recognizing rent expense as $2,400 plus one ninth of the rent deposit payment this month. The going concern concept would say that the rent deposit should not be recognized as expense until the ninth month." Comment on his statement.

c. Jack Kingsly McQueen, the theater group's manager, says, "Revenue measurement is confusing. The difference between the cash basis revenue and accrual basis revenue appears to be significant. Which is right?" Calculate both cash basis and accrual basis revenue. Explain why they are different and which is most appropriate.

## 5–6. Adjusting Ledger Accounts and Preparing Financial Statements

The trial balance of the Lake Corporation as of December 31, 1992, was as follows:

|  | *Debit* | *Credit* |
|---|---|---|
| Cash | 18,000 | |
| Accounts receivable | 42,000 | |
| Merchandise inventory | 68,000 | |
| Supplies inventory | 7,500 | |
| Prepaid insurance | 2,500 | |
| Notes receivable (due 1999) | 60,000 | |
| Buildings | 81,000 | |
| Accumulated depreciation | | 5,000 |
| Sales revenue | | 123,000 |
| Service fee revenue | | 12,000 |
| Interest revenue | | 4,800 |
| Salaries expense | 25,000 | |
| Insurance expense | 6,000 | |
| Service fee expenses | 9,000 | |
| Capital stock | | 130,000 |
| Retained earnings | | 44,200 |
| | 319,000 | 319,000 |

The accountant for Lake Corporation also made available the following information as of December 31, 1992:

1. A count of merchandise inventory indicated that $20,000 was on hand at year-end.

2. An additional $4,500 of salaries was earned by the employees, although it had not been paid to them.
3. Royalty payments on merchandise sold were estimated to be $7,500. Lake will have to pay these royalties on February 1, 1993.
4. At year-end all of the supplies had been used.
5. The buildings were being depreciated at a rate of $1,000 per year.
6. There was only one insurance policy in force on December 31. This policy cost $6,000 and runs from April 1, 1992 to March 31, 1993.
7. $2,500 of the service fee revenue was for advance payments and was unearned at December 31.
8. The annual interest rate was 12 percent on the notes receivable. Interest is collected three times a year—on February 1, June 1, and October 1.

**Required:**

a. Prepare ledger (T) accounts for all accounts in the trial balance and record the existing balances.
b. Record all adjustments directly to the ledger accounts. Use additional accounts if necessary.
c. Prepare an income statement and balance sheet at year-end.

**5–7. Reconstructing Adjusting Entries**

The Dayton Services Corporation was organized on January 1, 1990. The chief accountant provides you with the following information:

1. *Unadjusted* trial balance, December 31, 1990:

|  | Debit | Credit |
|---|---|---|
| Cash | 25,000 | |
| Fees receivable | 12,000 | |
| Notes receivable | 15,000 | |
| Office supplies | 1,800 | |
| Prepaid insurance | 2,200 | |
| Land | 24,000 | |
| Furniture and equipment | 55,000 | |
| Accumulated depreciation | | –0– |
| Accounts payable | | 13,000 |
| Capital stock | | 109,000 |
| Fees earned | | 45,000 |
| Rent expense | 9,500 | |
| Office salaries expense | 22,500 | |
|  | 167,000 | 167,000 |

2. 1990 income statement:

**DAYTON SERVICES CORPORATION**
**Income Statement**
**For the Year Ended December 31, 1990**

| Revenues: | | |
|---|---|---|
| Fees earned | $49,400 | |
| Interest | 1,500 | $50,900 |
| Operating expenses: | | |
| Depreciation | $ 5,500 | |
| Rent | 8,700 | |
| Insurance | 1,800 | |
| Office supplies | 1,500 | |
| Office salaries | 24,000 | 41,500 |
| Net income | | $ 9,400 |

**Required:**

a. Prepare all the adjusting journal entries which Dayton Services Corporation *must have made* on December 31, 1990.

b. Compare the methods used to record and adjust insurance with those used to record and adjust rent. Was the same procedure used for both sets of accounts?

## 5–8. Completing the Accounting Cycle

The McNeil Clothing Company began business on April 1, 1992. The following data summarize the transactions for the first month of operations:

1. Stockholders invest $95,000 in cash and $15,000 in marketable securities.
2. Furniture and fixtures are acquired at a cost of $27,000, paid in cash.
3. Inventory is acquired on account at a cost of $55,000.
4. $18,000 of rent is paid.
5. Sales are $64,000 on account and $9,500 for cash.
6. Cash payments to suppliers for inventory total $44,000.
7. Collections of accounts receivable amount to $32,000.
8. Advertising expenditures are $2,400, paid in cash.
9. Monthly insurance premium paid is $250.

**Additional Information:**

10. Interest of $125 has been earned on the securities during April.
11. Advertising supplies costing $400, purchased as part of transaction 8, remain unused on April 30.
12. Sales commissions equal to 15 percent of April sales are to be paid in early May.
13. The rent payment was for a 12-month period.
14. $15,000 of inventory remains on April 30.
15. Furniture and fixtures are estimated to have a 10-year life.

**Required:**

a. Prepare journal entries to record the April transactions numbered 1 through 9.
b. Post your journal entries to ledger (T) accounts.
c. Journalize and post adjusting entries for items 10 through 15.
d. Prepare an income statement for April and a balance sheet as of April 30, 1992.
e. Journalize and post closing entries.

**5–9. Analyzing Adjustment Errors**

The controller of the Bloomington Company asks you to analyze four situations which do not appear to have been handled correctly. He furnishes accounts from the December 31, 1991 trial balance, adjusted trial balance, and supporting information. He says, "Tell me what the adjusting entry should have been and how to correct it."

1.

| Rent | December 31 Unadjusted Trial Balance | December 31 Adjusted Trial Balance |
|---|---|---|
| Rent expense . . . . . . . . . . . . . . . . . | 2,400 | 8,400 |
| Prepaid rent . . . . . . . . . . . . . . . . . | 6,000 | –0– |

Rent is paid on two buildings. The office building has a monthly rental of $200. The warehouse lease began on July 1 of the current year and is $500 per month, paid in advance.

2.

| Insurance | December 31 Unadjusted Trial Balance | December 31 Adjusted Trial Balance |
|---|---|---|
| Insurance expense . . . . . . . . . . . . . . | 3,000 | 8,000 |
| Prepaid insurance . . . . . . . . . . . . . . | 14,600 | 9,600 |

There was no prepaid insurance at the beginning of the year. Insurance expense is related to four policies that have the following provisions:

*Policy 1.* January 1 to December 31, 1991—Premium $3,000
*Policy 2.* March 1, 1991 to February 28, 1992—Premium $6,000
*Policy 3.* July 1, 1991 to June 30, 1993—Premium $5,000
*Policy 4.* November 1, 1991 to October 31, 1994—Premium $3,600

3.

| Royalties | December 31 Unadjusted Trial Balance | December 31 Adjusted Trial Balance |
|---|---|---|
| Royalties receivable . . . . . . . . . . . . . | 5,250 | –0– |
| Royalty revenue . . . . . . . . . . . . . . . | 15,000 | 9,750 |

The company earns royalties at a rate of 15 percent on sales. Royalty sales in 1990 were $70,000, but the company had been paid for only one half of the royalty amount during 1990. Royalty sales during the current year were $80,000. One cash payment for royalties had been received on December 29, 1991 for $15,000.

4.

| | Interest | December 31 Unadjusted Trial Balance | December 31 Adjusted Trial Balance |
|---|---|---|---|
| Interest receivable . . . . . . . . . . . . . . . . | | –0– | –0– |
| Interest revenue . . . . . . . . . . . . . . . . | | 1,875 | 1,875 |

The company held the following three notes during the year:

*Note 1.* 2 year—$120,000 @ 10%—dated March 1, 1991
*Note 2.* 3 year—$200,000 @ 12%—dated October 1, 1991
*Note 3.* 3 month—$50,000 @ 15%—dated June 1, 1991

Interest on all notes is paid on the maturity date.

**Required:**

*a.* For each of these situations determine what the adjusting journal entry *should have been.*

*b.* For each situation, prepare the journal entry that will *correct* the current adjusted balances in the accounts.

**5–10. Evaluating Internal Control Weaknesses**

The following situations describe weaknesses in internal control, particularly with respect to a firm's safeguarding of its assets.

1. At the Able Company, inventory clerks are required to count one twelfth of the inventory monthly so that by year-end all inventory items will have been counted. After finishing a month's count, the clerks compare their count with the inventory records to determine agreement. If a difference exists, the clerks prepare a document from which an entry is made to adjust the inventory account. They then send the adjusting entry document to the general ledger clerk for posting.

2. For efficiency, the treasurer at the Baker Company is expected to reconcile the bank account monthly. As the company president said, "This makes sense because the treasurer prepares and signs checks, deposits the cash and checks received, and keeps the cash records. Who knows this account better?"

3. The Carlson Company uses a petty cash account for making payments for small miscellaneous purchases. Each purchase must not exceed $15 for payment from the petty cash funds. The total of the petty cash fund available for use is $500. The accounting manager feels that the fund is small enough so that any of the seven accounting department employees may make the payments by taking the funds as needed from the desk of the secretary. If possible when a payment is made, the employee is to jot down a note indicating the purpose of the disbursement.

4. The internal auditor at Dodson Company is organizationally assigned to report to the controller. The chief executive officer made the assignment because the internal auditor will be reviewing mainly the controller's records and feels that "this should make for a closer working relationship."

5. Efficiency in the manufacturing process is aided by a smooth flow of inventory to the manufacturing floor. To accomplish an efficient flow, the Eads Company

has factory workers enter the warehouse and take inventory whenever needed. Then, at the end of the day workers are to prepare a report of inventory taken and give it to the inventory clerk before leaving for home.

**Required:**

For each of the situations described above:

*a.* Identify and explain the weakness(es) that appear to exist.

*b.* Explain how you would change the situation to overcome the weakness(es) and add control.

**5–11. Evaluating Internal Control Weaknesses**

The following situations describe weaknesses in internal control.

1. The cashier for Farr Company is the focal point for cash collection and recording. Sales clerks send him cash from sales transactions. The cashier also opens the mail to receive payments. He makes daily deposits and prepares the journal entry for debiting Cash and crediting Sales and/or Accounts Receivable.
2. When inventory is received at the Gordon Company, the warehouse personnel compare the quantities received with a copy of the purchase order. The warehouse personnel then prepare an entry debiting Inventory and crediting Accounts Payable and post it to the general ledger accounts.
3. The Highland Company's factory employees punch in and out using a time clock. At the end of each week, the clock cards are approved and signed by each department supervisor. The cards are then sent to the payroll department for paycheck preparation. The paychecks are then returned to each supervisor for distribution to employees.
4. The accounts payable clerk at Intellect Company prepares checks for payment of invoices received from the firm's suppliers. Documents supporting the preparation of checks are sent, with the checks, to the treasurer for signature. The checks and documents are returned to the accounts payable clerk for mailing and filing.
5. At the end of each shift, the clerks who check out customers at the Jackson Company Discount Store count the money in their cash register drawers. They compare the cash count with the tape in the register, record the cash receipts on a special form, and deliver the cash with the form to the cashier. The clerks then discard the register tapes to clear their machines for the next person's use.

**Required:**

For each of the situations described above:

*a.* Identify and explain the weakness(es) that appear to exist.

*b.* Explain how you would change the situation to overcome the weakness(es) and add control.

**5–12. Cash Basis and Accrual Basis Statements**

On January 1, 1991 Wanda Forbes began a new business, Forbes Stereo Center, to sell, install, and repair stereo systems. She sold some of her IBM stock to have cash for starting the business. On December 31, she asks you to prepare financial statements for her. The business appears simple enough, but you are not sure whether to use the cash basis or the accrual basis.

You examine the bank statements and checks written during the year and prepare the following summary of transactions that have taken place:

1. *Cash receipts:*
   a. Sale of IBM stock—$100,000.
   b. Sales of:
      (1) stereo systems—$287,500.
      (2) system installations—$63,200.
      (3) component repairs—$22,300.
2. *Cash disbursements:*
   a. Purchases of system inventory—$315,000.
   b. Purchases of repair parts—$32,000.
   c. Purchase of tools—$7,800.
   d. Purchase of test equipment—$23,800.
   e. Rent at $150 per month—$1,800.
   f. Selling expenses—$1,600.
   g. UPS delivery expenses—$1,500.
   h. Administrative expenses—$75,100.

After closely examining the documents on hand and making inquiry of Forbes, you learn the following additional items of information:

1. Three customers purchased systems totaling $4,500 for Christmas but were unable to pay in cash. They signed six-month notes with payments beginning in March.
2. $87,000 of system inventory is still on hand at December 31.
3. $19,500 of repair parts are on hand at December 31.
4. Administrative expenses include the wages for the three sales clerks who are each paid $400 per month on the 15th of each month. In addition, 3 technical personnel are paid on the first of each month and have monthly salaries totaling $4,800.
5. Administrative expenses include $2,400 for a two-year fire insurance policy which began on April 1 of the current year.
6. Tools and test equipment were purchased in the first week of January. The tools have an expected life of five years and the test equipment, an expected life of seven years.

**Required:**

a. Prepare an income statement and a balance sheet using the cash basis method.
b. Prepare an income statement and a balance sheet using the accrual basis method.
c. Explain which method best depicts the results of the current year for Forbes Stereo Center.

**Casette 5–1.  Completing the Accounting Cycle**
The Sherman Corporation began operations on November 1, 1991. The following transactions took place in November:

Nov.  1   Issued capital stock for cash of $60,000 and for a building valued at $45,000 for use as corporate offices. The office building had a remaining useful life of 25 years.

      1   Paid two months' rent on warehouse space, $3,000.

      1   Purchased equipment with a useful life of 10 years for cash, $24,000.

      2   Purchased inventory from Northport, Inc., $10,000 on account.

      3   Sold inventory on account, $12,950 ($10,000 to Johnson & Smith Co. and $2,950 to Wilson Corporation).

      4   Cash sales, $8,400.

      6   Purchased supplies on account, $3,450 ($1,800 from Broom Chemical Co. and $1,650 from Northport, Inc.).

      8   Paid Beaver Express for freight charges on goods sold to customers, $950.

      9   Purchased inventory from Northport, Inc., $13,000 on account.

    12   Received a check from Wilson Corporation in full payment of its account.

    15   Paid $15,000 to Northport, Inc.

    16   Sold inventory to Basset Company on account, $13,600.

    16   Paid salaries of $5,500 in cash for the first half of November.

    16   Purchased a delivery truck with a useful life of five years from Smart Motors, Inc., for $12,000 cash.

    21   Received $2,000 from Johnson & Smith.

    28   Paid Northport, Inc., for the supplies purchased on November 6.

**Additional Information:**

1. On November 30, there were $1,600 of supplies and $7,300 of inventory on hand.
2. Salaries for the period November 16–30 were $5,500 and were to be paid on December 2.

**Required:**

*a*. Journalize the above transactions in a general journal. Include columns for date, explanation, posting reference, debits, and credits.

*b*. Prepare ledger (T) accounts for both the general and subsidiary ledgers. Assign numbers to the accounts with 100–199 for assets, 200–299 for liabilities, 300–399 for stockholders' equity, 400–499 for revenues, and 500–599 for expenses.

*c*. Prepare a trial balance and schedules of subsidiary account balances for accounts receivable and accounts payable. Prove the balances in the subsidiary and control accounts.

*d*. Review the transactions and additional information. Journalize and post all adjusting entries.

*e*. Prepare an adjusted trial balance.

*f*. Prepare an income statement and a balance sheet.

*g*. Journalize and post closing entries.

### Casette 5–2. Completing the Accounting Cycle

In Casette 3–2 you were asked to identify the assets and equities that relate to your acquisition of a par-three golf course. In Casette 4–1 you were asked to identify the revenue and expense accounts you would expect to use in accounting for the golf course. In this casette, you will complete the recording and preparation of financial statements for your golf course during the first six months of operation.

Recall, you inherited a large sum of money and for $200,000 purchased the par-three golf course. The purchase was completed on April 1.

A. The following summary transactions relate to the first six months of operations:

   1. You paid $200,000 in cash for the following assets:
      *a.* Land, $85,000.
      *b.* Main building, $40,000.
      *c.* Maintenance shed, $15,000.
      *d.* Lighting equipment, $30,000.
      *e.* Golf carts, $18,000.
      *f.* Food inventory, $4,000.
      *g.* Pro shop inventory, $8,000.

   2. On April 1 you opened a checking account and deposited $15,000.

   3. Sales, for cash, during the six months were:
      *a.* Greens fees, $35,000.
      *b.* Cart rentals, $12,000.
      *c.* Snack shop sales, $14,000.
      *d.* Pro shop sales, $18,000.

   4. Expenses during the six months were:
      *a.* Utilities paid: Outdoor lighting, $4,500; Course watering, $2,750; Snack and pro shops, $3,000; Office, $800.
      *b.* Salaries paid: Snack and pro shops, $9,000; Cart maintenance, $3,700; Course maintenance, $10,500.
      *c.* Purchases on credit: Food inventory, $6,000; Pro shop inventory, $10,500; Fertilizer and spray, $7,500.
      *d.* Cart maintenance paid: $4,500.
      *e.* Insurance policy paid: $12,000.

B. On September 30 the following additional accounting information was determined:

   1. Asset values consumed: Main building, $500; Maintenance shed, $300; Golf carts, $2,000; Outdoor lighting, $1,500.

   2. An inventory was taken September 30 and the on-hand quantities were: Food, $5,000; Pro shop, $7,000.

   3. The insurance policy was for one year and was purchased on July 1.

   4. The employees had earned $1,500 which would not be paid until October 15. This amount applies as follows: Snack and pro shops, $500; Cart maintenance, $300; Course maintenance, $700.

   5. The firm contacted the utility company, and it was agreed that an overpayment had been made for outdoor lighting of $800. The overpayment is to be applied to future charges for lighting.

**Required:**

*a.* Prepare journal entries for the events listed in (A) above. Create ledger (T) accounts and post your journal entries to these accounts. Select your own account titles to reflect the substance of the events.

  *b.* Prepare a trial balance of the ledger accounts.

  *c.* Prepare adjusting journal entries for the items listed in B above and post the entries to the ledger accounts.

  *d.* Prepare an income statement for the six months and a balance sheet as of September 30.

**Casette 5–3.  Reconstructing a Trial Balance**

The accounting cycle proceeds from the trial balance through the adjusting entries to the preparation of the financial statements and finally to closing entries. Based on your understanding of this process, reconstruct the December 31, 1991 trial balance of the Reverse Detail Company from the facts given below.

The financial statements at December 31 were:

**REVERSE DETAIL COMPANY**
**Income Statement**
**For the Year Ending December 31, 1991**

| | | |
|---|---:|---:|
| Sales revenue . . . . . . . . . . | | $35,000 |
| Operating expenses: | | |
| Cost of goods sold . . . . . . . . | $16,000 | |
| Rent expense . . . . . . . . . . . | 3,000 | |
| Insurance expense . . . . . . . . . | 1,500 | |
| Salaries expense . . . . . . . . . | 7,500 | |
| Utilities expense . . . . . . . . . | 400 | |
| Depreciation expense . . . . . . . | 3,000 | 31,400 |
| Net income. . . . . . . . . . . . . | | $ 3,600 |

**REVERSE DETAIL COMPANY**
**Balance Sheet**
**December 31, 1991**

| **Assets** | | | | **Equities** | | |
|---|---:|---:|---|---|---:|---:|
| Current: | | | | Current liabilities: | | |
| Cash . . . . . . . . . . . . | | $  4,000 | | Accounts payable . . . . . . . . | | $    400 |
| Accounts receivable . . . . . . | | 35,000 | | Accrued salary payable. . . . . . | | 1,500 |
| Inventory. . . . . . . . . . . | | 10,000 | | Total current liabilities . . . . . | | 1,900 |
| Prepaid insurance . . . . . . . | | 2,000 | | | | |
| Prepaid rent . . . . . . . . . | | 8,000 | | Stockholders' equity: | | |
| Noncurrent: | | | | Capital stock . . . . . . . . . | | 100,000 |
| Building . . . . . . . . . . | $68,000 | | | Retained earnings . . . . . . . | | 19,100 |
| Less: Accumulated | | | | Total stockholders' equity. . . . | | 119,100 |
| depreciation . . . . . | 6,000 | 62,000 | | | | |
| Total assets . . . . . . . . . . | | $121,000 | | Total equities. . . . . . . . . . | | $121,000 |

**Additional Information:**

1. The accounts that appeared in the trial balance at December 31 *before making adjusting entries* are shown following:

|  | *Debit* | *Credit* |
|---|---|---|
| Cash | | |
| Accounts receivable | | |
| Inventory | | |
| Prepaid rent | | |
| Building | | |
| Accumulated depreciation | | |
| Capital stock | | |
| Retained earnings | | |
| Sales revenue | | |
| Salaries expense | | |
| Insurance expense | | |

2. *Adjusting Entry Information:*

   a. The company sold and shipped $5,000 of inventory on December 29. An invoice for $8,000 was sent to the customer on January 3, 1992. An adjustment was recorded for this sale. The company counted inventory on December 31.

   b. Employees had earned $1,500 in salary as of December 31, but it will not be paid until the end of the first week in January 1992.

   c. The company received its December 1991 utility bills on January 5, 1992.

**Required:**

*a.* Analyze the income statement and reconstruct the *closing entries* which must have been made.

*b.* Reconstruct the *unadjusted trial balance* on December 31. Use the accounts listed in 1 above and the explanations in 2 to determine the balances which were in the accounts. To complete your analysis, reconstruct the adjusting entries that were necessary to produce the financial statements. Add accounts to the trial balance listing as necessary. (Hint: Create adjusted trial balance columns to the right of the unadjusted accounts listing—remember, you are working backwards.)

# Chapter 6

# Accounting Concepts of Income

In the preceding chapters we discussed the conceptual framework of accounting and examined several important procedures used to measure accounting income. According to our basic assumptions regarding accounting income, revenues are recorded when they are earned, and expired asset costs (expenses) are matched with the revenues they helped to generate in order to determine net income. In this chapter, we discuss some expansions and elaborations of the accounting income concept as well as some of the problems associated with it. First, let us tie together some of the threads of thought developed in earlier chapters that relate to income measurement.

## REVIEW OF THE MATCHING CONCEPT

The accounting concept of income rests on the relationship between assets received and assets consumed in the operating activities of the business. Asset inflows, usually of cash or accounts receivable, from the sale of goods or services provide a monetary measure of the *accomplishment* of the firm in satisfying customer needs. Similarly, the various assets consumed in the process of earning revenues afford a monetary expression of the *effort expended* in satisfying those same needs. When the inflow and outflow of assets are matched for particular time intervals, periodic readings about the performance of the business entity result. This accomplishment-effort relationship that exists under the matching concept is lacking if we look only at inflows and outflows of cash during the period.

Beginning with an initial equality of assets and equities, we observed that changes in assets associated with operating activities cause similar changes in owners' equity. We introduced revenue accounts to record the increases in owners' equity as assets flow into the business from operations. *Revenue transactions record sources of assets.* In turn, we set up various expense accounts to record the decreases in owners' equity as assets are consumed in the production of revenues. *Expense transactions record the outflows or uses of assets.*

The heart of the accounting concept of income consists of matching asset inflows with outflows during designated time periods. In its conceptual statement on elements of financial statements, the FASB formally defines revenues and expenses in terms of asset flows:[1]

> Revenues are inflows or other enhancements of assets of an entity . . . during a period from delivering or producing goods, rendering services, or other activities that constitute the entity's ongoing major or central operations. Expenses are outflows or other using up of assets . . . during a period from delivering or producing goods, rendering services, or carrying out other activities that constitute the entity's ongoing major or central operations.

However, in double-entry bookkeeping the actual implementation of the matching concept involves associating the owners' equity accounts (revenue and expense accounts) that reflect the relevant asset changes.

The matching concept presumes that the accountant is able to do two things—to relate earned revenues to specific periods of time and to relate the appropriate expired costs (expenses) with the revenues. Virtually all of the problems of conventional accounting theory emanate from the fact that at best we can do these tasks only imperfectly, particularly when it comes to measuring which costs have expired. Chapter 7 addresses the practical problems of revenue recognition. This chapter begins the discussion of the practical difficulties associated with the matching of particular costs against revenues. Out of this discussion comes the concept of period expenses.

A second portion of this chapter focuses on the restrictive nature of the matching concept as a measure of an entity's performance. The revenue-expense model does not clearly encompass all changes in owners' equity (net assets) during a period. Out of this discussion comes an expansion of the income concept to include other non-owner transactions and events beyond just revenues and expenses.

## PERIOD EXPENSES

Not all expired asset costs can be matched easily with specific dollars of revenue. Therefore, to implement the matching concept, accountants have developed a hierarchy for the association of costs with revenues. Costs that become classified as expenses fall into one of three categories:

1. Expenses *directly traceable to units sold* or specific revenue transactions.
2. Expenses *systematically allocable to time periods* in which the revenue is recognized.
3. Expenses for which *no measurable future benefit can be discerned.*

---

[1] FASB, *Statement of Financial Accounting Concepts No. 3*, "Elements of Financial Statements of Business Enterprises" (Stamford, Conn., December 1980), page xii. Copyright © by the Financial Accounting Standards Board, High Ridge Park, Stamford, Connecticut 06905, U.S.A. Quoted with permission. Copies of the completed document are available from the FASB.

When costs are closely associated with the sale of a product, they are relatively easy to match with the revenue they help to produce. For instance, the costs of merchandise inventory purchased for resale are attached to specific units of product. These costs are called *product costs* because they are directly related to units of product. They become part of the "cost of goods sold" expense whenever the product is sold. In this way, the costs are fairly accurately matched against the proper revenues.

Another example of a direct measure of cause and effect is sales commissions. Sales commissions expense arises at the time a sale is made, and the expense can be identified directly with the revenue produced from the sale.

The second and third categories of expired costs cannot be traced directly to specific units of product but can be identified as expenses incurred during an accounting period. Appropriately, these are called *period costs*. Expenses in the second category are systematically and rationally assigned to particular time periods. Depreciation expense, insurance expense, rent expense, and interest expense are examples. These costs benefit operations in one or more specific accounting periods, and they are associated with the revenues of those identifiable periods rather than particular units of revenue. If more than one accounting period is involved, the accountant estimates a period of future benefit and a pattern of relationship between costs incurred and benefits received. Then the costs are allocated to expense according to those estimates.

Expenses in the third category include period costs that cannot be closely identified with specific units of product, identifiable revenue transactions, or even determinable future time periods. Examples of this third type of cost include administrative salaries, training costs, advertising, and operating costs of the firm's computer system.

## Measurement Problems with Period Costs

Period costs clearly represent the use of resources; the problem is one of determining when the benefit from their use is received. Under ideal matching conditions, we would determine what portion of the cost is applicable to future periods, which future periods receive benefit, and to what extent each period benefits. Unfortunately, measurement difficulties make this goal unreachable for certain types of costs.

As a consequence, those period costs that cannot be systematically allocated to time periods *are treated as expenses of the period in which they are incurred*. For example, the cost of conducting an institutional advertising campaign is debited to Advertising Expense each period for the amount of advertising cost incurred. Theoretically, a portion of the advertising cost should be deferred to future periods as it will stimulate revenues in those periods. However, the amount and length of future benefit would be practically impossible to measure. The costs of market surveys, public relations, corporate planning, and legal and accounting services are handled in the same way.

Although the treatment of certain costs as period expenses is admittedly somewhat inaccurate, the practice is justified on two grounds. First, often no feasible alternative is available. Second, many of these types of expense are recurring costs, and the difference between immediate expensing and allocating is likely to be *immaterial*.

In the first case, the consumption of resources bears no discernible relation to future products, services, or revenues. Neither is there any rational basis for a systematic allocation to future periods. To carry forward an asset value without a clearly demonstrable and measurable future benefit would violate the qualitative guideline of *verifiability* and the constraint of *conservatism*.

The immaterial difference between immediate expensing and allocating in the second case can be illustrated by the current salary of the company president. Ideally, a portion of it should be allocated to future periods for efforts such as planning that benefit those periods. However, any such portion is counterbalanced approximately by portions of salary cost that were incurred in past periods but are applicable to the current period. When this same type of expenditure is incurred every period in about the same amount, no material distortion arises in measuring the expense.

## Research and Development Costs

Accounting for research and development costs (R&D) has been a troublesome task for accountants because of the difficulty in associating expenditures with specific revenues. These costs include salaries of scientists, engineers, technicians, and research administrators as well as supplies, tools, perishable equipment, and other indirect costs. Ideally these costs should be matched against the revenues to which they give rise. On the other hand, no costs should be deferred as assets unless there is a bona fide expectation that they will actually generate future revenues. The link between R&D expenditures and future revenues often is weakened by uncertainty and extended periods of time. Accounting difficulties arise in determining whether any asset has been created and, if so, which future periods will benefit.

Prior to 1974, firms recorded R&D costs in one of three ways: (1) collected by individual project in asset accounts and expensed on a case-by-case basis, (2) deferred as an intangible asset and expensed over an arbitrary time period, and (3) written off as an expense in the period incurred.

In 1974, the Financial Accounting Standards Board rejected alternatives (1) and (2) for recording R&D costs as assets. The board chose the expense alternative, which was the one most commonly used. It concluded that "all research and development costs . . . shall be charged to expense when incurred."[2] This treatment is based on three major considerations: (1) future

---

[2] FASB, *Statement of Financial Accounting Standards No. 2*, "Accounting for Research and Development Costs" (Stamford, Conn., October 1974), par. 12.

benefits are highly uncertain, (2) a causal relationship between expenditures and benefits is often lacking, and (3) R&D expenditures do not qualify as assets because future benefits cannot be identified and objectively measured.[3]

Generally accepted accounting principles now require almost all R&D costs to be treated as period expenses. Many accountants object, however, to the broad extension of this approach to R&D expenditures that are irregular in size, timing, and actually do give rise to future benefits. Those accountants argue that immediate expensing may result in a significant understatement of balance sheet assets, a violation of representational faithfulness. Moreover, because R&D expenses are largely discretionary, this approach may allow management to manipulate periodic net income. Net income can be increased by a cut in R&D expenditures. Unless readers study the detail on the total R&D costs charged to expense each period (a disclosure required by the FASB), they may not understand the way in which income was manipulated.

The difficulty in treating R&D costs stems from (1) differences in the nature and purpose of the costs for particular projects and (2) difficult measurement problems. Pure research costs probably should be handled differently from project-oriented costs. Constant recurring costs may be justifiably expensed but not fluctuating, one-shot costs. Nevertheless, even if detailed classifications are made, accountants still face measuring *whether* there is any future benefit, *how much* cost is applicable to the future, and in *what pattern* benefits will be received.

## OTHER EQUITY CHANGES RELATED TO PERIOD OPERATIONS

Period costs represent only one problem encountered when the matching concept is applied to real-world transactions. The matching concept assumes a normal causal relationship between the earning of revenues and the incurrence of expenses. However, certain other events may affect owners' equity during an accounting period. Many of these events relate to the use of assets and the conduct of business operations but do not fit neatly into the scope of the activities we have introduced so far.

Consequently, additional temporary owners' equity accounts are needed to record these other changes. Our concept of net income may also have to be modified and expanded to encompass some of these events. In this section we discuss some of these special accounts—gains, losses, interest, taxes, and dividends.

---

[3] An exception to this general treatment exists for research and development costs specifically reimbursable under a contractual agreement. Thus, the costs of developing a specialized microcomputer chip under a specific contract could allowably and logically be deferred.

To examine these accounts, we will use a continuing example. Assume that National Converters, Inc., has the following ledger balances at December 15, 1991:

|  | Debit | Credit |
|---|---|---|
| Cash . . . . . . . . . . . . . . . . . . . . | 1,018,100 |  |
| Accounts receivable . . . . . . . . . . . . . | 1,330,100 |  |
| Merchandise inventory . . . . . . . . . . . . | 863,500 |  |
| Investments. . . . . . . . . . . . . . . . . | 250,000 |  |
| Land . . . . . . . . . . . . . . . . . . . . | 475,000 |  |
| Building . . . . . . . . . . . . . . . . . . | 395,200 |  |
| Accounts payable . . . . . . . . . . . . . . |  | 392,200 |
| Notes payable. . . . . . . . . . . . . . . . |  | 161,000 |
| Capital stock . . . . . . . . . . . . . . . . |  | 1,750,000 |
| Retained earnings . . . . . . . . . . . . . . |  | 1,796,300 |
| Sales revenue . . . . . . . . . . . . . . . . |  | 1,260,200 |
| Rent revenue . . . . . . . . . . . . . . . . |  | 16,300 |
| Dividend revenue . . . . . . . . . . . . . . |  | 90,400 |
| Cost of goods sold . . . . . . . . . . . . . . | 686,500 |  |
| Selling expenses. . . . . . . . . . . . . . . | 210,200 |  |
| Administrative expenses . . . . . . . . . . . | 176,000 |  |
| Depreciation expense . . . . . . . . . . . . . | 61,800 |  |
|  | 5,466,400 | 5,466,400 |

The company's accounting period ends on December 31, 1991.

## Gains

Gains represent increases in owners' equity other than revenues or investments by owners. Sometimes peripheral or incidental transactions or other events during the period impact positively on owners' equity (net assets). Gains represent asset increases from favorable transactions and events other than those associated with selling goods and services. The term *revenue* is used to describe the latter asset increases.

For example, assume that on December 16, National Converters sells a parcel of its land. The land originally cost $300,000, and is sold for $384,900 in cash. This transaction would be recorded by the following entry:

| Dec. 16 | Cash . . . . . . . . . . . . . . . . . | 384,900 |  |
|---|---|---|---|
|  | Land . . . . . . . . . . . . . . . . |  | 300,000 |
|  | Gain on Sale of Land . . . . . . . . |  | 84,900 |

The Gain on Sale of Land account reflects an addition to owners' equity because net assets have increased other than through owners' investment or revenues. Gain accounts are closed to Income Summary and appear on the income statement.

The example above illustrates a gain resulting from the disposition of noninventory assets. The advantageous settlement of liabilities, the winning of a lawsuit, and the receipt of donations or gifts are also events that may give rise to gains.

## Losses

Losses are the opposite of gains. They are decreases in owners' equity other than expenses or distributions to the owners. Like gains, losses usually are associated with nonrecurring or unusual activities of a firm or with environmental circumstances largely beyond a firm's control.

Most losses occur when assets disappear or decrease with no corresponding contribution to the ordinary operations of the business. Expenses, on the other hand, are measures of assets consumed in order to generate revenue during the period. Examples of losses include the undepreciated cost of scrapped equipment, the uninsured cost of merchandise destroyed by fire, uninsured cash embezzled by an employee, and damages levied by a court.

Assume that National Converters has an investment of $150,000, representing partial ownership in the stock of the Fisher Transmission Co. The investment was made two years ago with the expectation that National eventually would acquire all of the stock. Conditions have changed and National decides to sell its interest on December 18 to an investor who offers only $100,900, cash. The sale would be recorded as follows:

| | | | |
|---|---|---:|---:|
| Dec. 18 | Cash | 100,900 | |
| | Loss on Sale of Investments | 49,100 | |
| | Investments | | 150,000 |

## Interest

In addition to operations, a major concern for management is the financing of the firm's activities. If assets are acquired through the incurrence of interest-bearing liabilities, then an additional legal claim on the firm's assets, for interest, accrues as time passes. The increase in the interest liability causes a corresponding decrease in owners' equity. When cash is actually distributed to the creditors, the liability is liquidated.

For instance, assume that National Converters borrowed $161,000 from the bank on January 1. In exchange, they signed a two-year, 10 percent note payable. When this year's accounting period ends on December 31, the following adjusting entry will record the twelve months' accrued interest:

| | | | |
|---|---|---:|---:|
| Dec. 31 | Interest Expense | 16,100 | |
| | Interest Payable | | 16,100 |
| | ($161,000 × .10 × 1 year) | | |

Interest Expense is the temporary retained earnings account used to accumulate the total compensation for the use of funds supplied by creditors during a period. Interest Payable represents the unpaid portion of that claim as of any particular date.

**Interest Conventions and Short-Term Notes.**   Notes payable (and notes receivable) usually result from short-term transactions with a single creditor (debtor). They can arise directly from a purchase transaction when the credit period is longer than the typical 30-to-60-day charge account. Sometimes they arise indirectly from substitution for an account payable (receivable) if the usual credit period is extended. Notes payable may also result from a direct loan from a bank or other creditor as in the previous example. In any case the note represents a signed promise by the borrower to pay a certain sum on a particular date to the lender. The written document indicates the rate of interest that must be paid by the borrower.

Because of the short time period (usually one year or less), the charge for use of the money is calculated under the simple interest formula,

$$I = P \times R \times T$$

Interest = Principal × Rate × Time

and the interest normally is paid at the time the principal is paid.

Businesses employ a number of conventions related to the simple interest formula. First, unless stated otherwise, the interest rate is assumed to be an annual rate. Secondly, if the time period is expressed in days, then the time period begins with the day after the date of the note and runs up to and includes the maturity date. For example, a 30-day note dated December 15 is due on January 14; a one-month note dated December 15 is due on January 15. Because of differing numbers of days in various months, most notes for less than a year are expressed in terms of days rather than months. A third convention that often influences interest calculations states that for interest purposes the year consists of 360 days. Thus, if we borrow money for 60 days, the time period is 60/360, or one sixth of a year.

To illustrate the accounting for a short-term note and its interest, assume that a firm buys machinery on March 15 for $10,000 and gives a 15 percent, 90-day note in exchange. This note promises payment on June 13 (the maturity date) of $10,000 plus interest at the rate of 15 percent, namely $375 ($10,000 × 0.15 × 90/360). The initial value of this note is its face value of $10,000. The present value will grow to $10,375 by the end of 90 days.[4] In making entries for this note payable, we must be sure to accrue the interest for the time passed in an adjusting entry whenever an accounting period ends.

---

[4] The conceptual valuation base for interest-bearing claims is called "present value." Present value concepts and procedures are explained in the Appendix to Chapter 11 and are applied to other types of liabilities in Chapter 11.

Because the legal document explicitly recognizes interest as a separate item, accountants accrue the contractual interest in a separate liability account.

If a firm's accounting period ends on May 31, the following entries would be made in connection with the preceding note:

| | | | |
|---|---|---|---|
| March 15 | Machinery . . . . . . . . . . . . | 10,000.00 | |
| | Notes Payable . . . . . . . | | 10,000.00 |
| | To record purchase of machinery in exchange for a 15 percent, 90-day note. | | |
| May 31 | Interest Expense. . . . . . . . . | 320.83 | |
| | Interest Payable . . . . . . . | | 320.83 |
| | To accrue interest at 15 percent for 77 days (16 days in March, 30 days in April, and 31 days in May). | | |
| June 13 | Interest Expense. . . . . . . . . | 54.17 | |
| | Interest Payable . . . . . . . | | 54.17 |
| | To accrue interest at 15 percent for 13 days. | | |
| | Interest Payable . . . . . . . . . | 375.00 | |
| | Notes Payable . . . . . . . . . | 10,000.00 | |
| | Cash . . . . . . . . . . . . | | 10,375.00 |
| | To record the payment of liabilities for interest and principal. | | |

## Taxes

Taxes are various governmental claims on a business's assets. We concern ourselves here with the more common types, such as property taxes and the corporate income tax. The latter tax is perhaps the most important and serves as our example.

As a tax liability accrues, there is a concomitant decrease in owners' equity. This decrease is recorded in a special nominal account. Assume that National Converters determines that their earnings for the year will result in a tax liability of $137,000. The entry to record these taxes would be:

| | | | |
|---|---|---|---|
| Dec. 31 | Income Taxes . . . . . . . . . . . . . . . | 137,000 | |
| | Income Taxes Payable . . . . . . . | | 137,000 |
| | To accrue income taxes for the year. | | |

Taxes in some ways are similar to an expense. In a broad sense, they can be viewed as a payment for government services consumed during the period or as a necessary expense for the privilege of conducting business as a corporation. On the other hand, the amount of assets eventually distributed to the government bears, at best, only an indirect and varying relationship to the amount of service received. Some accountants argue, therefore, that taxes are not like other expenses that measure assets used up in the production of revenues. They would treat taxes as a nonreciprocal transfer of wealth to the taxing authority. Probably there are elements of both concepts in tax charges.

One conclusion is sure. There can be no net increase in owners' equity from the activities of the period until the tax claims are provided for. Accordingly, most businesses treat taxes as an expense. Also, the FASB, in its *Statement of Financial Accounting Concepts No. 3,* specifically included taxes as an expense element. We will do likewise.

## Dividends

Dividends involve a distribution of assets by a corporation to its stockholders. If National Converters declares and pays immediately a $93,800 dividend, the entry is:

| | | |
|---|---|---|
| Dividends Declared | 93,800 | |
| Cash | | 93,800 |

Dividends are not expenses of the period but are pro rata distributions of assets previously reflected as earned income.

More commonly, the dividend is declared at one date, but payment occurs later. At the time of declaration, the corporation creates a legal obligation to distribute assets to its stockholders. If National Converters had made such a declaration, the entry to record it would be:

| | | |
|---|---|---|
| Dividends Declared | 93,800 | |
| Dividends Payable | | 93,800 |

Unlike interest, dividends do not accrue merely with the passage of time. When declared, however, the dividend represents a decrease in retained earnings and a corresponding increase in a current liability. The actual distribution of assets subsequent to the dividend declaration simply liquidates the current liability. The entry to record the payment would be:

| | | |
|---|---|---|
| Dividends Payable | 93,800 | |
| Cash | | 93,800 |

The Dividend Declared account records the decline in retained earnings when assets are withdrawn by the owners of the business or are promised to them. During the closing process, the Dividends Declared account will be credited, and a matching debit made to Retained Earnings. This entry transfers the amount of the Dividends Declared to Retained Earnings, thereby reducing its balance.

## Summary of Period Activities

The special-purpose accounts studied so far include the following:

| *Increases in Owners' Equity* | *Decreases in Owners' Equity* |
|---|---|
| Revenues | Operating Expenses |
| Gains | Losses |
| | Interest |
| | Taxes |
| | Dividends |

Each of the accounts listed have one trait in common—they all reflect periodic increases or decreases in retained earnings. The reason for the change differs with each type of account. Revenues, operating expenses, gains, losses, interest, and taxes each represent a particular aspect of periodic performance; together they affect the net change in retained earnings *via the final net income figure.* Dividends are treated as a *distribution* of a portion of the income to the owners; they are not an expense affecting the *determination* of net income.

These new temporary owners' equity accounts fit conveniently into our basic balance sheet framework. What began in Chapter 3 as a simple accounting equation now can be expanded to include the different components of the income statement. The following schema shows the relationship between the flows of the income statement and the stocks of the balance sheet.

Assets = Liabilities + Owners' equity = { Contributed capital + Ending retained earnings = { Beginning retained earnings + Net income − Dividends } } Net income = { Revenues + Gains − Operating expenses − Losses − Taxes − Interest }

## AN EXPANDED CONCEPT OF ACCOUNTING INCOME

Up to this chapter, our concept of accounting income has encompassed only revenues and expenses. Having introduced additional owners' equity changes, we must now address two additional questions:

1. How broadly or narrowly should periodic business income be defined?
2. How should these various changes in retained earnings be displayed on the financial statements?

The first question asks whether information about all activities that produce changes in retained earnings during the period should be reported on the income statement, or whether the income statement should be restricted only to the main, profit-directed activities. The Financial Accounting Standards Board has coined the term *comprehensive income* to describe "the change in equity (net assets) of an entity during a period from transactions and other events and circumstances . . . except those resulting from investments by owners and distributions to owners."[5] However, the Board has left to other authoritative pronouncements, some issued and some yet to be issued, the specifications of which elements of comprehensive income should comprise *net income* in accounting reports.

The second question recognizes that, even within the array of owners' equity changes selected for inclusion in the calculation of reported net income, several relevant subtotals could be singled out for emphasis. An "operating income" figure derived from "normal" revenues and expenses could be separately disclosed. Many firms claim that an income subtotal before and after income taxes is relevant. Moreover, reporting procedures must be developed to communicate information about changes in retained earnings that are not included in net income.

There are no simple answers to these two questions. Conceivably, we may have a whole series of different income figures and formats, depending on the view or the purposes of the user. Without attempting to resolve these questions (if indeed there is a resolution), we will consider some of the basic ideas and procedures involved in the definition of income and the reporting of owners' equity changes. The first section, Reporting of Unusual Items, provides some background for the first question. The second section, Income Statement Formats, addresses the question of alternative disclosures in the financial statement. Chapter 16 discusses in much greater detail the specific problems in defining net income and reporting unusual items.

## Reporting Unusual Items

One extremely perplexing problem related to income statement preparation is the reporting of unusual increases and decreases in retained earnings during a period. In a realistic situation, any or all of the following types of events not related to normal operations might occur during the current year:

1. Worn-out equipment is sold for more than its book value.
2. An entire plant is demolished by a tornado.
3. A tax refund is received in the current period, resulting from tax litigation relating to income from three years ago.

---

[5] FASB, *Concepts No. 3,* par. 56.

4. Plant assets purchased two years ago were erroneously charged as maintenance expense. The error is discovered and corrected in the current period.
5. An engineering firm evaluates the structural properties of the administrative headquarters and, based on the evaluation, the depreciation life for the building is revised downward from 50 years to 30 years.

Where and how should these items be reported? Each of the events causes a change in owners' equity during the current period; they are all part of comprehensive income. However, should they all enter into the determination of *current net income*? If not, how should they be reported? Which ones would you include in net income?

These questions illustrate the basic dilemma of financial reporting in serving a number of different objectives and audiences. Should the income statement show only transactions arising from normal, recurring operating activities during the current period or do we show all transactions even though some of them are unusual, nonrecurring, or involve activities of prior accounting periods? Those accountants who believe that net income measures the total change in stockholders' wealth include all transactions in the current period's income. Conversely, those supporting net income as an earnings predictor or performance measurement favor showing only the result of *current* operating transactions. Both interpretations appear relevant to the overall objectives set forth in Chapter 2.

Since 1966, the Accounting Principles Board and the Financial Accounting Standards Board have issued five major opinions and standards in an attempt to eliminate the diverse practices in reporting unusual events affecting retained earnings. In general, these pronouncements are consistent with the view that net income should be all-inclusive. The income statement of the current period should reflect all transactions, normal or unusual, affecting the owners' equity during the period—except transactions in capital stock and dividends. In this way, a series of income statements gives a complete history of the retained earnings account.

Special changes in retained earnings fall into various categories—for example, unusual charges and credits (tax refunds), extraordinary items (tornado losses), accounting errors (plant acquisitions charged as maintenance expenses), and changes in accounting estimates (changes in useful life). Detailed procedures are prescribed for reporting each category in financial statements. They will be discussed in Chapter 16.

## Income Statement Formats

In addition to the question of whether certain unusual items should be included in calculating net income, accountants must wrestle with a second issue. What format is best for displaying information on the income statement? Two general approaches have surfaced in accounting practice. They are called "single-step" and "multiple-step" formats. We will illustrate these formats using the National Converters example begun earlier in this chapter.

The income statements reflect the balances in the accounts shown earlier after updating them for the entries given for gains, losses, interest, taxes, and dividends. The adjusted balances of December 31 would be:

|  | *Debit* | *Credit* |
|---|---|---|
| Cash | 1,410,100 | |
| Accounts receivable | 1,330,100 | |
| Merchandise inventory | 863,500 | |
| Investments | 100,000 | |
| Land | 175,000 | |
| Building | 395,200 | |
| Accounts payable | | 392,200 |
| Notes payable | | 161,000 |
| Capital stock | | 1,750,000 |
| Retained earnings | | 1,796,300 |
| Sales revenue | | 1,260,200 |
| Rent revenue | | 16,300 |
| Dividend revenue | | 90,400 |
| Cost of goods sold | 686,500 | |
| Selling expenses | 210,200 | |
| Administrative expenses | 176,000 | |
| Depreciation expenses | 61,800 | |
| Gain on sale of land | | 84,900 |
| Loss on sale of investment | 49,100 | |
| Interest expense | 16,100 | |
| Interest payable | | 16,100 |
| Income taxes | 137,000 | |
| Income taxes payable | | 137,000 |
| Dividend declared | 93,800 | |
| | 5,704,400 | 5,704,400 |

Figures 6–1 and 6–2 illustrate the two income statement formats. Both statements use the most common heading, "Statement of Income." However, other titles frequently encountered are "Statement of Earnings" and "Statement of Operations."

**Single-Step Income Statements.** The format shown in Figure 6–1 is the more common of the two. All revenues and gains are grouped together, as are the revenue deductions. Although other subtotals besides the single net income figure may be helpful for some purposes, advocates of the single-step form reason that the simplified presentation focuses attention on the most important figure while allowing intelligent readers of the statement to use the figures in whatever ways are appropriate for *their* purposes.

**FIGURE 6–1**   Single-Step Income Statement

### NATIONAL CONVERTERS, INC.
### Statement of Income
### For the Year Ended December 31, 1991
### ($000)

Revenues and gains:

| | |
|---|---|
| Sales revenue | $1,260.2 |
| Dividend revenue | 90.4 |
| Rent revenue | 16.3 |
| Gain on sale of land | 84.9 |
| | 1,451.8 |

Expenses and losses:

| | |
|---|---|
| Cost of goods sold | 686.5 |
| Selling expenses | 210.2 |
| Administrative expenses | 176.0 |
| Depreciation expense | 61.8 |
| Loss on sale of investments | 49.1 |
| Interest expense | 16.1 |
| Income taxes | 137.0 |
| | 1,336.7 |
| Net income | $ 115.1 |

**Multiple-Step Income Statements.**   This approach follows the view that the purpose of the income statement is to communicate information for a number of different purposes. Therefore, data are arranged to highlight significant relationships and subtotals on the statement. Notice the various "income" subtotals in Figure 6–2. The operating income figure, for example, reflects the performance from the firm's main business activities.

Many analysts see the multiple-step income statement as a way of dealing with the requirements of an all-inclusive income statement. Operating income from main activities can be segregated from the impact of peripheral activities. The effect on income from abnormal or unusual events can be distinguished, and the special nature of income taxes can be highlighted. Investors and creditors will thus be better able to assess the amounts, timing, and uncertainty of the future cash flows of the enterprise.

As we shall see in Chapter 16, many authoritative pronouncements require that certain unusual events be segregated on the income statement. To this extent, some form of the multiple-step approach may be mandated. In fact, a slight drift toward multiple-step approaches seems to be building in accounting practice. Most published financial statements follow formats somewhere between the two extremes. Indeed even most single-step statements report income taxes as a separate deduction.

**FIGURE 6–2**   Multiple-Step Income Statement

**NATIONAL CONVERTERS, INC.**
**Statement of Income**
**For the Year Ended December 31, 1991**
**($000)**

| | | |
|---|---:|---:|
| Sales | | $1,260.2 |
| Cost of goods sold | | 686.5 |
| Gross margin | | 573.7 |
| Operating expenses: | | |
| Selling | $210.2 | |
| Administrative | 176.0 | |
| Depreciation | 61.8 | 448.0 |
| Operating income | | 125.7 |
| Other revenue and (expense): | | |
| Dividend revenue | 90.4 | |
| Rent revenue | 16.3 | |
| Interest expense | (16.1) | 90.6 |
| Income from recurring activities | | 216.3 |
| Gains and (losses): | | |
| Gain on sale of land | 84.9 | |
| Loss on sale of investments | (49.1) | 35.8 |
| Income before income taxes | | 252.1 |
| Income taxes | | 137.0 |
| Net income | | $  115.1 |

**Statement of Retained Earnings.**   To reconcile completely the period's change in retained earnings with the balances on the comparative position statements, most firms introduce a separate statement of retained earnings. The statement starts with the balance of retained earnings at the beginning of the year, adds the amount of net income shown on the income statement, and deducts dividends. In addition, other very rare direct debits or credits to retained earnings or adjustments associated with capital stock transactions may be reported there. An example of such a statement is assumed for National Converters, Inc., in Figure 6–3.

## Income Statement Analysis

One advantage claimed for the multiple-step income statement is the ease of spotting significant relationships. Analysts compute a number of income

---

**FIGURE 6–3**    Example of Statement of Retained Earnings

---

**NATIONAL CONVERTERS, INC.**
**Statement of Retained Earnings**
**For the Year Ended December 31, 1991**
**($000)**

| | |
|---|---:|
| Retained earnings, December 31, 1990 . . . . . . . . . . . . . | $1,796.3 |
| Correction of accounting error from prior period. . . . . . . . . | 47.2 |
| Balance as adjusted . . . . . . . . . . . . . . . . . . . . . | 1,843.5 |
| 1991 Net income  . . . . . . . . . . . . . . . . . . . . . . | 115.1 |
| | 1,958.6 |
| Dividends . . . . . . . . . . . . . . . . . . . . . . . . . | 93.8 |
| Retained earnings, December 31, 1991 . . . . . . . . . . . . . | $1,864.8 |

---

statement ratios and compare them across companies and time periods. A
few of the more common income statement ratios are:

1. Gross margin (or gross profit) to sales ratio
2. Operating income to sales ratio
3. Net income to sales ratio
4. Effective tax rate percentage

We can illustrate these computations using the National Converters multiple-step income statement in Figure 6–2. It is apparent in the statement that
the figures are stated in millions of dollars. Large quantities are difficult to
put into an easy frame of reference. Ratios help.

The gross margin ratio is calculated as:

$$\frac{\text{Gross margin}}{\text{Sales}} = \frac{573.7}{1,260.2} = 45.5\%$$

This ratio provides a measure indicating the percentage of each sale dollar
remaining after deducting the cost of inventory distributed to generate the
sales. In our case 45+ cents of each sales dollar is available for covering
other expenses and generating net income.

The ratio shown above only relates to the inventory cost incurred to generate sales. Other expenses such as selling, administrative, and depreciation
must also be covered to earn income. Another ratio is used to express the
percentage of each sales dollar remaining after covering all operating
expenses. This operating income ratio is calculated as:

$$\frac{\text{Operating income}}{\text{Sales}} = \frac{125.7}{1,260.2} = 10.0\%$$

This ratio indicates that the firm retains $.10 from each dollar of sales after
covering all recurring operating expenses. This ratio is a profitability measure showing management's ability to generate income.

Several other revenue and expense items, gains, losses, and income taxes also appear on the income statement. Each of these items will ultimately increase or decrease the final net income for the period. A third ratio can be used to express the final profitability after considering all of these items. The net income ratio is calculated as:

$$\frac{\text{Net income}}{\text{Sales}} = \frac{115.1}{1,260.2} = 9.1\%$$

This measure indicates the ultimate profitability related to the current period's operations. Management, in this instance, has generated a 9.1 percent return on each dollar of sales.

Individual items from the statement may be examined to gain an insight into their meanings. For example, income taxes can be analyzed in at least two different ways. First, we can calculate income taxes as a percentage of sales. This ratio is calculated as:

$$\frac{\text{Income taxes}}{\text{Sales}} = \frac{137.0}{1,260.2} = 10.9\%$$

This ratio indicates that almost 11 percent, or 11 cents, of each sales dollar is paid in taxes. A second ratio computes the effective tax rate which the entity actually paid. Taxes are based on the income before taxes. Therefore, if we relate the dollars of tax to that income, we can determine the effective rate the entity is paying. The effective tax rate percentage is calculated as:

$$\frac{\text{Income taxes}}{\text{Income before taxes}} = \frac{137.0}{252.1} = 54.3\%$$

This ratio reveals that the tax rate for National Converters was over 54 percent this period. In other words, although the company paid only 10.9 percent of sales in taxes, it paid 54.3 percent of its income dollars.

Ratio analysis allows us to express income statement dollars in a more manageable and meaningful form. Each of the ratios calculated can be compared to the same ratios in other accounting periods to determine the trends and changes in the composition of the income statement. Because the income statement reports on the results of operations of the business, these ratio comparisons should provide useful information about the performance of the company. Through them, an analyst gains insight into the operations of the firm.

# AN INTRODUCTION TO THE KIMBERLY-CLARK ANNUAL REPORT

National Converters, Inc., used as an example in this chapter, is a hypothetical company, and its statements are simplified and condensed. In the Appendix to this chapter, the most important financial portions of the 1987

Annual Report of Kimberly-Clark Corporation have been reproduced. This material comprises pages 10–11 and 16–37 in that annual report.

Kimberly-Clark is a worldwide business engaged in employing advanced technologies in absorbency, fiber-forming, and other fields. The corporation manufactures and markets a wide range of products for personal care, health care, business, and industry. It also produces and markets papers requiring specialized technology, as well as traditional papers and related products, for newspaper publishing and other communication needs. A subsidiary company, Midwest Express Airlines, operates a commercial airline.

The Kimberly-Clark accounting statements and other financial information are used as a continuing example throughout the rest of this book. Beginning in this chapter and appearing in subsequent chapters will be sections devoted to discussions of the Kimberly-Clark statements and the underlying accounting procedures. A portion of each chapter will contain a descriptive elaboration of this real-world example, relating the subject matter of that chapter to Kimberly-Clark's published statements. Our goal is to show that what is being discussed in the chapters is directly applicable to your understanding and use of actual financial reports.[6]

## An Overview of the Annual Report

Kimberly-Clark's annual report is distributed each year to stockholders and other interested parties. In addition to the financial section, the 1987 annual report contains (1) a letter to the stockholders from the chief executive officer, (2) a quarter-by-quarter profile of significant events related to the company's performance in 1987, (3) some financial highlights and selected data for the years 1985, 1986, and 1987, and (4) a major section providing an operating and financial review made by the company. None of this information has been reproduced except for four pages from the latter section.

The financial section contains the financial statements, their eleven notes, the independent auditor's opinion, a letter from the audit committee of the board of directors, and a statement of management's responsibilities. We refer to these annual report elements in subsequent chapters. However, before leaving this chapter, let us review briefly several elements in the report.

**1.** Management's responsibility for the conduct of the business includes preparing financial statements and maintaining a system of internal controls to safeguard assets and ensure integrity in financial reporting. Management also

---

[6] The authors appreciate the cooperation of Kimberly-Clark and its willingness to let us use the annual report for this purpose. Kimberly-Clark was selected because, while its financial reporting is reasonably complex, the statements are presented in a straightforward manner, and the disclosures are quite complete. The accounting procedures and reporting practices used by Kimberly-Clark are chosen solely for illustration. They are not intended to represent either desirable or undesirable reporting practices.

indicates that policies for lawful and ethical conduct of business affairs and for preserving the confidentiality of information and ideas have been adopted.

**2.** The auditor's opinion contains the professional judgment of the company's independent certified public accountant (CPA) concerning the financial statements. Management has stated its responsibility for the accuracy and fairness of the information in the statements. The auditor serves as an independent check on management's representations and, through the printed opinion, lends credibility to the statements for outside readers.

**3.** Kimberly-Clark presents the three primary financial statements we have introduced. These are the statement of income, statement of changes in financial position, and the balance sheet. Note that the statement of changes in financial position shows the cash flows during the year.[7] In the statement titles, the term *consolidated* is used. This means that Kimberly-Clark owns a number of other companies (such as the airline), and their results have been combined in the financial statements.

**4.** The eleven notes to the financial statements provide extended interpretations and elaborations of the financial statement information. They identify many of the accounting principles employed, disclose the financial impact of many accounting procedures used, and explain other important elements, thus making the financial statements more meaningful. The notes are crucial to understanding some of the complex reporting issues discussed in later chapters.

## An Overview of the Financial Statements

The three primary financial statements can be reviewed in light of our discussion in previous chapters. Our review here will be a general one, inasmuch as later we explore many items in detail. Notice that all of the statements are presented in comparative form; 1987's financial information is presented alongside that from 1986 and in some cases from 1985 also.

**Income Statement.** Kimberly-Clark uses a condensed multi-step format for the income statement. The gross profit section of the statement focuses the reader's attention on the matching of primary operating revenues (net sales) with the primary product costs (cost of products sold and distribution expense). Period expenses (advertising, research, and general) are then grouped and deducted to provide a measure of the income from primary business operations (operating profit). Then non-operating items such as interest income, interest expense, and other items are applied to obtain

---

[7] As we noted in Chapter 1, the statement of changes in financial position is no longer a generally accepted financial statement. It has been replaced by the statement of cash flows beginning in 1988. Kimberly-Clark uses the old title in 1987 but has modified most of the statement to conform to the new reporting requirements for cash flows.

income before taxes. Subtraction of the provision for income taxes results in the net income for the corporation.

Under GAAP, Kimberly-Clark must present its per share net income at the bottom of the income statement. The accounting policies that influence the calculation of net income are indicated as part of Note 1, as are the specific elements used for the earnings per share calculation.

**Balance Sheet.**    Kimberly-Clark's balance sheet employs the account form, with assets on one page and equities (liabilities and stockholders' equity) on the facing page. Its assets are classified into four categories. The current assets are typical with cash, accounts receivable, and inventories making up the category. Detailed information related to these assets is found in Note 9.

The second category contains the noncurrent properties owned by the corporation. Land and Timberlands appear as separate components. The nature of the fiber business results in timberland being a major productive resource quite different from land used for buildings. Accordingly, the accounting process reports these two significant resources separately.

The third and fourth categories are single lines showing Kimberly-Clark's investment in other companies and other assets that could not be classified in the previous categories. Normally this latter classification is used for miscellaneous assets.

The liabilities are divided into current and long-term. The former classification contains typical short-term debt and liability payments the firm anticipates paying within the next year. The long-term debt classification covers extended debt payments that will be met over a number of years. The details of the long-term debt are presented in Note 4 to the financial statements. Notice that the portion of long-term debt that is payable in 1988 appears as a current liability rather than as a long-term liability.

Deferred income taxes represent the amounts the company expects to pay to the government in future years. The accounting concept that gives rise to this account is discussed in Chapter 13. Minority owners' interest represents the equity (sources of assets) of shareholders other than Kimberly-Clark in other companies not completely owned by Kimberly-Clark. It is discussed in Chapter 15.

The shareholders' equity is quite complicated. There is common stock outstanding, some shares repurchased by the company (treasury stock), amounts that reflect decreases in ownership due to negative foreign currency translation adjustments, and retained earnings. All of these items are discussed in later chapters.

## Statement of Changes in Financial Position (Statement of Cash Flows)

We have briefly introduced this statement in earlier chapters. A detailed discussion will be completed in Chapter 17. This statement shows the major sources and uses of cash. The three areas of interest are operating, investing, and financing activities. Within each of these sections, the major events that provide cash inflows or require cash outflows are shown.

# A REFLECTION ON ACCOUNTING INCOME

Much of the discussion in this chapter emphasizes the tentative nature of income measurement. The problems we have discussed are associated with implementing the matching concept. These problems lead to uncertainty as to what exactly constitutes "net income" and require all readers to examine carefully the components of any amount so labeled.

Net income is no more accurate than the concepts on which it is founded. Inasmuch as this chapter completes the first section on fundamental concepts and procedures, a brief review of the relationship between the conceptual framework and the financial statements is useful.

## Problems with the Conceptual Framework

Implicit in much of our discussion of accounting theory is the belief that accounting produces useful information. Statements of objectives, assumptions about audience characteristics, qualitative guidelines, and generally accepted accounting principles all exist to enhance the statements' usefulness in decision making. We have introduced the state-of-the-art thinking about a conceptual framework. However, this is only a beginning. A number of fundamental issues and questions still need to be addressed.

**1.** *Identification of Users.*   Who are the primary users of financial statements? Are they homogeneous in their goals and other characteristics? Can a single set of generalized statements serve their needs? Inconsistencies remain in accounting that can be traced to a failure to distinguish between the needs of sophisticated and unsophisticated users. The notion of general-purpose statements designed to serve common needs continually conflicts with the notion of differential disclosures designed to recognize heterogeneous needs.

**2.** *Specification of Information Needs.*   What are the information needs of the user groups? Which needs can financial statements most effectively fulfill? Are existing statements the appropriate media for communicating this information? How is financial accounting information currently being used?

**3.** *Purpose of the Income Figure.*   Can a single net income concept or a single income statement serve all the purposes that users require? The income figure is used to (a) evaluate management's performance, (b) predict future income, dividends, and cash flows, (c) determine a firm's debt paying ability, and (d) measure changes in the wealth of an enterprise. Which of these uses should be the principle guide to developing accounting theory and practice?

**4.** *Resolution of Conflicts.*   If objectives or principles conflict, how can accounting accommodate the differences? Can the qualitative guidelines be made operational? We will find numerous examples where the difficulty of making trade-offs among qualitative guides and among measurement principles contributes to the complexity found in accounting practice.

**5.** *Investor Reaction to Accounting Data.* How do accountants determine whether financial statements contain useful information? Are investors misled by errors, differences, or changes in accounting methods? A growing body of empirical research suggests that investors see through changes and differences in accounting methods. The stock market seems to process new information quickly and without bias. Does this suggest that "disclosure issues" are more important than "measurement issues"?

## Accounting Income: Cash Flows versus Accrual Flows

Accounting income is determined largely by the assumptions used to determine when assets from operations are to be recognized as inflows (revenues) and outflows (expenses). We have made the case for recognizing revenue at the point where it is earned and expenses at the point where they have been incurred. This measurement approach, called "accrual basis accounting," is used for most corporate income statements. Alternatively, accounting income can be determined by measuring revenues at the points where cash is received and expenses are paid. This approach uses cash movements as the criteria for measurement and is called "cash basis accounting."

In the long run both methods result in the same income measurement. However, because income statements are prepared for short-run assessments of managerial performance, accountants generally feel that the accrual basis produces a more meaningful reflection of the current results of operations. Accrual basis accounting produces a more accurate measure of the firm's *performance* because it concentrates on measuring revenue inflows, whether cash or receivable, and expense incurrence, whether cash or payable, in the periods when the economic activity occurs.

The superiority of accrual basis measures does not mean that cash flows are unimportant—quite the contrary. Ultimately, cash is the liquid medium produced by accounts receivable and with which accounts payable must be paid. Cash flows, then, are important for two reasons. First, they determine the liquidity status of the firm. Indeed, the statement of cash flows shows whether the firm is generating sufficient cash flows to meet debt obligations, to maintain its level of operations, and to take advantage of future opportunities.

The second reason for the importance of cash flows is that they represent the ultimate measure of business activity and of accounting concern. The success of a business eventually rests on its ability to generate net cash flows. Similarly, as clearly stated in the objectives of financial reporting discussed in Chapter 2, measuring and predicting this ability to generate net cash flows is of paramount importance to accounting. Accountants are concerned with the relationship between accrual numbers and cash flow numbers and with the impact of transactions on cash flows.

However, for short periods of time, cash flows are more volatile than accrual measures and consequently may not faithfully represent economic performance. So, somewhat paradoxically, an "interest in an enterprise's future cash flows . . . leads primarily to an interest in information about its earnings rather than information directly about its cash flows. Information about enterprise earnings . . . generally provides a better indication of enterprise performance than information about current cash receipts and payments."[8]

It should be clear that accounting income and cash flows are two different, though related, measures of results. They complement each other. Both are important and should be evaluated regularly. Hence, GAAP requires accountants to prepare both income statements and statements of cash flows.

## Influence of Basic Assumptions

Finally, let us review the interrelationships between the extant conceptual framework and the financial statements.

In Chapter 2 we saw that seven fundamental assumptions form the basic fabric into which are woven the many principles and procedures of financial accounting. These assumptions are declaratory assertions, not discovered truths. As such, they exert an influence on financial statements only so long as and to the extent that they are accepted by the accounting profession and ultimately by the users of financial statements.

**Environmental Assumptions.** Three basic assumptions—entity concept, going-concern concept, and monetary concept—describe the environmental elements of financial accounting. The first two help set the stage for financial statements. Their initial impact is obvious. The *separate-entity concept* defines the organizational unit covered by the statements and hence determines which items are included in assets, liabilities, and so on, and which transactions get recorded. The *going-concern concept* supplies the rationale behind the matching concept. Specifically, it focuses attention away from periodic liquidation values for assets and allows for the allocation of costs, such as depreciation, over the useful lives of the noncurrent assets.

The *monetary concept* obviously supports the use of dollar amounts in the communication process. It also asserts that dollars of different vintages can be added together. Only by assuming that fluctuations in the value of the dollar can be ignored or are insignificant are we able to sum the cash in the bank, the cost of the merchandise bought in December of last year, and the amount spent on constructing a building 10 years ago into a single amount called "total assets." Although the monetary postulate aids the meaningful presentation of information, it may impair interpretation in times of monetary instability. If there is an increase in the general price level, causing the size of the measuring unit to decline, the various asset items really cannot

---

[8] FASB, *Concepts No. 1,* par. 43 and 44.

be added together. The yardstick with which the accountant measures dollar amounts changes over time. Ignoring price-level changes in conventional accounting statements has become increasingly limiting.

**Operational Assumptions.**    The remaining four assumptions relate closely to the process of income measurement. The *matching concept* provides the major foundation for the income statement. It asserts that resources consumed during the period which have a direct association (as does merchandise) or an indirect association (as do office salaries) with the revenue of the period should be related to those revenues in the calculation of periodic net income. As a corollary, any unexpired resources appear as assets on the position statement.

The particular matching concept underlying conventional financial accounting (matching of acquisition cost and revenue) derives from the *cost principle* for asset valuation discussed in Chapter 3. This principle in turn results from the *exchange-price concept,* which states that resources entering the accounting process should be assigned monetary values based on the prices implicit in the original exchange transactions. Expense recognition principles result from the interface of the matching and exchange-price concepts. The former determines when expenses are recognized, and the latter provides how much.

The matching concept is only one of several approaches to income measurement. Conventional accounting rejects, as too uncertain and subjective, concepts of "economic income" based on *expectations* about future cash flows, even though such future events are doubtless relevant to current decision making. Rather, the matching concept presumes that the basic subject matter of financial accounting is actual transactions, usually with outside parties. Therefore, it emphasizes primarily a *historical* perspective. Because of their objective tone, accounting reports may also have predictive value, but these income projections are left to the judgment of the individual user.

In the area of *revenue recognition,* financial accounting usually insists on a market transaction in which the firm supplies some good or service to a consuming unit outside the entity before recognition is given to value changes in the assets. However, increases and decreases in the value of assets do not suddenly come into economic being as the firm acquires various input factors and uses them to produce a salable output. By insisting that revenue be earned and reliably measured before being recognized, financial accounting may exaggerate the importance of the sales transaction and may tend to delay the recognition of accretion in values beyond the time of their occurrence. Also, different revenue recognition expedients may cause the timing of income to vary, since revenue recognition is the initiating event in the matching process.

*The periodicity concept* also exerts a direct impact on the financial statements. By establishing a time framework within which matching occurs, it ensures that the income statement is always prepared for a specific time period. In a sense, the classifications of current and noncurrent on the position statement also spring from the concept of the accounting period. The concept of the accounting period routinely causes numerous measurement problems that limit the precision of accounting net income. Although our basic data—revenues and expenses—result from market transactions, fitting them into an arbitrary time framework requires judgment. The adjusting entries for accruals and prepayments and the period cost concept are two examples of such judgments. In future chapters, some additional estimating procedures and assumptions are introduced, primarily for the purpose of matching costs and revenues within a specified time period. On the one hand, the periodicity concept requires the accrual basis of accounting. On the other hand, it increases the tentativeness of the income calculation. At best, the income figure serves only as an index of a continuing stream of economic and financial activity.

## A FINAL NOTE

All of the basic assumptions of financial accounting serve simultaneously to enhance and limit the usefulness of the statements. They are not immutable decrees; neither are they random assertions. They lead to some reasonable and useful, albeit tentative, conclusions about the nature and management of a firm's resources. They certainly do not produce precise figures or even "correct" figures according to other standards. To view the financial statements apart from the assumptions on which they rest or to use accounting measurements without being aware of their limitations is foolhardy.

One other point concerning the conventional accounting concept of income should be kept in mind. Although it is perhaps more certain and less subjective overall than alternative income systems, it is still a concept, not a precise measurement. A potential hazard to the unwary reader of an income statement is that different methods can be used for matching particular costs against revenues. Faced with inconclusive evidence as to the exact relationships between costs and revenues and uncertain as to how the end result is used, accountants have adopted a number of reasonable yet arbitrary procedures to implement the matching concept. The handling of period costs is one example encountered so far; many others are discussed in later chapters. If there is no single "right way" for handling particular items, there can hardly be any single resultant figure that represents "the correct" net income.

The purpose of this chapter and of this first section is to provide an insight into the items that appear on conventional financial accounting statements, particularly the income statement. With an understanding of the meaning and implications of these terms and concepts and given sufficient information through explanation or disclosure, the reader should be able to ascertain the elements comprising a particular net income figure, evaluate its usefulness, and possibly modify it for a specific purpose.

In the next section we talk in greater detail about specific problems in the measurement of accounting income. There the reader has occasion to employ many of the accounts and concepts discussed in this chapter and section.

# *Appendix: The 1987 Kimberly-Clark Annual Report*

*REVIEW OF OPERATIONS*

Sales, operating profit, net income and earnings per share all set records in 1987.

Volume increases were broadly based, accounting for more than half of the 14 percent improvement in consolidated sales, compared with a year ago. Top volume gainers were:

- Disposable diapers and tissue products in the U.S.,
- Consumer and service operations outside the U.S., especially in Canada, Korea, the United Kingdom and continental Europe, and
- Feminine care and adult incontinence products in the U.S.

Consolidated operating profit, which grew 21 percent, improved in most businesses. Major increases came from:

- Consumer and service operations outside the U.S., notably those in Canada, the United Kingdom, Brazil and continental Europe,
- Disposable diapers in the U.S., which benefited from increased volume and selling prices, reversing a one-year decline in 1986,
- Improved volume and selling prices for tobacco industry and correspondence papers,
- Higher newsprint selling prices,
- Operating efficiencies achieved in pulp-producing facilities, and
- Midwest Express Airlines, Inc., the company's commercial airline.

Other comments on sales and operating profit are in the product class sections, beginning on page 12.

Because 1986 net income from equity companies included an $8.2 million gain from the sale of the company's interest in Jujo Kimberly K.K. to its Japanese partner, Kimberly-Clark's share of net income from equity companies was down slightly in 1987. From an operating standpoint, however, equity company earnings were up 23 percent over 1986, with Kimberly-Clark de Mexico, S.A. de C.V. providing most of the improvement.

The effective income tax rate for 1987 was 43 percent, unchanged from 1986, despite the decline in the U.S. statutory income tax rate from 46 percent in 1986 to 40 percent in 1987. Major factors affecting the rate comparison were:

- The phaseout of the U.S. investment tax credit by the Tax Reform Act of 1986.
- Tax rates outside the U.S. that generally were lower than the U.S. statutory rate in 1986, but higher in 1987.

As a result of two share repurchase programs completed in 1987 and described more fully on page 11, earnings per share increased faster than net income (27 percent versus 21 percent, respectively).

*REVIEW OF LIQUIDITY AND CAPITAL RESOURCES*

Cash provided by operations increased 51 percent in 1987. Major factors affecting the increase were:

- Record 1987 earnings,
- Lower operating working capital, and
- Timing of income tax payments.

During 1987, the company repurchased 13 percent of its common stock on the open market.

- 12 million shares were acquired at a total cost of $632 million, or an average cost of $52.63 per share.
- After completing the share repurchase programs, the company retired 14.5 million shares of common stock held in treasury.

In 1987, long-term debt increased $261 million or 61 percent. Noteworthy changes in long-term financings during the year were:

- $100 million of 9⅛ percent notes were issued in the U.S. public market in the second quarter.
- $200 million of commercial paper was classified as long-term debt at year-end because it was refinanced by issuance of long-term obligations in the first quarter of 1988.

The ratio of total debt to adjusted capital increased to 36 percent at the end of 1987, compared with 22 percent a year earlier. The ratio is expected to be close to the company's target range of 28 to 32 percent by the end of 1988. (Adjusted capital is the sum of total debt, minority owners' interests in subsidiaries and stockholders' equity.)

The company's long-term debt securities have a double-A rating, and its commercial paper is rated in the top category. Unused credit facilities, capacity to issue long-term debt and the ability of operations to generate cash are believed adequate to fund working capital, capital spending and other needs in the foreseeable future.

Dividends were increased for the 15th consecutive year. The quarterly rate was increased by 16 percent to 36 cents per share from 31 cents per share in 1986.

(Continued)

*TRENDS IN THE LAST THREE YEARS*

More than half of the 35 percent increase in consolidated sales during the last three years was a result of growth in volume. Kleenex Huggies diapers were a major factor; diaper volume in 1987 exceeded volume in each of the last two years, although 1986 volume was less than 1985. Volumes of facial tissue and feminine care products in the U.S. increased in each of the last three years.

Diaper sales, which increased 60 percent for the three-year period, represented 25 percent of consolidated sales in 1987, compared with 26 percent in both 1986 and 1985. Household and other tissue-based products, while increasing in dollar amount each year, represented 29 percent of consolidated sales in both 1987 and 1985, and 28 percent in 1986.

Consolidated operating margins were 12 percent in 1987, 11.3 percent in 1986 and 11.9 percent in 1985. The 1987 performance represented the best operating margin since 1978. Advertising, promotion and selling expenses as a percentage of sales declined from 14.1 percent in 1985 to 13.8 percent in 1987. Historically, this percentage has ranged from 13.5 percent to 15.5 percent. During the three-year period, efficiencies were realized from a shift to single-brand advertising for Kleenex facial tissue.

The level of research expense has remained essentially unchanged from 1985 through 1987 after increasing more than 40 percent from 1984. The company remains committed to an intensive research effort, but now has focused more of its research activities on products and improvements utilizing known technologies. Research spending is expected to increase in 1988.

Over the three-year period, net income grew at a slower rate than operating profit (44.5 percent compared to 56 percent) because of an extraordinary gain of $7.5 million and high investment tax credits in 1984. Investment tax credits reduced 1984's effective income tax rate by about seven percentage points to 38.2 percent. The effective tax rate for the three years ending in 1987 has remained constant at about 43 percent.

## NEW ACCOUNTING STANDARDS

At the end of 1987, two new accounting standards that will affect the company were issued by the Financial Accounting Standards Board. These new rules, summarized below, have not yet been adopted by the company.

SFAS No. 95, Statement of Cash Flows, must be adopted by the end of 1988. It requires the Consolidated Statement of Changes in Financial Position to be changed to a Consolidated Cash Flow Statement and that most line items on the new statement be presented on a cash basis. Adoption of the standard will not have a material effect on the company's financial statements.

SFAS No. 96, Accounting for Income Taxes, must be adopted by the beginning of 1989. It requires that deferred income taxes be recorded on a liability method and adjusted periodically when income tax rates change. The company's deferred income tax balances are presently recorded based on the rates in effect when the transactions giving rise to the deferred tax occur, and deferred tax balances are not adjusted when income tax rates change. The new income tax rule can be adopted either by restating prior year financial statements or by recording the entire effect of adopting the rule in net income in the year the rule is first applied. The company has not yet determined when or how it will adopt the new rule. Based on rough estimates made to date, adoption of the new rule in 1988 or 1989 for consolidated operations is expected to decrease the company's deferred income tax balance and increase stockholders' equity by $75 million to $100 million.

Kimberly-Clark Corporation and Subsidiaries

| (Millions of dollars except per share amounts) | Year Ended December 31 | | |
| --- | --- | --- | --- |
| | 1987 | 1986 | 1985 |
| NET SALES | $4,884.7 | $4,303.1 | $4,072.9 |
| Cost of products sold | 3,065.9 | 2,712.2 | 2,511.5 |
| Distribution expense | 181.2 | 166.2 | 168.9 |
| GROSS PROFIT | 1,637.6 | 1,424.7 | 1,392.5 |
| Advertising, promotion and selling expense | 674.9 | 595.2 | 576.3 |
| Research expense | 110.5 | 111.0 | 109.4 |
| General expense | 266.1 | 233.6 | 220.5 |
| OPERATING PROFIT | 586.1 | 484.9 | 486.3 |
| Interest income | 7.2 | 5.6 | 6.0 |
| Other income | 26.2 | 22.8 | 20.5 |
| Interest expense | (65.6) | (62.8) | (59.0) |
| Other expense | (19.8) | (17.5) | (14.5) |
| INCOME BEFORE INCOME TAXES | 534.1 | 433.0 | 439.3 |
| Provision for income taxes (Note 2) | 230.5 | 186.5 | 189.4 |
| INCOME BEFORE | 303.6 | 246.5 | 249.9 |
| Share of net income of equity companies (Note 11) | 35.3 | 37.0 | 31.7 |
| Minority owners' interests in subsidiaries' net income | (13.7) | (14.1) | (14.5) |
| NET INCOME | $ 325.2 | $ 269.4 | $ 267.1 |
| NET INCOME PER SHARE | $ 3.73 | $ 2.93 | $ 2.92 |

See Notes to Financial Statements.

| *(Millions of dollars)* | *Year Ended December 31* | | |
|---|---|---|---|
| | 1987 | 1986 | 1985 |
| **OPERATIONS** | | | |
| Net income . . . . . . . . . . | $ 325.2 | $ 269.4 | $ 267.1 |
| Noncash items included in income: | | | |
| Depreciation . . . . . . . | 186.0 | 169.3 | 140.3 |
| Deferred income taxes . . . . | 85.0 | 52.6 | 87.2 |
| Unremitted net income of equity companies . . . . | (17.2) | (14.0) | (17.7) |
| Minority owners' interests in subsidiaries' net income . . . . | 13.7 | 14.1 | 14.5 |
| Other . . . . . | 18.6 | 3.0 | 6.6 |
| Cash provided by income . . . . . | 611.3 | 494.4 | 498.0 |
| Changes in operating working capital *(Note 9)* . . . . | 45.3 | (59.9) | 85.5 |
| Cash provided by operations . . . . . | 656.6 | 434.5 | 583.5 |
| **INVESTING** | | | |
| Capital spending . . . . . | (247.3) | (282.4) | (425.8) |
| Disposals of property . . . . . | 34.5 | 18.8 | 15.7 |
| Other . . . . | (20.8) | 20.6 | (4.4) |
| Cash used for investing . . . . | (233.6) | (243.0) | (414.5) |
| **CASH PROVIDED BEFORE FINANCING** . . . . | $ 423.0 | $ 191.5 | $ 169.0 |
| **FINANCING SUMMARY** | | | |
| Cash dividends paid . . . . | $(124.1) | $(112.0) | $(104.8) |
| Acquisitions of common stock for the treasury . . . . | (632.2) | (1.0) | (.7) |
| Changes in debt payable within one year . . . . | 116.0 | 11.7 | (24.3) |
| Increases in long-term debt . . . . | 314.9 | 35.2 | 20.7 |
| Decreases in long-term debt . . . . | (54.3) | (118.1) | (53.0) |
| Increase in cash and cash equivalents . . . . | (43.3) | (7.3) | (6.9) |
| **NET DECREASE IN FINANCING** . . . . | $(423.0) | $(191.5) | $(169.0) |

*See Notes to Financial Statements.*

Kimberly-Clark Corporation and Subsidiaries

|  | December 31 | |
| --- | --- | --- |
| *(Millions of dollars)* | 1987 | 1986 |
| **ASSETS** | | |
| *CURRENT ASSETS* | | |
| Cash and cash equivalents | $ 89.7 | $ 46.4 |
| Accounts receivable *(Note 9)* | 519.9 | 455.2 |
| Inventories *(Note 9)* | 525.4 | 531.3 |
| Total current assets | 1,135.0 | 1,032.9 |
| *PROPERTY* | | |
| Land | 25.6 | 24.7 |
| Timberlands | 56.3 | 55.9 |
| Buildings | 621.7 | 591.3 |
| Machinery and equipment | 2,961.4 | 2,765.5 |
| Construction in progress | 103.0 | 66.8 |
|  | 3,768.0 | 3,504.2 |
| Less accumulated depreciation | 1,431.2 | 1,241.2 |
| Net property | 2,336.8 | 2,263.0 |
| *INVESTMENTS IN EQUITY COMPANIES (Note 11)* | 264.8 | 243.8 |
| *DEFERRED CHARGES AND OTHER ASSETS* | 149.1 | 136.3 |
|  | $3,885.7 | $3,676.0 |

*See Notes to Financial Statements.*

| (Millions of dollars) | December 31 | |
|---|---|---|
| | 1987 | 1986 |

## LIABILITIES AND STOCKHOLDERS' EQUITY

### CURRENT LIABILITIES

| | | |
|---|---|---|
| Debt payable within one year *(Note 4)* | $ 250.0 | $ 134.0 |
| Accounts payable and accrued liabilities *(Note 9)* | 619.9 | 577.6 |
| Accrued income taxes | 96.7 | 64.7 |
| Dividends payable | 29.5 | 28.5 |
| Total current liabilities | 996.1 | 804.8 |
| *LONG-TERM DEBT (Note 4)* | 686.9 | 426.3 |
| *DEFERRED INCOME TAXES* | 548.2 | 448.5 |
| *MINORITY OWNERS' INTERESTS IN SUBSIDIARIES* | 82.6 | 76.5 |

### STOCKHOLDERS' EQUITY *(Notes 5, 6, and 8)*

| | | |
|---|---|---|
| Common stock — $1.25 par value — authorized 300.0 million shares; issued 81.0 million shares at December 31, 1987 and 95.5 million shares at December 31, 1986 | 101.2 | 119.3 |
| Additional paid-in capital | 144.5 | 168.5 |
| Cost of common stock in treasury | (39.3) | (61.8) |
| Unrealized currency translation adjustments | (85.9) | (163.8) |
| Retained earnings | 1,451.4 | 1,857.7 |
| Total stockholders' equity | 1,571.9 | 1,919.9 |
| | $3,885.7 | $3,676.0 |

*NOTE 1. ACCOUNTING POLICIES*

Kimberly-Clark Corporation's accounting policies conform to generally accepted accounting principles. Significant policies followed are described below.

**Basis of Presentation**

The consolidated financial statements include the accounts of Kimberly-Clark Corporation and all significant subsidiaries which are more than 50 percent owned and controlled. Investments in nonconsolidated companies which are at least 20 percent owned are stated at cost plus equity in undistributed net income. These companies are referred to as equity companies.

**Investment Tax Credits**

The Tax Reform Act of 1986 eliminated the U.S. investment tax credit retroactive to January 1, 1986. Certain assets, however, were entitled to the investment tax credit under the transition rules of the Act. Investment tax credits are treated as reductions of income tax expense in the year in which the credits arise.

**Start-Up and Preoperating Expenses**

Significant expenses incurred in bringing new or expanded facilities into operation are recorded as deferred charges and amortized to income over periods of not more than five years.

**Advertising and Promotion Expenses**

Advertising expenses are charged to income during the year in which they are incurred. Promotion expenses are charged to income over the period of the promotional campaign.

**Net Income Per Share**

Net income per share is based on the weighted average number of common shares outstanding, which were 87.2 million, 91.8 million and 91.5 million for the years ended December 31, 1987, 1986 and 1985, respectively.

**Inventories**

Most U.S. inventories which qualify to be valued at cost on the Last-In, First-Out (LIFO) method for U.S. income tax purposes are so valued for accounting purposes. The balance of the U.S. inventories and inventories of consolidated operations outside the U.S. are valued at the lower of cost on the First-In, First-Out (FIFO) method or market.

**Property and Depreciation**

Property, plant and equipment are stated at cost. Depreciable property is generally depreciated on a straight-line or unit-of-production method for accounting purposes and on an accelerated method for income tax purposes. The cost of property sold or retired is credited to the asset account, and the related depreciation is charged to the accumulated depreciation account. Profit or loss resulting from the sale or retirement is included in income.

## NOTE 2. INCOME TAXES

Provisions for income taxes were as follows:

| (Millions of dollars) | Year Ended December 31 | | |
|---|---|---|---|
| | 1987 | 1986 | 1985 |
| **Current income taxes:** | | | |
| United States | $ 67.0 | $ 81.7 | $ 74.1 |
| State | 14.6 | 12.7 | 15.6 |
| Other countries | 66.3 | 52.5 | 42.1 |
| Investment tax credits | (2.4) | (13.0) | (29.6) |
| | 145.5 | 133.9 | 102.2 |
| **Deferred income taxes due to:** | | | |
| Depreciation | | | |
| United States | 47.4 | 63.8 | 72.2 |
| State | 13.3 | 7.2 | 9.1 |
| Other countries | 19.2 | 1.7 | (3.6) |
| Obsolescence allowance | | | |
| United States | (2.1) | (4.6) | (3.5) |
| State | (.7) | (.3) | (.5) |
| Other | | | |
| United States | 4.3 | (13.4) | 9.8 |
| Other | 3.6 | (1.8) | 3.7 |
| | 85.0 | 52.6 | 87.2 |
| Total | $230.5 | $186.5 | $189.4 |

Income before income taxes included $190.8 million in 1987, $105.3 million in 1986 and $80.0 million in 1985 representing income from subsidiaries outside the U.S.

An analysis of the Corporation's effective income tax rates follows:

| | % of Income Before Taxes | | |
|---|---|---|---|
| | 1987 | 1986 | 1985 |
| Federal statutory rates | 40.0% | 46.0% | 46.0% |
| State income taxes, net of federal income tax benefit | 2.7 | 2.6 | 3.1 |
| Investment tax credits | – | (2.7) | (6.7) |
| Non-U.S. rates over (under) federal statutory rate | .4 | (1.2) | (.5) |
| All other factors — net | .1 | (1.6) | 1.2 |
| Effective income tax rates | 43.2% | 43.1% | 43.1% |

Income taxes have not been provided on $545.4 million of unremitted net income of operations outside the U.S. which had been permanently invested as of December 31, 1987.

*NOTE 3. RETIREMENT PLANS AND TRUSTS*

The Corporation and most of its major subsidiaries have defined benefit retirement plans covering substantially all their salaried and hourly employees. All plans are noncontributory except for Kimberly-Clark Limited (United Kingdom). Retirement benefits are based on years of service and generally on the average compensation earned in the highest five of the last 15 years of service except for the United Kingdom plan which bases benefits on the highest year during the last five years. Benefits are paid from pension trusts and, in certain cases, are supplemented by direct payments by the Corporation. The funding practice is to contribute to trusts at least the minimum amount required by governmental agencies. Assets of the trusts are comprised principally of common stocks, high-grade corporate and government bonds, guaranteed income contracts and cash investments.

Statement of Financial Accounting Standards (SFAS) No. 87, Employers' Accounting for Pensions, was adopted for the principal North American plans effective January 1, 1986, and for the United Kingdom plan effective January 1, 1987. The effect of adopting SFAS No. 87 in North America was to reduce 1986 pension expense by $11.1 million and to increase net income and net income per share by $5.4 million and 6 cents, respectively. The effect of adopting SFAS No. 87 in the United Kingdom was to reduce 1987 pension expense by $4.1 million and to increase net income and net income per share by $2.7 million and 3 cents, respectively.

The components of pension expense were as follows:

| (Millions of dollars) | Year Ended December 31 | | |
|---|---|---|---|
| | 1987 | 1986 | 1985 |
| Benefits earned . . . . . . . . . . . . . . . . . . . . . . | $30.9 | $24.1 | $ – |
| Interest on projected benefit obligation . . . . . . . | 73.1 | 61.9 | – |
| Amortization of transition adjustment . . . . . . . | (.9) | .2 | – |
| Special early retirement benefits* . . . . . . . . . | 3.3 | 5.4 | – |
| Pension expense determined under accounting pronouncements other than SFAS No. 87 . . . . | 1.4 | 3.2 | 29.1 |
| | 107.8 | 94.8 | 29.1 |
| Less expected return on plan assets (Actual return on plan assets was $143.7 million in 1987 and $83.0 million in 1986.) . . . . . . . . | 83.7 | 67.4 | – |
| Pension expense . . . . . . . . . . . . . . . . . . . . | $24.1 | $27.4 | $29.1 |

*Special early retirement benefits were offered to eligible employees at Spruce Falls Power and Paper Company, Limited in 1987 and at Terrace Bay and Longlac, Ont., in 1986.*

The funded status of the principal plans follows:

| *(Millions of dollars)* | December 31 | |
| --- | ---: | ---: |
| | 1987 | 1986 |
| Actuarial present value of plan benefits: | | |
| Vested . . . . . . . . . . . . . . . . . . . . . . . . . . . . . | $639.6 | $606.7 |
| Nonvested . . . . . . . . . . . . . . . . . . . . . . . . . . | 18.6 | 20.7 |
| Accumulated benefit obligation . . . . . . . . . . . . . . | $658.2 | $627.4 |
| Projected benefit obligation . . . . . . . . . . . . . . . . . | $836.2 | $796.6 |
| Plan assets at fair value . . . . . . . . . . . . . . . . . . . . | 936.1 | 769.7 |
| Plan assets in excess of (less than) projected benefit obligation . . . . . . . . . . . . . . . . . . . . . . . . . . . | $ 99.9 | $ (26.9) |
| Consisting of: | | |
| Favorable (unfavorable) actuarial experience not being amortized . . . . . . . . . . . . . . . . . . . . . | $ 77.7 | $ (31.6) |
| Unamortized transition adjustment . . . . . . . . . . | 13.0 | 9.7 |
| Net prepaid (accrued) pension expense . . . . . . . . | 9.2 | (5.0) |
| Total . . . . . . . . . . . . . . . . . . . . . . . . . . . | $ 99.9 | $ (26.9) |

The projected benefit obligation was based on assumed discount rates of 10% to 10.5% in 1987 and 9% to 10% in 1986 and assumed long-term rates of compensation increases of 6% to 7.5% in 1987 and 5.25% to 7.5% in 1986.

The assumed average long-term rate of return on pension assets was 11% in 1987 and 1986. The transition adjustment is being amortized to pension expense on the straight-line method over 14 to 18 years.

*NOTE 4. DEBT*

The major issues of long-term debt were:

| (Millions of dollars) | December 31 1987 | 1986 |
|---|---|---|
| Kimberly-Clark Corporation | | |
| Commercial paper to be refinanced . . . . . . . . . . . . | $200.0 | $ – |
| 9⅛% Notes due 1997 . . . . . . . . . . . . . . . . . . . . | 100.0 | – |
| 12% Notes due 1994 . . . . . . . . . . . . . . . . . . . . | 100.0 | 100.0 |
| 11½% Sinking Fund Debentures due 2013 . . . . . . . | 60.5 | 60.5 |
| 10.35% Notes due 1987 . . . . . . . . . . . . . . . . . . | – | 25.0 |
| 11⅛% Notes due 1990 . . . . . . . . . . . . . . . . . . . | 99.8 | 99.8 |
| 6⅛% to 9.67% Pollution Control and Industrial | | |
|    Development Revenue Bonds maturing to 2005 . . | 33.8 | 33.8 |
| Other . . . . . . . . . . . . . . . . . . . . . . . . . . . . | 18.1 | 15.3 |
| | 612.2 | 334.4 |
| Subsidiaries | | |
| Bank loans in various currencies at variable rates (8% | | |
|    to 11% at December 31, 1987) maturing to 1993 . | 54.3 | 92.1 |
| Bank loans in various currencies at fixed rates (9% to | | |
|    18% at December 31, 1987) maturing to 1996 . . . | 12.0 | 13.9 |
| Other . . . . . . . . . . . . . . . . . . . . . . . . . . . . | 16.5 | 15.6 |
| | 695.0 | 456.0 |
| Less current portion . . . . . . . . . . . . . . . . . . . . | 8.1 | 29.7 |
| Total . . . . . . . . . . . . . . . . . . . . . . . . . . . . | $686.9 | $426.3 |

At December 31, 1987, $200 million of commercial paper was classified as long-term debt. In January 1988, the Corporation issued $100 million of First Series Medium-Term Notes due in four to six years, with interest rates from 8.35% to 8.75%. The proceeds from this financing were used to retire $100 million of commercial paper. Also, $100 million of commercial paper will be repaid with the proceeds from a January 1988 offering of $100 million principal amount of 9½% Sinking Fund Debentures due in 2018.

Maturities of long-term debt, including the medium-term notes described above, are $23.8 million in 1989, $121.7 million in 1990, $53.5 million in 1991 and $62.1 million in 1992.

At December 31, 1987, the Corporation had $475 million of revolving credit facilities with a group of U.S. banks. These facilities, which were unused at December 31, 1987, permit borrowing at competitive interest rates and are available for general corporate purposes, including backup for commercial paper borrowings. The Corporation pays commitment fees on the unused portion but may cancel the facilities without penalty at any time prior to their expiration on October 1, 1989.

Debt payable within one year:

| (Millions of dollars) | December 31 1987 | 1986 |
|---|---|---|
| Commercial paper | $212.9 | $ 78.0 |
| Current portion of long-term debt | 8.1 | 29.7 |
| Other short-term debt | 29.0 | 26.3 |
| Total | $250.0 | $134.0 |

## NOTE 5. FOREIGN CURRENCY TRANSLATION

Assets and liabilities of foreign operations are translated into U.S. dollars at period-end exchange rates except for operations in the highly inflationary economies of Mexico, Brazil and Colombia where the functional currency is the U.S. dollar. Gains or losses on such translations are reflected as unrealized currency translation adjustments in stockholders' equity. Income and expense accounts are translated into U.S. dollars at rates of exchange in effect each month.

Unrealized currency translation adjustments:

| (Millions of dollars) | 1987 | 1986 |
|---|---|---|
| Balance, January 1 | $(163.8) | $(179.2) |
| Adjustments for the year: | | |
| Canadian Dollar | 21.3 | 3.8 |
| British Pound | 30.6 | 2.4 |
| French Franc | 12.3 | 7.9 |
| German Mark | 5.5 | 5.8 |
| Other | 8.2 | 7.8 |
| | 77.9 | 27.7 |
| Sale of Jujo Kimberly K.K. (Japan) | – | (12.3) |
| Balance, December 31 | $ (85.9) | $(163.8) |

The net loss reflected in the determination of net income pertaining to currency transactions and translation of balance sheets of operations in hyperinflationary economies was $13.4 million in 1987 and $3.5 million in 1985, compared to a gain of $.7 million in 1986.

### NOTE 6. EQUITY PARTICIPATION PLANS

The 1976 and 1986 Plans provide for awards of participation shares and stock options to key employees of the Corporation and its subsidiaries. The Plans are more fully described in the Corporation's proxy statement.

At maturity, participation shares result in cash payments determined by the increase in the book value of the Corporation's common stock. Participants are not entitled to dividends on the participation shares, but their accounts are credited with dividend shares which are payable in cash to the participant at the time the related participation shares become payable. Neither participation nor dividend shares are shares of common stock.

Data concerning participation shares and dividend shares follow:

| *Participation and Dividend Shares* | 1987 | 1986 | 1985 |
|---|---|---|---|
| Outstanding — Beginning of year | 2,037,492 | 1,873,674 | 1,651,250 |
| Awarded . . . . . . . . . . . . . . . | 46,000 | 269,000 | 300,400 |
| Dividend shares credited — net . | 108,930 | 102,118 | 90,366 |
| Matured or forfeited . . . . . . . . | (404,667) | (207,300) | (168,342) |
| Outstanding — End of year . . . . | 1,787,755 | 2,037,492 | 1,873,674 |

Stock options are granted at not less than market value, become exercisable over a period of three years from date of grant and expire 10 years after the date of the grant. Stock appreciation rights (SARs) have been granted to certain participants which allow them, in lieu of option exercise, to receive cash equal to the difference between the option price and the market price of the Corporation's common stock at the date of conversion. As a condition of SAR conversion, a participant is required to exercise an equal number of option shares.

Data concerning stock options and SARs follow:

| | 1987 Price Range | Number of Options | | |
| --- | --- | --- | --- | --- |
| | | 1987 | 1986 | 1985 |
| Outstanding — Beginning of year | $12.00-43.81 | 1,706,556 | 1,499,438 | 1,513,718 |
| Granted | $56.44 | 12,000 | 538,000 | 300,400 |
| Exercised* | $12.00-43.81 | (277,440) | (313,542) | (232,534) |
| Cancelled or expired | $30.44-43.81 | (18,300) | (17,340) | (82,146) |
| Outstanding — End of year* | $12.00-56.44 | 1,422,816 | 1,706,556 | 1,499,438 |
| Exercisable | $12.00-43.81 | 930,556 | 939,876 | 1,083,798 |

*Options outstanding on December 31, 1987, 1986 and 1985 included 33,650 shares, 128,920 shares and 138,820 shares, respectively, with related stock appreciation rights. Price ranges for shares exercised in 1986 were $10.06 to $30.44 and in 1985 were $10.06 to $24.44.

At December 31, 1987, the number of additional shares of common stock of the Corporation available for option and sale under the 1986 Plan was 2,461,600 shares; in the aggregate, the number of such shares available plus the number of participation shares which could be awarded at such date under the 1986 Plan was 3,161,800 shares. The 1976 Plan has expired and no additional grants will be made under that Plan. Amounts expensed under the Plans in 1987, 1986 and 1985 were $8.8 million, $5.4 million and $6.0 million, respectively.

### NOTE 7. LEASES

Future minimum rental payments under operating leases as of December 31, 1987 were:

(Millions of dollars)

| Year Ending December 31: | |
| --- | --- |
| 1988 | $15.9 |
| 1989 | 10.0 |
| 1990 | 6.7 |
| 1991 | 3.9 |
| 1992 | 3.2 |
| Thereafter | 21.2 |
| Total | $60.9 |

Consolidated rental expense under operating leases was $52.5 million in 1987, $48.0 million in 1986 and $44.5 million in 1985.

## NOTE 8. STOCKHOLDERS' EQUITY

Changes in common stock issued, treasury stock, additional paid-in capital and retained earnings are shown below:

| (Millions of dollars except share amounts) | Common Stock Issued Shares | Amount | Treasury Stock Shares | Amount | Additional Paid-In Capital | Retained Earnings |
|---|---|---|---|---|---|---|
| Balance at December 31, 1984 | 95,453,272 | $119.3 | 4,038,770 | $ (67.1) | $165.7 | $1,541.3 |
| Exercise of stock options | – | – | (232,534) | 2.9 | .8 | – |
| Purchased for treasury | – | – | 27,812 | (.7) | – | – |
| Net income | – | – | – | – | – | 267.1 |
| Cash dividends declared | – | – | – | – | – | (106.2) |
| Balance at December 31, 1985 | 95,453,272 | 119.3 | 3,834,048 | (64.9) | 166.5 | 1,702.2 |
| Exercise of stock options | – | – | (313,542) | 4.1 | 2.0 | – |
| Purchased for treasury | – | – | 23,154 | (1.0) | – | – |
| Net income | – | – | – | – | – | 269.4 |
| Cash dividends declared | – | – | – | – | – | (113.9) |
| Balance at December 31, 1986 | 95,453,272 | 119.3 | 3,543,660 | (61.8) | 168.5 | 1,857.7 |
| Exercise of stock options | – | – | (277,440) | 4.3 | 1.9 | – |
| Purchased for treasury | – | – | 12,012,790 | (632.2) | – | – |
| Retirement of treasury shares | (14,500,000) | (18.1) | (14,500,000) | 650.4 | (25.9) | (606.4) |
| Net income | – | – | – | – | – | 325.2 |
| Cash dividends declared | – | – | – | – | – | (125.1) |
| Balance at December 31, 1987 | 80,953,272 | $101.2 | 779,010 | $ (39.3) | $144.5 | $1,451.4 |

On April 16, 1987, the stockholders adopted an amendment to the Corporation's Restated Certificate of Incorporation: (a) increasing the authorized shares of common stock from 100 million shares to 300 million shares and the authorized shares of preferred stock from 10 million shares to 20 million shares; (b) reducing the par value of the common stock from $2.50 per share to $1.25 per share; and (c) splitting each issued share of common stock into two shares of common stock. Accordingly, all numbers of common shares and per share data for the current and prior periods presented in these financial statements have been restated to reflect the stock split.

During 1987, the Corporation completed the acquisition of 12 million shares of its common stock for $631.6 million under two separate six million share repurchase programs announced on January 27 and October 21, 1987.

On December 17, 1987, the board of directors authorized the retirement of 14.5 million shares of treasury stock which became authorized but unissued shares.

The Corporation has 20 million shares of authorized preferred stock with no par value, none of which has been issued.

At December 31, 1987, unremitted net income of equity companies included in consolidated retained earnings was $226.5 million.

## NOTE 9. SUPPLEMENTARY DATA *(Millions of dollars)*

| Summary of Cash Flow Effects of Changes in Operating Working Capital | Year Ended December 31 | | |
|---|---|---|---|
| | 1987 | 1986 | 1985 |
| Accounts receivable . . . . . . . . . . . . . . . | $ (64.7) | $ (14.5) | $ (28.4) |
| Inventories . . . . . . . . . . . . . . . . . . . . . | 5.9 | (54.3) | (3.0) |
| Accounts payable and accrued liabilities . . | 42.3 | 13.0 | 82.6 |
| Accrued income taxes . . . . . . . . . . . . . . | 32.0 | (15.0) | 31.7 |
| Currency rate changes . . . . . . . . . . . . . | 29.8 | 10.9 | 2.6 |
| Changes in operating working capital . . . . | $ 45.3 | $ (59.9) | $ 85.5 |

| Summary of Accounts Receivable and Inventories | December 31 | |
|---|---|---|
| | 1987 | 1986 |
| **Accounts Receivable:** | | |
| From customers . . . . . . . . . . . . . . . . . . . . . . . . | $490.5 | $440.3 |
| Other . . . . . . . . . . . . . . . . . . . . . . . . . . . . . . . | 39.3 | 25.4 |
| Less allowances for doubtful accounts and sales discounts . . . . . . . . . . . . . . . . . . . . . . . | (9.9) | (10.5) |
| Total . . . . . . . . . . . . . . . . . . . . . . . . . . | $519.9 | $455.2 |
| **Inventories By Major Class:** | | |
| At the lower of cost on the First-In, First-Out (FIFO) method or market: | | |
| Raw materials . . . . . . . . . . . . . . . . . . . . . . . . | $173.3 | $169.1 |
| Work in process . . . . . . . . . . . . . . . . . . . . . . . | 122.6 | 116.6 |
| Finished goods . . . . . . . . . . . . . . . . . . . . . . . | 241.7 | 262.7 |
| Supplies and other . . . . . . . . . . . . . . . . . . . . . | 107.4 | 104.9 |
| | 645.0 | 653.3 |
| Excess of FIFO cost over Last-In, First-Out (LIFO) cost . . . . . . . . . . . . . . . . . . . . . . . . . | (119.6) | (122.0) |
| Total . . . . . . . . . . . . . . . . . . . . . . . . . . . . . . . | $525.4 | $531.3 |

Inventories which were valued on the LIFO method at December 31, 1987 and 1986, were $190.4 million and $229.8 million, respectively.

*NOTE 9. (Continued)*

|  | December 31 | |
| --- | --- | --- |
| *Summary of Accounts Payable and Accrued Liabilities* | 1987 | 1986 |
| Accounts payable to suppliers . . . . . . . . . . . . . . . . . | $191.2 | $165.9 |
| Other accounts payable . . . . . . . . . . . . . . . . . . . . . | 90.4 | 80.0 |
| Total accounts payable . . . . . . . . . . . . . . . . . . . | 281.6 | 245.9 |
| Accrued advertising and promotion expense . . . . . . . . | 69.4 | 96.2 |
| Accrued salaries and wages . . . . . . . . . . . . . . . . . . | 85.7 | 87.1 |
| Accrued pension expense . . . . . . . . . . . . . . . . . . . . | 17.4 | 23.1 |
| Other accrued liabilities . . . . . . . . . . . . . . . . . . . . . | 165.8 | 125.3 |
| Total . . . . . . . . . . . . . . . . . . . . . . . . . . . . | $619.9 | $577.6 |

|  | Year Ended December 31 | | |
| --- | --- | --- | --- |
| *Other* | 1987 | 1986 | 1985 |
| Maintenance and repairs expense . . . . . . . | $247.4 | $234.7 | $211.2 |
| Advertising expense . . . . . . . . . . . . . . . . | 87.0 | 89.9 | 92.5 |
| Interest capitalized . . . . . . . . . . . . . . . . | 1.5 | 3.3 | 13.9 |

Please refer to the discussion of New Accounting Standards on page 17 of the Operating/Financial Review for information concerning the effects of recently issued accounting rules not yet adopted by the company.

*NOTE 10. UNAUDITED QUARTERLY DATA*

| (Millions of dollars except per share amounts) | 1987 | | | | 1986 | | | |
| --- | --- | --- | --- | --- | --- | --- | --- | --- |
|  | *Fourth* | *Third* | *Second* | *First* | *Fourth* | *Third* | *Second* | *First* |
| Net sales . . . . . . . . . . | $1,253.9 | $1,223.2 | $1,224.4 | $1,183.2 | $1,113.2 | $1,065.0 | $1,087.7 | $1,037.2 |
| Gross profit . . . . . . . . . | 414.1 | 410.5 | 404.2 | 408.8 | 337.5 | 348.4 | 373.0 | 365.8 |
| Operating profit . . . . . . . | 157.8 | 146.5 | 139.6 | 142.2 | 117.3 | 112.9 | 122.9 | 131.8 |
| Net income . . . . . . . . . . | 82.2 | 84.1 | 83.8 | 75.1 | 64.3 | 63.0 | 68.8 | 73.3 |
| Net income per share . . . | $ .99 | $ .98 | $ .94 | $ .82 | $ .70 | $ .68 | $ .75 | $ .80 |

## NOTE 11. PRODUCT CLASS AND GEOGRAPHIC DATA

The business and products of the Corporation and its subsidiaries are described on the inside front cover of this report. For reporting purposes, products are assigned to three product classes. Class I principally includes household and institutional tissues; feminine, infant and incontinence care products; industrial and commercial wipers; hospital and home health care products; and related products and by-products. Class II principally contains premium business and correspondence papers, tobacco industry papers and products, newsprint and other printing papers, technical and specialty papers, and related products and by-products. Class III comprises aircraft services, air transportation, and other miscellaneous products and services.

Information about consolidated operations by product class and geographic area, as well as data for equity companies, is presented in the tables below and on the following pages:

### Consolidated Operations by Product Class

| (Millions of dollars) | Sales | | | Operating Profit | | |
|---|---|---|---|---|---|---|
| | 1987 | 1986 | 1985 | 1987 | 1986 | 1985 |
| Class I | $3,808.7 | $3,369.7 | $3,171.8 | $433.9 | $362.6 | $361.2 |
| Class II | 1,000.4 | 876.4 | 855.9 | 177.3 | 144.9 | 162.1 |
| Class III | 125.3 | 98.8 | 118.3 | 13.1 | 9.0 | 2.1 |
| Combined | 4,934.4 | 4,344.9 | 4,146.0 | 624.3 | 516.5 | 525.4 |
| Interclass sales | (49.7) | (41.8) | (73.1) | – | – | – |
| Unallocated expenses | – | – | – | (38.2) | (31.6) | (39.1) |
| Consolidated | $4,884.7 | $4,303.1 | $4,072.9 | $586.1 | $484.9 | $486.3 |

| (Millions of dollars) | Assets | | | Depreciation | | | Capital Spending | | |
|---|---|---|---|---|---|---|---|---|---|
| | 1987 | 1986 | 1985 | 1987 | 1986 | 1985 | 1987 | 1986 | 1985 |
| Class I | $2,765.0 | $2,680.7 | $2,489.9 | $144.4 | $134.5 | $110.1 | $180.8 | $210.3 | $364.1 |
| Class II | 709.3 | 652.6 | 616.2 | 30.5 | 27.6 | 23.6 | 43.0 | 64.4 | 35.6 |
| Class III | 84.9 | 69.0 | 77.3 | 2.9 | 2.3 | 1.8 | 9.1 | 6.6 | 9.6 |
| Combined | 3,559.2 | 3,402.3 | 3,183.4 | 177.8 | 164.4 | 135.5 | 232.9 | 281.3 | 409.3 |
| Unallocated | 363.7* | 329.2* | 393.5* | 8.2 | 4.9 | 4.8 | 14.4 | 1.1 | 16.5 |
| Interclass assets | (37.2) | (55.5) | (73.1) | – | – | – | – | – | – |
| Consolidated | $3,885.7 | $3,676.0 | $3,503.8 | $186.0 | $169.3 | $140.3 | $247.3 | $282.4 | $425.8 |

*Included investments in equity companies of $264.8 million, $243.8 million and $253.8 million in 1987, 1986 and 1985, respectively.

NOTE 11. (Continued)

**Consolidated Operations by Geographic Area**

| (Millions of dollars) | Sales 1987 | Sales 1986 | Sales 1985 | Operating Profit 1987 | Operating Profit 1986 | Operating Profit 1985 | Assets 1987 | Assets 1986 | Assets 1985 |
|---|---|---|---|---|---|---|---|---|---|
| United States . . . . . . | $3,475.8 | $3,112.7 | $3,042.2 | $417.4 | $393.7 | $419.5 | $2,252.5 | $2,261.5 | $2,098.1 |
| Canada . . . . . . . . . . | 646.3 | 560.8 | 543.8 | 88.7 | 39.4 | 36.6 | 622.3 | 572.1 | 568.0 |
| Europe . . . . . . . . . . | 673.9 | 561.8 | 436.6 | 77.1 | 55.9 | 40.8 | 496.2 | 379.0 | 349.3 |
| Latin/South America . | 60.6 | 41.6 | 44.6 | 15.5 | 6.4 | 9.7 | 61.0 | 55.6 | 51.2 |
| Far East . . . . . . . . . | 150.9 | 120.5 | 109.9 | 25.6 | 21.1 | 18.8 | 119.7 | 102.3 | 84.2 |
| Combined . . . . . . . . | 5,007.5 | 4,397.4 | 4,177.1 | 624.3 | 516.5 | 525.4 | 3,551.7 | 3,370.5 | 3,150.8 |
| Intergeographic sales* | (122.8) | (94.3) | (104.2) | – | – | – | – | – | – |
| Unallocated expenses | – | – | – | (38.2) | (31.6) | (39.1) | – | – | – |
| Unallocated assets** | – | – | – | – | – | – | 363.7 | 329.2 | 393.5 |
| Intergeographic assets | – | – | – | – | – | – | (29.7) | (23.7) | (40.5) |
| Consolidated . . . . . . | $4,884.7 | $4,303.1 | $4,072.9 | $586.1 | $484.9 | $486.3 | $3,885.7 | $3,676.0 | $3,503.8 |

*Included sales of $99.0 million, $75.8 million and $85.9 million by operations in Canada to other geographic areas and all other intergeographic sales (primarily United States) of $23.8 million, $18.5 million and $18.3 million in 1987, 1986 and 1985, respectively.
**Included investments in equity companies of $264.8 million, $243.8 million and $253.8 million in 1987, 1986 and 1985, respectively.

| (Millions of dollars) | Net Income 1987 | Net Income 1986 | Net Income 1985 | Kimberly-Clark's Share of Net Income 1987 | Kimberly-Clark's Share of Net Income 1986 | Kimberly-Clark's Share of Net Income 1985 |
|---|---|---|---|---|---|---|
| United States . . . . . . . . . . . . . . . . . . . . . . . . . . . . . . . | $187.8 | $176.2 | $200.7 | $187.8 | $176.1 | $200.5 |
| Canada . . . . . . . . . . . . . . . . . . . . . . . . . . . . . . . . . . . . . | 45.0 | 18.4 | 17.4 | 38.4 | 10.9 | 8.2 |
| Europe . . . . . . . . . . . . . . . . . . . . . . . . . . . . . . . . . . . . . | 45.9 | 36.3 | 17.5 | 44.3 | 34.6 | 16.4 |
| Latin/South America . . . . . . . . . . . . . . . . . . . . . . . . . . . | 8.9 | 2.3 | 3.5 | 8.3 | 1.7 | 2.9 |
| Far East . . . . . . . . . . . . . . . . . . . . . . . . . . . . . . . . . . . . | 16.0 | 13.3 | 10.8 | 11.1 | 9.1 | 7.4 |
| Consolidated . . . . . . . . . . . . . . . . . . . . . . . . . . . . . . . . | $303.6 | $246.5 | $249.9 | $289.9 | $232.4 | $235.4 |

Sales of products between classes and geographic areas are made at market prices and are referred to as interclass sales and intergeographic sales.

Assets reported by product class and geographic area represent assets which are directly used and an allocated portion of jointly used assets. These assets include receivables from other product classes or geographic areas, and are referred to as interclass or intergeographic assets. Assets and expenses that cannot be associated with classes or geographic areas are referred to as unallocated assets or unallocated expenses.

With the exception of 1987, which benefited from increased pulp selling prices, the company's pulp manufacturing mill at Terrace Bay, Ont., has been unprofitable for the past nine years. The related woodlands operation at Longlac, Ont., has been unprofitable for all nine years.

In 1986, a survival plan was adopted. Two key features of the plan were to control manufacturing costs at the pulp mill and the woodlands operation and to resolve environmental issues. Since inception of the survival plan, total employment at the two operations has been reduced by more than 400 people. Other labor issues, however, remain a concern. Negotiations with the wood-workers union began early in the fourth quarter and a union contract with pulp mill employees expires on April 30, 1988. In 1987, the government of Ontario issued a new environmental control order which expires in October 1989.

Although mill operations have improved, the technological difficulties of complying with environmental regulations, including those contained in the control order, coupled with the excessive wood costs and the uncertain outcome of the labor negotiations, leave management of the Corporation unable to predict whether full recovery of the approximately $300 million net carrying amount of the facilities will occur.

## Equity Companies' Data by Geographic Area

| (Millions of dollars) | Current Assets | Non-current Assets | Current Liabilities | Non-current Liabilities | Stock-holders' Equity | Net Sales | Gross Profit | Operating Profit | Net Income | Kimberly-Clark's Share of Net Income |
|---|---|---|---|---|---|---|---|---|---|---|
| **December 31, 1987** | | | | | | | | | | |
| Latin/South America .... | $273.8 | $389.4 | $104.2 | $ 53.6 | $505.4 | $543.9 | $189.7 | $128.8 | $60.1 | $26.2 |
| Far East and Australia ... | 54.7 | 94.7 | 45.3 | 35.6 | 68.5 | 197.3 | 69.9 | 31.5 | 15.4 | 7.7 |
| Africa.............. | 35.3 | 33.1 | 24.1 | 18.3 | 26.0 | 108.9 | 34.3 | 8.7 | 3.5 | 1.4 |
| Total ............ | $363.8 | $517.2 | $173.6 | $107.5 | $599.9 | $850.1 | $293.9 | $169.0 | $79.0 | $35.3 |
| **December 31, 1986** | | | | | | | | | | |
| Latin/South America .... | $237.1 | $374.3 | $ 60.5 | $ 74.4 | $476.5 | $431.6 | $134.3 | $ 85.8 | $45.9 | $20.1 |
| Far East and Australia* .. | 47.8 | 70.8 | 39.4 | 23.8 | 55.4 | 333.0 | 135.1 | 33.7 | 23.0 | 15.5 |
| Africa.............. | 29.1 | 29.9 | 19.2 | 17.7 | 22.1 | 86.8 | 28.2 | 8.5 | 3.6 | 1.4 |
| Total ............ | $314.0 | $475.0 | $119.1 | $115.9 | $554.0 | $851.4 | $297.6 | $128.0 | $72.5 | $37.0 |
| **December 31, 1985** | | | | | | | | | | |
| Latin/South America .... | $245.1 | $383.8 | $ 64.8 | $ 93.1 | $471.0 | $446.2 | $154.5 | $101.3 | $56.6 | $24.6 |
| Far East and Australia ... | 86.3 | 121.8 | 97.4 | 24.5 | 86.2 | 289.5 | 109.5 | 26.2 | 11.3 | 5.6 |
| Africa.............. | 20.5 | 24.3 | 14.5 | 13.3 | 17.0 | 81.5 | 27.2 | 8.6 | 3.8 | 1.5 |
| Total ............ | $351.9 | $529.9 | $176.7 | $130.9 | $574.2 | $817.2 | $291.2 | $136.1 | $71.7 | $31.7 |

*In December 1986, the Corporation sold its interest in Jujo Kimberly K.K. (Japan).

The name and the percent of common stock owned of each company are shown on page 38.

## INDEPENDENT AUDITORS' OPINION

Kimberly-Clark Corporation, Its Directors and Stockholders:

We have examined the consolidated balance sheets of Kimberly-Clark Corporation and Subsidiaries as of December 31, 1987 and 1986, and the related consolidated statements of income and changes in financial position for each of the three years in the period ended December 31, 1987. Our examinations were made in accordance with generally accepted auditing standards and, accordingly, included such tests of the accounting records and such other auditing procedures as we considered necessary in the circumstances.

In our opinion, such consolidated financial statements of Kimberly-Clark Corporation and Subsidiaries present fairly the financial position of the companies at December 31, 1987 and 1986, and the results of their operations and the changes in their financial position for each of the three years in the period ended December 31, 1987, in conformity with generally accepted accounting principles applied on a consistent basis.

*Deloitte Haskins & Sells*

*Certified Public Accountants*
*Dallas, Texas*                                    *January 27, 1988*

## AUDIT COMMITTEE CHAIRMAN'S LETTER

The Audit Committee is selected by the board of directors and consists of five outside directors. The members of the Audit Committee are shown on page 39 of this annual report. The committee met three times during the year ended December 31, 1987.

The Audit Committee oversees the financial reporting process on behalf of the board of directors. As part of that responsibility, the committee recommended to the board of directors, subject to stockholder approval, the selection of the Corporation's independent public accountants. The Audit Committee discussed the overall scope and specific plans for audits with the internal auditor and Deloitte Haskins & Sells. The committee also discussed the Corporation's consolidated financial statements and the adequacy of its internal controls. The committee met regularly with the Corporation's internal auditor and Deloitte Haskins & Sells, without management present, to discuss the results of their examinations, their evaluations of the Corporation's internal controls, and the overall quality of the Corporation's financial reporting. The meetings also were designed to facilitate any private communication with the committee desired by the internal auditor or independent public accountants.

*John P. Raynor, S.J.*

*Rev. John P. Raynor, S.J.*
*Chairman, Audit Committee*                      *January 27, 1988*

Management of Kimberly-Clark is responsible for conducting all aspects of the business, including preparation of all information in this annual report and the audited financial statements. These financial statements have been prepared using generally accepted accounting principles considered appropriate in the circumstances to present fairly the Corporation's financial position, its results of operations and changes in financial position on a consistent basis.

As can be expected in a complex and dynamic business environment, some financial statement amounts are based on management's estimates and informed judgments. Even though estimates and judgments are used, readers of Kimberly-Clark's financial information should be aware of the measures that have been taken to ensure the integrity of this financial report. These measures include an effective control-oriented environment, in which the Internal Audit Department plays an important role, independent audits and an Audit Committee of the board of directors which oversees the quality of financial reporting.

One characteristic of a control-oriented environment is a system of internal controls which provides reasonable assurance that assets are safeguarded, transactions are appropriately authorized, recorded and reported, and that financial statements are reliable and fraudulent financial reporting is prevented or detected. This system is supported with written policies and procedures, and the Internal Audit Department monitors the system to help ensure that it is working effectively.

In addition, the Corporation has adopted policies with respect to conducting business affairs in a lawful and ethical manner in each country in which it does business, to potential conflicts of interest, and to confidentiality of information and business ideas. Internal controls have been developed and instituted to provide assurance that these policies are followed.

The financial statements have been audited by independent accountants, Deloitte Haskins & Sells, whose report appears on the facing page. Their examination included a review of the system of internal controls, tests of the accounting records and other auditing procedures which they considered necessary to form an opinion as to the fairness of the financial statements. In the course of their examination, the independent accountants were given unrestricted access to all financial records and related data, including minutes of all meetings of stockholders and the board of directors and all committees thereof. Furthermore, management believes that all representations made to the independent accountants during their audit were valid and appropriate.

Information about the Audit Committee is contained in the Audit Committee Chairman's letter shown on the facing page.

During the examinations conducted by both the independent accountants and the Internal Audit Department, management received recommendations to strengthen or modify internal controls as business develops and changes. Management has adopted or is in the process of adopting all such recommendations which are cost effective in the circumstances. Management believes that the Corporation's internal control system is adequate to accomplish the objectives for which it was designed.

Darwin E. Smith
*Chairman of the Board and*
*Chief Executive Officer*

Brendan M. O'Neill
*Senior Vice President and*
*Chief Financial Officer*

*January 27, 1988*

# PROBLEMS AND CASETTES

### 6–1. Recording Organization Costs

Wilson Company has been a family-owned business for 35 years. John Wilson, the president and son of the company's founder, decides to incorporate the firm and to issue stock to raise additional investment capital. The following costs are incurred to make the proper arrangements to incorporate the business:

| | |
|---|---:|
| Attorneys' fees—corporate application | $28,500 |
| Accountants' fees—system development | 19,750 |
| Annual Audit fee—independent accountants | 13,000 |
| Corporate filing fee | 5,000 |
| Printing costs—stock certificates | 3,200 |
| Key officer insurance policy | 25,000 |
| Underwriter's fee—stock issuance | 1,800 |
| Audit update—required by underwriter | 2,500 |
| Other organization costs | 6,300 |

Wilson says, "We can't write these costs off as expenses this year because it will wipe out most of our income. Figure out some legal way to delay showing these expenses."

### Required:

a. Explain to John Wilson how each of the costs should be handled. Indicate which costs can be deferred because they relate to the future life and value of the company and which costs must be charged to the current period. Prepare a list and a total cost of each type.

b. Assume that the firm decides to record the deferred costs from part *a* in an account titled "Organization Costs" and that these costs will be amortized over 20 years. Prepare the journal entry to record amortization for the first year.

c. Show how you would present the organization costs on the balance sheet after recording the journal entry in *b* above.

### 6–2. Assessing the Impact of Accounting Assumptions

Conventional financial accounting statements cannot be interpreted apart from the concepts on which they rest. Listed below are the seven basic assumptions introduced in Chapter 2 and reviewed in Chapter 6. Indicate the concept(s) that are directly responsible for each of the following items or procedures associated with the financial statements. Briefly explain the relationship.

#### Basic Assumptions

Entity concept
Going-concern concept
Monetary concept
Matching concept
Accounting period concept
Revenue recognition concept
Exchange-price concept

1. The balance sheet shows deferred training costs as a noncurrent asset.

2. Among the current liabilities on the balance sheet is an account labeled "Customers' Paid Orders." This account is credited when customers make deposits on orders to be delivered in the future.

3. On July 31, 3,000 shares of the firm's stock changes hands at various prices on the New York Stock Exchange; yet, the balance sheet on July 31 does not show any change in the capital stock account.

4. The balance sheet shows $1,800,000 for two laboratory buildings. The first building was purchased in 1970 at a cost of $675,000; the second building, built to match the first building identically, was completed in 1985 at a cost of $1,125,000.

5. The income statement heading contains the phrase, "for the year ended December 31, 1990."

6. Patents are shown as intangible assets in the amount of $8 million, although they could be sold readily for twice that amount.

7. Even though net income is extremely low, the company still records depreciation expense.

8. The word *accrued* precedes the account titles for a number of current assets and current liabilities.

9. Some specialized equipment appears on the balance sheet for $475,000. The plant manager admits that if the firm tried to sell it, only its scrap value of $45,000 would be received.

10. Ty Coon is the president of a corporation and sole owner of its capital stock. Ty also owns a few bonds issued by the corporation and has personally guaranteed all of the other outstanding long-term bond debt of the company. During the year, the company made substantial cash payments to him. Some payments are recorded as salary expense, some as interest expense, and some as dividends—even though all of the money is paid to Ty.

11. Inventory is shown on the balance sheet at $230,500, although the sales manager believes that it will be sold in the next accounting period for $280,000 to $310,000.

12. The salary for the vice president of corporate planning is shown on the income statement as salary expense, although he spends almost all of his time working on the five-year strategic plan for the company.

## 6–3. Income Statement Classification

Flibinite Corporation prepares a classified income statement using a multiple-step format as follows:

| | |
|---|---|
| Operating revenues | (A) |
| Operating expenses: | |
| Cost of goods sold | (B) |
| Selling expenses | (C) |
| Administrative expenses | (D) |
| Operating income: | |
| Other revenue | (E) |
| Other expenses | (F) |
| Income before gains and losses and unusual items: | |
| Gains | (G) |
| Losses | (H) |
| Unusual charges and credits | (I) |
| Net income | |

**Required:**

Using the preceding format, indicate where you would show each of the following items on the income statement using one of the key letters (A thru I). If the item would not appear on the income statement, identify it using the letter "X."

1. Annual depreciation on selling equipment.
2. Excess of the cash received from the sale of land over its cost.
3. Administrative salaries.
4. Cash dividends paid on capital stock.
5. Dividends received on long-term investments.
6. Costs associated with a strike.
7. Increase in the market value of temporary investments above their cost.
8. Vacation pay for office staff.
9. Rental fees received from the sublet of a portion of the company's warehouse.
10. Damages awarded to the firm under an antitrust settlement.
11. Expenditures on advertising.
12. Excess of the book value of equipment over the salvage value received when the equipment was scrapped.
13. Cost of office supplies used.
14. Proceeds from selling shares of the company's own stock.
15. Insurance settlement received from the insurance company for a fire that destroyed an entire warehouse. Because the insured values were based on replacement cost, the proceeds substantially exceeded the book value of the assets destroyed.
16. Costs of delivering the company's products to customers.
17. Proceeds received from a life insurance policy upon the death of an important officer in the company.
18. Sales commissions.
19. Cost of some inventory that had to be destroyed according to a new government regulation that had found the material hazardous to human health.
20. Interest paid on long-term notes payable.

## 6–4. Recording Transactions

The Fogler Athletic Shoe Company was organized on July 31. The activities listed below took place during August. Prepare journal entries to record the transactions for the month.

1. Issued capital stock for cash, $50,000.
2. Purchased a store building paying $10,000 cash and assuming a $60,000 mortgage that bears interest at the rate of 10 percent per year.
3. Paid cash for legal services, incorporation fees, printing of stock certificates, and other costs of organizing the corporation, $1,000.
4. Purchased furniture and fixtures for cash, $8,000.
5. Purchased athletic shoes, on account, $50,000.
6. Bought U.S. government bonds with excess cash, $10,000.
7. Purchased a delivery truck, on account, $5,000.
8. In unloading furniture and fixtures, the employees dropped a display case costing $300, completely ruining it.

9. Sales of shoes on account, $21,000; for cash, $31,000.
10. Recorded the cost of the shoes sold in 9. The selling price of shoes is calculated by marking them up 25 percent above cost.
11. The government bonds were sold for $10,350 plus accrued interest of $50.
12. Payment of salaries, $7,500.
13. Paid monthly merchant's tax to the city, $1,000.
14. Received an advance order from the state university for 50 pairs of special shoes that cost $67.50 per pair. The shoes were to be delivered in November. The order was accompanied by a cash deposit of $2,000.
15. The delivery truck was involved in an accident and required $800 of repairs, paid in cash.
16. Depreciation for the month on building, $200; on furniture and fixtures, $50; and on delivery truck, $100.
17. Interest for the month was accrued on the mortgage.
18. Income taxes applicable to August were accrued at a rate of 35 percent.
19. Dividends were declared, $100.
20. Received an offer to sell the entire business for $100,000.

## 6–5. Financial Statement Preparation

The controller of the Roosevelt Company is trying to decide whether the single-step or multiple-step income statement is most appropriate. She asks you to help her by preparing income statements using the following accounts taken from the trial balance as of December 31, 1990:

|  | Debit | Credit |
|---|---|---|
| Cash | 300 | |
| Accrued interest receivable | 800 | |
| Supplies used | 400 | |
| Goods delivered to customers | | 50,000 |
| Cost of goods delivered | 28,000 | |
| Salaries | 10,000 | |
| Interest earned | | 2,000 |
| U.S. government bonds | 40,000 | |
| Goodwill | 12,000 | |
| Gain on sale of building | | 3,500 |
| State taxes | 1,800 | |
| Interest | 1,000 | |
| Retained earnings, January 1, 1990 | | 32,000 |
| Fire damage to inventory | 200 | |
| Dividends | 700 | |
| Accrued payroll | | 1,100 |
| Depreciation | 2,300 | |
| Federal income taxes | 4,000 | |

**Required:**

*a.* Prepare a single-step income statement using the format of Figure 6–1.
*b.* Prepare a multiple-step income statement using the format of Figure 6–2.

 *c.* Prepare a statement of retained earnings using the format of Figure 6–3.

 *d.* Use your multiple-step income statement prepared in *b* and calculate:
  1. Gross margin as a percentage of sales
  2. Operating income as a percentage of sales
  3. Net income as a percentage of sales
  4. Effective tax rate

### 6–6. Accounting for Period Costs

J. R. Ewing Corporation listed Unamortized Preoperating Expense of $443,000 in its annual report for the fiscal year 1990. The amounts as of the end of the fiscal years 1989 and 1988 were $996,000 and $694,000, respectively. In its statements of income for fiscal 1990 and 1989, $665,000 and $392,000 were deducted as amortization expense to charge these costs against revenue. Net income was $7,536,000 in 1990 and $5,632,000 in 1989.

 The following note accompanied the financial statements:

> Research and development expenditures related to present and future products are expensed as incurred. Preoperating costs related to new companies and major facilities are generally deferred and amortized over three years.

**Required:**

 *a.* Calculate the amount of preoperating costs J. R. Ewing actually incurred in 1990 and 1989.

 *b.* List examples of costs which would be considered as preoperating. Explain whether you agree with the company's policy.

 *c.* Determine what net income would have been for 1990 and 1989 if the firm had charged the preoperating costs as period expenses at the time they were incurred. Assume an income tax rate of 40 percent.

 *d.* Is there any inconsistency in the treatment given to research and development costs in comparison to the treatment for preoperating costs? Explain.

### 6–7. Multiple- and Single-Step Income Statements

The accounts listed below have been taken from the adjusted trial balance of Titus Canbe Company at the end of 1990.

| | |
|---|---:|
| Administrative expense . . . . . . . . . . . . . . . . . . . . . . . . . . . . | $ 265,600 |
| Cost of goods lost from shoplifting . . . . . . . . . . . . . . . . . . . . . | 54,000 |
| Cost of goods sold to customers . . . . . . . . . . . . . . . . . . . . . . . | 1,824,000 |
| Correction of prior years understatement of depreciation* . . . . . . . . . | 53,800 |
| Dividends declared . . . . . . . . . . . . . . . . . . . . . . . . . . . . . | 120,000 |
| Dividends received . . . . . . . . . . . . . . . . . . . . . . . . . . . . . | 96,000 |
| Gain on sale of marketable securities . . . . . . . . . . . . . . . . . . . | 58,400 |
| Income taxes . . . . . . . . . . . . . . . . . . . . . . . . . . . . . . . . | 102,600 |
| Interest charges . . . . . . . . . . . . . . . . . . . . . . . . . . . . . . | 39,000 |
| Loss on sale of equipment . . . . . . . . . . . . . . . . . . . . . . . . . | 100,400 |

*GAAP requires that this item be reported in the statement of retained earnings as an adjustment of the opening balance.

| Real estate taxes | $ 33,000 |
|---|---|
| Rent revenue | 37,600 |
| Research and development costs | 104,000 |
| Retained earnings, January 1, 1990 | 780,200 |
| Sales | 2,940,000 |
| Selling expenses | 283,200 |

**Required:**

a. Prepare an income statement for 1990 using the multiple-step form and a separate statement of retained earnings.

b. Prepare an income statement for 1990 using the single-step form and a separate statement of retained earnings.

c. Discuss the advantages and disadvantages of the multiple-step and single-step formats. Which do you think is preferable?

## 6–8. Preparing Journal Entries for Annual Activities

The Boomorbust Bomb Shelter Distributing Company was incorporated on July 1, 1989. Prepare general journal entries to record the following transactions that summarize the activities of the company for the fiscal year ended June 30, 1990.

1. Capital stock was issued for $300,000 cash.
2. The following assets were acquired in exchange for cash and a $100,000 10-year mortgage: land, $45,000; buildings, $90,000; and equipment, $148,500. The mortgage liability was dated July 1, 1989, and bore a 12 percent rate of interest.
3. Insurance expense for the year paid in cash, $4,500.
4. Merchandise acquired on account, $742,500.
5. Promotional and entertainment costs were $89,000, paid in cash.
6. All sales of the product were made to a single foreign government, Middle Iamurpalia. A check for $75,000 was received early in the year to apply as a deposit against future deliveries.
7. Boomorbust sold some vacant land (acquired in transaction 2 for $25,000) for $37,300 cash.
8. General office and administrative work was done during the year at a cost of $54,000, paid in cash.
9. Property taxes paid in cash, $36,000.
10. Deliveries of products during the year totaled $1,312,000.
11. The cost of merchandise sold was $697,500.
12. Selling commissions were $39,300 of which $10,200 was unpaid at the end of the year.
13. Some equipment exploded while being tested. The cost of the equipment was $18,000. The loss was partially covered by insurance, and the company collected cash equal to 80 percent of the loss from the insurance company.
14. Additional equipment costing $22,000 was purchased on March 17, 1990. A cash payment of $7,000 was made, and a 10 percent, one-year note payable for $15,000 was given to the supplier.
15. Collections of cash from Middle Iamurpalia amounted to $1,222,500.
16. Depreciation amounted to $7,400 on equipment and $3,800 on the building.
17. Interest on the mortgage in transaction 2 and on the note in transaction 14 was accrued on June 30, 1990.

18. Payments to suppliers were $709,800.
19. On June 30, 1990, the board of directors declared a dividend of $100,000, payable on July 15, 1990.
20. Income taxes applicable to the fiscal year were accrued at a rate of 30 percent.

**6–9. Accounting Policy and Intangible Assets**

The Dravo Corporation included the following item related to intangible assets on its 1986 balance sheet:

|  | 1986 | 1985 |
|---|---|---|
| Drawings, patents, and other intangible assets . . . . . . . | $405,000 | $8,679,000 |

Note 1 to the financial statements states, "Intangible assets, including purchased patents, drawings, agreements, and goodwill are amortized on a straight-line basis over their estimated useful lives of from five to ten years."

**Required:**

*a.* Explain why Dravo Corporation would prepare this explanation on intangible assets when presenting its note on significant accounting policies. Do you feel this is a *significant* accounting policy?

*b.* Is materiality important in determining whether this note should be presented? Is it possible that the note is more important to one of the reporting years than it is to the other? Explain.

*c.* What does the term *amortized* mean in this note? Which basic accounting concept(s) are involved in the firm's treatment of these intangible assets?

*d.* What circumstances make it appropriate to defer these costs as assets rather than to treat them as period expenses?

**6–10. Preparing Statements Using the Cash and Accrual Bases**

Marcia and Michael opened a children's store called Wee World. They are partners and share in income and losses equally. They are not familiar with accounting and do not maintain double-entry records. They figure that if they have cash in the bank account, they must be making a profit. As the end of 1990 approaches, they ask you to prepare financial statements from their checkbook, deposit slips, and other records. They present you with a list of things they have paid for and the balance sheet prepared at the end of the previous year by a bookkeeper who worked for them on a part-time basis.

1. The bookkeeper's balance sheet on December 31, 1989 appeared as:

| Assets | | Equities | | |
|---|---|---|---|---|
| Cash . . . . . . . . . . . | $ 56,300 | Partnership equities: | | |
| Marketable securities . . . . | 14,600 | Marcia . . . . . . | $ | 56,700 |
| Inventory . . . . . . . . . | 27,000 | Michael . . . . . | | 56,000 |
| Store fixtures . . . . . . . | 14,800 | | | |
| Total assets . . . . . . . | $112,700 | Total equities . . . . | | $112,700 |

2. Cash receipts for the year 1990 are summarized as follows:

| | |
|---|---:|
| Advances from customers | $ 1,400 |
| Cash sales and collections from customers | 264,200 |
| Cash invested by Marcia. | 12,000 |
| Collection on note from customer: | |
| For interest | 300 |
| For principal | 2,000 |
| Cash borrowed from bank (90-day note, at 12 percent, dated 12/31/90) | 10,000 |
| Sale of 200 shares of ITT stock | 16,000 |
| | $305,900 |

3. A summary of checks written during 1990 shows:

| | |
|---|---:|
| Insurance premiums | $ 5,500 |
| Purchase of merchandise. | 181,100 |
| Purchase of fixtures. | 21,000 |
| Salaries paid to employees | 51,900 |
| Utilities | 3,700 |
| Withdrawals by partners: | |
| Marcia | 25,000 |
| Michael | 25,000 |
| | $313,200 |

**Required:**

a. Prepare an income statement under the *cash basis*.
b. Marcia and Michael present you with the following list of other financial information that also existed on *December 31, 1989:*

| | |
|---|---:|
| 200 shares of ITT stock owned by the firm | $14,600 |
| Accounts owed to the firm. | 39,300 |
| Outstanding note receivable | 3,000 |
| Interest on the note receivable | 100 |
| Total value of inventory on hand | 54,000 |
| Estimated portion of fixtures worn-out | 6,600 |
| Account balances the firm owes. | 27,000 |
| Advances from customers | 1,800 |
| Salaries owed to employees on 12/31/89 | 1,700 |

Prepare a *corrected* balance sheet as of December 31, *1989.*

c. On December 31, 1990 you determine the following:

| | |
|---|---:|
| Accounts receivable | $37,900 |
| Interest receivable | 50 |
| Inventory. | 62,100 |
| Insurance prepayments | 1,400 |
| Accounts payable | 21,300 |
| Advances from customers | 1,100 |
| Accrued salaries | 3,600 |

Depreciation should recognize the wearing away of fixtures at the rate of 20 percent per year; however, only one-half-year's depreciation is charged on fixtures acquired during the year.

Prepare an income statement under the *accrual basis* for 1990. Also, prepare a balance sheet as of December 31, 1990.

**6–11. Reconstructing Beginning Financial Statements from Completed Transactions**
The following financial statements have been prepared for Eastinghouse, Inc. at the end of the current period: a single-step income statement for the year 1990, a balance sheet as of December 31, 1990, and a statement of cash receipts and disbursements for the year 1990.

**Income Statement**
**For the Year Ended December 31, 1990**

| | | |
|---|---:|---:|
| Sales revenue. . . . . . . . . . . . . . . . . . . . . . . . | | $700,000 |
| Rent revenue . . . . . . . . . . . . . . . . . . . . . . . | | 80,000 |
| Gain on sale of marketable securities . . . . . . . . . . . . | | 26,000 |
| | | 806,000 |
| Less: Expenses, losses, and taxes: | | |
| Cost of goods sold. . . . . . . . . . . . . . . . . . . . | $456,000 | |
| Depreciation expense. . . . . . . . . . . . . . . . . . . | 10,600 | |
| Insurance expense. . . . . . . . . . . . . . . . . . . . | 8,000 | |
| Salaries and wages . . . . . . . . . . . . . . . . . . . | 170,400 | |
| Interest expense. . . . . . . . . . . . . . . . . . . . . | 4,800 | |
| Loss on sale of land . . . . . . . . . . . . . . . . . . . | 12,000 | |
| Income tax expense . . . . . . . . . . . . . . . . . . . | 48,000 | 709,800 |
| Net income. . . . . . . . . . . . . . . . . . . . . . . . | | $ 96,200 |

Note: $18,000 of dividends were declared in 1990.

**Balance Sheet**
**As of December 31, 1990**

| Assets | | Equities | |
|---|---:|---|---:|
| Cash . . . . . . . . . . . | $ 55,000 | Accounts payable. . . . . . | $ 87,600 |
| Marketable securities. . . . . | 70,000 | Interest payable . . . . . . | 1,200 |
| Accounts receivable . . . . . | 127,600 | Taxes payable . . . . . . . | 14,000 |
| Inventory . . . . . . . . . | 105,000 | Rent received in advance. . . | 30,000 |
| Prepaid insurance . . . . . . | 10,400 | Long-term notes payable . . . | 80,000 |
| Land . . . . . . . . . . . | 30,000 | Capital stock. . . . . . . . | 120,000 |
| Buildings and equipment . . . | 110,000 | Retained earnings. . . . . . | 119,200 |
| Accumulated depreciation . . . | (56,000) | | |
| | $452,000 | | $452,000 |

**Statement of Cash Receipts and Disbursements**
**For the Year Ended December 31, 1990**

Cash receipts:

| | |
|---|---|
| Cash sales | $ 56,400 |
| Collections from charge customers | 525,000 |
| Collections from tenants | 108,000 |
| Sale of marketable securities | 56,000 |
| Sale of land | 16,000 |
| Total cash receipts | 761,400 |

Cash disbursements:

| | |
|---|---|
| Payments to suppliers of merchandise | 448,000 |
| Payments to insurance companies | 7,800 |
| Payments to employees | 171,400 |
| Payments of interest | 4,200 |
| Payments of taxes | 46,400 |
| Payments of dividends | 20,000 |
| Purchase of equipment | 28,000 |
| Total cash disbursements | 725,800 |
| Excess of receipts over disbursements | $ 35,600 |

### Required:

Use the end of period information to reconstruct the balance sheet as of *January 1, 1990*. You might consider using T accounts as an analytical device to reconstruct the transactions that occurred during the period. Assume that purchases of inventory during the period were $444,600, all on account, and that only inventory purchases were recorded in Accounts Payable.

**Casette 6–1.  Georgia-Pacific Corporation**

In the appendix at the end of the book is a complete set of financial statements of Georgia-Pacific Corporation taken from its annual report of 1987.

Answer the following questions related to those financial statements and supporting information.

1. The Statements of Income for Georgia-Pacific are presented for the three years 1985–1987.

    *a.* Are these income statements prepared using the single-step or multiple-step structure? Explain the reasons for your conclusion.

    *b.* These statements do not show a calculated figure for the firm's gross margin. Prepare the gross margin computations for each of the three years.

    *c.* Examine the accounts used to prepare the Statements of Income and identify those accounts that are "period" costs, "product" costs, and difficult to identify. Explain why each account should be included in the indicated category.

2. Use the numbers from the Statements of Income to calculate the following ratios for the years 1985, 1986, and 1987 (carry your computations to one decimal place) and interpret your calculations:

    *a.* Gross margin ratio. What has the pattern been for this ratio? Explain what "gross margin" means and what the pattern indicates for Georgia-Pacific.

    *b.* Operating income ratio. What percentage of sales is the operating income? What does this percentage show? Is this percentage improving or worsening?

    *c.* Net income ratio. How does this ratio differ from the operating income ratio? Is this percentage improving or worsening? Explain how the rate of change in this ratio compares to the rate of change in the operating income ratio.

    *d.* Effective tax rate (income tax expense as a percentage of income before tax). Is the effective rate of tax paid each year constant? If it is constant, explain why the rate would remain constant. If the rate is not constant, explain why the rate might vary (see Note 8).

3. Note 2 to the financial statements is titled "Unusual Items." The note discloses details of several items that resulted in realized gains.

    *a.* What does the term *realized gains* mean?

    *b.* In 1986 and 1987 gains are reported from the liquidation of investments. Prepare the journal entries that would have been made to record the transactions that resulted in the gains reported.

4. Georgia-Pacific declared dividends in 1986 and 1987.

    *a.* What was the dollar amount of dividends *declared* in 1986 and 1987? Where did you find this information?

    *b.* What dollar amount of dividends were *paid* in those years? Where did you find this information?

    *c.* When a firm declares dividends in a larger dollar amount than it pays during a year, where would you expect to find the difference reported and how would you expect to find it reported?

5. Note 11 to the financial statements describes an extraordinary item experienced by Georgia-Pacific. Describe what this item was and why it would be described as an extraordinary item. Based on the description given, prepare the journal entry that would have been made to record this item.

### Casette 6–2. Analyzing the Impact of Intangible Asset Charges

The 1986 financial statements of Scientific Micro Systems, Inc. presented the following information:

#### Consolidated Balance Sheets

| | 1986 | 1985 |
|---|---|---|
| Total current assets | $30,108,000 | $22,380,000 |
| Note receivable and deposits | — | 369,000 |
| Property, equipment, and capitalized software, at cost less accumulated depreciation and amortization | 6,402,000 | 5,199,000 |
| Purchased technology, less accumulated amortization of $1,957,000 and $1,286,000 | 1,398,000 | 2,069,000 |
| Goodwill and other intangible assets, less accumulated amortization of $1,201,000 and $796,000 | 3,684,000 | 4,089,000 |
| | $41,592,000 | $34,106,000 |

**Consolidated Statements of Operations**

|  | 1986 | 1985 | 1984 |
|---|---|---|---|
| Net sales. . . . . . . . . . . . . . | $65,273,000 | $39,469,000 | $41,103,000 |
| Cost of goods sold. . . . . . . . . . | 46,458,000 | 28,429,000 | 24,168,000 |
| Gross profit on sales . . . . . . . . | 18,815,000 | 11,040,000 | 16,935,000 |
| Less other costs and expenses: | | | |
|   Research, development and engineering | 4,841,000 | 4,705,000 | 3,816,000 |
|   Selling, general and administrative . . | 9,030,000 | 7,658,000 | 6,033,000 |
|   Interest and other expense (income). . | (34,000) | 79,000 | 603,000 |
|   Amortization of goodwill and | | | |
|     purchased technology . . . . . . | 1,076,000 | 1,085,000 | 996,000 |
| Income (loss) before provision | | | |
|   for income taxes . . . . . . . . . | $ 3,902,000 | $ (2,487,000) | $ 5,487,000 |

Notes — Significant Accounting Policies:
Intangible assets:
The excess of the company's investment in an acquired business over the fair value of net assets acquired (goodwill) is being amortized on a straight-line basis over its estimated useful life, twelve years. Technology acquired in connection with a business acquisition is being amortized on a straight-line basis over its estimated useful life, five years.

## Required:

a. Use the balance sheet accounts to reconstruct and verify the $1,076,000 charge on the statements of operations listed as "Amortization of goodwill and purchased technology." Prepare the journal entries that must have been made in 1986.

b. The notes to the financial statements indicate that amortization is being made on a straight-line basis. Assuming that the current year's rate of amortization will remain constant, how many years will be required to complete the write-off of goodwill and purchased technology?

c. What effect did these charges for intangible assets have on the cash flow of Scientific Micro Systems? Calculate the percentage impact they had on net income for each of the three years 1984–1986. Discuss whether you believe the company's treatment is the most appropriate way to handle these charges.

d. The company spends significant sums on research to develop its technology further. How would these costs be reported on the financial statements? Is their treatment consistent with that given to purchased technology? Explain.

e. The balance sheet also shows another asset that includes *capitalized software* being amortized. Explain what conditions would make software costs eligible for capitalization and amortization. What are the problems related to software capitalization?

# Further Aspects of Financial Measurement—Assets

# Chapter 7

# Revenue Recognition and Receivables Measurement

Revenue recognition controls the determination of periodic income. Revenues first must be assigned to accounting periods. Then the costs incurred to produce the assigned revenues can be measured, with appropriate accrual or deferral where necessary, and matched against them. Besides its role in measuring income, the revenue figure also indicates the current volume of business activity and the relative size and growth of business entities.

Accountants typically record revenue from products whenever a sale is made. A temporary retained earnings account, Sales Revenue, is credited. If the sale does not result in the immediate receipt of cash, the debit is made to a current asset, Accounts Receivable. This account consists of all the open charge accounts used by the individual customers of a firm. Collectively, they are known as *trade* receivables to distinguish them from other receivables such as loans to officers and employees, advances to other companies, deposits with utility companies, and so on.

Similar entries are made for nonsale revenues, such as interest and rent. These revenues usually are recognized upon the receipt of cash or by year-end accrual. In any case, the inflows of assets to the business are recorded as debits, and credits to the revenue accounts measure the increase in owners' equity.

In a realistic business setting, complexities arise. Revenue can be recognized at times other than the point of sale. Amounts billed to customers may include charges in addition to those for products or services—for example, sales taxes. Cash eventually collected from accounts receivable may be less than the amount billed because of returned merchandise, customers' failure to pay, or discounts offered for prompt payment. All of these possibilities suggest that our existing concepts, procedures, and accounts have to be clarified and expanded.

This chapter looks at the problems and procedures associated with the definition, recognition, and measurement of revenue. Separate sections of the chapter present (1) a closer look at the concept of revenue, (2) a more detailed explanation of the meaning and implications of the revenue recognition concept, (3) a study of some of its special applications, and (4) a description of the procedures used when revenue is modified by events subsequent to the time of sale.

## THE CONCEPT OF REVENUE

In earlier chapters we defined revenue as the inflow of assets to the business entity from the provision of goods and services. Businesses engage in various activities leading to the delivery of products or the rendering of services. Revenue is the enterprise's *reward* for performing these activities. Whether the revenue is from a major undertaking (e.g., the sale of a product) or from a lesser, nonoperating service (e.g., the lending of money), one factor is common to all revenue flows.[1] The firm is being *compensated for efforts* expended during the period in satisfying consumer wants. This factor distinguishes revenues from other inflows of assets—capital contributions, gifts, gains, and tax refunds.

### Revenue and Cash Receipts

Revenue, therefore, is the reward to a business for efforts expended during the period. How is that reward (asset inflow) to be valued? The following observations may be helpful. The total reward over the life of the business normally cannot exceed the amount of cash collected from customers. Merchandise that is never delivered to customers and receivables that are never collected provide no compensation to the firm. The receivable arising from a revenue transaction has no intrinsic value per se. Its value, as we have seen in Chapter 3, is in its convertibility into cash. Indeed, our objective is to report accounts receivable on the balance sheet at the amount expected to be collected in cash.

These observations suggest that revenue should be defined in terms of ultimate cash receipts: "Revenues represent actual or expected cash inflows (or the equivalent) that have occurred or will eventuate as a result of the enterprise's ongoing major or central operations during the period."[2] Until it is turned into cash, revenue is just an estimate. It may be represented by an

---

[1] Some authors use the term *income* synonymously with *revenue* for such items as interest and rent. We generally employ the term *revenue* for gross inflows of assets and reserve the term *income* for net flows (after various subtractions) such as operating income, income before taxes, and net income.

[2] FASB, *Statement of Financial Accounting Concepts No. 3*, "Elements of Financial Statements of Business Enterprises" (Stamford, Conn., December 1980), par. 64.

inflow of assets other than cash, but the *value* of that inflow is determined by the cash equivalent price of the assets received by the firm. Our concept of revenue for a period, then, will be *the cash received, cash to be received, or cash needs satisfied as a result of the firm's performance during the period.*[3]

An important word of caution is necessary. The definition of revenue in terms of cash receipts does not imply that cash collections during a period equal the revenues of that period. Only under the cash basis of accounting will cash collections equal revenues, and we already have observed that the cash basis does not reflect economic activity well for complex businesses. Revenue should be the compensation for *performance* during the period. Receipt of cash may occur prior to the expenditure of effort, concurrent with it, or subsequent to it. Under accrual accounting, the timing of revenue recognition is determined by when the critical efforts necessary to provide goods and services were expended, not when the cash is actually collected.[4] However, the existence and amount of the *eventual cash receipt* do determine how much total revenue can be recognized.

## Adjustments for Nonrevenue Receipts

This more precise concept of revenue is helpful in later sections, where we explore the revenue recognition assumption and some associated measurement problems. Even now, however, it should be clear that only those amounts received from customers *in exchange for goods or services* can be considered revenues. Amounts billed or collected for sales taxes, customer deposits on containers, or some transportation costs are not rewards for the firm's efforts, even though a cash receipt results.

For example, a firm delivers merchandise having a sales price of $5,000. A state sales tax of 5 percent must be collected from the customer as well. The proper entry is:

| | | |
|---|---|---|
| Accounts Receivable. . . . . . . . . . . . . . . . . | 5,250 | |
| Sales Revenue . . . . . . . . . . . . . . . . . | | 5,000 |
| Liability for Sales Tax . . . . . . . . . . . . . . . | | 250 |
| To record sale on account plus sales tax. | | |

---

[3] "Cash needs satisfied" refers to those rare situations when the reward for efforts expended takes the form of a cancellation of a liability or a receipt of a tangible asset that can be used directly in the business. In such cases, the revenue is measured by the amount of cash that otherwise would have been paid out, that is, the cash needs fulfilled.

[4] If a significant time period exists before cash is collected, the eventual cash receipts probably include compensation for waiting (interest) as well as for the current period's efforts. The interest element, as the reward for waiting, should be allocated to the waiting period. In this situation, the revenue for the current period is actually the present value of the cash to be received. Present value concepts and procedures are explained further in Chapter 11 and in the Appendix to Chapter 11.

When the $250 is remitted to the state tax authorities, the liability will be debited. The sales tax represents neither a revenue nor an expense to the business entity. The entity serves only as a collection agent for the government.

Another example is found with deposits on beverage containers. Suppose a beverage wholesaler sells 100 cases of cola to a delicatessen. Each case contains 24 bottles, and each bottle has a 5 cent deposit on it. The cost per case is $15 plus bottle deposit. The wholesaler would make the following entry:

| | | |
|---|---|---|
| Cash (or Accounts Receivable) . . . . . . . . . . . . | 1,620 | |
| Sales (100 × $15). . . . . . . . . . . . . . . . . . | | 1,500 |
| Container Deposits (100 × 24 × $.05) . . . . . . . | | 120 |

To record cash receipt for sale and container deposit.

When the bottles are returned, the liability account, Container Deposits, will be reduced as cash is refunded to the retailer. Until then the $120 appears as a current liability on the balance sheet, not as a revenue on the income statement.

## CRITERIA FOR REVENUE RECOGNITION

We have specified in Chapter 1 two criteria for recognizing revenue. One concerns the economics of earning revenue and the other, the practical problem of measuring it. Our assumption states that *revenue should be recognized only when it has been earned and can be measured with a reasonable degree of reliability*. The first criterion is implicit in the definition of revenue. Because revenue is the reward for productive efforts expended, it cannot exist until all or a substantial portion of the earning efforts have been performed. However, during an accounting period, many efforts are exerted for which the rewards are to be received in subsequent periods. Only if these rewards are susceptible to reasonably precise measurement can the revenue be recognized and recorded in the period earned.

This dual approach attempts to strike a balance between the qualitative guidelines of relevance and reliability. The earning criterion relates revenue to the period in which the economic functions are performed. This provides timely and, hence, relevant monetary measures of the results of the period's efforts. The criterion of measurability confirms that a significant level of verifiability is also necessary if accounting information is to meet the guideline of reliability.

### Earning Criterion

Each cash receipt from a particular sale or revenue event represents the joint reward for a combination of earning efforts—organizing, purchasing, producing, selling, delivering, collecting, and others. These activities collectively are called the "earning process." Because the earning process is carried out over time, revenue may relate to activities in several accounting periods. Only that portion of the ultimate cash receipt that is compensation for efforts exerted during an accounting period should be reported as revenue for that period.

When all the earning efforts are not performed in one accounting period, the ultimate cash receipts (revenue) may have to be allocated to the various periods in which the earning process occurred. Conceptually, this allocation should reflect the relative importance of each function to the total efforts required for the creation and marketing of goods and services. Accountants traditionally consider cost to be a measure of effort. If a large portion of cost has not yet been incurred, some function associated with the production of particular revenues is still unperformed. Thus, the revenue has not yet been substantially earned. With the sale of products, "substantially earned" usually means that the risks and rewards of ownership of the goods pass from the seller to the buyer.

The basic principle regarding earning can be summarized as follows: *Revenues should be recognized only to the extent that the earning process has been completed. The earning process is substantially complete when all necessary costs have been incurred or can be reliably estimated.*

## Measurability Criterion

A measurement of the revenue earned in periods prior to the actual cash receipt requires a prediction of how much cash will be received. The second part of the dual standard for revenue states that this estimate must be reliable. The two aspects of reliability from Chapter 2 relevant here are verifiability and representational faithfulness.

As a characteristic of revenue recognition, verifiability refers to the minimization of measurer bias. Artificial delay or advancement of the time of revenue recognition introduces a bias. Likewise, personal biases of management, whether optimistic or pessimistic, could affect the revenue estimate. Verifiability requires that the estimate be free from distortion and subject to independent confirmation. Consequently, accountants traditionally have accorded great weight to market transactions and arm's-length negotiations with outside parties.

Here, representational faithfulness concerns the probability that the revenue measure will equal the ultimate cash receipt. Three questions must be answered affirmatively by the accountant. Is the sales value ascertainable? Can the amount that eventually will be collected from the customer be estimated? When more than one accounting period is involved, can the amount of revenue attributable to (earned during) each period be determined?

Of course, absolute certainty in the measure of revenue would have to wait until the final receipt of cash. What accountants search for is sufficient assurance that the amount of revenue being recorded is reasonably exact.

Again, they often find such assurance in market transactions and the receipt from customers of cash, receivables, or some other asset capable of being measured (valued) accurately.

## Realization

The foregoing discussion focuses on criteria for revenue *recognition*. In accounting literature and practice, *realization* is the term most commonly associated with revenue. You often hear, for example, that revenues should not be recognized until they are realized. Unfortunately, this declaration signifies little, for "realization" means different things to different people.

Historically, realization first was used to mean the conversion of assets into cash. The concept arose in response to income tax and dividend laws, which stressed ability to pay and possession of assets in distributable form. However, its use soon broadened to include other ideas as well—liquidity (convertibility of assets into monetary assets), measurability (predictability of ultimate cash to be received), and severability (ability of the asset to be separated from the business via an exchange with an external party).

Although most accountants use the term and subscribe to a realization criterion, the concept lacks a common meaning. For some it means earning, for others it implies measurability, and for still others it signifies a sale. Some writers use the term to cover all of the criteria for revenue recognition, and a few still use it in its narrowest sense of cash conversion. Care must be taken to interpret it in the correct context. Accordingly, we use the less common but more interpretable term, *recognition,* when talking about revenue.

## APPLICATION OF THE REVENUE POSTULATE

Our earning criterion asserts that the ultimate cash receipt is a joint product of many activities and that revenue is earned in relation to the importance and completion of these activities. Conceptually, revenue recognition should be continuous. As each stage in the earning process is completed, some increase in the value of the products being produced and sold by the business entity should be recorded. Gradually, the goods would move from cost to full retail price.

As a practical matter, continuous revenue recognition is impossible. Reliable determination of how much revenue is attributable to any single earning activity is extremely difficult. Therefore, accountants normally visualize revenue as arising at a particular point in the earning cycle. In a sense, this expedient meshes with the measurability criterion. The longer one postpones revenue measurement, the more certain that measurement will be. The risk of recognizing unearned revenue or of recording revenue inaccurately is minimized. However, postponing recognition also increases the likelihood of earned revenue being left unrecognized.

Two conclusions follow. First, the selection of a single point for revenue recognition is a useful expedient only if it does not unduly magnify either of these measurement errors. If it does, then an alternative method that recognizes revenue in stages should be adopted. Second, the optimum point of measurement would be that which minimizes the total effect of the offsetting errors—recognition of unearned or inaccurate revenue and failure to recognize earned revenue. The *earliest* point of revenue recognition is when (1) the major revenue-producing activity has been performed *and* (2) the ultimate cash receipt can be estimated within a small margin of error.

Based on these criteria, we find the following revenue recognition procedures widely used in accounting practice.

1. Revenue from the sale of products is recognized at the "point of sale"—when the goods are delivered to the customer.
2. Revenue from the sale of services is recognized when the services have been performed and the seller is allowed to send a bill.
3. Revenue from the use of other assets of the entity (rent, interest, royalties) is recognized either in relation to the passage of time or to the use of the assets.

However, there are other practices and varying applications. We need to look at some of them and their bases of support in the revenue recognition concept. The alternatives we look at in addition to point-of-sale recognition include completed contract, percentage of completion, and the installment method.

## Point-of-Sale Recognition

Recognition of revenue at the point of sale is common because selling is a principal activity in the earning process for most businesses. Once the sale is made, the probability of unearned revenue being recognized is substantially reduced. By the time of sale, practically all of the costs associated with producing the revenue have been incurred.

The accuracy of revenue measurement also is significantly enhanced at the point of sale. At any earlier point, the expected exchange price of goods and services and/or the probability of selling them is undetermined. At the point of sale, on the other hand, the customer either has paid cash or pledged, via an account receivable, that he or she will pay cash within a short time. Adjustments for uncollectibles, returns, and discounts can usually be estimated with a sufficient degree of assurance to satisfy the measurement criteria. These adjustments and the procedures for recording them are covered later in this chapter.

**Customer Advances.**   A special case in the application of point-of-sale recognition is the customer advance. In particular, the importance of the earning criterion can be seen. When customers pay cash before product delivery or service performance, we can measure the revenue reliably but have not earned it yet. For example, a customer pays $6,000 in advance for a delivery van to be manufactured and delivered later. Accountants for the van manufacturer should not recognize the $6,000 as revenue. Rather, the following journal entry should be made:

Cash . . . . . . . . . . . . . . . . . . . . . . . 6,000
    Customer Advances . . . . . . . . . . . . . . . .     6,000
  To record liability for unearned revenue.

Then, when the van is manufactured and delivered, the revenue will have been earned and can be recognized:

Customer Advances . . . . . . . . . . . . . . . . . 6,000
    Sales . . . . . . . . . . . . . . . . . . . . . .     6,000
  To recognize revenue upon delivery of the product.

The Customer Advances account represents a liability, one that probably will be satisfied by the delivery of goods or the performance of a service. Nevertheless, the customer has a claim against the assets of the firm. If the goods are not supplied or the service is not performed, the customer usually can claim a cash refund.

Similar situations exist with the sale of custom-made equipment, bus tokens, and magazine subscriptions. In each case, the cash collected represents not revenue but simply an advance payment for services or goods to be provided in the future. The liability accounts that are credited often are given special account names—Customers' Paid Orders, Tokens Outstanding, and Unexpired Subscriptions.

**Credit Card Sales.**   Another special application of point-of-sale recording is the credit card sale. One of the hallmarks of our modern society is our extensive use of credit cards to acquire goods and services. Major retail chains and oil companies issue their own credit cards. Banks throughout the nation sponsor MasterCard and VISA credit cards. Then, too, there are private companies, such as American Express and Carte Blanche, that have their own cards. We are indeed a society of plastic money.

How does the retailer record credit card sales? The answer depends on the type of card. When a firm uses its own credit card, the sale is recorded as a regular sale on open account. The credit card activates entries to Accounts Receivable. The local J.C. Penney's store will record a sale of $280 to a customer having a Penney's charge card as follows:

Accounts Receivable . . . . . . . . . . . . . . . . . . 280
    Sales . . . . . . . . . . . . . . . . . . . . . . .     280
  To record credit sale.

Any risk of nonpayment still rests with J.C. Penney.

In the case of bank cards and national credit card companies, the customer establishes credit with the issuer of the card (lender). As long as established procedures (validation of the card number, date, etc.) are followed, the retailer is able to transfer the risk of nonpayment and the expenses of collection to the lender. Moreover, the retailer does not have money tied up in receivable balances. For these services, the issuer of the card charges a fee, which usually ranges from 2 to 5 percent of credit card sales.

The specific entries depend on whether bank cards or national credit cards are involved. In many places, MasterCard sales invoices are treated the same as cash. They are deposited in the bank just as if they were checks. Then, usually monthly, the bank reduces the retailer's bank balance by the amount of the credit card service fee. Assume that the sale for $280 referred to above was processed using a MasterCard. The entry by the retailer to record the sale would be:

| | | |
|---|---:|---:|
| Cash | 280 | |
|    Sales | | 280 |
|      To record MasterCard sale. | | |

Moreover, assume that additional MasterCard sales for the month totaled $18,620 and that the fee is 3 percent. All other MasterCard sales would be recorded in a similar manner. The entry for the credit card service fees would be:

| | | |
|---|---:|---:|
| Credit Card Service Expense | 567 | |
|    Cash ($18,900 × .03 = $567). | | 567 |
|      To record MasterCard service fees. | | |

For purchases made with credit cards like American Express and Diners Club, the retailer must wait for remittance from the card issuer. A receivable is set up from the credit card company, and the retailer's invoices are sent periodically to the company. The credit card company remits to the retailer the amount minus the credit card fee. If the purchases in the preceding paragraph were made with American Express cards, the following entries would be appropriate:

| | | |
|---|---:|---:|
| Accounts Receivable—American Express | 18,900 | |
|    Sales | | 18,900 |
|      To record charge sale on American Express card. | | |
| Cash | 18,333 | |
| Credit Card Service Expense | 567 | |
|    Accounts Receivable—American Express | | 18,900 |
|      To record remittance from American Express. | | |

**Some Problem Areas.**　Point-of-sale recognition dominates revenue recording in most situations. So accustomed have accountants become to recognizing revenue at the point of sale that sometimes the underlying criteria are overlooked. For instance, overemphasizing the point-of-sale concept resulted in some questionable revenue recognition practices among land

development companies, franchising firms, and suppliers of long-term services during the 1960s and 1970s. The net result of these practices was a
"front-loading" of revenue—the recognition of too much revenue too early
in the earning cycle. Both the AICPA and FASB have issued recommendations to guide the recording of revenue in these industries in accordance
with the underlying criteria of earning and measurability.

## Completed Production

Recognition of sales revenue before products are sold normally cannot be
justified. The revenue is substantially unearned and is susceptible to unreliable measurement. However, in some cases, these conditions can be met
when production is completed but before actual delivery. For example,
completed production may be an appropriate point for revenue recognition
for companies that produce special orders under a binding contract or retain
goods that already have been sold in inventory for future delivery. No additional selling effort is required, and the amount of revenue can be determined as soon as production is completed.

The amount of revenue recognized is the market price for the completed
units less any direct marketing costs yet to be incurred. This amount is *net
realizable value*. For example, Gulf & Western Industries in 1983 showed
$39,796,000 of inventories labeled "Sugar Sold but Not Shipped" on its bal-
ance sheet. The inventory was stated at "estimated sales price less estimated
costs of disposal." *Assume* the *cost* of sugar sold was $39,000,000. The
summary entries that were made appear below:

| | | |
|---|---|---|
| Sugar Sold but Not Shipped. . . . . . . . . | 39,796,000 | |
| Sales  . . . . . . . . . . . . . . . . | | 39,796,000 |

To recognize revenue upon completion of
production by setting up a new inventory
account at net realizable value.

| | | |
|---|---|---|
| Cost of Goods Sold  . . . . . . . . . . . | 39,000,000 | |
| Sugar Inventory, at cost  . . . . . . . . | | 39,000,000 |

To recognize the old inventory cost as an
expense.

In the restricted circumstances outlined above, our dual criteria are met.
When it is *unnecessary* to locate a buyer and convince him or her to purchase at a negotiated price, revenue is substantially earned when production
is completed. Likewise, the selling price is a certainty. The costs of any
additional functions, such as delivery, storage, servicing, and collection,
either are immaterial or can be estimated and the revenue figure appropriately adjusted to net realizable value.

The completed production basis also has applications where a ready market exists to absorb all completed production at a quoted price. Examples

include the extraction of precious metals or the harvesting of grains and certain other agricultural products. A farmer may value wheat, corn, or other staple crops at net selling prices because the local grain exchange provides a ready market. The farmer can dispose of the entire output at a nearly fixed price with little additional effort. Income is recognized in the period of production, not in the period of delivery. The cash reward from the production efforts can be predicted reliably at the point of completed production. Location of a buyer, estimation of a sales price, incurrence of material marketing costs, and other functions normally part of the earning process are of no consequence in this situation.[5]

## Percentage of Completion

The percentage-of-completion expedient also relates revenue recognition to production rather than to sale. However, it provides for the recording of revenue as work progresses rather than when production is completed. Percentage of completion generally is employed for individual projects involving substantial amounts of revenue and considerable periods of time to complete. Such projects include the manufacturing of airplanes and ships and the construction of roads and bridges.

When the work span covers numerous accounting periods, reporting all of the revenue in any single period may be misleading as a measure of business activity and performance. Furthermore, waiting until delivery occurs may not be always necessary for reliable measurement. Unlike conventional sales orders, which may be modified or canceled, a long-term construction contract usually represents a firm commitment. The amount of revenue is either established in the contract or related directly to the cost incurred. Interim cash collections of portions of the sales price frequently are made as work is completed on the project.

Under this recognition expedient, the *amount of revenue earned each period is based on the percentage of work done during that period.* Often the percentage of completion (work done) is measured by the ratio of the costs of the current period to the total estimated contract costs.

**Illustration.**   A construction company entered into a long-term contract for a total price of $9 million. Estimated costs of the contract amounted to $8 million. During the first year, $3,200,000 of construction costs were

---

[5] If the harvested product can be sold in the current market with practically no additional effort, a seller choosing not to do so really is speculating on possible future price changes. Any gain or loss attributable to speculation properly belongs to the period between the point of completed production and the point of final sale. However, the revenue the seller earns by *raising the product* is reliably measured by the current market price at the time production is complete.

**TABLE 7–1**    Revenue Recognition under Percentage of Completion

|  | Year 1 | Year 2 | Year 3 | Total |
|---|---|---|---|---|
| Percentage of completion (work done) | 40% (3.2/8) | 50% (4/8) | 10% (.8/8) | 100% |
| Revenue to be recognized ($9,000,000 × %) | $3,600,000 | $4,500,000 | $900,000 | $9,000,000 |
| Construction costs incurred | 3,200,000 | 4,000,000 | 800,000 | 8,000,000 |
| Gross margin | $ 400,000 | $ 500,000 | $100,000 | $1,000,000 |

incurred; in the second year, $4,000,000 of such costs were incurred. The remaining work was completed in the third year at a cost of $800,000. Table 7–1 summarizes the revenue and gross margin results when percentage of completion is used.

If no revenue were recognized until the third year, the first two years would show no income, while the third year would show $1,000,000. Percentage of completion spreads revenue recognition over the period of construction activity in a reasonable manner.

The percentage-of-completion method is clearly preferable when (1) reasonably dependable estimates of work done can be made, (2) the contract specifies the rights of both buyer and seller, and (3) both parties can be expected to live up to the terms of the contract.[6] If estimates of work done or costs to complete the project are highly uncertain or if the other two criteria are not met, then revenue estimates would be too unreliable. Postponement of revenue recognition until the contract is completed would be required.

In a later section of this chapter, we contrast in greater detail the methods of handling long-term construction contracts. That section discusses some of the recording problems and illustrates the accounts and journal entries that could be employed.

## Installment Method

Some businesses engage in sales transactions requiring only a nominal down payment, with the balance to be paid in monthly installments. Sometimes with these installment sales, recognition of revenue is postponed until *after* the point of sale. *Revenue is recognized only in proportion to the cash received each period.* For example, land costing $10,000 is sold for $25,000,

---

[6] American Institute of Certified Public Accountants, *Statement of Position 81–1,* "Accounting for Performance of Construction-Type and Certain Production-Type Contracts" (New York, July 1981).

payable $5,000 each year over the next five years. Under the installment method, $3,000, or one fifth of the $15,000 ($25,000 − $10,000) gross margin on the sale, is recorded as income each year.

Under the installment method, the emphasis rests on the collection of receivables instead of on their origin. Two possible justifications might be cited for these situations. First, the collection costs may be large and the waiting period long. Hence, collecting and financing become major parts of the earning process. Therefore, revenue is substantially *unearned* at the point of sale. The second justification is that collectibility may be uncertain. Measurements may be too unreliable for revenue recognition at the point of sale because of the unpredictable estimates associated with the ultimate cash receipt. For example, in real estate transactions, the installment method is often advocated because the firm cannot estimate the collectibility of the sales price.

For most sales, however, these justifications are *not* applicable. First, a separate interest charge accompanies most installment sales. This charge, not the sales price, represents the compensation for the financing and collecting functions, which are not yet performed. Second, although a great degree of uncollectibility may be present with the installment sale, the relevant matter is the *ability to predict* the ultimate cash receipt. As long as reasonable estimates of uncollectible accounts can be made, deferral is not proper, even though the estimates may be large.

The installment method is permitted for some *income tax purposes*. Also, in financial accounting it is applied in some situations involving franchise fees and retail land sales. For these reasons, the mechanics of the method are included in the Appendix to this chapter. Nevertheless, except in very restricted circumstances, it should not be used for *financial reporting*. It postpones revenue recognition needlessly.

## MEASUREMENT ADJUSTMENTS OF REVENUE

Even following the revenue recognition concept strictly does not automatically solve all accounting problems involving revenue. The original debit to Accounts Receivable and credit to Sales Revenue are at best provisional figures subject to later modification in the amount of cash to be received. This section deals with the accounting procedures necessary to handle three specific modifications—uncollectible accounts, returns, and discounts. Decreases in revenues and receivables related to these modifications are often given special attention in the accounting records by means of contra accounts.

### Uncollectible Accounts

No matter how many precautions a firm takes to extend credit only to customers who will pay, some accounts receivable are never collected. To the extent that this happens, both the trade accounts receivable at the end of the period and the sales revenue for the period are overstated. Uncollectible accounts do not represent a valid claim to cash. Likewise, the sale turns out actually to have been made for nothing.

One approach to the problem is called the *direct write-off* procedure. An expense or loss is recorded when specific accounts receivable are identified as uncollectible. For example, if management in a retail store determines that $500 of accounts receivable will not be collected, the following entry would be made:

| | | |
|---|---|---|
| Uncollectible Accounts Expense . . . . . . . . . . . . . | 500 | |
| Accounts Receivable. . . . . . . . . . . . . . . | | 500 |

To record reduction in accounts receivable under the direct write-off method.

Unfortunately, a firm usually can identify specific uncollectible accounts only after time has elapsed and repeated efforts at collection have failed — in short, in an accounting period later than the one in which the sale was recorded. To wait until a later period to make an adjustment, as is done under direct write-off, is contrary to both the revenue concept and the periodicity concept. The revenue and income of the period in which the sale was made is overstated, not the income of the period in which the uncollectible account is discovered. Moreover, to ignore doubtful accounts until they can be specifically identified leads to an incorrect position statement. Because of the overstatement of accounts receivable, that asset would not represent the amount actually expected to be collected in cash.

The *allowance method* attempts to answer this timing dilemma. Although businesses cannot predict at the time of sale which specific customers will not pay, many of them can estimate, with a reasonable degree of accuracy, the aggregate amount of uncollectible accounts arising from a period's sales. By estimating doubtful accounts, the firm can adjust sales and accounts receivable in the current period.

Usually a direct relationship exists between the amount of uncollectibles (bad debts) and the amount of credit sales for a period of time or the amount of unpaid customer balances at a point in time. The estimate of doubtful accounts is based on past experience with these relationships. A firm can use its own past experience or, in the case of a new firm, the experience of similar companies in its particular line of business.

**Recognition of Doubtful Accounts.**  Assume that a company has credit sales of $250,000 during 1990, and collections during the year amount to $225,000. This leaves an outstanding balance of $25,000 in accounts receivable. Assume also that past experience indicates that one half of 1 percent of credit sales turns out to be uncollectible. The estimate of doubtful accounts would be $1,250 (.005 × $250,000). An entry at the end of the period adjusts both sales and accounts receivable:

    Dec. 31   Sales Uncollectibles. . . . . . . . . . . . . .   1,250
                   Allowance for Doubtful Accounts . . . . .            1,250
              To record estimate of uncollectibles for 1990.

For the purpose of a more complete reporting of financial information, the $1,250 decrease in revenue is segregated in a special *contra revenue* account called "Sales Uncollectibles." Similarly, accounts receivable are overstated and need to be reduced by $1,250. Rather than reduce the asset directly, however, accountants record the credit in a separate *contra asset* account called "Allowance for Doubtful Accounts" (hence, the name "allowance method"). The reason in this case is a practical one. Accounts Receivable is a general ledger account controlling numerous individual charge accounts in a subsidiary ledger. If we credit Accounts Receivable directly, it would no longer be in agreement with the total of the subsidiary ledger, unless we also reduce some specific individual accounts. However, at this point we are unable to identify the individuals who will not pay. All that can be said now is that of the $25,000 owed to us we expect not to collect $1,250. This is exactly the meaning of the balance in the contra asset account.

Sales and Sales Uncollectibles, being temporary accounts, are closed at the end of the period and appear on the income statement. Allowance for Doubtful Accounts (alternatively called "Allowance for Uncollectibles") appears on the balance sheet as a subtraction from Accounts Receivable. An alternative reporting treatment would be to show the net amount of receivables on the statement and the amount of the contra account in parentheses.

**Identification of Specific Uncollectible Accounts.**   The end-of-period adjusting entry made on December 31, 1990, reduces both sales and accounts receivable by $1,250. During the following year specific individual charge accounts will be identified as uncollectible. Assume that $750 of specific uncollectible accounts are discovered during 1991. The entry to write them off will be:

Allowance for Doubtful Accounts  . . . . . . . . . . . .   750
     Accounts Receivable. . . . . . . . . . . . . . . . .            750
         To write off specific uncollectible accounts.

We initially used a contra asset account because of our inability to pinpoint particular subsidiary accounts as uncollectible. We therefore reduced receivables indirectly by crediting the contra account. However, in later periods when the subsidiary accounts can be pinpointed, the need for the contra account disappears. The effect of the above entry is simply to remove the credit from the contra account and enter it in the main account. Corresponding credits are entered in the subsidiary ledger accounts also.

Under the allowance method, accounts receivable and net income are reduced only by the original estimate. Unlike the direct write-off method, *writing off an account causes no net change in assets or owners' equity.* There is no additional reduction in sales; the write-off entry only confirms an event that was anticipated when the allowance was established. To see the neutral effect of this entry, compare the following accounts receivable and allowance accounts before and after the write-off.

|  | *Before* | *After* |
|---|---|---|
| Accounts receivable . . . . . . . . . . . . . . . | $25,000 | $24,250 |
| Less: Allowance for doubtful accounts . . . . . . | 1,250 | 500 |
| Realizable value of accounts receivable . . . . . . | $23,750 | $23,750 |

The account balances after the entry simply say that of the $24,250 still owed, only $23,750 is expected to be realized in cash. The firm is still unable specifically to identify the remaining $500 of individual accounts that are estimated to be uncollectible.

In our illustration, we assumed that no individual accounts were written off until the years following the year of sale. This is the normal sequence. In some instances, however, specific accounts can be identified as bad debts in the period of sale. An account arising in January may be written off in July. In fact, if enough of these early write-offs are made, the contra asset, Allowance for Doubtful Accounts, could temporarily have a debit balance. Nevertheless, as soon as the estimating entry for that year's uncollectibles is recorded, the income statement and balance sheet will be accurate.

**Recovery of Accounts Deemed Uncollectible.**   What happens when a receivable that has previously been written off as a specific uncollectible account is collected? One very common treatment attributes the recovery to a premature write-off. The account really never was a bad debt. Suppose that the $750 of receivables written off during 1991 includes one account of $80 which ends up being collected in December. The write-off entry should be reversed and the cash treated as an ordinary collection of a receivable:

| | | |
|---|---|---|
| Accounts Receivable . . . . . . . . . . . . . . . . . . . . . | 80 | |
|     Allowance for Doubtful Accounts . . . . . . . . . . . | | 80 |
|     To reverse entry for incorrect write-off. | | |

| | | |
|---|---|---|
| Cash . . . . . . . . . . . . . . . . . . . . . . . . . . . . | 80 | |
|     Accounts Receivable . . . . . . . . . . . . . . . . . . . | | 80 |
|     To record collection of account receivable. | | |

Entries would also be made in the subsidiary ledger so that a complete record of the eventual collection of the account exists.

This procedure is particularly appropriate when arbitrary policies are followed in the naming of an account as uncollectible. For example, a firm's policy might be to write off all accounts with balances over one year old.

This policy may result in some accounts being erroneously identified as uncollectible.

Note that the recovery of an individual account does not imply that the estimate being used is inaccurate. Rather, the *write-off was a mistake;* this recovered account was not one of those inherent in the estimate.

**Adjustment Based on Credit Sales.**    In our example, we assume that bad debts are a direct function of credit sales. Consequently, the estimate of doubtful accounts was one half of 1 percent of credit sales. Let us pursue our example one more year. In 1991, the firm has sales on open account of $375,000 and cash collections of $345,000. The adjustment for doubtful accounts at the end of 1991 is one half of 1 percent of the credit sales for the period or $1,875 ($375,000 × .005).

Dec. 31   Sales Uncollectibles . . . . . . . . . . . . . 1,875
                 Allowance for Doubtful Accounts . . . . .      1,875
                 To record estimate of uncollectibles for 1991.

The year-end treatment of the accounts is the same as before. Sales and Sales Uncollectibles are closed. The T accounts below show the effect on Accounts Receivable and on Allowance for Doubtful Accounts from all entries in 1990 and 1991.

**Accounts Receivable**

| | | | |
|---|---|---|---|
| 1990 sales | 250,000 | 1990 collections | 225,000 |
| √ 12/31/90 | 25,000 | 1991 collections | 345,000 |
| 1991 sales | 375,000 | 1991 write-off | 750 |
| 1991 recovery of write-off | 80 | 1991 cash recovery | 80 |
| √ 12/31/91 | 54,250 | | |

**Allowance for Doubtful Accounts**

| | | | |
|---|---|---|---|
| | | 1990 provision | 1,250 |
| 1991 write-off | 750 | √ 12/31/90 | 1,250 |
| | | 1991 recovery of write-off | 80 |
| | | 1991 provision | 1,875 |
| | | √ 12/31/91 | 2,455 |

Both of these accounts appear on the balance sheet prepared at the end of 1991.

Accounts receivable . . . . . . . . . . . . . . . . . . . $54,250
    Less: Allowance for doubtful accounts . . . . . . . .    2,455   $51,795

Of the $54,250 owed by customers, the firm expects not to collect $2,455. The specific individual subsidiary accounts that are uncollectible will be identified in 1992 and subsequent years.

Under this method of adjustment, the estimate is based directly on the income statement figure of credit sales. The asset adjustment is the by-product of the revenue adjustment. This estimate based on sales is appropriate for companies that have a large number of customers with relatively small receivable balances. In these cases, one would expect that amounts lost through nonpayment would vary with credit sales in a reasonably stable manner from period to period. One potential defect of this approach is that the Allowance for Doubtful Accounts could grow too large or too small in relation to the end-of-period receivables if the estimate is faulty.

**Adjustment Based on Accounts Receivable.** To estimate the amount of uncollectibles, accountants frequently use an alternative procedure that adjusts the Allowance for Doubtful Accounts to equal a preestablished percentage of the accounts receivable at the end of each period. The focus is on an accurate measurement of accounts receivable, and the adjustment of sales is the by-product. Taking the preceding example, assume that past experience indicates that of the outstanding receivables existing at the *end* of any given year, 5 percent is never realized in cash. Instead of applying a percentage to total credit sales, we determine our adjustment for doubtful accounts by valuing the ending accounts receivable. Of the $25,000 of receivables outstanding at the end of 1990, 5 percent, or $1,250, is expected never to be collected. Therefore, $1,250 is the balance we desire to have in the Allowance for Doubtful Accounts to show the net realizable value of the trade receivables. Inasmuch as the contra asset account has no balance prior to the estimating entry for 1990, $1,250 is also the amount of the adjustment for doubtful accounts.

The estimate for 1991 is a little more complex. At the end of 1991, the balance in Accounts Receivable is $54,250. The estimate of 5 percent would suggest that $2,713 of this is uncollectible. Because a credit balance of $580 ($1,250 − $750 + $80) already is in the allowance account, we would make a $2,133 ($2,713 − $580) credit to Allowance for Doubtful Accounts and debit to Sales Uncollectibles for 1991.

The accounts receivable approach is widely used. Analysis of the individual accounts is particularly appropriate when some very large or unusual accounts are included in the total or when economic changes (such as a recession) occur. Estimates based on accounts receivable eliminate the possibility of a disproportionate relationship developing between the asset and the contra account. At the end of each accounting period, the contra account is adjusted by *whatever amount* is necessary to make it conform to the uncollectibility situation at that time.

**Aging of Accounts Receivable.** In the interests of greater accuracy, the individual accounts receivable often are aged. Aging is the process of classifying account balances according to the length of time they have been unpaid. Then, instead of an *average* uncollectible percentage like the 5 percent used above, a different percentage is applied to each age group.

**TABLE 7–2** Aging Schedule for Accounts Receivable as of December 31, 1991

| Customer Name | Total Balance | Age of Balance in Days | | | |
|---|---|---|---|---|---|
| | | 0–60 | 61–120 | 121–360 | Over 360 |
| Anderson, K. | $ 2,700 | $ 2,100 | $ 300 | $ 300 | — |
| Baker, L. | 8,150 | 1,600 | 2,400 | 4,150 | — |
| Black, J. | 4,200 | 4,200 | — | — | — |
| Daube, K. | 6,400 | 4,400 | 1,500 | 500 | — |
| Light, S. | 5,250 | 4,000 | 800 | 450 | — |
| Mason, P. | 8,300 | 6,200 | 2,100 | — | — |
| Nord, Z. | 3,950 | — | 2,000 | 1,400 | $ 550 |
| Rebele, J. | 5,400 | 5,400 | — | — | — |
| Smith, S. | 6,000 | 1,000 | 2,000 | 2,500 | 500 |
| Wilson, G. | 3,900 | 1,600 | 2,300 | — | — |
| Total | $54,250 | $30,500 | $13,400 | $9,300 | $1,050 |
| Uncollectible percentage | | 1% | 5% | 10% | 50% |
| Desired balance in allowance | $ 2,430 | $ 305 | $ 670 | $ 930 | $ 525 |
| Existing credit balance | 580 | | | | |
| 1991 estimate | $ 1,850 | | | | |

Table 7–2 shows a hypothetical aging of the $54,250 account balances outstanding at the end of 1991. The increasing uncollectibility percentages reflect the general relationship between the length of time a balance is outstanding and the likelihood that the account will be collected. Aging facilitates more accurate estimates of doubtful accounts than overall percentages, because it is more sensitive to the actual condition of the accounts receivable. The aging schedule also can present information to be used by management in evaluating credit-granting policies and collection efforts.

**Summary.** An adjustment based on sales asks the question, "How much of this year's sales will not be collected?" An adjustment based on accounts receivable asks the question, "How much of the year-end balance of accounts receivable will not be collected?" However, regardless of the method used for estimation, the interpretation of the accounts is the same. Sales Uncollectibles reflects the revenue adjustment applicable to the current period's sales. The Allowance for Doubtful Accounts measures the estimated amount of uncollectibles associated with the outstanding receivables, regardless of their year of origin.

The contra asset account is increased by each period's adjustment for doubtful accounts and is decreased when individual uncollectible accounts are identified. The balance in the contra account, therefore, should bear a

---

**TABLE 7–3**    Summary of Approaches and Entries Regarding Uncollectibles

1. Direct write-off method (uncollectible accounts recognized at the time they are judged to be uncollectible)

Uncollectible Accounts Expense
Accounts Receivable

2. Allowance method (estimate of uncollectible accounts matched with appropriate revenues)
   a. Entry is:

Sales Uncollectibles (Uncollectible Accounts Expense)
Allowance for Doubtful Accounts

   b. Estimate of uncollectible revenues is made by applying a rate to sales on account
   c. Estimate of uncollectibles in ending receivables is made by:
      (1) Applying an overall rate to ending receivables, or
      (2) Applying varying rates to an aging of receivables
   d. Entry to record specific identification of an uncollectible account is:

Allowance for Doubtful Accounts
Accounts Receivable

   e. Entries for recovery of uncollectible accounts are:

Accounts Receivable
Allowance for Doubtful Accounts
Cash
Accounts Receivable

---

fairly close relationship to the balance in the asset account, provided the original estimate remains accurate. Table 7–3 summarizes the entries we have discussed.

The allowance method assumes that the original entries recording sales on account are tentative. Revenue is equal to the amount of cash that will ultimately be collected, not the original sales price. Because uncollectible accounts have a net realizable value of zero, these sales provide no revenue. Hence, we deduct the estimate of uncollectibles from gross sales to obtain the adjusted net revenue figure.

Many accountants and business managers view uncollectible accounts as *expenses*. In practice, an Uncollectible Accounts Expense is used instead of the contra revenue, Sales Uncollectibles. The justification for this treatment is that a certain amount of uncollectibles is inevitable when business is conducted on credit. Management's decision to extend credit is based on the belief that the income from the expanded sales caused by offering credit will far outweigh the possible uncollectible amounts.

Nevertheless, uncollectibles are not like other expenses; *they represent revenue never received rather than costs incurred in the generation of revenues*. The treatment of bad debts as an expense views the original debits to Accounts Receivable as an absolute measure of value. It seems more logical to us not to divorce the value of the claim to cash from the amount of cash expected to be received.

Whether the debit entry resulting from the estimate of doubtful accounts is treated as a contra revenue or as an expense, the same net income results. Classification of this deduction on the income statement is not a major accounting issue.

What may be an issue is whether the use of any estimate introduces too much subjectivity into the recording process. The direct write-off procedure may appear to be more reliable. However, direct write-off actually may be *less objective.* The determination of when an account is uncollectible depends on managerial judgment. Under direct write-off, how management exercises this judgment affects income. The estimate procedure, on the other hand, allows for the specific write-off of an account without any effect on income. It thereby removes a potential distortion in income measurement arising from the purposeful speeding up or postponement of the identification of specific uncollectible accounts by management.[7]

## Sales Returns and Allowances

In addition to customers who never pay their accounts, the accountant must also deal with some customers who return the merchandise they have purchased. If the returned goods are accepted by the seller, the sale is canceled, and the accounts receivable claim disappears. The possibility of sales returns raises three questions that we will address in this section:

1. How do accountants record sales returns?
2. What about sales made at the end of the current accounting period that will be returned in the next accounting period?
3. What implications does the return privilege have for the timing of revenue recognition?

**Recording Sales Returns.**    Assume that a customer returns merchandise sold originally for $900. The return nullifies the original debit to Accounts Receivable and credit to Sales. Sometimes when the cause of customer dissatisfaction is minor imperfections in the merchandise, the seller and purchaser will agree on a price reduction (allowance) in lieu of a return. The entry to record either is

Sales Returns and Allowances . . . . . . . . . . . . . .    900
    Accounts Receivable . . . . . . . . . . . . . . . .    900
    To record cancellation of sale because of return.

---

[7] For many years the allowance (reserve) method was allowed for income tax purposes. Unfortunately, the Tax Reform Act of 1986 repealed this provision. Now only the direct write-off (specific charge-off) method can be used for tax purposes. Tax law is contrary to both generally accepted accounting principles and to economic reality.

The contra revenue account segregates these particular decreases in revenue and highlights them for management's attention. Changes in the level of sales returns and allowances vis-à-vis sales from period to period may reflect trends in customer tastes and/or changes in the quality of merchandise or service.

Because we know the exact customers who are returning the merchandise, we normally do not need a contra asset account. When the Accounts Receivable control account is credited as in the entry above, a credit is also made in the particular customer's charge account in the subsidiary ledger.

**Estimated Sales Returns.** What about sales made at the end of the current accounting period that will be returned in the next accounting period? If we debit a contra revenue account when the return actually takes place, cancellations of this period's sales will actually offset next period's sales. Moreover, the value assigned to accounts receivable on the year-end balance sheet will be overstated.

In some industries, the amount of estimated returns is significant. In these cases, accuracy in revenue recognition is enhanced by estimating the amount of current sales that will normally be cancelled by returns taking place in the next period. Then an adjusting entry is made, similar to the adjustment for doubtful accounts, with a credit to a contra asset, Allowance for Sales Returns.

The adjustment for estimated returns differs, however, from the adjustment for uncollectibles because a judgment must be made concerning the *cost* of merchandise that is estimated to be returned. For example, assume that anticipated returns, based on past experience, equal about 15 percent of outstanding accounts receivable at year-end. Moreover, the cost of the returned merchandise averages 66.7 percent of the selling prices. If accounts receivable at the end of an accounting period amount to $150,000, the proper adjusting entries would be:

| | | |
|---|---|---|
| Sales Returns and Allowances | 22,500 | |
|     Allowance for Sales Returns | | 22,500 |
|   To record estimated sales returns. | | |
| | | |
| Inventory—Estimated Returns | 15,000 | |
|     Cost of Goods Sold | | 15,000 |
|   To record cost of estimated inventory to be returned. | | |

These entries reduce sales by $22,500 and net income by $7,500—the original gross margin on the sales. Total assets also decline by $7,500; accounts receivable decreases by the $22,500 credited to the contra asset account; and the estimated inventory asset increases $15,000.

The foregoing adjustment is not an acceptable procedure for income tax purposes. Furthermore, for some firms, the amount of estimated returns is small and relatively constant from year to year. For practical reasons, then, these firms do not adjust for estimated returns. If estimated returns are material, however, the adjustment is strongly recommended.

**Deferral of Revenue Recognition.** In some circumstances, the existence of a right of return calls into question the appropriateness of recognizing revenue at the point of sale. A retail firm may have a right to return to the wholesaler or manufacturer merchandise that cannot be resold to the ultimate customers. Bookstores and record stores often have this right. In these cases, the risks of ownership of the merchandise have not really passed to the retailer. The manufacturer or wholesaler has not substantially earned the revenue until the return privilege expires, nor is there likely to be a reliable measure of the ultimate cash receipt until then.

If a significant right to return a product exists, no revenue can be recognized at the point of sale unless all of the following conditions are met:[8]

1. The price is fixed or determinable at the date of sale.
2. The buyer's obligation to pay the seller is not contingent on the buyer's resale of the product.
3. Theft or destruction of the product would not change the buyer's obligation to pay the seller.
4. The buyer has economic substance apart from the seller.
5. The seller has no obligation for resale.
6. The amount of returns can be estimated.

If all conditions are satisfied, it is acceptable to recognize revenue at the point of sale and to establish an allowance for estimated returns, as described in the preceding section. If one or more of the conditions is not satisfied, revenue recognition should be postponed until the return privilege expires. For example, in 1985 Intel Corporation had over $72 million in a liability account called "Deferred Sales to Distributors." In a note, it explained:

> Certain of Intel's sales are made to distributors under agreements allowing price protection and right of return on merchandise unsold by the distributors. Because of frequent sales price reductions and rapid technological obsolescence in the industry, Intel defers recognition on such sales until the merchandise is sold by the distributor.

## Sales Discounts

Another recording problem that may arise in purchase-sale transactions concerns cash discounts offered for the prompt payment of accounts. Particularly in the wholesale trade, the seller often allows a discount from the billed amount if payment is made within a certain time. Cash discounts are offered to encourage early payment, which reduces billing and collection costs and, more importantly, lessens the risk of uncollectibles.

---

[8] FASB, *Statement of Financial Accounting Standards No. 48*, "Revenue Recognition When Right of Return Exists" (Stamford, Conn., June 1981), par. 6.

The invoice price is referred to as the "gross price." The price after the discount for prompt payment is termed the "net price." Which amount of revenue is to be recorded at the time of the initial sale? Sales are recorded more commonly at gross prices than at net prices, but both methods are used in practice. Both methods usually also require later adjustments. If sales are entered at gross prices, then modifications are necessary whenever customers take the discount. If sales are initially recorded at net prices, then adjustments are necessary for all discounts lost by customers.

**Example.** Suppose two sales of $10,000 each (gross price) are made on October 1. One account is paid on October 9; the other is paid on November 21. Further, let us assume that the firm sells on terms that allow a 3 percent discount if the customer pays the account within 15 days of the invoice date. Otherwise, the full gross price is due within 60 days. These terms are abbreviated 3/15, n/60.

The journal entries in Table 7–4 show how these transactions are handled under both the gross and the net methods. Of course, an individual firm

---

**TABLE 7–4**  Comparison of Sales Recorded at Gross and at Net Prices

**Gross Price Recording**

| Oct. 1 | Accounts Receivable | 20,000 | |
| | Sales | | 20,000 |

*Collection within Discount Period*

| Oct. 9 | Cash | 9,700 | |
| | Sales Discounts | 300 | |
| | Accounts Receivable | | 10,000 |

*Collection after Discount Period*

| Nov. 21 | Cash | 10,000 | |
| | Accounts Receivable | | 10,000 |

**Net Price Recording**

| Oct. 1 | Accounts Receivable | 19,400 | |
| | Sales ($20,000 less 3%) | | 19,400 |

*Collection within Discount Period*

| Oct. 9 | Cash | 9,700 | |
| | Accounts Receivable | | 9,700 |

*Collection after Discount Period*

| Nov. 21 | Cash | 10,000 | |
| | Accounts Receivable | | 9,700 |
| | Sales Discount Revenue | | 300 |

would employ only one or the other. Under the gross method, payment within the discount period necessitates an adjustment to revenue by means of a debit to a contra revenue account, Sales Discounts. When payment in the gross amount is made after the discount period, no adjustment is normally made, as gross is the basis for the original entry.

In essence, the opposite occurs under the net method. No adjustment of revenue is necessary on October 9; the sale has been recorded under the correct assumption that the customer would take the discount. Gross payments after the discount period has expired, however, require recognition of an additional $300 of revenue from those customers who elected the deferred payment privilege.

Despite the greater usage of the gross method in business practice, logic seems to favor the net method. Loss of the cash discount is actually a penalty charged for late payment. Customers who pay on time do not have to remit that amount. The revenue expected from the sale of the merchandise is the "cash" price or net price. Under the net method, Sales is credited only with the cash price of the product. A separate revenue account is credited whenever additional cash is collected for late payment. Under the gross method these revenues are combined in the Sales account. Both methods, of course, record the same total revenue.

# LONG-TERM CONSTRUCTION CONTRACTS

Long-term construction contracts, such as those for buildings, ships, highways, and other major projects, present some special problems of revenue recognition. Two approaches are used in practice. *Percentage of completion* calls for periodic revenue recognition as the work progresses. Income is accrued over the life of the contract in proportion to the amount earned each period. We discussed the general theory behind this method earlier in the chapter.

A second approach, *completed contract,* conforms more closely to the traditional sales basis. During construction, the costs incurred are accumulated in an inventory account. They are matched against recognized revenue only in the period when the contract is completed and the constructed asset is "delivered" to the customer.

Long-term construction contracts contain other features that require careful treatment in the accounts. Under the terms of most contracts, the contractor may bill the customer periodically for partial payment. These *progress billings* may or may not conform to the amount of work completed. In addition, of the amounts billed, the customer commonly withholds a specified percentage until final completion as a guarantee of performance.

To contrast the recording procedures for completed contract and percentage of completion, we will use a single numerical example and the most common type of contract, the *fixed-price contract.*[9] Assume that a builder contracts to construct a two-story apartment building. The total contract price is $3.0 million. The estimated total cost of construction over the two and a half years' expected completion time is $2 million. The contract calls for three equal periodic billings — when the basement and foundation are completed, when the first story is completed, and when the entire project is completed. Each billing is collectible within 90 days, except for a 5 percent retainer to be paid upon final acceptance by the purchaser. Table 7–5 summarizes data pertaining to the construction period.

## Completed Contract

Summary entries to be made during each of the three years under the completed contract method appear in Table 7–6.

During Years 1 and 2, the income statement will show only $50,000 administrative expense. In Year 3, net income will be $900,000 ($950,000 gross margin from the contract minus $50,000 administrative expense). On the position statement, Accounts Receivable and Contract in Progress would be disclosed in the current asset section, the latter as a specially identified item of inventory.

The most troublesome account to classify is Progress Billings. The logical treatment is to show it as a current liability, a type of construction advance. Inasmuch as revenue is being recognized only at the completion of the contract, amounts collected from customers represent claims against assets that will be satisfied by subsequent delivery of the product. In practice, most companies treat the credit arising from progress billings as an off-

---

**TABLE 7–5**    Data for Illustration of Contract Accounting ($000)

|  | *Year 1* | *Year 2* | *Year 3* |
|---|---|---|---|
| Construction costs incurred | $ 800 | $ 600 | $ 650 |
| Estimated costs to complete | 1,200 | 700 | — |
| Progress billings | 1,000 | 1,000 | 1,000 |
| Collections on progress billings | — | 950 | 1,900 |
| Collection of retainer | — | — | 150 |
| Administrative expense (period charge) | 50 | 50 | 50 |

---

[9] On a fixed-price contract, the ultimate gross margin may be positive or negative, depending on the amount of costs. Two other types of contracts provide for revenue equal to costs incurred plus a fee and thus guarantee a positive gross margin. One, called cost-plus-fixed fee, specifies the fee as a fixed-dollar amount, often subject, however, to incentive or penalty provisions. The other, known as cost-plus-a-percentage, calculates the fee as a percentage of cost.

**TABLE 7–6**    Entries under Completed Contract ($000)

| Entry to Record | Year 1 | | Year 2 | | Year 3 | |
|---|---|---|---|---|---|---|
| 1. Construction costs: | | | | | | |
|    Contract in Progress . . . . . . . . . . | 800 | | 600 | | 650 | |
|    Cash, Materials, etc. . . . . . . . . . | | 800 | | 600 | | 650 |
| 2. Administrative expenses: | | | | | | |
|    Administrative Expenses. . . . . . . . | 50 | | 50 | | 50 | |
|    Cash, Payables, etc. . . . . . . . . | | 50 | | 50 | | 50 |
| 3. Progress billings: | | | | | | |
|    Accounts Receivable . . . . . . . . . | 1,000 | | 1,000 | | 1,000 | |
|    Progress Billings . . . . . . . . . . | | 1,000 | | 1,000 | | 1,000 |
| 4. Collections of billings: | | | | | | |
|    Cash . . . . . . . . . | | | 950 | | 1,900 | |
|    Accounts Receivable . . . . . . . . | | | | 950 | | 1,900 |
| 5. Collection of retainer: | | | | | | |
|    Cash . . . . . . . . . | | | | | 150 | |
|    Accounts Receivable . . . . . . . . | | | | | | 150 |
| 6. Revenue and expense:* | | | | | | |
|    Progress Billings . . . . . . . . . . | | | | | 3,000 | |
|    Construction Revenue . . . . . . . . | | | | | | 3,000 |
|    Cost of Construction Contract . . . . . | | | | | 2,050 | |
|    Contract in Progress . . . . . . . . | | | | | | 2,050 |

*Sometimes in practice, the revenue and expense are not recognized separately. Only the difference between them, or gross margin, appears in the accounts. A single journal entry is made upon completion of the job ($000):

| | |
|---|---|
| Progress Billings . . . . . . . . . . . . . . . . . . . . . . . . . . . . . . . . . . . . . . . . . . . . . . . . . . . . . . . . . . . . | 3,000 |
| Contract in Progress . . . . . . . . . . . . . . . . . . . . . . . . . . . . . . . . . . . . . . . . . . . . . . . . . . . . . . | 2,050 |
| Gross Margin on Construction Contracts . . . . . . . . . . . . . . . . . . . . . . . . . . . . . . . . . . . . . . . . | 950 |

However, the *Audit and Accounting Guide for Construction Contractors* published by the AICPA recommends the more meaningful practice of a separate recording for revenues and expenses.

set to Contract in Progress. The net differences between construction costs and progress billings are shown as a current asset (amount of uncompleted contracts in excess of related billings) or as a current liability (billings on uncompleted contracts in excess of related costs). The reasoning behind this offsetting of assets and liabilities is obscure.

## Percentage of Completion

Several slightly differing methods of recording under percentage of completion exist. The more common method uses the same framework of accounts as completed contract but includes a periodic revaluation of the construction in progress to reflect the earned gross margin element. This method will be illustrated. The unique feature of all methods used for percentage of completion is that the total contract price of $3.0 million is allocated over the three-year period in the ratio of costs incurred to total costs as shown in Table 7–7.

The $950,000 gross margin on the contract ($3,000,000 − $2,050,000) is likewise spread over the three-year period. With percentage of completion, entries 1–5 in Table 7–6 would remain the same. Entry 6 to recognize revenue and expense each year would appear as shown in Table 7–8.

The Construction Revenue and the Cost of Construction accounts record full sales and expense information. They provide information concerning the volume of construction activity during the period.

Both are closed to Income Summary each year and appear on the income statement. Table 7–9 contrasts the financial statements under percentage of completion with those resulting from completed contract.

**TABLE 7–7**  Determination of Annual Revenue under Percentage of Completion ($000)

|  | Year 1 | Year 2 | Year 3 |
|---|---|---|---|
| Actual cost incurred to date . . . . . . | $ 800 | $1,400 | $2,050 |
| Estimated cost to complete. . . . . . . | 1,200 | 700 | — |
| Total cost of contract . . . . . . . . . | $2,000 | $2,100 | $2,050 |
| Percentage earned to date . . . . . . . | $\dfrac{\$800}{\$2,000} = 40\%$ | $\dfrac{\$1,400}{\$2,100} = 66.7\%$ | 100% |
| Total revenue earned to date . . . . . . | $1,200 (40%) | $2,000 (66.7%) | $3,000 (100%) |
| Revenue recognized in prior periods . . . | — | 1,200 | 2,000 |
| Revenue to be recognized this period . . | $1,200 | $ 800 | $1,000 |

**TABLE 7–8**  Entries under Percentage of Completion ($000)

|  | Year 1 | | Year 2 | | Year 3 | |
|---|---|---|---|---|---|---|
| 6. Revenue and expense: | | | | | | |
| Contract in Progress . . . . . . . . . . . . . . . | 1,200 | | 800 | | 1,000 | |
|     Construction Revenue . . . . . . . . . . . . | | 1,200 | | 800 | | 1,000 |
| Cost of Construction Contract . . . . . . . . . | 800 | | 600 | | 650 | |
|     Contract in Progress . . . . . . . . . . . . . | | 800 | | 600 | | 650 |
| Progress Billings . . . . . . . . . . . . . | | | | | 3,000 | |
|     Contract in Progress . . . . . . . . . . . . . | | | | | | 3,000 |

**TABLE 7–9**   Comparative Financial Statement Information: Percentage of Completion and Completed Contract Methods ($000)

| | Percentage of Completion | | | Completed Contract | | |
|---|---|---|---|---|---|---|
| | Year 1 | Year 2 | Year 3 | Year 1 | Year 2 | Year 3 |
| Income statement: | | | | | | |
| Construction revenue . . . . . . . . | $1,200 | $ 800 | $1,000 | — | — | $3,000 |
| Cost of contract . . . . . . . . . | 800 | 600 | 650 | — | — | 2,050 |
| Gross margin . . . . . . . . . . | 400 | 200 | 350 | — | — | 950 |
| Administrative expense . . . . . . | 50 | 50 | 50 | 50 | 50 | 50 |
| Net income (loss) . . . . . . . . | $ 350 | $ 150 | $ 300 | $ (50) | $ (50) | $ 900 |
| Balance sheet (December 31): | | | | | | |
| Current assets: | | | | | | |
| Accounts receivable . . . . . . | $1,000 | $1,050 | — | $1,000 | $1,050 | — |
| Amount of uncompleted contracts in excess of related billings . . . . . . . | $ 200 | — | — | — | — | — |
| Current liabilities: | | | | | | |
| Billings on uncompleted contracts in excess of related costs . . . | — | — | — | $ 200 | $ 600 | — |

The entries in Table 7–8 cause the inventory account, Contract in Progress, to be valued at sales price earned to date rather than at cost. For example, in Year 1, the entries increase the asset from its $800,000 cost amount to $1,200,000, thereby reflecting the $400,000 income element recognized in Year 1.[10] On the balance sheet, the Progress Billings account would be netted against the Contract in Progress account as under completed contract. With percentage of completion, the procedure has more logic behind it, however. Progress Billings is a contra asset to the inventory. The process of billing has transferred the *sales* reflected in the inventory account to a receivable account.[11]

---

[10] The two entries in Table 7–8 could be combined into a single entry that would clearly reveal the upward revaluation of assets. For example, the first year would be:

| Cost of Construction Contract. . . . . . . . . . . . . . . . . . . . . . | 800 | |
| Contract in Progress. . . . . . . . . . . . . . . . . . . . . . . . . | 400 | |
| Construction Revenue . . . . . . . . . . . . . . . . . . . . . . | | 1,200 |

[11] Under one alternative procedure used by some firms in implementing the percentage-of-completion method, an account called Accounts Receivable Unbilled is used. Its balance equals the net difference between the credit balance in Progress Billings and the debit balance in Contract in Progress (at sales value).

## Choice of Method

At one time the choice between completed contract and percentage of completion was left to the individual company with little formal guidance. A comparison of the two methods will clearly reveal the superiority of percentage of completion in reflecting the *earning* criterion. The completed-contract method frequently does not reflect current productive activity. The only factor that might prevent the use of percentage of completion in *all* long-term construction contracts is *measurability*. When dependable estimates are lacking or no signed contract exists, completed contract would be acceptable.

Basically, these guidelines have now been incorporated in official accounting standards.[12] Percentage of completion is the preferred method. There must be strong evidence that estimates of cost to complete and degree of completion are not dependable before completed contract can be used. Moreover, the choice between the methods must be made on a contract-by-contract basis.

Because it postpones recognition of income, completed contract has been widely used for income tax purposes. However, new tax regulations in 1986 and 1987 restricted its use. Approximately 70 percent of each long-term contract must be reported on the tax return using percentage of completion.

## Measurement Problems

Measurement problems can occur in any of four areas: (1) determination of total revenue, (2) prediction of collectibility, (3) measurement of percentage of completion, and (4) estimation of costs. The latter two probably cause more problems than the first two.

Sufficiently reliable measurement of total revenue normally can be found in the contractual relationship between buyer and seller. The existence of an outside purchaser provides verifiability. The total price is known in advance in a fixed-price contract or is determinable by the terms of the contract in cost-plus arrangements.

Reliable measurement also requires that we can predict with reasonable accuracy the collectibility of the ultimate cash receipts. Normally, the likelihood of not being able to collect from the purchaser is small. A construction project requires sizable long-term risks on the part of the contractor. These are not undertaken without a thorough review of the credit standing and reputation of the customer. Large financially established firms and governmental bodies tend to be the ones that qualify. The risk of uncollectibility is further reduced by progress billings.

---

[12] AICPA, *Statement of Position 81–1*, "Accounting for Performance of Construction-Type and Certain Production-Type Contracts." These views were reaffirmed in *FASB No. 56*.

The third aspect of reliable measurement concerns how accurately the earned portion of total revenue may be measured. For fixed-price and cost-plus-fixed-fee contracts, some estimate of the portion earned is necessary so that the revenue or fixed fee can be allocated.

In the examples so far, we measure the portion earned according to the percentage of total cost incurred. In doing so, we assume that every dollar of cost earns an equal amount of revenue. Such an assumption may not be appropriate in all cases. If the construction consists of identical or very similar items and varying costs are incurred on different items, it may be more reasonable to assume that each item produces equal revenue. Similarly, if substantial material costs or subcontracting costs are involved, large or irregular costs could distort the measurement of the prime contractor's contribution.

Because of these potential limitations on cost as a measure of the portion earned, other measures of earning are sometimes used. These include engineering or architectural estimates of the percentage of work completed, physical measures of completion (e.g., miles of highway), contract milestones reached (e.g., number of floors erected), and payroll cost or labor-hours expended. Progress billings usually are not a satisfactory measure of work done because they tend to be dictated by financial rather than production considerations.

If cost incurred as a percentage of total cost is used as an estimate of the percentage of completion, a fourth measurement problem arises. The accuracy of the estimate depends directly on the predictability of the total cost of the project. This prediction may be inaccurate, as in the illustration shown in Table 7–7. The particular procedure used there to determine each period's allocation of revenue contains an automatic error-correction mechanism. By estimating *total revenue earned to date* and then subtracting the portion previously recognized, we include in any particular year the portion earned that year plus any corrections of prior periods, all based on the most recent cost estimates.[13]

In those cases where the cost estimates are subject to large errors, percentage of completion may not provide sufficiently reliable measurements, particularly for fixed-price contracts. Keep in mind, however, that the alternative may be completed contract, wherein no revenue is recognized until completion. The accountant must decide which error is more important— failure to recognize the reward for efforts expended (as under completed

---

[13] When the current estimate of total contract cost indicates a loss, a debit to a loss account and a credit to Contract in Progress should be recorded for the *full* amount of the anticipated loss. Inventory should never be valued at more than its net realizable value, the net amount for which it can be sold. If a portion of the cost of the asset cannot be recovered through sale, then that portion represents a cost that has no future value. Charging the entire anticipated loss against the Contract in Progress account ensures that its value will never exceed net realizable value, provided that the new cost estimates are accurate. More is said about this concept in Chapter 9, in the section dealing with lower-of-cost-or-market valuation of inventories.

contract) or inaccurate and perhaps misleading measurement of periodic revenue (as under percentage of completion when cost estimates are not dependable).

## LONG-TERM SERVICE CONTRACTS

Our discussions so far have concerned the sale of products. Some interesting revenue recognition problems also exist with the sale of services to be provided under long-term contracts. Correspondence schools offer courses for a fixed fee; research and development laboratories provide research services under long-term contracts; health clubs supply a variety of services to members in exchange for membership fees paid in advance; maintenance firms sign contracts to clean offices or service equipment; and computer service bureaus process data under long-term contracts.

In these situations, there is a point of sale at which a contract is signed. The services, however, are provided later. The earning criterion strongly suggests that the point of sale is not the proper point for revenue recognition.

With long-term service contracts, sometimes revenue recognition practices have abused the underlying concepts. These abuses tended to recognize revenue as soon as possible—called "front loading" of revenue. Such practices fell into three major categories:

**1.** All revenue was recorded at the time the contract was signed. None was deferred to future periods, when services were actually performed. Indeed, in some cases not even the estimated costs of providing the services were accrued.

**2.** Many such service contracts specified long periods in which the customer could cancel and receive a full or partial refund. However, no adjustment was made for this contingency.

**3.** Cash collections were not always reasonably assured, and uncollectible accounts were not capable of being reliably estimated. Again, no reflection was given to this fact in the revenue measure.

A single authoritative solution to these problems has not been formulated. However, a number of worthwhile suggestions have been made by the American Institute of Certified Public Accountants through its Accounting Standards Committee. With respect to the timing and pattern of revenue recognition, the AICPA proposes a variety of solutions suited to differing circumstances of specific contracts. These alternatives involve practical applications of the earning criterion.

If the service transaction is a single act or consists of a series of incidental services followed by a major act, revenue should be recognized upon completion of the single or major act. For example, an employment agency that receives a fee for locating and placing an employee would recognize revenue at the time the employee is placed.

In most other long-term service contracts, revenue should be recognized in accordance with some variant of the *proportional performance method*. Proportional performance measurement is the service counterpart to percentage of completion. Revenue is recognized in relation to some measure of performance or earning. The measure of performance may vary, but the underlying concept is the same.

If performance consists of a number of identical or similar acts, the total revenue under the contract would be apportioned in relation to the number of acts performed. Service bureaus that process computerized payrolls for customers or mortgage bankers who process mortgage payments would use this method. If performance consists of a number of defined but *not identical* acts (e.g., a correspondence school's provision of lessons, progress evaluations, examinations, and grading), then the ratio of direct costs incurred to total estimated direct costs of the contract could be used. This procedure is exactly the same as the one illustrated earlier in connection with percentage of completion. Finally, if performance consists of an unspecified number of acts within a fixed time period, revenue should be recognized on a straight-line method over the specified time. Hence, a health spa that sells two-year memberships for $1,500 would recognize revenue of $62.50 per month on each membership.

Often for long-term service contracts, the costs associated with negotiating and starting the service agreements are significant. These costs—which would include commissions, legal fees, costs of credit investigation, among others—are called "initial direct costs." In accordance with the matching concept, these costs usually would be deferred and expensed in proportion to revenue recognition.

With respect to the second and third problems mentioned earlier, the recommendations agree with our intuitions. If the buyer has the right to obtain a partial refund or if such refunds are industry practice, an allowance for expected refunds should be recorded as a reduction in revenue. Similar adjustments for estimated uncollectibles would also be required. If there is a *significant* degree of uncertainty as to the collectibility of the revenue, the installment method of recognition would have to be used.

# DISCUSSION OF THE KIMBERLY-CLARK ANNUAL REPORT

Few special revenue problems are disclosed in the Kimberly-Clark Company financial statements introduced in Chapter 5. The three-year income statement shows a sizeable increase in net sales (13.5%) that occurred from 1986 to 1987. This followed a 5.7 percent increase in sales from 1985 to 1986. Of course, increases in dollar sales can result from volume increases or price increases. Elsewhere in the annual report, the company indicates that over half of the increase was the result of growth in volume. This particularly meaningful disclosure is presented for some of its product classes as well.

Notice that net sales are shown as the major operating revenue. Interest revenue and other revenue (Kimberly-Clark uses the term *income* instead of *revenue*) are reported in a non-operating segment of the income statement.

The notes to the financial statements provide no special information about Kimberly-Clark's revenue recognition policies. Accordingly, we may assume that sales revenues are recognized generally at the time of delivery, and other revenues, when they are earned and become measurable. In accordance with the required segment disclosures to be discussed in Chapter 16, the company shows in Note 11 the sales revenue attributable to each of its three product classes and to each of its major geographical areas.

On the balance sheet, Kimberly-Clark shows net accounts receivable of $519.9 million and $459.2 million at the end of 1987 and 1986, respectively. These amounts represent the cash expected to be realized. Note 9 provides more detail. In both years, over 90 percent of the accounts receivable were trade receivables arising from sales in the ordinary conduct of business. An allowance for doubtful accounts and sales discounts has been subtracted.[14] This contra asset reflects estimates of accounts that will not be collected and sales discounts that will be taken when the accounts are collected. From the latter deduction, we can infer that the company uses the gross method of recording sales revenue.

A common relationship that analysts review is that between sales and trade receivables. This ratio is called the "turnover of receivables." It provides a measure of the liquidity of the receivables. How long before an average trade receivable is collected and converted into cash? For Kimberly-Clark, the ratio in 1987 is calculated by dividing net sales by average trade receivables:

Turnover of receivables = 10.5 times [$4,884.7/(($490.5 + $440.3)/2)]

Often the turnover is divided into 365 days to determine the *average collection period*. Kimberly-Clark is collecting its receivables in 35 days (365/10.5). Both the turnover and average collection periods would need to be compared with similar calculations for prior years or with other companies before meaningful conclusions could be drawn.

## SUMMARY

This chapter focuses attention on three issues: (1) what constitutes revenue, (2) when revenue should be recognized, and (3) how much revenue should be recognized.

---

[14] Form 10-K filed by Kimberly-Clark with the SEC reveals that on December 31, 1987 the Allowance for Doubtful Accounts was $5.1 million and the Allowance for Sales Discounts was $4.8 million.

We answer the first question by defining *revenue* as the cash received, cash to be received, or cash needs satisfied during a period as a result of the firm's efforts associated with supplying goods and services to customers. This definition has three elements: (1) revenue is a period concept, (2) it measures the reward resulting from productive activity during the period, and (3) the reward is expressed in terms of ultimate cash receipts or the equivalent.

The definition of revenue provides guidelines for what to recognize and the maximum amount to be recognized. The second question, concerning the timing of revenue recognition, is satisfied by the revenue recognition concept. Two conditions have to be met before revenue is recorded in financial accounting. Revenue must have been earned, and it must be measurable with a reasonable degree of reliability. *Earned* means that the business has exerted its major sales/production efforts and that a major portion of the costs has been incurred. *Measurable* means that the total amount of revenue is verifiable, that its assignment to different accounting periods (if applicable) is both objective and reliable, and that the estimated amount of the ultimate cash collection is reasonably assured.

We illustrate how the revenue recognition concept attempts to balance desirable but conflicting guidelines—timeliness, verifiability, and representational faithfulness. We also explore the application of this postulate to revenue recognition at times other than the point of sale as well as to special situations existing at the point of sale.

The final question of how much revenue to recognize is answered in part by the definition of revenue and the revenue recognition assumption. However, there are instances that require an adjustment of the original measurement. These adjustments fall into three categories. First, part of the cash receipt may represent something other than a reward for activities associated with the supplying of goods and services to customers and hence may not be revenue—for example, sales and excise taxes and container deposits. Secondly, the cash received or to be received may not yet have been earned because additional efforts are required on the part of the firm after the initial entry—for example, production, storage, financing, and servicing. Finally, events subsequent to the initial entry may alter the amount of cash eventually to be received—for example, uncollectibles, returns, and discounts.

The theory behind each of these types of adjustments is discussed, and illustrative entries are presented. In the case of uncollectibles, returns, and discounts, contra revenue accounts are used to segregate the particular decreases in revenues for informational purposes. In some cases, contra asset accounts also are used to reduce overstated trade accounts receivable. Most firms, in presenting their income statements to external audiences, condense the sales and contra revenue accounts. As a consequence, the vast majority of income statements begin with the caption "net sales," the returns and discounts already having been subtracted.

# Appendix: Accounting under the Installment Method

The installment method of accounting is briefly discussed in Chapter 7. However, the method generally is not appropriate for external financial reporting. Most installment sales are recorded as revenue at the time the goods are delivered to the buyer. Except for the use of a separate installment receivables category and the accruing of interest on the unpaid balances, there is little to distinguish the recording of installment sales from the recording of any other sales.

However, the *installment method* of recognizing income has been employed for tax purposes for a long time. It also has been reinstated as part of generally accepted accounting principles to handle problem areas in retail land sales and initial franchise fees where collecting the cash may be a major earning function and/or collectibility is highly uncertain. The example below illustrates its use in a land sale. As you follow through the entries, note how the recognition of gross margin or gross income (sales less cost of sales) parallels the receipt of cash.

## Illustration

Assume that a developer sells plots of land in a new subdivision on installment contracts. Let us follow two sales. On July 1, 1991 the company sells one plot of land having a cost of $48,000 to a customer for $60,000. The $60,000 is to be paid in five installments of $12,000.[15] The first installment is due immediately; the subsequent payments are due every six months on December 31 and June 30. On April 1, 1992, the company sells another plot of land having a cost of $70,000 to a customer for $100,000, payable in five installments of $20,000.

## Journal Entries

The following entries are made in 1991:

### July 1, 1991

| | | |
|---|---|---|
| Installment Accounts Receivable — 1991 | 60,000 | |
|     Installment Sales | | 60,000 |
|     To record sale of land. | | |
| Cost of Installment Sales | 48,000 | |
|     Inventory of Unsold Land | | 48,000 |
|     To record cost of land sold. | | |
| Cash | 12,000 | |
|     Installment Accounts Receivable — 1991 | | 12,000 |
|     To record receipt of first installment. | | |

---

[15] This example excludes any interest charges on the unpaid balances. In most cases, each payment has an interest element added to it. As indicated earlier, this interest revenue is the compensation for delayed payment and collection efforts.

December 31, 1991

Cash . . . . . . . . . . . . . . . . . . . . . . . . . . . . . . . . .  12,000
      Installment Accounts Receivable — 1991. . . . . . . . . . .      12,000
   To record receipt of second installment.

Installment Sales . . . . . . . . . . . . . . . . . . . . . . . . .  60,000
      Cost of Installment Sales . . . . . . . . . . . . . . . . .      48,000
      Deferred Gross Margin — 1991 . . . . . . . . . . . . . .      12,000
   To close installment sales and cost of sales for the year.

Deferred Gross Margin — 1991 . . . . . . . . . . . . . . . .  4,800
      Realized Gross Margin — 1991. . . . . . . . . . . . . . .      4,800
   To recognize the gross margin realized in 1991 based on
   cash collected.

Twenty percent of the total sales price ($12,000/$60,000) is gross margin. Therefore, 20 percent of each dollar of cash receipt is deemed to be gross margin. The gross margin percentage is applied to the cash collections to calculate realized gross margin (20% × $24,000 = $4,800).[16] There is another way of arriving at the same result. Because 40 percent of the total expected cash collections ($24,000/$60,000) is received in 1991, 40 percent of the gross margin is recognized in 1991 (40% × $12,000 = $4,800). The entries for 1992 are similar:

April 1, 1992

Installment Accounts Receivable — 1992. . . . . . . . . . . .  100,000
      Installment Sales . . . . . . . . . . . . . . . . . . . .    100,000
   To record sale of land.

Cost of Installment Sales . . . . . . . . . . . . . . . . . . .  70,000
      Inventory of Unsold Land. . . . . . . . . . . . . . . . .     70,000
   To record cost of land sold.

Cash . . . . . . . . . . . . . . . . . . . . . . . . . . . . . . .  20,000
      Installment Accounts Receivable — 1992. . . . . . . . . .     20,000
   To record receipt of first installment from 1992 sale.

June 30, 1992

Cash . . . . . . . . . . . . . . . . . . . . . . . . . . . . . . .  12,000
      Installment Accounts Receivable — 1991. . . . . . . . . .     12,000
   To record receipt of third installment from 1991 sale.

September 30, 1992

Cash . . . . . . . . . . . . . . . . . . . . . . . . . . . . . . .  20,000
      Installment Accounts Receivable — 1992. . . . . . . . . .     20,000
   To record receipt of second installment from 1992 sale.

---

[16] If many sales are involved, the gross margin percentage is an average of all installment sales for 1991. This average is applied to all cash collections of 1991 installment receivables, regardless of when the cash is received. In future years, cash receipts would have to be identified by year so that the gross margin percentage appropriate for each particular year could be applied.

December 31, 1992

| | | |
|---|---|---|
| Cash . . . . . . . . . . . . . . . . . . . . . . . . . . . . . . . . . . . . | 12,000 | |
| Installment Accounts Receivable — 1991 . . . . . . . . . | | 12,000 |
| To record receipt of fourth installment from 1991 sale. | | |
| Installment Sales . . . . . . . . . . . . . . . . . . . . . . . . . . . | 100,000 | |
| Cost of Installment Sales . . . . . . . . . . . . . . . . . | | 70,000 |
| Deferred Gross Margin — 1992 . . . . . . . . . . . . . . | | 30,000 |
| To close installment sales and cost of sales for the year. | | |
| Deferred Gross Margin — 1992 . . . . . . . . . . . . . . . | 12,000 | |
| Realized Gross Margin . . . . . . . . . . . . . . . . . . . | | 12,000 |
| To recognize 1992 gross margin realized in 1992 based on cash collections ($40,000 cash collected × 30% gross margin percentage for 1992). | | |
| Deferred Gross Margin — 1991 . . . . . . . . . . . . . . . | 4,800 | |
| Realized Gross Margin . . . . . . . . . . . . . . . . . . . | | 4,800 |
| To recognize 1991 gross margin realized in 1992 based on cash collections ($24,000 cash collected × 20% gross margin percentage for 1991). | | |

## Financial Statements

The Realized Gross Margin account appears on the income statement as a type of net revenue. However, the amount of installment sales and cost of sales each period should be disclosed if they are significant. Table 7A–1 shows how the top part of the income statement would look and how the installment receivables would appear on the balance sheet.

**TABLE 7A–1**    Financial Statement Presentation under the Installment Method

| | *1991* | *1992* |
|---|---|---|
| Income Statement: | | |
| Sales | $60,000 | $100,000 |
| Cost of goods sold | 48,000 | 70,000 |
| Gross margin | $12,000 | $ 30,000 |
| Less: Deferred gross margin of the current year | 7,200 | 18,000 |
| Realized gross margin on current year sales | $ 4,800 | $ 12,000 |
| Realized gross margin from prior year sales | — | 4,800 |
| Gross margin realized | $ 4,800 | $ 16,800 |
| Current Assets Section of Balance Sheet: | | |
| Installment receivables | $36,000 | $ 72,000 |
| Less: Deferred gross margin | 7,200 | 20,400 |
| | $28,800 | $ 51,600 |

The balance in the Deferred Gross Margin account should appear on the balance sheet as a contra asset to Installment Receivables. Sometimes it appears on the equity side among the liabilities—a curious classification because the customer has no claim against the firm's assets. Offsetting the Deferred Gross Margin reduces the balance of receivables to an amount equal to the unrecovered cost of the items sold. This is the only asset value that can exist and still be consistent with nonrecognition of gross margin at the time of sale. No increased asset value is appropriate, because no income associated with the uncollected cash has been recognized under this method.

# PROBLEMS AND CASETTES

### 7–1. Treatment of Advance Ticket Sales

Happy Jack's Funfair Amusement Park is open from April 1 through September 30 of each year. Customers can purchase books of admission tickets at $40 per book. The book contains 10 tickets good for admission any time from April through December. The regular admission price is $5. The following statements are prepared for April, May, and June:

|  | *April* | *May* | *June* |
|---|---|---|---|
| Sales . . . . . . . . . . . . . . . | $14,650 | $28,350 | $37,750 |
| Expenses. . . . . . . . . . . . . | 7,940 | 12,180 | 13,780 |
| Net income . . . . . . . . . . . | $ 6,710 | $16,170 | $23,970 |

Sales include the cash received from the sale of coupon books during each month. The number of books sold was 120 in April, 375 in May, and 525 in June. An analysis of admissions reveals that 660, 2,430, and 5,115 admission-book tickets have been presented in the three months, respectively. No entries have been made for these individual tickets.

### Required:

a. Prepare corrected income statements for each of the three months. Also, determine the liability for tickets outstanding at the end of each month.
b. What would you do with any balance remaining in the liability account on September 30 when the park closes down?

### 7–2. Comparison of Estimation Methods for Uncollectible Accounts

The following information is taken from the accounting records of Boltog Company on December 31, 1989 before annual adjusting entries are made:

| | |
|---|---|
| Sales . . . . . . . . . . . . . . . . . . . . . . . . . . . . . | $818,700 credit |
| Accounts receivable . . . . . . . . . . . . . . . . . . . . | 378,900 debit |
| Allowance for doubtful accounts . . . . . . . . . . . . . | 4,450 credit |

**Required:**

*a.* Prepare journal entries to record the estimate of uncollectibles for 1989 assuming:

1. Uncollectibles are estimated to be 2% of sales.
2. Uncollectibles are estimated to be 5% of the gross accounts receivable outstanding.
3. Uncollectibles are to be based on an aging schedule using the following percentages: 0–30 days, .8 of 1 percent; 31–60 days, 2 percent; 61–120 days, 5 percent; and Over 120 days, 40 percent. The ages of the accounts are as follows:

| | |
|---|---:|
| 0–30 days . . . . . . . . . . . . . . . . . . . . . . . . . . . . . . . . . | $251,000 |
| 31–60 days . . . . . . . . . . . . . . . . . . . . . . . . . . . . . . . | 68,500 |
| 61–120 days . . . . . . . . . . . . . . . . . . . . . . . . . . . . . | 33,000 |
| Over 120 days . . . . . . . . . . . . . . . . . . . . . . . . . . . | 26,400 |
| Total . . . . . . . . . . . . . . . . . . . . . . . . . . . . | $378,900 |

*b.* Assume that before the estimate for uncollectibles is made, $5,000 of specific accounts receivable are identified as being uncollectible and are written off. (The accounts written off are from the Over-120-days group.)

1. Prepare the journal entry to record the specific write-off.
2. How does this information affect your three estimates from part *a?*

**7–3. Accounting for Construction Contracts Using Percentage of Completion**
Sagging Suspension Bridge Corporation erects large spans over superhighways. Most projects require 15 to 22 months to complete. During the period 1990–92 the firm worked on four major projects. Relevant data applicable to each one are presented below (in thousands of dollars):

| Project Number | Contract Price | Total Estimated Cost | Cost Incurred 1990 | Cost Incurred 1991 | Cost Incurred 1992 | Year Completed |
|---|---|---|---|---|---|---|
| A510 | $750 | $700 | $700 | — | — | 1990 |
| A511 | 900 | 720 | 120 | $420 | $180 | 1992 |
| A513 | 680 | 600 | — | 300 | 300 | 1992 |
| A514 | 720 | 650 | — | 195 | 325 | 1993 |

**Required:**

*a.* Determine the amount of gross margin to be recognized in each year if percentage of completion is used to recognize revenue.
*b.* What would you do if the total of the actual costs incurred under the contract differed from the estimated cost?
*c.* The bookkeeper of Sagging Suspension drew up the following schedule of gross margin under "conventional" accounting (in thousands):

| | 1990 | 1991 | 1992 |
|---|---|---|---|
| Sales. . . . . . . . . . . . . . . . . . . . . . . . . . . . . . | $750 | $  0 | $1,580 |
| Construction costs . . . . . . . . . . . . . . . . | 820 | 915 | 805 |
| Gross margin . . . . . . . . . . . . . . . . . . . . | $(70) | $(915) | $  775 |

Do you agree that this is the result from conventional accounting? Explain. Revise the figures to show the margins under a proper interpretation of the conventional completed contract (sales) basis of accounting.

d. Explain why your revised figures in *c* are still an unsatisfactory measure of the firm's activity.

## 7–4. Recognition of Revenue in Unusual Transactions

The Harper Farm Equipment Company sells tractors and other farm apparatus primarily to individual farmers, sometimes in rather unusual deals. Three of those arrangements are described below:

1. In March, the firm exchanged a new tractor for a five-year lease on some adjacent ground to the east of its present location. The tractor cost Harper $7,200 and was listed to sell at $9,000. Harper needed the ground for storage and display of equipment. The firm could have leased similar land on its west side for $1,500 a year, but Harper would have had to spend $800 for grading.

2. On May 15, the company swapped a power tiller with a cost of $600 and a list price of $750 for 30 shares of stock in a regional cattle stockyard. At the time of the exchange, the shares had a market value of $23 per share. During the period from May 15 to December 31, Harper received dividends of $2.00 per share. The value of the stock was quoted at $24.50 per share on December 31.

3. Harper Farm Equipment in early September exchanged a corn picker for a claim on 4,000 bushels of corn. The machine cost Harper $5,800 and was priced to sell at $7,000. At harvest time in late September, the corn could be sold to the local grain exchange for $1.68 per bushel. Expecting that grain prices might go up, the management of Harper stored the grain until December and then sold it for $1.85 a bushel.

### Required

In each of these instances, how much revenue should Harper Farm Equipment record? Explain.

## 7–5. Calculation of Missing Amounts Related to Revenues, Receivables, and Uncollectibles

Some partial data for two independent companies are listed below. Supply the dollar amounts indicated by the numbers (1) through (8).

| | Company A | | Company B | |
|---|---|---|---|---|
| | *Jan. 1* | *Dec. 31* | *Jan. 1* | *Dec. 31* |
| Accounts receivable (gross) . . . . . | $75,000 | (2) | (5) | $135,000 |
| Accounts receivable (net) . . . . . . | (1) | 51,500 | $105,000 | 119,000 |
| Allowance for doubtful accounts . . . | 6,000 | 7,500 | 15,000 | (6) |
| Transactions during year: | | | | |
| Credit sales . . . . . . . . . . | | $537,000 | | (8) |
| Cash collections from | | | | |
| customers . . . . . . . . . | | (3) | | $767,500 |
| Estimated uncollectible | | | | |
| accounts . . . . . . . . . | | (4) | | 9,700 |
| Write-off of specific | | | | |
| uncollectibles . . . . . . . . | | 9,000 | | (7) |

### 7–6. Uncollectibles under the Allowance Method: Entries and Discussion

Perry Corporation prior to 1989 used the direct write-off method for uncollectible accounts. A Bad Debt Loss was recorded whenever an account was specifically identified as uncollectible. Upon the advice of its accountants, Perry installed an allowance system beginning on January 1, 1989. Each month Sales Uncollectibles would be debited and Allowance for Doubtful Accounts would be credited for 1.5 percent of credit sales. Specific write-offs were to be debited to the allowance account and recoveries were to be credited to the allowance account. Then at year-end, an adjusting entry would be made based on an aging of accounts receivable.

During 1989, credit sales were $5,000,000. Also during the year, $60,000 of specific uncollectibles were written off, and recoveries of accounts written off were $8,000. On December 31, 1989, there were $1,150,000 of outstanding accounts. A summary of the aging schedule and the respective uncollectibility percentages to be used are given below:

| Aging Category | Balance | Estimated Percent Uncollectibles |
|---|---|---|
| Under 90 days | $ 760,000 | 1% |
| 91–180 days | 310,000 | 5% |
| 181–300 days | 68,000 | 50% |
| Over 300 days | 12,000 | 90% |
| Total | $1,150,000 | |

**Required:**

a. Journalize the entries affecting the Allowance for Doubtful Accounts during 1989—the preliminary estimate based on credit sales, write-offs, and recoveries.
b. Prepare the adjusting entry based on the aging schedule at the end of the year.
c. Management is very surprised at the size of the adjustment made in part b. The estimate of 1.5 percent of credit sales and the estimates used in the aging schedule were thought to be very accurate. Management expected a very minor adjustment, no more than plus or minus $3,000. Can you explain why there could be such a large adjustment in 1989 even though the estimates were accurate?
d. Klaus Trophobia, the chief bookkeeper, wants to return to the direct write-off method used in 1988 and before. He says, "Accounting should record objective facts based on realized transactions, not guesses; recording a loss for accounts that we expect to go bad in the future is not sound accounting." Evaluate and reply to his argument.

### 7–7. Accounting for a Highway Contract Using Percentage of Completion

Rippling Road Construction Company entered into a contract for a 20-mile circumferential highway around town. The firm was to be responsible for grading and pouring concrete and for constructing 10 bridges. The contract price was $2,000,000, and the estimated cost was $1,600,000 ($60,000 per mile and $40,000 per bridge). Payments under the contract are received according to the following schedule: $80,000 per mile at the time each mile is finished and $20,000 per mile when the entire highway is completed and approved. Final approval takes place in 1991. Data related to the contract are summarized on the next page.

|                             | *1988*    | *1989*    | *1990*    |
|-----------------------------|-----------|-----------|-----------|
| Costs incurred . . . . . . . . . . . . . . . | $480,000  | $800,000  | $320,000  |
| Number of miles finished . . . . . . . . . . | 3         | 12        | 5         |
| Number of bridges constructed. . . . . . . . | 2         | 4         | 4         |

### Required:

*a.* Determine the amount of revenue and gross margin to be recognized in each year under the percentage-of-completion method using cost incurred as a percentage of total cost as the measure of work done.

*b.* Determine the amount of cash payment received by the company each year under the contract.

*c.* The controller recommends that revenue be recognized as each mile and bridge is completed. She suggests that this method does not delay recognition until cash is received but at the same time avoids the problem of making estimates inherent under percentage of completion. What would revenue be each year under her plan? Explain carefully how you arrived at your answer. What are the advantages and disadvantages of this plan relative to that in part *a*?

### 7–8. Calculating Revenue: Sales Basis and Installment Method

Short Circuit Appliance Company sells television sets, video recorders, and stereo systems on the installment-sales basis. Selected data for 1990 and 1991 are summarized below:

|                             | *1990*    | *1991*    |
|-----------------------------|-----------|-----------|
| Installment sales . . . . . . . . . . . . . . . . . . . | $200,000  | $270,000  |
| Cost of installment sales . . . . . . . . . . . . . . . | 130,000   | 189,000   |
| Selling and general expenses . . . . . . . . . . . . . | 31,000    | 42,000    |
| Cash collections from customers:                        |           |           |
| On 1990 sales . . . . . . . . . . . . . . . . . . . | 105,000   | 85,000    |
| On 1991 sales . . . . . . . . . . . . . . . . . . . |           | 140,000   |

### Required:

*a.* Calculate the amount of net income for 1990 and 1991, assuming that the company recognizes revenue at the time of sale.

*b.* Calculate the amount of net income for 1990 and 1991, assuming that the company recognizes revenue using the installment method.

*c.* Calculate the balance in the Deferred Gross Margin account(s) on December 31, 1991. Where should this be reported on the balance sheet? Why? (Knowledge of the appendix is required.)

### 7–9. Revenue Recognition in Unusual Situations

The following paragraphs describe different situations in which application of the revenue recognition concept is not clear.

1. An advertising agency in 1989 makes a number of one-minute spot advertisements for a local radio station. The latter planned to use the advertisements to

promote its own programs. The cost of development and recording to the advertising agency was $50,000. In exchange for the advertisements, the agency received a specified number of minutes of free air time from the radio station. There was a ready market for the air time, and the agency normally would have paid $80,000 for this amount of time. In 1990, the agency used the air time in advertising campaigns for other clients. Other costs of developing copy and placing ads for these clients totaled $25,000. It billed the clients $115,000. How much revenue and income should the advertising agency recognize in 1989 and 1990?

2. G. G. Wilson operates the family farm with his brother, Bert. G. G. has primary responsibility for actual growing operations, while Bert handles most marketing and other business activities associated with the farm. During the season, G. G. spent $265,000 in direct costs putting acreage into corn. His efforts resulted in a yield of 255,000 bushels of corn. At the time of harvest, the market price on the regional grain exchange was $3.30 per bushel. Bert decided to sell 180,000 bushels at that price immediately after harvest. Then he decided to wait and see what happened to corn prices before disposing of the remaining 75,000 bushels. The closing price on the exchange on the last day of the farm's fiscal year was $3.35. In the next fiscal year Bert sold 50,000 bushels of corn for $3.40 and 25,000 bushels for $3.20.

How much revenue and income should the Wilson Farm recognize in the first year? In the second year?

3. Winkum, Blinkum, and Nodd is a consulting firm that installs complex computer information systems. The firm signed a contract for $2,400,000 with a large manufacturing company. The contract calls for the firm to design the system, advise on the purchase of hardware, prepare all necessary software, implement the system, and test it. All of this is to be completed within a three-year period.

Discuss the method of revenue recognition that you feel the consulting firm should use on this engagement.

4. Silhouette Spa sells 30-month memberships in its health club facilities for $1,500. The total costs of servicing a membership are estimated to be $600. Currently, the company recognizes the membership fee as revenue in the year of sale and matches against it the estimated costs of $600. Its accountants have suggested that it recognize membership fee revenues and associated costs over the period of membership.

What is the difference between the two methods in terms of income measurement? Which do you prefer?

## 7–10. Recording Credit Card Sales

The Lost Horizon Novelty Shop accepts two types of credit cards from customers purchasing its merchandise. On VISA charges (a bank credit card), Lost Horizon deposits the charge slip in the bank at the face value less a 2 percent transaction fee. On Diners Club charges, the shop sends the invoices to the regional office of Diners Club, which remits 95 percent of all approved charges within four working days.

During September the following transactions took place:

Sept. 6   Total sales, $890. Cash sales were $80. VISA invoices amounted to $500, and Diners Club invoices amounted to $310.

9 Received payment from Diners Club for all charges except one for $60 which Lost Horizon erroneously had allowed to be charged on a canceled credit card.

15 Being unable to locate the customer with the canceled credit card, Lost Horizon wrote off the account to the Allowance for Doubtful Accounts.

**Required:**

a. Prepare journal entries to record the above transactions.

b. Where should the 2 percent transaction fee and the 5 percent discount appear on the income statement?

c. Assume you are a retailer who has been making credit sales for a number of years using your own credit card. MasterCard approaches you and suggests that you should accept MasterCard instead of your own credit card. What financial information would you use in deciding whether or not to change?

**7–11. Journal Entries and Year-End Adjustments Using the Sales Basis**

The financial statements for the first 11 months of the year for National Merchants Company show the following balances among the accounts:

|  | Debit | Credit |
|---|---|---|
| Sales | | $480,000 |
| Sales returns | $ 8,900 | |
| Sales discounts | 3,000 | |
| Provision for doubtful accounts | 9,422 | |
| Accounts receivable | 128,800 | |
| Allowance for doubtful accounts | | 20,600 |

The company sells on terms of 1 percent cash discount allowed for all accounts paid within 15 days of the invoice date. A monthly adjusting entry is made to reflect the fact that 2 percent of sales (after deducting returns) is not expected to be collected.

During December, the following transactions occur:

1. Sales of $108,000, of which $16,000 are cash sales.
2. Gross amounts of accounts collected, $156,000, of which $134,400 represents gross accounts collected within the discount period.
3. Gross amounts of returns, $2,200.
4. Accounts charged off as uncollectible, $11,700.
5. Recoveries made of accounts previously written off, $100.
6. The adjusting entry for doubtful accounts is made.

**Required:**

a. Journalize the December transactions.

b. A detailed study of the outstanding accounts receivable at year-end indicates that 15 percent of them will eventually prove uncollectible. Assuming this information is correct, what does this suggest about the accuracy of the firm's estimate for doubtful accounts? Can you suggest a possible reason for the disparity by reviewing how the estimate is made?

*c.* Assume that December sales were spread evenly over the month and that most customers do not pay until the 15th day. What adjustment could be made on December 31 with respect to sales discounts? Would you make it? Explain.

**7–12. Revenue Recognition under Long-term Contracts for Services**

Fixit Fast Maintenance Service enters into long-term contracts with manufacturers in high technology areas. For a fee of $8,000, payable in advance, Fixit Fast agrees to service a certain type of equipment for a two-year period. The maintenance contract covers routine maintenance and overhaul only; any fees for repairs arising from extraordinary events or damage are billed separately. Under the contract, Fixit Fast is required to adjust the equipment each month for five months and then to overhaul it in the sixth month. Thus, under each contract, Fixit will provide 20 adjustments and 4 overhauls. An adjustment costs about $150 in service labor time; an overhaul costs about $450 in labor and $300 in parts.

During 1990 and 1991, respectively, five and seven maintenance contracts were signed, and the advance payments were received. Fixit Fast performed all its contractual obligations under the contracts in both years. It made 40 service calls for adjustments in 1990 and 100 in 1991; it did 5 overhauls in 1990 and 17 in 1991.

The following costs were incurred in each of the two years:

|                          | 1990    | 1991     |
| ------------------------ | ------- | -------- |
| Service labor costs.     | $8,300  | $22,700  |
| Material costs.          | 1,400   | 5,200    |
| Other operating expenses | 2,200   | 4,600    |
| Administrative expenses  | 4,000   | 4,000    |

Fixit Fast Maintenance Service decides to recognize revenue under a proportional performance method in which $200 revenue is to be recognized for each adjustment performed and $1,000 is to be recognized for each overhaul performed.

**Required:**

*a.* How were the proportional performance criteria used to calculate the $200 and $1,000 revenue figures?

*b.* Using the company's accounting practices as described, prepare income statements for both 1990 and 1991.

*c.* What amounts would appear on the December 31, 1990 and 1991 balance sheets as Unearned Maintenance Revenue? How would this account be classified?

*d.* Evaluate the company's revenue recognition practices. What alternative practices might it have used? Are these better or worse than what it chose?

*e.* What accounting treatment would you recommend if commissions, legal fees, and other initial direct costs of securing the contracts had to be paid?

**7–13. Examining a Company's Policy on Revenue Recognition**

Baird Corporation includes the following note with its financial statements:

*E. Revenue Recognition:* In general, the Company and its subsidiaries recognize revenues on equipment sales when units are shipped. Shipment of a completed unit is sometimes delayed at the customer's request. However, in such instances, revenues are recognized when the customer accepts the related billing. With respect to large, multi-year, fixed-price contracts principally with the United States Government, the Company uses the percentage of completion method of accounting.

In those instances where the Company is responsible for installing equipment, the estimated costs for such services are accrued when revenue is recognized.

With respect to cost reimbursement type contracts with the United States Government, the Company recognizes revenue on the basis of allowable monthly incurred costs plus fee.

### Required:

*a.* Why does Baird Corporation use more than one method of revenue recognition?

*b.* When shipment is delayed at the customer's request, Baird Corporation recognizes revenue before the units are shipped. Does this practice violate the revenue recognition criteria? How does Baird's practice differ from the "completed production method?" What entries would it make for units billed but not shipped?

*c.* What is the difference between the accounting for the two types of contracts with the United States Government? On which is the measurement more reliable?

*d.* On installation contracts, estimated costs are accrued. Why? What journal entries are involved? Would a procedure of deferring recognition of some of the revenue until installation is complete be an appropriate alternative?

## 7–14. Comparing Revenue Calculations: Completed Production and Sales Basis

Wishy Washer Manufacturing Company manufactures automatic clothes washers and driers. It sells about 20,000 units a year under firm contract to Valley Appliance, a large appliance chain. The contract calls for a sales price of $200 per unit. (The manufacturing costs are $150 per unit.) The units are produced with Valley Appliance's brand name attached to them and are shipped to various locations as directed by Valley Appliance. Sometimes a unit may stay in Wishy Washer's inventory for two or three months. Valley Appliance is billed quarterly and is obligated to pay for all 20,000 units produced.

The contract production consumes about half of Wishy Washer's output, although the remaining output varies from month to month. The other units, which are virtually identical to the contract units except for the brand name, are sold to independent dealers.

During the month of September, Wishy Washer engages in the following transactions.

1. It makes 8,300 units, 5,000 units under the contract and 3,300 units under its own brand name.
2. It ships 3,500 of the contract units in September and 1,000 in October.
3. It sells 1,000 of its own units in September at an average price of $225 per unit and another 1,000 units in October at an average price of $240 per unit.

Assume that there were no units in inventory at the beginning of September. Wishy Washer recognizes revenue on a completion-of-production basis for the contract units and on a sales-delivery basis for the units sold under its own brand name.

### Required:

*a.* Calculate the amount of revenue and cost of goods sold that the company will show in September *and* October. Show the amounts for contract units and other units separately and then combine them in total amounts.

b. Calculate the amounts that the company will show in inventory at the end of September. Show the inventories of contract units separately from those of the other units. How does their valuation on the balance sheet differ?

c. What journal entry did Wishy Washer make in October when it shipped 1,000 units to Valley Appliance locations?

d. The bookkeeper has suggested that all units be handled the same way since the units are identical except for the nameplate. Do you agree?

**7–15. Journal Entries Using Percentage of Completion and Completed Contract**

Dru P. Cable Company signed a contract to construct an office building at a fixed price of $3.0 million. Estimated costs are $2.4 million. The financial agreement specified that the contractor was to receive $200,000 immediately. Progress billings were to be made at various times as specified in the contract based on approved work to date. However, 10 percent of each progress billing was to be retained until final approval of the building; 90 percent was due within 30 days of the billing date. The 10-percent retainer less the $200,000 initial advance was payable 60 days after final inspection.

Yearly data relating to this contract are summarized below (in thousands):

| Year | Costs Incurred | Estimated Cost to Complete | Progress Billings | Cash Collections |
|------|------|------|------|------|
| 1 | $ 560 | $1,900 | $ 500 | $ 520* |
| 2 | 1,200 | 800 | 1,400 | 1,100 |
| 3 | 860 | — | 1,100 | 1,020⁺ |

*Includes $200,000 initial advance.
⁺$360,000 cash was collected in Year 4.

**Required:**

a. Prepare journal entries for each year, assuming that the completed contract method was used. Indicate where and in what amounts each account (other than cash) would appear on the financial statements for each of the three years.

b. Repeat part a, assuming that the company uses percentage of completion.

**7–16. Revenue Recognition for Franchises**

Auntie Pasto, Inc., sells franchises to operate Italian restaurants under the name Auntie Pasto. The contracts with the franchisee provide for the following arrangements:

1. The franchisee pays an initial fee of $200,000, of which $80,000 is paid in cash at the time the franchise is signed. The balance is due in three annual payments of $40,000 each, plus interest at a realistic rate of 10 percent.

2. The franchisee may cancel the agreement any time. If cancellation occurs before the franchise is opened, the franchisee is entitled to receive back all amounts paid except $40,000, which is estimated to be equal to the value of services rendered. If cancellation occurs after the franchise is opened but before three years have expired, the franchisee is entitled to receive back 50 percent of the amounts paid. After three years, there is no refund upon cancellation.

3. In addition to the initial fee, the franchisee is required to pay to Auntie Pasto, Inc., a fee equal to 1 percent of gross sales.

4. Auntie Pasto, Inc., will render the following services to the franchisee—site selection, construction design and supervision, obtaining of financing, training of franchisee's employees, installation of accounting and quality control systems, and continuing advice on menus, promotion, and other management problems.

Four franchises were sold during 1990 as indicated below:

| Number | Date Sold | Date of Opening | Franchisee Sales in 1990 |
|---|---|---|---|
| 1 | Feb. 1 | Aug. 10 | $700,000 |
| 2 | July 1 | — | — |
| 3 | Aug. 1 | Nov. 18 | 97,000 |
| 4 | Nov. 1 | — | — |

The purchaser of the second franchise canceled, and appropriate amounts were refunded.

### Required:

a. Discuss how and when Auntie Pasto, Inc., should recognize revenue.

b. Prepare a schedule of revenue, classified by type (e.g., initial fee, continuing fees, interest), that you would recognize in 1990.

**7–17. Preparing Journal Entries and Adjustments for Estimated Uncollectibles and Returns**

The December 31, 1990 balance sheet of Highly Distinct Industries shows among its assets the following:

| | | |
|---|---:|---:|
| Accounts receivable | | $306,000 |
| Less: Allowance for uncollectibles | $14,000 | |
| Allowance for returns | 12,200 | 26,200 |
| | | $279,800 |

The transactions which took place in 1991 are summarized as follows:

| | |
|---|---:|
| Sales on account | $1,264,000 |
| Sales returns | 67,900 |
| Cash collected from customers | 1,086,200 |
| Accounts written off as uncollectible | 14,400 |

### Required:

a. Prepare journal entries to record the preceding transactions.

b. Prepare the adjusting entry for 1991 uncollectibles assuming that the company were to determine them under each of the following methods:

1. 1.5% of credit sales.

2. 5% of gross accounts receivable.

3. An aging of accounts receivable indicates that $23,000 will not be collected. Which of these methods do you prefer? Why?

    *c.* Highly Distinct's policy is to maintain its allowance for sales returns equal to 4 percent of gross accounts receivable. Make the journal entry to record the estimate for sales returns on December 31, 1991. (Your exact journal entry may be influenced by the particular entry you made in part *a* for sales returns.)

    *d.* Assume that in addition to the $14,400 of accounts written off during the year, two large customers owing a total of $67,400 went bankrupt when their businesses were completely wiped out as a result of severe forest fires in California. These had been old, established, and reliable customers. How would you record the write-off of these two accounts? Explain.

**7–18. Recording Transactions under the Installment Method**

(Knowledge of the appendix is necessary.) Industry Equipment Corporation sells large machinery installations on the installment plan. On September 1, 1989, Industry Equipment entered into an installment sales contract with Gigantic Production Company. The latter purchased a machinery installation with a sales price of $1,000,000. The cost of the installation to Industry Equipment was $835,000. The installment contract called for five equal annual payments of $200,000 due on September 1, beginning in 1989. In addition, an interest payment must be made on September 1, 1990 and subsequent years, equal to 12 percent of the unpaid balance.

**Required:**

    *a.* Prepare journal entries for the 1989 and 1990 transactions, assuming that Industry Equipment uses the installment method of recognizing revenue.

    *b.* How would the accounts you employed in *a* be classified on the financial statements in 1989 and 1990? What amounts would appear in these accounts?

    *c.* What amount of income as a result of the above transaction would Industry Equipment record in 1989 and 1990 under the conventional sales method of revenue recognition? Is this a better reflection of the firm's activities?

**7–19. Uncollectible Accounts: Entries, Aging, and Statement Presentation**

The Chaos Corporation has recently been turned down for a loan because of the "poor quality" of its accounts receivable. The president has called you in as a consultant. The following report that deals with the firm's credit sales, accounts receivable, and so forth since the firm's founding in 1987 has been prepared for you:

|  | *1987* | *1988* | *1989* |
|---|---|---|---|
| Sales on account . . . . . . . . . . . . . . | $165,000 | $247,500 | $157,500 |
| Cash collections: |  |  |  |
| From 1987 sales. . . . . . . . . . . . . | 135,000 | 24,700 | 2,300 |
| From 1988 sales. . . . . . . . . . . . . | — | 210,000 | 31,500 |
| From 1989 sales. . . . . . . . . . . . . | — | — | 135,000 |
| Estimate of bad debts . . . . . . . . . . . | 3,300 | 4,950 | 3,150 |
| Specific accounts written off: |  |  |  |
| From 1987 sales. . . . . . . . . . . . . | 300 | 2,400 | 300 |
| From 1988 sales. . . . . . . . . . . . . | — | 700 | 2,700 |
| From 1989 sales. . . . . . . . . . . . . | — | — | 300 |

**Required:**

a. Set up ledger accounts for Sales, Accounts Receivable, Cash, Sales Uncollectibles, and Allowance for Doubtful Accounts. Record the entries over the three-year period.

b. How would the accounts receivable be shown on a position statement at the end of each year?

c. How has the company been determining its estimate of bad debts?

d. An aging schedule of accounts receivable at the end of 1989 shows the following:

| Age | Amount |
|---|---|
| Current | $10,500 |
| 0–60 days past due | 4,500 |
| 60 days–6 months past due | 3,900 |
| 6 months–1 year past due | 3,300 |
| Over 1 year past due | 2,600 |
| Total | $24,800 |

You determine from experience with similar firms in the industry that the following uncollectibility percentages are reasonable for each category: 1 percent for current accounts; 5 percent for 0 to 60 days; 10 percent for 60 days to 6 months; 25 percent for 6 months to 1 year; and 50 percent for over 1 year.

Based on an aging analysis, what balance should be in the contra asset account? What does this suggest about the adequacy of the estimate in part c?

## 7–20. Revenue Recognition Policy at Walt Disney

Walt Disney Productions is a diversified company engaged in family entertainment and community development. It operates in four major business segments—entertainment and recreation, filmed entertainment, community development, and consumer products. Its annual report for 1986 contains the following note regarding revenue recognition:

> Generally, revenues are recorded when the earnings process is substantially complete and goods have been delivered or services performed. Revenues from participant/sponsors at the theme parks and Epcot Center are recorded over the period of the applicable agreements commencing with the opening of the attraction. Revenues from the theatrical distribution of motion pictures are recognized when motion pictures are exhibited domestically and when revenues are reported from foreign distributors; revenues from television licensing agreements are generally recorded when the film is available to the licensee and certain other conditions are met. Profit is recognized in full on sales of real estate when collectibility of the sales price is reasonably assured and the earnings process is virtually complete; if the sale does not meet requirements for recognition, profit is deferred until such requirements are met. Profit is recognized on residential unit sales at the time of closing.

**Required:**

a. Why does the company use so many different revenue recognition procedures? Would it be easier for stockholders to understand if all revenue were recognized at the point of sale?

*b*. Why is there a difference in timing of revenue recognition between films distributed to theaters and films licensed to television stations and networks?

*c*. Are there substantial differences in revenue recognition practices on sales of real estate and sales of residential units, which are also real estate? Why might these differences exist?

### Casette 7–1.  Georgia-Pacific Corporation

In the appendix at the end of the book is a complete set of financial statements of Georgia-Pacific Corporation taken from its annual report of 1987.

Answer the following questions related to sales revenue and accounts receivable on those statements:

1. What was the percentage increase in sales during the last year?
2. The company has a number of different product lines. What were the sales from each of the major product lines in 1987? Do they account for the total company sales?
3. By how much did the Allowance for Doubtful Accounts increase during 1987?
4. What percentage of accounts receivable at the end of 1986 and 1987 did the company expect to collect?
5. The 10–K report filed with the Securities and Exchange Commission by Georgia-Pacific shows a schedule detailing changes in the Allowance for Doubtful Accounts account. For 1987 the report shows (amounts in millions):

| | |
|---|---:|
| Balance at beginning of period | $21 |
| Additions | |
|     Charged to costs and expenses | 8 |
|     Charged to other accounts | 2* |
| Deductions | |
|     Accounts written off | (7) |
| Balance at end of period | $24 |

*Recoveries of accounts previously written off and $1 million acquired in the purchase of U.S. Plywood.

    *a*. Reconstruct in journal entry form or explain the transactions made in 1987 affecting Allowance for Doubtful Accounts.

    *b*. What percentage of sales is the 1987 provision for doubtful accounts?

6. Estimate the amount of cash collected from customers during 1987.
7. Calculate the turnover of accounts receivable in 1987. What is the average collection period? What assumptions regarding sales and accounts receivable are you making when you calculate and use this ratio?

### Casette 7–2.  Determining Revenue Recognition for an Advertising Agency

Slick-Flick Advertising Agency handles advertisements under contracts providing that the agency shall develop advertising copy and layouts and place ads in various media. The agency charges clients a commission of 18 percent of media costs as its fee. The agency makes advance billings to its clients of *estimated* media costs plus its 18 percent commission. Later adjustments of these advanced billings are usually minor. Often the billings and the receipt of cash from these billings occur before the period in which the advertising actually appears in the media.

Currently, the agency recognizes revenue at the time of the advanced billing on the grounds that it has a contract with clients for specified advertising, and thus income is earned when billed. At the time of billing, the agency establishes accounts receivable with clients and credits an estimated liability to the media and credits its commission earnings. At this time, the agency also estimates its expenses and establishes a liability for the estimated expense related to the client's billing. Adjusting entries are made later to record actual cost and revenue amounts when billings are received from media, when actual expenses are determined, and when statements are sent to clients.

It is industry practice not to consider the media cost as an expense of the agency. The agency simply serves as an intermediary collecting the media cost from the client and passing it on to the media. The only revenue the agency recognizes is its own fees and commissions. The expenses it recognizes include only its own costs and not those of the media.

**Required:**

*a.* Take the following situation as an illustration (this contract, however, would be one of perhaps 50 to 100 that the agency might work on).

Nov. 18, 1989—Signed contract with client and sent advanced billing for $354,000 (estimated media costs, $300,000 and estimated fee, $54,000). At this time the agency estimated that its own expenses on this contract would be $40,000.

Nov. 18–30, 1989—Actual layout and other costs incurred, $9,000.

December 1–31, 1989—Actual layout and other costs incurred, $27,000.

December 27, 1989—Received cash from client for $354,000.

January 1–10, 1990—Remaining layout and other costs incurred, $6,000.

January 15–31, 1990—Ads actually appear in media.

February 10, 1990—Billing received from media for actual media cost of $305,000.

February 15, 1990—Additional billing sent to client for $5,000 of additional media costs and $900 additional fees.

1. Make journal entries to record the above transactions under the agency's current accounting practices.
2. What accounts (including amounts) would appear on the December 31, 1989 balance sheet and how would they be classified (current asset, current liability, etc.)? How much income was recognized on this contract in 1989 and in 1990?
3. Evaluate the suitability of the agency's current method of revenue recognition and how effectively the current system matches costs and revenues.

*b.* Four other possible points at which revenue might be recognized are under consideration. These are: (1) when payment is received from the client, (2) when all layout and other costs of the agency have been incurred, (3) when the advertising appears in the media, and (4) when the bill for advertising is received from the media and the adjusted billing sent to the client. Compare the strengths and weaknesses of each of these alternative points of revenue recognition to the current method used.

c. Choose one alternative point of revenue recognition in *b* that you feel is most superior to the current method.
   1. Make journal entries to record the illustrative transactions given in part *a* consistent with the method of revenue recognition you have chosen.
   2. What accounts (including amounts) would appear on the December 31, 1989 balance sheet and how would they be classified? How much income would be recognized on this contract in 1989 and in 1990 under the method you prefer?

**Casette 7–3.    Subscriptions and Returns at Harper & Row**

Harper & Row, Publishers, Inc. is a major publisher of books and journals. Its annual report for the year ended April 30, 1986 shows the following accounts on the balance sheet (amounts in thousands):

|  | April 30 | |
|---|---|---|
|  | *1986* | *1985* |
| Current assets: | | |
| Accounts receivable less allowance for doubtful accounts of $1,517 in 1986 and $1,504 in 1985 and estimated future returns of $9,346 in 1986 and $10,128 in 1985 . . . . . . . . . . . . . . . . . . . . . | $54,369 | $46,376 |
| Long-term liabilities: | | |
| Unearned subscription income . . . . . . . . . . . . . . . | $14,829 | $12,147 |

The following notes accompany the financial statements:

(e) Reserve for Estimated Future Returns: The Company provides for estimated losses resulting from future returns of its publications at the time of their sale.
(f) Unearned Subscription Income: Income from medical journal subscriptions and certain loose-leaf sets is deferred at the time a subscriber is enrolled. Upon delivery of the journal or loose-leaf set, revenues and related costs are recognized based on a proportionate share of the gross subscription price. Procurement costs are expensed within the current year.

**Required:**

a. *Assume* that the income statement for 1986 showed $54,269,000 for Subscription Income (Subscription Revenue). How much *cash* was received in 1986 from subscriptions?
b. Why is Unearned Subscription Income classified among the long-term liabilities?
c. Does the practice of charging all procurement costs of subscriptions to expense as incurred agree with the matching concept? Explain why Harper & Row may follow this practice.
d. Evaluate the following two alternatives that Harper & Row might have used for subscription revenue: (1) recognize as revenue the cash received each period but set up an expense and liability for the estimated cost of the journals to be delivered in the future or (2) recognize 40 percent of the cash received as revenue on the grounds that selling the subscription is a major part of the earning function and defer the other 60 percent over the subscription period.

e. Calculate the percentage of *gross* accounts receivable represented by the Reserve for Estimated Future Returns on April 30, 1985 and 1986.

f. Why does Harper & Row use an account called Reserve for Estimated Future Returns? Is "reserve" a good title? How might the amount credited to the reserve be established?

g. *Assume* sales of books in 1986 were $136,395,000 and that returns are estimated to be 10 percent of sales. What journal entries were made in 1986 to the Reserve account?

## Casette 7–4. Comparisons of Long-Term Contract Accounting Practices

The following three excerpts have been taken from the notes in the annual reports of companies with long-term contracts.

### Addsco Industries (June 1986)

Revenues from contracts are recognized on the completed-contract method. The typical new construction contract is completed in approximately eighteen months and the typical repair and reconditioning contract is completed in approximately three months. The completed-contract method was selected because the inherent hazards relating to contract conditions may cause forecasts to be doubtful. A contract is considered complete when all costs, except insignificant items, have been incurred and the ship, barge, or vessel under construction or being repaired is operating according to specifications or has been accepted by the customer.

\* \* \* \* \*

Costs in excess of amounts billed are classified as current assets under costs in excess of billings on uncompleted contracts.

### Fluor Corporation (October 1986)

The company recognizes revenues on engineering and construction contracts on the percentage-of-completion method, primarily based on contract costs incurred to date compared with total estimated contract costs, and on manhours incurred to date compared with total estimated manhours for the construction of certain power plants. Contracts are segmented between engineering and construction efforts and, accordingly, gross margin related to each activity is recognized as those separate services are rendered. Changes to total estimated contract costs or manhours and losses, if any, are recognized in the period they are determined. Revenues recognized in excess of amounts billed are classified as current assets under contract work in progress. Amounts received from clients in excess of revenues recognized to date are classified as current liabilities under advance billings on contracts.

### Universal Voltronics Corporation (June 1986)

Percentage-of-completion accounting is applied to all contracts where (i) production takes more than three months, (ii) the customer has agreed to make substantial progress payments based upon achieved milestones and (iii) the aggregate contract sales price exceeds $100,000. In applying the percentage-of-completion method, earnings on contracts with a production term exceeding one year are based on the ratio of costs incurred to date on the contract to total estimated contract costs after providing for all known and anticipated costs. . . . In applying the percentage-of-completion method to all other contracts, earnings are recognized in proportion to actual labor costs incurred as compared with total estimated labor costs expected to be incurred on the entire contract.

**Required:**

a. Do you agree with the justification used by Addsco Industries for its use of completed contract? Could this same rationale apply to the other two companies?

b. Can you think of another justification that Addsco might use, particularly for repair and reconditioning contracts?

c. Fluor Corporation and Universal Voltronics Corporation both use percentage of completion. Yet each company uses two different methods of measuring percentage of completion. Are all of these practices appropriate? Why do you think each practice is used in the particular circumstance described?

d. Why does Universal not use percentage of completion on all contracts? Evaluate the reasonableness of the criteria it employs.

e. Addsco and Fluor both describe amounts that appear as *current assets* on their balance sheets. Explain in your own words the make-up of these current assets? How will they differ between the two companies?

f. Fluor Corporation states that "Changes to total estimated contract costs or man-hours . . . are recognized in the period they are determined." What do you think this sentence means?

## Chapter 8

# Cost Measurement

In Chapter 2 we introduced the *matching concept* as one of the fundamental ideas in financial accounting. Accountants measure net income by matching resources used against resources received from revenue-generating operations. The values of the resources used and received, according to the *exchange-price concept,* are measured by the prices agreed upon or implied in the exchanges in which the resources originated. From this concept and the concepts of the monetary unit and going concern, we derived in Chapter 3 the principle that assets generally should be recorded at their acquisition cost.

The acquisition cost of an asset includes all of the *necessary* and *reasonable* costs of acquiring the services of the asset—the cash price of the resource, the costs of transportation (freight, insurance) to its place of use, and the costs of preparation for its intended use. Necessary expenditures encompass all outlays that increase the use value of the asset. In economic terms, all costs that create form, place, or time utility are necessary costs. Reasonable costs include all outlays that a knowledgeable person would be willing to incur in an arm's-length transaction.[1]

This chapter applies the general concept of cost determination to four types of assets—labor services, purchased inventory, manufactured inventory, and noncurrent assets. Then, we take a brief look at modifications when the cost principle is applied to certain marketable securities. Also, we introduce some alternative approaches to cost determination that have appeared in the accounting literature.

## COST OF LABOR SERVICES

Labor services, like the various tangible properties a business uses, are a productive resource. However, this human resource rarely appears on a

---

[1] An *arm's-length transaction* is a term accountants use to describe an agreement between knowledgeable independent parties, both acting on behalf of their own interests.

position statement because employee work efforts leave no separate physical evidence. Labor efforts become an intangible part of other products and resources or are used immediately in revenue generation.

The accounting system attempts to measure and record the amounts paid in return for the labor services. These amounts constitute the cost of the labor efforts acquired. If we know that labor efforts will be consumed in generating revenue during the accounting period, we often debit an expense account directly when the services are acquired. Nevertheless, the amount of the expense is determined by the cost of the asset (human service potential) received.

There are two important factors to remember in the determination of total labor cost:

1. The wage and salary cost usually exceeds the amounts paid directly to employees.
2. *Total* labor costs include more than just the wage and salary cost.

The first point arises because employers act as collecting agents for other groups and withhold certain amounts from their employees' paychecks. For instance, employers are required by law to retain a portion of the earnings for employees' income taxes and social security taxes. On top of these mandatory withholdings, employees may authorize optional deductions for contributory insurance and supplemental retirement programs, bond-purchase and other savings plans, union dues, and so on. The *wage and salary cost* for an accounting period is the amount actually *earned* by the employees during that period, whether or not it is actually paid to them in cash. The amounts withheld must be recognized as liabilities, to be remitted periodically on behalf of the employees to the various governmental and other agencies concerned. From the company's point of view, the total wages and salaries earned are eventually paid out.

The second point results from the recognition that the cost of various fringe benefits is part of the total cost of maintaining a labor force. For example, *employers* must contribute an amount for social security independent from the social security withheld from the employee's pay. Employers also must pay unemployment compensation insurance and may spend additional sums for various employee pension and welfare programs in response to union contracts or company personnel policies.

## Recording Labor Costs

Let us assume that a company, in preparing its payroll for the week, encounters the following situation:

1. Total salaries earned are $30,000—$20,000 by salespersons and $10,000 by office employees.

2. The company is required to withhold 15 percent of employee earnings for income taxes and 7 percent for social security taxes.[2]

3. Certain employees have authorized the company to deduct from their salaries their contributions to the United Fund. These amount to $400. Also, each employee contributes 1 percent of his or her salary to the group life insurance program.

4. The company is required to match the employees' contributions for social security. It must also contribute an amount equal to 3.5 percent of gross salaries earned for the unemployment compensation insurance program (.8 percent to the federal government and 2.7 percent to the state government).

5. The company voluntarily contributes an additional amount equal to 2 percent of gross salaries earned to the employee group life insurance program plus 10 percent for a retirement program.

The following entry would be made to recognize the salary cost of labor services, the liability to employees for their net pay, and the liabilities to other agencies for the amounts withheld:

| | | |
|---|---|---|
| Sales Salaries Expense | 20,000 | |
| Office Salaries Expense | 10,000 | |
| Income Tax Withholdings Payable | | 4,500 (30,000 × .15) |
| Social Security Taxes Payable[3] | | 2,100 (30,000 × .07) |
| United Fund Withholdings Payable | | 400 |
| Group Life Insurance Premiums Payable | | 300 (30,000 × .01) |
| Wages Payable | | 22,700 |

Clearly, the manner of recording the debits would vary with the type of work performed and the degree of detail desired in expense classification. A single debit to Wage Expense might suffice for a small business.

Recall our second point above: the total labor cost also includes the employer's contribution to various fringe benefit programs. These costs and their related liabilities must also be recorded. The entries to accomplish this follow:

| | | |
|---|---|---|
| Payroll Tax Expense—Sales | 1,400 | |
| Payroll Tax Expense—Office | 700 | |
| Social Security Taxes Payable | | 2,100 (30,000 × .07) |

---

[2] The withholding rates used for these items are only approximations for illustrative purposes. The exact rates vary with the particular circumstances of each employee and with changes in legislation.

[3] This liability is often called FICA Taxes Payable (Federal Insurance Contributions Act).

| | | |
|---|---|---|
| Payroll Tax Expense—Sales. . . . . . . | 700 | |
| Payroll Tax Expense—Office . . . . . . | 350 | |
|     Federal Unemployment Taxes Payable | | 240 (30,000 × .008) |
|     State Unemployment Taxes Payable  . | | 810 (30,000 × .027) |
| | | |
| Employee Insurance Expense—Sales . . . | 400 | |
| Employee Insurance Expense—Office. . . | 200 | |
|     Group Life Insurance Premiums | | |
|         Payable . . . . . . . . . . . . . | | 600 (30,000 × .02) |
| | | |
| Pension Expense . . . . . . . . . . | 3,000 | |
|     Liability for Employee Pensions . . . | | 3,000 (30,000 × .10) |

The last four entries record costs over and above the basic salary costs. Accordingly, the total expense that is deducted on the income statement is $36,750. In addition to the $30,000 of salary expenses, there are $6,750 ($1,400 + $700 + $700 + $350 + $400 + $200 + $3,000) of payroll taxes and fringe benefit expenses. We have recorded them in separate expense accounts in order to supply additional information about the total labor cost, but conceptually they are costs incurred in the acquisition of labor services. They could have been debited to Sales Salaries Expense and Office Salaries Expense if we had chosen to do so.

The credits in the foregoing entries show the additional amounts owed to various groups for employer payroll taxes and employer-paid fringe benefits. They would appear as current liabilities on the balance sheet along with the liabilities for employee compensation and employee withholdings. Together they represent the total future outlays of cash that will be made to and for employees.

## COST OF PURCHASED INVENTORY

The costs necessary for acquiring inventory and preparing it for sale include the net invoice price, sales and excise taxes paid, freight charges to receive the inventory, and any handling costs incurred in unloading and storage. Each of these expenditures should be included as part of the total asset cost because each adds to the asset's usefulness in supplying its intended service. They are called *inventoriable costs*. When added to the beginning inventory, they make up a total pool of merchandise cost available for sale. This total eventually will be divided between the goods sold (expense) and the goods remaining on hand at the end of the period (asset).

Inventoriable costs must be distinguished from costs that on occasion may be incurred *unnecessarily* in the acquisition of an asset. Examples might include rehandling costs, lost discounts, and demurrage charges for the detention of ships or railroad cars beyond the time allowed for unloading. These expenditures do not increase the utility of the merchandise and should be treated as period expenses or losses, not as part of the cost of the asset.

## Recording the Elements of Inventory Cost

Assume that a firm begins the accounting period with a merchandise inventory of $10,600. During the period the following transactions (summarized) occur:

1. Merchandise is purchased for $60,000 at net invoice prices.
2. Freight charges of $3,600 are incurred on the incoming merchandise.
3. The firm incurs $1,200 of wage costs in unloading, unpacking, inspecting, and stocking the incoming merchandise.
4. In the receiving department, $7,000 of merchandise is discovered to be of the wrong size and is returned.

According to the cost concept, the first three items properly could be charged to the Merchandise Inventory account as asset increases. They are costs necessary to obtain the purchased merchandise and to ready it for sale. The returned merchandise signifies a reduction in the asset and could be credited directly to it. The same treatment would be applicable to price allowances for defects or damages; they reduce the cost of the asset purchased.

On the other hand, if all of these elements of inventory cost are lumped together in one account, some desirable managerial information may be hidden. For instance, the firm may wish to record the purchases separately in order to facilitate analysis. Comparisons between total purchases and total freight charges and handling costs on incoming merchandise would be helpful. Similarly, extensive purchase returns and allowances may indicate defects in ordering procedures or inefficiencies on the part of suppliers.

Therefore, many businesses record each element of inventory cost in a separate ledger account, as illustrated below for our example. This procedure provides the additional information needed for cost control and analysis. Purchases, Freight-In, and Handling Costs are *adjunct* accounts to the main asset account, Merchandise. They are segregated increases in the asset. Purchase Returns and Allowances is a *contra asset account*—a segregated decrease in the asset account.

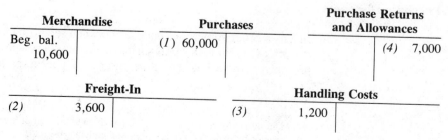

All of these accounts together make up the total cost of goods available for sale of $68,400 ($10,600 + $60,000 − $7,000 + $3,600 + $1,200). Assume that the ending inventory is counted and a cost of $15,200 (including applicable freight and handling cost) is determined for it. Then, cost of goods sold would be $53,200 determined as follows:

$$\text{Cost of Goods Sold} = \text{Beginning Inventory} + \text{Purchases}$$
$$- \text{Returns} + \text{Freight} + \text{Handling Cost}$$
$$- \text{Ending Inventory}$$

$$\$53,200 = \$10,600 + \$60,000 - \$7,000 + \$3,600$$
$$+ \$1,200 - \$15,200$$

In short, of the total cost pool of $68,400, an expense of $53,200 would appear on the income statement, and a current asset of $15,200 would appear on the balance sheet.

At the end of the accounting period, the contra and adjunct accounts, having served their purpose, are closed out (reset to zero). The adjusting entry to record the ending inventory, to close the contra and adjunct accounts, and to record the cost of goods sold would be:

| | | |
|---|---:|---:|
| Merchandise (ending balance) . . . . . . . . . . . . | 15,200 | |
| Cost of Goods Sold . . . . . . . . . . . . . . . | 53,200 | |
| Purchase Returns and Allowances . . . . . . . . . | 7,000 | |
| Merchandise (beginning balance). . . . . . . . . | | 10,600 |
| Purchases . . . . . . . . . . . . . . . . . . . | | 60,000 |
| Freight-In . . . . . . . . . . . . . . . . . . . | | 3,600 |
| Handling Costs . . . . . . . . . . . . . . . . | | 1,200 |

In concept, the cost of goods sold and the cost of the ending inventory should include all charges incurred in bringing the merchandise into its existing location and condition. Theoretically, this total would include the costs of ordering, receiving, inspecting, and warehousing. In practice, many of these costs are difficult to identify and trace and are relatively immaterial. Therefore, they are treated as period expenses or assigned solely to the goods sold. The *cost* of allocating them would exceed the *benefit* of increased accuracy from including them in inventoriable costs.[4]

## Purchase Discounts

Just as a seller sometimes chooses between recording sales at gross prices or net prices, a company purchasing from suppliers who allow a discount for prompt payment has the same choice. If purchases are recorded at gross

---

[4] The Tax Reform Act of 1986 requires companies with sales of more than $10 million to record all inventory-related costs and to add them to the cost of inventory. These inventoriable costs cannot be deducted for tax purposes until the inventory is sold. In some cases, these inventory capitalization rules result in some costs being treated as assets for tax purposes that are not capitalized for financial accounting purposes—for example, general and administrative costs related to inventory and warehousing.

prices initially, subsequent adjustment is necessary for discounts taken. If net prices are used, adjustments are needed whenever discounts are lost. For purchases, the net method seems to have all-around superiority over the gross method in terms of theoretical soundness, practicality, and managerial usefulness.

Conceptually, the net price is the cash equivalent exchange price of the inventory (and liability) on the purchase date. Any amount above the net price is related to how the acquisition of the asset is financed. If the gross price is eventually paid, the extra cash outlay represents a penalty for late payment—a type of financial or administrative charge—not the cost of an increase in the asset's usefulness. Recording gross prices initially overstates the asset, necessitating downward adjustment later for the amount of the discount.

From a practical viewpoint, management determines whether purchase discounts are taken or not. (In contrast, control over the taking of sales discounts rests with the customer.) Failure to take "cash discounts" on purchases is expensive[5] and adversely reflects upon the company's credit-worthiness. Management should expect to take all purchase discounts. Therefore, under the net price procedures, we have to account only for the discounts that are lost. Lost discounts are important to identify, but they are normally few. As a result, the bookkeeping procedure is simplified with few or no adjustments needed when the bills are paid.

**Recording at Net.**   As an example of the net method, assume a purchase of $8,000 gross is subject to a discount of 3 percent if paid within 15 days. Its payment within the discount period would be recorded as follows:

    Purchases . . . . . . . . . . . . . . . . . . . . . . . . . . .  7,760
        Accounts Payable . . . . . . . . . . . . . . . . . . . . .          7,760
        To record purchase (8,000 × .97 = 7,760).

    Accounts Payable . . . . . . . . . . . . . . . . . . . . . . .  7,760
        Cash . . . . . . . . . . . . . . . . . . . . . . . . . . .          7,760
        To record payment within discount period.

Now assume that the account in the preceding example is not paid within the 15-day period. This will illustrate an advantage of the net method that occurs whenever the discount is *not* taken. The entry under the net method would be:

    Accounts Payable . . . . . . . . . . . . . . . . . . . . . . .  7,760
    Purchase Discounts Lost (8,000 × .03) . . . . . . . . . .  240
        Cash . . . . . . . . . . . . . . . . . . . . . . . . . . .          8,000

---

[5] When it loses a discount, a firm buying $100 on terms calling for a 2 percent discount in 10 days or the full amount payable in 30 days has to pay 2 percent of the gross price for the privilege of waiting an additional 20 days to pay its bill. This is approximately equal to an annual interest charge of 36.7 percent (I = P × R × T; $2 = $98 × .367 × 20/360).

Management needs to know when resources have been wasted because of negligent delay on the part of the cashier's office in paying bills or because of insufficient cash being available for prompt payment of liabilities. Under the net price procedure, any amount in excess of the net invoice price is automatically isolated in a separate expense or loss account, Purchase Discounts Lost, as a natural part of the bookkeeping entry.

**Recording at Gross.**    One of the disadvantages of the net method is the difficulty encountered in maintaining subsidiary inventories at net prices. The invoice for $8,000 in the previous example may consist of 20 different items. In the detailed inventory records, each one would have to be recorded at 97 percent of its invoice price. If the gross price is used instead, the supplier's invoice agrees with the inventory records. The entries for the previous example, using the gross method, would be:

| | | |
|---|---|---|
| Purchases . . . . . . . . . . . . . . . . . . . . . . . | 8,000 | |
|     Accounts Payable . . . . . . . . . . . . . . . . | | 8,000 |
|     To record purchase. | | |
| | | |
| Accounts Payable . . . . . . . . . . . . . . . . . . | 8,000 | |
|     Cash . . . . . . . . . . . . . . . . . . . . . . | | 7,760 |
|     Purchase Discounts . . . . . . . . . . . . . . . . | | 240 |
|     To record payment *within* the discount period. | | |

To reduce the asset to its actual net cost, a credit to a *contra asset,* Purchase Discounts, is made when the account is paid.

When the discount is missed, the following entries would be made:

| | | |
|---|---|---|
| Accounts Payable . . . . . . . . . . . . . . . . . . | 8,000 | |
|     Cash . . . . . . . . . . . . . . . . . . . . . . | | 8,000 |
|     To record payment *after* the discount period. | | |
| | | |
| Purchase Discounts Lost . . . . . . . . . . . . . . . | 240 | |
|     Purchase Discounts . . . . . . . . . . . . . . . . | | 240 |
|     To record lost discounts. | | |

In the case of lost discounts under the gross method, a tendency exists to make only the entry paying off the gross liability. The second entry is not made, with the result that the inefficient use of resources is never highlighted for management's attention. The loss remains buried in an overstated asset. The net method automatically prevents this potential error.

## COST OF MANUFACTURED INVENTORY

Our illustrations so far involve merchandising concerns, in which most of the assets used up—merchandise, labor services, equipment, and so on—are consumed in an attempt to generate the current period's revenue. Consequently, we have focused our attention on two major stages in the life of an asset—acquisition (cost incurrence) and consumption (cost expiration). In a manufacturing firm, an additional aspect is introduced—*transformation or conversion*. Some assets are used not to produce revenue immediately but to produce another asset, the manufactured product. The costs of these assets are not recorded in expense accounts at the time of utilization. Instead, they become the cost of the new asset (product) being manufactured. In the accounting system, a clear separation of these three stages—acquisition, transformation, and consumption in the generation of revenues—is necessary.

Our purpose in this section is to set up the conceptual framework and introduce some new accounts and procedures appropriate for a manufacturing company. Specifically, we try to see how the cost measurement concept is implemented when the product is *made* rather than purchased.

## Nature of Manufacturing

Manufacturing consists of physically converting raw material, through the application of labor and other resources, into a finished product ready for sale. Cost accounting systems for manufacturing companies parallel this process. They record the flow of costs out of the accounts representing the assets used in the conversion process and into new accounts that correspond to the new forms of assets resulting from the manufacturing process. The cost of a manufactured product is developed through a careful tracing of the cost of assets used in production to the manufactured product.

The *costs of assets used in manufacturing affect net income (become expenses) only in the period when the products containing these costs are sold.* Consequently, the accounting system in manufacturing must be relatively detailed to allow for the accumulation of the various costs of making the product and the "storing" of these costs in inventory until the product is sold. Keep in mind that we are concerned only with those assets associated with the production process. Additional costs are incurred in selling or in general administration, but they are matched against the current period's revenues just as they are in a merchandising firm.

Manufacturing costs are inventoriable *product costs.* They are generally classified into three main categories—direct materials, direct labor, and manufacturing overhead.

*Direct materials* includes the cost of all raw material directly entering into the actual production of the physical units and becoming part of the specific product being manufactured. Iron ore for a steel company, lumber for a furniture firm, and steel for an automobile manufacturer are such raw materials. *Direct labor* includes the cost of labor directly identified with specific products—the cost of laborers who actually manufacture or assemble the product or operate the machines that do so.

*Manufacturing overhead* is a diverse category encompassing the costs of all other manufacturing resources except raw materials and direct labor. It includes indirect production costs that are not readily identified with any specific units but are necessary to the manufacturing process. Among these facilitating costs are the following:

1. Indirect labor—factory supervisors, maintenance employees, and production engineers.
2. Indirect materials—thread, nails, glue, wax, and other materials not readily traceable to particular units of product.
3. Factory supplies—oil, coal, and maintenance supplies.
4. Utility services for the manufacturing portion of the business—heat, light, power, and water.
5. Depreciation on factory buildings and equipment.
6. Repair and maintenance of factory equipment and facilities.

## Flow of Costs in Manufacturing

A typical cost accounting system for a manufacturing firm is depicted by the sequence of ledger accounts shown in Table 8–2. The numbers are developed from the data in Table 8–1 and can be traced from the journal entries in the next section. Separate production cost accounts are used to record the

**TABLE 8–1**    Data for Manufacturing Illustration

|  | | Transactions | |
| --- | --- | --- | --- |
|  | June 1 | During June | June 30 |
| 1. Inventories: | | | |
| Direct materials . . . . . . . . . | $21,600 | | $31,950 |
| Work in process. . . . . . . . . | 23,500 | | 17,800 |
| Finished goods . . . . . . . . | 48,600 | | 52,200 |
| 2. Direct material purchases . . . . . | | $205,200 | |
| 3. Wage and salary costs: | | | |
| Direct factory labor . . . . . . | | 139,500 | |
| Indirect factory labor. . . . . . | | 28,150 | |
| Sales salaries . . . . . . . . . | | 19,500 | |
| Executive salaries . . . . . . . | | 75,000 | |
| 4. Other factory costs: | | | |
| Depreciation on factory building . . . . . . . . . . | | 4,900 | |
| Depreciation on factory equipment . . . . . . . . . | | 6,100 | |
| Factory supplies used . . . . . | | 15,050 | |
| Heat, light, and power (80% applicable to production operations) . . . . . . . . . | | 12,000 | |

**TABLE 8–2** Product Cost Flow in Manufacturing

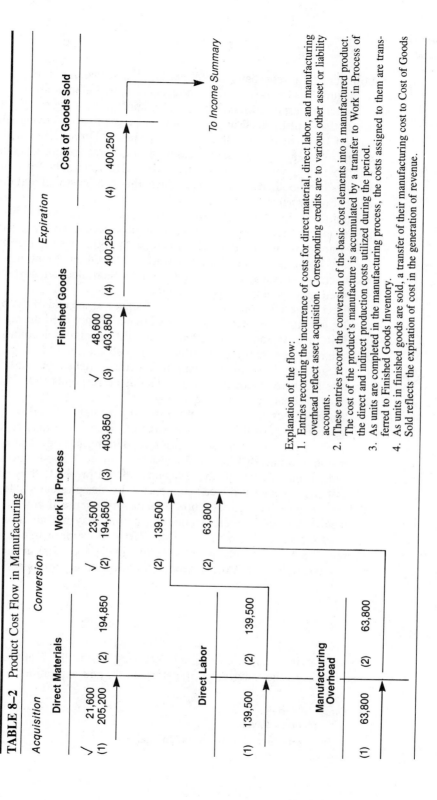

Explanation of the flow:

1. Entries recording the incurrence of costs for direct material, direct labor, and manufacturing overhead reflect asset acquisition. Corresponding credits are to various other asset or liability accounts.

2. These entries record the conversion of the basic cost elements into a manufactured product. The cost of the product's manufacture is accumulated by a transfer to Work in Process of the direct and indirect production costs utilized during the period.

3. As units are completed in the manufacturing process, the costs assigned to them are transferred to Finished Goods Inventory.

4. As units in finished goods are sold, a transfer of their manufacturing cost to Cost of Goods Sold reflects the expiration of cost in the generation of revenue.

utilization of direct materials, direct labor, and manufacturing overhead and to accumulate the cost of the products being manufactured.

Direct materials, direct labor, and manufacturing overhead all represent assets that will be used in production and costs that will eventually become part of the cost of the manufactured product. Direct labor and manufacturing overhead are temporary assets in that they are not physically stored and do not appear on the balance sheet. However, the cost of these resources is embodied in various products that can be stored and do appear as assets on the balance sheet.

Manufacturing Overhead serves as a summary account. Individual elements may be recorded first in separate cost accounts—for example, Indirect Labor, Indirect Materials, Factory Supplies Used, Depreciation of Factory Equipment, and Factory Utility Costs. Often, Manufacturing Overhead acts as a control account, and the individual, detailed cost elements are recorded in subsidiary ledger accounts.

Direct Materials commonly shows a balance at the end of the period. This ending inventory represents the cost of materials not used during the period. Work in Process and Finished Goods are also inventory accounts; their ending balances represent the manufacturing costs attached to the partially completed goods (Work in Process) and to the finished but unsold units of product (Finished Goods). Finished Goods corresponds to the Merchandise Inventory account in a merchandising firm.

Cost of Goods Sold is the only *expense* account in the flow of manufacturing costs. Part of the amount in Cost of Goods Sold may represent costs incurred in production in some prior accounting period. These costs have been stored as part of Work in Process and Finished Goods until the product is sold. Then, as part of the total cost of the product, they are matched against the revenue produced this period by the product's sale. Likewise, the direct materials, direct labor, and factory overhead costs acquired and utilized during the *present* accounting period may not all flow through to Cost of Goods Sold in this period. Part may remain in the inventories (Direct Materials, Work in Process, or Finished Goods) at the end of the period and will affect Cost of Goods Sold in future periods.

## Journal Entries

The following journal entries are necessary during the month or at month-end to record the incurrence, transformation, and expiration of the costs.

1. Direct Materials. . . . . . . . . . . . . . . .    205,200
       Accounts Payable . . . . . . . . . . . . . .        205,200
       To record the acquisition of additional
       direct materials.

2. Direct Labor . . . . . . . . . . . . . . . . . . . 139,500
    Manufacturing Overhead . . . . . . . . . . . . . 28,150
    Selling Expense. . . . . . . . . . . . . . . . . 19,500
    Administrative Expense . . . . . . . . . . . . . 75,000
        Wages and Salaries Payable . . . . . . . . . .    262,150
      To record the incurrence of labor costs for the
      month and to classify them by type.

3. Manufacturing Overhead . . . . . . . . . . . . . 26,050
    Accumulated Depreciation—
      Factory Building . . . . . . . . . . . . . .    4,900
    Accumulated Depreciation—
      Factory Equipment . . . . . . . . . . . . .    6,100
    Factory Supplies Inventory . . . . . . . . . . .    15,050
      To record other indirect factory costs in
      Manufacturing Overhead.

4. Manufacturing Overhead . . . . . . . . . . . . . 9,600
    Administrative Expense . . . . . . . . . . . . . 2,400
        Accounts Payable . . . . . . . . . . . . . .    12,000
      To allocate heat, light, and power costs
      for the month between manufacturing cost
      and general expense.

5. Work in Process . . . . . . . . . . . . . . . . . 194,850
        Direct Materials. . . . . . . . . . . . . . .    194,850
      To record the cost of direct materials
      put into production during the month
      ($21,600 + $205,200 − $31,950).

6. Work in Process . . . . . . . . . . . . . . . . . 203,300
        Direct Labor . . . . . . . . . . . . . . . .    139,500
        Manufacturing Overhead . . . . . . . . . .    63,800
      To transfer the direct labor and total
      manufacturing overhead costs to Work in Process
      to record the utilization of these assets in the
      manufacturing process.

7. Finished Goods . . . . . . . . . . . . . . . . . 403,850
        Work in Process . . . . . . . . . . . . . .    403,850
      To transfer the total manufacturing cost attached
      to the units of product completed during the month
      ($23,500 + $194,850 + $203,300 − $17,800).

8. Cost of Goods Sold . . . . . . . . . . . . . . . 400,250
        Finished Goods . . . . . . . . . . . . . . .    400,250
      To record the total manufacturing cost of
      the units of product sold during the month
      ($48,600 + $403,850 − $52,200).

**TABLE 8–3**    Statement of Cost of Goods Manufactured and Sold
For the Month of June 19--

| | | | |
|---|---:|---:|---:|
| Direct material inventory, June 1 . . . . . . . . . | | $ 21,600 | |
| Plus: Direct material purchases . . . . . . . . . | | 205,200 | |
| | | 226,800 | |
| Less: Direct material inventory, June 30 . . . . . | | 31,950 | |
| Cost of direct materials used . . . . . . . . . . . | | | $194,850 |
| Direct labor cost . . . . . . . . . . . . . . . | | | 139,500 |
| Manufacturing overhead costs: | | | |
| Indirect labor . . . . . . . . . . . . . . | | 28,150 | |
| Factory supplies . . . . . . . . . . . . . | | 15,050 | |
| Depreciation, building . . . . . . . . . . | | 4,900 | |
| Depreciation, equipment. . . . . . . . . . | | 6,100 | |
| Heat, light, and power . . . . . . . . . . | | 9,600 | 63,800 |
| **Total manufacturing costs** . . . . . . . . . . . | | | 398,150 |
| Plus: Work in process, June 1 . . . . . . . . . . | | | 23,500 |
| | | | 421,650 |
| Less: Work in process, June 30. . . . . . . . . | | | 17,800 |
| **Cost of goods completed** . . . . . . . . . . . . | | | 403,850 |
| Plus: Finished goods, June 1. . . . . . . . . . . | | | 48,600 |
| | | | 452,450 |
| Less: Finished goods, June 30 . . . . . . . . . | | | 52,200 |
| **Cost of goods sold**. . . . . . . . . . . . . . . | | | $400,250 |

## Statement of Cost of Goods Manufactured and Sold

Of the amounts included in the flow of costs, the income statement normally shows only the expense Cost of Goods Sold. A separate internal manufacturing cost report is prepared to summarize the production activity and to present detailed information concerning the determination of cost of goods manufactured and sold. Such a statement for the preceding illustration appears in Table 8–3.

The $398,150 total manufacturing costs represent the production costs incurred in June. Management focuses on this figure for monthly cost control. It is combined with the beginning inventories of Work in Process and Finished Goods to make up the total pool of manufacturing costs. This pool is divided among Cost of Goods Sold and the ending inventories of Work in Process and Finished Goods. The subtotal, Cost of Goods Completed, of $403,850 represents the cost of new salable products produced during the period. It is analogous to the amount in the Purchases account of a merchandising firm, except that in this case the cost is a production cost rather than a purchase cost. The final subtotal, Cost of Goods Sold, appears on the income statement, along with expenses associated with selling and administrative activities.

# COST OF NONCURRENT ASSETS

The same cost principle that we have applied to labor services and inventory also applies to noncurrent assets. This section explores some of the problems encountered in determining the cost of acquiring and preparing certain noncurrent assets for use.

## Land

The total initial acquisition cost of land consists of its purchase price (the amount of cash given up and any liabilities assumed) plus any other expenditures made for the purpose of acquiring ownership and use of land. Such expenditures might include legal fees for title search, costs of registration of deeds, brokerage commissions, and payments of liens for back taxes. Any costs incurred for permanent improvements to the land also are included in the Land account as charges necessary for rendering the property available for its intended purpose. Examples include the cost of additional surveying, clearing, grading, landscaping, and one-time special assessments for sewers and drainage systems. They increase the utility of the land and hence benefit all periods in which the land is used.

A situation that may tax the analytical skills of the accountant is the purchase of land with an existing structure on it. If the original intention is to acquire the land and the building as separate assets, the purchase price should be allocated between the two assets acquired. If the original intention is simply to acquire a flat piece of land, the subsequent cost of razing the old building is added to the cost of the land. It is a necessary expenditure to render the *land* available for *its* intended use. Rational management certainly considers this additional cost in reaching its decision to acquire a particular piece of property. However, sometimes management's original intention—whether to acquire two assets, land and building, or to acquire a single asset, land—is not clear. Suppose the firm uses the old building one or two years and then tears it down to make a parking lot. Is the razing cost part of the cost of the asset "land" or part of the loss on destruction of the asset "building"?

One reason care must be taken in establishing the cost of land is that this asset usually is not depreciable. Although the nondepreciable nature of land follows from its infinite service life, the same treatment does not apply to limited-life land improvements such as fences, pavements, sprinkler systems, and lighting systems. The costs of these items should be debited to a separate asset account, Land Improvements, and written off as expenses over their respective useful lives.

## Purchased Assets

The cost of equipment, machinery, furniture, and fixtures includes the net invoice price plus any costs necessary to bring the asset to the location and into the condition for the business to receive the intended service benefit. A machine that is delivered to the factory is more useful than one that rests on the supplier's loading dock. Likewise, a machine installed, tested, and ready for production is more effective than one sitting idle in the plant, waiting to be connected. Consequently, transportation, installation, and testing charges represent additional *necessary* costs and are properly charged to the asset account. A similar treatment would be accorded any costs of remodeling, renovating, or reconditioning a piece of used equipment that had been recently acquired.[6]

**Lump-Sum Acquisition.**    Sometimes a business will purchase at one time practically all of the assets of another business. When more than one asset is acquired by means of a single payment, the result is called a "basket" or "lump-sum" purchase. The accounting problem becomes one of reasonably allocating the total purchase cost among the individual assets acquired. No single solution to this problem will suffice for all cases. The accountant must look at various sources of evidence—replacement costs, appraisal values, insurable values, valuations for tax assessments—to find a way of approximating the "net cash cost" of each asset.

Assume that a company acquires the assets of a firm going out of business. Because it is willing to buy the entire group of assets—inventory, land, warehouse, and warehouse equipment—the company is able to purchase it for a total of $330,000. The inventory consists of commonly purchased items that could be acquired on the wholesale market for $42,000. The buyer has the other assets appraised by a competent appraisal firm, whose report shows the estimated values to be: land, $105,000; warehouse, $140,000; and warehouse equipment, $70,000. The following entry might be made to record the acquisition:

| | | |
|---|---:|---:|
| Inventory | 42,000 | |
| Land (105/315 of $288,000) | 96,000 | |
| Warehouse (140/315 of $288,000) | 128,000 | |
| Warehouse Equipment (70/315 of $288,000) | 64,000 | |
| Cash | | 330,000 |

---

[6]Noncurrent assets acquired other than through purchase—for example, donations, stockholder investments, exchanges for other noncash assets, and trade-ins—are generally recorded at fair market value. Under the *exchange-price concept,* this is the value that would have prevailed in a bona fide exchange for cash. Further explanation about noncurrent asset exchanges and trade-ins appears in Chapter 10.

In this case, the $42,000 wholesale cost reliably measures the current cash cost of the inventories. For the other assets, the accountant approximates the costs by allocating the remaining $288,000 cash paid among them in proportion to their appraised values.[7]

## Constructed Assets

Often a firm constructs some noncurrent asset for its own use. How do we determine the cost when there is no outright purchase? We apply concepts similar to those discussed earlier in connection with manufacturing. Just as the cost of a product being manufactured consists of the cost of the assets used in its production, the acquisition cost of a constructed noncurrent asset includes the cost of the resources utilized in its making.

If, for example, a firm decides to construct a building for its home office, a special asset account, Construction in Progress—Building is established to accumulate the various costs incurred in erecting it. Assume the following costs are incurred: (1) $640,000 for the cost of materials used, (2) $1,069,000 for the cost of labor services devoted to construction, (3) $51,000 for depreciation on long-term assets used in construction, and (4) $463,000 for subcontracting and other expenditures incurred for the purpose of creating the new asset. If these costs had been recorded in journal entries and posted to ledger accounts, the asset accounts would appear as follows:

| Construction in Progress—Building | | Office Building | |
|---|---|---|---|
| (1) | 640,000 | (5) | 2,223,000 |
| (2) | 1,069,000 | | |
| (3) | 51,000 | | |
| (4) | 463,000 | | |
| Bal. | 2,223,000 | 2,223,000 | (5) |

Upon completion of the construction project, an entry (5) is made and posted to transfer all relevant costs to the noncurrent asset.

Ideally, we should like to be able to identify each specific cost used in erecting the building. Practical problems of measurement often arise, how-

---

[7] Other accountants may prefer to allocate the $330,000 to all assets, including inventory, using the total fair market value of $357,000 as a base. In this case, $38,824 (42/357 of the $330,000) would be debited to inventories, $97,059 (105/357 of the $330,000) would be allocated to land, and so on. In our view, when the measurement of the fair market value of one or more assets is clearly more reliable, those measurements should carry more weight in the allocation process.

ever, when workers normally employed in manufacturing are temporarily assigned to construction work and some of the resources normally included in manufacturing overhead are diverted to the making of some noncurrent asset. Determination of the portion of these costs (indirect labor, power, supplies, etc.) that should be debited to Construction in Progress rather than to Work in Process may be difficult. At a minimum, any *increase* in overhead caused by the construction project should be assigned as part of its cost. Some accountants would stop at this point, arguing that management's decision to incur cost includes *only* the incremental costs. To charge regularly recurring manufacturing overhead to construction would reduce the costs charged to inventory and ultimately to cost of goods sold. Income would be higher in the period of construction.

On the other hand, the practice of charging only incremental costs seems to ignore the benefits received from the use of resources that otherwise would have been employed in other capacities or remained idle. Other accountants view all manufacturing overhead costs reasonably traceable to the construction project as additional costs. To allocate all overhead costs when the cost of manufactured inventory is determined but to charge only incremental overhead costs when calculating the cost of self-constructed assets seems inconsistent.[8]

## Financial Charges

Management's choice of how to finance the acquisition of an asset, whether by borrowed capital or stockholder capital, does not affect the service potential of that asset. Consequently, financing charges normally are excluded from the asset's cost. The "cash" price is the initial cost of the asset. Often, however, the financing charge is implicit in the means by which the asset is bought. For instance, a firm can acquire a machine by paying $450,000 cash or making 12 monthly payments of $40,000 ($480,000 total). If the latter alternative is accepted, the accountant has to go behind the scenes to pull out the $30,000 differential. This represents an interest charge for delayed payment, not part of the asset's cost.

For many years, the exclusion of financing charges from the cost of an asset was general practice. The theory was that interest expense relates to how a business acquires its financial capital and not to how much money must be expended to acquire a particular asset. Interest was treated as a general period expense, the cost of having sufficient financial capital to run the business.

---

[8] *Standard 404* issued by the Cost Accounting Standards Board requires the allocation of all costs to self-constructed assets for purposes of cost determination under government contracts.

The practice of charging interest expense to an asset account is called *capitalization of interest*. In the 1970s, the practice began to spread among industrial firms. With strong encouragement from the Securities and Exchange Commission, the Financial Accounting Standards Board studied the issue and in October of 1979 issued a standard recommending limited capitalization of interest costs.[9]

**FASB Standard.** Under this standard, an asset qualifies for interest capitalization only if a significant period of time will necessarily expire between the initial expenditure for the asset and its readiness for use. Plant assets acquired over time or constructed for internal use are examples. Assets manufactured for eventual sale under long-term construction contracts also qualify. Because the asset requires a significant preparation period, interest is viewed as a cost of getting the asset ready for its intended use.

The capitalization period begins when expenditures for the specific asset have been incurred, and it continues as long as activities to prepare the asset for use are in progress and interest costs are being incurred. Capitalization ends when the asset is substantially complete and ready for use.

The amount of interest to be capitalized is "that portion of the interest cost incurred during the assets' acquisition periods that theoretically could have been avoided . . . if expenditures for the assets had not been made."[10] The specific amount to be capitalized each accounting period by a company is the product of the average monthly accumulated expenditures on the asset and the company's capitalization rate. This rate is the interest rate actually incurred by the firm on specific borrowings related to the asset. If the average monthly accumulated expenditures exceed the amount of specific borrowings, the excess is multiplied by a weighted-average interest rate applicable to other borrowings of the company.

**Example.** Assume that during the current year a company spent $1,240,000 for the partial construction of its own new office building. The building will be completed in two more years. A $400,000 construction loan has been secured from a local bank at an interest rate of 12 percent. In addition, the firm has a number of interest-bearing liabilities outstanding with a weighted-average interest rate of 10 percent. The firm's *total* interest charges for the year are $518,300.

If the expenditures during the current year were to be made evenly throughout the year, the *average* accumulated expenditures would be $620,000

[9] FASB, *Statement of Financial Accounting Standards No. 34*, "Capitalization of Interest Cost" (Stamford, Conn., October 1979).
[10] FASB, *Statement No. 34*, par. 12.

($1,240,000/2). The interest to be capitalized on this building would be computed as follows:

*Construction Loan*

| | |
|---|---|
| $400,000 × 12% | $48,000 |
| *Excess Expenditures* | |
| $220,000 × 10% | 22,000 |
| Interest to Capitalize | $70,000 |

The summary entry to record interest for the year would be:

| | | |
|---|---|---|
| Interest Expense . . . . . . . . . . . . . . . . | 448,300 | |
| Construction in Progress—Building. . . . . . . . | 70,000 | |
| Cash (and/or Interest Payable) . . . . . . . . . | | 518,300 |

Only $448,300 of the total $518,300 interest is deducted on the income statement. The other $70,000 increases the asset on the balance sheet. It will become part of the cost of using the asset (depreciation expense) in future periods, after construction has been completed. The amount of interest capitalized must be disclosed in the financial statements.

Limited capitalization of interest is now required under generally accepted accounting principles. However, some accountants still find the practice objectionable. Different assets end up with different costs solely because they are financed differently. A building built with proceeds from the issuance of capital stock will have a lower cost than an identical building constructed with the proceeds from the issuance of bonds. In truth, it is extremely difficult to relate a particular source of cash to a particular project. *If* interest is to be treated as an asset cost, then the amount capitalized should represent the implicit cost of all financial capital tied up in the asset and not just the cost of borrowed money.

## Natural Resources

Natural resources such as oil fields and mines are unique in that the additional costs for exploration and development play a major role in cost determination. The original purchase price may be only a fraction of the total costs the firm has to incur. Subsequent expenditures for such purposes as geological tests, sinking of shafts, construction of tunnels, and removal of topsoil (in the case of strip mining) benefit future periods. These expenditures are part of the cost of the asset, for they enable the firm to use the acquired natural resources. Sometimes these costs are set up in asset accounts separate from the natural resource, particularly when the life of the development is different from the life of the natural resource. The services of a particular mine shaft may expire economically before the mine itself does. In this case, depreciation would be easier if the two were recorded separately.

**Successful Efforts versus Full Costing.**     A major difficulty in determining the cost of natural resources involves the handling of exploration and drilling expenditures when future benefit is uncertain. Many of the same considerations discussed in connection with research and development costs in Chapter 6 are relevant here. Should the cost of drilling oil wells, for example, be set up as an asset or be treated as a period expense? Varying circumstances may call for different answers. If the drilling is on scattered wildcat wells, many of which will be dry holes, then it is reasonable to treat drilling costs as an operating expense except in the case of a well that is completed as a producer. On the other hand, if the drilling costs are incurred in the development of an existing oil *area,* then all costs of drilling, whether or not they always result in a producing well, rightfully can be deemed *necessary* costs of preparing the asset *oil field* for its intended use. However, costs of developing unproductive fields are expensed.

Most major integrated refiners follow a policy called *successful-efforts costing.* Each individual well or identifiable mineral field is treated as a separate unit of account. The cost of dry holes or unproductive fields is charged to expense. Only those exploration and drilling costs traceable to successful wells or fields are set up as assets.

A number of other oil and gas firms, however, practice *full costing.* This procedure views all natural resource property within an area as a single asset unit. The Securities and Exchange Commission in *Accounting Series Release No. 258* requires that full costing be practiced on a country-by-country basis. Consequently, all expenditures made within a country, whether associated with unproductive or productive ventures, are treated as necessary asset costs. These costs enter into the determination of net income only over a substantial number of future years. As a result, yearly income would fluctuate much less than under successful efforts. Indeed, many proponents of full costing claimed that if they had to use successful efforts, they would be driven out of business. A company, particularly a small driller, could not stand to show dry holes as a direct expense, especially in a year when these were numerous, because it could not get financial support in the following year due to the previous year's poor income.

The Financial Accounting Standards Board grappled with this controversy during the 1970s. It opted for successful efforts despite the alleged unfavorable economic consequences. In addition to the full-costing method's reliance on an extremely broad asset concept, the FASB objected to "costs that are known not to have resulted in identifiable future benefits (being) nonetheless capitalized as part of the cost of assets to which they have no direct relationship."[11] For example, the cost of a dry hole in Wyoming would become part of the cost of an off-shore oil platform in Louisiana. Under full costing, a firm might not reflect on its income statement for many years the fact that it had an excessive number of dry holes and was relatively unsuccessful in exploration. The FASB felt that the financial statements should reflect the risk and uncertainty associated with oil- and gas-producing activities. Successful efforts faithfully represented that objective.

However, *Statement No. 19* never became effective. After much pressure and a three-year experiment by the SEC with alternative supplemental disclosures, the FASB restudied the whole issue. The result of this restudy was *Statement of Financial Accounting Standards No. 69* issued in the fall of 1982. Successful efforts and full costing continue to be acceptable alternatives. However, the following information has to be disclosed in the supplementary information to the financial statements:

1. The method being used.
2. Proved oil and gas reserve quantities.
3. Capitalized costs relating to oil- and gas-producing activities.
4. Costs incurred for property acquisition, exploration, and development activities.
5. Results of operations for oil- and gas-producing activities.
6. A standardized measure of discounted future net cash flows relating to proved oil and gas reserve quantities.[12]

The Board anticipates that these disclosures will assist users in assessing the degree of risk associated with different companies.

## Intangible Assets

Careful cost determination is just as important for intangible assets—patents, formulas, licenses, copyrights—as for tangible assets. The general principles are the same. When intangible assets are purchased, the amount paid is the initial measure of the asset's cost. To this amount are added any other costs that enhance the utility of the intangible. In the case of a patent, these would include the cost of a successful legal defense of the patent right.

Often intangible assets are acquired as part of a lump-sum purchase. For *specifically identifiable* intangible assets, accountants determine cost by estimating the fair value of the individual assets acquired, as in any lump-

---

[11] FASB, *Statement of Financial Accounting Standards No. 19*, "Financial Accounting and Reporting by Oil and Gas Producing Companies" (Stamford, Conn., December 1977), par. 144.

[12] FASB, *Statement of Financial Accounting Standards No. 69*, "Disclosures about Oil and Gas Producing Activities" (Stamford, Conn., November 1982), par. 7. Interestingly, three of the FASB members dissented from the issuance of this statement because they believed the sixth disclosure was completely lacking in *reliability*.

sum purchase. Any excess of the total purchase price over the sum of the market values of the tangible assets and the specifically identifiable intangible assets is recorded as a general intangible, Goodwill.

Many intangible assets are developed internally. Determining the cost of these assets is extremely difficult, and in fact often impossible. Some of the problems are discussed in Chapter 6 in the section on period costs. When these internal costs, other than research and development costs, can be specifically identified with a particular intangible, the cost of the asset includes all development costs traceable to it. However, the costs of internally developed intangibles that either "are not specifically identifiable, have indeterminate lives, or are inherent in a continuing business and related to an enterprise as a whole . . . should be deducted from income when incurred."[13] These would include expenditures for the development of a favorable standing in the community, a well-trained work force, a high-technology environment, and product recognition from effective advertising.

# VALUATION OF MARKETABLE EQUITY SECURITIES

The preceding discussions focus on the determination of acquisition cost as the essential first step in the recording of assets. Cost is the almost universal valuation measure used in financial accounting. Gains and losses are not recognized until the assets are sold or used in generating revenues. Such gains and losses are labeled "realized."

An important exception to the cost basis is required for certain marketable securities. The Financial Accounting Standards Board has ruled that in many circumstances marketable *equity* securities (shares of stock in other companies bought and sold on recognized stock exchanges) are to be reported in the balance sheet at the *lower of acquisition cost or current market value.*[14] Changes in the value of those securities classified as *current assets* are to be reflected in the determination of net income as *unrealized* gains and losses. Unrealized losses result when the aggregate market value declines below aggregate acquisition cost. Gains might occur if market values subsequently were to rise. However, the securities would not be reported at more than their aggregate acquisition cost.

## Recording Changes in Marketable Equity Securities

The collection of marketable equity securities is called a "portfolio." Let us examine how *FASB Statement No. 12* applies to the portfolio of the hypo-

---

[13] AICPA, *APB Opinion No. 17*, "Intangible Assets" (New York, August 1970), par. 24.

[14] FASB, *Statement of Financial Accounting Standards No. 12*, "Accounting for Certain Marketable Securities" (Stamford, Conn., December 1975).

**TABLE 8–4**   Portfolio of Current Marketable Equity Securities of Oard Corporation in 1990

| Security | Acquisition Cost* | Market Value | | | |
| --- | --- | --- | --- | --- | --- |
| | | March 31 | June 30 | September 30 | December 31 |
| Company A | $ 52,500 | $ 54,000 | $53,000 | $54,500 | $53,000 |
| Company B | 108,000 | 103,000 | † | — | — |
| Company C | 34,000 | 33,000 | 32,000 | 32,500 | 31,500 |
| | $194,500 | $190,000 | $85,000 | $87,000 | $84,500 |

*Security A, B, and C were all purchased during the first quarter.
†Security B was sold during the second quarter for $101,500.

thetical Oard Corporation. Table 8–4 shows the cost and 1990 market values of Oard's current securities. Assume that the company prepares quarterly financial statements for distribution to stockholders.

On March 31, an adjusting entry would be required to reflect as an unrealized loss the $4,500 excess of aggregate cost ($194,500) over aggregate market value ($190,000). The resultant credit goes to a *contra asset* account called "Allowance to Reduce Marketable Equity Securities to Market Value."

| | | |
| --- | --- | --- |
| Net Unrealized Loss from Decline in Value of Marketable Equity Securities . . . . . . . . . . . | 4,500 | |
| Allowance to Reduce Marketable Equity Securities to Market Value . . . . . . . . . . . | | 4,500 |

The carrying value of the securities becomes $190,000, the lower of cost or market. Note that the unrealized loss of $4,500 is applicable to the entire portfolio; its determination involves the offsetting of unrealized gains on A ($1,500) and unrealized losses on B ($5,000) and C ($1,000). The $4,500 reduces reported income in the first quarter.

During the second quarter, two entries are applicable to the current marketable securities. The first records the sale of Security B at a loss. This entry is made in the normal fashion.

| | | |
| --- | --- | --- |
| Cash . . . . . . . . . . . . . . . . . . | 101,500 | |
| Loss on Sale of Security B . . . . . . . . . . | 6,500 | |
| Marketable Equity Securities . . . . . . . . | | 108,000 |

The realized loss of $6,500 is the full difference between the original cost and the selling price. The loss will appear on the income statement for the second quarter. The other entry on June 30 adjusts the valuation (contra asset) account. The current credit balance in the Allowance account is $4,500, but it needs to be only $1,500. This is the excess of the $86,500 cost over the $85,000 current market value of the remaining securities, A and C. To reduce the Allowance account necessitates a debit of $3,000. The following entry accomplishes this adjustment.

> Allowance to Reduce Marketable Equity
>     Securities to Market Value . . . . . . . . . . . . . . 3,000
>       Recovery of Net Unrealized Losses
>        on Marketable Equity Securities . . . . . . . .         3,000

When the remaining balance of $1,500 in the contra asset is subtracted from the original cost of $86,500, the carrying value is $85,000. This is the lower current market figure. The credit to Recovery of Net Unrealizable Losses appears on the second-quarter income statement. Technically it is not a gain; it is a change in an estimate of an unrealized loss. Its effect on reported income is positive, as with a gain. The "recovery" is actually a combination of decreases in unrealized gains of $1,000 (A) and increases in unrealized losses of $1,000 (C) offset by the removal of the unrealized loss of $5,000 on Security B recorded in the first quarter. The *$5,000 unrealized loss* now has been recognized as part of the *realized loss of $6,500* in the second quarter.

By September 30, the market prices of the securities collectively have risen $2,000, to $500 more than their original cost. However, only a recovery of $1,500 is recorded, because the carrying value cannot exceed cost. The entry is:

> Allowance to Reduce Marketable Equity
>     Securities to Market Value . . . . . . . . . . . . . 1,500
>       Recovery of Net Unrealized Losses
>        on Marketable Equity Securities . . . . . . . .         1,500

The remaining balance in the contra asset account is eliminated, and the lower *cost* figure of $86,500 appears on the balance sheet.

By December 31, the two remaining securities had declined temporarily in value again. Because the total current market value was below cost, an entry similar to the first quarter is necessary.

> Net Unrealized Loss from Decline in Value
>     of Marketable Equity Securities . . . . . . . . . . . 2,000
>       Allowance to Reduce Marketable
>        Equity Securities to Market Value . . . . . . . .         2,000

An unrealized loss is recognized on the income statement, and the valuation balance of $2,000 is subtracted on the balance sheet.

Table 8–5 shows how the events recorded each quarter would appear on the quarterly income statements and balance sheets for Oard Corporation. For convenience we assume that operating income before considering marketable equity securities was $50,000 each quarter.

**Noncurrent Marketable Equity Securities.**   The previous discussion concerned marketable equity securities classified as current assets. If the securities were *noncurrent* assets, the basic entries are the same. The asset still appears on the balance sheet among the long-term investments valued at the lower of cost or market. However, the account Net Unrealized Losses on Noncurrent Marketable Equity Securities does not reduce reported

**TABLE 8–5**    Financial Statement Disclosures of Marketable Equity Securities for Oard Company

|  | First Quarter | Second Quarter | Third Quarter | Fourth Quarter |
|---|---|---|---|---|
| Income statement items: | | | | |
| Operating income . . . . . . . . . . . . . | $ 50,000 | $50,000 | $50,000 | $50,000 |
| Realized loss on sale of marketable securities . . . . . . . . . . . . . . . | | (6,500) | | |
| Net unrealized loss from decline in value of marketable equity securities* . . . . . . . . . . . . . . . | (4,500) | | | (2,000) |
| Recovery of net unrealized losses on marketable equity securities* . . . . . . . | | 3,000 | 1,500 | |
| Income before taxes . . . . . . . . . . . | $ 45,500 | $46,500 | $51,500 | $48,000 |
| Balance sheet items (current asset): | | | | |
| Marketable equity securities at cost . . . . . . | $194,500 | $86,500 | $86,500 | $86,500 |
| Allowance to reduce marketable equity securities to market value . . . . . . . . | (4,500) | (1,500) | — | (2,000) |
| Marketable equity securities, at lower of cost or market. . . . . . . . . . . . | $190,000 | $85,000 | $86,500 | $84,500 |

*Net unrealized gains and recoveries apply to the portfolio as a whole. However, *Statement No. 12* also requires that the total separate unrealized gains and the total separate unrealized losses be disclosed in notes to the financial statements.

income. Instead, it appears as a *direct* reduction in stockholders' equity on the balance sheet. The contra equity account and contra asset account will have the same balance. Presumably market declines on the noncurrent portfolio were considered not to be sufficiently imminent to be recognized in the determination of income.[15]

For example, assume that the securities for the Oard Corporation were classified as noncurrent assets. Then reported income before tax would be $50,000 except in the second quarter when the *realized* loss of $6,500 would reduce it to $43,500. The cumulative net unrealized losses and recoveries would be deducted from the total stockholders' equity. On December 31, if capital stock and retained earnings were $100,000 and $247,000 respectively, the stockholders' equity section would appear as follows:

---

[15] This statement applies only to *temporary* declines in market value. If there is a serious, permanent impairment in the value of the securities, the investment would be written down and the loss recognized in income.

**Oard Corporation**
**Stockholders' Equity**
**As of December 31**

| | |
|---|---:|
| Capital stock . . . . . . . . . . . . . . . . . . . . . . . . . . . . . . . . . . . . | $100,000 |
| Retained earnings . . . . . . . . . . . . . . . . . . . . . . . . . . . . . . . . . | 257,000 |
| Net unrealized losses on noncurrent marketable equity securities . . . . . . . . . . . . . . . . . . . . . . . . . . . . . . . . . | (2,000) |
| | $355,000 |

## Summary and Evaluation of FASB Statement No. 12

Briefly stated, the following procedures are involved in recording marketable equity securities:

1. Marketable equity securities are classified into two portfolios—current and noncurrent. Each portfolio is valued at the lower of aggregate cost or aggregate market.
2. The excess of aggregate cost over aggregate market is accounted for in a contra asset valuation account.
3. Periodic changes in the balance of the valuation account for *current* securities are included in the determination of net income as unrealized losses and gains. These are in addition to any realized losses or gains recognized at the time of sale of securities.
4. Periodic changes in the balance of the valuation account for *noncurrent* securities are reflected as direct adjustments to stockholders' equity in the form of changes in a contra equity account. They bypass the income statement until the securities are sold or reclassified as current assets.

*Statement No. 12* contains a number of logically objectionable provisions. For example, how a security is classified in the balance sheet determines whether changes in its value are reflected in income. Yet, the type of value change and the reliability of its measurement would seem to be more appropriate dominant factors. Also, some accountants object to the fact that increases in the market value of some current securities affect income while other increases do not. If the increases offset decreases and thereby cause a smaller net decrease, they affect income. If the increases come in a period subsequent to a decrease and thereby cause a recovery, they affect income. However, if securities increase in value so that aggregate market is above aggregate cost, they do not affect income. This inconsistency does not seem rooted in the qualitative guidelines of relevance or reliability.

It is not surprising, therefore, that *Statement No. 12* comes across as a somewhat inconsistent mixture of concepts. It deals solely with marketable *equity* securities, yet the same underlying reasoning would appear applicable to marketable *debt* securities. It does mandate the use of market values. However, it does so in a way that minimizes any major impact on income measurement. Unrealized losses and recoveries that are not based on completed transactions are included in reported income only in highly restricted circumstances.

Perhaps this ruling will be a forerunner of other reliably determined valuations as alternatives to acquisition cost. Some of these are explained in the next section.

# ALTERNATIVE CONCEPTS OF COST

The concept of cost we have been discussing embraces all actual dollar outlays necessary for acquiring resources. Under the exchange-price concept and the monetary postulate, this figure measures the effort of the firm. When significant price changes occur, however, the propriety of historic acquisition cost as the basis for the representation of assets is called into serious question. Some accountants would prefer using current replacement cost as the carrying value of assets. Others would retain historic outlays but restate them to reflect inflationary changes in general price levels.

These alternative approaches also match costs against revenues, as does conventional accounting, to provide an income figure after consideration of the recovery of capital committed to the various assets consumed. They differ, however, in their *measurement* of the recovery of capital.

A simple example will highlight the differences in these cost concepts. Merchandise is purchased at a cost of $3,000 when an index of the general price level stands at 100, is held until the end of the year, and then is sold for $5,000. At that time, the general price index stands at 120 and the *current* acquisition cost (replacement cost) of the merchandise is $3,800. What is income? Conventionally, we subtract the *original* acquisition cost of the asset consumed ($3,000) from the selling price of $5,000 and report an income of $2,000.

## Constant Dollar

Those who advocate the constant dollar alternative view the monetary postulate as faulty under conditions of general inflation (or deflation). The dollar is the accountant's measuring unit. When the general price level changes, the purchasing power of the monetary unit and hence its size changes also.

In our example, the $3,000 original acquisition cost and the $5,000 revenue are not comparable in their general purchasing power. Each dollar in the $3,000 represents a greater command over goods and services than does each dollar of revenue. This situation can be corrected by restatement of the cost in terms of the present general price level. The income calculation then would be:

| | | |
|---|---|---|
| Revenues . . . . . . . . . . . . . . . | $5,000 | |
| Expenses . . . . . . . . . . . . . . | 3,600 | ($3,000 × 120/100) |
| Income . . . . . . . . . . . . . . | $1,400 | |

Because prices *in general* have increased 20 percent, the $3,000 expended at the beginning of the year is equivalent to $3,600 of purchasing power at the end of the year. That latter amount must be recovered out of revenues measured at the end of the year for the firm to be as well off in terms of its pool of available purchasing power. Restatement of past costs in terms of present price levels, it is argued, provides a more meaningful measure of the preservation of capital. Conversely, use of unadjusted figures is analogous to subtracting apples from oranges—or Australian dollars from American dollars.

## Current Cost

The current cost approach departs from original dollar acquisition cost in favor of a more immediate measure of the asset's worth. Supply and demand conditions affecting a productive resource may cause its specific value relative to other goods and services to increase or decrease. The monetary representation of assets should reflect these changes in exchange value. Likewise, no income should result until the firm recovers the current value of asset services being consumed in the generation of its revenues. Under this concept the income statement might look like this:

| | |
|---|---|
| Revenues . . . . . . . . . . . . . . . | $5,000 |
| Expenses . . . . . . . . . . . . . . | 3,800 |
| Income . . . . . . . . . . . . . . . | $1,200 |

Because it would cost $3,800 currently to replace the asset used up, this figure provides a better measure of the real sacrifice (effort) involved in its use. The $3,800 represents the opportunity cost of the asset. Unless this amount is recovered through revenue generation, the *real* capital of the business has been eroded. Use of current cost highlights capital erosion.

A modification of this approach incorporates both original acquisition cost and current replacement cost. According to this suggestion, income consists of two parts—an operating income of $1,200, as previously calculated, and a price gain of $800 from holding the inventory during a time of dollar value increase, as calculated below:

| | |
|---|---:|
| Current replacement cost . . . . . . . . . . . . | $3,800 |
| Original acquisition cost . . . . . . . . . . . . | 3,000 |
| Price gain from holding inventory . . . . . . . . | $ 800 |

These brief excursions into the area of alternative cost concepts do not do justice to the many theoretical ramifications, practical complexities, recording problems, or possible uses of these alternatives. The purpose of the discussion is simply to acquaint you with some of the options that might be used in financial accounting. This background is helpful in Chapter 9 for an understanding of the LIFO inventory procedure, which rests to some extent on these alternative cost concepts.

None of them, however, is currently included in conventional financial statements because agreement is lacking about which concept should replace the existing assumptions, the absence of legal or tax recognition of these ideas, and the existence of difficulties in measurement. Nevertheless, these alternative approaches do seem to have the potential for supplying additional relevant information for the appraisal of managerial performance.

From 1976 to 1985, many large firms were required to include alternative cost information as supplementary disclosures accompanying the financial statements.[16] These requirements have since been dropped because they lacked demonstrated usefulness for external audiences and because of measurement difficulties. Also, Congress has recently experimented with limited use of price indices in the income tax laws. However, the permanence of those changes remains uncertain.

## DISCUSSION OF THE KIMBERLY-CLARK ANNUAL REPORT

The cost principle is very basic to the recording of assets. It is so ingrained in accounting practice that most financial statements do not emphasize it. Indeed, attention usually is given only to those situations in which assets have been recorded at other than acquisition cost. The only explicit reference to the cost principle in the Kimberly-Clark financial statements for 1987 is contained in Note 1 on Accounting Policies. There the company tells the reader that property, plant, and equipment are stated at cost.

---

[16] See SEC, *Accounting Series Release No. 190*, "Disclosure of Certain Replacement Cost Data" (Washington, D.C.: March 23, 1976); and FASB, *Statement of Financial Accounting Standards No. 33*, "Financial Reporting and Changing Prices" (Stamford, Conn., September 1979).

Nevertheless, the Kimberly-Clark statements do illustrate a number of the particular concepts, procedures, and practices discussed in this chapter.

Kimberly-Clark has over $525 million of inventories listed on its 1987 balance sheet (See Appendix to Chapter 6). In Note 1 the company indicates that the inventories are recorded using two different ways of establishing cost—last-in, first-out (LIFO) and first-in, first-out (FIFO). The precise meanings of these technical inventory terms are discussed in the next chapter. For now, simply note that the inventories are recorded at cost. In Note 9, Kimberly-Clark provides some additional useful information. If all of the inventory had been recorded under the first-in, first-out (FIFO) method, the inventory would have been $645.0 million in 1987 and $653.3 million in 1986.

Because Kimberly-Clark is a manufacturing company, it has more than one kind of inventory. Note 9 shows how much is raw materials, work in process, finished goods, and supplies.

The comparative balance sheet shows an increase in net plant assets from $2,263.0 million on December 31, 1986 to $2,336.8 million by the end of 1987. These amounts are after the deduction of accumulated depreciation. The original acquisition *costs* of the plant assets in service on these two dates were $3,504.2 million and $3,768.0 million, respectively.

## SUMMARY

In this chapter, we attempt to establish more detailed accounting procedures for determining the cost of specific productive resources. The general theme is that cost includes not only acquisition cost but also any necessary costs that contribute to the preparation of the asset for its intended use. In the case of most noncurrent assets, these costs are combined directly with the net purchase price in a single account. With labor services and inventory, the separate cost elements are accumulated in individual ledger accounts for management's attention and analysis.

For a merchandising firm, the recording process can be summarized as follows:

$$\text{Cost of goods sold} = \text{Beginning inventory} + \text{Net purchases} - \text{Ending inventory}$$

where

$$\text{Net purchases} = \text{Purchases} - \text{Returns and allowances} - \text{Discounts} + \text{Freight-in} + \text{Handling costs}$$

In a manufacturing firm, an elaborate recording system is set up to collect the product costs and assign them to units sold, units completed but not sold, and units partially completed. The recording process in summary form is:

$$\text{Cost of goods sold} = \text{Beginning inventory of finished goods}$$
$$+ \text{ Cost of goods completed}$$
$$- \text{ Ending inventory of finished goods}$$

where

$$\text{Cost of goods completed} = \text{Beginning inventory of work in process}$$
$$+ \text{ Material used} + \text{Direct labor}$$
$$+ \text{ Manufacturing overhead}$$
$$- \text{ Ending inventory of work in process}$$

In certain circumstances, modifications are made to the cost principle. Marketable equity securities are recorded at the lower of acquisition cost or current market value. Often the adjustment to reduce the acquisition cost to a lower market value or to increase the valuation to a higher market value (but not above cost) is handled by entries to a contra asset account. The changes in stockholders' equity corresponding to the changes in asset valuation are recorded as unrealized losses (gains) in the income statement if the marketable equity securities are classified as current assets. If they are classified as noncurrent assets, the changes in stockholders' equity flow directly to a contra equity account in the owners' equity section of the balance sheet.

Original dollar acquisition cost is not the only measure at which resources could be stated in the financial records. Constant dollar acquisition cost and current replacement cost are two measures that are sometimes suggested as alternatives.

# PROBLEMS AND CASETTES

### 8–1. Classifying Costs

For each of the following expenditures, indicate whether the item should be charged to Land, Buildings, Equipment, or some other account (indicate which other account).

1. Freight charges on a new machine recently purchased.
2. Legal fees in connection with a purchase of land.
3. Cost of a temporary building used as an on-site construction office during the building of a new sales office.
4. Architect's fees for a new sales office.
5. Cost of a special steel and concrete base for a new machine.
6. Cost of remodeling an old warehouse.
7. Insurance premium for a special policy to cover risks while a new piece of equipment was in transit.
8. Cost of blasting out limestone rock in construction of foundation and basement for a building.
9. Annual property taxes paid on machinery in the factory.
10. Tax assessment for improvement of city streets in front of the factory.
11. Delinquent property taxes assumed by the company in connection with the acquisition of land.

12. Expansion and modification of the elevator system in connection with the addition of a fourth story on a building.
13. Amount of a mortgage assumed in connection with the purchase of a warehouse.
14. Annual interest on the mortgage in item 13.
15. Costs of landscaping around the new office building.

## 8–2. Basic Payroll Entries

On December 31, 1989, the following account balances appeared among the liabilities of Soaper Company:

| | |
|---|---:|
| Wages payable . . . . . . . . . . . . . . . . . . . . | $54,720 |
| Social security taxes payable . . . . . . . . . . . . | 2,080 |
| Income tax withholdings payable . . . . . . . . . . | 8,800 |

The following selected transactions occurred during January 1990:

1. The total amount of gross wages for the month was $60,000. The company withheld 14 percent for employee income tax, 7 percent for social security taxes, and $1,200 under an employee stock purchase program. The $60,000 gross payroll was represented by $48,000 of direct labor wages, $6,000 of indirect labor wages, and $6,000 of administrative wages.
2. Fringe benefit costs were: employer's contribution to social security, 7 percent of gross payroll; employer's tax for unemployment compensation, 3 percent of gross payroll; employer's contribution to hospital insurance program, $2,400; and pension fund cost, $9,600. All fringe benefit costs are to be recorded as separate cost items (debit the social security and unemployment taxes to Payroll Taxes).
3. Checks drawn during the month:

| | |
|---|---:|
| Employee wage checks. . . . . . . . . . . . . . . . . . . | $99,980 |
| For income taxes withheld . . . . . . . . . . . . . . . | 16,600 |
| For social security contributions . . . . . . . . . . . . | 6,400 |

## Required:

a. Prepare journal entries for the month of January.
b. What liabilities and amounts would appear on the balance sheet as of January 31, 1990?
c. What would you do with the separate cost accounts that you established in connection with the recording of fringe benefits? On what financial statements, if any, would they appear?

## 8–3. Statement of Cost of Goods Manufactured and Sold

Hassell and Associates manufactures and sells sports equipment. Prepare a statement of cost of goods manufactured and sold for 1992 from the following costs and expenses incurred during the year. Use the format shown in Table 8–3.

| | |
|---|---:|
| Purchases of raw materials . . . . . . . . . . . . . . . . . . . . | $663,000 |
| Direct labor . . . . . . . . . . . . . . . . . . . . . . . . . . . . | 240,000 |
| Indirect labor . . . . . . . . . . . . . . . . . . . . . . . . . . . | 82,500 |

| | |
|---|---:|
| Depreciation of factory building . . . . . . . . . . . . . . . . . . . . . | 49,500 |
| Property taxes on factory building . . . . . . . . . . . . . . . . . . . | 6,000 |
| Depreciation on factory equipment . . . . . . . . . . . . . . . . . . | 39,000 |
| Light, heat, and power (60% applicable to manufacturing, | |
| 10% to selling, 30% to office) . . . . . . . . . . . . . . . . . . . | 25,000 |
| Salespersons' salaries . . . . . . . . . . . . . . . . . . . . . . . . | 78,000 |
| Maintenance costs on factory equipment . . . . . . . . . . . . . . . . | 1,900 |
| Office salaries  . . . . . . . . . . . . . . . . . . . . . . . . . . | 55,600 |
| Advertising supplies purchased and used . . . . . . . . . . . . . . . . | 7,200 |
| Factory supplies purchased . . . . . . . . . . . . . . . . . . . . . | 28,200 |
| Factory manager's salary . . . . . . . . . . . . . . . . . . . . . . | 37,000 |

Relevant inventory accounts show the following balances:

| | Jan. 1 | Dec. 31 |
|---|---:|---:|
| Raw materials . . . . . . . . . . . . | $ 43,500 | $ 61,500 |
| Goods in process . . . . . . . . . . . | 108,000 | 115,500 |
| Finished goods . . . . . . . . . . . . | 60,000 | 40,500 |
| Factory supplies  . . . . . . . . . . . | 5,800 | 7,700 |

### 8–4. Recording Purchases at Gross versus Net

The Modern Company buys merchandise from the New Company on terms of 3/10, n/30. Purchases during September 1990 are as follows (amounts are gross price figures):

| Purchase Date | Amount | Payment Date |
|---|---:|---|
| September  7 | $ 8,800 | September 15 |
| September 11 | 7,800 | September 20 |
| September 17 | 5,600 | $2,400 returned September 24; remainder paid October 10 |
| September 28 | 13,200 | October 12 |

### Required:

a. Using the net price method, record the entries that would be made on the books of the Modern Company for the months of September and October.
b. Repeat part a using gross prices.

### 8–5. Determination of Machinery Cost

Patterson Company acquired a machine with a list price of $80,000 and debited the Machinery account for that amount. The account was paid within the 30-day discount period, and the company took the 5 percent cash discount. A credit of $4,000 was made to Purchase Discounts. A credit of $4,000

Transportation costs of $1,600 were paid by Patterson Company and charged to Freight Expense. This amount included $200 for delayed delivery date charges. The company had agreed to take the machine earlier, but because there was no place to put it, Patterson had to pay a penalty for having the manufacturer hold the machine.

Installation was done by a consulting engineer outside the company assisted by a few of Patterson's own employees. The consulting engineer's fee of $2,000 was debited to the Machinery account; the wages of the employees, amounting to $800, were charged to Wage Expense.

Supplies of $600 were used in the installation, and raw materials of $400 were destroyed in testing. The former cost was debited to Supplies Expense; the latter cost, to Loss on Testing.

**Required:**

*a.* Prepare a schedule showing the total cost at which the machine should be recorded.
*b.* Prepare any adjusting entries necessary to correct the accounts.
*c.* Assume Patterson Company did not pay within the 30-day discount period. How would this affect the cost of the asset and the entries made?
*d.* Six months later, the Patterson Company decides to move the machinery to a different wing of the plant. The cost (primarily wages) is $3,000. How would you handle this relocation cost?

**8–6. Reporting Marketable Equity Securities**

Bennett Corporation had idle cash balances during the last quarter of 1990. It invested in the following portfolio of short-term marketable equity securities.

| Security | Number of Shares | Cost per Share | Total Cost | Market Value per Share 12/31/90 | Market Value per Share 3/31/91 |
|---|---|---|---|---|---|
| Fowler Company | 1,000 | $60 | $ 60,000 | $62 | — |
| Krauss Company | 1,500 | 50 | 75,000 | 48 | $51 |
| Cochran Company | 2,500 | 40 | 100,000 | 35 | 36 |

The market figures on December 31, 1990 and March 31, 1991 are also given. During the first quarter of 1991, all of the shares of Fowler Company were sold for $62,300.

**Required:**

*a.* Show how the marketable equity securities would appear on the balance sheet as of December 31, 1990. What amount would be reflected in the income statement for 1990?
*b.* Show how the marketable equity securities would appear on the balance sheet as of March 31, 1991. What amount would be reflected in the income statement for 1991?
*c.* What is the amount of unrealized gains and unrealized losses as of December 31, 1990? As of March 31, 1991?

### 8–7. Alternative Cost Concepts for Inventory

The following data are made available to you concerning the merchandise inventory of Grandma Crow's Discount Store:

|  | Cost |
|---|---|
| Inventory, January 1 . . . . . . . . . . . . . . | $ 57,000* |
| Purchases. . . . . . . . . . . . . . . . . . . | 562,600 |
| Cost of goods sold . . . . . . . . . . . . . . | 543,000† |
| Inventory, December 31 . . . . . . . . . . . . | 76,600‡ |

\*Wholesale cost on January 1, $66,000.
†Wholesale cost at date of sale, $651,000.
‡Wholesale cost at December 31, $90,000.

Total sales for the year were $770,000, and selling and administrative expenses were $100,000.

### Required:

*a.* Prepare an income statement employing conventional measures of cost.
*b.* Prepare a revised income statement employing a replacement cost concept and recognizing holding gains. What additional information does this statement provide?
*c.* The president of the company remarks that she prefers the approach in *b* because "it recognizes the impact of inflation." Comment on her view.

### 8–8. Identification of Costs for Noncurrent Assets

The Anderson Springs Company incurred the following costs related to its noncurrent assets. The bookkeeper recorded them all in a single account called Property, Plant, and Equipment.

| | |
|---|---|
| Land—Plot #18A . . . . . . . . . . . . . . . . . . . . . . . . . . . | $ 300,000 |
| Real estate commission paid on purchase of Plot #18A . . . . . . . . . | 18,000 |
| Legal fees for abstract and title search on Plot #18A . . . . . . . . . | 1,500 |
| Land—Plot #22C (total cost of land and two buildings. Building #1 will be razed to make room for new construction. Building #2 will be renovated. The appraisal value of Building #1 was $40,000; the appraisal value of Building #2 was $170,000) . . . . . . . . . . | 450,000 |
| Cost of tearing down Building #1 . . . . . . . . . . . . . . . . . | 9,000 |
| Excavation cost for new building on Plot #22C. . . . . . . . . . . . | 33,000 |
| Architectural fees for design of new building . . . . . . . . . . . . | 24,000 |
| Contract cost of new building on Plot #22C . . . . . . . . . . . . . | 450,000 |
| Contract cost for new parking lot on Plot #22C. . . . . . . . . . . | 90,000 |
| Painting, electrical, and construction costs during renovation of Building #2 . . . . . . . . . . . . . . . . . . . . . . . . . | 150,000 |
| Cost of trees, shrubs, and other landscaping around new building on Plot #22C . . . . . . . . . . . . . . . . . . . . . . | 12,600 |
| Invoice price of new equipment put in Building #2 (a cash discount of 3 percent was not taken) . . . . . . . . . . . | 96,500 |
| Unloading and installation costs of equipment. . . . . . . . . . . . | 6,600 |
| Royalty payments paid on products produced on the new equipment . . . . . . . . . . . . . . . . . . . . . . . . . . . | 3,100 |
| | $1,644,300 |

**Required:**

Prepare a schedule that will indicate the amount of cost to be recorded in each of the following *separate* noncurrent asset accounts:

Land
Buildings
Machinery and Equipment
Land Improvements (limited life)

## 8–9. Supply Missing Data about Manufacturing Costs

The following information has been taken from two *separate* manufacturing operations. Make the calculations necessary to supply the missing data (identified by letter) in each of these situations.

| | Case 1 | Case 2 |
|---|---|---|
| Direct materials, Jan. 1 | $ 32,000 | $ 2,000 |
| Direct materials, Dec. 31 | 46,000 | 2,800 |
| Work in process, Jan. 1 | 19,000 | D |
| Work in process, Dec. 31 | 20,900 | 27,100 |
| Finished goods, Jan. 1 | 57,000 | 17,200 |
| Finished goods, Dec. 31 | 68,800 | E |
| Cost of goods sold | A | 66,000 |
| Direct labor | B | 23,000 |
| Purchases of direct materials | 90,000 | 42,500 |
| Factory supplies used | 7,000 | 1,800 |
| Factory depreciation | 13,000 | 3,100 |
| Total manufacturing costs | 180,000 | 102,000 |
| Other factory overhead costs | 22,000 | F |
| Cost of goods completed | C | 107,000 |

## 8–10. Preparation of Payroll Entries

On July 31, the following account balances appear on the books of Haw Company:

| | |
|---|---|
| Accrued payroll | $15,000 |
| Employee income taxes payable | 5,000 |
| FICA taxes payable | 600 |

Payroll records for the month of August show the following:

| | |
|---|---|
| Employee: | |
| Gross wages | $30,000 |
| Withholding for income taxes | 2,300 |
| Withholding for FICA taxes | 1,800 |
| Withholding for union dues | 400 |
| Employer: | |
| FICA taxes | 1,800 |
| Premiums for group life insurance policy on employees | 150 |

Checks written during August are as follows:

| | |
|---|---:|
| Employees . . . . . . . . . . . . . . . . . . . . . | $36,500 |
| Union . . . . . . . . . . . . . . . . . . . . . . | 300 |
| Withholding taxes . . . . . . . . . . . . . . . . | 6,100 |
| FICA taxes . . . . . . . . . . . . . . . . . . . | 3,900 |
| Group life insurance premiums . . . . . . . . . . . | 150 |

### Required:

a. Prepare journal entries to record the wage and associated labor costs and the cash disbursements for August.
b. What was the amount of employees' take-home pay in August?
c. What was the total cost to Haw Company of maintaining a labor force during the month of August?

### 8–11. Ledger Entries for Elements of Inventory Cost

The Poorland Company begins operations on October 1, 1989. The following selected transactions relate to purchases and sales of inventory during October:

1. Merchandise purchases on account amount to $400,000 at gross prices.
2. Merchandise costing $16,000 is returned.
3. The accounts payable from merchandise purchases are paid; $4,400 of discounts are taken, and $2,000 of discounts are lost.
4. Bills of $20,000 are received for freight charges on incoming merchandise.
5. A bill for $600 is received for demurrage charges for failure to unload and return a railroad car within the allotted time.
6. The receiving department costs are $14,000 for the month consisting of $12,000 of labor cost and $2,000 of supplies.
7. Bills in the amount of $13,000 are received for freight charges on merchandise delivered to customers during October.
8. Ninety percent of the net merchandise purchased during October is sold on account at a price of $412,000.

### Required:

a. Record the selected transactions relating to inventory during October in general ledger (T) accounts. The company uses separate accounts for the individual cost elements. Include the necessary entries to determine cost of goods sold and the October 31 merchandise inventory.
b. What would be the impact on the accounts if Poorland treated the freight charges and receiving costs as period expenses?

### 8–12. Oil Exploration: Successful Efforts versus Full Costing

In 1990 and 1991 Grossbrecht Oil Company drilled a large number of oil wells on two tracts of land in Wyoming. The amounts spent and the results appear in the following schedule:

| Oil | Amount Spent | | |
|-----|------|------|---------|
| Well | 1990 | 1991 | Results |
| AD#1 | $350,000 | $200,000 | Found proven quantities of commercially feasible oil |
| AD#2 | 300,000 | 300,000 | Found proven quantities of commercially feasible oil |
| BK#1 | 400,000 | 250,000 | Found proven quantities of commercially feasible oil |
| AD#3 | 100,000 | 480,000 | Found limited quantities of low grade crude, not commercially feasible |
| BK#2 | 500,000 | — | Dry hole |
| BK#3 | 150,000 | 470,000 | Found proven quantities of commercially feasible oil |
| AD#4 | 50,000 | 530,000 | Found proven quantities of commercially feasible oil |
| AD#5 | — | 620,000 | Dry hole |
| BK#4 | — | 540,000 | Drilling operations abandoned as likely to be unfruitful |
| AD#6 | — | 410,000 | Found proven quantities of commercially feasible oil |

### Required:

a. Assume Grossbrecht uses the successful-efforts method. How much cost will appear on the income statements for 1990 and 1991 as an expense? At what amount will the asset Oil and Gas Properties appear on each of the year-end balance sheets?

b. Assume Grossbrecht uses the full-cost method. How much cost will appear on the income statement for 1990 and 1991 as an expense? At what amount will the asset Oil and Gas Properties appear on each of the year-end balance sheets?

c. Assume that well AD#6 was still in the process of being drilled at the end of 1991 so that no results are known at year-end. Explain how you would treat the $410,000 expended to date on the financial statements for 1991, assuming the company uses successful efforts.

**8–13. Determining Land and Building Costs (including Interest Capitalization)**

In 1990, the Hillandale Corporation acquired a parcel of farmland on the outskirts of town for the purpose of building a new plant. Hillandale used its own resources for most of the construction work in 1991 and 1992. The following information relates to these activities:

1. The property acquired included 150 acres of land, an old farmhouse to be razed, and a timber stand to be cut and leveled.

2. Hillandale paid $460,000 cash to the owner, paid $12,000 of unpaid back property taxes, and issued 2,000 shares of its stock to the owner of the farm. The current market value of the stock was $14 per share.

3. An appraisal report on the property listed the land at $480,000, the farmhouse at $18,000, and the timber tract at $50,000.

4. Labor costs incurred in razing the farmhouse were $20,000.
5. Cash was received in the amounts of $5,000 representing the value of material recovered from the farmhouse and $40,000 from a lumber mill representing the net proceeds to Hillandale from cutting the timber tract and removing all stumps.
6. Formal construction of the new building began on January 1, 1991, and was completed on June 30, 1992. The following costs were incurred (spread evenly over the 18-month construction period):

| | |
|---|---:|
| Architect's fees . . . . . . . . . . . . . . . . . . . . . . . . . . | $  210,000 |
| Labor costs . . . . . . . . . . . . . . . . . . . . . . . . . . | 1,200,000 |
| Materials . . . . . . . . . . . . . . . . . . . . . . . . | 600,000 |
| Subcontracting costs . . . . . . . . . . . . . . . . . . . . . . | 120,000 |
| Factory manager's salary (one half of the time spent supervising construction and the rest at the company's other plant) . . . . . . | 90,000 |

7. To help finance construction, the company borrowed $500,000 on January 1, 1991, and another $500,000 on January 1, 1992. Both of these borrowings were at 12 percent. In addition, the company had $3 million of bonds outstanding with an interest rate of 10 percent and $6 million of bonds with an interest rate of 9 percent.

**Required:**

*a.* What is the total cost to be assigned to the Land account?
*b.* What is the total cost, excluding interest charged during construction, of the new building? Explain how you treated any costs not charged to either the land or the building.
*c.* Calculate the total interest that would be capitalized during construction. What effect does interest capitalization have on the financial statements in 1991, 1992, and subsequent years?

**8–14. Reporting Marketable Equity Securities**
Ashly and Wooten, Inc. engage in the transactions related to marketable equity securities that are summarized in the table below:

| | | | | | Market Value, Dec. 31 | |
|---|---|---:|---|---:|---:|---:|
| Security | Date Acquired | Cost | Date Sold | Selling Price | 1989 | 1990 |
| Current: | | | | | | |
| M | 2/18/89 | $26,000 | | | $20,000 | $24,000 |
| N | 2/18/89 | 24,000 | 8/15/89 | $33,000 | | |
| O | 5/23/90 | 45,000 | | | | 50,000 |
| P | 5/23/90 | 33,000 | | | | 36,000 |
| Noncurrent: | | | | | | |
| Y | 2/23/89 | 73,000 | 8/22/90 | 60,000 | 67,000 | |
| Z | 2/23/89 | 59,000 | | | 55,000 | 67,000 |

**Required:**

a. How would these securities be presented on the balance sheets as of December 31, 1989 and December 31, 1990 so that they conform with *FASB Statement No. 12*? Indicate the accounts, amounts, and sections of balance sheets in which they would appear.

b. Calculate the impact of the transactions and events on income before taxes in both 1989 and 1990.

c. What is the amount of unrealized gains and unrealized losses on the *current* portfolio as of December 31, 1989 and December 31, 1990?

**8–15. Preparing Ledger Entries and Statements for Manufacturing**

On July 31, the following account balances existed for the Cosier Bowling Ball Manufacturing Company:

|  | Debit | Credit |
|---|---|---|
| Cash . . . . . . . . . . . . . . . . . . . . . . . . . . . . . . . . . . | $ 55,300 | |
| Raw materials . . . . . . . . . . . . . . . . . . . . . . . | 29,400 | |
| Work in process . . . . . . . . . . . . . . . . . . . . . | 29,700 | |
| Finished goods . . . . . . . . . . . . . . . . . . . . . . | 37,800 | |
| Building . . . . . . . . . . . . . . . . . . . . . . . . . . . . | 93,000 | |
| Accumulated depreciation on building . . . . . . . . . . . | | $ 19,000 |
| Factory equipment . . . . . . . . . . . . . . . . . . . . | 60,000 | |
| Accumulated depreciation on equipment . . . . . . . . . . | | 12,000 |
| Accounts payable . . . . . . . . . . . . . . . . . . . . | | 38,900 |
| Capital stock . . . . . . . . . . . . . . . . . . . . . . . | | 210,000 |
| Retained earnings . . . . . . . . . . . . . . . . . . . . | | 25,300 |
| | $305,200 | $305,200 |

During the month of August the following transactions took place:

1. Raw materials purchased on account, $120,600.
2. Raw materials used in production, $102,000.
3. Supplies (of all types) purchased on account, $42,000.
4. Supplies used, $25,100. Of this amount, $19,200 was used in production operations; $3,400 was used by the selling department; and $2,500 was used in the general office.
5. Wage and salary costs incurred: direct labor, $117,000; indirect labor, $45,000; sales department personnel, $55,500; and administration, $52,500. Amounts withheld by the company: 14 percent for federal income taxes and 7 percent for social security taxes.
6. Accrued the company's share of social security taxes and assigned it to the respective cost areas.
7. Depreciation on the building, $9,000.
8. Depreciation on factory equipment, $3,000.
9. Power cost for the month, $10,000 (credit Accounts Payable).
10. Sales on account were $472,800.

**Additional Information:**

1. The factory occupied three of the five floors in the building. The selling department occupied the first floor, and the general office took up the remaining floor.
2. Power cost was allocated on the basis of metered amounts: 80 percent to manufacturing, 5 percent to selling, and 15 percent to general administration.
3. Inventory of work in process and finished goods on August 31 amounted to $34,900 and $38,200, respectively.

**Required:**

a. Set up ledger (T) accounts and enter the opening balances. Record the entries during August, including any necessary entries based on the additional information provided. Use single accounts for Selling Expense, Administrative Expense, and Manufacturing Overhead.
b. Prepare a statement of cost of goods manufactured and sold and an income statement for August.

**8–16. Determining Land and Building Costs (including Interest Capitalization)**
On January 1, 1989, Lepok Corporation purchased a parcel of land with an old building on it for $900,000. The land was valued at $750,000, and the building, at $150,000. However, shortly after acquisition, the building was razed at a net cost of $112,500. Additional costs incurred by Lepok included real estate commissions of $54,000 and legal fees of $9,000.

Lepok entered into a $4,500,000 fixed-price contract with Hardin Construction Company on April 1, 1989, for the construction of an office building on the land. The building was completed and occupied on November 1, 1990. Additional costs incurred over and above the construction contract were:

| | |
|---|---:|
| Cost of clearing brush and tree stumps from land . . . . . . . . . . . . | $ 4,000 |
| Cost of building plans and permits . . . . . . | 18,000 |
| Architect's fees . . . . . . . . . . . . . . | 142,500 |

To finance the construction costs, Lepok borrowed $4,500,000 on April 1, 1989. The loan is payable in 15 annual installments of $300,000 plus interest at the rate of 12 percent. Lepok's average amounts of accumulated building construction expenditures were as follows:

| | |
|---|---:|
| From April 1 to December 31, 1989 . . . . . . | $1,350,000 |
| From January 1 to October 31, 1990 . . . . . . | 3,450,000 |

**Required:**

Prepare schedules that will indicate the cost elements that comprise the balances in the land account and in the office building account on October 31, 1990. Show supporting computations in good form.

## 8–17. Preparing Journal Entries for Inventory Transactions

On November 1, the inventory of Royal, Inc.—at net cost including applicable freight and handling costs—amounted to $66,000. The company records all purchases at gross prices and initially records all elements of inventory cost in separate accounts for purposes of analysis and control. During the month of November, the following transactions, in summary form, took place:

1. Inventory amounting to $254,000 gross invoice price was purchased on terms allowing a 2 percent discount if paid within 10 days.
2. The company discovered that $60,000 gross amount of inventory did not meet specifications. It returned $38,000 and was granted a purchase adjustment allowance of $6,000 by the vendor on the remaining amount.
3. The company ordered and received $30,000 gross amount of additional inventory (also subject to the 2 percent discount for prompt payment). This merchandise replaced part of that which was returned in transaction 2.
4. Transportation costs applicable to November purchases amounted to $4,000; transportation costs applicable to November sales were $9,000.
5. Wage payments made to the warehouse employees during the month were $10,000. It is estimated that 60 percent of the warehouse time is spent unloading and handling incoming purchases; the other 40 percent is spent loading and shipping merchandise sold.
6. The accounts payable were paid. All purchase discounts were taken except for a $700 discount that was lost.
7. Merchandise inventory on November 30 amounted to $51,400 at net invoice prices plus applicable transportation and handling costs.

### Required:

*a.* Journalize the above transactions.
*b.* The chief accountant recommends that the $30,000 in item 3 be debited to Purchase Returns, because it essentially cancels part of the original return. Evaluate this suggestion.

## 8–18. Accounting for Noncurrent Asset Expenditures

Select Products Corporation engaged in several activities during 1990 with respect to noncurrent assets. Several of them are described below. Briefly explain how you would have accounted for each of the following costs both initially and in future periods, if relevant.

1. Paid an advertising agency $500,000—$200,000 for recurring media advertising and the remainder for a consumer behavior study that was to provide a basis for marketing strategies during the next three or so years.
2. Hired a contractor to build a new warehouse. The contract price was $800,000. Of this amount, $600,000 was spent evenly over 1990, and the remaining $200,000 was paid during the first six months of 1991. Select Products borrowed $400,000 from a local bank at a 10 percent interest rate; the money was used explicitly for the warehouse. The other funds for the warehouse came from internal sources. Select Products has a $600,000 issue of bonds payable outstanding that carries an interest rate of 8 percent.

3. Accidentally discovered that an unused portion of the company's land contained a substantial copper deposit. Immediately spent $50,000 for the services of a consulting engineer to ascertain the feasibility of mining the ore commercially. Upon receipt of the engineer's affirmative report, spent $1.6 million to strip overburden and to develop the mine, plus another $210,000 for mining equipment.

4. Exchanged some marketable securities originally costing $180,000 for all the inventory and equipment of a small local business. The securities had a market price of $220,000 on the day of the exchange. The inventory and equipment on the books of the local company were recorded at $100,000 and $60,000 respectively. The replacement cost of the inventory is estimated to be $120,000. The equipment is in very bad condition. Select Products spends $56,000 for extensive overhauling, after which the machinery has an estimated current value of $160,000.

5. Paid $250,000 to a design firm for the creation of a new abstract logo to be used as a corporate identification and advertising symbol. Launched a broad 20-month media campaign costing $675,000 to promote the symbol. Paid $75,000 to a local firm that claimed to have developed and used the logo first. Rather than risk a court fight, Select Products bought the "rights."

## 8–19. Analysis of Errors in Manufacturing

You are engaged to audit the accounting records of Brand X Manufacturing Company. The following figures appear at the end of the period:

|  |  |
|---|---:|
| Work in process inventory . . . . . . . | $138,900 |
| Finished goods inventory . . . . . . . . | 92,500 |
| Net income . . . . . . . . . . . . . | 64,200 |

In the course of the investigation, you discover the following facts:

1. A purchase of raw materials in the amount of $6,000 has never been recorded, even though they have been used in production.
2. Depreciation of factory equipment has been overstated by $7,500.
3. The bookkeeper has failed to accrue $9,000 of indirect labor costs applicable to the period when making adjusting entries.
4. Direct labor costs of $15,000 have been incorrectly charged to administrative expense.
5. Rent costs of $12,000 have been charged to manufacturing overhead; 25 percent of this should have been allocated to selling and 25 percent to administration.

Of the production costs incurred in the period, one third are still in process. Of the finished goods manufactured during the year, 80 percent have been sold.

### Required:

Prepare a schedule showing the effect of these errors on the ending inventories and net income for the period and showing the correct amounts for these items. You may find it helpful to use the flow of costs through the manufacturing ledger accounts as an analytical device to help you trace through the effect of each error.

## 8–20. Journal Entries for Marketable Equity Securities

The table below summarizes information about the marketable equity securities of Nago Corporation during 1990 and 1991:

| Security | Date Acquired | Acquisition Cost | Sale Date | Sale Amount | Market Value 12/31/89 | Market Value 12/31/90 |
|---|---|---|---|---|---|---|
| **Current portfolio:** | | | | | | |
| Alpha | 1/8/89 | $240,000 | 11/7/89 | $250,000 | — | — |
| Beta | 2/6/89 | 385,000 | — | — | $380,000 | $387,000 |
| Gamma | 4/17/89 | 248,000 | 4/13/90 | 230,000 | 245,000 | — |
| Delta | 3/15/90 | 175,000 | — | — | — | 183,000 |
| Epsilon | 6/27/90 | 336,000 | — | — | — | 325,000 |
| Zeta | 9/10/90 | 118,000 | — | — | — | 115,000 |
| **Noncurrent portfolio:** | | | | | | |
| Eta | 5/10/89 | 125,000 | — | — | 120,000 | 127,000 |
| Theta | 9/15/89 | 262,000 | — | — | 251,000 | 258,000 |

### Required:

a. Prepare all journal entries relating to marketable equity securities during 1989 and 1990. The company prepares financial statements on December 31.

b. Show how the marketable equity securities would appear on the balance sheet as of December 31, 1989 and as of December 31, 1990.

c. Calculate the amount of unrealized gains and unrealized losses that would appear in the notes to the financial statements on December 31 of each year.

## 8–21. Determining the Costs of Self-Constructed Assets

Remoorg Corporation solicited bids from various equipment manufacturers for a new piece of special-purpose machinery. The lowest bid was $600,000, which was about 50 percent higher than Remoorg expected. Accordingly, it decided to manufacture the machine in its own machine shop, which was operating at less than full capacity.

The following list contains the items that were recorded in the Machinery account in connection with this machine:

Debit Entries:

1. Invoice cost of materials used in the construction of the machine, $120,000. Cash discounts received upon payment for these materials totaled $1,600 and were credited to Purchase Discounts. Freight charges on materials used in the machine, $17,000, were debited to Freight Expense.

2. Direct labor costs incurred in the machine shop to manufacture the new machine, $100,000.

3. Allocated manufacturing overhead during the period of construction, $180,000. Normal overhead for the period would have been $240,000. During construction, it increased to $360,000. Because the direct labor hours spent manufacturing the machine and those spent manufacturing regular products for sale were approximately equal, one half of the overhead was allocated to the new machine.

4. Cost of replacing the wooden floor with a cement one in the west wing of the building where the new machine is to be located, $68,000. Management felt

that this change, necessitated by the weight of the new machine, was a long overdue general improvement that had been contemplated for a number of years but never done.

5. Cost of electrical rewiring of the west wing of the building, $17,000. About $12,000 of this cost was incurred specifically for a new electrical line to service the new machine. The rest of the money was spent in general upgrading of conduits and outlets.

6. Amount paid to an engineering consulting company to install and test the new machine after it was built, $32,000.

7. Cost of products produced during the testing of the machine, $17,000. These products were scrapped.

8. Estimated profit of $79,000 on the manufacture of the new machine. This amount was the difference between the lowest outside bid of $600,000 and the *net* cost in the Machinery account. The effect of this entry is to increase the carrying value of the machine to $600,000. The corresponding $79,000 credit was to an account called Gain from Cost Savings on Self-Construction.

Credit Entries:

1. Value of lumber recovered from replacement of floors in west wing of building, $5,000. (See debit entry 4.)

2. Scrap value of products made during testing (see debit entry 7), $8,000.

**Required:**

a. Determine the proper amount at which the new machine should be recorded in the accounts. Show the individual elements of cost and explain your reasoning.

b. For each of the entries made to the Machinery account that you did not include in part a, explain how you would have accounted for the item.

**8–22. Applying Alternative Cost Concepts to Land**

The Cwagmire Realty Company speculates on land prices. It buys parcels of undeveloped land and holds them for a number of years. It subsequently either sells the undeveloped land or develops it by putting in streets and clearing trees and then sells individual lots to subdivision builders.

In 19x1, the company bought a piece of land for $200,000 when the general price index was 120. In 19x9, the undeveloped land could be sold for $300,000, and the general price index stood at 150.

**Required:**

a. If the company sells the undeveloped land in 19x9, what is the amount of gain in purchasing power?

b. If the company pays taxes at a rate of 30 percent of historical accounting income, for how much would it have to sell the undeveloped land in order to recover the original purchasing power invested?

c. Assume in 19x9, Cwagmire spends $60,000 on developing the land and sells the lots for $396,000. How much of the conventional accounting income of $136,000 ($396,000 − $200,000 − $60,000) is attributable to the actual development work (operating activity) and how much is the result of speculation (holding activity)?

### Casette 8–1.  Georgia-Pacific Corporation

In the Appendix at the end of the book is a complete set of financial statements of Georgia-Pacific Corporation taken from its annual report of 1987.

Answer the following questions related to cost determination as reflected in those statements.

1. Are there any nonmonetary assets not recorded at acquisition cost?
2. What is the total liability related to payroll accounts at the end of 1987?
3. Of the manufacturing inventories at the end of 1987, what percentage is raw materials, finished goods, and supplies? Why is there no work in process?
4. How does the company account for the costs related to its timber and timberlands?
5. Evaluate the change in policy effective January 1, 1986 regarding reforestation costs.
6. How much interest did the company capitalize in 1987? What would net income have been in 1987 if the interest had not been capitalized?
7. How much cost was added to property, plant, and equipment in 1987? In 1986? In what lines of business were these expenditures made?

### Casette 8–2.  Cost of Parking Lot

Duncan owned a supermarket that he leased to a food chain. The food chain needed more parking space and told Duncan it would not renew the lease if Duncan could not supply additional parking. The only adjacent land was residential, and its owners knew of Duncan's problem. The owners charged Duncan $150,000 for land having a current market value of $8,000 and residences having a current market value of $66,000. Duncan promptly demolished the residences at a cost of $28,000 and built a parking lot for $6,000.

### Required:

Discuss carefully how each amount should be handled on the books of Duncan to match costs and revenues properly. Indicate exactly what amounts would be involved, what accounts would be used, and how the items would be handled in future years.

### Casette 8–3.  Gas and Oil Accounting Policies

The following quotations are taken from the formal descriptions of accounting policies of two oil companies contained in their 1985 annual reports.

#### Standard Oil Company of Ohio

The successful efforts method of accounting is followed for costs incurred in oil and gas exploration and development operations.

Property acquisition costs for oil and gas properties are initially capitalized. The acquisition costs of all unproved properties that are not individually significant are aggregated, and the costs related to the portion of such properties estimated to be nonproductive based on past experience are amortized over their average holding period. . . . Any individually significant unproved properties are assessed at least annually on a property-by-property basis and any impairment in value is recognized currently.

Exploratory drilling costs are initially capitalized. If and when exploratory wells are determined to be nonproductive, the related costs are charged to expense. Other exploration costs, including geological, geophysical and carrying costs, are charged to expense as incurred.

When a property is determined to contain proved reserves, property acquisition costs and related exploratory drilling costs of successful wells are transferred to proved properties.

Development costs of proved properties, including producing wells and related facilities and any development dry holes, are capitalized.

### Tenneco

Tenneco and its subsidiaries follow the full-cost method of accounting whereby all productive and nonproductive costs incurred in connection with the acquisition, exploration and development of oil and gas reserves are capitalized and amortized over the companies' estimate of proved oil and gas reserves using the unit-of-production method. Cost centers for amortization purposes are determined on a country-by-country basis. Certain unevaluated properties are excluded for amortization purposes until the properties have been evaluated.

Under the full-cost method, unamortized capitalized costs may not exceed a "ceiling" based on the present value of future net revenues from proved reserves, less related income tax effects, in each case using each country of operations as a separate cost center. To the extent such costs for any cost center exceed the ceiling limitation for that cost center, the excess must be charged (as a non-cash item) to expense currently. Although Tenneco's unamortized capital costs have not previously exceeded the ceiling limitation in respect of any of its cost centers, it is probable that a material excess will occur in 1986 if price declines for oil and gas continue as experienced in early 1986.

Due to the progressive weakening of oil and gas prices, Tenneco is considering the option of changing from the full-cost method to the successful efforts method of oil and gas accounting in 1986. Under this acceptable alternative accounting method, certain non-productive costs are expensed currently rather than capitalized as under the full-cost method. Adoption of the successful efforts method would require a restatement of earnings for oil and gas producing activities for prior periods. Although the restatement would initially result in a material reduction in retained earnings, this effect would be offset in subsequent periods through lower amortization charged against future earnings. Cash flow would be unaffected by the change.

### Required:

a. Describe in your own words the difference between the successful-efforts method used by Standard Oil of Ohio and the full-cost method used by Tenneco.

b. Standard Oil of Ohio mentions a number of different types of costs. For each of the following costs, indicate how it is handled and the possible justification for its treatment.
   1. Property acquisition costs for unproved properties not individually significant
   2. Property acquisition costs for unproved properties individually significant
   3. Exploratory drilling costs
   4. Geological and geophysical costs
   5. Developmental costs of proved properties
   6. Cost of development dry holes

c. Standard Oil of Ohio initially treats the cost of exploratory wells as an asset and then writes it off as expense if unproductive. Would a better procedure be to treat the cost initially as an expense to be charged later to an asset if the wells prove productive? Explain.

d. Why does Tenneco use countries as costing units under full-costing? What other alternatives might be considered?

e. Comment on the exclusion of unevaluated properties from the amount of cost to be amortized (depreciated). Is this consistent with the theory of full-costing?

f. Explain the rationale underlying the "ceiling" described in Tenneco's second paragraph.

g. Why might Tenneco decide to change to successful efforts? What is the nature of the restatement that would have to be made?

**Chapter 9**

# Accounting for Inventories

One of the most important assets used in many businesses is the inventory of products manufactured or purchased. The process of selling and delivering inventory to customers frequently triggers the recognition of revenue. During the selling process, a firm records the cost of the inventory transferred to its customers as an expense, called "Cost of Goods Sold" or "Cost of Sales."

In the previous chapter, we discussed how inventory is valued at the time of acquisition or production. In this chapter, we examine the procedures necessary to trace those acquisition costs to the cost of goods sold and, for inventory items not sold, to the ending inventory. This chapter will consider the important decisions involved in assigning inventory costs, illustrate the effect on income when inventory errors occur, and discuss the modifications that are made to cost values when inventory market values change.

## INVENTORY FLOW

In most businesses, the receipt, storage, and issuance of inventory is a constant and revolving process. Physically, inventory is an asset that flows in and out of the business. The accounting system records information about inventory at each stage and tracks the flow through the inventory account to the cost of goods sold expense account.

The basic nature of the inventory flow is summarized in the following formula:

Beginning inventory balance + Net inventory purchased = Inventory available for sale − Ending inventory balance = Cost of inventory sold

We will use the following example to illustrate this inventory flow. Assume that a company had the following inventory facts:

1. Inventory on hand at April 1 is $10,000.
2. Inventory purchased in April is $30,000 (including freight and handling costs).
3. Inventory on hand at April 30 is $8,000.

If we examine the inventory account and the cost of goods sold account at April 30, we would find:

**Inventory**

| | | | |
|---|---|---|---|
| April 1 balance | 10,000 | | |
| April purchases | 30,000 | | |
| Amount available | 40,000 | Amount sold | 32,000 |
| April 30 balance | 8,000 | | |

**Cost of Goods Sold**

| | | |
|---|---|---|
| Amount sold | 32,000 | |

We can put this information in a form which uses the inventory formula as follows:

| | |
|---|---|
| Beginning inventory, April 1 . . . . . . . . . . | $10,000 |
| Add: Inventory purchased . . . . . . . . . . | 30,000 |
| Inventory available for sale . . . . . . . . | $40,000 |
| Deduct: Inventory on hand, April 30. . . . . . | (8,000) |
| Cost of goods (inventory) sold . . . . . . . . | $32,000 |

It should be evident from the example that by determining the cost of the ending inventory, we also determine the cost of goods sold. Of course, if we know the cost of goods sold, then the ending inventory may be determined. The cost of goods available for sale must end up as cost of goods sold or ending inventory. The latter figure appears on the balance sheet, and the cost of goods sold figure appears on the income statement. Both, therefore, are important for financial reporting.

# IMPACT OF INVENTORY ERRORS ON INCOME MEASUREMENT

The inventory formula serves as an effective tool for analyzing the impact of inventory errors on income. The inventory formula clearly shows that any error in beginning inventory, purchases, or ending inventory directly affects cost of goods sold. Because cost of goods sold is deducted from sales revenues in determining net income, an inventory error affects net income. Moreover, when an error occurs in the ending inventory of one accounting period, the error will be carried to the following period because the ending inventory of one period is the beginning inventory of the succeeding period.

We can use the inventory formula to trace the effects of many types of inventory errors on cost of goods sold and net income. Table 9–1 isolates the impact of two types of independent errors on cost of goods sold and net income.

1. *Ending Inventory Errors.*   When an error in counting and recording a period's ending inventory occurs, this error carries over to the succeeding period. This carryover reverses the effect of the error as shown below.

   a. *Overstated ending inventory of $5,000.*   Assume that $5,000 of inventory is counted twice when taking inventory at the end of an accounting period. This error results in an excessive deduction from the goods available for sale in Year 1. It also causes cost of goods sold to be understated and net income to be overstated. The impact on Year 2 is reversed by the same dollar amount because the ending inventory of Year 1 becomes the beginning inventory in Year 2. Goods available for sale and cost of goods sold are both overstated and net income is understated in that year if the correct ending inventory is taken at the end of Year 2.

   b. *Understated ending inventory of $2,000.*   Assume that $2,000 has not been unloaded from a rail car and is missed in counting inventory at year-end. This error results in a reduced deduction from the goods available for sale in Year 1. It also causes the cost of goods sold to be overstated and net income to be understated. The impact on Year 2 is reversed by the same dollar amount because the ending inventory of Year 1 becomes the beginning inventory in Year 2. Goods available

**TABLE 9–1**   Cost of Goods Sold and Net Income Effects of Inventory Errors

|  | *Error 1a* | | *Error 1b* | | *Error 2a* | | *Error 2b* | |
|---|---|---|---|---|---|---|---|---|
|  | *Year 1* | *Year 2* | *Year 1* | *Year 2* | *Year 1* | *Year 2* | *Year 1* | *Year 2* |
| Beginning inventory | 0 | +5,000 | 0 | −2,000 | 0 | 0 | 0 | 0 |
| Add: purchases | 0 | 0 | 0 | 0 | +6,000 | 0 | −4,000 | +4,000 |
| Inventory available | 0 | +5,000 | 0 | −2,000 | +6,000 | 0 | −4,000 | +4,000 |
| Less: ending inventory | +5,000 | 0 | −2,000 | 0 | 0 | 0 | 0 | 0 |
| Cost of goods sold | −5,000 | +5,000 | +2,000 | −2,000 | +6,000 | 0 | −4,000 | +4,000 |
| Net income effect | +5,000 | −5,000 | −2,000 | +2,000 | −6,000 | 0 | +4,000 | −4,000 |

  + means overstated as a result of the error
  − means understated as a result of the error
  0 means no effect as a result of the error

for sale and the cost of goods sold are both understated and net income is overstated in that year.

2. *Errors in Recording Purchases.*   Errors in recording purchases do not necessarily correct themselves as was shown with the inventory errors above. One type of recording error for purchases affects only a single period. A second type of error affects two periods. Both types are illustrated below.

   a. *Single period error.*   Assume that the bookkeeper erroneously records an inventory purchase as $16,000 when it should have been shown at $10,000. This error of $6,000 overstates inventory purchases and inflates both goods available for sale and cost of goods sold. Therefore, net income will be understated. No carryover to Year 2 will occur as the error is limited to the current period.

   b. *Multiple period error.*   Assume that $4,000 of inventory was received late in Year 1. The inventory is properly included in ending inventory, but the purchase is not recorded until Year 2 because the supplier did not send the invoice until January of Year 2. This error understates purchases, goods available for sale, and cost of goods sold, and overstates net income in Year 1. The impact on Year 2 is reversed because purchases, goods available for sale, and cost of goods sold are overstated, and the net income is understated.

Table 9–1 depicts how each of the errors affects the various components of the cost of goods sold calculation and net income. Observe that many inventory errors affect two accounting periods and have opposite effects in each period. Because such errors quickly correct themselves, it might seem tempting to view them as unimportant. However, inventory errors can cause substantial distortions in the net income of a single year and enormous deviations in the actual trend of earnings over several years.

The following example will demonstrate the important effects of inventory errors. Assume that a firm reports income before taxes of $68,000 in each year from 1990 to 1992. An audit of the records made at the end of 1992 uncovers the following errors:

1. Inventory valued at $4,000 was counted twice on December 31, 1990.
2. Inventory costing $5,000 was received late in 1990 and was not recorded as a purchase until early in 1991 but was included in ending inventory in 1990.
3. Inventory costing $3,000 was omitted from the count of inventory on December 31, 1991.

Table 9–2 analyzes the impact of these three errors on reported income. Although the corrected income is the same as the uncorrected income after three years, the apparent year-to-year stability has vanished.

---

**TABLE 9–2**   Correction of Inventory Errors and Effect on Income

| Explanation | 1990 Income | 1991 Income | 1992 Income | Total for 1990–1992 |
|---|---|---|---|---|
| Original pre-tax income | $68,000 | $68,000 | $68,000 | $204,000 |
| Correction of: | | | | |
| Error 1 | (4,000) | 4,000 | | |
| Error 2 | (5,000) | 5,000 | | |
| Error 3 | | 3,000 | (3,000) | |
| Corrected pre-tax income | $59,000 | $80,000 | $65,000 | $204,000 |

---

Although our example concerns errors in inventory, we can employ the same analytical framework to examine or predict the effect on net income of alternative costing methods or other changes in inventory determination.

## PERIODIC VERSUS PERPETUAL INVENTORY

The inventory formula:

$$\frac{\text{Beginning}}{\text{inventory}} + \frac{\text{Net}}{\text{purchases}} - \frac{\text{Ending}}{\text{inventory}} = \frac{\text{Cost of}}{\text{goods sold}}$$

applies to the inventory procedure called the *periodic inventory system*. The term *periodic* follows from the practice of computing the cost of goods sold only at the end of each accounting period. A physical count of the inventory on hand is taken. This ending inventory is subtracted from the sum of the beginning inventory plus net purchases to compute the cost of goods sold. Journal entries to implement the periodic inventory procedure were discussed in the last chapter.

The periodic method is used widely, particularly among merchandising concerns. Unfortunately, the procedure suffers from two disadvantages. First, it assumes that any inventory not on hand must have been sold. This automatically includes in cost of goods sold the cost of inventory that has been wasted, stolen, or otherwise lost. Little information to aid in the control of inventory usage is available under this accounting procedure. Second, the time-consuming job of taking a complete physical inventory before statements can be prepared effectively limits the frequency of accurate financial reporting.

Many companies, particularly manufacturing firms, use a *perpetual inventory system* to record inventory transactions. Cost of goods sold is computed and debited each time inventory is decreased through sale or use (i.e., perpetually). This method keeps a running, up-to-date record of the inventory on hand. With the cost of goods sold continuously known, the ending inventory is computed by restating the formula to:

$$\frac{\text{Beginning}}{\text{inventory}} + \frac{\text{Net}}{\text{purchases}} - \frac{\text{Cost of}}{\text{goods sold}} = \frac{\text{Ending}}{\text{inventory}}$$

The perpetual inventory system provides more timely and accurate information about inventory balances and withdrawals. This system enhances internal control over inventory because of the continuous attention given to inventory balances and the ability to reconcile physical quantities to the quantities in the inventory records. A physical inventory is taken with the perpetual inventory system, but it may be taken at any convenient time. As can be seen by the formula above, preparation of financial statements does not require a physical inventory count.

Perpetual inventory procedures involve detailed record-keeping. Therefore, until recently, its use was restricted to a few large firms with sufficient personnel to maintain the records or to firms with a few high-cost inventory items that were infrequently purchased and sold. Computerization of the detailed bookkeeping function has led to a wider usage of this technique.

# INVENTORY COSTING METHODS

Whether a firm employs perpetual or periodic inventory procedures, accountants must decide which costs to assign to the units sold and which to the units in ending inventory. A number of alternative methods are available for making the cost assignments. We examine four of the most commonly used methods. Because the periodic inventory formula better focuses attention on the relationship between cost of goods sold and ending inventory, we use it as our general framework for discussion. However, attention is drawn to points at which perpetual inventory procedures yield different results.

## Specific Identification

The costing method that might first come to mind is that of relating a specific purchase cost to each item acquired. Physically, we could attach to each unit purchased a tag or sticker indicating its cost. Alternatively, we could link inventory items with their invoices through serial numbers or other unique identifiers. Later when an inventory item is sold, its specific invoice cost can be identified and assigned to the expense account. For those items remaining unsold at the end of the period, a firm can easily determine the total cost of the ending inventory by adding the tags or relevant invoices.

Specific identification requires extensive records for each inventory item. For practical reasons, it is suitable primarily for high-unit-value merchandise that is purchased and sold infrequently. For instance, an automobile dealer would have a separate invoice for each automobile in inventory or an aircraft manufacturer would have serial numbers for each engine attached to an aircraft. Each car or engine can be separately identified and its individual cost determined. Assigning inventory costs to expense and to ending inventory becomes a mechanical process of identifying units and their costs. Appliances, jewelry, and furniture are other examples of inventories often costed by specific identification.

As a method of matching resources consumed against revenues generated, specific identification appears rational because it adheres to the actual physical flow of inventory. Nevertheless, two criticisms are raised against this method. First, specific identification may result in biased results for completely interchangeable units. If *identical* units have different costs, management, through deliberate choice of which units to deliver, can influence the size of the cost of goods sold and, in turn, manipulate the amount of income reported.

The second criticism is a practical one. Some goods cannot be kept physically separate or be specifically identified. Gasoline in underground tanks and items stored in bins are examples. Moreover, it is usually too costly to maintain separate records for each unit when the inventory consists of numerous small items of varying types. Even when it is feasible to maintain perpetual records of units received and used, identification of the *exact* unit sold and *its* specific cost may still be difficult.

Consequently, in most cases some assumption has to be made as to which costs should be assigned to the goods left on hand at the end of the accounting period and which to the goods sold. Some of the more common of these assumptions about inventory cost flows characterize the remaining methods of inventory costing to be discussed. They are:

1. *Weighted-average cost*—the units in ending inventory are assumed to be representative of all units purchased.
2. *First-in, First-out (FIFO)*—the units in ending inventory are assumed to be the last units purchased.
3. *Last-in, First-out (LIFO)*—the units in ending inventory are assumed to be the first units purchased.

The data in Table 9–3 are used to illustrate and contrast these three inventory costing procedures.

As the accompanying calculation shows, our problem is to determine how much of the $3,730 should be assigned to the 60 units of ending inventory and how much to the 250 units sold.

**TABLE 9–3** Data for Illustration and Comparison of Inventory Costing Methods

| | Number of Units | Unit Cost | Total Cost |
|---|---|---|---|
| Beginning inventory 1/1/91 . . . . . . . . . . | 50 | $10 | $ 500 |
| Add: 1991 purchases: | | | |
| March 1 . . . . . . . . . . . . | 60 | 11 | 660 |
| July 1 . . . . . . . . . . . . | 80 | 12 | 960 |
| September 1 . . . . . . . . . . . . | 70 | 13 | 910 |
| December 1 . . . . . . . . . . . . | 50 | 14 | 700 |
| Total purchases . . . . . . . . . . | 260 | | 3,230 |
| Cost of goods available for sale . . . . . . . | 310 | | $3,730 |
| Less: Ending inventory 12/31/91 . . . . . . | 60 | | |
| Cost of goods sold . . . . . . . . . . . . | 250 | | |

| | Units | Dollars |
|---|---|---|
| Beginning inventory . . . . . . . . . . . . . | 50 | $ 500 |
| Plus: Purchases . . . . . . . . . . . . . . | 260 | 3,230 |
| Goods available for sale . . . . . . . . . . . | 310 | 3,730 |
| Less: Ending inventory . . . . . . . . . . . | 60 | ? |
| Cost of goods sold . . . . . . . . . . . . . | 250 | ? |

## Weighted-Average Cost

One popular method for costing inventory assumes the units on hand and the units sold represent a mixture of all the units available for sale. This method might be particularly appropriate for liquids or items stored in bins. A *periodic* ending inventory under this assumption would be costed at a weighted-average unit cost. In our example, the following numbers would result:

| | |
|---|---|
| Cost of goods available for sale . . . . . . . . . . | $3,730 |
| Less: Ending inventory—60 units at a weight-average unit cost of $12.0323 ($3,730 goods available/310 units) . . . . . . . | 722 |
| Cost of goods sold . . . . . . . . . . . . . . . . . . | $3,008 |

Often the average cost method is used even when the units are not mixed physically. It is argued that average costing of interchangeable units minimizes possible distortions from short-term price fluctuations. If specific identification or some other alternative is used, cost of goods sold may fluctuate misleadingly from period to period. Average costing has the tendency to "normalize" the unit costs, particularly for short periods such as a month or a quarter.

Because the ending inventory under periodic average costing is assumed to be representative of all units purchased by the firm, costs incurred early in the period may influence its cost as much as or more than costs incurred near the end of the period. A *moving average cost,* as would be required if the average cost method were applied on a *perpetual* basis, would be more representative. With the moving average, a new average cost would be computed after each purchase. That average would be used for costing units sold until the next purchase occurs. However, this procedure requires many arithmetic calculations, particularly when frequent purchases are made. Both weighted-average (periodic) and moving-average (perpetual) cost methods are used, although they do not necessarily give identical results.

## First-In, First-Out

Among the criteria used to judge an *assumed* flow of costs, one factor that often receives mention is the *physical flow* of the inventory. In this view, the best inventory assumption is the one that most closely approximates the physical movement of the inventory. In most cases, this view leads to the first-in, first-out (FIFO) inventory costing method. The oldest inventory (first-in) is assumed to be sold first (first-out), and the ending inventory consists of the most recently purchased items.

In our example, the 250 units sold are assumed to be the beginning inventory, the March purchases, the July purchases, and 60 of the September purchases (50 + 60 + 80 + 60 = 250). The ending inventory, then, is costed at the prices of the newest merchandise. The results are:

| | | |
|---|---:|---:|
| Cost of goods available for sale . . . . . . . . . . . . . . | | $3,730 |
| Less: Ending inventory | | |
| 50 units @ $14 . . . . . . . . . . . . . . . . . . | 700 | |
| 10 units @ $13 . . . . . . . . . . . . . . . . . . | 130 | 830 |
| Cost of goods sold . . . . . . . . . . . . . . . . . . . . | | $2,900 |

In addition to its approximation of the physical flow of inventory, FIFO has the advantage of providing the same results whether applied on a perpetual or a periodic basis. As long as the oldest inventory is considered to be sold first, cost of sales is the same whether recorded at the end of the period or after each individual sale. Moreover, the inventory balance shown on the position statement under FIFO comes closer than the other inventory methods to the current replacement cost of the asset.

The major objection to FIFO is that price gains (or losses) from the *holding* of inventory are included as part of *operating income.* Assume that the firm in our example sold inventory in early December at a price of $21 or 150 percent of the most recent purchase cost of $14. The cost matched against it under FIFO was probably only $13 (the purchase cost on September 1). Many accountants would contend that instead of having a unit gross margin of $8 ($21 − $13), the firm has a unit gross margin of only $7 ($21 − $14) *plus a holding gain* of $1 ($14 − $13).

By assigning the oldest costs to the inventory sold, FIFO may match low-cost inventory against high selling prices during periods of rising prices and high-cost inventory against low selling prices in periods of falling prices. Under FIFO, gains (losses) from holding inventories that increase (decrease) in cost are reflected in net income through a *cost of goods sold* that is lower (higher) than the *current* cost of the resources used. This "inventory profit (loss)" is of a different nature from operating income and may result from external factors beyond management's influence.

## Last-In, First-Out

Last-in, first-out (LIFO) assumes that the cost of the most recently purchased merchandise should be matched against revenue as cost of goods sold. Correspondingly, the goods remaining on hand are assigned the cost of the oldest merchandise. By using the figures in Table 9–3 and applying LIFO on a periodic basis, we find the following results:

| | | |
|---|---:|---:|
| Cost of goods available for sale . . . . . . . . . . . . | | $3,730 |
| Less: Ending inventory | | |
| 50 units @ $10. . . . . . . . . . . . . . . | $500 | |
| 10 units @  11. . . . . . . . . . . . . . . | 110 | 610 |
| Cost of goods sold . . . . . . . . . . . . . . . . . . | | $3,120 |

The LIFO method gives us an ending inventory composed of layers. The base layer is the oldest inventory acquired, and each succeeding acquisition is then considered in order of purchase. The ending inventory in our example would be:

| | | | |
|---|---|---|---:|
| Layer 2 | First purchase after base layer . . . . . . . . | 10 units @ $11 | $110 |
| Layer 1 | Base LIFO layer . . . . . . . . . . . . | 50 units @  10 | 500 |
| | Ending inventory . . . . . . . . . . . . . . | 60 units | $610 |

Let us extend this example, and suppose that in Year 2 the following purchases are made:

| | | | |
|---|---|---|---:|
| March 1 . . . . . . . . . . . . . . . | 30 units @ $15 | $450 |
| June 1 . . . . . . . . . . . . . . . | 40 units @  16 | 640 |
| September 1 . . . . . . . . . . . . . . | 20 units @  17 | 340 |

If sales for the year are 60 units, then under the LIFO method the cost of goods sold is recorded at the cost of the September and June purchases. The March purchase remains on hand at the end of the year and is added to the beginning inventory as an additional layer. Therefore, the ending inventory for Year 2 is composed of these layers:

| | | | |
|---|---|---|---|
| Layer 3 | First purchase in Year 2 . . . . . . . . | 30 units @ $15 | $   450 |
| Layer 2 | First purchase after base layer . . . . . | 10 units @   11 | 110 |
| Layer 1 | Base LIFO layer  . . . . . . . . . . | 50 units @   10 | 500 |
| | Ending inventory . . . . . . . . . . . . . . | 90 units | $1,060 |

Now, suppose that in Year 3 the following purchases are made:

| | | |
|---|---|---|
| April 1 | 20 units @ $18  . . . . . . . . . . . | $360 |
| August 1 | 30 units @   19  . . . . . . . . . . . | 570 |

If sales for Year 3 are 85 units, then under LIFO the cost of goods sold is recorded as the sum of the purchases of the current year, Layer 3 from the beginning inventory, and 5 of the 10 units from Layer 2 of the beginning inventory. This leaves the ending inventory with the base layer and the remaining 5 units from the first layer as follows:

| | | | |
|---|---|---|---|
| Layer 2 | First purchase after base layer . . . . . . | 5 units @ $11 | $ 55 |
| Layer 1 | Base LIFO layer  . . . . . . . . . . . | 50 units @   10 | 500 |
| | Ending inventory . . . . . . . . . . . . . . | 55 units | $555 |

When the LIFO method for costing inventory is employed, increases in inventory are added as layers to the existing inventory. As the ending level of inventory is decreased, the most recent layer(s) is reduced. Accountants refer to the reduction in older LIFO layers as *liquidation*. Under LIFO, inventory is viewed as a quasi-fixed asset. As long as inventory levels remain constant or increase from year to year, early layers remain in ending inventory. However, if early inventory layers are liquidated, their lower costs in periods of rising prices will become part of cost of goods sold. The lower cost of goods sold generally creates higher income than the other methods.

LIFO clearly assumes a flow of costs that usually does not match the actual physical movement of the goods. However, many accountants and business executives claim that they can obtain more meaningful income figures by matching costs other than approximations of the acquisition cost of the actual units sold. They argue that the real cost of making a sale is the cost of *replacing* the inventory sold. While still using acquisition costs, LIFO approximates a valuation of cost of goods sold at replacement cost by using the cost of the most recently acquired units. So, in practice, LIFO approaches a *replacement cost method* in cases where physical inventories at the end of the period are equal to or greater than the beginning inventory. In these cases, the most recently incurred costs (the cost of replacing goods) are charged to expense.

This aspect of LIFO often is characterized by the phrase "matching current costs against current revenues." By matching approximate replacement costs against revenues, LIFO provides useful information for future decisions and projections of net income. When prices are rising, LIFO charges the higher purchase costs against the higher selling prices and thereby approximates the current cost-price margin. This figure, some claim, is more characteristic of current operating conditions than is the historic cost-price margin.

## Comparison of Inventory Costing Methods

We have seen that the three inventory-flow assumptions—weighted-average cost, FIFO, and LIFO—produce significantly different amounts for ending inventory and cost of goods sold. Specifically, the following variations exist:

|  | Weighted Average | FIFO | LIFO |
|---|---|---|---|
| Cost of goods available for sale . . . . . | $3,730 | $3,730 | $3,730 |
| Less: Ending inventory . . . . . . . . | 722 | 830 | 610 |
| Cost of goods sold . . . . . . . . . . | $3,008 | $2,900 | $3,120 |

The ending inventory sizes shown in the example—LIFO with the smallest value, FIFO with the largest value, and weighted-average between LIFO and FIFO—will *typically* prevail during a period when unit costs are increasing. Accordingly, the pattern exhibited is very likely to mirror that being experienced by most U.S. firms. Of the three methods, LIFO produces the highest cost of goods sold during a period of rising prices. Therefore, LIFO produces the lowest gross margin (gross profit) and net income. Conversely, FIFO, during periods of price upswings, results in the highest gross margin and net income. Of course, the above pattern would usually be reversed during a period of falling prices.

Even when prices are rising, however, the rankings can reverse when a firm is unable or unwilling to at least maintain the *physical volume* of inventory. Because the oldest inventory layers under LIFO have the lowest cost, a substantial depletion of inventory quantities will result in these lower cost layers being matched with current revenues. The resulting gross margin and net income will be high, just the reverse of what might be expected under LIFO. Depletion of inventory can be the result of voluntary manage-

ment action (e.g., in response to falling sales) or such outside factors as
strikes or material shortages.[1]

## LIFO Reporting Requirements

Entities that use the LIFO inventory method do so primarily for tax purposes. The tax advantage of LIFO during periods of rising prices derives
from the lower income the method produces. Lower income means lower
income taxes, so LIFO offers an opportunity to reinvest the cash that otherwise would have been paid in taxes. However, the Internal Revenue Service
regulations require all firms choosing to use LIFO for tax purposes to report
LIFO values on their annual financial statements as well. This *conformity
requirement* applies only to the LIFO inventory method.

Generally accepted accounting principles require firms to report the major
categories of inventory, the cost-flow methods used, the basis of valuation,
and any liquidation of LIFO inventory layers. The IRS permits a firm to disclose inventory, in footnotes or supplementary information, as if it had used
a method other than LIFO. However, the primary financial statements must
use the LIFO values.

Table 9–4 presents two examples illustrating different methods for reporting LIFO inventory values. The table shows that both the Brown Group,
Inc. and Trinity Industries, Inc. comply with the reporting requirements for
LIFO although each uses a different approach. Brown Group shows the difference between FIFO and LIFO cost in both the current assets section of
the balance sheet and in Note D to the financial statements. Had Brown
used FIFO amounts, the balance sheet inventories would have been higher
by $68.736 million in 1986 and $71.986 million in 1985. In turn, cost of
sales would have been higher by $3.25 million and income before taxes
would have been lower. Brown Group also discloses in Note D the effect
the liquidation of LIFO inventory had on company profits. The note indicates that this liquidation increased earnings by 10 cents per share in 1986
and 6 cents per share in 1985. This disclosure is required to aid readers in
determining the impact of matching the lower cost inventory values against
the current period's revenues.

Trinity Industries, Inc. reports its use of LIFO but shows the adjusted
inventory value in the balance sheet's current assets without any indication
of the FIFO-LIFO difference. The inventory note accompanying the financial statements discloses the adjustment. In the note, Trinity Industries
states the inventory value at cost and then deducts an allowance to reduce

---

[1] Since inventory depletions are more common over shorter periods of time, LIFO is used
on a *periodic* basis only. The likelihood of some early LIFO layers being depleted *temporarily*
during the year is high, and such depletions would have to be recognized under a perpetual
LIFO system.

**TABLE 9-4** LIFO Inventory Disclosures

### BROWN GROUP, INC. (000)

| | 1986 | 1985 |
|---|---|---|
| **Current assets** | | |
| Cash and cash investments | $ 36,200 | $ 25,943 |
| Receivables, net of allowances of $5,832 in 1986 and $6,302 in 1985 | 127,896 | 126,704 |
| Inventories, net of adjustment to last-in, first-out cost of $68,736 in 1986 and $71,986 in 1985 | 309,426 | 308,949 |
| Prepaid expenses and other current assets | 20,441 | 17,916 |
| Total current assets | $493,963 | $479,512 |

**Notes to Consolidated Financial Statements**

Note A (In Part): Summary of Significant Accounting Policies

Inventories

Substantially all inventories are valued at the lower of cost or market, determined under the last-in, first-out (LIFO) method.

Note D: Inventories

Inventories are valued at the lower of cost or market determined principally by the last-in, first-out (LIFO) method and consist of the following (in thousands):

| | November 1 1986 | November 2 1985 |
|---|---|---|
| Finished products | $285,517 | $281,768 |
| Work in process | 4,678 | 5,765 |
| Raw materials and supplies | 19,231 | 21,416 |
| | $309,426 | $308,949 |

If the first-in, first-out (FIFO) cost method had been used, inventories would have been $68,736,000 and $71,986,000 higher at November 1, 1986, and November 2, 1985, respectively.

As a result of reducing certain inventory quantities valued on the LIFO basis, profits from liquidation of inventories were recorded which increased earnings by $1,800,000 ($.10 per share) and $1,100,000 ($.06 per share) in 1986 and 1985, respectively.

### TRINITY INDUSTRIES, INC. (000)

| | 1986 | 1985 |
|---|---|---|
| **Current assets** | | |
| Cash and short-term investments | $ 7,484 | $ 4,609 |
| Accounts receivable, less allowance for doubtful accounts ($1,761 in 1986 and $1,719 in 1985) | 71,944 | 68,744 |
| Income tax refund receivable | — | 4,900 |
| Contract receivables not yet billed | 14,225 | 18,838 |
| Inventories | 78,150 | 112,495 |
| Prepaid retirement plans expense | 23,757 | — |
| Other current assets | 12,337 | 10,286 |
| Total current assets | $207,897 | $219,872 |

**Notes to Consolidated Financial Statements**

Summary of Accounting Policies (In Part)

Inventories and investments are valued at the lower of cost or market. Inventory cost is determined on a LIFO (last-in, first-out) method. Market is replacement cost or net realizable value.

Inventories (000)

| | March 31 1986 | 1985 |
|---|---|---|
| Finished goods | $11,003 | $ 23,915 |
| Work in process | 7,364 | 11,912 |
| Cost related to long-term contracts, net of progress billings of $518 and $1,264 at March 31, 1986 and 1985, respectively | 23,231 | 28,776 |
| Raw materials and supplies | 39,076 | 52,036 |
| Allowance to state inventories at LIFO cost | (2,524) | (4,144) |
| | $78,150 | $112,495 |

During fiscal 1984 certain inventory quantities were reduced. Such reduction resulted in liquidation of LIFO inventory quantities carried at lower costs prevailing in prior years as compared with purchases during those fiscal years, increasing net income by approximately $589,000.

Source: AICPA, *Accounting Trends and Techniques* (New York, 1987), pp. 128–130.

the inventory to its LIFO value. The use of an allowance account permits Trinity Industries to maintain its inventory records under its regular costing method. A separate adjustment by means of the allowance account shows the effect of using LIFO for tax purposes.

The last paragraph in the inventory note reveals that Trinity Industries in 1984 had liquidated a portion of its LIFO inventory layers from prior years. This disclosure indicates that the lower costs associated with that inventory increased net income by $589,000 in 1984. This disclosure aids analysts comparing 1984's net income with that of 1985 and 1986.

## Selection of Inventory Costing Methods

Because the great majority of firms are either unable or unwilling to use the specific identification procedure, they are faced with deciding among weighted-average cost, FIFO, and LIFO. A firm need not use the same inventory costing method for its entire inventory. Nevertheless, even those firms using more than one method must decide which ones to use and on what inventories to use them.

Ideally, a company should choose those inventory costing procedures that will lead to the most relevant and reliable set of financial statements. Unfortunately, such a determination cannot be made easily. The following issues first need to be addressed and resolved by the accounting profession and the financial community:

1. The meaning and purpose of the matching concept.
2. The relative importance of the balance sheet vis-à-vis the income statement.
3. The extent to which tax regulations should influence financial reporting.
4. The feasibility of selecting accounting procedures as a means of addressing the problem of changing prices.

**Matching.**    Although wide agreement exists that good matching occurs only when the costs incurred in earning revenues are deducted from those revenues, some disagreement exists concerning which costs, in the case of inventories, should be deducted. Some accountants believe that good matching can occur only if the inventory costing procedure that is adopted mirrors the actual flow of goods. Because in most businesses this flow is first-in, first-out, they argue that the supporters of matching should advocate the use of FIFO in most circumstances.

As noted earlier, LIFO supporters suggest an entirely different line of reasoning. They point out that many firms continuously replenish their inventory as sales are made. Therefore, a cost figure that is as close as possible to the cost of replacement should be matched against the sales revenue. The cost of the *last* purchase is likely to be closer to the cost of replacement than is the cost of the first purchase, so LIFO proponents consider their method preferable from a matching perspective.

Critics of LIFO raise two points in reply. First, even if the matching of current costs with current revenues accurately measures *operating income,* inventory price gains and losses are real economic changes and should not be ignored as they are under LIFO. They maintain that proper reporting on management's stewardship of entity resources requires that effective purchasing—buying at a low price merchandise that later increases in value—be reflected in a periodic measurement of income, perhaps as a separate component.

Second, through its inclusion of the increased cost of inventory replacement in cost of goods sold, LIFO implies that the income cycle is not complete until the investment is replaced. The general nature of business operations, however, is not from one investment to another investment but rather from uninvested funds back to uninvested funds available for reinvestment *or some other purpose.* Each new investment is an independent management decision based on *future* expectations. The amount and type of reinvestment are not automatically determined by the amount and type of past investment consumed. Thus LIFO, by implying reinvestment, confuses *income determination* with *income administration.* Income exists when the old investment is recovered. Whether that income is paid out in dividends or reinvested is a separate management decision dealing with the use of the income, not its measurement.

**Balance Sheet versus Income Statement.**    Accountants strive to prepare a relevant and reliable *set* of financial statements. Unfortunately, very few accounting methods provide realistic balance sheets *and* income statements. Even if LIFO results in better matching and a reliable gross margin for the income statement, such realism hardly carries through to a LIFO-based balance sheet.

Because the LIFO ending inventory amount represents the cost of old purchases made by the firm, the totals presented for current assets, working capital, and various other financial statistics become suspect. For example, a loan officer confronted with the position statement of a jewelry manufacturer who has used LIFO to cost the inventory of gold at $35 per ounce cannot really use the published amount to determine the firm's solvency or the collateral value of its assets. A FIFO-based balance sheet would add more realism by showing the gold inventory at the recent purchase prices of hundreds of dollars per ounce. However, LIFO proponents would allege that the corresponding FIFO income statement would present the loan officer with significantly overstated gross margin and net income amounts because of the matching of old costs with current revenues.

**Influence of Tax Regulations.**    Every firm that prepares financial statements for investors and creditors must also prepare a tax return for the Internal Revenue Service (IRS). A firm's taxable income is determined in accordance with the income tax regulations and almost never equals the book income reported in its published income statement. Such differences do not mean that the company has either misled its external readers or defrauded the government. Instead, a firm's two sets of books are viewed as the normal result of our tax regulations' greater concern for fund-raising and the promotion of certain social and economic behavior than for the proper matching of accrual-basis revenues and expenses.

In the case of inventories, however, we noted earlier that the IRS requires that companies using LIFO for tax purposes also use LIFO for published financial statements. LIFO has much appeal for tax purposes because it usually results in higher cost of goods sold, lower income, and lower taxes during inflationary times. Unfortunately, all such firms are then constrained to LIFO as the inventory costing method "chosen" for their financial statements.[2] To the extent that FIFO may have more accurately reflected the inventories, the tax code lessens the quality of financial reporting on the balance sheet.

**Changing Prices.** The existence of alternative accounting methods often has been welcomed by many who criticize the conventional historical cost accounting model. LIFO incorporates features of more than one income concept. It retains the use of historical costs employed in conventional accounting theory but at the same time attempts to address the problem of changing prices. However, LIFO costs reported on the income statement only approximate current (replacement) costs. Even when only a short time has elapsed between the product's purchase and sale, it is unlikely that the cost of the firm's latest purchases (what is expensed under LIFO) will equal the cost of its next purchase (replacement cost).

A complete replacement-cost system, unlike LIFO, recognizes inventory holding gains and losses as a separate element of income.[3] As a result, balance sheet measures of inventory reflect current replacement costs, not outmoded historical costs. Accordingly, supporters of a current cost model are not enamored with LIFO, although they may favor it over FIFO.

The double-digit inflation experienced in the mid-1970s created a great deal of concern over the apparent misinformation conveyed when accounting adhered to reporting on the basis of original costs. In response to requests for disclosure of inflation-adjusted information, the FASB required

---

[2] It is interesting to note that LIFO enjoys little popularity in Canada and the United Kingdom, where it is not acceptable for tax purposes, even though the rate of price increase in those countries rivals or exceeds that in the United States.

[3] A complete current cost system would also recognize holding gains or losses on units in the ending inventory. These are often referred to as "unrealized" holding gains or losses, "unrealized" because the units have not yet been sold. FIFO includes "realized" holding gains in the gross margin figure; LIFO attempts to exclude from income all holding gains, realized and unrealized.

firms to report supplementary information detailing the effect of changing prices on several elements in the financial statements. Inventory and cost of goods sold were included in the supplementary reporting. By the mid-1980s, however, the supplementary report requirements had been dropped.

Price-level adjusted information is referred to as "constant dollar accounting," and proponents of such accounting models would find LIFO lacking in certain respects. LIFO has to do with changes in *price structure*—the relative value of goods and services—an entirely different problem, as our example near the end of Chapter 8 illustrates. If general and specific prices move in different directions or at different rates, then LIFO fails to approximate the cost of goods sold that would be reported under a constant dollar model.

In summary, the selection of an inventory costing method can be fraught with frustration and contradiction. A firm must explicitly or implicitly address such issues as (1) the nature of the matching concept, (2) the trade-offs in realism between the balance sheet and the income statement, (3) the constraints on the selection process caused by a firm's desire legally to minimize its income taxes, and (4) the appropriateness of LIFO as a means of addressing the problem of changing prices.

Table 9–5 discloses the inventory methods used by a sample of 600 large U.S. companies for various years since 1973. A dramatic increase in the

**TABLE 9–5**  Inventory Methods Used by a Sample of 600 Large U.S. Firms for Selected Years 1973 through 1986

| | Number of Companies* | | | | |
|---|---|---|---|---|---|
| | *1973* | *1974* | *1979* | *1984* | *1986* |
| Methods: | | | | | |
| LIFO | 150 | 303 | 374 | 400 | 393 |
| FIFO | 394 | 375 | 390 | 377 | 383 |
| Average cost | 235 | 236 | 241 | 223 | 223 |
| Other† | 148 | 140 | 56 | 54 | 53 |
| Total disclosures | 927 | 1054 | 1061 | 1054 | 1052 |
| Use of LIFO: | | | | | |
| All inventories | 8 | 14 | 20 | 26 | 23 |
| 50 percent or more of inventories | 49 | 135 | 194 | 215 | 229 |
| Less than 50 percent of inventories | 68 | 67 | 94 | 82 | 74 |
| Extent not determinable | 25 | 87 | 66 | 77 | 67 |
| Companies using LIFO | 150 | 303 | 374 | 400 | 393 |

*Adds up to more than 600 because many sample companies used more than one method.
†Includes unique procedures applicable to specialized industries and situations.

Source: AICPA, *Accounting Trends & Techniques* (New York, 1974, 1975, 1980, 1985, and 1987).

number of LIFO users occurred in 1974 when inflation was running at double-digit levels. Many firms were convinced that they could no longer ignore the tax benefits provided from the use of LIFO. Having made the switch for tax purposes, the companies were required by IRS tax regulations to use LIFO for financial reporting also. Since 1974, the number of sample firms using LIFO and the extent of their use have remained steady and at a high level.

The LIFO-FIFO controversy highlights deficiencies in the existing accounting framework. Prices do change because of general inflationary pressures and specific movements in the supply/demand equilibrium for a particular product, and these changes often have great economic significance. However, the historical cost (exchange price) concept conceals the impact of certain specific price changes, and the monetary postulate ignores general price changes.

## LOWER OF COST OR MARKET

The inventory methods discussed in previous sections attempt to determine the *cost* of goods on hand and the *cost* of goods sold. Although they differ in the assumptions made as to which goods are sold, they all use acquisition cost figures. Under generally accepted accounting principles, inventory is actually valued according to a procedure known as *lower of cost or market* (LCM). It assigns to the ending inventory either a historical cost amount *or* a current market valuation, whichever is lower, and is applied regardless of which costing method is employed. Note in Table 9–4 that both Brown Group and Trinity Industries describe their inventory policies as lower of cost or market.

This procedure achieved prominence early in accounting practice, when the balance sheet was of prime importance and conservatism was a prized virtue. If market valuation declined below acquisition cost, a loss was assumed to have occurred. The writing down of inventory to the lower market figure "recognized" this loss and gave a more conservative value to the inventory in case the business had to be liquidated. In more recent years, as attention has shifted to the income statement and the matching concept, the interpretation of LCM appears to be that only costs possessing future use value should be carried forward as assets. Costs that cannot be recovered satisfactorily are seen to have lost their usefulness:

> A departure from the cost basis of pricing the inventory is required when the utility of the goods is no longer as great as its cost. Where there is evidence that the utility of goods, in their disposal in the ordinary course of business, will be less than cost, whether due to physical deterioration, obsolesence, changes in price levels, or other causes, the difference should be recognized as a loss of the current period. This is generally accomplished by stating such goods at a lower level commonly designated as market.[4]

---

[4] AICPA, *Accounting Research and Terminology Bulletins, Final Edition* (New York, 1961), p. 30.

## How LCM Operates

Assume that a physical inventory of 100 units exists at the end of the period. The original acquisition cost assigned to each unit is $160. Market at the end of the period is determined to be $130 per unit. Assume further that cost of goods available for sale amounts to $40,000. The effects of using lower of cost or market to value the ending inventory can be seen below:

|  | | *Cost* | | *LCM* |
|---|---|---|---|---|
| Cost of goods available for sale | | $40,000 | | $40,000 |
| Less: Ending inventory (100 @ $160) | | 16,000 | (100 @ $130) | 13,000 |
| Cost of goods sold | | $24,000 | | $27,000 |

This example shows that the $3,000 loss in inventory value has been included as a portion of the cost of goods sold. Of course, the inventory decline is unrelated to the goods sold; it pertains to the inventory still on hand. Logic would suggest that if the market decline is to be recognized, it should be segregated as a separate deduction. This method of presentation, however, is rarely used in accounting practice.

With respect to income measurement, lower of cost or market has the effect of shifting income from one accounting period to another. A write-down to market causes charges that otherwise would appear as expenses in future periods to be recorded in the current period. However, the reduced ending inventory value, which causes cost of goods sold to be higher and income to be lower this period, becomes the beginning inventory of the following period. It has an opposite effect on income then.[5] With respect to the balance sheet, LCM prevents the inventory from being stated at a figure above its future utility.

The lower-of-cost-or-market procedures applicable to inventory are almost identical to the rules set forth in the last chapter for *current* marketable equity securities. One exception is that inventories that are once written down to a lower market figure are not written back up if market prices recover. Also in the case of marketable equity securities, normally only one market price exists. However, as we shall see in the next section, different market prices can exist for inventory, depending on whether we are talking about the selling market or the purchase market. Consequently, the application of LCM to inventory is more complex and subjective than in the case of marketable equity securities.

---

[5] For *tax* purposes LIFO cannot be used to determine the cost element in LCM. Under LIFO any inventory value previously written down to market would remain, as long as a minimum inventory quantity was maintained, rather than flow through cost of goods sold in the following period. Consequently, lower of LIFO cost or market would result in a relatively permanent inventory value at the lowest purchase price that ever existed at the end of a period.

## Meaning of Market

The conceptual soundness of LCM depends to a large extent on the meaning of "utility" and on the measurement of "market." Two interpretations—one emphasizing exit values and one stressing entry values—have been advanced through the years.

**Net Realizable Value.**    One reasonable meaning of the term "utility" is what the company will receive upon disposal of the inventory. This exit-value amount, called "net realizable value," equals expected selling price reduced by any anticipated costs of completing and selling the inventory item. LCM, then, implies that inventory should not be stated at a figure greater than its *recoverable* cost. The inventory write-down or "loss of the current period" should include any portion of the acquisition cost that cannot be recovered out of anticipated revenue. This interpretation of market has commonly been employed for the recording of losses on damaged or obsolete merchandise in periods prior to their sale.

For example, suppose that a company develops and manufactures 500 pollution control units for automobiles. Because of the firm's inexperience, the manufacturing cost is $400 per unit. Management estimates that the selling price will have to be set at $350 to be competitive with that of other devices on the market. A 20 percent dealer commission is normal for this type of good. *Net realizable value* in this case is $280 ($350 − $70 commission). Of the $400 total cost per unit, $120 ($400 − $280) will not be recovered. Consequently, that portion has no future service potential and should not be carried forward as an asset.

**Replacement Cost.**    The more common definition of "market" is *replacement cost,* an entry-value amount. According to this interpretation, utility is the equivalent expenditure necessary to replace the item of inventory. Replacement cost is employed as evidence of realizability when there is a close association between purchase prices and selling prices. If replacement cost has fallen below acquisition cost, the contention is that net realizable value also has declined or will decline shortly.

The reader may consult the Appendix to this chapter for a more detailed analysis of alternative meanings of "market," the application of LCM under AICPA guidelines, and the theoretical implications of its many facets.

## Criticisms of LCM

The objections to cost or market, whichever is lower, include both theoretical and practical points. Some of the theoretical criticisms arise from variations in the concept of income implied by the alternative definitions of market. These are considered in depth in the Appendix to this chapter. Two, however, are of general import.

First, the charge of inconsistency plagues lower of cost or market. The inventory may be at cost one year and at market the following year, since market prices are deemed relevant only when they are *below* cost. It seems inconsistent to many to recognize losses before sale when replacement cost or net realizable value falls below cost, and yet at the same time to maintain that gains arising from the market's being above cost should be deferred until sale takes place.

Second, in some circumstances LCM will cause inventory to be written down even though the acquisition cost is still expected to be recovered out of future revenues. These circumstances occur when cost is less than net realizable value but greater than replacement cost. Many theorists argue that as long as the merchandise can be sold at some profit (net realizable value is above cost), no loss has occurred. Only a reduction in potential profit margin, not a loss, has taken place. The inventory write-down records a *hypothetical loss* for the current period and unnecessarily shifts income from one accounting period to another.

Three other criticisms denote practical limitations. First, LCM as practiced buries holding losses related to the *ending* inventory in cost of goods sold. Use of LCM thus may distort income statement relationships and may make year-to-year comparisons difficult. Second, a risk exists in using market figures at one particular moment to measure market because they may not be representative of the future. This risk is heightened if the moment of time is the end of an accounting period, when activity (purchasing and selling) may be at a low ebb. Finally, LCM will yield *varying* results depending on whether it is applied to the inventory as a whole or to each individual item.

# RETAIL INVENTORY METHOD

The preparation of monthly or quarterly financial statements requires either frequent physical inventory counts of the ending inventory or maintenance of perpetual inventory records. Both are arduous tasks for firms selling large quantities of many different products. Nevertheless, the need for interim financial information exists for these firms as well as for others.

Many merchandising concerns employ a method known as the retail inventory method to *estimate the dollar amount of ending inventory* when a physical count cannot conveniently be made. Retail establishments also use this procedure to find the *cost* of a physical inventory without having to go through the time-consuming job of sorting out the costs of a number of small, individual items. If the physical inventory has been taken at the current retail prices listed on the items, then the cost of that ending inventory can be estimated by means of the retail procedure. This method is also useful when insurers need to ascertain the approximate loss incurred as a result of fire or other casualty.

We can use the following monthly figures to illustrate:

|  | Cost | Retail |
|---|---|---|
| Beginning inventory . . . . . . . . . . . . . . . | $ 20,000 | $ 26,400 |
| Net purchases . . . . . . . . . . . . . . . . . . | 88,000 | 117,600 |
| Goods available for sale. . . . . . . . . . . . . . | $108,000 | $144,000 |

The retail method employs the relationship that exists between cost and retail prices. The method requires, therefore, that a firm keep track not only of the cost of its purchases but of the selling prices assigned to them as well. Then a relationship between the *cost* of goods available for sale and the *retail price* of goods available for sale can be established and applied to the retail value of the ending inventory for an estimate of its cost. This relationship, expressed as a *cost ratio,* is 75 percent ($108,000/$144,000) in our example.

If sales for the month are $84,000, the retail price of the ending inventory is $60,000 ($144,000 retail price of goods available for sale less $84,000 retail price of goods sold). Multiplying the $60,000 by the 75 percent cost ratio produces a $45,000 estimated cost for the ending inventory. The cost ratio can be applied either to an *estimate* of the ending inventory at retail prices, as in this case, or to an *actual physical count* of the ending inventory taken at retail prices.

Use of the ratio in the above manner approximates fairly accurately the *average cost* of the ending inventory if we can assume that the cost-retail relationship existing for goods available holds true for the goods sold and for the goods in the ending inventory. If different products have quite varying cost ratios and the product mix of the goods sold is not the same as the mix comprising the ending inventory, further refinements such as a partitioning of the inventory into homogeneous sections will be necessary for accurate results.[6]

## DISCUSSION OF THE KIMBERLY-CLARK ANNUAL REPORT

Kimberly-Clark's income statement shows a 1987 cost of products (goods) sold figure of $3,065.9 stated in millions of dollars. The balance sheet displays a December 31, 1987 inventory figure of $525.4 million. Additional disclosures related to inventory appear in Note 1 and Note 9 to the financial statements.

---

[6] The retail method becomes slightly more complicated when we take into consideration that changes often occur in the initial selling prices before the goods are sold. These changes are called "additional markups and markdowns." Because they modify the retail price, they can also affect the cost ratio. Coverage of the technical aspects of markups and markdowns is left to later courses.

Note 1 reveals that the company values most of its U.S. inventories at cost using the last-in, first-out (LIFO) method for both tax purposes and financial accounting purposes. The note also indicates that some United States inventory and all inventories of consolidated operations outside the U.S. are valued at the lower of cost or market using the first-in, first-out (FIFO) method. It appears that the rationale of management in selecting LIFO in the United States is for its tax advantages. The use of LIFO for tax purposes is not permitted in foreign countries and is therefore not selected by Kimberly-Clark. This information establishes the inventory principles that the corporation has elected to use and enables us to interpret the financial impact of the selected inventory method on the results of operations.

Note 9 shows several reporting disclosures related to inventory. Kimberly-Clark provides a breakdown of the total inventory into its major components—Raw Materials, Work in Process, Finished Goods, and Supplies. With the presentation in Note 9, we can also examine the changes, if any, in the composition of inventories. Comparing dollars in the millions is somewhat difficult so we convert the inventory amounts to percentages for easier analysis as follows:

|  | 1987 | | 1986 | |
| --- | --- | --- | --- | --- |
| Raw materials. | $173.3 | 26.9% | $169.1 | 25.9% |
| Work in process . | 122.6 | 19.0 | 116.6 | 17.8 |
| Finished goods | 241.7 | 37.5 | 262.7 | 40.2 |
| Supplies and others | 107.4 | 16.6 | 104.9 | 16.1 |

This analysis does not indicate any dramatic changes across the two years. There is a slight reduction in the finished goods on hand in 1987 with slightly more inventory partially finished. The important point to see is that reading the notes along with the financial statements permits us to extract more information than is presented with only dollar values.

The company first states its total inventory at the lower of cost or market using the first-in, first-out basis. This indicates that, had they used FIFO for all inventories, the ending inventory value would have been $645.0 million and the beginning inventory would have been $653.3 million. Because it used LIFO for tax purposes, the company had to report LIFO inventory values on the financial statements. Note 9 presents the value of the adjustment ($119.6 million for 1987 and $122.0 million for 1986) needed to reduce the FIFO inventory values to LIFO values. This second item of information permits us to see the dollar effect of the LIFO method while also being able to gauge the FIFO dollar value.

The 1987 LIFO adjustment of $119.6 million is a $2.4 million *decrease* from the 1986 adjustment ($122.0 − $119.6). This represents the inventory cost effect included in the cost of products sold in 1987 because of Kimberly-Clark's decision to use LIFO. We can determine this amount through the use of the inventory formula.

|                                                        | *LIFO*    | *FIFO*    |
| ------------------------------------------------------ | --------- | --------- |
| Beginning inventory (from Note 9) . . . . . . . . .    | $ 531.3   | $ 653.3   |
| Add: Purchases (calculated) . . . . . . . . . . . .    | 3,060.0   | 3,060.0   |
| Inventory available for sale (calculated) . . . . . .  | $3,591.3  | $3,713.3  |
| Less: Ending inventory (from Note 9) . . . . . . . .   | 525.4     | 645.0     |
| Cost of products sold:                                 |           |           |
| (from the Income Statement). . . . . . .               | $3,065.9  |           |
| (calculated). . . . . . . . . . . . . .                |           | $3,068.3  |

Difference:    FIFO − LIFO = $3,068.3 − $3,065.9 = $2.4

Notice that the inventory formula provides the framework to make the above calculations. Consider the LIFO column first. Initially, we insert the figures available from the income statement and Note 9. From these we infer that $3,060.0 million of purchases for the period must have been made ($3,591.3 − $531.3).

We then convert the LIFO values to a FIFO basis and compare the effect of the two inventory methods. The FIFO column shown above uses information from Note 9 and the LIFO computation column to determine the $3,068.3 million Cost of products sold on a FIFO basis.

The results shown here are unusual and probably different than would be expected. LIFO normally records a higher cost of products sold figure than is produced with the FIFO method. However, for Kimberly-Clark LIFO produces a *lower* income figure in 1987 than would FIFO. This means that LIFO *increased* income as compared with the FIFO method. This unusual result is probably caused by the liquidation of an older inventory layer. It should be noted that the ending inventory decreased from 1986 to 1987.

Finally, Note 9 discloses that since the adoption of LIFO, Kimberly-Clark has cumulatively charged the cost of products sold with $119.6 million more than would have been charged using the FIFO method. This LIFO charge has had the effect of reducing pre-tax income over those periods. Had the company not used LIFO, the $119.6 million would have increased income and would have been taxable. If Kimberly-Clark's effective tax rate during this period had been 46 percent, the firm saved paying the government about $55 million in taxes ($119.6 × .46) by using the LIFO inventory method. In summary, the reduction in income of $119.6 million was accompanied by a $55 million cash saving in income taxes.

As previously noted, total inventories are slightly lower in 1987 compared to 1986. We can conclude that the company is keeping control over its investment in inventory. The components of inventory are not changing dramatically, and these stable inventory levels have been maintained while sales have increased 13.5 percent.

Inventory assets are important to support a firm's ability to complete sales. The investment that is made in inventory must not be too large or too small. An investment that is too large ties up funds that can be used for more productive purposes. An investment that is too small results in stock outages and poor customer service or inefficient product production. Measuring a firm's inventory activity shows the intensity with which the firm is using its inventory to support sales generation. The inventory activity ratio is called "inventory turnover." This ratio measures a company's ability to sell and convert inventory into accounts receivable during an accounting period. The objective in business is to turn inventory over as frequently as possible. This turnover ratio is calculated as follows:

$$\text{Cost of goods sold/Inventory}^7 = \text{Number of turnovers}$$

We can then complete the analysis for 1987 and 1986:

$$1987 \quad \$3,065.9/\$645.0 = 4.75 \text{ times}$$
$$1986 \quad \$2,712.2/\$653.3 = 4.15 \text{ times}$$

This ratio can also be expressed in terms of the number of days it takes inventory to be sold by dividing 365 days by the number of turnovers. In Kimberly-Clark's case the calculation is:

$$1987 \quad 365 \text{ days/4.75 times} = 76.8 \text{ days}$$
$$1986 \quad 365 \text{ days/4.15 times} = 88.0 \text{ days}$$

These results indicate that the company is turning over its inventory every 2.5 to 3 months. More importantly, they have improved the turnover by 11.2 days during this year. Inventory turnover is an indication of efficiency, and this calculation shows a significant improvement by Kimberly-Clark. Each industry has unique inventory characteristics. Therefore, it is not the specific number of turnovers that is important but, rather, what is efficient for that type of industry. We would have to look at other firms in this industry to compare with Kimberly-Clark. Such a comparison with industry averages indicates that Kimberly-Clark is performing better than average.

## SUMMARY

In this chapter, we are primarily interested in how the pool of inventory cost is divided between the goods sold and the ending inventory. The inventory formula provides us with a helpful analytical tool for examining this and other inventory problems. In practice, a number of alternative procedures

---

[7] We have used the year-end balance sheet values for inventory for simplicity. A more appropriate and correct calculation would use the year-to-year average inventory values. Also, FIFO inventory values were used rather than LIFO values. The FIFO method reflects more current values in ending inventory than is shown by LIFO. These values are more appropriate for showing the turnover ratio because they reflect the values currently being paid by the firm. We will discuss these considerations in Chapter 18.

exist for dividing the cost pool. The effects of these choices on the income statement and position statement vary with the circumstances.

With so many alternatives, it behooves a firm to report clearly what its inventory policies are. Likewise, a user of financial information must understand the meaning of inventory terminology in order to assess the general impact of alternative procedures on the statements. This chapter lays the groundwork for a rational interpretation of financial statements in the inventory area.

The onset of double-digit inflation in 1974 led to an immediate and dramatic increase in the number of companies using LIFO for tax purposes. Because government regulations require conformity between book and tax inventory methods whenever LIFO is used, more firms now report unrealistically low balance sheet amounts for their inventories. Fortunately, voluntary disclosures of alternative inventory valuations, such as reported by Kimberly-Clark, have helped. These disclosures increase the probability that financial statement users can intelligently interpret the inventory data and make meaningful comparisons between firms.

# Appendix: Mechanics of Lower of Cost or Market

The notion of realizability or recoverability appears to underlie lower of cost or market (LCM). Nevertheless, the primary definition of market is replacement cost. The rationale for LCM, under this definition, appears to be as follows. If replacement cost has fallen below cost, then the net selling price of the merchandise on hand will probably decline also. Hence, the asset has lost part of its revenue-producing ability. This decline in value should be recognized as a loss upon incurrence.

## Limitations on Replacement Cost

This rationale contains some key assumptions. To the extent that these assumptions are not valid, the definition of market as replacement cost may lead to unreasonable results. Consequently, the AICPA, in formulating the cost-or-market principle, modifies replacement cost as the determinant of market by attaching upper and lower limits:

As used in the phrase *lower of cost or market* the term *market* means current replacement cost (by purchase or reproduction, as the case may be) except that:

(1) Market should not exceed the net realizable value (i.e., estimated selling price in the ordinary course of business less reasonably predictable costs of completion and disposal); and

(2) Market should not be less than net realizable value reduced by an allowance for an approximately normal profit margin.[8]

These modifications provide a floor and a ceiling to the measurement of "market." The ceiling is net realizable value; the floor is net realizable value less a normal profit. Market means replacement cost only as long as it lies between the floor and the ceiling.

**Upper Limit.**   When goods are obsolete or damaged, the cost of replacing them may actually be above both original cost and net realizable value. Consequently, no reduction would result under the normal definition of market as replacement cost. However, if net realizable value is below original cost, a portion of the cost cannot be recovered and a loss in this period should be recorded.

In this case, replacement cost does not measure the real loss in utility due to obsolescence. A loss equal to the difference between original cost and net realizable value ultimately will occur. Because the obsolescence or damage occurred in the current period, this loss should be recognized now by a decrease in the inventory to net realizable value, even though replacement cost has risen. A write-down to net realizable value measures the *minimum* loss suffered by the firm. Consequently, if replacement cost is above net realizable value, the latter is substituted for replacement cost as the meaning of market.

**Lower Limit.**   The floor placed on market attempts to resolve the problem that arises if the decline in selling prices is negligible or less than proportionate to the decline in replacement cost. In this case, a reduction in inventory to replacement cost would recognize a loss in the current period, only to show an *abnormal* income in the following period when the units are sold.

To avoid this absurdity, the AICPA has specified that if replacement cost is below net realizable value less a normal profit margin, the latter is used as the definition of market. Only a loss equal to the difference between cost and this lower limit is to be included in the cost of goods sold of the current period. Then, if the merchandise is sold in the following period as anticipated, a normal margin will be realized. Stated differently, so long as an item can be sold at a normal profit, no additional loss has occurred—even if replacement cost has declined more. A write-down to net realizable value less a normal profit presumably measures the *maximum* loss suffered by the firm.

## Analysis of Lower of Cost or Market

Thus, the lower-of-cost-or-market rule, as applied in accounting practice, actually offers four different concepts of utility for inventory items: (1) acquisition cost (AC), (2) current replacement cost (RC), (3) net realizable value (NRV), and (4) net realizable value less normal profit (NRV − NP). The last three represent alternative views of market, depending on particular circumstances. Conceivably, all three con-

---

[8] AICPA, *Accounting Research and Terminology Bulletins, Final Edition*, p. 31.

cepts of market could be used by a single company at the same time for different types of inventory or at different times for the same inventory. Of course, the market figure, however determined, is applicable only if it is below cost.

The information in Table 9A–1 relates to five items in an ending inventory. Assume that we are to determine the proper dollar amount *per unit* for each item in accordance with the LCM procedure, as interpreted by the AICPA. Table 9A–2 presents the results of the LCM procedure and serves as a focal point for the analysis of each alternative. The relevant market figure is shown in bold type.

**Item A: Cost.**    The ending inventory is valued at the acquisition cost of $6 per unit. The applicable market figure is the usual one, replacement cost, because it is between the floor and ceiling. Because it is still above cost, however, no adjustment is made. The inventory is deemed not to have suffered any decline in utility, even though the profit recognized in the next period will be only 80 cents ($6.80 NRV − $6.00 AC), less than the normal profit of $1.20.

**Item B: Net Realizable Value.**    In this case, the exit value (NRV) of the item on hand is less than its entry value (RC). Goods subject to major style or model

---

**TABLE 9A–1**    Data for Lower-of-Cost-or-Market Illustration

| Item | Acquisition Cost | Replacement Cost | Estimated Sale Price | Estimated Cost to Sell | Normal Profit |
|------|-----------------|------------------|---------------------|------------------------|---------------|
| A | $ 6.00 | $ 6.50 | $ 7.50 | $0.70 | $1.20 |
| B | 15.30 | 15.40 | 15.50 | 1.20 | 2.00 |
| C | 10.50 | 8.20 | 11.80 | 1.10 | 1.60 |
| D | 5.20 | 5.00 | 6.30 | 0.50 | 1.00 |
| E | 8.60 | 8.00 | 9.40 | 1.10 | 0.50 |

---

**TABLE 9A–2**    Computation of Lower of Cost or Market

| | Item | | | | |
|---|---|---|---|---|---|
| | A | B | C | D | E |
| Calculation of market: | | | | | |
| Ceiling—net realizable value (estimated selling price less estimated cost to sell) . . . . | $6.80 | **$14.30** | $10.70 | $5.80 | $8.30 |
| Replacement cost . . . . . . . | **6.50** | 15.40 | 8.20 | **5.00** | **8.00** |
| Floor—net realizable value less normal profit . . . . . . | 5.60 | 12.30 | **9.10** | 4.80 | 7.80 |
| Market—replacement cost as constrained by floor and ceiling . . . . . . . . . | 6.50 | 14.30 | 9.10 | 5.00 | 8.00 |
| Acquisition cost . . . . . . . . | 6.00 | 15.30 | 10.50 | 5.20 | 8.60 |
| Lower of cost or market . . . . . | 6.00 | 14.30 | 9.10 | 5.00 | 8.00 |

changes and those prone to breakage or deterioration may follow this pattern. The ceiling governs the determination of market. The firm is assumed to have suffered a loss of utility at *least* equal to $1 per unit ($15.30 − $14.30). Under LCM in this instance, the loss is recorded in this period—by write-down of the ending inventory to $14.30—instead of next period, when the goods are actually sold. No income or loss occurs in the next period when the goods are actually disposed of at a net selling price of $14.30.

Of the market alternatives under LCM, this one claims the greatest use and support. Most accountants agree that losses from damage, obsolescence, and similar causes are significant, measurable, economic events of the period in which they occur. Consequently, the notion that an *unrecoverable cost* is not an asset seems widely accepted. As we shall see in the next example, though, LCM often goes further than merely reducing inventory to net realizable value.

### Item C: Net Realizable Value less Normal Profit.

Here, replacement cost has declined proportionately more than selling prices. Replacement cost is below cost, but it is also below net realizable value less a normal profit. If the inventory value were reduced to replacement cost, a loss of $2.30 ($10.50 AC − $8.20 RC) would be recorded this period, and a profit of $2.50 ($10.70 NRV less the decreased inventory value of $8.20) would be recorded next period. This profit of $2.50 per unit would be much greater than the normal profit of $1.60. Therefore, the lower limit of net realizable value less normal profit becomes the applicable market figure. Through a reduction of the ending inventory to $9.10 and a concomitant charge to income this period of $1.40 ($10.50 AC less $9.10), a normal profit of $1.60 ($10.70 NRV − $9.10) is recorded in a later period.

Two major objections are raised against this result. First is the charge of profit manipulation mentioned in Chapter 9. The normal profit in the subsequent period results from an uncalled-for write-down of assets this period. Because net realizable value ($10.70) is above cost ($10.50), any "loss" recorded this period is entirely hypothetical in a conventional accounting sense. The second objection is a practical one. What, in fact, is a normal profit? The foregoing example assumes a *constant-dollar amount* regardless of changes in selling prices or costs. Should it be a *percentage* return on sales? Moreover, is normal profit a hoped-for figure, an average figure for this particular product, or an average return for the business as a whole? Grave doubts exist whether any practical quantification *could be* or *should be* given to a concept of "normal" in a dynamic business environment.

### Items D and E: Replacement Cost.

In both of these cases replacement cost is the applicable market figure because it is between the upper and lower limits. It is also the relevant figure for inventory valuation under LCM, because it is below the original acquisition cost. A write-down to replacement cost records a holding loss equal to the difference between acquisition cost and current cost. The precise nature of that loss depends on the circumstances. In the case of item D, the net realizable value of $5.80 remains above the acquisition cost of $5.20. Item D still will be disposed of at a profit, albeit not a normal one. Has the utility of the inventory fallen merely because an anticipated profit margin has shrunk? Even if we accept the viewpoint that unless the firm can sell at a normal profit it has suffered a loss, LCM in this instance does not achieve the objective of disposition at normal profit, either. After being reduced to a replacement-cost value of $5, the inventory will be sold at a net selling price of $5.80 for a profit of only 80 cents per unit rather than a normal profit of $1.

In the case of item E, the firm would incur an actual loss upon disposition of $0.30 per unit ($8.30 NRV less $8.60 AC). However, application of LCM results in a reduction of inventory to the replacement cost of $8. A loss of 60 cents per unit ($8.60 AC less $8 RC) is recognized in the current period, and a profit of 30 cents per unit ($8.30 NRV less the decreased inventory value of $8) will be recorded in the following period. In this case, LCM does not write the inventory down sufficiently far to allow for the normal profit of 50 cents nor does it accurately reflect the *actual* loss of 30 cents in item E in the current period.

## Summary of LCM

Lower of cost or market departs from a strict matching of original acquisition cost against revenues by recording losses on units which have not been sold. In so doing, it employs concepts of cost and income different from those which normally underlie financial accounting. These concepts, of course, are not unique to LCM, nor does their use necessarily imply a poor procedure. Actually, the real difficulty with LCM is that it adheres to no consistent concept of income. No fewer than three alternative concepts of inventory value in addition to cost—replacement cost, net realizable value, and net realizable value less normal profit—find their way into this procedure, none of them consistently.

The method basically uses replacement costs, which would imply a current cost approach to income. However, replacement cost is not used if it is above cost or below net realizable value less normal profit. The method also implies that part of an asset has expired if its original cost cannot be recovered. This argument, which also has validity, would result in a write-down to recoverable value (net realizable value). However, LCM sometimes goes further and reduces the inventory below net realizable value. The avowed purpose for a write-down below net realizable value is to allow for disposition at a normal profit later. This third procedure introduces a concept of loss that falls outside of either conventional accounting or economics. Moreover, LCM may not uniformly achieve that objective either, for, whenever replacement cost is above net realizable value less normal profit, the former is used.

Despite its inconsistencies and imprecision, lower of cost or market continues to be the most commonly used basis of valuation for inventories. In many cases, LCM may give the same results as the conventional cost method, because cost is normally lower than the applicable market figure. Unfortunately, the external reader does not know the extent of the write-downs, *if any*. By burying any inventory loss that does exist in cost of goods sold, most firms prevent the reader from knowing what impact LCM has had on the financial statements.

## PROBLEMS AND CASETTES

### 9–1. Using the Inventory Formula to Determine Missing Amounts
Use the inventory formula to determine the missing quantities for each of the independent cases shown following.

|  | Case 1 | Case 2 | Case 3 | Case 4 | Case 5 |
|---|---|---|---|---|---|
| Beginning inventory | $50,000 | $15,000 | $ 8,000 | $_____ | $13,000 |
| Ending inventory |  | 10,000 |  | 18,000 | 12,000 |
| Purchases | 30,000 |  | 38,000 | 20,000 | 40,000 |
| Inventory available |  |  | 40,000 | 37,000 |  |
| Purchase returns | 10,000 | 5,000 |  | 3,000 | 8,000 |
| Cost of goods sold | 40,000 | 25,000 | 15,000 |  |  |

## 9–2. Determining Net Income Effects of Inventory Errors

On December 31, 1990, the Park Company discovered the following errors in the costing of its ending merchandise inventory:

| | | |
|---|---|---|
| December 31, 1987 | $16,000 | overstatement |
| December 31, 1988 | 19,000 | understatement |
| December 31, 1989 | 4,200 | understatement |
| December 31, 1990 | 1,400 | understatement |

The reported pre-tax income for 1988, 1989, and 1990 was $23,200, $24,800, and $26,400, respectively. Each error was independent of the others, and none had been detected or corrected as of December 31, 1990.

### Required:

a. Using Table 9–2 as a guide, prepare a schedule showing the determination of corrected pre-tax income for 1988, 1989, and 1990.
b. Did the income for the 1988 to 1990 period change significantly as a result of your scheduled corrections in a? Why not? What purpose then does the schedule serve and what information does it reveal?

## 9–3. Identification of Different Inventory Costing Methods

The Bloom Company began business on January 1, 1990. Inventory purchases and retail sales of its products for the first month are shown in the following tabulation. All sales were made at a price of $50 per unit.

| | Purchases | | |
|---|---|---|---|
| Date | Tag Number | Cost per Unit | Units Sold (tag numbers) |
| January   1 | 17 | $30 | |
| 3 | 22, 26 | 32 | |
| 8 | 30, 31 | 36 | |
| 12 | | | 17 |
| 17 | 37 | 38 | 26 |
| 21 | 42, 43 | 37 | |
| 24 | | | 22, 42 |
| 31 | 52 | 41 | 43 |

In order to evaluate the effect of alternative inventory costing methods, management asked a bookkeeper to prepare a summary schedule of gross margins under various alternatives. The bookkeeper prepared the following:

|  | (1) | (2) | (3) | (4) |
|---|---|---|---|---|
| Sales . . . . . . . . . . . . . . . . . . . | $250 | $250 | $250 | $250 |
| Cost of goods sold. . . . . . . . . . . . . . . | 189 | 168 | 166 | 177 |
| Gross margin . . . . . . . . . . . . . . . . | $ 96 | $117 | $119 | $108 |

**Required:**

a. Unfortunately, the bookkeeper neglected to label the results. You have learned that the methods considered were FIFO, LIFO, weighted-average cost, and specific identification. *Without* making computations, can you match any of the bookkeeper's results with the inventory methods considered?

b. Calculate the cost of goods sold under each of the methods and match all of the bookkeeper's results with the inventory procedures analyzed.

c. If Bloom Company asked you to recommend just *one* inventory costing procedure, which would you suggest to them and why?

**9–4. Comparison of Inventory Methods Using the Periodic Procedure**

The books of the Whitney Corporation are closed monthly. The company uses the FIFO periodic method. The controller asks you to compare the FIFO method to the LIFO and weighted-average cost methods. The purchases and sales for the firm's first two months of operation are given below:

| Date | | Purchases Units | Cost per Unit | Units Sold |
|---|---|---|---|---|
| January | 1 | 12,000 | $ 7.00 | |
|  | 7 | | | 4,000 |
|  | 12 | 18,000 | 8.00 | |
|  | 15 | | | 11,000 |
|  | 21 | | | 9,000 |
|  | 23 | 7,000 | 9.00 | |
|  | 31 | | | 5,000 |
| February | 6 | 6,000 | 10.00 | |
|  | 11 | | | 7,000 |
|  | 16 | 10,000 | 12.00 | |
|  | 19 | | | 15,000 |
|  | 28 | 2,000 | 13.00 | |

**Required:**

a. Using the periodic inventory method, calculate the ending inventory as of January 31, and the January cost of goods sold using:
   1. the FIFO costing method.
   2. the LIFO costing method.

3. the weighted-average costing method (carry calculations to three decimal places).
   b. Continue the calculations from (*a*) and compute the ending inventory as of February 28, and the February cost of goods sold for each method using the periodic method.
   c. Assume that the replacement costs of the inventory are $10 and $12 on January 31 and February 28, respectively. Compute the inventory as of January 31 and as of February 28, using the lower of FIFO cost or market.

## 9–5. Comparison of Inventory Methods Using the Perpetual Procedure
Use the data shown in problem 9–4 to complete this problem. Use the *perpetual* inventory method.

**Required:**

a. Calculate the ending inventory as of January 31, and the January cost of goods sold using:
   1. the FIFO costing method.
   2. the LIFO costing method.
   3. the weighted-average costing method (carry calculations to three decimal places).
b. Continue the calculations from *a* and compute the ending inventory as of February 28, and the February cost of goods sold for each method using the perpetual method.

## 9–6. Use of the Retail Inventory Method
The following information is taken from the accounts and other records of Odana Department Store, Inc.:

|  | Cost | Retail |
|---|---|---|
| Beginning inventory | $ 20,000 | $ 32,000 |
| Purchases | 175,000 | 275,000 |
| Freight-in | 8,000 | |
| Purchase returns | 3,000 | 5,000 |
| Sales | | 260,000 |
| Sales returns | | 14,000 |

**Required:**

a. Use the retail inventory method to compute an ending inventory figure.
b. Discuss carefully the assumptions inherent in any use of the retail inventory method and their validity.

## 9–7. Adjusting Inventory to the Lower of Cost or Market
The following inventory information relates to the first four years of the Diamond Company's operations:

|                              | 1990      | 1991      | 1992      | 1993      |
|------------------------------|-----------|-----------|-----------|-----------|
| Net sales. . . . . . . . . . . . | $300,000  | $310,000  | $350,000  | $400,000  |
| Net purchases. . . . . . . . . | 210,000   | 230,000   | 240,000   | 225,000   |
| Ending inventory (at cost). . . . . | 100,000   | 125,000   | 130,000   | 120,000   |
| Ending inventory (at market) . . . | 98,000    | 126,000   | 125,000   | 119,000   |

### Required:

*a.* Determine the cost of goods sold for each year using the cost basis.

*b.* Prepare the journal entry for each year to adjust the ending inventory to the lower of cost or market.

*c.* Prepare an income statement for each year showing sales, cost of goods sold, and gross margin for each of the years on the:

  1. cost basis.
  2. lower-of-cost-or-market basis.

*d.* Indicate the amount of inventory that should appear on the balance sheet for each year using the lower-of-cost-or-market basis.

### 9–8. Converting a LIFO Statement to a FIFO Statement

Assume that the president of the Sheldon Company is in doubt about the accountant's use of LIFO and manner of presentation on the income statement. Sheldon states, "I need to see the gross margin for this company and your income statement does not show it. I also wonder about the impact of your use of LIFO. It seems to me that most of our inventory moves on a FIFO basis. I'd like to see your income statement redone on a FIFO basis."

Selected financial data from the firm's current statements (LIFO basis) appear below:

**Balance Sheet**
**(amounts in thousands)**

|                                                           | 1990       | 1989      |
|-----------------------------------------------------------|------------|-----------|
| Inventories—less adjustments from current costs to last-in, first-out costs of $34,417,000 in 1990 and $33,234,000 in 1989: |            |           |
| Finished products . . . . . . . . . . . . . . . . . . . . . | $ 60,540   | $58,274   |
| Work in process and materials . . . . . . . . . . . . . | 51,056     | 34,086    |
|                                                           | $111,596   | $92,360   |

**Income Statement**
**(amounts in thousands)**

|                                                        | 1990      |
|--------------------------------------------------------|-----------|
| Net sales . . . . . . . . . . . . . . . . . . . . . . . | $501,589  |
| Costs and expenses:                                    |           |
| Cost of sales . . . . . . . . . . . . . . . . . . . . . | $356,194  |
| Selling, administrative, and general expenses . . . . . . . | 105,562   |
| Interest . . . . . . . . . . . . . . . . . . . . . . . | 8,262     |
| Other (income) deductions—net . . . . . . . . . . . . . | (1,657)   |
|                                                        | $468,361  |
| Income before income taxes . . . . . . . . . . . . . . . | $ 33,228  |
| Federal and state taxes . . . . . . . . . . . . . . . . | 15,928    |
| Net income . . . . . . . . . . . . . . . . . . . . . . | $ 17,300  |

**Required:**

*a.* Use the selected data plus any additional computations to prepare the detail for the cost of goods sold (1) on the LIFO basis and (2) on the FIFO basis. Complete the schedule below.

|  | LIFO | FIFO |
|---|---|---|
| Beginning inventory . . . . . . . . . . . . . |  |  |
| Add: Purchases . . . . . . . . . . . . . . . |  |  |
| Goods available . . . . . . . . . . . . . . |  |  |
| Less: Ending inventory . . . . . . . . . . . |  |  |
| Cost of goods sold . . . . . . . . . . . . . |  |  |

*b.* Complete the partial income statements shown below on the LIFO and FIFO bases.

|  | LIFO | FIFO |
|---|---|---|
| Net sales . . . . . . . . . . . . . . . . . . |  |  |
| Cost of sales . . . . . . . . . . . . . . . . | $ | $ |
| Gross margin . . . . . . . . . . . . . . . . |  |  |
| Other expenses: |  |  |
| Selling, administrative and general expenses. . . . . |  |  |
| Interest. . . . . . . . . . . . . . . . . . . |  |  |
| Other (income) deductions — net . . . . . . . . . |  |  |
| Income before income taxes . . . . . . . . . . . | $ | $ |

*c.* Explain what importance the gross margin figure has in judging a firm's performance.

*d.* How would you respond to the president's concern over the use of LIFO rather than FIFO? Why would you use LIFO if the physical flow of the inventory was really in a FIFO pattern?

## 9–9. LIFO Perpetual and LIFO Periodic with Liquidation

The MEM Company maintains its inventory records using the perpetual LIFO method. The following data show the inventory transactions for April 1991:

| Date | Transaction | Purchases | Goods Sold | Inventory Units | Inventory Cost |
|---|---|---|---|---|---|
| 4/1 | Inventory balance |  |  | 250 | $9.00 |
|  |  |  |  | 300 | 9.50 |
| 4/5 | Sale |  | 200 @ $15.00 |  |  |
| 4/10 | Purchase | 150 @ $10.25 |  |  |  |
| 4/15 | Sale |  | 175 @ $15.00 |  |  |
| 4/20 | Purchase | 200 @ $10.50 |  |  |  |
| 4/27 | Sale |  | 150 @ $16.00 |  |  |
| 4/29 | Purchase | 300 @ $11.00 |  |  |  |

**Required:**

a. Use the LIFO perpetual inventory method to determine the figures necessary to complete the partial income statement shown below.

**MEM Company**
**Partial Income Statement**
**For the Month Ending April 30, 1991**

|  |  |  |  |
|---|---|---|---|
| Sales . . . . . . . . . . . . . . . . . . . . . . . . |  |  | $ |
| Cost of sales: |  |  |  |
|   Beginning inventory . . . . . . . . . . . . . . | $ |  |  |
|   Purchases . . . . . . . . . . . . . . . . . . |  |  |  |
|   Goods available . . . . . . . . . . . . . . . | $ |  |  |
|   Ending inventory . . . . . . . . . . . . . . |  |  |  |
|     Cost of goods sold . . . . . . . . . . . |  |  | $ |
| Gross margin . . . . . . . . . . . . . . . . . |  |  |  |

b. When the LIFO method is used, the periodic method computes a different value for ending inventory than does the perpetual method. What would the ending inventory value be if the periodic method is used? What impact would this value have on gross margin?

c. What is the cause of the differences between parts a and b? Does this result suggest reasons why LIFO is used on a periodic basis only?

**9–10. Using the Inventory Formula to Estimate Inventory**

Your firm, the Clothes Horse, suffered a disastrous fire during the night of July 1. Everything was destroyed with the exception of the accounting records that were stored in a fireproof vault.

You and the insurance adjuster are trying to make an estimate of your store's inventory loss. You need to determine the inventory cost prior to the fire to make an insurance claim.

The following information is shown in the records for the period January 1 through June 30:

| | |
|---|---|
| Inventory balance (at cost) on January 1 . . . . . . | $33,400 |
| Purchases. . . . . . . . . . . . . . . . . . . . . | 63,520 |
| Purchase returns . . . . . . . . . . . . . . . . . | 1,260 |
| Freight-in . . . . . . . . . . . . . . . . . . . . | 660 |
| Sales . . . . . . . . . . . . . . . . . . . . . . | 84,730 |
| Sales returns . . . . . . . . . . . . . . . . . . | 2,230 |

The monthly income statements for the past two years show that gross margin has been averaging 34 percent (sales less cost of sales/sales).

**Required:**

Prepare an analysis showing *your estimate of the cost of the store's inventory prior to the fire*. Use the inventory formula to determine (1) the inventory that was available for sale and (2) the cost of goods sold related to the period's sales. Then you can determine the value of the inventory prior to the fire.

### 9–11. Examining LIFO Inventory Policy

Recently the president of Progress, Inc. sent the following letter to the firm's stockholders:

Dear Stockholders:

Your firm is constantly attempting to improve the results of its operations and to increase your dividends.

In pursuing this objective, we have exhaustively reviewed the inventory environment within which we must make our purchases. Prices have moved up and down erratically over the last 5 years. As a consequence we have decided to switch to the LIFO inventory method. This method will reduce our tax payments every year because we are matching the latest purchases with current sales. Tax savings are an increased cash inflow to your firm and will assure you of increased dividend payments.

We have also decided that it makes sense to voluntarily report our new inventory methods in the annual report so that you will be able to see our improved financial position.

If inventory prices should begin declining, we will switch back to the previously used FIFO costing method for inventory. That will keep our profits up in a manner similar to the increased "cash profits" we are now going to pass on to you as dividends.

Sincerely,

I. M. Slick
President

### Required:

List and describe *all* of the misconceptions and misinformation conveyed by this letter to the stockholders.

### 9–12. Evaluation of Applications of LIFO and FIFO

Hershey Foods Corporation, a major producer of chocolate and confectionery products, also operates a chain of restaurants and is a producer of pasta products. Safeway Stores operates more than 2,000 food supermarkets in the United States and in many foreign countries. Excerpts from these companies' annual reports follow:

#### Hershey Foods Corporation

Substantially all of the Chocolate and Confectionery segment inventories are valued under the last-in, first-out (LIFO) method. . . . The remaining inventories are principally stated at the lower of first-in, first-out (FIFO) cost or market.

#### Safeway Stores

Approximately 60% of consolidated merchandise inventories are valued on a last-in, first-out (LIFO) basis. Inventories not valued on a LIFO basis are valued at the lower of cost on a first-in, first-out (FIFO) basis or replacement market. Inventories on a FIFO basis include meat and produce in the U.S. and all Canadian and overseas inventories.

**Required:**

a. "Safeway had to make an exception for its meat and produce inventories. Valuing those items on a last-in, first-out basis would have led to an incredible amount of spoilage." Do you agree with this statement?

b. Why do you believe Safeway excluded meat and produce inventories from the LIFO method?

c. What line of reasoning might have led Hershey Foods to conclude that its restaurant and pasta products inventories should be valued under FIFO rather than under the LIFO procedure used for chocolate and confectionery inventories?

**9–13. Analysis of Corporate Performance**

The performance of a corporation is related to its ability to increase sales revenue while keeping inventory costs under control. Several computations may be made to develop some indication of a firm's performance results. Selected information from the 1986 annual report of Premark International, Inc. is presented below (numbers in millions of dollars):

| | |
|---|---|
| Annual net sales for 1986 . . . . . . . . . . | $1,959.0 |
| Annual net sales for 1985 . . . . . . . . . . | 1,763.4 |
| Cost of products sold in 1986 . . . . . . . . | 1,109.2 |
| Cost of products sold in 1985 . . . . . . . . | 954.0 |
| Ending inventory for 1986 . . . . . . . . . . | 435.2 |
| Ending inventory for 1985 . . . . . . . . . . | 412.5 |

**Required:**

a. Complete the following computations:
   1. Percentage increase in net sales from 1985 to 1986.
   2. Percentage increase in the cost of products sold from 1985 to 1986.
   3. Percentage increase in the ending inventory on hand from 1985 to 1986.
   4. Percentage increase in the gross margin from 1985 to 1986.

b. Complete the following computations:
   1. Number of times inventory turned over (cost of goods sold/ending inventory) in 1985 and 1986.
   2. Number of days it took inventory to turn over in 1985 and 1986.

c. How would you summarize your conclusions about the performance of Premark in controlling their inventory costs?

**Casette 9–1.    Georgia-Pacific Corporation**

In the Appendix at the end of the book is a complete set of financial statements of the Georgia-Pacific Corporation taken from its annual report of 1987.

Answer the following questions with particular reference to its inventory figures and disclosures.

1. What inventory costing method(s) does Georgia-Pacific use for its inventory? Compute the dollar amount of inventory valued under each of the corporation's method(s).

2. Inventory increased from 1986 to 1987. Prepare computations and respond to the following questions related to the inventory change:
   a. What was the dollar value of the increase?
   b. What was the percentage growth of the increase?
   c. How much of the dollar value increase was represented by the acquisition of U.S. Plywood?
   d. Do inventories represent a greater or smaller proportion of total assets in 1987 than in 1986?
3. Inventory turnover is a measure that indicates the company's efficiency in using inventory. Answer the following questions related to Georgia-Pacific's inventory turnover (use the year-end inventory values for 1987 and 1986):
   a. How many times did inventory turn over in each year?
   b. How many days did it take inventory to turn over?
   c. What conclusions can you reach using the results of your calculations in *a* and *b*?
   d. What limitations do you see in using this relationship for Georgia-Pacific?
4. In Note 1, the company shows figures for an item titled "LIFO reserve."
   a. Explain what is meant by this term.
   b. What type of an account is this?
   c. Why is the account used?
   d. What is the journal entry which was made to this account in 1987?
5. Note 1 uses the term "(LIFO) dollar value pool method" when describing inventory valuation. Although this term was not discussed in the chapter, can you speculate on its meaning?

## Casette 9–2. Interpreting Statement Disclosures

Inventory disclosures for Burlington Industries, Inc. and Kraft, Inc. for 1986 were as follows:

### BURLINGTON INDUSTRIES
#### (in thousands)

|                                    | 1986      | 1985      |
|------------------------------------|-----------|-----------|
| Current assets:                    |           |           |
| Inventories (Note C) . . . . . . . | $327,286  | $368,330  |

Note C.  Inventories
    Inventories are summarized as follows (in thousands):

|                                          | 1986      | 1985      |
|------------------------------------------|-----------|-----------|
| Inventories at average cost:             |           |           |
| Raw materials . . . . . . . . . . .      | $ 54,124  | $ 66,248  |
| Stock in process. . . . . . . . . . .    | 124,599   | 131,359   |
| Produced goods . . . . . . . . . . .     | 259,576   | 325,575   |
| Dyes, chemicals, and supplies . . . .    | 33,024    | 37,389    |
|                                          | 471,323   | 560,571   |
| Less: Excess of average cost over LIFO . | 144,037   | 192,241   |
| Total . . . . . . . . . . . . . . . .    | $327,286  | $368,330  |

Inventories valued using the LIFO method comprised approximately 65% of consolidated inventories at September 27, 1986 and 76% at September 28, 1985.

The 1986 decrease in excess of average cost over LIFO was due to the liquidation of LIFO inventory quantities carried at lower costs prevailing in prior years, principally due to the sale of the company's Domestics division, and lower cotton prices. The effect of the liquidation of LIFO inventory quantities was to increase fiscal 1986 net earnings by approximately $8,875,000 or 32 cents per share of which $6,003,000 or 21 cents per share was related to the sale of the company's Domestics division.

**KRAFT, INC.**

**(dollars in millions)**

|  | Dec. 27, 1986 | Dec. 28, 1985 |
| --- | --- | --- |
| Inventories . . . . . . . . . . . . . . | $1,211.3 | $1,115.3 |

**Accounting Changes.** In 1985, the company changed its method of determining cost for substantially all domestic inventories from the first-in, first-out (FIFO) and average cost methods to the last-in, first-out (LIFO) method. The change was made because it results in a better matching of current costs and revenues. The effect of this change was to increase net income from continuing operations in 1985 by $16.8 million, or 12 cents per share. The adoption of LIFO had no effect on prior years' financial results.

**Inventories.** Inventories are valued at the lower of cost or market. Prior to 1985, cost was determined using the average cost method for food products and the FIFO cost method for most other products. Beginning in 1985, substantially all domestic inventories are valued on the LIFO cost method. For other inventories, approximately 43 percent, the FIFO cost method is generally used. Inventory cost includes cost of raw material, labor, and overhead.

At December 27, 1986 and December 28, 1985, if inventories valued on the LIFO method had been valued using the FIFO method, they would have been lower by approximately $21.6 million and $32.9 million, respectively.

**Required:**

*a.* In Note C, Burlington Industries presents an adjustment for each year, reducing inventories by the excess of average cost over LIFO. Why was this adjustment made? What kind of account is the "Excess of Average Cost over Lifo"?

*b.* Burlington Industries states that the decrease in the "excess of average cost over LIFO" in 1986 was due to "the liquidation of LIFO inventory quantities." Explain the meaning of this disclosure and why it *increased* 1986 net earnings by $8,875,000.

*c.* Kraft, Inc., in the note titled "Accounting Changes," indicates that the 1985 change in inventory methods to LIFO resulted in an increase to net income of $16.8 million. Explain the circumstances that would cause income to increase by making this change.

*d.* Why do you think Kraft values only its domestic inventories at LIFO?

*e.* In the Inventories note, Kraft, Inc. states that if LIFO inventories "had been valued using the FIFO method, they would have been lower by approximately

$21.6 million and $32.9 million." Should not FIFO ending inventories be *higher* than LIFO? Explain what circumstances Kraft could be experiencing to have the result disclosed.

f. Kraft showed cost of sales of $5,970.6 million on its 1986 income statement. Estimate what cost of sales would have been in 1986 if the company had been using FIFO continuously.

g. It appears that Kraft, Inc. could gain a greater tax advantage by using the FIFO inventory method. Ending inventories would be lower, cost of goods sold higher, and net income lower. Income taxes, therefore, would be lower than they are when using LIFO. Why does Kraft not change to the FIFO method to save taxes? Explain.

## Casette 9–3. Comparing FIFO with LIFO and Measurement of Holding Gains

The president of Willing-to-Change Corporation has asked you to assist in making a decision concerning inventory policy. Specifically, the company is considering whether to use LIFO or FIFO. He also has heard that "current cost" is the best, although LIFO often approximates current cost.

Below are the purchases and sales by quarter for 1991 and 1992:

| | | Purchases | | | Sales | | |
|---|---|---|---|---|---|---|---|
| | | Units | $/Unit | Total | Units | $/Unit | Total |
| Beginning inventory | | 3,000 | $4.00 | $12,000 | | | |
| 1991: | I | 2,000 | 4.40 | 8,800 | 3,000 | $5.50 | $16,500 |
| | II | 3,000 | 4.50 | 13,500 | 2,000 | 5.625 | 11,250 |
| | III | 1,000 | 4.70 | 4,700 | 2,000 | 5.875 | 11,750 |
| | IV | 2,000 | 5.00 | 10,000 | 1,000 | 6.25 | 6,250 |
| 1992: | I | 2,000 | 5.30 | 10,600 | 2,000 | 6.625 | 13,250 |
| | II | 3,000 | 5.40 | 16,200 | 2,000 | 6.75 | 13,500 |
| | III | 3,000 | 5.60 | 16,800 | 3,000 | 7.00 | 21,000 |
| | IV | 3,000 | 6.00 | 18,000 | 4,000 | 7.50 | 30,000 |

## Required:

a. Calculate cost of goods sold and ending inventory for the years 1991 and 1992 assuming the company uses:
  1. FIFO periodic inventory applied on an annual basis.
  2. LIFO periodic inventory applied on an annual basis.

b. Determine the amount of gross margin and the gross margin percentage (gross margin/sales) for each year under each method.

c. Compute cost of goods sold, gross margin, and gross margin percentage each year under current cost (defined as the current purchase price during the quarter the items were sold).

d. How closely do the FIFO and LIFO figures approximate gross margins under current cost? How much price gain or loss (holding gain or loss) is included in income each year under FIFO and LIFO?

e. Verify in detail the price (holding) gain for FIFO in 1991 that you calculated in d. Did LIFO completely eliminate the price gains from income in 1991 and 1992?

f. What would the ending inventories be each year if valued at current cost? How closely do the LIFO and FIFO figures approximate current cost valuations of ending inventory? Explain.

### 9A–1. Applying Lower-of-Cost-or-Market Procedures

You are the chief accountant for Washington Corporation. Your assistant gathered information about items in the ending inventory. You are to determine the proper dollar amount for each item and the total ending inventory in accordance with the lower-of-cost-or-market procedure, as interpreted by the American Institute of Certified Public Accountants.

| Item | Units | Original Cost | Replacement Cost | Estimated Selling Price | Estimated Cost to Sell | Normal Profit |
|------|-------|---------------|------------------|-------------------------|------------------------|---------------|
| A | 40 | $10.20 | $9.90 | $12.60 | $2.00 | $2.10 |
| B | 480 | 0.95 | 1.10 | 1.35 | 0.15 | 0.20 |
| C | 190 | 7.00 | 6.00 | 8.00 | 0.65 | 1.15 |
| D | 1,100 | 4.50 | 4.40 | 4.60 | 0.40 | 0.35 |
| E | 300 | 7.60 | 7.50 | 9.50 | 0.80 | 1.60 |

### 9A–2. Analyzing the Effect of the Lower-of-Cost-or-Market Method

Johnson Corporation uses the average cost method to assign dollar amounts to cost of goods sold and to ending inventory. Its income statement for 1990 appears below:

| | | |
|---|---:|---:|
| Sales (300,000 units at $1) . . . . . . . . . . . . . . . . | | $300,000 |
| Cost of goods sold: | | |
|   Beginning inventory . . . . . . . . . . . . . . . . . . . | $ 28,500 | |
|   Purchases . . . . . . . . . . . . . . . . . . . . . . | 143,750 | |
|   Goods available for sale (325,000 units at $0.53) . . . . . | 172,250 | |
|   Ending inventory (25,000 units at $0.53) . . . . . . . . | 13,250 | |
|     Cost of goods sold (300,000 at $0.53). . . . . . . . . | | 159,000 |
| Gross margin . . . . . . . . . . . . . . . . . . . . . . | | 141,000 |
| Selling expenses (300,000 at $0.20) . . . . . . . . . . . | | 60,000 |
| Net income (27% of sales revenue) . . . . . . . . . . . . | | $ 81,000 |

### Required:

For each situation described below, analyze the effect of lower of cost or market. Include in your analysis a calculation of the dollar impact on net income in 1990 *and* in 1991 if (1) market is defined as replacement cost or (2) if market is defined as net realizable value. Discuss the reasonableness of using each of these two definitions in the particular situation. Indicate how the AICPA rule would apply to each situation and why.

*a.* On December 31, 1990, the replacement cost of a unit of inventory is 44 cents and the selling price is only 85 cents. Selling expenses will increase from 20 to 25 cents per unit.

*b.* On December 31, 1990, the replacement cost of a unit of inventory is 52 cents and the selling price is only 71 cents. Selling expense remains at 20 cents per unit.

# Chapter 10

# Accounting for Long-Lived Assets

Accountants classify assets with more than one year of economic usefulness as noncurrent assets. Long-lived assets of this type typically fall into four major groupings—long-term investments, plant assets (property, plant, and equipment), natural resources (timber, oil, gas, coal, etc.), and intangibles (trademarks, patents, organization costs, etc.). This chapter shows how these costs are treated during the accounting periods following their acquisition.

We focus on the last three groups. Plant assets, natural resources, and long-term intangibles usually have limited periods of usefulness. In Chapter 8 we set forth the basic determinants of their cost. In this chapter, we study (1) methods of allocating the total acquisition cost from Chapter 8 among accounting periods to reflect the use of the assets, (2) journal entries made upon disposition of plant assets, and (3) the treatment of expenditures made after acquisition for the purposes of repairing, partially replacing, or improving plant assets.

## DEPRECIATION, DEPLETION, AND AMORTIZATION

*Depreciation, depletion,* and *amortization* are three accounting terms that relate to the same conceptual accounting procedure. Each term refers to the process of estimating the cost of noncurrent assets consumed during the current accounting period. Every productive resource a firm acquires represents a bundle of service potential that will be used over future time periods. The above terms describe the allocation of the cost of the noncurrent assets to the periods that the service potential is being used. This allocation of service potential cost complies with the matching concept we discussed in Chapter 2.

*Depreciation* is the accounting term given to the process of rationally and systematically allocating the cost of property, plant, and equipment. *Depletion* describes the allocation process for natural resources (wasting assets), and *amortization* defines the same process for intangible assets.[1] Productive noncurrent assets contribute to the generation of revenues in every accounting period in which they are used. Accordingly, part of their costs should be matched against (deducted from) revenues for those periods as part of the measure of the firm's effort.

We must emphasize that *depreciation refers only to a process of cost allocation. It is not a process of asset valuation.* People often refer to the decline in the market value of an asset as depreciation; for example, a new car "depreciated" by $500 after it was driven for a week. However, that is not how accountants use the term. They adhere to the cost concept and do not normally reflect the market value of a firm's resources on the books. In financial statements, depreciation refers to cost allocation.

Depreciation also is not a process that generates cash for the replacement of a particular asset. By matching depreciation expense against revenues, accountants attempt to recover the original investments in noncurrent assets made in the past. If revenues are sufficient to cover all expenses, dollar capital will be recovered. Nonetheless, revenues—not depreciation—are the source of the asset inflow. Furthermore, the depreciation process is not contingent on whether past investment is recovered or whether any of the recovered capital is used for replacement.

## Depreciation Base

The depreciation base (depletion base, amortization base) is the asset cost to be allocated to future accounting periods. In most cases, it is defined as:

$$\text{Depreciation base} = \text{Acquisition cost} - \text{Net residual value}$$

The depreciation base is the portion of an asset's cost that will be used in generating revenue. The net residual value is the estimated value that will be recovered (less the estimated costs of removal) when the entity disposes of the depreciable asset at the end of its useful life. Residual value is frequently called "salvage value." For natural resources, such as oil wells or mines, the net residual value consists of the estimated value of the remaining land. For some assets, a substantial amount is recovered when the asset is retired, either because the asset can supply use value to a new owner as in the case of trucks, aircraft, or office equipment or because salvage value is large as in the case of scrap copper, aluminum, or steel. In other cases, the assumption is frequently made that scrap value will be offset by the removal costs. Estimated net residual value is zero, and the acquisition cost becomes the depreciation base.

---

[1] *Amortization* is also used as a general term in accounting to describe the periodic allocation of any value.

# Major Problems in Determining Depreciation

Accountants encounter two problems when establishing a procedure for allocating the cost of noncurrent assets. They first must estimate the useful service life of the asset and then devise a systematic and rational way to spread the depreciation base over this service life.

The useful life of an asset is its period of service to the particular business entity, not necessarily its total conceivable life. Our entity concept restricts the determination of useful life to that economically justified period of service relevant to the business entity.

Even so, two factors affecting an asset's useful life have to be considered—physical limitations and economic limitations. Physical limitations can be caused by intensity of use (wear and tear), natural deterioration (decay caused by natural elements), adequacy of maintenance, and the passage of time (as with legal rights protected by law for a limited period). Economic limitations primarily stem from changes in technology, changes in demand for the products being produced, and changes in the business environment from growth and expansion. These may render an asset obsolete or inadequate even though physically the asset still can provide service.

The useful life of a particular asset is governed by the shortest time period derived from a consideration of these factors. Each asset may be affected differently. For a natural resource, useful life is probably most often determined by intensity of use. However, situations calling for alternative treatment can readily be imagined. For example, the useful life of an oil well may be determined by economics (it becomes uneconomical to continue operations when oil prices decrease) rather than by physical exhaustion. In contrast, the life of a building is primarily determined by action of natural elements, although in some cases obsolescence or inadequacy may be relevant. The legal life of a patent is 17 years, although economically its service potential may be exhausted much earlier because of technological change.

The point is that a determination of useful life requires careful consideration of a number of factors. Firms review their own records of property retirements and consult the experience of others in their industry. Even then, establishing an accurate useful life is a difficult task.

The second problem then arises. How should the cost of using the asset be allocated to the accounting periods contained in its useful life? Should each accounting period receive the same dollar charge, or should depreciation, depletion, or amortization cost be greater in some periods than in others? *The overriding consideration in selecting a depreciation method for financial accounting purposes is that it should result in a pattern of cost allocation that reasonably reflects the expiration pattern of the related services.* The pattern of service consumption may be impossible to determine precisely. Therefore, accountants approximate the expected pattern through the adoption of simplified formulas or depreciation methods.

## Depreciation Methods

Depreciation methods provide a rational way of systematically spreading the depreciation base over the life of an asset. There are four methods commonly encountered. These methods account for almost all of the depreciation policies used in accounting practice and can be classified by the type of periodic charge that results from their adoption:

1. Uniform charge per period—straight-line method.
2. Decreasing charge per period:
   *a.* Sum-of-the-years'-digits method.
   *b.* Declining-balance method.
3. Varying charge per period—activity method.

The term *depreciation methods* is used here in a general sense, inasmuch as the methods described are appropriate for various noncurrent assets. They are most often mentioned in connection with plant assets, but our discussion applies to wasting assets and intangibles as well.

Let us use the following situation to illustrate and compare the various depreciation methods. Assume that a machine has a total acquisition cost of $13,000 and an expected residual value of $1,000 at the end of a useful life of five years.

**Straight-Line Method.**   This method is the easiest to understand and compute. The depreciation base is spread evenly over the number of accounting periods in the asset's useful life. Each accounting period receives the same dollar charge for asset services consumed. The annual depreciation cost is determined by the formula:

$$\frac{\text{Cost} - \text{Residual value}}{\text{Useful life}} = \frac{\$13,000 - \$1,000}{5} = \$2,400$$

Table 10–1 summarizes the changes in the accounts.

The undepreciated cost at the end of each year, commonly called *book value,* is determined by subtracting the Accumulated Depreciation or Allowance for Depreciation account from the original cost recorded in the Machinery account. (See Chapter 5 for basic depreciation entries.) It represents the cost of that portion of the asset's services that has not been used and charged to operations. At the end of the fifth year, the asset's book value appears at $1,000, its expected residual value.

The straight-line method is widely used because of its simple concept and calculation. As a method of approximating the cost of using an asset's services, however, it implies a number of limiting assumptions. First, it presupposes that the services of the asset are consumed uniformly over its useful life. In addition, straight-line depreciation assumes that there is no impairment in the efficiency or quality of the service received from the asset as it becomes older. However, these assumptions may not hold for many

**TABLE 10–1**   Depreciation under Straight-Line Method

| Year | Annual Depreciation Cost* | At Year End Balance in Accumulated Depreciation Account | At Year End Remaining Undepreciated Cost or Book Value |
|---|---|---|---|
| 0 | — | — | $13,000 |
| 1 | $2,400 | $ 2,400 | 10,600 |
| 2 | 2,400 | 4,800 | 8,200 |
| 3 | 2,400 | 7,200 | 5,800 |
| 4 | 2,400 | 9,600 | 3,400 |
| 5 | 2,400 | 12,000 | 1,000 |

*The straight-line depreciation *rate* is expressed as a percentage. It is 20 percent of the depreciation base ($2,400/$12,000) or 18.46 percent of acquisition cost ($2,400/$13,000).

types of machinery and equipment. Conceptually, the straight-line method is most accurate when the passage of time is the most important element governing the expiration of the asset's service. It should be used when the asset supplies a service capacity for a limited period of time, and the availability of the service is more important than the actual extent of its use. For example, an office building may be depreciated under the straight-line method whether 100 people or 1,000 people actually use it during a particular year.

**Decreasing-Charge Methods.**   Two generally accepted methods result in a decreasing depreciation charge over the life of an asset. One method—sum-of-the-years' digits (SYD)—achieves a decreasing charge by applying a decreasing rate to a constant depreciation base. The other method—declining balance—applies a constant depreciation rate to a decreasing depreciation base. These two mathematical procedures have little justification in and of themselves, except that they are accepted and systematic ways of obtaining a decreasing charge.

The general rationale for a decreasing depreciation charge is that many assets contribute more service in the earlier years of their life than in their later years. Three situations fall under this rationale:

**1.** An asset becomes less actively used so that the *quantity* of service received from it each period declines. Example—as a machine gets older, it is used less for mainline production and more for peak needs only.

**2.** An asset becomes increasingly inefficient, so that the *quality* of services each period is less. Example—as a precision drill press becomes older, it has difficulty maintaining tolerances, thereby creating more rejects and causing more rework.

**3.** An increasing risk of obsolescence reduces the probability that services in the later years of an asset's life will ever reach fruition. Example—as an office building ages, the initial level of rentals becomes increasingly difficult to maintain, either because renters leave for newer buildings or because management must offer rental discounts to maintain full occupancy.

The effect of any one or a combination of these factors is that the contribution to operations and ultimately to the production of revenues lessens as many assets grow older. Inasmuch as depreciation attempts to measure the consumption of asset services, in these cases we ought to charge more depreciation in the earlier years of asset life.

Still another reason given for the use of *accelerated depreciation methods* is to compensate for increasing repair and maintenance costs over the life of the asset. The *total cost* of an asset's service is viewed as consisting of the depreciation base *plus* the other costs of the asset. If the amount of service received each period is the same, the total cost should be relatively constant. However, the depreciation portion should decline as the repair and maintenance portion rises.

**Sum-of-the-Years' Digits.**   This method starts by summing the digits in the expected useful life (N) of the asset.[2] If the expected service life is five years, the sum is 15 (5 + 4 + 3 + 2 + 1). The depreciation base of the asset is viewed as the cost of a number of service units adding up to this sum (SYD). These service units are assumed to expire in an order determined by the fractions N/SYD, (N − 1)/SYD, (N − 2)/SYD, . . . 1/SYD. Used in our example, this method gives the results summarized in Table 10–2.

---

**TABLE 10–2**   Depreciation under Sum-of-the-Years' Digits

| | | | At Year End | |
| Year | Depreciation Rate | Annual Depreciation Cost | Balance in Accumulated Depreciation Account | Remaining Undepreciated Cost or Book Value |
|---|---|---|---|---|
| 0 | — | — | — | $13,000 |
| 1 | 5/15 | $4,000 | $ 4,000 | 9,000 |
| 2 | 4/15 | 3,200 | 7,200 | 5,800 |
| 3 | 3/15 | 2,400 | 9,600 | 3,400 |
| 4 | 2/15 | 1,600 | 11,200 | 1,800 |
| 5 | 1/15 | 800 | 12,000 | 1,000 |

---

[2] A general shortcut in computing this sum for any asset is expressed by the formula: SYD = N(N + 1)/2

The depreciation base and the total depreciation cost over the asset's life both still equal $12,000 (cost less residual value), as with the straight-line method. However, through a decreasing depreciation rate each year, more cost has been systematically allocated to the earlier years of life.

**Declining Balance.** With this method, we apply a constant annual depreciation rate to a declining base. The depreciation base employed is the annual *book value* (cost less accumulated depreciation). Notice that *this base does not consider residual value*. Even though an asset cannot be depreciated below a reasonable residual value, a declining-balance method would seem inappropriate for assets that have large expected residual values. Two very common depreciation rates used with this method are 200 percent and 150 percent of the straight-line rate. These rates once corresponded to those allowed in the income tax laws for various classes of property, and their extension into financial accounting was inevitable. Although the tax law has changed, the methods are still used.

For our example, the straight-line rate is 20 percent (5-year life). Double-declining balance (DDB) would call for a 40 percent rate and the 150 percent declining balance would use 30 percent. These rates give the results shown in Table 10–3 (amounts are rounded to the nearest dollar). Neither of the declining-balance rates reduce the net asset precisely to the expected residual value. It is common to make an adjustment to the final year's depreciation to bring the book value into agreement with the expected residual value or to switch to the straight-line procedure toward the end of the asset's useful life.

**Activity Method.** This expedient takes a somewhat different approach. Instead of viewing depreciation initially as an allocation of cost to *time* periods, the activity method relates the cost first to some unit of asset service and then to periods of time. The asset's useful life is expressed in terms of *service units,* and the depreciation rate is expressed in dollars per service unit. Then the depreciation cost *per period* fluctuates with the activity of the asset. Service units can be expressed in any number of ways—hours, units of activity, units of output, and so on. Hence, this method also is labeled *the working-hours method, the production method, the output method,* and so forth—all of which share the same general objective of allocating cost in relation to asset activity.

Take our machine that costs $13,000. Assume that during its useful life it is expected to run 30,000 hours. The depreciation rate would be:

$$\frac{\text{Cost} - \text{Residual value}}{\text{Expected activity}} = \frac{\$13,000 - \$1,000}{30,000 \text{ Hours}} = \$.40 \text{ per hour}$$

Here the useful life is viewed as 30,000 service hours rather than five years. If the pattern of activity shown in Table 10–4 transpires, the relevant depreciation cost for each of the five years will be as indicated in that table. As

---

**TABLE 10–3** Depreciation under Declining-Balance Methods

*Double-Declining Balance*

| | | | At Year End | |
| | | | *Balance in* | *Remaining* |
| | | *Annual* | *Accumulated* | *Undepreciated* |
| | *Depreciation* | *Depreciation* | *Depreciation* | *Cost or* |
| *Year* | *Rate* | *Charge** | *Account* | *Book Value* |
|---|---|---|---|---|
| 0 | — | — | — | $13,000 |
| 1 | 40% | $5,200 | $ 5,200 | 7,800 |
| 2 | 40 | 3,120 | 8,320 | 4,680 |
| 3 | 40 | 1,872 | 10,192 | 2,808 |
| 4 | 40 | 1,123 | 11,315 | 1,685 |
| 5 | 40 | 674 | 11,989 | 1,011 |

*150 Percent-Declining Balance*

| | | | At Year End | |
| | | | *Balance in* | *Remaining* |
| | | *Annual* | *Accumulated* | *Undepreciated* |
| | *Depreciation* | *Depreciation* | *Depreciation* | *Cost or* |
| *Year* | *Rate* | *Charge** | *Account* | *Book Value* |
|---|---|---|---|---|
| 0 | — | — | — | $13,000 |
| 1 | 30% | $3,900 | $ 3,900 | 9,100 |
| 2 | 30 | 2,730 | 6,630 | 6,370 |
| 3 | 30 | 1,911 | 8,541 | 4,459 |
| 4 | 30 | 1,338 | 9,879 | 3,121 |
| 5 | 30 | 936 | 10,815 | 2,185 |

*Each year the amount is 40 percent (DDB) and 30 percent (150% DB) of the book value at the end of the preceding year.

---

with declining-balance methods, an adjustment to the final year's depreciation is often made to align the book value with the residual value when the estimate of total service units turns out to have been slightly inaccurate.

Although not used as widely as the other methods, the activity method seems particularly appropriate when physical use is the most important determinant of the expiration of asset services. For example, airplane engines are commonly depreciated on a flying-hour basis, and the lives of blast furnace linings are sometimes measured in terms of tons of metal produced. The cost of automobiles, trucks, or taxicabs can be allocated in relation to miles traveled during each period. Certain types of machinery—tools, dies, jigs, and patterns—for which intensity of use is a major factor also

**TABLE 10–4**   Depreciation under Activity Method

| | | | | At Year End | |
| --- | --- | --- | --- | --- | --- |
| Year | Hours Worked | Depreciation Rate | Annual Depreciation Charge | Balance in Accumulated Depreciation Account | Remaining Undepreciated Cost or Book Value |
| 0 | — | — | — | — | $13,000 |
| 1 | 8,000 | $.40/hr | $3,200 | $ 3,200 | 9,800 |
| 2 | 5,600 | .40/hr | 2,240 | 5,440 | 7,560 |
| 3 | 6,700 | .40/hr | 2,680 | 8,120 | 4,880 |
| 4 | 5,200 | .40/hr | 2,080 | 10,200 | 2,800 |
| 5 | 4,500 | .40/hr | 1,800 | 12,000 | 1,000 |

lend themselves quite readily to this expedient. The method probably has wider applicability than is currently recognized.

The major problems associated with it tend to be practical ones—difficulty in estimating life in service units and the extra effort involved in keeping track of the actual activity in each period. In addition, the activity method does not take into consideration declines in efficiency, although theoretically they could be compensated for through a declining rate per service unit. Moreover, if exclusive reliance is placed on service units when useful life is established, the economic factors of inadequacy and obsolescence may be ignored. However, if these other economic factors are used to establish an asset's life, then the activity method seems to give a very reasonable allocation of the depreciation base to the various accounting periods *within that life*.

## Depletion

The activity method is most widely used in the recording of depletion costs of natural resources. The cost allocation of a wasting asset bears a definite relationship to its physical exhaustion. To see how depletion works, assume that the total cost of acquiring and developing (exploration, drilling, etc.) a natural gas well is $6.8 million. Geologists estimate that the well contains 200 million cubic feet of natural gas that can be economically withdrawn. The residual value of the land is expected to be $800,000. The depletion rate would be $0.03 per cubic foot:

$$\frac{\text{Cost} - \text{Residual value}}{\text{Estimated production}} = \frac{\$6,800,000 - \$800,000}{200,000,000 \text{ Cubic feet}} = \$0.03 \text{ per Cubic foot}$$

Each year the depletion cost would vary with the amount of gas extracted. If during the first year, for instance, three million cubic feet were recovered, the entry to record depletion would be:

Depletion Cost . . . . . . . . . . . . . . . . . . 90,000
    Accumulated Depletion—Gas Well . . . . . . . .            90,000
      (3,000,000 × $0.03)

Depletion cost is an inventoriable cost. It represents the "material" portion of the gas extracted. Depletion costs plus labor and other direct costs become the total cost of the inventory of unsold gas. To the extent that the recovered gas is sold during the period, depletion cost is reflected on the income statement as an expense.

Two questions can be raised concerning the above practice of calculating depletion. First, the implication that each unit of output should have the same depletion cost may not be realistic if differing qualities of output may be recovered (e.g., high and low grades of ore) or if some units are easier and less costly to mine (e.g., ore in veins close to the surface). The second difficulty is the practical one of estimating the recoverable units contained in a natural resource. The original estimates are subject to great geological uncertainties, and the quantity of economically feasible production is a function of both future market conditions and technological changes. As a result, revisions in future estimated production ("recoverable reserves") and thus in the depletion rate are made periodically as additional knowledge becomes available.

## Amortization of Intangibles

Patents, copyrights, trademarks, franchises, and goodwill are typical of the many types of intangible assets that appear on the balance sheet. Many of the intangibles (goodwill being the major exception) represent specifically identifiable rights and privileges. The cost of intangible assets, whether acquired or developed internally, should be spread as expense over their estimated period of benefit.[3]

Estimating the period of benefit or useful life for these intangible assets often is a very difficult task. Some intangibles appear to have an unlimited term of existence (e.g., trade names, subscription lists, perpetual franchises, and organization costs). Others provide service benefits only during a useful life limited by legislation, regulation, or contract. Examples include patents, copyrights, licenses, and payments for a limited franchise. Even when the

---

[3] As we noted in Chapter 8, *internal* expenditures to develop or maintain intangibles *lacking specific identification* and most expenditures on research and development must be treated as period expenses according to *APB Opinion No. 17.* Consequently, the rest of our discussion relates to specifically identifiable intangible assets and externally purchased goodwill.

intangible appears to have a perpetual life or a specifically limited finite life, economic competition and obsolescence may introduce considerable fluctuations and uncertainty into the estimate. The result is that the lives of many intangibles are simply *indeterminate*.

Given this perplexing situation, the Accounting Principles Board established some arbitrary regulations. Reasoning that the service potential of all intangibles eventually disappears, the APB ruled that the cost of *all* intangibles must be amortized over some estimate of useful life. The estimate might vary with the type of intangible, but in no case can the period be longer than 40 years.[4]

*APB Opinion No. 17* requires straight-line amortization unless a company can demonstrate that some other method is more appropriate. The future service potential for many intangibles is highly uncertain. This fact might imply a decreasing charge for amortization. Furthermore, the amount of revenue directly attributable to an asset (e.g., royalties derived from a patent) may not be constant from period to period. Unfortunately, the accounting profession has not defined in more precise terms what is meant by the future service potential of an asset. Does a patent contribute equal service each period because it provides the same legal protection, or does it contribute decreasing service each period because the sales of the patentable item decline over time? Until more definite guidelines are established, straight-line amortization probably will prevail, particularly since this is the only *tax* method allowed for intangibles.

**Goodwill.**    One particularly thorny intangible is "purchased goodwill." Frequently in merger or acquisition transactions the price paid by the acquiring firm for the identifiable net assets of the acquired firm exceeds their fair market value. This excess is usually debited to an intangible asset called "excess cost applicable to acquired companies" or simply "goodwill." The account that receives this debit for "purchased goodwill" has been aptly described as a "master valuation" account. It is the difference between the total value of a business entity, taken as a whole, and the sum of the fair market values of its tangible and identifiable intangible assets. It is the combined value placed on the sources of future earning power that cannot be separately traced. It may include the value of trade names, a general reputation, an established clientele, strategic locations, a favorable regulatory climate, or simply a particular group of employees with special skills, knowledge, or managerial ability. In any case, the acquiring firm invests in it in order to possess the income-producing power of the acquired firm.

Under *APB Opinion No. 17*, purchased goodwill must be amortized over a period not longer than 40 years, although historically this view did not

---

[4] AICPA, *APB Opinion No. 17*, "Intangible Assets" (New York, August 1970), pars. 28 and 29.

always prevail. Goodwill more commonly was treated as a permanent asset, not subject to periodic amortization.[5] This practice was justified on the grounds that the intangible factors comprising goodwill either were not consumed or were replaced by subsequent expenditures recorded as period expenses. In contrast, more recent arguments have stressed the notion of purchased goodwill as a payment for certain economic factors that provide a transferable momentum to the new business. The payment for goodwill is the cost of the excess earnings accruing to the new owner as a result of this momentum built up in a going concern. As these future earnings arise, for the *new* owner they are a *recovery of investment,* not income. Amortization of the purchased goodwill reflects the fact that the momentum that produced these earnings will not persist indefinitely.

## Choice of Depreciation Methods

Under generally accepted accounting principles, a firm is permitted to choose any one of the alternative methods. They are considered equally acceptable. Consequently, the same firm may choose different methods for different assets. More disturbing and difficult to justify is the use of different methods for the same asset by different firms.

In a recent survey of 600 large companies, the methods listed in Table 10–5 were being used with the indicated frequency for at least a portion of their assets.

Tables 10–1 through 10–4 reveal that wide variations can occur in the amount of depreciation cost reported by a firm in any given year, depending

**TABLE 10–5**  Relative Use of Depreciation Methods

| Method | Number of Companies Indicating Usage* |
|---|---|
| Straight line | 561 |
| Declining balance | 49 |
| Sum-of-the-years' digits | 14 |
| Accelerated method (unspecified) | 77 |
| Activity | 48 |
| Other | 12 |

*Adds to more than 600 because many sample companies used more than one method.

Source: AICPA, *Accounting Trends & Techniques* (New York, 1987), p. 296.

---

[5] Such treatment is consistent with the position of current income tax regulations, which do not allow amortization of goodwill as a deductible expense.

on the method selected. Although a firm is free to choose any one of the four generally accepted methods, each one would seem to be particularly appropriate in certain circumstances. The idea behind the depreciation calculation is the matching concept. Therefore, the general principle is to select the depreciation method with a cost allocation pattern most closely corresponding to the pattern of service consumption of the asset. Implementing this theoretical concept, however, requires that accountants do two things. First, they must decide what is meant by "service potential"; second, they must be able to predict the expected consumption pattern of that service potential.

Until the accounting profession can generate some definite guidelines for these conceptual issues, practicing accountants must consider a variety of factors in determining an appropriate depreciation policy. Among these are:

1. Pattern and extent of asset usage.
2. Nature and amount of the asset's contribution to periodic revenue recognition.
3. Pattern of physical deterioration of the asset over time.
4. Expected influence of obsolescence.
5. Anticipated policy concerning repairs and maintenance and their expected timing and size of expenditure.
6. Degree of uncertainty concerning the asset's expected economic life.

**Depreciation and Income Taxes.**   Tax considerations were not included in the above list because—contrary to the case with inventory methods—companies may use different depreciation methods for financial reporting and tax reporting. Until 1981, most firms used one of the accelerated methods for income tax purposes, because greater depreciation expense meant lower taxable income in the early years of an asset's life. Even though more taxes would have to be paid in the later years, when depreciation deductions for tax purposes would be less, the company had use of the money in the interim. Normally one would prefer to pay taxes later rather than earlier because of the time value of money. Accelerated depreciation for tax purposes was a common means of accomplishing this objective. Fortunately, firms were free to select the proper depreciation method for the financial statements without being constrained by their attempts to minimize income taxes.

Tangible assets purchased after 1980 use new methods of tax depreciation. The accelerated cost recovery system (ACRS) applies to assets placed in service during 1981 through 1986, and the modified accelerated cost recovery system (MACRS) applies after 1986. Under both of these systems, assets are assigned to classes having arbitrarily established lives (recovery periods) of 3, 5, 7, 10, 15, or 20 years. These lives may bear little similarity to the lives that are used for financial reporting.

Within each asset class, an accelerated depreciation charge is computed as a percentage of cost. Residual value is completely ignored. The percentage varies with asset category and with the year the asset was placed in service. However, the rates are mandatory for all taxpayers.

The ACRS and MACRS hopefully will provide strong incentives for business leaders to invest in depreciable assets. At the same time, depreciation for tax purposes becomes greatly removed from the concept of depreciation for financial statement purposes.

# DISPOSITION OF NONCURRENT ASSETS

The second major problem to be discussed in this chapter arises when the business entity disposes of a noncurrent asset. Whether disposition occurs at or before the end of an asset's original useful life, and whether it is carried out with or without the acquisition of a replacement, the basic elements of the retirement entry are handled in the same way.

First, depreciation is recorded up to the date of retirement so that all charges for the asset's use are recorded. When the asset has been used for only part of a year, accountants record a fraction of the year's depreciation. Some firms simplify charging for part of a year by using the *half-year convention*, whereby all acquisitions and retirements are treated as if they occurred at midyear.

After updating an asset's depreciation expense, the old asset is retired by closing both the asset account and its associated accumulated depreciation account. Because the value of the asset is reflected in two accounts, the balances in both the asset and contra asset must be removed.

## Entries to Record Asset Retirement

The basic retirement process requires us to isolate the undepreciated cost of the asset plus other factors related to the determination of the total gain or loss on retirement. For example, any costs of removing or dismantling the asset increase the potential loss on retirement. Conversely, the amount of any scrap, reusable material, salvage value, or insurance proceeds (in the case of a casualty loss) represents a gain. The aggregate of all these factors is the net gain or loss.

Let us take the example in Table 10–2. Assume that at the end of the fourth year the machinery is retired. According to the depreciation schedule in Table 10–2, under sum-of-the-years' digits, $11,200 has been allocated to the four years in which the machine has been used. The entry to record the book value of $1,800 as part of the loss would be:

| | | |
|---|---|---|
| Loss on Retirement of Machinery . . . . . . . . . . . | 1,800 | |
| Accumulated Depreciation—Machinery . . . . . . . . | 11,200 | |
| Machinery . . . . . . . . . . . . . . . . . . . . . . . | | 13,000 |

To record the book value of machine retired as a loss.

In addition, assume that the firm incurs $400 of wage costs for removal and sells the dismantled machinery for $700 cash. The following entries would be made:

| | | |
|---|---|---|
| Loss on Retirement of Machinery . . . . . . . . . . | 400 | |
|     Wages Payable . . . . . . . . . . . . . . . | | 400 |
|     To increase the retirement loss by the amount of removal costs. | | |
| | | |
| Cash . . . . . . . . . . . . . . . . . . . . . | 700 | |
|     Loss on Retirement of Machinery . . . . . . . . | | 700 |
|     To reduce the retirement loss by the amount of resale value. | | |

The loss account now has a balance of $1,500, which represents the net decrease in owners' equity associated with the disposition of the asset. If all information about the retirement is known at the same time, a single journal entry could be made.

Any loss or gain on the sale of machinery is reported on the income statement of the period in which it is recognized. Although the gain or loss may be caused by an event happening in a period, the amount reported is primarily a function of the particular depreciation method originally selected by the business. For example, the firm in the example above would have reported a $3,100 loss on the sale if the straight-line method had been used rather than sum-of-the-years' digits. Accordingly, one must be careful when interpreting any gains or losses reported on the disposal of plant assets. In particular, the amount of the gain or loss reported may provide little insight into the question of whether the firm should have sold the plant asset when it did.

If the retirement of the asset is accompanied by a replacement purchase, we must be careful not to interpret the loss as part of the cost of the new asset. Two distinct transactions are occurring. The fact that the old asset has been retired to make way for the new one does not increase the service potential of the replacement asset. The loss, whether it be large or small, still is a measure of an asset that has disappeared without the firm's receiving full benefit from it. It should not be deferred as an expense of future periods by being buried in the acquisition cost of the new asset.

## Exchanges and Trade-Ins

An area where the separation of asset retirement from asset acquisition is particularly difficult is the exchange or trade-in. Here, two explicit events are telescoped into one. Further, the financial facts associated with trade-ins frequently mask the economic values involved in the exchange. The primary element to understand is that there are two events—a sale event and a purchase event—taking place simultaneously between the business entity and a single outside party. We must determine the economic values related to both transactions.

Assume that on January 1, 1991, a delivery truck is purchased for $12,000. The truck is to be depreciated by the straight-line method over a useful life of four years, and it is expected to have no residual value. On June 30, 1992, the company decides to trade in the truck toward the purchase of a new one with a *list price* of $19,800. The dealer will take the old truck in exchange and will allow $8,100 for it. The company has to pay the $11,700 difference in cash.

Before any entries for the exchange are made, we first would record a half-year's depreciation for the six months' use in 1992:

| | | |
|---|---|---|
| Depreciation Expense . . . . . . . . . . . . . . . . | 1,500 | |
| Accumulated Depreciation-Delivery Truck . . . . . . | | 1,500 |

Together with the $3,000 depreciation recorded for 1991, this entry brings the Accumulated Depreciation account to $4,500. The book value of the old truck is $7,500 ($12,000 − $4,500).

In theory, the economic substance of the transactions—both the disposition of the old truck and acquisition of the new one—should be based on current exchange values. The old truck is being sold at its present fair market value; likewise, the new truck is being bought for its cash purchase price. But in transactions involving trade-ins, the trade-in allowance may be an unreliable indicator of the current value of the old truck. Similarly, the sticker price of the new truck may be an unreliable indicator of the acquisition cost of the new truck. Adjustments to the initial list price are common in business. When a simultaneous purchase and sale are tied together, as they are in an exchange, an overallowance on the trade-in can be employed to disguise a price reduction on the new asset.

Assume that the old truck has a current market value of $5,700. This estimate may be determined from activities in a secondhand market or from a study of independent opportunities for selling the old asset. The following analysis shows the economic values being exchanged.

*New Truck*

| | | |
|---|---|---|
| List Price | $19,800 | |
| Less: Trade-in | 8,100 | |
| Cash Payment | $11,700 | *Economic Values Given for New Truck* |

*Old Truck*

| | | |
|---|---|---|
| | | $17,400 |
| Market Value | $ 5,700 | |
| Less: Book Value | 7,500 | |
| Loss on Exchange | $ (1,800) | |

The following entry would correctly reflect the disposal of the old truck and the acquisition of the new one as analyzed above.

| | | |
|---|---|---|
| Delivery Truck (new) . . . . . . . . . . . . . . . | 17,400 | |
| Accumulated Depreciation (old) . . . . . . . . . | 4,500 | |
| Loss on Exchange. . . . . . . . . . . . . . . . . | 1,800 | |
| Delivery Truck (old). . . . . . . . . . . . . | | 12,000 |
| Cash . . . . . . . . . . . . . . . . . . | | 11,700 |

If the old truck had been sold in a separate transaction, $5,700 would have been received with a loss of $1,800 recorded. The simultaneous acquisition of another truck should not be allowed to cloud the basic transaction. Furthermore, the real cost of the new truck consists of the current values exchanged for it. In this case, the company gives up $11,700 in cash and an old truck worth $5,700.

The above entry and analysis derive from the exchange-price concept, one of the fundamental concepts of financial accounting. When assets are acquired in exchange for nonmonetary considerations, the transaction should be based on the fair market values implicit in the exchange. This general principle is affirmed in *APB Opinion No. 29*.[6] Generally in an exchange situation, the *fair market value* of the old asset given up plus the cash paid measure the resources sacrificed for the acquisition of the new asset.

**Exchange of Similar Assets.**   An exception to the general rule, however, is required under *APB Opinion No. 29* whenever the exchange involves "similar" assets and would result in a gain being recorded.[7] Suppose that in our example the current market value of the old truck was $7,800. Adherence to the exchange-price concept would have resulted in a gain on disposition of $300 ($7,800 less $7,500 book value) and a cost of the new truck of $19,500 ($11,700 + $7,800). Because the exchange involved similar assets, however, the following entry would be required:

| | | |
|---|---|---|
| Delivery Truck (new) . . . . . . . . . . . . . . . . | 19,200 | |
| Accumulated Depreciation (old) . . . . . . . . . . | 4,500 | |
| Delivery Truck (old) . . . . . . . . . . . . . . . | | 12,000 |
| Cash . . . . . . . . . . . . . . . . . . . . . . | | 11,700 |

No gain on the disposition of the old truck is recognized, and the cost of the new truck is the cash paid plus the *book value* of the trade-in.

If the truck had been exchanged for a *dissimilar* asset, say a piece of land, fair market values would be used, and gains and losses would be recognized. If one truck were exchanged for another similar truck and a *loss* resulted, as in our first example, fair market values would be employed. However, when the trade-in of a *similar* asset would result in a *gain* on disposition of the old asset, then the use of book values is required.[8]

This exception is rationalized on the grounds that an exchange of similar productive assets does not represent the culmination of an earning process,

---

[6] AICPA, *APB Opinion No. 29*, "Accounting for Nonmonetary Transactions" (New York, May 1973), par. 18.

[7] A similar asset is one that is of the same general type, that performs the same function, or that is employed in the same line of business.

[8] This recording of an exchange using book values is known as the "income tax method." Its use is required for tax purposes for *all* exchanges of similar assets, whether a gain *or* loss results. This approach fails to distinguish between the two separate transactions making up the exchange. Gains and losses on disposition become buried in the cost of the new asset. Clearly this approach should be acceptable for financial reporting only when neither the real cost of the new asset nor the current value of the old is determinable.

while an exchange of dissimilar assets does. Without this exception, two tool and die shops could swap drill presses and each record a gain for the difference between the carrying value and the current market value. The APB reasoned that income should not increase simply from the substitution of one productive asset for a similar one. Earnings arise from the sale of goods and services made possible by the possession and use of productive assets.

## OTHER ASSET MODIFICATIONS

In Chapter 8, we introduce and illustrate the concept that all expenditures incurred to acquire a plant asset and to put it into use are charged to the asset account. These expenditures are said to have been *capitalized*. The use of many plant assets requires that additional amounts be spent periodically after acquisition. Whether these post-acquisition costs are capitalized depends on a number of theoretical and practical considerations.

Some of these expenditures simply keep the asset in good working condition but in no better condition than when it was purchased. These recurring maintenance and repair costs merely maintain the service initially expected from the asset. These costs are called *operating expenditures* (revenue expenditures). Costs of lubricating, cleaning, adjusting, and replacing worn-out or damaged small parts are operating expenditures. They are deemed to benefit only the current accounting period.

In contrast, other expenditures increase the quantity or quality of service through an addition to the asset, a partial replacement, or a major overhaul, with new components being substituted for old ones. These expenditures are called *capital expenditures*. They benefit future periods, and accordingly the costs should be treated as assets. Nevertheless, they frequently do not represent the acquisition of any new physical item or the complete replacement of one asset by another.

Different terms describe the modifications resulting from capital expenditures:

1. *Additions*—modifications that normally increase the physical size or capacity of the asset, such as an extension on a building or a labeling attachment connected to a bottle-filling machine.
2. *Improvements and betterments*—major modifications that increase the output of service, extend the useful life of the asset, or improve its economy of operation, such as the substitution of concrete for wooden floors or the acquisition of a new gear system to increase the speed or efficiency of a machine.
3. *Renewals and replacements*—substitutions, often of a more or less recurring nature, of essential units and parts for similar existing units and parts, such as the relining of the inside of a chemical tank every three years or the intermittent overhaul of pumps and filter systems.

In accounting practice, these terms are often employed interchangeably. They appear to differ primarily in the magnitude of the amounts involved and the economic or physical importance of the modification.

The conceptual objectives of recording subsequent expenditures related to plant assets are fairly clear. Operating expenditures (e.g., costs incurred to maintain the original estimated service) should be charged against operations in the period incurred. Costs that modify the service by lengthening useful life, by increasing capacity or efficiency, by reducing the cost of operating, or by replacing long-term service potential that has expired are capital expenditures. They should be treated as an addition to the stock of assets. In theory, any expenditure that benefits future accounting periods should be capitalized.

In practice, there are limitations. Each nut, bolt, or minor part cannot be set up as a separate asset. A benefit/cost criterion must be employed. Companies adopt policies specifying what costs are to be treated as capital expenditures and what ones, as operating expenditures. One way of making the distinction is in terms of dollar amount. Any expenditure over a pre-established amount, say $1,000, will be capitalized. Expenditures less than that are treated as period operating costs. Alternatively, if the modification of an existing asset costs more than a certain percentage of the original cost, it will be treated as an asset replacement; otherwise, it is handled as a repair cost.

Instead of establishing dollar-amount classifications, many firms define capital expenditures in terms of physical units, called "units of property." A depreciation unit is selected, and any subsequent modification short of the depreciation unit is handled as a periodic charge to operations. For example, trucking companies frequently classify truck bodies, tires, and engines as separate asset units. Telephone poles are an asset group for utility companies, as are the crossbars. The glass insulators attached to the crossbars are not. The replacement of a crossbar is a capital expenditure (asset replacement); costs of replacing the insulators are handled as repairs. Sometimes industry and trade groups will issue accounting guidelines specifying the commonly used units of property for that industry or trade.

As noted above, materiality plays a key role in this determination. Wastepaper baskets and pencil sharpeners, although they will probably last for more than one accounting period, are usually charged to expense. For practical purposes they are not defined as property units. Typewriters, on the other hand, frequently are a property unit, and expenditures for them are capitalized.

The establishment of policy regarding capital expenditures significantly influences income measurement. Sound policies must be formulated and consistently followed to achieve an equitable allocation of the total cost of services of noncurrent assets. Expenditures subsequent to acquisition are an integral part of this total cost. Care must be taken to see that these costs are not unreasonably charged against the revenues of a single period to distort income or treated as expenses one year but capitalized the next to manipulate income. Unless the expenditure is small or its future benefit is insignificant or unmeasurable, the presumption should be toward capitalizing the amount rather than expensing it. Unfortunately, the prospect of an immediate tax deduction and the modifying influence of conservatism often push accounting policies in the opposite direction. Also, if the same amount and type of capital expenditures are made each year, the results of a capitalize-and-depreciate policy may not be materially different from an immediate-expense policy.

## Noncurrent Asset Records

A firm's capitalization policy governs whether an asset is recognized as a result of a subsequent expenditure. Another closely related consideration is the degree of detail used in the recording of noncurrent assets. This factor determines whether the identified capitalizable costs are recorded in separate or combined asset accounts and also influences capitalization policy. As a general goal, accounting records for plant assets should be kept in detail whenever asset components have different life expectancies or are the object of separate management decisions.

Achievement of such a goal carries with it two major advantages. First, detailed asset records facilitate more accurate estimates of depreciation. Assume that a firm acquires a piece of machinery and a group of attachments. The economic life of the machine is 10 years, while the attachments have to be replaced at the end of 3 years. Recording the expenditure in two separate asset accounts would allow the cost of the machine itself to be allocated over 10 years and the cost of the attachments over 3. On the other hand, combining the machinery and attachments as one asset results in underdepreciation of the attachments.

The second advantage, directly germane to our discussion of asset modifications, is that the use of detailed asset records helps accountants to distinguish between maintenance and asset replacement. Determining which costs are classified as maintenance and repairs depends to a large extent on how accountants classify assets. If the attachments are part of the total cost of machinery, then their replacement could be treated as repairs—costs neccessary for maintenance of the asset service. The benefit from this expenditure though will certainly be received over more than one accounting period. If the degree of detail involved in asset records provides for the attachments to be set up as a separate asset, their replacement every three years is not a maintenance charge at all. It represents a retirement of one asset and the acquisition of a replacement.

## Recording Asset Modifications

Many additions and practically all improvements and betterments call for some change in the old asset. The enlargement of windows in the factory necessitates the complete removal of the old casements. The installation of a new air-conditioning system may require the removal of the old ducts. Even most periodic replacements—rebricking the inside of a blast furnace, for example—involve the removal of part of the old asset.

*Ideally,* if the old asset is partially removed, that part should be retired and replaced with the new one. The cost of the old part should be removed from the asset account, the accumulated depreciation on the portion displaced should be removed from the contra asset account, a gain or loss on retirement should be recognized if it has occurred, and the new cost should be debited to the asset account. Future periods are thus not burdened by depreciation charges on costs no longer in existence but are charged only with those expenditures that benefit operations in the future.

Assume that a building having a useful life of 20 years is constructed at a total cost of $280,000. Straight-line depreciation is used. After 10 years, the wood-shingle roof is replaced with a slate roof costing $36,000. A study of the original construction records reveals that $24,000 is an accurate estimate of the original cost of the wood-shingle roof. It would be erroneous simply to charge the $36,000 to the Building account without recognizing the underdepreciation on the old roof. The entries to record the partial replacement are:

| | | |
|---|---|---|
| Accumulated Depreciation—Building | 12,000 | |
| Loss on Retirement | 12,000 | |
|     Building | | 24,000 |
| To remove the shingle roof and its related depreciation. | | |

| | | |
|---|---|---|
| Building | 36,000 | |
|     Cash (or Accounts Payable) | | 36,000 |
| To record replacement with new slate roof. | | |

When these entries are posted, the Building account and its related contra will appear as follows:

| Building | | | Accumulated Depreciation | | |
|---|---|---|---|---|---|
| ✓ 280,000 | 24,000 | | | 12,000 | ✓ 140,000 |
| 36,000 | | | | | ✓ 128,000 |
| ✓ 292,000 | | | | | |

The book value of the asset has increased to $164,000 ($292,000 − $128,000). This represents the cost that should be depreciated over the next 10 years (we are assuming that the new roof does not increase the useful life of the building). Depreciation rates and amounts, of course, would be revised to reflect the major modification in the asset.

Perhaps a more accurate procedure would have been to record the various structural components—roof, foundation, heating system, and so on—of the building as separate assets and to depreciate the roof over 10 years rather than 20. If this had been done, the treatment of the new roof as an asset replacement would be obvious. The fact that it was not done, however, does not relieve the accountant of the responsibility to reflect accurately the exhaustion of the service potential of the old roof.

Whenever the carrying value (cost less accumulated depreciation) of the replaced asset (or portion thereof) is known or can be accurately approximated, the substitution method illustrated on the preceding page is the only appropriate method. Theoretically, all renewals and replacements, whether major or minor, should be handled this way. However, from a practical standpoint it may be difficult and probably unnecessary to record each substitution of a minor part for an asset as a replacement. Consequently, in practice accountants often treat minor modifications as operating expenditures (charged to repairs or maintenance) or capitalize them indirectly by charging them to the contra account (see discussion below).

**Charging Accumulated Depreciation.**    A hybrid treatment of replacements, renewals, and "extraordinary repairs" is to debit their cost to the Accumulated Depreciation account. Ostensibly, this approach reflects the rebuilding or recapture of service potential previously expired. It does recognize that the particular costs benefit future periods and should not be treated as costs of the current period only. Although this expedient departs from theoretical soundness, it is satisfactory when no significant gains and losses are involved. It is particularly useful when the accountant is unable to determine the original cost and accumulated depreciation related to the portion of the asset retired.

If the cost of the new roof in our example had been handled this way, the entry would have been:

```
Accumulated Depreciation—Building . . . . . . . . .  36,000
      Cash (or Accounts Payable) . . . . . . . . . . .           36,000
```

The *book value* of the asset increases by $36,000 to $176,000, although the asset account itself remains unchanged. Valid asset expenditures are brought in through the back door. The new depreciation charge will be $17,600 ([$280,000 − $104,000]/10 years remaining life).

The conceptual objection to this procedure is that it does not identify in the asset account the cost of the old asset (or portion thereof) removed from service and the cost of the new one added. It also leaves net assets overstated by $12,000, the amount of the loss not recognized on retirement. Any gain or loss on the old component remains buried in the asset account to be charged to future periods. In addition, this method ignores any difference between the cost of the replacement and that of the original part. Consequently, the asset account does not reflect the original cost of the plant *actually in service,* nor does the accumulated depreciation account provide an indication of the portion of that original cost charged to operations.

# DISCUSSION OF THE KIMBERLY-CLARK ANNUAL REPORT

The Accounting Principles Board recognized the significant effects company policies regarding depreciation and capitalization can have on financial position and income measurement. The Board issued *APB Opinion No. 12* in 1967 prescribing the disclosure of:

1. Depreciation expense for the period.
2. Balances of major classes of depreciable assets at the balance sheet date.
3. Accumulated depreciation, either by major classes of depreciable assets or in total at the balance sheet date.
4. A general description of the method or methods used in computing depreciation with respect to major classes of depreciable assets.

Let us examine the Kimberly-Clark financial statements to determine how it is implementing these disclosures. The financial statements of Kimberly-Clark are contained in the Appendix to Chapter 6. On the balance sheet, most of the noncurrent assets are listed under the caption "Property." The accompanying notes explain the accounting policies used by the corporation for its property. Note 1 on Accounting Policies indicates that property, plant, and equipment are stated at cost. Depreciable property is depreciated using the straight-line or unit-of-production method for financial statement purposes.

In addition, two other noncurrent asset categories are listed—Investments in Equity Companies and Deferred Charges and Other Assets. These two categories represent investments in other companies and start-up and preoperating expenses, respectively. According to Note 1, equity investments represent holdings of at least 20 percent but less than 50 percent of the stock in various companies. We discuss the detailed accounting procedures associated with them in Chapter 15. Deferred Charges and Other Assets are intangible assets. These expenditures were incurred to bring new facilities into operation and for certain advertising costs. Kimberly-Clark feels that these costs benefit future periods. Therefore, the charges are being deferred and will be allocated to the future periods. Note 1 indicates that these costs are amortized over periods of five years or less. Most companies treat these costs as period expenses because of the difficulty in determining the future periods of benefit. Kimberly-Clark uses a conservative five-year period to amortize these amounts, but it would have been informative to know the specific itemization of these costs.

The total value of property, at cost, is $3,504.2 million in 1986 and $3,768.0 million in 1987. The detailed listing of these noncurrent assets includes the traditional Land account that relates to the property on which the productive operating facilities and administrative offices are placed. A second account, Timberlands, represents timber being raised for producing many of the Kimberly-Clark products. This asset represents a renewable resource that takes many years to bring to maturity. Timberlands is also an account that will be depleted as the timber is harvested. The depletion cost then is included as part of the cost of products manufactured.

Analysts sometimes find it interesting and instructive to reconstruct the property accounts from one year to the next. Much of the needed information to do this for 1986 to 1987 can be found in the financial statements. However, a detailed analysis requires additional information that can be obtained only from the 10–K report filed with the Securities and Exchange Commission. The Form 10–K is a required annual filing with the SEC and supplements the published annual report of the company. We have not reproduced the 10–K report, but we show detailed information from that report to permit a reconstruction of the accounts.

Table 10–6 shows the reconstruction of the property cost figure and the accumulated depreciation figure. The table also indicates the source of the figures used to complete the computations.

**TABLE 10–6**   Reconstruction of Property Accounts

|  |  | *Source* |
|---|---|---|
| Total property cost, December 31, 1986 . . | $3,504.2 | Balance sheet |
| Additions: Capital spending, 1987  . . . . | 247.3 | Cash flow statement |
| Other* . . . . . . . . . . . | 110.7 | Form 10–K |
|  | 3,862.2 |  |
| Less: Retirements, 1987. . . . . . . . . | 94.2 | Form 10–K |
| Total property cost, December 31, 1987 . . | $3,768.0 | Balance sheet |
| Accumulated depreciation, December 31, 1986  . . . . . . . . . | $1,241.2 | Balance sheet |
| Additions: Depreciation expense, 1987. . . | 186.0 | Cash flow statement |
| Other* . . . . . . . . . . . | 68.8 | Form 10–K |
|  | 1,496.0 |  |
| Less: Retirements, 1987. . . . . . . . . | 64.8 | Form 10–K |
| Accumulated depreciation, December 31, 1987  . . . . . . . . . | $1,431.2 | Balance sheet |

*Other was footnoted in Form 10–K as: "Includes reclassifications, transfers and currency effects of translating property, plant and equipment at current rates under *SFAS No. 52.*"

Two observations can be made from Table 10–6. First, the financial statements in the annual report provide accurate financial information but condense several of the figures. Second, the SEC report contains the detail that can be used to gain additional insights into the published financial statements.

With the figures available from Table 10–6, we are able to compute the 1987 gain or loss on the retirement of property assets. This calculation appears as follows:

|  |  | Source |
|---|---|---|
| Cost of property retired . . . . . . . . . . . | $94.2 | Form 10–K |
| Less: Accumulated depreciation retired . . . | 64.8 | Form 10–K |
| Book value of property retired . . . . . . . | 29.4 | |
| Less: Cash inflow from disposal of property . . | 34.5 | Cash flow statement |
| Gain on sale of property . . . . . . . . . | $ 5.1 | |

The $5.1 million gain is included as a part of the $26.2 million of Other Income shown on the Kimberly-Clark income statement.

Kimberly-Clark is a very capital intensive company. This would intuitively seem to be correct as their primary products of paper and health products need sophisticated manufacturing equipment. The balance sheet supports this conclusion if we compare the total of net noncurrent property accounts to total assets. This comparison indicates that these accounts were 61.6 percent of total assets in 1986 ($2,263/$3,676) and 60.1 percent in 1987 ($2,336.8/$3,885.7).

In addition, if we look only at the noncurrent asset accounts and convert them from dollars to percentages, we can see the significant investment Kimberly-Clark has in machinery and equipment. The accounts appear as follows:

|  | December 31 | |
|---|---|---|
|  | 1987 | 1986 |
| Land . . . . . . . . . . . . . . . . . . . . . . . . . | .7% | .7% |
| Timberlands . . . . . . . . . . . . . . . . . . . . . | 1.5 | 1.6 |
| Buildings. . . . . . . . . . . . . . . . . . . . . . . | 16.5 | 16.9 |
| Machinery and equipment . . . . . . . . . . . . . . | 78.6 | 78.9 |
| Construction in progress . . . . . . . . . . . . . | 2.7 | 1.9 |
|  | 100.0% | 100.0% |

Kimberly-Clark does not show depreciation expense as a single number on the income statement. Its financial statement presentation parallels the form used by many corporations with the dollar value of depreciation included as a part of other accounts to which it relates. For instance, the cost of products sold includes depreciation on manufacturing equipment; general expense includes depreciation on administrative offices; and so on. The total depreciation appears on the statement of changes in financial position (cash flows) as $186 million in 1987 and $169.3 million in 1986.

In Note 1, Kimberly-Clark also discloses that accelerated depreciation methods are used for tax purposes. Accelerated methods increase the amount of depreciation expense on the tax return and lower taxable income. The company's cash payments in the current year are correspondingly reduced.

The effect of the different depreciation treatments for financial statement and tax purposes is shown in Note 2 on Income Taxes. The company is able to defer income tax payments to future years. This note shows that $47.4 million was deferred in 1987 and $63.8 million in 1986—both significant cash payment deferrals. We will take another look at this area in Chapter 13.

The statement of changes in financial position (statement of cash flows) indicates the cost of property acquired and also the proceeds received from property disposals. In 1987, Kimberly-Clark expended $247.3 million on new productive assets. In 1986 and 1985, $282.4 million and $425.8 million, respectively, were invested. During the three-year period, the corporation invested more than $955 million in new facilities. This statement provides an important disclosure about noncurrent assets and the company's direction in expansion, modernization, and development.

To complete our analysis of Kimberly-Clark's use of noncurrent assets, we need to calculate the *average* investment in assets. Previously, we used the end of period account balances in preparing our calculations. However, the use of average balances more closely represents the investment in resources during the period. Average amounts are particularly important when significant variations in the assets have occurred from period to period.

Kimberly-Clark presents the asset accounts for 1987 and 1986 in the balance sheet. We use these amounts to calculate the average asset value for 1987. Calculation of the average value for 1986 requires the balance for 1985. The company reports that amount in an unreproduced section of the annual report titled "Summary of Selected Financial Data." Kimberly-Clark reports total assets for 1985 as $3,503.8 million.

With the financial information available, we can draw some conclusions about the efficiency with which the company is using its assets—noncurrent as well as current. One measure used by analysts is the asset turnover. This computation divides sales by the amount of total assets. Kimberly-Clark's turnover for 1987 is:

$$\frac{1987 \text{ Sales}}{1987 \text{ Average assets}} = \frac{\$4,884.7}{(\$3,885.7 + \$3,676.0)/2} = 1.29 \text{ times}$$

The company was able to generate $1.29 in sales during the year for every dollar it had invested in assets. In 1986 the turnover was:

$$\frac{1986 \text{ Sales}}{1986 \text{ Average assets}} = \frac{\$4,303.1}{(\$3,676.0 + \$3,503.8)/2} = 1.20 \text{ times}$$

We can conclude that the company has used its assets more efficiently in 1987 than in 1986.

A second use of assets for performance measurement relates the net income earned to the assets used to earn the income. This is a calculation called "the rate of return on assets." The calculation divides net income by the average assets. For Kimberly-Clark the rates of return for 1987 and 1986 are:

$$\frac{\text{1987 Net income}}{\text{1987 Average assets}} = \frac{\$325.2}{(\$3,885.7 + \$3,676.0)/2} = 8.6\%$$

$$\frac{\text{1986 Net income}}{\text{1986 Average assets}} = \frac{\$269.4}{(\$3,676.0 + \$3,503.8)/2} = 7.5\%$$

Assets represent the invested resources in the corporation. In 1987, these resources generated an 8.6 percent return. In 1986, the return was 7.5 percent. It is clear that Kimberly-Clark used its assets more productively in 1987 than in 1986. A more detailed study of ratios and statement analysis will be made in Chapter 18. Nevertheless, we can see already that understanding the elements of financial statements permits us to make analyses to gain insights concerning a firm's performance which are not apparent from the dollar values alone.

## SUMMARY

This chapter concentrates on three major topics concerning noncurrent assets—periodic use, disposition, and expenditures for modifications. Each topic includes an exploration of major concepts, a presentation and analysis of alternative procedures, and a discussion of practical influences relevant to them. The interaction between the theoretical concepts and practical necessities of recordkeeping requires that accounting entities adopt policies to deal with each of these major problems:

1. Capitalization versus expensing at acquisition.
2. Estimates of useful life and residual value.
3. Choice of depreciation methods.
4. Distinction between repairs and replacements.
5. Treatment of trade-ins.

The accounting procedures and methods following from these policies have no effect on *total* noncurrent asset charges over the life of the asset. Their important impact is on the *timing* of these charges and the form they take—depreciation, repairs, or losses (gains) on retirement.

The relative lack of precision in these policy areas does not mean, however, that any old way will suffice. Sound policy must be formulated, consistently followed, and adequately disclosed if the ultimate communication purpose of the financial statements is to be fulfilled.

# *Appendix: Group Depreciation Procedures*

The depreciation methods described in Chapter 10 rest on the presumption that the cost of each asset is assigned *individually* to the accounting periods in which it is used. An estimate is made of each asset's expected useful life, and its specific depreciable cost is allocated in some reasonable manner over that period. If the asset is retired before the end of its useful life, a gain or loss is recorded, equal to the difference between the remaining book value (as shown in a separate subsidiary ledger account) and the amount received upon retirement. For many large, individual assets such a *unit depreciation* procedure is reasonable.

However, a firm's depreciable assets include numerous smaller items, often acquired in groups. Examples are the telephone poles of a utility company, the typewriters in a large office, tires acquired by a trucking company, and small tools used in a manufacturing concern. These expenditures benefit more than one accounting period and should be capitalized and depreciated. However, treating each telephone pole, tire, typewriter, or tool as a separate asset would be an almost insurmountable clerical chore. In addition, *unit depreciation* based on the average life of units in the group may distort periodic charges against revenues. With a large number of units, one would expect a mortality dispersion within the group around the average life. Unit depreciation fails to reflect this typical and often predictable dispersion. Unit depreciation indicates gains and losses on units retired before the average life, even though some were expected to be retired. Likewise, it records no more depreciation on units lasting longer than the average life, although, again, some might be expected to do so.

## Description of Group Depreciation

To overcome these two difficulties, many large firms employ *group depreciation* procedures. The chief characteristics of this method are as follows:

1. The individual costs of all units in a group are combined and treated as a single asset with one Accumulated Depreciation account.
2. A depreciation rate is based on the expected *average* life of the units in the group. The depreciation rate is applied to the asset balance in the group account for a determination of the periodic depreciation charge.
3. No gain or loss is recognized upon retirement of an individual unit from the group. This is the key procedural difference from unit depreciation.

*Example:* A typing service company purchases 50 electric typewriters, each costing $600. They are to be depreciated as a group over an average useful life of four years, each having an expected residual value of $120. Table 10A–1 shows the actual experience with the asset group.

**TABLE 10A–1**  Retirement Experience for Group of 50 Typewriters

| Year | | Retirements at End of Year | Residual Value per Typewriter |
|---|---|---|---|
| 1 | . . . . . . . . . . . . . . . . . . . . . . . | 4 | $240 |
| 2 | . . . . . . . . . . . . . . . . . . . . . . . | 8 | 200 |
| 3 | . . . . . . . . . . . . . . . . . . . . . . . | 8 | 120 |
| 4 | . . . . . . . . . . . . . . . . . . . . . . . | 11 | 120 |
| 5 | . . . . . . . . . . . . . . . . . . . . . . . | 9 | 120 |
| 6 | . . . . . . . . . . . . . . . . . . . . . . . | 5 | 50 |
| 7 | . . . . . . . . . . . . . . . . . . . . . . . | 3 | 0 |
| 8 | . . . . . . . . . . . . . . . . . . . . . . . | 2 | 0 |
| | | 50 | |

The following journal entries illustrate the basic features of the group method.

1. To record acquisition of the asset:

| | | |
|---|---|---|
| Typewriters (50 × $600). . . . . . . . . . . . . . | 30,000 | |
| Cash . . . . . . . . . . . . . . . . . . . . . . . | | 30,000 |

2. To record depreciation for first year:

| | | |
|---|---|---|
| Depreciation Expense—Typewriters . . . . . . . . . | 6,000 | |
| Accumulated Depreciation—Typewriters . . . . . . | | 6,000 |
| Cost . . . . . . . . . . . . . . . . . . . . . . . | $30,000 | |
| Residual value . . . . . . . . . . . . . . . . . . | 6,000 | |
| Depreciation base. . . . . . . . . . . . . . . . . | $24,000 | |
| Annual depreciation ($24,000/4) . . . . . . . . . . | 6,000 | |
| Depreciation rate ($6,000/$30,000) 20% of cost | | |

3. To record retirement of four units at the end of first year:

| | | |
|---|---|---|
| Cash (4 × $240) . . . . . . . . . . . . . . . . . | 960 | |
| Accumulated Depreciation—Typewriters ($2,400–$960) . . | 1,440 | |
| Typewriters (4 × $600) . . . . . . . . . . . . . . | | 2,400 |

4. To record depreciation for second year:

| | | |
|---|---|---|
| Depreciation Expense—Typewriters . . . . . . . . . . | 5,520 | |
| Accumulated Depreciation—Typewriters . . . . . . | | 5,520 |
| [20% × ($30,000 − $2,400)] | | |

5. To record retirement of eight units at end of second year:

| | | |
|---|---|---|
| Cash (8 × $200) . . . . . . . . . . . . . . . . . | 1,600 | |
| Accumulated Depreciation—Typewriters ($4,800–$1,600) . | 3,200 | |
| Typewriters (8 × $600) . . . . . . . . . . . . . . | | 4,800 |

Similar entries are made in each of the remaining six years. Depreciation expense calculated at 20 percent of the remaining gross asset balance each year is recorded as long as some asset units are still in service. No gain or loss is recog-

**TABLE 10A–2**   Summary of Changes in Asset and Contra Asset Accounts

| | Typewriters | | | Accumulated Depreciation—Typewriters | | | Year-End Asset Book Value |
| | Debit | Credit* | Year-End Balance | Debit* | Credit† | Year-End Balance | |
|---|---|---|---|---|---|---|---|
| Year | | | | | | | $30,000 |
| 0 . . | $30,000 | | $30,000 | | | | |
| 1 . . | | $2,400 | 27,600 | $1,440 | $6,000 | $4,560 | 23,040 |
| 2 . . | | 4,800 | 22,800 | 3,200 | 5,520 | 6,880 | 15,920 |
| 3 . . | | 4,800 | 18,000 | 3,840 | 4,560 | 7,600 | 10,400 |
| 4 . . | | 6,600 | 11,400 | 5,280 | 3,600 | 5,920 | 5,480 |
| 5 . . | | 5,400 | 6,000 | 4,320 | 2,280 | 3,880 | 2,120 |
| 6 . . | | 3,000 | 3,000 | 2,750 | 1,200 | 2,330 | 670 |
| 7 . . | | 1,800 | 1,200 | 1,800 | 600 | 1,130 | 70 |
| 8 . . | | 1,200 | 0 | 1,200 | 240 | 170 | (170) |

*These changes occur in connection with the retirement of typewriters at the end of each year. The credit to the asset account equals $600 times the number of typewriters retired. The debit to Accumulated Depreciation is the difference between the debit to Cash for the residual value received and the credit to Typewriters.
†The credit to Accumulated Depreciation is the annual depreciation expense equal to 20 percent of the asset balance.

nized on units retired; Accumulated Depreciation—Typewriters is debited for the difference between original cost and actual residual value (proceeds from the actual disposal). Under the group method, these early retirements were expected; consequently, more of the early years' depreciation expense applied to these units than to the units that were expected to last longer than average. Indeed, the group method assumes that sufficient depreciation has been charged for each unit retired to reduce it to actual residual value. Gains and losses caused solely by expected variations in asset lives are not true gains and losses; they should not be recognized.

Based on the information given in the problem, the changes in the ledger accounts for the group asset, Typewriters, and its related contra asset account are given in Table 10A–2. At the end of eight years the asset account shows no balance. If all estimates had been entirely accurate, the accumulated depreciation account would show no balance either. The $170 balance remains because the average salvage value was slightly greater than $120 per typewriter. When the last unit in the group is retired, the balance could be closed out to a gain account.[9]

## Evaluation of Group Depreciation

The advantage of the group method in saving clerical effort is obvious. Detailed asset and contra asset accounts for each unit are not necessary, and entries upon the retirement of individual units are simplified.

---

[9] This statement is true only if the group account is a *closed-end* one. In an *open-end* group account, additions of similar assets are debited to the asset account, and the procedures described above go on indefinitely.

**More Accurate Periodic Depreciation.**   Perhaps not so obvious is the fact that, with a homogeneous group of items, the group depreciation method provides a more accurate assignment of cost to periods in which the items are actually used. Table 10A–3 compares the total charges against revenues under the unit depreciation method and under the group depreciation method. Under the unit method, depreciation expense is calculated only for four years, the average useful life. The retirement loss is the undepreciated cost of each typewriter less residual value at retirement. For example, at the end of Year 1, four typewriters are retired. The retirement entry for the units, *under the unit depreciation method,* would be:

| | | |
|---|---|---:|
| Cash . . . . . . . . . . . . . . . . . . . . . . . . . . . . | 960 | |
| Retirement Loss . . . . . . . . . . . . . . . . . . . . | 960 | |
| Accumulated Depreciation—Typewriters . . . . . . . . . . . . | 480 | |
| Typewriters . . . . . . . . . . . . . . . . . . . . . . . | | 2,400 |

The total charge over the eight years is the same under both methods. The group method, however, distributes this total cost in closer relation to the actual usage of the assets. With a dispersion of lives around the average useful life, a uniform write-off over the life of each individual item is almost impossible, except on a post-mortem basis. The significant retirement losses indicate the unattainability of this goal. In contrast, the group method attempts to achieve a *uniform charge per service year.* The group method expresses the life of the asset group as 200 years of service. Under a straight-line assumption, each *year of service* carries an equal charge.

$$\text{Depreciation per Service Year} = \frac{\$30,000 - \$6,000}{200 \text{ Years}} = \$120 \text{ per Year}$$

The total charge each year varies with the number of units in service that year.

**TABLE 10A–3**   Comparison of Annual Charges under Group and Unit Depreciation Methods

| Year | No. of Units in Use | Group Depr. Expense | Unit Depreciation Method | | |
|---|---|---|---|---|---|
| | | | Depr. Expense | Retirement Loss | Total Charge |
| 1 . . . | 50 | $ 6,000 | $6,000 | $  960 | $ 6,960 |
| 2 . . . | 46 | 5,520 | 5,520 | 1,280 | 6,800 |
| 3 . . . | 38 | 4,560 | 4,560 | 960 | 5,520 |
| 4 . . . | 30 | 3,600 | 3,600 | — | 3,600 |
| 5 . . . | 19 | 2,280 | — | — | — |
| 6 . . . | 10 | 1,200 | — | 350 | 350 |
| 7 . . . | 5 | 600 | — | 360 | 360 |
| 8 . . . | 2 | 70* | — | 240 | 240 |
| | | $23,830 | | | $23,830 |

*Includes $170 gain on retirement of group.

**Limitations of the Group Method.** Many of the conceptual underpinnings of the group method come from those used in insurance and actuarial calculations. The average age of an individual item is actuarially calculated just like the average life expectancy of human populations. The expected mortality distribution also is similar to that employed in life insurance computations. One limitation then is that the asset group must be sufficiently large and the units similar enough in nature so that the concepts of average life and mortality distribution have statistical validity.

The other major difficulty of the group depreciation method is that errors in average useful lives may go undetected for many years. With unit depreciation, a gain or loss on retirement of an individual unit may trigger a reexamination of depreciation rates and lives of similar assets. Under the group method, no such gain or loss on retirement is recorded until the last unit in the group is retired. The depreciation expense may be too large or too small for a substantial time period before the error in the depreciation estimate becomes apparent.

## Composite Depreciation

When applied to a collection of *heterogenous* assets differing in kind and useful life, the same procedure illustrated above is called "composite depreciation." The depreciation rate is based on a weighted-average life of the assets comprising the composite group. This calculation is illustrated for an Office Equipment account in Table 10A–4.

Depreciation expense each year would be 10 percent of the *gross asset balance,* and no gain or loss is recognized when a component of the account is retired. If $4,500 were received for the calculators upon their retirement at the end of four years, annual depreciation expense would be $6,500 for four years and the retirement entry would be:

```
Cash . . . . . . . . . . . . . . . . . . . . . . . . .   4,500
Accumulated Depreciation . . . . . . . . . . . . . . .  13,000
     Office Equipment. . . . . . . . . . . . . . . . .          17,500
```

---

**TABLE 10A–4**  Calculation of Composite Depreciation Rates

| Asset | Cost | Residual Value | Depreciation Base | Estimated Life | Straight-Line Depreciation |
|---|---|---|---|---|---|
| Calculators. . . . | $17,500 | $ 5,500 | $12,000 | 4 | $3,000 |
| Office desks . . . | 10,400 | 2,400 | 8,000 | 8 | 1,000 |
| Files . . . . . . | 16,500 | 1,500 | 15,000 | 10 | 1,500 |
| Book shelves . . . | 20,600 | 3,600 | 17,000 | 17 | 1,000 |
| | $65,000 | $13,000 | $52,000 | | $6,500 |

Weighted-average life: 8 years ($52,000 ÷ $6,500).
Composite depreciation rate: 10% ($6,500 ÷ $65,000) on original cost or 12½% ($6,500 ÷ $52,000) on depreciation base.

---

Depreciation for the fifth year would be only $4,750 [10% × ($65,000 − $17,500)]. Assume any replacement calculators are treated as a new group.

Unfortunately, the theoretical justification of the group method decreases as the heterogeneity of the assets in the composite account increases. The concept of an expected mortality dispersion around an average life applies only to groups consisting of large numbers of homogeneous units. The practical advantages of simplified record keeping, of course, are still present under the composite method.

# PROBLEMS AND CASETTES

### 10–1. Calculating Depreciation Expense
Myers Tool and Die Company bought a machine for $37,000. Its anticipated useful life is five years at which time the residual value is expected to be $1,750. The firm expects to produce 75,000 units of output before the machine needs replacement.

**Required:**

a. Use the format of Tables 10–1, 10–2, 10–3, and 10–4 to calculate the depreciation expense for each of the first three years of the machine's life, using (1) straight-line; (2) double-declining balance; (3) sum-of-the-years' digits; and (4) the activity method. For the activity method assume that the units produced in years one, two, and three were 17,500, 15,000, and 18,700, respectively.

b. Prepare the journal entries to record depreciation expense, *for year one only,* for all four methods.

c. Specify what the balances are in the equipment cost account, the accumulated depreciation account, and the depreciation expense account at the end of the third year for each method.

d. Why does the accumulated depreciation account and the depreciation expense account have the same balance only at the end of the first period?

### 10–2. Using Account Balances to Determine Related Data
The following noncurrent asset account balances have been taken from the CNN Corporation's *adjusted* trial balance as of December 31, 1990:

|  | Debit | Credit |
|---|---|---|
| Land . . . . . . . . . . . . . . . . . . . | 50,000 | |
| Building . . . . . . . . . . . . . . . . . | 960,000 | |
| Accumulated depreciation—building . . . . . | | 182,000 |
| Equipment . . . . . . . . . . . . . . . | 32,000 | |
| Accumulated depreciation—equipment. . . . . | | 10,500 |
| Machinery . . . . . . . . . . . . . . . | 76,000 | |
| Accumulated depreciation—machinery. . . . . | | 18,000 |
| Furniture and fixtures. . . . . . . . . . . | 14,000 | |
| Accumulated depreciation—F&F . . . . . . . | | 6,300 |
| Patents—net . . . . . . . . . . . . . . | 27,000 | |

All assets are depreciated using the straight-line method. Answer the following questions concerning these assets. Show calculations where necessary.

**Required:**

a. Why are there no contra accounts used with Land and Patents?
b. The building has an estimated service life of 35 years from date of purchase and an expected net residual value of $50,000. In which year was the building purchased?
c. The equipment was purchased on July 1, 1987, and has an estimated service life of 10 years. What is the estimated net residual value of the equipment at the end of its useful life?
d. The machinery was purchased on January 1, 1988, at which time it had an expected net residual value of $4,000. What is its useful life?
e. On December 31, *1989,* Furniture and Fixtures showed a balance of $16,000 with accumulated depreciation of $5,700. No new furniture or fixtures were purchased during 1990 and all furniture and fixtures retired were fully depreciated. What was the depreciation expense for 1990?
f. On December 31, *1989,* Patents showed a net balance of $30,000. Patents are amortized over a useful life of 15 years with no expected net residual value. When were the patents acquired and how much did they originally cost?

**10–3. Examining Alternative Depreciation Methods**

Wescott Real Estate Corporation acquired a four-year-old apartment building on January 1, 1990, for $1,750,000. On the same day, the firm purchased a maintenance truck for $20,500. Wescott is considering the use of straight-line depreciation for the apartment building and sum-of-the-years' digits for the truck.

**Required:**

a. Assume that Wescott adopts the depreciation methods it was considering. The truck has a six-year life and no residual value. The apartment has a remaining life of 35 years and an estimated residual value of $175,000. Calculate the depreciation expense, accumulated depreciation, and book value for each asset at the end of 1990 and 1991.
b. An assistant controller has proposed an alternative set of depreciation methods. The building would be depreciated using the declining-balance method at a rate of 150 percent of the straight-line rate. The truck would be depreciated using the activity method based on the miles driven. The total estimated mileage is 75,000 miles over the six-year life. Mileage in 1990 and 1991 is 18,000 and 16,300 miles, respectively. Calculate the depreciation expense, accumulated depreciation, and book value for each asset at the end of 1990 and 1991.
c. "The choice of depreciation methods is influenced by both the quantity and quality of asset services." Explain this quotation. What relation might it have to choosing which alternative depreciation methods in *a* and *b* would be best?

**10–4. Determining Capital and Operating Expenditures**

The Hunt Corporation had the following transactions during the current year. Indicate how you would reflect each of these events in the accounting records, both initially (as a capital or operating expenditure) and in future accounting periods, if applicable. Indicate the factors you considered in reaching your decisions.

1. Incurred the following costs for projects related to its existing $3.5 million factory building:
   *a.* Replaced broken slate roofing tiles with new slate tiles, $35,000.
   *b.* Installed heavier grates in a molding furnace, $23,000.
   *c.* Waterproofed the factory walls below ground level, $7,700.
   *d.* Replaced all original windows with energy efficient windows, $105,000.
   *e.* Repainted the entire interior of the factory, $18,000.
2. Purchased a used delivery truck from a local dealer for $6,000. Arranged with a garage to have the delivery truck fixed up and to have similar trucks already owned by the company serviced. The following expenditures were made:
   *a.* License and insurance on the "new" truck, $975.
   *b.* Replacing spark plugs and tuning the other trucks, $545.
   *c.* Installing a new battery in the "new" truck, $52.
   *d.* Replacing the engine in one of the other trucks, $1,200.
   *e.* Repainting the "new" truck with the firm's colors and lettering the company name on the doors, $225.
3. Purchased a new machine for $17,000 to replace one that originally had cost $19,000. The new machine had a lower-rated capacity than the old one. Removal costs of the old machine were $1,900. The cost incurred to adapt the floor of the factory building for the installation of the new machine was $3,500.
4. Replaced the specially designed lining of a tank used to store acids. The relining cost $14,000, including $1,500 to remove the old lining. The storage tank itself had been built 10 years earlier at a cost of $138,000 and was being depreciated over an estimated life of 50 years. Relining is necessary every 10 years, or so.

## 10–5. Misconceptions about Depreciation

The president's letter in an annual report to stockholders made the following comments on the company's depreciation policy:

> The depreciation policy of your company has been very sound. The directors realize that it is necessary to charge depreciation in order to show the resale value of assets correctly. We use the straight-line method for both tax return and financial statement purposes. Stockholders, therefore, are not deceived by the accounting fraud of having two sets of books—one for the tax authorities and another for the stockholders. In addition, stockholders can be assured that the balance in the accumulated depreciation account assures funds for the replacement of assets when that time arises.
>
> You have undoubtedly read, in the financial press, the New York securities analysts' statements that our sizable depreciation charges have resulted in large cash flows. The analysts' statements reinforce our feeling that the cash in accumulated depreciation will protect the firm's current strong position by enabling us to meet the certain higher costs for replacement assets.

### Required:

List and explain *all* of the misconceptions evidenced in the president's comments.

## 10–6. Interpreting Gains and Losses on Disposal

The presidents of the Fast Corporation and the Slow Corporation recently had lunch. In the course of their conversation, it was discovered that both firms had just disposed of identical machines which each company had purchased two years before for $34,000. At the time of acquisition, both machines were expected to have eight-year lives and no residual value. Following lunch, a friendly argument broke out concerning which president should pay the check. The president of Fast Corporation told Slow's executive that she should pay because she sold her machine for $12,500—exactly $500 more than he had received for his machine. The president of Slow Corporation disagreed. She felt that Fast's executive was in a better position to pay. "You used the sum-of-the-years'-digits method to be able to record a gain of $2,083 on the disposal. I used the straight-line method and had a loss of $250 on disposal," she said.

**Required:**

a. Prepare a calculation to show the book value of each machine before its disposal.
b. Prepare the journal entries that would have been made by each firm to reflect the disposal of its machine.
c. Explain how the firm which received the most money on the machine disposal appears to have come out worse on that disposal. Did it come out worse?

### 10–7. Depreciating a Landfill

The OBIPU (Our Business Is Picking Up) Trash-Hauling Company purchased an abandoned quarry for $275,000 for use as a sanitary landfill. Several other trash-hauling companies bid on the quarry because the location was favorable and dumping could proceed without exhaustive preliminary preparation of the land. The management of OBIPU anticipated that the value of the quarry land would be considerably less after it was filled, because most people would not want to build on a landfill. The quarry land perhaps could only be sold for $15,000 after it was filled. OBIPU's accountant suggested that this quarry land should be depreciated as the hole was filling up with trash. However, the firm's treasurer objected, citing the "accounting and tax principle that land is not depreciable."

**Required:**

a. Comment on the treasurer's observation that "land is not depreciable." What is the objective of depreciation? How does depreciation apply to land?
b. Do you believe that the quarry land is different from other long-term assets? When the land was being quarried, should it have been depreciated? Now that the land is being filled, should it be depreciated again?
c. If the quarry land is depreciated, how should the accountant determine the rate for depreciation? Explain.

### 10–8. Recording Nonmonetary Exchanges of Assets

Barnac and Blake, Inc., has an old milling machine that originally cost $40,000 and has accumulated depreciation of $28,000. Prepare the journal entry to record the exchange of this machine under each of the following circumstances. Assume each situation is independent of the others and *APB Opinion No. 29* is followed.

1. The machine's fair market value is realistically determined to be $18,000. It is exchanged for a forklift truck with a list price of $30,000. Barnac and Blake pays $9,000 in cash, and the truck dealer allows $21,000 for the old machine.

2. The machine's fair market value is realistically determined to be $8,000. It is exchanged for a new milling machine with a list price of $46,000. Barnac and Blake pays $34,600 in cash, and the seller allows $11,400 on the old machine.
3. The machine's fair market value is realistically determined to be $9,600. It is exchanged for a forklift truck with a list price of $24,000. Barnac and Blake pays $13,000 in cash, and the truck dealer allows $11,000 for the old machine.
4. There is no realistic estimate of the fair market value of the old machine. It is exchanged for a new milling machine with a price of $50,000. Barnac and Blake pays $40,000 in cash, and the seller allows $10,000 for the old machine.
5. The machine's fair market value is realistically determined to be $15,000. It is exchanged for a new milling machine with a list price of $32,000. Barnac and Blake pays $16,000 in cash, and the seller allows $16,000 for the old machine.

## 10–9. Analysis to Determine Missing Numbers

Use your understanding of the accounting process for recording plant assets, depreciation expense, and for selling plant assets to determine the missing values in the data below.

Use the top portion of the data to determine the balance sheet values for property, plant, and equipment. In the lower portion of the data are the results from transactions that occurred during each year. Some of the figures dealing with the transactions will have to be determined prior to calculating the balance sheet values. You may find it helpful to create T accounts and to prepare appropriate journal entries to aid in determining the missing values (in thousands).

| Balance Sheet Accounts | Beginning of Year 1 | End of Year 1 | End of Year 2 | End of Year 3 |
| --- | --- | --- | --- | --- |
| Property, plant, and equipment . . . . . | 20.0 | 28.0 | ? | ? |
| Accumulated depreciation. . . . . . . . | ? | 12.3 | ? | 24.9 |
| Net property, plant, and equipment . . . . | ? | ? | ? | ? |

| Balances from Annual Transactions | During Year 1 | During Year 2 | During Year 3 |
| --- | --- | --- | --- |
| Depreciation expense . . . . . . . . . . . . | 6.0 | 8.0 | ? |
| New plant assets purchased . . . . . . . . . . . | ? | 5.0 | 10.0 |
| Original cost of plant assets sold . . . . . . . . . | 5.0 | 3.0 | 5.0 |
| Accumulated depreciation of plant assets sold . . . . | 4.8 | 1.8 | ? |
| Gain on sale of plant assets . . . . . . . . . . | ? | 4.0 | –0– |
| Loss on sale of plant assets . . . . . . . . . . . | ? | –0– | 1.4 |
| Cash received from sale of plant assets . . . . . . | .2 | ? | 3.0 |

## 10–10. Recording Asset Exchanges with Trade-Ins

The S. A. Louis Company purchased a new machine on January 1, 1990, and traded in an older machine of a similar type. The old machine was acquired on January 1, 1980 at a cost of $124,000. Both old and new machines had an estimated 15-year life and a $7,000 residual value. The terms of the purchase provided for a trade-in allowance of $58,000 (the fair market value of the used machine was $35,000) and called for either an immediate cash payment of $115,000 or 12 monthly payments of

$12,000 each, with the first payment due in one month. S. A. Louis chose to accept the latter alternative. Other costs incurred in connection with the exchange were:

| | | |
|---|---:|---:|
| Wage costs for: | | |
|   Removal of old machine . . . . . . . . . | $1,500 | |
|   Repairs to factory floor . . . . . . . . . | 1,000 | |
|   Installation of new machine . . . . . . . . | 2,300 | $4,800 |
| Invoices received: | | |
|   Freight-in for new machine . . . . . . . . | $2,700 | |
|   Freight-out for old machine . . . . . . . . | 2,300 | 5,000 |

**Required:**

a. Why did the firm receive a $58,000 trade-in allowance on a machine with a fair market value of only $35,000?

b. "The list price of the new machine must be $202,000, because S. A. Louis will pay $144,000 after receiving a $58,000 trade-in allowance." Is this statement correct? Explain.

c. "Of the five cost items listed above, the repairs to the factory floor pose the greatest problem with respect to proper accounting treatment." Do you agree? Why or why not? How would you account for the floor-repair costs?

d. Prepare journal entries to reflect the exchange of machines on the books of S. A. Louis Corporation. The old machine was being depreciated on a straight-line basis.

**10–11. Estimating Depletion Charges**

Wild Cat Oil Corporation specializes in speculative drilling ventures. During 1990, the company signed a lease with the owner of a farm, acquiring the rights to drill for oil for the next five years. The terms of the lease called for (1) an immediate payment of $100,000, (2) a payment of $1 for each barrel of oil sold during a year, and (3) a provision that Wild Cat would clean up and restore the land to its original condition for farming at the end of the five years (estimated cost of cleanup is $80,000).

No drilling activity occurred in 1990. Early in 1991, a successful well was drilled at a cost of $400,000. Total oil reserves in the well were estimated to be 1.5 million barrels. Of these, 250,000 barrels were pumped and sold in 1991, and 280,000 were pumped and sold in 1992. Operating costs were $60,000 in 1991 and $45,000 in 1992. The selling price was $10 per barrel.

**Required:**

a. Calculate the total receipts the landowner will receive each year.

b. Prepare an income statement for Wild Cat for 1991 and for 1992. Explain carefully the depletion and other accounting policies you adopt.

c. Indicate what accounts and amounts related to the above items would appear on the position statement as of December 31, 1992. Indicate how they would be classified.

d. At the beginning of 1993, a new geological study indicates that remaining recoverable oil reserves in the well are estimated to be 1.2 million barrels. What would be the revised depletion rate?

## 10–12. Justification of Amortization Procedures

During December 1989, a television station paid $450,000 for the local broadcast rights to the Barney Miller sitcom series. Under the terms of the agreement, the station is entitled to 5 runs, or showings, of each of the 200 different programs in the series. All runs must be completed no later than December 31, 1993. Beginning January 1, 1990, the station began showing the episodes in the order in which they originally were aired on ABC. The series ran Monday through Friday, so all 200 titles aired at least once during 1990, and 60 of these were shown for a second time.

At the end of 1990, the station's accountants got into a squabble concerning the proper procedure for amortization of the $450,000 contract cost. The chief accountant argued that this was a four-year contract payment so the same cost should be applied to each year using the straight-line method. One other staff member lobbied for accelerating the charges because viewers would find the series popular initially but would lose interest as the episodes were repeated. Therefore, he favored using the sum-of-the-years'-digits method. Each accountant argued that his method was a generally accepted method and so should be used.

### Required:

a. Calculate the dollar charges for the four years under each of the suggested methods. If you had to choose one of these methods, which would you favor? Explain your reasoning.

b. The controller objects to both methods because they "failed to incorporate the rate at which the broadcast rights were being used up." He proposes an activity charge of $432.69 per showing or a total charge of $112,500 for 1990. Determine how the controller derived the activity charge and annual charge. Evaluate the controller's suggestion.

c. How would you change the charging if the series loses viewers in later years? Can you develop a cost charging method that is more appropriate to reflect declining viewership? Explain.

## 10–13. Reporting Intangible Assets

The general ledger of Hoffman Company on December 31, 1990, contains the following accounts under the heading Intangible Assets:

| | |
|---|---:|
| Deferred rearrangement costs | $ 25,000 |
| Franchise fees | 205,000 |
| Trademark | 75,000 |
| Noncompetition agreement | 45,000 |
| | $350,000 |

The accounts reflect balances *before* year-end entries have been made for 1990. An examination of contracts and records reveals the following information:

1. The balance in the Deferred Rearrangement Costs account consists primarily of payments made in 1990 to a consulting firm for the design of a more efficient man-machine configuration in one of the firm's manufacturing plants. Every five years or so, the company undertakes such a study.

2. The firm paid a franchisor $205,000 for the *exclusive* rights to use the nationally known name and symbol of the franchisor on a certain line of products distributed in the sparsely populated states of North Dakota, Wyoming, and Montana. The agreement calls for Hoffman to pay a fee of 1 percent of its sales of such products. Late in 1989, the district court ruled that such exclusive territories were in restraint of trade. Henceforth, the franchisor must allow its franchisees the right to operate in any of the 50 states.

3. The balance in the Trademark account represents the cost of a trademark purchased early in 1990. Hoffman Company believes that the trademark has an indefinite life and therefore should not be amortized.

4. In 1988, the company took over the business activities of a very successful local retailer. As part of the acquisition agreement, $63,000 was paid to the owner in exchange for a promise not to start up any competing retailing business for a period of three years and not to locate a competing business within a radius of 20 miles for a period of seven years. The amount is being amortized on a straight-line basis over the seven-year period.

**Required:**

Explain how you would report each of these accounts in the financial statements for 1990. In preparing your explanation, use dollar amounts where possible, indicate the classification on the financial statements affected, and indicate both whether and why a footnote would seem necessary with any item.

**10–14. Recording Asset Acquisition, Depreciation, and Loss**

The EAS Corporation purchased a new mainframe computer system that was delivered and installed by Big Blue Computer Corporation in early January 1987. The equipment had an invoice cost of $1.5 million. Freight charges were $140,000; insurance, $25,000; and sales taxes, $35,000. The equipment was to be depreciated on a straight-line basis over eight years. The firm has a policy of charging one-half year's depreciation in the year of acquisition and in the year of disposal. The salvage value is estimated at $225,000.

The computer was upgraded in 1989 by the addition of a series of new switching boards and high-speed memory. The cost of the new add-on components was $265,000. Salvage value did not change, but two years were added to the system's life expectancy.

Unfortunately, provision for fire protection was not properly planned and on June 30, 1991, a fire completely destroyed the computing facility including the mainframe. The EAS company had an insurance policy that would pay 80 percent of the computer's book value on the date of loss. The insurance payment was received on July 15.

**Required:**

*a.* Determine the original cost of the computer system and prepare a journal entry to record the transaction.

*b.* Determine the depreciation charges for 1987 and 1988. Prepare journal entries to record depreciation for each year. The fiscal year ends on December 31.

c. Prepare a calculation to show the adjusted depreciation for the computer system after system upgrading in 1989. Prepare journal entries for 1989 and 1990 to record an adjustment to the computer cost and for the depreciation charges.

d. Prepare a calculation to determine the book value of the equipment on the date of the fire and the 80 percent value of the insurance reimbursement. Prepare journal entries to record the insurance receipt and asset retirement.

**Casette 10–1. Georgia-Pacific Corporation**

In the Appendix at the end of the book is a complete set of financial statements of Georgia-Pacific Corporation taken from its annual report of 1987.

Answer the following questions related to the noncurrent assets on those statements.

1. Changes in property, plant, and equipment:
   a. Determine the change in (a) the cost of property, plant, and equipment, (b) accumulated depreciation, and (c) the net amount (asset cost less accumulated depreciation) of property, plant, and equipment from 1986 to 1987.
   b. Is the *net* asset change from 1986 to 1987 higher or lower than similar changes in prior years? (Refer to the corporation's summary of Five-year Selected Financial Data.)
   c. How much did Georgia-Pacific spend in 1987 on new property, plant, and equipment? How much was added as a result of Georgia-Pacific's acquisition of U.S. Plywood?
   d. What conclusion can you reach regarding Georgia-Pacific's investment in property, plant, and equipment? Does the firm's investment seem to reflect a program of improvement and modernization?

2. What percentage of total assets were net property, plant, and equipment in 1986 and 1987? Based on your calculation, would you say that this corporation is a "capital intensive" firm? Explain.

3. What are the major classes of property, plant, and equipment reported by the firm? Which class has had the greatest change from 1986?

4. What is Georgia-Pacific's policy regarding asset replacements? Where did you find that policy explained? In the explanation, what is meant by the terms "capitalized" and "charge to expense"?

5. What depreciation method(s) is used by Georgia-Pacific? Does the firm use the same depreciation method for both financial and taxation purposes? (See the note on Income Taxes.)

6. What is the policy of the firm regarding the recording of gains or losses on the disposal of property, plant, and equipment?
   a. How does this policy relate to the firm's depreciation policy? (Knowledge of the material in the Appendix to Chapter 10 is required.)
   b. Assume that Georgia-Pacific had a $400,000 machine that had an expected $50,000 salvage value. The firm is disposing of the machine after taking $325,000 of depreciation, and a buyer is paying $60,000 for the machine. Record the disposal using Georgia-Pacific's policy.

7. Georgia-Pacific indicates that it "capitalizes" interest on certain projects and "defers" certain operating costs.
   a. Explain what is meant by these disclosures.
   b. Explain how the value of fixed assets is influenced by these procedures.

    *c.* How do these procedures influence the computation of depreciation expense?

    *d.* What is Georgia-Pacific's rationale for these procedures? Do you agree?

8. How much was charged for depreciation expense and how much for depletion expense in 1987? Where did you find this information? Why would Georgia-Pacific have both types of charge?

### Casette 10–2. Using a Variable Depreciation Method in the Steel Industry

The 1986 annual report of Wheeling-Pittsburgh Steel Corporation showed the following amounts for depreciation (in thousands) on the income statement:

|  | 1986 | 1985 | 1984 |
|---|---|---|---|
| Depreciation . . . . . | $48,804 | $45,209 | $48,729 |

The following notes accompanied the financial statements:

**Accounting Policies (in part)**

Depreciation is computed on the modified units of production method for financial statement purposes and accelerated methods for income tax purposes.

**Note G (In Part): Property, Plant, and Equipment**

The Corporation utilized the modified units of production method of depreciation which recognizes that the depreciation of steelmaking machinery is related to the physical wear of the equipment as well as a time factor. The modified units of production method provides for straight-line depreciation charges modified (adjusted) by the level of production activity. On an annual basis, adjustments may not exceed a range of 60% (minimum) to 110% (maximum) of related straight line depreciation. The adjustments are based on the ratio of actual production to a predetermined norm. Eighty-five percent of capacity is considered the norm for the Corporation's primary steelmaking facilities; eighty percent of capacity is considered the norm for finishing facilities. No adjustment is made when the production level is equal to norm. In 1986 depreciation under the modified units of production method exceeded straight-line depreciation by $1.5 million or 3.2%. For 1985 and 1984 aggregate straight-line depreciation exceeded that recorded under the modified units of production method by $10.1 million or 18.3%, $7.0 million or 12.6%, respectively.

**Required:**

*a.* Do you agree that depreciation methods should recognize the "related physical wear of the equipment as well as a time factor"? Explain why or why not. If both of these items should be recognized, why do you believe this method is not used by more firms?

*b.* Comment on the limitations imposed on the range of adjustment by the company. Why would Wheeling-Pittsburgh impose such a limit?

*c.* Use Wheeling-Pittsburgh's notes to the financial statements and calculate what the straight-line depreciation (before adjustment) must have been.

*d.* The company indicates that they use accelerated depreciation methods for tax purposes. Assume that they use double-declining balance depreciation. Would you expect to see twice as many dollars of depreciation on the company's tax return as you determined in *c* above? Explain why or why not.

**Casette 10–3. Justifying Changes in Accounting for Capital Assets**

Owens-Illinois, Inc. is a major producer of glassware products for business and consumer use. In the early 1980s, the company listed the following account among its liabilities and stockholders' equity items (amounts in millions):

|  | December 31 | | |
|---|---|---|---|
|  | *1982* | *1981* | *1980* |
| Reserve for rebuilding furnaces . . . . . . | — | 93.3 | 83.8 |

A note was included with the annual report explaining the account, the company's change in its use, and the reason it was reduced to zero:

> Effective January 1, 1982, the Company's domestic operations adopted the capital method of accounting for the cost of rebuilding glass melting furnaces, where such costs are capitalized and depreciated over the estimated service of the rebuild. In the past, the Company established a reserve for future rebuilding costs of its glass melting furnaces through a charge against earnings during each period between dates of rebuilds. The Company changed to the capital method for furnace rebuilding costs because that method is used by its major competitors in the glass container industry. The change to the capital method also achieves consistency in accounting for furnace rebuilding costs within the Owens-Illinois consolidated group.

**Required:**

a. Examine the reserve account and answer the following questions:
   1. Assume the 1981 charge against earnings was $25.7 million and the rebuilding costs in 1981 were $16.2 million. The previous practice was being used in 1981. Prepare the journal entries that must have been made to adjust the reserve.
   2. How should the reserve be classified on the firm's balance sheet?
   3. The reserve account was reduced to zero in 1982. Prepare the journal entry to accomplish this reduction. How should this elimination of the reserve affect the current year's income? Explain.
b. Assume that in 1982 the company incurred $27.9 million of cost in rebuilding their glass furnaces and that rebuilding is required every six years.
   1. Prepare the journal entry to record the 1982 costs.
   2. Prepare the journal entry to depreciate the 1982 costs.
   3. How should these accounts appear on the financial statements?
c. Compare and contrast the old and new approaches with respect to reliability of measurement and the matching of rebuilding costs against revenues.
d. Examine the rationale given by the company for making the change in accounting method. Do you believe that its reasoning for the change is an adequate explanation? Has it served the financial statement readers well by making this change? Explain.

**10A–1. Determining Group Depreciation**

Bumba Corporation owns numerous computer terminals. Although the terminals differ slightly, they all have approximately a four-year service life and are sufficiently similar to be treated together as an open-ended asset group (i.e., new additions are added into the same group). Expected residual value is estimated at 10 percent of original cost. On December 31, 1990, the account balances were:

Computer terminals (at cost). . . . . . . . .    $ 55,000
Accumulated depreciation. . . . . . . . . .    (20,000)

For depreciation purposes, all acquisitions and retirements during a year are treated as if they occurred on January 1. The following schedule sets forth pertinent data concerning subsequent activity in the account:

| Year | Additions at Cost | Retirements Cost | Retirements Salvage |
|------|-------------------|------------------|---------------------|
| 1991 | $ 8,000 | $ 6,100 | $ 850 |
| 1992 | 16,500 | 15,700 | 1,500 |
| 1993 | 14,700 | 18,500 | 2,000 |
| 1994 | 9,700 | 12,000 | 1,350 |

**Required:**

a. Is the use of a group depreciation method appropriate for the situation faced by Bumba Corporation? Explain.
b. For 1991 through 1994, prepare journal entries to record the additions and retirements and to reflect the yearly depreciation expense.
c. How would the account balances appear on the December 31, 1994 balance sheet?
d. Would you expect that the depreciation figures from your entries under the group method would be more accurate than those that would have resulted had the unit method been followed? Explain.

**10A–2. Determining Composite Depreciation Amounts and Entries**

Root Corporation purchases four new machines on January 1, 1989. Although the machines are quite dissimilar, the company decides to depreciate them as a composite group. Relevant information concerning them is given below:

| Machine | Estimated Life | Cost | Residual Value |
|---------|----------------|------|----------------|
| 1 | 5 years | $ 32,000 | $ 5,000 |
| 2 | 12 years | 44,000 | 6,000 |
| 3 | 8 years | 30,000 | 2,000 |
| 4 | 10 years | 26,000 | 3,000 |
| | | $132,000 | $16,000 |

**Required:**

a. Compute the composite life and the composite depreciation rate as a percentage of cost for the group of machines.
b. Prepare the journal entry to record depreciation expense in 1989 under the composite straight-line method.
c. If Machine No. 1 were sold at the end of three years for $8,000, what entry would be made?
d. What would the depreciation expense be for the fourth year if Machine No. 1 were sold as in part (c)?

# Further Aspects of Financial Measurement—Equities

# Chapter 11

# Bonds and Notes

This chapter marks the beginning of Section III, which is devoted to a further development of the concepts, recording procedures, and statement presentation of *equities*. The treatment accorded monetary claims in the form of notes and bonds constitutes an important part of this area, for they represent a major way in which companies borrow cash.

Notes and bonds are represented by formal, legal documents having definite maturity dates and bearing interest. Historically, notes have been associated with relatively short-term claims and with a single creditor, whereas bonds have been used with long-term borrowings, often from a number of individuals. However, those distinctions have blurred in modern financial practice.

The procedures associated with bonds are slightly different from those employed with notes, but the general concepts are the same. The major concepts concern the element of interest and the resultant recording of monetary claims at their *present value*. Indeed, the impact of the present value concept is the thread connecting the discussions of notes and bonds. Consequently, we begin the chapter with a brief explanation of present value and its relationship to the valuation of liabilities.[1] Then we discuss the use of present value techniques and other procedures in the recording of bond liabilities. This analysis is extended to the recording practices for notes payable and receivable. The concluding section discusses the relevant annual report disclosures of Kimberly-Clark.

---

[1] The first Appendix at the end of the chapter explores present value concepts in a formal fashion. Readers are encouraged to consult this Appendix first if the concepts of future and present value are not familiar subjects or if the review provided in the body of the chapter does not suffice.

## LIABILITIES AND THE PRESENT VALUE CONCEPT

Liabilities represent the amounts that the business entity owes to creditors. They represent both sources of and claims against the assets of the enterprise. Their incurrence brings assets into the firm. At some future time, though, an outlay of assets (usually cash) must be made in settlement of each liability. The *timing* of the cash disbursement has an important bearing on the recording of liabilities. In Chapter 3, liabilities are classified as current or long term, according to the date of payment. Even more fundamental, however, is that the date of payment may influence the *valuation* of the liability.

Because liabilities involve future disbursements, the force of interest often must be recognized. Ask yourself the question, "Would I rather have a dollar now or a dollar a year from now?" Obviously, your preference will be for a dollar now. Why? Because you can earn something with the dollar during the coming year if you have it now. Money is worth more now than at some time in the future because of the interest factor, the earning potential of the money. Put in another way, a promise of money at some future date is not worth that same amount today. Rather, its *present value* is less because the future amount includes the interest element, the charge for delayed payment.

Because money has this time value, the face amount of most liabilities probably includes some amount of interest. Theoretically, reported liabilities should represent the amount owed at a particular time. If the liability promises to pay a future amount, the real claim against assets *now* is measured by the cash equivalent that effectively would discharge the obligation as of the balance sheet date, even though payment may actually be delayed. We can ascertain this cash equivalent (present value) directly in some cases or measure it by excluding the interest element included in the future payments. The process of reducing future payments to present value is called "discounting," and the discount rate is the effective rate of interest inherent in the transaction. Discounting is explained more fully in the next section and in the first Appendix to this chapter.

Because the waiting period between incurrence of the liability and future payment is very short for many current liabilities, the element of interest is negligible. Usually no explicit recognition is given to it. For these obligations—trade accounts payable, taxes payable, wages payable, and so on—the face values of the liabilities are reasonable approximations of their theoretical present values. However, if the interest factor is specifically recognized in the transaction or if long time spans cause the amount of interest to be significant, *liabilities should be recorded at the present value of the future payments necessary to liquidate them.*

### Introduction to Present Value

An easy way to grasp the concept of present value is to think first about the process of *interest accumulation* or *compounding*. A typical savings account is a good example. Suppose that on January 1, 1990, you deposit $792.10 in a bank paying 6 percent interest compounded annually. The growth in your bank account is depicted below:

| Year | Amount at Beginning of Year | Interest Earned During Year | Amount at End of Year |
|------|------------------------------|------------------------------|------------------------|
| 1990 | $792.10 | $47.52 ($792.10 × 0.06) | $ 839.62 |
| 1991 | 839.62 | 50.38 ($839.63 × 0.06) | 890.00 |
| 1992 | 890.00 | 53.40 ($890.00 × 0.06) | 943.40 |
| 1993 | 943.40 | 56.60 ($943.40 × 0.06) | 1000.00 |

During the first year, $47.52 interest is added to the principal amount in the account. During the second year, 6 percent is earned not only on the $792.10 but also on the first year's interest of $47.52. This interest-on-interest phenomenon is called "compound interest" and causes the bank account to grow to $1,000 by the end of the fourth year.

The concept of present value reverses this process. In other words, $792.10 is the present value of $1,000 four years from now, discounted at 6 percent. Rather than indicating how much will accumulate in four years if $792.10 is deposited, present value shows how much *has to be deposited now* in order for a specified amount ($1,000) to be reached four years from now. The present value of some future amount is the dollar value you would be willing to accept *today* in lieu of the larger amount at a later date.

## Present Value of a Future Amount

There are two present value concepts that relate to interest-bearing liabilities. The first is the one we just discussed—the present value of a promise to pay a single amount at some specific time in the future. For example, how much are you willing to accept now instead of receiving $2,000 in five years or, stated another way, how much would you pay now for a promise of $2,000 in five years?

The answers to these questions depend on what could be earned with the money now. Let us assume an earning rate of 10 percent. If the $2,000 were due in one year, we could determine its present value by dividing $2,000 by 110 percent. Similarly, if we were to receive the $2,000 two years from now, its present value would be $2,000/(1.10)^2. Thus, the present value of $2,000 due in five years at 10 percent interest is $2,000/(1.10)^5. The answer of $1,241.80 is the amount that would accumulate to $2,000 in five years if invested now at a 10 percent annual return. If we could earn 10 percent on our money, we should be indifferent between accepting $1,241.80 now or $2,000 five years from now. Similarly, we would be willing to pay $1,241.80 now in exchange for a promise of $2,000 in five years.

Fortunately, this type of present value calculation has been worked out in Table 11A–8 in the first Appendix. This table gives the present value of $1 due in various periods of time for a sampling of interest rates. To determine the present value of any specified amount, simply find the present value of $1 for the relevant period and interest rate and multiply by the specified amount. Notice that the number shown in Table 11A–8 for five periods and 10 percent is 0.6209, signifying that the promise to receive $1 five years from now, discounted at 10 percent, is worth slightly more than 62 cents today. Consequently, a promise of $2,000 would have a present value of $1,241.80 ($2,000 × 0.6209).

## Present Value of an Annuity

The second present value concept builds on the first. It deals with the present value of a series of equal amounts due in each of a number of future periods. Such a series is called an *annuity*. The question of the present value of an annuity might be phrased in either of two ways: How much are you willing to accept now in lieu of receiving $1,000 per year for the next five years, or how much are you willing to pay now for a promise of $1,000 per year for five years?

One way of determining the answer is to calculate the present value of each $1,000 payment. The sum of these individual present values would be the present value of the series. For example, at an earning rate of 10 percent, the present value of the first payment, which is one year away, is $1,000/1.10, or $909.[2] The second payment, which is two years away, has a present value of $826[$1,000/(1.10^2)]. Similar computations for the remaining payments are shown in Table 11–1. Each succeeding payment has a lower present value because it is to be received further in the future.

The total of these present values, $3,790, is the current worth (present value) of the series of $1,000 payments. Although the above computations are far simpler to deal with than denominators such as $(1.10)^5$, the calculations can be simplified even further. In Table 11A–9, factors are presented for the Present Value of an Annuity of $1. Table 11A–9 directly reveals that the present value of $1 per period for five periods at 10 percent interest is $3.7908. The present value of the series of five $1,000 payments is found to be $3,790 ($1,000 × 3.7908); the identical figure is calculated less efficiently in Table 11–1 with the single-period factors from Table 11A–8.

The present value concepts for a single sum and for an annuity are used in the next section to establish the initial liability for bonds payable. The mathematical formulas for these concepts, as well as a more extensive

---

[2] In this illustration and many subsequent ones, we have taken the liberty of rounding all amounts to the nearest dollar. Our tables are carried only to four decimal places, so some rounding in the examples is inevitable.

---

**TABLE 11–1** Present Value at 10 Percent for a Five-Year, $1,000 Annuity

| *Present Value (at 10%)* | *Present Value Factor from Table 11A–8 (10% column)* | *Amount to Be Received at End of Year* | | | | |
|---|---|---|---|---|---|---|
| | | *1* | *2* | *3* | *4* | *5* |
| $ 909 | 0.9091 | $1,000 | | | | |
| 826 | 0.8264 | | $1,000 | | | |
| 751 | 0.7513 | | | $1,000 | | |
| 683 | 0.6830 | | | | $1,000 | |
| 621 | 0.6209 | | | | | $1,000 |
| $3,790 | 3.7907 | | | | | |

---

explanation of their derivations and other applications, are covered in the first Appendix to this chapter.

# BONDS PAYABLE

Bond issues represent the second largest source of corporate capital, being exceeded only by the issuance of stock. Investors purchase bonds in much the same manner that they acquire stock, and ownership of each security is evidenced by a certificate. Trading activity is not as extensively publicized in the bond market as in the stock market; this difference probably reflects the fact that fewer individuals invest regularly in bonds, each of which usually has a $1,000 denomination.

Nevertheless, most large firms have issued bonds. In fact, some $1.3 trillion of corporate bonds were estimated to be outstanding on December 31, 1985. In 1986 alone, over $300 billion of new bonds were issued domestically.[3] If an entire bond issue is acquired by a single lender, such as a pension fund or an insurance company, the issue is said to be *privately placed*. During 1986, 25 percent of the new corporate bonds issued were privately placed.[4] However, that percentage fluctuates from one year to the next.

The essence of most bonds is found in a group of legal promises the issuing company makes in exchange for the receipt of money from investors in the bond issue. The formal bond contract or *indenture* contains provisions, called *covenants*, which the borrower must respect and fulfill. A trustee acts on behalf of the bondholders to assure compliance with these promises. The two most important promises, from an accounting standpoint, are the prom-

---

[3] "Domestic Financial Statistics," *Federal Reserve Bulletin,* October 1987, p. A34.
[4] Ibid.

ise to pay a specified sum—the face or maturity amount—sometime in the future and the promise to pay interest periodically on the borrowed money.[5]

The interest rate actually stated in the bond contract is called the *nominal* or *stated* rate. In a private placement, this contractual rate is negotiated directly between the individual lender and the borrowing company. When bonds are issued publicly, the firm cannot negotiate with each individual investor. Therefore, it unilaterally must set the nominal rate (as a percentage of the face amount of the bonds). This rate may or may not equal the *market rate* (*effective* or *yield* rate), the one that lenders in the money markets actually require for the use of their money.

Corporations usually do not deliberately set out to establish a nominal rate which they know in advance will differ from the market rate on the bond-issuance date. The nominal rate represents the firm's best estimate of what the market rate will be for investments of similar risk. However, changes in general economic conditions and/or the riskiness of the firm during the two to four months between the dates of bond authorization, printing, and issuance often create disparities between the two rates. For example, the average market rate of interest on new industrial bonds rated A increased from 9.91 percent to 11.14 percent during the three-month period from July to October 1987. The nominal rate is already printed on the bonds and cannot be changed; at the same time, lenders will not purchase bonds that do not offer an appropriate rate of return in light of *current* market conditions. As we shall see shortly, the issue price of a bond in these cases is adjusted so that the effective yield for the investor equals the current *market* rate of interest.

In the following major sections of this chapter, we focus on three accounting and recording areas associated with bond liabilities: (1) the initial issuance (sale) of the bonds, (2) the periodic accrual and payment of interest, and (3) the possible extinguishment of the bonds prior to maturity.[6]

To understand the bond-recording process fully, the accountant needs to understand the relationship of present value concepts to the valuation of bonds. In the following examples, keep in mind that the nominal or stated rate of interest determines only the dollar amount of the interest payment/ receipt. It is not the rate used in the present value calculations. Only the market interest rate measures the time value of money to investors.

---

[5] Most books on business finance contain detailed descriptions of the various types of bonds (e.g., debenture, mortgage, and convertible) and the alternative ways in which they can be issued (e.g., through private placement, through underwriters, and through competitive bidding). Those books also discuss other covenants—such as restrictions on payment of dividends, provisions for sinking (retirement) funds, restrictions on the issuance of additional bonds, specification of minimum financial ratios, and so on.

[6] In the second Appendix to the chapter, entries made by the bond purchaser are summarized.

## Bonds and Present Value

The connection between bonds and present value is direct and logical. A bond consists of two basic promises—to pay a specified sum (face or maturity amount) at the end of a period of time and to pay a specified sum (interest) in each period for a certain number of periods. If the reasoning in the first section of this chapter is sound, a bond should be worth the total of the present values of these two promises at the market rate of interest.

If the nominal rate of interest is the same as the market interest rate, the bond will initially sell at the face or maturity amount. Take, for example, a $10,000, five-year bond, paying interest annually at a nominal rate of 10 percent. The promises represented by this bond are to repay $10,000 in five years and to pay $1,000 in interest (10% × $10,000) each year for five years. If the *market* rate of interest is also 10 percent, the investor will be willing to pay the present value of these promises at a 10 percent earning rate:

| | |
|---|---:|
| Present value of $10,000 due in five years at 10% ($10,000 × 0.6209, Table 11A–8 factor). . . . . . . . . . | $ 6,209 |
| Present value of $1,000 per year for five years at 10% ($1,000 × 3.7908, Table 11A–9 factor) . . . . . . . . . . | 3,791 |
| Total present value . . . . . . . . . . . . . . . . . . . | $10,000 |

What happens if the rate required by investors in the financial markets differs from that offered in the bond contract? If the market rate is higher than the stated rate, the investor would insist on a purchase price that is below face amount; the bond sells at a *discount*. This seems only logical; you would be unwilling to pay face value for a bond giving you a 10 percent return on your investment when you can earn, for example, a 12 percent return on other investments of equal risk. Instead, you would pay some lesser amount, so that your effective return (yield) would be 12 percent. You can determine this amount by valuing the bond promises above at an interest rate of 12 percent:

| | |
|---|---:|
| Present value of $10,000 due in five years at 12% ($10,000 × 0.5674, Table 11A–8 factor). . . . . . . . . . | $5,674 |
| Present value of $1,000 per year for five years at 12% ($1,000 × 3.6048, Table 11A–9 factor) . . . . . . . . . . | 3,605 |
| Total present value . . . . . . . . . . . . . . . . . . | $9,279 |

Part of the bondholder's return would be periodic payments of $1,000 and part would be the payment at the maturity date of $721 more than the amount originally paid for the bond ($10,000 − $9,279).

This bond sold at a discount of $721 because of the difference between the market rate of interest and the rate promised in the bond contract. An alternative view of the bond discount is in terms of an interest deficiency. Given the market rate of 12 percent, the issuer would have to offer *$1,200* annual interest to sell the bond at its face amount of $10,000. However, the issuer *must* pay exactly the 10 percent nominal rate, or $1,000, as the annual interest payment. Therefore, investors attach a discount equal to the present value of the $200 annual interest deficiency. The present value of $200 per year for five years at 12 percent equals the $721 discount ($200 × 3.6048, Table 11A–9 factor).

Conversely, if the market rate of interest is below the nominal rate, the bond will sell for more than face amount, the excess being called a *premium*. A lender who can only earn an 8 percent return on investments of similar risk would be willing to pay more than face value for a bond contract offering a 10 percent rate. The amount paid is calculated as follows:

Present value of $10,000 due in five years at 8%
    ($10,000 × 0.6806, Table 11A–8 factor). . . . . . . . . . .     $ 6,806
Present value of $1,000 per year for five years at 8%
    ($1,000 × 3.9927, Table 11A–9 factor) . . . . . . . . . . .     3,993
        Total present value . . . . . . . . . . . . . . . . . . .     $10,799

The bond sells at a premium of $799 because the nominal rate of interest is higher than the market rate set by competition among borrowers and lenders. With an 8 percent market rate, the issuer would have to offer only *$800* annual interest in order to sell the bond at its $10,000 face amount. Because the 10 percent nominal rate dictates that $1,000 be the annual interest payment, investors will pay a premium equal to the present value of the $200 annual "excess interest." The present value of $200 per year for five years at 8 percent equals the $799 premium ($200 × 3.9927, Table 11A–9 factor). A portion of the $1,000 received each year is a return of part of this "excess interest" investment the investor has made.

Table 11–2 summarizes the three variations in the above bond example. The critical role of the market rate of interest in the determination of the bond's issue price becomes very apparent. The present value factors, used to restate the bond's future promises into present dollars, always come from the table column representing the market rate. We can observe an inverse relationship between market rate and issue price, with the bond's selling price decreasing as market interest rates increase.

## Bond Prices and Interest Rates

In actual investment decisions, bond investors do not use individual present value tables to determine what to pay for a bond. The two present value

**TABLE 11–2**  Issue Price of Five-Year, 10 Percent Nominal Rate Bond at Various Market Interest Rates

| | Market Rate of Interest | | |
| --- | --- | --- | --- |
| | 8% | 10% | 12% |
| Present value of promise to pay $10,000 at the end of five years. . . | $10,000 × 0.6806 = $ 6,806 | 0.6209 = $ 6,209 | 0.5674 = $5,674 |
| Present value of promise to pay $1,000 at the end of each of the next five years. . . . . | $ 1,000 × 3.9927 = 3,993 | 3.7908 = 3,791 | 3.6048 = 3,605 |
| Issue price . . . . . . | $10,799 | $10,000 | $9,279 |

tables are combined and reflected in *bond tables*. These tables indicate the price (expressed as a percentage of face amount) of various bonds—depending on their stated interest rate, length of life, and the market rate of interest. For example, a bond table for five-year bonds indicates that a 10 percent, five-year bond would sell for 92.79 percent of face value in a 12 percent market and for 107.99 percent in an 8 percent market. The prices quoted in the bond market for subsequent transfers between lenders typically are stated as a percentage of face value also.

For illustrative purposes, three different assumptions are made in Table 11–2 with respect to the market interest rate at the date of bond issuance. In an actual situation, only one market rate exists for a particular bond issue at its date of issuance. The market rate is the yield to maturity that bondholders actually earn on their investment. It is set by the interaction of the supply and demand for loanable funds in the investment markets.

On the other hand, different market rates exist for different bond issues at the same point in time or for a particular bond issue over time. Interest rates vary with general economic conditions (loose money or tight money) and with the financial community's perception of the riskiness of the bond investment.

The benchmark interest rates for long-term lenders are the rates on long-term government securities—treasury notes and bonds. These rates come close to representing the "pure" interest rate, the true time value of money based on economic conditions. Risk here is minimal. We can view the interest rate on corporate bonds as the pure interest rate plus a risk premium. The amount of the risk premium varies with the degree of risk. As the risk of nonpayment of interest and/or default of principal increases, the required return increases, usually more than proportionally to the increase in risk.

Long-term bonds typically have higher yields to maturity than do short-term bonds. Investors consider long-term securities more risky than short-term ones. A greater time period exists in which the issuer could experience financial difficulty and hence not be able to pay interest or principal. Also, the investor has less flexibility with long-term investments to respond to changing economic and financial-market conditions. Investors, therefore, demand extra compensation in the form of a higher interest rate for investing their money in long-term bonds.

Thus, there are different market rates of interest for different risk classifications. Standard & Poor's Corporation (S&P) and Moody's Investors Services, Inc. are the most visible bond-rating agencies; S&P, for example, utilizes a 12-category scale, ranging from AAA (the highest grade or lowest risk) to D (in default with little salvage value).[7] During the week of July 27 to July 31, 1987, the interest rates for AAA bonds were 9.50 percent; for AA bonds, 9.87 percent; and for A bonds, 10.16 percent. These rates illustrate the different risk premiums.

In addition, market interest rates change through time. As we have seen, bond prices are the result of present value calculations using market rates of interest. When market rates change, bond prices change. Specifically, if market interest rates increase, bond prices will fall and vice versa. The longer the time to maturity of the bond, the greater will be the magnitude of response to a given interest rate change.[8] Thus, generally the prices of long-term bonds are more volatile.

## RECORDING THE ISSUANCE OF BONDS

Practically speaking, the valuation of bonds is of secondary concern to accountants. Their primary interest is recording the issuance of bonds after the investor has bought them at a particular price. A single principle applies at the time of issuance and throughout the life of the bond: *The carrying value of the liability should be the present value of the obligations to repay principal and to pay interest discounted at the market rate of interest at the time the bonds were issued.* If the market rate of interest and the nominal rate are the same, we know that present value equals maturity value. The entry to record this case is straightforward.

Cash . . . . . . . . . . . . . . . . . . . . . . . . 10,000
    Bonds Payable . . . . . . . . . . . . . . . . . .          10,000
    To record bond issued when the stated rate of
    interest equals the effective rate.

If bonds are issued between interest dates, the purchaser is required to pay for any interest that has accrued. The bond price is quoted as 100 percent plus accrued interest.

---

[7] For further information on the bond-rating process with particular reference to the role of accounting information, see Morton Backer and Martin L. Gosman, *Financial Reporting and Business Liquidity* (New York: National Association of Accountants, 1978).

[8] This differential reaction is inherent in the present value calculations; present value factors for a given interest rate are smaller for longer time periods.

## Bonds Issued at a Discount

A discount indicates that the investor is demanding a higher interest return than the particular bond in question promises to pay. Take, for example, the 10 percent, five-year bond being issued at a time when the market rate for bonds of similar risk is 12 percent. The cash received by the company is $9,279, which also represents the present value of its liability. The initial liability is the amount of money committed by lenders now, not the $10,000 due in five years. Accountants conventionally record this situation through the use of two accounts—the maturity value in one account offset by a *contra liability* called "Discount on Bonds Payable."

| | | |
|---|---|---|
| Cash . . . . . . . . . . . . . . . . . . . . . . . . . . . | 9,279 | |
| Discount on Bonds Payable . . . . . . . . . . . . . . . | 721 | |
| Bonds Payable . . . . . . . . . . . . . . . . . . . . | | 10,000 |
| To record bond issued when the stated rate of interest is less than the effective rate. | | |

The Discount on Bonds Payable account should be shown on the position statement as a deduction from bonds payable. It is not an asset. Although the liability at maturity will be $10,000, the source of assets at the issuance date is only $9,279, the amount borrowed. This is the present value of the obligations under the bond contract. The discount represents the portion of the total interest charge that will not be paid or collected until the maturity date. Since the discount is a phenomenon of interest, it becomes a liability only gradually as time passes and interest is earned at the effective rate.

## Bonds Issued at a Premium

If the 10 percent, five-year bond is sold in a market where the effective return is only 8 percent, investors would pay more than face value for it, namely, $10,799. Again, the initial liability is the amount borrowed. This liability gradually will be reduced over time, so that at the end of five years it will be only $10,000. Nevertheless, at this moment the equity is the present value of the obligations under the bond contract, $10,799. The face amount is recorded in one liability account and the excess or premium in a *liability adjunct* account.

| | | |
|---|---|---|
| Cash . . . . . . . . . . . . . . . . . . . . . . . . . | 10,799 | |
| Bonds Payable . . . . . . . . . . . . . . . . . . . | | 10,000 |
| Premium on Bonds Payable . . . . . . . . . . . . . | | 799 |
| To record bond issued when the stated rate of interest is greater than the effective rate. | | |

Premium on Bonds Payable represents the portion of the liability that will be returned to the investor over the life of the bond issue via periodic "interest" payments that are larger than those required by the investor.

**Bond Issue Costs.** Businesses may incur additional costs in issuing bonds. These, in some cases, run as high as 5 percent of the principal amount being issued. Examples include fees of auditors, charges for legal services, printing of the bonds, registration and filing fees for the Securities and Exchange Commission and stock exchanges, and commissions and other distribution fees to the underwriters who actually sell the bonds to the investing public. These collectively are called "bond issue costs" and represent an intangible asset.[9] They are an expenditure of funds for which benefit is received over the life of the bond issue. At the end of each period, accountants make an adjusting entry to amortize a portion of the bond issue costs as an expense of that period.

## RECORDING PERIODIC INTEREST EXPENSE

In the recording of interest, the guiding principle is that *interest cost is the charge for using borrowed money during a period of time.* The calculation of interest is completed by multiplying the amount of money actually used (the principal) by the market rate of interest that existed at the time the bond was issued. An interest rate is an annual rate, and the computation just cited would calculate the annual amount of interest. When the interest calculation is for a period shorter than one year, an adjustment is made for the length of the period. This results in a computation which can be expressed as:

$$\frac{\text{Interest}}{\text{expense}} = \frac{\text{Bond}}{\text{principal}} \times \frac{\text{Effective}}{\text{interest rate}} \times \frac{\text{Time}}{\text{period}}$$

If the bonds are issued at face value, then the stated rate of interest equals the effective rate, and face value is the amount actually borrowed. *In this case only,* the contractual interest payment equals the interest charge.

$$\frac{\text{Contractual}}{\text{interest payment}} = \frac{\text{Face}}{\text{value}} \times \frac{\text{Stated}}{\text{interest rate}} \times \frac{\text{Time}}{\text{period}}$$

In each period, an entry is made debiting Interest Expense and crediting Interest Payable (or Cash).

When bonds are issued at a discount or premium, the effective interest rate is not the same as the stated rate being paid in cash each year. Indeed, the disparity between nominal and market rates of interest is the precise reason why for some bonds the principal does not equal face value. This disparity complicates the interest entries in that the periodic interest expense no

---

[9] AICPA, *APB Opinion No. 21*, "Interest on Receivables and Payables" (New York, August 1971), par. 16. However, the Financial Accounting Standards Board suggested in *Statement of Financial Accounting Concepts No. 3* that bond issue costs simply reduce the proceeds from the bond issue and accordingly increase the effective interest rate. Under this view, they would be recorded as a reduction in the related liability and not as an asset that provides future economic benefit.

longer equals the periodic contractual interest payment. However, it does not change the basic principle: Interest expense = Principal × Effective rate × Time.

## Interest on Bonds Issued at a Discount

When bonds are issued at a discount, the effective interest rate is greater than the stated rate in the bond contract. As a consequence, the interest expense must be more than the nominal interest payment. Part of the interest cost each period is deferred until the maturity date, when the borrower repays more than originally received. The bond discount represents an additional interest expense to be recognized over the life of the bond.

For example, assume that the bond issued at a discount in the previous section is dated January 1, with interest payable once each year thereafter.[10] Although the bond bears a 10 percent coupon rate, the effective interest the bondholder charges for lending funds is 12 percent. The total interest for the five years consists of the difference between total payments and the total received, or $5,721:

| | | |
|---|---:|---:|
| Total payments: | | |
| Coupon interest ($1,000 × 5) . . . . . . . . . . . | $ 5,000 | |
| Repayment at maturity . . . . . . . . . . . | 10,000 | $15,000 |
| Total received at issuance . . . . . . . . . . . | | 9,279 |
| Total interest cost for five years . . . . . . . . . | | $ 5,721 |

By knowing the effective rate of interest and the amount borrowed, the accountant can spread this total charge over the five-year period in such a manner that each period's actual interest charges are recorded.

Although the final repayment will be $10,000, the principal amount actually borrowed during the first year is only $9,279. Consequently, on December 31, the company accrues interest for the year of $1,113 ($9,279 × 12% × 1 year). The amount of the lender's money actually invested during the year is multiplied by the *effective rate* of interest. However, the annual cash payment is only $1,000, determined by applying the *nominal rate* to the face amount of the bond. The $113 difference represents interest earned by investors and owed by the borrower, but not paid immediately. The company adds it to its long-term liability. The entry to do this is:

| | | | |
|---|---|---:|---:|
| Dec. 31 | Interest Expense . . . . . . . . . . . . . . . | 1,113 | |
| | Interest Payable . . . . . . . . . . . | | 1,000 |
| | Discount on Bonds Payable . . . . . . . . | | 113 |
| | To accrue interest on bonds issued at a discount. | | |

---

[10] Most corporate bonds pay interest semiannually. In that case, we would use half the yearly interest rate and twice the number of yearly periods making up the life of the bond. Interest entries would then be made every six months. To keep our example less complicated, we use yearly periods.

To increase the company's liability, we credit (reduce) the contra liability account, Discount on Bonds Payable. The borrower's liability is always the difference between Bonds Payable and the balance in the contra liability, so the net liability has increased by $113. It is now $10,000 less $608 (the new balance in Discount on Bonds Payable), or $9,392. The $113 is often called the *amortization of bond discount*.

On January 1 of the second year, the contractual interest would actually be paid in cash:

| | | |
|---|---|---|
| Interest Payable. . . . . . . . . . . . . . . . . . . . . . | 1,000 | |
| Cash . . . . . . . . . . . . . . . . . . . . . . . | | 1,000 |

On December 31 of the second year, another entry accruing that year's interest would be made. Again, the true interest expense is calculated as the market rate of interest multiplied by the amount of money actually borrowed. However, this amount is larger during the second year than during the first. The company's liability grew by the amount of the interest earned but not paid in the first period ($113). The entry would be:

| | | | |
|---|---|---|---|
| Dec. 31 | Interest Expense ($9,392 × 12%) . . . . . . . | 1,127 | |
| | Interest Payable . . . . . . . . . . . . . | | 1,000 |
| | Discount on Bonds Payable. . . . . . . . | | 127 |
| | To accrue interest for second year on | | |
| | discount bond. | | |

This same procedure is followed every year for the life of the bond issue.[11] As a result, each period is charged for its effective interest cost. Followed consistently, this method will leave Discount on Bonds Payable with no balance at the last interest payment date. At that time, the liability will be represented only by the balance of $10,000 in the Bonds Payable account. Table 11–3 shows the effective interest expense for each of the five years, along with the periodic amortization of bond discount and the resulting net liability.

At any time during the five-year period, the carrying value of the bond is the difference between Bonds Payable and Discount on Bonds Payable. For instance, at the end of the third year, the balance sheet would show under long-term liabilities:

| | |
|---|---|
| Bonds payable . . . . . . . . . . . . . . . . . . | $10,000 |
| Less: Unamortized discount. . . . . . . . . . . . | 338 |
| | $ 9,662 |

---

[11] A slight complication is introduced when the accounting period ends within an interest period. An adjusting entry to accrue interest for the elapsed time is necessary. First, determine what the total entry would be for the *interest* period. Then merely divide this basic entry to conform to the *accounting* period involved.

**TABLE 11–3**   Schedule of Interest Expense and Discount Amortization for a $10,000, 10 Percent Bond Sold at an Effective Rate of 12 Percent

| Year | (a) Interest Expense | (b) Cash Payments | (c) Credit to Bond Discount | (d) Ending Balance of Bond Discount | (e) Year-End Carrying Value (Net Liability) |
|---|---|---|---|---|---|
| 0 | — | — | — | $721 | $ 9,279 |
| 1 | $1,113 | $1,000 | $113 | 608 | 9,392 |
| 2 | 1,127 | 1,000 | 127 | 481 | 9,519 |
| 3 | 1,143 | 1,000 | 143 | 338 | 9,662 |
| 4 | 1,159 | 1,000 | 159 | 179 | 9,821 |
| 5 | 1,179 | 1,000 | 179 | — | 10,000 |
|  | $5,721 | $5,000 | $721 |  |  |

Note:   Column [a] is 12 percent of the net liability existing at the beginning of the year. Column [b] is the face value multiplied by the nominal rate of interest [$10,000 × 10%]. Column [c] equals [a] − [b]. Column [d] equals the preceding year's unamortized discount less [c]. Column [e] is the maturity value of $10,000 less the balance in the Discount on Bonds Payable account [d].

The carrying amount always will represent the present value of the two promises remaining under the bond contract *discounted using the effective rate of interest when the bond was first issued.*

Present value of $10,000 due in two years at 12%
($10,000 × 0.7972, Table 11A–8 factor). . . . . . . . . . . .   $7,972
Present value of $1,000 per year for two years at 12%
($1,000 × 1.6901, Table 11A–9 factor) . . . . . . . . . . . .   1,690
Total present value . . . . . . . . . . . . . . . . . .   $9,662

Sometimes the unamortized discount is subtracted directly from the face amount. For example, Brunswick Corporation listed the following bond among its long-term liabilities as of December 31, 1986:

Sinking Fund Debentures, 9 7/8% due 2016,
net of discount of $1,081,000 . . . . . . . . . . . . . .   $98,919,000

## Interest on Bonds Issued at a Premium

When bonds are issued at a premium, the nominal interest rate on the bond is greater than the market rate. The cash the borrower legally pays every period is more than the interest *expense* actually transacted with the investor. The real interest expense can be calculated as the amount of funds used during the particular period in question multiplied by the effective rate of interest.

The 10 percent, five-year bond issued in an 8 percent money market serves as a good example. When the bond is issued, cash of $10,799 is received because the investor purchases part of the interest *receipts* in advance. The total interest cost for the five years can be measured by the difference between amounts paid out and amounts received. This difference of $4,201 equals the interest payments less the bond premium:

| | | |
|---|---:|---:|
| Total payments: | | |
|     Coupon interest ($1,000 × 5) . . . . . . . . . . | $ 5,000 | |
|     Repayment at maturity . . . . . . . . . . . . | 10,000 | $15,000 |
| Total received at issuance . . . . . . . . . . . . . | | 10,799 |
| Total interest cost for five years . . . . . . . . . . | | $ 4,201 |

The bond premium represents a reduction in interest expense to be recognized over the life of the bond.

On the first interest date, the company writes a check for $1,000. However, the real interest expense is only $864 ($10,799 × 8%). From January 1 to December 31 the borrower has used $10,799 of the investor's funds at an effective rate of 8 percent. The excess payment represents a return to the lender of a portion of the initial amount borrowed. The liability is gradually reduced in each period by debits to the liability adjunct account, Premium on Bonds Payable:

| | | |
|---|---:|---:|
| Interest Expense . . . . . . . . . . . . . . . . . . . | 864 | |
| Premium on Bonds Payable . . . . . . . . . . . . . . | 136 | |
|     Cash . . . . . . . . . . . . . . . . . . . . . | | 1,000 |
|     To recognize interest on bond issued at a premium. | | |

Table 11–4 summarizes the information the accountant would use in making entries over the five-year period. Notice that each year the interest expense declines and the bond premium repaid (amortization of bond premium) increases. The interest expense decreases because a portion of the original amount borrowed is returned to the investor with each interest payment. Therefore, the amount of money used in each succeeding year decreases. By the end of the fifth year, all of the bond premium will have been returned to the investor. The only liability remaining at maturity is the $10,000 balance in Bonds Payable.

At any time until maturity, the net liability or carrying value is the balance in Bonds Payable plus the balance in the liability adjunct account, Premium on Bonds Payable. For instance, the balance sheet at the end of Year 3 would show under long-term liabilities:

| | |
|---|---:|
| Bonds payable . . . . . . . . . . . . . . . | $10,000 |
|     Plus: Unamortized premium . . . . . . . . | 357 |
| | $10,357 |

We leave as an exercise for the reader to prove that $10,357 is the present value at 8 percent of the remaining obligations under the bond contract.

**TABLE 11–4** Schedule of Interest Expense and Premium Amortization for a $10,000, 10 Percent Bond Sold at an Effective Rate of 8 Percent

| Year | (a) Interest Expense | (b) Cash Payments | (c) Debit to Bond Premium | (d) Ending Balance of Bond Premium | (e) Year-End Carrying Value (Net Liability) |
|------|---------|---------|---------|---------|---------|
| 0 | — | — | — | $799 | $10,799 |
| 1 | $ 864 | $1,000 | $136 | 663 | 10,663 |
| 2 | 853 | 1,000 | 147 | 516 | 10,516 |
| 3 | 841 | 1,000 | 159 | 357 | 10,357 |
| 4 | 829 | 1,000 | 171 | 186 | 10,186 |
| 5 | 814 | 1,000 | 186 | — | 10,000 |
| | $4,201 | $5,000 | $799 | | |

Note: Column [a] is 8 percent of the net liability existing at the beginning of the year. Column [b] is the face value multiplied by the nominal rate of interest [$10,000 × 10%]. Column [c] equals [b] − [a]. Column [d] equals the preceding year's unamortized premium less [c]. Column [e] is the maturity value of $10,000 plus the balance in the Premium on Bonds Payable account [d].

## Straight-Line Amortization

The above method of recording interest is called the *effective interest method*. It charges each period with an amount of interest directly related to the market rate at the date the bonds were issued and the actual amount of money being used. Under this method, the interest expense varies in each period, although the yield rate is constant. Amortization schedules similar to Tables 11–3 and 11–4 can be calculated and printed in a matter of minutes by a computer.

In accounting practice, however, a less accurate procedure is sometimes used. This procedure amortizes the premium or discount over the life of the bond issue on a *straight-line* basis. *Each period receives the same amount of interest expense,* which we determine by taking the nominal interest (cash payment) plus/minus an equal portion of the bond discount/premium. For the five-year, 10 percent bond sold at an effective rate of 8 percent, the annual entries for interest under the two amortization procedures are as follows for Year 1:

| | *Effective Interest* | | *Straight-Line* | |
|---|---|---|---|---|
| Interest Expense . . | 864 ($10,799 × 8%) | | 840# | |
| Premium on Bonds Payable . . . . | 136* | | 160 ($799/5) | |
| Cash . . . . | | 1,000 | | 1,000 |

*1,000 − 864.
#1,000 − 160.

Although simple to carry out, the straight-line procedure lacks conceptual soundness. Table 11–4 illustrates that the $840 of Interest Expense recorded for each of the five years of the bond's life approximates the true interest expense only in the third year. If the straight-line method is followed, the carrying amount shown for the bond in each financial statement will no longer equal the present value of the remaining bond promises. Because of these deficiencies in the straight-line approach, the effective interest method is preferred and required in many circumstances.

## Zero-Coupon Bonds

Generally the amount of any bond premium or bond discount is small in relation to the face value of the bond (usually less than 5 percent). Occasionally, companies will issue deep-discount bonds. The nominal rate of interest is zero. All of the interest earned is in the form of a discount from face value and is paid at the maturity date when the lender receives significantly more in cash than was originally loaned.

These bonds were especially popular in the early 1980s, particularly among tax-exempt investors or investors outside of the United States. The corporation could deduct the accrued interest expense each year on its tax return, even though the cash payment was deferred until maturity. The tax-exempt investor would be locked into an acceptable effective yield with little fear that the company would retire the bond issue prior to its maturity.

The same present value concepts apply to deep-discount bonds as to other issues. The issuance price is equal to the present value of the future cash payments. In this case, the future cash payment is only the payment at maturity. Consider the case of Caterpillar, Inc. Early in 1982, it issued $140 million of zero-coupon notes due in 1994. The effective annual interest rate then was 13 percent, so the bonds were issued at an original discount of $112 million (the present value of $140 million due in thirteen years at 13 percent is $28 million). Caterpillar's entry in 1982 was:

| | | |
|---|---|---|
| Cash . . . . . . . . . . . . . . . . . . | 28,000,000 | |
| Unamortized Note Discount . . . . . . . . . | 112,000,000 | |
|     Long-term Notes Payable . . . . . . . | | 140,000,000 |
| To record issuance of zero-coupon notes. | | |

The entry to record the first and second years' interest would be:

| | First Year | | Second Year | |
|---|---|---|---|---|
| Interest Expense . . . | 3,640,000* | | 4,113,200[#] | |
|   Unamortized Note | | | | |
|     Discount. . . . | | 3,640,000 | | 4,113,200 |
| To accrue interest based on effective rate of 13%. | | | | |

*$28,000,000 × .13
[#]($28,000,000 + $3,640,000) × .13

Although no cash is paid out, there is an interest charge for the use of money each year. The $112 million discount is recognized as interest expense over the life of the note. Each year's interest is 13 percent times the carrying value of the note. The carrying value of the note increases each year by the amount of interest earned but not paid.

By *1994*, the Unamortized Note Discount will have a zero balance; the liability will be the $140 million face value. In the intervening years, the liability is reported at the present value of the $140 million. For example, the note appears as long-term debt on the Caterpillar balance sheets as follows (in millions):

|  | December 31 | | |
|---|---|---|---|
|  | *1986* | *1985* | *1984* |
| Notes—zero-coupon due 1994 . . . . . . . . . . | $54 | $47 | $41 |

In 1987, there were over 25 zero-coupon bonds from more than 15 different companies traded on the New York Bond Exchange. Some of the prominent companies that have issued them include J. C. Penney, Allied Corporation, McDonalds, and Pepsico, Inc. In addition, other companies have issued bonds with low stated rates; these bonds, of course, are issued at large discounts.

# EXTINGUISHING THE BOND LIABILITY PRIOR TO MATURITY

Although bonds are issued for relatively long periods of time, the liability can be extinguished prior to maturity. Most bond issues contain a *call provision,* whereby the borrower can redeem the issue at certain set prices during its life. Usually the redemption price includes a *call premium* to compensate the investor for having to give up his or her investment prematurely. In addition to retiring bonds by call, a company also can purchase its own bonds in the securities markets.

Some other bonds, known as *convertible bonds,* contain a provision allowing the bonds to be exchanged for capital stock at the holder's option. This conversion feature offers the investor an opportunity to gain if the market price of the capital stock increases. Until it is converted, though, the bond provides creditors with protection and a preferential return. From the company's viewpoint, the conversion option may allow the bonds to be issued at a lower market rate of interest or to be used as an indirect way of issuing capital stock. If all or part of a bond issue is converted into capital stock, the liability disappears, and owners' equity replaces it.

Our primary interest lies in analyzing the basic transaction that occurs when bonds are extinguished. Regardless of whether this is accomplished by call, by open-market purchase, or through conversion, and whether the issue is retired in total or only partially, the analysis remains the same.

Therefore, a simple example is used to illustrate redemption or conversion. Assume that the account balances relating to a bond issue are as follows on the date of retirement or conversion:

|  | Debit | Credit |
|---|---|---|
| Bonds payable . . . . . . . . . . . . |  | $100,000 |
| Discount on bonds payable . . . . . . | $6,000 |  |
| Unamortized bond issue costs . . . . . | 300 |  |

The balances in the contra liability account, Discount on Bonds Payable, and in the asset account, Unamortized Bond Issue Costs, are not the original amounts. Each has been partially amortized during the period the bond issue has been outstanding.

## Redemption

The redemption price (call price) is usually expressed as a percentage of maturity value. The excess above maturity value is referred to as the "call premium" and is the extra payment required of the business for the privilege of retiring the bonds early. If, for example, this bond issue is callable at a price of 104, the company has to pay 104 percent of face value, or $104,000. The entry to record this retirement is:

| | | |
|---|---|---|
| Bonds Payable . . . . . . . . . . . . . . . . . . | 100,000 | |
| Loss on Bond Redemption . . . . . . . . . . . . | 10,300 | |
| Discount on Bonds Payable . . . . . . . . . | | 6,000 |
| Unamortized Bond Issue Costs. . . . . . . . | | 300 |
| Cash . . . . . . . . . . . . . . . . . . . | | 104,000 |

The loss on redemption arises from two factors: (1) the company has to pay $10,000 more than the carrying value shown on the books [$104,000 − ($100,000 − $6,000)] and (2) an asset of $300 is written off. In many respects the Loss on Bond Redemption account is an adjustment to prior years' earnings. Because the life of the bond issue is shorter than anticipated, the interest expense and amortization of bond issue costs during past years have been too low. The loss is reported as an *extraordinary item* in the period of redemption.[12]

## Refunding

Issuance of a new bond and use of its proceeds to redeem an old one, often to take advantage of lower interest rates, is called *refunding*. For instance,

---

[12] FASB, *Statement of Financial Accounting Standards No. 4*, "Reporting Gains and Losses from Extinguishment of Debt" (Stamford, Conn., March 1975), par. 8. See Chapter 16 for a complete discussion of the concept of an extraordinary item.

an existing 12 percent bond may be called prior to its maturity and a new 9 percent bond sold to take its place. In many ways, this situation is analogous to an exchange of noncurrent assets. The refunding should be treated similarly—as two separate transactions: (1) retiring the old bond issue as illustrated above and (2) recording the issuance of the new one as illustrated earlier. The old bond issue is being terminated because it has become comparatively uneconomical. The costs of ending the liability—unamortized discount, unamortized bond issue costs, and call premium—are part of the loss recognized upon elimination of the old bond.[13]

## Conversion

When bonds are converted into stock, the retirement of the bond liability is accompanied by a concomitant increase in contributed capital. The most commonly used procedure increases capital stock by the amount of the *carrying value* of the bond liability.

Suppose the bond issue described above contains a conversion option entitling each $1,000 bond to be converted into stock at a price of $50 per share. The entire bond issue, if converted, could be exchanged for 2,000 shares ($100,000/$50) of stock. If the stock price rises above $50 per share, bondholders may decide to convert. The entry to record complete conversion would be:

| | | |
|---|---:|---:|
| Bonds Payable . . . . . . . . . . . . . . . . . . | 100,000 | |
| Discount on Bonds Payable . . . . . . . . . . | | 6,000 |
| Capital Stock . . . . . . . . . . . . . . . . | | 94,000 |

Unlike a bond refunding, a bond conversion does *not* consist of two independent events. The initial proceeds of the bond issue reflected the fact that the bonds could be converted into stock. The actual conversion simply completes what was contemplated originally. The bond issued is canceled, and stockholders' equity takes its place. There is no change in assets, only a shifting among the equities. This treatment also draws support from the fact that under the income tax laws a bond conversion is a nontaxable exchange.

In the early 1980s, a number of prominent companies engaged in "debt-for-equity swaps." *Nonconvertible* bonds would be purchased on the bond market by a third party, often a brokerage firm. The brokerage firm then would approach the company to exchange the bonds for an equal value of capital stock in a tax-free exchange. Subsequently, the brokerage firm would sell the capital stock on the stock market. In this case, generally accepted accounting principles allowed the companies to treat the transaction as two independent events: (1) the retirement of the bond issue (almost always at a gain) and (2) the issuance of capital stock. U.S. Steel, Kroger

---

[13] AICPA, *APB Opinion No. 26,* "Early Extinguishment of Debt" (New York, October 1972), par. 20.

Company, Sherwin-Williams Company, and Revlon, Inc. all pumped up their reported earnings in this manner. Yet, the substance of the debt-for-equity swap appears to differ little from that of the bond conversion.

## In-Substance Defeasance

With simple bond retirements, refundings, conversions, and debt-for-equity swaps, the old bond issue disappears as a legal liability. Another form of extinguishing a bond liability prior to its maturity is called "in-substance defeasance." "Defeasance" means the legal voiding of an agreement, in this case, release of a debtor from payment. The term *in-substance* refers to the fact that economically the borrower may have paid off the liability, but legally it has not been retired.

Exxon Corporation championed this creative form of debt retirement in 1982 when interest rates were very high. Other companies followed suit. The following describes what happened in Exxon's case. Exxon purchased $313 million of U.S. Government securities earning interest at a double-digit rate. It then placed these securities in an irrevocable trust to be used only to pay the interest and maturing principle on six of its own outstanding bond issues that had been issued at low interest rates (around 6 to 7 percent) in the past. Because of the high yield on the government securities, the $313 million would generate cash inflows sufficient to pay all future interest and principle payments on $515 million face value of the six bond issues.

Exxon made the following entries:

| | | |
|---|---|---|
| U.S. Government Securities | 313 | |
| Cash | | 313 |

To purchase $313 million of risk-free securities.

| | | |
|---|---|---|
| Bonds Payable | 515 | |
| U.S. Government Securities | | 313 |
| Gain on Extinguishment of Bonds Payable | | 202 |

To place securities in an irrevocable trust, to remove the
debt issues from the balance sheet, and to record a gain
on bond extinguishment.

In brief, Exxon recorded the events as a bond retirement. After allowing for income taxes and other adjustments, a net gain of $132 million was reported on the income statement for the second quarter of 1982. By extinguishing the bond liability in this manner, Exxon avoided any call premiums and expenses of acquiring publicly held bonds. Hence, its "gain on retirement" was larger than if it had actually tried to repurchase the six bond issues at market prices.

The question is, "Is an in-substance defeasance the equivalent of an early bond retirement?" Exxon and others argued that it was. The substance of the transaction is that the borrower will not be required to make any future cash payments associated with the bond issues. In terms of legal form, however, the borrower has not been released from its obligation. Setting aside assets in an irrevocable trust fund does not legally retire the bonds; it merely ensures that the debt will be serviced.

Accountants usually insist on substance over form. It is one aspect of representational faithfulness. After much argument and debate, which incidentally still continues today, the Financial Accounting Standards Board ruled that the economic substance was that of an early bond retirement.[14] The borrower must place *cash or risk-free securities in an irrevocable trust solely for the purpose of satisfying the cash requirements of the debt* and be virtually assured that no future cash payments will be required.

# NOTES PAYABLE AND RECEIVABLE

Simple *short-term* notes payable are discussed in Chapter 6 in connection with the introduction of the Interest Expense account. The liability is recorded at face value, and interest is accrued as time passes. The recording of promissory notes receivable parallels that for notes payable. If the note is explicitly interest-bearing, entries may be made periodically to record the accruing of an asset, interest receivable, and the earning of interest revenue.

Observe, however, that notes—like bonds—are recorded at their present value. The amount borrowed on a note is its present value; the amount paid at the due date is its *maturity value;* and the difference is interest, the charge for the use of money. For example, if one were to borrow $6,000 and give a 9 percent, one-year note in exchange, the initial present value of the note is its face value of $6,000. The interest or growth in present value over the year will be $540, and the maturity value is $6,540. That the note's face value equals its present value can be demonstrated by discounting the maturity amount (face value plus interest) at 9 percent ($6,540/1.09 = $6,000). There is no premium or discount because the stated rate of interest on the note equals the market rate of interest. The transaction is between a single lender and a single borrower. Unless strong evidence exists to the contrary, the rate of interest they agree upon presumably represents a validly transacted effective rate.

*Long-term* notes are recorded almost identically to bonds. Instead of the face value being recorded in an account called "10% Debenture Bonds Payable," the account might be called "10% 15-Year Notes Payable." All other recording concepts and procedures are the same, and little is to be gained by

---

[14] FASB, *Statement of Financial Accounting Standards No. 76,* "Extinguishment of Debt" (Stamford, Conn., November 1983). Some international companies tried to establish instantaneous defeasance. They would borrow at a low interest rate in one world financial market and simultaneously invest in risk-free assets that yielded a higher rate in a different world financial market. This practice was *not* allowed to be treated as a retirement of the borrowing at a gain.

repeating them again. Instead, we will discuss in this section two somewhat unique aspects of notes—(1) installment notes and (2) interest imputation.

## Installment Notes

An installment note is paid off periodically over its life. Each installment consists of a portion representing interest and a portion representing principal repayment. Sometimes the legal document refers only to the total amount due. Nonetheless, an interest factor is present and included in the total amount due under the note. The amount of money actually borrowed, or the present value, is less than the amount of the note.

Assume a small manufacturer wishes to borrow $15,000 from its local bank to acquire some machinery. The borrower signs a note payable promising to pay $18,960 in 48 monthly installments of $395. The total interest charge over the five years is $3,960 ($18,960 − $15,000); the annual interest rate is 12 percent. The present value of $395 per period for 48 periods at a monthly interest rate of 1 percent is equal to $15,000.

**Notes Payable.**    The initial entry on the books of the manufacturer would be:

| | | |
|---|---|---|
| Cash . . . . . . . . . . . . . . . . . . . . . . . . . . | 15,000 | |
|     Notes Payable . . . . . . . . . . . . . . . . . . | | 15,000 |

Each monthly cash payment of $395 would consist of interest (.01 × the balance in the Notes Payable account) with the remainder as a partial reduction in the liability. The first three payments are recorded below:

| | First Payment | | Second Payment | | Third Payment | |
|---|---|---|---|---|---|---|
| Interest Expense | 150.00[a] | | 147.55[b] | | 145.08[c] | |
| Notes Payable | 245.00 | | 247.45 | | 249.92 | |
|     Cash | | 395.00 | | 395.00 | | 395.00 |

[a]$15,000 × .01
[b]($15,000 − $245) × .01
[c]($15,000 − $245 − $247.45) × .01

Similar entries for the next 45 months would result in the complete liquidation of the liability. The total debits to Interest Expense would sum to $3,960.

Notice that in this direct approach, the liability is recorded at its present value of $15,000, not the face amount of the note of $18,960. Liabilities represent a source of assets; in this case, the source is only $15,000.

Another common method of recording this type of transaction calls for crediting the note at its face value and making an offsetting debit to a contra liability account:

| | | |
|---|---|---|
| Cash . . . . . . . . . . . . . . . . . . . . . . . | 15,000 | |
| Notes Payable—Discount . . . . . . . . . . . . . . | 3,960 | |
|     Notes Payable . . . . . . . . . . . . . . . . . . | | 18,960 |

Each installment payment would be recorded in a manner similar to the first one which is illustrated below:

| | | |
|---|---|---|
| Notes Payable . . . . . . . . . . . . . . . . . . . | 395 | |
|     Cash . . . . . . . . . . . . . . . . . . . . . | | 395 |

| | | |
|---|---|---|
| Interest Expense . . . . . . . . . . . . . . . . | 150 | |
|     Notes Payable—Discount . . . . . . . . . . . . | | 150 |

When the Notes Payable—Discount is subtracted on the balance sheet from the main liability, the effect of the two entries above is to reduce the liability by $245.

| | *Before First Payment* | *After First Payment* |
|---|---|---|
| Notes payable . . . . . . . . | $18,960 | $18,565 |
| Less notes payable discount . . | 3,960 | 3,810 |
| Carrying value of the liability . . | $15,000 | $14,755 |

**Notes Receivable.** The holder of the installment note receivable may either record the present value directly or use a contra account approach. The bank in the above example could record the initial note and the first two monthly cash receipts in either of the ways shown in Table 11–5. The contra account procedure is more common. If this approach is used, Unearned Discount (Notes Receivable—Discount) is a contra asset representing the

**TABLE 11–5**  Recording of Installment Notes Receivable

| | *Direct Approach* | | *Contra Account Approach* | |
|---|---|---|---|---|
| Initial receipt of note: | | | | |
|   Notes Receivable . . . . . | 15,000 | | 18,960 | |
|     Unearned Discount . . . . | | | | 3,960 |
|     Cash . . . . . . . . . | | 15,000 | | 15,000 |
| First cash receipt: | | | | |
|   Cash . . . . . . . . . | 395 | | 395 | |
|   Unearned Discount . . . . . | | | 150 | |
|     Notes Receivable . . . . | | 245 | | 395 |
|     Interest Revenue . . . . . | | 150 | | 150 |
| Second cash receipt: | | | | |
|   Cash . . . . . . . . . | 395.00 | | 395.00 | |
|   Unearned Discount . . . . . | | | 147.55 | |
|     Notes Receivable . . . . | | 247.45 | | 395.00 |
|     Interest Revenue . . . . . | | 147.55 | | 147.55 |

amount of interest that will be earned if the note is held to maturity. On the position statement, it should be subtracted from the balance in the notes receivable account.

## Imputation of Interest

The valuation principle governing the recording of notes is that they be measured at their present value. If the stated interest rate on the note approximates the going market rate of interest, face value represents present value. If the note is exchanged for cash, the cash received or paid measures the present value of the note. Any difference between present value and face value should be recorded as a discount or premium to be amortized as part of the interest calculation over the life of the note.

However, when a note is received or issued in exchange for property, goods, and services, the face value of the note may not represent present value, and the stated interest rate may not reflect the effective rate. Such is the case whenever (1) no interest rate is stated, (2) the stated interest rate differs significantly from rates prevailing for similar debt instruments, or (3) the face value of the note is materially different from the current cash equivalent of the goods or services received in exchange. The Accounting Principles Board ruled that in these circumstances the receivables and payables must be recorded at present value even if a discount must be imputed to the debt instrument.[15]

**Example of Interest Imputation.** Sometimes companies sell products or services in exchange for long-term notes with low or no stated rates. Land development companies are a prominent example. Assume that Desert Sands Realty Company received $8,000 cash plus a three-year promissory note for $50,000 in exchange for a parcel of land. The note bears interest at an annual rate of 4 percent, or $2,000 per year. Clearly, the present value of the note is less than its face value of $50,000, because the going rate of interest is much higher than 4 percent. Likewise, land sales revenue is overstated if recorded at $58,000. *APB Opinion No. 21* provides that if either the fair market value of the land or the market value of the note can be measured independently, whichever one is more clearly determinable can be used to establish the present value of the note. In the absence of such evidence, one should establish the present value of the note by discounting future payments at an *imputed* rate of interest.

Assume that the fair market value of the land is not readily determinable and that the note is not readily marketable. In light of the credit rating of the customer, the small down payment, and the prevailing market rates of inter-

---

[15] AICPA, *APB Opinion No. 21*. This opinion applies to most *monetary* receivables and payables with terms longer than one year.

est for similar types of financing, a 12 percent interest rate is determined to be appropriate. The present value of the note at a 12 percent imputed rate is $40,393:

Present value of $50,000 due in three years at 12%
($50,000 × 0.7118, Table 11A–8 factor) . . . . . . . . . . . . $35,590
Present value of $2,000 per year for three years at 12%
($2,000 × 2.4018, Table 11–9 factor) . . . . . . . . . . . . 4,803
Present value of note . . . . . . . . . . . . . . . . . . $40,393

The journal entries by Desert Sands Realty Company to record the sale and interest accrued at the end of the first year follow:

Cash . . . . . . . . . . . . . . . . . . . . . . . . 8,000
Notes Receivable from Sale of Property . . . . . . . . . 50,000
  Unamortized Discount on Notes Receivable . . . . 9,607
  Sales ($8,000 cash + $40,393 value of note) . . . . 48,393
   To record sale of land—4 percent interest-bearing
  note receivable valued at an imputed rate of 12 percent.

Cash . . . . . . . . . . . . . . . . . . . . . . . . 2,000
Unamortized Discount on Notes Receivable . . . . . . . 2,847
  Interest Revenue ($40,393 × .12) . . . . . . . . 4,847
   To accrue interest at an imputed rate of 12 percent on
  $40,393, the present value of the note.

Similar entries for interest revenue of $5,189 and $5,571 would occur at the end of the following two years. As shown below, the discount is amortized by means of the effective interest method:

| Year | Interest Revenue (12%) | 4 Percent Interest Received | Discount Amortization | Unamortized Discount | Net Receivable |
|------|------|------|------|------|------|
| 0 | | | | $9,607 | $40,393 |
| 1 | $4,847 | $2,000 | $2,847 | 6,760 | 43,240 |
| 2 | 5,189 | 2,000 | 3,189 | 3,571 | 46,429 |
| 3 | 5,571 | 2,000 | 3,571 | — | 50,000 |

The purchaser would follow a parallel pattern, starting with a *liability* that has an initial present value of $40,393. The *Unamortized Discount on Notes Payable* would be reflected as interest expense over the three-year period at the imputed rate of 12 percent.

# DISCLOSURE OF DEBT INFORMATION

The preceding discussions focus primarily on the *valuation* of notes and bonds in accordance with present value concepts. Although fundamental to the accountant's task, valuation represents only one aspect of the information to be communicated about long- and short-term debt. Because of the complexity of many debt instruments and borrowing arrangements, full disclosure requires the inclusion of additional information so that users can make informed judgments about the liquidity and financial strength of the business entity.

With respect to long-term debt, companies provide a supplementary schedule showing the essential details of each obligation. Essential details include interest rates, maturity dates, conversion privileges, call features, special retirement provisions, and any restrictions imposed on the firm. Restrictions may relate to the declaration of dividends, the sale of plant assets, the issuance of additional securities, or the merger or liquidation of the firm.

Any portion of the long-term debt that matures within one year should be reported as a current liability unless there is convincing evidence that the debt will be refunded or repaid with assets classified as noncurrent (e.g., a bond retirement fund). Also required is a schedule summarizing the expected payments of long-term debt over the next five years necessitated by maturities and other mandatory retirements.[16]

In November 1973, the Securities and Exchange Commission issued *Accounting Series Release No. 148,* requiring disclosure of additional information relating to both short- and long-term debt. Although many of these disclosures technically are required only in reports like the 10–K filed with the SEC, notes containing them are appearing with increasing frequency in the annual reports to shareholders. The disclosures include (1) a breakdown of short-term debt into bank borrowings and commercial paper;[17] (2) the average interest rate and terms for these borrowings at the balance sheet date; (3) the average interest rate, average outstanding borrowings, and maximum month-end outstanding borrowings for short-term debt during the period; and (4) amounts and terms of unused lines of short-term credit and unused commitments for long-term financing arrangements.

*ASR No. 148* also requires disclosure of any compensating balance agreements the firm has. A *compensating balance* is that portion of the asset, Cash in Bank, that a firm agrees to maintain at all times in order to obtain a particular loan or line of credit. For example, a firm borrows $200,000 from a bank, exchanging a one-year, 9 percent note payable. The agreement calls for a 15 percent compensating balance. Consequently, $30,000 of the amount borrowed cannot be spent by the business entity; it must remain as an idle asset. The impact on the business is two-fold: (1) a portion of the cash

---

[16] FASB, *Statement of Financial Accounting Standards No. 47,* "Disclosure of Long-term Obligations" (Stamford, Conn., March 1981), par. 10.

[17] Commercial paper is defined in the money market as unsecured promissory notes issued by well-established corporations to meet their short-term seasonal borrowing requirements. These notes usually are issued in specific denominations arranged to suit the buyer with maturities ranging from a few days to nine months.

account is not really a current asset because it cannot be used for normal operating purposes and (2) the effective interest cost on the loan is 10.6 percent, since the firm must pay $18,000 interest for usable funds of only $170,000. Particularly during periods of tight monetary credit, compensating balance arrangements often are significant.

# DISCUSSION OF THE KIMBERLY-CLARK ANNUAL REPORT

We focus our discussion here only on the long-term debt and the debt payable within one year shown on the Kimberly-Clark balance sheet. Note 4 provides detailed information about both classifications of debt.

Let us look at short-term debt first. The total amount is $250 million on December 31, 1987. Of this amount, $29 million represents short-term notes payable to banks, $8.1 million consists of the current portion of long-term debt, and the rest is commercial paper the company has issued. The amount of commercial paper outstanding increased substantially during 1987 causing total short-term debt to increase by $116 million ($250 − $134) or 87 percent.

To enable the reader to judge financial flexibility, Kimberly-Clark points out that it could borrow an additional $475 million if needed under unused revolving credit agreements. The fact that the company can secure such a line of credit provides some evidence of its financial soundness despite the alarming increase in short-term debt. However, as noted, Kimberly-Clark has to pay a commitment fee on the entire $475 million for this financial flexibility. Commitment fees, which usually are less than one-quarter of 1 percent, add to the firm's interest expense.

Kimberly-Clark has elected not to include in its annual report the SEC-mandated disclosures regarding short-term debt. Table 11–6 reproduces the schedule taken from its 10–K report filed with the Securities and Exchange Commission.

Analysts would use this information to evaluate short-term financial strength and liquidity during the year as well as at year-end and to compare short-term debt policies and financing costs over the last three years.

Total *long-term debt* rose during 1987 from $426.3 million to $686.9 million, a significant increase. The Consolidated Statement of Changes in Financial Position (statement of cash flows) indicates that the net increase resulted from $314.9 million of new long-term debt, a $54.3 million reduction resulting from some long-term notes maturing in 1987, and a decrease in long-term bank loans. The statement of cash flows indicates that much of this new borrowing was used to buy back shares of Kimberly-Clark stock (more on that in Chapter 14).

In some cases, analysts might be concerned over the classification of $200 million of commercial paper as long-term debt. Commercial paper is almost always short-term in character. Kimberly-Clark's classification is based

**TABLE 11–6**    Schedule of Short-Term Borrowings of Kimberly-Clark Corporation

| Category of Aggregate Short-Term Borrowings | Balance at End of Period | Weighted-Average Interest Rate | Maximum Amount Outstanding at Any Month-End during the Period | Average Daily Amount Outstanding during the Period | Weighted-Average Interest Rate during the Period |
|---|---|---|---|---|---|
| **December 31, 1987** | | | | | |
| Holders of | | | | | |
| commercial paper . . . | $ 412.9 | 7.7% | $412.9 | $149.7 | 7.1% |
| Less commercial paper to | | | | | |
| be refinanced . . . . . | (200.0) | — | — | — | — |
| Other short-term | | | | | |
| debt . . . . . . . . . | 29.0 | 10.3 | 32.8 | 32.4 | 12.4 |
| | $ 241.9 | | | | |
| | | | | | |
| **December 31, 1986** | | | | | |
| Holders of | | | | | |
| commercial paper . . . | $   78.0 | 6.9% | $ 78.0 | $ 46.8 | 7.1% |
| Other short-term | | | | | |
| debt . . . . . . . . . | 26.3 | 9.4 | 54.9 | 32.7 | 13.6 |
| | $ 104.3 | | | | |
| | | | | | |
| **December 31, 1985** | | | | | |
| Holders of | | | | | |
| commercial paper . . . | $   52.9 | 8.0% | $ 78.3 | $ 58.5 | 8.2% |
| Other short-term | | | | | |
| debt . . . . . . . . . | 31.1 | 10.9 | 41.8 | 36.6 | 13.8 |
| | $   84.0 | | | | |

Source: Schedule IX of Form 10–K filed by Kimberly-Clark Corporation for the year ended December 31, 1987.

on the fact that these borrowings were actually refinanced in January 1988 on a long-term basis. The company's intention always was that this debt be long-term. Short-term commercial paper was simply a temporary means of achieving this goal. Because the long-term refinancing had taken place by the time the statements were issued (note that the auditors' opinion is dated January 27, 1988), the auditors agreed with the classification.

Note 4 details the composition of the long-term debt. Apart from the commercial paper, most of the long-term debt consists of long-term notes, long-term bank loans, and two bond issues ($60.5 million of Sinking Fund Debentures and $33.8 million of Revenue Bonds). Note 4 also serves the useful purpose of revealing just how long term the long-term debt is. Scheduled maturities for the four years after 1988 are indicated. Although a very small portion ($8.1 million) of Kimberly-Clark's existing long-term debt matures in 1988, $261.1 million falls due between 1989 and 1992.

Kimberly-Clark has a balance sheet goal of total debt being 28 to 32 percent of adjusted capital (sum of total debt, stockholders' equity, and the equity of minority stockholders in some of the subsidiary companies). The narrative "Review of Liquidity and Capital Resources" notes that this ratio increased from 22 percent on December 31, 1986 to 36 percent a year later. These percentages are derived below:

|  | *1987* | *1986* |
|---|---|---|
| Total debt | $936.9 <br> ($250.0 + $686.9) | $560.3 <br> ($134.0 + $426.3) |
| Adjusted capital | $2,591.4 <br> ($936.9 + $82.6 + $1,571.9) | $2,556.7 <br> ($560.3 + $76.5 + $1,919.9) |
| Ratio | 36.2% <br> ($936.9/$2,591.4) | 21.9% <br> ($560.3/$2,556.7) |

This ratio is a measure of financial solvency. (See Chapter 18 for other ways of looking at the relationship between borrowed capital and owners' capital.) The large increase in debt coupled with a large decrease in stockholders' equity caused by the retirement of stock caused the big jump in the ratio. Management feels that by the end of 1988, the ratio should be back within the desired range. An analyst could compare this range with other similar companies to evaluate its adequacy as a desirable financial target. The fact that Kimberly-Clark's bonds and commercial paper are rated high suggests that the other external evaluators are not concerned about the temporary jump outside of the desired range.

## SUMMARY

The accounting for bonds and notes rests on two basic concepts: *interest is the charge for the use of money* and *present value is the valuation basis for monetary liabilities and assets*. These principles sometimes seem masked in the recording process. Accountants, for example, often record maturity values and face values of bonds and notes in main accounts and use contra and adjunct accounts to reflect their present values.

Nevertheless, the amount recorded for monetary assets and liabilities should equal the present value of the cash flows promised under the contracts. Present value, not the ultimate maturity value, represents the amount of money actually borrowed or loaned and the claim as of any specific time. This principal amount borrowed, multiplied by the *effective* interest rate

**FIGURE 11–1**   Pattern of Changes in Present Value of Various Liabilities

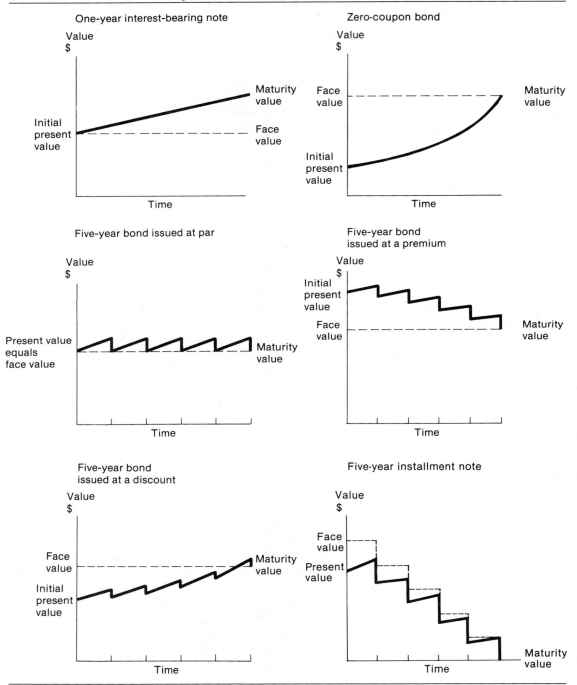

gives the periodic interest expense and growth in the liability. As the interest accrues with time, the present value of the note or bond moves toward its maturity value.

Figure 11–1 shows schematically the change in present value over time for each of the major monetary liabilities we have discussed. The sawtooth patterns on the bonds reflect the yearly accruals of interest and cash payments at year-end. In the case of the discount bond, the payment is less than the yearly interest charge; the residual present value increases to maturity value. With the premium bond, the cash payments exceed the yearly buildup of interest; the residual present value declines to maturity value. A similar, but more exaggerated, pattern to the premium bond exists for the installment note. Here the cash payments cover the interest accrual as well as reduce the residual present value to zero. The zero-coupon bond shows only a gradual increase from a low initial present value to maturity value. No sawtooth pattern exists because no periodic cash payments are made.

When bonds (and notes) are extinguished before maturity, a difference often exists between their carrying values and the amount needed to liquidate them. This difference is normally recognized as a gain or loss on bond retirement. Recognition of a gain or loss is allowed not only for simple early retirements but also for bond refundings, in-substance defeasances, and debt-for-equity swaps. However, no gains or losses are recognized when bonds are converted directly to capital stock.

# Appendix A: Compound Interest and Present Value

This Appendix has two purposes. First, it presents the basic elements of compound interest in a formal manner. Included are discussions of both compound interest and present value formulas, an explanation of the use of present value tables, and some elaboration of the basic concepts. Second, some uses of present value techniques beyond those described in Chapter 11 are outlined in an attempt to acquaint the reader with this common and valuable analytical aid in decision making.

## Compound Interest

Interest is the growth of an amount of money during a time period. It is the price that must be paid (received) for the use of money over time. Thus, if $1,000 is deposited at an interest rate of 5 percent, the amount receivable at the end of the year is $1,050. This example illustrates *simple interest*, that is, interest for one period only. The basic formula is:

$$F = P + iP = P(1 + i)$$

where $F$ equals the future amount of money accumulated, $P$ is the principal or the present amount invested, and $i$ is the rate of interest per time period.

Any growth in amount during the year, if not withdrawn, becomes part of the invested sum. Therefore, in future periods the interest element from past years will also draw interest. This phenomenon is called *compounding*. It lies at the heart of many financial decisions involving sums of money borrowed or invested for more than a single time period.

**Future Amount of a $1 Present Value.**    The future amount of $1 at compound interest is the sum of money to which the $1 will grow. We might ask the question: To what amount would a sum of money accumulate in *n* periods if invested now at *i* rate of interest? Our knowledge of simple interest would indicate that the amount at the end of a single period would be $1 plus the interest earned on it ($F_1 = 1 + i$). If the amount is left to accumulate, the compound interest phenomenon becomes operative. During the second period, the entire sum at the end of the first period earns interest. Therefore,

$$F_2 = F_1(1 + i) = (1 + i)(1 + i) = (1 + i)^2$$

A continuation of this process would lead to a general formula:

$$F_n = (1 + i)^n = (F/P, n, i)$$

where $(F/P, n, i)$ is the future amount of a $1 present sum invested for *n* periods at *i* rate of interest. The $(1 + i)^n$ is called the *accumulation factor*.[18]

*Example:*    $5,000 is invested for five years at 12 percent compounded annually. The accumulated amount at the end of five years is determined below. A timeline representation of the problem shows the equivalence of the $8,812 future value at the end of five years to the $5,000 present value.

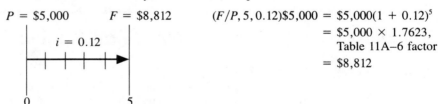

$P = \$5,000$    $F = \$8,812$    $(F/P, 5, 0.12)\$5,000 = \$5,000(1 + 0.12)^5$
$$= \$5,000 \times 1.7623,$$
Table 11A–6 factor
$$= \$8,812$$

$i = 0.12$

0    5

If interest were *compounded semiannually*, we would calculate the amount for 10 six-month periods at 6 percent per period.

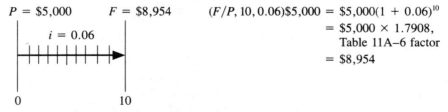

$P = \$5,000$    $F = \$8,954$    $(F/P, 10, 0.06)\$5,000 = \$5,000(1 + 0.06)^{10}$
$$= \$5,000 \times 1.7908,$$
Table 11A–6 factor
$$= \$8,954$$

$i = 0.06$

0    10

---

[18] In deriving and using formulas involving compound interest and present value, users find it easier to work in terms of a single dollar. Expressions and tables for values of $1 provide a generalized form that can be used in problems having different dollar amounts. Simply multiply the compound interest or present value factor for $1 by the actual amount in the problem.

Notice that the future amount is greater in this case because we have more opportunity to earn "interest on interest" than with annual compounding. A 12 percent interest rate compounded semiannually exceeds an annual 12 percent rate. If interest were only compounded annually, it would take the equivalent of a 12.36 percent annual rate to provide the same future value $(F/P, 5, 0.1236)\$5,000 = \$8,954.$[19]

### Future Amount of an Annuity of $1.

A natural extension of the concept of the future amount of $1 is the future amount of $1 per period. This concept deals with the growth of a *series* of equal investments made at the end of equal time intervals. The term *annuity* is used to describe a series of periodic deposits, receipts, or payments of this type. The basic question underlying the amount of an annuity might be phrased as follows: to what amount would a periodic deposit of money accumulate in $n$ years if a deposit is made at the *end* of each of the $n$ years and earns at $i$ rate of interest? We will use the abbreviation $(F/A, n, i)$ for the future amount of an annuity.

The derivation of a generalized formula for the future amount of an annuity is not so straightforward as that for a single investment. However, the general concept is the same. For example, $1 is deposited at the end of each year for four years. The growth of each year's deposit is summarized in Table 11A–1. Being made at the *end* of the first year, the first year's deposit earns compound interest only for three years — Years 2, 3, and 4.

**TABLE 11A–1   Generalized Formulas for Growth of a Four-Year Annuity**

| End-of-Year Deposit | *Accumulated Value at End of Year* | | | | |
|---|---|---|---|---|---|
| | *1* | *2* | *3* | *4* | *For n Years* |
| First . . . . . . . . . . | $1 | $(1 + i)$ | $(1 + i)^2$ | $(1 + i)^3$ | $(1 + i)^{n-1}$ |
| Second . . . . . . . . . | | 1 | $(1 + i)$ | $(1 + i)^2$ | $(1 + i)^{n-2}$ |
| Third . . . . . . . . . . | | | 1 | $(1 + i)$ | $(1 + i)^{n-3}$ |
| Fourth. . . . . . . . . . | | | | 1 | $(1 + i)^{n-4}$ |

The last year's deposit has earned no interest and adds only its original quantity to the total amount.

The amount of this annuity at the end of four years is the total of the accumulated value column for Year 4. The generalized notation at the right indicates that the future amount of any annuity of $1 for $n$ years is:

$$(1 + i)^{n-1} + (1 + i)^{n-2} + (1 + i)^{n-3} + \cdots + (1 + i) + 1$$

---

[19] The following formula will provide the effective *annually* compounded rate equivalent to a rate compounded more frequently:

$$(1 + i/n)^n - 1$$

where $i$ is the annual interest rate and $n$ is the number of compounding periods within a year.

This expression is a geometric series, the sum of which is:

$$(F/A, n, i) = \left[\frac{(1 + i)^n - 1}{i}\right]$$

The formula for the future amount of an annuity of $1 per period can be used in any situation in which there are regular periodic payments or receipts.

*Example:*   A firm has entered into a contract under which it receives $2,000 for its services at the end of every six months for five years. The buyer has asked the firm how much it would be willing to accept in a lump-sum amount at the end of five years in lieu of the periodic fees. Assume that the firm can earn 12 percent interest compounded semiannually.

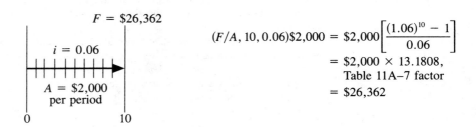

$$(F/A, 10, 0.06)\$2,000 = \$2,000\left[\frac{(1.06)^{10} - 1}{0.06}\right]$$
$$= \$2,000 \times 13.1808,$$
$$\text{Table 11A–7 factor}$$
$$= \$26,362$$

**Future Amount of Annuity Due.**   The preceding discussion assumed that all deposits were made at the end of the interest period. Such a series is called an *ordinary annuity* or *annuity in arrears*. If payments occur at the beginning of the periods, the series is called an *annuity due* or an *annuity in advance*. For the calculations of future amounts, there are five interest periods in a five-year annuity due; this equals the number of interest periods in a *six-year* ordinary annuity, since payments there are not made until the end of the year. Generalizing from this, we can conclude that the amount of an *annuity due* for *n* years is equal to $(F/A, n + 1, i) - 1$. The last item in the formula reflects the fact that no payment occurs at the end of the *n*th year. The above simple conversion allows us to deal with situations involving receipts or payments either at the beginning or the end of the period through use of the same annuity table. The above formula when applied to Table 11A–7 indicates, for example, that the factor for a five-year *annuity due* is calculated by subtracting 1.0000 from the factor found on line 6 in the appropriate interest column.

**Compound Interest Tables.**   Tables are available for both the future amount of $1 present value and the future amount of an annuity of $1. These tables simplify the calculations by presenting the results for varying interest rates and time periods. Brief extracts from such tables are presented in Tables 11A–6 and 11A–7 at the end of this Appendix. They show the ratio of future values to a present sum or to a series of sums, respectively.

There are essentially four elements—annuity amount, interest rate, number of periods, and future amount—in the above compounding formula. If any three of the four factors are specified, the fourth can be derived from the same basic formula and tables.[20]

# Present Value

The concept of present value is the opposite of compound interest. Instead of showing how much a single payment or series of payments will increase over time, present value indicates how much you have to pay now in order to have a certain amount or series of amounts in future periods. Present value is the current cash equivalent of some designated future amount or amounts.

**Present Value of a $1 Future Amount.**   The formula for the present value of $1 received $n$ periods in the future at an interest rate of $i$ percent $(P/F, n, i)$ can be derived from the formula for the amount of $1. If we let $x$ equal the present value of $1 $n$ years in the future, we can solve for $x$ as follows:

$$(F/P, n, i)x = x(1 + i)^n = 1$$

$$x = \frac{1}{(1 + i)^n} = (1 + i)^{-n} = (P/F, n, i)$$

In brief, a reciprocal relationship exists between the present value of a $1 future amount and the future amount of a $1 present value. The *discount factor* is $(1 + i)^{-n}$.

*Example:*   A customer owes you $7,500, due in six years, and approaches you about the possibility of paying off the debt early with a single payment now. What is the minimum amount you would be willing to accept now if the interest rate is 10 percent?

$P = \$4,234$       $F = \$7,500$

$i = 0.10$

0                           6

$(P/F, 6, 0.10)\$7,500 = \$7,500(1.10)^{-6}$
$= \$7,500 \times 0.5645,$
Table 11A–8 factor
$= \$4,234$

**Present Value of an Annuity of $1.**   Commonly, business and financial problems involve a series of equal amounts spaced at approximately equal intervals in the

---

[20] The explanation and example focused on determination of the future amount of an annuity $(F/A, n, i)$. Another use would be to find the *annuity* that will accumulate to (is equivalent to) a specified future amount $(A/F, n, i)$. This is the reciprocal of the formula derived above.

$$(A/F, n, i) = i/[1 + i)^n - 1] = 1/(F/A, n, i)$$

This reciprocal calculation is sufficiently common to warrant a special name, *sinking-fund factor,* and often the construction of separate tables.

future. What single cash receipt (or payment) now is equivalent to a series of cash receipts (or payments) to be made at the end of each of $n$ years if the earning value of money is $i$? The abbreviation $(P/A, n, i)$ is used for the present value of an annuity.

The present value of an annuity of $1 is closely related to the present value of $1 and to the future amount of an annuity of $1. It is the sum of a series of individual calculations of the present value of $1. Likewise, the present value of an annuity is the reverse of the future amount of an annuity. Consequently, its formula can be derived from either of these other concepts.

For example, $(F/A, n, i)$, the future amount of an annuity of $1 for $n$ years at $i$ rate of interest, was derived as $([1 + i]^n - 1)/i$. This is the single future amount that is the equivalent of the annuity. If we desire the single present amount that is the equivalent of the annuity, we must take the present value of the future amount. We can determine the present value of any future amount by multiplying it by $(1 + i)^{-n}$. Putting these facts together gives us the following when $A = \$1$:

$$(P/A, n, i) = (P/F, n, i)\,(F/A, n, i)$$

$$= [(1 + i)^{-n}]\left[\frac{(1 + i)^n - 1}{i}\right]$$

$$= \left[\frac{1 - (1 + i)^{-n}}{i}\right]$$

Using this formula, we can solve for the present value of any annuity or for other variables (interest rate, periodic payment) in which we are interested.[21]

*Example:* A customer owes you $1,250 at the end of each year for the next six years.[22] What is the minimum amount you would be willing to accept now in payment of the debt if the interest rate is 10 percent.

$P = \$5,444$

$i = 0.10$

$A = \$1,250$
per period

$0 \qquad 6$

$$(P/A, 6, 0.10)\$1,250 = \$1,250\left[\frac{1 - (1 + i)^{-n}}{i}\right]$$

$$= \$1,250 \times 4.3553,$$
Table 11A–9 factor

$$= \$5,444$$

---

[21] The reciprocal of this formula can be used to calculate the *annuity* that is equivalent to a specified present sum $(A/P, n, i)$.

$$(A/P, n, i) = 1/(P/A, n, i) = i/[1 - (1 + i)^{-n}] = \left[\frac{i(1 + i)^n}{(1 + i)^n - 1}\right]$$

$(A/P, n, i)$ is commonly called the *capital recovery factor* and frequently appears in separate tables.

[22] Notice that this example is quite similar to the previous one, except that in this case the $7,500 is payable in six yearly payments rather than in one payment at the end of six years. Because the series of receipts is not as distant as the single receipt, the present value of the annuity is larger than that of the single receipt six years hence ($5,444 versus $4,234), even though the total number of dollars is the same.

---

**TABLE 11A–2  Demonstration of the Present Value of an Annuity**

| Period | (a) Amount Invested at Beginning of Period | (b) Interest Earned at 10 percent | (c) Payment | (d) Amount Invested at End of Period |
|--------|---------------------------------------------|------------------------------------|-------------|---------------------------------------|
| 1. . . . . | $5,444.00 | $544.40 | $1,250.00 | $4,738.40 |
| 2. . . . . | 4,738.40 | 473.84 | 1,250.00 | 3,962.24 |
| 3. . . . . | 3,962.24 | 396.22 | 1,250.00 | 3,108.46 |
| 4. . . . . | 3,108.46 | 310.85 | 1,250.00 | 2,169.31 |
| 5. . . . . | 2,169.31 | 216.93 | 1,250.00 | 1,136.24 |
| 6. . . . . | 1,136.24 | 113.76* | 1,250.00 | — |

Note: Column *(d)* = Column *(a)* + Column *(b)* − Column *(c)*.
* Adjusted to compensate for rounding errors.

---

That the present value of an annuity of six payments of $1,250 at 10 percent is $5,444 is shown in Table 11A–2.

**Present Value of an Annuity Due.**  For the calculation of present value, there are only four interest periods in a five-year annuity due, since payments made at the beginning of Years 2 through 5 are the equivalent of payments made at the end of Years 1 through 4. Accordingly, the present value amount of an *annuity due* for *n* years is equal to $(P/A, n - 1, i) + 1$. The last item in the formula reflects the fact that the initial payment is received immediately (at the beginning of Year 1) and therefore is already stated at its present value. As applied to Table 11A–9, the above formula suggests, for example, that the factor for a five-year annuity due is calculated by adding 1.0000 to the factor found on line 4 in the appropriate interest column.

**Present Value Tables.**  Present value tables for $1 are presented in Tables 11A–8 and 11A–9 and supply us with the factors to use in expressing any dollar figures in terms of their present values. Table 11A–8 gives the amount a person would have to invest now at various interest rates in order to have $1 at the end of various time periods in the future. Table 11A–9 gives the amount a person would have to invest now at various interest rates in order to withdraw $1 at the end of each period for various time periods.

**Infinite Annuity.**  If annuity payments (receipts) continue for a large number of periods, the *n* in the present value formula below would become very large.

$$(P/A, n, i) = \frac{1 - (1 + i)^{-n}}{i}$$

As a result, the expression $(1 + i)^{-n}$ would become very small. In fact, as *n* approaches perpetuity, $(1 + i)^{-n}$ would approach zero, and the whole formula would approach the reciprocal of the interest rate $(1/i)$. By dividing the annuity payment (receipt) by the interest rate, we can calculate its present value, assuming an indefinite time period. If *n* exceeds 40 to 50 periods, the infinite annuity is a very close approximation.

**Continuous Discounting.** With shorter compounding intervals, the future amount of any given quantity of money becomes greater. The opposite is true with respect to the discounting of amounts to present value: the shorter the interest period, the smaller the present value. With more frequent interest accumulations, more interest is earned on prior interest accumulations. Consequently, it is necessary to invest a smaller sum now if interest is compounded monthly than if it is compounded only annually. Consequently, the current cash equivalent or present value is lower.

When the compounding period becomes infinitely short, the entire present value formula becomes $1/e^{in}$. The process giving rise to this formula is called *continuous discounting;* interest is accumulated and added to principal continuously rather than only intermittently. Some authors rightly contend that continuous discounting is more accurate when future cash receipts or payments consist of continuous flows throughout a time interval rather than of discrete quantities at specified intervals.[23]

Compound interest concepts can be used whenever managerial or investment decisions require a comparison of dollar amounts at two different points in time. In these cases, consideration must be given to the time value of money. Conversion of amounts to their equivalents either in future values, or more commonly, present values, provides a meaningful base of comparison for decisions involving time as a factor. The examples in the following sections briefly illustrate the application of compound interest techniques in some accounting and financial areas and provide an opportunity for using the interest tables.

## Asset Valuation

Assets are acquired to produce future economic benefits. Presumably, in deciding to acquire an asset, an investor makes a comparison between the present outflow to acquire an asset and the future inflows from the asset. Ideally, the value placed on the asset should be equal to the present value of the expected future net receipts derived from it. Two examples follow:

*Example 1—Bank Loan and Note Receivable:*   A bank is considering lending money through the acquisition of a $50,000 face value, five-year note to be issued by a nearby municipality. The note will be held to maturity as an investment. It bears no interest explicitly, but is being offered to the bank at a price of $30,000. The bank can invest its funds in alternative opportunities yielding 8 percent. Compound interest techniques can be used in a number of ways to help the bank decide whether to lend money on this note. First, if the bank invests its $30,000 in other opportunities, the $30,000 would grow to only $44,079 [$(F/P, 5, 0.08)$

---

[23] Continuous discounting (compounding) is more useful in mathematical operations involving calculus. Theoretically, it may be more accurate for certain types of investment decisions, but it is not used for most financial transactions—borrowing and lending. Practically, it does not produce results materially different from that of annual or semiannual discounting when interest rates are not unduly high or time periods excessively long. Therefore, tables like those presented in this Appendix are more widely employed and are suitable for most situations.

$30,000 = $30,000 × 1.4693 = $44,079], which is significantly less than the $50,000 it would receive from the municipality. Alternatively, the bank could determine the present value of the note to be $34,030 [($P/F$, 5, 0.08) $50,000 = $50,000 × 0.6806 = $34,030]. If the bank wishes to earn 8 percent, it could lend up to $34,030. Since the bank has to lend only $30,000 to earn the $50,000 dollar return, the value of the asset to management ($34,030) is greater than its cost ($30,000).

*Example 2—Equipment:*   Present value techniques play a large role in analyses of capital expenditures on plant assets. Take the following example. By purchasing a new piece of machinery for $70,000, a manufacturing firm could process its product one stage further. The more valuable product would command a higher selling price and cause sales to increase by $22,000 a year. The only other cost would be $12,000 of wages for an operator. The company believes that it can sell the machine for $5,000 at the end of its useful life of 10 years. The company will not undertake this investment unless it can earn a return of 10 percent. The maximum amount that the company should offer for the equipment is the present value of the expected returns from the equipment, discounted at 10 percent. The future values consist of a net return of $10,000 each year for 10 years ($22,000 of additional sales minus $12,000 for wages) and $5,000 at the end of 10 years.

$$\text{Present value of machine} = (P/A,\ 10,\ 0.10)\$10,000 + (P/F,\ 10,\ 0.10)\$5,000$$
$$= 6.1446(\$10,000) + 0.3855(\$5,000)$$
$$= \$63,374$$

Consequently, the firm would not pay $70,000 for this asset.[24]

# Financing Decisions

We have already explored the relationship between present value concepts and bonds and notes payable. These same concepts can be extended to the valuation of other types of liabilities, such as leases, pensions, and various alternative forms of financing. Leases and pensions are discussed in Chapter 12. A few examples of the application of present value to installment contracts and deferred payment plans are given in this section.

*Example 1—Determination of Installment Payments:*   A delivery service can acquire a new truck costing $7,200 from a dealer by signing an installment note. The note is to be liquidated over a 15-month period with interest at a rate of 1 percent per month. For financial planning, management wishes to know what the monthly installment payments will be. The face amount of the note can be

---

[24] This approach is called the *net present value* method of analysis. For simplicity, we have ignored the many difficulties involved in actually determining future returns in realistic situations, including the impact of income taxes. An alternative approach, called the *discounted or time-adjusted rate of return*, solves for the interest rate that will make the present value of future receipts exactly equal to $70,000. In this case, the rate is approximately 8 percent, substantially below the desired 10 percent rate.

viewed as the present value of a series of payments of $x$ amount for 15 periods at 1 percent per period.

$$(A/P, \ 15, \ 0.01) \ \$7,200 = \$7,200/(P/A, \ 15, \ 0.01)$$
$$= \$7,200 \div 13.8651$$
$$= \$519.29$$

As a separate exercise the reader can verify that 15 payments of $519.29 will, in fact, repay the $7,200 debt plus interest at 1 percent per month.

*Example 2—Calculation of Effective Interest Rates:*   A metal fabricator purchases a stamping press costing $50,000. A deferred payment plan is arranged under which the purchaser will make a $10,000 down payment and a $46,658 payment at the end of the second year. What effective rate of interest is inherent in this arrangement? The general analysis can be set forth in terms of present value formulas as follows:

$$\$50,000 = \$10,000 + (P/F, \ 2, \ i)\$46,658$$

$$(P/F, \ 2, \ i)\$46,658 = \$40,000$$

$$(P/F, \ 2, \ i) = \$40,000 \ /\$46,658 = 0.8573$$

$$i = 8 \text{ percent (on line 2 of Table 11A–8,}$$
$$0.8573 \text{ is found in 8 percent column)}$$

*Example 3—Comparison of Financing Plans:*   A real estate developer owns a piece of land at the edge of the city. Two companies have offered to purchase it under varying financial plans, as described below:

Offer 1:   $10,000 payment at the beginning of each year for five years.
Offer 2:   $8,000 down payment plus a four-year note for $35,000 face amount, bearing interest at the rate of 12 percent payable annually (i.e., $4,200 per year).

Money is worth 16 percent to the company. If the same risk is inherent in each offer, the best one is that which has the greater present value. A comparison of Tables 11A–3 and 11A–4 indictaes that Offer 2 is the more advantageous.

---

**TABLE 11A–3**    Analysis of Offer 1 (Five-Year Annuity Due)

Total present value of cash inflows is $37,982
$(P/A, \ 4, \ 0.16) \ \$10,000 + \$10,000$ (first payment)
$(2.7982) \ (\$10,000) + \$10,000$

---

**TABLE 11A–4**    Analysis of Offer 2

Total present value of cash inflows is $39,083
$\$8,000 + (P/A, \ 4, \ 0.16) \ (\$4,200) + (P/F, \ 4, \ 0.16) \ (\$35,000)$
$\$8,000 + (2.7982) \ (\$4.200) + (0.5523) \ (\$35,000)$

# Summary

There is an old adage that time is money. Compound interest and present value concepts simply put this adage into formulas and tables. The fundamental point is that differences in the timing of cash inflows and outflows must be considered when those flows are evaluated and compared. When we are determining the future amount that is equivalent to a given sum now, compound interest is involved. When the focal point is the amount at present (at present, of course, can be any specified point in time) which is equivalent to a given sum in the future, present value is employed. Often a time-line representation similar to those employed in this Appendix helps to organize the cash flows involved and to establish the proper time frame of reference.

Varying symbols and names are used to describe and express compound amounts and present values. Some authors use $s$ (sum) or $a$ (amount) instead of $F$, $r$ (rate) instead of $i$, or $S$ (series) instead of $A$. Alternative names include future sum, future value, future worth, compound amount, and present worth. The ones used in this Appendix are either commonly employed and/or recommended by the Standardization Committee of the Engineering Economy Division of the American Society for Engineering Education. The reader should be alert, however, to the use of other symbols. In most instances, the context of the problem or the magnitude of the interest factor will reveal whether future amounts or present values are involved.

Table 11A–5 summarizes the four major interest concepts and symbols discussed in this Appendix.

**TABLE 11A–5**    Summary of Symbols and Formulas

| Table | Name | Symbol | Formula | Alternative Symbol |
|-------|------|--------|---------|--------------------|
| 11A–6 | Future Amount of a $1 Present Value | $(F/P, n, i)$ | $(1 + i)^n$ | $a$ or $a_{\overline{n}|i}$ |
| 11A–7 | Future Amount of an Annuity of $1 | $(F/A, n, i)$ | $\dfrac{(1 + i)^n - 1}{i}$ | $A$ or $A_{\overline{n}|i}$ |
| 11A–8 | Present Value of a $1 Future Amount | $(P/F, n, i)$ | $\dfrac{1}{(1 + i)^n}$ | $p$ or $p_{\overline{n}|i}$ |
| 11A–9 | Present Value of an Annuity of $1 | $(P/A, n, i)$ | $\dfrac{1 - (1 + i)^{-n}}{i}$ | $P$ or $P_{\overline{n}|i}$ |

**TABLE 11A–6** Future Amount of $1 [F/P, n, i]

| Number of Periods | Rate of Interest | | | | | | | | |
|---|---|---|---|---|---|---|---|---|---|
| | 1% | 3% | 4% | 5% | 6% | 8% | 10% | 12% | 16% |
| 1 | 1.0100 | 1.0300 | 1.0400 | 1.0500 | 1.0600 | 1.0800 | 1.1000 | 1.1200 | 1.1600 |
| 2 | 1.0201 | 1.0609 | 1.0816 | 1.1025 | 1.1236 | 1.1664 | 1.2100 | 1.2544 | 1.3456 |
| 3 | 1.0303 | 1.0927 | 1.1249 | 1.1576 | 1.1910 | 1.2597 | 1.3310 | 1.4049 | 1.5609 |
| 4 | 1.0406 | 1.1255 | 1.1699 | 1.2155 | 1.2625 | 1.3605 | 1.4641 | 1.5735 | 1.8106 |
| 5 | 1.0510 | 1.1593 | 1.2167 | 1.2763 | 1.3382 | 1.4693 | 1.6105 | 1.7623 | 2.1003 |
| 6 | 1.0615 | 1.1941 | 1.2653 | 1.3401 | 1.4185 | 1.5869 | 1.7716 | 1.9738 | 2.4364 |
| 7 | 1.0721 | 1.2299 | 1.3159 | 1.4071 | 1.5036 | 1.7138 | 1.9487 | 2.2107 | 2.8262 |
| 8 | 1.0829 | 1.2668 | 1.3686 | 1.4775 | 1.5938 | 1.8509 | 2.1436 | 2.4760 | 3.2784 |
| 9 | 1.0937 | 1.3048 | 1.4233 | 1.5513 | 1.6895 | 1.9990 | 2.3579 | 2.7731 | 3.8030 |
| 10 | 1.1046 | 1.3439 | 1.4802 | 1.6289 | 1.7908 | 2.1589 | 2.5937 | 3.1059 | 4.4114 |
| 11 | 1.1157 | 1.3842 | 1.5395 | 1.7103 | 1.8983 | 2.3316 | 2.8531 | 3.4786 | 5.1173 |
| 12 | 1.1268 | 1.4258 | 1.6010 | 1.7959 | 2.0122 | 2.5182 | 3.1384 | 3.8960 | 5.9360 |
| 13 | 1.1381 | 1.4685 | 1.6651 | 1.8856 | 2.1329 | 2.7196 | 3.4523 | 4.3635 | 6.8858 |
| 14 | 1.1495 | 1.5126 | 1.7317 | 1.9799 | 2.2609 | 2.9372 | 3.7975 | 4.8871 | 7.9875 |
| 15 | 1.1610 | 1.5580 | 1.8009 | 2.0789 | 2.3966 | 3.1722 | 4.1773 | 5.4736 | 9.2655 |
| 20 | 1.2202 | 1.8061 | 2.1911 | 2.6533 | 3.2071 | 4.6610 | 6.7275 | 9.6463 | 19.4608 |
| 30 | 1.3478 | 2.4273 | 3.2434 | 4.3219 | 5.7435 | 10.0627 | 17.4494 | 29.9599 | 85.8499 |

**TABLE 11A–7** Future Amount of an Annuity of $1 [F/A, n, i]

| Number of Periods | Rate of Interest | | | | | | | | |
|---|---|---|---|---|---|---|---|---|---|
| | 1% | 3% | 4% | 5% | 6% | 8% | 10% | 12% | 16% |
| 1 | 1.0000 | 1.0000 | 1.0000 | 1.0000 | 1.0000 | 1.0000 | 1.0000 | 1.0000 | 1.0000 |
| 2 | 2.0100 | 2.0300 | 2.0400 | 2.0500 | 2.0600 | 2.0800 | 2.1000 | 2.1200 | 2.1600 |
| 3 | 3.0301 | 3.0909 | 3.1216 | 3.1525 | 3.1836 | 3.2464 | 3.3100 | 3.3744 | 3.5056 |
| 4 | 4.0604 | 4.1836 | 4.2465 | 4.3101 | 4.3746 | 4.5061 | 4.6410 | 4.7793 | 5.0665 |
| 5 | 5.1010 | 5.3091 | 5.4163 | 5.5256 | 5.6371 | 5.8666 | 6.1051 | 6.3529 | 6.8771 |
| 6 | 6.1520 | 6.4684 | 6.6330 | 6.8019 | 6.9753 | 7.3359 | 7.7156 | 8.1152 | 8.9775 |
| 7 | 7.2135 | 7.6625 | 7.8983 | 8.1420 | 8.3938 | 8.9228 | 9.4872 | 10.0890 | 11.4139 |
| 8 | 8.2857 | 8.8923 | 9.2142 | 9.5491 | 9.8975 | 10.6366 | 11.4359 | 12.2997 | 14.2401 |
| 9 | 9.3685 | 10.1591 | 10.5828 | 11.0266 | 11.4913 | 12.4876 | 13.5795 | 14.7757 | 17.5185 |
| 10 | 10.4622 | 11.4639 | 12.0061 | 12.5779 | 13.1808 | 14.4866 | 15.9374 | 17.5487 | 21.3215 |
| 11 | 11.5668 | 12.8078 | 13.4864 | 14.2068 | 14.9716 | 16.6455 | 18.5312 | 20.6546 | 25.7329 |
| 12 | 12.6825 | 14.1920 | 15.0258 | 15.9171 | 16.8699 | 18.9771 | 21.3843 | 24.1331 | 30.8502 |
| 13 | 13.8093 | 15.6178 | 16.6268 | 17.7130 | 18.8821 | 21.4953 | 24.5227 | 28.0291 | 36.7862 |
| 14 | 14.9474 | 17.0863 | 18.2919 | 19.5986 | 21.0151 | 24.2149 | 27.9750 | 32.3926 | 43.6720 |
| 15 | 16.0969 | 18.5989 | 20.0236 | 21.5786 | 23.2760 | 27.1521 | 31.7725 | 37.2797 | 51.6595 |
| 20 | 22.0190 | 26.8704 | 29.7781 | 33.0660 | 36.7856 | 45.7620 | 57.2750 | 72.0524 | 115.3797 |
| 30 | 34.7849 | 47.5754 | 56.0849 | 66.4388 | 79.0582 | 113.2832 | 164.4940 | 241.3327 | 530.3117 |

Note: For an annuity due, take one more period and subtract 1.0000.

**TABLE 11A–8**  Present Value of $1 $[P/F, n, i]$

| Number of Periods | Rate of Interest | | | | | | | | |
|---|---|---|---|---|---|---|---|---|---|
| | *1%* | *3%* | *4%* | *5%* | *6%* | *8%* | *10%* | *12%* | *16%* |
| 1 | 0.9901 | 0.9709 | 0.9615 | 0.9524 | 0.9434 | 0.9259 | 0.9091 | 0.8929 | 0.8621 |
| 2 | 0.9803 | 0.9426 | 0.9246 | 0.9070 | 0.8900 | 0.8573 | 0.8264 | 0.7972 | 0.7432 |
| 3 | 0.9706 | 0.9151 | 0.8890 | 0.8638 | 0.8396 | 0.7938 | 0.7513 | 0.7118 | 0.6407 |
| 4 | 0.9610 | 0.8885 | 0.8548 | 0.8227 | 0.7921 | 0.7350 | 0.6830 | 0.6355 | 0.5523 |
| 5 | 0.9515 | 0.8626 | 0.8219 | 0.7835 | 0.7473 | 0.6806 | 0.6209 | 0.5674 | 0.4761 |
| 6 | 0.9420 | 0.8375 | 0.7903 | 0.7462 | 0.7050 | 0.6302 | 0.5645 | 0.5066 | 0.4104 |
| 7 | 0.9327 | 0.8131 | 0.7599 | 0.7107 | 0.6651 | 0.5835 | 0.5132 | 0.4524 | 0.3538 |
| 8 | 0.9235 | 0.7894 | 0.7307 | 0.6768 | 0.6274 | 0.5403 | 0.4665 | 0.4039 | 0.3050 |
| 9 | 0.9143 | 0.7664 | 0.7026 | 0.6446 | 0.5919 | 0.5002 | 0.4241 | 0.3606 | 0.2630 |
| 10 | 0.9053 | 0.7441 | 0.6756 | 0.6139 | 0.5584 | 0.4632 | 0.3855 | 0.3220 | 0.2267 |
| 11 | 0.8963 | 0.7224 | 0.6496 | 0.5847 | 0.5268 | 0.4289 | 0.3505 | 0.2875 | 0.1954 |
| 12 | 0.8874 | 0.7014 | 0.6246 | 0.5568 | 0.4970 | 0.3971 | 0.3186 | 0.2567 | 0.1685 |
| 13 | 0.8787 | 0.6810 | 0.6006 | 0.5303 | 0.4688 | 0.3677 | 0.2897 | 0.2292 | 0.1452 |
| 14 | 0.8700 | 0.6611 | 0.5775 | 0.5051 | 0.4423 | 0.3405 | 0.2633 | 0.2046 | 0.1252 |
| 15 | 0.8613 | 0.6419 | 0.5553 | 0.4810 | 0.4173 | 0.3152 | 0.2394 | 0.1827 | 0.1079 |
| 20 | 0.8195 | 0.5537 | 0.4564 | 0.3769 | 0.3118 | 0.2146 | 0.1486 | 0.1037 | 0.0514 |
| 30 | 0.7419 | 0.4120 | 0.3083 | 0.2314 | 0.1741 | 0.0994 | 0.0573 | 0.0334 | 0.0116 |

**TABLE 11A–9**  Present Value of an Annuity of $1 $[P/A, n, i]$

| Number of Periods | Rate of Interest | | | | | | | | |
|---|---|---|---|---|---|---|---|---|---|
| | *1%* | *3%* | *4%* | *5%* | *6%* | *8%* | *10%* | *12%* | *16%* |
| 1 | 0.9901 | 0.9709 | 0.9615 | 0.9524 | 0.9434 | 0.9259 | 0.9091 | 0.8929 | 0.8621 |
| 2 | 1.9704 | 1.9135 | 1.8861 | 1.8594 | 1.8334 | 1.7833 | 1.7355 | 1.6901 | 1.6052 |
| 3 | 2.9410 | 2.8286 | 2.7751 | 2.7232 | 2.6730 | 2.5771 | 2.4869 | 2.4018 | 2.2459 |
| 4 | 3.9020 | 3.7171 | 3.6299 | 3.5460 | 3.4651 | 3.3121 | 3.1699 | 3.0374 | 2.7982 |
| 5 | 4.8534 | 4.5797 | 4.4518 | 4.3295 | 4.2124 | 3.9927 | 3.7908 | 3.6048 | 3.2743 |
| 6 | 5.7955 | 5.4172 | 5.2421 | 5.0757 | 4.9173 | 4.6229 | 4.3553 | 4.1114 | 3.6847 |
| 7 | 6.7282 | 6.2303 | 6.0021 | 5.7864 | 5.5824 | 5.2064 | 4.8684 | 4.5638 | 4.0386 |
| 8 | 7.6517 | 7.0197 | 6.7327 | 6.4632 | 6.2098 | 5.7466 | 5.3349 | 4.9676 | 4.3436 |
| 9 | 8.5660 | 7.7861 | 7.4353 | 7.1078 | 6.8017 | 6.2469 | 5.7590 | 5.3283 | 4.6065 |
| 10 | 9.4713 | 8.5302 | 8.1109 | 7.7217 | 7.3601 | 6.7101 | 6.1446 | 5.6502 | 4.8332 |
| 11 | 10.3676 | 9.2526 | 8.7605 | 8.3064 | 7.8869 | 7.1390 | 6.4951 | 5.9377 | 5.0286 |
| 12 | 11.2551 | 9.9540 | 9.3851 | 8.8633 | 8.3838 | 7.5361 | 6.8137 | 6.1944 | 5.1971 |
| 13 | 12.1337 | 10.6450 | 9.9856 | 9.3936 | 8.8527 | 7.9038 | 7.1034 | 6.4236 | 5.3423 |
| 14 | 13.0037 | 11.2961 | 10.5631 | 9.8986 | 9.2950 | 8.2442 | 7.3667 | 6.6282 | 5.4675 |
| 15 | 13.8651 | 11.9379 | 11.1184 | 10.3797 | 9.7123 | 8.5595 | 7.6061 | 6.8109 | 5.5755 |
| 20 | 18.0455 | 14.8775 | 13.5903 | 12.4622 | 11.4699 | 9.8182 | 8.5136 | 7.4694 | 5.9288 |
| 30 | 25.8077 | 19.6004 | 17.2920 | 15.3725 | 13.7648 | 11.2578 | 9.4269 | 8.0552 | 6.1772 |

Note: For an annuity due, take one less period and add 1.0000.

# Appendix B: Accounting for Bonds on Investor's Books

Chapter 11 focuses on liabilities, particularly bond liabilities. This Appendix illustrates how bond transactions would be reflected in the lender's accounts.

Because the bond purchaser is simply on the other side of the coin from the bond issuer, much symmetry can be expected and, in fact, does exist. The bond represents simultaneously a liability to the issuer and an asset to the purchaser. The issuer incurs interest expense, while the investor earns interest revenue. The cash payments made by the issuer equal the cash received by the investor. The underlying concepts of present value and interest are the same.

Nevertheless, the symmetry of bond accounting on the issuer's and investor's books is not complete. Four specific differences in procedure may be present:

1. Often many different individuals or institutions purchase portions of a corporate bond issue. Accordingly, the dollar amounts on the investor's books may represent only a small fraction of their counterparts on the issuer's books. Only in a private placement where the lender acquired the entire bond issue would the two amounts coincide.

2. The investor includes as part of the cost of the bond investment the amount of the broker's commission incurred upon the purchase. The asset cost to the lender may be slightly more than the proportionate proceeds to the borrower. Therefore, the effective interest yield may be slightly less for the former than the effective interest cost incurred by the latter.

3. The amortization methods followed by both parties to the bond transaction may be different. Perhaps the investor could employ the straight-line procedure without materially changing the results obtainable under the effective interest approach.

4. Investors traditionally do not establish a separate account for the bond premium or discount. Any amortization takes place through direct adjustment of the bond asset account.

Table 11B–1 shows the bond accounting on the investor's books for the two $10,000, 10 percent bond issues illustrated in Tables 11–3 and 11–4. Recall that the bond selling at a discount had an effective rate of 12 percent, and the bond selling at a premium had an effective rate of 8 percent. The investor is assumed to have acquired one fifth ($2,000 face value) of the bonds. To simplify matters, brokers' commissions and underwriters' costs are assumed away. However, let's assume that the effective interest method is used for the bond purchased at a discount, and the straight-line method is used for the bond purchased at a premium.

In the case of the first bond, the investor earns at the effective rate of 12 percent times the amount actually loaned ($1,856 in the first year and $1,879 in the second). Only part of the revenue is received in cash. The rest is added to the bond asset as its present value moves from the initial amount of $1,856 to the maturity value of $2,000. Just as the carrying value of the issuer's liability gradually grows over time with a discount bond, the investor's asset increases for the same reasons. The increase in liability is recorded indirectly through a reduction in bond discount; the increase in the asset value is recorded directly, but the underlying concept is the same.

The investor would show on the balance sheet Investment in Bonds of $1,904 ($1,856 + $23 + $25) among its noncurrent assets at the end of the second year.

**TABLE 11B-1**   Bond Accounting from the Perspective of the Investor

| | Discount Bond | | | Premium Bond | | |
|---|---|---|---|---|---|---|
| Jan. 1 | Investment in Bonds<br>  Cash<br>  (20% × $9279) | 1856 | 1856 | Investment in Bonds<br>  Cash<br>  (20% × $10,799) | 2160 | 2160 |
| Dec. 31<br>First Year | Cash<br>Investment in Bonds<br>  Interest Revenue<br>  $2000 × .10  = $200<br>  $1856 × .12  = $223<br>  $ 223 − $200 = $ 23 | 200<br>23 | 223 | Cash<br>  Interest Revenue<br>  Investment in Bonds<br>  $2000 × .10 = $200<br>  $ 160/5     = $ 32<br>  $ 200 − $32 = $168 | 200 | 168<br>32 |
| Dec. 31<br>Second Year | Cash<br>Investment in Bonds<br>  Interest Revenue<br>  $2000 × .10   = $200<br>  ($1856 + $23)<br>   × .12      = $225<br>  $225 − $200  = $ 25 | 200<br>25 | 225 | Cash<br>  Interest Revenue<br>  Investment in Bonds<br>  $2000 × .10 = $200<br>  $160/5      = $ 32<br><br>  $200 − $32  = $168 | 200 | 168<br>32 |

Notice that this equals 20 percent of the carrying value of the liability (20% × $9,519 = $1,904) of the issuer of the bonds at the end of Year 2 (see Table 11–3).

The carrying value of the bond investment purchased at a premium gradually moves from its initial value of $2,160 to its maturity value of $2,000. A portion of each year's cash receipt is a return of the initial investment. At the end of the second year, the investment would appear on the balance sheet at $2,096 ($2,160 − $32 − $32). Of course, in this case, the carrying value does not equate exactly to 20 percent of the borrower's liability because straight-line amortization is being used by the investor.

# PROBLEMS AND CASETTES

## 11–1. Interpretation of Bond Quotations and Valuations
Included among the listing of bonds trading on the New York Exchange in *The Wall Street Journal* on Tuesday, December 8, 1987 were seven separate issues of AT&T. A portion of the information presented for those bond issues appears below (items deliberately omitted are indicated by letters).

| Bond Description | | Closing Price as a Percentage |
|---|---|---|
| Interest Rate | Due Date | of Face Value on December 7 |
| 8 5/8% | 2026 | (A) |
| 8 5/8% | 2007 | 89 3/8% |
| (B) | 2005 | 91 3/4% |
| 7 1/8% | 2003 | 78% |
| 7% | 2001 | 78 7/8% |
| 8 3/4% | 2000 | 94 3/8% |
| 3 7/8% | 1990 | 91 1/4% |

**Required:**

Answer each of the following questions and explain your reasoning.

a. A securities broker tells you that you can buy AT&T's 7 1/8 percent bond issue due in the year 2003 at "78 plus accrued interest." Explain in your own words what the phrase in quotation marks means.

b. "The 8 3/4 percent issue due in the year 2000 is selling at 94 3/8 because, of all the bond issues, it was originally issued at the smallest discount." Comment on the accuracy of this statement.

c. The missing market price (A) is either 85 3/8 percent or 92 3/8 percent. Which one do you think it is and why?

d. The missing nominal interest rate (B) is either 8 3/5 percent or 8 4/5 percent. Which one do you think it is and why?

e. A friend confides in you that he cannot understand how a 3 7/8 percent bond can sell at a higher price (91 1/4) than a 7 percent bond sells for (78 7/8). He thinks the bond market knows nothing about present value concepts. Provide an explanation to resolve this misunderstanding.

f. The prices of all of AT&T's bond issues are below face value. Is this necessarily a reflection of a negative view of AT&T's credit rating by the bond market?

## 11–2. Bond Valuation and Entries

On January 1, 1990, the Scotch Company issued $800,000 face amount of 15-year, 8 percent bonds. The bonds were priced to yield investors an effective interest rate of 10 percent. Interest is paid annually on January 1. The Scotch Company closes its books annually on December 31.

**Required:**

a. Calculate the price at which the bonds were issued on January 1, 1990.

b. Prepare all journal entries necessary on Scotch Company's books during 1990 in connection with the bond issue. Use effective interest amortization.

c. Indicate what amounts and accounts would appear among the long-term liabilities in connection with these bonds on a balance sheet prepared on January 1, *1995*. Calculate the amounts directly; do not prepare a complete amortization schedule year by year.

d. Assume that bonds with similar risk to Scotch's are yielding a market rate of interest of 15 percent on January 1, 1995. Would your answer to c change?

## 11–3. Simple Bond Retirement

The Monroe Corporation issued $100,000 face value of 14 percent bonds for $107,000 cash on January 1, 1989. Interest is paid annually, and the effective interest rate was 12 percent. The bonds are callable at 108 during the first five years. Toward the end of 1990, a new president of the company is selected. He is opposed to the use of large amounts of borrowed money and insists that the bonds be retired immediately. The bonds are called in and retired on January 1, 1991.

**Required:**

a. Record the bond issuance on January 1, 1989.

b. Record the payment of interest on January 1, 1990 and January 1, 1991.

c. Record the retirement of the bonds on January 1, 1991.

## 11-4. Installment Notes

Pressler Motors, Inc. borrowed $500,000 from the local bank to finance its inventory of automobiles. The company agreed to pay the loan in twelve *monthly* installments of $44,424.30. The payments are made at the end of each month.

### Required:

a. Demonstrate that the effective interest rate on the loan is 1 percent a month.
b. Prepare journal entries to record the borrowing and the first two monthly payments on the books of Pressler Motors. Assume the company uses a direct recording of the liability.
c. Repeat part b but assume the company employs a contra account (Notes Payable—Discount) approach.
d. Record the loan and the first two monthly receipts on the books of the bank. Use the contra account approach.

## 11-5. Completion and Interpretation of Bond Amortization Table

The following is a partially completed amortization table prepared by Metcalf Corporation to account for its issuance of $100,000 face amount of bonds. Amounts in the table have been rounded to the nearest dollar. These bonds mature in five years and pay interest annually.

| Year | Interest Expense | Interest Paid | Premium Amortization | Unamortized Premium | Year-End Carrying Amount |
|------|------------------|---------------|----------------------|---------------------|--------------------------|
| 0 | | | | $4,213 | $104,213 |
| 1 | $6,253 | $7,000 | _____ | _____ | _____ |
| 2 | _____ | _____ | _____ | _____ | _____ |

### Required:

a. What is the stated or coupon rate of interest on this bond issue?
b. What was the effective market rate of interest when the bonds were issued?
c. Is the company using the effective interest method or the straight-line method for the calculation of interest expense and premium amortization? How do you know?
d. Determine the correct amount for each of the eight blank spaces in the table using the effective interest method.
e. Explain why interest *expense* in Year 2 is less than in Year 1.
f. The vice president of finance has suggested that the issuance of the bonds should be recorded as follows:

| | | |
|---|---|---|
| Cash . . . . . . . . . . . . . . . . . . . . . . . . . . . . | 104,213 | |
| Bonds Payable . . . . . . . . . . . . . . . . . . . | | 100,000 |
| Gain on Issuance of Bonds . . . . . . . . . . . . . | | 4,213 |

Explain why this entry is not appropriate.

## 11-6. Supply Missing Data for Bond Issues

The following table contains partial information on three separate bond issues. From the information given, calculate the missing items identified by the letters (A) through (F). Assume interest is paid annually.

|                              | *Issue #1*  | *Issue #2* | *Issue #3* |
|------------------------------|-------------|------------|------------|
| Face value                   | $100,000    | $50,000    | (F)        |
| Nominal interest rate        | 8%          | 12%        | 10         |
| Life of bond                 | 10 years    | (D)        | 20         |
| Effective interest rate      | 10%         | (C)        | (E)        |
| Issue price                  | (A)         | $57,607    | $170,128   |
| Interest expense—first year  | (B)         | $ 5,761    | $ 20,415   |

### 11–7. Entries for Bonds Issued at Discount

On July 1, 1990, the Lederer Company issued $300,000 face amount of 10 percent, 10-year bonds. The bonds were issued when the market rate of interest was slightly over 12 percent (6 percent each six months). Lederer Company received $265,588 for the bonds. Interest is payable *semiannually* on July 1 and January 1.

**Required:**

a. Derive the $265,588 issue price by using the present value tables in the Appendix to this chapter.
b. Prepare journal entries for the Lederer Company as follows: July 1, 1990; December 31, 1990 (end of accounting period); January 1, 1991; and July 1, 1991.
c. If Lederer were to prepare a balance sheet on July 1, 1995, what accounts and amounts would appear concerning the bonds? (Calculate amounts directly; do not prepare a complete amortization schedule.)

### 11–8. Implied and Imputed Interest on Notes Payable

On January 1, 1990, Middleton Construction Company entered into the following two contracts:

1. Purchased land having a $75,000 market value. Middleton pays $15,000 cash now and promises to pay $23,282 on December 31 in each of the next three years.
2. Purchased equipment by issuing a 5 percent, six-year note for $25,000. The interest of $1,250 is paid annually on January 1 and the principal is due on January 1, 1996.

**Required:**

a. Determine the implied interest rate in the first contract and prepare the general journal entry to record the land purchase on January 1, 1990.
b. Prepare the journal entry for the December 31, 1990 payment on the contract for land.
c. Assume that Middleton's best alternative source of funds for acquiring the equipment would entail an interest charge of 10 percent. Record the acquisition of the equipment using a 10 percent imputed interest rate.
d. Prepare the journal entry for the January 1, 1991 payment on the contract for equipment.

## 11–9. Correction of Erroneous Entry for Bond Refunding

RES Corporation shows the following accounts on its trial balance at the end of 1990.

| | | |
|---|---:|---|
| Bonds payable, 10% (due in 2000) | $200,000 | Cr. |
| Unamortized bond premium | 6,400 | Cr. |
| Unamortized bond issue costs | 1,800 | Dr. |

The bonds are callable at 104 percent of face value. The company has an opportunity to borrow money from an insurance company. The terms require issuing a 20-year, 6 percent bond for $220,000 to be purchased by the insurance company for $176,800. Not only does the new bond carry a lower interest rate, but it also contains fewer restrictions on the company's dividend policies.

Accordingly, RES calls in and retires the old bond and issues the new one to the insurance company. The chief accountant makes the following entry:

| | | |
|---|---:|---:|
| Bonds Payable, 10% | 200,000 | |
| Unamortized Bond Premium | 6,400 | |
| Cost of Successful Refunding | 49,600 | |
| Unamortized Bond Issue Costs | | 1,800 |
| Bonds Payable, 6% | | 220,000 |
| Cash | | 34,200 |

The credit to Cash is the difference between the $208,000 disbursed to call the old bonds and the $176,800 received from the issuance of the new bonds, plus $2,000 in costs involved in calling the old bonds and $1,000 in fees associated with issuing the new ones.

### Required:

*a.* Determine the effective interest rate being charged by the insurance company.

*b.* Prepare journal entries to record the refunding of the bonds in accordance with generally accepted accounting principles.

*c.* The chief accountant describes the Cost of Successful Refunding account as an intangible asset to be amortized over the next 10 years, the remaining life of the old bond issue. Based on your entry in *b*, determine exactly what elements comprise the $49,600. How should each of these elements be treated and why?

## 11–10. Entries for Bond Issuance and Conversion

The Cooper Corporation issued $100,000 of seven-year, 10 percent convertible bonds on January 1, 1990. Interest is payable *semiannually* on July 1 and January 1. The bonds were issued at 90.7 percent of their face amount to yield an effective interest rate of 12 percent. Each $1,000 bond is convertible into 30 shares of Cooper Corporation common stock. On January 1, 1993, holders of $40,000 face amount of the bonds decide to convert their bonds into common stock. The common stock has a current market value of $40 per share on the conversion date.

**Required:**

a. Use present value tables to verify that the effective interest rate is 12 percent per year (6 percent per six months).

b. Prepare the journal entries during 1990 in connection with this bond issue. Cooper's accounting period ends on December 31.

c. Use present value tables to demonstrate that the carrying value of the entire bond issue on January 1, 1993 was $93,789.

d. Prepare the journal entry to reflect the conversion on January 1, 1993.

**11–11. Journal Entries for Installment Note**

Dursluk Company purchased a delivery truck for $10,000 on July 1, 1990. The purchase was financed by an installment note in the total amount of $11,787.84. This amount is to be paid in 36 monthly installments of $327.44, beginning August 1. The annual interest rate is 11.011 percent (.9176 percent per month). The note contains a provision allowing Dursluk to increase the size of the monthly payment to pay off the note before the end of 36 months.

**Required:**

a. Prepare journal entries for Dursluk on July 1 and also to record payments on August 1 and September 1. Use the direct method of recording the liability.

b. Repeat part *a* but use the indirect (contra account) method of recording the installment note.

c. Beginning with the October 1 payment, Dursluk Company decided to increase the monthly amount to $400. Prepare the journal entries on October 1 and on November 1 using the direct method of recording.

**11–12. Zero-Coupon Bonds**

Amereeh Corporation issued $500,000 face value of zero-coupon bonds on January 1, 1991. The bonds mature on January 1, 2001.

**Required:**

a. Explain why an investor would be willing to buy bonds that pay zero interest.

b. If at the time the bonds were issued investors could earn 16 percent on bonds of similar risk, how much would a rational investor be willing to pay for a $1,000 face value bond of Amereeh.

c. Assume that Amereeh received $161,000 from issuance of the bonds. Prepare the journal entry to record the sale of the bonds on January 1, 1991.

d. At what effective rate were the bonds issued? Prepare the journal entry on December 31, 1991 to record accrued interest expense.

**11–13. Choice of Nominal Interest Rates for Bond Issue**

The board of directors of Nodice Corporation is trying to decide whether to issue its $5 million of seven-year bonds with a *nominal* rate of 8 percent or 12 percent. The vice president of finance indicates that the current *market* rate of interest for bonds of similar type and risk is 10 percent. Interest would be payable annually.

**Required:**

a. Calculate the proceeds from the bond issue if it is printed with a nominal rate of (1) 8 percent and (2) 12 percent.

b. Should Nodice Corporation select the 12 percent nominal rate, in light of the fact that it produces greater proceeds with no greater face amount of bonds or market rate of interest?

c. Calculate the interest expense for the first two years under each of the coupon arrangements. Explain why the interest expense declines in the second year in one case but increases in the second year in the other.

## 11–14. Zero-Coupon Notes

Odnumelet Group Inc. offered for sale on August 15, 1990 the following two issues of long-term notes:

| | |
|---|---|
| $10,500,000 | Zero-Coupon Senior Notes due August 15, 1995; Price, 61.39% |
| $11,500,000 | Zero-Coupon Junior Notes due August 15, 1996; Price, 49.70% |

**Required:**

a. Give two reasons why the price of the 1996 notes is lower than that of the 1995 notes.

b. What is the effective interest rate for each of the notes? (Use six-month interest periods.)

c. What are the total proceeds received by Odnumelet from issuing the notes? Prepare the journal entry to record their issuance.

d. Prepare journal entries to record the interest expense on each note for the first year.

e. What was Odnumelet's interest expense on the 1995 notes in the second year?

f. What was Odnumelet's interest expense on the 1996 notes in the *last* year?

g. What is the total interest expense over the six-year period?

## 11–15. Entries and Interpretation of Bond Refunding

The Orrison Company issued 15-year bonds with a face value of $1 million on January 1, 1986. The nominal rate of interest was 10 percent. The bonds were issued on an annual-yield basis of 12 percent, so that the original issue discount was $136,210. Interest is paid annually, and the company uses the effective interest method for amortization of bond discount.

On December 31, 1992 the bonds appeared on the balance sheet as follows:

| | |
|---|---:|
| Bonds payable . . . . . . . . . . . . . . . . . . | $1,000,000 |
| Less: Unamortized bond discount . . . . . . . . | 99,336 |
| | $ 900,664 |

Other elements in the company's financial structure included $380,000 of current liabilities and $1,030,000 of stockholders' equity.

Because of an increase in market rates of interest, the market price of the bonds has dropped to 87.5 percent of face value. The company has an opportunity to borrow money from an insurance company. The terms would be an 8-year, 13.5 percent note for $875,000 to be acquired by the insurance company at face value. Accordingly, Orrison issues the long-term note to the insurance company and uses the proceeds to buy back and retire its bonds.

**Required:**

a. Show how the carrying value of the bond on December 31, 1992 could be calculated directly using present value tables. (Your answer may not be exact because of rounding in the present value tables.)

b. Prepare journal entries to record the refunding (retirement of the old bonds and issuance of the new long-term note) in accordance with generally accepted accounting principles.

c. What was the ratio of total liabilities to total assets (total liabilities plus stockholders' equity) before and after the refunding?

d. Is the refunding decision a good one for the company? If not, then why does the entry in b show a gain and why does the ratio in c show a decline?

**11–16. In-Substance Defeasance of Debt**

On December 31, 1989 Rellit Company issued $300,000 of 10-year bonds. The bonds carried a 12 percent coupon interest rate and were issued at a slight premium. On December 31, 1991 the carrying value of the bonds is:

| | | |
|---|---|---|
| 12% Bonds Payable due 1999 . . . . . . . . | $300,000 | |
| Premium on bonds payable . . . . . . . . . | 6,200 | $306,200 |

On December 31, 1991, Rellit purchases U.S. government securities for $288,000. The securities have a face value of $300,000, carry a 12 percent coupon interest rate, and mature on December 31, 1999. The securities are placed in an irrevocable trust with the interest and maturity amounts to be used solely to satisfy the bond obligations.

**Required:**

a. Prepare the journal entry to record the transactions on December 31, 1991.

b. Why was Rellit able to purchase the U.S. government securities at a discount?

c. Why might Rellit have chosen an in-substance defeasance instead of simply calling the bonds in for a simple retirement?

**11–17. Convertible Bonds**

On January 1, 1990 Nago Corporation issued $500,000 of convertible bonds with a 10-year maturity value. The bonds earned a 10 percent nominal interest rate to be paid annually; they were sold at $426,260 to yield 12 percent. The bonds are convertible into Nago Corporation capital stock according to the following terms:

From 1990 to 1994, each $1,000 bond can be exchanged for
50 shares of capital stock.
From 1995 to maturity, each $1,000 bond can be exchanged for
40 shares of common stock.

The bonds are redeemable at par value at the company's option at any time.

The following transactions occurred in subsequent years in connection with these bonds.

1. On January 1, 1992, bonds having a maturity value of $200,000 were converted into capital stock. The current market price of the stock was $25 per share.
2. On January 1, 1994, bonds having a maturity value of $200,000 were converted into capital stock. The current market price of the stock was $31 per share.
3. On January 1, 1997, Nago called the remaining $100,000 maturity value of bonds for redemption. Ninety percent of the bonds were immediately converted into common stock. The current market price of the stock was $35 per share. The other $10,000 of the bonds were retired.

**Required:**

a. Prepare the journal entry to record the conversion of bonds on January 1, 1992. In calculating the carrying value of the bonds, assume Nago uses the straight-line method for amortization of bond discount.
b. Did the bondholders who converted gain from the conversion? If so, should Nago show a "loss on bond conversion"?
c. Prepare the journal entry to record the conversion of bonds on January 1, 1994. Again assume straight-line amortization of bond discount.
d. Prepare the journal entry to record the conversion and retirement of bonds on January 1, 1997.
e. Why did some bondholders not convert before 1997? What advantage did the call provision provide to Nago Corporation?

## 11–18. Imputed Interest on Notes Receivable

Hettenshed, Inc. decided to close one of its plants and to sell the land and building. Hettenshed received a three-year, $900,000 note receivable bearing interest at a nominal rate of 2 percent. The following entry was made to record the sale on January 1, 1991:

| | | |
|---|---:|---:|
| Notes Receivable. . . . . . . . . . . . . | 900,000 | |
| Accumulated Depreciation . . . . . . . . | 690,000 | |
| Land. . . . . . . . . . . . . . . . | | 210,000 |
| Building . . . . . . . . . . . . . | | 1,155,000 |
| Gain on Sale of Plant . . . . . . . . | | 225,000 |

Assume that 10 percent is a reasonable interest rate to be imputed to the note.

**Required:**

a. Determine the present value of the note receivable using an imputed interest rate of 10 percent.
b. What was the real gain on sale of the plant? Prepare an *adjusting* entry to *correct* the sales entry actually made.
c. Prepare journal entries to recognize the interest earned and interest collected each year and to record the collection of the note on January 1, 1994.

## 11–19. Actual In-Substance Defeasance

Baxter Travenol Laboratories and Burlington Industries were two of a number of companies that entered into in-substance defeasances of bond issues during 1984.

The notes to their 1984 financial statements describing these transactions are reproduced below:

### Burlington Industries, Inc. (September 1984)

During fiscal 1984, United States Government securities were purchased at a cost of $10,317,000 and deposited in an irrevocable trust to satisfy scheduled principal and interest payments on $5,000,000 of the 4.75% sinking fund debentures due in 1989 and 1990, $5,720,000 of the 4.125% notes due in 1989 and $4,280,000 of the 4.70% notes due in 1989. The debt issues and government securities were removed from the balance sheet in an in-substance defeasance transaction resulting in a net after-tax gain of $2,316,000 or 8 cents per share. During fiscal 1984, none of this debt was retired by the trustee.

### Baxter Travenol Laboratories, Inc. (December 1984)

In February, 1984, a wholly owned subsidiary of the company issued 200,000,000 Deutsche Mark ("DM") 7.25% bonds due in 1994, which are guaranteed by the company. The proceeds were used to purchase an approximate equivalent amount of German government securities maturing in 1994, yielding 8.25%. In September, 1984, the company extinguished the DM bonds (approximately $65,700,000) through an in-substance defeasance. This in-substance defeasance was accomplished by placing the German government securities in an irrevocable trust from which principal and interest payments will be made on the DM bonds. The company recognized a gain of $800,000 after taxes from this transaction.

## Required:

*a.* Prepare the journal entries associated with the in-substance defeasance done by Burlington Industries.

*b.* The bonds and notes extinguished by Burlington carried a very low nominal interest rate. Consequently, they were selling at large discounts in the 1984 bond markets. Why did Burlington not just buy the bonds in the bond market and realize an even larger gain?

*c.* What is the meaning of the last sentence of Burlington's note about none of the bonds being retired?

*d.* The annual reporting package of Baxter Travenol consisted of the 1983 balance sheet, the 1984 balance sheet, and the 1984 income statement. How was the bond issue and in-substance defeasance reflected in those statements?

*e.* How was the company able to issue the bonds at one interest rate and invest the proceeds at a higher interest rate?

*f.* Do you believe companies should be allowed to issue debt and then almost immediately extinguish it through an in-substance defeasance?

**Casette 11–1.   Questions about Georgia-Pacific Corporation**

At the back of the text is the complete set of financial statements of Georgia-Pacific Corporation taken from its annual report of 1987.

Answer the following questions related to the long-term debt shown on those statements.

1. By how much did the long-term debt change from 1986 to 1987?
2. What percentage of total assets was long-term debt on December 31, 1987? How does this compare to the same ratio at the end of 1986?

3. What is the difference between zero-coupon debentures and discount term debentures?

4. What do the amounts shown in Note 4 for zero-coupon debentures and discount term debentures represent? How might the effectiveness of these presentations be improved?

5. Is it appropriate for Georgia-Pacific to classify commercial paper and other short-term notes as long-term debt?

6. Prepare the journal entries that Georgia-Pacific made in *1986* to record the redemption of its 5.25 percent convertible subordinated debentures and the conversion of that debt into common stock.

7. Why does the Company devote so much space to a description of its credit agreements? Why are these important to the statement reader? Why are the credit agreements not included in the long-term debt?

8. Loan agreements require the Company to maintain a minimum of $250 million of working capital. How close is the company to this minimum on December 31, 1987?

## Casette 11–2. Issuance of Long-term Notes at a Premium

The July 14, 1987 issue of the *Wall Street Journal* contained announcements by two major corporations concerning the issuance of three-year Australian dollar notes. The information below is abstracted from those announcements.

|  | *Pepsico, Inc.* | *General Mills, Inc.* |
|---|---|---|
| Face amount | A $50,000,000 | A $100,000,000 |
| Stated interest rate | 13.5% | 14% |
| Issue date | July 22, 1987 | July 27, 1987 |
| Due date | July 22, 1990 | July 27, 1990 |
| Price | 101% plus accrued interest, if any, from July 22, 1987 | 101.8% plus accrued interest, if any, from July 27, 1987 |

### Required:

a. Calculate the proceeds that each company received from the issuance of its notes.

b. What does the phrase "plus accrued interest, if any" mean? Why is it part of the price quotation?

c. Prepare journal entries to record the issuance of the notes.

d. Suggest some reasons why the issue by General Mills would sell at a higher price.

e. Is the effective interest rate implicit in each of the notes more or less than the stated interest rate? How do you know? Estimate what it is for each of these notes. (Interest is paid semiannually.)

f. *Assume* that the answer to part e is 13 percent. Prepare the journal entries to record interest expense and interest paid on January 22, 1988 and July 22, 1988 for the Pepsico note.

g. Making the same assumption, repeat part f for the interest entries on January 27, 1988 and July 27, 1988 for the General Mills note.

## Casette 11–3. Zero-Coupon Notes and Discount Bonds

The following information is taken from Note 4 on Indebtedness contained in the annual report of Baker International Corporation for the fiscal year ending on September 30, 1983.

Long-term debt at September 30, 1983 and 1982 consisted of $533,078,000 and $608,607,000, respectively. Included in these totals were the following two items:

|  | September 30 | |
|---|---|---|
|  | *1983* | *1982* |
| Zero-Coupon Guaranteed Notes due 1992 with an effective interest rate of 14.48%, net of unamortized discount of $155,328,000 ($164,420,000 in 1982) | $ 69,672,000 | $ 60,580,000 |
| 6.00% Debentures due 2002 with an effective interest rate of 14.66%, net of unamortized discount of $123,152,000 ($124,440,000 in 1982) | 101,848,000 | 100,560,000 |

Both of these issues can be redeemed at the option of the company at any time at par. Also, "the zero-coupon notes due 1992 may be redeemed prior to maturity at prices (expressed as a percentage of principal amount) beginning with 24.70% and scaling upward overtime to 86.95% . . . in the event of certain changes affecting United States or Netherlands Antilles taxation."

### Required:

*a.* What is the principal (par) amount of the zero-coupon notes and of the 6.00 percent debentures?

*b.* Given that your answer in part *a* showed the same principal amount for both issues, why is the carrying value of the zero-coupon bonds so much lower?

*c.* Prepare the journal entries to record the accrual of interest on each issue for fiscal 1984. Why was the amortization of bond discount less for the 6.00 percent debenture bonds?

*d.* Prepare the journal entries to record the accrual of interest on each issue for fiscal 1985. What will be the carrying value of each issue on September 30, 1985?

*e.* Is it likely that either issue will be redeemed in the near future? Explain.

*f.* Speculate on the purpose of the sliding scale of redemption prices for the zero-coupon notes. What change in taxation might be at issue here?

## 11A–1. Finding Unknowns Related to Present and Future Values

Each line below represents a separate situation. Find the unknown amount (x) using Tables 11A–6, 11A–7, 11A–8, and 11A–9. Assume interest is compounded annually.

| *a.* | Present Value (P/F, n, i) | Future Value (F/P, n, i) | Interest Rate (i) | Number of Years (n) |
|---|---|---|---|---|
| 1. | x | $1,500 | 5% | 5 |
| 2. | $800 | x | 3% | 13 |
| 3. | $200 | $ 518.74 | x | 10 |
| 4. | $542.49 | $1,300 | 6% | x |
| 5. | $748.32 | $1,065.08 | x | 9 |
| 6. | $125.89 | $ 355.79 | 16% | x |

| b. | Present or Future Value of Annuity | Amount (A) | Interest Rate (i) | Number of Years (n) |
|---|---|---|---|---|
| 1. | $(P/A, n, i) = x$ | $5,000 | 8% | 10 |
| 2. | $(F/A, n, i) = x$ | $ 100 | 6% | 11 |
| 3. | $(P/A, n, i) = \$2,725.48$ | x | 10% | 12 |
| 4. | $(F/A, n, i) = \$1,333.85$ | x | 3% | 8 |
| 5. | $(P/A, n, i) = \$1,493.88$ | $ 200 | x | 20 |
| 6. | $(F/A, n, i) = \$4,310.10$ | $1,000 | x | 4 |
| 7. | $(P/A, n, i) = \$2,775.32$ | $ 753.20 | 16% | x |
| 8. | $(F/A, n, i) = \$ 178.35$ | $ 8.10 | 1% | x |

## 11A–2. Exercises in the Use of Future Value Tables

Compute the future amount for each of the following cases. Use Tables 11A–6 and 11A–7.

a. $700 to be deposited at the end of each of the next four years. Interest is compounded annually at 6 percent. Verify your answer by calculating the size of the fund year by year.

b. $4,000 to be deposited immediately. Interest at 24 percent is compounded quarterly for five years.

c. $2,000 to be deposited immediately. Interest at 12 percent is compounded semi-annually for the first four years, and then interest at 10 percent is compounded annually for the next four years.

d. $3,000 to be deposited at the end of each of the next five years. No additional deposits after that. Interest is compounded annually at 8 percent for 10 years.

## 11A–3. Exercises in the Use of Present Value Tables

Answer each of the following exercises. Use Tables 11A–8 and 11A–9.

a. Determine the present value of $400 under each of the following conditions:

| | Year of Receipt | Interest Rate |
|---|---|---|
| 1. | 3 | 6% |
| 2. | 6 | 10 |
| 3. | 10 | 8 |

Verify your answer to Condition No. 1 by showing that a fund in the amount of your answer will indeed accumulate to $400 at the end of three years if invested at 6 percent.

b. Determine the present value of an annuity of $500 payable *semiannually* under the following conditions (assume *semiannual* discounting):

| | No. of Years | Interest Rate |
|---|---|---|
| 1. | 4 | 12% |
| 2. | 7 | 20 |

Verify your answer to Condition No. 1 by preparing a table similar to Table 11A–2.

c. If you invest the sum specified in the first column, you will receive a single or a series of $100 payments in the year or years indicated in the second column. For each case, determine the actual annual rate of interest earned.

|  | *Invested* | *Year(s) of Receipt* |
|---|---|---|
| 1. | $ 40.39 | 8 |
| 2. | 31.18 | 20 |
| 3. | 624.69 | 1–9 |
| 4. | 91.33 | 21–25 |

d. In Table 11A–8, the present values become smaller as one moves either down or across the table. Carefully explain why.

## 11A–4. Alternative Repayment Plans

Pedro Alvarez borrows $40,000 to be used in remodeling his clothing store. The loan will be repaid in periodic installments covering interest and principal.

### Required:

a. If the loan were to be repaid in four annual payments, the first payment being made in one year at an interest rate of 12 percent, what would be the amount of each payment?

b. If the loan were to be repaid in eight semiannual payments, the first payment being made in six months at an interest rate of 12 percent compounded semiannually, what would be the amount of each payment?

c. If the loan were to be repaid in twelve quarterly payments, the first payment being made in three months at an interest rate of 12 percent compounded quarterly, what would be the amount of each payment?

d. Alvarez determines that he can pay about $9,500 every six months. If the lender requires an interest rate of 12 percent compounded semiannually, how long will it take Alvarez to pay off the loan?

e. Alvarez determines that he will have only $4,000 available each quarter for the next five years to make payments. If the lender requires an interest rate of 12 percent compounded quarterly, how much could Alvarez borrow?

## 11A–5. Present Value Analysis of Investment Opportunities

Assume that your firm wishes to earn 12 percent on all investments in new equipment. It has under consideration the following three proposals. Assume that all *annual* cash flows occur at the end of the year and ignore income taxes.

| Project | Immediate Cash Outlay | Cash Receipts Amount | Cash Receipts Years |
|---|---|---|---|
| A. . . . | $ 75,000 | $13,000 | 1–7 |
| B. . . . | 100,000 | ⎰17,000<br>⎱27,000 | 1–8<br>9 |
| C. . . . | 16,500 | ⎰ 2,500<br>⎱ 4,000 | 1–4<br>5–9 |

### Required:

*a.* Advise the company which of these projects it should accept and which it should reject. Show your calculations.

*b.* Would your answers in *a* change if the desired earning rate was only 8 percent?

*c.* What rate of return will the company earn on its money if it invests in Project B?

*d.* What is the maximum amount the company could afford to invest in Project C and still earn 12 percent?

### 11A–6. Automobile Rebates and Financing

Alena Pearlman faced a dilemma after she found a new car she wished to purchase for $10,000. The automobile dealer offered Alena *either* (1) 4 percent financing ($350.83 monthly installments for 30 months), (2) 6 percent financing ($359.79 monthly installments for 30 months) and an immediate cash rebate of $300, or (3) an immediate cash rebate of $500 if she paid the $9,500 net amount in cash immediately. Alena checked with her local bank and learned that it was charging 12 percent (1% per month) on 30-month automobile loans.

### Required:

*a.* Demonstrate that the bank would require monthly payments of $368.11 over the next 30 months in return for lending Alena the $9,500 she desired.

*b.* Should Alena opt for the 4 percent financing and no rebate, the 6 percent financing and $300 rebate, or the $500 rebate? Explain your reasoning.

### 11A–7. Comparison of Alternative Investments

Ty Coon inherited $50,000. He is considering four alternative investments in financial instruments for the next three years. These alternatives are described below.

1. Put the money in a savings account. Ty will receive a quarterly interest check of $500 and will withdraw the $50,000 at the end of the three years.
2. Put the funds in money market certificates. Ty will receive semiannual interest of $2,000, and the certificates have a maturity date three years from now.
3. Invest the money in corporate bonds. He will receive an interest check of $5,000 annually, and the bonds mature three years from now.
4. Buy 1,000 shares of stock in Nacirema Corporation for $50 a share. Dividends on the stock are paid quarterly and are expected to be $.80 per share. Ty estimates that he will be able to sell the stock for $60 a share in three years.

### Required:

*a.* Using present value tables compute the effective annual yield for each investment. (The effective annual yield is the rate that will make the present value of future cash receipts equal to $50,000.)

*b.* Which investment has the highest yield? Is this necessarily the best investment? What other factors should he consider?

### 11A–8. Purchase or Lease Decision Using Annuity Due

A warehouse company is negotiating for a building to use for storage. The building can be purchased for $600,000 cash or can be acquired under a 10-year lease at an annual rental of $70,000, payable at the *beginning* of each year. The building's estimated resale value at the end of 10 years is $40,000. Under either arrangement, the warehouse company would pay all operating costs, maintenance, and property taxes.

Which plan is better if the interest rate is assumed to be 8 percent? (Ignore income taxes.)

**11A–9. Future Value Analysis of Individual Retirement Account**

Susan Fischel recently read a bank advertisement for an Individual Retirement Account (IRA). The bank's ad stated, "Start an IRA with us today and retire as a millionaire." Susan is 30 years old. She could easily set aside $1,000 a year in an IRA and probably could manage to contribute the maximum amount of $2,000 for single wage earners.

**Required:**

*a.* If she contributes $1,000 at the end of each year for the next 30 years to an IRA and the account earns 16 percent, will she have a million dollars by age 60?

*b.* How much would she have to contribute each year to be a "millionaire" by age 60?

*c.* If the bank only pays 10 percent interest each year, can Susan reach her goal by contributing the maximum $2,000 each year?

*d.* If Susan marries David and they both work, the family could set aside $4,000 a year in an IRA. At 16 percent, how many years would they have to work before the family accumulates a million dollars? At 12 percent?

**11A–10. Present Value Analysis of Completing an MBA**

Andrew Kim has just received his undergraduate degree in engineering and has a job offer with a large manufacturing company. However, Andrew is contemplating spending the next two years in an M.B.A. program. He has been admitted to one of the finest programs, and the M.B.A. degree should enhance his future earning potential. The cost of tuition and books would be $10,000 a year. The following schedule shows Andrew's projected salaries with and without an M.B.A.

| | Salary per Year | |
| --- | --- | --- |
| Years | with B.S. only | with M.B.A. |
| 1 and 2 | $25,000 | — |
| 3–5 | 30,000 | $32,000 |
| 6–10 | 35,000 | 40,000 |
| 11–15 | 40,000 | 50,000 |
| 16–20 | 50,000 | 65,000 |

**Required:**

*a.* If 6 percent is an appropriate discount rate for Andrew Kim to use, should he continue on for an M.B.A. on purely financial grounds? For convenience, assume that all cash flows occur at the end of the year.

*b.* Does your answer change if the appropriate discount rate is 10 percent?

*c.* At the 6 percent rate, how many years before the two options would be equal in present value terms?

## 11B–1. Journal Entries for Bond Investments

Alice Smith, a wealthy investor, purchases two hundred $1,000 bonds of Heavenly Hotel, Inc. on June 30, 1990. The bonds bear interest at a stated rate of 10 percent, payable annually on December 31, and mature on December 31, 2005. Alice pays $211,000 plus accrued interest of $10,000 for a half-year. Brokerage fees and other costs of acquisition amount to an additional $4,500.

### Required:

a. Prepare the journal entry to record the purchase of the bonds (plus accrued interest) as an investment.

b. Record the receipt of interest on December 31, 1990 and December 31, 1991. Use the straight-line method of premium amortization over 15.5 years to recognize interest revenue.

c. Assume that on January 1, 1992, Alice sells half of the bonds at a price of $108,000. Make the journal entry to record the sale.

## 11B–2. Completion and Interpretation of Amortization Table for Bond Investment

The following is a partially completed amortization table prepared by Murray Tamarking to account for his investment in $100,000 face amount of Sherry Corporation bonds. Amounts in the table have been rounded to the nearest dollar. The bonds mature five years from the date of purchase and pay interest annually.

| Year | Interest Revenue | Interest Received | Discount Amortization | Unamortized Discount | Year-End Carrying Amount |
|------|------------------|-------------------|-----------------------|----------------------|--------------------------|
| 0    |                  |                   |                       | $3,991               | $96,009                  |
| 1    | $7,681           | $7,000            | $681                  | 3,310                | 96,690                   |
| 2    |                  |                   |                       |                      |                          |
| 5    |                  |                   | 926                   |                      |                          |

### Required:

a. Which amortization method is Murray Tamarking using? How do you know?

b. Determine the correct amount for each of the nine blank spaces in the table.

c. Why did Murray buy the Sherry Corporation bonds at a discount?

d. Prepare the journal entries made by Murray to record the purchase of the bonds as an investment and to reflect interest revenue for Year 1.

e. What would the interest revenue have been for Murray Company if it had chosen to follow the other amortization procedure?

## 11B–3. Bond Investments

On October 1, 1990, Hamilton Investment Company purchased a long-term bond as an investment for $1,185,900. The 16 percent bonds have a par value of $1,000,000, mature on October 1, 1997, and pay interest semiannually on April 1 and October 1. Hamilton Investment Company's accounting period ends on December 31. It uses the straight-line method for amortization of the premium.

**Required:**

a. Demonstrate that the effective rate of interest that Hamilton will earn on this investment is 12 percent (6 percent semiannually), if the bonds are held to maturity.

b. Prepare the required journal entries on the following dates:
   1. October 1, 1990
   2. December 31, 1990
   3. April 1, 1991
   4. October 1, 1991
   5. December 31, 1991

c. How will the investment account appear on the balance sheet on December 31, 1990 and December 31, 1991?

d. What interest rate (expressed as an annual rate) would Hamilton show is being earned on the investment in 1991? Why is this rate not 12 percent?

# Chapter 12

# Complex Areas of Liability Measurement: Leases and Pensions

Chapter 11 explores some of the basic concepts and accounting problems associated with interest-bearing liabilities. Although notes and bonds represent legal claims, we should remember that the concept of a liability extends beyond specifically determinable legal obligations. Liabilities encompass all measurable future outlays of cash or other assets that result from past or current transactions.

When a significant time period exists between the incurrence of a liability and its ultimate payment, the total cash payments include an interest charge for the delayed payment. Valuation of a liability at the present value of the future payments removes the element of interest and records the liability at the current cash equivalent needed to discharge the debt.

This chapter discusses the accounting for leases and pensions. Both areas employ present value concepts as measurement guides. However, their applications are more difficult because of complexities associated with lease and pension liabilities. In fact, both areas raise the fundamental question: To what extent do leases and pensions satisfy the definition of a liability and meet the criteria for recognition in the accounts?

The first part of the chapter discusses leases, and the second explores pension reporting. The common thread between the two is the use of present value methodology. The chapter then concludes with an analysis of Kimberly-Clark Corporation's disclosures.

## NATURE OF LEASES

A conventional lease agreement conveys the right to use property from its legal owner (the *lessor*) to a second party (the *lessee*) in exchange for a periodic cash payment (rent). The typical rental agreement for an apartment is a common example. The length of time the property may be used, any restrictions on its use, the amount and timing of the payments, and other pertinent features normally are specified in the lease contract. The length of time the lease covers may vary from a few hours or days (e.g., renting a truck to move your household belongings) to the entire life of the asset (e.g., leasing a store building for 40 years).

Leasing has become a popular means for businesses to acquire a variety of asset services. In 1980, the volume of new equipment leased was $43.5 billion. By 1985, this amount had more than doubled.[1] Not only are airplanes, computers, and machinery leased, but recently farmers have begun to lease cows; restaurants have leased plants and flowers; and some corporations have even leased clothes for their executives.

The diversity in lease property and terms is matched by the diverse motivations behind the people or firms who desire to lease. Some companies view leasing as a way of reducing the risk of obsolescence, avoiding the problems of maintenance, and maximizing tax benefits (e.g., under some circumstances, payments for land under a lease are tax deductible, but purchased land cannot be depreciated). Still other firms find that leasing offers a way to secure asset services without a large down payment. A lease may offer almost 100 percent financing and is often a more flexible, less restrictive arrangement than conventional borrowing. Moreover, the lessee may incur a financial obligation that is not recognized on the balance sheet. The issue of *off-balance-sheet financing* is at the heart of the accounting controversies involving leases.

In the first part of this chapter, we examine how lease arrangements should be reflected in the financial statements of lessees.[2] In particular, we address the questions of how and when accountants should recognize the right to use property and the related obligation to make rental payments that exist under many leases. Must a company be the legal owner of each item it reports as an asset on its balance sheet? Do differences exist between the obligation to make periodic payments on a note or mortgage payable and the commitment existing under a noncancelable lease?

### The Basic Issue

Often the nature of a lease arrangement suggests the economic substance of the transaction. For example, consider the difference between the rental of

---

[1] "A Boom in Lease Financing," *New York Times,* March 13, 1985, Section D, p. 1.

[2] In the Appendix at the end of this chapter, we look at the recording problems of the lessor.

an apartment by its occupant for one year and the leasing of machinery by a firm for that asset's expected useful life. The former appears to be a straight short-term rental arrangement. The latter, although in the form of a rental, is in substance a sale by the lessor and an installment purchase by the lessee.

The *basic issue* in accounting for leases is determining *whether a particular lease is a temporary rental of asset services or the acquisition of an asset through long-term financing*. A *capital lease* exists when the economic substance of the lease transaction suggests that the lessee is, in effect, acquiring the property being leased under a long-term installment purchase. All leases that do not meet the criteria for being capital leases are considered to be *operating leases*. Lease classification is important because it greatly influences several key elements on the financial statements and, hence, the resulting financial ratios. The qualitative guideline of representational faithfulness stresses that the economic substance of the lease transaction, not the legal form, should govern lease classification.

The accounting treatment for a capital lease differs greatly from the recording procedures for an operating lease. The economic substance of a capital lease consists of the acquisition of a future economic benefit and the creation of a long-term obligation. Accordingly, an asset and a liability must be reflected in the lessee's accounts. The lease is said to have been *capitalized*. The leased property and lease obligation should be placed on the lessee's balance sheet at an amount equal to the present value of the minimum lease payments required during the term of the lease. The income statement reflects depreciation of the leased asset and interest expense on the capital lease obligation. Each lease payment is recorded as we recorded installment notes in Chapter 11—partially as interest expense and partially as a payment of the liability.

An operating lease, in contrast, is viewed as a straight rental arrangement. There are no long-term property rights or financing arrangements implicit in the lease agreement. The cash payments for rentals are usually expensed as they become due over the term of the lease. No balance sheet asset and liability are recognized by the lessee for operating leases; the *lessor* continues to show the property on its balance sheet.

## Criteria for Capital Leases

Only with great difficulty can capital leases be distinguished from operating leases, because lease contracts have an almost infinite variety of payment terms, renewal privileges, purchase options, and other provisions and guarantees. Prior to 1976, the authoritative pronouncements were vague and ineffective. The recording was often governed by the form of the lease arrangement rather than by its economic substance. The guidelines that did exist were easily manipulated to avoid recording leases as capital leases, and off-balance-sheet financing seemed to dominate.

The FASB issued a relatively comprehensive leasing standard, *FASB Statement No. 13,* late in 1976.[3] It constituted a significant effort to improve lease recording. The FASB searched for reasonable and practical criteria that could be used in making the classification decision. *Statement No. 13* specified that a lease shall be classified as a capital lease if at its inception *at least one* of the following criteria is met:

1. The lease transfers ownership of the property to the lessee by the end of the lease term.
2. The lease contains a bargain purchase option.
3. The lease term is equal to 75 percent or more of the estimated economic life of the leased property.
4. The present value at the beginning of the lease term of the minimum lease payments . . . equals or exceeds 90 percent of the . . . fair value of the leased property to the lessor at the inception of the lease.[4]

Although cutoffs such as 75 and 90 percent are inevitably arbitrary, the above four conditions make sense. No lessee is going to receive either a free transfer of ownership or a bargain purchase option from a rational lessor unless the lease payments have in essence already paid for most of the asset's services. Similarly, an economically rational lessee who uses property for most of that asset's life or who commits, in present value terms, to paying close to the outright purchase price of the leased property must in substance be acquiring the asset by a long-term installment purchase.

# ILLUSTRATION OF ACCOUNTING BY LESSEE

Suppose that Laural Corporation can acquire some machinery either for an immediate cash payment of $41,114 or for a $10,000 payment each December 31 under a six-year, noncancelable lease.[5] The machinery has a useful life of six years and no expected residual value. The effective interest rate implicit in the lease is 12 percent because the present value of the six payments at 12 percent is equal to the cash purchase price [(P/A, 6, .12) $10,000 = $41,114]. If Laural decides to lease the machinery as of January 1, 1989, it would prepare *one* of the sets of journal entries that appear in Table 12–1 for 1989 and 1990, the first two years of the lease.

As you examine Table 12–1, keep in mind that Laural *cannot* actually choose which recording to use. It must follow the left set of entries, as this

---

[3] FASB, *Statement of Financial Accounting Standards No. 13,* "Accounting for Leases" (Stamford, Conn., November 1976).

[4] *FASB Statement No. 13,* par. 7.

[5] In business practice, lease payments are usually made at the beginning of the period. To facilitate calculations, we have assumed payments at year-end.

**TABLE 12–1**  Effect of Lease Classification on Lessee's Accounting

| *If Considered a Capital Lease:* | | | *If Considered an Operating Lease:* | |
|---|---|---|---|---|
| Jan. 1, 1989—beginning of lease term | | | | |
| Leased Property under | | | | |
|    Capital Leases. . . . . | 41,114 | | No entry | |
|     Obligations under | | | | |
|       Capital Leases. . . . | | 41,114 | | |
| Dec. 31, 1989—end of first year of lease | | | | |
| Interest Expense . . . . . | 4,934 | | Lease Rental Expense . . . | 10,000 | |
| Obligations under | | |    Cash . . . . . . . . | |
|    Capital Leases. . . . . | 5,066 | | | 10,000 |
|     Cash. . . . . . . . | | 10,000 | | |
|    12% × \$41,114 = \$4,934. | | | | |
| Depreciation Expense. . . . | 6,852 | | No entry | |
|    Accumulated | | | | |
|      Depreciation . . . . | | 6,852 | | |
|    Straight-line, 1/6 of \$41,114. | | | | |
| Dec. 31, 1990—end of second year of lease | | | | |
| Interest Expense . . . . . | 4,326 | | Lease Rental Expense . . . | 10,000 | |
| Obligations under | | |    Cash . . . . . . . . | |
|    Capital Leases. . . . . | 5,674 | | | 10,000 |
|     Cash. . . . . . . . | | 10,000 | | |
|    \$41,114 − \$5,066 = \$36,048. | | | | |
|    12% × \$36,048 = \$4,326. | | | | |
| Depreciation Expense. . . . | 6,852 | | No entry | |
|    Accumulated | | | | |
|      Depreciation . . . . | | 6,852 | | |

transaction more than qualifies as a capital lease. The lease covers much more than 75 percent of the estimated life of the asset (Criteria 3), and the present value of the minimum lease payments accounts for over 90 percent of the asset's initial fair value (Criteria 4). Prior to the issuance of *FASB Statement No. 13,* Laural probably could have interpreted the then-existing lease pronouncements to permit recording the machinery acquisition as an operating lease.

Nevertheless, by contrasting the entries recording the lease as a capital lease with those recording it as an operating lease, we can see clearly the differing impacts the two methods have. Table 12–2 summarizes the leases' results on the financial statements for the first two years. It reveals why lessees generally prefer that leases be classified and recorded as operating

**TABLE 12–2**    Effect of Lease Classification on Lessee's Financial Statements

| | | If Considered as a | | | | |
|---|---|---|---|---|---|---|
| | Capital Lease | | | Operating Lease | | |
| **Income Statement** | 1989 | 1990 | | 1989 | 1990 | |
| Interest expense | $ 4,934 | $ 4,326 | | | | |
| Depreciation expense | 6,852 | 6,852 | | | | |
| Rent expense | | | | $10,000 | $10,000 | |
| Total expense | $11,786 | $11,178 | | $10,000 | $10,000 | |
| **Balance Sheet** | 1/1/89 | 12/31/89 | 12/31/90 | 1/1/89 | 12/31/89 | 12/31/90 |
| Machinery | $41,114 | $41,114 | $41,114 | 0 | 0 | 0 |
| Accumulated depreciation | — | 6,852 | 13,704 | 0 | 0 | 0 |
| | $41,114 | $34,262 | $27,410 | 0 | 0 | 0 |
| Lease obligations | $41,114 | $36,048 | $30,374 | 0 | 0 | 0 |

leases. The requirement to recognize the economic event as a capital lease results in Laural's reporting:

1. More expense and less income during the early years of the lease, although total expense over the six years is the same.
2. More assets during all six years of the lease.
3. As a result of 1 and 2, a lower return on investment (income/assets) in *all* six years of the lease, with the decline most pronounced in the early years.
4. More liabilities during all six years of the lease. Operating leases record no liabilities; this is off-balance-sheet financing.
5. As a result of 1 and 4, a higher ratio of liabilities as a percentage of total equities during all six years of the lease.

The figures shown in Table 12–2 for the Lease Obligations on the balance sheet can be used to illustrate the critical role of present value analysis in the valuation process. The cost of the asset equals the value of the liability. The value of the liability equals the present value of the cash payments promised under the lease. Table 12–3 tracks the transactions associated with repaying the lease liability.

The Lease Obligations account continues to show the present value of the remaining debt throughout its life. For example, according to Table 12–3, the liability has a balance of $24,019 at the end of 1991. There are three remaining payments of $10,000 to be made. With a 12 percent interest fac-

**TABLE 12–3**   Repayment Schedule for Lease Liability

| Payment on Dec. 31 | Liability Balance prior to Payment | Debits | | Credit Cash | Liability Balance after Payment# |
|---|---|---|---|---|---|
| | | Interest Expense* | Liability | | |
| 1989 . . . . . . . . | $41,114 | $4,934 | $5,066 | $10,000 | $36,048 |
| 1990 . . . . . . . . | 36,048 | 4,326 | 5,674 | 10,000 | 30,374 |
| 1991 . . . . . . . . | 30,374 | 3,645 | 6,355 | 10,000 | 24,019 |
| 1992 . . . . . . . . | 24,019 | 2,882 | 7,118 | 10,000 | 16,901 |
| 1993 . . . . . . . . | 16,901 | 2,028 | 7,972 | 10,000 | 8,929 |
| 1994 . . . . . . . . | 8,929 | 1,071 | 8,929 | 10,000 | 0 |

*Interest expense equals 12 percent multiplied by the liability balance prior to payment.
#Ending liability balance equals beginning balance less debit to the liability account.

tor, the present value of three $10,000 payments is $24,019 (adjusted for rounding):

| | |
|---|---|
| Annuity amount . . . . . . . . . . . . . . . . . . . . . . | $ 10,000 |
| Present-value factor, Line 3, 12% Column, from Table 11A–9 . . . . . . . . . . . . . . . | × 2.4018 |
| | $ 24,018 |

# EVALUATION OF LEASE CAPITALIZATION

Although many observers regard *FASB Statement 13* as an improvement in the quantity and quality of lease disclosures, some believe the FASB has gone too far, and others feel that not enough progress has been made. There is a continuum of beliefs—do not capitalize any leases, capitalize only leases that are clearly disguised installment purchases (transfer of ownership or bargain purchase), capitalize all leases that transfer substantially all of the benefits and risks associated with ownership, and capitalize all long-term noncancelable leases. *FASB Statement No. 13* basically endorses the middle two positions.

## Objections to Capitalization of Leases

Those who favor the first two beliefs raise numerous objections to the capitalization of leases on the balance sheet of the lessee. One group of objections centers around unfavorable consequences that might result from disclosing leases as assets and liabilities. They voice fears that lessees, by reporting more debt and less earnings, would suffer an impairment in their borrowing ability and a decline in their stock prices.

Unfortunately, the above view ignores the important issue of whether capitalization best reflects the nature of many lease transactions and their impact on financial position and operating performance. Accountants should not be deterred from disclosing economic substance rather than legal form, even if the increased lease capitalizations mandated by *Statement No. 13* have an effect on the lessee's stock and bond prices. Interestingly, a major research study discovered that the capitalization of leases had no such significant effects.[6]

A second set of objections to capitalization questions the accuracy in measuring asset and liability amounts. Estimates must be made of the portion of lease rentals that are payments for the asset and the portion representing payments for other continuing services such as maintenance and real estate taxes. The latter are not included in the minimum lease payments that are capitalized. Similarly, the rate to be used in discounting and the frequency of discounting may not be known with precision. However, the judgments and estimates involved would seem to fall well within the tolerances existing for other areas in accounting. The discount rate, if not explicit in the lease contract, can be determined by comparing lease prices and purchase prices, if the latter are available, or by objectively determining the market rate of interest for leases.

The fundamental view that capital leases represent assets and liabilities to the lessee is the point of attack of the third set of objections. Some of these objections define assets narrowly, equating them with legal ownership or, at least, eventual ownership. Others claim that lease obligations are not debt because courts traditionally have treated leases differently from other liabilities in cases of bankruptcy or reorganization. This idea, however, is premised on a liquidation concept rather than on a going-concern assumption.

The most perplexing argument in this category states that leases are in substance *executory contracts,* both sides of which are equally unperformed. Performance by the lessor is viewed as a continuous concept involving either an implicit approval each period of the use of the asset by the lessee or a replacement of a faulty, destroyed, or obsolete asset. If the lessor does not continuously perform, the lessee has no obligation to pay. Therefore, leases should be recorded as are other executory contracts, such as long-term employment contracts or purchase commitments. In these cases, an asset is recorded only if a prepayment is made; a liability is recorded only when services actually are received.

Advocates of limited capitalization argue that the presumption that leases are executory contracts should be overturned only when the evidence is

---

[6] A. Rashad Abdel-khalik, "The Economic Effects on Lessees of *FASB Statement No. 13,* 'Accounting for Leases,'" *Research Report* (Stamford, Conn.: FASB, 1981).

clear that the economic effect of the lease is that of an installment purchase. This happens *only* when the lease transfers to the lessee substantially all ownership rights and benefits.

## Support for Increased Capitalization

Despite the merit that the above arguments may possess, many observers favor the capitalization of even more leases than are presently required to be capitalized. These accountants advocate that all *long-term noncancelable* leases should be capitalized. The economic substance of these leasing transactions is the transfer to the lessee of the right to use the property for a specified time period. The lessee has acquired the service potential to be gained from using the asset, conditioned only by the lessee's lack of residual rights at the end of the lease period.

Delivery of the leased asset constitutes a service completely performed by the lessor. A lease is different from other executory contracts where *substantial* future performance must occur. For services requiring continuous or periodic performance in the future, an asset and liability do not exist. However, that description does not apply to the basic service potential in the property; it has been relinquished by the lessor to the lessee. The noncurrent assets utilized by the lessee should be shown in order for financial statement users to appraise correctly the scale of the lessee's business and its return on investment (net income/average assets).

In a similar fashion, the lease payments, save for the portion applicable to additional services, constitute an agreement to pay for these user rights. The lessee has an irrevocable obligation to make the lease payments, which include the interest element inherent in any deferred payment arrangement. The lessee's obligation to make periodic lease payments for the use of leased assets strikes proponents as no less a liability than the obligation to make periodic payments on a long-term note or mortgage. Certainly, knowledge of the commitments made on all long-term noncancelable leases is an essential input to any complete analysis of the magnitude and timing of future cash flows.

In addition to the conceptual claim that *FASB Statement No. 13* does not go far enough, critics point to ambiguities and loopholes in the statement. The criteria in the statement used to determine if a lease is a capital lease, in particular the first three, can be manipulated easily to avoid capitalization— and they have been. The ingenuity of lessors eager to please prospective lessees has created a large number of leases that do not meet any of the four criteria and yet probably do conform to the spirit of a capital lease.[7]

---

[7] *FASB Statement No. 13* comes close to setting a record for authoritative pronouncements in terms of modifications. It has been formally amended at least a half-dozen times. In addition, the FASB has issued an equal number of "technical interpretations." As soon as one ambiguity or problem area is resolved, a new lease arrangement arises that opens a new loophole.

## Disclosure Requirements

*FASB Statement No. 13* imposes certain requirements for disclosure of lease information in notes to the financial statements. Some of the major disclosures are:

1. A general description of leasing arrangements by both lessees and lessors.
2. Future minimum lease payments to be paid or received in connection with capital leases *and* operating leases for each of the next five years.
3. Rental expense (lessee) and rental revenue (lessor) under operating leases, with separate amounts for minimum rentals, contingent rentals, and sublease rentals.
4. The gross amount of assets recorded under capital leases by the lessee.

The current capitalization rules plus the additional disclosures hopefully come close to satisfying the information needs of the majority of users. Yet, given the variety of possible arrangements, one suspects that the last word has not been written regarding how to report leases.

# NATURE OF PENSIONS

As Chapter 8 points out, the overall cost of labor services includes the cost of various fringe benefits. Among the most important of these are retirement programs and pension plans. They have grown significantly over the last 30 years and show every sign of continuing. The Employee Retirement Income Security Act of 1976 (ERISA) generally requires employers who offer pension programs to make participation available to all employees over age 25 who have at least one year of service. At the time of the stock market crash in October 1987, over $2 trillion was invested in pension funds.[8]

In its simplest terms, a pension plan is an agreement between a business entity and its employees whereby the former agrees to pay benefits to the latter after their retirement. Most pension arrangements also provide for an intermediary, the pension fund, as depicted in Figure 12–1. The employer makes periodic contributions to the pension fund, generally during the working lives of the employees. Those persons in charge of the pension fund have an obligation to invest the contributions and to administer the distribution of benefits to retired employees.

In the long run, of course, there should be a correspondence between the cost of the pension program to the employer (the contributions) and the benefits promised to the employees. In the short run and in some legal contexts, however, the business is obligated directly to the pension fund and only indirectly to the employees. The pension fund normally is a separate legal and accounting entity.

---

[8] Randall Smith, "Heard on the Street," *Wall Street Journal,* October 27, 1987, p. 69.

**FIGURE 12–1**    Typical Relationships between Parties to a Pension Plan

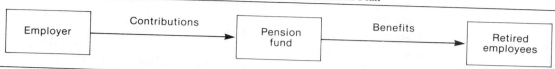

## Pension Complexities

In economic terms, a pension is a type of deferred compensation plan. The employer offers future compensation in exchange for employee services rendered in the present. Accordingly, the cost of the pension plan should accrue over the years when employees render service, even though the pension payments actually are made many years later. The financial accounting procedures and measurements necessary to accomplish this treatment of pension costs involve numerous complexities.

First, there is a great diversity of plans. Some, called *defined contribution plans,* limit the employer's payments to a fixed sum; for example, so much per ton of coal mined or per hour worked. Pension expense simply equals the required contributions. No specific pension benefits are promised other than those the pension fund contributions will provide. The more common form is a *defined benefit plan,* wherein a specific schedule of pension benefits is established. The employer must contribute amounts sufficient to provide those benefits. Some defined benefit plans are "contributory plans," wherein the employer's payments may be augmented by amounts withheld from the employees' earnings. Because our major concern in accounting for pensions is determining cost to the business entity, we focus only on noncontributory, defined benefit plans. Here the measurement problems are the most difficult.

A second source of measurement problems arises from differences in the way pension benefits are calculated, the so-called benefit formula. Most pension plans provide benefits based on a formula that includes a benefit percentage, compensation level, and number of years of service. For example, the pension benefit might be 1 percent of the employee's average compensation for each year with the company. One of the major points of contention is whether the pension benefits earned each year should be measured according to current compensation levels or be based on an estimate of future compensation. The former is called an "accumulated benefits approach"; the latter is a "projected benefit approach."

An additional complexity concerns *funding* of the pension program. Funding is the actual contribution of cash to some fiduciary agency. Under an *insured* plan the payments go to an insurance company, which invests the funds until they are needed. In *trusteed* plans, a bank or trust company receives the payments from the employer. Completely unfunded plans are almost nonexistent, but the pattern of funding varies significantly among plans. Because pension costs, like all business expenses, must be reported on an accrual basis, the amount *funded* in any particular period does not necessarily determine the amount of pension *expense* recognized that period. Nevertheless, the manner in which a firm contributes cash to its pension plan does influence the *total* pension cost, and hence it also influences periodic expense measurement.

Complexities in concept, terminology, and procedure also are introduced into pension calculations by insurance technicalities. Pension calculations necessarily require judgments and estimates about future events. These estimates normally demand the expertise of an actuary—a professional trained in the science of compound interest, probability, mortality distributions, and other aspects of insurance. The assumptions that actuaries tentatively make about future uncertainties affecting pension cost are called *actuarial assumptions*. Some of the more important assumptions concern future levels of compensation to the extent that they influence the amount of future benefits; the proportions of the employee group who will withdraw from the plan, die, become disabled, reach retirement age, and so on; the rate of interest or earnings to be generated from the pension fund; and the amount and timing of *vested benefits* (employee benefits that are no longer contingent on the employee's future work for the employer).

The actuary must make assumptions about these and similar subjects in order to estimate the benefits that will be paid under a pension plan. The estimates of benefits, in turn, provide the starting point for calculating the amount of contribution necessary for funding and the amount of pension expense for accounting purposes. We will take the actuarial assumptions for granted for the most part, although in practice they represent a whole separate set of potential difficulties and adjustments.

## The Regulatory Environment

In spite of these complexities and the profusion of terms and practices, the goals of the accounting procedures are relatively clear and simple. Inasmuch as pensions involve dollar claims payable in the future, accounting for them should utilize present value concepts. Pension cost each period ideally should be the present value of future benefits earned by employees during the period. The pension liability at the end of any period should be the *unfunded* present value of the benefits that have been earned to date. The practical problem is to accomplish these objectives in a manner that is rational and systematic.

Prior to 1966, the accounting for pension costs and liabilities followed no single pattern. Consequently, in November 1966, the Accounting Principles Board (APB) issued *Opinion No. 8,* the objective of which was to narrow the range of practices significantly and to prevent distortion in the accounting for pensions.[9] The general approach of the APB was to require that pension costs be systematically accrued by means of rational and consistently applied present value procedures. Even within this general recommendation for accrual accounting, however, definitive guidelines on the amount of pension cost to be accounted for—and specifically how it should be recorded—still required complex answers.

The problems created by the diversity of pension plans and funding arrangements did not go unnoticed by Congress. Employee rights to equitable retirement benefits sometimes were abused. In 1974, therefore, Congress passed the Employee Retirement Income Security Act (ERISA). Technically, the law relates to the pension plans themselves and not to the accounting by employers. However, it affects many of the elements that determine the employer's cost of the pension plan, and hence, it influences current recording practices. For example, under ERISA, companies must actually fund their pension plans in accordance with sound actuarial methods. In addition to minimum funding requirements, the law establishes minimum vesting provisions, sets requirements for including or excluding employees, and extends an employer's liability in the event a pension plan is terminated. Trustees of pension plans are required to make certain financial disclosures and meet other fiduciary responsibilities.

In 1980, the FASB issued two statements.[10] *Statement No. 35* contained standards for financial reporting by the pension fund *as a separate entity. Statement No. 36* modified and expanded the requirements for footnote disclosure by employers who have defined benefit plans.

Then the FASB issued *Statement No. 87* which went into effect in 1987.[11] It came after years of debate and discussion and was approved only amid great controversy. Its purpose was to reduce even further management's discretion in pension accounting and, in some cases, to recognize an increased pension liability. We look at some of its requirements later in the chapter, but its complex details are beyond the scope of our introductory discussion here.

---

[9] AICPA, *APB Opinion No. 8,* "Accounting for the Cost of Pension Plans" (New York, November 1966).

[10] FASB, *Statement of Financial Accounting Standards No. 35,* "Accounting and Reporting by Defined Benefit Pension Plans" (Stamford, Conn., March 1980); and *Statement of Financial Accounting Standards No. 36,* "Disclosure of Pension Information" (Stamford, Conn., May 1980).

[11] FASB, *Statement of Financial Accounting Standards No. 87,* "Employers' Accounting for Pensions" (Stamford, Conn., December 1985).

# PENSION ILLUSTRATION

The following discussion starts from the idea that pension costs are a cost of employment associated with the *present* work force. In accordance with the accrual basis of accounting and the matching concept, pension expense should be recorded in the periods during which the firm benefits from that work force. Through a simplified illustration, we examine some of the technical factors and present value concepts that are necessary to an understanding of pension accounting.

**Basic Data**

Assume that the employee group of L & B Corporation numbers 100 persons. They all begin work on January 1, 1990 at age 30. The company has established a noncontributory pension plan for its employees. The plan provides that each employee will receive an annual pension for life beginning one year after mandatory retirement at age 60. Assume that the life expectancy of each employee after retirement is exactly 10 years. The amount of the pension will be 1 percent of the employee's average earnings for each year with the company. If each employee receives average annual compensation of $30,000 over the 30-year period, he or she would receive an annual pension of $9,000 (1% × 30 years × $30,000).

Obviously, the equivalent of some *actuarial assumptions* already has been introduced. Employees do not form a single group. They do not all start to work at the same time and are not all the same age. Neither do they all work the same length of time, earn the same wages, retire at the same time, and live the same amount of time after retirement. Actuarial or insurance assumptions provide averages for a group. These assumptions cover factors that determine average working life, average retirement life, and average wage base for pension purposes. Perhaps thinking of our simplified figures as the result of actuarial assumptions may add an element of reality to the illustration.

Annual pension payments will be $900,000, beginning January 1, 2021. How large a pension fund must be built up over the 30 years of employee working life to permit the withdrawal of $900,000 each year for 10 years? The required size of the fund depends on the interest rate that can be earned on invested assets in the fund. This too is an actuarial assumption; we shall use 8 percent in this example. The desired pension fund equals the present value of an annuity equal to the yearly pensions:

$$\text{Pension fund on Jan. 1, 2020} = (P/A, 10, 0.08)\$900,000$$
$$= 6.7101 \times \$900,000$$
$$= \$6,039,090$$

If the firm builds up a fund of $6,039,090 by the end of the 30-year period, it will be able to satisfy its pension obligations.

## Normal Cost (Service Cost)

Part of the total fund needs of $6,039,090 will come from interest earned on pension fund investments. The rest must come from employer contributions and thus represents the cost of the pension plan to the employer. The problem of determining periodic pension *expense* involves calculating the portion of this total that is applicable to each of the 30 years.

**Actuarial Cost Methods.** Ideally, the amount of pension expense recognized each year ought to be related to the amount of pension benefits earned each year. However, one could assume any number of different earnings patterns. These alternative assumptions are called "actuarial cost methods." Different actuarial cost methods can cause significant variations in periodic pension expense.

Originally, the Accounting Principles Board specifically endorsed as reasonable five commonly used methods. In *Statement No. 87,* the Financial Accounting Standards Board decided that comparability in pension expense measurement and understandability of pension accounting in general would be improved if it required a single approach. The one selected is a projected benefit approach called *projected unit credit method* or benefits/years of service approach. It will be illustrated shortly. The important aspect of this method is that pension expense and obligations are computed taking into consideration *future* compensation levels. Generally, it gives a gradually rising pension expense over an employee's working life.

**Calculation of Normal Cost.** In our example, we want to build an amount of $6,039,090 by the end of 30 years. The amount of pension benefits attributable to each year is $201,303 ($6,039,090/30 years), and the pension expense each year would be the present value of this amount. For example, the pension expense for the first five years would be calculated as follows:

| Year | Benefit Attributable | Present Value[12] Factors | Pension Expense |
|------|------|------|------|
| 1990 . . . . . | $201,303 | (P/F, 29, .08 ) = .1073 | $ 21,600 |
| 1991 . . . . . | $201,303 | (P/F, 28, .08 ) = .1159 | 23,331 |
| 1992 . . . . . | $201,303 | (P/F, 27, .08 ) = .1252 | 25,203 |
| 1993 . . . . . | $201,303 | (P/F, 26, .08 ) = .1353 | 27,236 |
| 1994 . . . . . | $201,303 | (P/F, 25, .08 ) = .1460 | 29,390 |
| | | | $126,760 |

[12] These present value factors are not available in Table 11A–8. They would be the factors in the 8% column for years 25 to 29.

The annual pension expense in the last column is called "normal cost" or "service cost." It is the major component of pension cost. In fact, in our simple example, normal cost will be the only pension expense *if* two events occur. First, the pension expense each year must be funded. That is, an amount equal to the annual expense must be contributed in cash to a pension fund to earn interest. Second, the pension fund must earn at the rate of 8 percent.

We can see the importance of these two factors if we look at the present value of the benefits earned to date at the end of five years. This amount is called the *actuarial liability* or *projected benefit obligation*. At the end of the fifth year, the employee group has earned five years of benefits or $1,006,515 (5 × $201,303). However, this $1,006,515 is not payable for 25 years, so its present value is only $146,951 [(P/F, 25, .08 )$1,006,515 = .1460 × $1,006,515].

How do we reconcile the $146,951 present value of total benefits earned with the $126,760 of pension expense? The answer is interest. *If* the annual pension expense were contributed to a pension fund that earned 8 percent, the pension fund would have a balance of $146,951 at the end of 1994 equal to the projected benefit obligation. To the extent, then, that the normal cost is *not* funded, pension expense will be higher in future years to provide for the interest not earned. To the extent that the pension fund earns more or less than 8 percent, total pension expense in the future may be less or more than normal cost. We will see a little later how these ideas are incorporated into *FASB Statement No. 87.*

## Prior Service Cost (Retroactive Benefits)

Now let us make a major change in our example. Assume that at the end of five years, the pension plan is modified. The pension benefits are increased to *1.5 percent* of the employee's average earnings multiplied by the number of years of service with the company. All other conditions and assumptions remain the same. In determining the amount of future pension benefits, pension plans commonly recognize years of employee service *prior* to the change in the plan. In other words, the new benefits will be based on 30 years of service, not just the 25 years following the amendment of the plan.

A new actuarial evaluation needs to be made at the end of 1994. When the additional one half of 1 percent of average earnings is applied retroactively to the employees' benefits for the years 1990 to 1994, the projected benefit obligation (or actuarial liability) at the end of 1994 is $220,427 instead of the $146,951 calculated when benefits were limited to 1 percent of average salary. The $220,427 is the present value of five years' benefits earned as calculated under the new benefit formula.

The increase in the actuarial liability because of the amendment of the pension plan is called "prior service cost."[13] In our example, it is $73,476 ($220,427 − $146,951). It is an additional cost of the pension plan that should be recognized as expense.

To some extent, the label *prior service cost* is a misnomer. It is a future cost, not a correction of past periods' expense. The employer would not amend the plan and grant retroactive benefits except in contemplation of future benefits from the employees. The cost of pension benefits, whether prior costs or normal costs, fundamentally are related to specific individuals. Because they are the ones who will receive the pensions measured by prior service, it is reasonable that the period of benefit to the company is related to the time period between the amendment of the plan and the retirement of the existing employee group. Therefore, prior service cost should be spread over the future years comprising the remaining average employee working life. In our illustration, the $73,476 should be allocated to the 25 service years left in our employee group. Prior service cost adds $2,939 ($73,476/25 years) to the annual pension expense for the years 1995 to 2020.

We should take note of two other changes caused by the modification of the pension plan. First, if the $73,476 of prior service cost is not funded immediately, which commonly is the case, an interest element will also be added to pension expense in future years to compensate for the current underfunding on which interest could have been earned.[14] Second, because yearly pension benefits earned in the future are higher, normal cost must be recalculated to reflect the higher cost.

# REPORTING STANDARDS

The process of determining pension expense and pension liabilities, although governed by present value concepts, still does not lead to a single precise result. A number of judgments, any of which can materially influence the amounts shown as pension expense and pension liability, must be made within the overall principles. In addition, other areas of pension

---

[13] When a pension plan is first adopted, companies commonly recognize years of employee service prior to the adoption of the plan. An employee who has 10 years of service before the pension plan goes into effect and who then works 20 more years before retiring would receive retirement benefits based on *30* years of employment. In this case, the initial accrued actuarial liability is called "past service costs." It is determined in basically the same way as prior service cost and causes the same accounting problems. We will use the general term of prior service cost to cover both situations.

[14] Under the Employee Retirement Income Security Act of 1974, normal costs must be funded each year and most prior service costs must be funded over a maximum period of 30 years.

accounting also cause problems and disputes. In this section, we discuss some of these judgments and problem areas and how they are currently resolved under *FASB Statement No. 87.*

## Pension Expense

Pension expense commonly consists of the following four elements:

> Normal or service cost
> \+ Interest on beginning of the year actuarial liability
> − Expected return earned on fund assets
> \+ Amortization of prior service cost

**Normal Cost.** The present value of benefits earned by employees for the current year of service is the starting point. As noted earlier, *FASB Statement No. 87* requires the use of a single actuarial cost method for all employers in order to enhance comparability. For pension plans that define benefits in terms of future salary levels, the actuarial method must consider salary progression in measuring pension costs. The required method is the projected unit credit method we illustrated in the previous section. The benefits earned are discounted to their present values using a discount rate called a "settlement rate."

**Interest.** The calculation of pension expense provides for the use of two different interest assumptions—a rate used to discount pension benefits and a rate of return on pension fund assets. We noted earlier that *if* all pension costs were funded and *if* the pension fund assets earned the discount rate, the value of the fund assets would equal the projected benefit obligation at any point in time. Using two separate rates allows for either or both of these conditions not to occur. First, the actuarial liability could be more or less than the amount set aside in pension plan assets. For example, prior service cost increases the actuarial liability immediately but may be funded over a 30-year period. Second, the rate of return on plan assets may be more or less than the discount rate used to value liabilities.

The discount rate used to measure pension obligations and their periodic increases should be a realistic rate at which the obligations effectively could be settled (e.g., the rate on high-quality, fixed-income investments currently available). The choice of the interest factor can be significant. For instance, if in our example the interest factor were 10 percent instead of 8 percent, the normal cost for the first five years would have ranged from $12,129 to $17,771 instead of from $21,600 to $29,390. Moreover, past service cost would amount to $44,427 instead of $73,476. The discount rate is multiplied by the actuarial liability at the beginning of the period. The resulting "interest expense" element reflects the increase in obligations due to the passage of time.

The rate of return on pension fund assets should reflect the expected long-term rate of return.[15] This rate of return is multiplied by the fair market value of the pension plan assets at the beginning of the period to determine a type of "interest revenue." The latter reduces the net pension expense.

**Prior Service Cost.** The initial start-up or subsequent modification of a pension plan often grants retroactive benefits to employees. This creates an immediate increase in the actuarial obligation and a future pension cost to be amortized, as we saw in our earlier example. Under the new reporting standards, companies must amortize prior service cost over the future service lives of the particular employees active at the time the prior service cost arises. Because of differing employee service lives and turnover, such assignment usually results in a declining pattern of amortization. Alternatively, the prior service cost can be amortized straight line over the *average* remaining service life of the employee group.

## Prior Service Cost as a Liability

When a pension plan is modified, often a big jump occurs in the projected benefit obligation (actuarial liability). A major question with pensions is whether an *accounting* liability should be recognized if this actuarial liability exceeds the fair value of the pension fund assets. Does the existence of unfunded prior service costs create a recognizable obligation?

The Accounting Principles Board previously had taken a strict future-accrual approach to both expense and liability recognition. Unfunded prior service costs generally did *not* appear as a liability. The contention was that an employee earns pension benefits through future years of work. Employees receive pensions, including retroactive awards, not because they have worked, but because they will continue to work until retirement. As with wages, fringe benefits should be accrued as the employee works. Consequently, the only liability normally appearing on the balance sheet would be the difference between the amounts accrued as expense and the amounts funded.

The foregoing viewpoint reflects a primary emphasis on expense measurement. The only employer liability is to contribute to the pension fund. If more expense is accrued than is funded, then a liability results. However, the accounting by the employer is not concerned with any ultimate obligations to the employees.

An alternative viewpoint stresses liability measurement. This accounting looks through the pension fund to the obligation of providing the defined

---

[15] Actually, *Statement No. 87* uses the actual rate of return but then adjusts pension expense by the amount caused by any difference between the actual rate of return and the expected rate of return.

benefits to employees. An actuarial valuation measures the present value of future pension payments based on years of service already rendered, including prior service costs granted when the plan was initiated or amended. To some, this represents the employer's gross obligation. A fully funded plan is one in which pension *fund assets* equal or exceed this obligation. To the extent that the gross actuarial liability is unfunded, the employer should record a liability.

There is some evidence that members of the Financial Accounting Standards Board leaned toward the second view. However, in the final analysis, *FASB Statement No. 87* was a giant compromise on this point. A "minimum" liability must be reported only if the *accumulated benefit obligation* exceeds the fair value of the pension fund assets. Recall that accumulated benefit obligations measure the actuarial liability for pension benefits earned *not considering the impact of future salary progression.*[16]

## Actuarial Gains and Losses

When the actuarial assumptions underlying the pension calculations are modified to meet changing conditions or when actual experience differs from the original expectations, actuarial gains and losses result. The Pension Reform Act of 1974 (ERISA) called them "experience gains and losses"; *FASB Statement No. 87* simply calls them "gains and losses." They can result from mortality and turnover assumptions as well as from differences between the actual return on plan assets and the expected return on plan assets. Immediate recognition of these gains and losses would cause significant fluctuations in the year-to-year charge for pension expense.

Accordingly, *FASB Statement No. 87* provides for delayed recognition in expense over future years. Any significant unrecognized net gain or loss would be "amortized" to pension expense over the average remaining service life of the employees. Therefore, in some circumstances, a fifth element would be added to the four components of pension expense shown earlier.

## Transition Problems

Companies reporting on a calendar year basis must follow most of *FASB Statement No. 87* beginning in 1987. They could apply it in 1986, and many

---

[16]Recognition of this minimum liability for "underfunded" plans usually will result in a debit to an intangible asset up to the amount of the unamortized prior service cost, and to stockholders' equity for any excess. These adjustments and their rationale are complex and beyond the scope of our discussion. It should be noted that changes in the minimum liability, intangible asset, or owners' equity adjustment would not directly affect the determination of annual pension expense. They would have an impact only on the balance sheet.

companies did, particularly if it reduced pension expense. What happens to over- or underfunded pension plans when companies switch accounting principles?

If a company's projected benefit obligation differs from the fair market value of the plan assets at the time of change to *Statement No. 87,* an unrecognized net obligation or an unrecognized net asset arises. This *transition amount* must be expensed over either the average remaining service lives of the employees or 15 years. As with unrecognized prior service cost and unrecognized net gains, the transition amount never appears on the balance sheet. It does add another element to the pension expense calculation, however.

Sometimes this transition amount can significantly distort pension expense in the first few years after adoption of the new standard. For example, Caterpillar, Inc. estimated that the change to *FASB Statement No. 87* reduced its 1986 pension expense by about $10 million. Its table of pension expense components (in millions) appears below.

| | | |
|---|---:|---:|
| Service cost—benefits earned during period | | $ 65 |
| Interest on projected benefit obligation. | | 254 |
| Actual return on plan assets | $(645) | |
| Less: Difference between actual and expected return | 383 | |
| Expected return on plan assets | | (262) |
| Amortization: | | |
| Prior service cost | | 7 |
| Net transition asset. | | (19) |
| Pension expense. | | $ 45 |

Caterpillar's pension plans had assets exceeding projected benefit obligations by $288 million at the date of the switch to the new standard. The $19 million reduction in pension expense is the amortization of the $288 million applicable to 1986.

## Disclosure Requirements

Because of the complexities and alternatives accompanying pension calculations, informed readers need more disclosure about the significant factors affecting pensions than just the amounts on the financial statements. *FASB Statement No. 87* mandated some extensive disclosures to be presented in the notes. For single-employer defined benefit plans, these include:

1. A description of the plan identifying the employee groups covered, the type of benefit formula, funding policies, and the type of assets held in the plan.
2. The components of pension expense (net periodic pension cost) for the period. These include service cost + interest − expected return on plan

assets + amortization of prior service cost + amortization of unrecognized gains and losses + amortization of the transition amount.

3. The projected benefit obligation with a separate breakdown of the vested benefits and the accumulated benefit obligation.

4. Fair value of plan assets.

5. The amounts of any unrecognized prior service costs, unrecognized net gain or loss, and any unrecognized transition amount.

6. The discount rate (settlement rate) assumption used to value the actuarial liabilities, the assumed rate of return on plan assets, and the salary progression assumption.

7. A reconciliation of the funded status of the pension plan with the amount of any prepaid pension asset or accrued pension liability recognized on the balance sheet.

For the knowledgeable reader, these disclosures provide the detail behind many of the calculations and hopefully remove some of the mysteries about accounting for pensions.

## DISCUSSION OF THE KIMBERLY-CLARK ANNUAL REPORT

Notes 3 and 7 to the financial statements contain the detailed disclosures of Kimberly-Clark concerning pension plans and leases (see the Appendix to Chapter 6). Let us deal with leases first.

### Leases

Kimberly-Clark appears to have no capital lease liabilities. Note 7 provides information only about operating leases. In addition, we find no evidence of assets acquired through capital leases being combined with other property or lease obligations being combined with other long-term debt in Note 4. However, a review of the *1986* annual report reveals that in 1986, assets acquired through capital leases amounted to $6.4 million and were combined with other property. This makes economic sense because a capital lease represents in substance the purchase of tangible property. The capital lease is a financing device; there is no difference between assets financed by a capital lease and those financed by other forms of borrowing. Some companies, on the other hand, do adopt an acceptable alternative of reporting leased property as a separate intangible asset.

In *1986*, Kimberly-Clark included $7.4 million of capital lease obligations along with its other long-term debt. (Note the difference between the valuation of the liability in 1986 and the valuation of the asset in 1986 mentioned in the above paragraph.) Evidently, by 1987 the capital leases were all paid off or were so immaterial that the disclosure requirements no longer applied.

*FASB Statement No. 13* requires disclosure of schedules showing the minimum rental payments required under operating leases and capital leases. As noted, the latter are very small or nonexistent at the end of 1987 for Kimberly-Clark. Its Note 7 reports operating lease information only. Such information allows readers to better judge future cash flows. Remember, however, that the $60.9 million that Kimberly-Clark shows in Note 7 does not appear as an accounting liability. Operating leases are treated as executory contracts.

There is a material difference between the rental payments of $15.9 million required in 1988 and the rental expense under operating leases of $52.5 million in 1987. The schedule contains only the *minimum* required rental payments. Rent expense includes all rental payments for the period including contingent rentals based on various performance indices (e.g., sales volume) during the year.

## Pensions

All of the information that Kimberly-Clark reports about its pension and retirement plans is contained in Note 3. This information follows the guidelines of *Statement No. 87*, which the company adopted in 1986 for its pension plans in North America and in 1987 for its plan in the United Kingdom. The pension expense figures are not comparable across the three years being reported because of this change in standards.

Kimberly-Clark estimates for the reader that adoption of the new standard reduced pension expense by $11.1 million in 1986 and by another $4.1 million in 1987. The reason for the decline is not indicated. One might speculate that the settlement discount rates used to value the pension obligations have increased compared to 1985. Higher discount rates mean a lower present value of obligations on which interest is accrued.

Let us take a look at the components of the $24.1 million of pension expense for 1987. Benefits earned (service cost or normal cost) of $30.9 million and interest of $73.1 million on the actuarial liability (projected benefit obligation) at the beginning of the year are common elements of pension cost. To this is added $3.3 million of special early retirement benefits and $1.4 million of other pension expense. Subtracted is $900,000 of amortization of transition adjustment. At the times of adoption of *Statement No. 87*, the pension plans were slightly overfunded (more assets than projected benefit obligations). This excess "unrecognized asset" is spread over 14 to 18 years as a reduction in pension expense.

The major subtraction in the calculation of pension expense is the expected return on plan assets of $83.7 million. Kimberly-Clark assumes an 11 percent average long-run rate of return. The actual return of $143.7 million exceeded the expected return and is disclosed parenthetically. The difference between the actual return and the expected return in the current year becomes part of the unrecognized experience (actuarial) gain of the following period, possibly to be amortized. There was no amortization of actuarial gains and losses in 1987 (or in 1986) for reasons we will discuss shortly.

The second page of Note 3 contains the additional disclosures we mentioned in the preceding section of this chapter. Kimberly-Clark uses interest rates of 10 to 10.5 percent to discount its benefit obligations to present value. The amount of the accumulated benefit obligations is $658.2 million, and the amount of the projected benefit obligations is $836.2 million. These are the present values of pension benefits promised to all employees based on service rendered to date. These figures reflect not only the discount rate but other actuarial assumptions regarding such events as death, disability, and withdrawal. The difference between these two numbers reflects the impact of future compensation which Kimberly-Clark assumes will increase at a rate of 6 to 7.5 percent a year.[17]

On December 31, 1987, the fair value of the assets in the pension plans exceed the projected benefits earned to date by $99.9 million. In an economic sense, this represents a type of net asset of the plan. The reconciliation below explains that this "net asset" or "favorable situation" (at least at this particular point in time) results from three factors.

**1.** The greatest factor accounting for the net asset status is favorable actuarial experience. We have already noted that the actual rate of return in both 1986 and 1987 exceeded the expected rate of return. The total excess for the two years of $75.6 million accounts almost entirely for the favorable actuarial experience. Actuarial gains normally must be amortized as a reduction in pension expense over the remaining service lives of the employee group. That requirement, however, applies only to significant actuarial gains. Significant actuarial gains, according to *FASB Statement No. 87,* are those that exceed 10 percent of the greater of the pension assets or obligations. Because $77.7 is less than 10 percent, Kimberly-Clark does not amortize it. However, if the favorable experience continues, this "unrecognized asset" would begin to be amortized.

**2.** We already mentioned the favorable transition adjustment. The initial overfunding of the pension plan also is an "unrecognized asset." It, however, must be and is being amortized. The remaining transition amount is $13 million.

**3.** Finally, among the other assets on the balance sheet is $9.2 million of Prepaid Pension Cost. This amount arose because Kimberly-Clark contributed $9.2 million more over time than it charged to pension expense. Of course, cash payments greater than periodic pension expense contributes to the pension plan being overfunded. This is the only reconciliation item that actually appears on the books of Kimberly-Clark.

---

[17] Different interest rate assumptions and compensation progression assumptions exist because there are numerous pension plans for different employee groups.

This second schedule allows readers to evaluate the financial soundness of the pension plan, to assess the nature and types of *liabilities of the pension plan,* and highlights the differences between the financial status of the plan and the financial status of the company with respect to the plan as revealed by its balance sheet.

# SUMMARY

This chapter considers two advanced topics in the area of accounting liabilities and related expenses. It is evident from the discussions in the chapter that the problems of lease and pension accounting are complex. Each area has its theoretical controversies, practical compromises, and baffling detail. *FASB Statement No. 13* on leases ranks near the top in terms of subsequent modifications, amendments, and interpretations; *FASB Statement No. 87* on pensions tops the scale in terms of complexity and difficulty in understandability. Present value measurements and methodology provide the connecting thread between these two areas.

There are normally two parties to a lease transaction. The lessee uses the asset and pays rent for it; the lessor holds legal title to the asset and receives the rental amounts. A critical accounting issue focuses on detecting those leasing transactions that are in substance, if not in form, installment purchases of the leased property from the lessor by the lessee. An asset and a liability must be reflected for such capital leases on the lessee's books. An operating lease, on the other hand, is viewed by the lessee as a straight rental arrangement. The lessee records only rent expense.

The FASB, in its *Statement No. 13,* has formulated criteria for use in making the lease-classification decision. This decision substantially affects the financial statements of the lessee. A capital lease, in comparison to an operating lease, results in greater assets and debt, generally lower income, and lower return on investment. The current criteria have made it more difficult for a lessee's purchase through leasing to escape its balance sheet. Nevertheless, the arguments put forth for expanded capitalization of leases seem more persuasive than those calling for the capitalization of fewer leases.

Pension expense begins with a determination of service cost. This amount equals the present value of the pension benefits earned during the year. The benefit formula and the various actuarial assumptions concerning future events, including salary progression, determine the amount earned. The annual service cost is increased by interest on the actuarial liability at the beginning of the year, increased by the amortization of prior service cost to recognize the cost of benefits granted retroactively, decreased by the expected return on pension fund assets, and adjusted for amortization of experience gains and losses and amortization of the initial net asset or liability at the time of adoption of *Statement No. 87.*

The new pension reporting requirements went into effect in 1987. Certainly they will reduce management's discretion. Only one actuarial cost method is allowed, and guidelines are given for the choice of discount rates and periods of amortization for prior service costs. Generally, pension expense will be lower than previously recorded because most settlement discount rates used to value the pension obligations are higher than the rates previously used. Also, transition assets and experience gains are amortized faster than before. However, the pension expense may fluctuate more because the settlement discount rate can change from year to year.

Our simplified calculations and examples illustrate how present values are used in the valuation of lease liabilities and how this methodology underlies the fundamental nature of pension expense and liabilities. In the case of capital leases, the present values of the future payments are recorded as liabilities. In the case of pensions, the present value of pensions earned by employees during the period directly affects the measurement of pension expense. However, only in select and complicated circumstances does the unfunded present value of benefits that are earned to date appear as a liability.

Whether particular present values are recorded as accounting liabilities or expenses may depend on other criteria and definitions. However, the valuation methodology is unmistakably clear in each of these areas. There is ample room with both leases and pensions for further refinements of both concept and procedure. A mastery of the basic principles now will help us understand future developments that inevitably will come.

# APPENDIX: *Accounting for Leases by the Lessor*

In one sense, accounting for leases by the lessor is the opposite side of the coin from accounting for the lessee. When the latter records a lease liability and periodic interest expense under a capital lease, the lessor should record a lease receivable and periodic interest revenue. Similarly, under an operating lease, the lessee records rent expense, and the lessor should record rent revenue. This symmetry basically holds, but recording is slightly more complex for the lessor in both concept and procedure.

At times, the economic facts surrounding the lease transaction suggest that the lessor is basically a manufacturer or dealer who is using the leasing mechanism as a means of selling a product under a long-term sales contract. On other occasions, the lessor essentially finances a long-term purchase of property that the lessor has already acquired from a manufacturer or dealer. At other times, the lessor is merely entering into a short-term rental arrangement. These three different situations involving lessors are referred to, respectively, as sales-type, direct-financing, and operating leases. The operating lease is, once again, a residual category; in other words, all lessor leases that cannot be considered either sales-type or direct-financing leases are considered to be operating leases.

Both sales-type and direct-financing leases involve the capitalization of lease *receipts* as an asset. The leased property is removed from the lessor's balance sheet (to appear on the lessee's balance sheet) and is replaced by an interest-bearing receivable. The difference between the two types of lease capitalization hinges on whether or not the lease creates a manufacturer's or dealer's profit for the lessor. If it does, the lease is a sales-type. Otherwise, it is a direct-financing lease. For example, if a lessor leases a computer under a capital-type lease, it is likely to be a sales-type lease if the lessor is IBM, but it will probably be a direct-financing lease if the lessor is the leasing department of a bank that bought the computer from IBM.

As its name implies, a sales-type lease is viewed as a sale, so the manufacturer or dealer lessor must record sales revenue and cost of goods sold at the initiation of the lease and then reflect over the lease term the interest revenue earned from the *financing* aspect of the transaction. Under a direct-financing lease, a receivable is established whose *present value* equals the cost of the property being transferred to the lessee. The difference between the present value of the lease receivable and the total cash receipts represents interest to be reflected as revenue over the term of the lease. Each lease payment consists of two elements — interest revenue and a partial collection of the receivable.

## Illustration

Let us use the facts previously given in the illustration of accounting by the lessee. Laural Corporation entered into a six-year lease of some machinery. The machinery has a useful life of six years and no expected residual value. The annual lease payments are $10,000. Assume that the machinery, which had a cash price of $41,114, was manufactured by a lessor, Suma Corporation, at a cost of $30,000. Table 12A–1 reveals how Suma would record the lease events under both the sales-type and operating-lease assumptions. Recall that 12 percent was the approximate effective interest rate implicit in the lease. In the far right column of Table 12A–1, the assumption that Suma manufactured the leased machinery is dropped. There, we assume that Suma is a leasing division of a large bank and has recently made an outright cash purchase of the machinery for $41,114 from the manufacturer.

Under an operating lease, the only revenue reported is rental revenue. Also, the leased property is kept on the lessor's books and depreciated there. The lessor's treatment of an operating lease parallels that of the lessee.

How can sales-type, direct-financing, and operating leases be distinguished from one another for recording purposes? The FASB specifies in *Statement No. 13* that a lease will be *either* a sales-type or a direct-financing lease if:

1. It meets at least one of the four conditions for a capital lease previously discussed.
2. It also meets both of the following conditions:
   a. Collectibility of the minimum lease payments is reasonably predictable.
   b. No important uncertainties surround the amount of unreimbursable costs yet to be incurred by the lessor under the lease.

All leases not meeting the above criteria are operating leases.

These conditions specifying the proper classification of lessor leases appear reasonable. The reference to the capital lease criteria enhances consistency in the

**TABLE 12A–1**  Effect of Lease Classification on Lessor's Accounting Entries

| | *If Lease is Considered* | | |
| --- | --- | --- | --- |
| | *Sales Type* | *Operating* | *Direct Financing* |
| **Jan. 1, 1989—Beginning of lease term** | Lease Payments Receivable............ 60,000<br>  Sales............ 41,114<br>  Unearned Interest Revenue............ 18,886<br>Cost of Goods Sold............ 30,000<br>  Merchandise Inventory............ 30,000 | No entry<br><br>Property Leased to Others............ 30,000<br>  Merchandise Inventory............ 30,000 | Lease Payments Receivable............ 60,000<br>  Machinery............ 41,114<br>  Unearned Interest Revenue............ 18,886 |
| **Dec. 31, 1989—End of first year of lease** | Cash............ 10,000<br>  Lease Payments Receivable............ 10,000<br>Unearned Interest Revenue............ 4,934<br>  Interest Revenue............ 4,934<br>$60,000 − $18,886 = $41,114 net receivable; 12% of $41,114 = $4,934 | Cash............ 10,000<br>  Lease Rental Revenue............ 10,000<br>Depreciation Expense............ 5,000<br>  Accumulated Depreciation............ 5,000<br>straight-line, 1/6 of $30,000. | Cash............ 10,000<br>  Lease Payments Receivable............ 10,000<br>Unearned Interest Revenue............ 4,934<br>  Interest Revenue............ 4,934<br>$60,000 − $18,886 = $41,114 net receivable; 12% of $41,114 = $4,934 |
| **Dec. 31, 1990—End of second year of lease** | Cash............ 10,000<br>  Lease Payments Receivable............ 10,000<br>Unearned Interest Revenue............ 4,326<br>  Interest Revenue............ 4,326<br>$50,000 − $13,952 = $36,048 net receivable; 12% of $36,048 = $4,326 | Cash............ 10,000<br>  Lease Rental Revenue............ 10,000<br>Depreciation Expense............ 5,000<br>  Accumulated Depreciation............ 5,000 | Cash............ 10,000<br>  Lease Payments Receivable............ 10,000<br>Unearned Interest Revenue............ 4,326<br>  Interest Revenue............ 4,326<br>$50,000 − $13,952 = $36,048 net receivable; 12% of $36,048 = $4,326 |

recording of the lease by both parties. The additional conditions simply ensure that the lessor's performance is essentially complete when the asset is transferred to the lessee, as would in fact be the case if the lessor had sold the asset to the lessee.

*FASB Statement No. 13* specifies that lessors under capital leases should establish any needed receivable account at the total dollar amount of future rentals to be received. The $60,000 shown in Table 12A–1 as the initial Lease Payments Receivable for the sales-type and direct-financing leases consists of the $41,114 discounted present value of the rental receipts and $18,886 of as yet unearned interest revenue. Because the valuation of the receivable is its present value, the Unearned Interest Revenue account must be treated as a *contra asset account* to the Lease Payments Receivable account on the lessor's balance sheet.

Interest revenue becomes earned and recognized over the six-year term of the lease and is accompanied by reductions in the Unearned Interest Revenue account. Because the lessor establishes the receivable for the gross payments due (including interest), this account can be reduced each year by $10,000, which is the full amount of the annual lease receipt. A comparison of the *net* receivable (Lease Payments Receivable less Unearned Interest Revenue) over the two years reveals that it has declined $5,066 and $5,674 in 1989 and 1990, respectively. These amounts are the same as the decline recorded directly in the liability account in Table 12–1.

As implied by its title, the *sales-type lessor* records sales revenue and cost of goods sold at the lease inception date. Merchandise Inventory is reduced, and $11,114 of gross profit ($41,114 − $30,000) is reflected immediately in income. The *direct-financing lessor* is not considered to have made a sale. Accordingly, no gross profit is recorded, and its revenue from the lease will include only the interest revenue, which the sales-type lessor also recognizes. The leased property remains on the books of the *operating lessor,* so it is the only lessor in Table 12A–1 that records Depreciation Expense. In the operating lease situation, the lessor records Lease Rental Revenue in place of gross profit and interest revenue.

Of course, Suma *cannot* choose among the three sets of journal entries exhibited in Table 12A–1. If (1) Suma is the manufacturer of the leased machinery, and (2) the capital-type lease conditions are met, then the journal entries in the left-most column of Table 12A–1 *must* be followed. The event qualifies as a sales-type lease. In a similar fashion, changed circumstances would dictate treatment as either a direct-financing or an operating lease.

Table 12A–2 illustrates the impact of the three leases on the financial statements.

Lessors tend to prefer capital-lease treatment rather than operating-lease treatment. Manufacturers and dealers prefer to structure their lease transactions as sales-types so they can recognize a gross profit in the year of sale. Total *income* over the lease is the same, but sales-type leases allocate more of it to the year of sale. Similarly, a financial institution generally prefers the transaction to be structured as a direct-financing lease rather than as an operating lease because more of the same income stream over the six years is allocated to the early years of the lease period.[18]

---

[18] This tendency is not clear in Table 12A–2 because the operating lease assumes that the asset cost $30,000 while the direct-financing lease assumes that the asset cost $41,114. For the same asset cost, a direct-financing lease will provide a declining earnings stream over time that is higher in the earlier years. For example, *if* the asset had cost $41,114 under the operating lease, annual depreciation expense would have been $6,852 ($41,114/6 years). Net income would have been only $3,148 each year, lower than in the first two years of a direct-financing lease.

**TABLE 12A–2**    Effect of Lease Classification on Lessor's Financial Statements

| Income Statement | *Lease-Related Revenues and Expenses* | | | | | |
| | *Revenues* | | | *Expenses* | | *Net Income* |
| | *Sales* | *Interest* | *Rental* | *Cost of Goods Sold* | *Depreciation* | |
| 1989: | | | | | | |
| Sales-type . . . . . . | $41,114 | $4,934 | –0– | $(30,000) | –0– | $16,048 |
| Operating. . . . . . . | –0– | –0– | $10,000 | –0– | $(5,000) | 5,000 |
| Direct-financing . . . . | –0– | 4,934 | –0– | –0– | –0– | 4,934 |
| 1990: | | | | | | |
| Sales-type . . . . . . | –0– | 4,326 | –0– | –0– | –0– | 4,326 |
| Operating. . . . . . . | –0– | –0– | 10,000 | –0– | (5,000) | 5,000 |
| Direct-financing . . . . | –0– | 4,326 | –0– | –0– | –0– | 4,326 |

| Balance Sheet | *Property Leased to Others (net)* | *Present Value of Lease Payments Receivable* |
| --- | --- | --- |
| January 1, 1989: | | |
| Sales-type . . . . . . . . . . . . . . . . . . . . | –0– | $41,114 ($60,000 − $18,886) |
| Operating. . . . . . . . . . . . . . . . . . . . . | $30,000 | –0– |
| Direct-financing . . . . . . . . . . . . . . . . . . | –0– | 41,114 ($60,000 − $18,886) |
| December 31, 1989: | | |
| Sales-type . . . . . . . . . . . . . . . . . . . . | –0– | 36,048 ($50,000 − $13,952) |
| Operating. . . . . . . . . . . . . . . . . . . . . | 25,000 | –0– |
| Direct-financing . . . . . . . . . . . . . . . . . . | –0– | 36,048 ($50,000 − $13,952) |
| December 31, 1990: | | |
| Sales-type . . . . . . . . . . . . . . . . . . . . | –0– | 30,374 ($40,000 − $ 9,626) |
| Operating. . . . . . . . . . . . . . . . . . . . . | 20,000 | –0– |
| Direct-financing . . . . . . . . . . . . . . . . . . | –0– | 30,374 ($40,000 − $ 9,626) |

# Summary

From the lessor's perspective, a determination must be made as to whether the leasing transaction constitutes a sale by a manufacturer or dealer, a transfer of property and direct financing arrangement by a lessor who is not a manufacturer or dealer, or a simple rental situation. In the first two cases, the lessor records an interest-bearing receivable. In the first case, the manufacturer/dealer records a gross margin on the sale and interest revenue from the financing of the sale through the lease. In the second case, only interest revenue is recognized by the lessor. Under an operating lease, the lessor records only rental revenue and depreciation expense on the leased asset.

The conceptual guideline for making these distinctions is representational faithfulness. What treatment best describes the economic substance of the relationship? Does a particular lease effectively transfer the long-term control and major risks of ownership from the lessor to the lessee? *FASB Statement No. 13* currently provides the criteria for answering these questions and governs the disclosures that lessors have to make.

# PROBLEMS AND CASETTES

### Lease Problems:

## 12–1. Classification of Leases

Silvers Department Store has a number of stores located throughout the Midwest. Most of the stores are leased. Based on the information given below, explain whether the following six leases would be classified as operating leases or capital leases using the criteria of *FASB No. 13*. Assume that all lease payments are made at the end of the year and that 16 percent is the appropriate interest rate.

| Store Number | Fair Value of Property at Beginning of Lease | Economic Life | Lease Term | Lease Payment | Disposition at End of Lease |
|---|---|---|---|---|---|
| #316 | $1,000,000 | 10 | 8 | $210,000 | Reverts to lessor |
| #425 | 1,500,000 | 12 | 6 | $350,000 | Reverts to lessor |
| #509 | 2,300,000 | 12 | 10 | $430,000 | Title passes to lessee |
| #632 | 2,500,000 | 15 | 10 | $450,000 | Reverts to lessor |
| #657 | 3,000,000 | 15 | 12 | $500,000 | Lessee can purchase for $100 |
| #710 | 4,000,000 | 15 | 9 | $800,000 | Reverts to lessor |

## 12–2. Supply Missing Amounts about Capital Leases

The following schedule presents partial information regarding four capital leases of Esog Corporation. In each case, assume that the lease payments are made at the end of each year and that the company depreciates the leased property using the straight-line method.

| | Capital Lease | | | |
|---|---|---|---|---|
| | #1 | #2 | #3 | #4 |
| Life of lease (in years) . . . . . . . . | (A) | 9 | 8 | (J) |
| Annual lease payment . . . . . . . . | $ 5,000 | (D) | $ 7,500 | $9,000 |
| Interest rate . . . . . . . . . . | 10% | 8% | (G) | 16% |
| Present value of lease payments . . . . . . . . | $30,723 | (E) | $37,257 | (K) |
| Interest expense in Year 1. . . . . . . . | (B) | (F) | (H) | $5,816 |
| Depreciation expense in Year 1. . . . . . . . . . . . | (C) | $4,167 | (I) | (L) |

Calculate the number that should replace each of the letters in the above schedule. (All amounts are rounded to the nearest dollar.)

## 12–3. Calculations and Entries for Lessee

On January 1, 1990, Ro Corporation signs a five-year lease with Henry Company for some equipment. The equipment has a cash cost (fair market value) of $200,000, a useful life of five years, and no residual value. The lease is noncancelable, requires payments at the end of each year, and contains no renewal or bargain purchase options. Ro Corporation uses the straight-line method of depreciation for this type of equipment.

### Required:

*a.* If the interest rate implicit in the lease is 12 percent, demonstrate that the annual lease payment is about $55,480.

*b.* Prepare a repayment schedule for the lease liability similar to Table 12–3.

*c.* Prepare all journal entries for 1990 and 1991 in connection with the lease and equipment in the accounts of Ro as the lessee.

### 12–4. Classification, Calculations, and Entries for Lessee

On January 1, 1990, the Pinta Corporation signed an eight-year, noncancelable lease agreement for the use of some equipment. The equipment has a cash cost of $95,000, a useful life of about eight years, and no residual value. The contract calls for payments of $17,807 to be made at the end of each year. The firm capitalizes the lease rights and related obligations.

### Required:

*a.* Under generally accepted accounting principles, why is Pinta Corporation required to record this arrangement as a capital lease?

*b.* Demonstrate that the effective interest rate implicit in the lease is approximately 10 percent.

*c.* Prepare all the journal entries necessary on Pinta's books during 1990 and 1991 in connection with the lease. Management selects the sum-of-the-years'-digits method for the amortization of the lease rights.

*d.* Are you troubled by the fact that your entries in *c* show the asset account decreasing by lesser amounts in each successive year while the liability account decreases by larger amounts in each successive year? Explain.

*e.* What accounts and amounts will appear on the December 31, 1991 balance sheet relative to this lease?

### 12–5. Entries for Lessee and Executory Costs

On January 1, 1990, Monpere Corporation entered into a noncancelable, six-year lease for equipment. Annual lease payments of $55,000 are payable at the end of each year. The lease payments include not only the basic cost for the use of the equipment but also executory costs amounting to $4,000 that cover insurance, maintenance, and taxes. The latter costs are paid by the lessor, but are the obligation of Monpere Corporation. The effective interest rate inherent in the lease is 16 percent. Legal title reverts to Monpere at the end of the lease, at which time Monpere assumes responsibility for all executory costs. The equipment has an estimated life of 10 years with no salvage value.

The lease is recorded as a capital lease at an amount of $187,920. Sum-of-the-years'-digits depreciation is used.

### Required:

*a.* Why is this lease treated as a capital lease? How was the $187,920 amount calculated?

*b.* Prepare the journal entry on January 1, 1990 to record the lease.

*c*. Prepare the journal entries on December 31, 1990 to record the lease payment and to amortize the leased equipment.

*d*. Repeat the entries in part *c* for December 31, 1991.

### 12–6. Lease Payments at Beginning of Year

On January 1, 1991, National Trucking Company leased six trucks from American Leasing, Inc. to be used in its operations. The lease is to run for seven years with payments of $15,685 to be made at the *beginning* of each year. National is responsible for all maintenance, insurance, and taxes. However, the trucks revert to the lessor upon termination of the lease. The lessor is to earn a 10 percent return on its investment of $14,000 in each truck.

### Required:

*a*. Show how the $15,685 annual lease payment was derived.

*b*. Assume that the lease is treated as a capital lease by National (the lessee). Prepare the journal entries needed in 1991 and 1992. Assume straight-line depreciation.

*c*. Assume the lease is treated as an operating lease by National. What entries would it make in 1991 and 1992?

*d*. How should the lease be recorded by National? Why?

### 12–7. Comparison of Leasing and Borrowing

Adderly Company plans to acquire a new computerized data processing system. The manufacturer has offered to sell the system for $500,000. Adderly could borrow the $500,000 from an insurance company. Repayment would be via a five-year installment note bearing interest at a rate of 10 percent. The installment payments would be $131,900, payable at the end of each year. The system has a residual value of $100,000 and would be depreciated straight line over a five-year period.

Alternatively, the manufacturer will lease the equipment to Adderly under a five-year, noncancelable lease with an implicit interest rate of 10 percent. The lease payments of $115,520 are due at the end of each year. There are no bargain purchase or renewal options. The lease rights would be amortized straight line over the five years.

### Required:

*a*. Demonstrate that the capitalized lease rights and obligation would be $437,913 if the lease were treated as a capital lease.

*b*. For the first year, compare the total expenses of the (1) buy/borrow alternative (interest and depreciation), (2) treatment as a capital lease (interest and amortization), and (3) treatment as an operating lease (rent).

*c*. What is the total five-year expense for each of the three alternatives mentioned in *b*?

*d*. Assume that the company currently has $1,500,000 of assets, $500,000 of debt, and $1,000,000 of stockholders' equity. How is the ratio of total debt to total assets changed immediately after acquisition if the computer system were purchased, leased as a capital lease, or leased as an operating lease?

*e*. In your judgment, should this lease be a capital lease or an operating lease?

### 12–8. Off-Balance-Sheet Financing with Leases

Black Corporation reported the following assets and equities on December 31, 1989 (amounts in millions of dollars):

| **Assets** | | **Equities** | |
|---|---|---|---|
| Current . . . . . . . . . . | $ 20.4 | Current liabilities . . . . . . | $ 11.6 |
| Plant assets (net) . . . . . . | 115.0 | Long-term liabilities . . . . . | 89.9 |
| | | Common stock . . . . . . . | 20.0 |
| | | Retained earnings . . . . . . | 13.9 |
| Total assets . . . . . . . | $135.4 | Total equities. . . . . . . . | $135.4 |

The company recently approached its local bank and requested a loan to finance the purchase of $1.5 million of new equipment having an estimated useful life of 12 years. The bank refused to grant the firm the eight-year loan, even at the 15 percent interest rate Black Corporation was willing to pay. The company had almost given up, when the equipment dealer offered to structure an eight-year lease that "won't mess up your balance sheet and will only carry a 12 percent interest rate."

The firm enters into the lease on January 1, 1990. Payments of $268,741 are due each December 31.

**Required:**

*a.* Explain why the bank may have been reluctant to approve Black Corporation's application for a loan.

*b.* How could the dealer/lessor afford to offer Black a lease interest rate of 12 percent, a full 3 percent below the bank's rate?

*c.* How could the acquisition of this equipment have messed up Black's balance sheet? Has the lessor structured the lease agreement so as to avoid such an occurrence? Explain, showing calculations.

*d.* Prepare all journal entries necessary on Black's books for 1990 in connection with the lease.

*e.* Evaluate the representational faithfulness of Black's financial statements.

### 12–9. Impact of Leasing on Financial Statements

Memorial Corporation manufactures equipment used in demolition work. Fish Company wishes to buy a special type of crane from Memorial but cannot obtain sufficient financing. Memorial offers the crane to Fish on a noncancelable lease for 12 years, which is the crane's useful life.

The lease agreement is signed January 1, 1989 and calls for a $22,000 payment to be made at the end of each year. The crane cost Memorial $120,000 to manufacture, and it has a normal sales price of $136,277.

Fish Company's projected balance sheet as of December 31, 1989 and estimated income statement for 1989 are shown following (excluding any impact from the lease):

**Projected Balance Sheet**
**As of December 31, 1989**

| Assets | | Equities | |
|---|---|---|---|
| Current assets. . . . . | $ 270,000 | Current liabilities . . . . . . . | $180,000 |
| Land . . . . . . . . . | 50,000 | Long-term debt. . . . . . | 80,000 |
| Plant assets. . . . . . . | 400,000 | Stockholders' equity. . . . | 330,000 |
| Accumulated depreciation . . . . . | (130,000) | | |
| | $ 590,000 | | $590,000 |

**Projected Income Statement**
**For the Year 1989**

| | | |
|---|---|---|
| Sales . . . . . . . . . . . . . . . . . . . . . . . . . . . . . . . . | | $1,200,000 |
| Operating expenses . . . . . . . . . . . . . . . . . . . . . . | $740,000 | |
| Depreciation . . . . . . . . . . . . . . . . . . . . . . . . . | 70,000 | |
| Other expenses . . . . . . . . . . . . . . . . . . . . . . . | 210,000 | 1,020,000 |
| Income before taxes . . . . . . . . . . . . . . . . . . . | | $ 180,000 |
| Income taxes (40%) . . . . . . . . . . . . . . . . . . . . | | 72,000 |
| Net income. . . . . . . . . . . . . . . . . . . . . . . . . | | $ 108,000 |

## Required:

*a.* Calculate the effective interest rate implicit in this lease agreement.

*b.* Recast the financial statements for 1989 assuming that Fish records the lease as a capital lease. Assume the firm uses sum-of-the-years'-digits method to amortize the lease rights. Also assume no change in sales or expenses other than those caused by the lease.

*c.* Assume that Fish is able to reflect this transaction as an operating lease. Recast the financial statements for 1989 under this assumption.

*d.* Which set of statements would Fish prefer? Which best reflects the economic reality of the situation? Explain.

## Pension Problems:

**12–10. Basic Pension Calculations and Entries**

The Barbarajo Record Company sponsors a defined benefit pension program for its employees. The following information relates to the year 1991:

1. The present value of benefits attributable to services rendered by employees in 1991 is $150,000 using the projected unit credit method.
2. As of January 1, 1991, the pension plan had a projected benefit obligation of $2,800,000 and pension plan assets having a fair market value of $2,400,000.
3. The interest rate on the actuarial liability (settlement rate) is 8 percent; the return on plan assets is 10 percent.
4. Unrecognized prior service cost of $200,000 is being amortized over an average remaining service life for the participants of 10 years.
5. The company funds $120,000 during 1991.

**Required:**

*a.* Determine the total pension expense to be recognized in 1991. Identify its components.

*b.* Prepare the journal entries to record pension expense and the contribution to the pension trust fund for 1991.

**12–11. Basic Pension Calculations and Entries**

On January 1, 1991, Gerit Corporation adopts a defined benefit pension plan. Credit is given to employees for prior service. The present value of past service benefits is $240,000. (This is also the initial projected benefit obligation.) This amount will be amortized over 24 years, the average projected service life of the plan participants. The present value of benefits attributable to services rendered in 1991 and 1992 were $82,000 and $86,000, respectively. Interest on the projected benefit obligation accrues at the rate of 6 percent. An amount equal to the annual pension expense is contributed to the trustee of the pension plan at the end of each year and is invested by the trustee. These pension fund assets are expected to earn 8 percent.

**Required:**

*a.* Determine the total pension expense to be recognized in 1991. Identify its components.

*b.* Determine the total pension expense to be recognized in 1992. Identify its components.

*c.* Prepare the journal entries related to pension expense and pension contributions in both 1991 and 1992 on the books of Gerit Corporation.

**12–12. Pension Calculations for One Employee**

Macmo Company has one employee, Lauren, not covered by any pension program. The company decided to establish an individual plan for him. Lauren has worked for the company for 10 years, all of which counts toward his pension benefits. Other information related to Lauren and the pension plan appear below:

| | |
|---|---|
| Lauren's current age | 40 years |
| Retirement age | 60 years |
| Estimated life expectancy | 80 years |
| Pension benefit upon retirement | $30,000 per year, payable at the end of the year |
| Interest rate for both pension fund assets and actuarial liability | 12 percent |

**Required:**

*a.* Calculate the size of the pension fund that is needed when Lauren retires at age 60 in order to provide him with an annual pension of $30,000 per year.

*b.* Using the projected benefit actuarial method, calculate the normal cost for the first year after the plan is adopted (the 11th year actuarially). $(P/F, 19, .12) = .1161$.

*c.* Calculate the prior service cost at the time the plan is adopted. (This equals the actuarial liability after 10 years.)

*d.* Assume that the prior service cost will be amortized over the remaining 20 years of Lauren's service. Calculate the total pension expense for the first year of the program.

## 12–13. Calculation of Normal and Prior Service Costs

Makowski and Sons, Inc. initiates a pension program for its 10 employees. The firm makes the following actuarial assumptions:

1. Each employee will receive a pension payment of $5,000 per year upon retirement. The cash payments are made at the end of the year.
2. The average employee will live 12 years after retirement.
3. The average employee will retire 15 years after adoption of the pension plan.
4. The appropriate interest rate to use is 12 percent.

### Required:

*a.* Calculate the size of the pension fund needed in 15 years to provide the pension benefits to retired employees.
*b.* Assume that the answer to part *a* is $300,000. Determine the normal cost for the first five years.
*c.* What is the projected benefit obligation (actuarial liability) at the end of three years?
*d.* Assume that at the end of three years, Makowski and Sons, Inc. modifies the pension plan by increasing the annual pension by $500 to $5,500 per year. Calculate the prior service costs (change in the projected benefit obligation).

## 12–14. Pension Expense Calculations and Entries

Bubbling Beverage Company first adopted a formal pension plan on January 1, 1990. Credit toward benefits was given for prior service. The company's actuary estimated the initial projected benefit obligation (prior service cost) to be $350,000. Other information about the plan is given below:

|  | 1990 | 1991 |
|---|---|---|
| Normal service cost | $125,000 | $162,500 |
| Accumulated benefit obligation at year-end | 418,000 | 591,000 |
| Projected benefit obligation at year-end | 575,000 | 765,000 |
| Fair value of plan assets at year-end | 360,000 | 490,000 |
| Expected asset return rate | 10% | 10% |
| Current settlement rate | 12% | 8% |
| Funding contribution during year | $350,000 | $150,000 |
| Unrecognized actuarial gains (losses) at year-end | 45,000 | (76,000) |

Prior service cost and unrecognized actuarial gains and losses are to be amortized over 10 years, the average remaining service life of the employees.

### Required:

*a.* Calculate the amount of net pension expense that the company would recognize in 1990 and 1991.

*b.* Prepare the journal entries to record the expense and funding contribution in 1990 and 1991.

## 12–15. Interpretation of Pension Information

Harbour Company adopted the provisions of *FASB No. 87* at the beginning of 1989. Sy Clops, the assistant controller, is reviewing the information shown below on the pension plan for 1989 and 1990:

|  | *December 31* | | |
|---|---|---|---|
|  | *1988* | *1989* | *1990* |
| Accumulated benefit obligation . . . . . | $ 900,000 | $ 980,000 | $ 930,000 |
| Projected benefit obligation . . . . . . . | 1,160,000 | 1,280,000 | 1,210,000 |
| Fair value of pension assets . . . . . . . | 1,050,000 | 1,115,000 | 1,290,000 |

|  | *1989* | *1990* |
|---|---|---|
| Components of Net Pension Expense: | | |
| Service cost . . . . . . . . . . . . . . . . . . | $26,000 | $28,000 |
| Interest cost . . . . . . . . . . . . . . . . . | 87,000 | 94,800 |
| Expected return on plan assets . . . . . . . . . . . . | (84,000) | (89,200) |
| Amortization of transition amount . . . . . . . . . | 10,000 | 10,000 |
|  | $39,000 | $43,600 |

### Required:

*a.* Explain why the accumulated benefit obligation and projected benefit obligation increased from 1988 to 1989. Why did the two not increase by the same amount? (What is the difference between them?)

*b.* Sy does not understand how the projected benefit obligation can *decrease* from 1989 to 1990. Explain.

*c.* What rate of return is expected on plan assets? Is it the same for 1989 and 1990?

*d.* What is the interest rate (settlement rate) used to evaluate actuarial liabilities? Is it the same for 1989 and 1990?

*e.* Sy does not understand the amortization of the transition amount. Show him how the amount was calculated, and explain why it is part of the pension expense.

## 12–16. Calculation of Net Pension Expense

The trustee of the pension plan for Umberto Production Company provided the following information concerning the operation of the plan:

|  | *December 31* | | |
|---|---|---|---|
|  | *1987* | *1988* | *1989* |
| Accumulated benefit obligation . . . . . | $380,000 | $420,000 | $536,500 |
| Projected benefit obligation . . . . . . . | 480,000 | 550,000 | 677,500 |
| Fair value of plan assets . . . . . . . . | 112,000 | 280,000 | 398,000 |
| Normal service cost . . . . . . . . . . | | 100,000 | 125,000 |
| Prior service costs . . . . . . . . . . . | | — | 24,000 |
| Actuarial losses . . . . . . . . . . . . | | 10,000 | 18,000 |

The company adopted the provisions of *FASB No. 87* effective January 1, 1988. It modified the pension benefits in 1989, which gave rise to prior service costs. The expected rate of return on plan assets is 8 percent; the discount rate on the projected benefit obligation is 10 percent. The remaining average service life of employees is 20 years.

**Required:**

a. Explain what actuarial losses are and why they are relevant to calculating pension expense.
b. Explain what prior service costs are and why they are relevant to calculating pension expense.
c. Why does normal service cost increase from 1988 to 1989?
d. Calculate the initial transition amount to be amortized.
e. Calculate the net pension expense, divided into components, for 1988 and 1989.

**12–17. Reconciliation of Pension Expense and Balance Sheet Disclosure**
The following information relates to the pension program of Castillero Corporation as of December 3, 1991:

| | |
|---|---:|
| Projected benefit obligation | $405,000 |
| Accumulated benefit obligation | 375,000 |
| Fair value of plan assets | 300,000 |
| Unrecognized prior service cost to be amortized to expense | 60,000 |
| Unamortized actuarial loss | 7,000 |
| Pension expense recognized in 1991 | 70,000 |
| Cash contribution to plan during 1991 | 55,000 |

Assume no pension asset or liability existed at the beginning of the year on the balance sheet of Castillero.

**Required:**

a. What amount of asset/liability would appear on the balance sheet as of December 31, 1991?
b. Prepare the entries that were made during 1991 and the adjustments needed at the end of 1991.
c. Explain the nature of unamortized actuarial losses and the rationale for its treatment on the financial statements.
d. Explain the nature of unrecognized prior service costs and the rationale for its treatment on the financial statements.

**12–18. Calculation of Pension Estimates for a Complete Plan**
The Doleful Company established a pension plan on January 1, 1990. Annual benefits under the plan equal 2 percent of a retiree's average salary times the number of years of employment. Therefore, if an employee had an average salary of $20,000 and had worked for 10 years, the annual pension would be $4,000 ($20,000 × 0.02 × 10).

All costs of the plan are to be born by Doleful. Funding will be accomplished through payments to an independent trust fund.

The independent actuaries working with Doleful on the plan provide the following information and actuarial estimates:

1. Number of employees—100.
2. Percentage of employees who will retire under the plan—80 percent.
3. Average age on January 1, 1990—35.
4. Average years of eligible service prior to adoption of the plan—5.
5. Average age at retirement—65.
6. Average life expectancy after retirement—15.
7. Actuarial cost method—projected unit credit.
8. Interest rate to be used in actuarial calculations—10 percent.
9. Average salary of average employee:
   As of January 1, 1990—$10,000.
   As of December 31, 1990—$10,500.
   As of retirement date—$25,000.
10. (P/F, 29, .10) = .06304.

In all your computations, assume that cash payments are made at the end of the year.

**Required:**

a. Calculate the amount that needs to be on deposit at the average date of retirement for the employee group (December 31, 2019).
b. Without prejudice to your own answer, assume the answer in part *a* is $10,500,000. Now calculate the projected benefit obligation (prior service cost) as of January 1, 1990.
c. Also calculate the normal service cost applicable to 1990.
d. Without prejudice to your own answers, assume the answers in parts *b* and *c* are $86,000 and $19,000 respectively. Calculate total net pension expense for 1990.
e. Calculate the accumulated benefit obligation as of December 31, 1990. What role does this amount play in accounting for pension costs and liabilities?

**Casette 12–1. Georgia-Pacific Corporation**

In the Appendix at the end of the book is a complete set of financial statements of Georgia-Pacific Corporation taken from its annual report of 1987.

Answer the following questions related to the lease and pension disclosures shown on those statements.

a. Does Georgia-Pacific have any capitalized leases? How do you know? Where do they appear on the balance sheet?
b. Georgia-Pacific has no schedule of estimated payments under capital leases and under operating leases. Why?
c. Note 5 contains information about the company's defined benefit pension plans. What was the net pension expense during the last three years? Are these numbers comparable?
d. What are the components of the 1987 pension expense? Explain what each of them represents.
e. Why does an unrecognized net loss and an unrecognized prior service cost arise in 1986?

f.  Why are the discount rates used in determining the projected benefit obligation different each year? What impact does this change have?

g.  Can you reconstruct the journal entries that Georgia-Pacific made in 1986 and 1987 relevant to its defined benefit pension plan?

h.  What is the difference between a defined benefit plan and a defined contribution plan? Why would a company have both?

i.  Why are the pension disclosures much less extensive for the defined contribution plan than for the defined benefit plan?

**Casette 12–2.  Conversion of a Lease to Off-Balance-Sheet Financing***

Glass Bottle Company has perfected a new process for manufacturing small plastic bottles at half the cost of any comparable product. Glass has been actively promoting its new process and the response has been enthusiastic.

One of Glass's potential customers, International Drugs, could use so many plastic bottles that Glass would need to build a plant specifically to fill its orders. Glass does not have much capital and wants International to finance the construction. International refuses to put up cash, but wants the bottles and is agreeable to almost any financing plan.

Initially, Glass offered to create a new subsidiary, Plastics, to build the plant, finance it with a 100 percent bank loan, and lease it to International for 30 years. Lease payments would be substantially equal to the payments on the bank loan, which would be collateralized by the plant and by the lease agreement. Glass would have a 30-year management contract to operate the plant for a fee. The plan looked good, and it certainly was convenient. The bottle plant was to be built next to International's main manufacturing facility, and a conveyor belt was to carry the bottles into International's packing room.

But a snag soon appeared. International's auditors said that under Financial Accounting Standards Board Statement No. 13 on leases, the Plastics lease would require capitalization and the related additional "debt" would put International into default on its debt/equity requirement. Their conclusion was based on the fact that the proposed lease provided for minimum lease payments with a present value in excess of 90 percent of the fair value of the leased property. And so, International asked Glass to try again.

Now Glass has a new plan. Once again a new subsidiary (Plastics) would construct and finance the plant. This time, however, International would not be required to sign a lease but would simply be required to sign a purchase agreement. Under the purchase agreement, International would express its intention to buy all of its bottles from Plastics, paying a unit price which at normal capacity would cover labor, material, and overhead, the Glass operating fee, and the debt service requirement on the plant. That expected unit price is substantially lower than the current market price. Also, under the agreement, if International takes less than the normal production in any one year, and if the excess bottles are not sold at a high enough price on the open market, International is to make up any cash shortfall so that Plastics can make the payments on its debt and retain a profit to the extent of the man-

---

* Taken from Case 4 in *Accounting and Auditing Case Studies* (The Trueblood Professors' Seminar), The Touche Ross Foundation and the American Accounting Association, 1983, pp. 21–22.

agement fee. The bank will be willing to loan the money for the plant, taking the plant and the purchase agreement as collateral.

ating the plant and a guaranteed source of funds sufficient to service the obligation for the plant. International has an assured source of supply without incurring any obligation. The bank has its loan and feels secure. Glass's only concern is that International's auditor might object at the last minute. Glass's controller explains, "They were going to make International capitalize that lease, but surely they can't make International capitalize a purchase agreement. But just to be on the safe side, I'd like *you* to study this deal and tell me what you think. I'd like to be able to tell International that our auditors agree that this contract need not be recognized as an asset, or as a debt."

**Required:**

*a.* Evaluate Glass's new plan.
*b.* Does International have an asset and debt to record?

**Casette 12–3. Capital and Operating Leases of Caesars World**

Caesars World, Inc., is a major corporation in the entertainment industry. It showed the following information in its annual report for the fiscal year ending July 31, 1986 (amounts in thousands):

|  | 1986 | 1985 |
|---|---|---|
| Property under capital leases | $ 9,055 | $ 9,055 |
| Land | 45,740 | 45,739 |
| Buildings | 11,556 | 12,261 |
| Furniture, fixtures, and equipment | 1,180 | 1,357 |
| Current maturities of obligations under capital leases | 44,399 | 45,479 |
| Obligations under capital leases, net of current maturities | | |

**Note 8: Leases**

The Company leases land, buildings and equipment under noncancelable lease agreements which expire at various dates through 2076. The leases generally provide that the Company pay the taxes, insurance and maintenance expenses related to the leased assets. Major leased assets, which have been capitalized, include a portion of the Caesars Atlantic City facility and the land on which the hotel/casino is situated.

Caesars Atlantic City's primary lease expires in 2008, and is renewable for two additional 30-year periods. The Company has the right to purchase this property for $38,667,000 between 1989 and 1993 and a right to match any purchase offers for the property or the lease. The lease provides for a minimum rental of $2,820,000 for the lease year beginning June 1, 1986, increasing by up to $73,000 per year in each subsequent year, and a percentage rental of 19.3% of the hotel/casino's net profit (as defined). The percentage rental amounted to $6,432,000, $3,202,000 and $6,708,000 in 1986, 1985 and 1984, respectively.

The Caesars Tahoe land and building are leased pursuant to an operating lease which expires in 2004 and is renewable for two additional 25-year periods. The lease provides for a minimum rent of $1,931,000 for fiscal 1986, increasing by $75,000 per year in each subsequent year, and a percentage rental of 20% of the net profit (as defined). Additionally, the lease arrangements require an $11,857,000 payment in fiscal 1989, which is being amortized over the estimated useful life of the building. There was no percentage rental expense in 1986, 1985 or 1984.

Future minimum lease payments for all leases at July 31, 1986, are as follows (in thousands):

| | Year ending July 31 | Operating | Capital |
|---|---|---|---|
| | 1987 . . . | $ 7,359 | $ 6,141 |
| | 1988 . . . | 6,034 | 6,137 |
| | 1989 . . . | 17,566 | 6,091 |
| | 1990 . . . | 3,196 | 6,037 |
| | 1991 . . . | 3,150 | 6,010 |
| | Thereafter . | 46,834 | 153,260 |
| Total minimum lease payments. . . . . . | | $84,139 | 183,676 |
| Less amount representing interest. . . . . . | | | 138,097 |
| Less current maturities of obligations under capital leases. . . . . . | | | 45,579 |
| Long-term obligations under capital leases . . . . . . . . . . . . . | | | 1,180 |
| | | | $ 44,399 |

Minimum lease payments have not been reduced by future minimum sublease rentals of $1,830,000.

## Required:

a. Why is $138,097,000 subtracted from the future payments required under capital leases to obtain the amount that appears on the balance sheet?

b. Where does the total minimum lease payments of $84,139,000 for operating leases appear on the financial statements? Do you agree?

c. Caesar's Atlantic City facility is recorded as a capital lease while its Tahoe facility is recorded as an operating lease. What differences do you see between these leases that would justify different accounting treatments? Where does the incidence (risks and benefits) of ownership rest?

d. Separate contra accounts for accumulated depreciation and amortization of leased assets are not presented in the annual report. If such amounts were subtracted from the property under capital leases, would you expect the net amounts to equal the total amount shown as obligations under capital leases? Explain.

e. Explain how Caesars World will record the $11,857,000 payment in 1989 in connection with its Tahoe land and building. Is this consistent with treatment as an operating lease?

**Casette 12–4. Pillsbury Company as a Lessee and a Lessor**

Pillsbury, a major food company, has a fiscal year ending May 31. The following notes are taken from its annual report for the year ending May 31, 1986. They describe Pillsbury's activities as a lessee and as a lessor.

### 8. Investments as lessor

Restaurant subsidiaries lease buildings and land to franchisees. The building portions of the leases are direct financing leases while the land portions are operating leases. Substantially all leases are for 15 to 20 years, provide for minimum and contingent rentals, and require the franchisee to pay executory costs.

Minimum Future Lease Payments To Be Received during the
Fiscal Years Ending May 31:

| | Direct Financing Leases | Operating Leases |
|---|---|---|
| | *(in millions)* | |
| 1987 | $ 29.7 | $ 29.7 |
| 1988 | 30.2 | 28.9 |
| 1989 | 31.0 | 28.5 |
| 1990 | 31.0 | 27.0 |
| 1991 | 30.7 | 26.4 |
| Later | 307.3 | 275.0 |
| | $459.9 | $415.5 |

Net Investment in Direct Financing Leases at May 31:

| | 1986 | 1985 |
|---|---|---|
| | *(in millions)* | |
| Minimum lease payments receivable | $459.9 | $420.9 |
| Allowance for uncollectibles. | (4.4) | (4.0) |
| Estimated unguaranteed residual value. | 3.8 | 3.8 |
| Unearned amount representing interest. | (261.4) | (226.9) |
| Net investment | 197.9 | 193.8 |
| Current portion included in receivables | (4.6) | (4.5) |
| Net investment in direct financing leases. | 193.3 | 189.3 |

| Rental Income: | Year Ended May 31 | | |
|---|---|---|---|
| | 1986 | 1985 | 1984 |
| | *(in millions)* | | |
| Minimum rental income | $31.7 | $26.6 | $23.9 |
| Contingent rental income (a). | 32.3 | 32.8 | 27.9 |
| | $64.0 | $59.4 | $51.8 |

.(a) Includes contingent rentals on both owned and leased property under direct financing and operating leases.

## 9. Commitments as lessee

Capital leases cover restaurant buildings and transportation, computer and manufacturing equipment.

Operating leases cover land; manufacturing, warehousing and administrative facilities; grain handling and storage facilities; and manufacturing and transportation equipment.

Minimum Future Obligations on Leases with an Initial Term
Greater Than One Year (for the fiscal years ending May 31):

| | Capital Leases | Operating Leases (a) |
|---|---|---|
| | *(in millions)* | |
| 1987 | $ 15.7 | $ 69.1 |
| 1988 | 14.2 | 62.5 |
| 1989 | 13.1 | 59.4 |
| 1990 | 12.2 | 54.9 |
| 1991 | 11.6 | 49.3 |
| Later | 71.8 | 488.9 |
| Total minimum obligations (b) | 138.6 | 784.1 |
| Executory costs | (.8) | (6.3) |
| Net minimum obligations | 137.8 | $777.8(c) |
| Amount representing interest | (60.6) | |
| Present value of net minimum obligations | $ 77.2 | |
| Current portion | $ 7.2 | |

(a) Does not include obligations under term freight agreements for 1,860 barge loads in Fiscal 1987, decreasing to 1,360 in Fiscal 1989 and ending in Fiscal 1991.
(b) Minimum lease obligations have not been reduced by minimum sublease rentals. In addition to minimum obligations, contingent rentals may be paid under certain restaurant and grain facility leases on the basis of percentage of sales and volume, respectively.
(c) The present value of the net minimum future obligations under operating leases, calculated using the Company's incremental borrowing rate at the inception of the leases, is $362.9 million.

| Rental Expense: | 1986 | 1985 | 1984 |
|---|---|---|---|
| | *(in millions)* | | |
| Minimum rental expense (a) | $112.2 | $89.0 | $82.9 |
| Contingent rental expense (b) | 12.0 | 9.1 | 8.1 |
| Transportation equipment sublease income | (5.9) | (6.7) | (7.9) |
| | $118.3 | $91.4 | $83.1 |

(a) Includes rentals under leases with terms of one year or less. Payments under term freight agreements of $15.6 million, $21.9 million, and $26.1 million for Fiscal 1986, 1985 and 1984, respectively, are not included.
(b) Includes contingent rental expense under both capital and operating leases.

### Required:

*a*. Inasmuch as Pillsbury is a lessor and a lessee, would it be appropriate to offset the $193.3 million Net Investment in Direct Financing Leases against the $77.2 million Net Minimum Lease Obligations? Explain.
*b*. In Note 8, explain why building leases are direct financing leases while land leases are operating leases?
*c*. The balance sheet as of May 31, 1986 shows $193.3 million of Net Investment in Direct Financing Leases. Yet according to Note 8, Pillsbury expects to receive $459.9 million in cash receipts. Explain each of the items necessary to reconcile these two amounts.
*d*. Why does Pillsbury use direct financing leases instead of sales-type leases?
*e*. The total payments under capital leases in Note 9 are $138.6 million, but only $77.2 appears among the liabilities. Explain why.
*f*. The total net payments under operating leases in Note 9 are $777.8 million. Their present value is $362.9. Where does this amount appear on the balance sheet? Why did Pillsbury not employ the same disclosure schedule for operating leases as for capital leases?

### Casette 12–5.  Pension Accounting in the Telephone Industry

On January 1, 1984, American Telephone & Telegraph was required to divest part of the Bell System operating companies. The result was the existence of seven new telephone companies in addition to AT&T.

The selected quotations below are taken from the 1987 annual reports of two of those companies. All amounts are in millions.

#### AT&T

The company's pension contributions are made to trust funds, which are held for the sole benefit of pension plan participants. Contributions are determined in accordance with the aggregate cost method, an acceptable funding method under the Employee Retirement Income Security Act of 1974, and with appropriate Internal Revenue Service regulations. For purposes of determining contributions, rates of investment return are assumed and the weighted average of such rates was 7.6%, 7.8%, and 6.7% for 1987, 1986, and 1985, respectively.

Effective January 1, 1986, AT&T adopted the Statement of Financial Accounting Standards No. 87 (FAS 87), "Employers' Accounting for Pensions." Adoption of FAS 87 required AT&T to change from the aggregate cost method to the projected unit credit method for determining pension cost for financial reporting purposes. Additionally, FAS 87 required that the effects of retroactively applying the new method be amortized over the average remaining service period of active employees, which is estimated to be 15.9 years. Pension cost computed in accordance with FAS 87 was negative and amounted to $316 and $258 for 1987 and 1986, respectively, resulting in a pension credit (i.e., pension income). Pension cost for 1985 using the aggregate cost method was $657. If FAS 87 had not been adopted in 1986, pension cost computed using the aggregate cost method would have been $88 and $327 in 1987 and 1986, respectively.

Pension cost includes the following components:

|  | | 1987 | | 1986 |
|---|---|---|---|---|
| Service cost-benefits earned during the period . . . . . . . . . | | $ 446 | | $ 419 |
| Interest cost on projected benefit obligation . . . . . . . . . | | 1,351 | | 1,296 |
| Amortization of unrecognized prior service costs* . . . . . . . . | | 22 | | 13 |
| Less: Return on plan assets | | | | |
| Actual. . . . . . . . . . . . . | $1,412 | | $ 3,917 | |
| Deferred portion . . . . . . . . | 239 | | (2,415) | |
| Expected return . . . . . . . . . | | 1,651 | | 1,502 |
| Amortization of transition asset . . . | | 484 | | 484 |
| Pension credit . . . . . . . . . . . | | $ 316 | | $ 258 |

*These costs pertain to plan amendments in 1987 and prior years and are amortized on a straight-line basis over the average remaining service period of active employees.

The funded status of the plan was as follows:

| At December 31 | 1987 | 1986 |
|---|---|---|
| Actuarial present value of accumulated benefit obligation, including vested benefits of $14,623 and $14,222, respectively. . . . . . | $16,484 | $16,169 |
| Plan assets at market value . . . . . . . . . . | $26,590 | $26,379 |
| Less: Actuarial present value of projected benefit obligation . . . . . . | 17,696 | 17,481 |
| Excess of assets over projected benefit obligation. . . . . . . . . . . . | 8,894 | 8,898 |
| Unrecognized prior service costs . . . . . . . | 467 | 333 |
| Less: Unrecognized transition asset. . . . . . | 6,728 | 7,211 |
| Unrecognized net gain . . . . . . . . | 1,607 | 1,359 |
| Prepaid pension cost . . . . . . . . . . . | $ 1,026 | $ 661 |

The projected benefit obligation was determined using discount rates of 8.25% and 8.0% at December 31, 1987 and 1986, respectively, and an assumed long-term rate of compensation increase of 5.0%. The expected long-term rate of return on plan assets used in determining pension cost was 8.0% for 1987 and 1986. Plan assets consist primarily of listed stock, corporate and governmental debt, and real estate investment.

## Southwestern Bell

The Corporation's objectives in funding the plans, in combination with standards of the Employee Retirement Income Security Act of 1974 (ERISA), are to accumulate funds sufficient to provide for all promised benefits and to maintain a relatively stable contribution level in the future.

Pension cost for 1987 and 1986 was determined in accordance with Statement of Financial Accounting Standards No. 87, "Employers' Accounting for Pensions" ("Statement No. 87"), which requires the use of the projected unit credit method for pension cost determination and disclosure. The change in pension cost for 1987 over the prior year reflects the refinement of actuarial calculations associated with the implementation of Statement No. 87, a change in the discount rate and asset gains. Pension cost for 1986 reflects the change in accounting method required by the Corporation's adoption of Statement No. 87. The net effect of the change was to reduce pension cost for 1986, when compared to 1985, by approximately $166.8 and increase net income and earnings per common share by approximately $78.9 and $0.26, respectively. Pension cost for 1985 was determined under the provisions of Accounting Principles Board Opinion No. 8 utilizing the aggregate cost method.

Pension cost includes the following components:

|  | 1987 | 1986 |
|---|---|---|
| Service cost—benefits earned during the period | $ 91.5 | $ 90.0 |
| Interest cost on projected benefit obligation | 272.7 | 276.6 |
| Actual return on plan assets | (166.9) | (878.1) |
| Other—net | (301.0) | 452.6 |
| Pension cost | $(103.7) | $ (58.9) |

Statement No. 87 requires certain disclosures to be made reconciling the fair value of the plans' assets with amounts reported in the Corporation's balance sheets. This comparison, while intended to provide a general indication of the soundness of the pension plans' financial status, should be cautiously viewed, as the pension plans' assets are not general assets of the Corporation but are instead entrusted to irrevocable trust funds to provide retirement and survivor benefits.

A point-in-time comparison of the fair value of the plans' net assets to the estimated projected benefit obligation also has certain limitations. Market conditions will result in fluctuations in the fair value of the plans' net assets while having no direct effect on the actual benefits to be paid. In addition, the projected benefit obligation is based on assumptions concerning future events, conditions and payments covering a time period equivalent to the estimated life span of the existing employee work force. If actual experience differs from expectations, the benefit obligation will be affected.

The following table sets forth the defined benefit plans' funded status and amounts recognized as other assets in the Corporation's Consolidated Balance Sheets as of December 31:

|  | 1987 | 1986 |
|---|---|---|
| Fair value of plan assets | $ 5,678.6 | $ 5,599.1 |
| Adjusted for: |  |  |
| Unrecognized net gain | (377.3) | (530.6) |
| Unamortized difference between the fair value of plan assets and the projected benefit obligation at the transition date | (1,454.6) | (1,411.3) |
| Adjusted value of plan assets | 3,846.7 | 3,657.2 |

| Estimated amounts of assets required to provide funds for future payments of projected benefit obligation . . . . . . . . . . . | 3,831.6 | 4,081.8 |
|---|---|---|
| Adjusted for: | | |
| Unrecognized prior service cost . . . . . | (126.8) | (98.5) |
| Unrecognized net loss . . . . . . . . . . | (204.1) | (479.2) |
| Adjusted projected benefit obligation . . . . | 3,500.7 | 3,504.1 |
| Prepaid pension cost. . . . . . . . . . . | $   346.0 | $   153.1 |

Pension costs are determined using the actuarial assumptions at the beginning of the year. The funded status is determined using the actuarial assumptions as of the end of the year.

### Required:

a. Both AT&T and Southwestern Bell have negative pension expense in 1987 and 1986. How can pension expense be negative, particularly in light of the fact that a change was made from the aggregate cost method to the projected unit credit method?

b. AT&T uses different rate-of-return assumptions and actuarial cost methods for the purpose of determining periodic contributions to the trust funds than it does for determining pension expense. Is this appropriate? Why does AT&T do so?

c. Do you agree with Southwestern Bell's comments about the limitations of point-of-time comparisons and reconciliations of plan assets and benefits? What difference does it make that plan assets belong to irrevocable trust funds?

d. Both AT&T and Southwestern Bell present schedules disclosing the determination of pension expense and setting forth the funded status of the plan. The formats of these schedules are different. Which do you prefer? Why?

e. What was the amount of the original transition asset on January 1, 1986 for each corporation?

f. Southwestern Bell used discount rates of 8.0 percent in 1987 and 7.5 percent in 1986. It assumed a 7 percent rate of increase in future compensation in both years. Its expected long-term rate of return on plan assets was 7.5 percent in 1987 and 8.5 percent in 1986. Is it appropriate for Southwestern Bell to use different actuarial assumptions from AT&T? Discuss the implications of these differences on the determination of pension costs and pension liabilities if all other factors were constant between the two companies.

## 12A–1. Classification and Recording by Lessor

Stevens Automobile Mart sells and leases automobiles on a long-term basis. On January 1, 1991, it leases a car under a noncancelable, four-year lease. The fair value of the car is $17,751; it cost Stevens $12,200. Legal title passes to the customer upon termination of the lease. Stevens Automobile Mart desires an interest rate of 10 percent. Lease payments are made at the end of each year.

### Required:

a. How should Stevens record this lease? What other conditions would need to be satisfied?

   *b.* Calculate the required lease payments.
   *c.* Prepare a collection schedule for all four years. (Pattern your answer after Table 12–3 but from the lessor's viewpoint showing a receivable and interest revenue.)
   *d.* Prepare journal entries for Stevens in 1991 and 1992 to record the lease, the receipt of lease payments, and interest revenue.

## 12A–2. Entries under Direct-Financing Lease

Smile-Bright is a professional corporation of five dentists who operate a joint practice. They would like to acquire $200,000 of new equipment. However, the manufacturer will not sell the equipment to the corporation on credit unless each dentist personally guarantees repayment. However, the leasing department of the local Washington County Bank agrees to buy the equipment and then lease it to the dental corporation under the following terms:

1. Date of the lease is January 1, 1991.
2. Annual lease payments are $43,825, payable at the end of each year.
3. Lease is noncancelable for a period of seven years, at which time legal title passes to the corporation.
4. All executory costs are paid directly by the lessee.
5. The equipment has an estimated economic life of ten years.

### Required:

   *a.* Demonstrate that the bank will earn an effective interest rate of approximately 12 percent on its investment.
   *b.* Prepare journal entries in the accounting records of the bank (lessor) for the signing of the lease and the receipt of the first two lease payments.
   *c.* How would the recording be different if the original manufacturer had been the lessor?

## 12A–3. Financing Lease Received at Beginning of Year

Refer to the leasing situation introduced in Problem 12–6.

### Required:

   *a.* Assume that the lease is treated as a capital lease by American Leasing (the lessor). Prepare the journal entries needed during 1991 and 1992.
   *b.* Assume that the lease is treated as an operating lease by American Leasing. What entries would it make in 1991 and 1992?

## 12A–4. Sales-Type versus Operating Lease

The Mineral Point Computer Manufacturing Company makes and sells a computer model, Series 6318. The cost to Mineral Point is $1,600,000. Customers can acquire the computer at a cash price of $2,027,700, or they can acquire it under a 10-year lease. The lease is noncancelable and requires cash payments of $300,000 to be made at the *beginning* of each of the 10 years. The computer normally has a useful life of 10 years. At the end of the lease, the lessee assumes title to the computer.

On January 1, 1990, the West Company acquired one of the Series 6318 computers under the lease arrangement. Collectibility is reasonably predictable, and no uncertainties exist concerning unreimbursed lessor costs. West assumes all costs of maintenance, insurance, and taxes.

### Required:

*a.* Demonstrate that the effective interest rate implied in the lease is 10 percent.

*b.* Assuming that Mineral Point treats the transaction as a sales-type lease, what amounts and accounts would appear on its income statement for 1990 and 1991?

*c.* As a sales-type lease, what amounts and accounts would appear on the balance sheet of Mineral Point as of December 31, 1990 and 1991?

*d.* Now assume that the recording is for an operating lease. What amounts and accounts would appear on the income statement for 1990 and 1991? (Mineral Point depreciates assets under operating leases using the sum-of-the-years'-digits method.)

*e.* As an operating lease, what amounts and accounts would appear on the balance sheet of Mineral Point as of December 31, 1990 and 1991?

# Chapter 13

# Accounting for Income Taxes

Corporate income taxes are periodic charges levied by federal, state, and foreign governments on the taxable income of incorporated business entities. Taxable income is defined by the tax laws of each taxing authority. Taxes are treated in financial accounting as an expense and are recorded as a reduction in stockholders' equity (a debit to Income Taxes) and an increase in a liability (a credit to Income Taxes Payable). The liability is eliminated when cash is paid to the governmental units.

An accounting problem arises when the determination of taxable income is not identical to the determination of financial income.[1] Taxable income is a legal concept. Governmental units use the tax laws to accomplish a number of objectives in addition to providing cash to run government operations. Tax regulations also are used to promote or discourage different types of economic and social activity. Consequently, for a number of revenue and expense items, tax codes permit a variety of special handlings that run counter to generally accepted accounting principles. Tax laws, therefore, use accounting data but do not necessarily adhere to the objective of properly matching costs and revenues to measure business income. The regulations underlying tax accounting do not necessarily coincide with the informational needs of investors and the basic concepts of financial accounting.

## DIFFERENCES BETWEEN FINANCIAL INCOME AND TAXABLE INCOME

On the surface, the differences between accounting income and taxable income appear to be minimal. The Internal Revenue Code, in Section 446, requires that taxable income be computed according to the method of

---

[1] In this chapter we shall use the term *taxable income* to refer to the number calculated according to income tax regulations and *financial income* to refer to financial accounting income *before tax* calculated according to generally accepted accounting principles. The latter figure often is called "book income."

accounting regularly employed by the taxpayer, if that method clearly reflects income. However, authorized throughout the Code and in the regulations interpreting the law are many exceptions and special provisions that reflect either policy goals of Congress, to be attained through the income tax law, or administrative rulings to make implementing the law convenient. For example, procedures designed to regulate business activity, to encourage or discourage particular industries, to stimulate economic development, to maintain a perceived equity among taxpayers, and to time tax levies to coincide closely with cash receipts are reflected in the income tax law. Thus, the complex nature of income tax rules arises from goals other than just the measurement of business income. Once these tax options are written into the law, however, companies deliberately take advantage of them to minimize current taxable income.

The differences between taxable income and financial income tend to fall into three categories: (1) permanent differences, (2) temporary differences, and (3) operating loss carryovers.

## Permanent Differences

Certain revenues and gains are excluded by law from income taxes. Interest revenue from state and municipal bonds, for instance, is not taxed but is properly recognized as accounting revenue on the income statement. A portion of the dividends received by a corporation from other taxable domestic corporations is treated in much the same way.

Particular deductions also may be treated differently for tax and financial accounting purposes. For example, goodwill is not subject to amortization under current tax regulations but must be written off periodically as an expense on the financial statements. Similarly, life insurance premiums paid on insurance policies of employees are not tax deductible if the corporation is the beneficiary under the policy. Nevertheless, they are a valid expense on the firm's income statement.

Unless and until the statutory provisions of the tax laws are changed, these permanent differences *always* will be a cause of disparity between tax accounting and financial accounting. There is nothing special to do about them. Still, permanent differences may cause difficulties in interpretation because of the lack of reconciliation between the effective tax rate as indicated by the income statement and the statutory federal income tax rate. Consequently, it is important to disclose any material, permanent differences; more is said on disclosure at the end of the chapter.

## Temporary Differences

In contrast to the permanent differences, some events are reported for both financial accounting purposes and tax purposes, but in different accounting periods. Differences between taxable income and financial income for any year that are not caused by permanent factors, are called "temporary" differences. Differences between the carrying value of assets and liabilities for tax purposes and the amounts reported on the financial statements give rise to the temporary differences.

Most temporary differences result from differences in timing. Over a sufficiently long period, any individual timing difference should disappear; total taxable income should equal total financial income.[2] Accordingly, temporary differences do raise important financial reporting questions concerning how they should be accounted for on a *periodic* basis.

Let us review some of the major causes of temporary differences related to timing:

**1.** *Revenue* is recognized in financial income *before* it is recognized in taxable income. Examples include revenue recognized at the time of sale but being reported for tax purposes in installments, so that the taxation of the revenue is deferred until later periods when the cash is actually received. A similar situation exists when a company recognizes income according to percentage of completion for financial income purposes but reports at least part of the income for tax purposes only when contracts are completed.

**2.** *Revenue* is recognized in financial income *after* its inclusion on the tax return. If a corporation receives prepayments for rent or royalties or cash advances for goods and services, under certain circumstances such cash receipts are taxable before the services are rendered or the goods are delivered. However, in the accounting statements some of these receipts normally are treated as liabilities. They are recognized as revenue in future periods when the earning process occurs.

**3.** *Expense* is recognized in the accounting records *before* it is deducted on the tax return. Tax regulations do not allow a current tax deduction for certain types of expenses (and losses) recognized in the current period. For instance, some financial income deductions that create estimated liabilities—for example, estimated provisions for product warranties, litigation losses, and some deferred compensation amounts—must be reported on the tax return only when the cash is actually paid. Similarly, estimated provisions for uncollectibles, sales returns, and discounts are reflected in financial income before they can be reflected in taxable income.

**4.** *Expense* is recognized in the accounting records *after* its deduction on the tax return. The most prevalent example is depreciation. As noted in Chapter 10, firms must use the Accelerated Cost Recovery System (ACRS) or a modified version of it (MACRS) for tax purposes for all property placed in service after 1980. For plant assets acquired before 1981, most companies use declining-balance or sum-of-the-years'-digits methods, for tax purposes.

---

[2] Even though the differences disappear in the long run, the present value of these differences may be significant. It is for this reason that companies try to minimize current taxes, even though in so doing they may be adding equally to future taxes.

However, the great majority of firms use the straight-line depreciation method for financial reporting purposes (see Table 10–5). Accordingly, depreciation deductions on the tax return normally exceed those on the income statement in the early years of the asset's life. The book value of the depreciable asset is higher in the financial accounting records than in the tax records. Of course, there is an offsetting effect in later years; that is why the difference is temporary. Similar results occur if pension expenditures or other costs are deductible for tax purposes in the year incurred but are spread over some future period for financial accounting purposes.

Given the disparate objectives of tax accounting and financial accounting, it is not surprising that taxable income may deviate temporarily from financial income. However, a firm's financial statements must somehow accommodate these differences in its reports. The impact of the temporary differences means that in any accounting period, the tax liability to the government (Current Income Taxes Payable) differs from the tax expense that would have been incurred had the tax code adhered to GAAP. Should the income tax expense on the income statement be determined necessarily from the legal liability shown on the tax return for the period, or should it be related to the events reported on the income statement? This question lies at the heart of a procedure called *deferred tax accounting*. It is the focal point for much of this chapter and will be answered as we proceed.

## Operating Loss Carryovers

Current tax regulations allow corporations to deduct certain operating losses incurred in one year from the taxable income of prior and subsequent years. If income taxes were assessed only on an annual basis, a potential inequity can result between a corporation earning taxable income each year and one having a larger taxable income in some years but losses in other years. For the latter firm, taxes could be higher under a strict annual accounting even if the average yearly earnings of the two firms were the same.

To help alleviate such problems, many taxing authorities allow a deduction for a net operating loss. This deduction permits a corporation to offset the operating loss (unused tax deductions) incurred in one particular year against the taxable income of other years. Specifically, the operating losses can be carried back for three years and offset against the income for those years. If an unused loss still remains, it then can be carried forward for as many as 15 additional years.[3]

---

[3] A corporation with taxable income during the preceding three years can, if it wishes, elect to carry all of the loss forward and none back. Because such elections are rare, it will be assumed for the purposes of this discussion that the carryback option will be exercised first. Also, the accounting loss is subject to various adjustments before it becomes a carryback or carryforward operating loss. For most corporations, however, these adjustments are minor and specialized. Consequently, they are ignored in subsequent discussions.

Of course, an operating loss from one year would never appear as an expense on the income statement of another year. Therefore, operating loss carryovers provide another type of difference between taxable income and financial income. The financial accounting question becomes how and when the tax effects of operating loss carryovers should be recorded and reported in the financial statements.

This chapter focuses on two major issues, those caused by temporary differences and those related to the carryback and carryforward of net operating losses. The first issue is more important and pervasive than the second because temporary differences affect a large number of businesses.

However, we discuss carryovers first because out of that discussion will emerge some useful concepts and techniques that will help us understand how to treat temporary differences. The operating loss deduction creates a claim for a tax refund in the case of a carryback or a future, potential tax savings in the case of a carryforward. Under what conditions should these carryover tax benefits be recognized as assets and hence reductions in tax expense? If they are assets, should they be recognized in the period of loss or in the periods in which income tax is actually reduced? These questions, of course, apply only to corporations that have experienced a loss.

# A HISTORICAL NOTE

Prior to 1989, the official pronouncement covering income tax reporting had been *APB Opinion No. 11* issued in 1967.[4] However, the requirements related to the accounting for income taxes had been undergoing extended review since 1982.

After having finished a six-year review, the Financial Accounting Standards Board issued *FASB Statement No. 96,* "Accounting for Income Taxes."[5] The FASB encouraged early adoption of its requirements but initially set the mandatory effective date as all fiscal years beginning after December 15, 1988 (effectively, 1989 calendar years). Computations specified by the new pronouncement were more involved and complex than the APB's existing opinion. Bowing to pressure from accountants and auditors, the FASB subsequently delayed the effective date of *FASB Statement No. 96* for two years.

Therefore, the accounting environment was in transition from 1987 to 1991. Most firms used the old opinion in 1987 and 1988 and gradually changed to the FASB requirements during 1990 and 1991. However, a few firms adopted the new requirements in 1989 or 1990. In this chapter, we discuss the reporting requirements of *FASB Statement No. 96* because it will be

---

[4] AICPA, *Opinion of the Accounting Principles Board No. 11,* "Accounting for Income Taxes" (New York, December 1967).

[5] FASB, *Statement of Financial Accounting Standards No. 96,* "Accounting for Income Taxes" (Stamford, Conn., December 1987).

in effect for everyone in 1991 and beyond. The analyst must exercise care in doing historical comparisons extending back into the 1980s, however, for the methods used for income taxes then are not the same now. Likewise, the reader is encouraged to be alert to future modifications in the reporting requirements as tax code changes become effective and as complexities in the current pronouncements are addressed by the FASB.

Both *APB Opinion No. 11* and *FASB Statement No. 96* share a common thread. Each attempts to recognize in the tax calculations for financial income purposes the tax effects of all events recognized in the financial statements for the period. Both result in deferred tax expenses and deferred tax accounts on the balance sheet as a way of accounting for the tax effects of temporary differences. Therefore, we can understand and partially analyze many of the tax disclosures under *APB Opinion No. 11* using the concepts of *FASB Statement No. 96*. We will try to do this at the end of the chapter when we look at the *1987* annual report of Kimberly-Clark, which officially was prepared according to *APB Opinion No. 11*.

Nevertheless, the underlying philosophies and detailed procedures of the two authoritative pronouncements are quite different, even though in some cases they may end up with the same result. The issuance of *FASB Statement No. 96* changes the entire focus of accounting for taxes and moves the analysis and recording toward a more conceptually sound basis.

# CARRYBACK AND CARRYFORWARD OF OPERATING LOSSES

As noted earlier, corporations are allowed to carry back operating losses for 3 years and receive a refund of taxes paid in prior years. If the operating loss is not exhausted through the carryback, it can be carried forward for 15 years. It then offsets future income and causes a reduction in the future taxes payable. Our question is how to record the tax consequences of an operating loss carryover. Specifically, with a loss carryback, should the tax refund be treated as a reduction in the current period's loss (in effect, a negative income tax charge) or as a correction of prior years' taxes? Similarly, should the tax savings associated with a loss carryforward be recognized immediately as a reduction in the loss or only in future periods when taxes are actually reduced?

## Carryback Case

Generally, income tax effects should be reported in the same accounting period as the events causing them provided that any claims for tax refunds meet the accepted definition of accounting assets. Applying this concept to operating loss carrybacks leads to the conclusion that the *tax benefits from carrybacks should be recognized in the year the causative net loss is incurred.*

The operating loss this period creates a tax benefit in the form of an allowable, measurable claim for refund. This claim for refund meets the tests for an accounting asset. It is a future economic benefit that is measurable in dollars with a reasonable degree of reliability, and it arises from transactions and events that have already occurred. The creation of this asset should be considered in measuring the net results of the current period.

For example, assume that a corporation has averaged $80,000 for taxable income in each of the three preceding years from 1988 to 1990. In 1991, a net loss of $180,000 is incurred. This loss can be carried back to offset the taxable income of the prior years. If taxes for those years had been paid at a rate of 34 percent, the corporation would enter a claim for a tax refund and make the following entry in 1991:

```
Income Tax Refund Receivable ($180,000 × .34) . . . . .  61,200
    Income Tax Operating Loss Carryback Credit. . . .            61,200
```

The credit account is a type of contra expense or negative expense and would be closed to Income Summary for the year. It would be reported on the income statement for 1991 as follows:

| | |
|---|---:|
| Loss before income tax effect . . . . . . . . . . . . . . . . | $(180,000) |
| Less: Income tax operating loss carryback credit . . . . . . . | 61,200 |
| Net loss after income tax effect. . . . . . . . . . . . . . . | $(118,800) |

## Carryforward Case

Assume that the loss in 1991 is $380,000 instead of $180,000. In this case, $240,000 of the loss can be carried back, completely offsetting the income of 1988 to 1990 and giving rise to a tax refund claim of $81,600 (34 percent × $240,000). The other $140,000 of the loss can be carried forward as an unused tax deduction to offset taxable income for the next 15 years. When should the tax effect of the $140,000 operating loss carryforward be recognized, and how should it be reported on the income statement?

Some accountants believe that it is proper also to recognize the future tax savings of $47,600 (34 percent × $140,000) as an asset and to reduce the current year's loss accordingly. Under this approach, a Future Tax Benefit asset of $47,600 would appear on the balance sheet, and a similar amount would be deducted from the loss on the income statement in the current year. Because the loss in 1991 causes the reduction in taxes, the tax savings should be reported in 1991 rather than in future years. This treatment follows the concept illustrated in connection with the carryback.

If we assume, perhaps based on the going-concern assumption, that sufficient taxable income will exist over the next 15 years to realize the future tax benefit, then the potential offset against future tax liabilities is a valid asset. However, it is this *important factor of "realizability" that causes the*

*FASB to require deferral of recognition of an operating loss carryforward unless and until it actually is used to offset future taxes.* The future value of the carryforward depends directly on the existence of taxable income during the next 15 years. The fact that the company has already experienced a loss may cast doubt on its ability to generate sufficient income in future years. Because of the uncertainty of realization and the difficulty in measuring the amount of future benefit, the FASB ruled in *Statement No. 96* that the *income tax advantage of a loss carryforward is not an asset.* It reasoned that the benefit is contingent on a future event, the earning of taxable income, that is not automatically assured under the going-concern assumption. The current operating loss may have created a right to a future benefit, but the value of that benefit depends on future events.

Therefore, under generally accepted accounting principles, the operating loss in 1991 is reported without consideration of any potential tax savings from the carryforward. If and when taxable income does arise in the future, the tax benefits of the carryforward should be reported as a separate component of income tax expense to the extent it is actually realized.

In our example, the $140,000 of the $380,000 current year's loss that the firm was unable to carryback will be reflected only if and when the company earns its first $140,000 of income during the 15-year carryforward period. Assume that in 1992 the company rebounded economically and earned $300,000 of taxable income. If the tax rate remains at 34 percent, the following entry would be made:

| | | |
|---|---:|---:|
| Income Tax Expense ($300,000 × .34) . . . . . . . | 102,000 | |
| Current Income Taxes Payable. . . . . . . . . | | 54,400 |
| Income Tax Operating Loss Carryforward | | |
| Credit ($140,000 × .34) . . . . . . . . . . | | 47,600 |
| To accrue tax expense for 1992 and to recognize | | |
| favorable tax impact of the operating loss | | |
| carryforward actually realized. | | |

Both the income tax expense of $102,000 and the carryforward credit are reported on the 1992 income statement as follows:

| | | |
|---|---:|---:|
| Income before tax . . . . . . . . . . . . . | | $300,000 |
| Less:  Income tax expense. . . . . . . . . . | $102,000 | |
| Income tax operating loss | | |
| carryforward credit . . . . . . . | (47,600) | 54,400 |
| Net income . . . . . . . . . . . . . . | | $245,600 |

The realized carryforward tax credit is treated as a negative component of income tax expense.[6]

---

[6] Under *APB Opinion No. 11,* the realized carryforward tax credit was reported as an extraordinary item. See Chapter 16 for a complete discussion of extraordinary items. This disclosure is no longer acceptable beginning in 1991.

The refusal on the part of the FASB to recognize any asset value associated with an operating loss carryforward has been met with significant opposition from many accountants and companies. They believe that too strict an asset test is applied to the carryforward credit. Often other assets are recorded on the books if their value is assured beyond a reasonable doubt. These assets are written down only when evidence arises negating their future value. A similar perspective should be taken for loss carryforwards, these critics claim. Tax benefits should be recorded in the loss period *unless* specific doubts exist concerning their future realizability.

## DEFERRED TAXES FROM TEMPORARY DIFFERENCES

Temporary differences reflect the variance between the carrying value of the assets or liabilities for income tax purposes and the carrying value of the assets and liabilities for financial reporting purposes. These differences will result in taxable or deductible amounts in future years when the assets are recovered or the liabilities are settled. Temporary differences cause a variation between financial income and taxable income in the current year that will "reverse" in later years. Most temporary differences result from timing differences, and it is that group that we look at in detail.[7]

How should a firm account for income tax expense when timing differences cause pre-tax financial income to differ from taxable income? The accounting profession has wrestled with this question for decades, resolving it in favor of what is called "deferred tax accounting" or "interperiod tax allocation." Ignoring permanent differences, we know that in total the same revenues and expenses eventually are reported for both tax and financial accounting purposes. Temporary differences merely result in period-to-period variations when reporting these common items. Accordingly, it is a simple extension of our matching and periodicity concepts to say that the income tax consequences of an event should be recognized in the same accounting period that the event appears in the financial statements. The actual income tax consequences of some events are deferred to future periods when the related assets are collected or the liabilities settled. However, accrual accounting requires recognition of the deferred tax consequences of these temporary differences in the period the events appear on the financial statements.

---

[7] Other temporary differences exist when assets and liabilities in a merger are recorded at fair market values in the financial statements, but are kept at book value for tax purposes or in special circumstances involving foreign currency differences, certain tax credits, indexation of the tax basis of assets for inflation, and a few other areas. In these cases, deferred tax liabilities may have to be recognized in a manner similar to that described in the text for timing differences. However, we do not discuss or illustrate these other temporary differences.

## A Basic Example

Assume that the Dry Cell Battery Company had $15,000 of sales revenue in 1990, $5,000 of which was collected in cash. Using accrual accounting, Dry Cell would record the transaction as:

| | | |
|---|---|---|
| Cash | 5,000 | |
| Accounts Receivable | 10,000 | |
| Sales Revenue | | 15,000 |

If Dry Cell is allowed to use the cash basis for reporting income taxes, only $5,000 of revenue would be shown on the firm's tax return. For simplicity, assume no other expenses or revenues are involved. If the firm has a 34 percent tax rate, the tax liability would be $1,700. The $10,000 receivable represents a temporary difference between the carrying value of the asset for tax purposes ($0) and the carrying value of the asset on the balance sheet ($10,000).

If we assume that the temporary difference reverses in the following year (1991) when the receivable is collected, the $10,000 becomes taxable then. However, financial accounting has recorded the $10,000 of income in 1990. Therefore, its deferred tax effect of $3,400 ($10,000 × .34) should be recognized as a deferred tax liability in 1990. The income tax expense for 1990 is the sum of the taxes currently payable plus the amount of any taxes payable in future years caused by a temporary difference originating that year. The journal entry to be made in 1990 is:

| | | |
|---|---|---|
| Income Tax Expense ($1,700 + $3,400) | 5,100 | |
| Current Income Taxes Payable | | 1,700 |
| Deferred Tax Liability | | 3,400 |

To record income tax expense for 1990 and to recognize a deferred tax liability for temporary differences that will reverse in 1991.

## Basic Concepts in Deferred Tax Accounting

It is clear from this simple example that the objective of deferred tax accounting under *Statement No. 96* is to measure and record future tax consequences during the year in which their causal transactions or events are recorded. Deferred tax liabilities (and in some cases, deferred tax assets) reflect the future tax consequences. The goal is to present on the balance sheet the correct amount of current and deferred taxes payable or refundable as a result of all events recognized in the financial statements.

**Definitions.**   Let us review some of the basic terminology associated with deferred tax accounting. This will enable us to explain procedures clearly and to understand published financial statements in the future.

1. *Temporary timing difference*—A difference between the carrying value of an asset or liability for tax purposes and its reported amount in the financial statements that will result in taxable or deductible amounts in future years when the asset is recovered or the liability is settled.

2. *Deferred tax consequences*—The future effects on income taxes caused by temporary differences existing at the end of the current year.

3. *Deferred tax liability*—The amount of deferred tax consequences from temporary timing differences that will result in *net taxable amounts* in future years.

4. *Deferred tax assets*—The amount of deferred tax consequences from temporary differences that will result in *net tax deductions* in future years, provided that they could be recovered under operating loss carryback provisions by a refund of taxes paid in the current or prior years.

5. *Deferred tax expense (benefit)*—The net change during the year in the firm's deferred tax liabilities and assets.

6. *Income tax expense* (benefit)—The sum of the current taxes paid or payable (refundable) for the year based on the tax return and the deferred tax expense (benefit).

**Procedures.** In the examples that follow, we use a fairly well-established procedure for calculating the deferred tax liabilities and assets, the current income taxes paid or payable, and the total income tax expense.

1. Identify all temporary differences between the financial reporting basis and the tax basis of assets and liabilities existing at the end of the year.

2. Determine the particular future years in which the temporary differences will reverse and become taxable or deductible.

3. Prepare a schedule by year of expected reversals of temporary differences and compute the *net* taxable or deductible amounts for each future year.

4. If a future year has a net deductible amount, carry back or carry forward that amount as permitted by existing tax regulations to offset net taxable amounts that are scheduled to occur in prior years or subsequent years.

5. Determine the amount of the deferred tax *asset* that should be disclosed at the end of the period. It equals the tax benefit of any net *deductible* amounts that could be realized by a *carryback* from future years to reduce taxes paid in the current or prior years.

6. Determine the amount of the deferred tax *liability* that should be disclosed at the end of the period. It is calculated by applying presently enacted tax rates for future years to the remaining net *taxable* amounts that are expected to occur in future years.

7. Calculate the deferred tax expense (benefit) by comparing the balances in the deferred tax liabilities and assets at the end of the year, determined in steps 5 and 6, with those at the beginning of the year.

8. Determine income tax expense by adding the deferred tax expense to the current tax expense from the tax return.

**Assumptions.** The FASB in *Statement No. 96* specifies that these procedures be carried out under certain assumptions that it claims reflect the underlying conceptual structure of financial accounting. The assumptions deal with the impact of future events on the calculations. Some of the more critical of these assumptions are outlined below:

**1.** The amount of assets and liabilities shown on the balance sheet will be recovered or settled in future years through use, sale, or payment. It is implicit in the reporting of assets on the balance sheet that the assets will be collected or used in future periods. Similarly, the fact that accountants show liabilities on the balance sheet implies that those liabilities will be settled.

**2.** Based on the first assumption, we also can assume that any differences between the income tax basis of an asset or a liability and its reported basis on the balance sheet (i.e., temporary timing differences) will result in taxable or deductible amounts in future years. In other words, the reversal of temporary differences can be assumed to occur regardless of the existence of other future events.

**3.** Deferred tax accounting *cannot* assume the earning of income in future years. Therefore, measurement of deferred tax liabilities and assets must be based on the assumption that the reversal of temporary differences will be the *only* taxable or deductible amounts in future years. It is not appropriate for accountants to anticipate future income.

**4.** Similar to the third assumption, it is not appropriate to anticipate the future enactment of changes in the tax law or in the tax rates. Measurements must be made based on the provisions of currently enacted income tax laws.

**5.** Because current tax laws allow carrybacks and carryforwards of operating losses, these factors should be considered in calculating the *net amount* of taxable and deductible amounts in future years caused by the reversal of temporary differences.

**6.** However, because generally accepted accounting principles recognize an asset only for operating loss carrybacks, a deferred tax asset can be recognized only for net deductible amounts that can be carried back to current or prior years.

## Deferred Tax Illustrations

Let us apply the procedures outlined above using the definitions and assumptions set forth by the Financial Accounting Standards Board. We use four simple examples.

**Example 1—Deferred Tax Liability with Multiple Temporary Differences.** Shirley Court Company is computing its tax expense for the year 1991. Before 1991, financial income and taxable income have been the same. In 1991, financial income is $9,000 and taxable income is only $4,000 because of two temporary differences that originated that year. In

1991, Shirley Court purchased a depreciable asset for $90,000. For financial accounting purposes, the asset is depreciated over a four-year life using an activity method. For tax purposes, it is depreciated over a four-year life using the modified accelerated cost recovery system. The expected depreciation expense figures are shown below:

|      | Financial Depreciation | Income Tax Depreciation |
|------|------------------------|-------------------------|
| 1991 | $20,000                | $30,000                 |
| 1992 | 45,000                 | 40,000                  |
| 1993 | 15,000                 | 13,300                  |
| 1994 | 10,000                 | 6,700                   |
|      | $90,000                | $90,000                 |

Therefore, the book value of the asset at the end of 1991 is $70,000 ($90,000 − $20,000) but is $60,000 ($90,000 − $30,000) for tax purposes. The $10,000 difference in the carrying value of the asset will reverse over the next three years as the asset is depreciated. The amount of the reversal is equal to the difference between the depreciation expenses in 1992, 1993, and 1994. These reversals will result in taxable amounts in future years. Because depreciation for accounting purposes will be greater than depreciation for tax purposes, taxable income must exceed financial income.

The other temporary difference is a $5,000 deduction for warranty expense that is reported on the income statement in 1991 and shown as an estimated liability on the balance sheet. However, for tax purposes it will not be deductible until it is actually paid in future years. Therefore, the 1991 balance sheet book value of the estimated liability for warranties is $5,000, but it is $0 for tax purposes. The $5,000 difference in the carrying value of the liability will reverse over the next three years as the liability is settled. The amount of the reversal is equal to the expected payments in 1992, 1993, and 1994; let's assume they are $3,000; $1,000; and $1,000, respectively. These reversals result in deductible amounts in future years.

With this background, let us apply the procedures outlined in the previous section. Table 13–1 organizes the data for us.

We first identify the two timing differences—depreciation and warranty expense. Steps 2 and 3 involve identifying and scheduling the expected years of reversal for each of the temporary differences. When the depreciation differences reverse, the result is a taxable amount in future years because tax depreciation will be less than book depreciation. So even if there is zero financial income in the future (see Assumption 3 in the preceding section), there will be *taxable income* caused by the reversal. Similarly, the reversal of the temporary difference caused by the warranty liability results in a deductible amount for tax purposes. This is true even if financial income is zero in 1992, 1993, and 1994.

In future years, the reversal of temporary differences results in net taxable amounts. Accordingly, Steps 4 and 5 are not applicable to this example. Be-

**TABLE 13–1**   Computation of Deferred Tax Balances for Example 1

|  | *Actual* | *Projected* | | |
|---|---|---|---|---|
|  | *1991* | *1992* | *1993* | *1994* |
| Financial income . . . . . . | 9,000 | | | |
| Temporary differences: | | | | |
|   Depreciation . . . . . . . | (10,000) | 5,000 | 1,700 | 3,300 |
|   Warranty expense . . . . . | 5,000 | (3,000) | (1,000) | (1,000) |
| Current taxable income . . . . | 4,000 | | | |
| Net taxable (deductible) | | | | |
|   amounts . . . . . . . . . | | 2,000 | 700 | 2,300 |
| Enacted tax rates . . . . . . | 25% | 25% | 25% | 25% |
| Current taxes payable. . . . . | 1,000 | | | |
| Deferred taxes payable . . . . | | 500 | 175 | 575 |

cause the temporary differences arose in 1991 and appear on its financial statements, the future tax consequences must be recognized as a deferred tax liability. The future tax consequences are measured by multiplying the $2,000 in 1992; $700 in 1993; and $2,300 in 1994 by the tax rate enacted in the current law for those years. We assume a 25 percent rate.

The deferred tax liability totals $1,250 ($500 + $175 + $575). Deferred tax expense (Step 7) is the change in the balance in the deferred tax accounts. Because no temporary differences existed before 1991, no deferred tax accounts had any balances. Therefore, the deferred tax expense is $1,250 ($1,250 balance at the end of the year less $0 balance at beginning of year). Income tax expense (Step 8) equals the sum of the current tax expense of $1,000 and the deferred tax expense of $1,250. The journal entry for 1991 would be:

```
Income Tax Expense ($1,000 + $1,250)  . . . . . . . . .  2,250
      Current Income Taxes Payable. . . . . . . . . . .        1,000
      Deferred Tax Liability . . . . . . . . . . . . . .        1,250
   To recognize current and deferred income taxes in 1991.
```

Note that this entry results in $2,250 of income tax expense (.25 × $9,000) being matched against the $9,000 of pre-tax financial income on the income statement. Of the $2,250 expense applicable to 1991, $1,250 will not be paid until future years. However, the tenets of accrual accounting and the matching concept require that all $2,250 be recognized in 1991.

**Example 2—Deferred Tax Liability with Carrybacks and Changes in Tax Rates.**   In this example, the facts are the same as in Example 1 except for an additional temporary difference in 1991. Assume Shirley Court Company made the following entry to record an estimated loss resulting from legal proceedings against it:

Loss from Lawsuit . . . . . . . . . . . . . . . . 3,000
Estimated Liability for Damages . . . . . . . . .        3,000

This $3,000 amount is expected to be paid in 1995; at that time it will be deductible for tax purposes. In addition, we assume that a new tax law was passed in 1991 that reduces the tax rate to 20 percent in 1994 and beyond.

Table 13–2 presents the data for the revised situation. Financial income is reduced to $6,000 because of the loss. We now have three temporary differences. In the table, we have scheduled the future years in which the depreciable assets will be recovered and the liabilities for warranties and legal damages will be settled. In the case of the Estimated Liability for Damages, its carrying value for financial accounting purposes is $3,000, while its carrying value for tax purposes is $0. This temporary difference reverses in 1995 when the liability is settled. At that time a $3,000 deductible amount results for tax purposes *even if no financial income appears in 1995*.

If we assume no other revenues and expenses in future years, 1995 will experience a $3,000 loss because of the temporary difference. Step 4 of our procedures allows us to carry back this potential loss three years based on the existing carryback laws we discussed in the first part of this chapter. The carryback, of course, can go back only three years, but it wipes out the net taxable amounts in 1992 and 1993 and $300 of that applicable to 1994. The rationale is as follows: Ignoring all other future income, the loss that will occur in 1995 because of temporary differences could be carried back to recover the taxes that would be paid in 1992, in 1993, and partially in 1994 because of temporary differences.

**TABLE 13–2**    Computation of Deferred Tax Balances for Example 2

|  | Actual | Projected | | | |
|---|---|---|---|---|---|
|  | 1991 | 1992 | 1993 | 1994 | 1995 |
| Financial income. . . . . . . . . . . . . . | 6,000 |  |  |  |  |
| Temporary differences: |  |  |  |  |  |
| Depreciation . . . . . . . . . . . . . | (10,000) | 5,000 | 1,700 | 3,300 |  |
| Warranty expense . . . . . . . . . . | 5,000 | (3,000) | (1,000) | (1,000) |  |
| Lawsuit loss . . . . . . . . . . . | 3,000 |  |  |  | (3,000) |
| Current taxable income . . . . . . . . . | 4,000 |  |  |  |  |
| Net taxable (deductible) amounts . . . . . |  | 2,000 | 700 | 2,300 | (3,000) |
| Carrybacks . . . . . . . . . . . . . . |  | (2,000) | (700) | (300) | 3,000 |
| Net future taxable (deductible) amounts . . |  | 0 | 0 | 2,000 | 0 |
| Enacted tax rates. . . . . . . . . . . . | 25% |  |  | 20% |  |
| Current taxes payable. . . . . . . . . . | 1,000 |  |  |  |  |
| Deferred taxes payable . . . . . . . . . |  |  |  | 400 |  |

The net result, then, of temporary differences originating in 1991 is a net taxable amount in 1994. Application of the *currently enacted* tax rate of 20 percent for that year results in a deferred tax liability of $400. Because there is no existing deferred tax liability account balance prior to 1991, the net change in the company's account is $400. The deferred tax expense for 1991 is $400.[8] Income tax expense in total is $1,400. It would be recorded as follows in 1991:

```
Income Tax Expense ($1,000 + $400) . . . . . . . . .   1,400
        Current Income Taxes Payable. . . . . . . . . .          1,000
        Deferred Tax Liability . . . . . . . . . . . . .            400
```

In this case, the tax expense is *not* 25 percent of the $6,000 financial income. Part of the tax consequences of events in 1991 results in a payment in 1994 when the *known* tax rate will be only 20 percent. Notice, however, that the deferred tax accounting procedure records in 1991 the tax consequences of all events recognized on the income statement in 1991, whether or not the tax consequences actually are payable in 1991 at that year's tax rate.

### Example 3—Deferred Tax Asset from Carrybacks and Deferred Tax Liability.

Let us modify our example again. Assume that the estimated lawsuit loss is $8,000 in 1991 instead of only $3,000. Also, assume that the expected settlement date is during 1994 rather than in 1995, and that there is again a 25 percent tax rate in each year.

Table 13–3 shows the analysis of the deferred tax amounts. Financial income is now only $1,000 because of the additional $5,000 added to the loss. Steps 1, 2, and 3 are basically the same as before—identify the temporary differences, determine the years in which they are expected to reverse, and prepare a schedule by year of the expected reversals to compute the net taxable (deductible) amount for each future year.

Under this scenario and consistent with the assumption of no anticipation of other future revenues and expenses, 1994 will experience a net tax-deductible amount of $5,700 because of the temporary differences. As in Example 2, this loss could be carried back three years. The earliest carryback year is 1991, the current year. The carryback from 1994 would result in an actual recovery of the $1,000 in taxes paid in 1991 ($4,000 × 25%). Accordingly, Step 5 allows us to record a deferred tax *asset* for the tax benefit. We cannot record a reduction in current taxes payable in 1991 because the carryback has not actually occurred yet. Nevertheless, we know that the tax deduction will occur in 1994 (Assumptions 1 and 2) and that it will be allowed to be carried back under existing tax laws (Assumption 3). Therefore, a deferred tax benefit does exist. This deferred tax benefit is the

---

[8] If, for example, the company had a $150 balance in the deferred liability account prior to 1991 because some of the temporary differences originated before 1991, deferred tax expense for 1991 would be only $250. The deferred tax liability account changes by $250 ($400 balance at the end of 1991 less the $150 recorded balance at the beginning of 1991).

**TABLE 13-3**    Computation of Deferred Tax Balances for Example 3

|  | Actual | Projected | | |
|---|---|---|---|---|
|  | 1991 | 1992 | 1993 | 1994 |
| Financial income . . . . . . | 1,000 |  |  |  |
| Temporary differences: |  |  |  |  |
|   Depreciation . . . . . . . | (10,000) | 5,000 | 1,700 | 3,300 |
|   Warranty expense . . . . . | 5,000 | (3,000) | (1,000) | (1,000) |
|   Lawsuit loss . . . . . . . | 8,000 |  |  | (8,000) |
| Current taxable income . . . . | 4,000 |  |  |  |
| Net taxable (deductible) |  |  |  |  |
|   amounts . . . . . . . . . |  | 2,000 | 700 | (5,700) |
| Carrybacks . . . . . . . . . | (4,000) | (1,700) |  | 5,700 |
| Amounts recoverable |  |  |  |  |
|   from current and |  |  |  |  |
|   prior years . . . . . . . . | (4,000) |  |  |  |
| Net future taxable |  |  |  |  |
|   (deductible) amounts . . . . |  | 300 | 700 | 0 |
| Enacted tax rates . . . . . . | 25% | 25% | 25% |  |
| Deferred tax asset . . . . . . | (1,000) |  |  |  |
| Deferred taxes payable . . . . |  | 75 | 175 |  |

result of events reflected in the 1991 income statement. Consequently, the tax benefit should be reflected in 1991 also.

The carryback to 1991 does not exhaust the $5,700 net deductible item from 1994. Therefore, as in Example 3, the other $1,700 is carried back to 1992 and wipes out $1,700 of the $2,000 net taxable amounts in 1992. The company is left with net taxable amounts of $300 in 1992 and $700 in 1993. Consequently, the deferred tax liability is $250 [(.25 × $300) + (.25 × $700)].

The following journal entry would reflect the result of these calculations:

```
Income Tax Expense ($1,000 − $750) . . . . . . . . .    250
Deferred Tax Asset ($4,000 × .25). . . . . . . . . . .  1,000
      Current Income Taxes Payable ($4,000 × .25) . . . .        1,000
      Deferred Income Taxes Payable ($75 + $175) . . . .          250
```

The income tax expense is 25 percent of the financial income of $1,000. A deferred tax asset is recognized in 1991 because the lawsuit loss is recognized in 1991. When the corresponding liability is settled in 1994, a refund of the taxes from 1991 will result. That tax consequence should be recognized the same year as the loss is recognized. Similarly, net temporary differences existing at the end of 1991 will result in negative tax consequences in 1992 and 1993. The deferred tax liability also recognizes these consequences in 1991.

## Example 4—Deferred Tax Asset with Carrybacks and Carryforwards.

This last example makes two modifications in the facts from Example 3. First, assume that the lawsuit loss is $10,000 in 1991 instead of $8,000. As a result, financial income is a $1,000 *loss*. Second, assume that the depreciation reverses over the next four years in a pattern of $5,000; $1,700; $4,300; and $1,000.[9]

Table 13–4 depicts the deferred tax consequences of this set of circumstances.

The analysis and rationale in this example basically parallels the previous one. We assume no future income or expense. However, we do assume that assets and liabilities shown on the 1991 balance sheet will be recovered or settled in future years. The use of the assets and the settlement of the liabilities of 1991 will result in taxable and deductible amounts in future years as scheduled in Table 13–4.

**TABLE 13–4**  Computation of Deferred Tax Balances for Example 4

| | Actual 1991 | Projected 1992 | 1993 | 1994 | 1995 |
|---|---|---|---|---|---|
| Financial income (loss) . . . . | (1,000) | | | | |
| Temporary differences: | | | | | |
| Depreciation . . | (10,000) | 5,000 | 1,700 | 2,300 | 1,000 |
| Warranty expense . . . | 5,000 | (3,000) | (1,000) | (1,000) | |
| Lawsuit loss . . | 10,000 | | | (10,000) | |
| Current taxable income . . . . | 4,000 | | | | |
| Net taxable (deductible) amount . . . . | | 2,000 | 700 | (8,700) | 1,000 |
| Carrybacks . . . . | (4,000) | (2,000) | (700) | 6,700 | |
| Carryforwards. . . | | | | 1,000 | (1,000) |
| Amounts recoverable from current and prior years . . . | (4,000) | | | | |
| Net future deductible amount . . . . | | 0 | 0 | (1,000) | 0 |
| Enacted tax rates . | 25% | | | | |
| Deferred tax asset . | (1,000) | | | | |

---

[9] This pattern is not in keeping with the current MACRS schedules. However, for purposes of illustration, we assume it is.

Temporary differences reversing in 1994 result in $8,700 of net deductible amounts. Under current tax laws, this deduction—when it actually appears in 1994—could be carried back three years. Therefore, for purposes of computing deferred tax effects, the $8,700 is carried back and wipes out the potential deferred tax liabilities in 1992 and 1993. Also, as in Example 3, it offsets $4,000 of 1991 income, thereby creating a deferred tax asset.

Even after the carryback, there still exists $2,000 of net deductible amounts scheduled for 1994. Under current tax laws, these will be able to be carried forward. Because 1995 shows a potential taxable amount of $1,000, an equal amount of 1994's deductions is carried forward to wipe out 1995. The remaining $1,000 of potential carryforward is *not recognized* as a tax benefit. Why? The FASB's position on operating loss carryforwards is that they cannot be recognized before their actual offsetting of future income. The same position is taken here. The remaining $1,000 deduction in 1994 cannot be used in the computation because there are no *known* net taxable items in future years. Future income cannot be anticipated beyond that associated with the reversal of temporary differences. A deferred tax asset cannot be recognized on this remaining $1,000 because an asset can be recognized only on items carried back. The $1,000 is treated in future deferred tax calculations as a net operating loss carryforward.

Using the information and analysis above, the tax entry for 1991 can be prepared.

Deferred Tax Asset ($4,000 × .25). . . . . . . . . . .   1,000
  Current Income Taxes Payable ($4,000 × .25) . . . .        1,000

There is no income tax expense for 1991. Income tax expense is the amount of current taxes payable for 1991 of $1,000 less the change in the deferred tax accounts of $1,000. At first glance, we might expect to have a $250 negative tax expense in 1991 (25% × $1,000 loss). However, that does not happen because the tax loss carryforward is not allowed to be recognized as a deferred tax asset.

## Summary of Deferred Taxes

A careful study of these four examples is necessary to see how the basic principles and assumptions of deferred tax accounting are implemented with the procedures outlined earlier.

Before we move on to an evaluation of deferred tax accounting, a brief review of the basic concepts may be helpful. Deferred tax accounting aims to recognize a tax liability or asset for the tax consequences of amounts that will become taxable or deductible in future years as a result of transactions or events recognized in current or past financial statements. The balances in the deferred tax liability and asset accounts are calculated directly at the end of each period by scheduling the future years in which temporary differences become taxable or deductible. Although accountants assume that the reversal of timing differences will occur in the future, they cannot anticipate future financial accounting income.

The deferred tax liability is measured using known tax rates applicable to the types of taxable income that are expected to arise in future years. However, a deferred tax asset is recognized only for the benefits of future tax deductions that could be realized by carryback from the future year to reduce taxes paid in the current or a prior year.

The balances in the deferred tax liability (asset) accounts calculated at the end of the year are compared to similar balances at the beginning of the year. The sum of the changes in the deferred tax liability (asset) accounts equals the amount of deferred tax expense. Taxes currently paid or payable plus (minus) the deferred tax expense (benefit) is the income tax expense for the year. In short, liability recognition determines the amount of expense that can be recognized.

## Changes in Tax Rates

The calculations in the preceding examples used the currently enacted income tax rates that will exist when the temporary differences reverse. This approach is consistent with the liability orientation taken by *FASB No. 96*. Deferred tax liabilities should be measured using the most accurate estimates of future cash outflows.

On the other hand, if the credit balance resulting from deferred tax accounting is a liability, then an *actual* reduction in tax rates at some future time results in an overstated liability. Conversely, if tax rates should increase, the credit balance in Deferred Tax Liability is less than the cash payments necessary in future years. In either case, an adjustment to the liability account is required both in concept and under *FASB No. 96*.

For example, suppose that the Deferred Tax Liability account on January 1, 1995 has a balance of $5,000. This amount represents the tax consequences of $20,000 of net temporary differences originating in 1994 and prior years that will reverse in future years. These tax consequences were measured with a tax rate of 25 percent, as in our examples. Twenty-five percent was used because according to current tax law, it is the rate expected to be in existence in future years. However, if Congress passes a law in 1995 increasing the tax rate from 25 percent to 30 percent for 1995 and subsequent years, the deferred tax liability on January 1, 1995 should be $6,000 ($20,000 × .30). The deferred tax liability must be increased and an additional income tax charge recognized. The journal entry to accomplish this would be:

| | | |
|---|---|---|
| Income Tax Expense. . . . . . . . . . . . . . . . . . . . . | 1,000 | |
|     Deferred Tax Liability . . . . . . . . . . . . . . . . . | | 1,000 |
|   To adjust the deferred tax liability for increase in income tax rate. | | |

Generally accepted accounting principles mandate that the $1,000 debit be reported as a separately disclosed element of the income tax expense for 1995.

A parallel entry debiting the Deferred Tax Liability and crediting Income Tax Expense (Benefit) would be appropriate if tax rates were reduced from 25 percent. Note, however, that these adjustments apply only for actually enacted changes in tax rates, not for anticipated tax rate changes.

### Present Value Recording

In Chapters 11 and 12, we employed the concept of present value in the valuation of liabilities. Notes and bonds, capital leases, and pension obligations are recorded at the present value of their future cash outlays. Some accountants have suggested that this concept is equally applicable to the deferred tax liability. Because the payment is postponed until the future, the current obligation is only the present value of the postponed amounts. In subsequent years, interest expense is debited and the Deferred Tax Liability is credited to reflect the increase in the present value of the liability.

The major point at issue is what interest rate to use in discounting. The more commonly accepted view is that the appropriate interest rate for the deferred tax liability is zero; therefore, the present value is the same as future value. Accountants record bonds and notes at present value, using the rate of interest that is explicitly stated or implicitly indicated in the negotiations between borrower and lender. With tax deferrals, the circumstances are not the same. The government charges no explicit interest rate on its "loan," and no rate is implicit in the transaction. To use an opportunity interest rate not related to the transaction would be to sanction a procedure that is *not* used for valuing other liabilities.

The Financial Accounting Standards Board, while adhering strongly to the liability argument, decided not to require discounting of deferred tax liabilities at the present time. It viewed discounting as a separate broad measurement issue apart from the recording of income tax expense and related liabilities.

## EVALUATION OF DEFERRED TAXES

Accounting for the impact of temporary differences has been one of the most controversial issues in accounting in the last three decades. Consequently, it seems appropriate to evaluate the pros and cons of deferred tax accounting. To a large extent, the case *for* has already been made in our earlier descriptions of assumptions and procedures.

To summarize, proponents of deferred tax accounting, including the FASB, view it as an extension of accrual accounting in two respects. First, they view income tax as an expense that should be recognized in the same accounting periods as the events that cause it. The income tax consequences are deferred for some events (temporary differences). However, under the matching and periodicity concepts, tax expense should be accrued and matched with the events that give rise to the tax, regardless of when it has to be paid. Second, accrual accounting implicitly assumes that assets and liabilities reported on the balance sheet will be recovered or settled. Otherwise, they should not appear as economic resources and obligations. Therefore, we must assume that any temporary differences associated with reported assets and liabilities will result in taxable and deductible amounts in future periods. Although anticipating income from future revenues and expenses is not consistent with accrual accounting, anticipating the reversal of temporary differences, and hence recognizing their tax consequences, does follow accrual accounting.

Finally, proponents of deferred tax accounting argue that the amounts recognized as a deferred tax liability and a deferred tax asset meet the accounting requirements for those elements. For instance, a deferred tax liability represents a measurable obligation that has arisen from transactions in past or current periods. The deferred tax obligation derives from existing tax law requirements and will involve a probable future payment of assets to the government. The taxes relating to the net taxable amounts resulting from the reversal of temporary differences in future years must be paid in those future years.

In a parallel manner, an analysis of the deferred tax asset reveals that it meets the characteristics of an accounting asset. It represents a probable economic resource in the form of a future cash inflow (or reduction in cash outflow); its benefit accrues to the specific business entity; it results from past transactions or events; and it can be measured with a reasonable degree of reliability. Recall that the only deferred tax asset recognized results from the *carryback* of a net deductible amount in future years caused by existing temporary differences. The benefit is measurable because current or past periods show earned taxable income. The *carryforward* benefits of temporary differences are not recognized as an accounting asset because their amounts (measurability) depend on the earning of future taxable income (a future rather than a past event).

## Objections to Deferred Tax Accounting

Opponents of deferred tax accounting concentrate on three lines of argument: (1) the debit and credit balances recorded on the balance sheet are not accounting assets and liabilities; (2) tax charges are unlike other expenses and should be viewed as distributions of income to the government; and (3) deferred tax accounting may result in a permanent or an ever increasing deferred tax liability that in the aggregate never has to be paid. Let us consider each of these points more fully.

Many accountants have difficulty fitting the deferred tax accounts into the conventional asset-liability framework. The government recognizes no legal or contractual claim against the corporation for the deferred tax liability, and the corporation cannot demand payment from the government for any deferred tax asset. Payment of taxes equal to the amount shown on the income tax return effectively discharges all legal claims of the tax authorities. Moreover, even if we ignore the lack of legal recognition, the uncertainties surrounding future tax payments rule out an objective valuation of the "liability." Recognition of deferred taxes as a liability depends, opponents of tax allocation claim, on tenuous assumptions about tax rates, the similarity of tax regulations in the future, and the inevitability that temporary differences will reverse.

This first argument rests on a legalistic concept of liability and measurement. Such a concept is not necessarily employed with other items commonly treated as liabilities. For example, estimated liabilities for warranties, pensions, and certain leases that are capitalized also do not lend themselves to precise measurement, nor are they necessarily legal claims on the firm. However, like deferred taxes, they do fit the broader concept of liability suggested in Chapter 2 and reviewed in the above sections. The assumptions about the future that are made to measure the liability do not seem unrealistic. The procedures necessary for estimating other liabilities, depreciating plant assets, or adjusting for uncollectibles are based on the current period's best estimates of future events. They also assume that existing balance sheet assets and liabilities will be collected (used) and settled, respectively.

The second objection to deferred tax accounting concerns the fundamental nature of income taxes. The argument states that income tax is *not* an expense similar to other expenses. Income taxes do not directly contribute to the generation of revenue. Instead, they are more like a periodic, involuntary distribution of income made in recognition of society's contributions to the firm. Furthermore, the continually changing concepts that form the basis of the legal claim are under governmental control. These concepts increasingly rest on factors alien to the concepts underlying financial accounting income. As a consequence, opponents argue, the period's tax charge is best measured by the actual levy. If the government levies a reduced amount in a particular year with no *explicit* future repayment, the accounting statements should reflect a reduced tax charge. In short, income taxes relate only to taxable income and not to financial income.

Factors such as ACRS and MACRS depreciation have resulted in an increasing divergence between taxable and financial income. These and other differences have made this second argument more difficult to rebut. Nevertheless, close scrutiny of the tax code reveals that financial income and taxable income, except for permanent differences, basically *are* the same *over time*.

The third objection to deferred tax accounting focuses on whether there will be any future tax payment. Detractors claim that tax deferral often actually amounts to a permanent tax reduction. For instance, many firms that are required to use ACRS or MACRS depreciation for tax purposes continually make new investments, replacing old assets with new ones. Because the new assets are acquired at higher price levels or result from net expansion of the company, the temporary differences from depreciation that originate each year more than offset the temporary differences from depreciation that reverse. Therefore, as long as a firm maintains a regular policy of investing in new assets, the deferred tax liability account *in total* never will be reduced and in fact may grow larger each year. A similar situation arises when the installment method is used for recognizing sales for tax purposes. The deferred tax liability account is never reduced through payment as long as the cumulative temporary differences do not decrease, that is, as long as new installment receivables more than replace those collected.

**Partial Tax Allocation.** In brief, these critics claim that comprehensive deferred tax accounting, as required by *FASB No. 96*, results in the reversal of temporary differences being offset by originating temporary differences. The tax consequences of the temporary differences are continually deferred and never really paid. As a result, the financial statements lose representational faithfulness. A company that is able continually to postpone payment of taxes appears no different from one that has to pay all of its taxes currently. Moreover, the accounting statements are not indicative of future cash flows because the deferred taxes will never be paid off or at least not for a long, long time.

Advocates of this position prefer *partial* deferred tax accounting. As implied by the name, deferred tax accounting under this system would apply only to specific, nonrecurring temporary differences that can be expected to reverse within a relatively short time. Partial tax allocation (as it often is called) would not reflect as a deferred liability those temporary differences that are continually perpetuated in the aggregate.[10]

Critics of comprehensive deferred tax accounting view the deferred tax account as a single amount. In contrast, Deferred Tax Liability actually acts as a control account for the deferral pattern of each *individual* temporary difference the firm has. Therefore, although the total balance may remain constant or even grow, tax liabilities caused by specific temporary differences are being paid while other tax liabilities caused by new differences are being created. This process is somewhat analogous to the continual turnover in other liabilities, such as accounts payable. In a growing firm, total accounts payable may increase, but individual accounts do mature and are replaced by new accounts. The fact that different creditors are involved

---

[10] The FASB generally disagreed with this line of reasoning. However, for a few specific temporary differences where there was strong evidence of "indefinite reversal," no deferred taxes are required.

should not change the principle involved. An expense should not be ignored simply because the related liability may be replaced by another liability in the future, even if this process should go on for an indeterminable time.

# COMPLEXITIES

So far we have discussed two major issues regarding the accounting for income taxes—the treatment of operating loss carryovers and the handling of temporary differences through deferred tax accounting. We deliberately have kept the two discussions separate to emphasize the underlying concepts and procedures. One of the difficulties faced by some companies involves calculating income tax expense when actual operating loss carryforwards coexist with temporary differences. Tables like 13–1 through 13–4 become more complex. Operating loss carryforwards must be explicitly dealt with in those tables *before* the carryback and carryforward of net deductible amounts from temporary differences are considered.

Another complexity arises from the need to anticipate the expected reversal times of temporary differences. As long as enacted tax rates are the same in every future period and no discounting to present value is appropriate, no problem exists. However, if and when tax rates differ among future periods, then whether a temporary difference reverses in 1996, or 1997, or some other year, becomes important. Enacted tax rates can differ because of explicit changes in the tax law or because of the existence of graduated tax rates. A temporary difference, for instance, that results in net taxable income of $50,000 results in a deferred tax liability of $7,500 ($50,000 × .15) if it is the only reversal in that year. However, if the $50,000 is one element of a total $150,000 reversal, the deferred tax liability is calculated using the marginal tax rate of 39 percent ($50,000 × .39 = $19,500).

The two complexities above, while irksome to our calculations, pale in significance to the practical problems caused by different tax jurisdictions and different tax systems. Generally accepted accounting principles require that deferred tax accounting be calculated separately for each tax-levying entity and for each tax system.

A large multinational company may file an income tax return in the United States, one in Canada, and perhaps a dozen others in various foreign countries. In addition, many of the states in the United States levy a corporate income tax. Therefore, such a company may file 20 or more different income tax returns. Each jurisdiction has different tax laws. Consequently, many differences between the tax basis of assets and liabilities and their financial accounting basis can exist, and these differences are not measured the same across the many tax jurisdictions. As a consequence, numerous temporary differences must be tracked separately for each tax-levying entity. The procedure we illustrated earlier, in essence, must be repeated for each separate deferred tax calculation.

Even for federal tax purposes, we have assumed only one set of tax regulations. However, this is not the case. The Tax Reform Act of 1986 established for corporations (and individuals) a parallel tax system to the regular one. This *alternative minimum tax* (AMT) was designed to ensure that successful corporations pay more equitable amounts of income taxes. A corporation must pay the higher of its AMT or its regular income tax. The detailed calculations of AMT are beyond our scope. However, it not only affects a company's current income tax liability but also influences the calculation of deferred tax liabilities. The alternative minimum tax takes into consideration some, but not all, temporary differences. Moreover, it has its own set of carryforward credits.

Deferred income tax accounting, although premised on some basic concepts, is difficult to implement even in the simple situations described in the preceding section. When placed in more complex real-world settings, the difficulties grow exponentially. There is no question that the delay in implementation of *FASB No. 96* for two years was directly related to complaints about its complexity.

## DISCLOSURE REQUIREMENTS

With the areas of bonds, leases, and pensions discussed in Chapters 11 and 12, the entries to record the expenses and liabilities are only part of the story. Extensive disclosures in notes accompanying the financial statements are necessary to explain details behind the entries and accounts and to allow the analyst to interpret the amounts and the concepts on which they rest. Such disclosures are also an integral part of the accounting for income taxes. This section addresses a number of classification and disclosure matters.

The first issue concerns how deferred income tax accounts should be classified on the balance sheet. Generally accepted accounting principles make it abundantly clear that these accounts are legitimate accounting liabilities and assets. *FASB No. 96* gives further guidance. Generally, deferred tax liabilities and assets are classified as current or noncurrent depending on when the underlying temporary differences result in future taxable or deductible amounts. Generally, the deferred tax consequences of temporary differences expected to reverse in the next year are considered current. Also, a deferred tax account related to an asset or liability that appears as current on the balance sheet also is classified as current. All other deferred tax accounts are reported as noncurrent liabilities and assets.

Second, we have seen that the amount of income tax expense shown on the income statement is affected by a number of different factors. Accordingly, in a separate schedule, income tax expense must be subdivided into its significant components, four of which we have mentioned and/or illustrated.

1. Current income tax expense taken from the tax return.
2. Deferred income tax as measured by the change in the balances in the deferred tax accounts from the beginning to the end of the year.

3. Operating loss carryover benefits realized during the current period and recorded as reductions in income tax expense.
4. Adjustments to the balances in deferred tax liability and asset accounts from changes in enacted tax rates or laws.

These four components all wind up in income tax expense. However, they reflect very different economic events and may have different implications for the assessment of the firm's performance and the prediction of its future earnings and cash flows.

A third issue concerns a requirement that income tax expense on the income statement be reconciled to the amount of income tax expense that would have resulted from applying domestic statutory tax rates to financial income. Statement readers presumably know that since 1987 most corporate income is taxed at about 34 percent. Therefore, their expectation is that income tax expense should be around 34 percent of pre-tax financial income. Companies are required to present a schedule that explains any major differences between their income tax expense and what it would be under the statutory tax rates. Such a schedule highlights any permanent differences between financial income and taxable income. It also discloses the impact of state and foreign income taxes, which could cause the total income tax expense to exceed the federal statutory rate.

Temporary differences clearly are very important to an understanding of deferred taxes. Therefore, companies also must disclose the types of temporary differences that give rise to significant portions of the deferred tax liability and/or asset accounts. Moreover, *FASB Statement No. 96* mandates supplementary information about the amounts and expiration dates of unused loss carryforwards and about the nature and amounts of indefinite reversal items for which no deferred taxes have been provided. All of these disclosures enhance the reader's ability to estimate the timing and uncertainty of future cash payments associated with income taxes.

## DISCUSSION OF THE KIMBERLY-CLARK ANNUAL REPORT

The Appendix to Chapter 6 contains the financial statements of Kimberly-Clark Corporation. Information pertaining to its income taxes is found in the financial statements and in Note 2 of its 1987 annual report. The firm's disclosures concern (1) a breakdown of income tax expense into current and deferred, (2) a listing of the major components of current income tax expense, (3) the specific temporary differences that contributed to the yearly build-up in the deferred tax liability account, and (4) the factors responsible for producing an effective tax rate that was higher in 1987 than the statutory rate but lower in 1985 and 1986.

We noted at the outset of this chapter that *FASB Statement No. 96* is mandatory beginning in 1991 (originally 1989). Kimberly-Clark has not elected to adopt its requirements early. Therefore, the deferred tax accounting that it practices under *APB Opinion No. 11* differs somewhat from what we have described. However, the Kimberly-Clark statements still are understandable, although perhaps not as complete as in the context of the new standard. Note that in its report (page 199 in text), the company discusses the general impact of the new standard. When it is adopted, Kimberly-Clark will record a decrease of $75 to $100 million in its Deferred Tax Liability accounts. The credit would go to a special stockholders' equity account. The major reason for this change is that the existing deferred tax liability accounts reflect tax rates of around 46 percent. Corporate tax rates were reduced to around 34 percent in 1986, and the new standard requires that the currently enacted tax rates be used to value the liability. Therefore, the reported liability in 1987 is overstated and will have to be corrected.

Kimberly-Clark's income statement reveals a total Provision for Income Taxes (Income Tax Expense) of $230.5 million in 1987. The portion deferred and the portion currently payable to various governments is also disclosed in Note 2. The firm apparently made the following summary journal entry for 1987 income taxes:

| | | |
|---|---|---|
| Income Tax Expense. . . . . . . . . . . . . . . . . . . . . | 230.5 | |
| Federal Income Taxes Payable ($67.0 − $2.4) . . . . . . . | | 64.6 |
| State Income Taxes Payable. . . . . . . . . . . . . . . | | 14.6 |
| Foreign Income Taxes Payable. . . . . . . . . . . . . | | 66.3 |
| Deferred Income Taxes—Federal ($47.4 − $2.1 + $4.3). . | | 49.6 |
| Deferred Income Taxes—State ($13.3 − $.7) . . . . . . | | 12.6 |
| Deferred Income Taxes—Foreign ($19.2 + $3.6) . . . . . | | 22.8 |

## Temporary Differences Influencing Deferred Taxes

Deferred Income Taxes appears among the equities in Kimberly-Clark's balance sheet. During 1987, the account balance rose from $448.5 million to $548.2 million. The major factor contributing to the $99.7 million increase in the deferred accounts was the $85 million credited in the above journal entry; the remaining $14.7 million is not explained.

As noted earlier in the chapter, capital-intensive firms commonly show yearly increases in the balance for Deferred Income Taxes. This phenomenon occurs when the firm depreciates its plant assets more quickly for tax purposes than for financial accounting purposes. (Remember that the company's accounting policies indicate the use of straight-line and unit-of-production methods of depreciation on the books and accelerated methods on the tax return.) Kimberly-Clark reveals in Note 2 that $79.9 ($47.4 + $13.3 + $19.2) million of the $85 million increase in Deferred Income Taxes resulted from temporary differences caused by an excess of tax over book depreciation.

Kimberly-Clark also shows an obsolescence allowance as a temporary difference in Note 2. In this case, the temporary difference reflects the fact that financial income is less than taxable income. Two possible explanations could account for this result. First, in some year or years prior to 1985, Kimberly-Clark took an obsolescence loss (or expense) on its tax return. Then from 1985 to 1987, the company records the deduction as a financial accounting expense on the income statement. This situation is similar to accelerated depreciation. Here in the early years (prior to 1985), tax obsolescence expense exceeded book expense, but now in the later years, book obsolescence expense exceeds tax expense. The alternative explanation is that from 1985 to 1987, the firm has been recording an obsolescence loss or expense on the books that is not immediately deductible for tax purposes. Because the obsolescence events recorded from 1985 through 1987 give rise to future tax deductions, those benefits are recorded as reductions in the deferred tax expense.

Other temporary differences caused deferred income tax expenses to increase in 1985 and 1987 and to decrease in 1986. These temporary differences are probably related to differences in the treatment in financial income and taxable income of items such as start-up and preoperating expense, advertising and promotional expenses, and perhaps pension expense.[11]

One other disclosure regarding deferred taxes appears at the very bottom of Note 2 in the annual report. Kimberly-Clark notes that in past years a total of $545.4 million of income from companies it owns outside of the United States has been included on its income statement. Under current tax laws, this income does not appear on the tax return until it is remitted to Kimberly-Clark (usually in the form of dividends). This situation, therefore, would appear to be a temporary difference; income has been recorded in financial income that will appear as taxable income in future years. Because an event recognized currently on the income statement gives rise to future taxable amounts, deferred taxes are called for. However, none has been provided based on the indefinite reversal exception. Because these amounts have been permanently reinvested overseas, they will never be paid as dividends. If the probability of being paid as dividends is very low, then they will probably never become taxable. The temporary differences may not reverse until some indefinite time in the future.

## Reconciliation between Effective and Statutory Tax Rates

The other major disclosure in Note 2 is a reconciliation between the effective income tax rate incurred by the company and the statutory income tax rate. This disclosure is required by the accounting profession and the SEC.

---

[11] An interesting difference in disclosure policies is relevant here. Under *APB Opinion No. 11* followed by Kimberly-Clark, the firm must disclose the major types of temporary differences that give rise to the $85 million deferred tax *expense*. Under *FASB Statement No. 96*, the firm will have to disclose the major types of temporary differences that give rise to the $548.2 million *liability* on the balance sheet.

As noted earlier, Kimberly-Clark reported $230.5 million of income tax expense for 1987; this amount represents 43.2 percent of the $534.1 million of before-tax income reported on the income statement. The corporate statutory income tax rate was 40 percent in 1987 (46 percent in 1985 and 1986) for companies with income the size of Kimberly-Clark's. The reconciliation presented in Note 2 lists those factors that caused Kimberly-Clark to incur an effective tax rate of 43.2 percent (43.1 percent in 1985 and 1986) rather than 40 percent (46 percent in 1985 and 1986).

Frequently, such a reconciliation schedule reveals the *permanent* differences that account for the difference in rates. Such factors, if they exist, are not significant. In 1985 and 1986, investment tax credits reduced Kimberly-Clark's effective tax rate by 2.6 percent and 3.1 percent respectively. These credits were virtually eliminated during 1987 and had no material impact.

State income taxes were $27.2 ($14.6 + $13.30 − $.7) million in 1987. They represent about 5 percent ($27.2/$534.1) of the before-tax income. However, the state income taxes are a deductible expense on the federal tax return, so the full amount of state income tax is not added. Only the state income tax percentage after subtracting the savings in federal income tax increases the effective tax rate. The net increase is only 2.7 percent.

The effective tax rate also was increased in 1987 (decreased in 1985 and 1986) by an additional 0.4 percent because Kimberly-Clark experienced a tax rate slightly above (below in 1985 and 1986) the U.S. rate on the foreign income included on its income statement.

# SUMMARY

An old saying states that nothing in this world is certain except death and taxes. In light of the discussion in this chapter, we might extend the adage to include financial accounting problems caused by taxes. Income tax authorities, admittedly a separate audience for accounting reports, nevertheless provide a source of thorny problems in preparing financial statements for other external users.

Two of those problems form the focal points of this chapter. The concept used in approaching both of them is that income taxes are caused by certain transactions and events of the firm. Under accrual accounting, the tax consequences of these transactions and events should be recognized in the same accounting period in which these items are reported in the financial statements. However, any balance sheet accounts resulting from income tax measurements should meet the criteria of accounting assets and liabilities.

By considering these concepts, we reach the following conclusions regarding operating loss carryovers. The tax reductions (refunds) from net operating loss carrybacks should be recognized as a benefit of the year the net loss is incurred. However, the tax benefit from operating loss carryforwards should not be recognized until future periods when they are realized.

When employing these concepts, we derive some fairly complex procedures called "deferred tax accounting" to handle temporary differences that arise when the tax basis and financial-accounting basis of assets and liabilities differ. These procedures are designed to recognize tax liabilities or assets for the tax consequences of amounts that will become taxable or deductible in future years as a result of past transactions and events. In summary, deferred tax calculations require the following steps:

1. Schedule for each future year the expected taxable or deductible amounts arising from temporary differences between the financial-reporting basis and tax-reporting basis of assets and liabilities existing at the end of the current year.
2. Determine the net taxable or deductible amounts for each future year using allowable tax carryover rules.
3. Apply presently enacted tax rates to these net amounts to determine any deferred tax liability and/or asset.
4. Compare the balances in the deferred tax liability and/or asset with amounts currently existing in those accounts. The change is the deferred tax expense.
5. Add the deferred tax expense to the current tax expense for the year to determine total tax expense.

In applying these procedures, accountants must remember that deferred tax assets can be recognized only if the future tax benefits can be realized through carryback provisions and that no future income can be anticipated. Otherwise, some basic elements of an accounting asset will be missing.

Because of the complexities and controversies surrounding the accounting for income tax expense, a number of items require disclosure in notes. The most important of these is a schedule of the major temporary differences underlying the deferred tax accounts shown on the balance sheet and a reconciliation between the effective income tax rate and the statutory federal income tax rate.

*Statement of Financial Accounting Standards No. 96* hopefully places the measurement of income tax expense on a more sound conceptual basis than before. These procedures are justified by the matching concept underlying accrual accounting and by representational faithfulness to the concepts of accounting assets and liabilities. However, given the furor attending its release in 1987 and the subsequent deferment of its application until 1991, the last word on the accounting for income taxes probably has not been written. This chapter, nevertheless, should lay the foundation for an understanding of the changes and refinements that are to come.

# PROBLEMS AND CASETTES

**13–1. Classification of Differences between Financial Income and Taxable Income**
Listed below are several items that represent differences between accounting income and taxable income (or between the tax basis of assets and liabilities and their finan-

cial accounting basis) for the year 1991. For each item, indicate whether it is a permanent or a temporary difference. If the latter, indicate whether the item causes taxable amounts or deductible amounts in future years.

1. Goodwill amortization of $50,000 is deducted on the income statement but not on the tax return.
2. Sales of $125,000 are recognized on the income statement, but the installment method is used for tax purposes.
3. Estimated warranty costs of $16,000 applicable to 1991 sales are accrued for financial accounting purposes but are deducted only as incurred for tax purposes.
4. Life insurance premiums of $4,000 on officers' lives are expensed on the income statement but are not deductible for tax purposes.
5. MACRS depreciation used for tax purposes exceeds straight-line depreciation used for financial accounting purposes by $60,000.
6. Income of $150,000 on a long-term contract is included in financial income using the percentage-of-completion method, but part of it will be recognized in taxable income using completed contract.
7. Interest revenue of $18,000 earned on an investment in municipal bonds is recorded in the income statement of 1991 but not on the tax return.
8. Unearned service revenue of $25,000 is included in taxable income when received in 1991 but is properly deferred on the books because performance will not occur until 1992 and 1993.
9. Pension expense deducted on the income statement exceeds by $24,000 the amount funded and therefore deductible for tax purposes in 1991.
10. Interest of $32,000 is capitalized during 1991 as part of the cost of a constructed asset for financial accounting purposes but is deducted as incurred for tax purposes.

## 13–2. Operating Loss Carrybacks

Hedges Company began operations in 1990 and reported the following amounts of pre-tax financial income and taxable income:

| | |
|---|---|
| 1990. . . . . | $ 110,000 |
| 1991. . . . . | 98,000 |
| 1992. . . . . | 86,000 |
| 1993. . . . . | (220,000) |

The applicable tax rate for all years is 30 percent.

### Required:

a. Prepare the journal entry to record income tax expense for the years 1992 and 1993.
b. Prepare the lower portion of the comparative income statement for 1992 and 1993, beginning with income before taxes.
c. How would the situation be handled if the loss in 1993 were $320,000 instead of $220,000?

### 13–3. Deferred Taxes for a Single Temporary Difference

At the end of 1990, Baker Company reported its financial income before taxes as $214,000 and its taxable income as $188,000 because of a single temporary difference. The tax rate for 1990 and future years is 30 percent. Because of this one temporary difference, taxable income will exceed financial income over the next three years as follows:

|       |          |
|-------|----------|
| 1991. . . . . . | $14,000 |
| 1992. . . . . . | 8,000 |
| 1993. . . . . . | 4,000 |

**Required:**

*a.* Calculate the two components of income tax expense for 1990.
*b.* Prepare the journal entry to record income tax expense for 1990.

### 13–4. Deferred Tax Liability Adjustment with Different Tax Rates

For financial accounting purposes, Southern Corporation recognizes sales revenue in the period of sale. For tax purposes, it uses the installment method. On December 31, 1990, Southern reported a deferred tax liability of $19,000 related to the temporary difference at that time. Unrecognized gross margin related to the installment receivables on the December 31, 1991 balance sheet amounted to $125,000; this amount is expected to be recognized equally over the next five years as the accounts are collected. The enacted tax rate was 25 percent for 1990 but was changed early in 1991 to 30 percent for all subsequent years.

**Required:**

*a.* Calculate the *total* adjustment to the deferred tax liability account at the end of 1991.
*b.* Identify two separate components of this total adjustment.

### 13–5. Correction of Deferred Tax Entries

You have been assigned to review the financial statements of Caroline James and Co. at the end of its first year of operations. The bookkeeper made the following entry regarding income tax expense:

| | | |
|---|---|---|
| Income Tax Expense . . . . . . . . . . . . . . . . . . . . . . . . . | 203,000 | |
|     Current Income Taxes Payable . . . . . . . . . . . . . | | 133,000 |
|     Deferred Tax Liability. . . . . . . . . . . . . . . . | | 70,000 |

Upon your request, he produces the following schedule to support his tax calculation:

|  | Year 1 | Year 2 | Year 3 | Year 4 | Year 5 |
|---|---|---|---|---|---|
| Financial income . . . . | 500,000 | | | | |
| Temporary differences: | | | | | |
|   Depreciation . . . . . | (200,000) | (40,000) | 120,000 | 80,000 | 40,000 |
|   Litigation liability . . . | 80,000 | | | | (80,000) |
| Taxable income . . . . . | 380,000 | (40,000) | 120,000 | 80,000 | (40,000) |
| Income tax rate . . . . . | 35% | 35% | 35% | 35% | 35% |
| Income tax liability: | | | | | |
|   Current . . . . . . . | 133,000 | | | | |
|   Deferred. . . . . . . | | — | 42,000 | 28,000 | — |

You determine that the financial income figure is accurate, that the temporary differences are valid, and that their periods of reversal have been accurately determined. Current tax laws call for a decline in the tax rate to 30 percent in Year 3, and Congress is deliberating whether to cut rates to 25 percent beginning in Year 5.

**Required:**

a. Why does the depreciation reversal have a negative amount in Year 2 and a positive amount in Years 3, 4, and 5?

b. Why does the litigation loss result in a negative amount in Year 5?

c. List and discuss all the items that the bookkeeper has handled incorrectly in the preceding schedule.

d. Prepare a revised schedule of deferred taxes for Year 1.

e. Prepare a journal entry to *correct* the financial accounting records.

**13–6. Single Temporary Difference over Time with Change in Tax Rates**

Leap Year Calendar Corporation undertook a major advertising program to smooth out its sales volume, which tended to be quite cyclical in nature. The campaign cost $200,000 and was deducted on the company's tax return in 1995. However, on its financial statements the firm decided to reflect the amount as an asset, amortizing it to expense over a four-year period beginning in 1996.

In 1995, the company reported taxable income of $100,000, which was taxed at a rate of 40 percent (financial income was $300,000). Because of this difference originating in 1995, the following differences also appeared in 1996 and 1997:

|  | Taxable Income | Financial Income |
|---|---|---|
| 1996. . . . . . | $180,000 | $130,000 |
| 1997. . . . . . | 150,000 | 100,000 |

Early in 1997, the enacted tax rate was reduced from 40 to 30 percent for 1997 and subsequent years.

**Required:**

a. Prepare journal entries to record income tax expense, current income taxes payable, and deferred tax liability in 1995 and 1996.

b. Prepare the adjusting entry at the beginning of 1997 to reflect the change in tax rate.

c. Prepare the journal entry to record income tax expense, current income taxes payable, and deferred tax liability at the end of 1997.

d. What amount appears as income tax expense on the 1997 income statement?

**13–7. Operating Loss Carryovers**

Cromer, Inc. reported the following amounts of financial and taxable income (loss) for its first four years of operation:

| Year | Income before Tax |
|---|---|
| 1992 . . . . | $ 54,000 |
| 1993 . . . . | (45,000) |
| 1994 . . . . | (76,000) |
| 1995 . . . . | 160,000 |

No permanent or temporary differences existed in any of the years.

**Required:**

a. Calculate the amount of income tax expense (benefit) to be reported for each of the four years. Assume a tax rate of 25 percent.

b. Prepare the lower portion of the income statements for each year, beginning with income before taxes.

**13–8.  Temporary Differences from Depreciation**

At the beginning of 1994, Prince Corporation acquired for $450,000 some assets with an average life of three years. The firm decided to depreciate the $450,000 for financial accounting purposes by the straight-line method. For tax purposes, the assets were depreciated under an accelerated method.

The table below shows relevant information for 1994 to 1996. Assume that there are no other differences between financial income and taxable income. The tax rate remains at 30 percent throughout this period.

|  | Book Depreciation | Tax Depreciation | Temporary Difference | Income before Depreciation and Taxes |
|---|---|---|---|---|
| 1994 | $150,000 | $200,000 | $(50,000) | $400,000 |
| 1995 | 150,000 | 225,000 | (75,000) | 400,000 |
| 1996 | 150,000 | 25,000 | 125,000 | 300,000 |

**Required:**

a. Compute the annual taxable income and current taxes payable for the three years.

b. Compute the financial accounting income before tax and make journal entries for income tax expense using deferred tax accounting procedures.

c. Prepare a T account for Deferred Tax Liability and post the entries in *b* to it for the three years.

d. What would happen to the balance in the Deferred Tax Liability account if Prince Corporation were to spend on similar assets $450,000 per year indefinitely? Assume it begins in 1994 and all assets are depreciated in the same ways as outlined above.

e. What implications, if any, do the results in *d* have for your interpretation of the nature of the Deferred Tax Liability account?

**13–9.  Operating Loss Carryovers**

Mineral Corporation began operations in 1993. Earnings for the first four years of operations are shown below:

| | |
|---|---|
| 1993. . . . . . | $25,000 |
| 1994. . . . . . | 18,000 |
| 1995. . . . . . | 10,000 |
| 1996. . . . . . | 3,000 |

The income tax rate has been 25 percent for each year, and the firm has no permanent or temporary tax differences. The downturn in profits continued during 1997, with Mineral Corporation actually losing $57,000 during that year. At the end of 1997, the chief accountant for the firm made the following income tax journal entry:

| | | |
|---|---|---|
| Tax Refund Receivable . . . . . . . . . . . . . . . . . . . . . . . . . | 14,250 | |
| Reduction in Loss Due to Loss Carryovers . . . . . . . . | | 14,250 |

The accountant's assistant objected, arguing that the correct amount for the above entry was only $7,750.

**Required:**

a. How did the chief accountant come up with the $14,250 amount? What modifications, if any, would you make in the journal entry?

b. Is the assistant correct in stating that the correct amount for the journal entry should be only $7,750? Explain.

c. If the $6,500 in dispute is not reflected in the formal accounts, where, if at all, should the financial statement reader be alerted to it?

d. Assume that Mineral Corporation's fortunes experienced a dramatic turnaround during 1998, with the firm earning a profit of $30,000. Prepare the journal entry necessary to reflect income tax expense for that year under generally accepted accounting principles.

### 13–10. Deferred Tax Asset

In 1990, Hernandez, Inc. reports pre-tax financial income of $89,000 and taxable income of $101,000, due to two temporary differences. First, Hernandez deducted an expense of $72,000 for expected warranty costs. However, this amount is not deductible for tax purposes until it is paid. Expenditures are expected to be $25,000 in 1991; $30,000 in 1992; and $17,000 in 1993. Second, for tax purposes, the company recognizes income from some sales on the installment method. Accordingly, $60,000 of 1990's income was deferred to future tax years. Hernandez expects to recognize for tax purposes $20,000 of this amount in 1991, 1992, and 1993. The enacted tax rate for all years is 30 percent.

**Required:**

a. Prepare a schedule of future taxable and deductible amounts and calculate the amount of any current and deferred tax liabilities (assets).

b. Prepare the journal entry to record income taxes for 1990.

### 13–11. Temporary Difference from Construction Contracts

Babcock Corporation is engaged in the building of condominiums and apartment houses. Most projects take from two to three years to complete. Consequently, revenue is recognized on a percentage-of-completion basis for external reporting. However, for income tax purposes the firm elects to use the completed-contract method. Assume a tax rate of 30 percent.

During its first three years, the company worked on four different contracts. Information related to them is given below:

| | Contract Number | | | |
|---|---|---|---|---|
| | *1* | *2* | *3* | *4* |
| Contract price . . . . . . . . | $300,000 | $900,000 | $600,000 | $700,000 |
| Total cost . . . . . . . . . . | 150,000 | 500,000 | 450,000 | 500,000 |
| Year completed . . . . . . . . | Year 2 | Year 2 | Year 3 | |
| Percentage of work completed during: | | | | |
| Year 1. . . . . . . . . . . | 80% | 50% | 20% | |
| Year 2. . . . . . . . . . . | 20% | 50% | 60% | 30% |
| Year 3. . . . . . . . . . . | | | 20% | 50% |

### Required:

a. Determine income before taxes for each of the three years for financial accounting purposes.

b. Determine taxable income for each of the three years.

c. Prepare journal entries to record income tax expense each year under deferred tax accounting.

d. What is the balance in the Deferred Tax Liability account at the end of Year 3? What does it represent?

e. What would you do if at the beginning of Year 4 the enacted tax rate were raised to 35 percent?

**13–12. Operating Loss Carryovers**

Neverlite Bulb Manufacturing Company began operations in 1981 and operated profitably for 10 years. In 1991, the company introduced a photographers' new "whitelite" darkroom bulb. The bulb allowed film to be processed in full light. Unfortunately, this characteristic of the bulb did not have permanence, so that after a few hours of use, any film exposed under it was ruined. Consequently, the bulb was withdrawn from the market after three months.

The company suffered large losses from the disposal of inventory and settlement of claims. As a result, the income statement for 1991 showed a net loss of $120,000. The loss could be carried back to offset the taxable income of 1988, 1989, and 1990. The company is subject to a tax rate of 30 percent. Earnings since 1988 are shown below:

|        | Income before Tax | Income Tax |
|--------|-------------------|------------|
| 1988 . . . . | $ 25,000      | $7,500     |
| 1989 . . . . | 30,000        | 9,000      |
| 1990 . . . . | 21,000        | 6,300      |
| 1991 . . . . | (120,000) loss |           |

Because the tax loss carryback exhausted only $76,000 of the loss, giving rise to a refund of $22,800, there is a tax loss carryforward of $44,000 that can be offset against income for the next fifteen years. The potential future tax savings from this carryforward is $13,200.

The president wishes to record both the $22,800 and the $13,200 as an asset at the end of 1991. He proposes the following journal entry for 1991:

| | | |
|---|---|---|
| Current Tax Receivable . . . . . . . . . . . . . . . . . . . . . . | 22,800 | |
| Future Tax Receivable. . . . . . . . . . . . . . . . . . . . . . . | 13,200 | |
| Revenue from Tax Loss . . . . . . . . . . . . . . . . . . | | 36,000 |

As a result of the additional revenue of $36,000, the loss in 1991 would be only $84,000.

The president argues, "Because of a special provision in the tax law, our loss in 1991 earned us $36,000 in tax benefits—$22,800 which we collect now and $13,200 which we collect in the future. But collectibility is beyond a shadow of a doubt. We have been profitable in the past and we will be profitable in the future. Our loss in 1991 was the result of a fluke and will not happen again. As I understand generally accepted accounting principles, we can recognize revenue when it has been earned and measured with a reasonable degree of reliability. My entry is consistent with GAAP."

**Required:**

a. Evaluate the argument put forth by the president. In what areas do you agree or disagree with him?
b. Prepare the journal entry for 1991 that you believe is required under generally accepted accounting principles.
c. Assume the company's financial income before tax in subsequent years is 1992—$17,000, 1993—$21,000, and 1994—$28,000. What journal entries would you recommend to record income taxes in those years?
d. Do the results in part c strengthen the president's argument? Explain.

## 13–13. Permanent and Multiple Temporary Differences

Skarknitz Company has computed its financial income before taxes for 1990 to be $134,000. A reconciliation of this amount with taxable income revealed the following five differences:

1. Assets purchased in 1990 are being written off on an accelerated basis for income tax purposes, resulting in an excess of depreciation for tax purposes of $19,000. This amount is expected to reverse over the next four years at the rate of $4,000, $4,300, $5,700, and $5,000 respectively.
2. Warranty expense was deducted on the income statement in the amount of $15,300. This amount will be deductible for tax purposes when the warranty costs are paid in future years; the expectation is equal payment in 1991, 1992, and 1993.
3. Goodwill amortization of $3,200 was recorded in the accounting records.
4. Revenue of $8,000 was received in advance and is taxable in 1990 but will be included in financial income in 1991 when it is earned.
5. A legal claim (loss and estimated liability) of $31,500 was recognized on the 1990 financial statements. It is expected to be deductible for tax purposes in 1993 when the lawsuit finally is settled.

The enacted income tax rates are 25 percent for 1990, 1991, and 1992; and 30 percent for 1993 and 1994.

**Required:**

a. Prepare an analysis (similar to Tables 13–3 and 13–4) of future taxable and deductible amounts that would assist Skarknitz in calculating its income tax expense for 1990.
b. Prepare the journal entry to record income tax expense for 1990.
c. What would be the impact on your entry in b if Skarknitz expected to settle the legal claim in 1992 instead of 1993?
d. What disclosures relative to income taxes would accompany the 1990 financial statements?

**13–14. Two-Year Analysis of Temporary and Permanent Differences**

The following information relates to Sadler Company for 1991 and 1992:

|  | Pre-tax Financial Income | Taxable Income |
|---|---|---|
| 1991 . . . . . . | $204,000 | $152,000 |
| 1992 . . . . . . | 66,000 | 129,000 |

All elements of income are the same for book and tax purposes in all prior years and in 1991 and 1992 except for the following items:

1. During 1991, depreciable assets were purchased. First-year depreciation on the tax return was $60,000 more than the amount deducted on the income statement. However, for the next four years after 1991, financial income depreciation will exceed tax depreciation by $15,000 per year.
2. Amortization of goodwill is $8,000 each year; this amount is not deductible for tax purposes.
3. A litigation loss of $40,000 was recognized in 1992 on the income statement but will not appear on the tax return until 1993.

The enacted tax rates are 35 percent for 1991 and 30 percent for 1992 and beyond.

**Required:**

a. Prepare schedules similar to those illustrated in the chapter to be used in determining the amount of income tax expense for 1991 and 1992.
b. Prepare journal entries to record income tax expense in 1991 and 1992.
c. What is the effective income tax rate for 1991? Why does it differ from 35 percent?

**13–15. Multiple Temporary Differences over Time**

The following figures are taken from the financial accounting records and income tax return of the Gilman Company for the period from 1990 to 1992:

| Year | Earnings before Taxes on the Income Statement | Taxable Income on the Tax Return |
|---|---|---|
| 1990 . . . . . . | $360,000 | $290,000 |
| 1991 . . . . . . | 285,000 | 320,000 |
| 1992 . . . . . . | 330,000 | 385,000 |

Revenues and expenses are the same on the tax return as in the financial accounting records in each of the years, with the following exceptions:

1. Because of different depreciation methods being used for book and tax purposes on plant assets purchased in *1988,* the depreciation expense figures differ as follows:

|  | Financial Statement Depreciation | Tax Return Depreciation |
|---|---|---|
| 1990 . . . . . . | $30,000 | $ 40,000 |
| 1991 . . . . . . | 30,000 | 15,000 |
| 1992 . . . . . . | 15,000 | 5,000 |

2. In 1990, a $60,000 gain was recognized for financial reporting purposes. This gain will be recognized for tax purposes in the amount of $20,000 annually, beginning in *1991*.
3. In 1992, the company accrued a $25,000 expense on its books. For income tax purposes, this expense cannot be deducted until 1993 when the cash is actually disbursed.

The tax rate is 40 percent for all years, and the company has a balance of $6,000 in a Deferred Tax Liability account at the end of *1989*.

### Required:

*a.* Calculate the amount of income tax legally owed for each year.
*b.* Prepare journal entries to record income tax expense in each of the three years under deferred income tax procedures. Show supporting calculations.
*c.* Explain how the original balance of $6,000 in the Deferred Tax Liability account originated. What does it represent?

### 13–16. Entries Based on Reversal Schedules

L & J Enterprises has four temporary differences between financial income and taxable income for 1990 and 1991 (financial income and taxable income were the same before 1990):

1. Different depreciation methods are used on the tax returns than on the income statement.
2. Royalty revenue is taxed when received but is recognized in later periods in financial income when it is earned.
3. Income from installment sales is taxed in later years when received in cash but appears on the income statement in the year of sale.
4. A litigation loss was recognized in 1991 but is not deductible until the suit finally is settled, which is expected to be in 1994.

Data regarding these temporary differences are presented in the table below:

| | Annual Excess of Financial Income over Taxable Income | Cumulative Excess | Future Tax Consequences | | | |
|---|---|---|---|---|---|---|
| | | | 1991 | 1992 | 1993 | 1994 |
| **1990** | | | | | | |
| Depreciation | 130,000 | 130,000 | (50,000) | 40,000 | 60,000 | 80,000 |
| Royalty | (40,000) | (40,000) | (20,000) | (20,000) | | |
| Installment | 15,000 | 15,000 | 5,000 | 5,000 | 5,000 | |
| **1991** | | | | | | |
| Depreciation | 60,000 | 190,000 | | 40,000 | 65,000 | 85,000 |
| Royalty | (20,000) | (60,000) | | (40,000) | (20,000) | |
| Installment | 25,000 | 40,000 | | 15,000 | 15,000 | 10,000 |
| Litigation | (10,000) | (10,000) | | | | (10,000) |

The enacted tax rates are 30 percent for 1990 and 1991 and 35 percent thereafter. Financial income before taxes is $120,000 in 1990 and $140,000 in 1991.

**Required:**

*a.* Calculate taxable income and current taxes payable for 1990 and 1991.

*b.* Compute the amount of *new* temporary differences applicable to depreciation, royalty revenue, and installment income *originating in 1991*.

*c.* Prepare journal entries to record income tax expense in 1990 and 1991. Include appropriate schedules to support the calculations of deferred taxes payable and deferred tax expense.

**Casette 13–1. Questions about Georgia-Pacific Corporation**

At the back of the text is a complete set of financial statements of Georgia-Pacific Corporation taken from its annual report of 1987.

Answer the following questions relating to its income tax expense and deferred tax disclosures. Keep in mind that Georgia-Pacific prepared its statements under *APB Opinion No. 11* rather than *FASB Statement No. 96,* so the disclosures differ somewhat from those described in the chapter.

1. What is the total amount of income tax expense for 1987? How much of this amount was currently payable and how much was deferred? How much was actually paid in cash during 1987?
2. Prepare a journal entry that summarizes the recording of income taxes done by Georgia-Pacific during 1987. Do these amounts reconcile with the balance sheet accounts?
3. Verify that the income tax rate for Georgia-Pacific was 42.6 percent. Explain *in your own words* why this rate was higher than the 40 percent federal statutory rate. Explain *in your own words* why this rate was higher than the 39 percent effective rate in 1986, even though statutory rates declined.
4. What were the major temporary differences (Georgia-Pacific commonly refers to them as "timing differences") that existed in 1987? Explain in your own words, for as many of the items as you can, why each difference caused deferred tax expense to increase or to decrease.
5. At the end of Note 8, the company discusses implementation of *Statement of Financial Accounting Standards No. 96.* If Georgia-Pacific adopts the new standards in 1989, what journal entry (without numbers) will it make? Explain why the company expects this particular result.

**Casette 13–2. Reconciliation between Financial Income and Taxable Income**

The Vermont Apex Corporation reported financial accounting income before any income taxes of $3,830,000 for 1994.* Additional information follows:

1. The corporation's pre-tax accounting income includes $200,000 of tax-exempt interest from municipal bonds.

---

* Adapted from a case originally prepared by Leonard Morrissey, Professor Emeritus of The Amos Tuck School of Business Administration at Dartmouth College.

2. The corporation's pre-tax accounting income includes $160,000 of capital gains from ordinary disposals of plant assets. Such gains are subject to a preferential federal income tax rate of 30 percent, instead of 35 percent.

3. Pre-tax accounting income includes $460,000 earned in Puerto Rico where the corporation is exempt from all federal income taxes until 1995.

4. The corporation's state income tax for 1994 is $230,000. This amount is payable currently and is a deductible expense on the 1994 federal income tax return.

5. The corporation uses straight-line depreciation for accounting purposes, while it uses MACRS for income tax purposes. In 1994, depreciation was $1,320,000 (financial accounting) and $1,968,000 (tax return). This temporary difference will reverse equally over the next four years.

6. The corporation guarantees its products for two years following sale to a customer. In 1994, the corporation credited an Estimated Warranty Liability account for $620,000, debiting Warranty Liability Expense. The corporation during 1994 incurred expenditures of $400,000 to meet warranty claims; that amount was debited to the Estimated Warranty Liability account. Warranty expenses can be deducted for tax purposes only when the expenditures actually are incurred. The remaining $220,000 of warranty expenditures are expected to be incurred in 1995 and 1996 in the amounts of $150,000 and $70,000 respectively.

7. The corporation's pre-tax accounting income includes income of $320,000 earned in a foreign country and subject to income tax in that country at 25 percent. (In general, while the regulations are exceedingly complex, a U.S. corporation must pay federal income tax on overseas income in the year earned, regardless of the disposition of that income. However, a tax credit against the gross federal income tax liability may be claimed for any foreign income tax payable.)

**Required:**

a. Determine the amount of income tax at the statutory federal income tax rate of 35 percent applied to the pre-tax financial accounting income.

b. Determine the actual federal income tax currently payable for 1994.

c. Determine the provision (expense) for income tax to appear on the income statement for 1994. (This provision should include both federal and nonfederal income taxes.) Given the result, calculate the firm's effective income tax rate for 1994.

d. Prepare a detailed reconciliation of the differences in both dollar and percentage amounts between the results in *a* and *c*.

e. Prepare a journal entry (or entries) to record *all* income taxes on the books for 1994.

**Casette 13–3. Three-Year Comprehensive Analysis of Income Taxes**

Prior to 1992, financial accounting income and taxable income of the firm Howe, Dewey, Duit, Inc. were the same. The amounts of income tax expense reported on the tax return and on the income statement were as follows:

| | |
|---|---|
| 1989. . . . . . | $30,000 |
| 1990. . . . . . | 2,000 |
| 1991. . . . . . | 5,000 |

The following table contains information about pre-tax financial income and taxable income for the next three years. Below the table is some additional information for each year:

| | *1992* | *1993* | *1994* |
|---|---|---|---|
| Pre-tax financial income (loss) . . . . . . . . | $13,000 | $ (8,000) | $15,000 |
| Amortization of goodwill . . . . . . . . . | 10,000 | 10,000 | 10,000 |
| Excess of tax depreciation | | | |
| over book depreciation—net. . . . . . . | (27,000) | (15,000) | 17,000 |
| Advance rental—net . . . . . . . . . . . | 16,000 | 8,000 | (16,000) |
| Installment gain . . . . . . . . . . . . . | | (12,000) | 6,000 |
| Interest on municipal securities. . . . . . . | | (4,000) | (5,000) |
| Litigation loss . . . . . . . . . . . . . | | | 40,000 |
| Taxable income (loss) . . . . . . . . . . | $12,000 | $(21,000) | $67,000 |

## 1992:

1. Goodwill was amortized beginning in 1992. This expense is not deductible for tax purposes.
2. Assets acquired in 1992 are depreciated on an accelerated basis for tax purposes. This resulted in $27,000 more depreciation being deducted on the tax return than on the income statement. However, in the next three years, book depreciation will exceed tax depreciation by $9,000 each year.
3. Howe, Dewey, Duit collected $16,000 in advance rental on some equipment. The advance rental covers the years 1993 and 1994 but was reported as taxable income in 1992.

## 1993:

1. Amortization of goodwill continued.
2. Assets acquired in 1993 are depreciated on an accelerated basis for tax purposes. This resulted in $24,000 more depreciation being deducted on the tax return than on the income statement. This difference will balance out over the next three years when book depreciation will exceed tax depreciation by $8,000 per year. The $24,000 depreciation difference on new assets was partially offset by a $9,000 difference on 1992's acquisitions.
3. Again in 1993 the company received $16,000 advance rental for some equipment. The advance rental covers the next two years, 1994 and 1995. However, it was taxable in 1993. On the other hand, $8,000 of the advance rental from 1992 was recognized as revenue in 1993 but was not taxed then.
4. Late in 1993, the firm sold some land at a gain of $12,000. The gain was reported in full on the 1993 income statement but will be reported in two installments of $6,000 on the tax returns of 1994 and 1995, respectively. The gain is taxed as ordinary income.
5. The firm invested in some municipal securities in 1993 and earned $4,000 of nontaxable interest which appeared on the income statement of 1993.

**1994:**

1. Amortization of goodwill continued.
2. No new depreciable assets were purchased in 1994. Depreciation on the tax return was less than on the income statement by $17,000—$9,000 related to the acquisitions of 1992 and $8,000 related to the acquisitions of 1993.
3. $16,000 of rental revenue was recognized in 1994—$8,000 from the advance received in 1992 and $8,000 from the advance received in 1993. However, having already been taxed in the year of receipt, these amounts did not appear on the tax return in 1994.
4. One half of the gain on the sale of land from 1993 did appear on the tax return in 1994 under the installment method.
5. An additional amount of $5,000 interest revenue from the municipal securities appeared on the income statement of 1994 but not on its tax return.
6. A litigation loss of $40,000 reduced financial income in 1994, but it is not expected to be deducted for tax purposes until 1995.

The enacted tax rates under the 1989 law were 25 percent.

**Required:**

a. Prepare journal entries to record income tax expense for 1992, 1993, and 1994. Support your calculations for each year with a schedule of the future tax consequences due to temporary differences.
b. If applicable, divide the total income tax expense for each year in part *a* into its major component parts.
c. What amounts related to income taxes would appear on the balance sheet prepared at the end of 1992, 1993, and 1994? How would these items be classified?
d. Prepare disclosures that will explain the reasons for any balances in the deferred tax accounts that appear on the balance sheet in *b*.
e. Assume the enacted tax rate is changed to 30 percent early in 1995. What entry would you make?

# Chapter 14

# Stockholders' Equity

When the accounting system records equities, it separates them by source. Hence, liabilities (claims on assets by outside interests) are distinguished from owners' equity accounts (the source of assets from the owners). Further, accountants subdivide owners' equity to distinguish between contributed or invested capital (capital stock) and earned capital (retained earnings). Knowing what portion of the assets were contributed directly by the owners and what portion of the assets arose from a business's earning activities helps readers interpret the historical development and current position of the firm. It also clarifies the status of any asset distributions in the form of dividends, that is, whether they represent earnings or are a return of some portion of invested capital.

In this chapter, we examine the accounting considerations related to the stockholders' equity accounts. First, we explore the issuance of shares of stock. Second, we consider the payment of dividends to holders of stock. We then discuss accounting for a corporation's repurchase of its own shares of capital stock. The chapter concludes with a discussion of the impact on stockholders' equity related to foreign currency transactions by corporations having international operations.

## THE CORPORATION

A corporation is a separate *legal* entity. It comes into being when its founders draw up *articles of incorporation* and the corporation receives a state charter. The charter, in conjunction with the applicable state laws, endows the corporation with certain rights, powers, and obligations. One of the most significant of these legal attributes is the *limited liability* of stockholders. This means that creditors' claims are on the corporation's assets and do not carry over to the assets of the individual stockholders. Unlike partners and single proprietors, the owners of a corporation (stockholders) are not personally liable for the firm's debts. Stockholders' losses are limited to the amount invested in the corporation.

Most states require that a minimum amount of capital per share be invested. The investment is called *legal* (or *stated*) capital and cannot be reduced by voluntary action of the board of directors. Legal capital serves as a buffer to protect the claims of the corporation's creditors. Stockholders' equity cannot be reduced below legal capital through the payment of dividends or repurchase of capital stock by the corporation.[1]

At first glance, one might think that legal capital would automatically correspond to the total contributed capital, the relatively permanent investment made by the owners in exchange for shares of stock. This is not the case. The market value of a share of stock on the date it is issued reflects market forces, not legal considerations. It usually differs from the stated or legal value. Stated capital is a legal concept, specifically and variously defined in each state. This legal concept and the various definitions of stated capital influence the recording procedures for stockholders' equity.

In addition to the legal elements, many financial intricacies, conventions, and policies are also reflected in our accounting practices. We will see a number of practices that seem more a matter of financial convention than of accounting policy. Yet, it is in the accounting records that these matters find their final expression. Consequently, we need to understand how these factors affect stockholders' equity accounts as well.

## ISSUANCE OF STOCK

The legal expression of the owners' investment in a corporation is the share of stock. To individual stockholders, shares of stock represent personal assets. The owner of a share of stock has the right to share in earnings through dividends (if and when declared), the right to share in any residual assets in liquidation, the right to vote and share indirectly in management through election of the board of directors, plus other rights specified under corporate law. Usually, these rights have a market value.

To corporations, on the other hand, shares of stock are merely a representation of an ownership interest. State charters authorize corporations to issue a certain number of shares. *Authorized stock,* however, has no accounting significance. Only when stock is issued and assets actually flow into the firm do accountants record the increase in stockholders' equity. At that time, entries also are made in the stockholder ledger, the subsidiary ledger to the capital stock account, for the specified number of shares issued to

---

[1] Of course, unprofitable operations could deplete the owners' equity in a business. Stated capital is intended to protect creditors against voluntary withdrawals of capital by the owners, not against dissipation of assets through continued losses.

each investor and represented by the stock certificates. Therefore, the accounting process focuses on *outstanding stock* (or *issued stock*).

## Preferred Stock

Heretofore we have assumed that only one kind of ownership interest is present, that represented by capital stock. Actually, there are two major types of capital stock, *common* and *preferred*. The former corresponds to what we have been calling capital stock. It represents the residual ownership and control of the corporation. Preferred stock represents a special type of ownership interest that has certain modifications in the basic rights inherent in common stock.[2]

The term *preferred* refers to a priority position over common stock. There are two customary preferences. First, preferred stock usually has a *preference over common stock in the payment of dividends* and, second, it usually has a *prior claim on assets in the event of an entity's liquidation*. The latter provision need not concern us here because we are recording under the going-concern concept. The dividend preference modifies the risk of the preferred stock. *If* dividends are declared, they must first be paid to the preferred stockholders up to the amount stated in the preferred-stock contract. Usually the return is fixed, however. Once the preferred dividends are paid, any remaining dividends declared are applicable only to the common stock. Also, in most cases preferred dividends are *cumulative;* that is, before dividends can be paid on common stock, *all* preferred dividends, including any skipped in past years, must be paid.

Preferred stock is a hybrid security. Economically and financially, it is very similar to long-term debt except that dividends are not tax deductible to the corporation. Preferred stock has less risk than common stock, as reflected in its prior but limited claim on earnings. It is often callable, like a bond issue. On the other hand, *legally* it resembles common stock. Its claim on earnings is not mandatory; only if dividends are declared does preferred stock have a prior claim. There is neither an accrued liability for the payment of preferred dividends, as is the case with interest, nor a specific maturity date on a preferred stock issue.[3] As a hybrid equity element, preferred stock logically could be reported in a separate category between liabilities and common stock equity on the balance sheet. Typically, however, legal convention prevails, and it is included along with the common in an overall category labeled "stockholders' equity."

---

[2] We refer the reader to books on business finance for detailed descriptions of various provisions pertaining to preferred stock. We limit our discussion here to some of the basic and more usual differences between preferred and common stock, particularly those that have accounting implications.

[3] An exception exists for those preferred issues that feature a *mandatory* call provision. For all practical purposes, they are debt and should not be included in stockholders' equity.

## Par Value, Stated Value, and No-Par-Value Stock

Legal capital is generally recognized by assigning an arbitrary amount to each share of stock. This amount, called *par value,* is legally designated at the time of incorporation and is printed on each stock certificate. Par value may be any amount and is selected at the time a firm is incorporated. Historically, a popular par value was $100. This was clearly an arbitrary amount and did not determine the stock's market value when issued, or its subsequent value. Market value is governed by investors' appraisal of the future earning potential of the business.

The reason for the heavy use of par value stock lies in its legal significance. *Par value defines the amount of legal capital per share.* Creditors can presume that an amount equivalent to the par value of the shares issued is permanently invested by the stockholders. Issuing stock initially at a price below par value is illegal in practically all states because of the impairment of legal capital (defined as par value). To avoid the possibility that market value at issuance will be below par value, many corporations currently use a low par value ($1, $5, $10).

Legal capital has been responsible for two other practices associated with stock issuance. Some states allow the issuance of stock that has *no par value* printed on the certificates. This practice avoids the problem of market value being below par value. The total asset value invested measures the legal capital of the shares. No-par stock has the advantage of avoiding any implication that par value represents the real worth of the stock.

A second technique applied in many states and related to no-par-value stock requires the board of directors to assign a *stated value* to the no-par shares. The stated value is then treated in a manner similar to shares having a printed par value. The use of stated value with no-par stock is designed ostensibly to protect the creditors by evidencing that there is some *minimum stated* capital. With stated value, legal capital again becomes something distinct from invested capital.


## Entries to Record Stock Issues

For accounting and financial purposes, the important consideration is the increase in resources arising from the issuance of capital stock. The real increase in stockholders' equity, the amount of contributed capital, is determined by the amount of assets actually invested, not by any par or stated value arbitrarily assigned to the shares. Generally, the issuance of no-par shares involves little difficulty. Cash is debited and either Common Stock or Preferred Stock is credited for the total amount received. When par values or stated values are present, however, they are practically always recognized in the accounts.

The three entries following record the issuance of 2,000 shares of par value common stock, no-par-value common stock, and par value preferred stock, respectively. In each instance, investors contribute cash to the corporation according to the value they attach to the ownership represented by the 2,000 shares. Assets and owners' equity increase by the amount of assets received. The increase in stockholders' equity is conventionally reflected in two accounts.

### Entry 1: $10 Par Value Common Stock Issued for $30 per Share

```
Cash (2,000 × $30) . . . . . . . . . . . . . . .   60,000
    Common Stock—$10 Par (2,000 × $10) . . . . .           20,000
    Additional Paid-In Capital—Common. . . . . . .         40,000
```

### Entry 2: No-Par-Value with $15 Stated Value Common Stock Issued for $20 per Share

```
Cash (2,000 × $20) . . . . . . . . . . . . . . .   40,000
    No-Par Common Stock—$15 Stated Value
        (2,000 × $15) . . . . . . . . . . . . . .         30,000
    Additional Paid-In Capital—Common. . . . . . .         10,000
```

### Entry 3: $50 Par Value Preferred Stock Issued for $60 per Share

```
Cash (2,000 × $60) . . . . . . . . . . . . . .   120,000
    Preferred Stock—$50 Par (2,000 × $50) . . . .         100,000
    Additional Paid-In Capital—Preferred. . . . . .         20,000
```

The additional paid-in capital accounts are called "equity adjunct" accounts. They represent a part of the total contributed capital of the firm. They are not gains. A corporation does not generate income by issuing its own shares of stock in a capital-raising transaction. Additional paid-in capital reflects the portion of invested capital over and above the arbitrary amount that has been segregated as legal capital. Accountants frequently use other titles in practice for this account—*Premium* (particularly when preferred stock is sold above par) or *Excess over Par*. At one time Capital Surplus and Paid-In Surplus were also used. However, the connotation of the word *surplus* as indicating excess or supplementary funds that can be made available to creditors or stockholders is clearly inappropriate.

## Stock Split

The preceding entries illustrate the issuance of shares in exchange for an inflow of assets. The number of shares outstanding may also be increased by a stock split. A split results in the corporation distributing additional shares to stockholders for which no additional investment is required. Total contributed capital does not change, nor do total assets. The entire stockholders' equity remains constant in dollar amount. However, the equity is now represented by a larger number of shares, so each share accounts for a proportionately smaller interest.

The stock split is a financial mechanism used to increase the investor appeal for stock by reducing its market price and to broaden ownership by having more shares outstanding. Assume a company has 300,000 shares of stock outstanding. Then, a two-for-one stock split calls for distribution of an additional 300,000 shares. Each stockholder holds two shares for each share previously owned. If the market price of the stock is $70 per share before the split, theoretically it should fall to $35 per share after the split.[4] Because no change in resources or financial interests occurs, no substantive accounting entry is needed. However, if the capital stock has a par value, the stock split usually requires a reduction in par value to maintain total legal capital. For example, the entry to record a split for a $20 par value stock would be:

Common Stock—$20 Par. . . . . . . . . . .    6,000,000
     Common Stock—$10 Par. . . . . . . . .                6,000,000
To record issuance of 300,000 additional shares
under a two-for-one stock split and the
corresponding reduction in par value from $20
to $10 per share.

# DETERMINING THE AMOUNT OF CAPITAL RECEIVED

Usually the dollar increase in stockholders' equity is determined by measuring the value of the assets received in exchange for the shares issued. If the asset received from the issuance of a single security is cash, no measurement problem results. Whether one or more capital accounts are used to record owner's equity, the total net increase is the amount of cash received. In contrast, the measurements sometimes are ambiguous when shares of common stock are issued in exchange for noncash assets, in combination with other securities, or in exchange for other securities.

## Noncash Assets

In accordance with the *exchange-price* principle, shares of stock issued when noncash assets are invested should be recorded at the fair market value of the assets received. For example, if a stockholder invests land hav-

---

[4] Often the market price does not fall exactly to the theoretical level. If the dividend amount per share is maintained on the new shares, the stock split is a way of increasing dividend payout. The market price may also rise after the split because the lower price makes the stock attractive to more buyers. Neither of these increases in value is the direct result of the split; they are the result of other factors—increased dividends or greater demand for the stock.

ing a fair market value of $50,000 in exchange for 2,000 shares of $20 par value common stock, the entry should be:

| | | |
|---|---|---|
| Land . . . . . . . . . . . . . . . . . . . . . . | 50,000 | |
| Common Stock—$20 Par (2,000 × $20) . . . . . | | 40,000 |
| Additional Paid-in Capital—Common . . . . . . . | | 10,000 |

The fair market value of the noncash asset may be determined by referring to quoted market prices, cash transactions for similar assets, or independent appraisals. When accountants encounter difficulty in establishing the fair market value of certain noncash assets, they may look to the market value of the stock issued. Practically speaking, therefore, fair market value may be measured by a valuation of the shares of stock given up in exchange rather than the value of the asset received. The practical measurement problem boils down to a question of relative reliability. Ideally, we like to determine the value of the asset received and let that govern the amount credited to stockholders' equity. Sometimes, however, we find more accurate and verifiable measurement in the fair market value of the equity shares and use that in making the debit to the asset.[5]

### Package Issues and Stock Purchase Rights and Warrants

Corporations occasionally issue securities containing multiple instruments. For example, bonds may be issued with some shares of preferred or common stock attached, or with a certificate called a "stock right" or "stock warrant" that provides the right to purchase common stock at some later date. The same general procedure governs the recording in both cases.

When multiple security instruments are issued, we call the result a "package issue." Package issues increase the attractiveness of security issues and add flexibility to capital-raising efforts. Each security element is accounted for separately. Total proceeds are allocated among the security elements for accounting purposes, usually in proportion to their relative market values. Market value, however, is not always an easily determined or clearly attainable measure. Where market values are known for only one of the securities, that value should be assigned to the security and the remainder distributed to the other instrument.

A stock right or warrant entitles the owner to acquire shares of stock at specific prices. Rights and warrants both have similar characteristics and are

---

[5] Of course, using the market value of outstanding stock is not without its pitfalls. The market price on an organized stock exchange on any particular date may be distorted by temporary influences. Also, one cannot extend a price per share that is paid for a few shares to determine accurately the fair market value of a large block of stock. Transaction costs need to be considered too. Nevertheless, heavy reliance is frequently placed on the market value of the stock when a firm acquires another entire business through an exchange of stock. Further discussion of the recording complexities of mergers is contained in Chapter 15.

used for several different purposes. Employee stock purchase plans may use rights to provide employees an opportunity to purchase shares. Rights and warrants may be attached to bond instruments to strengthen their attractiveness, or they may be used to protect against hostile corporate takeovers. The right to acquire additional shares has a market value, and the rights and warrants often are traded in a manner similar to trading capital stock.

If the stock purchase rights are distributed with no consideration being received in exchange, no accounting problems accompany their issuance. No assets flow into the corporation. However, if the rights or warrants attach to some other security, then the same problem exists as with a package issue. The total proceeds must be allocated between the main security and the rights or warrants.

## Stock Options

Developing the measure of invested capital is somewhat involved when stock is issued in exchange partially or completely for employee services. A stock option plan gives employees the opportunity to purchase shares of the corporation's stock. The corporation's objectives include raising capital, increasing ownership, or providing compensation for services rendered to the firm. Stock option plans are classified as either *noncompensatory* or *compensatory*.

Noncompensatory stock option plans simply offer employees a chance to purchase the corporation's stock. As its name implies, no compensation for services is involved. The exercise of the option rights results in asset inflows to the corporation in a manner identical to any direct sale of stock. In fact, a hallmark of noncompensatory plans is that the option price (purchase price) approximates the fair market value of the stock. The accounting treatment for these plans requires no entry until the stock is purchased. At that time, the journal entry will result in the normal debit to Cash with credits to the Common Stock—Par and Additional Paid-In Capital accounts.

Compensatory option programs require measurements of the compensation being paid to employees. The value of the employee services, as measured by the compensation, together with the asset inflows when the options are executed constitute the total contributed capital. The purpose of these option plans is to extend stock ownership at attractive prices to employees as a part of their compensation. The accounting system must measure the total amount of compensation expense and, if more than one accounting period is involved, determine the appropriate periodic allocation.

Assume that a firm has a stock option plan for its key executives. The plan allows the executives to purchase $10 par value common stock at $30 per share. On December 31, 1989 the company grants an option to its chief executive officer to purchase 5,000 shares. The CEO cannot exercise the option (actually purchase the shares) for two years; must exercise it by

December 31, 1995; and must be employed by the firm when the option is exercised. The corporation's stock is selling for $45 on December 31, 1989.

Compensation is recorded only when the option price is less than the market price of the option shares. In this case, the compensation element is $15 per share ($45 market price less $30 option price) and totals $75,000 (5,000 shares × $15). It is evident that the CEO must work for two years (1990 and 1991) before being able to exercise the option. This period is called the "service period," and the compensation element is allocated over that period. The following entries will be made over the life of the option:

1. December 31, 1989—date of option grant:

| | | |
|---|---|---|
| Deferred Compensation Expense. . . . . . . . . . | 75,000 | |
|    Contributed Capital—Stock Options . . . . . . | | 75,000 |

2. December 31, 1990—end of first year of service period:

| | | |
|---|---|---|
| Compensation Expense . . . . . . . . . . . . | 37,500 | |
|    Deferred Compensation Expense. . . . . . . . | | 37,500 |

3. December 31, 1991—end of second year of service period:

| | | |
|---|---|---|
| Compensation Expense . . . . . . . . . . . . . | 37,500 | |
|    Deferred Compensation Expense. . . . . . . . | | 37,500 |

4. CEO exercises the option in February 1992:

| | | |
|---|---|---|
| Cash (5,000 shares × $30) . . . . . . . . . . . | 150,000 | |
| Contributed Capital—Stock Options . . . . . . . . | 75,000 | |
|    Common Stock—Par $10 . . . . . . . . . | | 50,000 |
|    Contributed Capital in Excess of Par . . . . . . | | 175,000 |

Each year the compensation expense related to the option plus the salary paid to the CEO would constitute the total value of employee services. Some accountants claim, however, that although the above procedures are required by the FASB, they usually cause compensation expense to be significantly understated. Many plans set the option price at or above the existing market price on the grant date. Under these circumstances, the required approach attaches no value to the option and records no compensation expense. Nevertheless, the option offers the recipient an opportunity for great gain by allowing shares to be acquired at a fixed price sometime in the future. This right possesses a value certainly greater than zero.

Account balances for Deferred Compensation and Contributed Capital from Stock Options are reported at the end of an accounting period in the contributed capital section of stockholders' equity. Deferred Compensation is a contra account deducted from Contributed Capital—Stock Options. The balance sheet accounts for the example above would appear on December 31, 1990 as follows:

| | | |
|---|---|---|
| Contributed capital—stock options . . . . . . . . . | $75,000 | |
| Less: Deferred compensation expense . . . . . . . . | 37,500 | $37,500 |

Because only one year of the service period has expired, the CEO is assumed to have invested only one year's services valued at $37,500. The net contributed capital, therefore, should be only $37,500—the amount that results from subtracting the contra equity account.

Current reporting standards require that the status of stock option plans be disclosed at the end of each accounting period. Status includes the number of shares granted, their option price, the number of options exercised, and the number of shares issued during the period. Normally firms make these disclosures in notes accompanying the financial statements.

The following stock option plan disclosure appeared in the 1986 Premark International Annual Report:

### Note 8: Stock Option Plans

The company established a stock option plan for key employees effective November 1, 1986. There were 4,000,000 shares reserved for issuance under the plan. During the year, options were granted to 300 employees (including officers) to purchase an aggregate of 2,858,000 shares at $19.65 per share. The options have a maximum term of ten years and one day and are generally exercisable proratably over five years after date of grant. At December 27, 1986, all options granted during the year were outstanding, none were exercisable and none were canceled. There were 1,142,000 shares reserved for future grants. No charges have been reflected in income for any period with respect to these options to purchase shares.

The last line of the note implies that this plan is noncompensatory and that the option price approximated the market value of the shares on the date of grant.

## Conversion of Preferred Stock

Often preferred stock, like some bond issues, contains a provision allowing the owners of the stock to convert into common stock. If conversion takes place, the transaction simply involves swapping one kind of equity for another. Common stock equity increases by the amount that preferred stock equity decreases, and total corporate assets remain the same.

On February 11, a corporation issues 2,000 shares of convertible preferred stock at $95 per share. The stock has a par value of $50 and can be converted at any time into five shares of $15 par value common stock. By October 25, the common stock has increased in market value to $20 per share, and holders of 500 preferred shares elect to convert them to common stock. The entries on February 11 and October 25 are:

| | | | |
|---|---|---|---|
| Feb. 11 | Cash (2,000 × $95) . . . . . . . . . . . | 190,000 | |
| | Preferred Stock—$50 Par | | |
| | (2,000 × $50) . . . . . . . . . | | 100,000 |
| | Additional Paid-in Capital—Preferred. . | | 90,000 |
| | To record issuance of preferred stock. | | |

| Oct. 25 | Preferred Stock—$50 Par (500 × $50) . . . | 25,000 | |
| | Additional Paid-in Capital—Preferred. . . . | 22,500 | |
| | Common Stock—$15 par | | |
| | (2,500 × $15) . . . . . . . . . . | | 37,500 |
| | Additional Paid-in Capital—Common. . | | 10,000 |

To record conversion of 500 shares of
preferred stock into 2,500 shares of
common stock.

Obviously, the preferred stockholders have elected to convert because the market value of the common stock has risen. However, as far as the corporate entity is concerned, no increase in equities or assets is recorded. One fourth of the preferred stock is canceled, and common stock equity takes its place. The total sources of capital remain constant.

# DIVIDENDS

Dividends are asset distributions to a firm's stockholders. A dividend results in decreases in both assets and stockholders' equity. The declaration and payment of dividends are governed by both legal and financial considerations. Legal requirements place limitations on which stockholders' equity accounts can be decreased so that dividends will not impair the legal capital of the firm. As a *general* rule, dividends represent earnings that are not retained in the business. Consequently, a credit balance in Retained Earnings is normally a requisite to dividend declaration.[6] However, the existence of retained earnings does not guarantee that the firm has cash available for dividend payments. The *financial* requirement for dividends is that there be some distributable asset, usually cash.

## Dividend Declaration and Payment

A firm planning to pay dividends would normally follow the procedure outlined below, providing that it has sufficient retained earnings and cash to fulfill the legal and financial requirements. The board of directors makes a formal announcement declaring the dividend; for example, "On July 2, 1991, the Board of Directors of Able Corporation declared a quarterly cash dividend of $0.50 per share on common stock payable on August 1, 1991, to stockholders of record on July 15, 1991."

---

[6] This is only a very rough guide. Many states allow dividends to be declared out of additional paid-in capital. Because this represents part of the invested capital, sound accounting requires that any decrease in this account caused by dividends be disclosed as a liquidating dividend, a return of contributed capital.

Since dividends are discretionary, no liability exists until the *date of declaration*. If 40,000 shares of common are outstanding on July 2, the entry is:

Dividends Declared—Common Stock . . . . . . . . . 20,000
    Common Dividends Payable. . . . . . . . . . . 20,000

Dividends Declared—Common Stock is a temporary owners' equity account reflecting the distribution of income; it is closed to Retained Earnings at the end of the year. Sometimes the procedure is streamlined, the initial debit being made directly to Retained Earnings.

July 15, in this case, is called the *date of record*. All stockholders owning stock on that date are entitled to receive the dividend. No additional accounting entries are necessary, however, until the *date of payment*. On August 1, the dividend checks are mailed, and the following entry is made:

Common Dividends Payable. . . . . . . . . . . . 20,000
    Cash . . . . . . . . . . . . . . . . . . . . . 20,000

Dividends paid in *noncash* assets (usually securities of other corporations or inventory) should be recorded at the fair market value of the assets transferred, and a gain or loss equal to the difference between fair market value and carrying value should be recognized on the disposition.[7]

**Preferred Stock Dividends.** The same general procedure is followed with preferred stock. The dividend rate is stated in the preferred stock contract as a fixed dollar amount per share for no-par stock or as a fixed percentage of par for par value stock. As with common dividends, there is no obligation to pay preferred dividends until they are declared. The dividend preference simply states that the preferred dividends have to be paid before common dividends, but not at any specific time.

This fact raises a major question concerning *preferred dividends in arrears*. If the preferred stock is cumulative and dividends in the past have been skipped, they must be paid before common dividends can be declared and paid. However, until they are declared, even preferred dividends in arrears represent only a first claim on any future dividend declaration and not a liability. Therefore, they are not reflected on the formal financial statements, despite their importance to the common stockholders. Arrearages represent a shadow hanging over any future earnings. A note to the financial statements should disclose this contingency.

---

[7] AICPA, *APB Opinion No. 29*, "Accounting for Nonmonetary Transactions" (New York, May 1973), par. 18.

## Stock Dividends

Sometimes corporations declare dividends payable in their own shares of stock. Additional shares are issued pro rata to the stockholders, but no assets are distributed or received by the corporation. The term *dividend* for this situation is a misnomer. Stock dividends really are not dividends at all but a type of small stock split. No change in total assets or total equities results. The dividend shares transfer no asset values to stockholders. They end up with more shares, but each share represents a proportionately smaller interest in the existing net assets. For example, an individual owning 2,000 shares of a corporation with total outstanding stock of 40,000 shares has a 5 percent ownership interest. If the company declares a 10 percent stock dividend, 200 shares will be given to the stockholder. However, the total number of shares outstanding is now 44,000, and the stockholder's interest remains at 5 percent (2,200/44,000). The investor has received no real income by having the extra shares. Indeed, an individual selling the dividend shares simply liquidates a portion of the investment.[8]

**Capitalization of Retained Earnings.**   One factor differentiates a stock dividend from a stock split in the accounting process. A stock dividend is accompanied by a transfer from retained earnings to the contributed capital accounts. This procedure is called "capitalizing retained earnings." The common stockholders' total financial interest remains the same; all that results is a transfer from one stockholders' equity account to another. The capitalization permanently removes a portion of retained earnings from dividend availability.

What amount of retained earnings should be capitalized per share? Possible alternatives include the par or stated value of the shares, the average contributed capital per share, the average book value (shareholders' equity) per share, or the current market value of a share. State statutes require as a minimum the capitalization of the par or stated value of the additional shares issued to maintain legal capital and may specify more. Beyond that, there is no clear and logical answer to this question in accounting theory.

The FASB requires the use of *market value* to determine the amount to be capitalized for stock dividends when the new shares being issued amount to less than 20 to 25 percent of the outstanding shares. For larger stock dividends, only the legal requirement needs to be capitalized. The reasoning is that large stock dividends clearly will be interpreted for what they are—stock splits. However, in the case of small stock dividends, stockholders view the dividend shares as income equivalent to their fair market value.

---

[8] As in the case of stock splits, changes in market prices caused by other factors—for example, disguised dividend increases or simply irrational reactions on the part of the investing public—may mask the small decline in market price that logically should accompany a small stock dividend.

Therefore, this should be the amount transferred out of retained earnings.[9] Another argument for the use of market value is that the end result agrees with what the situation would have been had the corporation paid cash dividends and the stockholders turned around and reinvested the cash in the newly issued shares.

If the 4,000 shares issued on the preceding page as a 10 percent stock dividend have a par value of $5 and a market value of $17, GAAP would sanction the following entry when the dividend shares are issued:

| | | |
|---|---:|---:|
| Retained Earnings (4,000 × $17) | 68,000 | |
|     Common Stock—$5 Par | | 20,000 |
|     Additional Paid-in Capital—Common | | 48,000 |

To record issuance of 4,000 shares as a 10 percent stock dividend to holders of the 40,000 shares outstanding.

If the 4,000 shares constituted a 50 percent stock dividend, then Retained Earnings and Common Stock—$5 Par would be debited and credited, respectively, for only $20,000, the par amount.

## REACQUISITION OF SHARES

A corporation may enter the stock market and reacquire shares of its own stock. The repurchased stock is called *treasury stock*. Formally defined, *treasury shares are shares of a company's own stock that have been previously issued, reacquired, and are not legally retired.* Many reasons are offered for why companies buy back their own stock. Some firms may need shares for use in employee stock option plans, for use in acquiring other companies, or for use when converting bonds and preferred stock. Other firms may have excess cash and view the repurchase of its own shares as a wise use of cash now to obtain a future reduction in dividend payments. In recent years, many companies acquired treasury shares to combat merger attempts. Reducing the number of shares outstanding normally increases the price of the remaining shares and increases the percentage of ownership represented by the outstanding shares.

---

[9] It is somewhat ironic that in the AICPA bulletin this particular justification follows a strong and sound argument that a stock dividend is not income. The result is an inconsistency—an admonition that stock dividends do not constitute income to the recipient, followed by a recommendation that they be treated in the accounting records in a particular way because stockholders may think they are income. See AICPA, *Accounting Research Bulletin No. 43,* "Restatement and Revision of Accounting Research Bulletins" (New York, 1953), chap. vii(b), for a complete discussion of the reasoning of the Committee on Accounting Procedure relating to both stock dividends and stock splits. Some authors have suggested that the requirement for capitalization of market value rather than par value was instituted more as a penalty provision than as an accounting principle, since it was designed to discourage companies with low earnings from declaring numerous stock dividends, which might mislead investors.

Treasury stock, economically and financially, is similar to unissued stock. It possesses no basic rights to vote, to receive dividends, or to receive payments upon liquidation. Legally, however, treasury stock is interpreted differently from unissued stock; nevertheless, these slight legal differences should not overshadow the fundamental effect on assets and equities.

When a corporation buys back shares of its own stock, essentially the reverse of a stock-issuing transaction occurs. When shares are issued, assets and stockholders' equity increase. Conversely, when shares are reacquired, assets and stockholders' equity decrease. The acquisition of treasury shares represents a contraction of capital—perhaps a partial and temporary one but a disinvestment of capital nevertheless. Reacquired shares may either be canceled (e.g., retired) or be held for subsequent reissue.

Two acceptable methods are employed to record treasury stock transactions. We will examine the *par value method* first and then the more widely used *cost method*. To illustrate these methods, assume that the Fox Corporation had the following stockholders' equity section on its balance sheet:

| | |
|---|---:|
| Common stock—$5 par, 20,000 shares authorized, issued, and outstanding . . . . . . . | $100,000 |
| Additional paid-in capital—common. . . . . . . . | 300,000 |
| Retained earnings . . . . . . . . . . . . . . . | 75,000 |
| | $475,000 |

### Treasury Stock—Par Value Method

Assume that the corporation buys 2,000 of its shares in the market. The book value per share is $23.75 ($475,000/20,000 shares). If Fox buys back the shares at book value, they would pay $47,500 ($23.75 × 2,000 shares). Cash would decrease by $47,500 and the total shareholders' equity would drop by a like amount. One way to record this effect is to reduce each stockholders' equity account proportionately:

| | | |
|---|---:|---:|
| Treasury Stock—$5 Par . . . . . . . . . . . . . | 10,000 | |
| Additional Paid-in Capital—Common . . . . . . . . | 30,000 | |
| Retained Earnings . . . . . . . . . . . . . . . | 7,500 | |
|     Cash . . . . . . . . . . . . . . . . . . . | | 47,500 |

To show that the shares are not permanently retired, the debit of $10,000 is made to a contra account, Treasury Stock—$5 Par, rather than directly to Common Stock. The Treasury Stock account appears as a deduction from Common Stock on the balance sheet. If the company pays more than book value for the shares, the adjustment normally takes place in Retained Earnings.

As treasury stock, the shares can be reissued at some later time. As a potential source of capital, they differ little from unissued stock. Assume the 2,000 shares are reissued later for $27 per share. The entry would be the same as with unissued stock.

| | | |
|---|---|---|
| Cash ($27 × 2,000 shares) . . . . . . . . . . . . . | 54,000 | |
| Treasury Stock—$5 Par . . . . . . . . . . . . | | 10,000 |
| Additional Paid-In Capital—Common . . . . . . . | | 44,000 |

This approach to the recording of treasury stock takes the position that treasury stock transactions should be no different in effect from a retirement and later issuance of new shares.

## Treasury Stock—Cost Method

The par value method, although theoretically sound, is not as widely used in current practice as the simpler *cost method,* particularly for shares that remain in the treasury only a short time before they are reissued. Instead of separate debits to each stockholders' equity account, a single debit is made to a *general contra equity account* called "Treasury Stock."

Under the cost method, the entry to reflect reacquisition of the 2,000 shares of stock at $23.75 (book value) would be:

| | | |
|---|---|---|
| Treasury Stock (2,000 shares × $23.75) . . . . . . . . | 47,500 | |
| Cash . . . . . . . . . . . . . . . . . . . . . | | 47,500 |

This method views the acquisition and subsequent reissuance of the treasury shares as a continuous transaction. The corporation serves as an intermediary between the retiring stockholder and the new stockholder. The entry records a temporary contraction in total capital that will shortly be reinstated. Consequently, no need exists to reduce each of the stockholders' equity accounts directly. Treasury stock is debited in lieu of each account individually as an indirect way of decreasing stockholders' equity through the use of a contra account.

The cost method easily accommodates repurchases at a price more or less than book value. Whatever amount is paid out in cash reduces stockholders' equity by that amount. Accordingly, Treasury Stock is debited for its "cost," whether that be book value or some other amount.

Unfortunately, the Treasury Stock account, on rare occasions, finds its way to the asset side of the balance sheet on the grounds that the shares can be resold. Such an interpretation is erroneous. Treasury shares are no more an asset than are all the unissued shares. At best, they represent possible sources of additional capital funds. Until they are issued, however, the corporation has received no asset. A firm cannot create an asset by *returning* cash to its stockholders. Treasury stock under the cost method should be shown as a deduction from total contributed capital and retained earnings on the position statement, as an unapportioned contraction of total capital.

**Reissuance of Treasury Stock under Cost Method.**    If treasury stock is not an asset, there can be no gain or loss on its reissuance. Income or loss arises from the *utilization* of assets, not from the issuance of stock. Issuing shares of stock, whether from unissued or from treasury stock, is a capital-raising transaction. If the treasury shares had been repurchased at book value ($23.75 per share) and are reissued for $24.50 per share, the entry is:

| | | |
|---|---:|---:|
| Cash ($24.50 × 2,000 shares). . . . . . . . . . . . | 49,000 | |
| Treasury Stock ($23.75 × 2,000 shares). . . . . . | | 47,500 |
| Additional Paid-in Capital—Common | | |
| ([$24.50 − $23.75] × 2,000 shares) . . . . . . | | 1,500 |

Cash increases by $49,000; contributed capital increases $49,000—part of it recorded as a cancellation of a contra equity and part of it as an increase in the Additional Paid-in Capital account. If the treasury stock is reissued at a price below its acquisition price, the difference can be debited to the Additional Paid-in Capital account, if there is one, or to Retained Earnings. The latter entry is justified on the grounds that the net result of the continuous transaction (reacquisition and reissuance) has been such that a part of the entity assets have been distributed as a special kind of dividend.

The acquisition of treasury stock reduces not only contributed capital but also stated or legal capital. Consequently, state laws governing corporations usually place fairly stringent, detailed limitations on when, how, and in what amount a company can repurchase its own shares. Often retained earnings must be restricted (made unavailable for dividends) in an amount equal to the cost of the treasury stock purchased.

## Retirement of Preferred Stock

Normally, when preferred stock is reacquired by a firm, the shares are retired rather than held in the treasury for possible reissue. Like bonds, preferred stock issues usually are subject to call, or they can be repurchased on the stock market. For example, assume that we have $90,000 of par value preferred stock outstanding, and it was originally issued at $5,000 over par. By contract, the preferred stock issue can be called in for retirement at a price equal to 108 percent of par value. The following entry would be necessary to record the retirement:

| | | |
|---|---:|---:|
| Preferred Stock—Par   . . . . . . . . . . . . . . . | 90,000 | |
| Additional Paid-in Capital—Preferred . . . . . . . . . | 5,000 | |
| Retained earnings . . . . . . . . . . . . . . . . | 2,200 | |
| Cash (108% × $90,000) . . . . . . . . . . . . | | 97,200 |

The excess of the $97,200 redemption price over the $95,000 contributed capital is debited to Retained Earnings to reflect the decrease in the total common stock equity—a special type of dividend to the preferred stockholders. In practice, the extra $2,200 debit is made to some Additional

Paid-in Capital account (either preferred, if it has a balance, or common), thereby eliminating the need for a debit to Retained Earnings. Likewise, if preferred stock were retired for less than book value, the difference would be credited to Additional Paid-in Capital — Common.

# FOREIGN CURRENCY ACCOUNTING ISSUES

Firms dealing with foreign companies or controlling divisions operating in foreign countries enter into transactions expressed in currencies other than the dollar—for example, francs, marks, or pounds. When financial statements are prepared, the results of foreign operations must be stated in terms of U.S. currency to enable statement users to properly analyze the firm's performance. Specific accounting procedures that affect the stockholders' equity accounts are used to record the conversion of foreign currency transactions and balances.

Currency conversion is completed by applying the ratio between foreign currencies and the U.S. dollar to transactions and account balances. The conversion ratios (called exchange rates) are ever changing. Shifts in the exchange rates lead to problems in choosing the rates to use and in recognizing any gains or losses. Actually there are two types of foreign currency problems—*transaction gains and losses* and *translation adjustments*. The former arise from explicit transactions involving the sale or purchase of merchandise and the borrowing or lending of funds during a period when exchange rates change. The latter arise in the process of restating ending account balances that are recorded in a foreign currency. Often the two types of problems are discussed together, although the treatment of transaction gains and losses has been much less controversial than the treatment of translation adjustments.

## Transaction Gains and Losses

Let us assume, for example, that a U.S. firm buys equipment from a French seller, promising to pay 6,000 francs at a time when one franc equals $0.167. The equipment account would be debited and accounts payable credited for $1,000—the dollar equivalent of the 6,000 francs (6,000 francs × $0.167). If, however, the exchange value of one franc is $0.184 when payment is due, the U.S. firm will have to spend $1,104 to acquire the 6,000 francs necessary (6,000 francs × $0.184) to settle the debt. Its journal entry will be:

| | | |
|---|---|---|
| Accounts Payable | 1,000 | |
| Foreign Currency Transaction Loss | 104 | |
| Cash | | 1,104 |

These currency adjustments result from explicit transactions denominated in a foreign currency. The domestic firm must settle, at a later date, a monetary claim expressed in a different unit of measure. In the interim, the value of that foreign currency shifts in relation to the dollar.

The FASB's current pronouncement, *Statement No. 52,* mandates that the gain or loss realized on the settlement of a foreign currency transaction be apportioned to all of the years that have passed since the transaction was initiated.[10] In the preceding example, therefore, the $104 foreign currency transaction loss might actually be apportioned to several income statements, if the equipment were paid for in a later accounting period than the period in which it was acquired.

## Translation Adjustments

These adjustments arise only when a firm has foreign branches or divisions. At the end of an accounting period, account balances on a foreign division's books are the net balances from transactions that occurred at times when differing exchange rates prevailed. What rate(s) should be used to restate these accounts to dollars at the date of the financial statements? In the past, the choice of exchange rates boiled down to selecting either the current exchange rate (the rate in existence at the date of the current statements) or an historic rate (the rate in existence at the time particular statement items were transacted). If current rates are used each period and the rate changes from a prior period, translation adjustments arise.

Historical exchange rates have the advantage of keeping assets recorded at an amount equivalent to what the *dollar* cost would have been at the date of acquisition. Therefore, contributed capital would be reflected at the equivalent dollar amount originally invested. Alternatively, current rates reflect current economic conditions. Translation of foreign accounts into dollars at current rates of exchange indicate the dollars that would be realized if the foreign *book* values could be liquidated and converted into dollars as of the statement date.

FASB *Statement No. 52* settles this question by requiring most firms to translate *all* assets and liabilities denominated in non-U.S. currencies by using *year-end* exchange rates.[11] However, *translation* gains and losses are not included in the income statement because they have not been realized through completed transactions. They are "disclosed and accumulated in a separate component of stockholders' equity until sale or until complete or substantially complete liquidation of the net investment in the foreign entity takes place."[12] Disclosure of the translation gains and losses is presented as

---

[10] FASB, *Statement of Financial Accounting Standards No. 52,* "Foreign Currency Translation" (Stamford, Conn., December 1981), par. 15. See par. 20 for two types of transaction gains and losses that need not be included in net income.

[11] FASB *Statement No. 52,* par. 12.

[12] Ibid., pars. 13 and 14.

either an adjunct (gains) or contra (losses) to stockholders' equity. The FASB has reasoned that the exclusion of translation gains and losses from income is appropriate because those gains and losses do not reflect cash flows. One major reporting objective, as discussed in Chapter 1, is to enable users to assess the cash flows of an enterprise.

# DISCUSSION OF THE KIMBERLY-CLARK ANNUAL REPORT

Kimberly-Clark's stockholders' equity information (in the Appendix to Chapter 6) illustrates many of the accounting elements discussed in this chapter. The basic data is found in the balance sheet's equity section, and supporting detail appears in Notes 5, 6, and 8.

## Stock Transactions and Adjustments

Examination of the balance sheet shows that the company has common stock ($1.25 par value), additional paid-in capital, treasury stock, foreign currency adjustments, and retained earnings. But if we limit our examination to the balance sheet, we miss several important additional items of information concerning stockholders' equity. The notes provide additional information.

A review of Note 8 indicates that during 1987, Kimberly-Clark's stockholders agreed to amend the corporate certificate to allow an increase in the authorized shares of common stock from 100 million to 300 million shares. Further, 10 million additional preferred shares were authorized. However, none of the preferred stock has been issued. That explains the absence of preferred stock from the balance sheet where issued shares are of greatest importance. Note 8 also explains that Kimberly-Clark had a two-for-one common stock split in 1987. Accordingly, the par value was reduced from $2.50 to $1.25 per share. Neither the stock split nor the par value reduction changed the total amount of contributed capital. Therefore, they are reported in Note 8 and not on the balance sheet.

Total stockholders' equity has decreased rather dramatically from $1,919.9 million in 1986 to $1,571.9 million in 1987. The income statement shows $325.2 million of net income. Clearly, the decrease is not due to operating losses, so the statements will have to be analyzed to explain the source of this decrease.

The common stock listing on the balance sheet describes the number of shares issued as 95.5 million in 1986 but only 81.0 million in 1987. This suggests that the equity decrease may be associated with the retirement of shares. Note 8 shows that in 1987 the firm paid $632.2 million for about 12 million treasury shares and retired $650.4 million worth of treasury stock (14.5 million shares). We can reconstruct the entries that apply to both the purchase and retirement of the shares. The purchase of treasury stock was recorded under the cost method as follows:

| | | |
|---|---|---|
| Treasury Stock | 632.2 | |
| Cash | | 632.2 |

This entry is also reflected in the statement of changes in financial position (cash flows). The section headed "Financing Summary" shows that cash was disbursed for the "Acquisition of common stock for the treasury" in the amount of $632.2 million. The repurchase of the treasury stock caused both stockholders' equity and cash to decrease.

Note 8 indicates that the retirement of the treasury shares was recorded as:

| | | |
|---|---|---|
| Common Stock | 18.1 | |
| Additional Paid-In Capital | 25.9 | |
| Retained Earnings | 606.4 | |
| Treasury Stock | | 650.4 |

Kimberly-Clark must have paid $606.4 million more for the reacquisition of these shares than was originally received when they were first sold. The inflow of assets at the time of original sale was $44.0 million ($18.1 + $25.9), but the treasury stock was repurchased for $650.4 million. This difference resulted in the $606.4 million charge to retained earnings. Note, however, that the retirement entry causes no net change in stockholders' equity because there has been no outflow of assets. The outflows of assets occurred when the treasury shares were repurchased.

Like other major corporations, Kimberly-Clark has a stock option plan as well as other "Equity Participation Plans." A general summary of these plans is found in Note 6, which also directs the reader to the company's proxy statement for detailed information.

This note describes Kimberly-Clark's use of the unusual techniques of participation shares and dividend shares. Though the term *shares* has been used, these are not real stock shares but rather a fairly complex way of providing cash bonuses that are tied to the growth in the book value per share of the company's stock. No entry is made when these shares are awarded, but an expense is debited and cash is credited when the cash value of the shares becomes payable.

The stock option plan is described in the second part of Note 6. This note indicates that stock options were exercised for 277,440 shares. This same number of shares is also found in the Stockholders' Equity schedule in Note 8. The exercise of stock options used treasury stock and was recorded as:

| | | |
|---|---|---|
| Cash | 6.2 | |
| Treasury Stock | | 4.3 |
| Additional Paid-In Capital | | 1.9 |

The average exercise price in 1987 was $22.35 per share ($6.2 million/ 277,440 shares). Note 6 states that the "Stock options are granted at not less than market value." Therefore, no compensation expense is ever recorded.

Yet, the employees undoubtedly must have felt that they received substantial benefit from buying stock at $22.35 per share in 1987 rather than at the market prices existing during the year. Market prices ranged between $40 and $63 per share. This illustrates the earlier comment that current recording practices for options probably understate compensation expense.

## Foreign Currency Disclosures

Kimberly-Clark operates in a number of foreign countries. Consequently, it is subject to currency transaction gains and losses as well as translation gains and losses. Note 5, "Foreign Currency Translation," indicates the effect of currency *translations* for Canadian, British, French, German, and other currencies. When current exchange rates were used to translate foreign balance sheet accounts into dollars on December 31, 1986, the loss in value was $163.8 million compared to the historic exchange rates existing at the time the foreign assets and liabilities arose. In 1987, the U.S. dollar strengthened in world trade compared to these other currencies. Therefore, when December 31, 1987 exchange rates were used, the loss in value was only $85.9 million. Net asset values and, hence, stockholders' equity increased $77.9 million because of the change in exchange rates. This improvement, just as the losses in prior years, did not appear on the income statement. The changes in stockholders' equity were made directly by adjusting the special contra equity account called "Unrealized Currency Translation Adjustments." Note 5 details these changes by country.

Note 5 also calls attention to the fact that during 1987 Kimberly-Clark experienced a loss of $13.4 million in currency *transactions* (including some special translation adjustments that are recorded in income). This loss did appear in the 1987 income statement, probably under "Other Expense."

Kimberly-Clark's stockholders' equity section on the balance sheet is clear and explains the company's activity during the year. It appears that Kimberly-Clark has been successful (net income), has paid dividends regularly, and is acquiring and retiring its common stock. This final action is undoubtedly related, to some extent, to an interesting situation confronting the corporation. In today's business environment, successful firms are frequently the target of takeover activities. As discussed earlier in the chapter, firms may issue special stock rights for the purchase of additional shares to counter takeover efforts. Kimberly-Clark has addressed this threatened takeover activity as explained below:

Kimberly-Clark Corp., which has been the subject of takeover rumors, said its directors adopted a share purchase rights plan that is intended to protect against hostile takeovers. The company said the rights will be issued July 1 to shareholders of record that day. . . . If the company is merged or acquired by a bidder owning 20% of the company's stock, or if a group acquires 80% of the stock, the rights entitle shareholders to buy stock in the remaining company at half price. In addition, Kimberly-Clark said that if a person or group acquires between 20% and 50% of its stock, its board may exchange the right for shares of the company's stock on a one-for-one basis, excluding the hostile bidder's shares.[13]

This article illustrates an additional insight into the use of the stockholders' equity elements by management and the need for complete disclosure in the financial statements.

## SUMMARY

We have discussed a number of problems associated with stockholders' equity. Each has some direct impact on the concepts, accounts, or terminology of the financial statements. Still, only the surface has been scratched. Space does not permit a discussion of all the possible ways certain entries may be recorded in practice. Moreover, variations in terminology are numerous. The terms *par, no-par,* and *stated value; additional paid-in capital;* and *retained earnings* are the key terms of stockholders' equity, but they represent only some of the commonly used titles.

Most of the problems in stockholders' equity involve questions of *classification* rather than of valuation or of measurement. Usually the total change in owners' equity is determined by measurable changes in other assets and liabilities. The primary accounting problem becomes how to divide up this total change among the various accounts in stockholders' equity. The fundamental division is between invested capital and retained earnings. We have seen that this distinction blurs in the case of stock dividends. Other desirable objectives in classifying stockholders' equity are to distinguish the interests of different classes of investor, such as preferred stockholders and common stockholders, and to separate legal capital from any excess amounts. Legal capital consists of the par value, the stated value for no-par stock, or the total contributed capital when the shares are no-par with no stated value.

Usually, making these classifications is not complex. In some special circumstances—conversions, retirements, and treasury stock transactions—the objectives conflict, and the recording problems become more difficult. Perhaps what is needed is a threefold classification of stockholders' equity—contributed capital (reflecting the type of stockholder and any legal distinctions), retained earnings, and other sources and adjustments.

Certainly, little doubt exists that major changes in all stockholders' equity accounts should be disclosed and explained. In fact, in *Opinion No. 12* the Accounting Principles Board requires that changes in the individual

---

[13] "Kimberly-Clark Corp. Adopts a Rights Plan As Takeover Defense," *The Wall Street Journal,* June 23, 1988.

accounts making up stockholders' equity and in the number of shares of stock are to be disclosed either in notes to the statements or in separate schedules (as in Kimberly-Clark's annual report). Before changes can be classified, however, the intricacies of some common events affecting owners' equity must be understood. From this chapter, the reader should acquire a basic ability to analyze stockholders' equity transactions. Such analysis often involves looking behind the facade of legal and financial convention.

# PROBLEMS AND CASETTES

### 14–1. Supplying Missing Figures in Stockholders' Equity

Complete the following table of independent stockholders' equity sections by using the numbers in each section and the additional descriptive data shown below the table (all amounts in thousands):

| | *Stockholders' Equity Sections* | | | | |
| | *1* | *2* | *3* | *4* | *5* |
|---|---|---|---|---|---|
| Preferred stock—par . . . . . . | $___ | $___ | $___ | $___ | $___ |
| Common stock—par . . . . . . | | | | 125 | |
| Additional paid-in capital: | | | | | |
|   Preferred . . . . . . . . . | 10 | | | | |
|   Common . . . . . . . . . | | 100 | | | |
| Retained earnings . . . . . . . | 5 | | | | |
| Total stockholders' equity . . . . | 500 | | 300 | | |

Use the following additional information with the matching section number listed above:

1. a. The total preferred stock is 10 percent of the total stockholders' equity.
   b. There are 100,000 shares of common stock with a $2 par value.
2. a. There are 10,000 shares of preferred stock with a $5 par value.
   b. The total invested in common stock is five times the preferred stock par value.
   c. Retained earnings is one half the size of common stock paid-in capital.
   d. Preferred stock paid-in capital is 25 percent of common stock paid-in capital.
3. a. Retained earnings is 15 percent of total stockholders' equity.
   b. Preferred stock paid-in capital is two times retained earnings.
   c. The total received when the preferred stock was sold was $143,000.
   d. Common stock par value is 25 percent of the total invested in common stock.
4. a. Common stock paid-in capital is two times the common stock par value.
   b. Total stockholders' equity is two times the amount invested in common stock.
   c. Retained earnings is 10 percent of total stockholders' equity.
   d. Preferred stock par value is equal to 10 percent of common stock paid-in capital.
5. a. Preferred stock is 1,000 shares of par value $50.
   b. Common stock is 100,000 shares of par value $5.
   c. Paid-in capital for each type of stock is two times their par value.
   d. Total stockholders' equity is $1,500,000.

### 14–2. Comparison of Cash and Stock Dividends

The president of HiRise Corporation made the following announcement in a letter to the stockholders:

> In years past, the company has paid a cash dividend of 10 percent of par value and purchased new assets with any remaining cash out of net income. These reinvestment policies are now beginning to reap additional benefits in the form of increased profits. As a consequence, your board of directors has decided to increase the dividend payout. Beginning this year, a 10 percent stock dividend will be added to the 10 percent cash dividend. In this way, the firm can continue to expand as in the past. Yet, you as stockholders will have additional assets in the form of the shares distributed, and they are not taxed by the IRS! You can convert the stock into cash, if necessary. By selling your dividend shares, you can increase the payout from the corporation to 20 percent.

### Required:

*a.* Assume HiRise has 500,000 shares of $15 par value common stock outstanding at the beginning of the year. The market price of the stock is $80 per share. Prepare journal entries to record the declaration and "payment" of the cash dividend and the stock dividend.

*b.* Evaluate the president's letter. List and comment on *all* the misunderstandings and inaccuracies contained in the letter.

*c.* One of your close friends has recently purchased 2,500 shares of HiRise stock at $75 per share. He said that with the cash dividend of $3,750 (2,500 shares at $1.50) plus the stock dividend worth $20,000 (250 shares at $80), he will already have earned over 12.67 percent on his investment ($23,750/$187,500). Comment on your friend's reasoning and calculations.

### 14–3. Recording Stockholders' Equity Transactions

The following *selected* transactions occurred during the first year of the Master Corporation's operations.

1. On February 10, issued 30,000 shares of $2.50 par value common stock for $9.00 per share.
2. On February 12, issued 4,000 shares of common stock to the Headley Company in exchange for a warehouse. Headley had purchased the warehouse eight years earlier and showed it among its fixed assets at $27,000.
3. On March 15, issued 400 shares of common stock in exchange for some used equipment. The seller had depreciated the assets down to salvage value, $4,000. However, the board of directors of Master estimated the equipment's current fair market value to be $4,700. The firm's common stock was currently being traded at $12 per share.
4. Declared a cash dividend of $1.25 per share on April 30.
5. Paid the cash dividend on May 15.
6. Declared and issued a 5 percent stock dividend on June 30. The current market price of Master's stock was $14 per share.
7. On July 10, purchased 700 shares of stock from one of Master's original shareholders at a price of $15 per share. The stock is to be held in the treasury either for resale or for issuance under the firm's new employee stock option plan.
8. Sold 200 of the treasury shares for $16 per share, on August 1.

9. Sold 200 of the treasury shares for $14 per share, on September 15.
10. Declared and paid a $1.30 cash dividend on October 31.

### Required:

a. Prepare journal entries to record the above transactions.
b. Prepare the stockholders' equity section of the balance sheet at the end of the current year. Assume that the net income for the year was $259,250.

## 14–4. Treasury Stock Transactions

The stockholders' equity of Bard Corporation appeared as follows:

**BARD CORPORATION**
**Stockholders' Equity**
**As of December 31, 1990**

| | |
|---|---:|
| Common stock—$3.50 par (500,000 shares authorized, 375,000 issued) | $1,312,500 |
| Additional paid-in capital | 4,593,750 |
| Retained earnings | 2,355,968 |
| Treasury stock (54,200 shares) | (934,950) |
| Total stockholders' equity | $7,327,268 |

### Required:

a. Determine the number of shares that are *outstanding*.
b. What was the average price received by Bard for the common stock issued?
c. What average price did Bard pay for the purchase of the treasury stock?
d. Prepare the journal entry that was made when the treasury stock was purchased.
e. Prepare the journal entry that Bard would prepare if the treasury shares were retired.
f. Assume that Bard does not retire the treasury shares but issues 65,000 shares at $18.50 per share. Of these shares 54,200 are the treasury shares and the remainder are previously unissued shares. Prepare the journal entry for this transaction.
g. Prepare a statement of the stockholders' equity section after the issuance of the shares in *f* above.

## 14–5. Package Issue of Securities and Subsequent Retirement of Preferred Stock

On July 1, 1992, Bangup Steel Corporation issued a package of securities. Each package consisted of two shares of 12 percent, $100 par value preferred stock and three shares of $5 par value common stock. The total price of the package was $340, and the firm received $170,000 from the issuance of 500 such packages.

The preferred stock was not sufficiently traded after issuance to establish any independent market price. Prior to this issuance, 200,000 shares of common stock were outstanding, and the common stock was widely traded. The closing price on June 30 of the common stock was $42 per share.

On December 31, 1993, as part of an overall recapitalization, Bangup Steel called in the preferred stock for retirement. The redemption price was $110.

**Required:**

a. Make entries to record the issuance of the package of securities on July 1, 1992. Comment on the procedure you used to allocate the total amount received among the two types of securities.

b. Prepare the journal entry on December 31, 1993 to retire the preferred stock. What impact does this entry have on total stockholders' equity? On common stockholders' equity?

**14–6. Analyzing and Recording Foreign Exchange**

During the first six months of 1990, John Ross Trading Company engaged in the following transactions with firms in foreign countries.

1. Purchased goods on open account from a French supplier for 100,000 francs (1 franc = $0.12).

2. Sold merchandise to a Portuguese customer receiving in exchange a 10 percent, three-month note for 1,200,000 escudos (1 escudo = $0.008).

3. Sold merchandise to a Spanish customer for 100,000 pesetas on open account (1 peseta = $0.0065).

4. Received from the Portuguese customer 1,230,000 escudos in payment of the note in item 2 plus interest. John Ross Trading Company converted the escudos into dollars at the rate of 1 escudo = $0.0079.

5. Purchased 100,000 francs at a bank for delivery to the suppliers in item 1 to settle the open account. The exchange rate was 1 franc = $0.122.

6. The exchange rate on June 30, 1990, when financial statements are to be prepared, is 1 peseta = $0.0073.

**Required:**

a. Prepare journal entries on the books of John Ross Trading Company to record the above transactions and events.

b. If consideration is given to changes in exchange rates, what real rate of interest was earned on the note in item 2?

c. What difference would there be if the purchase agreement in item 1 were denominated as $12,000?

**14–7. Recording Options**

On January 1, 1992, the Slapshot Corporation entered into a contract with Stanley Cup to obtain Cup's services as its chief executive officer for the next two years. The contract specified that Cup will receive a salary of $100,000 in cash per year and granted him an option to acquire 2,000 shares of stock at the end of *each* year at a cash price of $18 per share. The market price of the stock was $27 per share at the time the agreement was reached.

On December 31, 1992, Stanley Cup exercises his option to acquire 2,000 shares. The market price of the stock was $32 at the date he acquired it. Because of a decline in the fortunes of the company and in the stock market, the price of the shares declined to $15 by the end of 1993. Consequently, Cup did not exercise his option for the 2,000 shares in 1993 and the option expired.

**Required:**

a. Prepare any journal entries necessary to record the granting, exercise, and lapsing of the stock option.

b. How would your entries be modified if the option price had been set at the market price of $27 per share? Why might it be claimed that the conventional treatment in this case understates compensation expense?

c. A member of the board of directors of Slapshot Corporation was heard to say, "Stock options are a wonderful device. They can be used to compensate a highly valued employee, yet they cost the company nothing." Comment.

## 14–8. Recording a Stock Dividend

Designcraft Industries, Incorporated included the following Statement of Changes in Stockholders' Equity in its annual report (dollar amounts shown in thousands):

| | Common Stock ($.02 Par Value) | | Capital in Excess of Par Value | Retained Earnings (Deficit) | Treasury Stock | |
|---|---|---|---|---|---|---|
| | Shares | Amount | | | Shares | Amount |
| Balance—Feb. 29, 1984 . . . . | 1,212,968 | $24.26 | $4,939.6 | $1,316.5 | (54,548) | $(188.5) |
| Net income . . . . . . . . . | | | | 1,030.6 | | |
| 10% stock dividend . . . . . | 61,294 | 1.23 | 809.4 | (999.7) | 54,548 | 188.5 |
| Shares issued for services rendered . . . . . . . . . | 2,500 | .05 | 26.8 | | | |
| Balance—Feb. 28, 1985 . . . . | 1,276,762 | $25.54 | $5,775.8 | $1,347.4 | –0– | –0– |

**Required:**

a. Calculate the number of shares that were outstanding at the time the stock dividend was declared and paid. If Designcraft Industries followed generally accepted accounting principles, what must have been the market price of its shares at the time of the stock dividend?

b. Prepare the journal entry that was made to record the issuance of the stock dividend. What was the net change in stockholders' equity?

c. Prepare the journal entry that was made to issue the shares for the "services rendered." Assume the services were for legal work in defending one of the company's patents. What is your estimate of the market price of Designcraft shares at the time they were issued for services rendered?

## 14–9. Stock Rights and Retirement of Preferred Stock

In March 1990, the Murphy Trading Company issued 4,000 shares of preferred stock with a par value of $50 per share. Each share of preferred carried with it two detachable rights to acquire two shares of the firm's common stock at $25 at any time before July 15, 1990. The average market price of the common stock during March was $30 per share. The preferred stock (with the detachable rights) was sold at a price of $62. Both the preferred stock and the rights were traded on the stock market separately.

On July 11, 1990, when the firm's common stock was selling at $41 per share, 7,600 rights were exercised. The other 400 rights were never exercised, and they therefore lapsed. The common stock is no-par.

On December 31, 1992, Murphy Trading Company repurchased 2,000 shares of the preferred stock on the stock market at a price of $55 per share. The shares were then retired.

**Required:**

a. For what price would you expect the stock rights to be traded on the stock market immediately following the issuance of the 4,000 preferred shares?

b. Prepare the journal entry to record the issuance of the preferred with the stock rights. (Use a separate Capital Received—Stock Rights account.) Assume that immediately after issue of the preferred stock, it was quoted on the stock market at a price of $53, and the right to purchase one share of common was quoted at $5.50.

c. What journal entry would you make when the rights were exercised? When the rights lapsed? Did you make use of the $41 common stock market value in your entries? Why or why not?

d. Prepare the journal entry on December 31, 1992 to retire half of the preferred stock.

**14–10. Recording Equity Transactions**

On January 1, the stockholders' equity of Lombardi Company consisted of the following items:

| | |
|---|---:|
| 6% cumulative, convertible preferred stock $100 par value . . . . . . . . . | $   200,000 |
| Additional paid-in capital—preferred . . . . . . . . . . . . . . . . | 20,000 |
| Common stock—no par ($5 stated value) . . . . . . . . . . . . . | 2,200,000 |
| Additional paid-in capital—common . . . . . . . . . . . . . . . | 264,000 |
| Retained earnings . . . . . . . . . . . . . . . . . . . . . | 530,000 |
| Total . . . . . . . . . . . . . . . . . . . . . . . . . . | $3,214,000 |

During the year, the following transactions affecting stockholders' equity took place:

March 20 Declared the normal *quarterly* dividend on preferred stock and a $.25 per share dividend on common stock.

April  5 Paid the dividends declared on March 20.

       7 Half of the preferred stock was converted into common at the rate of five shares of common for each share of preferred.

May  7 Purchased 6,000 shares of its own common stock for $7.50 per share. The shares will be held in the treasury.

June 20 Declared *quarterly* dividends identical to those on March 20.

July  5 Paid the dividends declared on June 20.

August  4 Issued the 6,000 shares of treasury stock in exchange for patent rights held by another firm. The market value of the firm's stock was $7.00 per share.

**Required:**

*a.* Prepare journal entries to record the above transactions.

*b.* Prepare the stockholders' equity section of the balance sheet as of December 31. Assume that the firm had a net loss of $175,000 for the year.

*c.* Did the fact that the preferred stock is cumulative influence any of the items or amounts you included in your answer to part *b*? Why? (Recall that quarterly dividends were not declared on September 20 and December 20.)

**14–11. Foreign Exchange Translation**

Quest Corporation is a multinational corporation domiciled in the United States. On January 1, 1995, the company opened a branch in South America. Quest invested $50,000. At that time the exchange rate was one peso (P) for $0.10.

Each year Quest Company prepares financial statements for all branches together. The first step in this process is to convert the branch accounts from pesos to dollars so they can be combined with the other accounts.

The trial balance of the South American branch expressed in pesos is given below:

|  | January 1, 1995 | | December 31, 1995 | |
|---|---|---|---|---|
|  | Dr. | Cr. | Dr. | Cr. |
| Cash . . . . . . . . . . | P  50,000 |  | P  48,000 |  |
| Accounts receivable . . . . |  |  | 125,000 |  |
| Inventory . . . . . . . . |  50,000 |  | 112,000 |  |
| Plant and equipment . . . . | 400,000 |  | 400,000 |  |
| Accumulated depreciation. . |  |  |  | 20,000 |
| Accounts payable . . . . . |  |  |  | 66,000 |
| Sales . . . . . . . . . . |  |  |  | 370,000 |
| Cost of goods sold. . . . . |  |  | 200,000 |  |
| Operating expense . . . . . |  |  | 51,000 |  |
| Depreciation expense. . . . |  |  | 20,000 |  |
| Equity balance . . . . . . |  | P 500,000 |  | P 500,000 |
|  | P 500,000 | P 500,000 | P 956,000 | P 956,000 |

The exchange rate on December 31, 1995 was $0.06 per peso.

**Required:**

*a.* Translate the trial balance as of January 1, 1995 from pesos into dollars.

*b.* Translate the trial balance as of December 31, 1995 from pesos into dollars.

*c.* What is the amount of foreign currency translation gain or loss? How would Quest Corporation report it on its financial statements?

**14–12. Cash and Noncash Dividends**

Amoco Oil Corporation included the following excerpt from the Statement of Shareholders' Equity in its 1985 annual report and notes to the report (dollar amounts in millions):

| | Common Stock | Earnings Retained and Invested in the Business | Foreign Currency Translation Adjustment | Treasury Shares | Total |
|---|---|---|---|---|---|
| Balance on Dec. 31, 1984 . . . . . . . . | $2,238 | $12,273 | $(206) | $(1,781) | $12,524 |
| Net income . . . . . . . . . . . . . . | | 1,953 | | | 1,953 |
| Dividends paid: | | | | | |
| Cash dividends of $3.30 per share. . . . | | (872) | | | (872) |
| Distribution of | | | | | |
| Cyprus Minerals Company. . . . . . | | (1,212) | 4 | | (1,208) |
| Foreign currency translation adjustment . . | | | 1 | | 1 |
| Acquisitions of treasury shares . . . . . . | (4) | | | (806) | (810) |
| Balance on Dec. 31, 1985 . . . . . . . . | $2,234 | $12,142 | $(201) | $(2,587) | $11,588 |

## NOTES TO FINANCIAL STATEMENTS

### Asset Dispositions

Effective July 1, 1985, the corporation spun off to its shareholders its minerals subsidiary, Cyprus Minerals Company, in a tax-free distribution. The spun-off operations included all majority-owned metals, coal, and industrial minerals activities. The transaction resulted in a reduction of shareholders' equity of $1,208 million, the net assets of the spun-off operations.

### Required:

a. Does the distribution of a subsidiary to the shareholders present any special accounting problems? Explain.

b. Prepare the journal entry to record the distribution of the shares of Cypress Minerals.

c. Why would the distribution of the subsidiary involve an adjustment to the foreign currency equity item? Explain.

d. On average, how many shares of stock must have been outstanding on which cash dividends were paid? Prepare the journal entry to record the cash dividend payment.

## 14–13. Recording Stock Options

Toward the end of 1992, the Peffer Company adopted a stock option plan for its top managers. Under the plan, executives who qualify receive the right to acquire 1,000 shares of $10 par value common stock at a specified option price. The option is not transferable and, if not exercised, expires five years from the date of grant. The option cannot be exercised for two years from the date of grant and then only if the executives are still employees of the company.

On January 1, 1993, options were granted for 6,000 shares at a price of $18 per share. At that time, the stock was selling at $22 per share. Half of the options were exercised on January 1, 1995, and the other half on December 31, 1995.

### Required:

a. Compute the total amount of compensation cost you would attribute to the option. Over what period of time should this compensation be assigned as expense? Explain.

*b.* Prepare the journal entries, *if any*, necessary to reflect the option at the following times:
1. Adoption of the plan in 1992.
2. January 1, 1993.
3. End of 1993 and 1994.
4. January 1, 1995.
5. December 31, 1995.

*c.* Assume that the market price of Peffer Company stock dropped to $15 per share in 1993 and never rose above that level. Consequently, none of the options were ever exercised. Did the company incur a cost for executive compensation? Discuss how you would handle this possibility in the accounting records.

**14–14.** **Accounting for Stockholders' Equity Transactions**

The McCoy Corporation was organized on July 1, 1990. In its charter, it was authorized to issue 50,000 shares of 8 percent cumulative preferred stock with a stated value of $15 per share, and 500,000 shares of common stock with a par value of $5 per share. Each share of preferred stock was convertible into 3 shares of common stock and was also callable at the firm's discretion at $35 per share. The following are *selected* transactions of the corporation:

**1990 Transactions:**

July  2 Issued 25,000 shares of preferred stock at $30 per share.
      2 Issued 70,000 shares of common stock; 65,000 shares were issued for $650,000 and the remaining 5,000 were issued to a variety of professionals who provided legal and accounting assistance in organizing the firm.
Aug.  4 Issued 30,000 shares of common stock at $12 per share.
     15 Exchanged 2,000 shares of common stock for some used machinery. The seller had originally purchased the machinery for $19,000 and depreciated it down to $15,000 on its books. The local tax assessor has indicated that the machinery will be assessed at $21,000 for tax purposes.
Dec. 31 Declared preferred dividends for six months.

**1991 Transactions:**

Jan. 15 Paid the preferred dividends declared on December 31.
Mar.  2 Purchased 5,000 shares of its own common stock at $9.50. The stock is to be held in the treasury.
July  1 Declared a six-month dividend on preferred stock and a $2.00 dividend per share on common stock. Both dividends will be paid on July 15.
      1 Announced a call of the preferred stock for retirement at $35. The call would be effective on August 15. Sixty percent of the preferred stockholders converted their shares into common stock immediately. The price of the common stock was $13.00.
Aug. 15 On this date, 40 percent of the preferred stockholders surrendered their shares at the call price.
Aug. 19 Issued 10,000 shares of common stock at $15.00 per share. One half of these shares represented the shares acquired on March 2; the rest were previously unissued shares.

Oct.  4 A two-for-one stock split was declared on the common stock. The par value was formally reduced to $2.50 per share.

Dec. 31 Dividends of $1.15 per share were declared on the common stock.

### Required:

*a*. Prepare journal entries for the 1990 transactions.

*b*. Prepare a stockholders' equity section of the balance sheet at December 31, 1990. Assume that net income for the six months since the firm was organized was $215,000.

*c*. Prepare journal entries for the 1991 transactions.

*d*. Prepare a stockholders' equity section of the balance sheet at December 31, 1991. Assume that net income for the year was $430,000.

**Casette 14–1.** **Georgia-Pacific Corporation**

At the end of the book is a complete set of financial statements of Georgia-Pacific Corporation taken from its annual report of 1987. Use those financial statements and supporting information to answer the following questions related to the firm's stockholders' equity.

1. Refer to the Balance Sheets:

   *a*. Note that Georgia-Pacific has two types of stock outstanding in 1986. Why is preferred stock listed "without par value" while common stock is listed as having "par value $.80." What is par value?

   *b*. Use the values in the Common Shareholders' Equity section to determine the number of shares which were "outstanding" as opposed to "authorized" and "issued." Explain what each of these terms means.

   *c*. Which method is being used to account for treasury stock? Explain how your answer is supported after examining the handling of treasury stock in the Statements of Common Shareholders' Equity.

2. Refer to Note 6. Redeemable Preferred Stock: The corporation indicates that the three series of Adjustable Rate Convertible Preferred Stock were called for redemption in 1987. Conversion is on a one-for-one basis to Georgia-Pacific common stock. The note indicates that 1,624,000 Series A; 522,000 Series B; and 1,038,000 Series C shares, respectively, were converted.

   *a*. Prepare a calculation verifying that the total of these shares was converted into common stock. In completing the calculation, refer to the Statements of Common Shareholders' Equity.

   *b*. Reconstruct the journal entry that was made by Georgia-Pacific when the conversion to common stock was recorded. Assume that each type of convertible preferred stock was in a separate account.

3. Refer to Note 7. Common Stock: The corporation states that it has an Employee Stock Option Plan that provides for granting stock options to officers and employees. Common stock is purchased as treasury shares for making grants under the terms of the stock option plan. Further, cash awards—payable upon exercise of an option—are also granted.

   *a*. Prepare a calculation verifying the average purchase price of $41.25 per share the company claims was paid for the 6,182,000 common shares purchased for the treasury in 1987.

    *b*. Reconstruct a summary journal entry to show how Georgia-Pacific recorded compensation expense and the exercise of options during 1987. Refer to the Statements of Common Shareholders' Equity to complete this entry.

4. Dividends: The Georgia-Pacific report indicates that dividends were declared and paid in 1987 and 1986.

    *a*. What were the dollar amounts for dividends *declared* in 1987 and 1986? Where did you find this information in the annual report?

    *b*. What were the dollar amounts for dividends *paid* in 1987 and 1986? Where did you find this information in the annual report?

    *c*. Prepare a summary journal entry to reflect the declaration and payment of dividends in both 1987 and 1986. Use separate accounts for preferred and common dividends.

## Casette 14–2. Analyzing Stockholders' Equity

    The following statement was included in the annual report of Russ Togs, Inc., for the fiscal year ending January 31, 1986 (dollars in thousands):

### RUSS TOGS, INC.
### Statement of Stockholders' Equity

|  | Year Ended | | |
|---|---|---|---|
|  | Jan. 31, 1986 | Jan. 31, 1985 | Jan. 31, 1984 |
| Capital stock—$1 par value |  |  |  |
| Preferred: |  |  |  |
|   Balance at beginning of year . . . . . . . | $ 277 | $ 280 | $ 215 |
|   Adjustment to stated value . . . . . . . . |  |  | 65 |
|   Converted to common stock . . . . . . . . | (29) | (3) |  |
|   Balance at end of year . . . . . . . . . . | 248 | 277 | 280 |
| Common: |  |  |  |
|   Balance at beginning of year . . . . . . . | 5,124 | 5,121 | 4,114 |
|   Treasury shares canceled . . . . . . . . . |  |  | (699) |
|   Three-for-two stock split . . . . . . . . . |  |  | 1,706 |
|   Conversion of preferred stock . . . . . . . | 29 | 3 |  |
|   Balance at end of year . . . . . . . . . | 5,153 | 5,124 | 5,121 |
| Additional paid-in capital: |  |  |  |
|   Balance at beginning of year . . . . . . . | 1,242 | 1,242 | 10,088 |
|   Excess of cost over par value |  |  |  |
|     of treasury shares canceled . . . . . . . |  |  | (7,061) |
|   Par value of shares issued and |  |  |  |
|     cash paid in lieu of fractional |  |  |  |
|     shares on three-for-two stock split . . . . . |  |  | (1,720) |
|   Adjustment to stated value of |  |  |  |
|     preferred shares . . . . . . . . . . . . . . |  |  | (65) |
|   Balance at end of year . . . . . . . . . . | 1,242 | 1,242 | 1,242 |
| Retained earnings: |  |  |  |
|   Balance at beginning of year . . . . . . . . | 83,110 | 76,297 | 68,363 |
|   Net earnings . . . . . . . . . . . . . . | 10,986 | 11,113 | 12,114 |
|     Total . . . . . . . . . . . . . . . . | 94,096 | 87,410 | 80,477 |

|  | Year Ended | | |
|---|---|---|---|
|  | *Jan. 31, 1986* | *Jan. 31, 1985* | *Jan. 31, 1984* |
| Less cash dividends: | | | |
| Common ($.76 in 1986 and 1985 and $.7367 a share in 1984) . . . . . . . . | $ 3,903 | $ 3,893 | $ 3,772 |
| Preferred ($1.90 a share) . . . . . . . . . . | 387 | 407 | 408 |
| Total . . . . . . . . . . . . . | 4,290 | 4,300 | 4,180 |
| Balance at end of year . . . . . . . . . . . | 89,806 | 83,110 | 76,297 |
| Treasury stock: | | | |
| Balance at beginning of year . . . . . . . | — | — | (7,760) |
| Purchase of common stock for treasury (126,025 shares) . . . . . . . . | (2,914) | | |
| Treasury shares canceled . . . . . . . . . | | | 7,760 |
| Balance at end of year . . . . . . . . . | (2,914) | — | — |
| Total stockholders' equity. . . . . . . . . . | $93,535 | $89,753 | $82,940 |

## Required:

*a.* Reconstruct the journal entry that was made to purchase the treasury stock in 1986.

*b.* Reconstruct the journal entry that was made to cancel the treasury shares in 1984. Compute the price paid for these treasury shares when they had been purchased prior to 1984.

*c.* Preferred stock was converted to common stock in 1985 and 1986. Reconstruct the journal entries that were made to accomplish the conversions.

*d.* In 1984, a three-for-two stock split was distributed. Prepare a calculation to show that the correct dollar amount was used and reconstruct the journal entry for the stock split distribution.

*e.* Why would Russ Toggs use a three-for-two stock split instead of simply issuing a 50 percent stock dividend?

*f.* In 1984, a $65,000 transfer was made from paid-in capital to the Preferred Stock—Par account. Explain why you think such a transfer would have been made.

## Casette 14–3. Analyzing the Impact of Redeemable Preferred Stock at CMI Corporation

The 1985 annual report of CMI Corporation contained the following disclosures in the stockholders' equity section and related note on preferred stock. All dollar amounts are in thousands.

|  | *1985* | *1984* |
|---|---|---|
| Redeemable preferred stock: | | |
| Redemption value—$4,800 . . . . . . . . . . . . . . | $ 3,804 | — |
| Shareholders' equity: | | |
| Convertible preferred stock . . . . . . . . . . . . . . | — | 534 |
| Common stock . . . . . . . . . . . . . . . . . . . | 1,368 | 1,208 |
| Shares issued: 13,681,762 in 1985; 12,080,059 in 1984 | | |
| Additional paid-in capital . . . . . . . . . . . . . . . | 44,914 | 40,681 |
| Retained earnings (deficit) . . . . . . . . . . . . . . | 938 | (8,008) |
| Cumulative foreign currency adjustment . . . . . . . . | 202 | — |
| Less cost of treasury stock—12,199 shares . . . . . . . | (56) | (56) |
| Total shareholders' equity. . . . . . . . . . . . . . . | $47,366 | $34,359 |

### Redeemable Preferred Stock

In connection with the acquisition of RayGo, the Company issued 4,800 shares of 7% Series B Preferred Stock with a $4,800,000 redemption value. The preferred stock accrues dividends at the rate of $70 per share per year. The cumulative dividends are payable each January and July commencing in 1986, and must be fully paid or declared with funds set aside for payment before any dividend can be declared or paid on any other class of the Company's stock. The preferred stock carries mandatory redemption rights of $1,000 per share and must be redeemed according to the following redemption schedule: 300 shares on December 31, 1988; 500 shares on December 31, 1989; 750 shares on each December 31, from 1990 through 1994; and 250 shares on December 31, 1995. In addition to the normal voting rights of the common stock, the preferred stock carries special voting rights relating to a default in dividend payments or scheduled redemption payments. The difference between the redemption value and the carrying value is being accreted over the redemption period.

## Required:

a. Prepare the journal entry CMI must have made when they issued the Redeemable Preferred Stock. How much did they receive per share for this stock?

b. Calculate the *total* dollar amount of the difference between the redemption value and the carrying value that will need to be "accreted" over the redemption period. Where did the company get this value? Explain.

c. Prepare a schedule showing the number of shares, by year, that must be redeemed and the amount of additional value that will be required each year. Use the following headings in preparing your schedule:

| Year | Number of Shares to be Redeemed | Original Value Received | Value Needed at Redemption | Accretion Required |
|------|--------------------------------|-------------------------|----------------------------|--------------------|

d. The preferred stock accrues dividends at the rate of $70 per share per year. Prepare a schedule showing the required annual amount, by year, for dividends which will be required if the firm retires preferred stock in accordance with the schedule. Use the following headings in preparing your schedule:

| Year | Total Shares at the Beginning of the Year | Dividends Required | Number of Shares to be Redeemed | Total Shares at the End of the Year |
|------|-------------------------------------------|--------------------|---------------------------------|-------------------------------------|

e. Determine the total cash requirements, by year, for CMI to meet both the redemption payments (part c) and dividend payments (part d).

f. Assume that CMI paid no dividends in 1985. What must their net income have been in 1985? How large must retained earnings be in 1986 for CMI to be able to declare dividends to any class of stock other than the Redeemable Preferred Stock? Do the prospects for dividends seem very good for common stockholders? Explain.

g. Why does CMI classify the Redeemable Preferred Stock outside of the category of shareholders' equity?

# Financial Statements—Problems of Analysis, Disclosure, and Interpretation

# Chapter 15

# *Intercompany Ownership and Consolidation*

Many corporate businesses invest substantial sums to acquire the capital stock of other corporations. Sometimes corporate investors, like individual investors, purchase shares solely as investments in order to earn a return in the form of dividends and market value appreciation. In many cases, however, the purpose behind the intercorporate stockholdings is to affect or control the other firm. A corporation, through its substantial ownership of stock of other companies, may *significantly influence* the latters' operating and financial policies.

The owner of the shares is called the *investor* corporation; the corporations whose shares are held by the investor are called *investee* corporations. If the investor corporation owns more than half of the voting common stock of the investees, it is called a *parent* company. It has the ability to *determine* the operating and financial policies of the controlled companies, which are called *subsidiary* companies.

A parent company and its subsidiaries (and major investees) often are called *affiliated* companies. Groupings of affiliated companies are created for a variety of reasons:

1. To serve as a source of raw materials for the parent.
2. To provide outlets for the parent's finished products.
3. To gain production and distribution economies through integration of the operations of the subsidiaries and the parent.
4. To penetrate into new markets or to enlarge existing ones.
5. To reduce the overall variability of profits and the risk of the affiliate group when the intercorporate ownership results in a conglomerate of companies in different industries.
6. To gain control over new technologies or management skills and to obtain legal, political, or tax advantages.

Whatever its reasons, the parent/investor's acquisition of stock in another company results in an initial debit to an asset account called "Investment in Stock of XYZ Company." If the shares are purchased for cash, the Cash account is credited. However, other credits may reflect various noncash considerations exchanged for the shares. For example, the parent/investor may distribute its own shares of common stock, issue bonds or preferred stock, or exchange combinations of cash and securities for the voting stock of the investee. Indeed, the acquisition and merger mania of recent decades has fostered more alternatives than could possibly be described here.

This chapter explores three aspects of the accounting for intercorporate ownership and subsequent handling of the investment account.

**1.** The first section examines the proper accounting for intercompany investments when the intercompany holding is less than a controlling one. The investor and investee companies are treated as separate accounting entities. The *equity method* and the *cost method* are contrasted as techniques for recording the investment relationship in the investor's accounts.

**2.** If the parent company owns substantially all of the stock of the subsidiary, it may liquidate the subsidiary and legally transfer all its assets to the parent. Such a combination is called a *merger*. The investment account disappears, and the actual assets and liabilities of the acquired company take its place. The acquired company ceases to exist as a separate *legal* entity, although it often operates intact as a division of the combined company. The second section of this chapter considers the valuation and recording problems encountered when businesses merge or combine through an exchange of shares. Two recording procedures, called *purchase* and *pooling of interests*, constitute the focal point in this section.

**3.** If the parent owns a controlling interest in the stock of the subsidiary, it may choose to operate the latter as a separate corporation in harmony with the overall objectives of the parent. There are valid legal, tax, and business reasons to retain separate legal entities for different parts of the business, particularly parts with differing risk characteristics. Still, investors need financial information for the group of companies operating as a single *economic* entity. The third section of this chapter concerns the preparation of *consolidated financial statements*, which treat the legally separate parent and subsidiary companies as if they were a single company.

## NONCONTROLLING INVESTMENTS

Sometimes one company owns a substantial stock interest in another corporation but without majority control. The investor company reports the investee affiliates as investment assets on its balance sheet and income from them on its income statement. The investor corporation must employ either the equity method or the cost method for recording this type of investment.

## Cost Method

Under the cost method, the investment account is recorded at cost, as is any asset. The investment account basically remains at cost despite any future increases or decreases in the underlying net assets of the investee that result from its periodic operations. The only exception is when the stock of the investee has a market price that declines below cost. Then the procedures described in Chapter 8 to record the noncurrent marketable equity securities at the lower of cost or market would apply.

Under the cost method, no revenue is recognized by the investor unless and until the subsidiary pays a dividend.

For example, assume that on January 1, 1990 Price Corporation acquires 40 percent (20,000 shares) of the 50,000 shares of common stock of Ross Company for their book value of $10 per share. During the next three years, Ross Company's net income and dividends are:

|  | Net Income | Dividends |
|---|---|---|
| 1990 | $ 50,000 | $20,000 |
| 1991 | (10,000) | — |
| 1992 | 15,000 | 5,000 |
|  | $ 55,000 | $25,000 |

On January 1, 1990, Price Corporation would make the following entry to record the initial stock purchase:

| Investment in Ross Company | 200,000 | |
| Cash | | 200,000 |

Then, each year Price Corporation debits Cash and credits Dividend Revenue for the dividends (40 percent) that it receives—$8,000 in 1990, $0 in 1991, and $2,000 in 1992.

## Equity Method

Under the equity method, the investment account begins with the same amount as was shown for the cost method. However, in subsequent periods it will reflect changes in the underlying net assets resulting from investee operations. Income or loss appears on the books of the investor in the period it is earned by the investee. If the latter operates profitably, the investor debits the investment account and credits income for its share of the net income of the investee. The reverse procedure is followed when the investee operates at a loss. A dividend represents a recovery of the investment.

**Entries under the Equity Method.** The following journal entries illustrate the effect of the equity method on the amount and timing of income and on the valuation of the investment using the same events employed to illustrate the cost method:

1. January 1, 1990—acquisition of 20,000 shares of Ross Company:

| | | |
|---|---:|---:|
| Investment in Ross Company | 200,000 | |
| Cash | | 200,000 |

2. Entries during 1990:

| | | |
|---|---:|---:|
| Investment in Ross Company | 20,000 | |
| Equity in Investee Income | | 20,000 |
| To record 40 percent of investee income. | | |

| | | |
|---|---:|---:|
| Cash | 8,000 | |
| Investment in Ross Company | | 8,000 |
| To record receipt of $8,000 in dividends from investee. | | |

3. Entries during 1991:

| | | |
|---|---:|---:|
| Equity in Investee Income (Loss) | 4,000 | |
| Investment in Ross Company | | 4,000 |
| To record 40 percent of investee loss. | | |

4. Entries during 1992:

| | | |
|---|---:|---:|
| Investment in Ross Company | 6,000 | |
| Equity in Investee Income | | 6,000 |
| To record 40 percent of investee income. | | |

| | | |
|---|---:|---:|
| Cash | 2,000 | |
| Investment in Ross Company | | 2,000 |
| To record receipt of $2,000 in dividends from investee. | | |

The Equity in Investee Income appears each year as a separate element of income (or as a deduction in the case of investee losses) on the income statement of the investor. The equity method recognizes total earnings of $22,000 ($20,000 − $4,000 + $6,000) over the three-year period. The parent recognizes its share of the income in the period when the income is *earned* by the subsidiary.

Dividends received from the subsidiary are credited to the Investment account. For example, inasmuch as $20,000 of subsidiary income in 1990 was recognized by the parent, inclusion of the $8,000 dividend distribution as additional income would result in double counting. Rather, because the dividends reduce the net assets of the subsidiary, they are shown as a reduction in the parent's investment account. Dividends represent a conversion of the investment into cash.

Investment in Ross Company will appear among the noncurrent assets of Price Company. Its balance on December 31, 1992, is $212,000. The net increase of $12,000 from January 1, 1990, represents the investor's interest in investee earnings that have *not* been distributed as dividends. A separate position statement of Ross Company would show a retained earnings balance $30,000 larger than on January 1, 1990. Because the net assets of the subsidiary have increased $30,000, the investment account properly reflects the parent's 40 percent interest in this increase.

**Analysis of the Equity Method.**    Two major arguments support the equity method. First, the results shown by the investor company bear a direct relationship to the periodic operations of the investee. While still treating the investor and investee as separate companies, the equity method recognizes the existence of a significant economic relationship between them. The investor's financial statements, if drawn up according to the equity method, give a more useful picture of this relationship. The investor benefits from the asset growth in the investee. The equity method reflects this benefit. Second, often the investor company can significantly influence the dividend policy of the investee. The cost method, under which income is recorded only when dividends are received, enables the management of the investor company to exercise considerable influence over how much dividend revenue is recognized and when. By taking the investee's earnings onto the investor company's books as earned and treating dividends simply as a reduction in the amount invested, the equity method avoids this possible pitfall. Thus, it better satisfies the qualitative guidelines of timeliness and representational faithfulness.

The substance of both these arguments is that dividends poorly measure, in both timing and amount, the periodic benefit from some stock holdings. When investors can influence the dividend policy of the investee, dividends vary more with the cash needs of the investor and with income tax considerations than with the inherent profitability of the investment. The equity method simply extends the concepts of accrual accounting and revenue recognition to substantial intercompany investments. The investee's recognition of net income, measured according to generally accepted accounting principles, is deemed to meet satisfactorily the earnings criterion for revenue recognition by the investor company. Likewise, changes in the underlying net assets of the investee constitute sufficient reliability of measurement. A specific exchange of assets (dividend payment) adds little to fulfilling the revenue recognition criteria.

If the investor company were to pay more than book value for the investee shares, the difference between the cost of the investment and the underlying equity of the subsidiary must be written off over future periods as a reduction in Equity in Investee Income.

## Authoritative Standards

The rationale behind the equity method led the Accounting Principles Board to require it for intercompany investments where the investor can *influence significantly* the operating or financial decisions of the investee.[1] The ability to exercise considerable influence may of course be evidenced by many factors in addition to the amount of voting stock owned by the investor corporation. Nevertheless, the APB concluded that in the absence of compelling factors to the contrary, significant influence is presumed to exist with a 20 percent or more interest in the investee's voting common stock.[2]

Conversely, if the investor corporation owns less than 20 percent of the voting stock, the presumption is that the cost method is the appropriate procedure. The cost method assumes that the investor corporation, as only a minor owner of the investee, exercises little or no control over it. Revenue derived from the investment is recognized only in the periods when assets are actually distributed to the investor corporation in the form of dividends and only to the extent of the dividend amount.[3]

Unfortunately, the existence of relatively arbitrary distinctions between when the equity method must be used and when the cost method must be used has allowed a few companies to manipulate their earnings. For example, intercorporate holdings are kept below 20 percent when the investee is operating at a loss. When the latter begins to show consistent income, the investor will increase ownership to exceed the magic 20 percent level.

Some analysts object to the large gap that may exist between earnings reported under the equity method and the actual dividends received in cash. They claim that the equity method does not measure actual cash inflow. The prevailing argument, of course, is that if the investor does control the dividend policy of the investee, then the equity method measures *potential* cash inflows quite accurately.

**Disclosures.**  Because common stock investments carried on the equity basis may be significant in evaluating the investor corporation, *Opinion No. 18* also imposes some disclosure requirements. In notes or separate schedules, the investor corporation should indicate the percentage ownership of each investee, the accounting policies followed, and the excess, if any, of the Investment account balance over the underlying equity in net assets of the investee. Additionally, in some circumstances the market value of the investment, when available, must be disclosed.

---

[1] AICPA, *APB Opinion No. 18,* "The Equity Method of Accounting for Investments in Common Stock" (New York, March 1971).

[2] Factors that might overturn this presumption of significant influence include lack of representation on the investee Board of Directors, the other 80 percent of the shares being concentrated in a single controlling interest, or the investee viewing the intercompany holdings as a hostile acquisition.

[3] Firms usually use the cost method for tax purposes even when they use the equity method for financial accounting purposes. The difference in the amounts reported for tax and for book purposes may cause deferred tax problems similar to those described in Chapter 13.

# RECORDING MERGERS AND ACQUISITIONS

The transaction in which two companies join together is called a "merger," "acquisition," or "combination." When the merger is effected through the parent's cash purchase of the outstanding stock of the subsidiary, the situation is analogous to a lump-sum purchase of assets (discussed in Chapter 8). The cost assigned to the acquired shares is the amount of cash paid. The acquired company's shares are then retired. Because the shares of stock purchased represent the firm's net assets, the cost of the stock is allocated to the individual net assets—tangible and intangible—when they are combined with those of the acquirer.

For example, Jeckle, Inc., buys all of the outstanding stock of Hyde Company for $960,000 with the intent to merge the two companies. Hyde Company has tangible assets with a book value of $900,000 and a fair market value of $1,020,000; its liabilities are $190,000. The entries on Jeckle's books are:

| | | |
|---|---:|---:|
| Investment in Hyde Company Stock | 960,000 | |
|    Cash | | 960,000 |
|      To record purchase of stock. | | |
| | | |
| Tangible Assets (recorded in detail at their fair market value) | 1,020,000 | |
| Goodwill | 130,000 | |
|    Liabilities | | 190,000 |
|    Investment in Hyde Company Stock | | 960,000 |
|      To record the retirement of Hyde Company stock and the merging of its assets and liabilities into Jeckle, Inc. | | |

In brief, the only valuation problem is one of allocating the total cash consideration among the net assets acquired.

Some business combinations are accomplished through an exchange of shares rather than by an outright purchase for cash. The acquiring company offers to issue a certain number of its shares in exchange for the shares of the acquired company. Under most state laws, if a required percentage of each firm's stockholders agrees to the proposal, the exchange is binding and the firms are legally merged.

The question we address in this section is whether there is a different economic substance to the transaction when the parent corporation exchanges its own shares for those of the subsidiary instead of paying cash. Is a different method of accounting from that illustrated above appropriate?

In some circumstances, accountants answer this question in the affirmative. Two methods exist in accounting practice to account for business combinations effected through an exchange of shares. The *pooling of interests approach* is used when the parent company issues its own voting stock in exchange for substantially all the voting stock of the subsidiary. The *purchase approach* is used when any other combination of considerations is exchanged for the subsidiary shares. These two accounting procedures may have significantly different impacts on the financial statements, because they value the net assets acquired and record the increase in stockholders' equity differently.

## Illustrative Data

Assume that Jeckle, Inc.'s shares of stock have a current market value of $60 per share. Instead of making a $960,000 cash payment, Jeckle, Inc. issues 16,000 shares of its common stock worth $960,000 to the owners of Hyde Company in exchange for all the outstanding shares of that company. Jeckle promptly retires the Hyde shares, thereby liquidating and dissolving it as a separate corporation and formally consummating the merger.

Balance sheets for the two corporations immediately prior to the merger are given in Table 15–1. The Hyde Company's inventory of $120,000 is valued at average cost; its current replacement cost is $170,000. A recent appraisal of its buildings and equipment indicates a current value of about $530,000. The Hyde Company possesses a fine market reputation. Its brand names are well known, and the company is noted for turning out a quality product. In fact, one of the reasons that Jeckle, Inc., wishes to acquire Hyde Company is to obtain the benefits from this reputation.

**TABLE 15–1**   Premerger Balance Sheets ($000)

|  | Jeckle, Inc. | Hyde Co. |
|---|---|---|
| **Assets** | | |
| Cash | $ 110 | $ 20 |
| Accounts receivable | 770 | 100 |
| Inventory | 1,555 | 120 |
| Land | 305 | 200 |
| Buildings and equipment (net) | 3,360 | 460 |
| Total assets | $6,100 | $900 |
| **Equities** | | |
| Accounts payable | $1,540 | $190 |
| Capital stock—$10 par | 1,000 | 100 |
| Additional paid-in capital | 1,200 | 130 |
| Retained earnings | 2,360 | 480 |
| Total equities | $6,100 | $900 |
| Shares outstanding (thousands) | 100 | 10 |
| Market value per share | $ 60 | Not available |

## Purchase Approach

The journal entry below summarizes the entries made by Jeckle to effect the merger under the purchase approach:

| | | |
|---|---:|---:|
| Cash | 20,000 | |
| Accounts Receivable | 100,000 | |
| Inventory | 170,000 | |
| Land | 200,000 | |
| Buildings and Equipment | 530,000 | |
| Goodwill | 130,000 | |
| Accounts Payable | | 190,000 |
| Capital Stock—$100 Par | | 160,000 |
| Additional Paid-In Capital | | 800,000 |

To record issuance of 16,000 shares of Jeckle for 10,000 shares of Hyde and the subsequent liquidation of Hyde under purchase approach.

Under this approach the assets of Hyde Company, including any intangible assets being acquired, are recorded at their fair market values (their current acquisition costs), and the contributed capital accounts of Jeckle are credited.[4] The net result is the same as if the Jeckle shares first had been issued for cash and then the cash had been used to acquire the Hyde shares. Should the direct exchange of shares without an intermediate inflow and outflow of cash cause the acquisition to be recorded differently?

The purchase approach would say no. The negotiations between the two companies reasonably can be assumed to have been based on an equal exchange of values—the value of the net assets received by Jeckle and the value of the stock issued by it. Jeckle, Inc. has issued shares with a market value of $960,000 (16,000 shares at $60). Therefore, the net assets received are valued at $960,000. Each individual asset is stated at its fair market value, and the excess of $130,000 is assigned to Goodwill. The $960,000 increase in contributed capital is recorded in two accounts—the par value of the shares (16,000 × $10) in the Capital Stock account and the excess over par value in a separate Additional Paid-In Capital account.

The purchase approach views a business combination, *however consummated,* as primarily an acquisition of one company's assets by another company. The acquisition of assets is the result of a bargained exchange. The basis of accountability relevant to the new ownership is the values implicit in that exchange. The valuation of the assets should not differ from that associated with a cash purchase merely because shares of stock are the consideration exchanged. Similarly, the effect on stockholders' equity should not vary simply because noncash assets are received upon issuance of the stock.

---

[4] If the recorded values of the assets and liabilities acquired from Hyde differ from their values for tax purposes, a temporary difference exists as explained in Chapter 13. A deferred tax liability account in that instance would become part of the entry.

## Pooling of Interests Approach

This method calls for a simple combining of assets and equities. In a pooling of interests, the Investment account of the parent is valued at the *book value* of the stockholders' equity of the acquired firm. Then, when the investment is liquidated, the assets of the acquired firm are carried over to the acquiring firm at their book values. Likewise, the stockholders' equity amounts of the two firms are combined, including the respective retained earnings.

The *net* result of the combination with Hyde Company under pooling of interests can be expressed in the single journal entry below:

| | | |
|---|---:|---:|
| Cash | 20,000 | |
| Accounts Receivable | 100,000 | |
| Inventory | 120,000 | |
| Land | 200,000 | |
| Buildings and Equipment | 460,000 | |
|     Accounts Payable | | 190,000 |
|     Capital Stock—$10 Par | | 160,000 |
|     Additional Paid-In Capital | | 70,000 |
|     Retained Earnings | | 480,000 |

To record exchange of 16,000 Jeckle shares for 10,000 shares of Hyde and the subsequent liquidation of Hyde by combining its assets and equities with those of Jeckle.

Pooling of interests assumes a fusion, or marriage, of the two companies instead of an acquisition. The merged company is seen to be little different from the sum of the two companies prior to the merger. Total assets and stockholders' equity after the merger are the sums of the assets and stockholders' equity of each of the companies prior to the merger. The shareholders are also the same, as the Hyde Company shareholders are now shareholders in Jeckle, Inc. Notice that the only adjustment made reflects the par value of the shares issued by the acquiring firm. Because the additional contributed capital is now represented by 16,000 shares of Jeckle, Inc., stock with a total par value of $160,000—instead of 10,000 shares of Hyde Company stock with a total par value of $100,000—$60,000 of the $130,000 in the Additional Paid-In Capital account of Hyde has to be reclassified so that legal capital will conform to the number of shares issued.[5]

Advocates of the pooling of interest approach contend that nothing of substance has occurred in the combination to justify a new basis of account-

---

[5] If there were insufficient paid-in capital of the acquired company to accommodate the reclassification of stockholders' equity because of the increase in par value, then any additional paid-in capital of the acquiring company would be reduced. If the reclassification reduces the paid-in capital accounts of both companies to zero, then retained earnings would be reduced also. Outside of this minor legal adjustment, pooling basically calls for a simple combining of owners' equity accounts.

ability for the Hyde Company assets. The combined entity is nothing more than a combination of the two businesses formerly conducted separately. The assets and stockholders' interests remain the same, but they are now together instead of separate. Useful comparisons with past periods can be made if the accounting for the merged company is only a continuation of the combined accounts of the two companies.[6]

The conceptual arguments against pooling tend to be the same as those in favor of the purchase approach. First, the underlying rationale of pooling—that is, that two groups of stockholders owning businesses are coming together to operate henceforth as partners—just does not fit most business combinations. There is almost always a clearly identifiable acquiring company that is taking over the business of another company. One party is a continuing entity that exercises dominant control after the merger. Acquisition of another company is simply an alternative means of asset acquisition, and the accounting should be consistent with that resulting from other asset acquisitions. Second, something of substance does occur in most combinations. Two independent parties negotiate at arm's length to reach agreement on an exchange of values. To record the transfer of assets at book value seems to fly in the face of the agreement between the parties.

## Comparative Impact on the Financial Statements

The choice between purchase and pooling is extremely important because of the impact that each procedure has on the financial statements. The initial effect can be seen in our example. Balance sheets after the merger under the two approaches are presented in Table 15–2. In most instances, pooling of interests results in a balance sheet with lower figures than under the purchase approach.

Perhaps even more important is the impact on the measurement of future income. Under the purchase approach, with the newly acquired plant assets recorded at their current market values instead of at book values, subsequent depreciation charges are higher. Straight-line depreciation expense on the Hyde Company assets, if we assume that they have a remaining useful life of 5 years, will be $106,000 a year ($530,000/5 years) under the purchase approach but only $92,000 ($460,000/5) when the combination is accounted for as a pooling. Moreover, in accordance with *APB Opinion No. 17*, the acquiring company must also amortize the $130,000 goodwill recognized in the purchase. If we assume an amortization period of 10 years, postmerger earnings are reduced an additional $13,000 annually.

---

[6] Pooling also draws practical support from the fact that most exchanges of stock in conjunction with a merger are treated as tax-free exchanges under the income tax law. Consequently, for tax purposes the old asset values must be carried over.

**TABLE 15-2**    Postmerger Balance Sheets under Purchase and Pooling ($000)

|  | *Purchase* | *Pooling* |
|---|---:|---:|
| **Assets** | | |
| Cash . . . . . . . . . . . . . . . . . . . . . . . . | $ 130 | $ 130 |
| Accounts receivable . . . . . . . . . . . . . . . | 870 | 870 |
| Inventory. . . . . . . . . . . . . . . . | 1,725 | 1,675 |
| Land . . . . . . . . . . . . . . . . . . . | 505 | 505 |
| Buildings and equipment . . . . . . . . . . . . | 3,890 | 3,820 |
| Goodwill. . . . . . . . . . . . . . . . . . . . | 130 | — |
| Total assets . . . . . . . . . . . . . . . . . . . | $7,250 | $7,000 |
| **Equities** | | |
| Accounts payable . . . . . . . . . . . . . . . | $1,730 | $1,730 |
| Capital stock—$10 par . . . . . . . . . . . . . | 1,160 | 1,160 |
| Additional paid-in capital . . . . . . . . . . . | 2,000 | 1,270 |
| Retained earnings . . . . . . . . . . . . . | 2,360 | 2,840 |
| Total equities . . . . . . . . . . . . . . . | $7,250 | $7,000 |
| Shares outstanding (thousands) . . . . . . . . . . . | 116 | 116 |

Table 15–3 shows the income statement and other comparative results of the merged company. We assume that the total postmerger earnings of the two companies operating separately would be $1,000,000 before taxes; the tax rate is 40 percent. Pooling of interests, in contrast to a purchase, gives greater income and lower assets—a double infusion to return on investment. Theoretical reasons aside, one can understand why acquisition-minded companies prefer pooling of interests.

## Purchase-Pooling and the Entity Concept

Clearly the nature of the accounting entity lies at the heart of this recording problem. Purchase accounting presumes that the relevant entity is the acquiring company and that all recording should be viewed from its perspective. The ownership interests of the stockholders of the acquired company are significantly altered. In our example, for instance, Hyde stockholders cease to be a controlling group. On the other hand, pooling of interests asserts that a merger effected through an exchange of shares creates no new entity, merely a combination of two old entities. An exchange of shares is solely an arrangement between shareholders; it joins two ownership interests in a combined collection of assets.

Once the entity-identification issue is resolved, many of the other arguments fall into perspective. For instance, *if* the relevant entity is the

**TABLE 15–3**    Postmerger Income Statements Data under Purchase and
Pooling ($000)

|  | Purchase | Pooling |
|---|---|---|
| Postmerger earnings before adjustments and income taxes . . . . | $1,000.0 | $1,000 |
| Additional expenses: |  |  |
| Depreciation . . . . . . . . . . . . | 14.0 | — |
| Amortization of goodwill . . . . . . | 13.0 | — |
| Income before taxes . . . . . . . . | $ 973.0 | $1,000 |
| Income taxes . . . . . . . . . . . | 394.4* | 400 |
| Net income . . . . . . . . . . . . | $ 578.6 | $ 600 |
| Earnings per share . . . . . . . . . | $ 4.99 | $ 5.17 |
|  | ($578.6/116) | ($600/116) |
| Rate of return on assets . . . . . . . | 8% | 8.6% |
|  | ($578.6/$7,250) | ($600/$7,000) |

*Amortization of goodwill is not deductible for tax purposes. Under the purchase approach taxes are 40 percent of $986,000.

acquiring company, then the transfer of assets from one corporate entity to
another does necessitate a new basis of accountability for the assets. In *any*
acquisition of new assets—cash purchase or otherwise—the new assets are
recorded on the entity's books at the current acquisition costs, even though
other assets are valued at past purchase prices. Moreover, purchased goodwill is a real part of the transaction between the entity and an outside party,
even though internally developed goodwill goes unrecognized.

When viewed from the perspective of the acquiring entity, a merger
recorded under pooling of interests is unacceptable because of its implication that a firm can generate retained earnings simply by acquiring another
firm. Although the acquiring firm can buy another's assets and can assume
its liabilities, it cannot generate retained earnings in a capital-raising transaction. Retained earnings bear significance only to the entity that produced
the income. Thus, if we accept the *acquiring-entity interpretation of the
purchase approach,* the combination of owners' equity accounts under pooling of interests is nonsensical. On the other hand, the combining of all
assets and equities at book values is a logical extension of the *shared-entity
interpretation of the pooling approach.*

Therefore, the real issue centers on the nature of the entity that ultimately
exercises control over the acquired assets and the policies that govern their
use. The conceptual controversy is one of representational faithfulness.
What is the economic substance of the merger? Pooling conceptually would
seem to reflect an entity within which there is a truly mutual exchange of

risks and control by more or less equal parties. All previous owners remain with the intention of conducting a combined business *together.*

Except in rare instances, however, most business combinations are characterized by a single identifiable entity acquiring dominant (not shared) control over the assets of another firm. This control is accomplished through an exchange of shares based on an arm's length agreement. Such an exchange of shares is not solely an arrangement among shareholders. Control over assets passes from one group to another, and one of the original entities ceases to exist.

## Authoritative Standards

The accounting profession has long wrestled with the purchase-pooling issue. Two research studies sponsored by the Accounting Principles Board in the 1960s essentially recommended the abolition of pooling of interests accounting. However, in 1970, the APB issued a less extreme opinion, allowing both purchase and pooling but only under differing circumstances. Businesses cannot choose freely which method to use. Under *Opinion No. 16,* business combinations meeting rather specific criteria *must* be accounted for as poolings of interests; all other combinations *must* be handled as purchases.

Twelve specific conditions are set forth as requisite for the use of pooling of interests accounting.[7] The criteria can be summarized in the following five points:

1. The combination has to result from a single transaction completed within one year between independent companies that have been autonomous for at least two years.
2. Only voting common stock can be issued in exchange for substantially all (at least 90 percent) of the voting common stock of the acquired company.
3. No reacquisition of common stock or adjustments to its equity interest in contemplation of the combination can occur within two years before the merger.
4. There can be no major realignment of voting interests, restrictions on voting rights, or planned equity retirements after the combination.
5. There can be no disposition of assets after the combination except to eliminate duplicate assets.

Violation of any of these conditions evidences that one firm is *acquiring* another, in which case the purchase approach is the proper accounting method.

---

[7] AICPA, *APB Opinion No. 16,* "Business Combinations" (New York, August 1970), pars. 45–48.

Under these criteria, our Jeckle-Hyde merger probably would have to be recorded as a pooling of interests. Jeckle is issuing only its voting common stock in exchange for all the voting common stock of Hyde. What if Jeckle issues only 8,000 shares of its stock worth $480,000 for half of the Hyde shares and issues a bond with a present value of $480,000 or pays $480,000 in cash for the rest? In this instance, the merger would have to be recorded as a purchase. In both cases, $960,000 of values are exchanged for the Hyde shares. We return to the question posed before: Is there a different economic substance to the transaction? We think not.

# CONSOLIDATED FINANCIAL STATEMENTS

Many times the acquiring firm and the acquired firm do not merge formally. Each retains its legal identity as a separate corporation, and under state law each is required to maintain its own set of accounting records. Economically, however, the companies may closely coordinate their operations and financial positions as if they were one. Indeed, many large national and multi-national corporations in reality are parent corporations that own and control a number of subsidiary companies operating in different lines of business and/or in various countries.

Consolidated financial statements provide a comprehensive picture of this economic entity by meshing the accounts of the subsidiaries with those of the parent into a single set of statements. Consolidated statements indicate the results that would have transpired if all transactions had been recorded in a single set of accounts. The consolidated statements are concerned only with the transactions and relations between the affiliated companies, viewed as one, and the parties outside the family circle. Their purpose is to provide the management and stockholders of the parent company with an overall view of their company's activities and its related subsidiaries as one unit.

This picture typically is more meaningful than separate statements, because the legal entities frequently act in concert to achieve an overall goal for the parent company and its stockholders. In consolidated statements, investors in the parent company can see the results of their investment at work—directly and also indirectly through the parent's investments in other companies. Users of consolidated financial statements often can obtain a better picture of the financial and operating activities of the complex of companies. They get a better idea of the total asset investment subject to common control, the sales volume of the entire group of companies, and indirect financial arrangements (e.g., borrowing by subsidiary companies primarily on the credit of the parent company).

The mere existence of intercompany holdings of securities, however, does not automatically lead to the preparation of consolidated statements. For a group of firms to function as a single company, one of the group must have the ability to determine the operating activities and financial policies of the others. Consolidated statements are appropriate when there is clearly only one parent company and the parent company owns a majority interest in the subsidiaries. Consolidated statements should not be prepared if the parent's control is temporary or restricted in some major way. For example, sometimes foreign subsidiaries are not consolidated because of restrictions on the parent's control of subsidiary operations.

Historically, companies being consolidated were expected to be operationally related. If the types of assets and liabilities and the sources of revenue are radically dissimilar among the related entities, consolidation could provide less information than would individual reports of each company. However, three practices caused accountants to abandon the concept of homogeneity in operations:

**1.** Many businesses are significantly diversified and operate in numerous lines of business. Accordingly, the mere fact that a subsidiary operates in a different line of business from the parent is insufficient reason not to consolidate it. A seeming lack of similarity is irrelevant when the subsidiary is an organic part of the consolidated entity that is doing much of its operating business with other family members.

**2.** Homogeneous operations were inconsistently defined by different companies, thus resulting in a lack of comparability.

**3.** Many accountants and regulators felt that lack of homogeneous operations had been misused to justify off-balance-sheet financing. Subsidiary companies borrow substantial amounts often at the direction of the parent. However, the debt-laden subsidiaries are not consolidated, and the debt never shows up on the parent company's balance sheet.

Consequently, the FASB now requires the consolidation of all majority-owned subsidiaries.[8] The new standard is effective for fiscal years ending after December 15, 1988.

## Consolidated Balance Sheet

When consolidated statements are needed, the accountant works from the individual statements of the companies being consolidated, eliminating items that would not appear if the separate companies had been one company. Let us examine a few typical situations to see what we should eliminate to avoid double counting or to adjust for the effect of transactions solely within the family.

**Complete Ownership at Book Value.**    For the first example, assume that the parent company (P) acquires 100 percent of the common stock of the subsidiary (S) for $10,000 on December 31, 1989. The parent debits Invest-

---

[8] FASB, *Statement of Financial Accounting Standards No. 94,* "Consolidation of All Majority-Owned Subsidiaries" (Stamford, Conn., November 1987).

ment in Subsidiary and credits Cash. A consolidated balance sheet is desired. Presented below are the major accounts of each company. Because the parent has paid book value for its 100 percent ownership interest in the subsidiary, the $10,000 amount shown on the parent company books as Investment in Subsidiary equals the owners' equity (capital stock plus retained earnings) of the subsidiary.

|  | *Parent* | *Subsidiary* | *Eliminations* | *Combined* |
|---|---|---|---|---|
| Cash . . . . . . . | $10,000 | $ 5,000 |  | $15,000 |
| Accounts receivable. . | 5,000 | 2,000 |  | 7,000 |
| Land and other |  |  |  |  |
| assets . . . . . . | 25,000 | 8,000 |  | 33,000 |
| Investment in |  |  |  |  |
| subsidiary . . . . | 10,000 |  | 10,000 |  |
| Total assets . . . . | $50,000 | $15,000 |  | $55,000 |
|  |  |  |  |  |
| Accounts payable . . | $20,000 | $ 5,000 |  | $25,000 |
| Capital stock . . . . | 20,000 | 7,000 | 7,000 | 20,000 |
| Retained earnings . . | 10,000 | 3,000 | 3,000 | 10,000 |
| Total equities . . . | $50,000 | $15,000 |  | $55,000 |

The essence of what occurs when P buys the stock of S is that part of the parent's stockholders' equity is now invested in the subsidiary's assets. P's holding of the subsidiary stock is only a means through which P gains control over S's assets. Viewed from outside the family, the parent's investment account and the stockholders' equity of S have no significance. Only P's equity invested in S's assets matter.

In this simple case, then, the Investment in Subsidiary account on the parent's books and the Capital Stock and Retained Earnings accounts on the subsidiary's books need to be eliminated. The subsidiary's assets are counted as part of the consolidated assets, so it would be double counting to also consider the investment as a separate asset. Consolidation essentially substitutes the individual net assets of the subsidiary ($5,000 Cash + $2,000 Accounts Receivable + $8,000 Other Assets − $5,000 Accounts Payable) for the single $10,000 balance in the Investment account. Similarly, the double counting of assets is accompanied by a double counting of shareholders' equity. Both companies are financed only by the stockholders of the parent company. Inasmuch as the capital stock and retained earnings of the subsidiary do not represent relationships with those outside the family, they are eliminated.

**Minority Interest at Book Value.**     Assume now that the parent company purchases only 90 percent of the capital stock of the subsidiary, paying

$9,000 for it. The other 10 percent is called the "minority interest." Even though the subsidiary is not wholly owned, the parent company still controls its operation, and consolidation is therefore desirable.

The eliminations are basically the same, except that only 90 percent of the capital stock and retained earnings of the subsidiary is eliminated. This is the only portion represented by intercompany holdings of stock. The remaining 10 percent is not eliminated, because it represents a source of financing from a group outside the family. Because we wish to include all assets under common control (i.e., 100 percent of S's assets) in the consolidation, the financial interest of the minority stockholders in these assets rightfully belongs in the consolidated statement.

Accordingly, we would eliminate only $6,300 (90% × $7,000) of the subsidiary's capital stock and $2,700 (90% × $3,000) of the subsidiary's retained earnings to avoid double counting. The remaining $1,000 of equity interest ($700 capital stock and $300 retained earnings) in the subsidiary is segregated in a single figure called "minority interest." For the consolidated entity, it represents a special portion of owners' equity apart from the parent stockholders. Often it appears as a separate category between the total liabilities and the consolidated stockholders' equity of the parent company stockholders.

**Investment at More or Less than Book Value.** Acquisition of a subsidiary's stock at book value is likely only when the parent company establishes a new corporation as its subsidiary. When the parent acquires a controlling interest in a going concern, the subsidiary's stock usually does not sell at book value.

Assume that the parent company pays $10,800 to existing shareholders for 90 percent of the stock in the subsidiary. However, the subsidiary's books remain unchanged. The *book value* of the ownership interest to be eliminated is still $9,000 (90% × $10,000 total stockholders' equity at date of acquisition). The difference of $1,800 represents additional asset value that has no reciprocal element in the subsidiary's underlying equities. If the parent company is willing to pay $10,800 for the stock it acquires, there is reason to believe that it is acquiring an interest in assets worth $10,800. An additional $1,800 of tangible and/or intangible asset value presumably is present in the transaction. This excess cost of the stock investment to the parent company over its book value must be recognized as a *consolidated* asset.[9]

---

[9] If the parent company pays less than book value, then an Excess Book Value over Investment Cost would be required. This item recognizes an overstatement in the subsidiary assets, as measured by what the parent is willing to pay to acquire an interest in them. Unless the specific overvalued assets can be identified, this amount must be treated as a pro rata reduction in the values assigned to the noncurrent assets.

The excess may represent undervalued assets of the subsidiary—for example, LIFO inventory, appreciated land values recorded at original cost, or the value of unrecorded patents. Generally accepted accounting principles require that any portion of the excess attributable to specifically identifiable tangible or intangible assets be allocated to those asset accounts. The rest is treated as a general unidentified intangible asset, "Goodwill." Remember that these reclassifications are done *for consolidated statement purposes only.* And, for consolidation purposes, any amounts assigned to intangibles must be amortized, and any amounts assigned to plant assets must be depreciated.

**Other Intercompany Relationships.** Two other common eliminations exist. The first type involves intercompany receivables and payables. Whenever one company owes another company, on either a short- or long-term basis, and the two are to be consolidated, the resulting reciprocal asset and liability items should be eliminated. The receivable does not represent an asset to the consolidated entity; it is not an amount owed by an outsider. Neither does the payable represent an amount owed to an outside group. Intercompany accounts receivable, interest receivable, advances to subsidiary, and investment in subsidiary bonds would all be removed in measuring consolidated assets. Similarly, intercompany accounts payable, interest payable, advances from parent, and bonds payable to parent would all be removed in measuring consolidated liabilities.

The second type of other common eliminations involves the intercompany sale of assets that have not been sold to outsiders. If the assets are sold at cost, no problem arises. Similarly, if the assets are sold from one company to another and then resold to outsiders, no *balance sheet* problem arises, because the assets no longer appear in the accounts of any member of the consolidation. The problem occurs only when assets are sold at a gain or loss by the parent to the subsidiary, or vice versa, and the assets are not resold to outsiders.

If by consolidating we are to treat the two companies as if they were one, then no gain or loss should be recorded on the intercompany transfer of assets that are not resold to outsiders. For example, assume that the parent sells land to the subsidiary for $5,000. The land originally cost the parent $4,100. From the parent's view as a separate entity, a profit of $900 is realized. From the subsidiary company's perspective, an asset that cost $5,000 is purchased. However, from the viewpoint of the consolidated entity, the asset has simply gone from one member of the family to another. Before we add the land accounts of the parent and subsidiary together in consolidation, we need to adjust the subsidiary's land downward by $900. The cost of the land to the consolidated entity is only $4,100. Also, the parent company's retained earnings must be reduced by $900. Retained earnings is the balance sheet account where the gain on the sale has been reflected. Consolidated companies can realize gains or losses only on sales to outsiders.

## Consolidated Income Statement

When we are done, the balance sheet reports only the consolidated assets and equities, eliminating any, such as intercompany receivables and payables, that represent existing relationships between the individual companies that comprise the consolidated entity. In the same manner, the consolidated income statement should report only revenues and expenses arising out of transactions with outsiders during the period. If there are *no* intercompany sales, dividend payments, interest payments, and so on; the consolidation procedure simply combines the individual income statements comprising the consolidated entity.

**Intercompany Revenues and Expenses.**   Normally though, there are intercompany transactions that must be eliminated. The most frequent is the intercompany sale. Take the case of a subsidiary that has $50,000 of inventory and sells 100 percent of it to the parent company for $80,000. The parent resells to outsiders all that it buys from the subsidiary and makes no sales other than what it buys from the subsidiary. Assume also that the subsidiary rents a warehouse from the parent for $5,000 per year. The individual income statements, the necessary eliminations, and the resultant consolidated income statement are presented below:

|  | *Parent* | *Subsidiary* | *Eliminations* | *Combined* |
|---|---|---|---|---|
| Sales revenue . . . . | $100,000 | $80,000 | 80,000 | $100,000 |
| Rent revenue . . . . | 5,000 | — | 5,000 | — |
| Total . . . . . . | $105,000 | $80,000 | | $100,000 |
| Cost of goods sold . . | $ 80,000 | $50,000 | 80,000 | $ 50,000 |
| Operating expenses . . | 10,000 | 20,000 | 5,000 | 25,000 |
| Total . . . . . . | $ 90,000 | $70,000 | | $ 75,000 |
| Net income . . . . . | $ 15,000 | $10,000 | | $ 25,000 |

In our consolidated statement, we have removed the double-counting effect of the intercompany purchase and sale. From a consolidated viewpoint, these are merely interfirm transfers, not revenue and expense items. The cost of inventory to the consolidated group is only $50,000. Selling it to the parent for $80,000 does not increase the value of the inventory or the amount of assets in the consolidated group. It merely shifts the inventory physically from the subsidiary to the parent and transfers $80,000 in cash from the parent to the subsidiary.

Therefore, the $80,000 of sales revenue on the subsidiary's records is a fiction that needs to be eliminated. Similarly, the increase in the parent's cost of goods sold is fictional. By contrast, the $100,000 of sales to outsiders does bring new assets to the consolidated group and should be matched with the $50,000 actual inventory cost given up by the consolidated group.

Similarly, we must correct for the overstatement of revenue and expense related to the warehouse rental. Revenues and expenses cannot arise from dealing with oneself. The increase in subsidiary income caused by elimination of $5,000 of its rent expense is offset by a decrease in parent net income caused by elimination of its rent revenue of like amount.

**Incomplete Reselling.** A more complicated case arises when we assume that the parent company does not resell all it buys from the subsidiary. In addition, let us relax our assumptions that the subsidiary makes no sales directly to outside customers and that the parent has no additional sales of its own. Suppose that a subsidiary sells only 50 percent of its products to the parent and the other 50 percent directly to outsiders. The parent resells 80 percent of what it purchases from the subsidiary, as well as some merchandise purchased from other sources. The resultant income statements for this example and the consolidation procedures are summarized below:

|  | *Parent* | *Subsidiary* | *Eliminations* | *Combined* |
|---|---|---|---|---|
| Sales revenue . . . . | $200,000 | $80,000 | 40,000 | $240,000 |
| Rent revenue . . . . | 5,000 | — | 5,000 | — |
| Total . . . . . . | $205,000 | $80,000 |  | $240,000 |
| Cost of goods sold . . | $150,000 | $50,000 | $\left\{ \begin{matrix} +3,000 \\ -40,000 \end{matrix} \right\}$ | $163,000 |
| Operating expenses . . | 30,000 | 20,000 | 5,000 | 45,000 |
| Total . . . . . . | $180,000 | $70,000 |  | $208,000 |
| Net income . . . . . | $ 25,000 | $10,000 |  | $ 32,000 |

Before studying the eliminations in detail, let us step back and ask intuitively what the *consolidated* sales and cost of goods sold *should* be. The consolidated revenues include only asset inflows to the group from outsiders:

| | |
|---|---|
| Sales by parent to outsiders . . . . . . . . . . . . | $200,000 |
| Sales by subsidiary to outsiders | |
| (50% × $80,000 subsidiary sales . . . . . . . . | 40,000 |
| Total consolidated sales . . . . . . . . . . . . | $240,000 |

The elimination of the 50 percent of the subsidiary's sales ($40,000) made to the parent accomplishes the desired results.

Cost of sales for the consolidated group should represent the *cost* of all inventory delivered to outside parties. The $163,000 consists of three elements:

Cost of goods purchased by parent
    from outsiders and sold to outsiders:

| | | |
|---|---:|---:|
| Parent cost of sales. . . . . . . . . . . . . . . . | $150,000 | |
| Less: Amount purchased from subsidiary | | |
|     and resold ($40,000 × 80%). . . . . . . . . | 32,000 | $118,000 |

Cost of goods purchased by parent
    from subsidiary and resold:

| | | |
|---|---:|---:|
| Parent purchases at sales price . . . . . . . . . . | $ 40,000 | |
| Profit element. . . . . . . . . . . . . . . . . | 15,000 | |
| Parent purchases at cost. . . . . . . . . . . . | $ 25,000 | |
| Portion sold   . . . . . . . . . . . . . . . . | ×      .80 | 20,000 |

Cost of goods sold directly to outside parties
    by subsidiary:

| | | |
|---|---:|---:|
| ($50,000 × 50%) . . . . . . . . . . . . . . . | | 25,000 |
| | | $163,000 |

The adjustments shown to arrive at the $163,000 from the total of the two companies' cost of goods sold can be understood best by considering the inventory formula:

| | | |
|---|---|---:|
| Beginning inventory | | |
| + Purchases | overstated | $40,000 |
| − Ending inventory | overstated | 3,000 |
| = Cost of goods sold | overstated | $37,000 |

If the consolidated entity were a single company, purchases and cost of goods sold are overstated by the $40,000 of intercompany purchases. The $3,000 adjustment represents the impact on cost of goods sold of the parent's *ending* inventory which was acquired from the subsidiary. Twenty percent, or $8,000, of the intercompany purchases rests in the parent's ending inventory. This inventory actually represents a consolidated cost of only $5,000 (20 percent of $25,000). Because the ending inventory is overstated by the $3,000 unrealized profit element, cost of goods sold is correspondingly understated.[10]

***

[10] An alternate set of eliminations preferred by some accountants would be:

| | |
|---|---:|
| Total cost of goods sold (parent and subsidiary) . . . . . . . . . . . . . . . . | $200,000 |
| Less: Parent company cost of sales purchased from | |
|     the subsidiary ($80,000 × .50 × .80) . . . . . . . . . . . . . . | (32,000) |
| Less: Subsidiary cost of goods sold not resold by | |
|     the parent ($50,000 × .50 × .20) . . . . . . . . . . . . . . . | (5,000) |
| | $163,000 |

**Minority Interest in Income.**   We have seen that, after all adjustments, the consolidated income is $32,000. However, if the subsidiary is not wholly owned, not all of the $32,000 is attributable solely to the parent company shareholders even though the consolidated statement is prepared for them. Minority shareholders in the subsidiary have an interest in some of the $32,000.

Assume the parent owns only 90 percent of the subsidiary. The *consolidated view* of the subsidiary's income excludes unrealized portions arising from intercompany transactions:

| | |
|---|---:|
| Reported subsidiary income . . . . . . . . . . . . . . . . . | $10,000 |
| Add: Rent expense from intercompany transaction . . . . . . . . | 5,000 |
| Less: Gain on intercompany sale not resold to outsiders | |
| ($40,000 − $25,000 = $15,000; $15,000 × .20) . . . . . . | (3,000) |
| Subsidiary income as viewed by consolidated entity . . . . . . . | $12,000 |

Ten percent of the $12,000 is applicable to the minority interest. The $1,200 is the minority's interest in the income of the consolidated entity, *not its interest in the income of the legally separate subsidiary.*[11]

In published financial statements, the minority's interest often is buried among the expenses, although conceptually it is a distribution of income. In theory, the $32,000 income of the consolidated entity, which includes the interests of all stockholders, best measures the overall results of operations and should be related to total assets in calculating return on investment.

## Illustration

Let us bring the preceding discussions together in a single example as well as consider the preparation of the consolidated statements *after the date of acquisition.* The parent and subsidiary may operate as related units, but they maintain separate accounting records as individual entities.

Table 15–4 shows condensed financial information for Parenco and Subsico at the end of 1991. Parenco had acquired an 80 percent interest in Subsico on *January 1, 1991.* At that time, Subsico had common stock of $150,000 and retained earnings of $30,000. Parenco therefore paid $172,000 for $144,000 book value of Subsico ($150,000 + $30,000 = $180,000; $180,000 × .80 = $144,000). Of the excess cost over book value paid by Parenco, $15,000 is attributable to undervalued plant assets of Subsico, which have a remaining useful life of 15 years. The remaining $13,000 rep-

---

[11] Many authorities would only adjust for the $3,000 intercompany profit and calculate the minority interest in income as $700 [10% × ($10,000 − $3,000)]. The applications of slightly different theories of minority interest usually have no material impact on the consolidated income statement.

---

**TABLE 15–4**   Data for Consolidation Example after Date of Acquisition

### Balance Sheet

|  | December 31, 1991 | |
| --- | --- | --- |
|  | *Parenco* | *Subsico* |
| Current assets . . . . . . . . . . . . . . . . | $ 70,000 | $ 50,000 |
| Investment in Subsico, at cost . . . . . . . . | 172,000 | |
| Other tangible assets, net . . . . . . . . . . | 417,000 | 174,000 |
| Total assets . . . . . . . . . . . . . . . . . | $659,000 | $224,000 |
| Liabilities . . . . . . . . . . . . . . . . . | $130,000 | $ 29,500 |
| Common stock . . . . . . . . . . . . . . . . | 350,000 | 150,000 |
| Retained earnings . . . . . . . . . . . . . . | 179,000 | 44,500 |
| Total equities . . . . . . . . . . . . . . . . | $659,000 | $224,000 |

### Income Statement

|  | For the Year 1991 | |
| --- | --- | --- |
|  | *Parenco* | *Subsico* |
| Sales . . . . . . . . . . . . . . . . . . . . | $550,000 | $195,000 |
| Dividend revenue from subsidiary. . . . . . . . | 10,000 | — |
| Gain on sale of land . . . . . . . . . . . . . | — | 3,000 |
| Total . . . . . . . . . . . . . . . . | 560,000 | 198,000 |
| Cost of goods sold . . . . . . . . . . . . . . | 307,500 | 127,500 |
| Other expenses . . . . . . . . . . . . . . . | 201,500 | 43,500 |
| Total . . . . . . . . . . . . . . . . | 509,000 | 171,000 |
| Net income . . . . . . . . . . . . . . . . . | 51,000 | 27,000 |
| Dividends . . . . . . . . . . . . . . . . . | (25,000) | (12,500) |
| Increase in retained earnings . . . . . . . . . | $ 26,000 | $ 14,500 |

---

resents limited-life intangible assets. Management authorizes the amortization of these costs over a period of 10 years on the consolidated statements.

During 1991, Parenco sold products costing $20,000 to Subsico for $30,000. Half of these were resold during 1991 by Subsico to its customers; the rest is in Subsico's inventory as of December 31, 1991. Subsico still owes Parenco $6,000 in connection with these purchases. Also, Subsico sold some of its vacant land, which was on its books at $5,000, to Parenco for $8,000 cash.

Tables 15–5 and 15–6 present a set of consolidated statements. Following each statement is a line-by-line description of how each consolidated item was derived. We have used what might be called a "direct approach." Each item is calculated by asking the questions, "What would the amount be from

**TABLE 15–5**  Consolidated Balance Sheet for Parenco and Subsidiaries as of December 31, 1991

### Assets

| | |
|---|---:|
| Current assets (a) . . . . . . . . . . . . . . . . . . . . . . . . . | $109,000 |
| Other tangible assets (b) . . . . . . . . . . . . . . . . . . . | 602,000 |
| Excess cost over value of tangible assets (c) . . . . . . . . . . . | 11,700 |
| | $722,700 |

### Equities

| | |
|---|---:|
| Liabilities (d) . . . . . . . . . . . . . . . . . . . . . . . . . . | $153,500 |
| Minority interest (e) . . . . . . . . . . . . . . . . . . . . . . . | 38,300 |
| Common stock (f) . . . . . . . . . . . . . . . . . . . . . . . . . | 350,000 |
| Retained earnings (g) . . . . . . . . . . . . . . . . . . . . . . . | 180,900 |
| | $722,700 |

**TABLE 15–6**  Consolidated Income Statement for Parenco and Subsidiaries for the Year Ended December 31, 1991

| | | |
|---|---:|---:|
| Sales (h) . . . . . . . . . . . . . . . . . . . . . . | | $715,000 |
| Cost of goods sold (i) . . . . . . . . . . . . . . . . | | 410,000 |
| Gross margin . . . . . . . . . . . . . . . . . . . . . . | | $305,000 |
| Other expenses (j) . . . . . . . . . . . . . . . . . | $246,000 | |
| Amortization of excess cost (k) . . . . . . . . . . . | 1,300 | |
| Minority interest in income (l) . . . . . . . . . . . | 4,800 | 252,100 |
| Net income (m) . . . . . . . . . . . . . . . . . . . . | | $ 52,900 |
| Dividends (n) . . . . . . . . . . . . . . . . . . . . . | | 25,000 |
| Increase in retained earnings . . . . . . . . . . . . | | $ 27,900 |

the perspective of the relationship between the family of corporations and outside parties?" and "What items would not appear if this were a single company?"[12]

---

[12] In practice, accountants use consolidated worksheets to prepare the statements. "Elimination entries" are recorded in the accountant's working papers. Beginning readers often pay excessive attention to the entries (even trying to memorize them) and lose sight of the underlying concepts and purpose of consolidation. The direct approach focuses on the amounts that appear on the consolidated statements rather than on the procedures and process of consolidation. The Appendix to this chapter illustrates the use of consolidated worksheets to prepare the same consolidated statements for those who are interested.

(a) Two adjustments need to be made in the current assets. First, accounts receivable is overstated from a consolidated perspective because Parenco's receivables include $6,000 owed by Subsico. This is not a claim on an outside party. Second, Subsico's inventories are overstated by $5,000, the amount of the unrealized intercompany profit on the unsold goods. The inventories are recorded at $15,000, the cost to Subsico. However, these goods cost Parenco only $10,000. If this were a single company, the inventory would remain at $10,000 until sold to an outside customer. Accordingly, consolidated current assets are $109,000 ($70,000 + $50,000 − $6,000 intercompany receivable − $5,000 intercompany profit included in inventories).

(b) The Land account on Parenco's books is overstated by $3,000. The cost of the land to the consolidated entity was only $5,000. When it was transferred from Subsico to Parenco, it was revalued upward to $8,000. However, if this were a single company, no revaluation would have occurred. On the other hand, Parenco did make an additional payment of $15,000 *to outside parties* for Subsico's plant assets. At the date of acquisition, Subsico's plant assets were undervalued by $15,000. This additional cost is recognized in consolidation because of the explicit payment made by Parenco at the date of acquisition. Furthermore, because one year has passed since acquisition, the additional plant asset cost would be reduced by one year's depreciation charge. Therefore, other tangible assets on the consolidated balance sheet are $602,000 ($417,000 + $174,000 − $3,000 intercompany profit included in land + $15,000 excess cost attributable to plant assets − $1,000 accumulated depreciation on the excess plant cost).

(c) The Investment in Subsico account disappears because it represents a double counting of Subsico's net assets. It is not an interest in an outside company. However, to the extent that the $172,000 paid at acquisition exceeds Subsico's net assets, additional asset values must be recognized in consolidation. In (b) we recognize $15,000 as additional plant assets. The remaining $13,000 is recognized as an intangible asset called "Excess Cost over Value of Tangible Assets." This initial amount must be amortized over 10 years. On December 31, 1991, $11,700 would appear as a consolidated asset as calculated below:

| | |
|---|---:|
| Original investment cost | $172,000 |
| Less: Book value of assets purchased ($180,000 × .8) | 144,000 |
| Excess investment cost | $ 28,000 |
| Less: Amount applicable to plant assets | 15,000 |
| Amount attributable to intangible assets | $ 13,000 |
| Less: One year's amortization | 1,300 |
| Unamortized excess investment asset | $ 11,700 |

(d) For the same reason given in (a), the $6,000 intercompany payable must be eliminated from Subsico's liabilities to obtain consolidated liabilities of $153,500 ($130,000 + $29,500 − $6,000).

**(e)** Minority interest on the consolidated balance sheet represents the minority shareholders' equity in the subsidiary, *adjusted for any changes caused by the elimination of intercompany gains*. Stockholders' equity of Subsico is $194,500. However, this includes a $3,000 gain on sale of land. The adjusted stockholders' equity, therefore, is $191,500; the minority interest is 20 percent or $38,300.

**(f)** The only common stock that represents a relationship with outside parties is the common stock of Parenco.

**(g)** The consolidated retained earnings consist of Parenco's retained earnings, adjusted for any unrealized intercompany profit, plus Parenco's interest in the subsidiary's retained earnings *since acquisition*. Retained earnings of Subsico on the date of acquisition are eliminated to avoid double counting. Retained earnings, since acquisition, are not reflected in the parent's accounts and, consequently, should appear on the consolidated position statement—adjusted, of course, for any unrealized intercompany gains and divided between majority (parent company) and minority interests:

| | |
|---|---|
| $ 14,500 | Subsico's retained earnings since acquisition ($44,500 at December 31 − $30,000 at acquisition) |
| − 3,000 | Unrealized intercompany profit on sale of land |
| $ 11,500 | |
| × .8 | |
| $ 9,200 | Parenco's interest in retained earnings of Subsico since acquisition |
| 179,000 | Parenco's retained earnings |
| − 5,000 | Unrealized intercompany profit on sale of inventory |
| − 1,000 | Depreciation of additional plant cost |
| − 1,300 | Amortization of excess cost |
| $180,900 | Consolidated retained earnings |

**(h)** Consolidated sales would include only sales made to customers outside the family. It would eliminate the $30,000 intercompany sale ($550,000 + $195,000 − $30,000). Of course, neither the Dividend Revenue nor the Gain on Sale of Land would appear on the consolidated income statement, for these amounts would not exist if this were a single company.

**(i)** Consolidated cost of goods sold can be derived in two ways. First, simply total the *cost* of the merchandise that ended up in the hands of outside customers:

| | |
|---|---|
| Cost of goods sold to outsiders by Parenco ($307,500 − $20,000 cost of sales to Subsico) . . . . . . . . | $287,500 |
| Cost of goods sold to outsiders and purchased from outsiders by Subsico ($127,500 − $15,000 cost of goods sold that were purchased from Parenco) . . . . . . . . | 112,500 |
| Cost of goods sold by Parenco to Subsico and then to outsiders . . . . . . . . . . . . . . . . . . . . . . | 10,000 |
| | $410,000 |

Alternatively, we could use the inventory formula. If this were a single company, the combined purchases would be overstated by $30,000, the amount of the intercompany purchase, and ending inventory would be overstated by $5,000 (the intercompany profit included in inventory). Overstated purchases and overstated ending inventory would result in cost of goods sold being overstated by $25,000. Therefore, consolidated cost of sales is $410,000 ($307,500 + $127,500 − $25,000).

(j) Other expenses would need to be increased by $1,000 depreciation on the additional plant cost recognized in consolidation ($201,500 + $43,500 + $1,000).

(k) The excess cost attributed to intangibles was calculated as $13,000 in (c). Ten percent amortization would be $1,300.

(l) In (e) Subsico's adjusted income was $24,000 ($27,000 less a $3,000 unrealized gain on sale of land). The minority shareholders have an equity claim to 20 percent of this or $4,800. We have treated this deduction as a miscellaneous expense as do many companies in practice.

(m) Net income from the perspective of Parenco's shareholders consists of Parenco's adjusted income of $33,700 ($51,000 − $10,000 divided revenue − $5,000 unrealized intercompany profit on sale of inventory − $1,000 additional depreciation − $1,300 amortization) plus $19,200, which is an 80 percent interest in Subsico's adjusted income [.8 × ($27,000 − $3,000)].

(n) Only the dividends of Parenco paid to its shareholders appear as consolidated dividends. Subsico's dividends were eliminated to the extent that they were paid to Parenco or reduced the minority interest on the balance sheet to the extent that they were paid to the minority shareholders.

## Basic Considerations

Remember the two overriding objectives of consolidated statements. First, they are designed to provide the *parent company stockholders* with a picture of their investment in the parent and, through the parent, their investment in the subsidiary.

Second, the consolidated statements attempt to report on the two companies *as if they were a single entity*. In fact, when we think about the consolidated balance sheet, we realize that it differs little from that which would result if the companies had formally merged under the purchase approach. The assets of the subsidiary (acquired company) are restated to their fair market values in the consolidation process, and any excess purchase price (excess of the investment account over the value of the identifiable assets) is recorded as an intangible asset. Consolidated retained earnings include the retained earnings of the parent (acquiring company) and the parent's share of the subsidiary's retained earnings *since acquisition*—just as in the situation of a formal merger. The only difference is the recognition of minority interest when ownership is less than 100 percent.

# DISCUSSION OF THE KIMBERLY-CLARK ANNUAL REPORT

An aspect of the Kimberly-Clark financial statements we notice almost immediately is that they are consolidated. The first accounting policy described by Kimberly-Clark in Note 1 is its consolidation policy.

The economic entity that is Kimberly-Clark operates by means of a parent company and a number of legally separate subsidiary companies. However, they function as if they were a single company. On page 38 (not reproduced in the Appendix to Chapter 6), Kimberly-Clark lists 29 consolidated subsidiaries. Most of them are owned 100 percent by the parent company, but almost a third have some minority shareholders. We would know this because of the existence of $82.6 million of "Minority Owners' Interests in Subsidiaries" that appears on the consolidated balance sheet and $13.7 million representing "Minority Owners' Interests in Subsidiaries Net Income" on the income statement.

Kimberly-Clark employs the equity method for eight affiliates in foreign countries. The parent company has a noncontrolling but significant interest (between 30 percent and 50 percent) in these companies. Note 11 provides detailed financial information about these equity companies by geographic region. Notice that Kimberly-Clark's share of the equity companies' net income shown in Note 11 ($35.3 million in 1987, $37.0 in 1986, and $31.7 in 1985) agrees with the income item reported on the consolidated statement of income. In its Operating/Financial Review, management provides an explanation of the decline from 1986 to 1987.

The asset account, "Investments in Equity Companies," on the balance sheet increased only $21.0 million ($264.8 − $243.8) during 1987. The $35.3 million of income under the equity method would have caused an initial increase of that amount in the Investment account. Our first supposition might be that Kimberly-Clark received approximately $14.3 million in cash dividends ($35.3 − $21.0) from the equity companies. Of course, this is only a guess because we know nothing about additional investments in or sales of stock in the equity companies.

Interestingly, Kimberly-Clark reports a separate income subtotal on its statement of $303.6 million before adding income from equity companies or deducting minority interest in subsidiary income.

Kimberly-Clark makes no mention of mergers or acquisitions of other companies in the notes to the financial statements. In fact, a comparison of the subsidiaries in 1987 to those in 1986 reveals no change. Accordingly, applications of either purchase or pooling of interests approaches are not relevant. We know from the schedule of changes in stockholders' equity in Note 8 that no common shares were issued in connection with any acquisitions.

# SUMMARY

We talk about three aspects of intercorporate relationships in this chapter. They all concern the accounting problems encountered when one firm acquires a substantial holding of the common stock of another company. If the investor has a noncontrolling interest, how and when can the equity method be employed to account for the intercorporate relationship? If the acquired company is to be dissolved and merged, then is the acquisition a purchase or pooling of interests? Finally, if the subsidiary remains a separate legal entity, how should the consolidated statements be prepared?

The general conclusions reached are shown below:

| Condition | Accounting Treatment |
|---|---|
| 1. A acquires an active minority interest (between 20 and 50 percent) in the stock of B. | 1. Investment recorded under the equity method. |
| 2. A acquires a passive minority interest (less than 20 percent) in the stock of B. | 2. Investment recorded under the cost method (or lower of cost or market, if the shares are marketable). |
| 3. A acquires a majority interest (between 50 and 100 percent) in the stock of B. B is retained as a separate legal entity but A controls its operations. | 3. Subsidiary included as part of a consolidated statement. |
| 4. A and B are two independent companies that merge via an exchange of common stock for the purpose of mutually sharing risks and benefits. | 4. Merger recorded as a pooling of interests. |
| 5. A acquires the stock of B through issuance of its own securities, cash payments, or a combination of the two. B is dissolved and becomes an operating division of A. | 5. Merger recorded as a purchase. |

We discuss and illustrate procedures for each of these treatments. The equity method records increases and decreases in the investment account to correspond with changes in the underlying net assets of the investee. Income to the investor is recognized in the periods when it is earned by the investee.

Under pooling of interests, assets and equities are combined at book values. With a purchase, assets—including any intangible assets implicit in the transaction—are recorded at their fair market values.

The procedures for consolidation are founded on one underlying objective—to present the situation as if the companies were a single company. They therefore entail the elimination of intercompany relationships and transactions.

To keep the discussion manageable, we deal with these treatments independently. They may, however, exist together. For example, a company may use the equity method for handling its investment account for a subsidiary and yet still consolidate the subsidiary. Such a practice would not change the underlying concepts of consolidated statements. Similarly, we imply that purchase versus pooling is an issue concerning only legally merged subsidiaries. This is not always the case. Sometimes a firm will record the acquisition of another company as a pooling of interests but not actually liquidate it. Instead, the statements will show it as a consolidated subsidiary. The valuation of assets and the entries to stockholders' equity are the same, however, as with a merger; and the consolidated effect is the same as a pooling with a legally merged subsidiary.

These problems and complexities all involve the *entity concept*. The direct consequences of the entity concept are clear—we treat the entity as separate and distinct from groups associated with it. However, we must still resolve the antecedent problems of defining what the accounting entity should be, deciding when it starts and ceases, and identifying the relevant entity in given situations.

# Appendix: Worksheet Method for Preparation of Consolidated Statements

The example of Parenco and Subsico discussed earlier was a simple one. Therefore, we prepared the consolidated statements in as straightforward a manner as possible. In this way we could illustrate the basic concepts and results of consolidation.

A company with many subsidiaries, some of which were acquired years ago, or with numerous intercompany transactions that influence many years could not efficiently consolidate using our procedure. Instead, accountants employ two related techniques—consolidated journal entries and consolidated working papers (worksheets).

## Consolidated Journal Entries

For analytical purposes, the eliminations necessary for consolidation can be presented in the form of journal entries. Accountants commonly cast eliminations in a form similar to adjusting entries to take advantage of the self-balancing debit-credit framework. By assuring themselves that all eliminations have equal debits and credits, accountants are less likely to omit an adjustment or elimination.

Three examples taken from the Parenco-Subsico example are given below:

1. To eliminate the investment account and the internally held portion of the subsidiary's stockholders' equity at the date of acquisition and to recognize the excess amount paid over book value:

| | | |
|---|---:|---:|
| Common Stock—Subsico | 120,000 | |
| Retained Earnings—Subsico | 24,000 | |
| Excess Cost over Book Value | 28,000 | |
|     Investment in Subsico | | 172,000 |

2. To eliminate intercompany receivables and payables:

Accounts Payable—Subsico . . . . . . . . . . . . . .   6,000
  Accounts Receivable—Parenco . . . . . . . . . . .       6,000

3. To eliminate intercompany gain on sale of land and to restore land to its consolidated cost:

Gain on Sale of Land—Subsico . . . . . . . . . . . .   3,000
  Land—Parenco . . . . . . . . . . . . . . . . . .       3,000

The complete set of elimination entries is given later in this Appendix.

It is important to recognize that these "elimination entries" are not recorded in any company's formal accounting records. Each corporation keeps its own set of books as a separate entity. The accountant prepares the elimination entries only as a way of organizing the data to be used in preparing the consolidated statements. They appear only in the accountant's working papers.

## Consolidated Worksheets

To facilitate the organizing and adjusting of the individual company accounts that lead to preparing consolidated statements, accountants use a columnar device called a "worksheet." Its sole purpose is to help arrange the data used in preparing the statements. The worksheet serves as the accountant's scratch paper (although much neater, better organized, and more formal).

Worksheets are of many forms and types, depending on the complexity of the consolidation and on the personal preferences of the individual accountant. One common approach uses separate worksheets for the balance sheet and for the income statement. A more modern format uses a single-tiered worksheet to adjust all financial statements simultaneously. We will employ the latter version.

Table 15A–1 presents the consolidated worksheet for Parenco and Subsico. Study the form of the worksheet. Moving from top to bottom, we find a section of the worksheet devoted to each of three statements—the income statement, the statement of retained earnings, and the balance sheet. The totals on the line labeled "net income" are carried down to the net income line in the statement of retained earnings. Similarly, the totals on the line for the ending balance of retained earnings are carried down to the balance sheet. Moving from left to right, beyond the column for accounting names, we find columns for each company to be consolidated. Then a set of debit and credit columns appear for the eliminations. The consolidated journal entries appear here. Each part of an entry has been keyed to the other parts and to an appropriate explanation. Finally, adding horizontally gives the figures for the consolidated statements.

## Explanation of Eliminations

(a) To eliminate intercompany investment and 80 percent of the common stock and retained earnings of Subsico at the date of acquisition and to recognize $28,000 excess of investment cost over book value of stockholders' equity acquired.

**TABLE 15A–1**   Consolidated Worksheet

| | Parenco | Subsico | Eliminations Dr. | Eliminations Cr. | Consolidated |
|---|---|---|---|---|---|
| **Income Statement:** | | | | | |
| Sales | 550,000 | 195,000 | (*f*)  30,000 | | 715,000 |
| Dividend revenue | 10,000 | | (*c*)  10,000 | | — |
| Gain on sale of land | | 3,000 | (*d*)  3,000 | | — |
| Cost of goods sold | (307,500) | (127,500) | (*g*)  5,000 | (*f*)  30,000 | (410,000) |
| Other expenses | (201,500) | (43,500) | (*h*)  1,000 | | (246,000) |
| Amortization of excess | | | (*i*)  1,300 | | (1,300) |
| Minority interest | | | | | |
| in income | | | (*k*)  4,800 | | (4,800) |
| Net income | 51,000 | 27,000 | 55,100 | 30,000 | 52,900 |
| **Statement of Retained Earnings:** | | | | | |
| Balance, Jan. 1, 1991: | | | | | |
| Parenco | 153,000 | | | | 153,000 |
| Subsico | | 30,000 | (*a*) ⎰24,000 | | — |
| | | | (*j*) ⎱ 6,000 | | |
| Net income — per above | 51,000 | 27,000 | 55,100 | 30,000 | 52,900 |
| Dividends | (25,000) | (12,500) | | (*c*)  12,500 | (25,000) |
| Balance, Dec. 31, | | | | | |
| 1991 | 179,000 | 44,500 | 85,100 | 42,500 | 180,900 |
| **Balance Sheet:** | | | | | |
| Current assets | 70,000 | 50,000 | | (*e*) ⎰6,000⎱ | 109,000 |
| | | | | (*g*) ⎱5,000⎰ | |
| Investment in Subsico | 172,000 | | | (*a*) 172,000 | — |
| Other tangible assets | 417,000 | 174,000 | (*b*)  15,000 | (*d*) ⎰3,000⎱ | 602,000 |
| | | | | (*h*) ⎱1,000⎰ | |
| Unamortized excess | | | | | |
| cost | | | (*a*)  28,000 | (*b*) 15,000⎱ | 11,700 |
| | | | | (*i*)  1,300⎰ | |
| | 659,000 | 224,000 | | | 722,700 |
| Liabilities | 130,000 | 29,500 | (*e*)  6,000 | | 153,500 |
| Common stock | | | | | |
| Parenco | 350,000 | | | | 350,000 |
| Subsico | | 150,000 | (*a*) ⎰120,000 | | — |
| | | | (*j*) ⎱ 30,000 | | |
| Retained earnings — | | | | | |
| per above | 179,000 | 44,500 | 85,100 | 42,500 | 180,900 |
| Minority interest | | | (*c*)  2,500 | (*j*)  36,000⎱ | 38,300 |
| | | | | (*k*)  4,800⎰ | |
| | 659,000 | 224,000 | 286,600 | 286,600 | 722,700 |

(*b*) To reclassify $15,000 of excess investment cost attributable to undervalued plant assets.

(*c*) To eliminate intercompany dividend revenue and dividends declared and to reclassify subsidiary dividends paid to minority stockholders as a reduction in minority interest.

(*d*) To eliminate the intercompany gain on sale of land and to restate land to its consolidated cost.

(*e*) To eliminate intercompany accounts receivable and accounts payable.

(*f*) To eliminate intercompany sales and purchases of merchandise. The $30,000 intercompany transfer overstates Parenco's sales and also was included in Subsico's purchases and thus increased its cost of goods sold.

(*g*) To eliminate *unrealized* intercompany profit of $5,000 on intercompany transfer of inventory that has not been resold to outsiders. The $5,000 causes Subsico's ending inventory to be overstated which, in turn, causes its cost of goods sold to be understated from a consolidated viewpoint.

(*h*) To record depreciation of $1,000 ($15,000/15 years) on additional plant recognized in consolidation.

(*i*) To record amortization for current year of $1,300 ($13,000/10 years) on excess of cost over value of tangible assets recognized in consolidation.

(*j*) To reclassify as minority interest 20 percent of the stockholders' equity of Subsico (common stock and retained earnings) at the date of acquisition.

(*k*) To segregate part of the 1991 income as being applicable to the minority interest. The $4,800 is the minority's interest in the income of the consolidated entity [20% × ($27,000 − $3,000)], not its interest in the income of the legally separate subsidiary.

# PROBLEMS AND CASETTES

### 15–1. Consolidated Balance Sheet at Date of Acquisition

Condensed balance sheets of Deluxe Company and Standard Company as of January 1, 1990, are shown below:

|  | Deluxe | Standard |
|---|---|---|
| **Assets** | | |
| Cash . . . . . . . . . . . . . . . . . . . . . . . . . . . . . . . . . . | $ 360,000 | $ 72,000 |
| Other assets . . . . . . . . . . . . . . . . . . . . . . . . . . . | 900,000 | 168,000 |
| Total assets. . . . . . . . . . . . . . . . . . . . . . . . . . . . | $1,260,000 | $240,000 |
| **Equities** | | |
| Liabilities . . . . . . . . . . . . . . . . . . . . . . . . . . . . . . | $ 300,000 | $ 24,000 |
| Capital stock . . . . . . . . . . . . . . . . . . . . . . . . . . . | 600,000 | 160,000 |
| Retained earnings . . . . . . . . . . . . . . . . . . . . . . . | 360,000 | 56,000 |
| Total equities . . . . . . . . . . . . . . . . . . . . . . . . . . | $1,260,000 | $240,000 |

**Required:**

Assume that Deluxe acquires a controlling interest in Standard under the conditions outlined below. Prepare a consolidated balance sheet for Deluxe and subsidiary as of January 1, 1990 for each alternative situation. Treat each situation independently.

a. Deluxe acquires all the capital stock of Standard for a cash payment of $240,000 made to Standard's stockholders.
b. Deluxe acquires 80 percent of the capital stock of Standard for a cash payment of $200,000.
c. Deluxe acquires 90 percent of the capital stock of Standard for a cash payment of $180,000.

## 15–2. Application of Criteria for Purchase or Pooling

Pratt Corporation has decided to acquire a controlling interest in McKinney Company at a time when the latter's balance sheet appears as follows:

**Assets**

| | |
|---|---:|
| Cash | $ 210,000 |
| Accounts receivable | 132,000 |
| Inventory | 467,000 |
| Equipment (net) | 574,000 |
| | $1,383,000 |

**Equities**

| | |
|---|---:|
| Accounts payable | $ 160,000 |
| Common stock | 500,000 |
| Retained earnings | 723,000 |
| | $1,383,000 |

McKinney's inventory and equipment have current market values of $500,000 and $700,000, respectively.

Pratt has total assets of $5,000,000, total liabilities of $2,000,000, and stockholders' equity of $3,000,000. The latter consists of $1,000,000 of $10 par value common stock, $700,000 additional paid-in capital, and $1,300,000 of retained earnings.

**Required:**

For each of the alternative scenarios below, indicate whether the acquisition would be treated as a purchase or as a pooling of interests. Also for each situation, indicate the amount that would be reported on a combined balance sheet as total assets.

a. Pratt pays $500,000 in cash and issues $1,000,000 in long-term notes to acquire all of the outstanding stock of McKinney.
b. Pratt issues 40,000 shares of its $10 par value common stock in exchange for all of the outstanding stock of McKinney. The Pratt shares have a market value of $1,500,000.

c. Pratt issues 36,000 shares of its $10 par value common stock in exchange for 90 percent of the outstanding stock of McKinney. The Pratt shares have a market value of $1,350,000. The remaining stockholders in McKinney receive cash payments from Pratt totaling $150,000.

d. Pratt issues 32,000 shares of its $10 par value common stock in exchange for 80 percent of the outstanding stock of McKinney. The Pratt shares have a market value of $1,200,000. The remaining stockholders in McKinney receive cash payments totaling $300,000.

## 15–3. Cost and Equity Methods

At the beginning of 1990, Williams Company acquired 30,000 shares of Rohn Corporation for a cash payment of $150,000. Rohn Corporation has 100,000 shares outstanding with a book value of $5 per share. Around the same time, Williams also purchased at book value 4,000 shares of Laswahl Corporation for $40,000. Laswahl has 40,000 shares of stock outstanding.

During 1990 and 1991, the two investees report the following information.

|  | Rohn | Laswahl |
|---|---|---|
| Net income—1990. | $200,000 | $100,000 |
| Dividends—1990 | 80,000 | 60,000 |
| Net income—1991. | (60,000) | (16,000) |
| Dividends—1991 | 40,000 | 12,000 |

### Required:

a. What method of accounting should Williams use for each of these investments?

b. What amount of income (revenue) will Williams show on each of these investments in 1990 and 1991?

c. How will the long-term investment in each company be reported on Williams's balance sheet as of December 31, *1991*?

## 15–4. Consolidated Balance Sheet at Date of Acquisition

On January 1, 1991, Sand Company acquired 90 percent of the common stock of Water Company. Immediately after acquisition, the balance sheet accounts of the two companies were as follows:

|  | Sand | Water |
|---|---|---|
| **Assets** |  |  |
| Cash | $ 130,000 | $ 20,000 |
| Accounts receivable | 120,000 | 130,000 |
| Inventory | 350,000 | 100,000 |
| Plant (net) | 650,000 | 200,000 |
| Investment in Water, at cost | 395,000 | — |
| Other assets | 15,000 | 40,000 |
|  | $1,660,000 | $490,000 |

| | Sand | Water |
|---|---|---|
| **Equities** | | |
| Accounts payable . . . . . . . . . . . . . . . . . . . . | $ 150,000 | $ 50,000 |
| Bonds payable . . . . . . . . . . . . . . . . . . . . | 190,000 | 40,000 |
| Common stock . . . . . . . . . . . . . . . . . . . | 300,000 | 100,000 |
| Additional paid-in capital . . . . . . . . . . . . . . | 250,000 | 180,000 |
| Retained earnings . . . . . . . . . . . . . . . . . | 770,000 | 120,000 |
| | $1,660,000 | $490,000 |

The accounts receivable of Water Company includes $5,000 owed by Sand Company. Also, the other assets of Sand Company includes $10,000 of Water Company bonds which Sand is holding as an investment. Assume that any excess cost is attributable to unrecognized intangible assets of Water Company.

**Required:**

a. Prepare a consolidated balance sheet in good form as of January 1, 1991.
b. Assume that Water's plant assets were understated by $20,000. How would this change your answer to part a?

**15–5. Journal Entries under Cost and Equity Methods**

On January 1, 1991, Bach Corporation purchased 20,000 of the 100,000 shares outstanding of Haydn Company. The shares were purchased at $18 per share, which was equal to the book value of Haydn's stock. During 1991, Haydn reported a net income of $250,000 and paid dividends of $100,000. In 1992, Haydn's income was $300,000, and dividends were $150,000.

**Required:**

a. Assume that Bach's 20 percent interest was *not* sufficient to allow it to exercise a significant influence over Haydn. Prepare the journal entries for 1991 and 1992 relevant to the investment.
b. Assume that Bach was able to exercise significant influence over Haydn's operating and financial policies. Prepare the journal entries for 1991 and 1992 relevant to the investment.
c. How would the Investment account in Haydn stock appear on the balance sheet of Bach as of December 31, 1991 in part a? In part b?

**15–6. Financial Statement Items under Purchase or Pooling**

On July 1, 1990, Mississippi River Corporation exchanged 20,000 of its $5 par common stock for all of the outstanding stock (30,000 shares, par value, $10) of Missouri Barge, Inc. At that time, Mississippi stock was selling at a market price of $40 per share. Missouri Barge's stock was not widely traded. After the exchange of shares, Missouri was formally merged into Mississippi and became an operating division.

Balance sheets drawn up for the two corporations *before* the merger showed the following:

| | Mississippi | Missouri |
|---|---|---|
| **Assets** | | |
| Total assets. . . . . . . . . . . . . . . . . . | $2,600,000 | $680,000 |
| **Equities** | | |
| Liabilities . . . . . . . . . . . . . . . . . . | $ 600,000 | $100,000 |
| Common stock—par . . . . . . . . . . . . . . | 400,000 | 300,000 |
| Common stock—excess over par . . . . . . . . . . | 600,000 | 150,000 |
| Retained earnings . . . . . . . . . . . . . . | 1,000,000 | 130,000 |
| Total equities . . . . . . . . . . . . . . . . | $2,600,000 | $680,000 |

Earnings for the two companies separately for 1990 were:

| | Mississippi | Missouri |
|---|---|---|
| January 1–June 30. . . . . . . . . . . . . . . . | $ 200,000 | $ 30,000 |
| July 1–December 31 . . . . . . . . . . . . . . . | 140,000 | 50,000 |
| | $ 340,000 | $ 80,000 |

The market value of Missouri's noncurrent assets is $120,000 above book value. These noncurrent assets have a remaining life of 6 years as of the date of the merger. Any goodwill recognized should be amortized over 10 years.

**Required:**

*a.* Fill in the blanks in the following table. Show calculations where necessary.

| | If Acquisition Were Recorded as— | |
|---|---|---|
| | Purchase | Pooling of Interests |
| Total assets, June 30 . . . . . . . . . . . . . . . . . . | | |
| Goodwill, June 30 . . . . . . . . . . . . . . . . | | |
| Retained earnings, June 30 . . . . . . . . . . . . . . . | | |
| Common stock—par, June 30 . . . . . . . . . . . . . | | |
| Common stock—excess over par, June 30 . . . . . . . . . | | |
| Net income for 1990 . . . . . . . . . . . . . . . . | | |
| Goodwill, December 31 . . . . . . . . . . . . . . | | |
| Retained earnings, December 31 . . . . . . . . . . . . | | |

*b.* Which method do you think would have to be followed in the merger of Missouri Barge into Mississippi River Corporation? Explain why.

## 15–7. Consolidated Balance Sheet One Year after Acquisition

The following represent the ledger account balances of Able Company and its subsidiary, the Baker Company, as of December 31, 1989 (in thousands of dollars):

|  | Able | Baker |
|---|---|---|
| Cash . . . . . . . . . . . . . . . . . | $ 160 | $ 24 |
| Accounts receivable . . . . . . . . . . . | 132 | 72 |
| Inventories . . . . . . . . . . . . . . | 160 | 200 |
| Investment in Baker stock . . . . . . . . . | 420 | — |
| Land . . . . . . . . . . . . . . . . | 180 | 88 |
| Plant . . . . . . . . . . . . . . . . | 600 | 240 |
| Accumulated depreciation . . . . . . . . . | (260) | (52) |
|  | $1,392 | $572 |
| | | |
| Accounts payable . . . . . . . . . . . . | $ 328 | $ 96 |
| Capital stock . . . . . . . . . . . . . | 700 | 320 |
| Retained earnings . . . . . . . . . . . . | 364 | 156 |
|  | $1,392 | $572 |

Able Company acquired 85 percent of the stock of the Baker Company on January 1, 1989 for $420,000 cash. The owners' equity accounts of Baker on that date were: capital stock, $320,000; retained earnings, $80,000.

During the year, Able Company sold merchandise costing $24,000 to the Baker Company for $36,000. The merchandise was still in the latter's inventory on December 31, 1989. Baker Company still owed Able Company $16,000 in connection with this purchase.

### Required:

a. Prepare a consolidated position statement in good form for the two companies. Assume any excess cost is attributable to intangible assets with a useful life of 10 years.

b. If Able Company had used the equity method of accounting for its investment in Baker, what entries would have been made on Able's books during 1989? How would the consolidation process and the consolidated balance sheet differ?

## 15–8. Elimination of Intercompany Purchases and Sales

Red Company owns all of the stock of Gold Company and prepares consolidated statements. The following information was taken from the income statements of the separate companies.

|  | Red | Gold |
|---|---|---|
| Sales . . . . . . . . . . . . . . . . | $320,000 | $466,000 |
| Cost of goods sold . . . . . . . . . . | 190,000 | 330,000 |

During the year, Red Company sold goods to Gold Company at a price of $100,000. The cost of those goods was $60,000.

**Required:**

  a. Assume that Gold Company resold to outside customers for $120,000 all of the goods purchased from Red Company. Compute the amount to be reported as consolidated sales and consolidated cost of goods sold.

  b. Assume that Gold Company resold to outsiders for $60,000 half of the goods purchased from Red Company. The other half are in the ending inventory of Gold Company at the end of the year. Compute the amount to be reported as consolidated sales and consolidated cost of goods sold. What adjustment would have to be made to report consolidated inventory on the balance sheet?

  c. How would your answers to *a* and *b* change if Red only owned 80 percent of the stock of Gold Company? Explain.

**15–9. Calculation of Consolidated Income, Minority Interest, and Retained Earnings**
Blue Company acquired an 80 percent stock ownership in Orange Company on January 1, 1990. The amount paid in cash by Blue was $200,000. Any excess cost is attributable to intangible assets with a useful life of 10 years.

  During 1990, Orange Company had net income of $45,000 and paid $30,000 in dividends. Blue Company, as a separate company, reported $105,000 as net income including dividend revenue of $24,000 representing the amount it received from Orange. Blue paid $60,000 in dividends during the year.

  The stockholders' equity sections of the balance sheets of each of the companies separately are shown below at the beginning and end of the year:

|  | *Blue Company* | | *Orange Company* | |
| --- | --- | --- | --- | --- |
|  | *Jan. 1, 1990* | *Dec. 31, 1990* | *Jan. 1, 1990* | *Dec. 31, 1990* |
| Common stock | $100,000 | $100,000 | $ 90,000 | $ 90,000 |
| Additional paid-in capital | 140,000 | 140,000 | 35,000 | 35,000 |
| Retained earnings | 660,000 | 705,000 | 95,000 | 110,000 |
|  | $900,000 | $945,000 | $220,000 | $235,000 |

There were no other transactions between the two companies during the year.

**Required:**

  a. Calculate the consolidated net income for 1990 (after deducting the minority interest in income).

  b. Calculate the amount at which minority interest would appear on the consolidated balance sheet as of December 31, 1990.

  c. Prepare the consolidated stockholders' equity section of the balance sheet as of December 31, 1990.

**15–10. Consolidated Balance Sheet after Acquisition**
Presented on the next page are the condensed balance sheets of Mammoth Corporation and its two subsidiaries, Little and Tiny, as of December 31, 1992:

| | Mammoth | Tiny | Little |
|---|---|---|---|
| **Assets** | | | |
| Current assets. . . . . . . . . . . . . | $300,000 | $120,000 | $ 60,000 |
| Investment in Tiny, at cost . . . . . . . . | 50,000 | | |
| Investment in Little, at cost . . . . . . . . | 19,000 | | |
| Other assets . . . . . . . . . . . . . | 431,000 | 80,000 | 40,000 |
| | $800,000 | $200,000 | $100,000 |
| **Equities** | | | |
| Current liabilities . . . . . . . . . . . . | $200,000 | $152,000 | $ 80,000 |
| Common stock, no par . . . . . . . . . . . | 400,000 | 40,000 | 15,000 |
| Retained earnings . . . . . . . . . . . | 200,000 | 8,000 | 5,000 |
| | $800,000 | $200,000 | $100,000 |

Mammoth owns 100 percent of the capital stock of Tiny. The stock of Tiny was acquired on January 1, 1991, when its retained earnings were $5,000.

Mammoth owns 90 percent of the capital stock of Little. The stock of Little was acquired on January 1, 1991, when its retained earnings were $3,000.

Any excess cost over book value is attributable to intangible assets, to be amortized over 20 years.

During 1992, Tiny Company sells land costing $20,000 to the Mammoth Corporation for $21,000. Also, on December 31, 1992, Tiny owes Little $10,000 in connection with a cash advance made earlier in the year.

### Required:

Prepare a consolidated position statement in good form as of December 31, 1992.

### 15–11. Equity Method with Excess Cost

On January 1, 1990, the Kirkwood Corporation acquired 30 percent of the outstanding stock of Parkway, a newly organized corporation, for a cost of $900,000.

On January 1, 1992, Kirkwood invested another $400,000 for an additional 10 percent of Parkway. The following table gives the results of Parkway's operations in the years 1990 through 1992:

| | Net Income Reported | Dividends Paid |
|---|---|---|
| 1990 . . . . . | $180,000 | $150,000 |
| 1991 . . . . . | 360,000 | 270,000 |
| 1992 . . . . . | 330,000 | 240,000 |

### Required:

a. Prepare journal entries to record the original investment and subsequent events, assuming that the equity method of accounting for unconsolidated subsidiaries is used. Assume that any excess book value is to be amortized over 20 years.
b. How much income would Kirkwood have recognized each year if the cost method of recording investments in other companies had been employed?

*c.* On December 31, 1991, Kirkwood describes its Investment account as being recorded at the underlying book value or equity in the subsidiary's assets. Show that this is true. Is the same description appropriate on December 31, 1992? Explain.

**15–12.** **Financial Statements under Purchase and Pooling of Interests**

At the end of 1989, Alpha Corporation began negotiations to acquire the net assets and business of Beta Corporation. Condensed balance sheets of the two companies as of December 31, 1989, contain the following accounts:

|  | *Alpha* | *Beta* |
|---|---|---|
| **Assets** | | |
| Cash. . . . . . . . . . . . . . | $ 180,000 | $ 70,000 |
| Inventory—at FIFO cost. . . . . . . | 330,000 | 150,000 |
| Buildings and equipment . . . . . . | 720,000 | 450,000 |
| Total assets . . . . . . . . . . . | $1,230,000 | $670,000 |
| **Equities** | | |
| Current liabilities. . . . . . . . . | $ 200,000 | $145,000 |
| Common stock—$10 par . . . . . . | 300,000 | — |
| Common stock—$1 par . . . . . . . | — | 100,000 |
| Paid-in capital . . . . . . . . . . | 500,000 | 200,000 |
| Retained earnings . . . . . . . . | 230,000 | 225,000 |
| Total equities . . . . . . . . . . | $1,230,000 | $670,000 |

Alpha is interested in how the proposed merger would affect its financial statements. Alpha is planning to offer—as of January 1, 1990—12,000 of its previously unissued stock to the stockholders of Beta in exchange for the 100,000 shares of Beta stock outstanding. The market price of Alpha Company shares is $55 per share. Management of Alpha Company attributes any value implicit in the offer in excess of the book values of Beta's net assets to the following assets: (1) inventory understated by $25,000; (2) additional value of equipment, $80,000; and (3) any remainder to goodwill.

Income statement data for the year 1989 for each of the companies appear below:

|  | *Alpha* | *Beta* |
|---|---|---|
| Sales. . . . . . . . . . . . . . | $1,350,000 | $720,000 |
| Expenses: | | |
| Cost of goods sold . . . . . . . . | 730,000 | 380,000 |
| Depreciation . . . . . . . . . . | 72,000 | 35,000 |
| Selling and general . . . . . . . . | 420,000 | 250,000 |
| Income taxes . . . . . . . . . . | 51,000 | 22,000 |
| Total expenses . . . . . . . . . | 1,273,000 | 687,000 |
| Net income . . . . . . . . . . . | $ 77,000 | $ 33,000 |

Management expects that revenues and expenses for both companies in 1990 will be the same as in 1989 except as affected by the accounting for the merger. If recognized, the additional value of the equipment would be depreciated over a remaining life of 10 years. Goodwill, if recorded, would be amortized over 20 years.

**Required:**

a. Prepare a balance sheet as of January 1, 1990, on the assumption that the acquisition is treated (1) as a purchase and (2) as a pooling of interests.
b. Prepare a projected income statement for 1990 using the data from 1989 and the assumption that the acquisition is treated (1) as a purchase and (2) as a pooling of interests.
c. Which procedure for recording the merger would have to be followed? How would your answer differ if Alpha were to offer only 8,000 of its shares plus $220,000 cash for the shares of Beta? How would your answer differ if Alpha were to sell its 12,000 shares for $660,000 ($55 a share) and then pay cash for the Beta shares?

**15–13. Consolidated Income Statement**

The Big Company owned 80 percent of the stock of the Little Company. During the year, Little Company—the subsidiary—sold $240,000 of goods to the parent. These goods had cost Little Company $180,000. The year-end inventories of the Big Company still included 20 percent of the goods it purchased during the year from Little Company. On December 31, Big sold some surplus equipment to Little for $40,000. The equipment had a book value of $30,000 to Big.

Income statements, in summary form, for the two companies are given below (in thousands of dollars):

|  | *Big* | *Little* |
|---|---|---|
| Sales | $900 | $400 |
| Gains and other revenues | 54 | 18 |
|  | 954 | 418 |
| Cost of goods sold | 640 | 280 |
| Other expenses | 191 | 58 |
|  | 831 | 338 |
| Net income | $123 | $ 80 |

**Required:**

Prepare a consolidated income statement in good form.

### 15–14. Consolidated Income Statement and Balance Sheet

Indicated below are the financial statements of Shanghai Corporation and its subsidiary, Wuhan Company, as of December 31, 1991 (in thousands of dollars).

|  | Shanghai | Wuhan |
|---|---|---|
| **Income Statement** | | |
| Sales . . . . . . . . . . . . . . . . . . . . . . . . . . . . . . . | $ 850 | $ 940 |
| Interest revenue . . . . . . . . . . . . . . . . . . . . . . . . . | 8 | 7 |
| Dividend revenue . . . . . . . . . . . . . . . . . . . . . . . . | 24 | — |
| Gain on sale of land . . . . . . . . . . . . . . . . . . . . . . | 4 | — |
| Cost of sales . . . . . . . . . . . . . . . . . . . . . . . . . . | (530) | (732) |
| Operating expenses . . . . . . . . . . . . . . . . . . . . . . | (240) | (155) |
| Interest expense . . . . . . . . . . . . . . . . . . . . . . . . . | (6) | (5) |
| Net income . . . . . . . . . . . . . . . . . . . . . . . . . . . . | $ 110 | $ 55 |
| Dividends . . . . . . . . . . . . . . . . . . . . . . . . . . . . . | 50 | 30 |
| Earnings retained in business . . . . . . . . . . . . . . . . | $ 60 | $ 25 |
| **Balance Sheet** | | |
| Cash . . . . . . . . . . . . . . . . . . . . . . . . . . . . . . . . | $ 75 | $ 78 |
| Accounts receivable . . . . . . . . . . . . . . . . . . . . . . | 227 | 221 |
| Interest receivable . . . . . . . . . . . . . . . . . . . . . . . | 4 | 3 |
| Inventory . . . . . . . . . . . . . . . . . . . . . . . . . . . . . | 180 | 48 |
| Investment in Wuhan, at cost . . . . . . . . . . . . . . . . | 240 | — |
| Land . . . . . . . . . . . . . . . . . . . . . . . . . . . . . . . . | 204 | 50 |
| Buildings and equipment, net . . . . . . . . . . . . . . . . | 700 | 120 |
|  | $1,630 | $ 520 |
| Accounts payable . . . . . . . . . . . . . . . . . . . . . . . . | $ 236 | $ 239 |
| Interest payable . . . . . . . . . . . . . . . . . . . . . . . . . | 2 | 1 |
| Common stock . . . . . . . . . . . . . . . . . . . . . . . . . . | 560 | 180 |
| Retained earnings . . . . . . . . . . . . . . . . . . . . . . . . | 832 | 100 |
|  | $1,630 | $ 520 |

### Additional Information:

1. Shanghai owns 80 percent of the common stock of Wuhan. It acquired its interest on January 1, 1991. Any excess cost paid by Shanghai is attributable as follows: $6,000 to land, which was recorded on Wuhan's books at less than its value on January 1, 1991, and the remainder to goodwill with a useful life of 20 years. (Remember, Wuhan's stockholders' equity was not $280,000 at the date of acquisition.)
2. During 1991, Wuhan Company made sales of $400,000 to Shanghai. This merchandise cost Wuhan $300,000. On December 31, 1991, Shanghai has 25 percent of this merchandise in its ending inventory.
3. On December 31, 1991, Shanghai still owes Wuhan $40,000 in connection with the merchandise purchase in item 2.
4. Shanghai makes temporary loans to Wuhan as needed during the year. No loans themselves are outstanding at year-end. However, as a result of activity during the year, Wuhan accrued $1,000 as interest expense, which is yet unpaid. Shanghai similarly accrued interest revenue.

5. During 1991, Shanghai transferred some land to Wuhan. The selling price was $16,000 cash. The land originally had cost Shanghai $12,000.
6. The Dividend Revenue recorded by Shanghai represents 80 percent of the dividends paid by Wuhan.

**Required:**

a. Prepare a consolidated income statement for 1991 and a consolidated balance sheet as of December 31, 1991 for Shanghai Corporation and its subsidiary.
b. What future consolidation problems would arise if Shanghai had sold depreciable assets to Wuhan instead of land in item 5 above?

**15–15. Equity Method with Excess Cost**

On January 1, 1990, the Sumner Corporation purchased for $250,000 cash 30 percent of the common stock of Winterthur Company. On this date, Winterthur's balance sheet showed total assets of $880,000; liabilities of $210,000; common stock of $350,000; and retained earnings of $320,000. Any difference between the purchase price and the book value acquired is attributable to assets having a remaining life of 20 years.

During 1990, Winterthur reported income of $120,000 and paid dividends of $64,000.

On January 1, 1991, Sumner Corporation sold half of its stock holdings in Winterthur for $140,000.

**Required:**

a. Prepare journal entries on the books of Sumner to record the purchase of the Winterthur shares, the recognition of investment income under the equity method, and the receipt of dividends from Winterthur.
b. Prepare the journal entry to record the sale of half of the Winterthur shares.
c. In what section of the income statement—revenues, other operating income, other income, and so on—would you report the account, Equity in Earnings of Investee? Why?
d. How should Sumner record transactions after January 1, 1991 relating to its investment in Winterthur?

**15–16. Merger through Acquisition or Creation of a New Corporation**

Halen Corporation and Hardy Company have been considering the possibility of a merger of their businesses. As of May 1, 1991, the condensed balance sheets of the two firms were as follows (in thousands):

| Assets | Halen | Hardy |
|---|---|---|
| Total assets . . . . . . . . . . | $1,607.4 | $402.4 |

| Equities | Halen | Hardy |
|---|---|---|
| Liabilities . . . . . . . . . . . | $  165.8 | $112.4 |
| Common stock, $1 par . . . . . | 200.0 | 100.0 |
| Excess over par . . . . . . . . | 780.0 | 54.0 |
| Retained earnings. . . . . . . . | 461.6 | 136.0 |
| Total equities . . . . . . . . . | $1,607.4 | $402.4 |

The market price of Halen Corporation common stock is very close to $9 a share; Hardy Company common stock is traded at $4.50 per share. An appraisal of the specifically identifiable assets of each company indicates their fair market values to be $1,750,000 for Halen and $500,000 for Hardy.

Two plans are under consideration. One calls for Halen Corporation to acquire the 100,000 outstanding shares of Hardy Company. Halen would pay $50,000 in cash, issue 400 shares of a new $100 par preferred stock carrying a market dividend rate of 12 percent, and issue 40,000 shares of its own common stock. Hardy Company would be liquidated as a separate legal entity and formally merged into Halen Corporation. The other plan calls for a new company called "Halenhardy Corporation" to be chartered. Its authorized capital would consist of 100,000 shares of $5 par value common stock. The new corporation would issue its shares to the stockholders of the two existing corporations in exchange for their stock. The exchange ratios would be 1 new share for each 5 shares of Halen and 1 new share for each 10 shares of Hardy. The two existing companies would be dissolved and their assets and liabilities transferred to the new corporation.

### Required:

*a.* Under the first plan, which method would have to be used to record the merger? Prepare a combined position statement for Halen Corporation under this plan.

*b.* Under the second plan, which method would have to be used to record the merger? Prepare a combined position statement for Halenhardy Corporation under this plan.

### Casette 15–1.  Georgia-Pacific Corporation

In the Appendix at the end of the book is a complete set of financial statements of Georgia-Pacific Corporation taken from its annual report of 1987. Answer the following questions related to those statements.

1. Does Georgia-Pacific prepare consolidated statements? How do you know?
2. Can you determine if the consolidated subsidiaries are wholly owned or only partially owned?
3. During the last three years, did Georgia-Pacific enter into any significant acquisitions/mergers that were recorded as a pooling of interests? As a purchase? How do you know?
4. Can you determine if Georgia-Pacific employs the equity method in accounting for any investments? What would you look for?

### Casette 15–2.  Consolidation Policy and Treatment of Investments

The consolidation policy of two companies are given below. Each statement has been taken from notes to the firm's financial statements for the year indicated.

#### Borg-Warner (12/31/85)

The consolidated financial statements include all subsidiaries except those in Mexico and South America, which are carried at cost due to political and economic uncertainty, the Air Conditioning operations and the Financial Services companies. Borg-Warner intends to distribute the shares of its Air Conditioning subsidiary to shareholders and therefore has reported it as a discontinued operation. Investments in the Financial Services companies are carried at equity in underlying net assets. Investments in affiliated companies, at least 20 percent owned by Borg-Warner, and in the Hughes Tool Company are carried at cost plus equity in undistributed earnings which generally approximates equity in underlying net assets.

### Chicago Pneumatic Tool (12/31/86)

Consolidated Financial Statements include the accounts of all majority-owned domestic and foreign subsidiaries except the Company's domestic finance subsidiary which is carried at the Company's equity in its net assets, in accordance with industry practice. Investments in affiliates and the domestic finance subsidiary are accounted for by the equity method. All significant intercompany transactions and balances have been eliminated from the consolidated statements.

FASB *Statement No. 94*, "Consolidation of All Majority-Owned Subsidiaries," is effective beginning in the 1988 calendar year. It will cause major changes in the consolidation policy of many companies.

### Required:

*a*. Borg-Warner in 1985 excluded from consolidation three groups of subsidiaries— those in Mexico and South America, the Air Conditioning operations, and the Financial Services companies. Evaluate Borg-Warner's rationale in each of these situations. In 1988 which, if any, of these groups of subsidiaries would the company be able to exclude?

*b*. Borg-Warner used the equity method for its Financial Services companies and for other investments. Should that method also be used for the subsidiaries in Mexico and South America?

*c*. Both Borg-Warner and Chicago Pneumatic Tool exclude their finance subsidiaries from consolidation. What would be their justification? Would these justifications be valid under *Statement No. 94*?

*d*. Borg-Warner states that its investments in affiliated companies "are carried at *cost plus equity in undistributed earnings* which generally approximates *equity in underlying net assets.*" Chicago Pneumatic Tool uses the phrase, "equity in net assets." How and why do these bases of reporting differ?

## Casette 15–3. Real-World Mergers and Acquisitions

The following descriptions of mergers and acquisitions are taken from the annual reports of three actual companies.

### Black and Decker (9/30/84)

On April 27, 1984, the Corporation acquired substantially all of the assets and businesses of General Electric Company's Housewares operations in exchange for cash, promissory notes, and shares of the Corporation's common stock for a total value of approximately $212,000. The acquisition was accounted for as a purchase transaction; and the assets acquired, liabilities assumed, and results of the Housewares operations from the date of acquisition are included in the accompanying financial statements.

The fair value assigned to assets acquired and liabilities assumed, excluding cash and marketable securities of $7,698, was as follows:

| | |
|---|---:|
| Accounts receivable . . . . . . . . | $ 8,048 |
| Inventories . . . . . . . . . . . . | 99,463 |
| Property, plant, and equipment . . . | 119,361 |
| Goodwill . . . . . . . . . . . | 91,303 |
| Other assets . . . . . . . . . . | 52,160 |
| Current liabilities . . . . . . . . | (116,358) |
| Other long-term liabilities . . . . . . | (49,597) |
| | $204,380 |

Goodwill represented the excess of total acquisition cost over the fair value of net assets acquired.

Other assets consisted primarily of patents and trademarks. Included in current liabilities and other long-term liabilities were amounts representing brand transition, redundancy, relocation and plant closing costs incident to the acquisition.

During fiscal 1985, the promissory notes and goodwill were reduced to adjust the purchase price pursuant to certain provisions of the purchase agreement, which guaranteed a minimum level of earnings for the year ended December 31, 1984 of one of the acquired foreign subsidiaries. The notes were further adjusted during 1985 for certain termination costs borne by the Corporation but chargeable to General Electric Company, as provided in the purchase agreement. The notes will be further adjusted for similar charges through April 1986.

Pro forma results of operations, assuming the acquisition occurred at the beginning of each period presented, are displayed in the following table. These pro forma results have been prepared for comparative purposes only and do not purport to be indicative of the results of operations which actually would have resulted had the combination been in effect on the dates indicated, or which may result in the future.

| | 1984 | 1983 |
|---|---:|---:|
| Net Sales . . . . . . . . . . . . . . . . . . . . . . | $1,780,234 | $1,634,044 |
| Earnings from Continuing Operations . . . . . . . . | 87,153 | 30,558 |
| Net Earnings . . . . . . . . . . . . . . . . . . . | 87,153 | 46,558 |
| Earnings per Share: | | |
|   Continuing Operations . . . . . . . . . . . . . | $ 1.72 | $ .66 |
|   Discontinued Operations . . . . . . . . . . . . | — | .35 |
|     Total . . . . . . . . . . . . . . . . . . . | $ 1.72 | $ 1.01 |
| Average Shares Outstanding . . . . . . . . . . . . | 50,700 | 46,200 |

### CMI Corporation (12/31/85)

On October 1, 1985, the Company acquired all of the outstanding capital stock of RayGo, Inc. and its wholly-owned subsidiary, R.G.B.A. Albaret Industries S.A. (RayGo), for $7,500,000. RayGo builds a broad line of soil and road compaction equipment.

The RayGo shareholders received from the Company 468,000 shares of common stock with a fair market value of $3,534,000; 4,800 shares of 7% Series B Preferred Stock with a fair market value of $3,766,000; and a $200,000 note due December 31, 1985. The preferred stock is more fully described in Note 6 of the notes to consolidated financial statements, "Redeemable Preferred Stock."

RayGo's assets, liabilities and results of operations since October 1, 1985, are included in the accompanying consolidated financial statements. The acquisition has been accounted for as a purchase and the purchase price has been assigned to the net assets acquired based on the fair value of such assets and liabilities at date of acquisition. The excess of cost over the net tangible assets acquired of $2,581,000 is included in deferred charges and other assets in the accompanying balance sheet and is being amortized over 25 years on a straight-line basis.

### Rubbermaid, Incorporated (12/31/85)

In December 1985, 2,266,449 Common Shares were issued in exchange for all the outstanding Common Shares of Gott Corporation, a manufacturer of insulated chests, beverage coolers and other molded plastic products.

The acquisition has been accounted for as a pooling of interests, and accordingly the accompanying financial information has been restated to include the accounts of Gott Corporation for all periods presented. Gott Corporation financial information included in the accompanying consolidated financial statements has been converted from a fiscal year ending September 30 to the Company's calendar year basis of reporting.

Net sales and net earnings of the separate companies for the periods preceding the acquisition were:

|  | *Eleven Months ended November 30, 1985* | *Years Ended December 31,* 1984 | 1983 |
|---|---|---|---|
| Net sales: |  |  |  |
| Rubbermaid | $570,337 | $566,429 | $479,584 |
| Gott | 55,996 | 42,706 | 32,124 |
| Combined | $626,333 | $609,135 | $511,708 |
| Net earnings: |  |  |  |
| Rubbermaid | $ 50,466 | $ 46,870 | $ 39,575 |
| Gott | 3,358 | 2,558 | 2,222 |
| Combined | $ 53,824 | $ 49,428 | $ 41,797 |

## Required:

a. Put in journal form the summary entries made by Black and Decker and CMI to record their acquisitions. The Black and Decker numbers are in thousands. Use an account called "Net Tangible Assets" in the CMI entry.

b. Black and Decker refer to adjustments made in 1985 and possible adjustments to be made in 1986. Why are they made and are they appropriate? Would they be present in a pooling of interests?

c. Rubbermaid's stock was selling at $33 per share on December 31, 1985. What was the approximate fair market value of Gott Company's net assets at the date of acquisition? Was this amount recorded in Rubbermaid's accounts?

d. Why are the operations acquired by Black and Decker included since the date of acquisition, while those acquired by Rubbermaid are included for 1983, 1984, and 1985? Explain Black and Decker's comment on the usefulness of the pro forma disclosures. Do you agree?

*e.* Why do Black and Decker and CMI have substantial increases in intangible assets such as goodwill, deferred charges, and cost in excess . . . when Rubbermaid does not?

### Casette 15–4.  Some Problem Areas with Investments

The creation of a meaningful method for recording investments in other companies has not been an easy matter in financial accounting. The following examples taken from actual company situations illustrate some of the problems.

#### Amerada Hess Corporation

The noncurrent section of its balance sheet lists an investment called The Louisiana Land and Exploration Company—at cost. Data relevant to that account for 1986, 1985, and 1984 follow:

|  | 1986 | 1985 | 1984 |
|---|---|---|---|
| Cost of investment at year-end | — | $    223,000 | $    506,000 |
| Market value of investment at year-end | — | 3,640,000 | 19,244,000 |
| Cost of investment sold each year | $   223,000 | 283,000 | 100,000 |
| Gain on sale | 3,407,000 | 10,113,000 | 42,469,000 |

#### Borg-Warner

Since 1974, Borg-Warner has owned shares of common stock of Hughes Tool Company. Excerpts from its 1985 annual report describe its holdings:

In 1980 Borg-Warner began recording its interest in earnings of Hughes Tool Company. The equity basis of accounting was adopted after exchanges of operating units to Hughes Tool dating back to 1974 increased the company's common stock ownership to 20.4 percent.

As of December 31, 1985 increases in total shares outstanding have reduced Borg-Warner's ownership percentage to 18.6 percent. The company has continued to account for its investments in Hughes Tool on an equity basis since the underlying relationship between the two companies has not changed.

The Hughes investment is accounted for at cost, adjusted for Borg-Warner's equity in undistributed earnings and dividends. The carrying value was $133.4 million at December 31, 1985. The equity in undistributed earnings of Hughes Tool exceeds the carrying value of the investment by $13.4 million as of December 31, 1985. The original excess is being credited to earnings on a straight-line basis over a remaining period of seven years.

Then in its 1986 annual report, Borg-Warner stated:

Borg-Warner's 18 percent investment in Hughes Tool Company is accounted for on the cost method as a long-term marketable security. Prior to 1986, this investment had been accounted for using the equity method. The change was made because the company felt it no longer could exercise significant influence over the affiliate's operations. . . . Accordingly, its carrying value of $91 million at December 31, 1986, based on quoted market prices, is net of an unrealized loss of $39.2 million that is recorded as a valuation reserve in shareholders' equity.

**Deluxe Check Printer Incorporated**

The following information contained in the 1985 annual report relates to the company's investment in Data Card:

|  | 1985 | 1984 |
|---|---|---|
| Investment in Data Card on balance sheet . . . . . . | $32,417,000 | $20,468,000 |
| Interest in outstanding stock . . . . . . . . . . . . | 41.58% | 42.41% |
| Equity in earnings of Data Card from income statement . . . . . . . . . . . . . . . | $ 4,226,000 | $ 2,925,000 |
| Dividends received . . . . . . . . . . . . . . . | 809,000 | 639,000 |
| Market value of common stock held . . . . . . . . | 74,988,000 | 43,922,000 |

**Greyhound**

In 1983, Greyhound sold the assets of one of its subsidiaries to ConAgra. Part of the consideration received was 5,100,000 shares of ConAgra common stock. In its 1985 annual report, Greyhound made the following statement:

In addition, the investment in ConAgra, Inc. (15% owned) is included in the accounts on the equity method. Greyhound's membership both on the Board of Directors of ConAgra and its substantial voting rights provide the ability to significantly influence the operating and financial affairs of ConAgra.

**Required:**

a. Does the great discrepancy between the cost and market value of the investment in Louisiana Land and Exploration Company cause a material distortion in the financial statements of Amerada Hess? Are its stockholders being deceived? Would the equity method solve this reporting problem?

b. Evaluate Borg-Warner's reporting of its investment in Hughes Tool. Is it appropriate to change methods from year to year? What is meant in 1985 by the references to "adjusted for equity in undistributed earnings" and "excess of equity in undistributed earnings over carrying value of the investment . . . being credited to earnings"? What entry was made on December 31, 1986 regarding Hughes Tool?

c. What entries did Deluxe Check Printers make in 1985 regarding its investment in Data Card? How could its interest decline during 1985 when the investment account increased?

d. Evaluate the appropriateness of the equity method for use by Greyhound in accounting for ConAgra.

**Casette 15–5. Maytag Company Pooling with Magic Chef, Inc.**

The following note was taken from the 1986 annual report of the Maytag Company:

On May 31, 1986, the Company issued 16,072,000 shares of its Common stock for all of the outstanding Common stock of Magic Chef, Inc., a manufacturer of home appliances and soft drink vending equipment. This merger has been accounted for as a pooling of interests and, accordingly, the consolidated financial statements have been restated for all periods prior to the acquisition to include the accounts and operations of Magic Chef. Magic

Chef was on a June fiscal year. The restated financial statements for the years ended December 31, 1986 and 1985 include both companies on a calendar year basis. . . . Separate sales, net income and dividends of Maytag and Magic Chef prior to the restatement are as follows (in thousands):

|  | Five Months Ended May 31, 1986 (Unaudited) | Year Ended December 31 1985 |
|---|---|---|
| Net Sales: |  |  |
| Maytag . . . . . . . . . . . . . . . . . . . . | $292,918 | $ 683,721 |
| Magic Chef . . . . . . . . . . . . . . . . . . | 398,677 | 975,084 |
| Combined . . . . . . . . . . . . . . . . . . . | $691,595 | $1,658,805 |
| Net Income: |  |  |
| Maytag . . . . . . . . . . . . . . . . . . . . | $ 30,677 | $ 71,840 |
| Magic Chef . . . . . . . . . . . . . . . . . . | 12,169 | 53,052 |
| Combined . . . . . . . . . . . . . . . . . . . | $ 42,846 | $ 124,892 |
| Cash Dividends: |  |  |
| Maytag . . . . . . . . . . . . . . . . . . . . | $ 26,418 | $ 44,788 |
| Magic Chef . . . . . . . . . . . . . . . . . . | 2,688 | 9,924 |
| Combined . . . . . . . . . . . . . . . . . . . | $ 29,106 | $ 54,712 |

The announcement of the merger was made in April 1986 and called for each share of Magic Chef common stock to be converted into 1.671 shares of Maytag common stock. On April 1, the market price of a Magic Chef common share was about $73. The market price of a Maytag common share was approximately $45 on April 1 and was $45.875 on May 30 when the merger was consummated.

The following schedule of stockholders' equity accounts of Maytag have been prepared from information in the 1985 and 1986 annual reports (in millions):

|  | As Originally Reported on December 31, 1985 | As Restated for the Merger as of December 31, 1985 |
|---|---|---|
| Common stock—$1.25 par value . . . . . | $ 36.0 | $ 56.0 |
| Additional paid-in capital . . . . . . . . | 21.6 | 95.7 |
| Retained earnings . . . . . . . . . . . | 227.7 | 436.8 |
| Treasury stock . . . . . . . . . . . . | (28.7) | (28.7) |
|  | $256.6 | $559.8 |

**Required:**

a. How do you think the boards of directors of the two companies arrived at the 1.671 exchange ratio of shares?

b. Approximately how many shares of Magic Chef stock were outstanding as of the date of the merger?

c. Assume the answer to part *b* is 9,618,000 shares. Each of those shares had a par value of $3.00 a share. Estimate the amount of additional paid-in capital and retained earnings recorded on the books of *Magic Chef as of December 31, 1985.*

d. Estimate the *book value* of the *net* assets (assets less liabilities) of Magic Chef acquired by Maytag on May 30, 1986. (Be sure to include the impact of the five months of operations between December 31, 1985 and May 30, 1986.

e. Estimate the *fair market value* of the *net* assets of Magic Chef acquired by Maytag on May 30, 1986 using the market value of the Maytag shares. How much asset value implicit in the exchange of shares was suppressed by Maytag's use of pooling of interests?

f. The financial statements have been restated to include the accounts of the pooled companies for 1986 and 1985 (actually for 1984 also). Explain why this is done consistent with the theory underlying pooling of interests.

## 15A–1. Analyzing a Worksheet for Consolidated Statements

The accountant for Rotten Lumber Company has prepared the consolidated worksheet for Rotten Lumber and its subsidiary, Warped Wood, Inc., as of December 31, 1993. It is shown below without any explanations. Amounts are in thousands of dollars. Rotten Lumber purchased a controlling interest in Warped Wood on January 1, 1993.

| | Rotten Lumber | Warped Wood | Eliminations Dr. | Eliminations Cr. | Consolidated |
|---|---|---|---|---|---|
| **Income Statement:** | | | | | |
| Sales . . . . . . . . . . . | 179.0 | 96.0 | (f) 30.2 | | 244.8 |
| Gain on sale of equipment . . . . | | 3.0 | (d) 3.0 | | — |
| Cost of goods sold . . . . . . . | (126.0) | (68.4) | | (f) 30.2 | (164.2) |
| Other expenses . . . . . . . | (30.0) | (15.6) | | | (45.6) |
| Amortization of excess . . . . . | | | (b) .4 | | (.4) |
| Loss on bond . . . . . . . . | | | (c) 2.0 | | (2.0) |
| Minority interest . . . . . . . | | | (h) 1.2 | | (1.2) |
| Net income . . . . . . . . . . | 23.0 | 15.0 | 36.8 | 30.2 | 31.4 |
| | | | | | |
| **Statement of Retained Earnings:** | | | | | |
| Balance, Jan. 1, 1993 | | | | | |
| Rotten . . . . . . . . . . | 70.0 | | | | 70.0 |
| Warped . . . . . . . . . | | 20.0 | { (a) 18.0 | | |
| | | | { (g) 2.0 | | |
| Net income—per above . . . . . | 23.0 | 15.0 | 36.8 | 30.2 | 31.4 |
| Dividends . . . . . . . . . | (15.0) | — | | | (15.0) |
| Balance, Dec. 31, 1993 . . . . . | 78.0 | 35.0 | 56.8 | 30.2 | 86.4 |

| | Rotten Lumber | Warped Wood | Eliminations Dr. | Eliminations Cr. | Consolidated |
|---|---|---|---|---|---|
| **Balance Sheet:** | | | | | |
| Current assets . . . . . . . . . | 57.0 | 45.0 | | | 102.0 |
| Investment in bonds . . . . . . | 8.0 | — | | (c)   8.0 | — |
| Investment in subsidiary (cost) . . | 85.0 | — | | (a) 85.0 | — |
| Loans to subsidiary. . . . . . . | 10.0 | — | | (e) 10.0 | — |
| Land . . . . . . . . . . . . | 23.0 | 13.0 | | | 36.0 |
| Plant and equipment . . . . . . | 250.0 | 150.0 | (d) 16.0 | (d) 10.0 | 406.0 |
| Accumulated depreciation . . . . | (113.0) | (45.0) | | (d)   9.0 | (167.0) |
| Excess cost over book value . . . | — | — | (a)   4.0 | (b)    .4 | 3.6 |
| | 320.0 | 163.0 | | | 380.6 |
| | | | | | |
| Current liabilities . . . . . . . | 47.0 | 36.0 | | | 83.0 |
| Bonds payable. . . . . . . . . | — | 12.0 | (c)   6.0 | | 6.0 |
| Advances from parent . . . . . | — | 10.0 | (e) 10.0 | | — |
| Capital stock—R . . . . . . . | 195.0 | — | | | 195.0 |
| Capital stock—W . . . . . . . | — | 70.0 | { (a) 63.0<br>{ (g)   7.0 | | |
| Retained earnings — per above. . . . . . . . . | 78.0 | 35.0 | 56.8 | 30.2 | 86.4 |
| Minority interest . . . . . . . . | | | | (g)   9.0 }<br>(h)   1.2 } | 10.2 |
| | 320.0 | 163.0 | 162.8 | 162.8 | 380.6 |

**Required:**

a. What percentage of Warped Wood's stock was acquired by Rotten Lumber? How do you know?

b. What period of amortization is being used for any excess cost paid by Rotten Lumber?

c. What is the amount of intercompany sales and purchases during 1993? Is any of this merchandise unsold to outside parties at year-end? How do you know?

d. Explain the nature of the intercompany transaction that caused the need for elimination (c).

e. Explain the nature of the intercompany transaction that caused the need for elimination (d).

f. How was the amount of elimination (h) determined?

**15A–2. Preparation of a Simple Consolidated Worksheet**
On January 1, 1992, First Company purchased 80 percent of the outstanding capital stock of Second Company for $178,000. At that date the stockholders' equity of Second Company consisted of Common Stock, $120,000 and Retained Earnings, $50,000. The excess purchase price over book value should be reflected as (1) an increase in inventories of $4,000 (all of which were sold to outside parties in 1992), (2) an increase in equipment of $8,000 (remaining useful life is 10 years), and (3) $30,000 as goodwill (to be amortized over 20 years).

The separate financial statements for the two companies at the end of 1992 are summarized below:

| | First Company | Second Company |
|---|---|---|
| **Income Statement (for 1992):** | | |
| Sales . . . . . . . . . . . . | $555,000 | $215,000 |
| Dividend revenue . . . . . . . . | 12,000 | — |
| Cost of goods sold. . . . . . . . | (335,000) | (123,000) |
| Selling and general expenses . . . . . . | (158,000) | (63,500) |
| Depreciation expense. . . . . . . . . | (9,000) | (3,500) |
| Net income. . . . . . . . . | $ 65,000 | $ 25,000 |
| **Statement of Retained Earnings (for 1992):** | | |
| Retained earnings, Jan. 1 . . . . . . . . . | $130,000 | $ 50,000 |
| Net income. . . . . . . . . . | 65,000 | 25,000 |
| Dividends . . . . . . . . . . . . | (25,000) | (15,000) |
| Retained earnings, Dec. 31 . . . . . . . . | $170,000 | $ 60,000 |
| **Balance Sheet (as of 12/31/92):** | | |
| Cash . . . . . . . . . . . . | $ 75,000 | $ 41,000 |
| Accounts receivable . . . . . . . . . | 88,000 | 33,000 |
| Inventories . . . . . . . . . . | 170,000 | 94,000 |
| Investment in Second Co., at cost . . . . . | 178,000 | — |
| Equipment . . . . . . . . . . | 200,000 | 70,000 |
| Other assets . . . . . . . . . . | 15,000 | 22,000 |
| | $726,000 | $260,000 |
| Accounts payable . . . . . . . . . . | $ 66,000 | $ 40,000 |
| Bonds payable . . . . . . . . . | 150,000 | 40,000 |
| Common stock . . . . . . . . . | 340,000 | 120,000 |
| Retained earnings . . . . . . . . . . | 170,000 | 60,000 |
| | $726,000 | $260,000 |

## Additional information:

1. On December 31, 1992, First Company owes $10,000 to Second Company on open account.
2. During 1992 Second Company sold merchandise costing $20,000 to First Company for $30,000. Half of this remains unsold in the inventory of First Company at the end of 1992.

## Required:

*a.* Prepare a consolidated worksheet for First and Second Companies. Identify all elimination entries by key letters.
*b.* Write a brief explanation for each elimination entry.
*c.* What is the amount of minority interest that will appear on the consolidated income statement and on the consolidated balance sheet?

# Chapter 16

# Disclosure Issues in Financial Reporting

As discussed in Chapter 2, completeness of financial statement disclosure is a subcomponent of the qualitative guideline of reliability. According to this concept, accounting reports should disclose fully and fairly the results of a business entity's transactions. In earlier chapters, we have seen repeated examples of reporting issues being intertwined with the conceptual and procedural aspects of the accounting process. Most of the authoritative guidelines for financial accounting—APB Opinions, FASB Statements, and SEC pronouncements—include disclosure recommendations or requirements. Disclosure is the final product of the accounting process.

In this chapter, we examine several important aspects of classification and presentation that are not covered elsewhere. First, we discuss the reporting of some special changes in retained earnings. A few of these were mentioned earlier, but we deferred a detailed discussion of their presentation in the financial statements until now. Second, we examine disclosure practices governing additional data designed for investors' use. Such disclosures include earnings per share, segment reporting, and interim financial statements. The third section analyzes the problems of reporting contingencies—possible losses or gains that depend partially or completely on some future event. The chapter concludes with an examination of Kimberly-Clark's reporting presentations.

## REPORTING OF SPECIAL ITEMS

The income statement is the most prominent of the financial statements, and net income probably is the single number most important to the majority of investors. Users look to the income statement and the net income figure for a measure of how the firm has performed during a period of time. A potential problem of interpretation arises, however, when during that period other events happen that cause changes in owners' equity—changes beyond those resulting from normal revenues, expenses, and dividends. Recurring but non-operating items have been covered in Chapter 6. These include interest expense, gains and losses on disposal of plant assets, and the like.

In this section, we discuss the following additional special items that cause increases and decreases in retained earnings:

1. *Extraordinary items*—material events that are characterized by *both* their unusual nature *and* their infrequent occurrence.
2. *Discontinued operations*—the discontinuance and disposal of an entire segment of a business.
3. *Prior period adjustments*—rare events and corrections of errors requiring direct adjustment to the retained earnings account and retroactive restatement of net income.
4. *Changes in accounting principles*—substitution of one current generally accepted accounting principle for another.
5. *Changes in estimates*—modification or adjustment in an accounting estimate as new information becomes available.

Note that these items have specific definitions that have evolved over time as authoritative opinions have been issued and revised. Users of accounting data should be careful not to substitute meanings taken from ordinary usage of the terms.

How these changes in retained earnings during the period are presented can have a profound effect on the income statement and net income, so accounting policy makers have spent significant time on these issues. The following subsections describe and illustrate the GAAP that have evolved to deal practically with each of these items. Inasmuch as each of these special items may have related tax effects, the proper treatment of the tax impact of these items is presented at the end of this section.

## Extraordinary Items

A comprehensive income figure would reflect all items of profit or loss recognized during the period. (The only exception would be for prior period adjustments, such as corrections of errors, defined and illustrated in a later section.) However, the results of certain transactions called "extraordinary items" are shown in a separate section of the income statement as a distinct element of net income for the period. To qualify as an extraordinary item, an event must be *both* unusual in nature and nonrecurring.[1] Consequently, usual and/or recurring events such as write-downs of receivables, invento-

---

[1] AICPA, *APB Opinion No. 30,* "Reporting the Results of Operations" (New York, June 1973), par. 20.

ries, or marketable securities would not qualify; nor would such non-operating events as the disposal of plant assets, the effect of strikes, or the impact of major currency devaluations. Events of this nature are only considered extraordinary if they are due to major casualties, government expropriations, or prohibitions under newly enacted laws.[2] Additionally, under a separate standard, a gain or loss on the retirement of a bond issue (Chapter 11) also is reported as an extraordinary item.

If an event qualifies as an extraordinary item, the income statement would highlight it as illustrated by the following excerpt from the 1987 annual report of Schlumberger Limited:

**TABLE 16–1**   Disclosure of Extraordinary Item by Schlumberger Limited (in thousands)

|  | 1987 | 1986 | 1985 |
|---|---|---|---|
| Income (loss) before extraordinary item . . . . . . . . . . | $282,560 | $(2,017,591) | $351,036 |
| Extraordinary item, less taxes and other expenses of $46 million . . . . . . . . . . . | 70,080 | — | — |
| Net income (loss) . . . . . . . . . . . . . . . . . . . | $352,640 | $(2,017,591) | $351,036 |

Extraordinary Item: In July 1987, Sedco Forex, the Company's drilling services operation, received an award from the Iran-U.S. Claims Tribunal of $116 million. This award arose from Iran's seizure of a SEDCO, Inc., drilling business in 1979 prior to its acquisition by the Company. After taxes and other expenses of $46 million, the award resulted in a net gain of $70 million.

Most non-operating, abnormal, *or* infrequent items are included in income *before* extraordinary items; only items meeting *both* of the characteristics mentioned earlier are considered to be extraordinary. Clearly, the APB intended to restrict severely the number of extraordinary items. It succeeded, as surveys have revealed that of 600 large corporations' income statements since 1981, less than 15 percent listed extraordinary items in each of the years surveyed.[3]

In one sense, the strict criteria for determining extraordinary items may have improved the quality of financial reporting by eliminating some past potential for manipulation. When firms were allowed maximum discretion in classifying their transactions, observers detected a tendency to identify losses as extraordinary and to report gains as ordinary. This treatment gave

---

[2] The environment in which the entity operates must be considered when assessing whether an item is unusual in nature and infrequent in occurrence. For example, tornado losses are more likely to be viewed as extraordinary in Maine or Oregon than they are in Kansas or Oklahoma. Similarly, losses from earthquakes would be extraordinary in Iowa but a common occurrence in southern California.

[3] AICPA, *Accounting Trends & Techniques* (New York, 1982–86.)

a most positive emphasis to operational results although final net income was not affected.

To many accountants, however, the APB may have overreacted. Items that are unusual but happen to be of a recurring nature can no longer appear as extraordinary. Although *Opinion 30* requires that such gains and losses be reported as a separate component of income *before* extraordinary items, they are more likely to be overlooked by analysts when treated this way than when categorized as extraordinary. More than ever, the analyst must examine closely the nature of income before extraordinary items to ferret out unusual but recurring items.

## Discontinued Operations

Accounting income statements present gains and losses from the recurring disposal of individual plant assets as a part of the income before extraordinary items. In many large firms, plant disposals are a necessary part of modernization and occur with regularity. Disposal of an entire segment of a business—a subsidiary, a division, or a separate major line of business—is a different matter. The accounting process recognizes the likely material impact of such an event.

The FASB requires special accounting treatment for discontinued operations, akin to that for extraordinary items. Discontinued operations must be reported in a separate section of the income statement. Its placement after income from continuing operations but before extraordinary items recognizes that such discontinuance is neither a direct measure of operations nor the result of unplanned occurrences. Rather, it is a planned management action requiring separate disclosure.

The income statement disclosure consists of two elements—the periodic income or loss from operating the segment up to the time of its discontinuance and the gain or loss on the segment's disposal. For example, the 1985 annual report of the Coca-Cola Company displayed the income statement elements and separate note appearing in Table 16–2.

Income from discontinued operations reflects the functioning of the disposed units up until the date (measurement date) that management committed itself to a formal plan of disposition. The disposed units were profitable in 1985, and the earlier years' results are presented for comparative purposes. The actual disposal transaction in 1985 resulted in a net gain of $35,733,000. This gain includes (1) the excess of the sales price over the book value of the net assets sold, (2) any estimated costs directly associated with the disposal, and (3) any further operating results after the measurement date. Note that the total gain was $55,985,000. Taxes of $20,252,000 were paid on this gain. The income statement discloses the tax amount and displays the resulting net amount.

**TABLE 16–2**   Partial Income Statement of Coca-Cola Company Reporting Discontinued Operations (in thousands)

| | *Year Ended December 31* | | |
| --- | --- | --- | --- |
| | *1985* | *1984* | *1983* |
| Income from continuing operations | | | |
| before income taxes . . . . . . . . . . . . . . . . . | $1,092,849 | $1,054,829 | $990,510 |
| Income taxes . . . . . . . . . . . . . . . . . . . | 415,283 | 433,071 | 437,566 |
| Income from continuing operations . . . . . . . . . . | 677,566 | 621,758 | 552,944 |
| Income from discontinued operations (net of applicable income taxes of $7,870 in 1985; $6,144 in 1984; and $4,920 in 1983). . . . . . . . . . | 9,000 | 7,060 | 5,843 |
| Gain on disposal of discontinued operations (net of applicable income taxes of $20,252). . . . . . . | 35,733 | — | — |
| Net income . . . . . . . . . . . . . . . . . . . . | $ 722,299 | $ 628,818 | $558,787 |

Note (in part): In December 1985, the Company sold Presto Products, Incorporated, and Winkler/Flexible Products, Inc., manufacturers of plastic products, for approximately $112 million. In November 1983, the Company sold its wine business for book value plus advances, amounting to approximately $230 million. Operating results for these companies have been reported as discontinued operations. Net revenues of discontinued operations were $235 million, $212 million and $350 million in 1985, 1984 and 1983, respectively.

As shown in Table 16–2, the gain or loss on the sale of the businesses is not considered to be an extraordinary item, although it is listed as a separate component for the interested reader. Coca-Cola's net income from the business segments sold is wisely segregated from the income figure resulting from continuing operations. The analyst desiring to use the 1985 income figure as a basis for forecasting future earnings needs the $677,566,000 number, which is not distorted by the earnings from the business units no longer owned by Coca-Cola.

## Prior Period Adjustments and Corrections of Errors

This category of unusual events is rarely encountered. Prior period adjustments are not reported on the income statement. Instead they are added to or are subtracted from the opening balance of retained earnings on the separate statement of retained earnings.

*FASB Statement No. 16* specifies that *only* the following events can be considered as prior period adjustments:[4]

1. Correction of an error in the financial statements of a prior period.

---

[4] FASB, *Statement of Financial Accounting Standards No. 16,* "Prior Period Adjustments" (Stamford, Conn., June 1977), par. 11.

2. Adjustments that result from realization of income tax benefits of preacquisition operating loss carryforwards of purchased subsidiaries.

Inasmuch as the second item is too specialized and technical for this book, we now focus exclusively on the correction of errors.

*APB Opinion No. 20,* issued in 1971, set forth the initial requirement that corrections of past errors be treated as direct adjustments to retained earnings.[5] The APB recognized that had the errors not occurred, the retained earnings balance would have been stated at a different level. At the same time, however, it wanted to preclude direct retained earnings charges for losses or other reductions that would reflect negatively on the firm and would be less obvious to the statement readers because they became buried in the retained earnings account. Accordingly, direct retained earnings charges for errors are limited to (1) oversights that resulted in failure to record transactions, (2) corrections of mathematical errors, and (3) the recording of changes from the use of an unacceptable to an acceptable accounting principle.

The concept of a subsequent correction of past error applies only to material, nonrecurring events. Also, accounting principles state that changes from one acceptable accounting principle to another acceptable principle and changes in accounting estimates resulting from new information are not considered to be corrections of errors.

The correction of errors involves an adjustment to an asset or liability and a corresponding increase or decrease in retained earnings. For example, assume that a firm fails to record depreciation of $300,000 on a new machine acquired in 1990. The error is discovered in 1991. The correcting entry in 1991 would be:

Correction of Prior Period
Unrecorded Depreciation . . . . . . . . . . . . 300,000
    Accumulated Depreciation . . . . . . . . . . . 300,000

The Correction account will be closed to Retained Earnings at the end of the period. The $300,000 would be recorded on the statement of retained earnings as a deduction from the balance at the beginning of the year. If comparative statements covering the period of the error are presented, they should be restated in the correct amounts.

## Changes in Accounting Principles

Most financial statements are prepared in accordance with generally accepted accounting principles. However, we have seen numerous examples of alternative procedures that are considered equally acceptable and instances where GAAP fails to come to grips with certain economic realities.

---

[5] AICPA, *APB Opinion No. 20,* "Accounting Changes" (New York, July 1971), par. 13.

Consequently, anyone who analyzes and compares financial statements without comprehending the accounting principles employed runs a risk of error and misinterpretation. Analysts may be unable to adjust the financial statements of a company so that the underlying accounting procedures and principles exactly correspond with those used by a second company. Nevertheless, they should at least be able to understand the general effects that alternative procedures may have on the statements.

Present standards of disclosure direct that the policies that are followed in most of the areas where alternatives exist be so indicated. *Opinion No. 22* requires that companies identify and describe their significant accounting policies as an integral part of the financial statements, preferably in a separate section preceding the notes or in the first note to the statements.[6] Examples of required disclosures include consolidation policies; depreciation methods; inventory costing methods; revenue recognition practices associated with construction, leasing, or franchising operations; procedures for recording pension plan costs; and any other practices that are unusual or will have a significant influence on interpreting the financial statements.

The reporting standard of consistency implies that the selected principles will remain the same from period to period. An obvious extension of the disclosure guidelines leads to the requirement that any *changes* in accounting principle must also be disclosed. *Opinion No. 20* contains that mandate. It goes further, however, and allows changes in accounting principles only if the new principle is preferable to the old. The firm assumes the burden not only of disclosing the change in accounting principle but also of justifying the change. Changes that fall under this requirement include changes in methods of inventory valuation (e.g., from FIFO to LIFO), those in methods of depreciation (e.g., from straight-line to sum-of-the-years'-digits), those in methods of revenue recognition (e.g., from percentage of completion to completed contract), and other similar changes. A change in principle refers to principles currently being used and does not include the adoption of a principle for new or substantially different transactions from those previously occurring.

Disclosure is not the only concern when accounting principles are changed. How should the impact of the change be reported on the financial statements? Should we record the change as we do a correction of error, that is, as a direct adjustment to the beginning balance of retained earnings with retroactive restatement of all comparative income statements? Alternatively, should we show the effect on retained earnings as a special item on the income statement similar to an extraordinary item?

In *Opinion No. 20,* the Accounting Principles Board generally opted for the second alternative. Aware of the "potential dilution of public confidence in financial statements resulting from restating financial statements of prior

---

[6] AICPA, *APB Opinion No. 22,* "Disclosure of Accounting Policies" (New York, April 1972), par. 15.

periods," the APB ruled that *most* changes should be recognized by inclusion of the cumulative effect of the change on retained earnings in the net income of the period of change.[7]

Several specific accounting changes that often are of substantial magnitude (e.g., a change *from* the LIFO method of inventory costing) must, however, be handled retroactively by restatement of the financial statements of prior periods.[8] Apparently the APB's concern was that a substantial cumulative effect, if placed on one income statement, could swamp all other statement items and distort the bottom line. Also, restatement of past financial statements sometimes is required or permitted for accounting changes mandated by official pronouncements.

For most accounting changes, the cumulative effect of the change is reported on the income statement between the captions "Extraordinary items" and "Net income." Although it is not an extraordinary item, the cumulative effect is reported in a similar manner. An example of this reporting can be seen in the partial income statements of Ingersoll-Rand Company appearing in Table 16–3.

As Table 16–3 shows, Ingersoll-Rand retroactively treated as product costs (included in inventory cost) some manufacturing costs that previously had been treated as period expenses. Inventory balances as of January 1, 1987 were increased. Expenses reported in prior years had been too high. New income tax returns for the prior years must be filed to reflect larger incomes. Therefore, income taxes payable increases. The net effect on stockholders' equity appears on the income statement. The journal entry on January 1, 1987 in summary form was:

| | | |
|---|---|---|
| Inventory | 18,759,000 | |
| Income Taxes Payable | | 9,004,000 |
| Cumulative Change in Accounting Principle | | 9,755,000 |

The Cumulative Change in Accounting Principle signifies the effect the accounting change had on net income after tax for years prior to 1987. It increased the net income and earnings per share by approximately 9 percent.

Notice that the disclosures accompanying the income statement include pro forma amounts to show what the incomes would have been had the newly adopted accounting principle been used in the preceding two years. Although past financial statements are not completely restated for this type of accounting change, the summary data on net income and earnings per share *are* restated. The pro forma information constitutes more meaningful trend data than do the three-year figures for income before the cumulative effect. The pro forma net income numbers were derived by holding the accounting

---

[7] *APB Opinion No. 20,* par. 18.

[8] Others include (1) a change in the method of accounting for long-term construction contracts and (2) a change to or from the full-cost method of accounting for natural resources.

**TABLE 16–3** Partial Comparative Income Statement of Ingersoll-Rand Company and Related Footnote, Showing Reporting of a Change in Accounting Principle (in thousands)

|  | Year Ended December 31 | | |
|---|---|---|---|
|  | *1987* | *1986* | *1985* |
| Earnings before extraordinary item and cumulative effect of accounting change . . . . . . . . . . . . . . . | $107,936 | $100,634 | $79,581 |
| Extraordinary item—(net of income tax benefit of $5,673) . . . . . . . . . . . . . . . . . . | — | (6,660) | — |
| Cumulative effect of accounting change—(net of income tax provision of $9,004) . . . . . . . . . . . | 9,755 | — | — |
| Net earnings . . . . . . . . . . . . . . . . . . | $117,691 | $ 93,974 | $79,581 |
| Earnings per share of common stock: | | | |
| Earnings before extraordinary item and cumulative effect of accounting change . . . . . . . . | $1.98 | $1.92 | $1.51 |
| Extraordinary item . . . . . . . . . . . . . . . . | — | (.13) | — |
| Cumulative effect of accounting change . . . . . . . . | .19 | — | — |
| Net earnings per share . . . . . . . . . . . . . | $2.17 | $1.79 | $1.51 |

Pro forma amounts, assuming the new method of accounting had been applied retroactively for 1987, 1986, and 1985, are $107.9 million ($1.98 per share), $100.1 million ($1.91 per share) and $78.1 million ($1.48 per share), respectively, for earnings before extraordinary item and $107.9 million ($1.98 per share), $93.4 million ($1.78 per share) and $78.1 million ($1.48 per share), respectively, for net earnings.

Note 1 (in part): Summary of Significant Accounting Policies:

*Accounting Changes:* Effective January 1, 1987, the company changed its method of accounting to include in inventory certain manufacturing overhead costs which were previously charged to operating expense. Among the more significant types of these costs are depreciation of manufacturing facilities and equipment, employee pensions and fringe benefits and certain other product-related costs. The company believes that this change is preferable because it provides a better matching of production costs with related revenues in reported operating results. The cumulative effect of this change for the years prior to January 1, 1987 amounted to a net benefit of $9,755,000. The change did not have a material effect on operating results for 1987.

methods constant and are much superior for trend analysis. For example, the $78.1 million figure for 1985 earnings *can* be meaningfully compared with 1987 income of $107.9 million, because *both* of these numbers assume that the additional manufacturing costs are treated as product costs.

## Changes in Accounting Estimates

Financial accounting is rife with estimates. Recall from the discussion in earlier chapters that estimates are used extensively to implement the matching concept. Estimates are made of useful lives and residual values for depreciable assets, uncollectible percentages for receivables, recoverable mineral reserves for assets subject to depletion, costs of future services for warranties, various actuarial factors for pensions, and many other figures. In most cases, the need for these judgments stems from the very essence of the accounting process. Therefore, changes in estimates are also a natural consequence of the accounting process. What happens if an accounting estimate is found to be wrong when new information becomes available?

In the preceding sections, we have illustrated two major ways of recording and reporting unusual items. One calls for a direct adjustment to retained earnings and a retroactive restatement of the comparative income statements, as in the case of corrections of errors. The second calls for a special charge in the current period's income statement for the cumulative effect of the item, as in the case of changes in accounting principle and extraordinary items. Which of these methods is appropriate for reporting the impact on income and retained earnings of changes in accounting estimates? In *Opinion No. 20,* the Accounting Principles Board ruled that neither approach is acceptable for changes in estimates. Rather, they must be handled *prospectively,* that is, as adjustments to the expenses or revenues of the current and/ or future periods. No correction of past periods or cumulative catch-up provision is allowed.

**Change in Depreciation Estimate.**    As an example of a change in accounting estimate, let us assume that the original life of 16 years for a large machine was being reduced to 10 years due to the recognized influence of changing technological obsolescence. The equipment cost $96,000, has an expected residual value of $4,000, and is being depreciated on a straight-line basis. Near the end of the seventh year, *before* adjusting entries are made, the firm realizes that the equipment will last only three more years. During the first six years, annual depreciation of $5,750(($96,000 − $4,000)/16) has been charged, and the balance in the Allowance for Depreciation account stands at $34,500 ($5,750 × 6). Based on the revised estimate of useful life, the annual depreciation expense should have been $9,200 ($92,000/10) and the balance at the end of Year 6 in the Allowance account should be $55,200 ($9,200 × 6) rather than the $34,500.

*Opinion No. 20* does *not* allow any retroactive adjustment for this $20,700 difference ($55,200 − $34,500). Rather, an adjustment to the current and future depreciation charges must be made to compensate for underdepreciation in the past. The adjustment uses the asset's unrecovered book value and expenses it over the remaining years of useful asset life. In the current example, this will result in an annual depreciation expense of $14,375 ($96,000 − $4,000 − $34,500 = $57,500; $57,500/4 = $14,375) in Years 7 through 10. By the end of the 10th year, the asset's $92,000 depreciation base will have been completely written off.[9]

---

[9]The only requirement for disclosure is a note in the year of change indicating the effect on income and earnings per share for a material change in estimate or for one that affects several periods.

The conceptual rationale for this requirement rests on the belief that estimation of future events is an inherent part of the process of preparing periodic financial statements. Therefore, the adjustments arising from changes in estimates constitute reaction to new events or experiences and not corrections of past mistakes. The practical justifications for the requirement are its simplicity, its required use for tax purposes, and its avoidance of any addition to the number of unusual items shown in the income statement.

As one looks back over the plethora of authoritative standards surrounding the reporting of special items, they seem highly technical and often conflicting. However, some general tendencies are evident. First, an all-inclusive approach to income statement reporting is favored for events occurring in the current period. Second, operations are not to be defined too narrowly or artificially. Third, completed periods generally are to be treated as history.

## Intraperiod Tax Allocation

In Chapter 13, we discussed deferred tax problems arising from temporary differences between financial accounting and tax code requirements. The issue there is how to determine the appropriate tax charge for an accounting period. A separate tax question is the proper *reporting* of the tax charge when special items exist in addition to operating income. As we have seen, according to the guidelines of *APB Opinions No. 20 and No. 30*, the income statement includes all special items except corrections of past errors, which are reported on a separate statement of retained earnings. On the income statement itself, extraordinary items, discontinued operations, and changes in accounting principles are segregated. However, all of these items affect the determination of the taxable income and tax charge for the period. *Intraperiod* tax allocation is the division of the total amount of income taxes for the period among sections of the income statement or between the income statement and the statement of retained earnings.

For instance, it would be quite misleading to report a favorable adjustment of prior years' income in the statement of retained earnings but to include the increased taxes that have to be paid because of the item as part of the tax expense on the income statement. If a special item is shown on a separate statement of retained earnings, then the tax charge or saving related to it should be shown there also. In effect, then, this procedure divides the tax charge for the period between the income statement and the retained earnings statement. The portion shown on the former would be the tax applicable to the income shown there. The additional tax (in the case of a favorable adjustment) or the estimated tax reduction (in the case of an unfavorable adjustment) is reported with the adjustment itself in the statement of retained earnings.

The same idea applies to items reported in separate categories of the income statement. *The tax effect modifies the special item rather than the normal income tax expense*. Examples of this type of intrastatement tax allocation can be seen in Table 16–2 for the Coca-Cola Company (income related to discontinued operations and gain on the sale of the discontinued operation) and in Table 16–3 for Ingersoll-Rand (extraordinary item and cumulative effect of a change in accounting principle). The total tax charge for the period is allocated among different parts of the income statement.

# EXPANDING THE DATA AVAILABLE TO INVESTORS

As a way of responding to the audience's needs, accountants often take steps to expand the information disclosed in order to make the financial reports more useful for decision making by investors. Often these presentations are formally incorporated in generally accepted accounting principles as required disclosures. This section describes several of the most important of these expanded presentations—earnings per share, segment reporting, and interim financial reports.

## Earnings per Share

In the financial press, the most popular measure of earning power is earnings per share (EPS). Investors hold, buy, and sell shares of stock, and earnings (income) per share relates a firm's success to their individual interests in the firm. Changes in EPS can be used to evaluate past managerial performance or to project the future growth and potential of the firm. A common comparison relates EPS to the current market price of the stock as an indicator of "inherent" value. If earnings per share are $5.00 and the market price of the stock is $44.25, we say that the *price-earnings ratio* is about 9 times ($44.25/$5.00) or that the stock market values (capitalizes) earnings at over 11 percent ($5.00/$44.25).

**Authoritative Standards.**   The importance of the earnings per share figure caused the Accounting Principles Board to issue two opinions on the subject and the FASB to issue one statement.[10] As a result, GAAP now explicitly requires that earnings per share be reported on the income statement. For simple capital structures, the calculation of EPS is straightforward. It is computed by dividing the net income available to common shareholders (net income minus preferred dividends) by the average number of common shares outstanding during the period. Separate EPS figures are

---

[10] AICPA, *APB Opinion No. 9*, "Reporting the Results of Operations" (New York, December 1966); *APB Opinion No. 15*, "Earnings per Share" (New York, May 1969); and FASB, *Statement of Financial Accounting Standards No. 55*, "Determining Whether a Convertible Security Is a Common Stock Equivalent" (Stamford, Conn., February 1982).

calculated for any special subtotals on the statement such as the cumulative effect of changes in accounting principles, net income before extraordinary items, net income, and so on.

Numerous intricacies are involved when a firm has a *complex financial structure,* one containing convertible securities, stock options, or stock purchase warrants. If these securities would have a *dilutive* effect on earnings per share—that is, if they would reduce EPS by 3 percent or more when the securities are converted or exercised—the APB requires that two earnings per share figures be disclosed. The following summaries highlight the components in these two EPS computations, which are called "primary earnings per share" and "fully diluted earnings per share."

**Primary Earnings per Share.**   This figure is net income available to common stock divided by the sum of the average common shares outstanding plus the number of *common stock equivalent* shares. Common stock equivalents are securities that have many of the characteristics of common stock but have not yet become common stock. Examples include stock options and warrants and convertible securities that meet certain criteria discussed below. Primary earnings per share is a hypothetical "what-if" calculation intended to provide the financial statement reader with an early warning of a possible future decline in the EPS figure if the complex-structure items do result in the issuance of additional common stock.

**Fully Diluted Earnings per Share.**   This per share figure measures the *maximum* dilution in earnings per share that could take place if all contingent issues of common stock were exercised. To determine the number of shares which would be outstanding, one assumes *full* conversion of bonds and preferred stock, exercise of warrants, and so on because they might have a future claim on net income. This is another prospective calculation showing what would occur under the most conservatively assumed circumstances. Options, warrants, convertible bonds, and preferred stock that do not meet the criteria for inclusion in the primary EPS are incorporated in the fully diluted number. Accordingly, fully diluted EPS figures are often significantly lower than the primary EPS figures.

**Illustration.**   Assume the following facts for the Ace Corporation for 1991:

1. 1991 net income after tax is $2,250,000.
2. As of January 1, 1991, 800,000 shares of common stock were issued and outstanding. On July 1, 200,000 additional shares were issued.
3. The market price per share remained at $30 throughout 1991.
4. Options have been granted to executives to purchase 60,000 shares any time prior to January 1, 1994, at $25 per share.
5. Eight percent convertible bonds—issued January 1, 1984 at their face amount of $2,400,000—mature in 1995. Each $1,000 bond is convertible into 50 common shares. The average Aa corporate bond yield was 14 percent on January 1, 1984.

6. Seventy-five thousand shares of 11 percent convertible preferred stock, $50 par, were issued on January 1, 1986 at par. Each share is convertible into four common shares. The average Aa corporate bond yield was 15 percent on January 1, 1986.

7. A 50 percent income tax rate is assumed.

The authoritative pronouncements contain detailed rules for classifying securities as common stock equivalents. Options and warrants are common stock equivalents because they derive their value from the common stock. Those convertible securities that derive their value primarily from the convertibility feature are also common stock equivalents. To achieve uniformity, the FASB arbitrarily ruled that convertible securities issued to provide a return less than two thirds of the average Aa corporate bond yield are common stock equivalents. The FASB reasoned that investors would accept such a relatively low interest rate only if, in fact, they really viewed the security as if it were common stock.

The determination of common stock equivalency status is made when the securities are issued, and that status cannot change as long as the convertible security is outstanding. For Ace Corporation, the 8 percent convertible bonds are considered to be a common stock equivalent (8 percent is less than two thirds of 14 percent), while the convertible preferred stock is not (11 percent is *not* less than two thirds of 15 percent). Accordingly, the convertible bonds are used to determine primary earnings per share whereas the convertible preferred stock is reserved for the fully diluted EPS.

Of course, the income figure in the EPS calculation must be consistent with the number of shares in the computation. For example, if a convertible bond issue is treated as if it were converted, then the income figure would have to be modified for the interest expense (and its related tax effect). Likewise, if stock options are treated as if they were exercised, then some assumption must be made about the use of the proceeds received upon exercise. To relieve the firm from having to estimate how much extra income would have resulted if the hypothetical option proceeds had been invested, the APB required that the EPS calculation assume that the firm uses those proceeds to acquire treasury stock.

*If* the capital structure of Ace Corporation had been simple, the computation of earnings per share for 1991 would be relatively easy. The simple EPS would be:

$$\frac{\text{Net income available to common shareholders*}}{\text{Weighted-average number of common shares}^\dagger}$$

$$= \frac{\$1,837,500}{900,000} = \$2.04 \text{ Simple EPS}$$

| *Net income | $2,250,000 | †Shares out-standing all year 200,000 shares for 6 months | 800,000 |
|---|---|---|---|
| Preferred dividends | (412,500) | | 100,000 |
| Net income to common | $1,837,500 | | 900,000 |

However, the capital structure of Ace Corporation is complex, and the impact of the convertible securities is dilutive. Therefore, *Opinion No. 15* requires the disclosure of both primary and fully diluted EPS figures instead of the simple $2.04 EPS number. Their determinations appear in Tables 16–4 and 16–5.

**Evaluation of Pronouncements.** Accounting thought is divided concerning the value of the primary earnings per share and the fully diluted earnings per share numbers. Some critics object to the hypothetical nature of both calculations. Many believe that the $2.04 simple EPS for 1991 represents the only "true" or "real" EPS amount. Others are willing to accept the primary EPS concept but find the fully diluted EPS number too conservative to be of any significant value.

Perhaps the needs of financial statement readers would be better served by the disclosure of both simple and primary EPS numbers rather than the present combination of primary and fully diluted EPS. Persons holding Ace Corporation stock options need only pay $25 for common shares that are currently selling for $30 per share. Those holding Ace's convertible bonds are earning a substandard interest return on those securities. These facts suggest that exercise of the stock options and conversion of the bonds could be expected in the near future. Although the "real" EPS may have been

---

**TABLE 16–4**  Calculation of Primary Earnings per Share

| | | |
|---|---:|---:|
| Net income available to common . . . . . . . . . | | $1,837,500 |
| Add: After-tax interest savings from assumed conversion of convertible bonds ($2,400,000 × .08 × .50) . . . . . . . . . . . | | 96,000 |
| Earnings applicable to common stock and equivalents . . . . . . . . . . . . . . . . | | $1,933,500 |
| Weighted-average common shares outstanding. . . . | | 900,000 |
| Add: Shares issuable upon assumed conversion of convertible bonds (2,400 bonds at 50 common shares each) . . . . . . . . . . . . . . . | | 120,000 |
| Add: Incremental shares arising from assumed exercise of stock options: | | |
| Shares issuable upon exercise of options . . . . . | 60,000 | |
| Less: Assumed buy-back of shares with option proceeds of $1,500,000. (60,000 × $25/$30). . . | 50,000 | 10,000 |
| Total shares. . . . . . . . . . . . . . . . . . | | 1,030,000 |

$$\text{Primary EPS} = \frac{\$1,933,500}{1,030,000} = \$1.88$$

---

**TABLE 16–5**   Calculation of Fully Diluted Earnings per Share

| | |
|---|---:|
| Net income available to common . . . . . . . . . . . . . . . . | $1,837,500 |
| Add: After-tax interest savings from assumed conversion of convertible bonds ($2,400,000 × .08 × .50) . . . . . . . . | 96,000 |
| Add: Dividend savings from assumed conversion of convertible preferred shares (75,000 × $50 × .11). . . . . . | 412,500 |
| Earning with full dilution . . . . . . . . . . . . . . . . . . | $2,346,000 |
| Weighted-average common shares outstanding. . . . . . . . | 900,000 |
| Add: Shares issuable upon assumed conversion of convertible bonds (2,400 bonds at 50 common shares each) . . | 120,000 |
| Add: Incremental shares arising from assumed exercise of options (see Table 16–4) . . . . . . . . . . . . . . . . | 10,000 |
| Add: Shares issuable upon assumed conversion of convertible preferred shares (75,000 shares at 4 common shares each). . . | 300,000 |
| Total shares. . . . . . . . . . . . . . . . . . . . . . . . | 1,330,000 |

$$\text{Fully diluted EPS} = \frac{\$2,346,000}{1,330,000} = \$1.76$$

---

$2.04 for 1991, financial statement readers deserve to know that it could decline by 8 percent to $1.88 (Table 16–4) just as soon as the options are exercised and the bonds are converted.

## Segment Reporting

During the last 30 years, an accelerating trend toward the development of large diversified conglomerate corporations has been apparent. These corporations have divisions that operate in widely diverse industries with separate manufacturing and marketing facilities. They are linked only by top management control and overall stock ownership.

Comparisons of the operating results of diversified companies with industry trends or competing companies are especially perplexing. The reporting of only a single income statement and balance sheet combining all the unrelated businesses causes three potential difficulties for the investor. First, the evaluation of management is made complex, because data for profitable and unprofitable lines may offset each other. A combined statement allows management to hide its mistakes and avoid external assessment of the costs and benefits from its diversification policy. Second, industry lines are blurred or disappear in conglomerate companies. Industry analysis is an essential element in evaluating past performance and even more crucial in predicting the future. The third difficulty concerns the impossibility of making meaningful comparisons among individual companies. A conglomerate is likely to compete with one or more firms in one line of business but with entirely different groups of firms in its other lines. To what (if anything) does the analyst compare the overall financial statements?

Numerous analysts and accountants have suggested as a solution that diversified companies be required to report separate income statements for each of their major lines of business or segments.

**Difficulties in Segment Reporting.**    Any company attempting to provide financial data by segments encounters numerous difficulties. One obvious problem is identifying the segments on which to report. If each firm were to report according to its peculiar organizational structure (geographic area, customer class, product line), comparability between firms would not necessarily be improved. A second difficulty involves measuring income by segment. Some expenses jointly serve a number of segments—advertising, interest costs, home office administrative expenses, research and development, taxes, and so on. Assignment of these common costs to individual lines of business can be accomplished only through the use of allocation procedures, some of which may be highly arbitrary. The assignment of assets and liabilities to segments may be even more difficult. The narrower the segments become, the more arbitrary are the allocated amounts. Accordingly, the results might simply mislead investors and provide them with very unreliable data for predicting the future.

An alternative often suggested is the segmental reporting of some intermediate income subtotal, such as "Contribution to Earnings before General Corporate Expenses." Only revenues and expenses directly assignable to segments would be included. This solution might aid in predicting the future, but resultant figures would, of course, not be comparable to those of other firms operating as separate entities. Additionally, some business executives oppose disclosure of this type of information for fear of aiding competitors or encouraging government regulatory actions.

**Governmental Activity.**    In 1974, the Federal Trade Commission ordered most corporations with more than $50 million in assets to start reporting profits, revenue, advertising, and R&D expenses by segments—defined in terms of the three-digit U.S. Standard Industrial Classification (SIC) code. Because firms were not being allowed any latitude in the selection and definition of reportable segments, many firms initiated court action, alleging invasion of privacy. Court actions dragged on for many years. The FTC ruling was formally scrapped in the early 1980s.

The Securities and Exchange Commission established less restrictive segment reporting requirements in the early 1970s. Later the SEC made its rules quite similar to the segment ruling enacted by the FASB.

*FASB Statement No. 14.*    The need for segment data seems obvious, yet the practical difficulties of drawing up reasonable requirements are large.

Since 1967, the Accounting Principles Board and its successor, the Financial Accounting Standards Board, have grappled with the problem. The result is a requirement that companies disclose certain data for all *industry segments* for which the revenue, operating income or loss, *or* identifiable assets are 10 percent or more of the company total.[11] The reportable segments should account for at least 75 percent of the combined sales. Industry segments can be determined by the management of the firm. For guidance in grouping products and services into industry segments, the FASB suggests that companies consider such factors as nature of product, nature of production process, and markets and marketing methods. Most firms have divided their operations into anywhere from three to six reportable segments.

In general, firms must disclose at least the following data for each reportable segment (and in the aggregate for the remainder of the operations):

1. Sales, including sales to unaffiliated customers and intersegment sales and transfers—the latter must be separately disclosed.
2. Operating profit or loss—operating expenses are to include both directly traceable segment expenses and operating expenses reasonably allocated to the segments but not general corporate expenses, interest expense, or income taxes.
3. Identifiable assets.
4. Other related disclosures—depreciation expense, capital expenditures, and so on.

The above information reported by segments must be reconciled with the related amounts shown in the overall financial statements.

In addition, firms deriving 10 percent or more of their sales from a single customer or from a domestic or foreign government must disclose that fact and the revenue amounts. Such information can prove useful in evaluating the underlying risk associated with the firm. Consider, for example, the cookie manufacturer that makes 35 percent of its sales to the Girl Scouts or the heavy machinery firm with sizable sales to a foreign government undergoing revolution or economic crises.

## Interim Financial Reports

The accounting period concept recognizes the need for information about time periods shorter than the life of the enterprise. The most common reporting period has been an annual one, either a calendar year or a fiscal (natural business) year. In recent years, however, increased attention has been focused on interim reporting—the presentation of accounting information at times other than the end of the year and for periods shorter than a year.

---

[11] FASB, *Statement of Financial Accounting Standards No. 14*, "Financial Reporting for Segments of a Business Enterprise" (Stamford, Conn., December 1976), par. 15.

In most instances, the concern has centered on *quarterly reports* that many companies issue to external users. In recognition of the fact that a year is too long for investors to wait for information, the New York Stock Exchange requires that companies with stock listed on the exchange supply quarterly reports to stockholders. Numerous empirical studies have demonstrated that stock market prices react to the release of quarterly earnings numbers.

**Problems in Interim Financial Statements.** As we know, with shorter reporting periods, accountants must increase the number of estimates made to deal with uncertainties. Adjustments for revenue earned under percentage of completion, expense accruals, and sales uncollectibles are more difficult to make for quarterly periods than for annual ones. Similarly, in interim reports the determination of lower of cost or market, the calculation of cost of goods sold in manufacturing firms or under LIFO, and the assignment of period expenses may lead to potentially misleading reports.

This high potential for inaccuracy in interim reports calls into question the more fundamental issue concerning the purpose of such reports. Is a quarterly statement to present the actual results of that particular three-month period as a separate time span or simply as one part of an annual period? The answer to this question influences the accounting for income taxes, where the annual effective rate may differ from the quarterly rate; the accruing of such expenses as bonuses, the existence of which may not be determinable until year-end; the handling of LIFO liquidation (sale of basic inventory layers) during an interim period; and many other accrual and deferral practices.

Closely related is the question of seasonality. Should the interim statements report on each quarter as it occurs or attempt to predict the year's results? Should an investor be able to multiply the quarterly income figures by four to arrive at the best estimate of yearly income figures? The answer to this question influences the amount of smoothing that is done in the recording of sales and particularly in the treatment of period expenses. The more each quarterly period is treated as an independent period, the less comparable are the quarters with one another because of seasonal factors, and the more unusual they may become because of the irregular occurrences of particular period expenses.

**Authoritative Standards.** Accounting bodies in both the public and private sectors have addressed themselves to the question of interim reporting. The Accounting Principles Board in *Opinion No. 28* provides guidelines and establishes minimum disclosure requirements.[12] The Securities and Exchange Commission in its *Accounting Series Release No. 177,* issued in

---

[12]AICPA, *APB Opinion No. 28,* "Interim Financial Reporting" (New York, May 1973).

September 1975, expands the information that must be contained in the quarterly Form 10–Q and requires that summarized quarterly data must appear in the notes to the annual financial statements of large publicly traded companies.[13]

*Opinion No. 28* begins from the express presumption that each interim period should be viewed primarily as an integral part of the annual period. Revenue is to be recorded in interim reports on the same basis as in the annual report, so seasonal factors do show. Likewise, expense recognition procedures used for interim reporting are essentially the same as the procedures used to prepare annual financial statements. However, certain modifications are allowed so that the interim results may better articulate with the annual results. The modifications for the measurement of cost of goods sold include using estimating procedures where physical inventory is taken only once a year, the use of estimated replacement cost when there is a temporary depletion of basic LIFO inventory layers, and the ignoring of write-downs to lower of cost or market when the market decline is thought to be temporary. Similarly, *Opinion No. 28* allows some period costs readily identifiable with more than one interim period to be allocated on some reasonable basis such as time expired, benefit received, or activity transpired. Income taxes are to be accrued in accordance with the best estimate of the effective rate for the year.

Although *Opinion No. 28* does not *require* companies to issue quarterly reports, it does set forth the general guidelines that must be followed when they are issued. Similarly, it mandates minimum disclosure requirements for the interim financial reports of *companies whose securities are publicly traded*. Such quarterly reports are to include at least gross revenues, provision for income taxes, net income, and earnings per share. Additionally, any extraordinary, unusual, or infrequently recurring items or any changes in accounting principles, estimates, or provisions for income taxes are to be reported.

The foregoing information is to be reported on a comparable basis with the preceding year for the current quarter and the year to date. Also, to prevent the possibility that a quarter heavily influenced by seasonal factors will be extrapolated to the whole year, *Opinion No. 28* requires that firms disclose seasonal patterns of revenue or expenses and strongly urges that companies supplement their interim reports with information for the last 12 months to date.

---

[13] The revised instructions for Form 10–Q now require quarterly income statements, balance sheets, and statements of cash flows plus a narrative analysis of results of operations. The statements may be presented in summarized form but must otherwise conform to the principles contained in *APB Opinion No. 28*. The quarterly data to be included in the *annual report* notes must include revenue, gross profit, net income, and earnings per share for each quarter of the last two years.

## CONTINGENCIES AND COMMITMENTS

As we have seen in previous chapters, financial statements are concerned primarily with reporting monetary amounts reflecting the results of completed transactions. However, accountants face another factor when preparing reports. This factor concerns current conditions that depend on events that have not yet occurred and may never occur. These situations present several interesting and difficult judgment problems. Even though precise transaction data is absent, information about the conditions may be important for an accurate reading and interpretation of the statements. These conditions are called "contingencies and commitments."

Contingencies relate to business transactions that *may* occur in the future. Because the transactions have not occurred, the dollar amounts related to the transactions clearly are difficult to measure, and the disclosure of these amounts in the company's financial statements may be misleading. As an example, one of the most frequently reported contingencies relates to ongoing litigation. The difficulty in reporting litigation contingencies arises from the fact that the outcome is unknown at the time the balance sheet is prepared. Therefore, the accountant is on the horns of a dilemma: it is important to know that the company is involved in litigation but to imply that the company will be successful or unsuccessful may be wrong and consequently misleading. The accountant faces crucial questions on what to report, when to report, and how to report contingencies.

Generally accepted accounting principles provide the requirements to be followed in reporting and recording contingencies. *Statement of Financial Accounting Standards No. 5*[14] defines a contingency as an existing circumstance that involves an uncertain but possible gain or loss. Further, it is anticipated that the uncertainty will be resolved when a future event occurs or fails to occur.

The FASB was more concerned with the disclosure of losses than of gains, so we focus our discussion on unfavorable contingencies.[15] *Statement No. 5* relates different requirements to the degree of likelihood that the future event will confirm the loss. Three levels of probability are described:

1. *Probable*—the future event is likely to occur.
2. *Reasonably possible*—the future event's occurrence is less than likely but more than remote.
3. *Remote*—the future event's occurrence is remote.

Recording and reporting loss contingencies involves considering two elements: whether a loss should be accrued and how the elements of the situ-

[14] FASB, *Statement of Financial Accounting Standards No. 5,* "Accounting for Contingencies" (Stamford, Conn., 1975).

[15] Gain contingencies are not recognized on the financial statements until they are realized. However, footnote disclosure can be employed so long as no misleading suggestion as to realization is given.

ation should be disclosed. Accountants must exercise significant accounting judgment. *Statement No. 5* sets forth two conditions for the recognition of losses by charges to income. If *both* conditions are met, then the loss contingency must be accrued:

**1.** Information prior to issuance of the financial statements must indicate that it is *probable* that an asset had been impaired or a liability had been incurred at the date of the financial statements. This condition implies that it must be probable that one or more future events will occur confirming the fact of the loss.

**2.** The amount of the loss can be reasonably estimated.[16]

Accounting for a liability when the loss is probable and can be estimated results in an entry similar to that shown below. Assume that a firm makes estimates of its product warranties and determines the current year estimate for future claims to be $850,000. The following entry would be made:

| | | |
|---|---|---|
| Loss on future warranty claims . . . . . . . . . | 850,000 | |
| Estimated liability for future | | |
| warranty claims . . . . . . . . . . . . . | | 850,000 |

The loss would appear on the income statement; the liability, on the balance sheet; and a note to the financial statements would discuss the warranty program. When warranty claims are processed, the liability will be reduced with an offsetting asset decrease.

If no accrual entry is actually made because the loss is considered only to be *reasonably possible,* not probable, or the amount cannot be reasonably estimated, the contingency must be described in a note to the financial statements. The note should give an estimate of the loss or range of loss if possible. Also, certain loss contingencies where the possibility of loss is remote still need to be disclosed to the reader in the notes. An example would be if one company guaranteed the debt of another company, agreeing to pay if the second company were unable to pay.

Contingencies, then, cover a broad set of conditions with unknown outcomes. An interesting way to look at contingencies is by classifying them into four sets:

1. Known situations whose financial impacts cannot be estimated (example: continuing litigation).
2. Known situations for which an estimated range of the financial impact may be made (example: estimating uncollectible accounts receivable).
3. Anticipated future situations whose financial impacts cannot be estimated (example: compliance with federal EPA regulations).
4. Anticipated future situations over which an estimated range of the financial impact may be made (example: guarantee of financial obligations).

The following illustrations of each situation show the contingency reporting used by several companies.

---

[16]*FASB Statement No. 5*, par. 8.

## Known Situation—Unknown Outcome

This set of factors requires disclosure only in the notes to the financial statements. Litigation is the most common example of this type of loss contingency wherein the suit is known but the outcome is unknown. The following note from the Amcast Industrial Corporation illustrates the disclosure required:

> In June 1985, a class action suit was filed on behalf of certain retired employees of the Ironton Division. The plaintiffs allege defendant's breach of contract relating to their medical and life insurance benefits. Plaintiffs are seeking reinstatement of benefits for the remainder of their lives which were discontinued on the day of the plant closing. The plaintiffs are seeking $35 million of compensatory damages and $40 million for punitive damages. Management believes these claims are without merit and the outcome of the case will not materially affect the financial position of the company.

## Known Situation—Estimated Outcome

This set of factors requires disclosure of the dollar impact of the situation on the statements and an explanation in the notes. For example, Southland Corporation disclosed the following information regarding its receivables:

Accounts and Notes Receivable (000's omitted):

|  | December 31 | |
| --- | --- | --- |
|  | *1985* | *1984* |
| Trade accounts and notes receivable . . . . . . . | $243,636 | $145,093 |
| Franchise accounts receivable . . . . . . . . . | 33,952 | 34,936 |
|  | 277,588 | 180,029 |
| Allowance for doubtful accounts . . . . . . . . | (12,665) | (11,962) |
|  | $264,923 | $168,067 |

> On December 28, 1984, the Company sold $250 million of accounts receivable under an agreement in which the purchaser will reinvest the proceeds collected in new receivables for a period of five years. Throughout 1985, the rollover of proceeds collected and reinvested in new accounts receivable aggregated $4.6 billion. As of December 31, 1985, $251 million of receivables were outstanding under the agreement. The Company is contingently liable for the collection of up to $25.5 million of these receivables; however, management believes that the allowance for doubtful accounts will be adequate and no additional liabilities will accrue.

## Future Situation—Unknown Outcome

Disclosures of this type appear in the notes and alert statement readers to the situation although specific dollar amounts cannot be associated with the situation. The following note is taken from Fansteel Inc.:

Processing of certain ores results in residues which are subject to storage and disposal regulations of the Nuclear Regulatory Commission. The Company intends to continue to store these residues at one of its processing plants. Maximum disposal costs, if any, cannot be reasonably estimated, but management believes they would not have a material effect on the consolidated financial position of the Company.

## Future Situation—Estimated Outcome

With these situations, the notes disclose the situation and indicate the range of potential amounts that could be involved. In the following disclosure of Nortek, Inc., the firm discloses both potential liabilities that cannot be estimated and guarantees which could range from $0 to $1 million dollars, depending on certain future events:

The Company and its subsidiaries are subject to legal proceedings and claims arising out of their businesses that cover a wide range of matters, including, among others, product liability, warranty and product recalls, and contract and employment claims. The amount of ultimate liability with respect to these proceedings and claims cannot reasonably be estimated. At December 31, 1985, the Company is contingently liable for obligations (approximately $19,000,000) under Industrial Revenue Bond agreements related to facilities which were sold. Management considers that any such liabilities would not materially affect the consolidated financial position of the Company nor its results of operations.

The Company has guaranteed a $1,000,000 term loan of the Nortek Foundation with a bank. Proceeds of the loan were used to purchase Nortek Common Stock.

As these few examples make clear, disclosing contingencies stretches accountants' judgment to the limit as they grapple with difficult decisions on how to report conditions that convey valuable information without creating undue expectations concerning the occurrence of possible events and results. Footnote disclosure is important and users should be prepared to read and interpret the notes on contingencies.

A further disclosure required by GAAP is called "commitments." It relates to *future contractual* obligations of the firm. Commitments need to be disclosed so that the statement reader will have sufficient information to interpret the statements in light of known future asset claims that will apply to the firm. Typically, these commitments apply to purchase contracts—although other commitments to restrict dividends, to meet employment contracts, fulfill sales agreements, deliver under production agreements, and the like are all important to interpreting the firm's future performance.

The following note by Capital Cities Communications, Inc./American Broadcasting Companies, Inc. illustrates the disclosure of important agreements that will have significant effects on future years' performance:

### Commitments

The Company (excluding ABC and disposed operations) has entered into agreements for future delivery of syndicated and feature film programming for its television stations, which aggregate $10,881,000, payable from 1986 through 1990.

At December 28, 1985, ABC is obligated for payments for the purchase of broadcast rights to various feature films, sports events, and other programming aggregating approximately $1.8 billion.

# DISCUSSION OF THE KIMBERLY-CLARK ANNUAL REPORT

Additional disclosure issues in the Kimberly-Clark annual report deal only with earnings per share, interim reporting, and segment reporting. Over the three-year period, the company had no extraordinary items, corrections of errors, discontinued operations, or changes in accounting principles.

## Earnings per Share

Kimberly-Clark's balance sheet contains a very basic stockholders' equity section. Determining the net income per share (EPS) shown on the statement of income requires the use of the average number of shares outstanding. Kimberly-Clark provides the statement reader with this information in Note 1. Under the heading "Net Income per Share," the average number of shares for the years ended 1987, 1986, and 1985 are given as 87.2 million, 91.8 million, and 91.5 million, respectively.

This disclosure permits the verification of the net income per share figures disclosed on the statement of income. The values are:

|  | *(in millions)* |  |  |  |  |
| --- | --- | --- | --- | --- | --- |
| *Year* | *Net Income* |  | *Average Shares* |  | *Net Income per Share* |
| 1987 | $325.2 | / | 87.2 | = | $3.73 |
| 1986 | 269.4 | / | 91.8 | = | 2.93 |
| 1985 | 267.1 | / | 91.5 | = | 2.92 |

Because the firm had no unusual or extraordinary items during this three-year period, a single net income per share figure is sufficient. In this instance, the firm also has no elements that could cause dilution of the per share figure, so a simple EPS suffices. Note that in 1987, the increase in EPS was caused by the combined action of higher net income and a reduced number of shares.

## Interim Reporting

A summary of the data reported quarterly by Kimberly-Clark for 1987 and 1986 appears in Note 10 to the financial statements. A steady, consistent, upward trend in net sales, except for the third quarter of 1986, may be observed during this period. Operating income and net income over this same period also show an upward trend but with more fluctuation than with net sales.

An examination of the gross profit percentage (gross profit/net sales) by quarter indicates that this percentage is quite steady at 33 to 34 percent. We can find similar patterns if percentages are calculated for operating profit and net income. Operating profits are consistently 11 to 12 percent per quarter and net income percentages are primarily in the 6.3 to 6.9 percent range. All of the computations indicate that the firm is not being affected by unusual events from quarter to quarter.

## Segment Reporting

Kimberly-Clark's annual report contains extensive descriptions (Note 11) of its product classes and geographic data. The first disclosure displays a breakdown of corporate sales, operating profit, assets, depreciation, and capital spending by class of products produced for each of the three years. Three classes are presented: I—household and institutional tissues, II—feminine and infant care products, and III—aircraft services and miscellaneous products. Totals for each item (sales, operating profit, and so on) may be tied back to the income statements and balance sheets.

The firm then reorders the display of this data to present it by geographic area of the world. The categories shown are the United States, Canada, Europe, Latin and South America, and the Far East. The statement elements of sales, operating profits, and assets are disclosed for each geographic area.

Finally, the corporation details the geographic distribution of the assets and income statement items for firms in which Kimberly-Clark has investments. These firms are not totally owned by Kimberly-Clark and are referred to as "equity companies." However, because Kimberly-Clark derives income from these investments, their geographical breakdown is a useful supplement in assessing the company's geographical sources of income.

The segment disclosures provide substantial insight into the product categories and their portion of the total business as well as the international distribution of the firm's operations. In addition, the detail provided permits analysis of the profitability of individual segments of the company's businesses and prevents the unprofitable operations of one segment from being covered up by the profitable operations of another. In Kimberly-Clark's case, all segments presented appear healthy.

Within Note 11 is an important disclosure concerning problems with one portion of the Canadian operation. Unprofitable operations are being addressed, but an additional environmental factor is described. The Canadian government has imposed stringent environmental regulations, and the firm has described its technical difficulties in complying. This information might be a significant indicator of future operational costs. Segment reporting highlights these types of important information.

## SUMMARY

This chapter considers a number of disclosure issues and presentations that must be incorporated in the financial statements. The earlier part of the chapter discusses accounting for various unusual items and changes that affect retained earnings.

Three general approaches have filtered down from authoritative bodies:

1. *Current reporting*—Report the cumulative effect on retained earnings as a separately identified item on the current period's income statement. This approach is used for extraordinary items, discontinued operations, and most changes in accounting principles.
2. *Retroactive adjustment*—Restate each income statement presented and show the remaining effect as an adjustment of the retained earnings balance at the beginning of the earliest year included in the report. This approach is required for prior period adjustments (e.g., correction of errors) and certain specific changes in accounting principles.
3. *Prospective correction*—Adjust the operating income of the current and future periods for the effect of the change. This approach applies to changes in accounting estimates.

Discussion in the latter part of the chapter then turns to issues related to the usefulness of accounting data. Most of these issues have been resolved at least temporarily through authoritative pronouncements. Earnings per share, interim reporting, segment reporting, and contingencies are significant among these issues.

In the discussion of these areas, the reader can sense the dynamic nature of financial accounting. New problems requiring applications of new principles or the development of new concepts continually appear on the horizon. The reader can also see how the qualitative guidelines of completeness, comparability, and consistency as well as the accounting principles based on our underlying framework of assumptions interact to provide a combined, interrelated approach to finding practical solutions to these problems.

## PROBLEMS AND CASETTES

### 16–1. Disclosure of Extraordinary Items and Discontinued Operations

St. Regis Corporation's 1991 income statement accounts appeared as follows:

|  | Dr. | Cr. |
|---|---|---|
| Sales . . . . . . . . . . . . . . . . . . . . . . . . . . . |  | $1,275,000 |
| Gain on sale of battery division . . . . . . . . . . . . . |  | 91,500 |
| Cost of goods sold. . . . . . . . . . . . . . . . . . . | $568,000 |  |
| Selling and administrative expense . . . . . . . . . . . | 379,300 |  |
| Loss from flood (after tax) . . . . . . . . . . . . . . . | 225,000 |  |
| Income tax expense . . . . . . . . . . . . . . . . . . . | 104,800 |  |

St. Regis was a longtime distributor of automobile parts. In 1985, in an attempt to diversify, it acquired a battery manufacturing plant. However, the battery division never was profitable. In 1991, St. Regis decided to sell it and return its attention to its major business activity, the wholesaling of automobile parts. Although the sale of the plant resulted in a gain, operations of the plant had a negative effect on 1991's income. The following amounts related to the battery division are included in the above income statement accounts:

| | |
|---|---:|
| Sales . . . . . . . . . . . . . . . . . | $ 52,400 |
| Cost of goods sold . . . . . . . . . . . | (41,700) |
| Selling and administrative expense . . . . | (36,300) |
| Loss . . . . . . . . . . . . . . . . . | $(25,600) |

Also in 1991, the firm experienced an uninsured flood loss of $300,000 before deducting the tax savings of 25 percent. The flood resulted from a "hundred-year" storm. Although the St. Regis facility stood on high ground, the collapse of a dam caused extensive damage to the building and destroyed most of the inventory.

### Required:

Prepare an income statement for St. Regis Corporation in a form that isolates the flood loss as an extraordinary item and that distinguishes between income from continuing operations and discontinued operations.

**16–2. Treatment of Unusual Items**

The following items relate to the Bolton Corporation for the year 1993. Indicate how each of these items would be reported on the *1993* financial statements. Assume that all amounts are material and ignore the effects of income tax.

1. Proceeds of $400,000 were received from a life insurance policy on an officer of the firm who died in 1993.
2. Bolton Corporation guarantees its products for a three-year period. It had set up an estimated liability equal to 4 percent of sales. The balance in the account as of January 1, 1993, was $190,000, and applicable sales in 1993 were $900,000. Based on detailed cost studies made in 1993, it was concluded that the estimate should be reduced to 2 percent of sales starting in 1993.
3. An analysis of outstanding insurance policies in 1993 reveals that on July 1, 1992, a four-year insurance policy costing $40,000 was debited to Insurance Expense. No adjusting entry was made on December 31 of that year.
4. Early in 1993 the company decided to abandon its sporting goods line, which accounted for about 30 percent of the firm's sales volume. The assets directly associated with that phase of activity were sold on August 14, 1993, at a loss of $360,000. Operating losses from January 1 to August 14, 1993 for the sporting goods line were $194,000.
5. The depreciation method on some machinery purchased in 1989 was changed in 1993 from the sum-of-the-years'-digits method to the straight-line method. The effect of the change was to reduce depreciation by the following amounts: $16,300 for 1989; $12,700 for 1990; $10,000 for 1991; $5,400 for 1992; and $2,100 for 1993.

6. During November and December, one of Bolton's major suppliers incurred a labor strike. As a result, low-cost LIFO inventory on Bolton's books was liquidated. This liquidation resulted in a $170,000 increase in net income over what would have been recorded if inventory could have been replenished by year-end.

### 16–3. Judgments Involved in Interim Reporting

Crosby Corporation has asked you for guidance in the preparation of its interim report for the first quarter of 1993. Selected information concerning the firm follows:

1. An employee strike was forecast for the upcoming second quarter. As a result, Crosby shipped twice as much as normal during the first quarter.
2. Crosby normally incurs approximately 65 percent of its annual heating costs during the first quarter.
3. The annual audit takes place during January.
4. Almost all of the equipment overhaul costs are incurred in the summer months, primarily in the third quarter.

The firm's management proposes to defer half of the sales until the quarter (second) in which they would have occurred had there been no strike. It wishes to assign only one fourth of the audit fee to the first quarter because it believes that the expenditure benefits the entire year. Similarly, the firm believes that only one fourth of the heating costs belongs on the first-quarter income statement. It reasons that heating the buildings during January to March helps operations throughout the year by "preventing pipes from freezing, machinery from breaking, and employees from quitting." Finally, Crosby proposes to accrue one fourth of the equipment overhaul costs slated for the third quarter to record as an expense during the first quarter.

### Required:

For each of these proposals, evaluate management's suggestions. Which would you support or not support? Why? Make your evaluation in light of your understanding of the purpose of interim reports and the requirements of *APB Opinion No. 28.*

### 16–4. Disclosure of Discontinued Operations

The board of directors of Oak Meadow Corporation decided to dispose of its Lombard Division. The Lombard Division, although marginally profitable, no longer fit into the long-run strategic plan of the corporation. The net assets of the Lombard Division on October 1, 1992, when the division was sold, amounted to $575,000. Oak Meadow received $455,000 in cash for them.

The results of operations for the year ended December 31, 1992, with the operations of the Lombard Division from January 1 through October 1 shown separately, are summarized below:

|  | *Rest of Business* | *Lombard Division* |
|---|---|---|
| Net sales. . . . . . . . . . . . . . . . . | $3,400,000 | $800,000 |
| Cost of goods sold. . . . . . . . . . . . | 1,300,000 | 500,000 |
| Operating expenses . . . . . . . . . . . | 900,000 | 200,000 |
| Interest expense . . . . . . . . . . . . . . | 120,000 | 30,000 |

Income taxes at the rate of 30 percent apply to all income items.

**Required:**

a. Prepare an income statement for 1992 in proper form. Be sure to include appropriate intrastatement tax allocation.

b. What disclosure modifications would be made if Oak Meadow were to report a comparative income statement for 1992 and 1991?

## 16–5. Treatment of Unusual Items

The following items relate to the Winder Corporation for the year 1991. Indicate how each item would be reported on the *1991* income statement or statement of retained earnings. Assume all amounts are material and ignore income tax effects.

1. Extra depreciation of $90,000 was taken in 1991 to compensate for the failure to take any depreciation on a machine acquired in 1989.

2. A patent purchased in 1987 for $510,000 was being amortized over its legal life of 17 years. In 1991, this policy was reevaluated, and the decision was made to shorten the life to a total period of 10 years.

3. All of the assets of the firm's foreign subsidiary were expropriated by a foreign government without compensation. The book value of the assets was $2,190,000.

4. A large portion of the inventory was found to be obsolete and was written down by $120,000 to net realizable value.

5. In 1991, Winder Corporation purchased some new equipment for $700,000. Because of great uncertainty concerning the future benefits to be derived, the firm decided to use the sum-of-the-years'-digits method with a four-year life. Other equipment is depreciated using straight-line depreciation, however.

6. A loss of $182,000 resulted from a very large customer going bankrupt and being unable to pay the account receivable. The bankruptcy was completely unexpected and unpredictable; consequently, the amount was not covered by the normal estimate of doubtful accounts.

7. A cash payment of $270,000 was made during 1991 to a visitor who was injured in 1988 during a plant tour. Damages of $500,000 were originally assessed by a lower court in 1989. Upon appeal, the state supreme court reduced the amount of damages to only $270,000. A loss and estimated liability for $500,000 had been recognized originally in 1989 when the lower court handed down its ruling.

## 16–6. Correction of Miscellaneous Errors

R. W. and Sons determined its 1990, 1991, and 1992 income figures to be $120,000, $135,000, and $150,000, respectively. You have been called in to review the company's financial statements. You uncover the following two errors:

1. The ending inventory on December 31, 1991 was understated because $22,000 of merchandise was not counted. As near as you can determine, the ending inventory on December 31, 1992 was determined correctly.

2. During 1990, some equipment with an original cost of $100,000 and accumulated depreciation of $70,000 was sold for $50,000 cash. The bookkeeper made the following entry:

| | | |
|---|---|---|
| Cash . . . . . . . . . | 50,000 | |
| Equipment . . . . . | | 50,000 |

The company calculates its depreciation expense by applying a rate of 20 percent to the original cost balance in the Equipment account at the end of each year.

**Required:**

*a.* Prepare a schedule that will show the determination of the correct income for 1990, 1991, and 1992. Ignore taxes.
*b.* Prepare the entries in *1993* to correct the accounts.
*c.* Assume instead that the errors were detected in *1992*. Describe how the error corrections would be reported on comparative financial statements covering both 1992 and 1991. Include a calculation of relevant amounts where possible.

**16–7. Disclosure of Contingencies**

You have been asked to advise the Gardner Corporation regarding the proper treatment of the following situations in its financial statements for 1992.

1. Early in 1992, Gardner Corporation experienced a toxic waste spill that resulted in significant pollution of the nearby Douglas River. The state and county governments filed a combined lawsuit for negligence against the company. Gardner's legal counsel believes it is highly probable that that company will lose the suit. The state and county are asking for $500,000 in damages. However, the lawyer hopes to limit the damage judgment to $200,000, although she believes the most probable outcome will be $350,000.
2. Gardner buys a specialized chemical from North Texas Company, a small manufacturer. North Texas experienced financial difficulties in 1991 and was on the verge of going out of business unless it could get additional financing. To secure a continued supply of the chemical, Gardner agreed to guarantee repayment of a $100,000 loan made by Texas Bank and Trust to North Texas on June 18, 1992. The loan comes due June 18, 1993; North Texas' financial situation does not seem to have improved.
3. On February 5, 1993, before the 1992 financial statements were completely audited and distributed, an explosion occurred in one of Gardner's chemical plants. The company estimated that $800,000 of damage was done to the plant. The company self-insures so that there will be no insurance recovery. In addition, individuals living around the plant are expected to file suits for damage done to the windows and perhaps the foundations of their homes.
4. During the months of April and May 1992, Gardner instituted a special promotional campaign directed at its agricultural customers. For each ten gallons of herbicide purchased, a customer received a coupon that could be exchanged for a bag of seed. During the promotion, 100,000 gallons of herbicide were sold, and 9,000 coupons were issued. In 1992, 5,000 coupons were exchanged for seed. The cost of a bag of seed is $20. Gardner Corporation estimated, based on past experience, that 80 percent of the coupons eventually would be redeemed.
5. During 1992, the corporation completed a government contract. The contract price was $800,000, and the amount was reflected in 1992's sales. However, the contract is subject to renegotiation. The corporation is arguing that certain costs were initially disallowed under the contract erroneously. If its position is upheld by the government auditors and Contract Renegotiation Board, Gardner would receive an additional $97,000 of revenues. Negotiations are currently underway at the end of 1992.

**Required:**

Indicate how each of these situations would be reported on the financial statements for 1992. Assume all amounts are material. If a journal entry is required, indicate the accounts to be debited and credited and where they would appear on the statements. Indicate also the nature of any disclosure you would make in notes to the financial statements.

### 16–8. Calculation of Earnings per Share

The Kipp Company has the following capital structure on December 31, 1994:

| | |
|---|---:|
| Convertible bonds, 7%, issued January 1, 1992, at the face amount, convertible into common stock at the rate of 40 shares per $1,000 bond | $150,000 |
| Convertible preferred stock, $10 par value, 9% dividend rate, issued January 1, 1991, convertible into common stock on a one-for-one basis | 300,000 |
| Common stock, $5 par value | 350,000 |
| Common stock, excess over par | 750,000 |

You have obtained the following information:

1. The 70,000 common shares outstanding on December 31, 1994 have been outstanding all year.
2. The convertible bonds are considered a common stock equivalent; the convertible preferred stock is not.
3. 1994 net income after interest and taxes is $800,000.
4. The income tax rate is 40 percent.

**Required:**

a. Calculate primary earnings per share for 1994.
b. Calculate fully diluted earnings per share for 1994.
c. An analyst exclaims, "Accountants are living in a dream world. Kipp Company's real earnings per share actually were over $11." Explain where the $11 figure came from. Do you agree with the statement?

### 16–9. Change in Depreciation Accounting Principles and Estimates

Dyme Corporation purchased a major machinery complex on January 1, 1989 for $114,000. The machinery complex has been depreciated on a straight-line basis over a 10-year useful life with an estimated residual value of $4,000. During 1992, management undertook a detailed study of its plant assets, with particular reference to the impact of a seemingly accelerated rate of obsolescence in the industry. As a result, two alternatives with respect to the machinery complex were suggested.

1. Change the depreciation method retroactively to sum-of-the-years'-digits.
2. Depreciate the machinery complex over a *total* life of 8 years instead of the original estimate of 10 years, and revise the anticipated residual value downward to zero.

You are called in to prepare the financial statements for the 1992 report. The report will show a comparative income statement for 1992 and 1991.

**Required:**

a. Prepare the journal entry to record depreciation expense on the complex in 1992 assuming alternative #1 is selected. Also prepare any other related entries, if applicable.

b. Prepare the journal entry to record depreciation expense on the complex in 1992 assuming alternative #2 is selected. Also prepare any other related entries, if applicable.

c. Indicate how each of the alternatives in a and b would be disclosed in the 1992 report.

d. Do you see any conceptual differences between the two alternatives? Why are they required to be handled differently?

**16–10. Reporting Problems with Interim Earnings**

The financial statement section of the interim report of Ocelok Industries to its stockholders for the second quarter of 1991 appears below:

**OCELOK INDUSTRIES**
**Consolidated Statement of Operations**

|  | Three Months Ended | | Six Months Ended | |
|---|---|---|---|---|
|  | June 30, 1991 | June 30, 1990 | June 30, 1991 | June 30, 1990 |
| Net sales. . . . . . . . . . . . | $379,014 | $260,403 | $919,524 | $424,620 |
| Cost and expenses: |  |  |  |  |
|   Cost of goods sold. . . . . . . | 197,799 | 157,257 | 502,587 | 256,842 |
|   Selling expenses . . . . . . . | 169,832 | 55,569 | 305,852 | 92,409 |
|   Administrative expenses . . . . | 16,231 | 9,111 | 29,114 | 14,514 |
|  | 383,862 | 221,937 | 837,553 | 363,765 |
| Earnings before income taxes . . . | (4,848) | 38,466 | 81,971 | 60,855 |
| Income tax provision. . . . . . . | (1,212) | 9,615 | 20,493 | 15,223 |
| Net earnings . . . . . . . . . . | $ (3,636) | $ 28,851 | $ 61,478 | $ 45,632 |
| Earnings per share . . . . . . . . | $ (.36) | $ 2.89 | $ 6.15 | $ 4.71 |

In preparing these statements, the company had to make judgments on four troublesome accounting issues:

1. The company gives quantity discounts based on total purchases for the year to selected large-volume customers. Because no customer has purchased enough merchandise yet to trigger the quantity discounts, none has been reflected in the above statements. Based on anticipated sales volumes for the year, however, quantity discounts for the year should average 2 percent of dollar sales. Typically, Ocelok records all quantity discounts in the fourth quarter.

2. Property taxes are $10,000 for the tax year ended June 30, 1991 and are *reliably* estimated to be $16,000 for the tax year beginning July 1, 1991. Ocelok shows $3,250 of property tax expense each quarter in the interim statements above.

3. In the second quarter of 1991, Ocelok spent $50,000 on a new advertising program for a product expected to be introduced in the fourth quarter. Because the money was spent in the second quarter, the amount has been included in selling expenses then.
4. The company uses the LIFO inventory method. During the second quarter, there was a liquidation of the base LIFO inventory layer caused by normal seasonal factors. However, Ocelok expects to complete the year with an ending inventory larger than the beginning inventory. On an *annual* basis, none of the low-cost, beginning inventory would be assumed to be sold. Therefore, cost of goods sold for the second quarter was recorded at current purchase prices rather than the artificially low costs in the beginning inventory.

**Required:**

*a.* Evaluate the treatment by the company of each of the four reporting issues. Which do you agree or disagree with?
*b.* Ocelok Corporation does not directly compare the first-quarter results with the second-quarter results. Is this a major omission? Why might such a comparison be useful?

**16–11. Interpretation of Segment Information**

American Brands, Inc. reported the following segment information for 1987 in its annual report of that year (amounts in millions):

| | Segment | | | | |
|---|---|---|---|---|---|
| | *Tobacco Products* | *Distilled Spirits* | *Hardware* | *Office Products* | *Other* |
| Net sales. . . . . . | $6,144.0 | $599.4 | $291.6 | $ 508.6 | $1,609.3 |
| Operating income . . . . . . | 673.8 | 68.3 | 42.1 | 26.5 | 91.5 |
| Identifiable assets . . . . . . . | 2,235.5 | 875.7 | 298.4 | 1,162.6 | 881.7 |
| Capital expenditures . . . . | 83.8 | 6.2 | 15.1 | 23.8 | 52.9 |
| Depreciation/ amortization . . . . | 55.0 | 16.9 | 8.9 | 20.6 | 39.5 |

**Required:**

*a.* Does this division of operations into segments seem reasonable? How were the segments determined and by whom?
*b.* Calculate a return on investment for each division by dividing operating income by identifiable assets. Which segment is most "profitable"? What limitations do you see in such comparisons?
*c.* Of what use is the disclosure of capital expenditures and depreciation by industry segment?

**16–12. Change in Accounting Principles for Inventory**

You have been called in to audit the records of Nickl Company for 1991. During that year, the company decided to change its method of inventory costing from first-in, first-out to average cost. The company was founded in 1988. Inventory computed according to each basis on December 31 for each year is:

| December 31 | Inventory at FIFO Cost | Inventory at Average Cost | Income Reported |
|---|---|---|---|
| 1988 . . . . . . . . . | $66,000 | $61,600 | $41,800 |
| 1989 . . . . . . . . . | 96,800 | 90,200 | 55,000 |
| 1990 . . . . . . . . . | 83,600 | 46,200 | 59,400 |
| 1991 . . . . . . . . . | 44,000 | 48,400 | 50,600 |

**Required:**

*a.* Prepare a schedule showing the adjusted income for each of the four years. Be sure to include the impact of inventory differences in both beginning and ending inventories. Ignore income tax considerations.

*b.* Prepare the entry necessary to adjust the accounts as of December 31, 1991. Assume the accounts have not been closed for 1991.

*c.* The financial report for 1991 will show comparative income statements and statements of retained earnings for 1991 and 1990. Indicate how this matter should be disclosed in the 1991 report. Be specific as to amounts and manner of presentation.

**16–13. Disclosure of Contingencies**

You have been called in by the Graves Company to examine its accounts prior to the issuance of financial statements for 1992. In the course of your examination, you learn about the following situations:

1. During 1991, Graves Company was sued by another firm for breach of contract. In 1992, a judgment was rendered against Graves Company. At the end of 1992, the case is still in litigation with respect to the amount of the damages to be awarded. The plaintiff is seeking damages of $1 million, while the lawyers for Graves Company contend that damages should not exceed $400,000.

2. The company owns a manufacturing plant in a foreign country which in 1992 announced its intention to expropriate all property owned by other than its own nationals. The expropriation would affect the Graves Company plant, which has a book value of $1.5 million and a market value of $2 million. The foreign government has announced that it will compensate the owner of expropriated property in an amount equal to 60 percent of fair market value.

3. Because of its large size and diversified operations, the company decided in 1992 to begin self-insuring its plant assets. Management felt that in the long run, the losses they would incur by not having insurance would be less than the $450,000 annual insurance premium they would have to pay for coverage.

4. The company leases over 50 stores which it uses for retail outlets. In 1992, management concluded that 16 of these stores would be discontinued because of their unprofitability. Management estimates that the company will suffer losses of $1.8 million because of this decision. The $1.8 million represents $500,000 write-off of leasehold improvements; $450,000 for liquidation of inventory; $250,000 for penalties associated with lease cancellations; and $600,000 for projected operating losses to dates of closing.

5. A customer filed a claim for $250,000 against Graves Company on October 15, 1992, as payment for injuries sustained in a fall on the company's premises. The customer contends that negligence on the part of the company resulted in the fall. The counsel for Graves Company believes the case is completely without merit and will never be brought to trial. However, if necessary, legal defenses are more than adequate to win the case in the opinion of the lawyers.

**Required:**

Indicate how each of these situations should be reflected on the financial statements for 1992, if at all. If a journal entry is required, indicate the accounts to be debited and credited and where they would appear on the statements. Also indicate the nature of any disclosure you would make in notes to the financial statements.

**16–14. Correction of Equipment Error**

You have been called in to audit the financial records of Penny Company for 1994. You discover that over the past four years certain purchases of new machinery were erroneously charged to repair expense. The machinery so charged should have been depreciated over a useful life of 10 years.

Selected information related to these errors is presented below:

| Year | Net Income Reported | Retained Earnings Balance at Dec. 31 | New Machinery Purchases Debited to Expense |
|------|------|------|------|
| 1991 . . . . . . | $210,600 | $ 741,100 | $80,000 |
| 1992 . . . . . . | 164,500 | 846,500 | 54,000 |
| 1993 . . . . . . | 161,700 | 963,900 | 60,000 |
| 1994 . . . . . . | 169,500 | 1,078,100 | 38,000 |

**Required:**

a. Prepare a schedule showing the corrected net income for each of the four years. Assume that a full year's depreciation expense is charged on new purchases in the year of acquisition. Ignore income tax considerations.
b. Prepare the adjusting entry necessary to correct the accounts as of December 31, 1994. Assume the accounts have not been closed for 1994.
c. The financial report for 1994 will show comparative income statements and statements of retained earnings for 1994 and 1993. Indicate how this matter should be disclosed in the 1994 report. Be specific as to amounts and manner of presentation.

**16–15. Preparation of Segment Reports**

Brigham Industries has three major product lines—industrial products, automotive products, and construction materials. The firm's income statement for 1992 appears on the next page:

**BRIGHAM INDUSTRIES**
**Income Statement for 1992**
**(in thousands)**

| | | |
|---|---:|---:|
| Sales . . . . . . . . . . | | $1,560 |
| Cost of goods sold . . . . . . . | | 809 |
| Gross margin . . . . . . . . . | | $ 751 |
| Operating expenses . . . . . . . | $368 | |
| Administrative expenses . . . . . | 190 | 558 |
| Income before taxes . . . . . . . | | $ 193 |
| Income taxes . . . . . . . . . | | 77 |
| Net income . . . . . . . . . | | $ 116 |

The following items can be traced directly to the three product lines and the central administrative headquarters:

| | Product Line | | | Central Headquarters |
|---|---:|---:|---:|---:|
| | *Industrial* | *Automotive* | *Construction* | |
| Sales . . . . . . . . . | $624 | $528 | $408 | — |
| Cost of goods sold. . . . | 324 | 274 | 211 | — |
| Operating expenses . . . | 71 | 68 | 56 | $173 |
| Administrative expenses . . | 27 | 32 | 14 | 117 |

Central headquarters costs consist of:

| | |
|---|---:|
| Advertising . . . . . . . . . . . . . . . | $100 |
| Research and development . . . . . . . . . | 33 |
| Salaries of operating personnel in the central office . . . . . . . . . . . . . | 40 |
| Salaries and expenses associated with the corporation as a whole . . . . . . . . | 60 |
| Interest . . . . . . . . . . . . . . . . | 57 |
| | $290 |

**Required:**

*a.* Which of the central headquarters costs are allocable to the segments under the guidelines of *FASB Standard No. 14*?

*b.* Compute operating income by segments for Brigham Industries assuming that the allocable central headquarters costs from part *a* are allocated to the product lines—
1. On the basis of sales volume.
2. Equally.

*c.* Calculate an operating income figure for each line of business excluding any allocated costs.

*d.* What are the advantages and disadvantages of each of the presentations in *b* and *c*? Which set of data do you prefer?

*e.* How would an analyst use segment information?

### 16–16. Calculation of Earnings per Share

Columbia Company's capital structure is as follows:

|  | December 31 | |
|---|---|---|
|  | *1992* | *1991* |
| Outstanding shares of stock: | | |
| Nonconvertible preferred stock. . . . . . . . . . . . . | 50,000 | 50,000 |
| Common stock . . . . . . . . . . . . . . . . . . . | 600,000 | 400,000 |
| 6% convertible bonds . . . . . . . . . . . . . . . . | $500,000 | $500,000 |

#### Additional Information:

1. On April 1, 1992, Columbia Company sold 200,000 additional shares of common stock.
2. The preferred stock dividend rate is $3.00 per share. All preferred dividends were paid in 1992.
3. When the preferred stock was issued, each share was accompanied by a warrant that entitled the holder to purchase a share of common stock at $20 per share anytime until 1995. All warrants still are outstanding on December 31, 1992.
4. The 6 percent convertible bonds were issued at par on July 1, 1990, when the average Aa corporate bond yield was 8 percent. Each $1,000 bond can be converted into 40 shares of common stock at any interest date. None of the bonds has been converted so far.
5. The market price of Columbia Company common stock was $28 during and at the end of 1992.
6. Reported net income for 1992 was $800,000, and the effective tax rate is 35 percent.

#### Required:

*a.* Should the stock purchase warrants and the convertible bonds be treated as common stock equivalents for the calculation of primary earnings per share? Explain your answer.
*b.* Without prejudice to your answer in *a*, assume that the warrants are common stock equivalents and that the convertible bonds are not. Compute the number of shares that should be used in calculating primary earnings per share for 1992.
*c.* Calculate primary earnings per share for 1992.
*d.* Compute the number of shares that should be used in calculating the fully diluted earnings per share for 1992.
*e.* Calculate the fully diluted earnings per share for 1992. Would this figure have to be disclosed?

### 16–17. Recording and Disclosure of Contingencies

Amoul Corporation is in a quandry regarding some legal proceedings and other special situations it experienced during 1993. Substantial debate and discussion have occurred among the financial staff and between them and the top management of the company. No entries have been made for any of these situations, described below:

1. An employee abruptly quit the company in July 1993 after being told in a semi-annual performance review that he was "brain dead but physically alive." The

employee subsequently filed an age discrimination lawsuit against Amoul for $100,000. Legal counsel did not think the suit had any merit. However, because the estimated costs of defending the suit would be $30,000 or $40,000, counsel suggested offering an out-of-court settlement of $10,000. The offer was accepted quickly by the employee in December 1993 and appropriate papers were signed. The money is to be paid at the rate of $2,500 a month beginning in January 1994.

2. Amoul sells annually about 500,000 pairs of football shoes, primarily to high schools and colleges. During 1993, it discovered a design defect in one of its models. The cleats would break off with the potential consequence of serious ankle or knee injuries. Sales of the model were discontinued in June of 1993, but inventory of $352,000 is still on the books. It will have to be destroyed. By December 31, 1993, eight lawsuits had been filed against Amoul, ranging in amounts from $3,000 to $30,000. Legal counsel has advised the company that it can expect to lose most of these cases. With out-of-court settlements and a few trials, damages actually paid should range between $20,000 and $50,000.

3. The corporation routinely endorses (guarantees) the bank borrowings of many of its small suppliers, who otherwise would not have access to credit from financial institutions at a reasonable cost. In fact, on December 31, 1993, Amoul is contingently liable on $600,000 of these notes payable to banks. In one case, the maker (Amoul's supplier) of a note for $75,000 has gone bankrupt. The referee in bankruptcy estimates that only 20 percent of the liabilities of the supplier will be paid. Therefore, Amoul will have to pay the other 80 percent of this note.

4. Amoul Corporation has a small plant located in Central America. The plant, which makes tennis shoes, is incorporated as a separate subsidiary company, Amoul owning all of the stock. Under a new law in the Central American country, all businesses operating in that country must be at least 60 percent owned by the foreign government. In November of 1993, Amoul receives an offer of $100,000 for 60 percent of the subsidiary's stock. The Investment in Subsidiary account appears in the accounting records at $650,000. The offer is a take-it-or-leave-it offer; no negotiation is possible. Amoul has decided to accept the offer rather than close the plant, but the arrangements have not been finalized.

5. In years past, the company has paid about $30,000 in insurance premiums to cover liability and collision claims on its fleet of delivery trucks. Actual losses averaged less than that, so in 1993, the company decided to assume this risk itself. Accordingly, it discontinued the insurance coverage on April 1, 1993. From then to December 31, 1993, actual losses were $12,300. These were charged to a loss account. The chief accountant, however, wants to make an entry as follows:

Self-Insurance Expense . . . . . . . . . . . . . . . . . . . . . . . .    30,000
    Reserve for Self-Insurance . . . . . . . . . . . . . . . . . . . .            30,000

Then the $12,300 would be charged to the reserve account. Similar entries would be made in future years, and all future losses would be charged to the reserve as well. He argues, "This approach maintains consistency with past accounting practices, but instead of paying the $30,000 premium to an insurance company, we pay it to ourselves. Moreover, the Reserve for Self-Insurance account provides a place to which losses can be charged and communicates to readers of our statements that the lack of insurance coverage is not a major problem for us."

**Required:**

You are called in to provide advice on each of these situations. Indicate for each the journal entry, if any, that you would make. Also, indicate how the item would be reported on the financial statements or in the notes thereto. Explain your reasoning.

**16–18. Change from Completed-Contract Method to Percentage-of-Completion Method**
Build-It Fast Construction Company has recorded its contracts under the completed-contract method of accounting since its inception in 1988. Its income statements for the first three years appear below:

|  | 1988 | 1989 | 1990 |
|---|---|---|---|
| Construction revenues from completed contracts . . . . . . . . . | $ 0 | $ 1,500,000 | $ 5,500,000 |
| Cost of completed contracts . . . . . . . | (0) | (1,280,000) | (4,650,000) |
| Other expenses . . . . . . . . . . . . . | (80,000) | (120,000) | (200,000) |
| Income before taxes . . . . . . . . . . | $(80,000) | $ 100,000 | $ 650,000 |

In 1991, management decided to change to the percentage-of-completion method. An analysis was made of the contracts worked on from 1988 to 1990, assuming that the percentage-of-completion method had been used:

|  | Contract Number | | | |
|---|---|---|---|---|
|  | 565 | 566 | 567 | 568 |
| Total revenue . . . . . . | $1,500,000 | $3,000,000 | $2,500,000 | $2,000,000 |
| Portion earned in: |  |  |  |  |
| 1988 . . . . . . . . | 60% | 20% | — | — |
| 1989 . . . . . . . . | 40% | 40% | 30% | 30% |
| 1990 . . . . . . . . | — | 40% | 70% | 50% |
| Costs incurred in: |  |  |  |  |
| 1988 . . . . . . . . | $ 800,000 | $ 500,000 | $ — | $ — |
| 1989 . . . . . . . . | 480,000 | 1,100,000 | 600,000 | 540,000 |
| 1990 . . . . . . . . | — | 1,050,000 | 1,400,000 | 750,000 |
| Date completed . . . . . | 1989 | 1990 | 1990 | 1991 |

**Required:**

a. Prepare a schedule that will show the amount of income before tax that would have been recognized each year under the percentage-of-completion method.
b. Prepare the journal entry to be made during 1991 to reflect the change in accounting principle. Assume a tax rate of 30 percent for all years.
c. If *only* 1991 financial statements were presented, how would the change in accounting principle be reported?
d. If comparative financial statements for 1990 and 1991 were presented, how would the change in accounting principle be reported?

**16–19. Calculation of Earnings per Share**

The Stockholders' Equity section for Piper Corporation on December 31, 1992, was as follows:

| | |
|---|---:|
| 9% convertible preferred, $100 par, 100,000 shares authorized; 30,000 issued and outstanding . . . . . . . . . | $ 3,000,000 |
| Additional paid-in capital—preferred . . . . . . . . . . . . . . | 900,000 |
| Common stock, no par, 500,000 shares authorized; 270,000 shares issued and outstanding. . . . . . . . . . . . . | 7,400,000 |
| Retained earnings . . . . . . . . . . . . . . . . . . . . . . . . . | 2,300,000 |
| Total stockholders' equity . . . . . . . . . . . . . . . . . . . . . | $13,600,000 |

**Additional Information:**

1. Piper issued in 1987 $2,400,000 of 9% convertible bonds at face amount. The bonds are due in 2002 and can be converted until then into 22 common shares per $1,000 bond. The average Aa corporate bond yield was 13 percent when the bonds were issued.
2. The preferred stock was issued in 1988 at $130 per share, when the average Aa corporate bond yield was 12 percent. The preferred is convertible at the rate of three shares of common stock for each share of *preferred*. No shares have yet been converted.
3. Unexercised stock options to purchase 30,000 shares of common stock at $15 per share are outstanding. The options expire in 1996.
4. Of the 270,000 shares of common, 250,000 were outstanding during all of 1992; the remaining 20,000 were not issued until October 1.
5. The market price of the common shares remained constant at $30 throughout 1992.
6. Net income for 1992 was $1,032,000.
7. A 40 percent tax rate is assumed.

**Required:**

*a.* Calculate simple earnings per share for 1992.
*b.* Are Piper's convertible bonds and convertible preferred stock considered to be common stock equivalents?
*c.* Assume that the convertible preferred stock is a common stock equivalent. Would you use it in calculating primary earnings per share? Explain carefully. Would your answer differ if the conversion ratio were four shares of common stock for each share of preferred?
*d.* Calculate primary earnings per share for 1992.
*e.* Calculate fully diluted earnings per share for 1992.

**16–20. Intraperiod Tax Allocation**

Unusual Enterprises, Inc. is located in the midwestern plains. The following information is taken from its records for the year 1995:

Credits:

| | |
|---|---:|
| Sales . . . . . . . . . . . . . . . . . . . . . . . . . . . . . . . . . . . . . | $690,000 |
| Rent revenues and other income . . . . . . . . . . . . . . . . . . . . | 33,000 |
| Gain on sale of building . . . . . . . . . . . . . . . . . . . . . . . | 24,000 |
| Correction of recording error made in 1992. . . . . . . . . . . . . . | 120,000 |
| Income adjustment—change to equity method . . . . . . . . . . . | 30,000 |

Debits:

| | |
|---|---:|
| Cost of goods sold. . . . . . . . . . . . . . . . . . . . . . . . . . | 350,000 |
| Selling and administrative expense . . . . . . . . . . . . . . . . . . | 150,000 |
| Loss on retirement of bonds . . . . . . . . . . . . . . . . . . . . . | 40,000 |
| Hurricane damages . . . . . . . . . . . . . . . . . . . . . . . . . . | 170,000 |
| Interest expense. . . . . . . . . . . . . . . . . . . . . . . . . . . . | 2,000 |
| Income tax charges . . . . . . . . . . . . . . . . . . . . . . . . . . | 55,400 |
| Dividends . . . . . . . . . . . . . . . . . . . . . . . . . . . . . . . | 25,000 |

Taxable items are subject to a tax rate of 40 percent except (1) the gain on sale of building, which is taxed at a rate of 30 percent; (2) the error correction, which is taxed at 1992's tax rate of 35 percent; and (3) the income adjustment from the change to the equity method, which is taxed at a rate of only 6 percent. The latter item represents the cumulative impact up to January 1, 1995, from a change to the equity method from the cost method for an unconsolidated subsidiary. The equity method was used in 1995. Retained earnings at the beginning of the year were $123,900.

## Required:

a. Show how the income tax figure of $55,400 was derived.
b. Prepare in good form separate statements of income and retained earnings for 1995. Classify unusual items in their appropriate places and employ proper tax allocation procedures within and between the statements.

## Casette 16–1. Questions about Georgia-Pacific Corporation

At the back of the text is a complete set of financial statements of Georgia-Pacific Corporation taken from its annual report of 1987.

Answer the following questions about its disclosures of special items and additional information.

1. The income statements for all three years have a category called "unusual items." What do these unusual items represent? How do they differ from the gains on sales of assets (see statement of cash flows) and from extraordinary items and disposals of discontinued operations? How does their *reporting* on the income statement differ from these other items?
2. In 1985, an extraordinary gain of $10 million was reported. Do you believe this properly is an extraordinary item? Why does the income statement show $10 million, but the statement of cash flows shows that actually $14 million was collected in cash in 1986?
3. In 1985, the corporation showed a loss from discontinued operations of $30 million. What does this figure represent? Do you agree with the classification of this item as a discontinued operation?

4. Effective January 1, 1986 Georgia-Pacific made two changes in accounting principle—one involving pensions (Note 5) and one involving timberlands (Note 1). Yet, nowhere on the income statement for 1986 is there a caption, "Cumulative Effect of Change in Accounting Principle." Explain why. Did these changes in accounting principle cause income to increase or decrease over what it otherwise would have been?

5. Earnings per share
   a. Verify the calculation of earnings per share for all three years.
   b. Georgia-Pacific shows 107 million as the average number of shares outstanding during the year. However, listed as issued on the balance sheet were almost 108 million shares at the beginning of the year and 111.2 million shares at the end of the year. How do you explain the discrepancy between these numbers and the average?
   c. Georgia-Pacific had convertible preferred stock outstanding during 1986 and 1987 and had outstanding stock options. These generally are aspects of a complex capital structure. Why then does the company not display primary earnings per share and fully diluted earnings per share?

6. Segment reporting
   a. How many segments does Georgia-Pacific have? What are they?
   b. What are the advantages of reporting sales with and without the inclusion of intersegment sales? How might an analyst use this information?
   c. Calculate a return on assets for each segment by dividing operating income by identifiable assets. What are the potential pitfalls in using this information?
   d. Which segment is expanding the fastest?

7. Does Georgia-Pacific have a seasonal pattern to its business as evidenced by quarter-to-quarter fluctuations in sales?

8. Calculate the gross profit percentage (gross profit/net sales) for each quarter in 1986 and 1987.

9. Commitments and contingencies
   a. Why do you think Georgia-Pacific shows a caption called *Commitments and Contingencies* on its balance sheet but without any dollar amounts?
   b. What major commitments and contingencies does the company have?
   c. Why does Georgia-Pacific claim that the likelihood of any obligation with respect to its guarantee of the debt on the Atlanta Headquarters complex is remote? Would you record a liability for it?

**Casette 16–2.  Comprehensive Analysis of Special Items**

The following information was obtained from the accounting records and other sources of Horseshoe Bend Corporation:

**Income Statements**
**Years Ended December 31**

|  | 1992<br>*Preliminary* | 1991<br>*As Previously Reported* |
|---|---|---|
| Sales . . . . . . . . . . . . . . . . . | $2,000,000 | $2,200,000 |
| Cost of goods sold. . . . . . . . . . . . | 1,200,000 | 1,300,000 |
| Gross margin . . . . . . . . . . . . . . | 800,000 | 900,000 |

|  | *1992* *Preliminary* | *1991* *As Previously Reported* |
|---|---|---|
| Operating expenses . . . . . . . . . . . . | $ 600,000 | $ 620,000 |
| Other losses (income), net . . . . . . . . | 148,000 | (64,000) |
| Income taxes . . . . . . . . . . . . . | 21,000 | 138,000 |
|  | 769,000 | 694,000 |
| Net income. . . . . . . . . . . . . . | $ 31,000 | $ 206,000 |

### Retained Earnings Statements
### Years Ended December 31

|  | *1992* *Preliminary* | *1991* *As Previously Reported* |
|---|---|---|
| Balance at beginning of year . . . . . . . | $1,306,000 | $1,200,000 |
| Add: Net income . . . . . . . . . . . . | 31,000 | 206,000 |
| Deduct dividends . . . . . . . . . . . | 100,000 | 100,000 |
| Balance at end of year . . . . . . . . . | $1,237,000 | $1,306,000 |

## Additional Information:

1. All sales are on credit.
2. The tax rate is 40 percent on all types of taxable income. Assume for purposes of this problem that all amounts and changes in financial accounting also are appropriate for tax purposes.
3. The company has decided to change its estimate of bad debts expense from 1 percent to .5 percent of credit sales. This change reflects better collection experience and more control over credit granting. The change has not yet been reflected on the company's books, but the company does want the change to be made beginning in 1992. Bad debt expense is included in the operating expense amounts shown above.
4. After the preliminary statements for 1992 were prepared, management discovered that a patent acquired in 1989 has never been amortized. The cost of the patent was $120,000, and it should have been amortized on a straight-line basis over a useful life of 12 years.
5. The company elected at the end of 1992 to change the method of depreciating plant assets retroactively from an accelerated method to the straight-line method. This change has *not* been made on the company's books, but management wants the change recorded in 1992. Accelerated depreciation was $200,000 for 1992 and $180,000 for 1991, whereas straight-line depreciation was $80,000 for 1992 and $70,000 for 1991. For years prior to 1991 and for assets still in service in 1991, accelerated depreciation exceeded straight-line depreciation by $600,000.
6. A schedule of the items making up Other Losses (Income) appears below:

|  | *1992* | *1991* |
|---|---|---|
| Gain on sale of plant assets . . . . . . . . . . . . . . | $(24,000) | $(98,000) |
| Loss from discontinuance of inventory styles . . . . . . | 8,000 | 34,000 |
| Loss from sale of health-care division . . . . . . . . | 80,000 | — |
| Losses from employee strike . . . . . . . . . . . . | 36,000 | — |
| Loss from destruction of inventory pursuant to government prohibition . . . . . . . . . . . . . . . . . . . | 48,000 | — |
| Loss (Income) . . . . . . . . . . . . . . . . . . | $148,000 | $(64,000) |

The gains on sale of plant assets represent normal disposals of used equipment.

The loss on discontinuance of inventory styles represents the annual write-off of obsolete inventory done at the end of each model season.

The health care division was sold intact during 1992. In 1992 and 1991, health-care sales were $80,000 and $100,000; cost of goods sold were $40,000 and $50,000; and operating expenses were $28,000 and $30,000 respectively.

From July 18 to August 10, 1992, the company's employees were on strike. The $36,000 represents the cost of overtime to supervisory employees and other costs associated with the strike.

Inventory costs of $48,000 were written off in 1992. The write-off was necessitated by an unusual and nonrecurring prohibition by the government on the sale of products containing hexydryoxylene. The inventory was destroyed under government supervision.

## Required:

a. Prepare the journal entries necessary to reflect the above changes and corrections and their related tax effects. Assume that the accounts for 1992 have not been closed.

b. Prepare in good form a two-year comparative income statement and a two-year comparative statement of retained earnings for the Horseshoe Bend Corporation.

# Chapter 17

# Statement of Cash Flows

In Chapter 2 we presented three statements that stand at the center of the reporting function in financial accounting. We have discussed various aspects of the balance sheet and income statement. Now we turn our attention to the statement of cash flows. It provides information about how an entity's cash receipts and cash disbursements are affected by the period's operating, financing, and investing activities.

Consider the information provided by the income statements and balance sheets of three different companies. The first company has operated profitably every year, and in some years has experienced a large net income. Yet, the company always seems to be in a cash bind and has a low credit rating because of its inability to pay debts on time. If the company consistently has reported net income, why is it unable to meet its obligations when they come due? The second company has increased its plant and equipment almost 40 percent each year for the last three years. Where did it get the money necessary to expand so rapidly? The third company recently created quite a stir in the financial markets when it sold the largest single issue of bonds ever placed by a company of its size in its industry. Why were the bonds issued and what happened to the cash that was received in exchange for the bonds?

The search for answers to these questions begins with the statement of cash flows. Of course, the income statement and comparative balance sheet provide some information but only in a limited manner. The income statement deals solely with operations and—under accrual accounting—is affected by asset changes that do not necessarily mirror cash flows. Comparative balance sheets show only *net* changes in assets and equities for all activities between balance sheet dates, and these are not classified by cause.

Because an important responsibility of management is to finance adequately the activities of the firm, a special report relating particularly to financing and investing activities is a desirable addition to the reporting package. Historically, such a statement was commonly called a "funds statement." In 1971, its name was changed to "statement of changes in financial position," and it became a required presentation.[1] Then in 1987 it was further refined and relabeled the "statement of cash flows."[2] The FASB defines cash to include cash equivalents such as money market funds, commercial paper, and short-term treasury bills.

## INTERPRETATION AND USE OF THE STATEMENT

In general, the statement of cash flows discloses how the cash position of the firm is affected by various activities. An adequate supply of cash and cash equivalents is essential to ensure the proper functioning of the business and to maintain its financial soundness. In explaining the basic causes of changes in cash resources, the statement reflects the major events and policy decisions during the period with respect to financing practices and asset expansion. Much of this information about the *causes of changes* in asset makeup, equity composition, or liquidity structure would not be available or readily apparent from an analysis of other financial statements.

### Objectives of the Statement of Cash Flows

Consistent with the major objective of financial reporting mentioned in Chapter 1, the overall purpose of the cash flow statement is to assist investors in assessing a company's ability to generate positive future net cash flows. It does this by providing feedback information about the firm's actual cash flow movements in current and past periods.

Specifically, cash flow information should aid analysts in making judgments about three areas:

1. *Liquidity*—the firm's ability to meet its obligations as they come due and to pay dividends.
2. *Financial flexibility*—the firm's ability to effectively change the amount and timing of cash flows as a response to unexpected needs and opportunities.
3. *Operating capability*—the firm's ability to maintain its level of operations and the role of operations in generating cash flows.

These three subobjectives are clearly interrelated. However, a brief discussion of them individually may underscore the relevance of the statement of cash flows.

---

[1] AICPA, *APB Opinion No. 19*, "Reporting Changes in Financial Position" (New York, March 1971).

[2] FASB, *Statement of Financial Accounting Standards No. 95*, "Statement of Cash Flows" (Stamford, Conn., November 1987).

**Liquidity.**   The maintenance of satisfactory liquidity is essential to financial health. An adequate amount of cash and equivalents provides a financial defense against emergencies or seasonal drains of cash, enhancing the firm's creditworthiness. The statement of cash flows may highlight the causes of a chronic liquidity problem or signal an imminent critical cash flow problem. This statement can answer questions such as: Is management depleting cash in order to finance needed expansion or to meet required debt payments? How much cash was generated by nonrecurring events (e.g., selling off plant assets) compared to normal operations?

**Financial Flexibility.**   Although liquidity is certainly part of financial flexibility, the latter term is broader. Financial flexibility also involves the ability to employ unused borrowing capability and to realize cash from assets other than those used regularly in the business. Financial flexibility enables management to operate efficiently. It allows a firm to take all purchase discounts, achieve an optimal balance between short-term and long-term financing, and time its borrowings so as to minimize its financing costs. Financial flexibility also allows a firm to take advantage of special favorable opportunities—for example, expansion or merger possibilities. The evaluation of financial flexibility requires an understanding of the company's investing and financing transactions, which of course are one focal point of the statement of cash flows.

**Operating Capability.**   The relationship between net income and cash flow from operations and between cash flow from operations and asset replacement lies at the heart of this concept. For example, are dividends being paid with internally generated cash or with borrowed cash? In the latter case, the company may be cannibalizing itself and failing to maintain its productive capability. Over time, operations should provide sufficient cash not only to pay dividends but also to provide for normal asset replacement. External users need to understand the differences between net income and associated cash receipts and disbursements. How close are these two measures in a particular period and from year to year? Some analysts claim that a high correlation between income and cash flow from operations means that the earnings are of "higher quality." This means that the net income number is not unduly distorted by the allocations, estimates, and choices of different accounting principles that accompany accrual accounting. For this same reason, cash flow from operations may be more comparable across different firms than is net income.

## Uses of the Statement of Cash Flows

The brief discussion of objectives points to three important areas that affect cash flows. These are operations, financing, and investing. Not surprisingly, they provide the structure for both the preparation and interpretation of the statement of cash flows.

**Operations.**    Cash from operations probably is the most important number on the statement. Operations should provide a large continuing source of cash. Other sources of cash tend to be intermittent and less subject to management control. Indeed, without a solid base in operations, more risky sources of cash from external financing may not even be available to a company.

A statement of cash flows may be used by external audiences to answer questions about the impact of operations on cash and about the relationship between income and cash flows. Some of these questions might be: Does the firm have existing cash-generating capability for adequate protection against financial embarrassment? How was the firm able to pay large dividends and/or increase its cash balances in a period of low earnings or operating losses? To what extent is the company able to finance growth in noncurrent assets through its internal operations?

**Financing.**    Activities in this category involve transactions with creditors and owners. Borrowing from creditors or issuing stock to owners are major financing events that provide cash. Similarly, debt repayment or reacquisition of stock are financing transactions that reduce a firm's cash. In addition, the return on owners' equity in the form of dividends paid is classified as a cash outflow from financing.

A statement of cash flows, then, may be used by external audiences to evaluate a firm's past financing policies. The statement may help answer questions similar to the following: How much reliance has been placed on external versus internal sources of cash or on creditor versus stockholder sources of cash? How did the firm manage to expand its plant and equipment without borrowing or while at the same time retiring debt? How were additions to plant and equipment financed?

**Investing.**    Activities in this category involve major changes in total assets and asset composition. The acquisition and sale of plant assets constitute the major events here. Also included would be long-term lendings or investments in securities of other companies.

Stockholders and creditors may use a statement of cash flows to see how management has channeled financial resources into alternative uses, particularly expansion of property, plant, and equipment. By showing how cash has been invested, the statement illuminates a number of pertinent questions: Why did dividends not increase with increased net income? How were the proceeds from a stock or bond issue used? How much was received from selling the plant assets of a particular division and what was done with the money? Why did the firm have to borrow money when it had a large income? Is management using its cash inflow for any single purpose, such as plant modernization? Is the company's expansion happening too fast in relation to its ability to generate cash?

A statement of cash flows can be used to answer questions such as these about the historical performance of the firm. It also can be used as a tool to facilitate the planning of future operations and to assess the liquidity and financial flexibility of the company in future periods. Using a forecast (pro forma) cash flow statement, management can see what financial plans must be made to ensure that the desired future level of operations, dividends, expansion, and so on is achieved.

Investors project cash flows using prior periods' cash flow statements in evaluating financial riskiness. Creditors use the statement in estimating a firm's ability to pay its debts. Indeed, the ratio of cash from operations to total liabilities has been suggested as one of the best predictors of financial distress. Backer and Gosman showed that the ratios of cash from operations to long-term debt and to total liabilities were widely used by bond-rating agencies and other credit evaluators to judge creditworthiness.[3]

In the next few sections of this chapter, we review the major sources and uses of cash. Then, we explore the issues and problems involved in preparing a statement of cash flows. The concluding section examines Kimberly-Clark's cash flow disclosures.

## INFLOWS AND OUTFLOWS OF CASH

Transactions and events that generate cash are called "inflows"; those that use cash are called "outflows." Our objectives are to measure the cash effect of these transactions; to classify them into operating, financing, and investing categories; and to report them in an understandable manner. Figure 17–1 depicts the major events that fall under each of these three categories. As you can see, each category includes events that both provide and use cash.

### Inflows of Cash

Those events that result in an increase in cash are shown on the left side of Figure 17–1.

In the first category, the inflow of cash from operations comes from sales and other revenues. However, we must remember that revenues are measured by the amount of *assets,* not necessarily cash, received from the sale of goods and services. To obtain the cash inflow from sales of product, for example, we must measure collections from customers. That is the source of cash corresponding to the accrual-based sales figure. If accounts receivable has increased significantly during the period, cash collections will be smaller than sales.

---

[3] Morton Backer and Martin L. Gosman, *Financial Reporting and Business Liquidity* (New York: National Association of Accountants, 1978).

**FIGURE 17–1** Inflows and Outflows of Cash

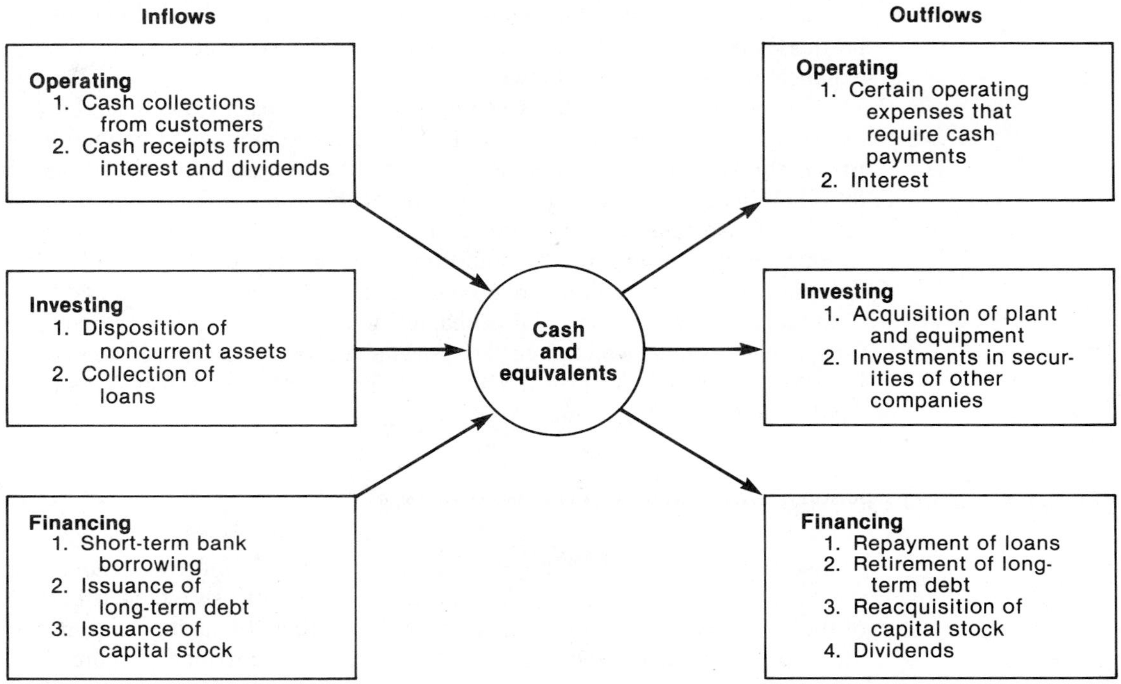

The major source in the investing category involves the sale of noncurrent assets. Whether the noncurrent asset is sold at a gain or at a loss does not affect the cash flow. For instance, assume that a firm sells for $18,000 in cash some excess land that originally cost $22,000. The journal entry to record this sale would be:

```
Cash . . . . . . . . . . . . . . . . . . . . . . . .   18,000
Loss on Sale of Land  . . . . . . . . . . . . . . . .    4,000
    Land . . . . . . . . . . . . . . . . . . . . . .            22,000
```

The loss indicates the decrease in owners' equity because total assets decrease (land decreases more than cash increases). However, this transaction, *although reducing total assets, increases cash*. Therefore, it should appear on the statement of cash flows as an inflow in the amount of $18,000.

Short- and long-term financing is a third major type of cash inflow. If a company engages in bank borrowing or issues additional bonds or stock, cash usually increases. For example, if a company issues for $202,000 bonds with a face value of $200,000, then cash increases $202,000. The offsetting credits are to noncurrent liability accounts, Bonds Payable and

Premium on Bonds Payable. This event is an inflow. The issuance of preferred stock or common stock could be analyzed in a similar manner. Note that the amount of change in the par or face value of the shares issued does not govern the amount of cash inflow resulting from the transaction. The total proceeds of the sale received in cash are recorded on the statement of cash flows.

## Outflows of Cash

Typical events that result in an outflow of cash are shown on the right side of Figure 17–1. Again we have grouped them under the operating, investing, and financing categories.

Expenses record decreases in owners' equity as assets are used in the process of generating revenues. However, only those expenses that involve a current outflow of cash are relevant for the statement of cash flows. Some expenses—such as depreciation expense, amortization of patents, and depletion expense—represent solely allocations of costs incurred in prior periods. These expenses decrease owners' equity and decrease a *noncurrent* asset; therefore, they are called "noncash" expenses. Other operating expenses such as cost of goods sold, labor expense, and rent expense are related to current cash flows. However, like sales revenue, they must be converted from an accrual basis to their cash flow counterparts—cash payments to suppliers for purchased inventory, cash disbursements to employees, and cash expenditures for rent. Procedures to accomplish this conversion are discussed and illustrated later in the chapter.

The second type of transaction that decreases cash is the acquisition of noncurrent assets, such as land, plant assets, or intangibles. These acquisitions frequently cause a concomitant decrease in cash. Also included as uses of cash for investing would be increased investments in the capital stock and bonds of other companies or additional cash loans made to others.

When cash is used to retire bonds or preferred stock or to acquire treasury stock, an outflow of cash from financing activities occurs. The face value or par amount retired is not significant from a cash flow viewpoint. Only the amount of the decrease in cash is relevant. Financing uses also encompass dividend payments.[4] This transaction usually involves a debit to an owners' equity account (Preferred Dividends or Common Dividends) and a credit to

---

[4] Three of the seven members of the Financial Accounting Standards Board dissented to the issuance of *FASB Statement No. 95*. They believed that interest payments should be classified as an outflow from financing rather than as a cash outflow from operations. We are sympathetic to the conceptual argument that both interest and dividends represent recurring payments to investors arising from financing decisions and not operating decisions. However, we illustrate the required method of classification. The same three members also would have classified interest and dividend receipts under investing rather than operations.

cash. To the extent that dividends declared by the board of directors have not been paid in cash, the Dividends Payable account will increase, and the amount of dividends declared must be adjusted to a cash basis. The procedure is similar to that for operating expenses.

## STATEMENT OF CASH FLOWS

The statement of cash flows for Cardinal Company is shown in Table 17–1. In the next section, we will talk about how accountants prepare such a statement. But first, let us look at the end result.

Notice that like the income statement, the statement of cash flows is prepared for a period of time, for the year 1990 in this case. It is divided into three major sections—operating, investing, and financing. Within each section, the major inflows and outflows are listed. The net effect of those flows

---

**TABLE 17–1**

### CARDINAL CORPORATION
#### Statement of Cash Flows
#### For the Year 1990

| | | | |
|---|---|---:|---:|
| **Net cash flow provided by operating activities:*** | | | $ 37,300 |
| **Cash flows from investing activities:** | | | |
| Acquisition of land | | $ (30,000) | |
| Acquisition of equipment | | (54,000) | |
| Proceeds from sale of equipment | | 19,200 | |
| Proceeds from sale of investment securities | | 60,000 | |
| Net cash used in investing activities | | | (4,800) |
| **Cash flows from financing activities:** | | | |
| Proceeds from increase in bank loans | | $ 6,000 | |
| Payments to retire bonds | | (186,800) | |
| Proceeds from issuing preferred stock | | 88,000 | |
| Proceeds from issuing common stock | | 30,000 | |
| Dividends paid: | | | |
| Preferred | $ (6,000) | | |
| Common | (50,000) | (56,000) | |
| Net cash used in financing activities | | | (118,800) |
| Net decrease in cash | | | $ (86,300) |
| Cash and cash equivalents at beginning of year | | | 108,700 |
| Cash and cash equivalents at end of year | | | $ 22,400 |

*Normally there would be a schedule that would provide a detailed derivation of this amount. The schedule would either appear in the body of the statement or accompany it. We will provide such a schedule later in our discussion.

reconciles the beginning and ending balances of cash and cash equivalents on the balance sheet.

In actual annual reports, the statement would be shown in comparative form for two or three years so readers could analyze trends and components over time. Nevertheless, even the single-year statement reveals some interesting information. For instance, net cash flow from operating activities is only $37,300—insufficient to cover the dividends of $56,000 during the year. Yet, if we glance ahead at Table 17–3, we note that net income was $79,000. Evidently, at least in 1990, cash flow from operations did not track closely with net income. The reasons for this will become clear as we look at the calculation of the $37,300 figure.

Cardinal Corporation engaged in a number of major investing activities in 1990. Proceeds from the sale of equipment and the liquidation of long-term investments more than offset the plant expansion. Perhaps the company deliberately had built up its investments over the years with the intention of cashing them to pay for plant expansion. A review of past years' statements of cash flows might reveal whether or not this supposition is accurate.

The major cash outflows were in the financing area. In addition to dividends, $186,800 of cash was needed to retire bonds in 1990. Some of this money was raised through the issuance of preferred stock and common stock. Normally the substitution of stockholders' equity for bonds improves the long-term financial solvency of the business. In this case, the substitution was not complete; the result was a fairly large drain on cash balances. Again, perhaps the company had increased its cash balances in prior years in anticipation of the bond retirement. We would want to look at statements of cash flows for 1989 and perhaps 1988.

In brief, we can summarize 1990's results as follows: Cash balances were significantly reduced primarily to provide for dividends not fully funded by operations and to provide for the bonds retired that were not funded by the issuance of stockholder capital. If this cash drain had been anticipated, our concern would not be great. However, if the decrease is from a normal level of cash balances, then a significant adverse effect on liquidity and financial flexibility has occurred. In any case, external audiences might be worried about the relationship between cash flow from operations and dividends, particularly if similar patterns appeared in prior years.

## PREPARATION OF THE STATEMENT

Having set forth the general framework for the statement of cash flows and having discussed the usefulness of the statement, we now illustrate its preparation. Tables 17–2 and 17–3 contain the financial statements of Cardinal Corporation. Included are a comparative balance sheet as of the end of 1989 and 1990 and a combined statement of income and retained earnings

## TABLE 17–2

### CARDINAL CORPORATION
### Comparative Balance Sheet
### As of December 31, 1989 and 1990

|  | 1990 | 1989 |
|---|---:|---:|
| **Assets** | | |
| Current assets: | | |
| Cash. | $ 22,400 | $ 108,700 |
| Accounts receivable | 107,700 | 97,600 |
| Interest receivable | 1,500 | 1,300 |
| Inventories | 159,600 | 130,000 |
| Prepaid insurance | 4,600 | 6,000 |
| Total current assets. | 295,800 | 343,600 |
| Land | 290,000 | 260,000 |
| Plant and equipment*. | 684,000 | 660,000 |
| Accumulated depreciation | (162,000) | (144,000) |
| Investments—at cost | 40,000 | 100,000 |
| Goodwill (net of amortization) | 38,000 | 42,000 |
| Total assets. | $1,185,800 | $1,261,600 |
| **Equities** | | |
| Current liabilities: | | |
| Accounts payable (merchandise) | $ 186,000 | $ 218,000 |
| Wages and salaries payable | 8,000 | 6,000 |
| Interest payable | 6,000 | 4,000 |
| Income taxes payable. | 1,000 | 500 |
| Bank loans payable. | 28,000 | 22,000 |
| Other accrued liabilities | 5,000 | 2,500 |
| Total current liabilities | 234,000 | 253,000 |
| Deferred income taxes | 15,200 | 13,000 |
| Bonds payable. | 200,000 | 400,000 |
| Total liabilities | 449,200 | 666,000 |
| Stockholders' equity: | | |
| Preferred stock | 148,000 | 60,000 |
| Common stock | 480,000 | 450,000 |
| Retained earnings | 108,600 | 85,600 |
| Total stockholders' equity | 736,600 | 595,600 |
| Total equities | $1,185,800 | $1,261,600 |

*Management indicates that the capital expenditures for new plant and equipment during 1990 were $54,000.

**TABLE 17–3**

### CARDINAL CORPORATION
#### Combined Statement of Income and Retained Earnings
#### For the Year 1990

| | | |
|---|---:|---:|
| Revenues from net sales | | $565,700 |
| Operating expenses: | | |
|   Cost of goods sold | $336,000 | |
|   Wage and salary expense | 68,000 | |
|   Advertising expense | 2,000 | |
|   Insurance expense | 3,600 | |
|   Depreciation expense | 24,000 | |
|   Amortization of goodwill | 4,000 | |
|   Other operating expenses | 32,000 | |
|     Total operating expenses | | 469,600 |
| Operating income | | $ 96,100 |
| Nonoperating items: | | |
|   Interest and dividend revenue | $(23,100) | |
|   Interest expense | 26,000 | |
|   Loss on sale of equipment | 4,800 | |
|     Total nonoperating deductions | | 7,700 |
| Income before income taxes | | $ 88,400 |
| Income taxes | | 19,300 |
| Income before extraordinary item | | $ 69,100 |
| Extraordinary item: Gain on retirement of bonds of $13,200, | | |
|   minus applicable income taxes of $3,300 | | 9,900 |
| Net income | | $ 79,000 |
| Retained earnings, January 1 | | 85,600 |
| | | $164,600 |
| Dividends: | | |
|   Preferred | $ 6,000 | |
|   Common | 50,000 | |
|     Total dividends | | 56,000 |
| Retained earnings, December 31 | | $108,600 |

for 1990. From these and some other items of information, we shall construct the statement of cash flows which appeared as Table 17–1.

A thorough knowledge of the material covered in Chapters 1 through 11 and 13 through 14 will help you understand this section. Advanced topics such as leases (Chapter 12), parent investments in unconsolidated subsidiaries (Chapter 15), and foreign currency adjustments (Chapter 16) are discussed in the section, Treatment of Complex Items.

## Cash Flows from Operations

A major source of cash for most companies is operations. Because the income statement summarizes the operations of the firm, we look to it for the information necessary to calculate cash flows related to this area. Cash from operations is a net flow, consisting of the excess of cash inflows associated with revenue transactions over those cash outflows associated with certain expense transactions. Special analysis is frequently required for determining the full impact of extraordinary items on cash. Consequently, we focus our attention primarily on the items included in income before income taxes and on income tax expense.

Two types of adjustments are necessary to convert the $69,100 income before extraordinary items of Cardinal Corporation to cash flow from operations. First, expenses that do not involve current cash outlays should be ignored. Depreciation expense and amortization of goodwill are noncash deductions. They represent decreases in noncurrent assets and do reduce net income, but they do not affect cash this period.

Second, we must convert each revenue and the rest of the expenses from an accrual to a cash basis. This means adjusting each item for the effect of changes in the current assets or liabilities operationally related to it. Operationally related current assets and liabilities are those that directly affect the measurement of income statement items. Items like accounts receivable, merchandise inventory, and wages and salaries payable are examples. For Cardinal Company, the only current asset or current liability that does not directly affect operating activity is Bank Loans Payable. Changes in it are considered under financing.

**Cash Receipts from Customers.** Sales during 1990 were $565,700. However, if accounts receivable changed during the year, cash collected from customers will be more or less than the sales. For example, if cash received from customers (credits to Accounts Receivable) were exactly equal to sales revenue (debits to Accounts Receivable), accounts receivable would not change during the period. However, if accounts receivable decreased during the year, then the company collected an amount of cash equal to the sales revenue plus an additional amount of cash equal to the reduction in accounts receivable. The relationship between sales and cash collections may be seen as follows:

$$\text{Sales} \begin{cases} - \text{ Increase in accounts receivable} \\ + \text{ Decrease in accounts receivable} \end{cases} = \text{Cash collections from customers}$$

Cardinal Corporation's accounts receivable increased $10,100 during 1990. Collections from customers must have been less than the $565,700 of sales. Consequently, the source of cash from customer collections is actually $555,600 ($565,700 − $10,100).

**Interest and Dividends Received in Cash.**   The income statement reveals interest and dividend revenue of $23,100. This is a potential source of cash. However, like sales, it must be converted from an accrual basis to a cash basis. Interest receivable increased $200 in 1990 (from $1,300 to $1,500). Interest collected in cash must have been less than interest earned. Accordingly, the cash receipt from interest and dividends is only $22,900 ($23,100 − $200).

**Cash Payments to Suppliers.**   With cost of goods sold, we must consider both changes in inventory levels and changes in the amount of accounts payable related to inventory purchases. The amount desired in the end is cash payments for purchases. Its relationship to cost of goods sold is summarized below:

$$\text{Cost of goods sold } \begin{Bmatrix} + & \text{Increase in inventory} \\ - & \text{Decrease in inventory} \end{Bmatrix} = \begin{matrix} \text{Merchandise} \\ \text{purchases} \end{matrix}$$

$$\begin{matrix} \text{Merchandise} \\ \text{purchases} \end{matrix} \begin{Bmatrix} - & \text{Increase in accounts payable} \\ + & \text{Decrease in accounts payable} \end{Bmatrix} = \begin{matrix} \text{Cash payments} \\ \text{for purchases} \end{matrix}$$

For Cardinal Corporation, we note from Table 17–2 that inventories increased $29,600 and that accounts payable related to inventory purchases decreased $32,000. These facts indicate that merchandise purchases exceeded goods sold and cash payments exceeded the amount of purchases. The outflow of cash can be calculated as follows:

| | |
|---|---:|
| Cost of goods sold. . . . . . . . . . . . . . . | $336,000 |
| Add: Increase in inventory . . . . . . . . . . | 29,600 |
| Merchandise purchases . . . . . . . . . . . . | 365,600 |
| Add: Decrease in accounts payable . . . . . . . | 32,000 |
| Cash payments for purchases . . . . . . . . . | $397,600 |

**Cash Payment to Employees.**   Because Wages and Salaries Payable increased $2,000, we can infer that cash payments to employees were only $66,000—$2,000 less than the $68,000 expense. The general procedure for adjustment is shown below:

$$\text{Labor expense } \begin{Bmatrix} - & \text{Increase in wages payable} \\ + & \text{Decrease in wages payable} \end{Bmatrix} = \begin{matrix} \text{Cash payments} \\ \text{to employees} \end{matrix}$$

**Cash Payments for Insurance.**   Although insurance expense was \$3,600 in 1990, we want a measure of the cash outlay for insurance premiums. The following adjustment needs to be made:

$$\text{Insurance expense} \left\{ \begin{array}{l} + \quad \text{Increase in prepaid insurance} \\ - \quad \text{Decrease in prepaid insurance} \end{array} \right\} = \begin{array}{l} \text{Cash outlay} \\ \text{for premiums} \end{array}$$

A similar adjustment would be appropriate for any operating expense related to a specific prepayment. For Cardinal Corporation, the decrease in Prepaid Insurance of \$1,400 means that cash disbursements for insurance premiums were only \$2,200 (\$3,600 − \$1,400).

**Other Cash Related Expenses.**   Assume that "other accrued expenses" on the balance sheet refers to the various accruals related to advertising and other operating expenses. Because this liability increased \$2,500 during the period, the total of these expenses must have exceeded the cash expenditures for the items by that amount. Consequently, the use of cash is \$31,500 (\$2,000 + \$32,000 − \$2,500). The general approach to adjustment is:

$$\text{Expense} \left\{ \begin{array}{l} - \quad \text{Increase in accrued liability} \\ + \quad \text{Decrease in accrued liability} \end{array} \right\} = \text{Cash expenditures}$$

**Cash Payments for Interest.**   The payment of interest represents an outflow of cash. Interest expense of \$26,000 can be found on the income statement in Table 17–3. The balance sheet shows that interest payable increased \$2,000 during the year. Using the approach for accrued expenses discussed in the previous section, we can deduce that the cash payments for interest were only \$24,000 (\$26,000 − \$2,000 increase in the accrued liability).

**Income Tax Disbursements.**   Total income taxes for Cardinal Corporation are influenced by operating items, nonoperating items, and extraordinary items. The cash effects of some of these events are reported elsewhere in the statement of cash flows. However, the Financial Accounting Standards Board requires that all income taxes *paid* be included in determining net cash flow from operating activities. The Board reasoned that although accrued tax *expense* might be directly associated with specific transactions, *taxes paid* could not be.

Income taxes on an accrual basis are \$22,600 (\$19,300 + \$3,300 applicable to the gain on retirement of bonds). However, the portion of income taxes that results in an increase in the *deferred* income tax liability is a non-cash deduction. As noted in Chapter 13, a Deferred Taxes account is established at the initiation of a temporary difference and is usually credited for the difference between the debit to Income Tax Expense and the credit to Current Income Taxes Payable. If Cardinal Corporation recorded a total of \$22,600 of income taxes on its 1990 income statement (including the tax resulting from the extraordinary gain) and simultaneously increased the

Deferred Income Taxes liability by $2,200 on its balance sheet, the following entry must have been made:

| | | |
|---|---:|---:|
| Income Tax Expense. | 22,600 | |
|     Current Income Taxes Payable. | | 20,400 |
|     Deferred Income Taxes. | | 2,200 |

Although the *current* portion of the income tax expense is $20,400, this amount is not necessarily paid in cash. What is the cash outlay for taxes? Only $19,900. We obtain this by adjusting the current portion of the tax expense of $20,400 by the increase of $500 in the balance of the current tax liability owed to the IRS on the position statement ($1,000 − $500). Although income for 1990 is properly reduced by the entire $22,600 of income tax expense, the cash effect is only $19,900.

In summary, the two-stage adjustment for income taxes is as follows:

$$\text{Income tax expense} \begin{Bmatrix} - & \text{Increase in deferred taxes} \\ + & \text{Decrease in deferred taxes} \end{Bmatrix} = \text{Current portion of tax expense}$$

$$\text{Current portion of tax expense} \begin{Bmatrix} - & \text{Increase in current taxes payable} \\ + & \text{Decrease in current taxes payable} \end{Bmatrix} = \text{Cash outlay for taxes}$$

Table 17–4 summarizes the cash flow from operations. The $37,300 net cash flow from operations derives from a restatement of individual revenues and expenses on a cash basis. Such a schedule illustrates what is called the "direct approach" to the reporting of operating cash flows.

Practically, it may be difficult to relate specific current assets and current liabilities to particular revenue and expenses on the income statement. The one-to-one correspondence, although helpful in understanding the derivation

---

**TABLE 17–4**    Direct Reporting of Cash from Operations

| | | |
|---|---:|---:|
| **Cash inflows:** | | |
| Collections from customers | $555,600 | |
| Interest and dividends received . | 22,900 | $578,500 |
| **Cash outflows:** | | |
| For merchandise purchases | $397,600 | |
| For employee services | 66,000 | |
| For insurance premiums. | 2,200 | |
| For advertising and other operating expenses . | 31,500 | |
| For interest payments. | 24,000 | |
| For income taxes | 19,900 | 541,200 |
| Net cash inflow from operations | | $ 37,300 |

of cash flow from operations, is not really necessary if we only wish to focus on the net result. Therefore, most companies employ an alternative procedure for reporting cash from operations.

This procedure is called the "indirect" or "reconciliation approach." It begins with the net income figure and adjusts for those items not related to cash and for gains and losses resulting from investing and financing transactions. An adjustment is also made in total for the changes in the current assets and current liabilities related to operations. This approach for Cardinal Corporation is shown in Table 17–5. Such a computation would appear either in the body of the statement or in a separate schedule.

The advantage of the indirect approach is that it ties together the income statement and the statement of cash flows, addressing the relationship between net income and cash flows from operations. Earlier we noted that the statement of cash flows allows readers to assess the reasons for differences between net income and net cash flow from operating activities.

The primary disadvantage of the indirect approach is the possibility of confusion and misinterpretation. Depreciation, amortization, and taxes deferred are *not sources* of cash. They are added back because the initial starting figure, net income, is understated from a cash standpoint. Unfortunately, these

**TABLE 17–5** Indirect Reporting of Cash from Operations

| | | |
|---|---:|---:|
| Net income | | $ 79,000 |
| Adjustments to reconcile net income to | | |
| net cash provided by operating activities: | | |
| Expenses not using cash or related to | | |
| investing and financing cash flows: | | |
| Depreciation expense | $ 24,000 | |
| Amortization of goodwill | 4,000 | |
| Increase in deferred taxes | 2,200 | |
| Loss on sale of equipment | 4,800 | |
| Gain on retirement of bonds | (13,200) | 21,800 |
| Adjustments to convert to a cash basis: | | |
| Increase in accounts receivable | $(10,100) | |
| Increase in interest receivable | (200) | |
| Increase in inventories | (29,600) | |
| Decrease in prepaid insurance | 1,400 | |
| Decrease in accounts payable | (32,000) | |
| Increase in wages and salaries payable | 2,000 | |
| Increase in interest payable | 2,000 | |
| Increase in income taxes payable | 500 | |
| Increase in other accrued liabilities | 2,500 | (63,500) |
| Net cash flow from operations | | $ 37,300 |

items, particularly depreciation, are all too frequently looked upon as generating cash simply because they appear to be an addition to net income.

## Analysis of Changes in Other Accounts

Apart from cash generated by operations, the statement of cash flows primarily conveys information about investing and financing activities. The very nature of these activities points us to an analysis of other balance sheet accounts. The acquisition or sale of noncurrent assets will affect these accounts. Similarly, long-term liabilities, owners' equity items, and current liabilities not related to operations will reflect the issuance or retirement of stocks and bonds, short-term borrowing, and other financing flows. Consequently, a careful analysis of the changes in other accounts, as revealed by the comparative balance sheet, is a logical next step in preparing a statement of cash flows.

An examination of Table 17–2 reveals the following changes in these accounts:

| Account | Increase | Decrease |
|---|---|---|
| Land . . . . . . . . . . . . . . . . . . . . . . . . | $30,000 | |
| Plant and equipment . . . . . . . . . . . . . . | 24,000 | |
| Accumulated depreciation . . . . . . . . . . . | 18,000 | |
| Investments. . . . . . . . . . . . . . . . . . . | | $ 60,000 |
| Goodwill . . . . . . . . . . . . . . . . . . . . | | 4,000 |
| Bank loans payable . . . . . . . . . . . . . | 6,000 | |
| Deferred income taxes . . . . . . . . . . . . | 2,200 | |
| Bonds payable . . . . . . . . . . . . . . . | | 200,000 |
| Preferred stock . . . . . . . . . . . . . . . | 88,000 | |
| Common stock . . . . . . . . . . . . . . . . | 30,000 | |
| Retained earnings . . . . . . . . . . . . . . | 23,000 | |

If we can explain each of these changes, we most likely will have considered all of the events that have affected Cardinal Corporation's cash. Indeed, if we can account for the change in all asset, liability, and owners' equity accounts other than Cash, because of the accounting equation we will have accounted for the change in cash.

The earlier discussion of cash from operations provides explanations for the entire change in Goodwill (amortization of $4,000) and Deferred Income Taxes (expense exceeding current taxes payable by $2,200). We also explained one component of the change in Accumulated Depreciation (depreciation expense of $24,000) and one factor influencing the net increase in Retained Earnings (net income of $79,000). Let us take the remaining changes and fit them into our investing and financing framework.

## Investing Activities

As you will recall, investing activities include two major types of events—acquisition and sale of noncurrent assets, and lending money and collecting loans.

**Sale of Noncurrent Assets.**    To determine whether cash has been generated through the sale of noncurrent assets, we have to investigate three areas: (1) noncurrent asset decreases as revealed by the comparative position statement, (2) gains or losses on the income statement indicating that noncurrent assets have been sold, and (3) other information relating to asset acquisitions and retirements that accompanies the financial statements. When we do this for Cardinal Corporation, we find two inflows—$60,000 from investments and $19,200 from the sale of plant and equipment. Each figure is derived below.

Table 17–2 reveals a $60,000 decrease in the Investments account. Typically, this account decreases by sale. Unless the notes to the financial statements provide an alternative explanation, a reasonable conclusion is that $60,000 of investments have been sold. Because no gain or loss is reported, we presume that the sale is at book value. Thus, sale of investments is one inflow of cash appearing in the investing section.

A Loss on Sale of Equipment account appears on the income statement for the year. Accordingly, a sale of equipment must have occurred. Furthermore, Table 17–2 shows a net increase in the Accumulated Depreciation account of only $18,000; this is less than the $24,000 of Depreciation Expense. Similarly, the Plant and Equipment account increased by an amount which is smaller than the capital expenditures of $54,000 for 1990 (see the note on Table 17–2). All of these facts strongly suggest the presence of asset retirements.

However, as we noted before, the net proceeds, not the gain or loss, is the cash effect. The loss discloses only that total assets decreased as the result of the transaction; the cash flow statement is concerned with the increase in cash associated with the proceeds from the sale. To find the source of cash, we must reconstruct the journal entry that was made when the equipment was sold. Combining our information into normal journal entry form, we can infer that cash was increased by $19,200 at the time of plant retirement:

| | | |
|---|---|---|
| Cash . . . . . . . . . . . . . . . . . . . . . . . . . | 19,200 | |
| Accumulated Depreciation . . . . . . . . . . . . . | 6,000 | |
| Loss on Sale of Equipment . . . . . . . . . . . . . | 4,800 | |
| Plant and Equipment . . . . . . . . . . . . . . . | | 30,000 |

The loss on sale is found on the income statement. The rest of the entry, except for cash, is derived from the following reconstruction of ledger accounts:

| **Accumulated Depreciation** | | | **Plant and Equipment** | | |
|---|---|---|---|---|---|
| (x) Total depreciation on retirements | 144,000 | Beginning balance | Beginning balance | 660,000 | (y) Original cost of retirements |
| | 24,000 | Depreciation expense added during 1990—see income statement | New equipment purchases— given | 54,000 | |
| | 162,000 | Ending balance | Ending balance | 684,000 | |

$$\$144{,}000 + \$24{,}000 - x = \$162{,}000 \qquad \$660{,}000 + \$54{,}000 - y = \$684{,}000$$
$$x = \$\ \ 6{,}000 \qquad\qquad\qquad y = \$\ \ 30{,}000$$

In order to account for the net changes of only $18,000 in Accumulated Depreciation and only $24,000 in Plant and Equipment, we assume that the former account must have been debited $6,000 and the latter credited for $30,000 when the equipment was sold.

**Acquisition of Noncurrent Assets.** An analysis of the noncurrent assets on the comparative balance sheet again is the starting point for this major category of cash usage. However, the net change in a noncurrent asset may not reveal the full amount of cash spent. Consideration must be given to the effect of retirements in a computation of the *gross* additions to noncurrent assets.

In the Cardinal Corporation example, the gross equipment purchases are given as an additional piece of direct information at the bottom of Table 17–2. Keep in mind, however, that in some cases this figure could be derived through a reconstruction of the entries made in the Plant and Equipment account, if we had supplementary information about retirements. In addition to the $54,000 purchase of equipment, there was a $30,000 increase in the Land account. We can reasonably assume that cash was used to purchase land.

## Financing Activities

Major changes in cash from financing events are usually relatively easy to find. Look at the comparative position statement to see if short-term borrowings, long-term liabilities, or capital stock accounts have changed. If they have increased, there probably has been an inflow of cash. If they have decreased, cash probably has been disbursed. We do need to check to see if the increase or decrease is the result of a netting of retirements against new issues. Also remember that changes in the Treasury Stock account, although not present in Cardinal Corporation, may signal significant cash outflows or inflows in other companies.

**Issuance of Stock and Borrowing.** For Cardinal Corporation, long-term debt has decreased. Short-term bank loans along with preferred stock and common stock have increased. These latter three events represent inflows of cash in the amounts of $6,000, $88,000, and $30,000, respectively.

Three words of caution are in order. First, if the $6,000 increase in bank loans results from material netting of new bank borrowings against repayments to banks, Cardinal Corporation should show the gross receipts and gross disbursements separately. Second, recall from the discussion in Chapter 14 that proceeds from stock issuances often are credited to two balance sheet accounts—the stock account for the par or stated value and an additional paid-in capital account for the excess over par or stated value. Under such circumstances, the increases in both of the accounts reflect the total proceeds from the sale of the stock and should be combined into *one* inflow of cash.

Third, the issuance of a stock dividend (in contrast to a cash dividend) involves no new financing. The entry only involves a debit to Retained Earnings and a credit to Common Stock and, probably, to Additional Paid-in Capital. If evidence of a stock dividend exists, the analyst must be careful not to infer too quickly that the entire change in the capital stock accounts represents an inflow of cash. The amount of the stock dividend must be deducted from the increase in these accounts before the actual amount of cash can be ascertained.

**Bond Retirement.** The only long-term equity of Cardinal Corporation that declined is bonds payable. The extraordinary gain on the income statement provides the reason—a retirement of part of the bond issue. A reconstruction of the retirement entry reveals a use of cash for return of invested capital of $186,000:

| | | |
|---|---:|---:|
| Bonds Payable . . . . . . . . . . . . . . . . . . . . | 200,000 | |
| Gain on Retirement of Bonds . . . . . . . . . | | 13,200 |
| Cash . . . . . . . . . . . . . . . . . . . . . | | 186,800 |

Had there been an unamortized discount or premium related to the bonds being retired, it would have been removed from the accounts at the same time as the bonds. The estimate of cash paid out would then change.

**Dividends.** Cash dividends represent a cash disbursement. The amounts of dividends *declared* can be found on the combined statement of income and retained earnings. For example, Table 17–3 reveals that Cardinal Corporation had declared dividends of $6,000 and $50,000 on preferred and common stock, respectively. The $79,000 net income minus the $56,000 of dividends equals the $23,000 net increase in Retained Earnings during 1990. The balance sheets show no dividends payable at the beginning or end of the year. Therefore, we infer that all the dividends declared were paid in cash during 1990.

## Summary of Preparation Procedures

For most situations, the approach illustrated in this chapter leads to an accurate statement of cash flows. Never lose sight of the original transaction; a reconstruction of the journal entry will reveal the effect on cash whenever ambiguity is encountered. In fact, preparation of the statement of cash flows almost always entails the reconstruction of some transactions and the analysis of some ledger accounts. However, if we understand the type of events in each of the categories (operating, financing, investing), we know where to begin looking for the details. Then the preparation is not difficult.

If we wish to explain changes in the cash account, we must account for the changes in all of the noncash accounts. If the noncash accounts are current assets and liabilities related to operations, they are used in adjusting operating revenues and expenses to a cash basis. Changes in other noncash accounts may suggest major investing and financing activities or adjustments needed to measure other cash flows.

# OTHER SIGNIFICANT FINANCING AND INVESTING ACTIVITIES

A detailed accounting for the changes in noncash assets and equities sometimes reveals the existence of significant financing and investing activities that do not flow through the cash account. Examples include the acquisition of assets in exchange for stock or debt, conversion of bonds into stock, and the exchange of noncurrent assets.

The FASB believes that these events provide relevant information about financing and investing activities of the firm. To complete the disclosures, the Board requires that these events be reported in separate schedules and notes, *but not on the statement of cash flows*.

Two such events to be discussed here are the acquisition of noncurrent assets through the issuance of securities and the conversion of bonds into stock. For the sake of illustration, let us assume that not all of the $88,000 of preferred stock shown in Table 17–1 was sold for cash. Suppose that $20,000 of it was issued in exchange for land and that $50,000 of preferred stock was issued as part of a conversion or retirement of the bond issue. Only $18,000 was sold for cash. The entries relating to land, preferred stock, and bonds *would have been:*

| | | |
|---|---|---|
| Land . . . . . . . . . . . . . . . . . . . . . . . . | 20,000 | |
|     Preferred Stock . . . . . . . . . . . . . . . . | | 20,000 |
| | | |
| Bonds Payable . . . . . . . . . . . . . . . . . . | 50,000 | |
|     Preferred Stock . . . . . . . . . . . . . . . . | | 50,000 |
| | | |
| Land . . . . . . . . . . . . . . . . . . . . . . . . | 10,000 | |
|     Cash . . . . . . . . . . . . . . . . . . . . . | | 10,000 |

| | | |
|---|---|---|
| Cash . . . . . . . . . . . . . . . . . . . . . . . . . . | 18,000 | |
| Preferred Stock . . . . . . . . . . . . . . . . . . | | 18,000 |

| | | |
|---|---|---|
| Bonds Payable . . . . . . . . . . . . . . . . . . . | 150,000 | |
| Gain on Retirement of Bonds . . . . . . . . . . | | 13,200 |
| Cash . . . . . . . . . . . . . . . . . . . . . . . | | 136,800 |

No cash is involved in the first two entries. Yet, the investment of land in exchange for preferred stock is an important financing step and a major asset expansion. Similarly, the conversion of bonds to preferred stock reflects a change in financial policy and in capital structure. These transactions, however, are disclosed separately from the statement of cash flows. The latter would show only a $10,000 outflow due to the acquisition of land under investing activities and an $18,000 inflow from the issuance of preferred stock and a $136,800 outflow for the retirement of bonds under financing activities.

## TREATMENT OF MORE COMPLEX ITEMS

This section discusses how four specialized items affect the statement of cash flows:

1. Bonds issued at a discount or premium
2. Leases
3. Parent investments in investees
4. Foreign currency adjustments

### Bonds Issued at a Discount or Premium

In the case of Cardinal Corporation, no bonds were issued during 1990. The bonds outstanding at the beginning of the year had been issued at face value. No premium or discount accounts appeared. Consequently, the interest expense on the income statement (adjusted by any change in the current liability, Interest Payable) corresponds directly to the outflow of cash.

When bonds are issued at a premium or discount, the initial impact on cash is measured by the proceeds of the issue, not by the face amount of the bonds. Assume two bond issues with a face value of $100,000 are sold. One is sold at a discount of $7,000 (its stated interest rate is less than the market rate of interest), and the other is sold at a premium of $3,000 (its stated interest rate exceeds the market rate of interest). The two entries are:

| | | |
|---|---|---|
| Cash . . . . . . . . . . . . . . . . . . . . . . . | 93,000 | |
| Discount on Bonds Payable . . . . . . . . . . . . | 7,000 | |
| Bonds Payable . . . . . . . . . . . . . . . . . . | | 100,000 |

| Cash . . . . . . . . . . . . . . . . . . . . . . . | 103,000 | |
|---|---|---|
| Bonds. . . . . . . . . . . . . . . . . . . . . | | 100,000 |
| Premium on Bonds Payable . . . . . . . . . . | | 3,000 |

The total receipt of cash is $196,000 and not $200,000. We can easily see this by referring to the journal entries used to record the issuance of the bonds.

In subsequent periods, additional adjustments to interest expense will be needed to reflect the periodic amortization of the bond discount or the bond premium. For instance, when bonds are issued at a discount, the current market rate of interest is greater than the nominal rate. In each period, the interest expense exceeds the amount actually credited to Cash. The remaining credit is made to Discount on Bonds Payable, a contra liability account.

For example, let us analyze the following hypothetical entry made for interest when bonds have been issued at a discount:

| Interest Expense . . . . . . . . . . . . . . . . . . . | 9,900 | |
|---|---|---|
| Cash . . . . . . . . . . . . . . . . . . . . . | | 9,000 |
| Discount on Bonds Payable . . . . . . . . . . . | | 900 |

Owners' equity is decreased by $9,900—the amount of the charge for use of the money. The decrease in owners' equity is offset by a $9,000 decrease in cash and a $900 increase in a long-term liability (actually recorded as a decrease in a contra liability account). From a cash viewpoint, the only payment is $9,000. Therefore, in reporting cash outlays for interest, one must take care to adjust the interest expense shown on the income statement for the decrease in Discount on Bonds Payable. Only a portion of the interest expense results in an actual decrease in cash.

When bonds have been issued at a premium, the analysis is the reverse. The effective interest charge for use of the money is less than the actual cash disbursed. Part of the periodic "interest" payment really represents a return of a portion of the bondholders' original investment. Assume the following hypothetical entry for the recording of interest on a bond originally issued at a premium:

| Interest Expense . . . . . . . . . . . . . . . . . | 9,400 | |
|---|---|---|
| Premium on Bonds Payable . . . . . . . . . . . . | 600 | |
| Cash . . . . . . . . . . . . . . . . . . . . . | | 10,000 |

The total cash outflow is $10,000. The $9,400 debited to interest expense will appear on the cash flow statement in cash from operations. The $600 amortization of bond premium would appear as a financing outflow.

## Leases

As noted in Chapter 12, *FASB Statement No. 13* has significantly increased the proportion of leases that must be accounted for as the equivalent of a long-term installment purchase of the leased property. Capital leases affect the statement of cash flows in several ways. When a capital lease is initially signed, the acquisition of the leased asset is a major investing event, and the incurrence of the lease obligation is a major financing event. In such circumstances, the lessee makes a journal entry similar to the following one:

| | | |
|---|---|---|
| Leased Property under Capital Leases . . . . . . . . | 150,000 | |
| Obligations under Capital Leases . . . . . . . . | | 150,000 |

Because no inflow or outflow of cash takes place, the event is disclosed apart from the statement of cash flows.

Because lease obligations constitute long-term debt, payments that reduce this liability represent an outlay of cash. So, for a company with capital leases, one would expect to see a separate use of cash called "payments on capital lease obligations." This item would appear in the financing activity section. Of course, the interest on the capital leases would be treated on the statement of cash flows in the same manner as all other interest payments.

If the cash from operations section begins with the net income number, any depreciation of leased property (amortization of leased rights) must be added back. This expense, like amortization of goodwill and depreciation of owned property, is a noncash item.

## Parent Investments in Investees

Chapter 15 includes a discussion of the equity method. This method is used to record intercompany investments when a parent/investor exerts significant influence over an investee corporation.

Recall that under the equity method, the Investment account is debited and Equity in Investee Income is credited each period for the investor's portion of the net income of the investee. The Investment in Subsidiary account is, of course, a noncurrent asset. Consequently, only the portion of the investee earnings actually remitted via dividend payments is an inflow of cash. For instance, assume that a 50 percent-owned investee earns $90,000 during the year and pays $50,000 in dividends. The following entries would appear on the *investor's* books.

| | | |
|---|---|---|
| Investment in Investee . . . . . . . . . . . . . . . | 45,000 | |
| Equity in Investee Income . . . . . . . . . . . | | 45,000 |
| | | |
| Cash . . . . . . . . . . . . . . . . . . . . . | 25,000 | |
| Investment in Investee . . . . . . . . . . . . . | | 25,000 |

Only $25,000 of the $45,000 that appears on the income statement should appear on the statement of cash flows. It would appear in the operating activities section along with other dividends and interest received. The cash impact can often be isolated by comparing the income statement item with the net change in the investment account. If the two are equal, then the entire Equity in Investee Income shown on the income statement is noncash.

### Foreign Currency Transactions

A company with international operations or with transactions involving foreign currencies has two unique problems. First, cash flow transactions may be denominated in foreign currencies. Second, changes in exchange rates can cause changes in the dollar equivalent of foreign cash balances. Problems similar to these were discussed in the last chapter.

The FASB addressed both of these issues. The statement of cash flows deals with the first point by reporting the dollar equivalent of foreign currency cash flows using the exchange rates in effect at the time of the cash flows. These cash flows would be classified as operating, investing, and financing just as if they had been measured in dollars. The second issue is resolved by reporting the effect of exchange rate changes on foreign cash balances as a separate reconciling item on the statement of cash flows.

## WORKING CAPITAL AND "CASH FLOW"

Until 1987, the statement designed to show financing and investing activities was called a statement of changes in financial position or funds statement. It attempted to measure and report those financial events that caused changes in financial position between two balance sheet dates.

Changes in financial position could be expressed in, or oriented around, any of several different concepts of funds. Until 1987, the term *funds* was never precisely defined in either accounting theory or practice. Two common definitions were used—cash or working capital (the difference between current assets and current liabilities). *Opinion No. 19* of the Accounting Principles Board allowed either concept to be used.

Until the early 1980s the concept of funds most widely used for external reporting was working capital (current assets minus current liabilities). The advantages of the working capital definition were twofold:

**1.** Working capital was a broader, more comprehensive measure of liquidity than cash. The exclusion of detailed fluctuations in the individual current asset and current liability accounts presumably allowed the external analyst to focus on the overall impact of long-term events on the short-term liquidity of the firm.

**2.** The working capital concept articulated better with other financial statements because it reflected many normal accrual accounting procedures.

Despite its wide usage, the working capital concept in the 1980s began to give way to a cash definition of funds. Among the reasons for the shift were the following:

**1.** Increasing numbers of individuals and groups questioned whether the predominance of the working capital funds statement was consistent with the accounting profession's increasing concern for the *cash* consequences of business events. Recall from Chapter 1 that one of the basic objectives of financial reporting is to provide users with information about cash inflows and outflows to help them assess future cash flows.

**2.** The working capital concept excluded too much. Changes in individual current assets and liabilities may be vital to external analysts' understanding of the firm's financial activities. Examples of potentially significant changes in current accounts include a large buildup of inventory, an increase in accounts receivable caused by a slowdown in collections, and short-term bank borrowings. The working capital funds statement could reveal a favorable flow, and yet the firm would be unable to pay its bills.

For these and other reasons, the FASB initially encouraged (but did not require) the use of the cash concept. The Financial Executives Institute also encouraged its members to switch to the cash approach. Finally, *FASB Standard No. 95* now requires the cash approach. The renaming of the statement reflects the new emphasis on cash. However, analysts reviewing historical reports through 1987 will frequently encounter statements of changes in financial position prepared on a working capital basis.

## The Concept of "Cash Flow"

In the preceding discussions we have used the term *cash flow* in a precise context—the inflow or outflow of cash from operations or some other event. However, historically and still today the popular financial press uses the term in a less precise manner. Businesses sometimes use it in reporting on the results of operations, and security analysts use it in their evaluations and recommendations concerning the common stock of various companies. As used in these situations, "cash flow" is commonly defined as net income plus depreciation and sometimes deferred taxes.

"Cash flow" is a misnomer if it is limited to net income plus depreciation and similar items. Net income computed on an accrual basis does not necessarily represent a net cash inflow. Adding back depreciation does not adjust for the other accrual items reflected in net income. Moreover, it carries the false implication that depreciation is a source of cash. All that net income plus depreciation may show is the increase in working capital, *not cash,* arising from the operation of the business.

Both the FASB and the SEC have frowned upon the presentation of isolated statistics of "cash flow from operations." Particularly nettlesome has been some users' practice of expressing "cash flow" in per share terms and suggesting it as a substitute for net income. "Cash flow" earnings are a misuse of both the concept of cash and the concept of earnings. *FASB Statement No. 95* specifies that cash flow per share may not be reported in financial statements. Even when cash flow from operations is calculated accurately and consistently among companies, it serves as a measure of liquidity and not profitability. In the view of the Board, "neither cash flow nor any component of it is an alternative to net income as an indicator of an enterprise's performance, as reporting per share amounts might imply."[5]

## DISCUSSION OF THE KIMBERLY-CLARK ANNUAL REPORT

*FASB Statement No. 95* was not issued until November of 1987. It becomes effective for 1988. Consequently, Kimberly-Clark has not followed its precise requirements. Its statement is called "Consolidated Statement of Changes in Financial Position." However, notice that financial position is defined in terms of cash. Also Kimberly-Clark has adopted the operating-financing-investing format.

Accordingly, the company notes in its annual report (page 199) that adoption of the new standard will not have a material effect on its financial statements. Perhaps the change will result in more detail in some categories, but most of the changes will concern format. Some of the more obvious of these changes in 1988 will include:

1. The statement title will become "Statement of Cash Flows."
2. The changes in working capital, currently shown in Note 9, would become an integral part of the statement if prepared using the indirect approach.
3. The lines labeled "Cash provided by income" (more about that later) and "Cash provided before financing" will be deleted.
4. The "Increase in cash and cash equivalents," currently shown as an outlay of cash from financing, will become the net effect of the cash flows from operations, financing, and investing. It will be added to the cash and cash equivalents at the beginning of the year to obtain the cash balances at year-end.
5. The $29.8 million shown in Note 9 as currency rate changes will be shown as a separate item on the statement, also as part of the reconciling of beginning and ending cash balances.

Keeping in mind these minor modifications required in 1988, let us look at Kimberly-Clark's statement much as we would a statement of cash flows.

### Cash from Operations

Kimberly-Clark uses the indirect approach to reporting cash from operations. Two general types of items are added to net income in much the same manner as our Cardinal Corporation example. One group consists of non-

---

[5] *FASB Statement No. 95*, par. 33.

cash revenues and expenses. The second group consists of changes in current assets and current liabilities related to operations. These adjustments are necessary to convert current accrual numbers to their equivalent cash numbers.

The net result is $656.6 million, which Kimberly-Clark calls "Cash Provided by Operations." If we removed the effect of currency rate changes, the figure becomes $626.8 ($656.6 − $29.8). The Company also displays a figure of $611.3 million called "Cash from Income." This is a misleading disclosure. The amount represents working capital from operations, not cash. So the item is mislabeled and is inconsistent with a statement purporting to measure cash flows.

**Noncash Add-Backs.**   Kimberly-Clark lists five noncash adjustments to net income. Many of these were discussed earlier in this chapter. Depreciation and deferred income taxes are the two most common noncash expenses. Depreciation represents the consumption of a noncurrent asset; deferred tax expense results in an increase in a long-term liability. In this case, the deferred tax expense of $85.0 is less than the balance sheet change of $99.7 million. Evidently, other events affecting the Deferred Income Taxes Liability account happened in 1987 also.

Kimberly-Clark employs the equity method for certain foreign affiliates (see Note 11). The income statement shows $35.3 million of equity income. The summary entry for 1987 was:

Investment in Equity Companies . . . . . . . . . . . . . . 35.3
    Share of Net Income of Equity Companies . . . . . . .        35.3

However, the $35.3 is not necessarily a cash inflow. Evidently only $18.1 million was received in cash ($35.3 − $17.2 *unremitted* net income of equity companies). The $35.3 million was included in net income. Therefore, it is overstated from a cash standpoint by the $17.2 noncash portion. This becomes a negative adjustment.

An amount of $13.7 million was deducted on the income statement as the minority owners' interests in subsidiaries' net income. But, no cash dividends were paid to the minority owners. Note that the $13.7 million equals the increase shown for minority interest on the comparative balance sheet. Accordingly, this noncash deduction must be added back to net income in deriving cash from operations.

The last add-back, Other, represents the net results of other minor adjustments to items on the income statement. We only can speculate, but some items that could be summarized under this heading are:

1. Gains and losses on sale of property and investments.
2. Amortization of start-up and preoperating expenses, which are charged to expense over five years (see Note 1 on Accounting Policies).
3. Allocation of some advertising and promotion costs incurred in prior years but charged as an expense in 1987 when the promotional campaign occurred (see Note 1 on Accounting Policies).

4. Adjustments related to pensions and losses on foreign currency transactions and translations.

**Changes in Operating Working Capital.**  Adjustments for noncash income items is insufficient to restate net income on a cash basis. Each of the current revenues and expenses must be adjusted to a cash basis. Kimberly-Clark does this with a single adjustment for all of the *operating* working capital. The individual current assets and liabilities are detailed in Note 9. All of them arise from or relate to revenues and operating transactions.

An analysis of each of them individually may help us to understand the $15.5 ($45.3 − $29.8 currency rate changes) net addition. Table 17–6 summarizes this analysis.

**TABLE 17–6**  Analysis of Changes in Operating Working Capital to Determine Impact on Cash Flows

| Item | Adjustment Needed to Net Income |
|---|---|
| 1. Accounts receivable increased $64.7 million during 1987. This means net sales on account exceeded by $64.7 the amount of cash collected in 1987. | −64.7 |
| 2. Inventories decreased $5.9 million in 1987. Purchases of inventories must have been less than cost of products sold. The expense deducted on the income statement is overstated from a cash standpoint. | + 5.9 |
| 3. Accounts payable and accrued liabilities: | |
|   a. Accounts payable to suppliers increased $25.3 million. That means that cash payments to suppliers were less than purchases. Again, cost of goods sold and other expenses were overstated in terms of cash outlays. | +25.3 |
|   b. Other accounts payable increased $10.4 million. By the same reasoning as in 3a, the expenses connected with these liabilities were greater than the concomitant cash outflow. | +10.4 |
|   c. Accrued advertising and promotion expense decreased $26.8 million. Cash payments for these purposes were greater than the corresponding expense included in income; therefore, the liability declined. The expense deducted is *understated* from a cash standpoint. | −26.8 |
|   d. Accrued salaries and wages also declined by $1.4 million. As in 3c, cash payments exceeded expense. Labor expense on the income statement was less than cash outlays to employees. | − 1.4 |

| Item | Adjustment Needed to Net Income |
|---|---:|
| **TABLE 17–6** *(concluded)* | |
| e. Accrued pension expense declined $5.7 million. Accordingly, cash outlays for payments to the pension trust must have been $5.7 million more than current pension expense. | − 5.7 |
| f. Other accrued liabilities *increased* $40.5 million. Interest expense and other accrued expenses were more than the cash payments. The income statement *deductions are overstated* from a cash standpoint. | +40.5 |
| 4. Accrued income taxes increased $32.0 million in 1987. Although current income tax expense was $145.5 (Note 2), cash payments for income taxes were $113.5 million, $32.0 million less. | +32.0 |
| Changes in operating working capital (exclusive of currency rate changes) | +15.5 |

## Cash Flow from Investing

Kimberly-Clark lists three items in this category. All are common. Included are cash outlays for property of $247.3 million, cash receipts from the disposition of property of $34.5 million, and an outflow of $20.8 million called "Other." This latter category probably reflects the net result of sales of investments and other assets, acquisitions of new investments in equity companies, and new expenditures for deferred charges (start-up and preoperating costs and certain advertising and promotion costs) and other assets. Under *FASB No. 95,* this category probably will have to be reported in a more disaggregated manner.

In the Cardinal Corporation example, we were able to reconcile the capital expenditures and disposals to changes in the balance sheet accounts for plant assets. Information contained in the Kimberly-Clark annual report is insufficient for this purpose. Other changes in property and accumulated depreciation took place besides capital expenditures and disposals. In particular, the currency effects of translating property accounts of foreign subsidiaries into dollars at current exchange rates was a major factor. Detailed information for the interested analyst is available in Form 10–K filed by the company with the Securities and Exchange Commission. From this information, we prepare the following reconciliations:

| Property | |
| --- | ---: |
| Balance, Dec. 31, 1986 . . . . . . . | $3,504.2 |
| Capital expenditures . . . . . . . . | 247.3 |
| Other additions . . . . . . . . . . | 110.7 |
| Original cost of asset retirements . . . | (94.2) |
| Balance, Dec. 31, 1987 . . . . . . . | $3,768.0 |

| Accumulated Depreciation | |
| --- | ---: |
| Balance, Dec. 31, 1986 . . . . . . . | $1,241.2 |
| Depreciation expense . . . . . . . . | 186.0 |
| Other additions . . . . . . . . . | 68.8 |
| Applicable to asset retirements . . . . | (64.8) |
| Balance, Dec. 31, 1988 . . . . . . . | $1,431.2 |

As noted above, the other additions in both accounts result primarily from changes in exchange rates. This reconciliation allows us to see clearly the relationship between items appearing on the statement of cash flows and changes in the balance sheet. It also allows us to surmise that gains totaling approximately $5.1 million on the disposal of plant assets were included in other income on the income statement.

| | | |
| --- | ---: | ---: |
| Cash . . . . . . . . . . . . . . . . . . . . . . . . . . . | 34.5 | |
| Accumulated Depreciation . . . . . . . . . . . . . . . . | 64.8 | |
| Gain on Disposal . . . . . . . . . . . . . . . . . . . | | 5.1 |
| Property . . . . . . . . . . . . . . . . . . . . . . . . | | 94.2 |

## Cash Flow from Financing

If we delete the $43.3 million increase in cash balances, the net cash flow from financing activities shown in the Financing Summary of Kimberly-Clark is a $379.7 outflow. Each of the items comprising this total can be traced to the other financial statements.

According to Note 8 on Stockholders' Equity, cash dividends declared in 1987 were $125.1 million. However, the amount of dividends payable on the comparative balance sheet increased from $28.5 million to $29.5 million. For this to happen, cash payments for dividends must have been $1 million less than dividends declared. The cash flow statement shows the lower figure of $124.1 million as an outflow.

Many different transactions affected the capital stock accounts during 1987. Again, all of these are summarized in Note 8, and they explain the total changes in stockholders' equity accounts reflected on the balance sheet. We are interested only in those events that involved cash. The only two such events involved treasury stock. A small amount of treasury stock was reissued in connection with the exercise of stock options, and a large amount of treasury stock was purchased for cash. In summary form, the journal entries were:

| | | |
| --- | ---: | ---: |
| Cash . . . . . . . . . . . . . . . . . . . . . . . . | 6.2 | |
| Treasury Stock . . . . . . . . . . . . . . . . . . | | 4.3 |
| Additional Paid-In Capital . . . . . . . . . . . . | | 1.9 |
| Exercise of stock options. | | |

Treasury Stock . . . . . . . . . . . . . . . . . . . 632.2
    Cash . . . . . . . . . . . . . . . . . . . . .     632.2
    Purchase of shares for treasury.

The $632.2 million appears as a cash outflow from financing on the statement. Presumably the $6.2 million was included in one of the "Other" categories on the statement.

The *net* change in debt payable within a year, according to the comparative balance sheet, is an increase of $116.0 million. This net amount appears as a cash inflow from financing. Under *FASB No. 95,* netting of inflows and outflows is allowed only for debts with original maturities of three months or less. The commercial paper and perhaps some of the other short-term debt (see Note 4) meet this criterion. The decrease in the current portion of long-term debt in the future, probably will be combined with other outflows for repayment of long-term debt.

The inflow and outflow associated with long-term debt are not netted against each other. Nevertheless, the $314.9 million increase (cash inflow) less the $54.3 million decrease (cash outflow) does explain the net increase of $260.6 million that appears on the balance sheet.

## SUMMARY

The general purpose of the statement of cash flows is to disclose a firm's major receipts and payments of cash during the period. In so doing, the statement provides information about major policy decisions affecting an entity's financing and investing activities. Such information can be used to make judgments about liquidity, financial flexibility, and operating capability.

Recommended formats for the statement group cash flow activities into three categories—operating, investing, and financing. The first area commonly is measured by adjusting net income for noncash revenues and expenses. Inflows of cash from investing activities come from the collection of loans or the sale of noncurrent assets, as revealed by decreases on the balance sheet and/or gains and losses in the income statement. Outflows of cash from investing activities arise from the acquisition of noncurrent assets, as revealed by gross changes in the balance sheet accounts. Cash flows from financing activities include dividends, short-term borrowings and repayments, and increases and decreases in long-term equities.

A careful analysis of common events in these three areas normally will reveal the needed information for preparing the statement. Reconstruction of journal entries or ledger accounts are often useful tools to the analyst in this task. He or she has two additional checks. First the cash inflows and outflows on the statement should articulate with the change in cash and cash equivalents revealed on the balance sheet. Second, an investigation to see that all changes in noncash assets and equities have been explained will preclude the omission of some major event and will identify relevant *noncash* exchanges that must be reported separately.

The statement of cash flows is an important analytical tool for investors and analysts. Although it is historical in nature, the cash flow statement is more forward looking than the balance sheet and income statement. In the process of explaining the causes for the change in cash balances, the statement provides insight into current investment and financing activities that may very well influence the firm's financial position and net income for many years in the future.

# PROBLEMS AND CASETTES

## 17–1. Identification and Classification of Cash Effects

The following list contains some selected accounting events. For each of these items, indicate whether it would result in an increase, a decrease, or no change in cash. For those events affecting cash, indicate whether the event would be reported as an operating, investing, or financing cash flow.

1. Issuance of a five-year note payable.
2. Sale of investment securities at more than their original cost.
3. Issuance of common stock in exchange for shares of preferred stock presented to the company for conversion.
4. Acquisition of a building through a cash down payment and the assumption of an existing mortgage on the property.
5. Collection of accounts receivable.
6. Recording depletion.
7. Purchase of treasury shares.
8. Mortgage payments, each consisting of interest and principal.
9. Write-off of goodwill.
10. Declaration of a cash dividend on common stock on December 15, payable on January 10.
11. Retirement of bonds payable at a gain.
12. Write-off of a specific uncollectible account.
13. Checks written to employees for labor services.
14. Sale of partially depreciated equipment at less than its book value.
15. Insurance premiums paid on new insurance policies taken out during the year.

## 17–2. Calculation of Cash from Operations

For each of the three independent cases below, calculate the amount of cash provided by operations.

|  | Company A | Company B | Company C |
|---|---|---|---|
| Net income (loss) . . . . . . . . . . . | $150,000 | $(30,000) | $85,000 |
| Depreciation expense. . . . . . . . . . | 25,000 | 20,000 | 60,000 |
| Gain (loss) on sale of equipment . . . . | 5,000 | (10,000) | (4,000) |
| Income taxes . . . . . . . . . . . . | 60,000 | — | 30,000 |

|  | Company A | Company B | Company C |
|---|---|---|---|
| Increase (decrease) in: |  |  |  |
| Accounts payable . . . . . . . . . | $ 25,000 | $ (6,000) | $ 12,000 |
| Accounts receivable . . . . . . . . | 35,000 | 2,000 | 43,000 |
| Current income taxes payable . . . . | 10,000 | (2,000) | (7,000) |
| Deferred income taxes payable. . . . | (8,000) | — | 5,000 |
| Inventories . . . . . . . . . . . . | 15,000 | 30,000 | (25,000) |

## 17–3. Preparation of Basic Cash Flow Statement

Fairway Bend Company has prepared its income statement and comparative balance sheet for 1991. This information is summarized below:

### Comparative Balance Sheet

|  | December 31 | |
|---|---|---|
| **Assets** | *1991* | *1990* |
| Cash . . . . . . . . . . . . . . . . . . . . . . . . . . . | $ 26,300 | $ 6,200 |
| Accounts receivable . . . . . . . . . . . . . . . . . . . | 26,000 | 22,500 |
| Inventory . . . . . . . . . . . . . . . . . . . . . . . . | 21,600 | 23,000 |
| Property, plant, and equipment (net) . . . . . . . . . . | 60,000 | 64,500 |
| Patent (net of amortization) . . . . . . . . . . . . . . . | 4,500 | 5,000 |
|  | $138,400 | $121,200 |

| **Liabilities and Stockholders' Equity** | | |
|---|---|---|
| Accounts payable . . . . . . . . . . . . . . . . . . . . . | $ 21,000 | $ 22,000 |
| Income taxes payable . . . . . . . . . . . . . . . . . . | 600 | 700 |
| Accrued liabilities . . . . . . . . . . . . . . . . . . . . . | 800 | 1,700 |
| Bonds payable . . . . . . . . . . . . . . . . . . . . . . | 28,000 | 18,000 |
| Capital stock . . . . . . . . . . . . . . . . . . . . . . . | 63,000 | 60,000 |
| Retained earnings . . . . . . . . . . . . . . . . . . . . | 25,000 | 18,800 |
|  | $138,400 | $121,200 |

### Income Statement
### For the Year Ended December 31, 1991

| Sales . . . . . . . . . . . . . . . . . . . . . . . . . . . | | $ 90,000 |
|---|---|---|
| Expenses: | | |
| Cost of goods sold. . . . . . . . . . . . . . . . . . . | $ 42,000 | |
| Depreciation expense. . . . . . . . . . . . . . . . . . | 6,000 | |
| Amortization of patent . . . . . . . . . . . . . . . . . | 500 | |
| Other operating expenses . . . . . . . . . . . . . . . | 27,000 | 75,500 |
| Income before tax . . . . . . . . . . . . . . . . . . . . | | $ 14,500 |
| Income tax expense . . . . . . . . . . . . . . . . . . | | 4,300 |
| Net income. . . . . . . . . . . . . . . . . . . . . . . . | | $ 10,200 |

## Other Information:

1. All property, plant, and equipment purchased in 1991 was paid for in cash. There were no retirements or disposals.
2. Dividends declared in 1991 were paid in cash.

**Required:**

Prepare a statement of cash flows for 1991 to complement the balance sheet and income statement.

## 17–4. Calculation of Cash Flow from Operations

The 1991 income statement for Visagismee Enterprises is as follows:

| | | |
|---|---:|---:|
| Sales revenue. . . . . . . . . . . . . . . . . . . . . . . . . . | | $612,500 |
| Interest revenue . . . . . . . . . . . . . . . . . . . . . . . . | | 24,000 |
| Total revenues . . . . . . . . . . . . . . . . . . . | | $636,500 |
| Expenses: | | |
| Cost of goods sold. . . . . . . . . . . . . . . . . . . | $428,800 | |
| Salaries and wages . . . . . . . . . . . . . . . . | 75,600 | |
| Depreciation . . . . . . . . . . . . . . . . . . . . | 18,000 | |
| Insurance . . . . . . . . . . . . . . . . . . . . . | 2,900 | |
| Amortization of patents. . . . . . . . . . . . . . . . | 2,700 | |
| Loss on sale of land . . . . . . . . . . . . . . . . . | 8,000 | |
| Interest . . . . . . . . . . . . . . . . . . . . . . | 23,800 | |
| Income taxes . . . . . . . . . . . . . . . . . . . . | 22,600 | |
| Total expenses . . . . . . . . . . . . . . . . . | | 582,400 |
| Net income. . . . . . . . . . . . . . . . . . . . . . . . . . | | $ 54,100 |

You uncover the following information:

1. All accounts receivable and payable relate to merchandise transactions.
2. Deferred taxes payable on the balance sheet were $3,600 at the beginning of the year and $6,900 at the end of the year.
3. Discount on Bonds Payable was $18,000 at the beginning of 1991 and $17,300 at the end of 1991. No new bonds were issued or retired.
4. Dividends declared were $12,000 in 1991.
5. Changes in current assets and current liabilities in 1991 were:

| | *Increase (Decrease)* |
|---|---:|
| Cash. . . . . . . . . . . . . . . . . . . . . . . . . . . . . . | $ 2,400 |
| Accounts receivable . . . . . . . . . . . . . . . . . . . . . . | (10,200) |
| Interest receivable . . . . . . . . . . . . . . . . . . . . . | 4,000 |
| Inventory. . . . . . . . . . . . . . . . . . . . . . . . . . . | 16,200 |
| Prepaid insurance . . . . . . . . . . . . . . . . . . . . . . | 4,400 |
| Accounts payable . . . . . . . . . . . . . . . . . . . . . . | 15,800 |
| Salaries and wages payable. . . . . . . . . . . . . . . . . | (1,400) |
| Interest payable . . . . . . . . . . . . . . . . . . . . . . | 5,000 |
| Dividends payable . . . . . . . . . . . . . . . . . . . . . | (3,000) |
| Current income taxes payable. . . . . . . . . . . . . . . . | 2,900 |

**Required:**

*a.* Calculate the amount of cash flow from operations in 1991 starting with net income and employing the indirect method.
*b.* Calculate the amount of cash flow from operations in 1991 using the direct method.

### 17–5. Analysis of Cash Impact of Transactions

The following descriptions concern transactions and events that took place in 1992.

1. The beginning and ending balances of plant and equipment were $1,650,000 and $2,720,000, respectively. The beginning and ending balances in accumulated depreciation were $400,000 and $474,000. The original cost of plant and equipment retired during 1992 was $310,000. The income statement shows depreciation expense of $245,000 and a gain on sale of plant and equipment of $57,000.

2. Bonds Payable—Face Value had a balance of $600,000 at the beginning of the year and $450,000 at the end of the year. Discount on Bonds Payable had a balance of $90,000 at the beginning of the year and $67,500 at the end of the year. Bonds with a face value of $160,000 were issued at par during the year. The bonds retired during the year had a *carrying value* of $290,000 and were retired at a loss of $18,000. Interest expense was $57,000.

3. On December 31, 1991 the balance in an account called "Investment in Zee Corporation Bonds" was $106,000, representing the cost of one hundred $1,000 bonds purchased on that date. This account balance grew during 1992 by $42,500. Forty more bonds were purchased at a 10 percent premium in 1992. There were no sales of bond investments. Interest revenue recorded in connection with these bonds was $11,500.

**Required:**

For each of the three descriptions above, calculate the cash flows for all the transactions and events involved in the description. Indicate where they would appear on a statement of cash flows.

### 17–6. Preparation of a Basic Statement of Cash Flows

Avista Stores showed the following income statement and balance sheet for 1992:

**Income Statement**
**For the Year Ended December 31, 1992**

| | | |
|---|---:|---:|
| Net sales. | | $760,000 |
| Cost of goods sold. | $ 455,000 | |
| Wages and salaries | 45,000 | |
| Other operating expenses | 38,000 | |
| Depreciation | 55,000 | |
| Loss on sale of equipment | 10,000 | |
| Interest expense. | 17,000 | 620,000 |
| Income before tax | | $140,000 |
| Income taxes. | | 52,000 |
| Net income. | | $ 88,000 |

**Comparative Balance Sheet**

|  | December 31 | |
|---|---|---|
|  | 1992 | 1991 |
| **Assets** | | |
| Cash . . . . . . . . . . . . . . . . . . . . . . . . . . | $ 78,000 | $ 80,000 |
| Accounts receivable, net . . . . . . . . . . . . . . . | 209,000 | 156,000 |
| Inventories . . . . . . . . . . . . . . . . . . . . . | 410,000 | 340,000 |
| Plant and equipment . . . . . . . . . . . . . . . . . | 835,000 | 650,000 |
| Accumulated depreciation . . . . . . . . . . . . . . | (278,000) | (250,000) |
| Investments . . . . . . . . . . . . . . . . . . . . . | 116,000 | — |
|  | $1,370,000 | $976,000 |
| **Equities** | | |
| Accounts payable . . . . . . . . . . . . . . . . . . | $ 85,500 | $107,500 |
| Wages payable . . . . . . . . . . . . . . . . . . . | 3,500 | 4,500 |
| Accrued expenses payable . . . . . . . . . . . . . | 15,400 | 14,600 |
| Taxes payable . . . . . . . . . . . . . . . . . . . | 34,000 | 27,000 |
| Bonds payable . . . . . . . . . . . . . . . . . . . | 150,000 | 100,000 |
| Capital stock — $100 par . . . . . . . . . . . . . . | 750,000 | 550,000 |
| Additional paid-in capital . . . . . . . . . . . . . . | 225,000 | 100,000 |
| Retained earnings . . . . . . . . . . . . . . . . . | 106,600 | 72,400 |
|  | $1,370,000 | $976,000 |

## Additional Information:

1. All dividends declared in 1992 were paid in cash.
2. Capital expenditures for new plant and equipment in 1992 were $225,000, all paid in cash.
3. Accounts receivable and accounts payable relate to inventory transactions, and accrued expenses payable relate to other operating expenses.

## Required:

Prepare in good form a statement of cash flows for Avista Stores for the year 1992.

## 17–7. Cash from Operations, Direct and Indirect Approaches

The Foster Company reported the following income statement for 1992:

| Revenues and gains: | | |
|---|---|---|
| Sales . . . . . . . . . . . . . . . . . . . . . . . . . . | $200,000 | |
| Rent revenue . . . . . . . . . . . . . . . . . . . . . | 20,000 | |
| Interest revenue . . . . . . . . . . . . . . . . . . . | 10,000 | |
| Gain on sale of investments . . . . . . . . . . . . . | 3,800 | $233,800 |

Expenses, losses, and taxes:

| | | |
|---|---:|---:|
| Cost of goods sold. . . . . . . . . . . . . . . . . . | $106,000 | |
| Labor expense . . . . . . . . . . . . . . . . | 52,000 | |
| Depreciation expense. . . . . . . . . . . . . . . | 16,000 | |
| Amortization of goodwill . . . . . . . . . . . . | 3,000 | |
| Other operating expenses . . . . . . . . . . . . | 17,000 | |
| Bad debt expense . . . . . . . . . . . . . . . | 2,000 | |
| Loss on sale of land . . . . . . . . . . . . . . | 4,700 | |
| Tax expense: | | |
| Current . . . . . . . . . . . . . . . . . . . | 13,000 | |
| Deferred . . . . . . . . . . . . . . . . . . . | 4,100 | $217,800 |
| Net income. . . . . . . . . . . . . . . . . . . . . | | $ 16,000 |

During 1992, the following changes occurred in the company's current assets and current liabilities:

| | *Increase* | *Decrease* |
|---|---:|---:|
| Current assets: | | |
| Cash . . . . . . . . . . . . . . . . . . . | $ 3,800 | |
| Accounts receivable . . . . . . . . . . . . . . . | 14,100 | |
| Allowance for doubtful accounts . . . . . . . . . . . | 1,000 | |
| Interest receivable . . . . . . . . . . . . . . . . . | | $1,500 |
| Inventories . . . . . . . . . . . . . . . | | 9,800 |
| Prepayments . . . . . . . . . . . . . . . . . | | 3,200 |
| Current liabilities: | | |
| Accounts payable . . . . . . . . . . . . . . . | | 2,000 |
| Wages payable . . . . . . . . . . . . . . . | 1,600 | |
| Rent received in advance . . . . . . . . . . . . . | 4,000 | |
| Bank loans payable . . . . . . . . . . . . . . | 10,000 | |
| Accrued liabilities . . . . . . . . . . . . . | 1,200 | |
| Current taxes payable . . . . . . . . . . . . . . . | | 5,600 |

Assume that all accounts payable relate to merchandise purchases. Also, prepaid expenses and accrued expenses are both included among the other operating expenses.

**Required:**

a. Prepare a schedule to determine cash from operations. Start with net income (indirect approach).
b. Prepare a similar schedule to part a using a direct approach.

## 17–8. Preparation and Use of Statement of Cash Flows

Sir Loin Stake, the distinguished chief executive officer of your firm, calls you on the telephone. He says quite irately, "The worse we do, the better off we get. We operated at a net loss of over $15 million, but cash increased by over $12 million. Can anyone around here explain to me what's going on?"

Financial information for the year is summarized below (in thousands):

## Income Statement

| | | |
|---|---:|---:|
| Sales revenue. . . . . . . . . . . . . | | $139,600 |
| Expenses: | | |
| Cost of goods sold . . . . . . . . . . | $ 83,600 | |
| Depreciation expense . . . . . . . . . | 4,100 | |
| Other expenses . . . . . . . . . . . . | 66,200 | |
| Loss on sale of equipment . . . . . . . | 900 | 154,800 |
| Net loss . . . . . . . . . . . . . . | | $(15,200) |

## Statement of Retained Earnings

| | | |
|---|---:|---:|
| Beginning balance. . . . . . . . . . . | | $ 30,000 |
| Net loss . . . . . . . . . . . . . . | $(15,200) | |
| Dividends . . . . . . . . . . . . . . | (6,000) | (21,200) |
| Ending balance . . . . . . . . . . . . | | $ 8,800 |

## Balance Sheet Comparative Data

| | End of Year | Beginning of Year |
|---|---:|---:|
| **Assets** | | |
| Cash . . . . . . . . . . . . . . . . | $30,600 | $ 18,100 |
| Marketable securities . . . . . . . . . | — | 600 |
| Accounts receivable . . . . . . . . . . | 18,400 | 24,300 |
| Inventory . . . . . . . . . . . . . . | 10,000 | 17,000 |
| Prepayments (current) . . . . . . . . . | 800 | 1,200 |
| Land . . . . . . . . . . . . . . . . | 9,500 | 9,500 |
| Plant assets . . . . . . . . . . . . . | 40,200 | 45,000 |
| Allowance for depreciation . . . . . . . | (24,200) | (22,600) |
| Total assets . . . . . . . . . . . . . | $ 85,300 | $ 93,100 |
| **Equities** | | |
| Accounts payable . . . . . . . . . . . | $ 15,100 | $ 19,100 |
| Accrued liabilities. . . . . . . . . . . | 1,400 | 700 |
| Dividends payable. . . . . . . . . . . | 1,500 | 1,300 |
| Long-term notes payable . . . . . . . . | 9,900 | 7,000 |
| Common stock . . . . . . . . . . . . | 31,300 | 31,000 |
| Additional paid-in capital . . . . . . . . | 17,300 | 4,000 |
| Retained earnings . . . . . . . . . . . | 8,800 | 30,000 |
| Total equities. . . . . . . . . . . . . | $ 85,300 | $ 93,100 |

**Required:**

*a.* Prepare a statement of cash flows for the year that will explain the increase in the cash balance.

*b.* Write a brief memo summarizing your major conclusions and explanations for "what's going on."

## 17–9.  Preparation of Statement of Cash Flows

The following data relate to the financial information included in the 1995 annual report of UMA Corporation:

**UMA CORPORATION**
**Comparative Balance Sheet**
**As of December 31**

|  | 1995 | 1994 |
|---|---|---|
| **Assets** | | |
| Cash | $ 92,800 | $ 26,900 |
| Accounts receivable (net) | 158,000 | 138,600 |
| Inventories | 113,900 | 88,700 |
| Plant assets | 504,600 | 497,000 |
| Accumulated depreciation | (104,000) | (91,300) |
| Total assets | $ 765,300 | $659,900 |
| **Equities** | | |
| Accounts payable | $ 163,400 | $116,500 |
| Mortgage payable | 37,000 | 45,800 |
| Deferred income taxes | 26,600 | 15,900 |
| Preferred stock | 4,000 | — |
| Common stock | 291,100 | 281,700 |
| Retained earnings | 243,200 | 200,000 |
| Total equities | $ 765,300 | $659,900 |

**UMA CORPORATION**
**Statement of Income and Changes in Retained Earnings**
**For 1995**

| | | |
|---|---:|---:|
| Sales revenue | | $580,000 |
| Less: | | |
|     Cost of goods sold | $397,000 | |
|     Selling and general expenses | 30,000 | |
|     Depreciation expense | 26,200 | |
|     Interest expense | 5,000 | 458,200 |
| Operating income | | 121,800 |
| Less: | | |
|     Loss on sale of plant assets | | 8,300 |
| Income before taxes | | 113,500 |
| Income taxes | | 53,500 |
| Net income | | 60,000 |
| Retained earnings, January 1 | | 200,000 |
| Total | | 260,000 |
| Less: | | |
|     Preferred dividends | 500 | |
|     Common dividends | 16,300 | 16,800 |
| Retained earnings, December 31 | | $243,200 |

### Additional Information:

The plant assets sold in 1995 had a *net book value* of $43,900.

### Required:

*a*. Prepare the journal entry to reflect the sale of plant assets in 1995. Assume a cash sale.

*b*. Prepare a statement of cash flows for 1995 in good form.

**17–10. Preparation of Statement of Cash Flows**

Condensed financial data for the Main Corporation are given below:

**THE MAIN CORPORATION**
**Comparative Position Statement Data**
**As of December 31**

|  | 1993 | 1992 |
|---|---|---|
| Cash | $ 31,400 | $ 7,900 |
| Marketable securities | 500 | 700 |
| Accounts receivable | 12,800 | 17,000 |
| Allowance for doubtful accounts | (3,000) | (1,500) |
| Land | 130,000 | 100,000 |
| Plant and equipment | 296,700 | 313,000 |
| Accumulated depreciation | (30,400) | (35,600) |
| Patent, net | 40,000 | 50,000 |
|  | $478,000 | $451,500 |
|  |  |  |
| Accounts payable | $ 9,100 | $ 9,000 |
| Accrued liabilities | 400 | 3,100 |
| Accrued interest payable | 900 | 600 |
| Accrued federal income tax | 3,000 | 5,900 |
| Mortgage notes payable—current | 4,000 | — |
| Bonds payable | 50,000 | 50,000 |
| Discount on bonds payable | (800) | (1,000) |
| Mortgage notes payable—noncurrent | 16,000 | — |
| Preferred stock, $100 par | 44,000 | 55,000 |
| Premium on preferred stock | 8,900 | 10,500 |
| Common stock, no par | 300,000 | 270,000 |
| Retained earnings | 42,500 | 48,400 |
|  | $478,000 | $451,500 |

**THE MAIN CORPORATION**
**Income Statement**
**For the Year 1993**

| | | |
|---|---|---|
| Sales revenue | | $300,100 |
| Less: | | |
| Returns | $ 12,000 | |
| Uncollectibles | 3,800 | 15,800 |
| Net sales | | $284,300 |

Less:

| | | |
|---|---:|---:|
| Cost of goods sold. | $174,000 | |
| Operating expenses | 66,400 | |
| Interest expense. | 6,600 | |
| Amortization of patent | 10,000 | $257,000 |
| Operating income | | $ 27,300 |
| Income taxes | | 13,000 |
| | | $ 14,300 |

Other income:

| | | |
|---|---:|---:|
| Gain on sale of plant. | $ 5,700 | |
| Gain on retirement of preferred stock | 1,400 | 7,100 |
| Net income. | | $ 21,400 |
| Preferred dividends | $ 5,900 | |
| Common dividends | 21,400 | 27,300 |
| Reduction in retained earnings | | $ (5,900) |

### Additional Information:

1. Equipment costing $80,000 was sold. The book value of the equipment on the date of sale was $59,500.
2. Depreciation expense is included in operating expenses.
3. Specific uncollectible accounts of $2,300 were charged off to the allowance for doubtful accounts.

### Required:

Prepare in good form a statement of cash flows for the year 1993.

**17–11.** **Preparation of Ending Balance Sheet from Other Statements**
Rebecca and William operate a retail store as partners, sharing profits equally. On December 31, 1993, shortly after financial statements had been prepared, a fire destroyed their accounting records. All that was saved was the balance sheet as of December 31, 1992, the income statement for 1993, and the statement of cash flows for 1993. These are reproduced below:

**REBECCA AND WILLIAM STORES**
**Balance Sheet**
**As of December 31, 1992**

**Assets**

Current assets:

| | | |
|---|---:|---:|
| Cash | $150,000 | |
| Accounts receivable | 62,000 | |
| Merchandise inventory | 115,000 | |
| Prepaid insurance | 1,800 | $328,800 |

Noncurrent assets:

| | | |
|---|---:|---:|
| Land | $ 75,000 | |
| Building | 100,000 | |
| Less: Accumulated depreciation | (35,000) | |
| Equipment | 40,000 | |
| Less: Accumulated depreciation | (12,000) | 168,000 |
| | | $496,800 |

## Equities

Current liabilities:

| | | |
|---|---:|---:|
| Accounts payable | $ 86,500 | |
| Advances from customers | 4,500 | |
| Salaries payable | 5,800 | $ 96,800 |

Partner equities:

| | | |
|---|---:|---:|
| Rebecca | $200,000 | |
| William | 200,000 | 400,000 |
| | | $496,800 |

## REBECCA AND WILLIAM STORES
### Income Statement
### For the Year 1993

Revenues:

| | | |
|---|---:|---:|
| Sales | $669,500 | |
| Gain on sale of equipment | 2,500 | $672,000 |

Expenses:

| | | |
|---|---:|---:|
| Cost of goods sold | $359,600 | |
| Salaries | 222,400 | |
| Utilities | 9,200 | |
| Insurance | 4,900 | |
| Depreciation—building | 5,000 | |
| Depreciation—equipment | 4,000 | 605,100 |
| Income before taxes | | $ 66,900 |
| Taxes on income | | 20,100 |
| Net income | | $ 46,800 |

## REBECCA AND WILLIAM STORES
### Statement of Cash Flows
### For the Year 1993

**Cash Flow from Operations:**

| | | |
|---|---:|---:|
| Collections of accounts receivable | $ 632,700 | |
| Advances from customers | 3,500 | |
| Payments on accounts payable for merchandise | (410,200) | |
| Salaries paid to employees | (215,300) | |
| Disbursements for insurance premiums | (4,200) | |
| Expenditures for utility services | (9,200) | |
| Payments for income taxes | (15,000) | |
| Net cash outflow from operations | | $(17,700) |

**Cash Flow from Investing Activities:**

| | | |
|---|---:|---:|
| Sale of equipment | $ 23,500 | |
| Purchase of equipment | (90,000) | |
| Addition to building | (23,000) | |
| Net cash outflow from investing | | (89,500) |

**Cash Flow from Financing Activities:**

Withdrawals by partners:

| | | |
|---|---:|---:|
| Rebecca | $ (30,000) | |
| William | (30,000) | |
| Proceeds from issuance of 120-day note to bank on December 31, 1993 | 50,000 | |
| Additional investment by Rebecca | 70,000 | |
| Net cash inflow from financing | | 60,000 |
| Net decrease in cash balances | | $(47,200) |

**Additional Information:**

1. Sales revenue includes $5,000 of products delivered to customers who had paid in advance.
2. Purchases of merchandise on account were $350,000.
3. The original cost of equipment sold in 1993 was $30,000; its book value was $21,000.

**Required:**

*a.* Reconstruct the journal entry made in connection with the sale of equipment.

*b.* Prepare the balance sheet as of December 31, 1993.

**17–12. Preparation of Projected Statement of Cash Flows**

Late in December 1991, the board of directors of National Products, Inc. was in the process of making plans for the coming year. Presented below are the actual balance sheet at December 31, 1991, and a projected (budgeted) income statement for 1992:

**NATIONAL PRODUCTS, INC.**
**Balance Sheet**
**December 31, 1991**

**Assets**

| | | |
|---|---:|---:|
| Current assets: | | |
| Cash | $196,000 | |
| Marketable securities | 125,000 | |
| Net receivables | 232,000 | |
| Inventories | 217,000 | |
| Total current assets | | $ 770,000 |
| Plant properties: | | |
| Land | $ 21,000 | |
| Buildings, net of depreciation | 387,000 | |
| Machinery and equipment, net of depreciation | 468,000 | |
| Net plant properties | | 876,000 |
| Total assets | | $1,646,000 |

**Equities**

| | | |
|---|---:|---:|
| Current liabilities: | | |
| Accounts payable | $129,000 | |
| Notes payable | 133,000 | |
| Income taxes payable | 135,000 | |
| Total current liabilities | | $ 397,000 |
| Deferred taxes payable | | 150,000 |
| Stockholders' equity: | | |
| Preferred stock, $100 par | $150,000 | |
| Common stock, $10 par | 250,000 | |
| Additional paid-in capital—common | 385,000 | |
| Retained earnings | 314,000 | |
| Total stockholders' equity | | 1,099,000 |
| Total equities | | $1,646,000 |

**Projected Income Statement**
**for 1992**

| | |
|---|---:|
| Net sales. . . . . . . . . . . . . . . . . . . . . . . . . . . . . . | $3,108,800 |
| Cost of goods sold. . . . . . . . . . . . . . . . . . . . . . . . | 1,955,800 |
| Gross margin . . . . . . . . . . . . . . . . . . . . . . . . . . | $1,153,000 |
| Depreciation . . . . . . . . . . . . . . . . . . . . . . . . . . | (107,000) |
| Other operating expenses . . . . . . . . . . . . . . . . . . | (575,600) |
| Operating income . . . . . . . . . . . . . . . . . . . . . . . | $ 470,400 |
| Other income (deductions): | |
| Interest expense . . . . . . . . . . . . . . . . . . . . . . . | (12,600) |
| Gain on sale of marketable securities . . . . . . . . . . . . | 17,000 |
| Loss on sale of machinery . . . . . . . . . . . . . . . . . | (54,000) |
| Income before taxes . . . . . . . . . . . . . . . . . . . . . | $ 420,800 |
| Income taxes | |
| Current . . . . . . . . . . . . . . . . . . . . . . . . . . . | (159,200) |
| Deferred . . . . . . . . . . . . . . . . . . . . . . . . . . . | (30,200) |
| Net income. . . . . . . . . . . . . . . . . . . . . . . . . . | $ 231,400 |

Management's financial plans for 1992 include the following actions:

1. Expenditures for new machinery and equipment, $232,000.
2. Retirement of all the preferred stock outstanding at a price of 110 percent of par value. Dividends to be paid on the preferred stock before redemption will be $8,000.
3. Sale of one half of the marketable securities.
4. Sale of machinery with an original cost and accumulated depreciation of $175,000 and $58,000, respectively.
5. A complete repayment of the short-term notes payable to the bank.
6. An increase in accounts receivable and inventories of 10 percent each.
7. Year-end current liabilities expected to be as follows:

| | |
|---|---:|
| Accounts payable . . . . . . . . . . . . . . . . . . . . . . . . | $140,000 |
| Interest payable . . . . . . . . . . . . . . . . . . . . . . . . | 2,000 |
| Income taxes payable . . . . . . . . . . . . . . . . . . . . . . | 110,000 |

8. If possible, the commencement of dividend payments on the common stock of $2 per share.

**Required:**

*a.* Prepare a projected statement of cash flows for 1992.
*b.* Will management be able to realize its objectives?
*c.* Management may be able to issue some mortgage bonds, if necessary. How many thousands of bonds would have to be issued at face value for National Products to achieve its objectives and maintain a minimum cash balance of $150,000 at the end of the year?
*d.* Determine the budgeted balance in retained earnings at December 31, 1992.

### 17–13. Preparation of Statement of Cash Flows
Presented below are the financial statements of Sykes Corporation for 1992:

**SYKES CORPORATION**
**Comparative Position Statement**

| | December 31 | |
| --- | --- | --- |
| | *1992* | *1991* |
| **Assets** | | |
| Current: | | |
| Cash . . . . . . . . . . . . . . . . . . . . . | $ 39,000 | $ 30,500 |
| Marketable securities. . . . . . . . . . . . . . . | 11,000 | 40,000 |
| Accounts receivable . . . . . . . . . . . . . . | 100,000 | 60,000 |
| Allowance for bad debts . . . . . . . . . . . . | (4,000) | (2,000) |
| Inventories . . . . . . . . . . . . . . . . . . . | 150,000 | 130,000 |
|    Total current assets . . . . . . . . . . . . . | $296,000 | $258,500 |
| | | |
| Noncurrent: | | |
| Buildings and equipment . . . . . . . . . . . . | $155,000 | $100,000 |
| Accumulated depreciation . . . . . . . . . . . . | (10,000) | (20,000) |
| Patents, net of amortization . . . . . . . . . . . | 20,000 | 15,000 |
|    Total noncurrent assets . . . . . . . . . . . . | $165,000 | $ 95,000 |
| Total assets. . . . . . . . . . . . . . . . . . . | $461,000 | $353,500 |
| | | |
| **Equities** | | |
| Current liabilities: | | |
| Accounts payable . . . . . . . . . . . . . . . | $182,000 | $120,000 |
| Salaries payable . . . . . . . . . . . . . . . . | 30,400 | 15,000 |
| Taxes payable . . . . . . . . . . . . . . . . . | 24,000 | 20,000 |
|    Total current liabilities . . . . . . . . . . . . | $236,400 | $155,000 |
| | | |
| Noncurrent liabilities: | | |
| Bonds payable, par . . . . . . . . . . . . . . | $ 20,000 | $ 20,000 |
| Bonds payable, discount . . . . . . . . . . . . . | (400) | (500) |
| Deferred income taxes . . . . . . . . . . . . . | 18,000 | 11,000 |
|    Total noncurrent liabilities . . . . . . . . . . | $ 37,600 | $ 30,500 |
| | | |
| Stockholders' equity: | | |
| Preferred stock . . . . . . . . . . . . . . . . | $ 60,000 | $ 50,000 |
| Common stock, no-par value . . . . . . . . . . | 110,000 | 90,000 |
| Retained earnings . . . . . . . . . . . . . . . | 35,000 | 28,000 |
| Cost of treasury stock . . . . . . . . . . . . . | (18,000) | 0 |
|    Total stockholders' equity . . . . . . . . . . . | $187,000 | $168,000 |
| Total equities . . . . . . . . . . . . . . . . . | $461,000 | $353,500 |

## SYKES CORPORATION
### Income Statement
### For the Year Ending December 31, 1992

| | | |
|---|---:|---:|
| Sales . . . . . . . . . . . . . . . . . . . . . . . . | | $413,000 |
| Less: | | |
| Returns and allowances. . . . . . . . . . . . . . . | $ 4,000 | |
| Provision for bad debts . . . . . . . . . . . . . . | 8,000 | 12,000 |
| Net sales. . . . . . . . . . . . . . . . . . . . . . | | $401,000 |
| Less: | | |
| Cost of goods sold. . . . . . . . . . . . . . | $230,000 | |
| Selling and general expense . . . . . . . . . . | 80,000 | |
| Depreciation expense. . . . . . . . . . . . | 6,000 | |
| Patent amortization expense . . . . . . . . . . | 5,000 | |
| Interest expense. . . . . . . . . . . . . . . . | 900 | 321,900 |
| Operating income . . . . . . . . . . . . . . . . | | $ 79,100 |
| Other income: | | |
| Gain on sale of equipment* . . . . . . . . . . | $ 10,000 | |
| Loss on sale of marketable securities† . . . . . . . . | (15,600) | (5,600) |
| Income before taxes . . . . . . . . . . . . . . | | $ 73,500 |
| Income taxes . . . . . . . . . . . . . . . . | | 39,000 |
| Net income. . . . . . . . . . . . . . . . . . | | $ 34,500 |
| Preferred dividends . . . . . . . . . . . . . | | 2,500 |
| Earnings of common stockholders . . . . . . . . . | | $ 32,000 |
| Common dividends—cash . . . . . . . . . . . . | $ 5,000 | |
| Common dividends—stock . . . . . . . . . . . | 20,000 | 25,000 |
| Earnings retained in the business . . . . . . . . . . . | | $ 7,000 |

*The original cost of the equipment sold in 1992 was $30,000.
†All marketable securities at the beginning of year were sold.

### Required:

*a.* Prepare a schedule showing cash from operations using the direct approach.
*b.* Prepare a statement of cash flows for 1992.

**17–14. Preparation of Statement of Cash Flows from Comparative Balance Sheet**
Comparative balance sheet data for the Fortune Corporation follow:

| | December 31 | |
|---|---:|---:|
| | *1994* | *1993* |
| Debit-balance accounts: | | |
| Cash . . . . . . . . . . . . . . . . . . . . . . | $ 30,000 | $ 50,000 |
| Marketable securities. . . . . . . . . . . . . . . | 15,000 | 18,000 |
| Accounts receivable . . . . . . . . . . . . . . . | 68,000 | 32,000 |
| Inventories. . . . . . . . . . . . . . . . . . . | 110,000 | 120,000 |
| Investment in Coe Corporation bonds . . . . . . . . . | 23,500 | 24,000 |
| Plant assets. . . . . . . . . . . . . . . . . . . | 660,000 | 700,000 |
| Totals . . . . . . . . . . . . . . . . . . . . | $906,500 | $944,000 |

|  | December 31 | |
|---|---|---|
|  | *1994* | *1993* |
| Credit-balance accounts: | | |
| Allowance for depreciation . . . . . . . . . . . . . . | $ 80,000 | $ 45,000 |
| Accounts payable . . . . . . . . . . . . . . . . | 55,000 | 115,000 |
| Dividends payable . . . . . . . . . . . . . . . . | 4,000 | 5,000 |
| Income taxes payable . . . . . . . . . . . . . . | 13,000 | 27,000 |
| Deferred income taxes . . . . . . . . . . . . . . | 4,000 | 2,000 |
| 7% bonds payable . . . . . . . . . . . . . . . | 160,000 | 200,000 |
| Premium on 7% bonds payable . . . . . . . . . . | 14,400 | 20,000 |
| Common stock, $5 par . . . . . . . . . . . . . . | 280,000 | 260,000 |
| Paid-in capital — common . . . . . . . . . . . . . | 170,000 | 130,000 |
| Retained earnings . . . . . . . . . . . . . . . . | 126,100 | 140,000 |
| Totals . . . . . . . . . . . . . . . . . . . . . | $906,500 | $944,000 |

### Additional Information:

1. On July 1, 1994, marketable securities costing $3,000 were sold for $4,500.
2. Some equipment was sold during 1994 at its book value of $80,000.
3. Cash dividends *declared* during 1994 amounted to $8,000.
4. Depreciation expense during 1994 amounted to $70,000.
5. Fortune Corporation purchased twenty $1,000 bonds of Coe Corporation on December 31, 1993, for $24,000. These bonds mature on December 31, 2001.
6. The 7 percent bonds payable mature on December 31, 2003. However, $40,000 of them were retired early on July 1, 1994 at 110. Premium on bonds payable is amortized straight line.
7. $10,000 of land was acquired on January 1, 1994, in exchange for 400 shares of Fortune Corporation stock.
8. A $20,000 stock dividend was declared on April 1, 1994, and distributed on May 1, 1994. 500 shares of Fortune stock were involved and the per share market price was $40 on April 1, 1994.

### Required:

*a*. Prepare schedules, T accounts, or journal entries to determine:
1. Net income ($14,100).
2. Premium amortization on bonds payable in 1994 ($1,800).
3. Loss on bond retirement ($200).
4. Cash provided by sale of stock ($30,000).
5. Cost of equipment sold ($115,000).
6. Cash used to purchase plant assets ($65,000).

*b*. Prepare a statement of cash flows for 1994 in good form.

*c*. How would you report the exchange of shares of stock for land?

**17–15. Preparation of Statement of Cash Flows—Complex**
The Warren Company's financial statements for fiscal 1995 show the following (all figures are in thousands of dollars):

**WARREN COMPANY**
**Consolidated Position Statement**

| | *June 30* | |
| --- | --- | --- |
| | *1995* | *1994* |
| **Assets** | | |
| Current assets: | | |
| Cash . . . . . . . . . . . . . . . . . . | $ 936 | $ 604 |
| Accounts receivable, net . . . . . . . . . . . . . . . . | 1,502 | 1,221 |
| Inventories . . . . . . . . . . . . . . . . . | 1,711 | 719 |
| Prepayments . . . . . . . . . . . . . . . . . | 30 | 50 |
| Total current assets . . . . . . . . . . . . . . | 4,179 | 2,594 |
| | | |
| Noncurrent assets: | | |
| Securities held for plant expansion . . . . . . . . . . . | — | 83 |
| Land . . . . . . . . . . . . . . . . . . . | 181 | 122 |
| Buildings and equipment . . . . . . . . . . . . . | 2,101 | 2,169 |
| Accumulated depreciation . . . . . . . . . . . . . | (640) | (400) |
| Rights to leased property, net . . . . . . . . . . . | 141 | — |
| Excess cost over book value . . . . . . . . . . . . | 200 | 240 |
| Total assets . . . . . . . . . . . . . . . . . | $6,162 | $4,808 |
| | | |
| **Equities** | | |
| Current liabilities: | | |
| Accounts payable . . . . . . . . . . . . . . . | $ 180 | $ 178 |
| Wages payable . . . . . . . . . . . . . . . | 100 | 110 |
| Interest payable . . . . . . . . . . . . . . . | 41 | — |
| Income taxes payable . . . . . . . . . . . . . | 18 | — |
| Notes payable to banks . . . . . . . . . . . . . | 34 | 20 |
| Total current liabilities . . . . . . . . . . . . . | 373 | 308 |
| | | |
| Long-term liabilities: | | |
| Bonds payable . . . . . . . . . . . . . . . | 1,000 | — |
| Discount on bonds payable . . . . . . . . . . . | (54) | — |
| Lease obligations . . . . . . . . . . . . . . | 147 | — |
| Deferred income taxes . . . . . . . . . . . . . | 156 | 210 |
| Deferred contract revenue . . . . . . . . . . . . | 60 | 80 |
| Total liabilities . . . . . . . . . . . . . . | 1,682 | 598 |
| Minority interest . . . . . . . . . . . . . . . | 304 | 281 |
| | | |
| Stockholders' equity: | | |
| Common stock . . . . . . . . . . . . . . . | 3,467 | 3,400 |
| Retained earnings . . . . . . . . . . . . . . | 919 | 913 |
| Cost of treasury shares . . . . . . . . . . . . . | (210) | (384) |
| Total equities . . . . . . . . . . . . . . . | $6,162 | $4,808 |

**WARREN COMPANY**
**Consolidated Income Statement**
**For the Year Ended June 30, 1995**

| | | |
|---|---:|---:|
| Sales . . . . . . . . . . . . . . . . . . . . . . . . . | | $2,520 |
| Contract revenue . . . . . . . . . . . . . . . . . . . . | | 129 |
| | | $2,649 |
| Deductions: | | |
| Cost of goods sold. . . . . . . . . . . . . . . . . . . . | $1,763 | |
| Selling and general expense . . . . . . . . . . . . . . . | 468 | |
| Other expenses, net . . . . . . . . . . . . . . . . . . . | 159 | |
| Interest . . . . . . . . . . . . . . . . . . . . . . . . | 76 | |
| Minority interest in earnings. . . . . . . . . . . . . . . | 23 | 2,489 |
| Income before taxes . . . . . . . . . . . . . . . . . . . | | 160 |
| Income taxes. . . . . . . . . . . . . . . . . . . . . . . | | 59 |
| Net income. . . . . . . . . . . . . . . . . . . . . . . . | | $    101 |

**WARREN COMPANY**
**Consolidated Statement of Retained Earnings**
**For the Year Ended June 30, 1995**

| | |
|---|---:|
| Retained earnings, July 1, 1994 . . . . . . . . . . . . . . | $  913 |
| Add: Net income . . . . . . . . . . . . . . . . . . . . . | 101 |
| | 1,014 |
| Deduct: | |
| Cash dividends on common stock. . . . . . . . . . . . . | (60) |
| Adjustment arising from reissuance of treasury | |
| stock below original acquisition cost . . . . . . . . . . | (35) |
| Retained earnings, June 30, 1995 . . . . . . . . . . . . . | $  919 |

**Additional Information:**

1. Depreciation of $449,000 is included among the various expense accounts.
2. Income tax expense includes $13,000 realization of a tax loss carryforward.
3. Buildings and equipment acquired during the year cost $458,000.
4. On April 1, 1995, the company entered into a noncancelable capital lease for office equipment. The lease had a present value of $150,000 and was capitalized at that figure. Amortization of lease rights is included in "Other expenses, net."
5. "Other expenses, net" on the income statement includes along with other items a loss on sale of securities held for expansion of $15,000 and a gain on sale of equipment of $10,000.
6. Of the treasury stock on hand at the beginning of the year, one half was reissued during the year in exchange for $59,000 worth of land and for cash. The other half is on hand at the end of the year along with additional treasury stock acquired during the year.
7. The bonds were issued January 1, 1995, at 94 percent of face value.

**Required:**

*a.* Prepare a statement of cash flows for fiscal 1995 in good form.
*b.* What major financing and investing activities are excluded from this statement? How would they be reported?

**17–16. Preparation of Cash Flow Statement—Complex**

Presented below are the balance sheet accounts of Schenberg and Associates as of December 31, 1994 and 1993, and the statement of income and retained earnings for the year ended December 31, 1994 (amounts are in thousands):

**SCHENBERG AND ASSOCIATES**
**Comparative Balance Sheet Accounts**

|  | December 31 1994 | December 31 1993 | Increase (Decrease) |
|---|---|---|---|
| **Assets** | | | |
| Cash | $ 33 | $ 44 | $ (11) |
| Accounts receivable | 1,260 | 460 | 800 |
| Allowance for doubtful accounts | (23) | (13) | (10) |
| Interest receivable | 2 | 1 | 1 |
| Inventories | 860 | 1,035 | (175) |
| Land | 2,300 | 2,090 | 210 |
| Buildings and machinery | 4,400 | 3,750 | 650 |
| Accumulated depreciation | (1,502) | (905) | (597) |
| Machine tools, net | 200 | 350 | (150) |
| Investment in common stock of Claypool | 720 | 880 | (160) |
| Investment in bonds of Nelson | 73 | 75 | (2) |
|  | $ 8,323 | $7,767 | $ 556 |
| **Equities** | | | |
| Accounts payable | $ 280 | $ 160 | $ 120 |
| Salaries payable | 20 | 15 | 5 |
| Interest payable | 45 | 30 | 15 |
| Notes payable to bank (short-term) | 23 | 34 | (11) |
| Long-term notes payable | 800 | 650 | 150 |
| Unamortized discount on long-term notes | (10) | (12) | 2 |
| Deferred taxes payable | 45 | 160 | (115) |
| Capital stock ($100 par) | 2,400 | 2,000 | 400 |
| Additional paid-in capital | 2,324 | 1,700 | 624 |
| Retained earnings | 3,227 | 3,919 | (692) |
| Treasury stock—at cost | (831) | (889) | 58 |
|  | $ 8,323 | $7,767 | $ 556 |

**SCHENBERG AND ASSOCIATES**
**Statement of Income and Retained Earnings**
**For the Year Ended December 31, 1994**

Revenues and gains:

| | | |
|---|---:|---:|
| Sales . . . . . . . . . . . . . . . . . . . . . . . . | $8,763 | |
| Interest revenue . . . . . . . . . . . . . . . . . . | 9 | |
| Gain on sale of machinery . . . . . . . . . . . . . | 6 | $8,778 |

Expenses and losses:

| | | |
|---|---:|---:|
| Cost of sales . . . . . . . . . . . . . . . . . . . . | $5,797 | |
| Salaries expenses . . . . . . . . . . . . . . . . . . | 2,075 | |
| Depreciation expense. . . . . . . . . . . . . . . . . | 933 | |
| Bad debt expense . . . . . . . . . . . . . . . . . . | 128 | |
| Interest expense. . . . . . . . . . . . . . . . . . . | 72 | |
| Equity in loss of Claypool . . . . . . . . . . . . . | 60 | |
| Tax expense . . . . . . . . . . . . . . . . . . . . . | (115) | 8,950 |
| Net loss . . . . . . . . . . . . . . . . . . . . . . . | | $ (172) |
| Retained earnings, January 1, 1994 . . . . . . . . . . . . . . | | 3,919 |
| | | $3,747 |
| 10% dividend, payable in shares of common stock. . . . . . . | | (520) |
| Retained earnings, December 31, 1994 . . . . . . . . . . . | | $3,227 |

**Additional Information:**

1. $23,000 was spent during 1994 on machine tools. The cost of used and discarded tools is included in depreciation expense.
2. Capital expenditures on buildings and machinery amounted to $832,000 in 1994.
3. The investment in Nelson bonds represents seven $10,000 bonds purchased initially at a cost of $76,500 and carried on the books on December 31, 1993 at an amortized cost of $75,000. None were sold during 1994.
4. $150,000 of new long-term notes payable were issued at face value in 1994.
5. There were 20,000 shares of capital stock issued as of the beginning of the year. Of these, a little over 7,600 shares were in the treasury. Capital stock transactions during 1994 were as follows:
    (i)   2,000 new shares were issued as a stock dividend when the market price of the shares was $260.
    (ii)  1,000 new shares were issued in exchange for the entire addition to land during 1994.
    (iii) 1,000 new shares were issued for cash at a price of $224 per share.
    (iv)  500 shares of treasury stock were reissued for cash at a price of $256 per share.

**Required:**

*a.* Reconstruct the entries that were made in the ledger accounts for Accumulated Depreciation and Buildings and Equipment. Prepare the journal entry that was made to record the sale of equipment.
*b.* Prepare the journal entries that must have been made in connection with the Investment in Common Stock of Claypool.

*c.* Reconstruct the four entries described in item 5 involving shares of capital stock.
*d.* Prepare a statement of cash flows for 1994 in good form.

**17–17. Preparation of Cash Flow Statement—Complex**

Presented below are the balance sheet accounts of Nrets Corporation as of December 31, 1994 and 1993, and the statement of income and retained earnings for the year ended December 31, 1994.

**NRETS CORPORATION**
**Comparative Balance Sheet Accounts**

| | December 31 1994 | December 31 1993 | Increase (Decrease) |
|---|---|---|---|
| **Assets** | | | |
| Cash . . . . . . . . . . . . . . . | $ 43,900 | $ 20,400 | $ 23,500 |
| Accounts receivable (net) . . . . . . . . . | 32,300 | 33,200 | (900) |
| Interest receivable . . . . . . . . . . . | 700 | 1,000 | (300) |
| Inventory . . . . . . . . . . . . . | 63,000 | 52,000 | 11,000 |
| Land . . . . . . . . . . . . . . | 50,000 | 35,000 | 15,000 |
| Buildings and equipment . . . . . . . . | 94,400 | 106,800 | (12,400) |
| Less: Accumulated depreciation . . . . . | (29,900) | (27,100) | (2,800) |
| Notes receivable (long-term). . . . . . . | 10,000 | 14,000 | (4,000) |
| Investment in Sregor (at equity) . . . . . | 14,300 | 11,400 | 2,900 |
| Goodwill . . . . . . . . . . . . . | 2,900 | 3,700 | (800) |
| | $ 281,600 | $ 250,400 | $ 31,200 |
| **Equities** | | | |
| Accounts payable . . . . . . . . . . | $ 63,200 | $ 58,400 | $ 4,800 |
| Wages payable . . . . . . . . . . . | 1,100 | 700 | 400 |
| Dividends payable—common . . . . . . . | 2,700 | 2,000 | 700 |
| Current taxes payable . . . . . . . . | 2,400 | 2,500 | (100) |
| Interest payable . . . . . . . . . . . | 1,500 | 1,800 | (300) |
| 12% bonds payable . . . . . . . . . | — | 30,000 | (30,000) |
| 10% bonds payable . . . . . . . . . | 35,000 | — | 35,000 |
| Discount on 10% bonds. . . . . . . . | (1,500) | — | (1,500) |
| Deferred income taxes . . . . . . . . . | 4,900 | 4,200 | 700 |
| Preferred stock . . . . . . . . . . | 15,000 | 10,000 | 5,000 |
| Additional paid-in capital—preferred . . . . | 3,000 | 2,000 | 1,000 |
| Common stock . . . . . . . . . . . | 57,000 | 55,000 | 2,000 |
| Additional paid-in capital— common . . . . | 33,600 | 31,200 | 2,400 |
| Retained earnings . . . . . . . . . . | 63,700 | 52,600 | 11,100 |
| | $ 281,600 | $ 250,400 | $ 31,200 |

**NRETS CORPORATION**
**Statement of Income and Retained Earnings**
**For the Year Ended December 31, 1994**

| | | |
|---|---:|---:|
| Net sales. . . . . . . . . . . . . . . . . . . . . . . . . | | $226,900 |
| Operating expenses: | | |
|    Cost of goods sold. . . . . . . . . . . . . . . . | $134,900 | |
|    Selling and administration. . . . . . . . . . . . | 52,500 | |
|    Depreciation . . . . . . . . . . . . . . . . . . | 7,400 | 194,800 |
| Operating income . . . . . . . . . . . . . . . . . . | | $ 32,100 |
| Other income and (expense): | | |
|    Interest revenue . . . . . . . . . . . . . . . . | $  1,200 | |
|    Equity in Sregor income . . . . . . . . . . . . | 3,500 | |
|    Loss on sale of equipment . . . . . . . . . . . | (700) | |
|    Interest expense. . . . . . . . . . . . . . . . | (3,700) | |
|    Amortization of goodwill . . . . . . . . . . . . | (800) | (500) |
| Income before taxes . . . . . . . . . . . . . . . . | | $ 31,600 |
|    Income tax expense . . . . . . . . . . . . . . | | 9,300 |
| Income before extraordinary item. . . . . . . . . . . | | $ 22,300 |
| Gain on retirement of bonds (less applicable income tax | | |
|    of $300) . . . . . . . . . . . . . . . . . . . . | | 600 |
| Net income. . . . . . . . . . . . . . . . . . . . | | $ 22,900 |
| Retained earnings, January 1, 1994 . . . . . . . . . . | | 52,600 |
| | | $ 75,500 |
| Preferred dividends . . . . . . . . . . . . . . . . | $  1,500 | |
| Common dividends . . . . . . . . . . . . . . . . | 10,300 | 11,800 |
| Retained earnings, December 31, 1994 . . . . . . . . . | | $ 63,700 |

**Additional Information:**

1. During the year Nrets sold equipment originally costing $16,000 for cash.
2. The 12 percent bonds payable, which were originally issued at face value, were purchased for cash on the bond market and retired.
3. The 10 percent bonds were issued at an original discount of $1,700 during 1994.

**Required:**

Prepare a statement that will explain why cash increased $23,500 in 1994. Arrange your data in proper form.

**Casette 17–1.  Questions about Georgia-Pacific Corporation**
At the back of the text is a complete set of financial statements of Georgia-Pacific Corporation taken from its annual report of 1987.

Answer the following questions with particular reference to its Statement of Cash Flows for 1987.

a. Give an overall summary of what caused Georgia-Pacific's cash to decline $10 million in 1987.

b. Why is $49 million of deferred income taxes added to net income in calculating cash provided by operations? Explain the relationship between the $49 million and the December 31, 1987 balance in the Deferred Income Taxes account on the balance sheet.

c. Why are the gains on sales of assets and on liquidations subtracted from net income? Did not these events provide cash?

d. In the section on cash provided by operations, Georgia-Pacific shows an unlabeled subtotal of $870 million. What does this figure represent? Why is it listed?

e. In calculating cash provided by operations, Georgia-Pacific subtracts $78 and $70 million, respectively, for receivables and inventories. These amounts do not equal the balance sheet changes in receivables and inventories. Explain why these amounts are subtracted and reconcile them to the balance sheet changes (see Note 9).

f. The financing section of the statement of cash flows shows repayments of long-term debt of $339 million and additions to long-term debt of $683 million, for a net increase in long-term debt of $344 million. Yet, the balance sheet shows long-term debt increasing $405 million ($1,298 − $893). Can you reconcile these changes? (Hint: Study the balance sheet carefully, as well as Notes 4 and 9.)

g. Georgia-Pacific indicates that it spent $255 million to acquire common stock for the treasury. Yet, the treasury stock account increased only $244 million on the balance sheet. Why?

h. Explain why the Timber and Timberlands, Net account increased from $844 million to $915 million?

i. Form 10–K filed by Georgia-Pacific with the Securities and Exchange Commission indicates that additions to the Property, Plant, and Equipment account were $717 million for new additions and $20 million resulting from reclassifications and foreign currency translation adjustments. Similarly, in addition to depreciation expense, $18 million was added to the Accumulated Depreciation account as a result of reclassifications.

   1. Explain why the $717 million figure differs from $592 million shown as capital expenditures on the statement of cash flows.

   2. Reconstruct the journal entry that would summarize the sale of plant assets in 1987. Why does this entry not balance?

**Casette 17–2. Rearrangement and Interpretation of the Statement of Changes in Financial Position**

Before the requirements of *FASB Statement No. 95* became mandatory, companies were required to present a statement of changes in financial position. Reproduced on the next page is such a statement taken from the 1986 annual report for American Maize-Products Company:

**AMERICAN MAIZE-PRODUCTS COMPANY**
**Statement of Changes in Financial Position**
**For the Year Ended December 31, 1986**
**(in thousands)**

| | |
|---|---:|
| **Funds provided by (used in):** | |
| **Operations:** | |
| Income before extraordinary charge. . . . . . . . . . . . . . . . | $ 10,231 |
| Charges to income not affecting funds: | |
| Depreciation and amortization . . . . . . . . . . . . . . . . . | 18,352 |
| Amortization of original issue discount on subordinated debentures . . | 252 |
| Deferred taxes and expenses. . . . . . . . . . . . . . . . . . | 9,666 |
| Minority interest in earnings of subsidiary . . . . . . . . . . . | 5,452 |
| Net loss on disposal of fixed assets . . . . . . . . . . . . . . | 688 |
| Funds provided by operations before extraordinary charge. . . . . | 44,641 |
| Extraordinary charge. . . . . . . . . . . . . . . . . . . . . . | (499) |
| Funds provided after extraordinary charge . . . . . . . . . . . . | 44,142 |
| **Working capital:** | |
| Accounts receivable, trade . . . . . . . . . . . . . . . . . . | (5,797) |
| Income tax refund receivable . . . . . . . . . . . . . . . . . | (1,341) |
| Inventories. . . . . . . . . . . . . . . . . . . . . . . . . | (26,906) |
| Accounts payable and accrued liabilities . . . . . . . . . . . . | 4,436 |
| Other working capital . . . . . . . . . . . . . . . . . . . . | 64 |
| **Additions to property, plant, and equipment** . . . . . . . . . . . | (19,762) |
| **Other sources** . . . . . . . . . . . . . . . . . . . . . . . . | 3,244 |
| | (1,920) |
| **Financing and investment activities:** | |
| Cash dividends . . . . . . . . . . . . . . . . . . . . . . . | (2,777) |
| Issuance of common stock upon conversion of long-term debt . . . . . | 4,779 |
| Business acquisitions: | |
| Fixed assets . . . . . . . . . . . . . . . . . . . . . . . . | (23,117) |
| Goodwill . . . . . . . . . . . . . . . . . . . . . . . . . . | (12,765) |
| Other assets . . . . . . . . . . . . . . . . . . . . . . . . | (5,285) |
| Debt transactions: | |
| Payments of short-term debt. . . . . . . . . . . . . . . . . . | (4,500) |
| Issuance of long-term debt . . . . . . . . . . . . . . . . . . | 161,538 |
| Payments of long-term debt . . . . . . . . . . . . . . . . . . | (115,588) |
| Conversion of long-term debt to common stock . . . . . . . . . . | (4,779) |
| Funds used in financing investment . . . . . . . . . . . . . . . | (2,494) |
| Change in cash and short-term investments . . . . . . . . . . . . | $ (4,414) |

## Required:

*a.* American Maize-Products lists five "charges to income not affecting funds." For each of these five, explain why it is added in deriving funds from operations.

*b.* The concept of funds being employed appears to be cash and short-term investments. The company shows $44,641,000 of funds from operations before extraordinary charge. Is this figure cash from operations? What is it? Calculate an estimate of cash from operations.

c. If financing activities and investing activities were to be separated as in *FASB No. 95*, what items would you classify under each heading? Calculate the net cash provided (used) by financing activities and the net cash provided (used) in investing activities.

d. In 1986, $4,779,000 of bonds were converted to common stock. This transaction is shown on the statement of changes in financial position as a source and use of funds. Why? How should it be reported under *FASB No. 95*? Do you agree?

**Casette 17–3. Rearrangement of the Statement of Changes in Financial Position of Digital Equipment**

Reproduced below is the comparative statement of changes in financial position reported by Digital Equipment in its 1987 annual report. This statement was prepared to explain the changes in cash and temporary cash investments. However, the disclosure standards of *FASB Statement No. 95* were not required at that time.

**DIGITAL EQUIPMENT CORPORATION**
**Statement of Changes in Financial Position**
**For the Years Ended**
**(in thousands)**

| | June 27, 1987 | June 28, 1986 |
|---|---|---|
| **Funds from Operations:** | | |
| Net income. | $1,137,435 | $ 617,420 |
| Add: Expenses not requiring funds in current period: | | |
| Depreciation and amortization (Notes A and G) | 436,118 | 384,044 |
| Disposal of property, plant, and equipment. | 53,456 | 44,112 |
| Restricted stock plans—charge to operations (Note I) | 20,653 | 21,155 |
| Deferred income tax provision (Note E) | (158) | (13,936) |
| Total funds from operations | 1,647,504 | 1,052,795 |
| **Funds Used to Support Operations:** | | |
| Increase (decrease) in working capital: | | |
| Accounts receivable | 408,901 | 364,332 |
| Inventories | 253,163 | (556,411) |
| Prepaid expenses | 33,919 | 20,705 |
| Accounts payable | (171,010) | (74,363) |
| Income taxes | (190,576) | 130,342 |
| Deferred revenues and customer advances | (222,135) | (93,685) |
| Other current liabilities | (174,573) | (93,685) |
| | (62,311) | (302,765) |
| Additions to property, plant, and equipment | 748,359 | 564,205 |
| Increase in other assets | 80,463 | — |
| Total funds used to support operations. | 766,511 | 261,440 |
| Net increase in funds from operations | 880,993 | 791,355 |

| | June 27, 1987 | June 28, 1986 |
|---|---|---|
| **Funds Provided (Used) by Financing Sources:** | | |
| Bank loans and current portion of long-term debt (Note H). . . . . . . . . . . . . . . . . | $ (17,324) | $ 8,535 |
| Long-term debt *(Note H)* . . . . . . . . . . . . | (863) | (144) |
| 9 3/8% Debentures due 2000 *(Note H)* . . . . . | (63,000) | (3,646) |
| 13% Debentures due 2014. . . . . . . . . . . | — | (100,000) |
| 8% Conv Sub Debentures due 2009. . . . . . . | — | (400,000) |
| Common stock issued under stock option and purchase plans *(Note I)*. . . . . . . . . . . | 189,346 | 138,932 |
| Common stock issued upon conversion of 8% Convertible Subordinated Debentures . . . . . | — | 395,721 |
| Purchase of Treasury stock *(Note I)*. . . . . . . | (781,790) | — |
| Total funds from financing sources . . . . . . | (673,631) | 39,398 |
| Net increase in cash and temporary cash investments . . . . . . . . . . . . . . . . | 207,362 | 830,753 |
| Cash and temporary cash investments at beginning of year . . . . . . . . . . . . . . . . . | 1,910,933 | 1,080,180 |
| Cash and temporary cash investments at end of year . . . . . . . . . . . . . . . . . . | $2,118,295 | $1,910,933 |

**Required:**

a. Assume that the $53,456,000 shown as Disposal of property, plant, and equipment in 1987 represents the actual cash proceeds. Comment on the classification of this item as part of funds from operations. Why might the company choose to classify it as an addition to net income?

b. Why are restricted stock options added to net income in deriving funds from operations? What journal entry was made in connection with this item?

c. Did the Deferred Tax Liability account on the balance sheet increase or decrease in 1987 and 1986?

d. What does Digital Equipment Corporation mean by the term, "operations"? What does the $1,647,504 shown as total funds from operations really represent? How about the $880,993 shown as net increase in funds from operations?

e. Describe in your own words the items that constitute funds used to support operations?

f. Recast the 1986 and 1987 statements to conform to the reporting standards of *FASB Statement No. 95.* How did you handle the conversion of 8 percent convertible debenture bonds in 1986?

g. Which statements, the original ones or those you prepared in part *f,* better aid readers' attempts to understand the causes of changes in cash?

# Chapter 18

# Analysis of Financial Statements

In the preceding chapters, we have developed a system for collecting and reporting financial information about the performance and position of a business entity. We have had one major goal in mind—the preparation of reports for external groups interested in the activities of the business. Nearly all decisions made by management ultimately are reflected on the financial statements. Hence, the statements provide major assistance to stockholders or creditors who are making judgments about the firm.

This chapter adds to the analyses made in earlier chapters and studies the financial statements from the user's viewpoint. We also develop some additional analytical procedures to make the statement figures more meaningful. The development of such procedures requires not only a knowledge of particular computational techniques but also an appreciation of the context in which statement analysis is carried out.

## OBJECTIVES OF STATEMENT ANALYSIS

The analysis of financial statements serves a number of different objectives— evaluation of past performance, appraisal of present condition, and prediction of future potential. Being basically historical, financial statements are better suited for the first two purposes. However, the majority of statement readers are interested in the future—the capacity of the firm to grow and prosper and the ability of the firm to adapt to varying conditions. Wisely used, financial statement analysis can provide a base for projection of the future and can supply insights on how the firm may respond to future economic developments.

Regardless of the relative emphasis placed on the past, present, and future, analysts generally desire information about the liquidity, financial strength, efficiency, and profitability of the business. Different statement users employ different analytical procedures and emphasize different information according to their individual purposes. For example, creditors (bankers, suppliers) and bond raters may be interested primarily in liquidity and financial strength. However, they cannot entirely ignore profitability, for in the long run a firm that continually operates unprofitably will encounter difficulty in acquiring sufficient financial capital to remain solvent. Stockholders and professional security analysts, on the other hand, presumably are more concerned with the firm's profitability. Nonetheless, they also are interested in determining if the business is financially sound. Managers must consider the effects of their decisions on all four areas.

Because of this overlap in interests among user groups, we present statement analysis in a general framework organized around the four major areas of liquidity, financial strength, efficiency, and profitability. These areas can be analyzed historically for answers to such questions as:

1. How has the financial condition of the firm changed over time?
2. In what areas has the firm exhibited success or failure?
3. Do the financial statements support management's opinion of the condition of the business?
4. How well has management performed as a steward of invested resources?

In addition, these same areas can be examined prospectively for answers to questions like:

1. How will management's plans for the future affect the financial statements?
2. Do the statements indicate difficulty in reaching future goals?
3. How will the firm be affected by a contraction or expansion of economic activity?
4. Do any areas show a deteriorating condition that may become critical in the future?

## COMPARISON—THE KEY POINT

Statement analysis entails the analyst's selection of particular items from the financial statements for detailed study. However, statement analysis cannot be done in a vacuum; it requires some basis for comparison. The way to determine whether an accounting number is adequate, improving or deteriorating, or in or out of proportion is to relate it to other items. The companion ideas of relationships and comparison have been implicit in our earlier discussions on consistency, disclosure, and accounting principles.

For example, a firm reports operating income of $800,000. Is this satisfactory? If last year the company reported only $700,000 of operating income, then $800,000 looks good. But, if industry profits have expanded an estimated 25 percent during the year, 14 percent does not look so good. On the other hand, if the firm generated the $800,000 of income with an asset investment of only $2.4 million, a 33 and 1/3 percent return on investment, even before tax, appears reasonable. Its reasonableness diminishes, however, if we discover that a major competitor was able to earn $400,000 operating income on an asset investment of $900,000—a before-tax return of almost 45 percent.

The major point is that some comparison is essential in order to put the analysis into perspective. Different bases of comparison are used in different circumstances, and they do not all necessarily lead to the same judgments. The starting point is to relate specific statement items to each other. The study of specific statement relationships is called "ratio analysis." We have already looked at some important ratios in earlier chapters. Nevertheless, this is only the starting point. The ratios themselves also must be compared with similar ratios. Three common bases of comparison are discussed below.

## Comparison with Prior Periods

One customary approach is to compare a firm's performance over time. Indeed, surveys of analysts suggest that comparison with past performance is the most common type. By looking at interperiod changes, users can spot trends as well as appraise current periods in the light of historical relationships.

We must make sure, however, that we are dealing with comparable data. Accounting methods may have changed; business entities may have been modified; or the measuring unit, the dollar, may have been altered because of changing price levels. Short-term changes and nonrecurring events from one year to the next must be detected and their effects removed from the comparison.

## Comparison with Predetermined Goals

A second basis of comparison is with a normative standard that has been set in advance. Internal management makes frequent use of this type of comparison when they compare actual amounts with the budgeted amounts for the period. Actual income is related to budgeted income; actual rate of return on investment is compared to a target percentage. Analysts often compare the actual results reflected in the financial statements with management projections. If predetermined goals are carefully formulated, this type of comparison is valuable, particularly when followed up by a detailed study to determine why the actual results differ from expectations.

External analysts sometimes use preestablished rules of thumb as guides in their analysis; for example, the ratio of current assets to current liabilities should be at least 2:1. However, in many instances such external guidelines are too general and fail to take into consideration changes in the operating, legal, or economic environment.

## Comparison with Other Companies

Another comparison, often made by investors, employs interfirm contrasts. Standards of comparison include ratios calculated from the financial statements of similar companies or average ratios for an industry.

A number of organizations publish financial statistics for individual firms and/or industry groups. Robert Morris Associates, a national association of bank loan and credit officers, publishes in its *Annual Statement Studies* 16 different ratios for a large number of lines of business. This information is classified by size of firm. Dun & Bradstreet, Inc., reports similar information on 14 ratios for 900 lines of business. Other sources of such data include investment advisory services (e.g., Standard and Poor's *Industry Surveys* and *Value Line Investment Service*), government reports (e.g., *The FTC Quarterly Financial Report*), professional magazines (e.g., *Business Week*'s quarterly "Corporate Scoreboard"), and trade associations.

Although this type of comparison can be valuable, the analyst must be cautious. In this case, the problems of noncomparable data are magnified. Differences in accounting procedures may mask real differences or significant similarities among firms. In addition, differences in the definition of items such as current assets, current liabilities, income, and investment also can distort comparisons. Mergers and diversification may make tenuous at best the classification of a firm in a particular industry or the identification of the major companies corresponding to it. Comparisons across firms of different sizes and industries are likely to be misleading.

# FINANCIAL STATEMENTS—THE RAW MATERIAL

Before turning their attention to specific methods of statement analysis, analysts first consider the nature and quality of their "raw material." The depth of possible analysis and the reliability of the results are related directly to the accuracy and soundness of the statements themselves. Any limitations in the financial statements carry over to the analysis.

Some of these limitations are inherent in the basic nature of financial accounting. For instance, most resources on the position statement are listed at amortized cost. Current market values may be more appropriate for many purposes. Moreover, the position statement represents only one moment in time. Any ratio developed from its accounts represents a relationship that existed only on that one date. If the position statement data were atypical at that one point in time or if they had been influenced by a major recent event, the relationship may not be a normal one. Similarly, the income statement may contain unusual items that could distort the analysis for particular purposes.

## Preliminary Steps

Still other limitations may be introduced into the analysis through inadequate or misunderstood accounting policies or reporting disclosures. To avoid errors and to become cognizant of such limitations, the analyst should begin with three preliminary steps: (1) read the auditor's report, (2) ascertain the accounting principles employed, and (3) review supplementary disclosures, including notes.

The auditor's report is discussed in Chapter 2. One attestation made there is that the financial statements are prepared in accordance with generally accepted accounting principles. Sound interpretations and meaningful comparisons require, at a minimum, knowledge of the general effects of the accounting principles actually applied in preparing the statements. Information concerning accounting policies and principles must be communicated in notes to the financial statements.

Additionally, these notes contain other information. Explanations of unusual items and major changes in accounting methods as well as their financial impact can be found there. Financial commitments, lease agreements, preferred dividends in arrears, changes in owners' equity accounts, and descriptions of contingencies are examples of disclosures mentioned in previous chapters.

Notes also call attention to material facts occurring after the date of the statements. The statements may be reliable as of the end of the year. However, they are published two or three months later. If major changes have occurred in capital stock, indebtedness, dividends, plant assets, and other such items, a note providing an explanation should accompany the statements. The reader will then be able to interpret the statements in the light of existing conditions materially different from those reflected in the statements.

Supplementary information of interest to the analyst also includes explanations of management required by the Securities and Exchange Commission. These explanations include information on lines of business and a narrative discussion of period-to-period changes in the major components of operations during the last three years. Such explanations and disclosures provide meaningful insights into the environmental factors and management policy decisions influencing the firm's performance.

## Percentage Comparisons of the Financial Statements

Most analysts begin their quantitative study of the financial statements with an examination of the general percentage relationships and changes shown on the comparative financial statements for a number of years. The financial statements of Sebago Company, a hypothetical concern, are presented in Tables 18–1 and 18–2. These tables illustrate the general percentage com-

**TABLE 18–1**

**SEBAGO COMPANY**
**Comparative Balance Sheet with Percentage Comparisons**
**As of December 31, 1989, and 1990**

| | Amounts | | Percentage of Total | | Increase (Decrease) 1990 over 1989 | |
|---|---|---|---|---|---|---|
| | *1990* | *1989* | *1990* | *1989* | *Dollars* | *Percent* |
| **Assets** | | | | | | |
| Current: | | | | | | |
| Cash. . . . . . . . . | $ 44,600 | $ 42,300 | 10.9% | 10.7% | $ 2,300 | 5.4% |
| Accounts receivable . . | 57,100 | 49,800 | 13.9 | 12.7 | 7,300 | 14.7 |
| Inventory. . . . . . | 88,700 | 85,900 | 21.6 | 21.8 | 2,800 | 3.3 |
| Prepaid expenses. . . . | 15,700 | 15,300 | 3.8 | 3.9 | 400 | 2.6 |
| Total current assets . . | 206,100 | 193,300 | 50.2 | 49.1 | 12,800 | 6.6 |
| Land . . . . . . . . | 61,000 | 61,000 | 14.9 | 15.5 | –0– | –0– |
| Buildings and equipment . . . . . | 212,900 | 199,100 | 51.9 | 50.5 | 13,800 | 6.9 |
| Less: Accumulated depreciation. . . . | (88,100) | (79,400) | (21.4) | (20.2) | 8,700 | 11.0 |
| Intangibles . . . . . . | 18,000 | 20,000 | 4.4 | 5.1 | (2,000) | (10.0) |
| Total assets . . . . . . | $409,900 | $394,000 | 100.0% | 100.0% | $15,900 | 4.0% |
| **Equities** | | | | | | |
| Liabilities: | | | | | | |
| Current: | | | | | | |
| Accounts payable . . | $ 61,600 | $ 54,900 | 15.0% | 13.9% | $ 6,700 | 12.2% |
| Taxes payable . . . . | 15,400 | 14,000 | 3.8 | 3.6 | 1,400 | 10.0 |
| Other accrued liabilities . . . . . | 22,000 | 19,600 | 5.4 | 5.0 | 2,400 | 12.2 |
| Total current liabilities . . . . | 99,000 | 88,500 | 24.2 | 22.5 | 10,500 | 11.9 |
| Bonds payable—11% . . | 66,000 | 72,000 | 16.1 | 18.2 | (6,000) | (8.3) |
| Total liabilities . . . | 165,000 | 160,500 | 40.3 | 40.7 | 4,500 | 2.8 |
| Stockholders' equity: | | | | | | |
| 12% preferred stock— $100 par . . . . . . | 30,000 | 30,000 | 7.3 | 7.6 | –0– | –0– |
| Common stock—$10 par . . . . . . . . | 70,000 | 70,000 | 17.1 | 17.8 | –0– | –0– |
| Additional paid-in capital—common . . | 90,000 | 90,000 | 21.9 | 22.9 | –0– | –0– |
| Retained earnings . . . | 54,900 | 43,500 | 13.4 | 11.0 | 11,400 | 26.2 |
| Total stockholders' equity . . . . . . | 244,900 | 233,500 | 59.7 | 59.3 | 11,400 | 4.9 |
| Total equities . . . . . . | $409,900 | $394,000 | 100.0% | 100.0% | $15,900 | 4.0% |

**TABLE 18–2**

### SEBAGO COMPANY
#### Comparative Statement of Income and Retained Earnings
#### With Percentage Comparisons
#### For the Years Ended December 31, 1989 and 1990

| | Amounts | | Percentage of Sales | | Increase (Decrease) 1990 over 1989 | |
|---|---|---|---|---|---|---|
| | *1990* | *1989* | *1990* | *1989* | *Dollars* | *Percent* |
| Sales . . . . . . . . . . | $502,500 | $480,000 | 100.0% | 100.0% | $22,500 | 4.7% |
| Cost of goods sold . . . . | 324,900 | 319,600 | 64.7 | 66.6 | 5,300 | 1.7 |
| Gross margin . . . . . . | 177,600 | 160,400 | 35.3 | 33.4 | 17,200 | 10.7 |
| Operating expenses: | | | | | | |
|   Selling . . . . . . . . | 90,700 | 76,300 | 18.0 | 15.9 | 14,400 | 18.9 |
|   Administrative . . . . . | 41,140 | 41,180 | 8.2 | 8.6 | (40) | (0.1) |
|     Total operating expenses . . . . . | 131,840 | 117,480 | 26.2 | 24.5 | 14,360 | 12.2 |
| Operating income . . . . | 45,760 | 42,920 | 9.1 | 8.9 | 2,840 | 6.6 |
| Interest expense . . . . . | 7,260 | 7,920 | 1.4 | 1.6 | (660) | (8.3) |
| Income before taxes . . . | 38,500 | 35,000 | 7.7 | 7.3 | 3,500 | 10.0 |
| Income taxes (40%) . . . | 15,400 | 14,000 | 3.1 | 2.9 | 1,400 | 10.0 |
| Net income . . . . . . . | 23,100 | 21,000 | 4.6% | 4.4% | 2,100 | 10.0 |
| Retained earnings, January 1 . . . . . . . | 43,500 | 32,900 | | | 10,600 | 32.2 |
| Total . . . . . . . . | 66,600 | 53,900 | | | 12,700 | 23.6 |
| Dividends declared: | | | | | | |
|   Preferred . . . . . . . | 3,600 | 3,600 | | | –0– | –0– |
|   Common . . . . . . . | 8,100 | 6,800 | | | 1,300 | 19.1 |
|     Total dividends . . . | 11,700 | 10,400 | | | 1,300 | 12.5 |
| Retained earnings, December 31 . . . . . | $ 54,900 | $ 43,500 | | | $11,400 | 26.2% |

parisons. Our subsequent discussion of specific ratios also draws upon these statements for illustration.

**Vertical Analysis.**    Vertical analysis restates the dollar values on the statements as percentages of some base item. On the income statement, all of the expenses and the net income are usually converted to percentages of net sales. On the balance sheet, total assets (total equities) serve as the base, and all individual assets and equities are translated into their relative percentages of the total. The resulting set of financial statements, called *common-size statements*, emphasize relative size rather than dollar amounts. They provide a means by which the reader can analyze the composition of the statements.

Common-size statements highlight relationships that could be masked by changing absolute dollar amounts. For example, selling expenses for Sebago Company absorbed only 15.9 percent of each sales dollar in 1989 but rose to 18.0 percent in 1990. Long-term debt decreased from 18.2 to 16.1 percent of total equities, even though the proportion of total liabilities in the capital structure remained about the same. The analyst may wonder why the company appears to be relying more on short-term sources of assets.

The Robert Morris Associates' data mentioned earlier also contain a vertical analysis for each of the industries surveyed. If Sebago Company were a wholesaler of appliances, the analyst could compare the middle set of columns in Tables 18–1 and 18–2 with information from a number of similar businesses.

**Horizontal Analysis.**   Horizontal analysis employs percentages to show how individual items change from year to year. A percentage increase or decrease from the prior year is calculated for each component on the current income and position statements. Such abstraction from the absolute dollar changes may add insights into developing trends.

As one example, horizontal analysis for Sebago Company reveals that accounts receivable increased 14.7 percent from 1989 to 1990, while net sales increased only 4.7 percent. Such a disproportionate change might suggest a decrease in the firm's attention to account collections, extension of credit to riskier customers, or, conversely, a change in the type of business conducted. Perhaps the firm has moved from being a heavily cash-oriented business to a credit-based one. Horizontal analysis will not provide direct answers to why the percentages changed but will highlight areas that should be examined.

# RATIO ANALYSIS

Ratio analysis is the study of specific relationships, and it forms the heart of statement analysis. Indeed, we will review many of the ratios we have already seen in earlier chapters. Ratios are used to link different parts of the financial statements to find clues about the status of particular aspects of the business. Specifically, ratio analysis helps us to make judgments about financial risk, short-term liquidity, long-term financial strength, efficiency in acquiring and using resources, and profitability (earning a satisfactory income in relation to the investment base).

Ratios conveniently capsulize the results of detailed recordings and often complex relationships in all of these areas. Their use is widespread throughout the financial community. Stockholders employ ratios to assess the risk of companies and to value their securities. Lenders also use ratios to assess risk in making loans. Often ratios are included in loan covenants, and lenders monitor them to make sure the company is meeting its commitments. For example, a bond issue may contain a requirement that the company maintain a level of earnings before interest and taxes at least eight times the interest expense. We call this a "times-interest-earned ratio," and the company may be required quarterly or semiannually to submit evidence that this ratio has been maintained.

In like manner, government agencies use ratios to monitor a company's conformance to regulatory goals established in financial terms. Rates of return on investment are common inputs into rate regulation, for instance. Other regulatory areas that sometimes employ ratios include guaranteed government loans and government contracts.

Ratios often are included as targets in management contracts and bonus arrangements. Comparisons of the actual ratios with the target ratios provide ways of evaluating management performance. The achievement of certain target ratios—for example, a rate of return on stockholders' equity greater than 20 percent—may trigger the awarding of bonuses to management.

Even auditors use ratios to reveal potential problem areas. In a procedure that auditors call "analytical review," the auditor compares some common relationships expressed in ratios from the current financial statements to similar relationships in prior years. Unexplained major shifts in one or more ratios from year to year may signify accounts that need more careful auditing. The potential for a recording errors may be larger in the accounts involved in the abnormal ratios.

Despite these widespread uses, it is easy to get carried away with an oversimplified use of ratios. Wise statement analysis involves knowing the objective of each calculation. Each ratio that we discuss provides information about a particular area. Although our coverage of ratios is broad, it does not exhaust all of the possible ratios that are computed or the numerous ways financial relationships are defined and expressed. Nevertheless, these matters of convention and individual preference are less important than our understanding of the purpose for each ratio.

Keep in mind also that ratios merely aid in evaluating a business; they do not substitute for sound judgment. The financial statements from which ratios are taken cannot present all the relevant information about the operations, management, and environment of an enterprise. Ratios represent past data and only can hint at the future. Moreover, few ratios signify improved performance indefinitely as they move in one direction. When closely analyzed, ratios are satisfactory within a middle range and become unsatisfactory out of this range in either direction. For example, too few current assets can hinder liquidity, but too much money tied up in current assets can hinder profitability.

What we hope for from an analysis of accounting reports is to spot exceptions and variations. Are there relationships that seem abnormal or trends which, if continued, might cause trouble? Ratios neither pinpoint precise problems nor indicate causes. They may, however, aid in decision making by highlighting problem areas that may require further investigation.

## Impact of Alternative Accounting Principles

We already have noted that the limitations of the financial statements carry over to the ratios calculated from them. Comparative analysis among companies is further confounded by the choice of accounting principles available to the managements of different companies. Consider for a moment the vast array of policies we have discussed in the preceding chapters:

1. Alternative times at which to recognize revenue.
2. Percentage of completion versus completed contract for long-term contracts.
3. FIFO versus LIFO inventory methods.
4. Accelerated versus straight-line depreciation.
5. Periods of amortization of intangible assets.
6. Capitalizing versus expensing of certain period costs.
7. Full-cost versus successful-efforts recording of drilling and development costs.
8. Lease capitalization, i.e., operating versus financial lease distinctions.
9. Pension accounting assumptions.
10. Cost versus equity methods for investees.
11. Purchase versus pooling in recording mergers.

We have seen how these and other accounting policy choices can modify materially the revenues, expenses, assets, liabilities, and shareholders' equity on the financial statements. Yet, these are the basic ingredients in the calculation of ratios. If these items are distorted or different between companies because of alternative accounting policies, the ratios also are likely to be distorted or different. Expressing a relationship as a ratio or as a percentage does not magically transform it into something that is necessarily meaningful or comparable.

In Chapter 12, we saw how the failure to capitalize long-term financing leases caused major differences in the relationship of debt to stockholders' equity, a common financial strength measure. In Chapter 15, we saw how the use of pooling of interests accounting usually causes a higher income figure and a lower asset base. Rate of return on investment (income/investment), a common profitability ratio, accordingly is distorted. Many other examples exist. Intelligent analysts need to ask themselves continually what impact accounting policies might have on specific ratios.

## LIQUIDITY

One group of ratios deals with the business' ability to meet creditors' short-run claims for repayment; we refer to these as liquidity measures.

*Some* indication of liquidity is provided by the working capital number, which equals current assets minus current liabilities. Unfortunately, the absolute nature of this measure precludes meaningful comparison among firms of different size.

To obtain a better indication of various companies' relative capacity to meet their currently maturing obligations, we calculate two ratios. The *current ratio* divides current assets by current liabilities. The *quick* ratio divides current monetary assets—cash, marketable securities, and accounts receivable—by current liabilities. It is a measure of more immediate liquidity because it does not rely on the conversion of inventories to cash through sale. For Sebago Company, the ratios are:

$$
\begin{array}{lll}
 & \underline{1990} & \underline{1989} \\
\text{Current ratio} = & \dfrac{\$206{,}100}{\$99{,}000} = 2.1 & \dfrac{\$193{,}300}{\$88{,}500} = 2.2 \\[2ex]
\text{Quick ratio} = & \dfrac{\$101{,}700}{\$99{,}000} = 1.0 & \dfrac{\$92{,}100}{\$88{,}500} = 1.0
\end{array}
$$

Both measures can be distorted by accounting conventions. A quick ratio calculated valuing marketable securities at cost, when market values are materially higher, is not going to be as useful as a ratio in which the securities are valued at market. Similarly, FIFO inventories tend to reflect current replacement costs on the balance sheet. Therefore, current ratios calculated using FIFO amounts generally indicate current liquidity better than LIFO inventories. The latter may reflect cost prices incurred many years previously.

These relationships are among the most widely used measures of current financial liquidity because in the short run a firm must look to its current assets and particularly to its monetary assets for debt-paying ability. The current and quick ratios measure the size of the short-term liquidity buffer. A satisfactory ratio means that the risk is low that the existing short-term creditors could not be paid even if current assets were to shrink in value. On the other hand, an extremely high ratio may indicate the presence of excessive receivables or unproductive inventories.

As static measures, both the current ratio and the quick ratio must be interpreted in relation to the character of the business, its industry, and its general economic condition. In industries or firms where the cash flow from operations is relatively stable (e.g., utilities), acceptable liquidity ratios are lower than in situations characterized by greater uncertainty. When interest rates reach very high levels, most firms attempt to reduce the levels of cash on hand and funds tied up in receivables and inventories. As a consequence, a current ratio as low as 1.4 or 1.5, while substantially below the 2.0 level normally desired by many, may nevertheless signify good financial management and compare favorably with industry averages.

## Turnover of Inventory and Receivables

How well the current and quick ratios indicate short-term debt-paying ability depends on how rapidly inventory and receivables can be converted into cash. Consequently, two supplementary ratios are computed to measure the movement of these current assets.

Inventory turnover is a calculation of how fast inventory on hand normally is sold and converted into accounts receivable. For Sebago Company, the formula in 1990 is:

$$\text{Turnover of inventory} =$$

$$\frac{\text{Cost of goods sold}}{\text{Average inventory}} = \frac{\$324,900}{(\$88,700 + \$85,900)/2} = 3.7 \text{ times/year}$$

Many analysts divide the inventory turnover into 365 days to measure the average number of days that units are in inventory—99 days in our example (365/3.7). Of course, an inventory turnover ratio calculated with LIFO costs in the denominator is relatively useless as a measure of how fast the inventory physically turns over. The cost of goods sold under LIFO reflects current cost levels; the ending inventories, on the other hand, usually are grossly understated. Dividing one by the other results in an overstated turnover of inventory and an average number of days that is much less than the actual.

The turnover of receivables provides information on the liquidity of the receivables. How fast are the accounts collected? It is computed as follows:

$$\text{Turnover of receivables} =$$

$$\frac{\text{Credit sales}}{\text{Average accounts receivable}} = \frac{\$502,500}{(\$57,100 + \$49,800)/2} = 9.4 \text{ times}$$

The higher the turnover of receivables, the shorter the time between sale and cash collection. Division of the turnover into 365 days yields an estimate of the average collection period. For Sebago Company, the estimate for 1990 is 39 days (365/9.4). By adding the inventory turnover period and collection period, the analyst gains an idea of the average elapsed time before an inventory item finally winds up as cash. The longer this time period, the weaker the current ratio becomes as an indicator of debt-paying ability.

# FINANCIAL STRENGTH

Another group of ratios focuses on long-term financial strength. These ratios reflect the business's ability to meet interest payments and to maintain a steady payment of preferred and common dividends.

## Equity Ratios

The relationship between borrowed capital and owners' equity is one common measure of long-term financial solvency and risk. This relationship is alternatively measured by developing several ratios referred to as *leverage ratios*. Indeed, research evidence shows a positive relationship between various leverage ratios and price volatility in the stock market.

Leverage ratios can be expressed in a number of ways, including the following:

|  |  |  | *1990* | *1989* |
|---|---|---|---|---|
| Stock-Equity ratio | = | $\dfrac{\text{Common stock equity}}{\text{Total equities}}$ | $\dfrac{\$214,900}{\$409,900}$ | $\dfrac{\$203,500}{\$394,000}$ |
|  |  |  | 52.4% | 51.6% |
| Debt-Equity ratio | = | $\dfrac{\text{Long-Term debt}}{\text{Total equities}}$ | $\dfrac{\$66,000}{\$409,900}$ | $\dfrac{\$72,000}{\$394,000}$ |
|  |  |  | 16.1% | 18.3% |
| Debt-Stock ratio | = | $\dfrac{\text{Long-Term debt}}{\text{Common stock equity}}$ | $\dfrac{\$66,000}{\$214,900}$ | $\dfrac{\$72,000}{\$203,500}$ |
|  |  |  | 30.7% | 35.4% |

Sometimes, the total equities denominator is replaced with an amount called *capitalization*. Current liabilities are excluded, and the focus is on the relatively permanent investment in the firm. If Sebago Company's ratios are adjusted to use capitalization as the denominator, the stock-equity and debt-equity ratios will reflect the following values:

|  |  |  | *1990* | *1989* |
|---|---|---|---|---|
| Stock-Equity ratio | = | $\dfrac{\text{Common stock equity}}{\text{Capitalization}}$ | $= \dfrac{\$214,900}{\$310,900}$ | $\dfrac{\$203,500}{\$305,500}$ |
|  |  |  | 69.1% | 66.6% |
| Debt-Equity ratio | = | $\dfrac{\text{Long-Term debt}}{\text{Capitalization}}$ | $= \dfrac{\$66,000}{\$310,900}$ | $\dfrac{\$72,000}{\$305,500}$ |
|  |  |  | 21.2% | 23.6% |

In this illustration, using capitalization does not present a different picture of the change between years from the picture using total equities. However, because current liabilities *in the aggregate* can constitute a significant and changing portion of a company's long-term capital from period to period, ratios based on capitalization may be misleading.

The stock-equity ratio tells what portion of the assets has been contributed by common stockholders. A higher ratio generally indicates greater long-term financial strength because less reliance is placed on long-term debt, which has definite maturity dates and mandatory periodic payments, and preferred stock. A common stockholder might calculate this ratio to judge the firm's ability to acquire additional funds in the future. A high ratio would indicate room for capital expansion via additional bond borrowing or preferred stock issuance; a low ratio might indicate that the firm is already "borrowed up." A bond holder might use the alternative version, the debt-equity ratio, to obtain an idea of the financial cushion—how much the corporation could lose in assets without the creditors' capital being endangered. The lower the ratio, the greater the margin of safety for existing bondholders.

What a proper equity ratio should be, of course, must be judged according to the type and size of the business, the stability of the firm's revenues and earnings, and its susceptibility to general economic fluctuations. In addition, the equity ratios are directly affected by accounting policies. Lease capitalization policy, bond retirement through in-substance defeasance, debt-for-equity swaps, and mechanisms for off-balance-sheet financing are examples.

Also, some aggressive managements deliberately adopt high leverage strategies. They elect to incur abnormal amounts of debt (compared to other companies in their industries) for purposes of expansion and merger. These companies believe that the additional risk is compensated by significantly higher returns to the stockholders. (See the discussion of financial leverage in the section on profitability.) The junk bond craze of the 1980s was one manifestation of this risk taking.

Nevertheless, whether the financial solvency risk arises from economic factors or deliberate management strategy, an astute analyst looks carefully at the equity ratios to assess this risk. Equity ratios are among the financial measures most stressed by bank lending officers and bond rating agencies.

## Coverage Ratios

A more direct measure of a firm's capacity to employ large amounts of financial capital from senior securities is its ability to pay the recurring fixed charges imposed. This ability is indicated by coverage ratios that express the relationship between what is normally available from periodic operations and the requirements for interest expense and preferred dividends. The *interest coverage* is calculated as follows:

$$\text{Interest coverage} = \frac{\text{Income before interest and taxes}}{\text{Interest expense}}$$

| 1990 | 1989 |
|------|------|
| $\dfrac{\$45{,}760}{\$7{,}260} = 6.3$ times | $\dfrac{\$42{,}920}{\$7{,}920} = 5.4$ times |

The number of times interest is protected (covered) by earnings gives an idea of the firm's ability to handle interest-bearing liabilities in the normal course of events. Because interest is an allowable deduction for income tax purposes, an income figure, before income taxes, is used in the numerator. If substantial amounts of interest are capitalized as noncurrent asset costs instead of being expensed, the denominator may be significantly understated.

Even if Sebago's income before interest and taxes were to shrink to one sixth of its 1990 amount, the firm still would be earning an amount equivalent to interest expense. To further appraise the solvency risk, some analysts calculate times-interest-earned for forecasted income or for the poorest year in the past. Still others use cash flow from operations before interest as the numerator.

When a firm has both debt and preferred stock outstanding, we can calculate a ratio for the *coverage of total fixed charges*. Failure to pay preferred dividends, while not legally harmful, is viewed by the financial community as a serious weakness. Before-tax earnings of Sebago Company could decline to one third of the 1990 level and still be sufficient to cover its fixed financial charges.[1]

$$\frac{\text{Income before interest and taxes}}{\text{Interest expense} + \text{Pre-tax preferred dividend requirements}}$$

$$1990 = \frac{\$45{,}760}{\$7{,}260 + (\$3{,}600/.6)} = \frac{\$45{,}760}{\$7{,}260 + \$6{,}000} = 3.5 \text{ times}$$

$$1989 = \frac{\$42{,}920}{\$7{,}920 + (\$3{,}600/.6)} = \frac{\$42{,}920}{\$7{,}920 + \$6{,}000} = 3.1 \text{ times}$$

---

[1]Because preferred dividends, unlike interest expense, are not deductible for tax purposes, the income before tax needed to cover preferred dividends is necessarily higher. Dividing the amount of preferred dividends by $(1 - \text{tax rate})$ gives the before-tax burden of preferred dividends. Note that subtraction of income taxes of 40 percent from the $6,000 of Income before Taxes leaves the $3,600 needed for preferred stock dividends. Many analysts ignore this tax adjustment unless the coverage is low. In fact, for a rough guide, some analysts use after-tax income in calculating all times-charges-earned ratios, although the results are not as logical or interpretable as those presented above.

## Cash Flow to Long-Term Debt

Another financial strength measure commonly stressed by both bond raters and bank lending officers compares cash flow from operations with the long-term debt total.

The computation for Sebago Company for 1990 is:

$$\frac{\text{Cash flow from operations}}{\text{Long-term debt}} = \frac{\$33,800}{\$66,000} = 51.2\%$$

Under current reporting standards, cash flow from operations would come directly from the statement of cash flows. In this case, we estimated it as follows:

| | |
|---|---:|
| Net income . . . . . . . . . . . . . . . . . . . . . . . . | $23,100 |
| Add: Noncash expenses: | |
| Depreciation expense (measured by change in accumulated depreciation account) . . . . . . . . . . . . . . . . . . | 8,700 |
| Amortization expense (measured by decrease in intangibles) . . . | 2,000 |
| | $33,800 |
| Adjustments to convert to a cash basis: | |
| Increase in accounts receivable . . . . . . . . . . . . . . | (7,300) |
| Increase in inventory . . . . . . . . . . . . . . . . | (2,800) |
| Increase in prepaid expenses . . . . . . . . . . . . . . . | (400) |
| Increase in accounts payable . . . . . . . . . . . . . . . | 6,700 |
| Increase in taxes payable . . . . . . . . . . . . . . | 1,400 |
| Increase in other accrued liabilities . . . . . . . . . . . | 2,400 |
| Cash flow from operations. . . . . . . . . . . . . . . . . | $33,800 |

## EFFICIENCY

Two aspects of efficiency may be of interest to an analyst—investment efficiency and operating efficiency. Investment efficiency concerns the degree of asset utilization or activity. Investment efficiency ratios relate the size of various asset investments to volume of activity. Operating efficiency concerns asset consumption in the generation of revenue.

## Investment Efficiency

The primary expression of investment activity is *turnover*. Various turnovers measure the efficiency with which specific assets or groups of assets are used.

**Turnover of Receivables.**   This turnover was introduced earlier as a supplementary measure of liquidity. It indicates the speed or slowness with which receivables are converted into cash. An average collection period that is significantly longer than that of other firms in the industry may result from a more liberal policy for granting credit and/or a poorer quality of receivables.[2]

The turnover of accounts receivable also can be used to assess efficiency in the collection of receivables and in the management of credit. For example, comparison of the average collection period with the *selling terms* may reveal poor credit selection or collection efforts. A series of years in which the turnover of receivables declines may disclose a situation that is getting out of control. With no change in selling terms, a growing investment in receivables relative to sales volume indicates either a deliberate change in policy, sales to more marginal customers, or insufficient effort being devoted to collection.

**Turnover of Inventory.**   In a manner similar to that employed with receivables, a study of inventory turnovers can be used to assess efficiency in management of inventory. A steadily decreasing turnover of inventories may denote an overinvestment in inventory. As a result, the firm incurs unnecessary carrying costs and a higher risk of loss from obsolescence. An unusually *high* inventory turnover may evidence an underinvestment in inventory relative to the current volume of sales. It may foretell a future loss of sales and customer goodwill because the firm may not be able to deliver promptly, or it may indicate the need for additional funds to rebuild the inventory level.

Whether the turnover of 3.7 times (or 99 days) calculated earlier for Sebago Company is satisfactory depends on the type of merchandise. Inventory turnover in a jewelry store is significantly lower than that in a supermarket. The analyst also must be on the lookout for distortions introduced into the turnover calculation by unusually high or low inventories at the beginning and end of the year. If available, average monthly or quarterly inventory figures may serve as a better indicator of overall inventory levels during the year.

**Turnover of Total Assets.**   A measure of overall investment efficiency is the turnover of total assets, computed as follows for 1990:

$$\frac{\text{Sales}}{\text{Average total assets}} = \frac{\$502,500}{(\$409,900 + \$394,000)/2} = 1.25 \text{ times}$$

---

[2] The National Association of Credit Management publishes collection periods for many industry groups.

This relationship shows how many dollars of recurring revenue are generated by each dollar of assets. If a firm's turnover is relatively low or if the trend is downward over a number of years, the analyst may suspect the presence of unnecessary assets (such as idle cash balances) or inefficiently used assets (such as obsolete equipment). On the other hand, a sudden jump in the turnover should not be always interpreted as a favorable sign. It may actually result from a sharp increase in sales volume and a temporary underinvestment in assets. In fact, if the increased volume of sales is to be maintained, additional investment in plant and inventories may be necessary.

## Operating Efficiency

In this area we are interested in income statement relationships. Most of them are expressed as a percentage of sales. A complete set of income statement relationships can be seen in the common-size income statement shown on Table 18–2. We highlight here only a few of the more commonly employed ratios. All of them can be significantly influenced by accounting policies that affect the calculation of expenses—for example, inventory and depreciation policies and capitalization versus expensing of equipment repairs and improvements.

**Operating Ratio.**    The ratio between *recurring* operating expenses and operating revenues (commonly only sales) measures the proportion of resource inflow, from sales, that is consumed by normal operating activities—manufacturing, marketing, administration, research, and so on. This ratio is expressed as:

$$Operating\ Expenses/Operating\ Revenue$$
$$1990 = (\$324{,}900 + \$90{,}700 + \$41{,}140)/\$502{,}500 = 90.9\%$$
$$1989 = (\$319{,}600 + \$76{,}300 + \$41{,}180)/\$480{,}000 = 91.1\%$$

Definitions of the revenue and expense activities that constitute *normal* operations vary among analysts. For Sebago Company, we are excluding interest expense and income taxes from operating expenses. When defined consistently and applied within industry lines, the operating ratio can provide a rough index of operating efficiency.

**Income or Profit Margins.**    Another approach to operating efficiency is to look at what remains after various expenses have been deducted. A number of margin figures can be computed according to the general formula, *income/revenue*. Each ratio attempts to measure what portion of the revenue dollar ends up as income. Revenue can be defined as sales only or can include all recurring revenues. Common numerators include gross margin (sales less cost of goods sold), operating income, income before interest and after taxes (the reward to the various suppliers of investor capital), and net earnings to common stockholders. Some of these were introduced and discussed in Chapter 6.

**Gross Margin Analysis.**     Retailers and wholesalers, in particular, frequently focus on the gross margin. As shown in Table 18–2, the gross margin percentage (gross margin/sales) increased from 33.4 percent in 1989 to 35.3 percent in 1990. These figures measure the average markup above the cost of the products sold. The level of the gross margin percentage may provide clues to the company's pricing policies and marketing strategies. How satisfactorily this measure performs these functions depends on the inventory method employed. Under LIFO, which matches relatively current costs against current revenues, movements in the ratio primarily reflect how changes in purchase prices are translated into changes in selling prices. Under FIFO, the gross margin reflects both pricing policy and, to a greater extent than under LIFO, the effect on income from holding inventory.

In addition to studying changes in the relationship of gross margin to sales, analysts also like to probe the causes of changes in the dollar amounts. For example, the increase in the gross margin of Sebago Company from 1989 to 1990 was $17,200. This results from an interplay among three major factors—selling prices (price), purchase prices (cost), and number of units sold (volume). Occasionally, an analyst sufficiently familiar with the industry will be able to approximate the separate impact of each factor on gross margin. Alternatively, management may provide information about changes in gross margin in terms of price, cost, and volume in its narrative report on the firm's operations.

**Operating Leverage.**     An important aspect of statement analysis is the attempt to shed light on the future, particularly future earnings. Operating leverage concerns the impact on operating profits caused by changes in volume of activity. A change in sales volume may result in a *more than proportional change* in operating income because of the existence of fixed costs among the business's operating expenses.

Broadly speaking, the operating expenses of a business tend to be either fixed or variable in relation to the number of units sold (i.e., volume). Fixed expenses are incurred in approximately the same amount regardless of the level of operations in the period. Salaries, rent, and most depreciation charges are examples of fixed expenses. Variable expenses change in total more or less proportionately with changes in the volume of operations in the period. Raw materials, hourly wages, and sales commissions are usually variable expenses.

The rate at which income changes with volume depends on the expense structure. If all expenses are variable and price remains unchanged, income will change at the same rate as volume. There is *no* operating leverage.

Because cost of goods sold is a variable expense in a retailing enterprise, one would expect the gross margin percentage to remain relatively constant in spite of volume changes. If some expenses are fixed, however, income will change at a rate *greater* than will volume because not all the expenses rise or fall as volume increases or decreases. The difference in rates of change between income and volume is magnified as fixed expenses become more significant.

Operating leverage, then, deals with the volatility of earnings with changes in volume. External analysts may be unable to measure the precise impact of operating leverage, because under current reporting practices the fixed and variable expenses are not distinguished in the annual report. Nevertheless, analysts may make rough estimates based on their knowledge of the firm. Even a general understanding of the expense structure and the concept of operating leverage may improve the accuracy of their projections.

**Discretionary Expenses.**  A vertical analysis of a comparative income statement reveals changes in the relationships between various expenses and sales. Some of these changes reflect the impact of operating leverage (the expense remains fixed but sales volume changes) or of changing environmental conditions (a new labor contract increases the ratio of labor expense to sales). In other instances, the change may result from deliberate policy decisions made by management regarding discretionary expenses. *Discretionary expenses are those that management can modify significantly in amount from period to period.* Research and development, advertising, and repair and maintenance expenses are among the items that fall into this category.

Analysts usually conduct a horizontal analysis of the income statement to monitor closely the level of expenditure on the major discretionary expenses. They can be postponed or otherwise manipulated readily in the short run. Thus, an increase in operating income achieved as the result of a substantial curtailment in spending for research and development or for repair and maintenance, for example, may be illusory in a longer-run context. For this reason, some analysts calculate the ratio of repair and maintenance expenses to sales or to plant assets each period to evaluate the adequacy or reasonableness of the company's policy compared to industry averages.

# PROFITABILITY

Generally the most important overall ratios are those that reflect the earning power of the enterprise. The ultimate test of the economic success of a firm is its ability to earn a return on the resources invested in it. Thus, the central measure of profitability is a percentage rate of return on investment (income/average investment). The precise definitions of income and investment to be used vary with the viewpoint and purpose of the analyst. Some of the more commonly used rates of return are discussed below—along with some other ratios often associated with profitability.

## Rate of Return on Total Capital Investment

To evaluate overall earnings performance, we begin with a rate of return on total capital investment. This percentage aids in the evaluation of operating management, for it measures how productively the total resources of the business have been employed, irrespective of how they are financed. Consequently, it facilitates comparisons between firms with different capital structures and comparisons within a single firm with a changing capital structure over time.

Two commonly used formulas are illustrated below for Sebago Company for 1990. The first defines investment as average total assets; the second views average investment as the relatively permanent capital supplied by stockholders and long-term creditors. The reasoning for the exclusion of current liabilities in this latter approach is that they usually are a fairly stable, somewhat automatic source of capital arising out of normal accruals and trade credit. Most managerial decisions concern the employment of assets from long-term sources.

*Rate of Return on Total Assets*

$$\frac{\text{Net income} + \text{Tax adjusted interest}}{\text{Average total assets}} =$$

$$\frac{\$23,100 + (\$7,260 \times 0.6)}{(\$409,900 + \$394,000)/2} =$$

$$\frac{\$23,100 + \$4,356}{\$401,950} = \frac{\$27,456}{\$401,950} = 6.8\%$$

*Rate of Return on Capitalization*

$$\frac{\text{Net income} + \text{Tax-adjusted interest}}{\text{Average capitalization}} =$$

$$\frac{\$23,100 + (\$7,260 \times 0.6)}{(\$409,900 - 99,000) + (\$394,000 - 88,500)/2} =$$

$$\frac{\$23,100 + \$4,356}{\$308,200} = \frac{\$27,456}{\$308,200} = 8.9\%$$

A few words of explanation about the numerator are in order. The income component should be consistent with the investment component. Therefore, if we are concerned with total assets or total long-term investment, the return should eliminate the effect of alternative financing arrangements. That is, the return calculation should be unaffected by how management has chosen to finance the total assets. However, if the $7,260 interest expense were eliminated in 1990, tax expense would increase by $2,904 ($7,260 × 40% tax rate). Therefore, instead of adding to net income the entire interest charge, we add only $4,356 ($7,260 − $2,904), the after-tax burden of the interest expense. The resultant figure is the amount of after-tax income that would have been generated if all assets (or long-term capital) had been supplied by the common stockholders.[3]

The denominator in this and other ratios consists of a simple average of the beginning and ending balances.[4] When there is reason to believe that such a simple average might not indicate the average amount available during the period, the analyst should make appropriate adjustments. For example, new assets invested shortly before year-end obviously were not available for use during the year and should be omitted entirely in the calculation of average total assets. If the objective of the calculation is a rate of return on assets available for *productive* use, then temporarily idle funds and construction in progress also might be excluded from the asset base.

In analyzing differences among firms or changes in the return on investment from one year to the next for one firm, we can visualize the rate of return as the product of two component parts—a profit margin and the previously discussed turnover of assets. Overall profitability is dependent upon both *operating efficiency* and *investment efficiency*. The 6.8 percent rate of return on total assets for Sebago Company for 1990 can be broken down as follows:

$$\underset{\substack{\textit{Return on Investment} \\ \dfrac{\text{Net income} + }{\dfrac{\text{Tax-adjusted interest}}{\text{Average total assets}}}}}{} = \underset{\substack{\textit{Margin} \\ \dfrac{\text{Net income} + }{\dfrac{\text{Tax-adjusted interest}}{\text{Sales revenue}}}}}{} \times \underset{\substack{\textit{Turnover} \\ \dfrac{\text{Sales revenue}}{\text{Average total assets}}}}{}$$

$$\frac{\$27{,}456}{\$401{,}950} = \frac{\$27{,}456}{\$502{,}500} \times \frac{\$502{,}500}{\$401{,}950}$$

$$6.8\% = 5.4\% \times 1.25 \text{ Times}$$

By studying the margin and turnover figures separately, we often can glean additional information about the basic causes of differences or changes in the total return on investment.

## Rate of Return on Common Stock Equity

Another application of the general concept of return on investment takes the viewpoint of the owners of the business. They are interested not only in how

---

[3] Many analysts do not worry about tax adjustments or internal consistency. Consequently, the reader will often see the numerator in the rate-of-return calculation defined as net income before interest, net income, or net income before interest and taxes. All of these are theoretically incorrect for measuring a return on total capital; but, employed consistently, they still can provide meaningful information in many instances.

[4] Many analysts ignore the theoretical refinement of averages and simply use investment figures as of the beginning or end of the period.

well management uses the total assets available but also in the profitability of their particular equity interest in the firm. How well in 1990 has Sebago Co. used the assets *and* modified the capital structure to benefit the common stockholders of the business?

$$\frac{\text{Net income to common stock equity}}{\text{Average common stock equity}} =$$

$$\frac{\$23,100 - \$3,600}{(\$214,900 + \$203,500)/2} = \frac{\$19,500}{\$209,200} = 9.3\%$$

The numerator in this case represents the amount of income from recurring sources that remains after provision has been made for rewarding sources of capital other than common stockholders. Hence, it consists of income after deductions for taxes, interest, and any *preferred* stock dividends. The investment denominator includes all portions of common stock equity—par or stated value of the outstanding common stock, the excess over par or stated value, and retained earnings, less treasury stock.

Rate of return on common stock equity is superior to earnings per share as a measure of the profitability of the owners' investment. It explicitly considers the increased investment from earnings retention. It is among the most significant financial measures examined by stockholders and financial analysts.

## Financial Leverage

Notice in the preceding calculations that the rates of return on investment and on owners' equity differ. Rate of return on total assets is 6.8 percent, while rate of return on common stock equity is 9.3 percent. The difference reflects the impact of *financial leverage*. With financial leverage, the use of debt or preferred stock capital modifies the rate of return on common stockholders' equity from what it otherwise would be.

Management may employ assets supplied by creditors and preferred stockholders in lieu of common stockholders in the expectation that the business will earn more on the noncommon capital than the fixed charges (interest and preferred dividends) associated with this capital. If so, the excess inures to the common stockholders, thereby increasing the rate of return on their investment. The firm experiences *favorable* financial leverage. On the other hand, the firm could earn at an overall rate that is less than the cost of the noncommon capital. Because the return to the bondholders and preferred stockholders is fixed, the deficiency reduces the earnings available to the common stockholders' equity. As a result of this *negative* financial leverage, the rate of return on common stocks is less than the overall earning rate.

The overall effect of favorable financial leverage on the 1990 rate of return on common equity for Sebago Company is illustrated in Table 18–3.

**TABLE 18–3**    Analysis of Favorable Financial Leverage in Sebago Company

| Source of Capital | Average Amount Available in 1990 | Overall Earnings Rate of 6.8307% | Payments to Suppliers of Funds | Benefit Remaining for Common |
|---|---|---|---|---|
| Current liabilities . . . . . . . . . . . . . | $ 93,750 | $ 6,404 | None | $ 6,404 |
| Bonds payable. . . . . . . . . . . . | 69,000 | 4,713 | $4,356 | 357 |
| Preferred stock . . . . . . . . . . . . | 30,000 | 2,049 | 3,600 | (1,551) |
| Total leverage capital . . . . . . . . . . | 192,750 | 13,166 | $7,956 | 5,210 |
| Common stock equity. . . . . . . . . . | 209,200 | 14,290 | | 14,290 |
| Total assets . . . . . . . . . . . . . . . | $401,950 | $27,456 | | $19,500 |

Sebago earned an average return of 6.8307 percent on total assets, which were financed in part by current liabilities, bonds, and preferred stock. Because the assets financed from current liabilities (for which no explicit interest charge is made) earned $6,404 during 1990, the common stockholders benefit by that amount. They benefit slightly from bonds-payable financing, since the $4,713 of earnings on the assets provided by bonds exceeds the *after-tax* interest expense ($7,260 × 0.6 = $4,356). The financial leverage from the preferred-stock financing is unfavorable; the 12 percent rate paid on such capital far exceeds the 6.8 percent earned on such funds. The $5,210 net amount generated from the current liabilities, bonds, and preferred stock for the benefit of common stockholders adds 2.5 percent ($5,210/$209,200) to the 6.8 percent return on average assets. The result is a 9.3 percent return on common equity ($19,500/$209,200).

The extent to which a firm employs financial leverage is a function of the *amount of fixed-charge securities in its capital structure*. How advantageous the financial leverage effect is, though, depends on the *differential between the earnings rate on total assets and the fixed-charge cost of debt and preferred stock*. Of course, the increased use of debt or preferred stock capital adds to the riskiness of the firm. Therefore, in making capital-structure decisions, management must consider the trade-off between potential increases in profitability through financial leverage and potential decreases in long-term financial strength reflected in a lower stock-equity ratio.

### Earnings and Dividend Measures

In Chapter 16, we discussed the most frequently cited measure of earning power—earnings per share (EPS). Quite commonly, EPS is related to the current market price of the stock by means of a *price-earnings ratio* (P/E ratio). Through studying movements in the price-earnings ratios of particular stocks, some investors attempt to identify over- and undervalued stock issues. Stock issues are undervalued when the stock market has not fully reflected the value of the firm's earnings in the market price (price-earnings ratios are low).[5] In any case, like many of the widely used measures, extreme price-earnings ratios or sudden changes in relative P/E ratios may signal situations that require the analyst's further attention. Interestingly, research has shown that some of the differences in price-earnings ratios between companies are due to alternative accounting practices. When earnings are adjusted to a common set of principles, the price-earnings ratios of the respective firms tend to converge.

*Dividends per share* supplements the earnings-per-share figure. It measures the *amount* of earnings actually distributed per share in the form of cash dividends to the common stockholders and is reported in most statements as historical fact. Adjustments are necessary only when dividends per share are presented in comparative form over time and the number of shares has been affected by stock dividends or stock splits. Then the past years' dividends should be restated in terms of the current equivalent number of shares. As with EPS, analysts commonly divide dividends per share by the current market price to obtain a *dividend yield* rate.

The future dividend stream from an investment in a common stock depends dually on the level of earnings and the *dividend-payout ratio*. The payment ratio measures the *proportion* of earnings distributed as cash dividends. It is calculated as follows for Sebago Company for 1990:

$$\frac{\text{Cash dividends to common}}{\text{Net income to common}} = \frac{\$8,100}{\$19,500} = 41.5\%$$

A company's payout ratio is influenced by its current financial condition (availability of cash), its capital structure (debt-equity ratios), and its need for cash for expansion.

---

[5] A growing body of research suggests that such searches for undervalued stocks are somewhat futile. In an efficient capital market, the market price of shares fully reflects all publicly available information. Moreover, market prices tend to react rapidly to the availability of new information. What individual investors may perceive as an undervaluation of a stock may only represent a difference in risk evaluation by the market.

## Quality of Earnings

All of the profitability ratios discussed in this section employ some measure of accounting earnings. Fairly pervasive evidence exists that earnings numbers from the accounting system capture significant amounts of information. The prices of securities on the stock exchanges appear to react to the release of accounting earnings figures, and their informational content becomes quickly impounded in security prices.

We also know, however, that accounting earnings have multiple sources and can be measured in different ways, even under GAAP. Therefore, many analysts supplement the quantitative analysis with qualitative judgments about the "quality of earnings." These users look behind the numbers and explore the bases on which they rest. They study the reasons for changes in earnings; some reasons are more important than others.

*High-quality earnings* are those that result from conservative accounting measurements and policies. In this context, for example, LIFO is preferred to FIFO, accelerated depreciation is preferred to straight-line depreciation, and amortization of goodwill over 10 years is better than over 40 years. Moreover, the emphasis on predicting future earnings and cash flows gives rise to two additional characteristics of high-quality earnings.

**1.** They are indicative of the future in the sense that they can be predicted easily. So, stable earnings over time are more desirous than fluctuating earnings. Indeed, companies sometimes use accounting principles and procedures to artificially smooth their reported income numbers. Also, earnings that derive from the ongoing fundamental activities of the business, in contrast to those from unusual or infrequent occurrences or those arising from accounting or tax law changes, are of higher quality.

**2.** They are distributable in cash or map closely with cash flows. As we have noted in Chapter 17, some analysts desire a close correspondence between operating income and cash flow from operations.

## STUDIES OF THE USEFULNESS OF FINANCIAL RATIOS

The discussions so far focus on normative descriptions of how financial statement relationships might be used by analysts. Since the early 1960s, a large number of studies of financial ratios have been conducted. Much of this research has focused on the use of ratios in predicting business failure or in credit-rating decisions. Some of these studies have investigated, through surveys and interviews, what ratios decision-makers actually use, how they use them, and whether the ratios actually help. Others have looked at the predictability of individual ratios or groups of ratios in quantitative models.

This section presents some of those findings. The studies tend to be in four areas: (1) bankruptcy prediction, (2) bond rating predictions, (3) analysis of bank loans, and (4) trade credit ratings.

## Bankruptcy and Financial Failure

Perhaps the best-known studies relating ratio levels to business failure were conducted by Beaver and Altman.[6] Beaver looked at six ratios for 79 firms that "failed" between 1954 and 1964 and an equal number of firms that had not failed. He found that the ratio of cash flow to total debt (financial strength), the ratio of net income to total assets (profitability), and the ratio of total debt to total assets (financial strength) had the strongest power to distinguish between failed and nonfailed firms.

While Beaver looked at each individual ratio's ability to predict financial failure, Altman developed a series of multiple discriminant statistical models to derive a combination of ratios that would predict bankruptcy in advance. Among the financial accounting ratios that appeared in combination to be highly predictive from one to five years before bankruptcy were:

1. Earnings before interest and taxes to total assets (profitability).
2. Earnings before interest and taxes to total interest payments (financial strength).
3. Current assets to current liabilities (liquidity).
4. Common equity to total capital (financial strength).

Other important variables were the stability of earnings, total assets (perhaps a proxy for size of company), and the relationship of retained earnings to total assets (perhaps a proxy for cumulative profitability over time).

The initial enthusiasm for these models subsided somewhat in later years. Subsequent research indicated that most ratio prediction models lost significant predictive power when applied to a different sample of firms in a different time period. Nevertheless, although a conclusive forecasting model has not been developed, the evidence does suggest that accounting ratios can be useful in predictions of this type.

---

[6] William H. Beaver, "Financial Ratios as Predictors of Failure," *Empirical Research in Accounting: Selected Studies, 1986,* Supplement to Volume 4, *Journal of Accounting Research,* pp. 71–111; Edward I. Altman, "Financial Ratios, Discriminant Analysis and the Prediction of Corporate Bankruptcy," *Journal of Finance,* September 1968, pp. 589–609; and Edward I. Altman, Robert G. Haldeman, and P. Narayanan, "Zeta Analysis: A New Model to Identify Bankruptcy Risk of Corporations," *Journal of Banking and Finance,* 1977, pp. 29–54.

## Bond Rating Predictions

A parallel group of studies focused on the use of financial ratios in predicting bond ratings.[7] Bonds are rated by a number of organizations, the primary ones being Moody's and Standard & Poor's. The ratings presumably reflect the investment quality of the bonds and/or the creditworthiness of the issuer with respect to the particular debt obligation. These bond ratings impact significantly the market rates of interest for different bond issues and even determine, in some cases, the securities in which banks and trusts can invest.

Many attempts have been made to generate and test quantitative models designed to duplicate or predict these bond ratings. The models employ various variables including financial accounting ratios. If successfully developed, such models could be used to eliminate inconsistencies in the rating process. Also, they would highlight the factors that appear to be important to the rating agencies. Management then could use these factors in structuring and evaluating their internal production and financial decisions. Investors could also use these factors to anticipate possible changes in ratings.

Most of the bond rating prediction models use multiple discriminant analysis. Unfortunately, the models are not perfect; they correctly classified only 60 to 70 percent of the bond issues to which they were applied. However, they do show that accounting data and financial ratios play an important role in this process. Particular ratios of importance include long-term debt to total capitalization, net income to total assets, and interest coverage.

## Analysis of Bank Loans

A limited number of studies have tried to duplicate the quality ratings of commercial bank loans in much the same manner as the previous studies did with bond ratings.[8] Again, the multiple discriminant models performed adequately, but not outstandingly, in classifying loans or predicting bank loan compliance. Among the financial ratios that in combination aid in predictions are the (1) quick ratio, (2) earnings before interest and taxes to total assets, (3) cash and marketable securities as a percentage of total assets, (4) total debt to total assets, and (5) working capital to net sales.

---

[7] This literature is quite substantial. Representative studies include: James O. Horrigan, "The Determination of Long-Term Credit Standing with Financial Ratios," *Empirical Research in Accounting: Selected Studies, 1966,* Supplement to Volume 4, *Journal of Accounting Research,* pp. 44–62; Thomas F. Pogue and Robert M. Soldofsky, "What's in a Bond Rating," *Journal of Financial and Quantitative Analysis,* June 1969, pp. 201–28; George E. Pinches and Kent A. Mingo, "A Multivariate Analysis of Industrial Bond Ratings," *The Journal of Finance,* March 1973, pp. 1–18; and Ahmed Belkaoui, *Industrial Bonds and The Rating Process* (Westport, Conn.: Quorum Books, 1983).

[8] See, for example, Delton L. Chessor, "Predicting Loan Noncompliance," *The Journal of Commercial Bank Lending,* August 1974, pp. 28–37.

---

**TABLE 18–4**   Important Ratios in Commercial Bank Loans

| *Most Significant to Bank Loan Officers* | *Most Frequent Inclusion in Loan Agreements* |
|---|---|
| Debt to equity | Debt to equity |
| Current ratio | Current ratio |
| Cash flow to current maturities of long-term debt | Dividend payout ratio |
| Fixed charge coverage | Cash flow to current maturities of long-term debt |
| After-tax profit margin | Fixed charge coverage |
| Times interest earned | Times interest earned |
| Before-tax profit margin | Degree of financial leverage |
| Degree of financial leverage | Equity to assets |
| Inventory turnover in days | Cash flow to total debt |
| Accounts receivable turnover in days | Quick ratio |

---

Source: Charles H. Gibson and Patricia A. Frishkoff, *Financial Statement Analysis* 2nd ed. (Boston, Mass.: Kent Publishing Co., 1983).

Other studies of commercial bank loans focused on surveys of banks and examinations of ratios appearing in loan agreements. Table 18–4 shows the 10 ratios perceived to be the most important by the 100 largest banks in the United States and the 10 ratios that most banks include in their loan agreements, as reported in a comprehensive study by Gibson.

## National Association of Accountants Study[9]

Another study, completed by Backer and Gosman in 1978 for the NAA, focused on the prediction of *financial distress*. Because changes in ratings received by a firm for its trade credit, bank loans, or bonds could signal the beginning of financial distress, Backer and Gosman looked at the use of financial measures in the credit-rating decisions of Dun & Bradstreet, federal and state bank examiners, and Standard & Poor's. Downgradings to a rating of 3 for trade credit, substandard for bank loans, and BB for bonds were considered to be capable of producing varying degrees of financial distress.

Senior executives at Dun & Bradstreet, 24 leading banks, and all 3 bond-rating agencies were asked how important financial ratios are in their credit-rating evaluations. The ratios stressed by the interviewees as having moderate to strong importance were then compared with ratios actually

---

[9] Morton Backer and Martin L. Gosman, *Financial Reporting and Business Liquidity* (New York: National Association of Accountants, 1978).

exhibiting significant deterioration prior to the downgrading actions of the credit raters.

The results are reported in Table 18–5. These findings reveal that:

1. The levels and trends of certain key financial measures do influence the probability that a firm will experience the downgrading of its bonds, bank loans, and trade credit and consequent financial distress.
2. The ratios stressed in actual credit downgradings were quite congruous with the bond analysts' and bankers' (but not trade credit raters') descriptions of their own decision models.

All of these research studies point to the fact that financial ratios do influence organizations and individuals outside the firm who often can significantly affect the company's financial flexibility and future outlook. The accounting profession continually should assess whether the financial statement amounts upon which most ratios are based truly measure what they should be measuring. Individual companies need to closely monitor the trends in their financial ratios and to prominently disclose and candidly discuss in their annual reports the existence and implication of such trends. Kimberly-Clark's efforts in this regard are reviewed in the next section of this chapter.

## DISCUSSION OF THE KIMBERLY-CLARK ANNUAL REPORT

Kimberly-Clark discloses an extensive array of ratios and other analytical information. Many of these presentations have not been reproduced in the material contained in the Appendix to Chapter 6. For example, the very first page of the annual report lists nine specific financial highlights during 1987. All of them involve percentage comparisons with 1986, and three of them employ ratios:

1. Net income as a percentage of stockholders' equity increased from 14.7 percent in 1986 to 18.6 percent in 1987.
2. Operating profit as a percentage of assets increased from 14.5 percent in 1986 to 16.6 percent in 1987.
3. Additional debt incurred during the year increased the ratio of debt to capital from 22 percent in 1986 to 36 percent in 1987.

An additional presentation of financial information appears in the *Financial Highlights* presented on pages 8 and 9 of the annual report (not included in the Appendix to Chapter 6). Tables 18–6 and 18–7 reproduce some of that information. In the first table, Kimberly-Clark organizes the information in two very useful ways. First, financial data is presented in several categories of analytical interest. Second, within each category, the percentage change from the preceding year is shown. The latter presentation represents a type of horizontal analysis for selected data items.

**TABLE 18–5**   Financial Ratios Stressed by Credit Raters

| *Ratios Stressed during Interviews* | *Ratios Exhibiting Significant Deterioration in Actual Credit Downgradings* |
|---|---|
| *Bonds:* | |
| Cash flow to long-term debt<br>Long-term debt to capitalization | Cash flow to long-term debt<br>Long-term debt to capitalization |
| Fixed-charge coverage | Net tangible assets to long-term debt<br>Return on tangible net worth<br>Return on sales<br>Return on total assets<br>Cash flow to senior debt<br>Long-term debt to property, plant, and equipment |
| *Bank loans:* | |
| Cash flow to total liabilities<br>Return on sales<br>Total liabilities to tangible net worth | Cash flow to total liabilities<br>Return on sales<br>Financial leverage |
| Working capital to sales | Gross margin<br>Return on equity<br>Fixed-charge coverage<br>Interest coverage<br>Cash flow to senior debt<br>Effective tax rate<br>Percentage sales growth<br>Inventory turnover<br>Current ratio<br>Quick ratio<br>Cash flow growth<br>Percentage profit growth |
| *Trade credit:*<br>Current liabilities to tangible net worth<br>Total debt to tangible net worth<br>Inventory to working capital<br>Long-term debt to working capital<br>Current ratio<br>Quick ratio | Return on tangible net worth<br>Percentage cash flow change<br>Return on working capital<br>Percentage profit change |

Note: Boxed items signify congruity between interviews and statistical findings.

Source: Morton Backer and Martin L. Gosman, *Financial Reporting and Business Liquidity* (New York: National Association of Accountants, 1978), p. 19.

**TABLE 18–6**    Financial Highlights of Kimberly-Clark (dollars in millions except per share amounts)

| | Year Ended December 31 | | | Change | |
|---|---|---|---|---|---|
| | | | | 1987 versus 1986 | 1986 versus 1985 |
| | 1987 | 1986 | 1985 | | |
| **Return on Investment:** | | | | | |
| Net income return on average stockholders' equity . . . . . | 18.6% | 14.7% | 16.1% | +27% | −9% |
| Operating profit return on average assets* . . . . . . . | 16.6% | 14.5% | 15.7% | +14% | −8% |
| **Operating Results:** | | | | | |
| Net sales . . . . . . . . . . | $4,884.7 | $4,303.1 | $4,072.9 | +14% | +6% |
| Operating profit . . . . . . . | 586.1 | 484.9 | 486.3 | +21% | 0% |
| Income before income taxes . . . | 534.1 | 433.0 | 439.3 | +23% | −1% |
| **Net Income:** . . . . . . . . . | 325.2 | 269.4 | 267.1 | +21% | +1% |
| **Working Capital:** . . . . . . . | 138.9 | 228.1 | 163.6 | −39% | +39% |
| **Capitalization:** | | | | | |
| Stockholders' equity . . . . . . | 1,574.9 | 1,919.9 | 1,743.9 | −18% | +10% |
| Total assets . . . . . . . . . | 3,885.7 | 3,676.0 | 3,503.8 | +6% | +5% |
| Long-term debt . . . . . . . | 686.9 | 426.3 | 509.2 | +61% | −16% |
| **Cash Flow:** | | | | | |
| Capital spending . . . . . . . | 247.3 | 282.4 | 425.8 | −12% | −34% |
| Depreciation . . . . . . . . | 186.0 | 169.3 | 140.3 | +10% | +21% |
| Cash provided by operations . . . | 686.6 | 434.5 | 583.5 | +51% | −26% |
| **Per Share Basis:** | | | | | |
| Net income . . . . . . . . . | 3.73 | 2.93 | 2.92 | +27% | 0% |
| Dividends declared . . . . . . | 1.44 | 1.24 | 1.16 | +16% | +7% |
| Book value . . . . . . . . . | 19.60 | 20.89 | 19.04 | −6% | +10% |
| Market value . . . . . . . . | 50.00 | 40.00 | 33.50 | +25% | +19% |

*Average assets excluding investments in equity companies.

Table 18–7 shows a horizontal and vertical analysis of the income statement. Kimberly-Clark titled this information *Distribution of Revenue Received*. It presents an alternative breakdown of expenses from that shown on the formal income statement. The vertical analysis shows the expenses and other distributions that account for 100 percent of the net sales during each of the last three years. The horizontal analysis presents the percentage change in each component from year to year.

## Liquidity

Financial measures indicative of Kimberly-Clark's liquidity are not prominently featured. Of course, all of the data necessary to calculate the com-

**TABLE 18–7**  Distribution of Revenue Received (Dollars in millions)

| | Year Ended December 31 | | | | | | Change | |
|---|---|---|---|---|---|---|---|---|
| | 1987 | | 1986 | | 1985 | | 1987 versus 1986 | 1986 versus 1985 |
| Wages, salaries, and benefits . . . . . . | $1,151 | 24% | $1,088 | 25% | $1,003 | 25% | +6% | +8% |
| Manufacturing materials . . . . . . . | 1,416 | 29 | 1,285 | 30 | 1,107 | 27 | +10 | +16 |
| Other manufacturing costs. . . . . . . . | 746 | 15 | 536 | 12 | 581 | 14 | +39 | −8 |
| Other business costs . . . | 903 | 18 | 827 | 19 | 828 | 20 | +9 | — |
| Income, payroll, and other taxes . . . . . | 344 | 7 | 298 | 7 | 287 | 7 | +15 | +4 |
| Dividends . . . . . . | 125 | 3 | 114 | 3 | 106 | 3 | +10 | +7 |
| Retained earnings . . . . | 200 | 4 | 155 | 4 | 161 | 4 | +29 | −3 |
| Net sales . . . . . . | $4,885 | 100% | $4,303 | 100% | $4,073 | 100% | +14% | +6% |

mon liquidity measures are available to the analyst in the annual report. In Table 18–8, we have prepared a summary of the key financial ratios, including liquidity measures, for Kimberly-Clark. Tracing each of the calculations to the numbers in the statements in the Appendix to Chapter 6 will be a good review.

The company does give attention to its cash provided by operations figure of $656.6 million in 1987 and $434.5 million in 1986. Kimberly-Clark experienced a 51 percent increase from 1986 after having a 26 percent decline from 1985. This impressive cash flow change in 1987 was accomplished with an increase in net sales of just 14 percent. As Table 18–8 reveals, both the turnover of inventories and receivables increased in 1987.

## Financial Strength

Kimberly-Clark substantially expanded its long-term debt during 1987. Management explained the need for this capital primarily in terms of asset expansion. This expansion included construction of manufacturing facilities, acquisition of new paper machinery, and a substantial growth in the firm's aircraft fleet used by Midwest Express Airlines.

Examination of the balance sheet reveals that long-term debt increased by $260.6 million during the year ($314.9 million increase less a $54.3 million decrease according to the statement of cash flows). At the same time, there was a substantial decline in stockholders' equity primarily due to the acquisition of $632 million of treasury stock. As a result, the ratio of *total debt to adjusted capital* as reported by the firm jumped from 22 percent in 1986 to 36 percent in 1987. Kimberly-Clark calculates this ratio as:

1987:    36%    ($686.9 + $250.0)/($686.9 + $250.0 + $82.6 + $1,571.9)

1986:    22%    ($426.3 + $134.0)/($426.3 + $134.0 + $76.5 + $1,919.9)

The numerator is long-term debt plus debt payable within one year. The denominator is total debt plus minority owners' interest in subsidiaries plus stockholders' equity. Other current liabilities and deferred taxes are excluded from both debt and adjusted capital.

Management calls the readers' attention to the fact that this ratio is on the high side and indicates its intention to reduce the ratio to a target range of 28 to 32 percent by the end of 1988. It also points out, in the *Review of Liquidity and Capital Resources,* that the increased debt has not caused any decline in the rating of its bonds at double-A or of its commercial paper in the top category.

Perhaps one reason for the fact that the large jump in this debt ratio does not seem to have had an adverse effect is the comparatively large interest coverage in 1987 of 9.1 times. Moreover, interest coverage improved from 1986 to 1987, despite the large increase in debt. These calculations and other financial strength ratios are presented in Table 18–8.

**Profitability**

Kimberly-Clark feels, quite rightfully, that it has used its assets well and has generated a substantial return from their use. Therefore, it emphasizes two return on investment ratios (see Table 18–6).

Instead of a rate of return on total assets, Kimberly-Clark uses an Operating Profit Return on Average Assets as a measure of overall profitability. This is, of course, a before-tax figure. The calculation uses operating profit from the income statement as a numerator. Miscellaneous nonoperating revenue and expense items, interest expense, equity in earnings of subsidiaries, minority interest in earnings, as well as income taxes are excluded. To be consistent, the denominator also excludes investments in equity companies from the average asset base. The calculation for 1987 was derived as follows:

*Operating Profit/Average Assets Excluding Equity Investments*

$586.1/.5[($3,885.7 − $264.8) + ($3,676.0 − $243.8)]

$586.1/.5($3,620.9 + $3,432.2)

16.6%

The other profitability ratio displayed is the familiar rate of return on common stockholders' equity. In 1987, net income of $325.2 million is divided by average stockholders' equity of $1,745.9 million to get the percentage rate of 18.6 percent. A similar calculation for 1986 appears in Table 18–8 along with other profitability measures such as rate of return on total assets.

The difference between the 16.6 percent operating profit ratio and the 18.6 percent net income return reflects a number of different factors—nonoperating income and expense, investment income and assets, income taxes, and financial leverage. The reader should also observe that the dramatic increase in rate of return on stockholders' equity from 14.7 percent in 1986 to 18.6 percent in 1987 was caused by two factors—an increase in net income and a decrease in stockholders' equity resulting from a significant purchase of treasury shares during 1987.

## Analysis of Kimberly-Clark Statements

In Table 18–8, we calculate the key financial ratios illustrated in this chapter for Kimberly-Clark. As the preceding review indicates, however, there are many alternative ways of looking at financial strength and profitability.

All denominators that are listed as "average" in Table 18–8 are simple averages of the beginning and end of the year. The 1987 averages may be determined readily from the balance sheet. The total assets and stockholders' equity as of December 31, 1985 are given in other parts of the report so that 1986 averages for these items can be calculated. However, to obtain the December 31, 1985 balances for accounts receivable and inventories, we made use of information contained in Note 9. The first schedule there summarizes the impact on cash flows from changes in working capital items. During 1986, both accounts receivable and inventories increased (i.e., they are deducted from operations to obtain cash flow). Accordingly, we can subtract these increases to obtain an estimate at the end of 1985 as follows:

|  | Accounts Receivable | Inventory |
|---|---|---|
| 1986 balance . . . . . . . . . . . . . | $455.2 | $531.3 |
| Less: Increase during 1986 . . . . . . | (14.5) | (54.3) |
| 1985 balance . . . . . . . . . . . . . | $440.7 | $477.0 |

**Return on Average Total Assets.** The numerator for this profitability ratio is net income plus tax-adjusted interest plus minority interest. Tax-adjusted interest expense is included in the numerator for the purpose of consistency between numerator and denominator. Many of the assets reflected in the denominator were financed through the use of long-term debt, and, accordingly, the numerator should be adjusted to eliminate the effect of this financing. Although Kimberly-Clark's effective tax rates were

**TABLE 18–8**   Summary of Key Financial Ratios for Kimberly-Clark

| Name of Ratio | Formula | | | Calculations |
|---|---|---|---|---|
| **A. Liquidity Measures:** | | | | |
| 1. Current ratio | $\dfrac{\text{Current assets}}{\text{Current liabilities}}$ | 1987:<br>1986: | 1.1<br>1.3 | ($1,135/$996.1)<br>($1,032.9/$804.8) |
| 2. Quick (Acid-test) ratio | $\dfrac{\text{Monetary current assets}}{\text{Current liabilities}}$ | 1987:<br>1986: | .6<br>.6 | ($609.6/$996.1)<br>($501.6/$804.8) |
| **B. Financial Strength (Solvency) Measures:** | | | | |
| 3. Stock-equity ratio | $\dfrac{\text{Stockholders' equity}}{\text{Total equities}}$<br>or<br>$\dfrac{\text{Stockholders' equity}}{\text{Total capitalization}}$ | 1987:<br>1986:<br><br>1987:<br>1986: | 40.4%<br>52.2%<br><br>54.4%<br>66.9% | ($1,571.9/$3,885.7)<br>($1,919.9/$3,676)<br><br>($1,571.9/$2,889.6)<br>($1,919.9/$2,871.2) |
| 4. Debt-equity ratio | $\dfrac{\text{Long-Term debt}}{\text{Total equities}}$<br>or<br>$\dfrac{\text{Long-Term debt}}{\text{Total capitalization}}$ | 1987:<br>1986:<br><br>1987:<br>1986: | 17.7%<br>11.6%<br><br>23.8%<br>14.8% | ($686.9/$3,885.7)<br>($426.3/$3,676)<br><br>($686.9/$2,889.6)<br>($426.3/$2,871.2) |
| 5. Interest coverage | $\dfrac{\text{Income before interest and taxes}}{\text{Interest expense}}$ | 1987:<br>1986: | 9.1<br>7.9 | ($599.7/$65.6)<br>($495.8/$62.8) |
| 6. Cash flow to debt | $\dfrac{\text{Cash flow from operations}}{\text{Long-Term debt}}$<br>or<br>$\dfrac{\text{Cash flow from operations}}{\text{Total debt (including deferred)}}$<br>taxes and current liabilities | 1987:<br>1986:<br><br>1987:<br>1986: | 95.6%<br>101.9%<br><br>29.4%<br>25.9% | ($656.6/$686.9)<br>($434.5/$426.3)<br><br>($656.6/$2,231.2)<br>($434.5/$1,679.6) |

## C. Investment Efficiency (Utilization) Measures:

7. Turnover of receivables $\dfrac{\text{Net sales}}{\text{Average accounts receivable}}$

   1987: 10.0 ($4,884.7/$487.55)
   1986: 9.6 ($4,303.1/$447.95)

8. Turnover of inventory $\dfrac{\text{Cost of goods sold}}{\text{Average inventory}}$

   1987: 5.8 ($3,065.9/$528.35)
   1986: 5.4 ($2,712.2/$504.15)

9. Turnover of total assets $\dfrac{\text{Net sales}}{\text{Average total assets}}$

   1987: 1.3 ($4,884.7/$3,780.85)
   1986: 1.2 ($4,303.4/$3,589.9)

## D. Operating Efficiency Measures:

10. Operating ratio $\dfrac{\text{Operating expenses}}{\text{Net sales}}$

    1987: 88.0% (4,298.6/$4,884.7)
    1986: 88.7% ($3,818.2/$4,303.1)

11. Income (profit) margin $\dfrac{\text{Net income}}{\text{Net sales}}$

    1987: 6.7% ($325.2/$4,884.7)
    1986: 6.3% ($264.4/$4,303.1)

12. Gross margin $\dfrac{\text{Gross profit}}{\text{Net sales}}$

    1987: 33.5% ($1,637.6/$4,884.7)
    1986: 33.1% ($1,424.7/$4,303.1)

## E. Overall Profitability and Performance Measures:

13. Rate of return on total assets $\dfrac{\text{Net income} + \text{Tax-adjusted interest} + \text{interest} + \text{Minority interest}}{\text{Average total assets}}$

    1987: 9.96% ($376.5/$3,780.85)
    1986: 8.8% ($315.8/$3,589.9)

14. Rate of return on common stock equity $\dfrac{\text{Net income to common}}{\text{Average common stock equity}}$

    1987: 18.63% ($325.2/$1,745.9)
    1986: 14.71% ($269.4/$1,831.9)

15. Dividend payout ratio $\dfrac{\text{Cash dividends to common}}{\text{Net income to common}}$

    1987: 38.5% ($125.1/$325.2)
    1986: 42.3% ($113.9/$269.4)

43.2 percent in 1987 and 43.1 percent in 1986, we have used an estimated *marginal* tax rate of 42.7 and 48.6 percent in 1987 and 1986, respectively (federal statutory rates plus state income taxes, net). The deduction of interest expense presumably has saved Kimberly-Clark $28.0 million in income taxes in 1987 ($65.6 × .427) and $30.5 million in 1986 ($62.8 × .486). If there had been no interest expense and related tax deduction, after-tax net income would have been greater by $37.6 ($65.6 − $28.0) in 1987 and $32.3 ($62.8 − $30.5) in 1986.

The addition of the minority interest in income to the numerator is also a way of ensuring consistency with the denominator. Recall from our discussion in Chapter 15 that Kimberly-Clark has a number of subsidiaries that are less than 100 percent owned. In the consolidated balance sheet, the assets of these subsidiaries are included in their entirety. On the consolidated income statement, however, the minorities' interest in income has been deducted (as an expense) so that the reported net income reflects only Kimberly-Clark's return. Because assets contributed by both the majority and minority interests are counted in the denominator, *all* the income produced by those assets belongs in the numerator. Accordingly, the $13.7 million in 1987 and $14.1 million in 1986 of minority interest in income that was previously deducted in the calculation of income must be added back.

Just as the return on investment for Sebago Company was dissected into its margin and turnover components, so can Kimberly-Clark's return on investment be decomposed. The income margin or *return on sales* demonstrates the firm's ability to convert sales dollars into profit. The measure has been adjusted, so it differs a little from the income margin reported in Table 18–8. The asset turnover can be taken directly from the table:

| Rate of return on total assets | | Tax-adjusted income margin (Return on sales) | | Asset turnover |
|---|---|---|---|---|
| 1987 ($376.5/$3,780.85) | = | ($376.2/$4,884.7) | × | ($4,884.7/$3,780.85) |
| 9.96% | = | 7.70% | × | 1.29 times |
| 1986 ($315.8/$3,589.9) | = | ($315.8/$4,303.1) | × | ($4,303.1/$3,589.9) |
| 8.8% | = | 7.34% | × | 1.2 times |

Both the income margin and asset turnover show only a slight improvement. The combination of the two components, however, results in an increase in the return on invested assets of more than one percent.

**Financial Leverage.** The rates shown above display returns in terms of overall assets and total income. The residual ownership group, that is the common stockholders, are interested in the return their investment earns and in the corporation's use of financial leverage. A comparison of the return on total assets with that on common stockholders' equity (see Table 18–8) shows:

|                               | *1987*  | *1986*  |
|-------------------------------|---------|---------|
| Return on total assets        | 9.96%   | 8.8%    |
| Return on stockholders' equity| 18.63%  | 14.71%  |

Kimberly-Clark experienced favorable leverage for both 1987 and 1986. It results from the firm carrying a substantial amount of noninterest-bearing current liabilities and deferred taxes. Also, the after-tax interest cost on the long-term debt was considerably below the 9.96 percent return on the average total assets.

# A CONCLUDING NOTE

The analysis of financial statements is truly problematic. On the one hand, it is one major reason for preparing accounting reports and certainly a logical capstone to a study of financial accounting. On the other hand, the area is fraught with difficulties and potential traps. The qualitative considerations mentioned throughout the chapter are as important as the quantitative aspects of statement analysis that receive the greater attention in the chapter.

As an analyst, you are faced with a variety of ratios and alternative definitions. You must select the relevant information and analytical procedures for your particular purposes. The techniques discussed provide a start in this direction. However, in computing and using ratios, keep four points in mind:

1. Ratios are only as valid as the statements themselves. Ratios reflect all the conventions and limitations underlying the basic accounting data. A detailed understanding of the financial statements is essential to an intelligent interpretation of the ratios and a meaningful explanation of changes in ratios.
2. Ratio analysis requires a basis for comparison.
3. Ratios are only a clue to areas needing further investigation. They can serve as screening devices, but they rarely supply answers and can never make decisions.
4. Ratio analysis is meaningful only if the user clearly understands the purpose of each relationship—short-term liquidity, long-term financial strength, efficiency, and profitability. The ratios used should make sense; some *a priori* reason or analytical purpose should exist to support the belief that the financial statement items chosen are related.

# PROBLEMS AND CASETTES

## 18–1. Effect of Accounting Transactions on Selected Ratios

Assume that you have just completed a ratio analysis of a company. As part of that analysis, you calculated the four ratios listed in the table at the end of the problem.

The notes to the financial statements disclose the following six material events happening after the date of the statements. State whether each of these transactions will cause the four ratios to increase (+), decrease (−), or remain the same (0). Explain your reasoning. Consider each transaction independently of all the others and assume no other changes.

1. Sold a building that had been used as a spare warehouse for cash at a price below book value.
2. Acquired 80 percent of the common stock of another company to be held as an investment. Issued 1,000 shares of treasury stock and paid $250,000 cash to acquire the investment shares.
3. Declared and paid an extra cash dividend of 30 cents on each share of common stock outstanding.
4. Entered into a long-term financial lease with an insurance company under which the firm acquired the use of a warehouse for 15 years.
5. Signed an agreement with a bank for a line of credit under which the firm could borrow up to $300,000. Borrowed $100,000 for six months under this agreement.
6. Completed an early retirement of mortgage bonds that would have matured in five years. An extraordinary gain resulted.

| | Original | *Effect of Transactions* | | | | | |
| *Ratio* | *Calculation* | *(1)* | *(2)* | *(3)* | *(4)* | *(5)* | *(6)* |
|---|---|---|---|---|---|---|---|
| Current ratio | 2.5 to 1 | —— | —— | —— | —— | —— | —— |
| Interest coverage | 8 times | —— | —— | —— | —— | —— | —— |
| Rate of return on assets | 22% | —— | —— | —— | —— | —— | —— |
| Stock-equity ratio | 40% | —— | —— | —— | —— | —— | —— |

## 18–2. Explain Purpose of Other Ratios

The following ratios have been taken from various authoritative sources. They represent relationships *not* described in the text. For each ratio explain the purpose or use that would be made of it.

1. Ratio of long-term debt to working capital.
2. Provision for doubtful accounts as a percent of gross trade receivables.
3. Ratio of sales to working capital.
4. Proportion of stockholders' equity represented by plant assets.
5. Percent of operating revenue absorbed by maintenance expense.
6. Ratio of current liabilities to inventory.
7. Ratio of plant assets to long-term debt.

## 18–3. Interrelationships among Ratios

Some selected ratios for 1991 and 1992 for Magnolia Enterprises are given below:

| | 1992 | 1991 |
|---|---|---|
| Turnover of accounts receivable . . . . . . . . . . . | 10.3 | 8.1 |
| Turnover of inventory . . . . . . . . . . . . . . . . | 5.7 | 6.8 |
| Turnover of total assets . . . . . . . . . . . . . . . | 2.1 | 2.2 |

|                                          | *1992* | *1991* |
|------------------------------------------|--------|--------|
| Current ratio . . . . . . . . . . . . . . . . . . . . . | 2.3 | 1.8 |
| Quick ratio . . . . . . . . . . . . . . . . . . . . | 1.5 | 1.0 |
| Debt-equity ratio . . . . . . . . . . . . . . . . | 30% | 43% |
| Operating ratio . . . . . . . . . . . . . . . . | 81.2% | 86.3% |
| Rate of return on total assets . . . . . . . . . . . . | 12.0% | 10.5% |
| Rate of return on common stock equity . . . . . . . | 14.8% | 14.7% |

Answer each of the questions below by interpreting and interrelating some of these ratios.

**Required:**

*a.* Both the current ratio and the quick ratio increased from 1991 to 1992. Which increase provides the greater assurance that short-term liquidity has improved?

*b.* Why has the rate of return on total assets increased from 1991 to 1992?

*c.* Why has the rate of return on common stock equity remained stable although the rate of return on assets has increased?

*d.* If the ratio, times interest earned, had been calculated, would you expect that it would increase or decrease from 1991 to 1992? Why?

**18–4. Impact of Accounting Transactions on Specific Ratios**

Seven independent transactions are shown below. Underneath each transaction there appear two ratios and their values *before* considering the impact of the transaction.

1. Purchase of merchandise inventory with entire purchase financed by a 120-day bank loan.
   Current ratio is 2.8 to 1.
   Quick ratio is 1.2 to 1.
2. Payment of an account payable in cash.
   Current ratio is 2.2 to 1.
   Quick ratio is .8 to 1.
3. Conversion of long-term debt to common stock.
   Stock-equity ratio is 60 percent.
   Rate of return on total assets is 21 percent.
4. Change from FIFO to the LIFO method of inventory during a period of rising prices.
   Inventory turnover is 7 times.
   Earnings per share is $3.40.
5. Issuance of common stock for cash at an amount greater than par value.
   Debt-equity ratio is 30 percent.
   Rate of return on common stock equity is 25 percent.
6. Acquisition of a warehouse with a 20 percent cash down payment and the other 80 percent represented by a long-term mortgage note.
   Current ratio is 2.7 to 1.
   Debt-equity ratio is 40 percent.
7. Sale of a machine for cash at a loss.
   Earnings per share is $2.80.
   Quick ratio is 1.2 to 1.

**Required:**

For each of the seven transactions, indicate whether the ratios indicated will increase, decrease, or stay the same. Confine your answers to the expected impact in the short run without assuming other events occur.

**18–5. Derive Missing Statement and Ratio Elements**
Fill in the following schedule:

1. Net sales __$50,000__
2. Operating income _____
3. Interest expense __$250__
4. Net income before tax __$2,750__
5. Income taxes _____
6. Net income _____
7. Stockholders' equity _____
8. Total assets __$12,500__
9. Operating income/sales _____
10. Net income/sales _____
11. Turnover of assets _____
12. Turnover of stockholders' equity __8.0__
13. Return on total investment _____
14. Return on stockholders' equity __26.4%__

**18–6. Calculation of Financial Leverage**
Selected data for two companies are presented below:

|  | James Company | Geary Company |
|---|---|---|
| Average current liabilities. . . . . . . . . . . . | $  100,000 | $  200,000 |
| Average long-term debt. . . . . . . . . . . . . | 100,000 | 500,000 |
| Average preferred stock equity. . . . . . . . . | 200,000 | 600,000 |
| Average common stock equity . . . . . . . . . | 800,000 | 400,000 |
| Average total assets . . . . . . . . . . . . | $1,200,000 | $1,700,000 |
| Earnings before interest and taxes  . . . . . . . | $  240,000 | $  340,000 |

Both companies are subject to an income tax rate of 40 percent. The long-term debt of James Company has an average interest rate of 8 percent while that of Geary Company carries an average rate of 10 percent. James Company declared and paid preferred dividends of $20,000 during the year; Geary Company paid $66,000.

**Required:**

a. Calculate the rate of return on total assets and the rate of return on common stock equity for each company.
b. Did each of the companies use financial leverage successfully? Support your answer with a detailed analysis similar to Table 18–3.

c. Which company employed financial leverage *more* successfully? Explain why.

d. Would your answer be the same to parts *b*, *c*, and *d* if the earnings before interest and taxes were $108,000 and $153,000 for James Company and Geary Company, respectively?

**18–7. Calculation of Ratios for One Company**

The condensed financial data for the Ruggles Company appear below (dollars in thousands):

**RUGGLES COMPANY**
**Balance Sheet**

| Assets | | Equities | |
|---|---|---|---|
| Cash . . . . . . . . . . . . | $ 44 | Accounts payable . . . . . . . | $102 |
| Marketable securities. . . . . . | 16 | Accrued liabilities. . . . . . . | 41 |
| Receivables . . . . . . . . . | 75 | 8% mortgage bonds . . . . . . | 80 |
| Inventories . . . . . . . . . | 170 | 10% preferred stock . . . . . . | 80 |
| Investment securities . . . . . . | 60 | Common stock . . . . . . . . | 200 |
| Plant assets (net) . . . . . . . | 229 | Retained earnings . . . . . . . | 91 |
| Total assets. . . . . . . . . | $594 | Total equities . . . . . . . . | $594 |

**RUGGLES COMPANY**
**Income Statement**

| | | |
|---|---|---|
| Net sales . . . . . . . . . . . . . . . . . . . | | $990 |
| Cost of goods sold . . . . . . . . . . . . . | $754 | |
| Operating expenses . . . . . . . . . . . . . | 146 | |
| Depreciation expense . . . . . . . . . . . . | 30 | 930 |
| Operating income . . . . . . . . . . . . . . | | 60 |
| Other income . . . . . . . . . . . . . . . . | 16 | |
| Other expense . . . . . . . . . . . . . . . . | (7) | |
| Interest expense . . . . . . . . . . . . . . | (6) | 3 |
| Interest before taxes . . . . . . . . . . . . | | 63 |
| Income taxes (40%) . . . . . . . . . . . . . | | 25 |
| Net income . . . . . . . . . . . . . . . . | | $ 38 |

Dividends on stock declared and paid during the year were $8,000 to preferred and $7,000 to common. At the beginning of the year, inventories were $210,000, total common stockholders' equity was $256,000, and the total assets were $545,000. Preferred stock was $80,000 throughout the year.

**Required:**

a. From the above information, calculate the following ratios:
   1. Current ratio.
   2. Quick ratio.
   3. Stock-equity ratio.
   4. Times-fixed-charges-earned.
   5. Average number of days' sales uncollected at year-end.

6. Turnover of merchandise.
7. Rate of return on total assets.
8. Rate of return on total common stockholders' equity.

b. Did the firm experience favorable or unfavorable financial leverage from its use of preferred stock? From its use of bonds? Show calculations to support your answer.

## 18–8. Identification of Companies through Ratios

The following ratios have been calculated from the financial statements of four companies. One of the companies is a utility, one is a manufacturer of consumer durables, one is a legal partnership, and the fourth is a retailer of consumer products.

| | Company | | | |
|---|---|---|---|---|
| | *A* | *B* | *C* | *D* |
| Current ratio | 1.99 | 0.65 | 1.81 | 1.12 |
| Stock-equity ratio | 59% | 28% | 53% | 69% |
| Turnover of average total assets | 1.72 times | 0.28 times | 2.57 times | 4.2 times |
| Margin | 3.9% | 20.8% | 3.2% | 6.3% |
| Rate of return on average total assets | 6.8% | 5.8% | 8.1% | 26.5% |

### Required:

a. From the differences in the ratios for the four firms, attempt to identify the utility, manufacturer, retailer, and law partnership.
b. Explain what industry conditions or other environmental factors might account for the differences in the ratios for the four different firms.

## 18–9. Analysis of Return on Investment and Its Components

The following data for the year 1990 relate to Krueger Company and Glidewell Company, companies in the same basic line of business:

| | *Krueger Company* | *Glidewell Company* |
|---|---|---|
| Sales revenue. . . . . . . . . . . . . . . . . | $3,800,000 | $2,000,000 |
| Net income. . . . . . . . . . . . . . . . | 76,000 | 80,000 |
| Interest expense. . . . . . . . . . . . . . . | 26,000 | 20,000 |
| Average total assets . . . . . . . . . . . . . | 700,000 | 900,000 |
| Average stockholders' equity . . . . . . . . . . | 420,000 | 650,000 |

Both companies are subject to a tax rate of 40 percent.

### Required:

a. Compare the two companies with respect to the following ratios: (1) rate of return on stockholders' equity, (2) rate of return on total assets, (3) asset turnover, and (4) income margin.

*b.* Explain in as great detail as the data will permit why one firm earns a substantially higher rate of return for its stockholders.

## 18–10. Forecasting Changes in Return on Investment

Refer to the facts in Problem 18–9. In addition, each of the companies contemplates the following actions for 1991. All other conditions are expected to remain the same as in 1990.

Krueger Company plans in 1991 to expand assets by $300,000. The expansion will take place uniformly throughout next year, and 50 percent will be financed through borrowing at an interest cost of 10 percent and 50 percent through an increase in stockholders' equity. Management expects that the asset expansion will generate $30,000 in additional income before tax next year and even greater amounts in future years.

Glidewell Company anticipates a 20 percent increase in sales volume next year. Seventy-five percent of its *operating* expenses are variable and 25 percent are fixed.

### Required:

*a.* What will be the *expected* rates of return on average total assets and on average stockholders' equity for Krueger Company for 1991?

*b.* What will happen in 1991 to the income margin, the turnover of assets, and the rate of return on total assets for Glidewell Company?

## 18–11. Impact of Accounting Policies on Ratios

Assume that two companies, Rectenwold Corporation and Kappas Company, are identical in all respects except that they use different accounting policies as indicated below:

| Accounting Policy Area | Rectenwold Corporation | Kappas Company |
|---|---|---|
| Inventory | FIFO | LIFO |
| Depreciation | Straight-line | Accelerated |
| Goodwill amortization | 10 years | 40 years |
| Oil drilling and development costs | Successful efforts | Full costing |
| Assumed rate of return on pension fund assets | 8% | 10% |

### Required:

*a.* Which of the two firms would you expect to have the:
  1. Greater turnover of inventory
  2. Larger rate of return on assets
  3. Larger gross margin
  4. Greater turnover of total assets
  5. Larger current ratio

  Explain carefully the basis for your conclusion by analyzing the impact of each accounting policy, if relevant, on each of the above ratios.

*b.* Which company in your judgment has the higher quality earnings? Explain.

## 18–12. Comparative Analysis of Two Companies

The information presented below is taken from the records of two companies in the same industry:

|  | Alphonse Co. | Gaston Co. |
|---|---|---|
| Cash . . . . . . . . . . . . . . | $   44,000 | $   74,000 |
| Receivables (net) . . . . . . . . | 76,000 | 116,000 |
| Inventories . . . . . . . . . . . | 248,000 | 185,000 |
| Plant assets (net) . . . . . . . . | 369,000 | 500,000 |
| Total assets . . . . . . . . . . | $ 737,000 | $ 875,000 |
|  |  |  |
| Accounts payable . . . . . . . . | $ 171,000 | $ 207,000 |
| Bonds payable . . . . . . . . . . | 134,000 | 200,000 |
| Common stock . . . . . . . . . . | 230,000 | 335,000 |
| Retained earnings . . . . . . . . | 202,000 | 133,000 |
| Total equities . . . . . . . . . . | $ 737,000 | $ 875,000 |
|  |  |  |
| Sales . . . . . . . . . . . . . . | $1,150,000 | $1,730,000 |
| Cost of goods sold . . . . . . . . | 820,000 | 1,350,000 |
| Other expenses . . . . . . . . . | 140,000 | 161,000 |
| Interest expense . . . . . . . . . | 12,000 | 15,000 |
| Income taxes . . . . . . . . . . | 71,000 | 82,000 |
| Dividends . . . . . . . . . . . . | 21,000 | 35,000 |

**Required:**

a. Answer each of the following questions by computing one or more relevant ratios:
  1. Which company is using the stockholders' investment more profitably?
  2. Which company is better able to meet its current debts?
  3. If you were going to buy the bonds of one firm, which one would you choose? (Assume you would buy them at the same yield.)
  4. Which firm collects its receivables faster?
  5. How long does it take each company to convert an investment in inventory to cash?
  6. Which company retains the larger proportion of income in the business?
b. Which company is earning the higher rate of return on its total asset investment? Explain the general reasons for the differences in terms of investment efficiency and operating efficiency.

## 18–13. Comparison and Analysis of Rates of Return

The following statistics for 1985 have been gathered for three supermarkets in the United States (all amounts are in millions of dollars):

|  | Big U Supermarkets | Kroger | Safeway |
|---|---|---|---|
| Sales . . . . . . . . . . . . . . | $560.63 | $17,123.53 | $19,650.54 |
| Interest expense . . . . . . . . . . | 2.15 | 105.15 | 172.91 |
| Net income. . . . . . . . . . . . | 5.74 | 180.75 | 231.30 |
| Average total assets . . . . . . . . | 110.12 | 2,001.13 | 4,840.61 |
| Average stockholders' equity . . . . . | 42.75 | 1,188.67 | 1,622.61 |

**Required:**

a. Compute a rate of return on average total asset investment as a product of margin and turnover for each of the firms. Assume a 46 percent tax rate.
b. Comment on the differences discovered in part a. Did the firms with lower margins achieve higher turnovers and vice versa?
c. Compute a rate of return on average stockholders' equity for each company.
d. "Each of the three companies is to be commended, for they all managed to employ favorable financial leverage." Is this true? Should they all be equally commended? Explain.

## 18–14. Ratio Analysis for a Short-Term Loan

The Ali Finance Company is attempting to evaluate an applicant for a *short-term* loan. The following information is furnished by the loan applicant:

|  | *December 31* | | |
|---|---|---|---|
|  | *1991* | *1990* | *1989* |
| Cash . . . . . . . . . . . . . | $ 3,000 | $ 5,000 |  |
| Marketable securities . . . . . . . | 3,500 | 9,000 |  |
| Receivables. . . . . . . . . . | 29,000 | 34,000 | $19,000 |
| Inventories . . . . . . . . . . | 40,000 | 35,000 | 30,000 |
| Prepayments . . . . . . . . . | 6,500 | 8,000 |  |
| Accounts payable . . . . . . . . | 32,000 | 49,000 | 27,000 |

|  | *Year Ended December 31* | |
|---|---|---|
|  | *1991* | *1990* |
| Sales . . . . . . . . . . . . | $115,000 | $106,000 |
| Cost of goods sold . . . . . . . . . . . | 85,000 | 79,000 |

**Required:**

a. Compute for 1990 and 1991 the following ratios: (1) current ratio, (2) quick ratio, (3) inventory turnover, and (4) receivables turnover.
b. Based on your findings in part a, would you recommend that Ali Finance Company grant the loan? Explain.
c. What limitations, if any, do you see in your analysis?
d. Would quarterly data have been helpful in this type of situation?
e. If the applicant were requesting a *long-term* loan instead of a short-term loan, is there any additional financial data that the Ali Finance Company should insist on seeing? Explain.

## 18–15. Comparison of Selected Ratios for Three Airlines

Selected financial information from the 1985 annual reports of three airlines is presented below (amounts in millions of dollars):

|  | *Delta* | *Republic* | *UAL* |
|---|---|---|---|
| 1985: |  |  |  |
| Sales revenue. . . . . . . . . . . . | $4,684.1 | $1,734.4 | $6,383.4 |
| Net earnings (loss) from operations . . . . . | 366.0 | 166.3 | (103.4) |
| Net earnings (loss). . . . . . . . . . . | 259.5 | 177.0 | 48.7 |

|  | Delta | Republic | UAL |
|---|---|---|---|
| December 31, 1985: |  |  |  |
| Receivables . . . . . . . . . . . . . . | $ 439.3 | $ 158.1 | $ 933.7 |
| Total current assets . . . . . . . . . . | 614.2 | 528.3 | 3,089.5 |
| Total assets. . . . . . . . . . | 3,626.8 | 1,286.3 | 7,874.2 |
| Air traffic liability . . . . . . . . . . . | 357.8 | 128.6 | 432.8 |
| Total current liabilities . . . . . . . . . | 940.8 | 415.7 | 3,153.1 |
| Total liabilities . . . . . . . . . . . . | 2,339.8 | 1,090.2 | 6,081.0 |

**Required:**

*a.* The "air traffic liability" is also referred to as "advance ticket sales" and "tickets outstanding." What procedure for revenue recognition is implied by the existence of this current liability?

*b.* Calculate the current ratio and the amount of working capital for each airline at December 31, 1985. Are such levels generally viewed as satisfactory? Are airlines' current ratios really quick ratios in disguise? Explain.

*c.* According to Delta, a negative working capital position is normal for Delta and the airline industry in general and does not indicate a lack of liquidity. Is negative working capital normal for the airline industry? If so, what factors contribute to this situation?

*d.* Compare and contrast the relationship among the airlines' net operating earnings (loss) vis-à-vis their net income numbers. What factors might have created the observed disparity? Which relationship would you pay more attention to in evaluating the relative profitability of the three firms? Explain.

*e.* Do the airlines differ in their use of financial leverage? Is their debt too high?

**18–16. Choice between Two Loans by a Bank**

You are the new small-loan officer at Mark Time State Bank. Two companies have submitted requests for one-year unsecured loans of $300,000. Because of lending limits imposed by bank policies on this type of loan, only *one* of the loans will probably be granted. Condensed financial information appears below (amounts are in thousands of dollars):

|  | Cape Co. | Cod Co. |
|---|---|---|
| Cash . . . . . . . . . . . . . . | $ 78.0 | $ 20.0 |
| Accounts receivable . . . . . . . . . | 153.6 | 171.2 |
| Inventories . . . . . . . . . . . | 400.0 | 480.0 |
| Plant assets (net) . . . . . . . . . | 460.0 | 463.2 |
| Total assets . . . . . . . . . . | $1,091.6 | $1,134.4 |
|  |  |  |
| Accounts payable . . . . . . . . . | $ 164.0 | $ 480.0 |
| Mortgage payable . . . . . . . . . | 372.0 | 400.0 |
| Stockholders' equity . . . . . . . . . | 555.6 | 254.4 |
| Total equities . . . . . . . . . | $1,091.6 | $1,134.4 |

|                          | *Cape Co.* | *Cod Co.* |
|--------------------------|-----------:|----------:|
| Sales . . . . . . . . . . . . . . . | $1,283.2 | $1,000.0 |
| Cost of goods sold . . . . . . . . . | (746.4) | (607.2) |
| Operating expenses . . . . . . . . . | (391.6) | (234.4) |
| Other expenses . . . . . . . . . . . | (95.2) | (40.0) |
| Net income before tax . . . . . . . . | 50.0 | 118.4 |
| Income tax . . . . . . . . . . . | (20.0) | (47.4) |
| Net income . . . . . . . . . . . | $   30.0 | $   71.0 |

**Required:**

*a.* As a loan officer considering these requests for one-year loans, are you equally concerned with the four areas of liquidity, financial strength, efficiency, and profitability? Explain.

*b.* Calculate some ratios that would be helpful to you in assessing the performance of both applicants in the priority areas you cited in your answer to *a*. Which *one* of the two companies would you recommend for the loan?

*c.* One of your assistants suggests that your ratio analysis in part *b* should really have been made on a pro forma basis, in other words, assuming that the loan request was granted. Do you agree?

*d.* Calculate the time it takes each firm to convert an investment in inventory to cash.

**18–17. Analysis of a Single Company over Time**

Comparative financial statements for Center Awning Company appear below:

**CENTER AWNING COMPANY**
**Income Statements**
**Year Ended December 31**

|                          | *1992* | *1991* | *1990* |
|--------------------------|-------:|-------:|-------:|
| Sales . . . . . . . . . . . . . . . . . | $60,000 | $49,000 | $45,000 |
| Cost of goods sold. . . . . . . . . . . . . | 39,000 | 32,800 | 28,000 |
| Selling expenses . . . . . . . . . . . | 6,400 | 4,000 | 3,600 |
| Administrative expenses . . . . . . . . . . | 9,100 | 5,000 | 7,100 |
| Total expenses . . . . . . . . . . . | 54,500 | 41,800 | 38,700 |
| Net income before tax . . . . . . . . . . . | 5,500 | 7,200 | 6,300 |
| Income taxes . . . . . . . . . . . . | 2,200 | 2,880 | 2,520 |
| Net income. . . . . . . . . . . . . | $ 3,300 | $ 4,320 | $ 3,780 |

**CENTER AWNING COMPANY**
**Balance Sheets**
**As of December 31**

|                          | *1992* | *1991* | *1990* |
|--------------------------|-------:|-------:|-------:|
| Cash . . . . . . . . . . . . . . . . . | $ 2,400 | $ 2,800 | $ 1,400 |
| Accounts receivable . . . . . . . . . . . . . | 7,000 | 7,200 | 3,100 |
| Inventory . . . . . . . . . . . . . . | 8,500 | 8,200 | 6,000 |
| Plant and equipment . . . . . . . . . . . | 9,000 | 11,400 | 12,900 |
| Total assets. . . . . . . . . . . . . | $26,900 | $29,600 | $23,400 |

|  | 1992 | 1991 | 1990 |
|---|---|---|---|
| Current liabilities . . . . . . . . . . . . . . . . | $ 6,800 | $ 6,400 | $ 2,900 |
| Bonds payable . . . . . . . . . . . . . . . . | 5,000 | 6,000 | 8,000 |
| Common stock . . . . . . . . . . . . . . . . | 11,000 | 12,000 | 9,000 |
| Retained earnings . . . . . . . . . . . . . . . | 4,100 | 5,200 | 3,500 |
| Total equities . . . . . . . . . . . . . . . . | $26,900 | $29,600 | $23,400 |

## Required:

*a.* Express the income statements and balance sheets in common-size percentages. Comment on any significant fluctuations.

*b.* Prepare a horizontal analysis, 1992 over 1991, for each item. Does this reveal any significant insights?

*c.* Calculate the following ratios for all three years and comment on your findings: (1) current ratio and (2) quick or acid-test ratio.

*d.* Calculate the following ratios for 1992 and 1991 only and comment on your findings: (1) rate of return on stockholders' equity, (2) turnover of total assets, (3) turnover of inventories, and (4) turnover of receivables.

**18–18. Comparison of Company and Industry Ratios**

Below are the comparative position statements and income statements of United Corporation for the years 1991 and 1992:

**UNITED CORPORATION**
**Comparative Position Statements**

|  | December 31 | |
|---|---|---|
|  | 1991 | 1992 |
| **Assets** | | |
| Current assets: | | |
| Cash . . . . . . . . . . . . . . . . . . . . | $ 8,800 | $ 12,300 |
| Receivables, net. . . . . . . . . . . . . . . . | 30,000 | 36,000 |
| Inventories . . . . . . . . . . . . . . . . . . | 46,200 | 60,800 |
| Total current assets . . . . . . . . . . . . . | 85,000 | 109,100 |
| Plant and equipment, net . . . . . . . . . . . | 95,000 | 151,000 |
| Total assets. . . . . . . . . . . . . . . . . | $180,000 | $260,100 |
| **Equities** | | |
| Current liabilities: | | |
| Accounts payable . . . . . . . . . . . . . . | $ 25,500 | $ 31,500 |
| Accrued liabilities . . . . . . . . . . . . . . | 1,000 | 1,200 |
| Other current . . . . . . . . . . . . . . . . | 21,500 | 26,000 |
| Total current liabilities . . . . . . . . . . . | 48,000 | 58,700 |
| Long-term debt . . . . . . . . . . . . . . . | 35,000 | 34,000 |
| Stockholders' equity: | | |
| Preferred stock . . . . . . . . . . . . . . . | — | 40,000 |
| Common stock . . . . . . . . . . . . . . . . | 70,000 | 100,000 |
| Retained earnings . . . . . . . . . . . . . . | 27,000 | 27,400 |
| Total equities . . . . . . . . . . . . . . . . | $180,000 | $260,100 |

**UNITED CORPORATION**
**Comparative Income Statements**
**For the Years Ended December 31**

|                          | 1991      | 1992      |
|--------------------------|-----------|-----------|
| Sales . . . . . . . . . . . . . . . . . . . . . . . | $175,000  | $225,000  |
| Cost of goods sold. . . . . . . . . . . . . . . . . | 108,500   | 152,500   |
| Selling expense . . . . . . . . . . . . . . . . . . | 24,900    | 29,500    |
| Administrative expense. . . . . . . . . . . . . . . | 12,000    | 14,800    |
| Research and development . . . . . . . . . . . . . . | 4,800     | 9,700     |
| Interest expense . . . . . . . . . . . . . . . . . . | 2,800     | 2,900     |
| Total expenses . . . . . . . . . . . . . . . . . . | 153,000   | 209,400   |
| Income before tax . . . . . . . . . . . . . . . . . | 22,000    | 15,600    |
| Income taxes . . . . . . . . . . . . . . . . . . . . | 8,800     | 6,200     |
| Net income. . . . . . . . . . . . . . . . . . . . . | $ 13,200  | $  9,400  |

Preferred dividends were $4,000 in 1992.

The following table shows some statistics representing the average company in the primary industry in which United Corporation operates.

|                                               | 1991       | 1992       |
|-----------------------------------------------|------------|------------|
| 1. Current ratio . . . . . . . . . . . . . . . . . . . . . | 2.1 to 1   | 2.2 to 1   |
| 2. Inventory turnover . . . . . . . . . . . . . . . . . . | 2.6 times  | 2.8 times  |
| 3. Collection period . . . . . . . . . . . . . . . . . . | 59 days    | 56 days    |
| 4. Total debt/stockholders' equity . . . . . . . . . | 42%        | 45%        |
| 5. Fixed-charge coverage before tax . . . . . . . . . | 10.7 times | 10.0 times |
| 6. Turnover of assets . . . . . . . . . . . . . . . . . | 1.4 times  | 1.35 times |
| 7. Income before tax/sales . . . . . . . . . . . . . . | 12.8%      | 11.9%      |
| 8. R&D/sales . . . . . . . . . . . . . . . . . . . . . | 2.6%       | 2.6%       |
| 9. Rate of return on stockholders' equity . . . . . . . . | 11.2%      | 10.9%      |

**Required:**

*a.* Calculate yearly ratios for United Corporation that are comparable to the industry statistics. Use year-end balance sheet figures in lieu of averages.

*b.* What is the purpose of each of these nine ratios? How does United compare with its industry?

*c.* What other ratios would you calculate to aid in an analysis of these statements?

**Casette 18–1. Questions about Georgia-Pacific Corporation**

At the back of the text is a complete set of financial statements of Georgia-Pacific Corporation taken from its annual report of 1987.

Answer the following questions about the analysis of its financial statements:

1. Calculate for 1987 for Georgia-Pacific Corporation the same 15 ratios shown in Table 18–8 for Kimberly-Clark.
2. Compare Georgia-Pacific's ratios with those of Kimberly-Clark. What conclusions can you draw? Is this a valid comparison?
3. Prepare a horizontal and vertical analysis of the balance sheet and income statements for 1986 and 1987.

4. In its financial highlights, Georgia-Pacific shows three ratios for 1987: Return on capital employed, 12.6 percent; Return on common stock equity, 18.7 percent; Total debt-to-capital, 31.4 percent. See if you can validate these calculations. (Note the definitions given in the Financial Glossary at the bottom of the page.) Do you believe these ratios are superior or inferior to the ones presented in the text? Explain.

5. Compare the company's inventory turnover for 1987 using average cost and LIFO inventory valuations in the denominator. Which calculation do you prefer? Why?

6. Does the policy of capitalizing interest on construction cause a distortion in the interest coverage ratio?

**Casette 18–2.  Analysis of Eli Lilly Financial Statements**
Figures 3–2 and 3–3 in Chapter 3 contain the balance sheets and income statements of Eli Lilly and Company for 1986 and 1987. The following questions relate to those statements.

1. Prepare a vertical analysis of the income statements and balance sheets for both years. Does this analysis reveal any significant changes in the composition of the statements from 1986 to 1987?

2. Prepare a horizontal analysis (percentage change from 1986 to 1987) for each element on the financial statements.
   *a.* Are current assets increasing faster than current liabilities?
   *b.* Is long-term debt increasing faster than stockholders' equity?
   *c.* Are sales and cost of goods sold increasing faster than receivables and inventories, respectively?

3. Calculate for Eli Lilly the 15 ratios shown in Table 18–8 for Kimberly-Clark. Use year-end investments instead of average investments. Eli Lilly's dividends were $289.4 million in 1987 and $257.6 million in 1986.

4. Can you validly compare the ratios from part 3 to those of Kimberly-Clark in Table 18–8?

**Casette 18–3.  Comparison of Two Companies**
Two companies, Grimes Corporation and Meyer Corporation, operate in the same line of business. The companies were started at the same time and operate competitively with one another. They follow the same accounting principles.

   Following are their balance sheets and income statements for 1992 (amounts are in thousands):

## Income Statements for 1992

|  | Grimes Corporation | Meyer Corporation |
|---|---|---|
| Net sales. . . . . . . . . . . . . . . . | $11,700 | $12,500 |
| Cost of goods sold. . . . . . . . . . . | 7,520 | 7,860 |
| Gross profit . . . . . . . . . . . . | $ 4,180 | $ 4,640 |
| Selling expenses . . . . . . . . . . | $ 1,691 | $ 1,835 |
| Administrative expenses . . . . . . . . | 819 | 933 |
| Total operating expenses . . . . . . | $ 2,510 | $ 2,768 |
| Operating income . . . . . . . . . . | $ 1,670 | $ 1,872 |
| Other revenue . . . . . . . . . . . | 139 | 143 |
| Interest expense. . . . . . . . . . . | (315) | (309) |
| Income before tax . . . . . . . . . . | $ 1,494 | $ 1,706 |
| Income tax . . . . . . . . . . . . . | 523 | 597 |
| Net income. . . . . . . . . . . . . | $    971 | $ 1,109 |
| Dividends in 1992: | | |
| Preferred . . . . . . . . . . . . . | $    120 | $    120 |
| Common . . . . . . . . . . . . . | 205 | 205 |

## Balance Sheets
## as of December 31, 1992

|  | Grimes Corporation | Meyer Corporation |
|---|---|---|
| Current assets: | | |
| Cash . . . . . . . . . . . . . . . | $    550 | $    555 |
| Marketable securities. . . . . . . . . | 125 | 220 |
| Accounts receivable . . . . . . . . . | 825 | 875 |
| Inventories . . . . . . . . . . . . . | 1,200 | 1,380 |
| Prepayments . . . . . . . . . . . . | 100 | 70 |
| Total current assets . . . . . . . . | $ 2,800 | $ 3,100 |
| Investments (long-term) . . . . . . . . | 475 | 450 |
| Property, plant, and equipment (net) . . . | 7,098 | 6,893 |
| Total assets. . . . . . . . . . . . | $10,373 | $10,443 |
| Current liabilities . . . . . . . . . . | $ 1,650 | $ 1,650 |
| Long-term debt . . . . . . . . . . . | 2,545 | 2,710 |
| Total liabilities . . . . . . . . . . | $ 4,195 | $ 4,360 |
| Preferred stock . . . . . . . . . . . | 1,500 | 1,500 |
| Common stock . . . . . . . . . . . | 1,500 | 1,500 |
| Retained earnings . . . . . . . . . . | 3,178 | 3,083 |
| Total stockholders' equity . . . . . . | $ 6,178 | $ 6,083 |
| Total equities . . . . . . . . . . . . | $10,373 | $10,443 |

**Required:**

*a.* Compare these two companies on the dimension of liquidity (short-term financial strength). Which would you rate as stronger?

*b.* Compare these two companies on the dimension of financial solvency (long-term financial strength). Which would you rate as stronger?

*c.* Compare these two companies on the dimensions of operating and investment efficiency. Which would you rate as stronger?

*d.* Compare these two companies on the dimension of profitability. Which would you rate as stronger?

*e.* Analyze each company's rate of return on total assets by examining the margin and turnover components. Are these components significantly different between the two companies?

*f.* Which company's common stockholders benefit more from financial leverage? Is this because the company uses more leverage capital or earns a higher differential on it, or both?

# *The 1987 Georgia-Pacific Annual Report*

| (Dollar amounts, except per share, and shares are in millions) | 1987 | 1986 | Change |
|---|---|---|---|
| Net sales | $8,603 | $7,223 | 19% |
| Net income | 458 | 296 | 55 |
| Income per common share | 4.23 | 2.70 | 57 |
| Depreciation and depletion | 387 | 339 | 14 |
| Cash provided by continuing operations | 781 | 575 | 36 |
| Cash dividends paid | 115 | 97 | 19 |
| Total assets at year end | 5,870 | 5,114 | 15 |
| Return on capital employed* | 12.6% | 10.4% | |
| Return on common equity* | 18.7% | 13.8% | |
| Total debt-to-capital* | 31.4% | 26.3% | |
| Cash dividends declared per share of common stock | $ 1.05 | $ .85 | 24% |
| Shares of common stock outstanding at year end | 105 | 107 | (2) |
| Number of common shareholders of record | 56,000 | 66,000 | (15) |
| Number of employees | 42,000 | 39,000 | 8 |

*The method of calculating this ratio is described in the Financial Glossary presented below.

**Financial Glossary**

*Book value per common share*
Common shareholders' equity minus the unamortized discount on redeemable preferred stock, divided by the number of common shares outstanding as of the end of the year.

*Current ratio*
Total current assets divided by total current liabilities as of the end of the year.

*Effective income tax rate*
Provision for income taxes divided by income from continuing operations before income taxes.

*Return on capital employed*
Income from continuing operations plus interest expense (net of taxes) and deferred income tax expense, divided by capital employed as of the beginning of the year. Capital employed is calculated as total assets, excluding net assets of discontinued operations, minus noninterest-bearing current liabilities.

*Return on common equity*
Income from continuing operations divided by common shareholders' equity as of the beginning of the year.

*Return on sales (industry segments)*
Segment operating profits divided by sales to unaffiliated customers.

*Total debt-to-capital*
Total debt divided by the sum of total debt, deferred income taxes, other long-term liabilities, redeemable preferred stock and common shareholders' equity as of the end of the year.

**Liquidity and Capital Resources**

*Cash Flow*

Cash provided by continuing operations increased to $781 million in 1987 from $575 million in 1986. The increase is primarily attributable to a $204 million increase in net income after adjustments for items not affecting cash. Cash from continuing operations, supplemented by additional debt, proceeds from the liquidation of investments and cash from other sources, was used to finance capital expenditures, purchases of our common stock, our investment in U.S. Plywood Corporation and dividend payments. Effective in the 1987 fourth quarter, the Board of Directors voted to increase the quarterly dividend on common stock from 25 cents to 30 cents per share.

During the first and second quarters of 1987, the Corporation received cash proceeds of $82 million from the liquidation of its remaining investment in preferred stock and warrants of Georgia Gulf Corporation, purchaser of the Corporation's commodity chemicals subsidiary in 1984. A $66 million pre-tax gain was recorded from these transactions.

*Debt*

Georgia-Pacific's total debt-to-capital ratio was 31.4 percent at December 31, 1987, compared with 26.3 percent at December 31, 1986. During 1987, total debt increased by $434 million. This increase was primarily used to fund the acquisition of U.S. Plywood Corporation for $208 million, other acquisitions and the purchase of 6,182,000 shares of common stock for $255 million at an average price of $41.25 per share. The Corporation has been authorized by its Board of Directors to purchase its common stock in the open market or in privately negotiated transactions, provided its total debt-to-capital ratio does not exceed 35 percent. With the total debt-to-capital ratio within this limit, the Corporation should have flexibility for both internal and external investment opportunities as they arise. Open market repurchases of the Corporation's common stock are continuing and, depending upon market conditions and other considerations, could involve substantial amounts.

At December 31, 1987, the Corporation had $500 million of debt securities registered with the Securities and Exchange Commission for sale under shelf registration statements. The purpose of a shelf registration is to enable the Corporation to react quickly to acquisition opportunities and favorable market conditions for restructuring existing debt.

On January 28, 1988, the Corporation issued $200 million of 9¾% sinking fund debentures due January 15, 2018 at a price of 97.75% plus accrued interest, pursuant to the shelf registration statements. On February 16, 1988, the Corporation issued $200 million of 9½% debentures due February 15, 2018 at a price of 98.15% plus accrued interest, also pursuant to the shelf registration statements. The net proceeds from the sales of the debentures were added to the Corporation's general funds and were used to reduce the Corporation's outstanding short-term borrowings and for other corporate purposes, including additional repurchases by the Corporation of its outstanding common stock.

The Corporation's committed bank lines of credit totaled $700 million at December 31, 1987, of which approximately $604 million was being used to support commercial paper and other short-term notes. These agreements establish unsecured lines of credit and do not expire until May 1, 1989. These committed lines of credit, together with other available financing sources and Georgia-Pacific's capacity to generate funds from operations, are adequate to finance the Corporation's capital expenditure program and meet operating and liquidity needs for the forseeable future.

In March 1987, the Corporation called for redemption on April 15, 1987 all of its outstanding preferred stock. Approximately 1,624,000 Series A, 522,000 Series B and 1,038,000 Series C shares were converted to shares of Georgia-Pacific common stock on a one-for-one basis. The remaining shares were redeemed at $39.00 per share plus accumulated dividends.

### Capital Expenditures

On June 12, 1987, the Corporation acquired all of the stock of U.S. Plywood Corporation for approximately $208 million in cash. In addition to the purchase price, the Corporation assumed debt of $81 million. U.S. Plywood was a nationwide manufacturer of industrial wood products and distributor of building materials with net sales in 1986 of $944 million.

Capital expenditures for 1987, including $125 million in the building products segment and $1 million in timber and timberlands for assets acquired in the purchase of U.S. Plywood Corporation, were as follows:

| (Millions) | Building Products | Pulp & Paper | Timber & Timber-lands | Other | Total |
|---|---|---|---|---|---|
| Capital expenditures before acquisitions | $154 | $359 | $ 18 | $ 19 | $550 |
| Plus acquisitions | 147 | 38 | 90 | — | 275 |
| | $301 | $397 | $108 | $ 19 | $825 |

Capital expenditures of approximately $900 million are projected for 1988, excluding acquisitions. This amount includes approximately $575 million for projects started prior to 1988.

At our Port Hudson, Louisiana pulp and paper mill, installation of a second white-paper machine and expansion of market pulp production capacity with a total cost of approximately $285 million are expected to be completed in the 1988 third quarter. A major project to increase linerboard capacity at our Monticello, Mississippi pulp and paper mill with a total cost of approximately $88 million is expected to be completed during the third quarter of 1988. Installation of a new recovery boiler at our Woodland, Maine pulp and paper mill will cost approximately $77 million and is expected to be completed in the first half of 1989. In the building products segment, construction of a new gypsum wallboard plant near Las Vegas, Nevada was completed in the fourth quarter of 1987. Construction of a new byproduct gypsum wallboard plant at Paradise, Kentucky is expected to be completed at the end of 1989.

### Income Taxes

Under the Tax Reform Act of 1986 (the Act), the statutory Federal tax rate on ordinary income declined to 40 percent in 1987 from 46 percent in 1986 and will decline to 34 percent in 1988. The rate at which capital gains are taxed, however, increased to 34 percent in 1987 from 28 percent in 1986. Certain other provisions of the Act repealed the investment tax credit (generally for property placed in service after December 31, 1985) and, after December 31, 1986, modified inventory capitalization rules, lengthened depreciable lives and established a new alternative minimum tax which limits the benefits of tax preference items.

The higher tax rates for capital gains and other rule changes more than offset benefits the Corporation would have otherwise realized from lower tax rates on ordinary income in 1987 as the new tax rates were phased in. The effect of the loss of the investment tax credit should be offset, to some extent, by lower ordinary tax rates on income in the future. Consequently, we do not think that the Act will have a significant impact on future capital investments.

In December 1987, the Financial Accounting Standards Board issued Statement of Financial Accounting Standards No. 96, "Accounting for Income Taxes" which, among other provisions, will change the method of accounting for deferred income taxes. For further discussion, see "Income Taxes," Note 8.

## Other

Working capital amounted to $733 million and $583 million, respectively, at December 31, 1987 and December 31, 1986. The current ratio was 1.7 to 1 at December 31, 1987 and December 31, 1986.

Due to inflation, the current costs of property, plant and equipment, and timber are higher than the historical values reported in the financial statements. Accordingly, depreciation and depletion expense would be higher if the costs of such assets were adjusted to a current cost basis. The adverse effects resulting from such an adjustment to income would be offset to some extent by a gain in purchasing power because the Corporation's monetary liabilities exceeded monetary assets.

### 1987 Compared with 1986

Georgia-Pacific's consolidated net sales of $8.6 billion in 1987 were 19.1 percent higher than the 1986 level of $7.2 billion. Net income increased 54.7 percent to $458 million in 1987 ($4.23 per share), compared with $296 million ($2.70 per share) in 1986.

Results included pre-tax gains of $66 million in 1987 and $33 million in 1986 from the liquidation of the Corporation's remaining investments in Georgia Gulf Corporation, purchaser of the Corporation's commodity chemicals subsidiary in 1984. These gains have been reported as "Unusual items" in the Corporation's financial statements and are excluded from segment operating results.

## Selected Industry Segment Data

| (Millions) | Year ended December 31 | 1987 | 1986 | 1985 |
|---|---|---|---|---|
| **Trade sales** | | | | |
| Building products | | $5,755 | $4,853 | $4,470 |
| Pulp and paper | | 2,810 | 2,281 | 2,134 |
| Other operations | | 38 | 89 | 112 |
| | | $8,603 | $7,223 | $6,716 |
| **Operating profits** | | | | |
| Building products | | $ 533 | $ 500 | $ 391 |
| Pulp and paper | | 383 | 146 | 29 |
| Other operations | | 10 | 35 | 35 |
| | | 926 | 681 | 455 |
| General corporate | | (70) | (91) | (33) |
| Interest expense | | (124) | (138) | (132) |
| Unusual items | | 66 | 33 | 19 |
| Income taxes | | (340) | (189) | (102) |
| | | $ 458 | $ 296 | $ 207 |

843

The remaining discussion refers to the "Selected Industry Segment Data" table.

The building products segment reported sales of $5.8 billion for 1987, up 18.6 percent from $4.9 billion in 1986. Operating profits of $533 million were 9.0 percent higher than in 1986 after excluding an $11 million pre-tax reduction of expense in 1986 due to a change in accounting for reforestation costs. Excluding this adjustment, returns on sales averaged 9.3% and 10.1% for 1987 and 1986, respectively. Demand for most building products in 1987 was affected by reduced housing starts; however, marketing efforts in the repair and remodeling sector have tended to reduce the Corporation's dependence on new residential construction. Average prices for both plywood and lumber were higher in 1987. Gypsum prices, adversely affected by reduced commercial construction, have shown a decline from 1986 levels. For 1988, we expect building products to receive continued support from the home improvement and export markets.

Sales in the pulp and paper segment reached $2.8 billion for 1987, 23.2 percent higher than the $2.3 billion recorded in 1986. Operating profits in 1987 increased by $237 million to $383 million, more than two and one-half times the 1986 level of $146 million. Returns on sales averaged 13.6% and 6.4% for 1987 and 1986, respectively. The improved results in 1987 are primarily attributable to strong demand in the commodity sector of the pulp and paper industry, particularly for linerboard and market pulp. Demand for products in export markets improved substantially throughout the year, reflecting favorable currency exchange rates. Pulp, linerboard and kraft paper prices were higher on average in 1987 than in 1986. Increased sales of printing and writing papers, which are higher-margin products, have also improved the results in this segment. Average prices for these products in 1987 were also higher than in 1986. We expect continued improvement in most of our pulp and paper markets in 1988, especially in commodity grades such as pulp, linerboard and uncoated freesheet paper.

General corporate charges decreased to $70 million in 1987 from $91 million in 1986. This decrease is primarily attributable to lower compensation expense for stock options. Pre-tax charges for obligations under stock option agreements with employees, which are adjusted for changes in common stock price, were $11 million in 1987 and $33 million in 1986.

The Corporation's interest expense in 1987 was $124 million, compared with $138 million in 1986. Both interest rates and debt levels were lower, on average, in 1987; however, debt levels were higher at the end of 1987.

The provision for income taxes was $340 million in 1987, based on a 42.6% effective tax rate on income before income taxes. A 39.0% rate was used in 1986. The provision for taxes currently payable increased in 1987 as the higher capital gains tax rate and the full impact of the repeal of the investment tax credit were realized. Timing differences arising in future years should result in lower provisions for deferred taxes because of lower statutory tax rates on ordinary income.

**1986 Compared with 1985**

Georgia-Pacific's consolidated net sales of $7.2 billion in 1986 were 7.5 percent higher than the 1985 level of $6.7 billion. Income from continuing operations increased 43.0 percent to $296 million in 1986 ($2.70 per share) from $207 million ($1.84 per share) in 1985. A $30 million loss from discontinued operations, which was partially offset by a $10 million extraordinary gain from settlement of a condemnation suit, lowered 1985 net income to $187 million ($1.65 per share).

Effective January 1, 1986, the Corporation adopted Statement of Financial Accounting Standards No. 87, "Employers' Accounting for Pensions." This change in accounting principle increased income from continuing operations by approximately $11 million in 1986. Also effective January 1, 1986, a new timber capitalization policy was adopted and applied retroactively, which had the cumulative effect of increasing 1986 income from continuing operations approximately $8 million.

Income from continuing operations also includes a $33 million pre-tax gain from liquidation of investments in 1986 and a $19 million pre-tax gain on the sale of certain Oregon timberlands in 1985. These gains are classified as "Unusual items" in the accompanying financial statements and excluded from segment operating results.

The impact of the Tax Reform Act of 1986 reduced 1986 income from continuing operations approximately $17 million through repealing the investment tax credit, although some credits were allowed in 1986 under transition rules. These lost investment tax credits were recorded in the 1986 fourth quarter and were the primary reason for a 39.0 percent effective tax rate for the year, compared with 33.0 percent in 1985.

The remaining discussion refers to the "Selected Industry Segment Data" table.

The building products segment reported sales of $4.9 billion in 1986, up 8.6 percent from $4.5 billion in 1985. Operating profits of $500 million in 1986 included an $11 million pre-tax reduction of expense due to the adoption of a new timber capitalization policy. Excluding this adjustment, operating profits increased to $489 million in 1986 from $391 million in 1985, as the returns on sales improved to 10.1 percent from 8.7 percent. Increased volume and reduced manufacturing costs were the major reasons for this segment's improved results. Average prices for plywood and lumber in 1986 were comparable to 1985 levels, while gypsum, roofing and thermosetting resins prices were lower on average in 1986 than in 1985.

Sales in the pulp and paper segment reached $2.3 billion in 1986, 6.9 percent higher than the 1985 level of $2.1 billion. Operating profits rose to $146 million in 1986 from the 1985 level of $29 million, as the returns on sales improved to 6.4 percent from 1.4 percent. The improved results in 1986 were due primarily to decreased inventories worldwide and the lower-valued U.S. dollar, as well as timely upgrading and modernization of mills and equipment. Results in the prior year were hampered by lost production time due to labor problems and several major equipment conversion projects. Average prices for pulp, linerboard, kraft paper and commercial tissue were higher in 1986 than in 1985. Prices for printing papers, corrugated boxes and multiwall packaging also strengthened during 1986, particularly late in the year, although average prices for the year were lower than in 1985.

General corporate charges increased to $91 million in 1986 from $33 million in 1985. This increase relates primarily to higher compensation expense for stock options due to stock price increases as well as losses from early retirements of high interest rate debt in 1986.

Total interest costs decreased to $147 million in 1986 from $162 million in 1985 as a result of reduced debt levels and lower interest rates. Interest expense of $138 million in 1986 was higher than the 1985 level of $132 million, due to less interest being capitalized on construction projects in 1986.

**Responsibility for Financial Statements**

*Georgia-Pacific Corporation and Subsidiaries*

The financial statements on the following pages, which consolidate the accounts of Georgia-Pacific Corporation and its subsidiaries, have been prepared in conformity with generally accepted accounting principles.

Management of Georgia-Pacific Corporation is responsible for the accurate and objective preparation of the consolidated financial statements. Accordingly, the Corporation maintains a system of policies, procedures and controls which is designed to provide reasonable assurance that assets are safeguarded and that accounting records are reliable. Management believes that the proper internal controls are in place and that the system is adequate and effective in safeguarding assets and providing reliable accounting records.

An independent evaluation of the system is performed by the Corporation's qualified internal audit staff in order to confirm that the system is adequate and operating effectively. As indicated in the Independent Auditors' Report, Arthur Andersen & Co. performs a separate independent examination of the Corporation's consolidated financial statements for the purpose of determining that the statements are presented fairly in accordance with generally accepted accounting principles applied on a consistent basis. Arthur Andersen & Co. is appointed by the Board of Directors and meets regularly with the Audit Committee of the Board.

The Audit Committee consists of five outside directors who provide oversight in a number of areas, review the work of the Corporation's internal auditors and independent public accountants and approve fees paid for audit and non-audit services.

The independent public accountants and internal audit staff have full and free access to the Audit Committee.

*James C. Van Meter*
*Executive Vice President*
*and Chief Financial Officer*

*T. Marshall Hahn, Jr.*
*Chairman and*
*Chief Executive Officer*

February 17, 1988

**Independent Auditors' Report**

To the Shareholders and Board of Directors of Georgia-Pacific Corporation:

We have examined the balance sheets of Georgia-Pacific Corporation (a Georgia corporation) and subsidiaries as of December 31, 1987 and 1986 and the related statements of income, common shareholders' equity and cash flows for each of the three years in the period ended December 31, 1987. Our examinations were made in accordance with generally accepted auditing standards and, accordingly, included such tests of the accounting records and such other auditing procedures as we considered necessary in the circumstances.

In our opinion, the financial statements referred to above present fairly the financial position of Georgia-Pacific Corporation and subsidiaries as of December 31, 1987 and 1986 and the results of their operations and cash flows for each of the three years in the period ended December 31, 1987, in conformity with generally accepted accounting principles consistently applied during the period except for the changes (with which we concur) made as of January 1, 1986 in the method of accounting for pensions described in Note 5 and the method of accounting for reforestation costs described in Note 1.

*Arthur Andersen & Co.*

Atlanta, Georgia
February 17, 1988

## Statements of Income

*Georgia-Pacific Corporation and Subsidiaries*

| (Millions, except per share amounts) Year ended December 31 | 1987 | 1986 | 1985 |
|---|---|---|---|
| *Net sales* | **$8,603** | $7,223 | $6,716 |
| *Costs and expenses* | | | |
| Cost of sales | **6,777** | 5,783 | 5,553 |
| Selling, general and administrative | **583** | 511 | 431 |
| Depreciation and depletion | **387** | 339 | 310 |
| Interest | **124** | 138 | 132 |
| | **7,871** | 6,771 | 6,426 |
| *Income from continuing operations before unusual items,* | | | |
| *income taxes and extraordinary item* | **732** | 452 | 290 |
| *Unusual items* | **66** | 33 | 19 |
| *Income from continuing operations before income taxes and* | | | |
| *extraordinary item* | **798** | 485 | 309 |
| *Provision for income taxes* | **340** | 189 | 102 |
| *Income from continuing operations before extraordinary item* | **458** | 296 | 207 |
| *(Loss) on disposal of discontinued operations, net of taxes* | **—** | — | (30) |
| *Income before extraordinary item* | **458** | 296 | 177 |
| *Settlement of condemnation suit, net of taxes* | **—** | — | 10 |
| *Net income* | **$ 458** | $ 296 | $ 187 |
| *Income per common share* | | | |
| Income from continuing operations before | | | |
| extraordinary item | **$ 4.23** | $ 2.70 | $ 1.84 |
| (Loss) on disposal of discontinued operations | **—** | — | (.29) |
| Income before extraordinary item | **4.23** | 2.70 | 1.55 |
| Settlement of condemnation suit | **—** | — | .10 |
| Net income | **$ 4.23** | $ 2.70 | $ 1.65 |
| *Average number of shares outstanding* | **107** | 104 | 103 |

*The accompanying notes are an integral part of these financial statements.*

## Statements of Cash Flows

*Georgia-Pacific Corporation and Subsidiaries*

| (Millions) | Year ended December 31 | 1987 | 1986 | 1985 |
|---|---|---|---|---|
| *Cash provided by (used for) continuing operations* | | | | |
| Income from continuing operations before | | | | |
| extraordinary item | | **$458** | $296 | $207 |
| Items in income not affecting cash | | | | |
| Depreciation | | **351** | 316 | 270 |
| Depletion | | **36** | 23 | 40 |
| Deferred income taxes | | **49** | 87 | 84 |
| Gain on sales of assets | | **(4)** | (30) | — |
| Gain on liquidation of investments | | **(66)** | (33) | — |
| Other | | **46** | 7 | 35 |
| | | **870** | 666 | 636 |
| Cash provided by (used for) working capital | | | | |
| Receivables | | **(78)** | (61) | 86 |
| Inventories | | **(70)** | (60) | 64 |
| Other current assets | | **(10)** | (15) | (9) |
| Accounts payable and accrued liabilities | | **69** | 45 | (6) |
| | | **(89)** | (91) | 135 |
| Cash provided by continuing operations | | **781** | 575 | 771 |
| *Cash provided by discontinued operations* | | **—** | 11 | 117 |
| *Cash provided by extraordinary item* | | **—** | 14 | — |
| *Cash provided by (used for) financing activities* | | | | |
| Repayments of long-term debt | | **(339)** | (661) | (481) |
| Additions to long-term debt | | **683** | 476 | 358 |
| Net increase (decrease) in bank overdrafts | | **(1)** | 79 | — |
| Net (decrease) in commercial paper | | | | |
| and other short-term notes | | **(15)** | (4) | (6) |
| Common stock purchased for treasury | | **(255)** | — | — |
| Preferred stock purchase offer | | **—** | (50) | (40) |
| Cash dividends paid | | **(115)** | (97) | (94) |
| Cash (used for) financing activities | | **(42)** | (257) | (263) |
| *Cash provided by (used for) investment activities* | | | | |
| Capital expenditures | | | | |
| Property, plant and equipment | | **(592)** | (426) | (619) |
| Timber and timberlands | | **(107)** | (56) | (23) |
| | | **(699)** | (482) | (642) |
| Investment in U.S. Plywood | | **(208)** | — | — |
| Proceeds from sales of assets | | **11** | 79 | 32 |
| Proceeds from liquidation of investments | | **125** | 92 | — |
| Other | | **22** | (14) | 11 |
| Cash (used for) investment activities | | **(749)** | (325) | (599) |
| *Increase (decrease) in cash* | | **(10)** | 18 | 26 |
| Balance at beginning of year | | **80** | 62 | 36 |
| Balance at end of year | | **$ 70** | $ 80 | $ 62 |

*The accompanying notes are an integral part of these financial statements.*

**Balance Sheets**

*Georgia-Pacific Corporation and Subsidiaries*

| (Millions, except shares and per share amounts) | December 31 | 1987 | 1986 |
|---|---|---|---|
| **Assets** | | | |
| *Current assets* | | | |
| Cash | | $ 70 | $ 80 |
| Receivables, less allowances of $24 and $21 | | 771 | 618 |
| Inventories | | 837 | 681 |
| Other current assets | | 51 | 41 |
| | | 1,729 | 1,420 |
| *Timber and timberlands, net* | | 915 | 844 |
| *Property, plant and equipment* | | | |
| Land and improvements, buildings, machinery and equipment, at cost | | 5,702 | 5,052 |
| Accumulated depreciation | | (2,654) | (2,361) |
| | | 3,048 | 2,691 |
| *Other assets* | | 178 | 159 |
| | | $5,870 | $5,114 |
| **Liabilities and Shareholders' Equity** | | | |
| *Current liabilities* | | | |
| Bank overdrafts, net | | $ 104 | $ 79 |
| Commercial paper and other short-term notes | | 85 | 100 |
| Current portion of long-term debt | | 153 | 134 |
| Accounts payable | | 355 | 295 |
| Accrued compensation | | 109 | 87 |
| Other current liabilities | | 190 | 142 |
| | | 996 | 837 |
| *Long-term debt, excluding current portion* | | 1,298 | 893 |
| *Deferred income taxes* | | 744 | 695 |
| *Other long-term liabilities* | | 152 | 124 |
| *Commitments and contingencies* | | | |
| *Redeemable preferred stock* | | | |
| Adjustable rate convertible preferred stock, without par value; authorized 10,000,000 shares (involuntary liquidating value $39.00 per share) | | — | 113 |
| *Common shareholders' equity* | | | |
| Common stock, par value $ .80; authorized 150,000,000 shares; 111,187,000 and 107,987,000 shares issued | | 89 | 86 |
| Additional paid-in capital | | 1,215 | 1,101 |
| Retained earnings | | 1,645 | 1,304 |
| Less—Common stock held in treasury, at cost; 6,448,000 and 639,000 shares | | (263) | (19) |
| Accumulated translation adjustments | | (6) | (20) |
| | | 2,680 | 2,452 |
| | | $5,870 | $5,114 |

*The accompanying notes are an integral part of these financial statements.*

## Statements of Common Shareholders' Equity

*Georgia-Pacific Corporation and Subsidiaries*

| *(Millions, except shares)* Common Stock Shares, Issued | Common Stock Shares, Treasury | | Total | Common Stock | Additional Paid-in Capital | Retained Earnings | Treasury Stock | Accumulated Translation Adjustments |
|---|---|---|---|---|---|---|---|---|
| 104,115,000 | 1,589,000 | *Balance at December 31, 1984* | $2,035 | $83 | $ 999 | $1,029 | $ (49) | $(27) |
| | | Net income | 187 | — | — | 187 | — | — |
| | | Cash dividends declared | | | | | | |
| | |   Common stock | (82) | — | — | (82) | — | — |
| | |   Preferred stock | (11) | — | — | (11) | — | — |
| | | Common stock issued | | | | | | |
| | (446,000) |   Stock option plans | 11 | — | — | (3) | 14 | — |
| 253,000 | |   Employee stock purchase plan | 5 | — | 5 | — | — | — |
| | |   Other | 2 | — | — | (6) | — | 8 |
| 104,368,000 | 1,143,000 | *Balance at December 31, 1985* | 2,147 | 83 | 1,004 | 1,114 | (35) | (19) |
| | | Net income | 296 | — | — | 296 | — | — |
| | | Cash dividends declared | | | | | | |
| | |   Common stock | (89) | — | — | (89) | — | — |
| | |   Preferred stock | (8) | — | — | (8) | — | — |
| | | Common stock issued | | | | | | |
| | (504,000) |   Stock option plans | 14 | — | — | (2) | 16 | — |
| 829,000 | |   Employee stock purchase plan | 14 | 1 | 13 | — | — | — |
| 2,790,000 | |   Conversion of debentures | 86 | 2 | 84 | — | — | — |
| | |   Other | (8) | — | — | (7) | — | (1) |
| 107,987,000 | 639,000 | *Balance at December 31, 1986* | 2,452 | 86 | 1,101 | 1,304 | (19) | (20) |
| | | Net income | 458 | — | — | 458 | — | — |
| | | Cash dividends declared | | | | | | |
| | |   Common stock | (113) | — | — | (113) | — | — |
| | |   Preferred stock | (2) | — | — | (2) | — | — |
| | | Common stock issued | | | | | | |
| | (373,000) |   Stock option plans | 17 | — | 6 | — | 11 | — |
| 3,184,000 | |   Conversion of preferred stock | 111 | 3 | 108 | — | — | — |
| 16,000 | |   Employee stock purchase plan | — | — | — | — | — | — |
| | 6,182,000 | Common stock purchased | (255) | — | — | — | (255) | — |
| | |   Other | 12 | — | — | (2) | — | 14 |
| **111,187,000** | **6,448,000** | *Balance at December 31, 1987* | **$ 2,680** | **$89** | **$1,215** | **$ 1,645** | **$(263)** | **$ (6)** |

*The accompanying notes are an integral part of these financial statements.*

## Notes to Financial Statements
*Georgia-Pacific Corporation and Subsidiaries*

### Note 1. Summary of Significant Accounting Policies
*Principles of Consolidation*

The consolidated financial statements include the accounts of Georgia-Pacific Corporation and subsidiaries (Corporation). All significant intercompany balances and transactions are eliminated in consolidation.

*Income Per Common Share*

Income per common share is computed based on income applicable to common stock (after preferred stock dividends and discount accretion) and the weighted average number of common shares outstanding. The effects of assuming issuance of common shares under stock option and stock purchase plans and conversion of redeemable preferred stock were antidilutive or insignificant. Income per common share amounts presented in 1986 and 1985 have been restated to conform with the 1987 presentation. The number of shares used in the income per common share computations were 107,480,000 in 1987, 104,069,000 in 1986 and 102,966,000 in 1985.

*Inventory Valuation*

Inventories are valued at the lower of average cost or market. Inventory includes costs of materials, labor and plant overhead. The major classes of inventories were as follows:

| (Millions) December 31 | 1987 | 1986 |
|---|---|---|
| Raw materials | $243 | $186 |
| Finished goods | 625 | 517 |
| Supplies | 81 | 77 |
| | 949 | 780 |
| LIFO reserve | (112) | (99) |
| | $837 | $681 |

The last-in, first-out (LIFO) dollar value pool method of inventory valuation is used for the majority of inventories at manufacturing facilities and the Corporation's manufactured inventories located at its building products distribution centers. The average cost method is used for all other inventories. Inventories valued using the LIFO method represented approximately 47% and 55%, respectively, of consolidated inventories at December 31, 1987 and 1986.

*Property, Plant and Equipment*

Property, plant and equipment are recorded at cost. Lease obligations for which the Corporation assumes substantially all the property rights and risks of ownership are capitalized. Replacements of major units of property are capitalized and the replaced properties retired. Maintenance, repairs and replacements of minor units of property are charged to expense as incurred.

The major classes of property, plant and equipment were as follows:

| (Millions) | December 31 | 1987 | 1986 |
|---|---|---|---|
| Land and improvements | | $ 135 | $ 123 |
| Buildings | | 610 | 549 |
| Machinery and equipment | | 4,705 | 4,318 |
| Construction in progress | | 252 | 62 |
| | | $5,702 | $5,052 |

Provisions for depreciation are computed using the straight-line method with composite rates based upon estimated service lives. The ranges of composite rates for the principal classes are: land improvements — 5% to 7%; buildings — 3% to 5%; and machinery and equipment — 5% to 20%.

No gain or loss is recognized on normal property dispositions; property cost is credited to the property accounts and charged to the accumulated depreciation accounts and any proceeds are credited to the accumulated depreciation accounts. When there are abnormal dispositions of property, the cost and related depreciation amounts are removed from the accounts and any gain or loss is reflected in income.

The Corporation capitalizes interest on projects where construction takes considerable time and entails major expenditures. Such interest is charged to the property, plant and equipment accounts and amortized over the approximate life of the related assets in order to properly match expenses with revenues resulting from the facilities. Interest capitalized, expensed and paid were as follows:

| (Millions) | Year ended December 31 | 1987 | 1986 | 1985 |
|---|---|---|---|---|
| Total interest | | $134 | $147 | $162 |
| Interest capitalized | | (10) | (9) | (30) |
| Interest expense | | $124 | $138 | $132 |
| Interest paid | | $116 | $136 | $153 |

The Corporation defers net operating costs on new construction projects during the start-up phase and amortizes the deferral over five years. The amounts deferred, which were not material in 1987, 1986 and 1985, are included in the property, plant and equipment accounts.

*Timber and Timberlands*
The Corporation depletes its investment in timber based on the total fiber that will be available during the estimated growth cycle. Timber carrying costs are expensed as incurred. Effective January 1, 1986, the Corporation changed its accounting for timber costs to capitalize certain reforestation costs previously expensed in order to achieve a better matching of these costs with the revenues realized from the eventual harvesting of the timber. This capitalization policy was applied retroactively and had the cumulative effect of increasing 1986 net income approximately $8 million. The new capitalization policy is not expected to materially affect depletion expense in future periods.

*Reclassifications*
Certain amounts have been reclassified in 1986 and 1985 to conform with the 1987 presentation.

**Note 2. Unusual Items**

The Corporation realized certain gains during the last three years which are considered to be unusual items:

| (Millions) | Year ended December 31 | 1987 | 1986 | 1985 |
|---|---|---|---|---|
| Liquidation of investments | | $66 | $33 | $— |
| Sale of timberlands | | — | — | 19 |
| | | $66 | $33 | $19 |

During the first and second quarters of 1987, the Corporation received cash proceeds of $82 million and recorded a pre-tax gain of $66 million from the liquidation of its remaining $16 million investment in preferred stock and warrants of Georgia Gulf Corporation, purchaser of the Corporation's commodity chemicals subsidiary in 1984.

In the 1986 fourth quarter, the Corporation received cash proceeds of $92 million and recorded a pre-tax gain of $33 million from the liquidation of portions of its investment in Georgia Gulf Corporation.

The Corporation has completed an agreement with an unrelated third party to sell or exchange approximately 134,000 acres of Oregon timberlands. A pre-tax gain of $19 million was recorded in 1985 from the sale of a portion of the timberlands under this agreement.

**Note 3. Industry Segment Information**

The Corporation's building products segment includes 144 manufacturing facilities and 153 distribution centers. Manufactured product lines primarily consist of wood panels (plywood, particleboard, hardboard, oriented strand board, etc.), lumber, gypsum products, roofing, formaldehyde and thermosetting resins.

The Corporation's pulp and paper segment includes 82 manufacturing facilities. Manufactured product lines primarily consist of containerboard and packaging (linerboard, kraft paper, corrugated boxes, etc.), tissue, printing and writing papers, market pulp and pulp mill by-product chemicals.

Certain industry segment information for the years 1985 through 1987 is presented on the following page. The Corporation's sales to foreign markets represented less than 10% of total sales to unaffiliated customers in each of those years. No single customer accounted for more than 10% of total sales to unaffiliated customers in any year during that period.

| Georgia-Pacific Corporation and Subsidiaries<br><br>(Millions) | Sales to Unaffiliated Customers | Intersegment Sales | Total Revenues | Operating Profits | Depreciation and Depletion | Capital Expenditures | Assets |
|---|---|---|---|---|---|---|---|
| **Year ended December 31, 1987** | | | | | | | |
| Building products | $5,755 | $ 274 | $6,029 | $ 533 | $188 | $301 | $2,134 |
| Pulp and paper | 2,810 | 81 | 2,891 | 383 | 191 | 397 | 2,561 |
| Other operations | 38 | 29 | 67 | 10 | 2 | 8 | 58 |
| | 8,603 | 384 | 8,987 | 926 | 381 | 706 | 4,753 |
| Eliminations and adjustments | | | | | | | |
| Intersegment sales | — | (384) | (384) | — | — | — | — |
| Timber and timberlands | — | — | — | — | — | 108 | 915 |
| Unusual items (Note 2) | — | — | — | 66 | — | — | — |
| General corporate | — | — | — | (70) | 6 | 11 | 202 |
| Interest expense | — | — | — | (124) | — | — | — |
| Income taxes | — | — | — | (340) | — | — | — |
| Total | **$8,603** | **$ —** | **$8,603** | **$ 458** | **$ 387** | **$ 825** | **$5,870** |
| **Year ended December 31, 1986** | | | | | | | |
| Building products | $4,853 | $ 235 | $5,088 | $ 500 | $153 | $192 | $1,694 |
| Pulp and paper | 2,281 | 77 | 2,358 | 146 | 176 | 213 | 2,253 |
| Other operations | 89 | 29 | 118 | 35 | 5 | 6 | 60 |
| | 7,223 | 341 | 7,564 | 681 | 334 | 411 | 4,007 |
| Eliminations and adjustments | | | | | | | |
| Intersegment sales | — | (341) | (341) | — | — | — | — |
| Timber and timberlands | — | — | — | — | — | 56 | 844 |
| Unusual items (Note 2) | — | — | — | 33 | — | — | — |
| General corporate | — | — | — | (91) | 5 | 15 | 263 |
| Interest expense | — | — | — | (138) | — | — | — |
| Income taxes | — | — | — | (189) | — | — | — |
| Total | **$7,223** | **$ —** | **$7,223** | **$ 296** | **$339** | **$482** | **$5,114** |
| **Year ended December 31, 1985** | | | | | | | |
| Building products | $ 4,470 | $ 188 | $4,658 | $ 391 | $145 | $164 | $ 1,623 |
| Pulp and paper | 2,134 | 76 | 2,210 | 29 | 149 | 435 | 2,175 |
| Other operations | 112 | 28 | 140 | 35 | 7 | 7 | 71 |
| | 6,716 | 292 | 7,008 | 455 | 301 | 606 | 3,869 |
| Eliminations and adjustments | | | | | | | |
| Intersegment sales | — | (292) | (292) | — | — | — | — |
| Timber and timberlands | — | — | — | — | — | 23 | 803 |
| Unusual items (Note 2) | — | — | — | 19 | — | — | — |
| General corporate | — | — | — | (33) | 9 | 13 | 183 |
| Interest expense | — | — | — | (132) | — | — | — |
| Income taxes | — | — | — | (102) | — | — | — |
| Continuing operations | 6,716 | — | 6,716 | 207 | 310 | 642 | 4,855 |
| Discontinued operations, net | — | — | — | (30) | — | — | 11 |
| Settlement of condemnation suit, net | — | — | — | 10 | — | — | — |
| Total | **$6,716** | **$ —** | **$6,716** | **$ 187** | **$310** | **$642** | **$4,866** |

*Intersegment sales are recorded at estimated fair values and income on such sales is included in operating profits.*

*Timber and timberlands have not been allocated to industry segments because they are managed jointly to supply raw materials to both the building products and pulp and paper segments. Logs and residual fiber are included at cost in the operating profits of the manufacturing facilities.*

*Capital expenditures in 1987 include $125 million in the building products segment and $1 million in timber and timberlands for assets acquired in the purchase of U.S. Plywood (Note 9).*

**Note 4. Indebtedness**

Long-term debt consisted of the following:

| (Millions)                                                                                                                               | Year ended December 31 | 1987 | 1986 |
|------------------------------------------------------------------------------------------------------------------------------------------|:----------------------:|-----:|-----:|
| Commercial paper and other short-term notes                                                                                              |                        | $ 519 | $ 175 |
| Notes                                                                                                                                     |                        |      |      |
|     Floating rate                                                                                                     |                        | —    | 32   |
|     Floating rate, currently 7.19%, due 1988                                                                          |                        | 50   | —    |
|     9¾% due 1992                                                                                                      |                        | 150  | —    |
|     13½% due 1994, redeemable after 1991                                                                             |                        | 100  | 100  |
|     15% due 1990, redeemable after 1987                                                                               |                        | 53   | 53   |
|     15.37% due 1988                                                                                                   |                        | 75   | 76   |
| Insurance companies                                                                                                                       |                        |      |      |
|     6⅝% term loan, payable in annual installments through 1989                                                       |                        | 1    | 3    |
|     9⅜% term loan, payable in annual installments through 1997                                                       |                        | 7    | 7    |
|     10½% term loan, payable in semiannual installments through 1996                                                  |                        | 4    | 4    |
|     10⅔% term loans, payable in semiannual installments through 1996                                                 |                        | 31   | 32   |
|     13.60% senior notes                                                                                               |                        | —    | 50   |
| Revenue bonds, average interest rate 6.73% with varying annual payments to 2014                                                           |                        | 143  | 153  |
| Purchase contracts and other, average interest rate 6.82% with varying payments to 2000                                                  |                        | 37   | 65   |
| Debentures                                                                                                                                |                        |      |      |
|     9¼% debentures due 2016, sinking fund payments commencing 1997                                                   |                        | 150  | 150  |
|     Zero coupon debentures, effective interest rates of 9.75% to 10.30%, maturing annually 1988 through 1990         |                        | 42   | 56   |
|     Discount term debentures, effective interest rate 11.30% due 2015, sinking fund payments commencing 1996, redeemable after June 14, 1990 |            | 125  | 125  |
|                                                                                                                                          |                        | 1,487 | 1,081 |
| Less: Current portion                                                                                                                     |                        | 153  | 134  |
|     Unamortized discount                                                                                              |                        | 36   | 54   |
|                                                                                                                                          |                        | $1,298 | $ 893 |

The scheduled maturities of long-term debt are as follows: $153 million in 1988, $8 million in 1989, $70 million in 1990, $28 million in 1991 and $161 million in 1992.

*Commercial Paper and Other Short-term Notes*

As of December 31, 1987, the Corporation had three bank revolving credit agreements providing for aggregate lines of credit of $700 million.

One of these agreements is with nine domestic money center banks and establishes a $385 million unsecured revolving line of credit until May 1, 1989, at which time the outstanding balance may be converted to a term loan repayable in eight equal semiannual installments beginning on June 30, 1989. Commitment fees during the revolving loan period are ¼ of 1 percent of the daily average unused available credit. The interest rates associated with this agreement are based on either the prime rate, certificate of deposit rate or the offshore rate.

A second agreement is with ten banks and establishes an unsecured revolving line of credit totaling $215 million until May 1, 1989. Commitment fees are ¼ of 1 percent of the daily average unused available credit. The interest rates associated with this agreement are based on either the prime rate, Federal funds rate or Eurodollar interbank offered rate.

A third agreement is with four banks and establishes a $100 million unsecured revolving line of credit until May 1, 1989. Commitment fees are ¼ of 1 percent of the daily average unused available credit. The interest rates associated with this agreement are based on either the prime rate or certificate of deposit rate.

The Corporation uses these three agreements to support commercial paper and other short-term notes. At December 31, 1987, $519 million of the total $604 million of commercial paper and other short-term borrowings, with an average interest rate of 6.94%, were classified as long-term debt. Management intends to refinance these borrowings on a long-term basis by either replacing them with long-term obligations or with equity securities or by renewing, extending or replacing them with short-term obligations.

*Notes*

In July 1987, the Corporation retired $50 million of 13.60% senior notes. The Corporation also retired $32 million of floating rate notes in October, 1987.

On October 28, 1987, the Corporation issued $150 million of 9¾% notes due November 1, 1992 at par.

The floating rate note is due in December 1988, although the Corporation has the option to redeem it prior to that date. The interest rate is adjustable daily to a rate equal to the Federal funds rate plus a specified premium.

*Debentures*

On June 15, 1987, $14 million of zero coupon debentures were retired as scheduled. The remaining zero coupon debentures may not be redeemed prior to maturity. The discount term debentures do not bear interest prior to June 15, 1990 but bear interest thereafter at 11.30%.

In 1986, the Corporation called for redemption its outstanding 5¼% convertible subordinated debentures. By the redemption date, 2,790,000 shares of common stock had been issued upon conversion of $86 million of debentures at $30.87 per share and $1 million cash had been paid for debentures that were redeemed.

*Other*

During 1987, the Corporation reduced debt classified as "purchase contracts and other" by $28 million, including retirement of a $25 million note in October. Long-term debt of $81 million, assumed in connection with the purchase of U.S. Plywood (Note 9), was also retired in 1987.

In 1986, the Corporation terminated two interest rate exchange agreements which were being used as hedges against anticipated future rollovers of $102 million of commercial paper borrowings. The Corporation paid $25 million in termination fees which are being amortized to interest expense over the periods from termination until the original 1991 maturity dates of the terminated agreements.

At December 31, 1987, $58 million of long-term debt was secured by property and timber with a net book value of $107 million, including $81 million net book value (original cost $140 million) relating to certain manufacturing and pollution control facilities which were financed with the proceeds from revenue bonds issued by local governmental units and guaranteed by the Corporation. The Corporation leases such facilities from the governmental units and pays all costs incidental to ownership of the properties.

Certain insurance company loan agreements place limitations on cash dividends that can be paid. The amount of retained earnings available for cash dividends under the most restrictive covenants of these agreements is approximately $1.1 billion. In addition, the agreements require the Corporation to maintain a minimum of $250 million of consolidated working capital and impose certain limitations on additional borrowings.

At December 31, 1987, the Corporation had registered for sale up to $500 million of debt securities under shelf registration statements with the Securities and Exchange Commission. For a discussion of debt issued after December 31, 1987, see "Management's Discussion and Analysis."

### Note 5. Retirement Plans

*Defined Benefit Pension Plans*

Most of the Corporation's employees participate in noncontributory defined benefit pension plans. These include plans which are administered solely by the Corporation, plans which are administered jointly by the Corporation and other employers or labor unions, and union-administered multiemployer plans. The Corporation's funding policy for solely administered plans is based on actuarial calculations and the applicable requirements of Federal law. Contributions to jointly administered and multiemployer plans are generally based on fixed hourly rates as set forth in negotiated labor contracts.

Benefits under the majority of plans for hourly employees (including multiemployer plans) are primarily related to years of service. The Corporation has separate plans for salaried employees and officers under which benefits are primarily related to earnings and years of service. The officers' plan is not funded and is nonqualified for Federal income tax purposes.

Effective January 1, 1986, the Corporation adopted Statement of Financial Accounting Standards No. 87, "Employers' Accounting for Pensions" (SFAS 87). This change in accounting principle reduced pension expense by approximately $22 million before income taxes in 1986, principally due to the initial excess of plan assets over the projected benefit obligation being amortized over the estimated remaining service periods ranging from 10 to 17 years. Net income increased approximately $11 million in 1986 as a result of this change.

The table below sets forth the funded status of the solely and jointly administered plans and the amounts recognized in the accompanying Balance Sheets.

| (Millions) | Year ended December 31, 1987 Plans Having Assets in Excess of Accumulated Benefits | Year ended December 31, 1987 Plans Having Accumulated Benefits in Excess of Assets | Year ended December 31, 1986 Plans Having Assets in Excess of Accumulated Benefits | Year ended December 31, 1986 Plans Having Accumulated Benefits in Excess of Assets |
|---|---|---|---|---|
| Accumulated benefit obligation at November 30 | | | | |
| Vested portion | $ 308 | $ 20 | $303 | $ 13 |
| Nonvested portion | 30 | 2 | 29 | 2 |
| | 338 | 22 | 332 | 15 |
| Effect of projected future compensation levels | 38 | 5 | 40 | 3 |
| Projected benefit obligation at November 30 | 376 | 27 | 372 | 18 |
| Plan assets at fair value at November 30 | 515 | 7 | 497 | 4 |
| Plan assets in excess of (less than) projected benefit obligation | 139 | (20) | 125 | (14) |
| Contributions made in December | — | — | 5 | — |
| Unrecognized net (gain) loss | (11) | 2 | 10 | 2 |
| Unrecognized prior service cost | 12 | 3 | 2 | — |
| Unrecognized net (asset) obligation from initial application of SFAS 87 | (114) | 1 | (120) | 1 |
| Adjustment required to recognize minimum liability | — | (1) | — | — |
| Prepaid (accrued) pension cost at December 31 | $ 26 | $(15) | $ 22 | $(11) |

The discount rates and rates of increase in future compensation levels used in determining the projected benefit obligation were, respectively, 9.0% and 6.0% at November 30, 1987 and 8.0% and 6.0% at November 30, 1986. Plan assets consist principally of common stocks, bonds, mortgage securities, guaranteed investment contracts, cash equivalents and real estate. At December 31, 1987 and 1986, respectively, $13 and $9 million of current prepaid pension cost was included in other current assets, with the remaining $13 million of noncurrent prepaid pension cost in each year included in other assets. The unfunded accrued pension cost of $15 million and $11 million, respectively, at December 31, 1987 and 1986, was included in other long-term liabilities.

Pension expense included the following components:

| (Millions) | 1987 | 1986 |
|---|---|---|
| Net periodic pension cost for solely | | |
| and jointly administered pension plans | | |
| Service cost of benefits earned | $ 30 | $22 |
| Interest cost on projected benefit obligation | 32 | 26 |
| Actual return on plan assets | (10) | (79) |
| Net amortization and deferral | (43) | 38 |
| | 9 | 7 |
| Contributions to multiemployer pension plans | 4 | 4 |
| | $ 13 | $11 |

The expected long-term rate of return on plan assets used in determining net periodic pension cost was increased to 8.5% in 1987, from 7.5% in 1986. The increase reduced 1987 pension expense by approximately $5 million. The Corporation's contributions to solely and jointly administered plans were $26 million in 1987 and $29 million in 1986. Prior to adopting SFAS 87, the Corporation's policy was to expense its annual pension contributions. The total expense recognized for defined benefit pension plans was $35 million in 1985.

*Defined Contribution Plan*
The Corporation also sponsors a Savings and Capital Growth Plan (Savings Plan) to provide eligible salaried employees with additional income upon retirement. The Corporation makes annual contributions to the Savings Plan equal to 3% of the first $100,000 of each participant's annual compensation, as defined. The Corporation also matches a portion of voluntary before-tax contributions up to a maximum matching contribution of approximately 3% of a participant's compensation. At November 30, 1987, approximately 11,600 employees were eligible to participate in the Savings Plan, which had net assets of approximately $272 million. The cost of the Savings Plan was $16 million in 1987, $15 million in 1986 and $13 million in 1985.

*Retiree Health Care and Life Insurance Benefits*
The Corporation also provides certain health care and life insurance benefits to eligible retired employees. The Corporation accrues currently the actuarially determined cost for retired employees and accrues over their estimated future service periods the actuarially determined cost for active employees' retirement benefits.

### Note 6. Redeemable Preferred Stock

| (Millions) | Adjustable Rate Convertible Preferred Stock | | | |
| --- | --- | --- | --- | --- |
| | Series A | Series B | Series C | Total |
| *Balance at December 31, 1984* | $119 | $34 | $37 | $190 |
| Shares repurchased | (32) | (8) | — | (40) |
| Amortization of the excess of involuntary liquidating value over fair value at issue date | 3 | — | 3 | 6 |
| *Balance at December 31, 1985* | 90 | 26 | 40 | 156 |
| Shares repurchased | (32) | (7) | (11) | (50) |
| Amortization of the excess of involuntary liquidating value over fair value at issue date | 3 | 1 | 3 | 7 |
| *Balance at December 31, 1986* | 61 | 20 | 32 | 113 |
| Shares converted to common stock | (61) | (18) | (32) | (111) |
| Shares redeemed | (1) | (2) | — | (3) |
| Shares repurchased | — | — | (1) | (1) |
| Amortization of the excess of involuntary liquidating value over fair value at issue date | 1 | — | 1 | 2 |
| *Balance at December 31, 1987* | $ — | $ — | $ — | $ — |

The number of shares of adjustable rate convertible preferred stock (preferred stock) issued and outstanding at December 31, 1986 were 1,656,000 of Series A, 573,000 of Series B and 1,049,000 of Series C. The preferred stock was recorded at fair market value on the date of issue. The excess of involuntary liquidating value over such fair market value was amortized by a charge to retained earnings and corresponding credit to preferred stock. Each share of preferred stock received cumulative quarterly cash dividends at the annual rate of $2.24.

In March 1987, the Corporation called for redemption on April 15, 1987 all of its outstanding preferred stock. Approximately 1,624,000 Series A, 522,000 Series B and 1,038,000 Series C shares were converted to shares of Georgia-Pacific common stock on a one-for-one basis. The remaining shares were redeemed at $39.00 per share plus accumulated dividends.

### Note 7. Common Stock

At December 31, 1987, the following authorized shares of the Corporation's common stock were reserved for issue:

| | |
| --- | --- |
| 1987 Employee Stock Purchase Plan | 773,000 |
| 1984 Employee Stock Option Plan | 3,293,000 |
| | 4,066,000 |

The Corporation purchased 6,182,000 shares of its common stock for the treasury during 1987 for $255 million at an average price of $41.25 per share.

In 1987, the Corporation called for redemption all of its outstanding preferred stock (Note 6). Approximately 3,184,000 shares of preferred stock were converted to shares of Georgia-Pacific common stock on a one-for-one basis. In 1986, the Corporation called its 5¼% convertible subordinated debentures, which resulted in the issuance of 2,790,000 common shares to holders who elected to convert their debentures into common stock at a conversion price of $30.87 per share (Note 4).

The Corporation adopted the 1987 Employee Stock Purchase Plan (Purchase Plan) in 1987. At December 31, 1987, the Purchase Plan reserved for issue 773,000 shares of common stock at a subscription price of $39.53. Subscribers have the option to receive their payments plus interest at the rate of 7% per annum in lieu of stock. Additional shares can no longer be subscribed under the Purchase Plan, which expires on March 31, 1989. At December 31, 1987, 6,200 subscribers remained in the Purchase Plan.

The Corporation issued 829,000 shares during 1986 under the 1984 Employee Stock Purchase Plan, which expired on October 31, 1986.

In connection with the 1984 Employee Stock Option Plan (Option Plan), 3,293,000 shares of common stock were reserved for issue. The Option Plan provides for the granting of stock options to certain officers and employees. Holders of stock options may be granted cash awards, payable upon exercise of an option, of an amount not to exceed the amount by which the market value of the common stock, as defined, exceeds the option price. In addition, holders may be granted rights to surrender all or part of the related stock option in exchange for common stock with a fair market value equal to the amount by which the market value of the common stock, as defined, exceeds the option price.

Compensation resulting from stock options and cash awards is initially measured at the grant date based on the market value of the common stock, with adjustments made in subsequent periods for market price fluctuations. The Corporation recognized stock options compensation expense of $11 million in 1987, $33 million in 1986 and $6 million in 1985.

Additional information relating to the Option Plan is as follows:

| *Year ended December 31* | **1987** | *1986* |
|---|---|---|
| Options outstanding at January 1 | **1,491,000** | 1,226,000 |
| Granted | **566,000** | 1,408,000 |
| Exercised/Surrendered | **(810,000)** | (1,107,000) |
| Cancelled | **(8,000)** | (36,000) |
| Options outstanding at December 31 | **1,239,000** | 1,491,000 |
| Options available for grant at December 31 | **2,054,000** | 2,612,000 |
| Total reserved shares | **3,293,000** | 4,103,000 |
| Options exercisable at December 31 | **679,000** | 115,000 |
| Option prices per share | | |
| Granted | **$46** | $26 |
| Exercised/Surrendered | **$21–$26** | $21–$25 |
| Cancelled | **$26–$46** | $21–$26 |

The shares and prices relating to the Purchase Plan and the Option Plan are subject to adjustment for certain changes in the capital structure, including common stock splits and stock dividends.

### Note 8. Income Taxes

The provision for income taxes is based on pretax financial income which differs from taxable income. Differences generally arise because certain items, such as depreciation and write-downs of certain assets, are reflected in different time periods for financial and tax purposes.

The Corporation used the flow-through method of accounting for investment tax credits. Under the flow-through method, investment tax credits are recognized as a reduction of income tax expense in the year the qualified investment is made.

The provision for income taxes and income taxes paid for continuing operations were as follows:

| (Millions)                    Year ended December 31 | 1987 | 1986 | 1985 |
|------------------------------------------------------|------|------|------|
| Federal income taxes, net of investment tax credit   |      |      |      |
|    Current                            | $243 | $ 79 | $ 13 |
|    Deferred                           | 49   | 87   | 84   |
| State income taxes                                   | 48   | 23   | 5    |
|                                                      | $340 | $189 | $102 |
|                                                      |      |      |      |
| Income taxes paid                                    | $255 | $119 | $ 3  |

The difference between the statutory Federal income tax rate and the Corporation's effective income tax rate for continuing operations is summarized as follows:

| Year ended December 31 | 1987 | 1986 | 1985 |
|------------------------|------|------|------|
| Federal income tax rate | 40.0% | 46.0% | 46.0% |
| Increase (decrease) as a result of |      |      |      |
|   Value of timber appreciation taxed at capital gains rate | (2.0) | (7.8) | (9.8) |
|   Investment tax credit | — | (2.9) | (10.2) |
|   State income tax, net of Federal benefit | 3.6 | 2.7 | 2.7 |
|   Other | 1.0 | 1.0 | 4.3 |
|                        | 42.6% | 39.0% | 33.0% |

The Tax Reform Act of 1986 reduced the statutory Federal income tax rate from 46% to 40% in 1987. However, the effective income tax rate increased in 1987 and 1986 primarily due to the repeal of the investment tax credit (although some credits were allowed in 1986 under the transition rules) and a higher capital gains tax rate in 1987.

The following is a summary of the components of the deferred tax provision for continuing operations:

| (Millions)                    Year ended December 31 | 1987 | 1986 | 1985 |
|------------------------------------------------------|------|------|------|
| Excess of tax depreciation over financial depreciation | $ 64 | $ 87 | $ 97 |
| Write-down of certain assets                         | (6)  | (15) | (6)  |
| Sale of tax benefits                                 | 2    | (12) | (13) |
| Fees paid to terminate interest rate exchange agreements | (2) | 12   | —    |
| Prepayment of pension expense                        | (2)  | 11   | —    |
| Deferred start-up costs, net                         | —    | 7    | 4    |
| Capitalized interest, net                            | (4)  | (4)  | 6    |
| Other                                                | (3)  | 1    | (4)  |
|                                                      | $ 49 | $ 87 | $ 84 |

In December 1987, the Financial Accounting Standards Board issued Statement of Financial Accounting Standards No. 96, "Accounting for Income Taxes" which, among other provisions, will change the method of accounting for deferred income taxes. Companies are required to adopt the new standard no later than for fiscal years beginning after December 15, 1988.

It is anticipated that the Corporation will adopt the new standard in 1989, that prior periods will not be restated, and that the cumulative effect of the accounting change will result in a reduction of deferred tax balances recorded on the balance sheet and an increase in reported net income in the year of adoption. The amount to be recorded will be dependent upon cumulative net timing differences and statutory tax rates existing at that time.

### Note 9. Acquisition

On June 12, 1987, the Corporation acquired all of the outstanding stock of U.S. Plywood Corporation for $208 million in cash in a transaction accounted for as a purchase. The assets acquired and liabilities assumed at the acquisition date were as follows:

*(Millions)*

| | |
|---|---:|
| Receivables | $ 75 |
| Inventories | 86 |
| Property, plant and equipment | 126 |
| Other assets | 91 |
| | 378 |
| Bank overdrafts, net | 26 |
| Accounts payable | 28 |
| Other current liabilities | 33 |
| Current portion of long-term debt | 81 |
| Other long-term liabilities | 2 |
| | 170 |
| | $208 |

The assets acquired included six manufacturing facilities along with distribution centers and shipping facilities located throughout the United States. The purchase price exceeded the $117 million fair value of net assets acquired by $91 million. The excess is included in other assets and is being amortized over 12 years.

The results of U.S. Plywood's operations have been included in the accompanying Statements of Income from the date of acquisition. Had the operations been acquired as of the beginning of 1987, the Corporation's operating profits for the year would not have been materially affected.

### Note 10. Discontinued Operations

Beginning in 1984, the Corporation disposed of certain lines of business, including all of its commodity chemicals and oil and gas operations. These dispositions were completed in the first quarter of 1986 with the sale of Georgia-Pacific Plastics, Inc., whose principal asset was an expandable polystyrene plant in Painesville, Ohio, for $13 million in cash.

In September 1985, the Corporation sold Exchange Oil & Gas Corporation (Exchange). After adjusting for cash received from Exchange prior to the sale, net cash proceeds were approximately $136 million at closing. Also during 1985, the Corporation sold Polymer, Inc., whose principal asset was a color concentrate plant in Farmingdale, New York, for $8 million in cash.

The Corporation's initial estimate in 1984 of the loss on disposal of discontinued operations was revised in 1985, at which time an additional $30 million loss, net of related income tax benefits of $14 million, was recorded.

Cash provided by discontinued operations consisted of the following:

| *(Millions)*     *Year ended December 31* | **1987** | *1986* | *1985* |
|---|---:|---:|---:|
| Cash provided by (used for) | | | |
|   Operating income (loss), net of taxes, noncash items and changes in working capital | $ — | $(2) | $(13) |
|   Capital expenditures prior to sale | — | — | (14) |
|   Proceeds from sale of assets | — | 13 | 144 |
| | $ — | $11 | $117 |

## Note 11. Extraordinary Item

In November 1986, pursuant to a court-approved settlement of a condemnation proceeding begun in 1975, the Corporation received approximately $14 million in cash. A $10 million extraordinary gain, net of related income taxes of $4 million, was recorded in 1985 upon entry of the judgment.

## Note 12. Commitments and Contingencies

The Corporation is a party to various legal proceedings generally incidental to its business. Although the ultimate disposition of these proceedings is not presently determinable, management does not believe that adverse determinations in any or all of such proceedings would have a material adverse effect upon the financial condition of the Corporation.

During 1986, the Corporation adopted a program to self-insure for general liability claims up to $25 million per claim. These risks were previously insured with a nominal deductible amount.

The Corporation is a 50% partner in a joint venture (GA-MET) with Metropolitan Life Insurance Company (Metropolitan). GA-MET owns and operates the Corporation's office headquarters complex in Atlanta, Georgia. The Corporation accounts for its investment in GA-MET under the equity method.

During 1986, GA-MET borrowed $170 million from Metropolitan for the primary purpose of retiring debt incurred from the acquisition and construction of the Atlanta headquarters complex. The note bears interest at 9½% and requires monthly payments of principal and interest with a final installment due in 2011. The note is secured by the land and building of the Atlanta headquarters complex. In the event of foreclosure, each partner has severally guaranteed payment of one-half of any shortfall of collateral value to the outstanding secured indebtedness. Based on present market conditions and building occupancy, the likelihood of any obligation to the Corporation with respect to this guarantee is considered remote.

## Note 13. Unaudited Selected Quarterly Financial Data

| *(Millions, except per share amounts)* | 1st Quarter | | 2nd Quarter | | 3rd Quarter | | 4th Quarter | |
|---|---|---|---|---|---|---|---|---|
| | **1987** | *1986* | **1987** | *1986* | **1987** | *1986* | **1987** | *1986* |
| Net sales | **$1,855** | $1,604 | **$2,095** | $1,929 | **$2,424** | $1,909 | **$2,229** | $1,781 |
| Gross profit (net sales minus cost of sales) | **403** | 287 | **446** | 374 | **486** | 411 | **491** | 368 |
| Net income | **80** | 30 | **148** | 86 | **118** | 97 | **112** | 83 |
| Income per common share | **.71** | .25 | **1.35** | .80 | **1.10** | .90 | **1.06** | .75 |
| Dividends declared per common share | **.25** | .20 | **.25** | .20 | **.25** | .20 | **.30** | .25 |
| Price range of common stock | | | | | | | | |
| High | **52.75** | 33.50 | **52.38** | 34.25 | **48.38** | 37.38 | **46.13** | 41.25 |
| Low | **37.00** | 24.75 | **40.25** | 28.00 | **39.75** | 29.00 | **22.75** | 35.63 |

*Net income includes:*
*– a $6 million pre-tax gain from the liquidation of investments in the 1987 first quarter (Note 2);*
*– a $60 million pre-tax gain from the liquidation of investments in the 1987 second quarter (Note 2);*
*– an $11 million pre-tax reduction in expense in the 1986 first quarter from adoption of a new timber capitalization policy (Note 1);*
*– a $33 million pre-tax gain from liquidation of investments in the 1986 fourth quarter (Note 2); and*
*– a $17 million increase in income tax expense in the 1986 fourth quarter due to the repeal of the investment tax credit under the Tax Reform Act of 1986 (Note 8).*

**Five-year Selected Financial Data**

*Georgia-Pacific Corporation and Subsidiaries*

| (Millions, except per share amounts)          Year ended December 31 | 1987 | 1986 | 1985 | 1984 | 1983 |
|---|---|---|---|---|---|
| *Operations* | | | | | |
| Net sales | $8,603 | $7,223 | $6,716 | $6,682 | $6,040 |
| Costs and expenses | | | | | |
| Cost of sales | 6,777 | 5,783 | 5,553 | 5,441 | 4,978 |
| Selling, general and administrative | 583 | 511 | 431 | 426 | 374 |
| Depreciation and depletion | 387 | 339 | 310 | 282 | 289 |
| Interest | 124 | 138 | 132 | 156 | 157 |
| Provision for restructuring operations | — | — | — | — | 135 |
| | 7,871 | 6,771 | 6,426 | 6,305 | 5,933 |
| Income from continuing operations before unusual items, income taxes and extraordinary item | 732 | 452 | 290 | 377 | 107 |
| Unusual items | 66 | 33 | 19 | 19 | — |
| Provision for income taxes | 340 | 189 | 102 | 143 | 32 |
| Income from continuing operations before extraordinary item | $ 458 | $ 296 | $ 207 | $ 253 | $ 75 |
| *Financial position, end of year* | | | | | |
| Current assets | $1,729 | $1,420 | $1,291 | $1,406 | $1,268 |
| Timber and timberlands, net | 915 | 844 | 804 | 840 | 753 |
| Property, plant and equipment, net | 3,048 | 2,691 | 2,606 | 2,270 | 1,989 |
| Net assets of discontinued operations | — | — | 11 | 158 | 653 |
| Other assets | 178 | 159 | 154 | 111 | 69 |
| Total assets | 5,870 | 5,114 | 4,866 | 4,785 | 4,732 |
| Current liabilities | 996 | 837 | 631 | 640 | 612 |
| Long-term debt | 1,298 | 893 | 1,257 | 1,383 | 1,453 |
| Deferred income taxes | 744 | 695 | 606 | 503 | 413 |
| Other long-term liabilities | 152 | 124 | 69 | 34 | 26 |
| Redeemable preferred stock | — | 113 | 156 | 190 | 215 |
| Total net assets | $2,680 | $2,452 | $2,147 | $2,035 | $2,013 |
| Working capital | $ 733 | $ 583 | $ 660 | $ 766 | $ 656 |
| *Other statistical data* | | | | | |
| Capital expenditures | $ 825 | $ 482 | $ 642 | $ 710 | $ 188 |
| Per common share | | | | | |
| Income from continuing operations before extraordinary item | 4.23 | 2.70 | 1.84 | 2.28 | .53 |
| Dividends declared | 1.05 | .85 | .80 | .70 | .60 |
| Market price: High | 52.75 | 41.25 | 27.38 | 25.75 | 31.88 |
| Low | 22.75 | 24.75 | 20.50 | 18.00 | 22.38 |
| Year end | 34.50 | 37.00 | 26.50 | 25.00 | 24.75 |
| Book value* | 25.59 | 22.70 | 20.59 | 19.58 | 19.48 |
| Shares of common stock outstanding at year end | 105 | 107 | 103 | 103 | 102 |
| Number of common shareholders of record (thousands) | 56 | 66 | 74 | 79 | 80 |
| Number of employees (thousands) | 42 | 39 | 39 | 40 | 39 |
| Effective income tax rate* | 42.6% | 39.0% | 33.0% | 36.1% | 29.9% |
| Return on capital employed* | 12.6% | 10.4% | 8.7% | 11.7% | 4.2% |
| Return on common equity* | 18.7% | 13.8% | 10.2% | 12.6% | 3.8% |
| Total debt-to-capital* | 31.4% | 26.3% | 32.0% | 35.7% | 37.4% |
| Current ratio* | 1.7 | 1.7 | 2.0 | 2.2 | 2.1 |

*The method of calculating this ratio is described in the Financial Glossary presented on page 1.

# *Glossary*

**accelerated cost recovery system (ACRS)**   Extremely accelerated method of depreciation, which must be used for tax purposes for all tangible assets placed in service during 1981 to 1986. It normally would not be acceptable for financial reporting purposes. (10)*

**accelerated depreciation**   Depreciation methods which take proportionately more of the asset's cost to depreciation expense in the earlier years of the asset's life. (10)

**account**   Summarizing device prepared for each asset, liability, owner's equity, revenue, and expense item. Collectively accounts constitute the firm's ledger and are used to accumulate and maintain current balances for all items. (4)

**accounting**   The concepts and processes by which financial and economic data, primarily quantitative in nature, are gathered and summarized in reports that are useful in decision making. (1)

**accounting cycle**   The established order in which the procedures in an accounting system are performed. The steps in this order include journalizing transactions, posting, preparing a trial balance, adjusting entries, preparing financial statements, and closing entries. (5)

**accounting equation**   Refers to the equality of assets and equities, or the equality of assets and the sum of liabilities and owners' equity. (3)

**accounting information systems**   The integrated set of personnel, equipment, and procedures which capture, process, and report accounting information to management. Accounting systems generate data primarily in economic terms to provide scorekeeping, attention-directing, and decision-making information to management. (5)

**accounting period concept**   Assumption that economic activity can be meaningfully divided into time periods which will facilitate the communication of relatively timely information. Also referred to as *periodicity concept*. (2)

---

*The numbers in parentheses after each definition refer to the chapter in which the term is prominently discussed.

**Accounting Principles Board**  Organization created by the AICPA in 1960 to issue authoritative opinions and to publish research studies. Dissolved in 1973 upon the establishment of the FASB. (1)

**Accounting Series Releases (ASRs)**  Policy statements issued by the SEC in which the Commission articulates standards for the reporting of financial information in SEC reports and firms' annual reports to stockholders. Name changed in 1982 to *Financial Reporting Releases*. (1)

**accrual basis accounting**  Basis of accounting which recognizes revenues when they are earned and recognizes expenses when they are incurred in earning revenue. The timing of the cash flows does not control the recording of revenues and expenses. (5)

**accrued liability**  Liability which grows progressively in amount until a payment date is reached, at which time the debt is liquidated. Wages Payable is an example. (3)

**accumulated depreciation**  Contra asset account which reflects the total depreciation expense taken on a plant asset since its date of acquisition. Also referred to as *allowance for depreciation*. (5)

**acquisition cost**  All reasonable and necessary costs of acquiring an asset, getting it to the place of business, and rendering it available and ready for the intended use. (8)

**activity method**  Depreciation method whereby the cost of the plant asset is first related directly to some unit of asset service and then to periods of time. Depreciation expense will only be constant from period to period if the asset's use is constant from period to period. Also referred to as *units of production method*. (10)

**actuarial assumptions**  The assumptions that actuaries make about future uncertainties affecting pension costs. Examples include estimates of employee turnover and the interest rate earned on pension fund assets. (12)

**actuarial cost methods**  Alternative assumptions used by actuaries for establishing the amount and incidence of the annual actuarial cost of pension plan benefits and of the related actuarial liability. (12)

**actuarial gains and losses**  Gains and losses which occur when the actuarial assumptions underlying pension calculations are modified to meet changing conditions or when actual experience differs from the original expectations. (12)

**actuarial liability (projected benefit obligation)**  Accumulated present value of the benefits earned by employees as of the end of each accounting period. (12)

**adjunct account**  An account whose balance is on the same side (debit or credit) as that of another related account to which it is added. Premiums on Bonds Payable is an example. (8)

**adjusting entries**  Those entries made at the end of the accounting period to record internal events that have taken place but have not yet been recorded and to revise entries that were made incorrectly. (5)

**advances**  Liability claims arising from the receipt of cash or other assets, which will be satisfied by delivery of products or services. Magazine subscriptions received in advance are an example of advances. (3)

**affiliated companies**   Reference to a group of companies composed of a parent company and its subsidiaries and major investees. (15)

**aging accounts receivable**   The process of classifying accounts receivable balances according to the length of time they have been outstanding and applying a different estimated uncollectible percentage to each age group. (7)

**allowance for doubtful accounts**   A contra to the Accounts Receivable account. Credited in an entry to estimate bad debts, it measures a firm's estimate of the amount of receivables that will probably prove to be uncollectible. (7)

**alternative minimum tax (AMT)**   Provision in the tax code to ensure that successful corporations pay equitable amounts of income taxes. A corporation must pay the higher of its AMT or its regular tax. (13)

**American Accounting Association**   Organization of accounting educators which conducts research into accounting problems and offers normative suggestions to the principle-setting process. (1)

**American Institute of Certified Public Accountants**   Professional organization of certified public accountants (CPAs) which oversees the professional conduct of CPAs, sets auditing standards, and offers extensive input to the FASB in the standard-setting process. (1)

**amortization**   The process of rationally and systematically allocating the cost of intangible assets over their useful service lives. (10)

**annuity**   A series of equal amounts due in each of a number of future periods. If the amounts are exchanged at the end of each period, it is referred to as an *ordinary annuity*. (11)

**annuity due**   A series of equal payments/receipts occurring at the beginning of each period. (11)

**assets**   Future economic benefits obtained or controlled by a particular entity as a result of past transactions or events. Assets consist of economic resources which arise in a transaction, can be measurable in monetary terms, and hold future economic benefit. (3)

**auditing**   The function of verifying and appraising the accuracy, integrity, and authenticity of the financial statements. (2)

**auditors' report (opinion)**   Report in which the company's independent certified public accountant (CPA) expresses professional judgment concerning the financial statements. It accompanies the financial statements in a firm's annual report. (2)

**audit trail**   Series of cross-references entered during posting journal entries to ledger accounts. (5)

**authorized stock**   Total number of shares of capital stock that the state charter permits a corporation to issue. (14)

**balance sheet**   Financial statement which presents the financial condition of the entity (assets, liabilities, and owners' equity) as of a moment in time. Also referred to as *statement of financial position*. (2)

**benefit-cost comparisons**   Constraint that guides the accounting process to prevent the requirement to process or report information where the cost of developing the information exceeds the value received from the information. (2)

**benefit formula**   The calculation which provides pension plan benefits based on a formula including benefit percentage, compensation level, and number of years' service. (12)

**bond**   Group of legal promises made in exchange for the receipt of money from investors. Primary promise is to repay principal funds borrowed and interest on those funds over extended future periods of the loan. (11)

**bond indenture**   Contract containing provisions (covenants) related to the legal conditions surrounding the borrowing and repayment of funds borrowed. (11)

**bond issue costs**   Costs expended to permit the issuance of bonds. Examples of the costs are audit fees, legal fees, printing costs, registration and filing fees, etc. (11)

**bookkeeping**   The system for recording and classifying accounting data. (1)

**book value**   The excess of the original cost of an asset over the balance in the Accumulated Depreciation account. (10)

**book value per share**   Total common stockholders' equity divided by number of shares of common stock outstanding. (3)

**call provision**   Provision in bond agreement which specifies that bonds can be redeemed by the issuer at certain set prices during their life. (11)

**capital expenditures**   Expenditures which increase the quantity or quality of service provided by an asset. They are treated as assets since they benefit future periods. Examples include a major engine overhaul and an addition to an asset. (10)

**capitalization of interest**   Charging some of the period's interest cost to an asset account. The interest cost will be charged to expense over future periods as the completed asset is depreciated. (8)

**capitalization of retained earnings**   Transfer of amounts from retained earnings to par value and additional paid-in capital accounts. This transfer removes retained earnings from dividend availability. This procedure is required in payments of stock dividends. (14)

**capital lease**   Leasing transaction whose economic substance suggests that the lessee is, in effect, acquiring the property being leased under a long-term installment contract. Leases meeting at least one of four specified criteria are considered to be capital leases from the lessee's perspective and are reflected on its books as an asset and a related obligation. (12)

**capital stock**   Owners' equity in a corporation arising from a direct commitment of capital. Shares of stock are issued as evidence of the investment. See common stock. (3)

**cash basis accounting**   Basis of accounting that recognizes revenues when cash is received and recognizes expenses when cash is paid. (5)

**cash flow to long-term debt**   A widely used measure of financial strength. Calculated by dividing cash flow from operations by long-term debt. (18)

**change in accounting estimates**   Changes which are implemented to adjust the accounting records in light of new information concerning the adequacy of previous estimates. They are recognized prospectively in the accounts. Examples include a change in the estimated useful life of a machine or the anticipated bad debt losses from credit sales. (16)

**change in accounting principles**  Substitution of one generally accepted accounting principle for another. Examples include changes from FIFO to LIFO and from straight-line to sum-of-the-years'-digits depreciation. They usually are reported in a separate section of the income statement. (16)

**chart of accounts**  A list which identifies the accounts used by a particular company as the components of its ledger. (5)

**closing entries**  Necessary entries prepared at the end of the accounting period to clear the revenue and expense accounts to zero and to transfer the net income or net loss for the period to the Retained Earnings account. (4)

**commercial paper**  Unsecured promissory notes issued by well-established corporations to meet their short-term seasonal borrowing requirements. These notes usually are issued in specific denominations arranged to suit the buyer, with maturities ranging from a few days to nine months. (11)

**commitments**  Future contractual obligations which need to be disclosed in the footnotes to the financial statements. Disclosure permits statement interpretation in light of known future asset claims. (16)

**common-size statements**  Financial statements resulting from vertical analysis, where all items are expressed in percentages rather than dollar amounts. (18)

**common stock**  All capital stock which is not preferred stock and represents the residual ownership and voting control over a corporation. (14)

**common stock equivalents**  Securities which have many of the characteristics of common stock but have not yet become common stock; important in EPS calculations. (16)

**comparability**  Reporting standard that calls for like events to be reported in the same manner and unlike events to be reported differently; facilitates analysis among firms and between accounting periods. (2)

**compensating balances**  Portion of cash asset that must be maintained on hand (on deposit) at all times to obtain a loan or line of credit. (11)

**completed production method**  Revenue recognition procedure (point) permitted when a ready market exists to absorb all completed production at a quoted price. Examples include the extraction of precious metals and the harvesting of grains. (7)

**completeness**  Reporting standard that requires financial accounting information to be fully disclosed. (2)

**complex financial structure**  A financial structure that contains convertible securities, stock options, or stock purchase warrants. Its existence requires the calculation of primary and fully diluted earnings per share. (16)

**compound interest**  Phenomenon whereby interest earned on an investment is not withdrawn but rather remains invested and earns interest itself. (11)

**comprehensive income**  The change in equity (net assets) of an entity during a period, from transactions and other events and circumstances, except those resulting from investments by owners and distributions to owners. (6)

**conservatism** When a decision requires judgment, accountants tend to select those procedures which result in smaller measures of assets or income. The consequences of overstating these items are more risky than those associated with an understatement. (2)

**consistency** Reporting standard that calls for accounting practices not to be changed unless a change would facilitate more accurate or correct reporting; an essential ingredient of comparability over time within a single firm. (2)

**consolidated financial statements** Financial statements which report a legally separate parent company and its subsidiary companies as if they were a single company. (15)

**constant dollar accounting** Asset valuation and income determination procedure which recognizes changes in the general level of prices and the impact of inflation in the accounts. (8)

**contingencies** Existing circumstance involving an uncertain but possible gain or loss. Uncertainty will be resolved when a future event occurs or fails to occur. (16)

**contingent liabilities** Potential liabilities whose existence is solely dependent upon future events. They do not presently appear on the balance sheet but are referred to in the footnotes to the financial statements. An example would be the guarantee of another's debts. (16)

**contra account** An account whose balance is on the opposite side of another related account from which it is subtracted. Examples include Allowance for Doubtful Accounts, Accumulated Depreciation, and Discount on Bonds Payable. (7)

**contributed capital** The portion of stockholders' equity that arises from the contribution of capital by stockholders. (14)

**control account** A general ledger account for which detailed information is maintained in a subsidiary ledger. Examples are accounts receivable and accounts payable. (5)

**convertible bonds** Bonds which contain a provision allowing them to be exchanged for capital stock at the holder's option. (11)

**cost method of accounting for investment in stock** Procedure used to account for an investment of less than 20 percent in the stock of another corporation. The acquiring firm maintains the Investment account on its books at acquisition cost and only reports income from its investment when dividends are received. (15)

**cost of goods sold** Cost of inventory sold during the period and matched with the revenues of the period to calculate gross margin (profit). (8)

**coverage of total fixed charges** A measure of the firm's ability to meet its interest obligations and the normally declared preferred dividends. Calculated by dividing income, before interest and taxes, by the sum of interest expense and normally declared preferred dividends. (18)

**credit** Right side of ledger account and right-hand amount column in a journal. Credits occur (amounts are entered on the right side) whenever assets decrease or liabilities and owner's equity increase. (4)

**currency exchange rates** Ratio applied to transaction and account balances expressed in foreign currencies to convert the amounts to U.S. dollars. (14)

**current assets**   Cash and other resources which will be converted into cash or used in the normal operations of the business within a relatively short period of time (usually one year). Examples include cash, accounts receivable, merchandise inventory, and prepayments. (3)

**current cost accounting**   Asset valuation and income determination procedure which recognizes changes in the specific level of prices and the gains and losses incurred from the holding of certain assets. (8)

**current liabilities**   Obligations that will be paid within one year (or within the operating cycle when that is longer). Examples include accounts payable and taxes payable. (3)

**current ratio**   A widely used measure of liquidity; equal to current assets divided by current liabilities. (18)

**debit**   Left side of ledger account and left-hand amount column in a journal. Debits occur (amounts are entered on the left side) whenever assets increase or liabilities and owners' equity decrease. (4)

**debt to equity ratio**   A widely used measure of financial strength. Calculated by dividing long-term debt by total equities. (18)

**declining-balance depreciation**   An accelerated depreciation procedure whereby a constant percentage (150 percent or 200 percent) of the straight-line depreciation rate is applied to the decreasing book value of the asset in order to calculate annual depreciation expense. (10)

**deferred tax accounting**   Method of accounting for income taxes in which the income tax consequences of an event are recognized in the same accounting period in which the event appears on the financial statements. The differences between income tax expense based on the income statement and current taxes payable based on the tax return are recognized as deferred liabilities or deferred assets. (13)

**deferred tax assets**   Deferred tax consequences from temporary differences that will result in net tax deductions in future years, provided that they can be recovered under operating loss carryback provisions by a refund of taxes paid in the current or prior years. (13)

**deferred tax consequences**   Future effects on income taxes, caused by temporary differences existing at the end of the current year. (13)

**deferred tax expense**   Net change during the year in the firm's deferred tax liabilities and assets. (13)

**deferred tax liability**   Amount of deferred tax consequences from temporary differences that will result in net taxable amounts in future years. (13)

**deficit**   Term used to describe a debit balance in the Retained Earnings account. (4)

**defined-benefit plans**   Pension plans which establish a specific schedule of pension benefits. The employer must contribute amounts sufficient to provide these benefits. (12)

**defined-contribution plans**   Pension plans which limit the employer's payments to a fixed sum. No specific pension benefits are promised except those provided by the pension fund contributions. (12)

**depletion** The process of rationally and systematically allocating the cost of natural resources (wasting assets) over their useful service lives. (10)

**depreciation** The process of rationally and systematically allocating the cost of plant assets over their useful service lives. (10)

**depreciation base** The asset cost to be allocated to the various periods in which the asset provides service. In most cases, it is equal to the acquisition cost minus the net residual value. (10)

**direct-financing lease** Leases meeting certain criteria when the lessee is purchasing the asset and the lessor is financing the purchase. (12)

**direct labor** Cost of labor services directly identified with specific products being manufactured. (8)

**direct material** Cost of raw materials directly entering into production of physical units. (8)

**direct write-off method** Procedure whereby an expense for bad debts is recorded only when specific uncollectible accounts are identified. No Allowance for Doubtful Accounts is established. Results in less accurate and perhaps less objective financial statements than under the Allowance method. (7)

**disbursement** The payment of money. (5)

**discontinued operations** The sale or abandonment of a significant component of the business. A separate income statement section is created to report (a) the periodic income or loss from operating the component until it was discontinued and (b) the gain or loss on its disposal. (16)

**discounted cash flows** The present value of the net future cash flows. (11)

**discount on bonds** Excess of face or maturity amount of a bond over its issue price. Occurs when the market rate of interest demanded by investors exceeds the nominal rate of interest offered by the corporation. Accounted for as an addition to the interest expense over the life of the bond. (11)

**discretionary expenses** Those period costs which management can significantly modify in amount from period to period. Examples include research and development and advertising. (18)

**dividend payout ratio** Measures the proportion of earnings distributed as cash dividends; calculated by dividing cash dividends to common stockholders by the net income available to common stockholders (after preferred dividends). (18)

**dividends** A pro rata distribution of assets by a corporation to its stockholders. Usually they are in the form of cash and represent a distribution of the firm's earnings. (6)

**double-entry bookkeeping** Method of recording in which every transaction has at least two aspects — a debit and a credit. (4)

**earning criterion** Criterion which asserts that revenue should not be recognized until it has been earned. In conjunction with the measurability criterion, influences the recognition of revenue. (7)

**earnings per share (EPS)** The earnings available for common stockholders divided by the number of shares outstanding. In more complex situations, very complicated calculations are made for primary and fully diluted earnings per share. (16)

**effective interest bond amortization**   Interest-recording procedure which charges each period with an amount of interest directly related to the market rate and the actual amount of money being used. The interest expense varies in each period of the bond's life, but the yield rate is constant. (11)

**effective interest rate**   The actual rate of interest paid for borrowed funds. Calculated by dividing the total interest expense by the principal amount borrowed. (11)

**effective tax rate**   Percentage calculated by dividing income tax expense by the income before taxes. (6)

**entity concept**   Assumption which states that accounting reports and records pertain to a specifically defined business entity, separate and distinct from the people or groups concerned with it. (2)

**equities**   Representing the source of assets, they measure the financial investment in or claim on the business by creditors (liabilities) and owners (owners' equity). (3)

**equity method of accounting for investment in stock**   Procedure used to account for an investment of between 20 and 50 percent in the stock of another corporation. The acquiring firm increases the Investment account for its share of the other firm's income and reduces it for its share of any dividends from that company. It reports income in relation to earnings reported, regardless of the extent to which earnings were received as dividends. (15)

**ERISA (Employee Retirement Income Security Act)**   Act passed by Congress in 1974. Affects funding, vesting procedures, and various other aspects of an employer's pension plan. (12)

**estimated liabilities**   Obligations or claims on a firm's assets when the amount owed and/or the identity of the claimant is not known precisely. The amount should be reasonably measured and shown as an estimated liability. Liability under product warranty programs is an example. (3)

**exchange-price (cost) concept**   Establishes the valuation measures to be applied as data enter the accounting process. The assets held by a firm and its liabilities are recorded at the prices (values) agreed upon or inherent in the exchanges in which they originated. This results in most assets being reported on the financial statements at their historical cost. (2)

**executory contracts**   Contracts which are traditionally not reflected in the formal accounting records, since they depend on equal future performance from both parties to the contract. Examples are long-term employment contracts and purchase commitments. (3)

**expenditure**   A monetary sacrifice to acquire a productive resource. Does not become an expense until the productive resource is consumed in the generation of revenues. (3)

**expenses**   The consumption or use of assets in the generation of revenues. Expenses measure the effort of the firm. (4)

**extraordinary items**   Material events which are characterized by both their unusual nature and their infrequent occurrence. Such items are shown in a separate section of the income statement as a distinct element of net income for the period. Examples include major casualties and government expropriations. (16)

**FIFO (first-in, first-out)**    Inventory costing procedure which assumes that the ending inventory consists of those goods most recently purchased. During a period of rising prices, it produces higher income than LIFO and a relatively current balance sheet amount for ending inventory. (9)

**financial accounting**    Accounting activity whose primary concern is the provision of information to investors and other groups not directly involved in operating the business or empowered to dictate the presentation and content of the reports prepared for them. (1)

**Financial Accounting Standards Board (FASB)**    The authoritative force in the private sector, since 1973, for setting the standards for financial accounting reports. (1)

**Financial Executives Institute**    Organization composed of top financial executives of large corporations which have direct interest in reporting principles imposed by the SEC and FASB. It presents the position of top management to the standard-setting process. (1)

**financial flexibility**    The ability of an enterprise to take effective actions to alter the amounts and timing of cash flows so that it can respond to unexpected needs and opportunities. (17)

**financial leverage**    The modification of the rate of return on common stockholders' equity from what it otherwise would be through the use of debt and/or preferred stock to finance the acquisition of part of the assets. (18)

**financial strength (solvency)**    Measure of firm's ability to meet its long-term obligations. (18)

**finished goods**    Inventory of merchandise for which the manufacturing process is completed. Merchandise is available for sale to customers. (8)

**fiscal year**    Another term for natural business year. (3)

**fixed expenses**    Expenses that are incurred in approximately the same total amount regardless of the level or volume of operations in the period. Examples include depreciation charges and many salaries. (18)

**foreign currency transaction gains and losses**    Gains and losses which result from explicit transactions denominated in a foreign currency. The value of the foreign currency, vis-à-vis the dollar, has changed between the initial recording and the eventual settlement of a business event. Such gains and losses appear on the income statement in the year in which they occurred. (14)

**foreign currency translation adjustments**    Adjustments arising when the accounts on the books of a foreign branch or subsidiary are translated at current year-end exchange rates that differ from the exchange rates in effect when the items arose. Such gains and losses appear as a contra or adjunct stockholders' equity item. (14)

**Form 10–K**    Annual report which firms under SEC jurisdiction must file with the Commission; includes a complete set of financial statements audited and prepared in accordance with guidelines set forth by the SEC in its Regulation S–X. (1)

**full costing**    Procedure whereby all expenditures for exploration and drilling, whether associated with productive or unproductive ventures, are treated as asset costs. (8)

**fully diluted earnings per share** A conservative measurement of the maximum dilution in earnings per share that hypothetically could take place if all contingent issues of common stock that could reduce earnings per share actually do take place. (16)

**future value** The future sum of money which is the equivalent of a smaller present amount. (11)

**gains** Events favorable from the stockholders' perspective and not connected with the main earning activities of the firm. Examples include the excess of selling price over acquisition cost of noncurrent assets and the advantageous settlement of liabilities. (6)

**general ledger** Single main set of accounts containing the major ledger accounts for asset, liability, and owners' equity items. A single account which is supported by subsidiary ledger accounts is called a *control account*. (5)

**generally accepted accounting principles (GAAP)** Elements in the framework on which financial accounting rests. GAAP consist of concepts and conventions that act as general guides in the identifying, measuring, classifying, and reporting processes. (1)

**general price changes** Changes in the overall level of prices for goods and services in the economy; caused by general inflation rather than shifts in the supply/demand relationship for particular goods or services. (8)

**going-concern concept** In the absence of evidence to the contrary, the entity is assumed to remain in operation sufficiently long enough to carry out its objectives and plans. Also referred to as *continuity concept*. (2)

**goodwill** Excess of the total purchase price over the sum of the separate market values of the tangible assets and the specifically identified intangible assets acquired in a business transaction; a general intangible which represents the cost of the unidentified intangible assets. (10)

**gross margin (profit)** The excess of sales revenue over the cost of goods sold. (6)

**gross margin ratio** Percentage calculated by dividing the gross margin by sales. (6)

**gross price** The invoice price before consideration of any discounts or adjustments. (8)

**group depreciation** Depreciation procedure whereby the individual costs of all units in a group are combined and treated as a single asset. There is only one Accumulated Depreciation account and one depreciation rate based on the average expected life. No loss is recognized on the retirement of individual units. (10)

**holding gains and losses** The value increase or decrease attributable to the holding of assets during a time of changing specific prices. Such holding activities are separated from operating activities under a full-fledged, current cost (replacement cost) reporting system. (9)

**horizontal analysis** Analysis that employs percentages to show how individual financial statement items have changed from year to year. A percentage increase or decrease from the prior year is calculated for each component on the current income and position statements. (18)

**imputed interest** Interest rate inferred when the evidence suggests that the stated interest rate on a note does not represent the effective rate. (11)

**income statement**   Financial statement that summarizes the major changes in the resources of the business as a result of operating or earning activities (revenues, expenses, gains, and losses). (2)

**installment method**   Revenue recognition procedure (point) whereby revenue is recognized later than the sale and then only in proportion to the cash received each period. It is widely used for tax purposes but cannot be used for financial reporting except where enormous uncertainty exists concerning amount and probability of payment. (7)

**in-substance defeasance**   Method to retire bonds by placing risk-free securities in trust and having the trust pay the interest and principal from the trust earnings. (11)

**intangible assets**   Nonphysical rights and privileges. Examples include patents and copyrights. (3)

**interest coverage**   A measure of the firm's ability to meet its interest obligations; calculated by dividing income before interest and taxes by interest expense. (18)

**interim financial reports**   Accounting reports prepared for periods shorter than a year, usually every three months. The disclosures are not as complete as those contained in the annual financial statements. (16)

**internal control**   The procedures and techniques to detect and correct unintentional mistakes (errors) and reduce opportunities for intentional mistakes (irregularities) in an accounting system. (5)

**interperiod tax allocation**   Another name for deferred tax accounting. (13)

**intraperiod tax allocation**   The allocation of the total tax expense of a given period among various sections of the income statement, with a portion perhaps going directly to the retained earnings statement. (13)

**inventoriable cost**   All costs necessary to acquire inventory and to place it for sale. Examples include net invoice price, freight charges into the firm, and handling costs incurred in unloading and storage. (8)

**inventory formula**   Beginning inventory plus net purchases equals cost of goods available for sale. Cost of goods available for sale less ending inventory equals cost of goods sold. (9)

**inventory profits**   The realized inventory holding gains; calculated by subtracting cost of goods sold at historical cost (using FIFO, LIFO, or weighted average) from cost of goods sold at replacement cost. (9)

**inventory turnover**   A measure of how fast inventory on hand normally is sold and converted into accounts receivable; calculated by dividing cost of goods sold by the average inventory balance. (18)

**investee corporation**   The corporation whose shares are owned by another corporation (the investor). (15)

**investment efficiency**   Measures the degree of asset utilization and relates the size of various asset investments to the volume of activity. Inventory and receivables turnovers are examples of such investment efficiency measures. (18)

**investor corporation**   The owner of the shares of stock of another corporation (the investee). (15)

**issued stock** The number of shares that have ever been issued by the corporation. Includes shares outstanding plus shares previously issued and then reacquired (treasury stock). (14)

**journal** Recording medium which maintains a separate record of each event so that a chronological history of the transactions that affected the business is preserved. (4)

**lease** An agreement conveying the right to use property from its legal owner (the lessor) to a second party (the lessee) in exchange for a periodic cash payment (rent). (12)

**ledger** Recording medium which facilitates the accumulation of the effects of various transactions on individual asset, liability, owners' equity, revenue, and expense elements. (4)

**legal (stated) capital** The minimum amount of originally invested capital which state laws specify may not be reduced by voluntary action of the board of directors. Because it is not available for dividends, it serves as a buffer to better protect the claims of creditors. (14)

**lessee** Party who receives the right to use a lessor's property in exchange for a periodic rent payment. (12)

**lessor** Party who grants the right to a lessee to use property in exchange for the receipt of a periodic rent payment. (12)

**liabilities** The debts and other amounts owed by the business to its creditors; one of the two major sources of assets and, accordingly, categories of equities. (3)

**LIFO (last-in, first-out)** Inventory costing procedure which assumes that the ending inventory consists of those goods that were purchased first. During a period of rising prices, LIFO produces the lowest income and income taxes and an unrealistically low balance sheet amount for ending inventory. It must be used for financial reporting if it is used for tax purposes. (9)

**LIFO reserve** A contra asset account that measures the excess amount of a firm's inventory valued at either FIFO or average cost over its LIFO cost. (9)

**liquidating dividend** Dividends that are not paid out of retained earnings and, accordingly, represent a return of contributed capital. (14)

**liquidity** Measure of firm's ability to meet its short-term obligations. (18)

**losses** Events unfavorable from the stockholders' perspective and not connected with the main earning activities of the firm. Examples include the excess of acquisition cost over selling price of noncurrent assets and cost of inventory destroyed in a fire. (6)

**lower-of-cost-or-market** Procedure whereby inventories or marketable equity securities are assigned either a historical cost amount or a current market valuation, whichever is lower. (9)

**managerial accounting** Accounting activity whose primary concern is the provision of information to management for use in controlling current operations and planning future operations. This branch of accounting includes the procedures and techniques for generating detailed operating data and projections. (1)

**manufacturing overhead** Costs of all manufacturing resources, other than direct materials and direct labor, entering the manufacturing process. (8)

**marketable equity securities**   Marketable securities that are to be reported in the balance sheet at the lower of acquisition cost or current-market value. (8)

**market bond interest rate**   The interest rate actually incurred by the corporation issuing the bonds. A function of the supply and demand for loanable funds of a given risk. It will differ from the nominal rate of interest in many cases, giving rise to bond discounts or premiums. Also referred to as the effective or yield interest rate. (11)

**matching concept**   The central operational assumption of financial accounting— net income is best measured by a matching (deduction) of costs against (from) the revenues to which the costs have given rise. (2)

**materiality**   Refers to the relative importance or magnitude of a piece of accounting information; any amount or transaction that has a significant (material) effect on the financial statements should be recorded correctly and reported. (2)

**maturity value**   The specified sum which the corporation must pay to the bondholder or noteholder at the maturity date. (11)

**measurability criterion**   Criterion which asserts that revenue should not be recognized until it can be measured with a reasonable degree of reliability. In conjunction with earnings criterion, it influences the recognition of revenue. (7)

**merger**   Joining of two companies, with the parent company acquiring the outstanding stock of a subsidiary company. The acquired shares are retired, and the subsidiary firm's net assets are combined with those of the parent. (15)

**minority interest**   The portion of the subsidiary company not owned by the parent company. It often appears on the consolidated balance sheet as a separate category between liabilities and stockholders' equity. (15)

**modified accelerated cost recovery system (MACRS)**   Extremely accelerated method of depreciation, used for tax purposes for tangible assets placed in service after 1986. (10)

**monetary assets**   Assets which are presently cash or which can be converted to cash rapidly such as short-term securities, accounts receivable, and notes receivable. (3)

**monetary concept**   Assumption containing two basic ideas about the unit of measurement used in accounting. First, because money is the common denominator for the expression of economic activity, it should be used to measure and analyze accounting events and transactions. Second, fluctuations in the value of the dollar can be ignored without significant impairment of the relevance of the financial statements. (2)

**multiple-step income statement**   Presentation that groups revenue and expense data in significant categories and shows various income subtotals before displaying net income. (6)

**National Association of Accountants**   Organization composed of internal management accountants, which researches and presents the position of management in the standard-setting process. (1)

**natural business year**   Accounting period that ends during some month other than December. (3)

**net assets** Excess of assets over liabilities; equal to owners' equity. (3)

**net income** The residual measure of the excess amount when asset increases (revenues) from operations exceed asset decreases (expenses) from operations. (3)

**net loss** The residual measure of the excess amount when asset decreases (expenses) from operations exceed asset increases (revenues) from operations. (3)

**net price** The price calculated by deducting the discount offered for prompt payment from the invoice price (8)

**net realizable value** Selling price reduced by the anticipated costs of completing and selling an asset. (9)

**neutrality** Qualitative characteristic which states that accounting policies should be chosen without any purpose other than measurement accuracy. Accounting judgments should be free of bias to allow the financial statements to present information fairly and impartially. (2)

**nominal bond interest rate** The interest rate actually stated in the bond contract; multiplied by the bond's maturity amount to determine the cash interest paid each year. Also referred to as the stated or contractual interest rate. (11)

**noncash expenses** Expenses which do not involve a current cash outlay. An example would be depreciation expense, which has no effect on cash but does affect accrual-based net income. (17)

**normal cost (service cost)** The present value of expected future payments to employees attributable to work performed during each year after the date of the pension plan adoption. (12)

**off-balance-sheet financing** Reporting techniques which allow a firm to acquire long-term assets through various types of borrowing without recognizing an accounting liability on the balance sheet. (12)

**operating cycle** The time needed by the business to acquire the product or service, sell it, and collect the receivables. (3)

**operating efficiency** Concerns asset consumption in the generation of revenue. The operating ratio and profit margins are among the factors calculated and examined. (18)

**operating expenditures** Expenditures which simply keep plant assets in good working condition but in no better condition than when they were purchased; these are expensed immediately, as they are deemed to benefit only the current accounting period. Examples include lubrication and other routine maintenance procedures. (10)

**operating income** Excess of gross margin over operating expenses. (6)

**operating lease** A residual category. It covers all leases from lessee's perspective that are not capital leases and all leases from lessor's perspective that are not sales-type or direct-financing leases. The depreciable leased asset remains on the lessor's books, and the periodic rental payments are reflected by the lessee as an expense. (12)

**operating leverage** A measure of the impact on operating profits caused by changes in volume of activity. It is greatly influenced by the proportion of fixed vis-à-vis variable expenses present in the firm. (18)

**operating ratio**    The ratio between recurring operating expenses and operating revenues (commonly only sales). It measures the proportion of resource inflows from sales that are consumed by normal operating activities. (18)

**outstanding stock**    The number of issued shares of stock that are in the possession of the stockholders at the current time. (14)

**owners' equity**    The residual interest in the assets of an entity that remains after deducting its liabilities. It is one of the two major sources of assets and, accordingly, categories of equities. Referred to as stockholders' equity in a corporation. (3)

**parent company**    A company which owns more than half of the voting stock in another corporation referred to as a *subsidiary*. (15)

**par value**    An arbitrary amount printed on each stock certificate and assigned to each share. In many states, it represents the legal or stated capital per share. The par value of shares issued is credited to the stock account directly. (14)

**percentage of completion method**    Revenue recognition procedure (point) used for individual projects involving substantial amounts of revenue and considerable periods of time from the inception of the project to its completion. Revenue is recorded as work progresses in proportion to the percentage of estimated total costs incurred. The method is useful for such businesses as airplane manufacture and highway construction. (7)

**period costs (expenses)**    Expired costs that cannot be traced directly to units of product and, accordingly, are expensed in the period in which they are incurred. Examples include rent expense and the president's salary. (6)

**periodic inventory system**    Ending inventory balance and cost of goods sold are recorded only at the end of the accounting period in the form of an adjusting entry removing the cost of goods sold from the inventory account. (9)

**permanent tax differences**    Differences between taxable income and accounting income created by certain items of revenue and expense, which enter into either taxable or accounting income without ever affecting the computation of the other. (13)

**perpetual inventory system**    Inventory balance is increased with each inventory purchase. Inventory balance is decreased, and cost of goods sold is recorded each time inventory is sold or used. (9)

**point-of-sale revenue recognition**    Revenue recognition procedure (point) when sale is completed. Selling activities are finished, revenue is earned, and accuracy of measurement is enhanced. (7)

**pooling-of-interests approach**    Procedures used to account for business combinations where the parent company issues its own voting stock in exchange for substantially all the voting stock of the subsidiary. All the subsidiary's asset accounts are carried over at book value, and no goodwill is recognized. The retained earnings of both firms are combined. (15)

**posting**    Transcribing the component parts of journal entries to individual ledger accounts. (4)

**preferred dividends in arrears**    Dividends which have been skipped in past periods on cumulative preferred stock. They do not represent a liability of the corporation but must be paid along with current preferred dividends before any common dividends can be declared. They are usually disclosed in a footnote to the statements. (14)

**preferred stock**  A special type of ownership interest with certain modifications of the basic rights inherent in common stock. It usually has a preference over common stock in the payment of dividends and usually has a prior claim on assets in the event of liquidation. (14)

**premium on bonds**  Excess of issue price of a bond over its face or maturity amount; occurs when the nominal rate of interest offered by the corporation exceeds the market rate of interest demanded by investors. It is accounted for as a reduction in interest expense over the life of the bond. (11)

**present value concept**  The current cash equivalent of some designated future amount or amounts. It is based on the observation that a smaller amount today is the equivalent of a larger amount in the future because today's amount can be invested and earn compound interest. (11)

**primary earnings per share**  The net income available to common stock (perhaps adjusted) divided by the sum of the average common shares outstanding and the number of common stock equivalent shares. (16)

**prior period adjustments**  Very rare events and corrections of errors that require direct adjustment to retained earnings and retroactive restatement of net income. (16)

**prior service costs**  The present value of expected future pension benefits attributable to employee service prior to the adoption or amendment date of a pension plan. Also called *past service costs*. (12)

**product costs (expenses)**  Expired costs which can be traced directly to units of product. Examples include the direct purchase price of merchandise and such indirect items as freight charges. (6)

**profit margin**  One component of return on assets (investment). Calculated by dividing net income plus tax-adjusted interest by sales revenue. (18)

**projected unit credit method**  The FASB-endorsed actuarial cost method that computes pension expense and obligations by considering years of service and future compensation levels. (12)

**property, plant, and equipment**  Land, buildings, machinery, equipment, and other fixed property used in the business. (3)

**proportional performance method**  The service counterpart to percentage of completion for revenue recognition. Total revenue is apportioned and recognized in relation to some measure of performance (e.g., magazines provided under the terms of a subscription). (7)

**purchase approach**  Procedure used to account for all business combinations where it is not possible to use the pooling-of-interests approach. Usually at least some cash is exchanged for the subsidiary's shares. The balance sheet items of the subsidiary are revalued, and goodwill is usually recognized. (15)

**qualified opinions**  Issued by the auditor whenever the scope of the examination has been limited or some other factor has prevented the issuance of an unqualified opinion. (2)

**quick (acid-test) ratio**   A widely used measure of liquidity. It has the same denominator as the current ratio, current liabilities, but uses only monetary assets in the numerator, excluding inventory and prepaid expenses. (18)

**rate of return on common stock equity**   A widely used measure of profitability that reveals how well the firm has used the assets and modified the capital structure to the benefit of the common stockholders. It is calculated by dividing net income available to common stockholders (after deduction of any preferred dividends) by the average common stockholders' equity balance. (18)

**rate of return on investment (total assets)**   A widely used measure of profitability. Calculated by dividing net income plus tax-adjusted interest by the balance of average total assets. It can be broken down into its profit-margin and asset-turnover components. Also referred to as *return on investment*. (18)

**ratio analysis**   Computations relating specific financial statement elements to each other to permit comparisons with prior periods, predetermined goals, and/or other companies. (18)

**raw materials**   Inventory of materials which have not yet entered the manufacturing process. Also called *direct materials*. (8)

**receivables turnover**   A measure of how fast accounts receivable are turned into cash. Calculated by dividing net (credit) sales by the average accounts receivable balance. (18)

**redemption (call) price**   Extra premium payment required for the privilege of retiring bonds before the maturity date. (11)

**refunding**   Issuance of a new bond and use of its proceeds to redeem an old bond. (11)

**regulatory accounting**   The accounting process which organizes accounting data in specific records and reports to comply with regulations of federal, state, and local governments. (1)

**relevance**   Qualitative guideline which states that accounting information should be responsive to the audience's information needs and capable of affecting its decisions. To be relevant, information must have either predictive or feedback value to the user and must be timely. (2)

**reliability**   Qualitative guideline which states that financial accounting information should be reasonably free from error and bias and should faithfully represent what it purports to represent. Two conditions which contribute to the existence of reliability are (a) representational faithfulness and (b) verifiability. (2)

**replacement cost**   The current acquisition cost of a previously purchased and currently held asset. (9)

**representational faithfulness**   One of several qualitative guidelines which contribute to the existence of reliability. It implies a correspondence between accounting measures and the underlying economic events they are representing. (2)

**residual value**   Portion of the asset's cost expected to be recovered at the end of its useful life to the firm. (10)

**retail inventory method**   Method of estimating the cost of ending inventory by applying the relationship between cost and retail prices for the goods available for sale to the ending inventory at retail prices. (9)

**retained earnings**  The additional owners' equity arising from the retention of earnings in the corporation. It is increased by net income and decreased by net losses and dividends. (3)

**revenue recognition concept**  Revenue should be recognized only when it has been earned and can be measured with a reasonable degree of reliability. (2)

**revenues**  Inflows of assets from business operations which reflect the sale of goods and services. Revenues reflect the accomplishment of the firm. (4)

**sales-type lease**  Leases meeting certain criteria which create, for the lessor, a manufacturer's or dealer's profit. Lessor removes property from its books, reflects gross margin on sale immediately, and reports interest revenue over the term of the lease purchase it is financing. (12)

**Securities and Exchange Commission (SEC)**  Federal agency established in the 1930s to regulate the nation's securities markets and to ensure that investors receive adequate information on which to base their investment decisions. (1)

**segment reporting**  Disclosure requirements that result in reporting certain data for each industry segment for which the revenue, operating income or loss, or identifiable assets are 10 percent or more of a company's total. Firms have considerable discretion in their definition of segments. (16)

**single-step income statement**  Presentation which groups all expense and loss accounts together and groups all revenue and gain accounts together. Net income is shown as a single subtraction of the total expenses from the total revenues. (6)

**specific identification**  Inventory costing method under which the various purchases made are segregated so that the goods remaining on hand at the end of the period can be specifically identified as having come from certain lots purchased. (9)

**specific price changes**  Changes in the number of dollars of a particular good or service; caused by changes over time in the interaction of supply and demand for the particular good or service. (8)

**statement of cash flows (SCF)**  Financial statement designed to disclose how the cash position of the firm is affected by the major sources of capital and the areas to which the resources were committed. The three important areas that affect cash flows are operations, financing, and investing. (17)

**statement of retained earnings**  A statement that reconciles the period's change in retained earnings with the balances on the comparative balance sheets. It begins with the beginning-of-period balance, adds income and deducts dividends, and ends up with the end-of-period balance. (6)

**Statements of Financial Accounting Concepts (SFAC)**  Publications issued by the FASB which attempt to lay the groundwork for a conceptual framework for financial accounting and reporting. (1)

**Statements of Financial Accounting Standards (SFAS)**  Authoritative statements issued by the FASB which spell out the current generally accepted accounting principles. (1)

**stewardship**  The responsibility of management for protecting funds and other properties committed to the firm, for using the resources for the purposes intended, and for periodic reporting. (2)

**stock dividends**   Dividends declared by corporations where the "payment" is made in additional shares of the firm's stock. No assets are transferred to the stockholders and all stockholders retain their same proportional ownership in the firm. (14)

**stock-equity ratio**   A widely used measure of financial strength; calculated by dividing the common stock equity by total equities. (18)

**stock option**   An agreement whereby selected employees can acquire shares of stock, after some date in the future, at a specified price per share. (14)

**stock split**   The corporation distributes additional shares of stock to shareholders for which the latter invest nothing. It represents a financial mechanism to reduce market price per share and increase the stock's appeal to investors. A stock split usually involves far more shares than a stock dividend. (14)

**stock warrants (rights)**   Rights given outright to stockholders or included with the sale of other securities such as bonds. Holders of the warrants are permitted to acquire new shares of common stock at a specified price, even if the market price per share is in excess of that amount. (14)

**straight-line bond amortization**   Interest-recording procedure which charges each period for the cash interest adjusted for a pro rata share of any bond premium or discount. The interest expense will be constant for each period of the bond's life. (11)

**straight-line depreciation**   Depreciation procedure whereby a uniform charge for depreciation expense is taken during each year of the asset's life. (10)

**subsidiary company**   A company which has more than half of its voting stock owned by another corporation, referred to as the *parent*. (15)

**subsidiary ledger**   A group of accounts in which detailed information about a particular general ledger account (a control account) is kept. (5)

**successful efforts**   Procedure whereby only those exploration and drilling costs traceable to successful wells or fields are set up as assets. The cost of dry holes or unproductive fields is immediately charged to expense. (8)

**sum-of-the-years'-digits (SYD) depreciation**   An accelerated depreciation procedure whereby a smaller fraction of the asset's depreciation base is charged as depreciation expense in each successive year. (10)

**tax accounting**   The accounting process which organizes accounting data in specific records and reports to comply with the laws and rules of the respective tax codes. (1)

**tax loss carrybacks and carryforwards**   Provisions in the tax code which permit firms to offset a current tax loss against taxable income of the prior 3 years and the following 15 years. (13)

**temporary tax differences**   Differences between taxable income and accounting income, created by certain items of revenue and expense, which affect the computation of taxable income in one year and the computation of accounting income during another year. (13)

**transactions**   Those financial activities and events involving the business entity which generate data concerning a measurable change in asset or equity accounts. (4)

**treasury stock** A corporation's own stock which has been previously issued and then reacquired but not legally retired. (14)

**treasury stock — cost method of recording** Recording the total cost paid to reacquire shares of capital stock outstanding in a single contra-equity account called *treasury stock*. (14)

**treasury stock — par value method of recording** Recording the cost of reacquiring shares of capital stock outstanding by reducing the par value, additional paid-in capital, and retained earnings accounts proportionally. (14)

**trial balance** A listing of ledger accounts and their balances, classified as debit or credit; a procedure to ascertain whether the equality of debits and credits has been maintained in the accounting records. (5)

**turnover of assets** One component of return on assets (investment); calculated by dividing sales revenue by average total assets. (18)

**uncollectible accounts (bad debts)** Accounts receivable which will never be collected because the customer is unable or unwilling to pay. (7)

**unit depreciation** Depreciation procedure whereby the cost of each asset is assigned individually to the accounting periods in which it is used. (10)

**unqualified ("clean") opinion** An auditors' report which provides positive assurance that there is a reliable basis for the representations shown by management on its financial statements. (2)

**variable expenses** Expenses which change in total amount more or less proportionally with changes in the volume of operations in the period. Examples include direct materials and sales commissions. (18)

**verifiability** Quality which suggests that accounting information and measurement models can be independently confirmed by other competent measurers. It is one of two conditions which contribute to the existence of reliability. (2)

**vertical analysis** Analysis which abstracts from the absolute amounts on the financial statements the relative magnitude of figures expressed as percentages of some base item. Total assets and net sales are usually the bases used for the balance sheet and income statement (called *common-size statements*). (18)

**vested benefits** Employee benefits, the right to which is no longer contingent on the employee's continuing to work for the employer. (12)

**weighted-average cost** Inventory costing method which assumes that the ending inventory is representative of all units available for sale during the period. It produces ending-inventory and cost-of-goods-sold figures between those resulting from FIFO and LIFO. (9)

**working capital** Excess of current assets over current liabilities. (3)

**work in process** Inventory of products for which the manufacturing process has been begun but not yet completed. (8)

**worksheet** A columnar device employed as a convenient and orderly way of organizing information to be used in the preparation of financial statements such as consolidations. (15)

**zero-coupon bonds** Bonds issued with a nominal interest rate of zero. Bonds are sold at deep discount, and all interest earned is in the maturity value paid at the maturity date of the bonds. (11)

# *Index*

# H–I